OXFORD INTERNATIONAL ARBITRATION SERIES

Series Editor: Loukas Mistelis

Professor of Transnational Commercial Law and Arbitration, Queen Mary, University of London

INTERNATIONAL INVESTMENT, POLITICAL RISK, AND DISPUTE RESOLUTION

OXFORD INTERNATIONAL ARBITRATION SERIES

Series Editor: Loukas Mistelis

The aim of this series is to publish works of quality and originality on specific issues in international commercial and investment arbitration. The series aims to provide a forum for the exploration of important emerging issues and those issues not adequately dealt with in leading works. It should be of interest to both practitioners and scholarly lawyers.

INTERNATIONAL INVESTMENT, POLITICAL RISK, AND DISPUTE RESOLUTION

A Practitioner's Guide

SECOND EDITION

NOAH RUBINS QC
THOMAS-NEKTARIOS PAPANASTASIOU
N. STEPHAN KINSELLA

OXFORD
UNIVERSITY PRESS

OXFORD
UNIVERSITY PRESS

Great Clarendon Street, Oxford, OX2 6DP,
United Kingdom

Oxford University Press is a department of the University of Oxford.
It furthers the University's objective of excellence in research, scholarship,
and education by publishing worldwide. Oxford is a registered trade mark of
Oxford University Press in the UK and in certain other countries

First Edition published in 2005
Second Edition published in 2020

Impression: 1

Published in the United States of America by Oxford University Press
198 Madison Avenue, New York, NY 10016, United States of America

British Library Cataloguing in Publication Data
Data available

Library of Congress Control Number: 2019934656

ISBN 978–0–19–880805–3

Printed and bound by
CPI Group (UK) Ltd, Croydon, CR0 4YY

SERIES EDITOR'S PREFACE

This series of monographs is dedicated to specific issues in international arbitration law and practice, and gives authors the opportunity and the challenge of a more in-depth treatment than is possible in leading generalist works. It also provides an international forum for the profound exploration of important practical and theoretical matters and will further the development of arbitration as a self-luminous academic discipline and major international legal practice area.

This twentieth book in the series is a second, fully updated and expanded edition of a successful book on international investment, political risk, and dispute resolution. The issue of political risk and its impact on dispute resolution is pervasive but has been in the limelight in recent years given, for example, the crisis in Venezuela, the annexation of Crimea by the Russian Federation, and several other events of political risk in other parts of the world. This new monograph for the series by Noah Rubins, Stephan Kinsella, and Thomas-Nektarios Papanastasiou aims to be the undisputed reference book on the topic. Indeed, while some articles exist on the topic this is the main book addressing all these critical issues.

International Investment is constantly exposed to legal and political risk. Political risk has been the source of increased concern for international investors: regime change, political instability, and civil unrest can and do have adverse impact on foreign investments. Both governments and the international business community wish to have clarity as to the relevant risk and how such risk may be insured. Since the first edition of this book in 2005, a great deal has happened: political risk has increased rather than diminished and although the original structure has been maintained, one chapter has been added and all other chapters have been significantly updated and amended.

The book is organised in three parts.

Part I, provides the context and foundations of the monograph: chapter 1 explores the concept and ontology of political risk, chapter 2 discusses how transactions may be arranged (structure of contracts, contract drafting and key clauses), to minimize political risk and chapter 3 looks at available investment insurance (OPIC, national insurance programmes, MIGA and available private insurance).

Part II is one of the two main parts of the monograph and is dedicated to the international law framework of investment protection and political risk. Chapter 4 focuses on state responsibility and remedies under customary international law (and also covers the issue of jurisdictional immunity of states), chapter 5 is dedicated to the history and evolution of customary international law of expropriation and investment protection while chapter 6 discusses the substantive law of contemporary international investment protection.

Part III addresses investment disputes, human rights, and political risk. Chapter 7 explores the establishment of arbitral jurisdiction, chapter 8 looks at arbitration procedure (including pursuant to ICSID and UNCITRAL Rules), and chapter 9 is dedicated to the mediation and conciliation of investment disputes. Chapter 10 focuses on the intervention of states in investment disputes (including a section on economic sanctions). Finally, chapter 11 explores the interaction between international investment law and human rights. Amongst the useful appendices there is an OPIC Contract of Insurance and a Sample Private Contract.

This is a substantially updated and enhanced version of the 2005 first edition of this book and contains a wealth of research and a systematic, balanced, and comprehensive analysis of all major issues associated with the topic. It is insightful and very relevant to practice and a most welcome addition to the series.

LM
London 7 June 2019

PREFACE

The first edition of our book *International Investment, Political Risk, and Dispute Resolution: A Practitioner's Guide* was warmly received by practitioners and scholars on its release well over a decade ago. But much has happened in law and international arbitral practice since the first edition. For this reason, a third co-author has been enlisted to contribute to this second edition.

Given the positive response and the increasing importance of the subject matter, we have long felt that there was a need to maintain the book as a current reference work by integrating contemporary issues related to international investment and political risk.

Political risk—the risk that a host government will interfere with the property rights of a foreign investor—remains a topic increasingly central to strategic discussions within both governments and the international business community. Our purpose is to explore the multi-layered legal framework for the protection of foreign investment against political risk, analyzing some of the key issues, such as structuring transactions to minimize political risk, political risk insurance, State responsibility, treaties protecting foreign investmentand international arbitration between States and investors.

Since the previous edition was released in 2005, far more attention has been paid to some of these issues, in particular investor–State arbitration. The original structure of this book remains unaffected. The present volume provides updated and expanded coverage of the issues addressed in the 2005 edition.

All chapters have been revised, updated, and some significantly reorganized, given the number of new arbitration awards that have come to light and the massive volume of commentary on the subject of international investment arbitration since the first edition. Dr. Papanastasiou's input was critical to the update. His additions to the text also expanded upon the original with entirely new sections and brought new material and commentary. We have taken into account the latest theoretical approaches to foreign investment protection and the most intellectually challenging awards issued in the intervening decade, as well as the most recent practical guidance on the procedural recourse available to investors who face political risks. Finally, this book is addressed to a wide audience, and is written to appeal to lawyers and non-lawyers alike. It is suitable as a primer for non-specialist practitioners (attorneys, in-house and outside counsel for corporations and investors) seeking to familiarize themselves with international law pertaining to political risk. While appropriate for practitioner use, this book is also suitable for undergraduate students or for graduates (as a textbook for one or two semesters) who intend to specialize in international investment law.

Before concluding, we would like to thank Emmanuel Giakoumakis, Associate Legal Officer to the President of the International Court of Justice, for his research assistance in reviewing recent developments in the work of investment treaty tribunals.

In this guide, we hope to provide our readers with the tools necessary to understand the international law of investment and its relationship to political risk. If we have succeeded in our task, the reader will be better equipped to understand political risks associated with foreign investments and how they are managed, negotiated, and safeguarded.

Noah Rubins
Thomas-Nektarios Papanastasiou
N. Stephan Kinsella
January 2020

SUMMARY OF CONTENTS

CONTENTS

PART III: INVESTMENT DISPUTES AND POLITICAL RISK

TABLE OF CASES

References are either to page numbers or paragraph numbers.

TABLE OF TREATIES, STATUTES AND REGULATORY MATERIALS

References are either to page numbers or paragraph numbers.

DOMESTIC LEGISLATION

Albania

Algeria

Argentina

Armenia

Australia

Belgium

Bulgaria

Canada

Cuba

Estonia

France

Germany

India

BIBLIOGRAPHY

BOOKS AND ARTICLES

Anne van Aaken, *Defragmentation of Public International Law through Interpretation: A Methodological Proposal*, 16(2) Indiana J. Global Leg. Stud. 483–512 (2009)

Manuel Abdala & Pablo Spiller, *Damage Valuation of Indirect Expropriation in International Arbitration Cases*, 14 Am. Rev. Int'l Arb. 447 (2003)

Abdel-Wahab, *Economic Development Agreements and Nationalization*, 30 U. Cincinnati L. Rev. 418, 440 (1961)

Hossein Abedian, *Judicial Review of Arbitral Awards in International Arbitration—A Case for an Efficient System of Judicial Review*, 28(6) J. Int'l Arb. 553 (2011)

Danny Abir, *Suing a Foreign Government: A Note on Siderman v. Republic of Argentina*, 15 Whittier L. Rev. 575, 580 (1994)

Pia Acconci, *Determining the Internationally Relevant Link between a State and a Corporate Investor*, 5 J. World Inv. & Trade 139 (2004)

Pia Acconci, *Most-Favored Nation Treatment*, in The Oxford Handbook of International Investment Law 363–406 (Peter Muchlinski et al. eds. 2008)

Ifeanyi Achebe, *The Legal Problems of Indigenization in Nigeria: A Lesson for Developing Countries*, 12 Hastings Int'l & Comp. LR 637, 659–62 (1989)

Libby Adler & Peer Zumbansen, *The Forgetfulness of Noblesse: A Critique of the German Foundation Law Compensating Slave and Forced Laborers of the Third Reich*, 39 Harv. J. Leg. 1, 2 (2002)).

Jai Prakash Agarwal, *Effect of Foreign Direct Investment on Employment in Home Countries*, 6 Transnat'l Corporations 1 (1997)

Vinod Agarwal, *Alternative Dispute Resolution Methods*, DFM Doc. No. 14 (March 2001), available at https://www.unitar.org/pft/sites/ unitar.org.pft/files/DocSeries14.pdf

Adeoye Akinsanya, *International Protection of Direct Foreign Investments in the Third World*, 36 Int'l & Comp. LQ 58, 70–75 (1987)

George Aldrich, The Jurisprudence of the Iran–U.S. Claims Tribunal 603–04 (1996)

George H. Aldrich, *The Selection of Arbitrators*, in The Iran-United States Claims Tribunal and the Process of International Claims Resolution (David Caron & John Crook eds. 2000)

Frank C. Alexander, Jr., *Production Sharing Contracts and Other Host Government Contracts* (46 Rocky Mt. Min. L. Inst. 20–1 (2000)), 3(1) OGEL (Mar. 2005) available at http://www.gasandoil.com/ogel

Frank C. Alexander, Jr., *The Three Pillars of Security of Investment under PSCs and other HGCs*, Fifty-Fourth Annual Institute on Oil and Gas Law (Institute for Energy Law of the Center for American and International Law, Publication 640, Release 54, 2003)

Stanimir Alexandrov, *Non-Appearance before the International Court of Justice*, 33 Colum. J. Transnat'l L. 41 (1995)

Stanimir A. Aleksandrov, *Introductory Note* to *SGS Societe Generale de Surveillance S.A. v. Pakistan*, ICSID Case No. ARB/01/13, 42 I.L.M. 1285, 1287 (2003)

Stanimir Alexandrov, *Breaches of Contract and Breaches of Treaty: The Jurisdiction of Treaty-based Arbitration Tribunals to Decide Breach of Contract Claims in SGS v. Pakistan and SGS v. Philippines*, 5 J. World Inv. 555 (2004)

Stanimir A. Alexandrov, *The "Baby Boom" of Treaty-Based Arbitrations and the Jurisdiction of ICSID Tribunals: Shareholders as Investors and Jurisdiction Ratione Temporis*, 4 L. & Pract. Int'l Cts. & Tribunals 19 (2005), available at https://heinonline.org/HOL/Page?collection=jo urnals&handle=hein.journals/lpict4&id=25&men_tab=srchresults

Stanimir Alexandrov, *Breach of Treaty Claims and Breach of Contract Claims: Is It Still Unknown Territory?* in Arbitration under International Investment Agreements: A Guide to the Key Issues 323 (Katia Yannaca-Small ed. 2010)

Stanimir Alexandrov, *The Evolution of the Full Protection and Security Standard*, in Building International Investment Law: The First 50 Years of ICSID (Meg Kinnear et al. eds. 2016)

Stanimir A. Alexandrov & James Mendenhall, *Breach of Treaty Claims and Breach of Contract Claims: Simplification of International Jurisprudence*, in Contemporary Issues in International Arbitration and Mediation: The Fordham Papers 2014 24–44

Edlira Aliaj, *Dispute Resolution through Ad Hoc and Institutional Arbitration*, 2(2) Ac. J. Bus. 241–50 (2016)

Carsten Alting, *Piercing the Corporate Veil in American and German Law—Liability of Individuals and Entities: A Comparative View*, Tulsa J. Comp. & Int'l L. 187 (1995)

Guillermo Aguilar Alvarez & William W. Park, *The New Face of Investment Arbitration: NAFTA Chapter 11*, Mealey's Int'l Arb. Rep. (*January 2004), at 39, 41*

José E. Alvarez, *Are Corporations Subjects of International Law?* 9 Santa Clara J. Int'l L. 1, 13 (2011)

José E. Alvarez, *The Use (and Misuse) of European Human Rights Law in Investor–State Dispute Settlement*, in The Impact of EU Law on International Commercial Arbitration 72 (Franco Ferrari ed. 2017), available at SSRN: https://papers.ssrn.com/sol3/papers.cfm?abstract_id=2875089

José E. Alvarez & Kathryn Khamsi, *The Argentine Crisis and Foreign Investors: A Glimpse into the Heart of the Investment Regime*, 2008–09 Yb. Int'l. Inv. L. & Pol'y. 441–48 (2009)

Henri C. Alvarez, *Setting Aside Additional Facility Awards: The Metalclad Case*, in Annulment of ICSID Awards 267 (Emmanuel Gaillard & Yas Banifatemi eds. 2004)

C.F. Amerasinghe, *State Breaches of Contracts with Aliens in International Law*, 58 AJIL 881 (1964)

C.F. Amerasinghe, State Responsibility for Injuries to Aliens 281–82 (1967)

C.F. Amerasinghe, *Submissions to the Jurisdiction of the International Centre for Settlement of Investment Disputes*, 5 J. Mar. L. & Comm. 211, 223 (1974)

C.F. Amerasinghe, *The International Centre for the Settlement of Investment Disputes and Development through the Multinational Corporation*, 9 Vand. J. Transnat'l L. 793, 809–10 (1976)

C.F. Amerasinghe, *Whither the Local Remedies Rule?* 5 ICSID Rev.—For. Inv. L.J. 292, 293–95 (1990)

C.F. Amerasinghe, *Issues of Compensation for the Taking of Alien Property in the Light of Recent Cases and Practice*, 41 ICLQ 22, 64 (1992)

C.F. Amerasinghe, Local Remedies in International Law (2004)

Austin Amissah, *The ACP/EEC Conciliation and Arbitration Rules*, 8 Arb. Int'l 167 (1992)

Bernardo Sepulveda Amor, *The NAFTA and the Claims of Mexican Jurisdiction*, 19 Hous. J. Int'l L. 565, 586–91 (1997)

Tang An, *The Law Applicable to a Transnational Economic Development Contract*, 21 J. World Trade 95 (1987)

Chandler P. Anderson, *Title to Foreign Confiscated Property*, 20 AJIL 528 (1926)
Aurélia Antonietti, *The 2006 Amendments to the ICSID Rules and Regulations and the Additional Facility Rules*, 21(2) ICSID Rev.—For. Inv. L.J. 427–48 (2006)
Carlos Ignacio Suarez Anzorena, *Vivendi v. Argentina: on the Admissibility of Requests for Partial Annulment and the Ground of a Manifest Excess of Powers*, in Annulment of ICSID Awards 267 (Emmanuel Gaillard & Yas Banifatemi eds. 2004)
Gaetano Arangio-Ruiz, *The Normative Role of the General Assembly of the United Nations and the Declaration of Principles of Friendly Relations*, 137 Recueil Des Cours 419, 434–518 (1972 III)
Julian Arato, *The Margin of Appreciation in International Investment Law*, 54 Va. J. Int'l. L. 546 (2013)
Jiménez de Aréchega, *L'Arbitrage entre les Etats et les Sociétés Privées Etrangères*, in Melanges En L'Honneur De Gilbert Gidel 367, 375 (1961)
Samuel Asante, *The Concept of the Good Corporate Citizen in International Business*, 4 ICSID Rev.—For. Inv. L.J. 1, 18–19 (1989)
Peter Ashford, The IBA Rules on the Taking of Evidence in International Arbitration: A Guide (2013)
Amazu Asouzu, *A Review and Critique of Arbitral Awards on Article 25(2)(b) of the ICSID Convention*, 3 J. World Inv. 397, 398 (2002)
Hans Bagner, *Jeremy Carver, Bohuslav Klein & Wolfgang Kühn, How to Avoid Conflicting Awards: The Lauder and CME Cases*, 5 J. World Inv. & Trade 7–35 (2004)
Stewart A. Baker & Mark D. Davis, *Establishment of an Arbitral Tribunal under the UNCITRAL Rules: The Experience of the Iran–United States Claims Tribunal*, 23 Int'l Law. 81 (1989)
Domitille Baizeau & Tessa Hayes, *The Arbitral Tribunal's Duty and Power to Address Corruption Sua Sponte*, in International Arbitration and the Rule of Law: Contribution and Conformity, ICCA Congress Series Vol. 19, 225–65 (Andrea Menaker ed. 2017)
Eric N. Baklanoff, Expropriation of U.S. Investment in Cuba, Mexico, and Chile (1975)
Filip Balcerzak, *Jurisdiction of Tribunals in Investor–State Arbitration and the Issue of Human Rights*, 29(1) ICSID Rev.—For. Inv. L.J. 216–30 (2014)
Filip Balcerzak, Investor–State Arbitration and Human Rights 110 (2017)
Markham Ball, *Just Do It—Drafting the Arbitration Clause in an International Agreement*, 10(4) J. Int'l Arb. 29 (1993)
Markham Ball, *Assessing Damages in Claims by Investors against States*, 16 ICSID Rev.—For. Inv. L.J. 408 (2001)
Markham Ball, *Probity Deconstructed: How Helpful, Really, are the New International Bar Association Guidelines on Conflicts of Interest in International Arbitration?* 21 Arb. Int'l 323, 326 (2005)
Yas Banifatemi, *The Law Applicable in Investment Treaty Arbitration*, in Arbitration under International Investment Agreements: A Guide to the Key Issues 191 *et seq.* (Katia Yannaca-Small ed. 2010)
Yas Banifatemi, *The Impact of Corruption on "Gateway Issues" of Arbitrability, Jurisdiction, Admissibility and Procedural Issues*, in Addressing Issues of Corruption in Commercial and Investment Arbitration, Dossiers of the ICC Institute of World Business Law 16 *et seq.* (Domitille Baizeau & Richard H. Kreindler eds. 2015)
James Barrows, *International Trends and Latest Changes in Oil Laws, Concession, and Production- Sharing Agreements Worldwide*, Inst. Int'l Oil & Gas L. A–1 (1983)
Russel Lawrence Barsh, *A Special Session of the U.N. General Assembly Rethinks the Economic Rights and Duties of States*, 85 AJIL 192, 192–93 (1991)

Lorand Bartels, *Jurisdictions and Applicable Law Clauses: Where Does a Tribunal Find the Principal Norms Applicable to the Case before It?* in Multi-Sourced Equivalent Norms in International Law 115 *et seq.* (Tomer Broude & Yuval Shany eds. 2011)
Lance Bartholomeusz, *The Amicus Curiae before International Courts and Tribunals*, 5 Non-St. Actors & Int'l L. 209 (2005);
S. Bastid, *La Commission de conciliation franco-siamoise*, 1 Etudes en l'Honneur de Georges Scelle 1 (1950)
Ian F.G. Baxter, *International Business Disputes*, 39 Int'l & Comp. LQ 288 (1990)
Joel C. Beauvais, *Student Article: Regulatory Expropriations under NAFTA: Emerging Principles and Lingering Doubts*, 10 NYU Envt'l L.J. 245 (2002)
Tim Bedford & Roger Cooke, Probabilistic Risk Analysis: Foundations and Methods (2001)
M. Bedjaoui, *Responsibility of States: Fault and Strict Liability*, 10 Encyclopaedia of Public International Law 359 (1987)
Christina L. Beharry, *Objections to Requests for Documents in International Arbitration: Emerging Practices from NAFTA Chapter 11*, 27(1) ICSID Rev.—For. Inv. L.J. 33–64 (2012)
Massimo V. Benedettelli, *To Bifurcate or Not to Bifurcate? That is the (Ambiguous) Question*, (3) Arb. Int'l. 493–506 (2013)
Evrett W. Benton, *The Libyan Expropriations: Further Developments on the Remedy of Invalidation of Title*, 11 Hous. L. Rev. 924, 935 (1974)
Jacob Bercovitch & Scott Sigmund Gartner, International Conflict Mediation: New Approaches and Findings 41 (2009)
Rudolf Bernhardt, 8 Encyclopedia of Public International Law 246 (1990)
Yearbook of Commercial Arbitration, vol. XXVI 18–23 (A.J. van den Berg ed. 2001)
Albert Jan van den Berg. interview with, on the First Session (video), (March 24, 2015), available at https://livestream.com/ICSID/events/3915475/ videos/81480656
Albert Jan van den Berg, *Dissenting Opinions by Party-Appointed Arbitrators*, in Investment Arbitration in Looking to the Future: Essays on International Law in Honor of W. Michael Reisman 821–43 (Mahnoush Arsanjani et al. eds. 2011)
Albert Jan van den Berg, *Time and Costs: Issues and Initiatives from an Arbitrator's Perspective*, 28(1) ICSID Rev.—For. Inv. L.J. 218–22 (2013)
Klaus P. Berger, *The New Multilateral Investment Guaranty Agency Globalizing the Investment Insurance Approach towards Development*, 15 Syr. J. Int'l L. & Com. 13 (1988), 31
C.F. Bergsten & E.M. Graham, *Needed: New International Rules for Foreign Direct Investment*, 7 Int'l Trade J. 15 (1992)
George A. Bermann, *Navigating EU law and the Law of International Arbitration*, 28 Arb. Int'l 397 (2012)
Nathalie Bernasconi-Osterwalder et al., *Arbitrator Independence and Impartiality: Examining the Dual Role of Arbitrator and Counsel*, IV Annual Forum for Developing Country Investment Negotiators, Background Papers, 8–16 (2010)
Peter Bernstein, Against the Gods: The Remarkable Story of Risk (1998)
Ana-Mita Betancourt, *OPIC Political Risk Insurance for Infrastructure Projects in Emerging Markets*, in Project Financing in Emerging Markets 179, 183–84 (1996)
Okan Beygo, *Nationality of Corporations in International Claims Arising Out of Foreign Investment Disputes*, 46 Revue Hellénique De Droit International 33 (1993)
Pieter H.F. Biekker, *The Oil Platforms Decision*, 91 AJIL 518 (1997)
Lord Justice Bingham, *The Problem of Delay in Arbitration*, 5(4) Arb. Int'l 333 (1989)
Elizabeth Birch, *Practical and Cultural Aspects of International Mediation*, in Contemporary Issues in International Arbitration and Mediation: The Fordham Papers 2013, 472–79 (2014)

Doak Bishop & Lucy Reed, *Practical Guidelines for Interviewing, Selecting, and Challenging Party-Appointed Arbitrators in International Commercial Arbitration*, 14 Arb. Int'l 395, 408–09 (1998)

Andrea K. Bjorklund, *Contract without Privity: Sovereign Offer and Investor Acceptance*, 2 Chi. J. Int'l L. 183 (2001)

Andrea K. Bjorklund, *Waiver and the Exhaustion of the Local Remedies Rule in NAFTA Jurisprudence*, in NAFTA Investment Law and Arbitration 253 (2004)

Andrea K. Bjorkland, *The Emerging Civilization of Investment Arbitration*, 113 Penn. State L. Rev. 169, 1280 (2009)

Nigel Blackaby et al., Redfern and Hunter on international arbitration (6th ed. 2015)

Susan Blake et al., The Jackson ADR Handbook 1–2 (2013)

Patrick Blanchard, *Electric and Gas Concessions and BOTs in the Ivory Coast: Innovating Attempts During the Nineties*, 7 Int'l Bus. L.J. 829 (2000)

Gordon Blanke, *Institutional versus* Ad Hoc *Arbitration: A European Perspective*, 9(2) ERA Forum 275–82 (2008)

Marc Blessing, *The Major Western and Soviet Arbitration Rules: A Comparison of the Rules of UNCITRAL, UNCITRAL Model Law, LCIA, ICC, AAA and the Rules of the USSR Chamber of Commerce and Industry*, 6(3) J. Int'l Arb. 8 (1989)

Keith W. Blinn et al., International Petroleum Exploration and Exploitation Agreements: Legal, Economic, and Policy Aspects (1986)

Guy Block et al., *A Remarkable Example of Promotion of Arbitration and ADR: The Resolution of Disputes in the Belgian Newly Liberalized Energy Sector*, 18 Arb. Int'l 401 (2002)

Karl-Heinz Böckstiegel, *The Relevance of National Arbitration Law for Arbitrations under the UNCITRAL Rules*, 1(3) J. Int'l Arb. 223, 232–36 (1984)

John Boloro, *Aspects of the Law on the Responsibility of a Host State for Injuries Caused to Foreign Investment During Internal Armed Conflcits: The ICSID Award in Asian Agricultural Products Limited (AAPL) v. Republic of Sri Lanka*, 18 S. African Yb. Int'l L. 105–26 (1992)

Brian Eric Bomstein & Julie M. Levitt, *Much Ado About 1782: A Look at Recent Problems with Discovery in the United States for Use in Foreign Litigation under 28 § 1782*, 20 U. Miami Inter-Am. L. Rev. 429 (1989)

Stephen R. Bond, *ICC Terms of Reference Rules Saves Time and Money While Promoting Common Understanding*, Mealey's Int'l Arb. Rep., Aug. 1991, at 33

Stephen R. Bond, *How to Draft an ICC Arbitration Clause*, 7 ICSID Rev.—For. Inv. L.J. 153, 157 (1992)

Jonathan Bonnitcha, Substantive Protection under Investment Treaties: A Legal and Economic Analysis 143 *et seq.* (2014)

Edwin Borchard, Diplomatic Protection of Citizens Abroad 817 (1915)

Gary B. Born, International Commercial Arbitration in the United States 5–8 (1994)

Gary B. Born, International Arbitration: Cases and Materials 246 (2d ed. 2015) *et seq.*

Gary Born & Michal Jorek, *Dallah and the New York Convention*, Apr. 7, 2011, Kluwer Arbitration Blog

Gary Born & Marija Scekic, *Pre-Arbitration Procedural Requirements: "A Dismal Swamp,"* in Practising Virtue Inside International Arbitration 234 *et seq.* (David D. Caron et al. eds. 2015)

Leo J. Bouchez, *The Prospects for International Arbitration: Disputes between States and Private Enterprises*, 8 J. Int'l Arb. 81, 100 (1991)

Derek William Bowett, *State Contracts with Aliens: Contemporary Developments on Compensation for Termination or Breach*, 59 Brit. Yb. Int'l L. 49, 54 (1988)

Tim Boyce, Commercial Risk Management (2003)

Eric de Brabandere, *Non-State Actors and Human Rights: Corporate Responsibility and the Attempts to Formalize the Role of Corporations as Participant in the International Legal System*, in Participants in the Internatioanl Legal System: Multiple Perspectives on Non-State Actors in International Law 268 (Jean d'Aspremont ed. 2011)

Eric de Brabandere, Investment Treaty Arbitration as Public International Law 115–16 (2014)

Ronald A. Brand, External Sovereignty and International Law, 18 1685, 1692 (1995)

David J. Branson & W.M. Tupman, *Selecting an Arbitral Forum: A Guide to Cost-Effective International Arbitration*, 24 Va. J. Int'l L. 4 (1984)

David J. Branson & Richard E. Wallace, Jr., *Choosing the Substantive Law to Apply in International Commercial Arbitration*, 27 Va. J. Int'l L. 39 (1986)

Martin Dietrich Brauch, *Exhaustion of Local Remedies in International Investment Law*, IISD Best Practices Series, 7–10 (2017)

Tillman Rudolf Braun, *Globalization: The Driving Force in International Investment Law*, in The Backlash Against Investment Arbitration (Michael Waibel et al. eds. 2010)

Stavros Brekoulakis, *Systemic Bias and the Institution of International Arbitration: A New Approach to Arbitral Decision-Making*, 4 J. Int'l Disp. Settlement 553 (2013)

Lorraine M. Brennan, *Preparing the Client in an International Mediation: What to Expect from the Process*, in Contemporary Issues in International Arbitration and Mediation: The Fordham Papers 2014 139–51 (Arthur W. Rovine ed. 2015)

Thomas L. Brewer, *International Investment Dispute Settlement Procedures: The Evolving Regime for Foreign Direct Investment*, 26 L. & Pol'y. Int'l Bus. 633 (1995), 634

Aron Broches, *The Convention on the Settlement of Investment Disputes between States and Nationals of Other States: Applicable Law and Default Procedure*, in International Arbitration Liber Amicorum for Martin Domke 12 (1967)

Aron Broches, *The Convention on the Settlement of Investment Disputes between States and Nationals of Other States*, 136 Recueil Des Cours 331, 359–60 (1972-II)

Aron Broches, *Bilateral Investment Protection Treaties and Arbitration of Investment Disputes*, in Selected Essays: World Bank, ICSID, and Other Subjects of Public and Private International Law 447, 455 (1995)

A.F. Brooke II, *Great Expectations: Assessing the Contract Damages of the Take-or-Pay Producer*, 70 Tex. L. Rev. 1469 (1992)

Charles N. Brower, *Current Developments in the Law of Expropriation and Compensation: A Preliminary Survey of Awards of the Iran–United States Claims Tribunal*, 21 Int'l Law. 643 (1987)

Charles N. Brower, *Investor–State Disputes Under NAFTA: The Empire Strikes Back*, 40 Colum. J. Transnat'l L. 43 (2001)

Charles N. Brower, *The Ethics of Arbitration: Perspectives from a Practicing International Arbitrator*, 5 Berkeley J. Int'l L. Publicist 1, 3 (2010)

Charles N. Brower & Jason Brueschke, The Iran–U.S. Claims Tribunal 644 (1998)

Charles N. Brower & Lee A. Steven, *NAFTA Chapter 11: Who Then Should Judge? Developing the International Rule of Law under NAFTA Chapter 11*, 2 Chi. J. Int'l L. 193 (2001)

Charles N. Brower & Jarrod Wong, *General Principles of Valuation: The Case of Santa Elena*, in International Investment Law and Arbitration: Leading Cases from the ICSID, NAFTA, Bilateral Treaties and Customary International Law 747–76 (Todd Weiler ed. 2005)

Henry Brown & Arthur Marriott, ADR Principles and Practice 108 (1993)
J. Jeffrey Brown, *The Jurisprudence of the Foreign Claims Settlement Commission: Viet Nam Claims*, 27 Va. J. Int'l L. 99, 100 (1986)
Ian Brownlie, International Law and the Use of Force by States 289 (1963)
Vienna Convention on the Law of Treaties, in Basic Documents of International Law 349 (Ian Brownlie ed. 1983), available at http://www.un.org/law/ilc
Ian Brownlie, System of the Law of the Nations 452 (1986)
Ian Brownlie, Principles of Public International Law 508–09 (2003)
Gianluca Brusco, *Eurocentrism and Political Conditionality: The Case of the Lomé Convention*, in Europe, Diplomacy and Development 103 (Carol Cosgrove-Sacks ed. & Carla Santos assist. ed. 2001)
Peter Buckley, The Strategy and Organization of International Business (1993)
Christian Bühring-Uhle, Arbitration and Mediation in International Business 273 (1996)
Jennifer M. Bund, Note and Comment, *Force Majeure Clauses: Drafting Advice for the CISG Practitioner*, 17 JL & Com. 381, 399–401 (1998)
M. Bunter, *Indonesia: From Concession to Contract*, published in Oil, Gas & Energy Law Intelligence (OGEL) "Special Feature: Production Sharing Contracts," in 3(1), available at http://www.gasandoil.com/ogel
Markus Burgstaller, Theories of Compliance with International Law (2004)
Markus Burgstaller, *Nationality of Corporate Investors and International Claims against the Investor's Own State*, 7 JWI 857–82 (2006)
Markus Burgstaller & Michael Waibel, "Investment Codes," in VI Max Planck Encyclopedia of Public International Law 300–09 (Rudiger Wolfrum ed. 2012)
F.N. Burton & Hisashi Inoue, *Expropriations of Foreign-Owned Firms in Developing Countries: A Cross-National Analysis*, 18 J. World Trade L. 396, 397 (1984)
Steven J. Burton, *Combining Conciliation with Arbitration of International Commercial Disputes*, 18 Hastings Int'l Comp. L. Rev. 637, 639 (1995)
T. Büthe & H. Milner, *Bilateral Investment Treaties and Foreign Direct Investment: A Political Analysis*, in The Effect of Treaties on Foreign Direct Investment—Bilateral Investment Treaties, Double Taxation Treaties, and Investment Flows 171 *et seq.* (Karl P. Sauvant & Lisa E. Sachs eds. 2009)
Nicholas Butler, *Arbitration and Conciliation Treaties*, in Max Planck Encyclopedia of Public International Law (2006)
Katherarina A. Byrne, *Regulatory Expropriation and State Intent*, Can. Yb. Int'l L. 89, 93 (2000)
James Cable, Gun boat Diplomacy: Political Applications of Limited Force (1981)
N. Jansen Calamita, *International Human Rights and the Interpretation of International Investment Treaties: Constitutional Considerations*, in Investment Law within International Law: Integrationist Perspectives 178 (Freya Baetens ed. 2013)
N. Jansen Calamita, *The Principle of Proportionality and the Problem of Indeterminacy in International Investment Treaties*, Yb. Int'l. Inv. L. & Pol'y. 157 (2013–14)
Peter D. Cameron, *Creating a Legal Framework for Investment in the Commonwealth of Independent States Energy Sector: Lessons from the Energy Charter Experiment*, 1 Tulsa J. Comp. & Int'l L. 233 (1994)
Peter D. Cameron, International Energy Investment Law: The Pursuit of Stability, paras 1.73–1.113 (2010)
Julien Cantegreil, *The Audacity of the Texaco/Calasiatic Award: René-Jean Dupuy and the Internationalization of Foreign Investment Law*, 22(2) EJIL 441, 444–48 (2011)
Thomas E. Carbonneau, Cases and Materials on the Law and Practice of Arbitration 27 (2000)

Andrea Carlevaris, *Preliminary Matters: Bi-furcation, Request for Provisional Measures*, in Litigating International Investment Arbitration Disputes: A Practitioner's Guide 180 (Chiara Giorgetti ed. 2014)
David D. Caron, *Reputation and Reality in the ICSID Annulment Process*, 7 ICSID Rev.—For. Inv. L.J. 21 (1992)
Dominique Carreau & Patrick Juillard, Droit International Economique 387 (2003)
Barry E. Carter, *International Economic Sanctions: Improving the Haphazard U.S. Legal Regime*, 75 Cal. L. Rev. 1159, 1173 (1987)
James H. Carter, *Dispute Resolution and International Agreements*, 703 PLI/ Comm. Law & Prac. Course Handbook Series 405 (1994)
Bruno de Cazalet, *Construction Contracts in the Framework of BOT Projects*, 1998 Int'l Bus. L.J. 405 (1998)
Carles Chatterjee, *The Use of the Discounted Cash Flow Method in the Assessment of Compensation: Comments on the Recent World Bank Guidelines on the Treatment of Foreign Direct Investment,* 10(4) J. Int'l Arb. 19 (1993)
Pratap Chatterjee, *The Convention Establishing the Multilateral Guarantee Agency*, 36 ICLQ 76 (1987)
Beng Cheng, General Principles of Law as Applied by International Courts and Tribunals 112–14 (1993)
Pat K. Chew, *Political Risk in U.S. Investments in China: Chimera of Protection and Predictability?*, 34 Va. J. Int'l L. 615, 669 (1994)
A.Z. El Chiati, *Protection of Investment in the Context of Petroleum Agreements*, 4 Recueil des Cours 9 (1988)
Yen Yee Chong, Investment Risk Management (2004)
Barnali Choudhury, *Evolution or Devolution? Defining Fair and Equitable Treatment in International Investment Law*, 6 J. World Inv. & Trade 297 (2005)
Gordon Christenson, *U.S.–Rumanian Agreement of March 30, 1960*, 55 AJIL 452 (1961)
G.C. Christie, *What Constitutes a Taking of Property under International Law*, 38 Brit. Yb. Int'l Law 307, 310–11 (1964)
Amy L. Chua, *The Privatization-Nationalization Cycle: The Link between Markets and Ethnicity in Developing Countries*, 95 Col. L. Rev. 223, 239 (1995)
Brice M. Clagett, *Present State of the International Law of Compensation for Expropriated Property and Repudiated State Contracts*, in Private Investors Abroad § 12.05[2][a] (Southwestern Legal Foundation ed. 1989)
Michael Clancy & Thomas W. Wälde, *Efficiency in Mediation: Solving a Complex Cross-Border Energy Infrastructure Dispute in the Shadow of Three Moving Regulatory Regimes*, 5 J. World Inv. & Trade 257 (2004)
Maria Nicole Cleis, The Independence and Impartiality of ICSID Arbitrators Current Case Law, Alternative Approaches, and Improvement Suggestions (2017)
Christopher Clement-Davies, *Public/ Private Partnerships in Central and Eastern Europe: Structuring the Concession Agreement*, 2001(1) Bus. L. Int'l 17 (2001), version available at https://heinonline.org/HOL/Page?collection=journals &handle=hein.journals/blawintnl2001&id=21&men_tab=srchresults
Margarita T.B. Coale, *Stabilization Clauses in International Petroleum Transactions*, 30 Denv. J. Int'l L. & Pol'y. 217 (2002)
Matthew B. Cobb, *The Development of Arbitration in Foreign Investment*, Mealey's Int'l Arb. Rep. (Apr. 2001)
Jack Coe, Jr., *Metalclad—A Retrospective*, in NAFTA Arbitration Reports 65 (Chris Thomas & Cameron Mowatt eds. 2002)

Jack Coe, Jr., *Taking Stock of NAFTA Chapter 11 in Its Tenth Year: An Interim Sketch of Selected Themes, Issues, and Methods*, 36 Vand. J. Transnat'l L 1381 (2003)
Jack Coe, Jr. & Noah Rubins, *Regulatory Expropriation and the Tecmed Case: Context and Contributions*, in International Investment Law and Arbitration 597 (Todd Weiler ed. 2005)
Dagmar Coester-Waltjen, *German Conflict Rules and the Multinational Enterprise*, 6 Ga. J. Int'l & Comp. L. 197–226 (1976)
Michael Collins, *Privacy and Confidentiality in Arbitration Proceedings*, 11 Arb. Int'l 321 (1995)
R. Collins, *Alternative Dispute Resolution: Choosing the Best Option*, 2(3) Australian Construction Law Newsletter 3 (1989)
Commerce, The Official Newsletter of the C.I.S.-American Chamber of Commerce (Fall 1995)
Anthony Connerty, *The Role of ADR in the Resolution of International Disputes*, 12 Arb. Int'l 47 (1996)
Silvia Constain, *Mediation in Investor–State Dispute Settlement: Government Policy and the Changing Landscape*, 29(1) ICSID Rev.—For. Inv. L.J. 25–40 (2014)
George Coombs, Jr., *International Dispute Resolution*, in Transnational Litigation 7–12 to 7–14 (1992)
Investment Protection and the Energy Charter Treaty (Graham Coop & Clarisse Ribeiro eds. 2008)
Carlos M. Correa, *Investment Protection in Bilateral and Free Trade Agreements: Implications for the Granting of Compulsory Licences*, 26 Mich. J. Int'l L. 331 (2004)
Carlos M. Correa & Jorge E. Viñuales, *Intellectual Property Rights as Protected Investments: How Open are the Gates?* 19(1) J. Int'l Econ. L. 91–120 (2016)
Jean-Pierre Cot, International Conciliation 193 (1972)
Jean-Pierre Cot, *Conciliation*, in Max Planck Encyclopedia of Public International Law, para. 3 (2006)
Lorenzo Cotula, *Reconciling Regulatory Stability and Evolution of Environmental Standards in Investment Contracts: Towards a Rethink of Stabilization Clauses*, 1 J. World Energy L. 158–79 (2008)
W. Laurence Craig et al., Annotated Guide to the 1998 ICC Arbitration Rules 3–18 (1998)
W. Laurence Craig et al., International Chamber of Commerce Arbitration 155–60 (3d ed. 2000)
William Craig, *Uses and Abuses of Appeal from Awards*, 4 Arb. Int'l 174 (1988)
James Crawford, *Second Report on State Responsibility*, 2 Yearbook of the International Law Commission, A/CN.4/SER.A/1999/Add.1 (Part 1), 83 (1999)
James Crawford, The International Law Commission's Articles on State Responsibility: Introduction, Text and Commentaries 96 (2002)
James Crawford, *Treaty and Contract in Investment Arbitration*, 24(3) Arb. Int'l 351–74 (2008)
The Law of International Responsibility (James Crawford et al. eds. 2010)
James Crawford, Brownlie's Principles of Public International Law 721 (8th ed. 2012)
Bernardo Cremades, *Global Mediation*, Israel Bar Ass'n. Newsletter (May 3, 2003), available at http://www.israelbar.org.il/article_inner.asp?catID=179&pgID=3559
Bernardo Cremades & David Cairns, *Transnational Policy in International Arbitral Decision-Making: The Cases of Bribery, Money Laundering and Fraud*, in Dossiers of the ICC Institute of World Business Law—Money Laundering, Corruption and Fraud 65 (2003)

John R. Crook, *Applicable Law in International Arbitration: The Iran–U.S. Claims Tribunal Experience*, 83 AJIL 278 (1989)

Luis Enrique Cuervo & Vernon Valentine Palmer, *Judicial Protection of Foreign Investors in Latin America: Exposé des Motifs*, 77 Tul. L. Rev. 1053, 1054 (2003)

Alvaro Cuervo-Cazurra, *Host Country Concerns and Policies toward State-Owned MNEs*, Columbia FDI Perspectives on Topical Foreign Direct Investment Issues, No. 237 (Oct. 22, 2018), available at http://ccsi.columbia.edu/files/2016/ 10/No-237-Cuervo-Cazurra-FINAL.pdf

Gennady M. Danilenko, *International Jus Cogens: Issues of Law-Making*, 2(1) Eur. J. Int'l L. 42 (1991), available at http://www.ejil.org/journal/Vol2/No1/art3.html

Frank Dawson & Burns Weston, *"Prompt Adequate and Effective": A Universal Standard of Compensation?*, 30 Fordham L. Rev. 727, 738 (1962)

Michail Dekastros, *Portfolio Investment: Reconceptualising the Notion of Investment under the ICSID Convention*, 14(2) JWIT 286–319 (2013)

Georges R. Delaume, *Convention on the Settlement of Investment Disputes between States and Nationals of Other States*, 1 Int'l Law. 64, 70 (1966)

Georges R. Delaume, Transnational Contracts: Applicable Law and Settlement of Disputes (1982)

Georges R. Delaume, *Le Centre International pour le Réglement des Différends Relatifs aux Investissements (CIRDI)*, 109 J. de Droit Int'l 775, 797 (1982)

Georges R. Delaume, *Sovereign Immunity and Transnational Arbitration*, 3 Int'l Arb. 28 (1987)

Georges R. Delaume, Law and Practice of Transnational Contracts 4–30 (1988)

Georges R. Delaume, *The Finality of Arbitration Involving States: Recent Developments*, 5 Arb. Int'l 21 (1989)

Georges R. Delaume, *How to Draft an ICSID Arbitration Clause*, 7 ICSID Rev.—For. Inv. L.J. 168 (1992)

Georges R. Delaume, *Consent to ICSID Arbitration*, in The Changing World of International Law in the Twenty-First Century 155, 174 (1998)

Joseph W. Dellapenna, *Foreign State Immunity in Europe*, 5 NY Int'l L. Rev. 51 (1992)

Eileen D. Denza & Shelagh B. Brooks, *International Protection of Investment Treaties*, 36 ICLQ 909 (1987)

Eileen Denza & Shelagh Brooks, *Investment Protection Treaties: United Kingdom Experience*, 36 ICLQ 908, 917 (1987); https://www.cambridge.org/core/journals/international-and-comparative-law-quarterly/issue/908B5E76F670D1AA407522739BF18F89?sort=canonical.position%3Aasc&pageNum=1&searchWithinIds=908B5E76F670D1AA407522739BF18F89&productType=JOURNAL_ARTICLE&template=cambridge-core%2Fjournal%2Farticle-listings%2Flistings-wrapper&hideArticleJournalMetaData=true&displayNasaAds=false

Yves Derains & Eric A. Schwartz, A Guide to ICC Arbitration 76–109 (2d ed. 2005)

V.S. Deshpande, *How International Arbitration Can Always Prevail over Litigation*, 4(4) J. Int'l Arb. 9 (1987)

Human Rights Obligations of Business: Beyond the Corporate Responsibility to Respect? (Surya Deva & David Bilchitz eds. 2013)

John S. Diaconis, *Political Risk Insurance: OPIC's Use of a "Fiduciary Agent" to Facilitate Resolution of Subrogation Claims*, 23 Int'l L. 271 (1989)

A.V. Dicey, Introduction to the Study of the Law of the Constitution (8th ed. 1982)

A.V. Dicey & J.H.C. Morris, Conflict of Laws (13th ed. 2000)

Michael Dickstein, *Revitalizing International Law Governing Concession Agreements*, 6 INT'L TAX & BUS. LAW. 54 (1988)

Rocío Digón & Marek Krasula, *The ICC's Role in Administering Investment Arbitration Disputes*, in CONTEMPORARY ISSUES IN INTERNATIONAL ARBITRATION AND MEDIATION: THE FORDHAM PAPERS (8) 2014 58 *et seq.* (Arthur W. Rovine ed. 2015)

ANGELOS DIMOPOULOS, EU FOREIGN INVESTMENT LAW 259 *et seq.* (2011)

Ricky H. Diwan, *Problems Associated with the Enforcement of Arbitral Awards Revisited*, 19 ARB. INT'L 55 (2003)

Angelos Dimopoulus, *EC Free Trade Agreements: An Alternative Model for Addressing Human Rights in Foreign Investment Regulation and Dispute Settlement?* in HUMAN RIGHTS IN INTERNATIONAL INVESTMENT LAW AND ARBITRATION 592 (PIERRE-MARIE DUPUY ET AL. EDS. 2009)

Yoram Dinstein, *Diplomatic Protection of Companies under International Law*, in INTERNATIONAL LAW: THEORY AND PRACTICE 505 (Karel Wellens ed. 1998)

Aïssatou Diop, *Objection under Rule 41(5) of the ICSID Arbitration Rules*, 25(2) ICSID REV.—FOR. INV. L.J. 312–36 (2010)

William S. Dodge, *Exhaustion of Remedies and Res Judicata under Chapter Eleven of NAFTA*, 23 HASTINGS INT'L & COMP. L. REV. 357, 361–62 (2000)

William S. Dodge, *International Decision: Metalclad Corp. v. Mexico*, 95 AJIL 910 (2001)

William S. Dodge, *Investor–State Dispute Settlement between Developed Countries: Reflections on the Australia–United States Free Trade Agreement*, 39(1) VAND. J. TRANSNAT'L L. 1–37 (2006)

Rudolf Dolzer, *Indirect Expropriation of Alien Property*, 1 ICSID REV.—FOR. INV. L.J. 41 (1986)

Rudolph Dolzer, *Indirect Expropriations: New Developments?* 11 NYU ENVIRON. L.J. 64, 65 (2003)

RUDOLF DOLZER & MARGRETE STEVENS, BILATERAL INVESTMENT TREATIES 81 (1995)

RUDOLF DOLZER & CHRISTOPH SCHREUER, PRINCIPLES OF INTERNATIONAL INVESTMENT LAW 7–8 (2d ed. 2012) ENCYCLOPEDIA OF PUBLIC INTERNATIONAL LAW 96 (Rudolf Dolzer et al. eds. 1987)

Lord Donaldson, *Alternative Dispute Resolution*, 58 Arb. 102 (1992)

Patrick J. Donovan, *Creeping Expropriation and MIGA: The Need for Tighter Regulation in the Political Risk Insurance Market*, 7 GONZ. J. INT'L L. 10 (2003–04), available at http://blogs.law.gonzaga.edu/gjil/2006/03/creeping-expropriation-and-miga-the-need-for- tighter-regulation-in-the-political-risk-insurance-mar/

Zachary Douglas, *The Hybrid Foundations of Investment Treaty Arbitration*, 74 BRIT. YB. INT'L L. 151, 282 (2003)

ZACHARY DOUGLAS, THE INTERNATIONAL LAW OF INVESTMENT CLAIMS 321 (4th ed. 2009) (Rule 37)

Zachary Douglas, *Property, Investment and the Scope of Investment Protection Obligations*, in THE FOUNDATIONS OF INTERNATIONAL INVESTMENT LAW: BRINGING THEORY INTO PRACTICE 377–78 (Zachary Douglas et al. eds. 2014)

Stephen J. Doyle, *International Boycotts*, in THE LAW OF TRANSNATIONAL BUSINESS TRANSACTIONS (Ved P. Nanda ed. 2005)

Matthew Duchesne, *The Continuous- Nationality-of-Claims Principle: Its Historical Development and Current Relevance to Investor–State Investment Disputes*, 36 GW INT'L L. REV. 783 (2004)

CHRISTOPHER DUGAN et al., INVESTOR–STATE ARBITRATION 491 (2012)

Patrick Dumberry, *The Quest to Define "Fair and Equitable Treatment" for Investors under International Law: The Case of the NAFTA Chapter 11 Pope & Talbot Awards*, 3 J. WORLD INV. 657 (2002)

Patrick Dumberry, *Are BITs Representing the "New" Customary International Law in International Investment Law?* 28(4) Penn. State Int'l L. Rev. 676–701 (2010)

Patrick Dumberry, *The Legal Standing of Shareholders before Arbitral Tribunals: Has Any Rule of Customary International Law Crystallized?* 18(3) Mich. J. Int'l L. 353 *et seq.* (2010)

Patrick Dumberry & Gabrielle Dumas-Aubin, *A Few Pragmatic Observations on How BITs should be Modified to Incorporate Human Rights Obligations*, 11(1) TDM 2 (2014)

Hew Dundas, *Mediation in the Oil and Gas Industry*, 2(3) Oil, Gas & Energy Law Intelligence 2 (July 2004)

Pierre-Marie Dupuy, *Unification Rather than Fragmentation of International Law? The Case of International Investment Law and Human Rights Law*, in Human Rights in International Investment Law and Arbitration 45–62 (Pierre-Marie Dupuy et al. eds. 2009)

Figueres Jiménes Dyalá, *Multi-Tiered Dispute Resolution Clauses in ICC Arbitration*, 14(1) ICC Int'l Ct. Arb. Bull. 71 (2003)

Roberto Echandi, *Complementing Investor–State Dispute Resolution: A Conceptual Framework for Investor–State Conflict Management*, in Prospects in International Investment Law and Policy 270 (Roberto Echandi & Pierre Suave eds. 2013)

Roberto Echandi & P. Kher, *Can International Investor–State Disputes Be Prevented? Empirical Evidence from Settlements in ICSID Arbitration*, 29(1) ICSID Rev.—For. Inv. L.J. 41 *et seq.* (2014)

ECT Secretariat, *Changing Dynamics of Investment Cases under the Energy Charter Treaty (ECT)* (May 18, 2018), available at https://energycharter.org/what-we-do/dispute-settlement/cases- up-to-18-may-2018/ (cases as of May 18, 2018)

Don't Sue, The Economist, Oct. 26, 2002, at 34

The Economist Intelligence Unit, Country Reports, available at http://www.eiu.com

The Economist Intelligence Unit, Country Risk Service, available at http://www.eiu.

Frédéric Eisemann, *La clause d'arbitrage pathologique*, in Arbitrage Commercial-Essais in Memoriam Eugenio Minolo 129 (1974)

Pierre Michel Eisemann, *The Court of Arbitration: Outline of its Changes from Inception to the Present Day*, in International Chamber of Commerce: 60 Years of ICC Arbitration 391, 397 (1984)

Cheri D. Eklund, *A Primer on the Arbitration of NAFTA Chapter Eleven Investor-State Disputes*, 11(4) J. Int'l Arb. 159, 135–171 (1994)

Troy Elder, *The Case against Awards of Specific Performance in Transnational Commercial Disputes*, 13(1) Arb. Int'l 1 (1997)

Mahmoud A. El-Gamal, *Interest and the Paradox of Contemporary Islamic Law and Finance*, 26 Fordham Int'l L.J. 108, 126 (2003)

Hamed El-Kady, *Towards a New Conceptualization of International Investment Agreements*, BCDR 3(2) Int'l Arb. Rev. 331 (2016)

Z. Elkins et al., *Competing for Capital: The Diffusion of Bilateral Investment Treaties, 1960–2000*, in The Backlash against Investment Arbitration: Perceptions and Reality 369–406 (Michael Waibel et al. eds. 2010)

Richard A. Epstein, Takings: Private Property and the Power of Eminent Domain (1985)

Claude B. Erb et al., *Political Risk, Financial Risk and Economic Risk*, 52(6) Financial Analysts J. 28 (Nov./Dec. 1996), available at http://www.duke.edu/~charvey/Country_risk/pol/pol.htm

Alejandro Escobar, *Requirements Ratione Materiae*, in Course on Dispute Settlement in International Trade, Investment and Intellectual Property 19 (2003)

Hélène Ruiz Fabri, *The Approach Taken by the European Court of Human Rights to the Assessment of Compensation for "Regulatory Expropriations" of the Property of Foreign Investors*, 11 NYU ENVIRON. L.J. 148 (2003)

Alexander P. Fachiri, *Expropriation in International Law*, 6 BRIT. YB. INT'L L. 159, 169–70 (1925)

Alexander P. Fachiri, *International Law and the Property of Aliens*, 10 BRIT. YB. INT'L L. 32 (1929)

Halliburton Fales, *A Comparison of Compensation for Nationalization of Alien Property with Standards of Compensation under United States Domestic Law*, 5 NORTHWESTERN J. INT'L L. & BUS. 871, 876 (1983)

Abdullah Al Faruque, *Creating Customary International Law through Bilateral Investment Treaties: a Critical Appraisal*, 44(2) INDIAN J. INT'L L. 292 (2004)

Nazila Fathi, *Conservatives in Iran Battle the Spread of Foreign Investment*, NY TIMES, Oct. 10, 2004, at 20

ARGHYRIS A. FATOUROS, GOVERNMENT GUARANTEES TO FOREIGN INVESTORS (1962)

J.E.S. Fawcett, *Some Foreign Effects of Nationalisation of Property*, 27 BRIT. YB. INT'L L. 355 (1950)

Mark Feldman, *The Annulment Proceedings and the Finality of ICSID Arbitral Awards*, 2 ICSID REV.—FOR. INV. L.J. 85 (1987)

A.A. de Fina, *Different Strokes for Different Folks: Institutional Appointment of Arbitrators*, ARB. & DISP. RES. L.J. 31–35 (2000)

J.D. Fine, *Continuum or Chasm? Can West Meet East? Commercial Arbitration and Alternative Dispute Resolution Techniques in the Western Nations of the LAWASIA Region*, 6(4) J. INT'L ARB. 27, 31–33 (1989)

Robert D. Fischer & Roger S. Haydock, *International Commercial Disputes: Drafting an Enforceable Arbitration Agreement*, 21 WM. MITCHELL L. REV. 941, 947–48 (1996)

Vincent Fischer- Zernin et al., *Arbitration and Mediation: Synthesis or Antithesis?* 5(1) J. INT'L ARB. 21 (1988)

ROGER FISHER ET AL., GETTING TO YES 42–55 (1991)

Talia Fisher, *Law and Economics of Alternative Dispute Resolution*, in 3 THE OXFORD HANDBOOK OF LAW & ECONOMICS, ch. 14 (Francesco Parisi ed. 2017)

Peter F. Fitzgerald, *Overview of Risks in International Financing*, 707 PLI/COMM. L. & PRAC. COURSE HANDBOOK SERIES 7 (1995)

Gerald Fitzmaurice, *The Problem of the Non-Appearing Defendant Government*, 51 BRIT. YB. INT'L L. 89 (1980)

ISI FOIGHEL, NATIONALIZATION: A STUDY IN THE PROTECTION OF ALIEN PROPERTY IN INTERNATIONAL LAW 19 (1957)

RALPH H. FOLSOM ET AL., INTERNATIONAL BUSINESS TRANSACTIONS (1992)

Emmanuel Fontaine, *Unforeseeability in BOT Contracts for Public Infrastructure*, 15 INT'L CONSTRUCTION L. REV. 504 (1998)

Foreign Claims Settlement Commission Announces the Commencement of the Albanian Claims Program, 6 WORLD ARB. & MED. REP. 171.

L. Yves Fortier, *The Occasionally Unwarranted Assumption of Confidentiality*, 15 ARB. INT'L 131 (1999)

L. Yves Fortier, *Caveat Investor: The Meaning of "Expropriation" and the Protection Afforded Investors under NAFTA*, NEWS FROM ICSID, Summer 2003, at 1, 10

L. Yves Fortier & Stephen L. Drymer, *Indirect Expropriation in the Law of International Investment: I Know It When I See It, or Caveat Investor*, 19 ICSID REV.— FOR. INV. L.J. 293 (2004)

ENFORCEMENT OF INVESTMENT TREATY ARBITRATION AWARDS: A GLOBAL GUIDE 121 *et seq.* (Julien Fouret ed. 2015)

Federal Reserve Bank of San Francisco, *Learning from Argentina's Crisis*, FRBSF Economic Letter 2002–31, Oct. 18, 2002, available at available at http://www.frbsf.org/publications/economics/letter/2002/el2002-31.html

Francesco Francioni, *Access to Justice, Denial of Justice and International Investment Law*, in HUMAN RIGHTS IN INTERNATIONAL INVESTMENT LAW AND ARBITRATION 64 (Pierre-Marie Dupuy et al. eds. 2009)

Susan D. Franck, *Rationalizing Costs in Investment Arbitration*, 88(4) WASH. UNIV. L. REV. 769 (2011)

Susan D. Franck & Anna Joubin-Bret, *Investor–State Mediation: A Simulation*, 29(1) ICSID REV.—FOR. INV. L.J. 90–111 (2014)

Susan D. Franck, *Using Investor–State Mediation Rules to Promote Conflict Management: An Introductory Guide*, 29(1) ICSID REV.—FOR. INV. L.J. 66–89 (2014)

Sarah François-Poncet & Caline Mouawad, *Observations on Nagel v. Czech Republic*, 2004(1) STOCKHOLM ARB. REP. 168

Steven Franklin & Gerald T. West, *The Overseas Private Investment Corporation Amendments Act of 1978: A Reaffirmation of the Developmental Role of Investment Insurance*, 14 TEX. INT'L L.J. 1 (1979)

Elyse M. Freeman, *Regulatory Expropriation under NAFTA Chapter 11: Some Lessons from the European Court of Human Rights*, 42 COLUM. J. TRANSNAT'L L. 177 (2003)

Jody Freeman, *The Contracting State*, 28 FLA. ST. U.L. REV. 155 (2000)

Paul Friedland & E. Wong, *Measuring Damages for the Deprivation of Income-Producing Property*, 6 ICSID REV.—FOR. INV. L.J. 400 (1991)

Paul Friedland, *AAPL v. Sri Lanka: Rethinking Protection and Security for 21st Century Claims (Arbitration Academy* 2016, *The Berthold Goldman Lecture)*, 3 LES CAHIERS DE L'ARBITRAGE/PARIS J. INT'L ARB. 605–29 (2016)

Aldo Frignani, *Drafting Arbitration Agreements*, 24(4) ARB. INT'L 561–70 (2008)

James D. Fry, *International Human Rights Law in Investment Arbitration: Evidence of International Law's Unity*, 18 DUKE J. COMP. & INT'L L. 102 (2007)

James D. Fry & Odysseas G. Repousis, *Towards a New World for Investor–State Arbitration Through Transparency*, 48 NYU J. INT'L L. & POL. 795 (2016)

JASON D. FRY et al., THE SECRETARIAT'S GUIDE TO ICC ARBITRATION paras. 3-32 and 3-120 (No. 729E, 2012)

Emmanuel Gaillard, *Some Notes on the Drafting of ICSID Arbitration Clauses*, 477 PLI/COMM. LAW & PRAC. COURSE HANDBOOK SERIES 33 (1988)

Emmanuel Gaillard, *Chronique des sentences arbitrales*, 126 J.D.I. 273, 292 (1999)

EMMANUEL GAILLARD, LA JURISPRUDENCE DU CIRDI 788 (2004)

Emmanuel Gaillard, *Investment Treaty Arbitration and Jurisdiction Over Contract Claims: the SGS Cases Considered*, in International Investment Law and Arbitration 325 (2005)

Emmanuel Gaillard & Yas Banifatemi, *The Meaning of "and" in Article 42(1), Second Sentence, of the Washington Convention: The Role of International Law in the ICSID Choice of Law Process*, 18 ICSID REV.—FOR. INV. L.J. 375 (2003)

Glenn Gallins, *Bilateral Investment Protection Treaties*, 2 J. ENERGY NAT. RESOURCES & ENVT'L L. 77 (1984)

Nick Gallus, *No Joy for British Mining Company at ICSID*, 2(4) OIL, GAS & ENERGY LAW INTELLIGENCE (2004)

David A. Gantz, *Symposium: Global Trade Issues in the New Millennium: Potential Conflicts between Investor Rights and Environmental Regulation under NAFTA's Chapter 11, 33 Geo. Wash. Int'l L. Rev.* 651, 721–23 (2001)

David A. Gantz, *The Evolution of FTA Investment Provisions: From NAFTA to the United States–Chile Free Trade Agreement*, 19 AM. U. INT'L L. REV. 679, 740–46 (2004)

F.V. García-Amador, *State Responsibility in Case of "Stabilization" Clauses*, 2 J. Transnat'l L. & Pol'y. 23, 50 (1993)
F.V. García-Amador, *The Proposed New International Economic Order: A New Approach to the Law Governing Nationalization and Compensation*, 12 Law. Americas—U. Miami J. Int'l L. 1 (1980)
David Gaukrodger, *Appointing Authorities and the Selection of Arbitrators in Investor–State Dispute Settlement: An Overview*, OECD Consultation Paper (March 2018)
David Gaukrodger & K. Gordon, *Investor–State Dispute Settlement: A Scoping Paper for the Investment Policy Community*, OECD Working Papers on International Investment, at 19, 2012/03, available at http://dx.doi.org/10.1787/5k46b1r85j6f-en
Tarcisio Gazzini, *The Role of Customary International Law in the Field of Foreign Investment*, 8(5) J. World Inv. 691–715 (2007)
Tarcisio Gazzini, *Nigeria and Morocco Move Towards a "New Generation" of Bilateral Investment Treaties*, *EJIL:Talk!*, May 8, 2017, available at https://www.ejiltalk.org/nigeria-and- morocco-move-towards-a-new-generation-of-bilateral-investment-treaties/
Michael A. Geist, *Toward a General Agreement on the Regulation of Foreign Direct Investment*, 26 L. & Pol'y. Int'l Bus. 673, 686–706 (1995)
Hamid Gharavi, The International Effectiveness of the Annulment of an Arbitration Award 29 (2002)
Judith Gill & M. Gearing, *Contractual Claims and Bilateral Investment Treaties: A Comparative Review of the SGS Cases*, J. Int'l Arb. 397 (2004)
Tom Ginsburg, *International Substitutes for Domestic Institutions: Bilateral Investment Treaties and Governance*, 25 Int'l Rev. L. & Economics 107, 119 (2005)
Chiara Giorgetti, *Challenges of International Investment Arbitrators: How Does it Work, and Does it Work?*, 7 World Arb. & Mediation Rev. 303 (2013)
Chiara Giorgetti, *Who Decides Who Decides in International Investment Arbitration?*, 35 U. Pa. J. Int'l. L. 431, 446 (2013)
Chiara Giorgetti, *The Arbitral Tribunal: Selection and Replacement of Arbitrators*, in Litigating International Investment Disputes: A Practitioner's Guide 143–72 (2014)
Teresa Giovannini, *Ex Officio Powers to Investigate: When Do Arbitrators Cross the Line?* in Stories from The Hearing Room: Experience from Arbitral Practice (Essays in Honour of Michael E. Schneider) 60 (Domitille Baizeau & Bernd Ehle eds. 2015)
Global Arbitration Review, *How Long Is Too Long to Wait for an Award?* (Feb. 18, 2016), available at https://vannin.com/press/pdfs/18-2-16_How_long_is_too_long_to_wait_for_an_ award_.pdf
Stanley J. Glod, *The Foreign Claims Settlement Commission of the United States: Resolutions of International Claims in the Nineties and Beyond*, 37 Fed. Bar News & J. 140 (1990)
George E. Glos, *The Effect of Foreign Decrees of Expropriation in the Courts of the Forum*, 19 S. Tex. L.J. 241 (1978)
Stephen B. Goldberg, *The Dynamic of Mediation: Is Creative Genius the Key to Successful Mediation?*, paper given at the WIPO Conference on Mediation in Geneva (Mar. 29, 1996), available at http://www.arbiter.wipo.int/events/conferences/1996/ goldberg.html.
Jean-Claude Goldsmith, *How to Draft Terms of Reference*, 3 Arb. Int'l 298 (1987
Heribert Golsong, *A Guide to Procedural Issues in International Arbitration*, 18 Int'l Law. 633, 634–35 (1984)
J. Gomez-Ibanez, *Private Infrastructure in Developing Countries: Lessons from Recent Experience*, paper presented to the Commission on Growth and Development at the Workshop "Global Trends and Challenges," New Haven, CT, Sept. 28–29, 2007

MICHAEL W. GORDON, THE CUBAN NATIONALIZATIONS: THE DEMISE OF FOREIGN PRIVATE PROPERTY 69–108 (1976)

Richard J. Graving, *The International Commercial Arbitration Institutions: How Good A Job Are They Doing?*, 4 AM. UJ INT'L L. & POL'Y. 319, 323 n.12 (1989)

Richard J. Graving, *Mini-Glossary of Treaty Terms* (1992), available from the Institute for Transnational Arbitration at http://www.cailaw.org/ita

Richard J. Graving, *Status of the New York Arbitration Convention: Some Gaps in Coverage by New Acceptances Confirm its Vitality*, 10 ICSID REV.—FOR. INV. L.J. 1, 8 (1995)

Cheryl W. Gray & William W. Jarosz, *Law and the Regulation of Foreign Direct Investment: The Experience from Central and Eastern Europe*, 33 COLUM. J. TRANSNAT'L L. 1 (1995)

Jonathan J. Green, *Managing Risks in International Power Projects*, 672 PLI/COMM. L. & PRAC. COURSE HANDBOOK SERIES 669 (1993)

Jonathan Clark Green, *Are International Institutions Doing Their Job?*, 90 AM. SOC'Y. INT'L L. PROC. 62, 70 (1996)

Simon Greenberg, *Arbitral Award Scrutiny under Scrutiny: An Assessment*, in ARBITRAL INSTITUTIONS UNDER SCRUTINY: ASA SPECIAL SERIES No. 40, 89 (Philipp Habegger et al. eds. 2013)

Christopher Greenwood, *State Responsibility for the Decisions of National Courts*, in ISSUES OF STATE RESPONSIBILITY BEFORE INTERNATIONAL JUDICIAL INSTITUTIONS 55, 61–68 (2004)

Lucy Greenwood, *Does Bifurcation Really Promote Efficiency?* 28(2) J. INT'L ARB. 105–11, 107 (2011)

Todd J. Grierson-Weiler & Ian A. Laird, *Standards of Treatment*, in THE OXFORD HANDBOOK OF INTERNATIONAL INVESTMENT LAW 261–304 (Peter Muchlinski et al. eds. 2008)

Gavan Griffith, *Constitution of Arbitral Tribunals: The Duty of Impartiality in Tribunals or Choose your Arbitrator Wisely*, 16 THE ARBITRATOR: J. OF THE INSTITUTE OF ARBITRATORS AUSTRALIA 229 (1998)

Gavan Griffith & Andrew D. Mitchell, *Contractual Dispute Resolution in International Trade: The UNCITRAL Arbitration Rules (*1976*) and the UNCITRAL Conciliation Rules (1980)*, 3(1) MELBOURNE J. INT'L. L. 197 *et seq.* (2002)

James H. Grossman & David M. Frost, *Foreign Claims Settlement Commission of the United States—A Paradigm for International Claims Resolution*, 21 INT'L BUS. LAW. 276, 276–77 (1993)

Hugo Grotius, de Jure Belli ac Pacis, ch. 1, § 2; ch. 2, § 13 (A.C. Campbell trans., 1814), available at http://www.constitution. org/gro/djbp.htm

Philippe Gruslin v. Malaysia, ICSID Case No. ARB/99/3, Award of Nov. 27, 2000, at para. 13.7

Scott K. Gudgeon, *United States Bilateral Investment Treaties: Comments on their Origin, Purposes and General Treatment Standards*, 4 INT'L TAX & BUS. LAW. 105, 124 (1986)

Omar Guerrero et al., *Piercing the Corporate Veil in Mexico*, COMP. L. YB. INT'L BUS. 375 (Dennis Campbell ed. 2004)

Andrew T. Guzman, *Why LDCs Sign Treaties that Hurt Them: Explaining the Popularity of Bilateral Investment Treaties*, 38 VA. J. INT'L L. 639, 669 (1998)

Peter M. Haas, *Why Comply, or Some Hypotheses in Search of an Analyst*, in INTERNATIONAL COMPLIANCE WITH NON-BINDING ACCORDS 21 (Edith Brown Weiss ed. 1997)

ECONOMIC SANCTIONS AND AMERICAN DIPLOMACY (RICHARD N. HAASS ed. 1998)

MAX HABICHT, POST WAR TREATIES FOR THE PACIFIC SETTLEMENT OF INTERNATIONAL DISPUTES 226 (1931)

Joseph P. Hadley, *Use of Political Risk Insurance in Connection with Project Financings*, in INTERNATIONAL INFRASTRUCTURE PROJECTS VIII-3 (1995)

Jacominj J. Van Haersolte-Van Hof & Anne K. Hoffmann, *The Relationship between International Tribunals and Domestic Courts*, in THE OXFORD HANDBOOK OF INTERNATIONAL INVESTMENT LAW, ch. 24, 991 (Peter Muchlinski et al. eds. 2008)

G. Winthrop Haight, *Libyan Nationalization of British Petroleum Company Assets*, 6 INT'L LAW. 541 (1972)

M. Hallward-Driemeier, *Do Bilateral Investment Treaties Attract Foreign Direct Investment? Only a Bit—and They Could Bite*, World Bank Policy Research Working Paper No. 3121 (2003), available at http://documents. worldbank.org/curated/en/ 113541468761706209/pdf/multi0page.pdf

Walid Ben Hamida, *The Mihaly v. Sri Lanka Case: Some Thoughts Relating to the Status of Pre-Investment Expenditures*, in INTERNATIONAL INVESTMENT LAW AND ARBITRATION (T. Weiler ed., 2005)

Bernard Hanotiau, *Non-Signatories in International Arbitration: Lessons from Thirty Years of Case Law*, in INTERNATIONAL ARBITRATION 2006: BACK TO BASICS? 341 (Albert Jan van den Berg ed. 2007)

Bernard Hanotiau, *The Law Applicable to Arbitrability*, 26 SINGAPORE ACADEMY L.J. 874–85 (2014)

Richard Happ, *Dispute Settlement under the Energy Charter Treaty*, 45 GERMAN YB. INT'L L. 331 (2003)

Inaamul Haque & Ruxandra Burdescu, *Monterey Consensus on Financing for Development: Response Sought from International Economic Law*, 27 BC ICLQ 219, 254 (2004)

PHILIPP HARMS, INTERNATIONAL INVESTMENT, POLITICAL RISK, AND GROWTH (2000)

Cedric Harris, *Abuse of the Arbitration Process-Delaying Tactics and Disruptions: A Respondent's Guide*, 9(2) J. INT'L ARB. 87 (1992)

Paul Harris, *NGOs: Public Pressure Forces Bechtel to Drop Water Case*, BN AMERICAS (Jan. 19, 2006), available at http://www.bnamericas.com/en/news/privatization/NGOs:_ Public_pressure_ forces_Bechtel_to_drop_water_case

James Harrison, *Human Rights Arguments in* Amicus Curiae *Submissions: Promoting Social Justice?*, in HUMAN RIGHTS IN INTERNATIONAL INVESTMENT LAW AND ARBITRATION 396–451 (Pierre-Marie Dupuy et al. eds. 2009)

H.L.A. HART, THE CONCEPT OF LAW (1961)

Dominique Hascher, *ICC Practice in Relation to the Appointment, Confirmation, Challenge and Replacement of Arbitrators*, 6(2) ICC INT'L CT. ARB. BULL. 4, 6 (November 19950)

Jean R. Haynes, *International Arbitration May Not Be as Confidential as You Think—or Want*, in CONFLICTING LEGAL CULTURES IN COMMERCIAL ARBITRATION 99 (Stefan M. Frommel & Barry Alexander Rider eds. 1999)

John N. Hazard, *Risks in Investing in the USSR: Can There Be Protection against Them?*, 11 NYL Sch. J. Int'l & Comp. L. 457, 458 (1990)

William Heinemann, APPIAN'S ROMAN HISTORY 409 (1912)

Veijo Heiskanen, *Comment on Andrea Marco Steingruber's Remarks on Veijo Heiskanen's Note "Menage a Trois? Jurisdiction, Admissibility and Competence in Investment Treaty Arbitration,"* 29(3) ICSID REV.—FOR. INV. L.J. (2014)

Veijo Heiskanen, *Key to Efficiency in International Arbitration*, 30(3) ICSID REV.—FOR. INV. L.J 481–85 (2015)

LOUIS HENKIN, HOW NATIONS BEHAVE 9–98 (2d ed. 1969)

Jarrod Hepburn & Vuyelwa Kuuya, *Corporate Social Responsibility and Investment Treaties*, in SUSTAINABLE DEVELOPMENT IN WORLD INVESTMENT LAW 607 (Marie-Claire Cordonier Segger et al. eds. 2011)

Jerrod Hepburn & Luke Nottage, *Case Note: Philip Morris v Australia*, Sydney Law School, Legal Studies Research Paper No. 16/86 (Sept. 2016), at 8, available at SSRN: http://ssrn.com/abstract=2842065

Gerold Hermann, *Commentary on the UNCITRAL Conciliation Rules*, 6 Yb. Comm. Arb. 170, 174 (1981)

Rosalyn Higgins, The Development of International Law through the Political Organs of the United Nations (1963)

Rosalyn Higgins, *Aspects of the Case Concerning the Barcelona Traction, Light & Power Company, Limited*, 11 Va. J. Int'l L. 327 (1971)

Rosalyn Higgins, *The Taking of Property by the State: Recent Developments in International Law*, 176 Recueil des Cours 259, 268 (1982)

Rosalyn Higgins, Problems and Process: International Law and How We Use It 298 *et seq.* (1994)

Ken Highet, *Nonappearance and Disappearance before the ICJ*, 81 AJIL 237 (1987)

Claire A. Hill, *How Investors React to Political Risk*, 8(2) Duke J. Comp. & Int'l L. 288–313 (1998)

Richard Hill, *Non-Adversarial Mediation*, 12(4) J. Int'l Arb. 135 (1995)

Richard Hill, *The Theoretical Basis of Mediation and Other Forms of ADR: Why They Work*, 14 Arb. Int'l 173 (1998)

Richard D. Hill, *The New Reality of Electronic Document Production in International Arbitration: A Catalyst for Convergence?*, 25(1) Arb. Int'l. 87–102 (2009)

Steffen Hindelang, *Bilateral Investment Treaties, Custom and a Healthy Investment Climate: The Question of Whether BITs Influence Customary International Law Revisited*, 5 J. World Inv. 789–809 (2004)

Jonathan Hines & Aset A. Shyngyssov, *Kazakhstan Enacts PSA Law: Summary Analysis of Its Terms*, 3 OGEL (2005)

Moshe Hirsch, The Arbitration Mechanism of the International Centre for the Settlement of Investment Disputes 59 (1993)

Moshe Hirsch, *Investment Tribunals and Human Rights: Divergent Paths*, in Human Rights in International Investment Law and Arbitration 107–13 (Pierre-Marie Dupuy et al. eds. 2009)

Kaj Hober, *The Energy Charter Treaty—An Overview*, 8 J. World Inv. & Trade 321 (2007)

Michael F. Hoellering, *How to Draft an AAA Arbitration Clause*, 7 ICSID Rev.—For. Inv. L.J. 141 (1992)

J.J. van Hof, Commentary on the UNCITRAL Arbitration Rules: The Application by the Iran–U.S. Claims Tribunal (1991)

F. Hoffmeister, *Litigating against the European Union and Its Member States—Who Responds under the ILC's Draft Articles on International Responsibility of International Organizations?* 21 EJIL 723 (2010)

Hans-Hermann Hoppe, *Fallacies of the Public Goods Theory and the Production of Security*, 9 J. Libertarian Stud. 27 (1989)

Hans-Hermann Hoppe, *Banking, Nation States and International Politics: A Sociological Reconstruction of the Present Economic Order*, 4(1) R. Austrian Econ. 55, 60–61 (1990), available at http://www. mises.org

Hans-Hermann Hoppe, *On Certainty and Uncertainty, Or: How Rational Can Our Expectations Be?* 10(1) R. Austrian Econ. 49–78 (1997), available at http://www.mises.org

Nina N. Hoque & J. Michael Robinson, *An Examination of the Build, Operate and Transfer Model for International Projects in Emerging Markets*, International Infrastructure Projects X–1 (1995)

ARBITRATING FOREIGN INVESTMENT DISPUTES, vol. 19 299 (Norbert Horn ed. 2004)
Robert Hornick, *The Mihaly Arbitration: Pre-Investment Expenditure as a Basis for ICSID Jurisdiction*, 20 J. INT'L ARB. 189, 189–90 (2003)
Gunther Horvath, *The Duty of the Tribunal to Render an Enforceable Award*, 18(2) J. INT'L ARB. 135 (2001)
GUERRILLA TACTICS IN INTERNATIONAL ARBITRATION (Günther J. Horvath & Stephan Wilske eds. 2013)
Martin B. Howard, *Military and Paramilitary Activities in and against Nicaragua: The International Court of Justice's Jurisdictional Dilemma*, 7 LOY. LA INT'L & COMP. L.J. 379 (1984)
Robert Howse & Efraim Chalamish, *The Use and Abuse of WTO Law in Investor—State Arbitration: A Reply to Jürgen Kurtz*, 20 EJIL 1087 (2010)
JAMES C. HSIUNG, LAW AND POLICY IN CHINA'S FOREIGN RELATIONS 141 (1972)
Martin Hunter, *Modern Trends in the Presentation of Evidence in International Commercial Arbitration*, 3 AM. REV. INT'L ARB. 204 (1992)
Martin Hunter & Jan Paulsson, *A Code of Ethics for Arbitrators in International Commercial Arbitration*, 13 INT'L BUS. LAW. 153, 155 (1985)
CHARLES HYDE, 3 INTERNATIONAL LAW 710–27 (1949)
Virtus C. Igbokwe, *Developing Countries and the Law Applicable to International Arbitration of Oil Investment Disputes*, 14 J. INT'L ARB. 99 (1997)
Motomichi Ikawa, *Introduction*, in INTERNATIONAL POLITICAL RISK MANAGEMENT: EXPLORING NEW FRONTIERS 2 (Theodor H. Moran ed. 2001)
Institute of International Law, RESOLUTION ON ARBITRATION BETWEEN STATES, STATE ENTERPRISES OR STATE ENTITIES, AND FOREIGN ENTERPRISES, 16 YB. COMM. ARB. 236 (1991), art. 8
International Bar Association, *Rules on the Taking of Evidence in International Arbitration* (the 2010 IBA Rules on the Taking of Evidence), available at https://www.ibanet.org/ENews_Archive/ IBA_30June_2010_Enews_Taking_of_Evidence_new_rules.aspx.
Multi-Tiered Dispute Resolution Clauses, International Bar Association Litigation Committee (2015)
INTERNATIONAL CHAMBER OF COMMERCE, BILATERAL TREATIES FOR INTERNATIONAL INVESTMENT 7–8 (1977)
International Chamber of Commerce, Outgoing Secretary General Bond Sees Greater Role for ICC Court, 2 WORLD ARBITRATION AND MEDIATION REP. 164, 165 (June 1991)
ICC Court Statistics 2017, available at https://www.flickr.com/photos/international-chamber-of-commerce/sets/72157694229086035
ICC, Effective Management of Arbitration—A Guide for In-House Counsel and Other Party Representatives, Commission on Arbitration and ADR, (2018), at 19, available at https:// cdn.iccwbo.org/content/uploads/sites/3/2017/05/effective-management-of-arbitration-icc-guide- english-version.pdf
ICCA Drafting Sourcebook for Organizing International Arbitrations, Draft of Mar. 1, 2014, available at https://www.arbitration-icca.org/ media/2/13963492574410/ 27032014_icca_draft_01_drafting_sourcebook_for_organising_inter-national_arbitrations.pdf.
ICSID, HISTORY OF THE ICSID CONVENTION: DOCUMENTS CONCERNING THE ORIGIN AND THE FORMULATION OF THE CONVENTION 3 (1968)
ICSID. 2 ANALYSIS OF DOCUMENTS CONCERNING THE ORIGIN AND THE FORMULATION OF THE ICSID CONVENTION 34, 257–58, 260, 497–99 (1970)
International Law Commission, *Report of the Int'l Law Comm'n. on the Work of Its Thirtieth Session*, U.N. Doc. No. A/ CN.4/SER.A/1978/Add.1, Part 2, at 30 (1978)

INTERNATIONAL MONETARY FUND, BALANCE OF PAYMENTS MANUAL, para. 408 at 136 (4th ed. 1977)
Kenneth S. Jacobs, *Reinvigorating ICSID with a New Mission and with Renewed Respect for Party Autonomy*, 33 VA. J. INT'L L. 123 (1992)
Mahir Jalili, *Kompetenz- Kompetenz: Recent U.S. and U.K. Developments*, 13(4) J. INT'L ARB. 169, 170 (1996)
Sigvard Jarvin, *Objections to Jurisdiction*, in THE LEADING ARBITRATORS' GUIDE TO INTERNATIONAL ARBITRATION 83, 88 (Lawrence W. Newman & Richard Hill eds. 2004)
COLLECTION OF ICC ARBITRAL AWARDS 1974–1985 8–9 (Sigvard Jarvin & Yves Derains eds. 1990)
Robert Jennings, *State Contracts in International Law*, 27 BRIT. YB. INT'L L. 156 (1961)
OPPENHEIM'S INTERNATIONAL LAW 927 (Sir Robert Jennings & Sir Arthur Watts eds. 1992)
Dyalá Jiménez-Figueres, *Amicable Means to Resolve Disputes: How the ICC ADR Rules Work*, 21(1) J. INT'L ARB. 91, 92 (2004)
DAVID A. JODICE, POLITICAL RISK ASSESSMENT: AN ANNOTATED BIBLIOGRAPHY (1985)
D.H.N. Johnson, *The Effect of Resolutions of the General Assembly of the U.N.*, 32 BRIT. YB. INT'L L. 97 (1955)
George F. Jones, *Termination of Declarations under the Optional Clause: Military and Paramilitary Activities in and Against Nicaragua*, 20 TEX. INT'L L.J. 557 (1985)
Tom Jones, *Five-Member ICC Panel Hears Multibillion-Dollar Case*, Global Arb. Rev. (May 30, 2018)
Tom Jones, *ICSID Unveils Draft of New Rules*, GLOBAL ARBITRATION REVIEW (Aug. 3, 2018) available at https://globalarbitrationreview.com/article/1172618/icsid-unveils-draft-of-new-rules.
Anna Joubin-Bret, *Investor–State Mediation (ISM): A Comparison of Recent Treaties and Rules*, in CONTEMPORARY ISSUES IN INTERNATIONAL ARBITRATION AND MEDIATION: THE FORDHAM PAPERS 2014, 152–56 (Arthur W. Rovine ed. 2015)
Christopher C. Joyner, *The Reality and Relevance of International Law in the Post-Cold War Era*, in THE GLOBAL AGENDA 211 (C.W. Kegley & E.R. Wittkopf eds. 1995)
Justice Department Announces Progress on Iran and Vietnam Claims, 6 WORLD ARB. & MEDIATION REP. 75 (1995)
Justice Department Announces Progress on Iran and Vietnam Claims, 6 WORLD ARB. & MED. REP. 75 (1995)
Justice Department Announces Progress on Iran and Vietnam Claims, 6 World Arb. & Med. Rep. 75 (1995).
Mark Kantor, *International Project Finance and Arbitration with Public Sector Entities: When Is Arbitrability a Fiction?*, 24 FORDHAM INT'L L.J. 1122, 1132 n.30 (2001)
JOHN P. KARALIS, INTERNATIONAL JOINT VENTURES: A PRACTICAL GUIDE 207 (1992)
MARKOS KARAVIAS, CORPORATE OBLIGATIONS UNDER INTERNATIONAL LAW (2013)
Pierre Karrer, *Arbitration Saves! Costs: Poker and Hide-and-Seek*, 3(1) J. INT'L ARB. 35, 39 (1986)
Gabrielle Kaufmann-Kohler, *Interpretive Powers of the Free Trade Commission and the Rule of Law*, in FIFTEEN YEARS OF NAFTA CHAPTER 11 ARBITRATION 174–94 (E. Gaillard ed. 2011)
PETER B. KENEN, THE INTERNATIONAL FINANCIAL ARCHITECTURE (2001)
Lionel Kennedy, *Enforcing International Commercial Arbitration Agreements and Awards Not Subject to the New York Convention*, 23 VA. J. INT'L L. 784 (1981)
Mohammed I. Khalil, *Treatment of Foreign Investment in Bilateral Investment Treaties*, 7 ICSID REV.—FOR. INV. L.J. 339, 355 (1992)

Dany Khayat, *Swembalt: When Less Is Not More—Expropriation and Compensation*, 2004(2) STOCKHOLM ARB. REP. 141

Vladimir Khvalei, *Using Red Flags to Prevent Arbitration from Becoming a Safe Harbor for Contracts that Disguise Corruption, 24* ICC INT'L. COURT ARB. BULL., Special Supplement 15 et seq. (2013)

Building International Investment Law: The First 50 Years of ICSID (Meg Kinnear et al. eds. 2015)

N. Stephan Kinsella, *A Civil Law to Common Law Dictionary*, 54 LA. L. REV. 1265 (1994), available at http://www.KinsellaLaw.com

N. Stephan Kinsella, *Legislation and the Discovery of Law in a Free Society*, 11 J. LIBERTARIAN STUD. 132 (1995), available at http://www.mises.org

Frederic L. Kirgis, *Enforcing International Law*, ASIL INSIGHTS, Jan. 1996, available at http://www.asil.org/insights/insight1.htm

Courtney Kirkma, *Fair and Equitable Treatment: Methanex v. United States and the Narrowing Scope of NAFTA Article 1105*, 34 L. & POL'Y. INT'L BUS. 343 (2002)

Bernard Kishoiyian, *The Utility of Bilateral Investment Treaties in the Formulation of Customary International Law*, 14 J. INT'L L. & BUS. 327 (1994)

L.T. Kissam & E.K. Leach, *Sovereign Expropriation of Property and Abrogation of Concession Contracts*, 28 FORDHAM L. REV. 177, 224 (1959)

HEGE ELISABETH KJOS, APPLICABLE LAW IN INVESTOR–STATE ARBITRATION 61 (2013)

ROLAND KLAGER, "FAIR AND EQUITABLE TREATMENT" IN INTERNATIONAL INVESTMENT LAW 117 *et seq.* (2011)

Nikolas Klein, *Human Rights and International Investment Law: Investment Protection as Human Right?*, 4(1) GOETTINGEN J. INT'L. L. 210–11 (2012)

FRANK H. KNIGHT, RISK, UNCERTAINTY AND PROFIT (1971 [1921]), esp. ch. 7, available at http://www.econlib.org

Ioana Knoll-Tudor, The Fair and Equitable Treatment Standard and Human Rights Norms, in HUMAN RIGHTS IN INTERNATIONAL INVESTMENT LAW AND ARBITRATION 338–39 (Pierre-Marie Dupuy et al. eds. 2009)

William H. Knull, III & Noah Rubins, *Betting the Farm on International Commercial Arbitration: Is It Time to Offer an Appeals Option?*, 11 AM. REV. INT'L ARB. 531, 538–41 (2000)

Christian Koller, *Die Schiedsvereinbarung*, in SCHIEDSVERFAHRENSRECHT, para. 3/259, 7 (Christoph Liebscher et al. eds. 2012)

Abba Kolo, *Transfer of Funds: The Interaction between the IMF Articles of Agreement and Modern Investment Treaties: a Comparative Law Perspective, in International Investment Law and Comparative Public Law 357* (Stephan W. Schill ed. 2010)

Vera Korzun, *The Right to Regulate in Investor–State Arbitration: Slicing and Dicing Regulatory Carve-Outs*, 50(2) VAND. J. TRANSNAT'L L. 375 (2017), available at http://ssrn.com/abstract=2950939

Ursula Kriebaum, *Privatizing Human Rights. The Interface between International Investment Protection and Human Rights*, in THE LAW OF INTERNATIONAL RELATIONS: LIBER AMICORUM HANSPETER NEUHOLD 180 (August Reinisch & Ursula Kriebaum eds. 2007)

Ursula Kriebaum, *Local Remedies and the Standards for the Protection of Foreign Investment*, in INTERNATIONAL INVESTMENT LAW FOR THE 21ST CENTURY: ESSAYS IN HONOUR OF CHRISTOPH SCHREUER 418 *et seq.* (C. Binder et al. eds. 2009)

Ursula Kriebaum, *Foreign Investments & Human Rights—the Actors and Their Different Roles*, 10(1) TDM 12 (2013)

Ursula Kriebaum, *Case Comment: The Rompetrol Group N.V. v. Romania*, 15 J. WORLD INV. & TR. 1030–31 (2014)

Ursula Kriebaum & Christopher Schreuer, *The Concept of Property in Human Rights Law and International Investment Law* (2007), at 1–20, available at http://www.univie.ac.at/intlaw/ wordpress/pdf/88_concept_property.pdf

Stefan Kröll, *Die schiedsrechtliche Rechtsprechung 2004*, SchiedsVZ 139, 141 (2005)

Jasper Krommendijk & John Morijn, *"Proportional" by What Measure(s)? Balancing Investor Interests and Human Rights by Way of Applying the Proportionality Principle in Investor–State Arbitration*, in Human Rights in International Investment Law and Arbitration 430 (Pierre- Marie Dupuy et al. eds. 2009)

Vivian Kube & Ernst-Ulrich Petersmann, *Human Rights Law in International Investment Arbitration*, 11(1) AJWH 99 (2016)

Andreas Kulick, Global Public Interest in International Investment Law 296–97 (2012)

Andreas Kulick, *Case Comments, Electrabel S.A. v. The Republic of Hungary, ICSID Case No. ARB/07/19, Decision on Jurisdiction, Applicable Law and Liability, 30 November 2012 (Gabrielle Kaufmann-Kohler, Brigitte Stern, V.V. Veeder)*, 15 J. World Investment & Trade 273–84 (2014)

Bjorn Kunoy, *Developments in Indirect Expropriation Case Law in ICSID Transnational Arbitration*, 6 J. World Inv. & Trade 467 (2005)

Jürgen Kurtz, *A General Investment Agreement in the WTO? Lessons from Chapter 11 of NAFTA and the OECD Multilateral Agreement on Investment*, 23 U. Pa. J. Int'l Econ. L. 713, 734 (2002)

Jurgen Kurtz, *Access to Justice, Denial of Justice and International Investment Law: A Reply to Francesco Francioni*, 20(4) EJIL 1077–1085, 1079 (2009)

Jürgen Kurtz, *The Use and Abuse of WTO Law in Investor—State Arbitration: Competition and Its Discontents*, 20 EJIL 749 (2010)

Jürgen Kurtz, *Building Legitimacy through Interpretation in Investor–State Arbitration: On Consistency, Coherence and the Identification of Applicable Law*, in The Foundations of International Investment Law 157 *et seq.* (Zachary Douglas et al. eds. 2014)

Edward M.A. Kwaw, *Trade Related Investment Measures in the Uruguay Round: Towards a GATT for Investment?* 16 NCJ Int'l Comm. & Reg. L. 309 (1991)

Ian A. Laird, *A Community of Destiny: The Barcelona Traction Case and the Development of Shareholder Rights to Bring Investment Claims*, in International Investment Law and Arbitration (T. Weiler ed, 2005) at 77

Ian A. Laird, *The Weakening of the International Rule of Law in the NAFTA Zone*, presentation prepared for May 3, 2002, CD Howe/Munk Centre Conference on NAFTA Chapter 11, at 12–14

Pierre Lalive, *The First "World Bank" Arbitration: Some Legal Problems*, 51 Brit. Yb. Int'l L. 123 (1980)

Carolyn Lamm & Abby Cohen-Smutny, 12(11) *The International Centre for Settlement of Investment Disputes: Responses to Problems and Changing Requirements*, Mealey's Int'l Arb. Rep. 20 (1997)

Ole Lando, *The Law Applicable to the Merits of the Dispute*, 2 Arb. Int'l 104 (1986)

Thomas J. Lang, *Satisfaction of Claims Against Viet Nam for the Expropriation of U.S. Citizens' Property in South Viet Nam in 1975*, 28 Cornell Int'l L.J. 265, 298 (1995)

Anton van Langelaar, *Establishing Settlement Ranges by using Subject Matter Experts and Probability Analysis*, 71 Arb. 1, 64 (2005)

Erik Langeland, *The Viability of Conciliation in International Dispute Resolution*, 50 Disp. Resol. J. 34 (1995)

Donald C. Langevoort, *Ego, Human Behavior, and Law*, 81 Va. L. Rev. 853 (1995)

Clifford Larsen, *International Commercial Arbitration*, ASIL INSIGHTS, 2 (April 1997), available at http://www.asil.org/insights/insight97041.pdf
BRITISH PRACTICE IN INTERNATIONAL LAW 202–06 (Eli Lauterpacht ed. 1964)
Elihu Lauterpacht, *Issues of Compensation and Nationality in the Taking of Energy Investments*, 8 J. ENERGY & NAT. RES. L. 241, 245–46 (1990)
Serge Lazareff, *The Language of Institutional Arbitration*, 8(1) ICC BULL. 18 (1997)
T.N. Leach, *Frey v. Amoco Production Co.: Payment of Mineral Royalties on Take-or-Pay Settlements in Louisiana*, 67 TUL. L. REV. 840 (1993)
Charles Leben, *Hans Kelsen and the Advancement of International Law*, 9 EUR. J. INT'L L. 287 (1998), available at http://www.ejil.org
Stephen Lee, *Title to Foreign Real Property in Transnational Money Claims*, 32 COLUM. J. TRANSNAT'L L. 607 (1995)
Barton Legum, *Federalism, NAFTA Chapter Eleven and the Jay Treaty of 1794*, NEWS FROM ICSID, Spring 2001
Stephanie Barbara Leinhardt, *Some Thoughts on Foreign Investors Responsibilities to Respect Human Rights*, 10(1) TDM 1 (2013)
Axelle Lemaire, *Le nouveau visage de l'arbitrage entre État et investisseur étranger: le chapitre 11 de l'ALENA*, janv.–mars REVUE DE L'ARBITRAGE 43, 59 (2001)
Gabriel M. Lentner, *Litigating Patents in Investment Arbitration: Eli Lilly v. Canada*, 12(10) J. INTEL. PROP. L. & PRACT. 815–16 (2017)
BRUNO LEONI, FREEDOM AND THE LAW 75 (3d ed. 1991)
Bruno Leurent, *Reflections on the International Effectiveness of Arbitration Awards*, 12 ARB. INT'L 269 (1996)
Judith Levine, *Dealing with Arbitrator "Issue Conflicts" in International Arbitration*, 61 DISP. RESOL. J. 60 (2006)
Tali Levy, *NAFTA's Provision for Compensation in the Event of Expropriation: A Reassessment of the "Prompt, Adequate and Affective" Standard*, 31 STAN. J. INT'L L. 423 (1995)
Catherine Li, *Evaluating the Various Non-Litigation Processes for Resolving Disputes: The Cost-Effectiveness Approach*, 18(4) J. INT'L ARB. 435 (2001)
William C. Lieblich, *Determining the Economic Value of Expropriated Income-Producing Property in International Expropriations*, 8 J. INT'L ARB. 37, 63 (1991)
Richard B. Lillich, *The United States–Bulgarian Claims Agreement of 1963*, 58 AJIL 187 (1964)
RICHARD B. LILLICH, PROTECTION OF FOREIGN INVESTMENT 117–46 (1965)
Richard B. Lillich, *Joint Ventures and the Law of International Claims*, 10 MICH. J. INT'L L. 430 n.28 (1989)
RICHARD B. LILLICH & BURNS H. WESTON, INTERNATIONAL CLAIMS: THEIR SETTLEMENT BY LUMP SUM AGREEMENT (1975)
Troland S. Link, *Foreign Sovereign Immunity, Expropriation, Act of State, and Comity*, 703 PLI/COMM. L. & PRAC. HANDBOOK SERIES 183 (1994)
Klaus Lionnet, *Arbitration and Mediation—Alternatives or Opposites*, 4(1) J. INT. ARB. 69 (1987)
DAVID B. LIPSKY & RONALD L. SEEBER, THE APPROPRIATE RESOLUTION OF CORPORATE DISPUTES 17 (1996)
Daniel R. Loritz, *Comment: Corporate Predators Attack Environmental Regulations: It's Time to Arbitrate Claims Filed under NAFTA Chapter 11*, 22 LOY. LA INT'L & COMP. L. REV. 533, 546–47 (2000)
Tamara Lothien & Katharina Pistor, *Local Institutions, Foreign Investment and Alternative Strategies of Development: Some Views from Practice*, 42 COLUM. J. TRANSNAT'L L. 101, 106
R.B. Love, *The Local Remedies Issue in Venezuelan Investment Treaty Disputes*, 5 TDM (2008)

William A. Lovett, *Lessons from the Recent Peso Crisis in Mexico*, 4 TUL. J. INT'L & COMP. L. 143 (1996)
Lucinda A. Low, *Coping with the Foreign Corrupt Practices Act: A Primer for Energy and Natural Resource Sectors*, 2(2) CEPMLP INTERNET J. (1997)
EXPROPRIATION IN THE AMERICAS (Andreas Lowenfeld ed. 1971)
A.F. LOWENFELD, INTERNATIONAL PRIVATE INVESTMENT (2d ed. 1982)
ANDREAS LOWENFELD, *The Party-Appointed Arbitrator in International Controversies*, 30 TEX. INT'L L.J. 59 (1995)
ANDREAS LOWENFELD, INTERNATIONAL ECONOMIC LAW (2002) 565–616
Andreas Lowenfeld, *Investment Agreements and International Law*, 42 COLUM. J. TRANSNAT'L L. 123 (2003)
J. Stewart McClendon, *Enforcement of Foreign Arbitral Awards in the United States*, 4 NW. J. INT'L L. & BUS. 58 (1982)
SURVEY OF INTERNATIONAL ARBITRATION SITES (J. Stewart McClendon ed. 1993)
TIMOTHY L. H. MCCORMACK, SELF-DEFENCE IN INTERNATIONAL LAW 240–83 (1996)
R. St. J. Macdonald, *The Margin of Appreciation*, in THE EUROPEAN SYSTEM FOR THE PROTECTION OF HUMAN RIGHTS 83, 111 (R. St. J. Macdonald et al. eds. 1993)
Peter M. McGowan, *Arbitration Clauses as Waivers of Immunity from Jurisdiction and Execution under the Foreign Sovereign Immunities Act of 1976*, 5 NYL SCH. J. INT'L & COMP. L. 409, 417–19 (1984)
Campbell McLachlan, *The Principle of Systemic Integration and Article 31(3)(c) of the Vienna Convention*, 54 INT'L. & COMP. LQ 279 (2005).
CAMPBELL MCLACHLAN et al., INTERNATIONAL INVESTMENT ARBITRATION: SUBSTANTIVE PRINCIPLES 416 (2d ed. 2017)
Douglas Earl McLaren, *Effective Use of International Commercial Arbitration: A Primer for In-house Counsel*, 19 J. INT'L ARB. 473, 473–76 (2002)
Douglas Earl McLaren, *The New ICC ADR Rules*, MEALEY'S INT'L ARB. REP. (Mar. 2002)
Douglas Earl McLaren, *Party-Appointed vs. List-Appointed Arbitrators*, 20 J. INT'L ARB. 233 (2003)
Lord Mcnair, THE LAW OF TREATIES 272–305 (1961)
Annette Magnusson & Hanna Larsson, *Recent Practice of the Arbitration Institute of the Stockholm Chamber of Commerce Prima Facie Decisions on Jurisdiction and Challenges of Arbitrators*, 2004(2) STOCKHOLM. ARB. REP. 47
Peter Malanczuk, *State-to-State and Investor-to-State Dispute Settlement in the OECD Draft Multilateral Investment Agreement*, in MULTILATERAL REGULATION OF INVESTMENT 137 (E.C. Nieuwenhuys & Marcel M.T.A. Brus eds. 2001)
Ali Malek & Christopher Harris, *A Pilgrimage to Paris: Dallah v. Pakistan*, 2(4) INT'L J. ARAB ARB. 23–55 (2010)
Marie-Hélène Maleville, *Pathologies des Clauses Compromissoires*, 1 RDAI/IBLJ 61 (2000)
G.I. Malumfashi, *Environmental and Social Due Diligence Vis-à-Vis Political Risk Insurance: An Assessment of the Role of the Multilateral Investment Guarantee Agency (MIGA)*, 2(1) OIL & GAS L. INTELLIGENCE (2004)
A.F.M. Maniruzzaman, *Expropriation of Alien Property and the Principle of Non-Discrimination in International Law of Foreign Investment: An Overview*, 8 J. TRANSNAT'L L. & POL'Y. 57 (1998)
A.F.M. Maniruzzaman, *Understanding Stabilization Techniques in Production Sharing Agreements: Some Remarks*, published in Oil, Gas & Energy Law Intelligence (OGEL) "Special Feature: Production Sharing Contracts," in 3(1), available at http://www.gasandoil.com/ogel
F.A. Mann, *The Protection of Shareholders' Interests in the Light of the Barcelona Traction Case*, 67 AJIL 259, 272–73 (1973)

F.A. Mann, *The Consequences of an International Wrong in International and National Law*, 48 Brit. Yb. Int'l L. 1, 60 n.1 (1977)

F.A. Mann, *British Treaties for the Promotion and Protection of Investment*, 52 Brit. Yb. Int'l L. 241, 249 (1981)

F.A. Mann, Further Studies in International Law 126 (1990)

Howard Mann, *NAFTA and the Environment: Lessons for the Future*, 13 Tul. Envt'l L.J. 387, 405–06 (2000)

D. Manning-Cabrol, *The Imminent Death of the Calvo Clause and the Rebirth of the Calvo Principle: Equality of Foreign and National Investors*, 26 L. Pol'y. Int'l Bus. 1169 (1995)

B. Thomas Mansbach, *Financing and Political Risk: Risk Sharing and Project Finance: The Programs of the Overseas Private Investment Corporation, State Bar of Texas Advanced International Law Institute, Investment and Trade with Emerging Economies*, B-1 (Houston, Texas, May 14, 1993)

Irmgard Marboe, *Compensation and Damages in International Law—The Limits of "Fair Market Value,"* 7(5) JWIT 723, 725 (2006)

Irmgard Marboe & August Reinisch, *Contracts between States and Foreign Private Law Persons*, in Max Planck Encyclopedia of Public International Law (2011)

Reto Marghitola, Document production in international arbitration (2015);

Fabrizio Marrella, *On the Changing Structure of International Investment Law: The Human Right to Water and ICSID Arbitration*, 12 Int'l Community Law Rev. 359 (2010)

Geoffrey Marston, *The Aminoil–Kuwait Arbitration*, 17 J. World Trade L. 177 (1983)

The Business and Human Rights Landscape: Moving Forward, Looking Back (Jena Martin & Karen E. Bravo eds. 2016)

Ramona Martinez, *Recognition and Enforcement of International Arbitral Awards under the United Nations Convention of 1958: The "Refusal" Provisions*, 24 Int'l Law. 487, 488 (1990)

Pedro J. Martinez-Fraga, *In Good Faith, Bad Faith, But Not Losing Faith: A Commentary on the 2010 IBA Rules on the Taking of Evidence in International Arbitration*, 43 Georgetown J. Int'l L. 411 (2012)

Arshad Masood, *Default Procedure in Arbitration under the World Bank Convention*, 22 L. Rev. 1 (1970)

Scott E. Masten & Keith J. Crocker, *Efficient Adaptation in Long-Term Contracts: Take-or-Pay Provisions for Natural Gas*, 75 Am. Econ. Rev. 1083 (1985)

Stefan Matiation, *Arbitration with Two Twists: Loewen v. United States and Free Trade Commission Intervention in NAFTA Chapter 11 Disputes*, 24 U. Penn. J. Int'l Econ. L. 451 (2003)

Tomoko Matsukawa & Odo Habeck, *Review of Risk Mitigation Instruments for Infrastructure*

Bernard Mayer, The Dynamics of Conflict Resolution: A Practitioners Guide (1st ed. 2000)

Hannah Mayer, *Political Risk Insurance and Its Effectiveness in Supporting Private Sector Investment in Fragile States*, Report of the LSE-Oxford Commission on State Fragility, Growth and Development (2018), at 10–11, available at https://www.theigc.org/wp-content/uploads/2018/05/ Political-risk-insurance.pdf

Wilf Mbanga, *Farmers Are Seeking Compensation*, The Zimbabwean, May 13, 2005

J. Michael Medina, *The Take-or-Pay Wars: A Cautionary Analysis for the Future*, 27 Tulsa L.J. 283 (1991)

George M. von Mehren & Claudia T. Salomon, *Submitting Evidence in International Arbitration: A Common Lawyer's Guide*, 20(3) J. Int'l Arb. 285 (2003)

Robert von Mehren & P. Nicholas Kourides, *International Arbitrations between States and Foreign Private Parties: The Libyan Nationalization Cases*, 75 AJIL 476, 523 (1981)

Maurice Mendelson, *What Price Expropriation? Compensation for Expropriation: The Case Law*, 79 AJIL 414 (1985)

Maurice Mendelson, *The Runaway Train: The "Continuous Nationality Rule" from the Panevezys- Saldutsikis Railway Case to Loewen*, in Maurice Mendelson, *The Runaway Train: The "Continuous Nationality Rule" from the Panevezys-Saldutsikis Railway Case to Loewen*, in INTERNATIONAL INVESTMENT LAW AND ARBITRATION 97, 123 (Todd Weiler ed. 2005)

THEODOR MERON, INVESTMENT INSURANCE IN INTERNATIONAL LAW 47 (1976)

J.G. MERRILLS, INTERNATIONAL DISPUTE SETTLEMENT 64–90 (4th ed. 2005)

T. Meshel, *Human Rights in Investor–State Arbitration: The Human Right to Water and Beyond*, 6(2) J. INT'L. DISP. SETT. 277–307 (2015).

Eleni Methymaki & Antonios Tzanakopoulos, *Masters of Puppets? Reassertion of Control through Joint Investment Treaty Interpretation*, in REASSERTION OF CONTROL OVER THE INVESTMENT TREATY REGIME 155–81 (Andreas Kulick ed. 2017)

Stanley D. Metzger, *Property in International Law*, 50 VA. L. REV. 594, 598–600 (1964)

MIGA, ANNUAL REPORT 1995, available at http:// www.miga.org

MIGA, ANNUAL REPORT 2004 (2004), https://www.miga.org/report/2004-annual-report, *Development Impact* section

MIGA, *World Investment and Political Risk Report 2010* (2011), available at http://documents.worldbank.org/curated/en/273261468332370710/World-investment-and-political-risk-2010

MIGA Investment Guarantee Guide (2015), https://www.miga.org/guide/investment- guarantee-guide

MIGA, *Operational Policies of the MIGA* (2015), http://www.miga.org/sites/default/files/archive/Documents/Operations-Regulations.pdf

RAYMOND F. MIKESELL, PETROLEUM COMPANY OPERATIONS AND AGREEMENTS IN THE DEVELOPING COUNTRIES (1984)

CAMERON A. MILES, PROVISIONAL MEASURES BEFORE INTERNATIONAL COURTS AND TRIBUNALS 159 *et seq.* (2017)

Wendy Miles, *International Arbitrator Appointment*, 57 DISP. RES. J. 36 (2002)

Wendy Miles, *Practical Issues for Appointment of Arbitrators*, 20 J. INT'L ARB. 219 (2003)

LUDWIG VON MISES, HUMAN ACTION (4th ed. 1996), esp. ch. VI, available at http://www.mises.org

RICHARD VON MISES, PROBABILITY, STATISTICS, AND TRUTH (1957), esp. chs. 1 and 3

Loukas A. Mistelis, *Reality Test: Current State of Affairs in Theory and Practice Relating to "Lex Arbitri"*, 17(2) AM. REV. INT'L ARB. 155 *et seq.* (2006)

Loukas A. Mistelis, *Arbitral Seats: Choices and Competition*, in INTERNATIONAL ARBITRATION AND INTERNATIONAL COMMERCIAL LAW: SYNERGY CONVERGENCE AND EVOLUTION 367 *et seq.* (Stefan Kröll et al. eds. 2011)

LOUKAS A. MISTELIS & STAVROS BREKOULAKIS, ARBITRABILITY: INTERNATIONAL AND COMPARATIVE PERSPECTIVES (2009)

Zhang Monan, *Investment Protectionism in the Name of National Security*, China– US Focus (Sept. 6. 2017), available at https://www.chinausfocus.com/finance-economy/investment-protectionism-in-the-name-of-national-security

Bertrand Montembault, *The Stabilisation of State Contracts Using the Example of Oil Contracts: A Return of the Gods of Olympia?* 6 INT'L BUS. L.J. 593 (2003)

Theodore H. Moran, *Political and Regulatory Risk in Infrastructure Investment in Developing Countries: Introduction and Overview*, 5(6) CEPMLP J. 3 (1999)

Mary L. Moreland, *"Foreign Control" and "Agreement" under ICSID Article 25(2)(b): Standards for Claims Brought by Locally Organized Subsidiaries against Host States*, 9 CURRENTS INT'L TRADE L.J. 18 (2000)

Michael L. Morkin, *How to Choose Arbitration*, in International Arbitration Checklists 209, 212–14 (Lawrence W. Newman & Grant Hanessian eds. 2004)
Glenn Morris, *Piercing the Corporate Veil in Louisiana*, 52 La. L. Rev. 271 (1991)
John Humphrey, Carlile Morris & G.C. Cheshire, *The Proper Law of a Contract in the Conflict of Laws*, 56 LQR 320 (1940)
John Humphrey & Carlile Morris, *Torts in the Conflict of Laws*, 12 Modern L. Rev. 248 (1949)
John Humphrey & Carlile Morris, *The Proper Law of a Tort*, 64 Harv. L. Rev. 881 (1951)
Margaret L. Moses, The Principles and Practice of International Commercial Arbitration 72–73 (2008)
Margaret L. Moses, *Is Good Faith in the IBA Evidence Rules Good?* Kluwer Arbitration Blog (Nov. 15, 2012), available at http://arbitrationblog.kluwerarbitration.com/2012/11/15/is-good-faith-in-the-iba-evidence-rules-good/
Richard M. Mosk, *Expropriation: What to Do About It?* 5 Cal. Int'l Pract. 11 (1993–94)
GG. Cordero Moss, *Contract or License? Regulation of Petroleum Investment in Russia and the Role of Foreign Legal Advice* (version also reprinted in 3(11) CEPMLP J.), published in Oil, Gas & Energy Law Intelligence (OGEL) "Special Feature: Production Sharing Contracts," in 3(1), available at http://www.gasandoil.com/ogel
G. Cordero Moss, *Full Protection and Security*, in Standards of Investment Protection 133–36 (August Reinisch ed. 2008)
Helen Mountfield, *Regulatory Expropriations in Europe: The Approach of the European Court of Human Rights*, 11 NYU Environ. L.J. 136 (2003)
Khaled Moyeed & Clare Montgomery, *Key Changes in the LCIA's new Arbitration Rules*, Kluwer Arbitration Blog (2014), available at http:// arbitrationblog.kluwerarbitration.com/2014/08/29/key-changes-in-the-lcias-new-arbitration-rules/
Peter T. Muchlinski, Multinational Enterprises and the Law 508 (1995)
Peter Muchlinski, *The Rise and Fall of the Multilateral Agreement on Investment*, in Foundations and Perspectives on International Trade Law 114 (Ian Fletcher ed. 2001)
Peter Muchlinski, *Corporate Social Responsibility*, in The Oxford Handbook of International Investment Law 637–84 (Peter Muchlinski et al. eds. 2008)
Eva Muller, *How Do International Institutions Select Arbitrators?* 17 J. Int'l Arb. 157 (2000)
Yayan Mulyana & Jan K. Schaefer, *Indonesia's New Framework for International Arbitration: A Critical Assessment of the Law and Its Application by the Courts*, 17 Mealey's Int'l Arb. Rep. 39, 57 (2002)
Alexandra Munoz, *The New ICC Mediation Rules of 2014: Evolution not Revolution*, 2 Cahiers de l'Arbitrage 325 (2014)
Sean D. Murphy, *The Security Council, Legitimacy, and the Concept of Collective Security after the Cold War*, 32 Colum. J. Transnat'l L. 201, 229, 249–51 (1994)
Sean D. Murphy, *Contemporary Practice of the United States relating to International Law*, 95 AJIL 873, 881–85 (2001)
Junji Nakagawa, Nationalization, Natural Resources and International Investment Law: Contractual Relationship as a Dynamic Bargaining Process 75–97 (2018)
The Law of Transnational Business Transactions, chs. 4 and 8 (Ved P. Nanda ed. 1994)
Ved P. Nanda & David K. Pansius, Litigation of International Disputes In U.S. Courts, chs. 8, 10 (1995)
Eva Nanopoulos & Rumiana Yotova, *"Repackaging" Plain Packaging in Europe: Strategic Litigation and Public Interest Considerations*, 19(1) J. Int'l Economic L. 175–210 (2016)
Horacio Grigera Naòn, *Foreign Investment Arbitration in Latin America: The New Environment*, American Bar Assn. Section of Int'l Law and Practice Newsletter (Winter 1995), at 14–23

Horacio Grigera Naòn, *The Settlement of Investment Disputes between States and Private Parties*, 1 J. World Inv. 59, 63 (2000)

Marian Nash (Leich), *U.S. Practice: Bilateral Investment Treaties*, 87 AJIL 433 (1993)

N.V.S.K. Nathan, *Submissions to the International Centre for Settlement of Investment Disputes in Breach of the Convention*, *12* J. Int'l Arb. 27, 29 (1995)

K.V.S.K. Nathan, The ICSID Convention: The Law of the International Centre for Settlement of Investment Disputes (2000)

Eric Neumayer et al., *Are Stricter Investment Rules Contagious? Host Country Competition for Foreign Direct Investment through International Agreements*, 152(1) Review of World Economics 177–213 (2015)

Andrew Newcombe & Luis Paradell, Law and Practice of Investment Treaties: Standards of Treatment 371 (2009)

A. Newcombe, *Investor Misconduct: Jurisdiction, Admissibility or Merits?*, in Evolution in Investment Treaty Law and Arbitration 187 (C. Brown and K. Miles eds. 2011)

NEXI Annual Report 7 (FY 2016), available at https://www.nexi.go.jp/corporate/booklet/pdf/annual2016-e.pdf

V.U. Nguyen, *Foreign Investment in Vietnam by Build Operate and Transfer Projects: An Update*, 9 Butterworth's J. Int'l Banking Fin. L. 482 (1994)

Frauke Nitschke, *The IBA's Investor–State Mediation Rules and the ICSID Dispute Settlement Framework*, 29(1) ICSID Rev.—For. Inv. L.J. 112–32 (2014)

Albert Jay Nock, Our Enemy, The State 3 (1973)

William Northcote, *Default, ex parte and Want of Prosecution Proceedings in International Commercial Arbitration*, 14 Advocate's Q. 319 (1992)

P. M. Norton, *Back to the Future: Expropriation and the Energy Charter Treaty*, in The Energy Charter Treaty: An East-West Gateway for Investment and Trade (T. Walde ed., 1996)

Patrick M. Norton, *A Law of the Future or a Law of the Past? Modern Tribunals and the International Law of Expropriation*, 85 AJIL 474, 495 (1991)

Grant Nulle, *IMF Ignores Causes of Crisis*, Financial Times, Aug. 18, 2003, at 10

Lester Nurick & Stephen Schnably, *The First ICSID Conciliation: Tesoro Petroleum Corp. v. Trinidad & Tobago*, 1 ICSID Rev.—For. Inv. L.J. 340, 343 (1986)

Bede O.N. Nwete, *To What Extent Can Stabilisation Clauses Mitigate the Investor's Risks in a Production Sharing Contract?* 3(1) OGEL (Mar. 2005), published in Oil, Gas & Energy Law Intelligence (OGEL) "Special Feature: Production Sharing Contracts," in 3(1), available at http://www.gasandoil.com/ogel

Amaechi David Nwokolo, *Is There a Legal and Functional Value for the Stabilization Clause in International Petroleum Agreements?* 2003–04(8) CEPMLP Ann. Rev. 8 (2004)

Eloïse Obadia, *ICSID, Investment Treaties and Arbitration: Current and Emerging Issues*, Investment Treaties and Arbitration, at 67, 70–71 (2002)

Eloïse Obadia & Frauke Nitschke, *Chapter 4: The Role of the Secretariat, Litigating International Investment Disputes*, in Litigating International Investment Arbitration Disputes: A Practitioner's Guide 80 (Chiara Giorgetti ed. 2014)

D.P. O'Connell, International Law 1035 (2d ed. 1970)

T. Modybo Ocran, Bilateral Investment Protection Treaties: A *Comparative Study*, 8 NYU J. Int'l & Comp. L. 401 (1987)

Organisation for Economic Cooperation and Development (OECD), Development Cooperation—1984 Review 64, Table IV-1 (1984)

OECD Directorate for Financial and Enterprise Affairs, *"Indirect Expropriation" and the "Right to Regulate" in International Investment Law*, Working Papers on International Investment, No. 2004/4 (September 2004), available at https://www.oecd.org/daf/inv/investment-policy/WP- 2004_4.pdf

Won-Suk Oh & Yongil Kim, *A Comparative Study on the Institutional Arbitration and* Ad Hoc *Arbitration*, 19(1) J. Arb. Stud. 25–44 (2009)

D. Christopher Ohly, *A Functional Analysis of Claimant Eligibility*, in International Law of State Responsibility for Injuries to Aliens 281, 291 (Richard B. Lillich ed. 1983)

Marie Öhrström, *Decisions by the SCC Institute Regarding Challenge of Arbitrators*, 1 Stockholm Arb. Rep. 35 (2002)

Andrew I. Okekeifere, *The UNCITRAL Model Law and the Problem of Delay in International Commercial Arbitration*, 14(1) J. Int'l Arb. 125 (1997)

Alexa Olesen, *Singapore to Ink Landmark Free Trade Pact with the United States*, Associated Press, May 4, 2003

David M. Ong, *Joint Development of Common Offshore Oil and Gas Deposits: "Mere" State Practice or Customary International Law?* 93 AJIL 771 (1999)

OPIC Annual Report 15 (1994).

OPIC Annual Report 2004 (Nov. 2003), at 3, available at https://www.opic.gov/sites/default/ files/docs/04_AnnualReport.pdf

OPIC Annual Report 10 (2017) available at: https://www.opic.gov/sites/default/files/files/

OPIC Annual_Report-2017_1.pdf

OPIC Program Handbook 1, available at https://www.opic.gov/who-we-are/faqs (as of Aug. 2018)

Franz Oppenheimer, The State 24–27 (1926)

Gary W. Orloff, *Private Political Risk Insurance for Energy Investors*, in Maclean International Energy Network, Going International Seminar (Dallas, Texas, July 28, 1993)

Pietro Ortolani, *Are Bondholders Investors? Sovereign Debt and Investment Arbitration after* Poštová, 30(2) LJIL 383–404 (2017)

Jerome Ortscheidt, La Réparation du Dommage dans L'Arbitrage Commercial International 199 (2001)

öSterreichische Zeitschrift für öffentliches Recht und Völkerrecht 17 (1994)

OXFAM, Running into the Sand, Why a Failure at the Cancun Trade Talks Threatens the World's Poorest People, OXFAM Briefing Paper No. 53 (Sept. 2, 2003), at 33, available at https://policy-practice.oxfam.org.uk/ publications/running-into-the-sand-why-failure-at-the-cancun-trade-talks-threatens-the-world- 114588

Kristine M. Paden, *Choice of Law, Choice of Forum and Arbitration Clauses Override U.S. Security Rights*, 6 Transnat'l L. 431 (1993)

S. Paksoy, *Foreign Investment and Exchange Regulations in Turkey*, 18 Comp. L. Yb. Int'l Bus. 241 (1996)

Matina Papadaki, *Compromissory Clauses as the Gatekeepers of the Law to Be "Used" in the ICJ and the PCIJ*, 5(3) J. Int'l. Dispute Settlement 560–604 (2014)

Thomas Nektarios Papanastasiou, *Protecting Foreign Investments against Expropriation: A Comparative Study of Japan's EPAs*, 1(2) Int'l J. Pub. L. & Pol'y. 171–201 (2011)

Thomas Nektarios Papanastasiou, *The Role of Economic Partnership Agreements in Protecting Foreign Investments against Political Risk: An Analysis of Japan's EPAs*, 21(4) J. Graduate School Asia-Pacific Studies 95– 124, 109–14 (2011)

Thomas-Nektarios Papanastasiou, The Legal Protection of Foreign Investments against Political Risk: Japanese Business in the Asian Energy Sector (2015)

Thomas-Nektarios Papanastasiou, Corruption in the Infrastructure Provision: The Role of Accountability Mechanisms in the Community Driven Development Projects of Indonesia (2016)

Thomas-Nektarios Papanastasiou, *Mediation in Japan (in Greek)*, 5–6 Epitheorisi Politikis Dikonomias J. 522–34 (2016)

Martins Paparinskis, *The Limits of Depoliticization in Contemporary Investor–State Arbitration*, 3 Select Proceedings of the European Society of International Law (2010)

Martins Paparinskis, The International Minimum Standard and Fair and Equitable Treatment 142–53 (2013)

Athena J. Pappas, *References on Bilateral Investment Treaties*, 4 ICSID Rev.—For. Inv. L.J. 189 (1989)

William W. Park, *Arbitration of International Contract Disputes*, 39 Bus. Law. 1783 (1984)

William W. Park, *Safeguarding Procedural Integrity in International Arbitration*, 63 Tul. L. Rev. 647, 707 (1989)

William W. Park, *The Arbitrability Dicta in First Options v. Kaplan: What Sort of Kompetenz-Kompetenz Has Crossed the Atlantic?* 12 Arb. Int'l 137, 138–39 (1996)

William W. Park, *The Specificity of International Arbitration: The Case for FAA Reform*, 36 Vand. J. Transnat'l L. 1241, 1258 n.69 (2003)

William W. Park, *Non-signatories and International Contracts: An Arbitrator's Dilemma*, in Multiple Party Actions in International Arbitration 1 (Belinda Macmahon ed. 2009)

Antonio Parra, *The Screening Power of the ICSID Secretary*, 2(1) News from ICSID 10 (1985)

Antonio Parra, *Principles Governing Foreign Investment as Reflected in National Investment Codes*, 7 ICSID Rev.—For. Inv. L.J. 428 (1992)

Antonio Parra, *The Scope of New Investment Laws and International Instruments*, in 4 Economic Development, Foreign Investment and the Law 27 (Robert Pritchard ed. 1996)

Antonio Parra, *Provisions on the Settlement of Investment Disputes in Modern Investment Laws, BITs, and Multilateral Instruments on Investment*, 12 ICSID Rev.—For. Inv. L.J. 287, 325 (1997)

Antonio R. Parra, The History of ICSID (2d ed. 2017)

Constantine Partasides, *The Art of Selecting the Right Arbitrator*, lecture, London School of Economics, London (Nov. 9, 2011)

Jan Paulsson, *Arbitration without Privity*, 10 ICSID Rev.—For. Inv. L.J. 232 (1995)

Jan Paulsson et al., The Freshfields Guide to Arbitration and ADR 49–66 (2d ed. 1999)

Jan Paulsson, *Continuous Nationality in Loewen*, 20 Arb. Int'l 213 (2004)

Jan Paulsson, Denial of Justice under in International Law (2005)

Jan Paulsson, *The Timely Arbitrator: Reflections on the Böckstiegel Method*, 22(1) Arb. Int'l. 19–26 (2006)

Opinion of Professor Jan Paulson, *In the Matter of an Arbitration under the Bilateral Investment Treaty between Ecuador and the United States of America and the 1976 Arbitration Rules of the United Nations Commission on International Trade Law* (Mar. 12, 2012), at 6–7, available at https://www.italaw.com/sites/default/files/case-documents/ita0176_0.pdf.

Jan Paulsson & Nigel Rawding, *The Trouble with Confidentiality*, 11(3) ICC Int'l Court Arb. Bull. 303–20 (1994)

Vratislav Pechota, *The 1981 U.S.–Czechoslovak Claims Settlement Agreement: An Epilogue to Postwar Nationalization and Expropriation Disputes*, 76 AJIL 639

Julianne Peck, *The U.N. and the Laws of War: How Can the World's Peacekeepers Be Held Accountable?*, 21 Syracuse J. Int'l L. & Com. 283, 291 (1995)

Edith Penrose et al., *Nationalization of Foreign-Owned Property for a Public Purpose: An Economic Perspective on Appropriate Compensation*, 55 Modern L. Rev. 351, 353 (1992)

Facundo Pérez-Aznar & Henrique Choer Moraes, *The Mercosur Protocol on Investment and Facilitation: Regionalizing an Innovative Approach to Investment Agreements*, EJIL

TALK!, EUR. J. INT'L L. (Sept. 2017), available at https://www.ejiltalk.org/the-mercosur-protocol-on-investment- cooperation-and-facilitation-regionalizing-an-innovative-approach-to-investment-agreements/

Saul Perloff, *The Ties that Bind: The Limits of Autonomy and Uniformity in International Commercial Arbitration*, 13 U. PA. J. INT'L BUS. L. 323, 333 (1987)

Maura B. Perry, *A Model for Efficient Foreign Aid: The Case for Political Risk Insurance Activities of the Overseas Private Investment Corporation*, 36 VA. J. INT'L L. 511 (1996)

Branko Pesel.j., *The New Yugoslav– American Claims Agreement*, 59 AJIL 362 (1965)

Chris M. Peter, *MIGA and GRIP: Two International Investment Insurance Programmes*, 12 WORLD COMPETITION: L. & ECONOMICS REV. 95 (1989)

P. Peters, *Exhaustion of Local Remedies: Ignored in Most Bilateral Investment Treaties*, 44(2) NETHERLANDS INT'L L. REV. 233 (1997)

Ernst-Ulrich Petersmann, *Constitutional Theories of International Economic Adjudication and Investor–State Arbitration*, in HUMAN RIGHTS IN INTERNATIONAL INVESTMENT LAW AND ARBITRATION 183 (Pierre-Marie Dupuy et al. eds. 2009)

Luke Eric Peterson & Kevin R. Gray, International Human Rights in Bilateral Investment Treaties and in Investment Treaty Arbitration, International Institute for Sustainable Development (IISD) (April 2003), at 10, available at https://www.iisd.org/pdf/2003/investment_int_human_ rights_bits.pdf

Elizabeth Pietanza, *Comment: Winning the Risky Global Business Game: Parrying the Thrusts from Terrorism with an International Insurance Coalition*, 34 CAL. W. INT'L L.J. 85 (2003)

Martina Polasek, *The Threshold for Registration of a Request for Arbitration under the ICSID Convention*, 5(2) DISP. RES. INT'L. 177 (2011)

Michael Polkinghorne, *Investor–State Dispute Resolution under the Energy Charter Treaty: Which Fork? Which Road?* MEALEY'S INT'L ARB. REP., April 2004, at 13

Daniel Q. Posin, *Recent Developments in ICSID Annulment Procedures*, 13 WORLD ARB. & MED. REP. 170, 171 (2002)

Eric Posner, *Probability Errors: Some Positive and Normative Implications for Tort and Contract Law*, U. Chic. L. & Econ., Olin Working Paper No. 161 (2002) (describing how excess optimism might interact with incentives in tort and contract law).

Michele Potestà, *The Interpretation of Consent to ICSID Arbitration Contained in DomesticInvestment Laws*, 27(2) ARB. INT'L 149–70 (2011)

Felix Praendl, *Measure of Damages in International Commercial Arbitration*, 23 STAN. J. INT'L L. 263 (1987)

The Press Association, *Zimbabwe: Attempted Farm Eviction*, NY TIMES, Aug. 15, 2002, at A13; Human Rights Watch, *Fast Track Land Reform in Zimbabwe* (Mar. 2002), http://www.hrw.org/ reports/2002/zimbabwe.

PRICEWATERHOUSECOOPERS, JAHRESBERICHT 2003. INVESTITIONSGARANTIEN DER BUNDESREPUBLIK DEUTSCHLAND: DIREKTINVESTITIONEN AUSLAND 13 (2004)

PANAYIOTIS M. PROTOPSALTIS, MULTILATERAL INVESTMENT GUARANTEE AGENCY *(MIGA)* (2014)

Raymond R. Probst, *"Good Offices" in International Relations in the Light of Swiss Practice and Experience*, 201 RECUEIL DES COURS 211 (1987).

Sergio Puig & Chester Brown, *The Secretary-General's Power to Refuse to Register a Request for Arbitration under the ICSID Convention*, 27(1) ICSID REV.—FOR. INV. L.J. 172–91 (2012)

RAMESH F. RAMSARAN, NEGOTIATING THE LOMÉ IV CONVENTION (1990)

William Rant et al., *ICSID's Emerging Jurisprudence: The Scope of ICSID's Jurisdiction*, 19 NYUJ INT'L L. & POL. 33, 36 (1986)

Nigel Rawding, *Protecting Investments under State Contracts: Some Legal and Ethical Issues*, 11 ARB. INT'L 341, 342–46 (1995)
Michael R. Reading, *The Bilateral Investment Treaty in ASEAN: A Comparative Analysis*, 42 DUKE L.J. 679 (1992)
Alan Redfern, *ICSID: Losing Its Appeal?* 3 ARB. INT'L 98 (1987)
Alan Redfern, *Dissenting Opinions in International Commercial Arbitration: The Good, the Bad, and the Ugly*, 20 ARB. INT'L 223 (2004)
ALAN REDFERN & MARTIN HUNTER, LAW AND PRACTICE OF INTERNATIONAL COMMERCIAL ARBITRATION 443 (3d and 4th ed. 1999)
Lucy Reed, *More on Corporate Criticism of International Arbitration*, KLUWER ARBITRATION BLOG (JULY 16, 2010)
Lucy Reed et al., Guide to ICSID Arbitration 35 (2004)
Lucy Reed & Daina Bray, *Fair and Equitable Treatment: Fairly and Equitably Applied in Lieu of Unlawful Indirect Expropriation?* in CONTEMPORARY ISSUES IN INTERNATIONAL ARBITRATION AND MEDIATION: THE FORDHAM PAPERS 2007 (Arthur W. Rovine ed. 2008)
Klaus Reichert, *Confidentiality in International Mediation*, 59 DISP. RESOL. J. 60 (2005)
Linda C. Reif, *Conciliation as a Mechanism for the Resolution of International Economic and Business Disputes*, 14 FORDHAM INT'L L.J. 578 (1991)
Clara Reiner & Christoph Schreuer, *Human Rights and International Investment Arbitration*, in Human Rights in INTERNATIONAL INVESTMENT LAW AND ARBITRATION 90–91 (Pierre-Marie Dupuy et al. eds. 2009)
AUGUST REINISCH, STANDARDS OF INVESTMENT PROTECTION 135 (2008)
August Reinisch & Loretta Malintoppi, *Methods of Dispute Resolution*, in THE OXFORD HANDBOOK OF INTERNATIONAL INVESTMENT LAW, ch. 18, 715–17 (Peter Muchlinski et al. eds. 2008)
Michael Reisman, *The Breakdown of the Control Mechanism in ICSID Arbitration*, 4 DUKE L.J. 739 (1989)
George L. Ridgeway, Merchants of Peace 325–26 (1938)
David Riesenberg, *Fee Shifting in Investor– State Arbitration: Doctrine and Policy Justifying Application of the English Rule*, 60(4) DUKE L.J. 990 (2011)
Stefan A. Riesenfeld, *The Ethiopia–United States Compensation Agreement: Dicey Ending to a Spicy Tale*, 5 INT'L TAX & BUS. LAW. 239, 240 (1987)
HEINS RINDLER, *The Insurance of Austrian Investment Abroad against Political Risk: A Comparative Approach with Special Regard to Developmental Aspects*, 47
SERGEY RIPINSKY & KEVIN WILLIAMS, DAMAGES IN INTERNATIONAL INVESTMENT LAW (2008)
Leonard L. Riskin, *Mediation and Lawyers*, 43 OHIO ST. L.J. 29 (1982)
David Rivkin, *IBA Rules on the Taking of Evidence in International Commercial Arbitration*, 24a YB. COMM. ARB. 408, 409 (1999)
Maryse Robert et al., *Negotiating Investment Rules*, in AN INTEGRATED APPROACH TO THE EUROPEAN UNION–MERCOSUR ASSOCIATION 265, 270–79 (Paolo Giordano ed. 2002)
Patricia Robin, *The BIT Won't Bite: The American Bilateral Investment Treaty Program*, 33 AM. UL REV. 931 n.93 (1984)
Myrna Robinson-Waters & Christopher Hamel-Smith, *The New Oil Tax Regime: Taxation or Expropriation?* BUSINESS GUARDIAN, July 21, 2005, available at http://library2.nalis.gov.tt/gsdl/ collect/news3/index/assoc/HASHb346/9a743359.dir/4290.jpg
Republic of Cyprus (Ministry of Energy, Commerce, Industry and Tourism), "Model Exploration and Production Sharing Contract," Nicosia, 2016, available at: http://www.mcit.gov.cy/mcit/hydrocarbon.nsf/All/EFCD315C63D1D2B2C2257FA2002794F4/$file/%CE%9A%CE%B1%CE%B8%CE%BF%CE%B4%CE%B7%CE%B3%CE%B7%CF%84%CE%B9%CE%BA%CF%8C%20%CE%A3%CE%B7%CE%BC%CE%B5%CE%AF%CF%89%CE%BC%CE%B1.pdf

João Ribeiro & Michael Douglas, *Transparency in Investor–State Arbitration: The Way Forward*, 11 Asian Int'l. Arb. J. 49–67 (2015)

Renato Ribeiro, Nationalization of Foreign Property in International Law i (1977)

William M. Richman & William L. Reynolds, Understanding Conflict of Laws (2002)

Anthea Roberts, *Clash of Paradigms: Actors and Analogies Shaping the Investment Treaty System*, 107 AJIL 66 (2013)

Patricia McKinstry Robin, *The BIT Won't Bite: The American Bilateral Investment Treaty Program*, 33 Am. UL Rev. 931, 947–48 (1984)

J. Michael Robinson, *The Build, Own, and Transfer Model for International Projects in Emerging Markets*, 8 int'l LQ 126 (1996)

Zvonko R. Rode, *The American–Polish Claims Settlement Agreement of March 30, 1960*, 55 AJIL 452 (1961)

Raymond Rody, International Business Negotiations: Strategies, Tactics and Practices (2002)

Catherine A. Rogers & José María de la Jara, *Generating Needed Information about Arbitrators, One Arbitration at a Time*, Kluwer Arbitration Blog (Sept. 15, 2018), available at http://arbitrationblog.kluwerarbitration.com/2018/09/15/generating-needed-information-about-arbitrators-one-arbitration-at-a-time/

George Rosenberg, *State as Party to Arbitration*, 20 Arb. Int'l 387, 393–403 (2004)

Robert Rosenstock, *The ILC and State Responsibility*, 96 AJIL 792 (2002), available at https://documents-dds-ny.un.org/doc/UNDOC/GEN/N01/557/81/img/N0155781.pdf?OpenElement

Murray N. Rothbard, Man, Economy, and State: A Treatise on Economic Principles (1962), at ch. 12, § 11 (pp. 850–78), available at http://www.mises.org

Murray N. Rothbard, What Has Government Done to Our Money? (4th ed. 1990), available at http://www.mises.org

Ronald D. Rotunda, *Cautionary Lessons from American Securities Arbitration: Litigation v. Arbitration*, 5 Arb. Int'l 199 (1989)

C. Rousseau, *Echec de la procédure d'enquête det de conciliation dans l'affaire du déroutement de l'avion transportant de Rabat à Tunis les chefs nationalistes algériens le 22 octobre 1956*, 62 RGDIP 691 (1958)

Malcolm D. Rowat, *Multilateral Approaches to Improving the Investment Climate in Developing Countries: The Cases of ICSID and MIGA*, 33 Harv. Int'l L.J. 104 (1992)

Kristin T. Roy, *The New York Convention and Saudi Arabia: Can a Country Use the Public Policy Defense to Refuse Enforcement of Non-Domestic Arbitral Awards?* 18 Fordham Int'l L.J. 925 (1995)

Andres Rozental, *The Charter of Economic Rights and Duties of States and the New International Economic Order*, 16 Va. J. Int'l L. 309 (1976)

Alfred Rubin, *Book Review—Application of the Rule of Exhaustion of Local Remedies in International Law*, 25 Harv. Int'l L.J. 517, 518 (1984)

Seymour J. Rubin, *Introductory Note [to the World Bank: Report to the Development Committee and Guidelines on the Treatment of Foreign Direct Investment]*, 31 ILM 1363 (1992)

Noah Rubins, *In God We Trust, All Others Pay Cash: Security for Costs in International Commercial Arbitration*, 11 Am. Rev. Int'l Arb. 307, 314–15 (2000)

Noah Rubins, *The Arbitral Seat is No Fiction*, Mealey's Int'l Arb. Rep. (Jan. 2001)

Noah Rubins, *Manifest Disregard of the Law and Vacatur of Arbitral Awards in the United States*, 12 Am. Rev. Int'l Arb. 363, 364–67 (2001)

Noah Rubins, *Must the Victorious Claimant Relinquish Title to Expropriated Property?*, 4 J. World Inv. 481 (2003)

Noah Rubins, *The Arbitral Innovations of Recent U.S. Free Trade Agreements: Two Steps Forward, One Step Back*, 8 Int'l Bus. L.J. 865 (2003)

Noah Rubins, *Swembalt: An Introduction and the Dilemma of Default*, 2004(2) Stockholm Arb. Rep. 119

Noah Rubins, *Swembalt v. Latvia: An Overview and the Dilemma of Default*, 2 Stock. Int'l Arb. Rep. 119 (2004)

Noah Rubins, *The Final Damages Award in CME v. Czech Republic, B.V. v. Czech Republic: An Overview*, Mealey's Int'l Arb. Rep., September 2003, at 35

Noah Rubins, *The Notion of Investment in International Investment Arbitration*, in Arbitrating Investment Disputes 283, 320–23 (Norbert Horn ed. 2004)

Noah Rubins, *Judicial Review of Investment Arbitration Awards*, in NAFTA: Investment Law and Arbitration 359 (Todd Weiler ed. 2004)

Noah Rubins, *Loewen v. United States: The Burial of an Investor–State Claim*, 21 Arb. Int'l 1, 32–36 (2005)

Noah Rubins & Bernhard Lauterburg, *Independence, Impartiality and Duty of Disclosure in Investment Arbitration*, in Investment and Commercial Arbitration: Similarites and Divergences 153 (Christina Knahr et al. eds. 2010)

Sharon D. Ruccolo, *The Foreign Sovereign Immunities Act: Encouraging Foreign Plaintiffs to Sue Foreign Sovereigns in American Courts*, 25 Rutgers L.J. 517 (1994)

Frank Ruddy, *Book Review: Foreign Investment in the Present and a New International Economic Order*, 84 AJIL 961, 962 (1990)

H.G. Ruse-Khan, *Litigating Intellectual Property Rights in Investor–State Arbitration: From Plain Packaging to Patent Revocation*, Paper No. 52/2014, Cambridge Legal Studies Research Papers Series

Henning Grosse Ruse-Khan, *The Protection of Intellectual Property and International Investment Law*, 19(1) J. Int'l Econ. L. 87–90 (2016)

Valerie H. Ruttenberg, *The United States Bilateral Investment Treaty Program: Variations on the Model*, 9 U. Pa. J. Int'l Bus. L. 121 (1987)

Georgio Sacerdoti, *The Source and Evolution of International Legal Protection for Infrastructure Investments Confronting Political and Regulatory Risks*, 5(7) CEPMLP J. 4–5 (2008)

Jeswald W. Salacuse, *Towards a New Treaty Framework for Direct Foreign Investment*, 50 J. Air L. & Comm. 969 (1985)

Jeswald W. Salacuse, *BIT by BIT: The Growth of Bilateral Investment Treaties and Their Impact on Foreign Investment in Developing Countries*, 24 Int'l Law. 655 (1990)

Jeswald W. Salacuse, The Global Negotiator: Making, Managing, and Mending Deals around the World in the Twenty-First Century 229–55 (2003)

Jeswald W. Salacuse, *Mediation In International Business*, in Studies in International Mediation: Essays in Honor of Jeffrey Z. Rubin (Jacob Bercovitch ed. 2003)

Jeswald Salacuse, *Towards a Global Treaty on Foreign Investment: The Search for a Grand Bargain*, in Arbitrating Foreign Investment Disputes 51, 63 (Norbert Horn ed. 2004)

Jeswald W. Salacuse, *Is There A Better Way? Alternative Methods of Treaty Based Investor–State Dispute Resolution*, 31(1) Fordham Int'l. L.J. 155 (2007)

Jeswald Salacuse, The Law of Investment Treaties 273 (2010)

Jeswald W. Salacuse, The Three Laws of International Investment: National, Contractual, and International Frameworks for Foreign Capital, ch. 6, sec. 8.2(a) (2013)

Claudia T. Salomon, *Selecting an International Arbitrator: Five Factors to Consider*, 17 Mealey's Int'l Arb. Rep. 25 (Oct. 2002)
Vincent Sama, *Problems in Enforcement of Foreign Arbitral Awards* (transcript of seminar), 6 World Arb. & Med. Rep. 77, 79 (1995)
Arb. 21 (1988);
Frank E.A. Sander, *Varieties of Dispute Processing*, 70 FRD 79, 114 (1976).
Gloria L. Sandrino, *The NAFTA Investment Chapter and Foreign Direct Investment in Mexico: A Third World Prospective*, 27 Vand. J. Transnat'l L. 259 n.276 (1994)
Mavluda Sattorova, *Denial of Justice Disguised? Investment Arbitration and the Protection of Foreign Investors from Judicial Misconduct*, 61(1) ICLQ 224, notes 1 and 2 (2012)
Karl P. Sauvant, *The Regulatory Framework for Investment: Where Are We Headed?* 15 Research in Global Strategic Management 407–33 (2011)
Sarah Schadendorf, *Human Rights Arguments in Amicus Curiae Submissions: Analysis of ICSID and NAFTA Investor-State Arbitrations*, 10(1) TDM 1, 16 (2013)
Thomas O. Schelling, *An Essay on Bargaining*, 46 Am. Econ. Rev. 281, 300 (1956)
Stephan W. Schill, *Illegal Investments in International Arbitration* (Jan. 4, 2012), at 5, available at https://papers.ssrn.com/sol3/papers.cfm?abstract_id=1979734
Stephan W. Schill, *Transparency as a Global Norm in International Investment Law*, Kluwer Arbitration Blog (Sept. 15, 2014)
Peter F. Schlosser, *Coordinated Transnational Interaction in Civil Litigation and Arbitration*, 12 Mich. J. Int'l L. 150, 170 n.84 (1990)
Michael E. Schneider, *The Terms of Reference*, ICC Bull. Supp. 26 (1997)
Michael E. Schneider, *Combining Arbitration with Conciliation*, 2(1) Oil, Gas & Energy Law Intelligence 1 (Mar. 2003)
Christoph Schreuer, *Commentary on the ICSID Convention*, 11 ICSID Rev.—For. Inv. L.J. 318 *et seq.* (1996)
Christoph Schreuer, *Travelling the BIT Route: of Waiting Periods, Umbrella Clauses and Forks in the Road*, 5(2) J. World Inv. & Trade 231 (2004)
Christoph Schreuer, *Three Generations of ICSID Annulment Proceedings*, in Annulment of ICSID Awards 267 (Emmanuel Gaillard & Yas Banifatemi eds. 2004)
Christoph Schreuer, *The Concept of Expropriation under the ETC and other Investment Protection Treaties*, 3 TDM (2005), at para. 82
Christoph Schreuer, *Fair and Equitable Treatment in Arbitral Practice*, 6 J. World Trade & Inv. 357 (2005)
Christoph Schreuer, *Calvo's Grandchildren: The Return of Local Remedies in Investment Arbitration*, in The Law and Practice of International Courts and Tribunals 1–17 (2005)
Christoph Schreuer, *Consent to Arbitration*, in The Oxford Handbook of International Investment Law, ch. 21, 830–67 (Peter Muchlinski et al. eds. 2008)
Christoph H. Schreuer et al., The ICSID Convention: A Commentary 92 (2009)
Christoph Schreuer, *Full Protection and Security*, 1(2) J. Int'l Dispute Settlement 353–69 (2010)
Christoph Schreuer, *Jurisdiction and Applicable Law in Investment Treaty Arbitration*, 1(1) McGill J. Disp. Res. 1 (2014)
Olivier De Schutter, *The Accountability of Multinationals for Human Rights Violations in European Law*, in Non-State Actors and Human Rights 227 (Philip Alston ed. 2005)
Karl Heinz Schwab & Gerhard Walter, Schiedsgerichtsbarkeit 25–26 (7th ed. 2005)

Eric A. Schwartz, *The Domain of Arbitration and Issues of Arbitrability: The View from the ICC*, 9 ICSID Rev—For. Inv. L.J. 17, 19 (1994)

Eric Schwartz, *International Conciliation and the ICC*, 5(2) ICC Int'l Court Arb. Bull. 5 (1994)

Johnson Schwartz, *Court-Assisted Discovery in Aid of International Commercial Arbitrations: Two Recent U.S. Cases Regarding the Applicability of 28 U.S.C. § 1782*, 15(9) J. Int'l Arb. 53 (1998)

Georg Schwarzenberger, *Equality and Discrimination in International Economic Law*, in The Yearbook of World Affairs 164 (1971)

Georg Schwarzenberger, *Principles and Standards of International Economic Law*, 117 Recueil des Cours 1, 71 (1966)

Stephen M. Schwebel, *The Story of the U.N.'s Declaration on Permanent Sovereignty over Natural Resources*, 49 ABAJ 463 (1963)

Stephen Schwebel, *On Whether the Breach by a State of a Contract with an Alien Is a Breach of International Law*, in International Law at the Time of Its Codification 401 (1987)

Steven Schwebel, *Arbitration and the Exhaustion of Local Remedies*, in Justice in International Law 171 (1994)

Stephen Schwebel, *The Influence of Bilateral Investment Treaties on Customary International Law*, Proceedings of the 98th Annual Meeting of the American Society of International Law (Mar. 31–Apr. 3, 2004)

S. Schwebel, *The Reshaping of the International Law of Foreign Investment by Concordant Bilateral Investment Treaties*, in Law in the Service of Human Dignity—Essays in Honour of Florentino Feliciano 241 (S. Charnovitz et al. eds. 2005)

Stephen M. Schwebel, *The Overwhelming Merits of Bilateral Investment Treaties*, 32 Suffolk Transnat'l L. Rev. 263 (2009)

Stephen Schwebel & J. Gillis Wetter, *Arbitration and the Exhaustion of Local Remedies*, 60 AJIL 484, 486 (1966)

Sarah Scofield, *A Report on The London Court of International Arbitration (LCIA): History, Practices, Past Procedures, and the New Rules*, World Arb. & Med. Rep., Oct. 1998, at 269

Eugene Scoles et al., Conflict of Laws (3d ed. 2000)

Georg von Segesser, *The IBA Rules on the Taking of Evidence in International Arbitration*, 28(4) ASA Bull. 735–52 (2010)

Jamal Seifi, *Investor–State Arbitration v. State- to-State Arbitration in Bilateral Investment Treaties*, 1(4) Oil, Gas & Energy Law Intelligence (Sept. 2003)

Robert B. Shanks, *Insuring Investment and Loans against Currency Inconvertibility, Expropriation, and Political Violence*, 9 Hastings Int'l & Comp. L. Rev. 417, 421 (1986)

Yuval Shany, *Towards a General Margin of Appreciation Doctrine in International Law?* 16 EJIL 907–40 (2005)

Malcolm N. Shaw, International Law 588–95 (7th ed. 2014)

Donald Shea, The Calvo Clause: A Problem of Inter-American and International Law and Diplomacy (1955)

The Oxford Handbook of International Human Rights Law (Dinah Shelton ed. 2013)

Audley Sheppard, *Arbitrator Independence in ICSID Arbitration*, in International Investment Law for the 21st Century: Essays in Honour of Christoph Schreuer 131, 133–36 (Christina Binder et al. eds. 2009)

Frederick E. Sherman & Steven C. Bennett, *Avoiding "Pathological" Arbitration Clauses*, The Practical Lawyer 43 (Aug. 2006)

Peter Sherwin et al., *Ch. 19. The Decision to Arbitrate*, in PROSKAUER ON INTERNATIONAL LITIGATION AND ARBITRATION: MANAGING, RESOLVING, AND AVOIDING CROSS-BORDER BUSINESS OR REGULATORY DISPUTES (2007)

Ibrahim F.I. Shihata, *Destination Embargo of Arab Oil: Its Legality under International Law*, 68 AJIL 591, 625 (1974)

Ibrahim F.I. Shihata, *Towards a Greater Depolitization of Investment Disputes: The Role of ICSID and MIGA*, 1 ICSID REV.—FOR. INV. L.J. 1 (1986)

Ibrahim Shihata, *The Settlement of Disputes Regarding Foreign Investment: The Role of the World Bank, With Particular Reference to ICSID and MIGA*, 1 AM. UJ INT'L L. & POL'Y. 97, 102–03 (1986)

Ibrahim F.I. Shihata, *Factors Influencing the Flow of Foreign Investment and the Relevance of a Multilateral Investment Guarantee Scheme*, 21 INT'L L. 671 (1987)

IBRAHIM F.I. SHIHATA, MIGA AND FOREIGN INVESTMENT—ORIGINS, OPERATIONS, POLICIES AND BASIC DOCUMENTS OF THE MULTILATERAL INVESTMENT GUARANTEE AGENCY (1988)

Ibrahim Shihata, Towards a Greater Depoliticization of Investment Disputes: The Roles of ICSID and MIGA 1–10 (1992)

Ibrahim Shihata, TOWARDS A GREATER DEPOLITICIZATION OF INVESTMENT DISPUTES: THE ROLES OF ICSID AND MIGA 1–10 (1992)

IBRAHIM SHIHATA, LEGAL TREATMENT OF FOREIGN INVESTMENT: THE WORLD BANK GUIDELINES 9 (1993)

Ibrahim F.I. Shihata, *Recent Trends Relating to Entry of Foreign Direct Investment*, 9 ICSID REV.—FOR. INV. L.J. 47 (1994)

Ibrahim Shihata & Antonio R. Parra, *Applicable Substantive Law in Disputes between States and Private Foreign Parties: The Case of Arbitration under the ICSID Convention*, 9 ICSID REV.—FOR. INV. L.J. 191 (1994)

Wesley Sholz, *International Regulation of Foreign Direct Investment*, 31 CORNELL INT'L L.J. 485, 486 (1998)

Laurence Shore & Kenneth Juan Figueroa, *Dissents, Concurrences and a Necessary Divide between Investment and Commercial Arbitration*, 3 GLOBAL ARB. REV. 18, 20 (2008) Daniel W. Shuman, *The Psychology of Deterrence in Tort Law*, 42 U. Kan. L. Rev. 115, 127–29 (1993)

Bruno Simma, *The Work of the International Law Commission at its 52nd Session, Report of the Ad Hoc Committee of Legal Advisers to the Council of Europe on International Law*, Sept. 4, 2000, at 24, published at https://www.coe.int/en/web/cahdi/20th- meeting-meeting-documents?p_p_id=101&p_p_lifecycle=0&p_p_state=maximized&p_p_col_ id=column-1&p_p_col_count=1&_101_struts_action=%2Fasset_publisher%2Fview_content&_ 101_assetEntryId=2785827&_101_type=content

Bruno Simma & Theodore Kill, *Harmonizing Investment Protection and International Human Rights: First Steps Towards a Methodology*, in INTERNATIONAL INVESTMENT LAW FOR THE 21ST CENTURY: ESSAYS IN HONOUR OF CHRISTOPH SCHREUER 678–707 (Christina Binder et al. eds. 2009)

Anthony Sinclair, *ICSID Arbitration: How Long Does It Take?* 4(5) GLOBAL ARB. REV. J. (2009)

Ian Sinclair, *Nationality of Claims: British Practice*, 27 BRIT. YB. INT'L L. 125 (1950)

LINDA R. SINGER, SETTLING DISPUTES 24–25 (1990)

Jose Luis Siqueiros, *Bilateral Treaties on the Reciprocal Protection of Foreign Investment*, 24 CAL. W. INT'L L.J. 255, 257 (1994)

F. Blaine Sloan, *The Binding Force of a "Recommendation" of the General Assembly of the United Nations*, 25 BRIT. YB. INT'L L. 1 (1948)

Ileana M. Smeureanu, Confidentiality in International Arbitration (2011)

Hans Smit, *The Future of International Arbitration: A Single Transnational Institution?* 25 Colum. J. Transnat'l L. 9 (1986)

Hans Smit, *Confidentiality*, 9 Am. Rev. Int'l Arb. 233 (1988)

Hans Smit, *American Assistance to Litigation in Foreign and International Tribunals: Section 1782 of Title 28 of the U.S.C. Revisited*, 25 Syr. J. Int'l L. & Com. 1, 5–8 (1998)

Robert H. Smit, *An Inside View of the ICC Court*, 10 Arb. Int'l 53 (1994)

Robert H. Smit et al., Comparison of International Arbitration Rules (4th ed. 2013)

David Smith, *Shifting Sands: Cost-and-Fee Allocation in International Investment Arbitration*, 51 Va. J. Int'l. L. 749 (2011)

Ernest E. Smith & John S. Dzienkowski, *A Fifty-Year Perspective on World Petroleum Arrangements*, 24 Tex. J. Int'l L. 13, 35 (1989)

Ernest E. Smith et al., International Petroleum Transactions (1993)

James F. Smith, *Mediation and the Principles of UNIDROIT*, in Contratación Internacional: Comentarios A Los Principios Sobre Los Contratos Comerciales Internacionales Del UNIDROIT 237 (1998)

Abby Cohen Smutny, *State Responsibility and Attribution: When Is a State Responsible for the Acts of State Enterprises?* in International Investment Law and Arbitration 17 (Todd Weiler ed. 2005)

Christer Söderlund, *The State as a Party in Arbitration and Issues of Sovereign Immunity* at 5, presented on Sept. 17, 2004 in Almaty, Kazakhstan (discussing SCC Case No. 38- 39/1997)

Manual of Public International Law 582 (Max Sørensen ed. 1958)

Neil Sorenson, *Bilateral Investment Treaties and Disputes*, Bilaterals.org (2001), available at http://www.bilaterals.org/article.php3?id_article=122

M. Sornarajah, *Power and Justice in Foreign Investment Arbitration*, 14 J. Int'l Arb. 103 (1997)

Ole Spiermann, *Individual Rights, State Interests and the Power to Waive ICSID Jurisdiction under Bilateral Investment Treaties*, 20 Arb. Int'l 179 (2004)

M. Sornarajah, The Settlement of Foreign Investment Disputes 223–78 (2000)

M. Sornarajah, International Law on Foreign Investment 47–60 (3d ed. 2010)

Standard & Poor's, *The Argentine Crisis: A Chronology of Events after the Sovereign Default*, Apr. 12, 2002, available at http://www.standardandpoors.com/eu- rope/francais/Fr_news/Argentine-Chronology-of-Events_12-04-02.html

Anna Spain, *Integration Matters: Rethinking the Architecture of International Dispute Resolution* 32(1) U. Pa. J. Int'l L. 19 (2010)

Ole Spiermann, *Investment Arbitration: Applicable Law*, in International Investment Law 1373 (Marc Bungenberg et al. eds. 2015)

Christopher Staker, *Diplomatic Protection of Private Business Companies: Determining Corporate Personality for International Law Purposes*, 61 Brit. Yb. Int'l L. 155 (1991)

Philip Stansbury, *Planning against Expropriation*, 24 Int'l Law. 677 (1990)

J.G. Starke, *Treaties as a "Source" of International Law*, 23 Brit. Yb. Int'l L. 341, 344 (1946)

Thomas R. Stauffer, *Valuation of Assets in International Takings*, 17 Energy L.J. 459–88 (1996)

Steven J. Stein & Daniel R. Wotman, International Commercial Arbitration in New York 87–96 (1986)

Charles R. Stevens & Kazunobu Takahashi, *The East Asian Preference for Conciliation: An Example in a Kabuki Play*, 5 Arb. Int'l 43 (1989)

Joseph E. Stiglitz, *Is there a Post-Washington Consensus*? in THE WASHINGTON CONSENSUS RECONSIDERED: TOWARDS A NEW GLOBAL GOVERNANCE (Narcís Serra & Joseph E. Stiglitz eds. 2008)

Stockholm Chamber of Commerce Arbitration Institute, *A Great Year for Investment Treaty Disputes*, available at http://www.sccinstitute.com/statistics/investment-disputes-2017/

Stockholm Chamber of Commerce Arbitration Institute, *The Administration of Investment Disputes*, available at http://www.sccinstitute.com/dispute-resolution/investment-disputes/

Stockholm Chamber of Commerce Arbitration Institute, *Calculator*, available at http://www.sccinstitute.com/dispute-resolution/calculator/

SUSAN STRANGE, THE RETREAT OF THE STATE: THE DIFFUSION OF POWER IN THE WORLD ECONOMY (1996)

SUSAN STRANGE, MAD MONEY: WHEN MARKETS OUTGROW GOVERNMENTS (1998)

Daniella Strik, *Investment Protection of Sovereign Debt and Its Implications on the Future of Investment Law in the EU*, 29(2) J. INT'L ARB. 183–204 (2012)

Pheng Low Sui, *The Influence of Chinese Philosophies on Mediation and Conciliation in the Far East*, 62(1) ARB. 16 (1996)

Edna Sussman, *The Advantages of Mediation and the Special Challenges to Its Utilization in Investor State Disputes* (Feb. 5, 2011), available at SSRN: https://ssrn.com/abstract=2372313

Erik Suy, *Innovations in International Law-Making Processes*, in THE INTERNATIONAL LAW AND POLICY OF HUMAN WELFARE 187, 190 (1978)

Alex Stone Sweet & Giacinto della Cananea, *Proportionality, General Principles of Law, and Investor–State Arbitration: A Response to Jose Alvarez*, 46 NYU J. INT'L. L. 911 (2014)

SANDRA SYNKOVÁ, COURTS' INQUIRY INTO ARBITRAL JURISDICTION AT THE PRE-AWARD STAGE: A COMPARATIVE ANALYSIS OF THE ENGLISH, GERMAN AND SWISS LEGAL ORDER 93–95 (2013)

Paul Szasz, *A Practical Guide to the Convention on the Settlement of Investment Disputes*, 1 CORNELL INT'L L.J. 1, 20 (1968)

KIM TALUS, EU ENERGY LAW AND POLICY: A CRITICAL ACCOUNT 228–30 (2013)

K. Tamas, *The ELSI Case and the Rule of the Exhaustion of Local Remedies*, in RESPONSIBILITY OF STATES—THESAURUS ACROASIUM 341 (1993)

Christian J. Tams & Alessandra Asteriti, *Transparency and Representation of the Public Interest in Investment Treaty Arbitration*, in INTERNATIONAL INVESTMENT LAW AND COMPARATIVE PUBLIC LAW (Stephan W. Schill ed. 2010)

Kenji Tashiro, *Conciliation or Mediation during the Arbitral Process: A Japanese View*, 12(2) J. INT'L ARB. 119 (1995)

Ted G. Telford & Heather A. Ures, *The Role of Incentives in Foreign Direct Investment*, 23 LOY. INT'L & COMP. LR 605, 615–16 (2001)

RAVI C. TENNEKOON, THE LAW AND REGULATION OF INTERNATIONAL FINANCE (1991)

WILLIAM TETLEY, INTERNATIONAL CONFLICT OF LAWS 10–11 (1994)

Patrick Thieffry, *Negotiating Settlement of Disputes Provisions in International Business Contracts: Recent Developments in Arbitration and Other Processes*, 45 BUS. LAW 577 (1990)

HUGH THIRLWAY, THE SOURCES OF INTERNATIONAL LAW 1–25 (2014)

J.C. Thomas, *Reflections on Article 1105 of NAFTA: History, State Practice and the Influence of Commentators*, 17 ICSID REV.—FOR. INV. L.J. 21 (2002)

Adam Thomson, *Argentina Defiant towards Private Creditors*, FINANCIAL TIMES, Mar. 11, 2004, at 11

Jennifer Tobin & Susan Rose-Ackerman, *Foreign Direct Investment and the Business Environment in Developing Countries: The Impact of Bilateral Investment Treaties*, Yale

Law & Economics Research Paper No. 293 (2004), available at http://papers.ssrn.com/sol3/papers.cfm?abstract_id=557121.

Mehmet Toral & Thomas Schultz, *The State, a Perpetual Respondent in Investment Arbitration? Some Unorthodox Considerations*, in The Backlash against Investment Arbitration: Perceptions and Reality 577–602 (Michael Waibel et al. eds. 2010)

Leon E. Trakman, *Confidentiality in International Commercial Arbitration*, 18(1) Arb. Int'l 1–18 (2002)

Johannes Trappe, *Conciliation in the Far East*, 5 Arb. Int'l 183 (1989)

Matias F. Travieso-Diaz, *Some Legal and Practical Issues in the Resolution of Cuban Nationals' Expropriation Claims against Cuba*, 16 U. Pa. J. Int'l Bus. L. 217, 229–30 (1995)

Matias F. Travieso-Diaz, *Alternative Recommendations for Dealing with Expropriated U.S. Property in Post-Castro Cuba*, 12 Cuba in Transition 101, 107 (ASCE 2002), available at https://ascecuba.org//c/wp-content/uploads/2014/09/v12-travieso2.pdf

Volker Triebel, *The Choice of Law in Commercial Relations: A German Perspective*, 37 ICLQ 935–45 (1988)

A.A. Cancado Trindade, The Application of the Rule of Exhaustion of Local Remedies in International Law: Its Rationale in the International Protection of Individual Rights (1983)

H. Tümpel & C. Sudborough, *ICC's ADR Rules 2001– 2010: Current Practices, Case Examples and Lessons Learned*, in II ADR in Business, Practice and Issues across Countries and Cultures (A. Ingenhousz ed. 2011)

W.M. Tupman, *Case Studies in the Jurisdiction of the International Centre for Investment Disputes*, 35 ICLQ 813, 816 (1986)

W. Michael Tupman, *Challenge and Disqualification of Arbitrators in International Commercial Arbitration*, 38 Int'l & Comp. LQ 26, 50 (1989)

Gillian Turner, *Investment Protection through Arbitration: The Dispute Resolution Provisions of the Energy Charter Treaty*, 1 Int'l Arb. L. Rev. 166, 167 (1998)

Inna Uchkunova, *Rule 41(5) of the ICSID Arbitration Rules: The Sleeping Beauty of the ICSID system*, Kluwer Arbitration Blog (2014), available at http://arbitrationblog.kluwerarbitration.com/2014/06/27/rule-415-of-the-icsid-arbitration-rules- the-sleeping-beauty-of-the-icsid-system/

Nicholas C. Ulmer, *Drafting the International Arbitration Clause*, 20 Int'l Law. 1335, 1339 (1986)

Nicolas Ulmer, *The Cost Conundrum*, 26(2) Arb. Int'l. 221–51 (2010)

U.N. Centre on Transnational Corporations, *The New Environment,* UNTC Current Studies, Series A, No. 16 (New York: United Nations, 1990), at 18

United Nations Commission on International Trade Law (UNCITRAL) Arbitration Rules, G.A.R. 98, U.N. GAOR, 31st Session, Supplement No. 39 at 182, U.N. Doc. A/31/39 (1976)

UNCITRAL, Notes on Organizing Arbitral Proceedings, U.N. Doc. A/CN.9/410, arts. 21–23, available at https://www.uncitral.org/pdf/english/texts/arbi- tration/arb-notes/arb-notes-e.pdf (2012) [hereinafter, the UNCITRAL Notes]

United Nations, International Law Commission, Report on the Work of its Fifty-Third Session (April 23–June 1 and July 2–Aug. 10, 2001), General Assembly, Official Records, Fifty- Fifth Session, Supplement No. 10 (A/56/10), available at http://legal.un.org/ilc/texts/instruments/ english/draft_articles/9_6_2001.pdf

U.N. Conference on Trade and Development (UNCTAD), Trends in International Investment Agreements: An Overview, UNCTAD/ITE/IIT/13, at 39 (1999), available at http://www.unctad.org/en/docs/iteiit13_en.pdf

UNCTAD/UNEP, Foreign Direct Investment and the Promotion of Sustainable Human Development (1999)

UNCTAD, THE SOCIAL RESPONSIBILITY OF TRANSNATIONAL CORPORATIONS (1999)
UNCTAD, Bilateral Investment Treaties 1959–1999, 3–4 (2000), available at http:\\www.unctad.org/en/docs/poiteiiad2.en.pdf
UNCTAD, 1 INTERNATIONAL INVESTMENT AGREEMENTS: KEY ISSUES 240–41 (2000)
UNCTAD, *Taking of Property*, UNCTAD/ITE/ IIT/15 (2000), available at http://www.unctad.org/en/docs/psiteiitd15.en.pdf, at 24 *et seq*
UNCTAD, World Investment Report, Geneva (2002)
UNCTAD, World Investment Report, 6–7 (2004), available at https://unctad.org/en/Docs/ wir2004overview_en.pdf
UNCTAD, World Investment Report 2006 (2006)
UNCTAD, Investor–State Disputes: Prevention and Alternatives to Arbitration (2010), at 16–18
UNCTAD, *Scope and Definition*, UNCTAD Series on Issues in International Investment Agreements II (2011)
U.N. Conference on Trade and Development, The Impact of International Investment Agreements on Foreign Direct Investment: An Overview of Empirical Studies 1998–2004, Working Draft (2014)
UNCTAD, World Investment Report: Investment and the Digital Economy (2017), at 111, available at http://unctad.org/en/PublicationsLibrary/wir2017_en.pdf
WILLIAM L. URY ET AL., GETTING DISPUTES RESOLVED: DESIGNING SYSTEMS TO CUT THE COSTS OF CONFLICT 3–19 (1988)
U.S. Dept. of State, *Investment Climate Brazil 2000*
Valentina Sara Vadi, *Reconciling Public Health and Investor Rights: The Case of Tobacco*, in HUMAN RIGHTS IN INTERNATIONAL INVESTMENT LAW AND ARBITRATION 453 (Pierre-Marie Dupuy et al. eds. 2009)
Detlev F. Vagts, *Coercion and Foreign Investment Rearrangements*, 72 AJIL 17 (1978)
Detlev F. Vagts, *Dispute-Resolution Mechanisms in International Business*, 3 RECUEIL DES COURS 9 (1987)
Detlev F. Vagts, *Protecting Foreign Investment: An International Law Perspective*, in FOREIGN DIRECT INVESTMENT IN THE 1990S: A NEW CLIMATE IN THE THIRD WORLD 109 (Cynthia Day Wallace ed. 1990)
Kenneth Vandevelde, *The Bilateral Treaty Program of the United States*, 21 CORNELL INT'L L.J. 21, 201 (1988)
KENNETH J. VANDEVELDE, UNITED STATES INVESTMENT TREATIES: POLICY AND PRACTICE (1992)
Kenneth J. Vandevelde, *U.S. Bilateral Investment Treaties: The Second Wave*, 14 MICH. J. INT'L L. 621 n.19 (1993)
TIBOR VÁRADY et al., INTERNATIONAL COMMERCIAL ARBITRATION 532 (1999)
Baiju S. Vasani & Shaun A. Palmer, *Challenge and Disqualification of Arbitrators at ICSID: A New Dawn?*, 30(1) ICSID REV.—FOR. INV. L.J. 1–23 (2014)
Stephen Vasciannie, *Bilateral Investment Treaties and Civil- Strife: The AAPL–Sri Lanka Arbitration*, 39 NETHERLANDS INT'L L. REV. 332–54 (1992)
Stephen Vasciannie, *The Fair and Equitable Treatment Standard in International Investment Law and Practice*, 70 BRIT. YB. INT'L L. 99 (2000)
Lori Y. Vassar, *Foreign Assets Control: Proposed Vesting of Viet Nam Assets*, 84 AJIL 539 (1990)
Carlos M. Vazquez, *Direct vs. Indirect Obligations of Corporations under International Law*, 43 COLUM. J. TRANSNAT'L L. 927 (2005)
V.V. VEEDER, *London Court of International Arbitration: The New 1998 LCIA Rules*, 23 YB. COMM. ARB. 366 (1998)
V.V. Veeder, *Lloyd George, Lenin and Cannibals: The Harriman Arbitration*, 16 ARB. INT'L 115 (2000)

Herman Verbist, *The Practice of the ICC International Court of Arbitration with Regard to the Fixing of the Place of Arbitration*, 12 Arb. Int'l 347 (1996)

Raymond Vernon, In the Hurricane's Eye: The Troubled Prospects of Multinational Enterprises 32–59 (1998)

Francisco Orrego Vicuna, *The International Regulation of Valuation Standards and Processes: A Reexamination of Third World Perspectives*, in 3 The Valuation of Nationalized Property in International Law 131–48 (Richard B. Lillich ed. 1975)

Francisco Orrego Vicuna, *Changing Approaches to the Nationality of Claims in the Context of Diplomatic Protection and International Dispute Settlement*, in Liber Amicorum Ibrahim F.I. Shihata: International Finance And Development Law 503 (S. Schlemmer-Schulte & K.-Y. Tung eds. 2001)

Francisco Orrego Vicuña, *Bilateral Investment Treaties and the Most-Favored-Nation Clause: Implications for Arbitration in the Light of a Recent ICSID Case*, Presentation to Swiss Arbitration Association Conference, Zurich, Jan. 25, 2002, at 2

Daniel E. Vielleville & Baiju Simal Vasani, *Sovereignty over Natural Resources Versus Rights under Investment Contracts: Which One Prevails?* 5(2) TDM 21 (2008)

Jorge E. Viñuales, *Human Rights and Investment Arbitration: The Role of Amici Curiae International Law*, 8 Revista Colombiana de Derecho Internacional 231–73 (2006).

Jorge E. Viñuales, *Sources of International Investment Law: Conceptual Foundations of Unruly Practices*, in The Oxford Handbook on the Sources of International Law 1069 (Jean d'Aspremont & Samantha Besson eds. 2017)

Paul H. Vishny, Guide to International Commercial Law §§ 5.23, 11.09 (1994)

Robert Volterra, *Mitigating Expropriation Risk for Oil & Gas Investment in the Caspian Region*, IEA Roundtable on Caspian Oil & Gas Scenarios (Apr. 15, 2003)

Tania Voon & Andrew D. Mitchell, *Philip Morris vs. Tobacco Control: Two Wins For Public Health, But Uncertainty Remains*, 182 Colum. FDI Perspectives 1 (2016)

Nathalie Voser & Neomi Rao, *Background Information on the IBA Guidelines on Conflicts of Interest in International Arbitration*, 5 Bus. L. Int'l 433, 442 (2004)

Shai Wade et al., A Commentary on the LCIA Arbitration Rules 2014 (2015)

Michael Waibel, *Opening Pandora's Box: Sovereign Bonds in International Arbitration*, 101 AJIL 711–59 (2007)

Michael Waibel, *Investment Arbitration: Jurisdiction and Admissibility* (2014), University of Cambridge Faculty of Law Research Paper No. 9/2014, at 34–38

Michael Waibel & Yanhui Wu, *Are Arbitrators Political?*, ASIL Research Forum 13 (Nov. 5, 2011)

Jeff Waincymer, *Balancing Property Rights and Human Rights in Expropriation*, in Human Rights in International Investment Law and Arbitration 277–84 (Pierre-Marie Dupuy et al. eds. 2009)

J.M. Wagner, *International Investment, Expropriation and Environmental Protection*, 29 Golden Gate UL Rev. 465 (1999)

The Energy Charter Treaty: An East– West Gateway for Investment and Trade (Thomas W. Wälde ed. 1996)

Thomas W. Wälde, *Investment Arbitration Under the Energy Charter Treaty—from Dispute Settlement to Treaty Implementation*, 12 Arb. Int'l 429 (1996)

Thomas W. Wälde & Todd Weiler, *Investment Arbitration under the Energy Charter Treaty in the Light of New NAFTA Precedents: Towards a Global Code of Conduct for Economic Regulation?* in Investment Treaties and Arbitration 159, 160–62 (Gabrielle Kaufmann-Kohler & Blaise Stucki eds. 2002)

Thomas W. Wälde, *The Treatment of the "Umbrella" or "Pacta Sunt Servanda" Clause in the SGS v. Pakistan Jurisdictional Decision (2003): Correct?* 1(5) OIL, GAS & ENERGY LAW INTELLIGENCE (December 2003)

Thomas W. Wälde, *Mediation/Alternative Dispute Resolution in Oil, Gas and Energy Transactions: Superior to Arbitration/Litigation from a Commercial and Management Perspective*, 13(8) CEPMLP J. (2003)

Thomas W. Wälde, *Pro-Active Mediation of International Business and Investment Disputes Involving Long-Term Contracts: From Zero-Sum Litigation to Efficient Dispute Management*, 1 OIL, GAS & ENERGY LAW INTELLIGENCE 2 (Sept. 2003)

Thomas W. Wälde, *Energy Charter Treaty-based Investment Arbitration: Controversial Issues*, 6 J. WORLD INV. & TRADE 373 (2004).

Thomas W. Wälde, *The "Umbrella" (or Sanctity of Contract/Pacta Sunt Servanda) Clause in Investment Arbitration: A Comment on Original Intentions and Recent Cases*, 1(4) TDM (2004)

Thomas W. W älde, *Investment Arbitration under the Energy Charter Treaty: An Overview of Key Issues*, 1 TDM (2004)

Thomas W. Wälde, *The "Umbrella" Clause in Investment Arbitration—A Comment on Original Intentions and Recent Cases*, 6 J. WORLD INV. & TRADE 184 (2005)

Thomas W. Wälde, *Efficient Management of Transnational Disputes: Mutual Gain by Mediation or Joint Loss in Litigation*, 22 ARB. INT'L. 205–33 (2006)

Thomas W. Wälde, *Chapter 12—Improving the Mechanisms for Treaty Negotiation and Investment Disputes, Competition and Choice as the Path to Quality and Legitimacy*, in YEARBOOK ON INTERNATIONAL INVESTMENT LAW & POLICY 2008–2009 535–36 (Karl Sauvant ed. 2009)

Thomas W. Wäelde & Abba Kolo, *Multilateral Investment Treaties and Environmental Expropriation of Foreign Investment*, Alexander's Gas and Oil Connection—Speeches (2002) available at https://www. ogel.org/article.asp?key=801

Thomas W. Wälde & George N'Di, *Stabilizing International Investment Commitments: International Law versus Contract Interpretation*, 1 CEPMLP J. (Professional Paper PP13) (1994), available at http://www.dundee.ac.uk/cepmlp

Thomas W. Wälde & George N'Di, *Stabilizing International Investment Commitments: International Law versus Contract Interpretation*, 31 TEX. INT'L L.J. 216, 236 n.83 (1996), version available at http://www. dundee.ac.uk/cepmlp

Thomas W. Walde & Borzu Sabahi, *Compensation, Damages, and Valuation*, in THE OXFORD HANDBOOK OF INTERNATIONAL INVESTMENT LAW 1069–70 (Peter Muchlinski et al. eds. 2008)

Andrew Walter, British Investment Treaties in South Asia: Current Status and Future Trends, 14 (2000)

André von Walter, *Oil Concession Disputes, Arbitration on*, in MAX PLANCK ENCYCLOPEDIA OF PUBLIC INTERNATIONAL LAW, paras. 11 and 43 (2008)

Jonathan Walters, *Caspian Oil and Gas: Mitigating Political Risks for Private Participation*, 7(5) CEPMLP J. 2–3 (2001), available at http://documents.worldbank.org/curated/en/ 152381468032950270/pdf/353700rev0Caspian0oil0prague2000a.pdf

Margaret Wang, *Are Alternative Dispute Resolution Methods Superior to Litigation in Resolving Disputes in International Commerce?* 16 ARB. INT'L 189 (2000)

Peter Watson, *Private Sector Investment in Development*, Aspen Institute (July 31, 2004), available at http://www.opic.gov

THOMAS H. WEBSTER & DR. MICHAEL BUHLER, HANDBOOK OF ICC ARBITRATION: COMMENTARY, PRECEDENTS, MATERIALS 111–21 (2014)

Philip R. Weems, *An Introduction to Upstream Government Petroleum Contracts: Their Evolution and Current Use* published in Oil, Gas & Energy Law Intelligence (OGEL)

"Special Feature: Production Sharing Contracts," in 3(1), available at http://www.gasandoil.com/ogel

Frank-Bernd Weigan, Practitioner's Handbook on International Commercial Arbitration, paras. 14.393 *et seq.* (2009)

Prosper Weil, *Problèmes relatifs aux contrats passés entre un Etat et un particulier*, 128 Recueil des Cours 94, 130 (1969)

The EU, The WTO and the NAFTA: Towards a Common Law of International Trade? (Joseph H.H. Weiler ed. 2000)

Todd Weiler, *NAFTA Article 1105 and the Free Trade Commission: Just Sour Grapes, Or Something More Serious?* 29 Int'l Bus. Law. 491 (2001)

Todd Weiler, *A First Look at the Interim Merits Award in S.D. Myers v. Canada*, 24 Hastings Int'l & Comp. L. Rev. 87 (2001)

Todd Weiler, *Metalclad and the Government of Mexico: A Play in Three Parts*, 2 J. World Invest. 685 (2001)

NAFTA Investment Law and Arbitration: Past Issues, Current Practice, Future Prospects (Todd Weiler ed. 2004)

Todd Weiler, *Prohibitions against Discrimation in NAFTA Chapter 11*, in NAFTA Investment Law and Arbitration 27 (Todd Weiler ed. 2004)

Todd Weiler, *Saving Oscar Chin* [sic]: *Non-Discrimination in International Investment Law*, in International Investment Law and Arbitration 557 (Todd Weiler ed. 2005)

Todd Weiler & Luis Miguel Diaz, *Causation and Damages in NAFTA Investor–State Arbitration*, in NAFTA Investment Law and Arbitration: Past Issues, Current Practice, Future Prospects 199 (Todd Weiler ed. 2004)

Louis T. Wells & Rafiq Ahmed, Making Foreign Investment Safe: Property Rights and National Sovereignty (2007)

Irene Welser & Susanne Molitoris, *The Scope of Arbitration Clauses—Or "All Disputes Arising out of or in Connection with this Contract,"* in Austrian Yearbook of International Arbitration 18 (Christian Klausegger et al. eds. 2012)

Nancy A. Welsh, *Mandatory Mediation and Its Variations*, in Investor–State Disputes: Prevention and Alternatives to Arbitration II, 108 *et seq.* (Susan D. Franck & Anna Joubin-Bret eds. 2011)

Nancy A. Welsh & Andrea Kupfer Schneider, *The Thoughtful Integration of Mediation into Bilateral Investment Treaty Arbitration,* 18 Harv. Neg. L. Rev. 71–142 (2003)

Nancy A. Welsh & Andrea K. Schneider, *Becoming "Investor–State Mediation,"* 1(1) Penn. St. JL & Int'l Af. 86–88 (2012)

Alexander Wentker, *Venezuela's Non-Participation be- fore the ICJ in the Dispute over the Essequibo Region*, EJIL:Talk! (June 29, 2018), available at https:// www.ejiltalk.org/venezuelas-non-participation-before-the-icj-in-the-dispute-over-the-essequibo- region/

Jacques Werner, *Dissenting Opinions: Beyond Fears*, 9(4) J. Int'l Arb. 23 (1992)

Gerald T. West, Investment Insurance and Developmental Impact 13 (2001)

John Westlake, A Treatise on Private International Law, with Principal Reference to its Practice in England 237 (2d ed. 1880)

Burns Weston, International Claims: Postwar French Practice 83 (1971)

Burns H. Weston, *"Constructive Takings" under International Law: A Modest Foray into the Problem of "Creeping Expropriation"*, 16 Va. J. Int'l L. 103, 170 (1975)

Burns H. Weston, *The Charter of Economic Rights and Duties of States and the Deprivation of Foreign-owned Wealth*, 75 AJIL 437, 445 (1981)

Burns H. Weston et al., International Claims: Their Settlement by Lump Sum Agreement 1975–95 (1999)

J. Gills Wetter, The International Arbitral Process 27–173 (1962)

J. Gillis Wetter, *The Conduct of the Arbitration*, 2(2) J. INT'L ARB. 20–23 (1985)
J. Gillis Wetter, *The Present Status of the International Court of Arbitration of the ICC: An Appraisal*, 1 AM. REV. INT'L ARB. 91 (1990)
Gillian White, *A New International Economic Order?* 16 VA. J. INT'L L. 323, 330 (1976)
MARJORIE M. WHITEMAN, 2 DAMAGES IN INTERNATIONAL LAW 827 (1937)
MARJORIE M. WHITEMAN, 3 DAMAGES IN INTERNATIONAL LAW 1694–703 (1943)
8 MARJORIE M. WHITEMAN, DIGEST OF INTERNATIONAL LAW 739–40 (1967)
David A.R. Williams QC, *Jurisdiction and Admissibility*, in THE OXFORD HANDBOOK OF INTERNATIONAL INVESTMENT LAW 893–97 (Peter Muchlinski et al. eds. 2008)
John Fischer Williams, *International Law and the Property of Aliens*, 9 BRIT. YB. INT'L L. 1, 28 (1928)
S. Linn Williams, *Political and Other Risk Insurance: OPIC, MIGA, Eximbank and Other Providers*, 5 PACE INT'L L. REV. 59 (1993)
Kent Wilson, *Savings Costs in International Arbitration*, 6 Arb. Int'l 151 (1990)
ROBERT R. WILSON, THE INTERNATIONAL LAW STANDARD IN TREATIES OF THE UNITED STATES 103–04 (1953)
Robert Wisner & Nick Gallus, *Nationality Requirements in Investor–State Arbitration*, 5 J.
Peter M. Wolrich, *ICC ADR Rules: The Latest Addition to ICC's Dispute Resolution Services*, ICC INT'L COURT ARB. BULL. 7, 8–9 (2001)
World Bank, *The Role of Foreign Direct Investment in Development*, Presentations to the 41st Meeting of the Development Committee, at 39 (1991)
WORLD BANK, LEGAL FRAMEWORK FOR THE TREATMENT OF FOREIGN INVESTMENT: SURVEY OF EXISTING INSTRUMENTS, PROGRESS REPORT AND BACKGROUND STUDIES 24 (1992)
World Bank, 1 WORLD DEBT TABLES 1992–93, at 20–21 (1992)
WORLD BANK, GUIDELINES ON THE TREATMENT OF FOREIGN DIRECT INVESTMENT (1992), 31 I.L.M. 1379 (1992), available at: https://www.italaw.com/documents/WorldBank.pdf
Financing and Recent Trends and Developments, Trends and Policy Options Paper No. 4, PPIAF, World Bank 7 (2007)
WORLD INV. & TRADE 927 (2004)
WORLD TRADE 99 (1994)
Non-Discrimination, Most-Favored-Nation Treatment and National Treatment, World Trade Organization Secretariat, Doc. WT/CTE/EDB/1 (2002)
Understanding the WTO: The Organization: Members and Observers, http://www.wto.org/english/thewto_e/whatis_e/tif_e/org6_ e.htm.
B.A. Wortley, EXPROPRIATION IN PUBLIC INTERNATIONAL LAW 1 (1959)
Jason Webb Yackee, *Do Bilateral Investment Treaties Promote Foreign Direct Investment? Some Hints from Alternative Evidence*, 51 VA. J. INT'L L. 397 (2010)
Farouk Yala, *Salini v. Morocco (Observations)*, 2003 CAHIERS DE L'ARBITRAGE/GAZETTE DU PALAIS 9
Farouk Yala, *Mihaly v. Sri Lanka (Observations)*, 2003 CAHIERS DE L'ARBITRAGE/GAZETTE DU PALAIS 15
Farouk Yala, *Joy Mining v. Egypt (Observations)*, 2004 Les CAHIERS DE L'ARBITRAGE/GAZETTE DU PALAIS 17
Farouk Yala, *Swembalt: The Notion of Investment and Attribution of State Responsibility under a BIT*, 2004(2) STOCKHOLM ARB. REP. 128
Farouk Yala, *Nagel v. Czech Republic (Observations)*, 2004 CAHIERS DE L'ARBITRAGE/GAZETTE DU PALAIS 15
Farouk Yala, *La notion d'investissement*, 2004(2) LES CAHIERS DE L'ARBITRAGE 15, 17–19
Farouk Yala, *The Notion of Investment in ICSID Case Law—Some Un-conventional Thoughts on Salini, SGS &Mihaly*, 22(2) J. INT'L ARB. 105 (2005)

Catherine Yannaca-Small, *"Indirect Expropriation" and the "Right to Regulate" in International Investment Law*, OECD Working Paper on International Investment No. 2004/4 (2004)

Katia Yannaca-Small, *Indirect Expropriation and the Right to Regulate: How to Draw the Line?* in Arbitration under International Investment Agreements: A Guide to the Key Issues 445–77 (Katia Yannaca-Small ed. 2010)

G.H. Yu, *China's Foreign Exchange Regulations and Direct Foreign Investment*, 28(6)

H.L. Yu & Lawrence Shore, *Independence, Impartiality and Immunity of Arbitrators—US and English Perspectives*, 52 Int'l & Comp. LQ 935, 963 (2003)

Mark R. Yzaguire, *Project Finance and Privatization: The Bolivian Experience*, 20 Hous. J. Int'l L. 597, 616–19 (1998)

H. Zakariye, *Insurance against Political Risks in Oil Development*, 4 J. Energy Nat. Resources & Envt'l L. 217 (1986)

Helge Elisabeth Zeitler, *The Guarantee of "Full Protection and Security" in Investment Treaties Regarding Harm Caused by Private Actors*, 1 Stockholm Int'l Arb. Rev. (2005)

J.X. Zhan, *The Spread of BITs and Their Changing Face,* 24 ICSID Rev.—For. Inv. L.J. *339* (2009)

Jie Zheng, *Competition between Arbitral Institutions in China—Fighting for a Better System?, Kluwer Arbitration Blog (2015),* available at http://arbitrationblog.kluwerarbitration.com/2015/10/16/competition-between-arbitral-institutions-in-china-fighting- for-a-better-system/

Jian Zhou, *National Treatment in Foreign Investment Law: A Comparative Study from a Chinese Perspective*, 10 Touro Int'l L. Rev. 39, 90 (2000)

Andreas R. Ziegler and Louis-Philippe Gratton, *Investment Insurance*, in The Oxford Handbook of International Investment Law 524–48 (Peter Muchlinski et al. eds. 2008)

Nassib G. Ziadé, *Achieving Efficiency in Arbitration: The Role of the Institutions*, 25(1) News from ICSID (2008)

INTRODUCTION

The twentieth century witnessed two important economic counter-currents affecting the international investment community. On the one hand, institutionalized respect for individual rights has spread swiftly across many parts of the globe. On the other hand, collectivist ideologies, political clashes, and misunderstandings between the developing and developed world[1] have led at times to massive nationalizations and confiscations of the property of investors from capital-exporting States.

Most of these nationalizations and confiscations were takings of property invested in developing states in the form of so-called "foreign direct investment" (FDI). Foreign direct investment refers to direct or indirect control of either assets or an enterprise in a foreign country through ownership of a substantial portion of the assets or enterprise.[2] It is "investment that is made to acquire a lasting interest in an enterprise operating in an economy other than that of an investor, the investor's purpose being to have an effective voice in the management of the enterprise."[3] One commentator defined FDI in the following terms:

> [Foreign direct investment] may best be defined as the creation, acquisition or endowment in the host country of enterprises, either incorporated as branches, subsidiaries, or associate companies, or in the form of unincorporated enterprises or joint ventures. The desired result is to acquire a lasting interest, with powers of management and control, where the investor's return depends upon the performance of the enterprise. [Foreign direct investment] flows include all funds provided by the investor, specifically, equity capital, reinvested earnings, and net borrowings.

---

[1] Developing States have often accused multinational corporations of adopting overly capital-intensive production techniques and making insufficient transfers of technology. Klaus P. Berger, *The New Multilateral Investment Guaranty Agency Globalizing the Investment Insurance Approach towards Development*, 15 SYR. J. INT'L L. & COM. 13, 31 (1988).

[2] Thomas L. Brewer, *International Investment Dispute Settlement Procedures: The Evolving Regime for Foreign Direct Investment*, 26 L. & POL'Y. INT'L Bus. 633, 634 (1995); *see also* Cheryl W. Gray & William W. Jarosz, *Law and the Regulation of Foreign Direct Investment: The Experience from Central and Eastern Europe*, 33 COLUM. J. TRANSNAT'L L. 1 (1995). Different countries use different threshold levels of ownership, usually between 10 and 25 percent, to distinguish FDI from so-called "portfolio investment." Brewer, *id.* at n.2.

[3] International Monetary Fund, BALANCE OF PAYMENTS MANUAL, para. 408 at 136 (4th ed. 1977). Thus, "[w]ith respect to foreign direct investment, a foreign investor retains at least part of the ownership and control, unlike [official development assistance] and private bank lending where the business is owned and controlled by local companies or entrepreneurs." Berger, *supra* note 1, at 17.

> Equity investment that does not meet this standard constitutes portfolio investment which is placed through the capital markets without entrepreneurial commitment and merely for the sake of capital yield.[4]

FDI as a mode of economic activity offers benefits for both investors and host States that cannot be gleaned from portfolio investment. From the private party's standpoint, FDI provides a platform for implementing improvements, seizing on potential efficiency and synergy gains, and otherwise gaining advantage from the investor's own initiative, innovation, and vision. From the government's perspective, FDI is a potential engine for development, as the foreigner employs and trains local personnel, indirectly encourages secondary service providers and producers of goods, pays taxes, and—in some cases—leaves behind valuable know-how.[5]

But FDI's benefits for all cannot come without concomitant risks. In order to obtain the necessary control over local operations, the investor must "invest himself," placing his money, equipment, personnel, and day-to-day operations within the sphere of the host State's local law, customs, and political vagaries.[6] For developing state governments, meanwhile, the political pressure to extract additional benefits for local constituents grows as the foreign-owned enterprise prospers. Particularly in times of social and economic instability, host governments may be tempted to redistribute some of the foreigner's property to achieve political gain. Such a shift of property may take any number of forms, from direct nationalization by fiat to increases in taxes, fees, or investment requirements.

Furthermore, the salubrious effect of FDI on the economy of developing countries is hardly undisputed.[7] Some argue that freedom of investment equals a

[4] Berger, *supra* note 1, at 17 (references omitted).

[5] *See generally* UNCTAD/UNEP, Foreign Direct Investment and the Promotion of Sustainable Human Development (1999); Jai Prakash Agarwal, *Effect of Foreign Direct Investment on Employment in Home Countries*, 6 Transnat'l Corporations 1 (1997); *see also* Running into the Sand, Why a Failure at the Cancun Trade Talks Threatens the World's Poorest People, OXFAM Briefing Paper No. 53 (Sept. 2, 2003), at 33, available at https://policy-practice.oxfam.org.uk/publications/running-into-the-sand-why-failure-at-the-cancun-trade-talks-threatens-the-world-114588 (FDI can play a crucial role in development by transferring capital, technology, and skills into developing countries; UNCTAD research indicates that the number of regulatory changes in the domestic foreign investment regulations of the relevant countries during the relevant period was over 1,300, 95 percent of which were aimed at facilitating foreign investment) (citing UNCTAD, World Investment Report, Geneva (2002)). Nevertheless, considering the impact of FDI on host States' economic development, various conflicting economic theories have been formulated. *See* M. Sornarajah, The International Law on Foreign Investment 47–60 (3d ed. 2010).

[6] The distinction between "investing" and "investing oneself' was best articulated by Professors Carreau and Juillard in Dominique Carreau & Patrick Juillard, Droit International Economique 387 (2003) ("Il faut non seulement que l'investisseur investisse, mais encore qu'il s'investisse").

[7] However, there is a growing demand for reformulated investment policies that would prioritize sustainable development for host States, sanction of environmental abuses, the protection of human rights and labor rights, and the like. Moreover, according to empirical studies, there is no consensus as to whether FDI inflows have uniformly had a positive impact on GDP growth, especially for developing economies; *see e.g.* Laza Kekic, *To What Extent has FDI Benefited the Transition*

license for multinational corporations to pillage the assets of poorer countries, buying resources for less than their true value and expatriating them to the home country.[8] At the very least, the influx of capital does not necessarily mean that the profits gained from that investment will remain in the developing host country. Between 1965 and 1986, "net transfers" on FDI, meaning the flow of investment adjusted for the repatriation of profits, was either negative or only slightly positive.[9] Therefore, some have argued that an increase in direct investment into a less-developed country may not necessarily provide substantial support for long-term development projects, infrastructure improvements, or other welfare-enhancing activities.[10] Additionally, the drain of repatriating profits may in fact harm a capital-importing country's balance of payments, if FDI flows are not consistently renewed and outward transfer of profits continues.

These concerns were part of the impetus that drove the "new international economic order" movement among developing countries. In 1974, as part of a movement that became known as the "New International Economic Order" (NIEO), a large number of States initiated a campaign against the prevailing norms of equal treatment for foreign investors, culminating in a U.N. resolution known as the Charter of Economic Rights and Duties of States.[11] These States advocated preferential treatment for local capital. The Charter set forth a new standard for the treatment of investments, although the standard was vehemently opposed by developed countries in the General Assembly: "Every State has and shall freely exercise full permanent sovereignty, including possession, use and disposal, over all its wealth, natural resources and economic activities."[12] While the general exhortatory provisions of the Charter were approved by a wide margin, the most controversial provision—article 2, which purported to remove the act of nationalization from the protections of international law—was passed over the objections of all the major industrialized nations, as well as several developing countries.[13]

Economies of Central and Eastern Europe?, Columbia FDI Perspectives on Topical Foreign Direct Investment Issues, No. 236 (Oct. 8, 2018), available at http://ccsi.columbia.edu/files/2016/10/No-236-Kekic-FINAL.pdf

[8] As a result, a number of recent investment agreements have attempted to refine the definition of "investments" in a way that reflects the economic priorities and social expectations of the host State, by requiring specific characteristics or linking the concept of "investment" to contributions to sustainable development; *see e.g.* Hamed El-Kady, *Towards a New Conceptualization of International Investment Agreements*, BCDR 3(2) Int'l Arb. Rev. 331 (2016).

[9] World Bank, 1 World Debt Tables 1992–93, at 20–21 (1992).

[10] Ibrahim Shihata, Legal Treatment of Foreign Investment: The World Bank Guidelines 9 (1993).

[11] G.A. Res. 3281, 29 U.N. GAOR Supp. (No. 31), at 50, 51–55, U.N. Doc. A/9631 (1974), *reprinted in* 14 I.L.M. 251, 252–60 (1975), available at www.un.org/documents/resga.htm. *See* Patricia Robin, *The BIT Won't Bite: The American Bilateral Investment Treaty Program*, 33 Am. UL Rev. 931 n.93 (1984).

[12] 29 U.N. GAOR Supp. (No. 31) at 52, 14 I.L.M. at 254–55, *supra* note 11.

[13] Robert von Mehren & P. Nicholas Kourides, *International Arbitrations between States and Foreign Private Parties: The Libyan Nationalization Cases*, 75 AJIL 476, 523 (1981).

In this atmosphere of conflicting interests, some governments in the Middle East and Africa turned to nationalization of foreign investment as an economic and political tool, in part as an assertion of "permanent sovereignty" over natural resources following de-colonialization.[14] Many of these expropriations took place despite elaborate, long-term concessions that the host States had granted to foreign investors.[15] Expropriations of foreign investment continued into the 1970s in States such as Uganda, Ethiopia, Pakistan, and Iran. By 1980, the only OPEC (Organization of Petroleum Exporting Countries) States where oil concessions benefitting multinational corporations remained in effect were the United Arab Emirates and Libya. This represented a substantial deterioration in stability from the middle part of the twentieth century.[16] (These historical developments are elaborated on in Chapter 5.)

However, the NIEO ultimately had little impact on targeted institutions such as the Bretton Woods system, the GATT, and the WTO. Subsequent attempts to include NIEO principles in documents elaborating development strategy also failed to obtain any consensus.[17] By the beginning of the 1990s, with the fall of Communist regimes in Europe and the onset of debt crises throughout the developing world, the NIEO appeared to have fallen into wide disfavor. In its place, a more balanced, pragmatic approach to foreign economic participation gained currency, one that recognized both the so-called humanitarian risks of unregulated capitalism and the simple fact that "less-developed countries compete on a worldwide scale for scarce private investment capital, and that capital will not come unless there is security and a good chance of profit making."[18]

States formerly hostile to foreign investment have enacted investment codes favorable to investors,[19] and have adopted legal and business methodologies familiar

---

[14] On the concept of permanent sovereignty and rights to oil deposits in international law, *see* David M. Ong, *Joint Development of Common Offshore Oil and Gas Deposits: "Mere" State Practice or Customary International Law?* 93 AJIL 771 (1999).

[15] *See* Vratislav Pechota, *The 1981 U.S.–Czechoslovak Claims Settlement Agreement: An Epilogue to Postwar Nationalization and Expropriation Disputes*, 76 AJIL 639. *See also* Rode, *The American–Polish Claims Settlement Agreement of March 30, 1960*, 55 AJIL 452 (1961); Gordon Christenson, *U.S.–Rumanian Agreement of March 30, 1960*, 55 AJIL 452 (1961); Richard B. Lillich, *The United States–Bulgarian Claims Agreement of 1963*, 58 AJIL 187 (1964); Branko Pesel.j., *The New Yugoslav–American Claims Agreement*, 59 AJIL 362 (1965); Expropriation in the Americas (Andreas Lowenfeld ed. 1971); Eric N. Baklanoff, Expropriation of U.S. Investment in Cuba, Mexico, and Chile (1975).

[16] Edith Penrose et al., *Nationalization of Foreign-Owned Property for a Public Purpose: An Economic Perspective on Appropriate Compensation*, 55 Modern L. Rev. 351, 353 (1992).

[17] Russel Lawrence Barsh, *A Special Session of the U.N. General Assembly Rethinks the Economic Rights and Duties of States*, 85 AJIL 192, 192–93 (1991).

[18] Frank Ruddy, *Book Review: Foreign Investment in the Present and a New International Economic Order*, 84 AJIL 961, 962 (1990).

[19] Ibrahim F.I. Shihata, *Recent Trends Relating to Entry of Foreign Direct Investment*, 9 ICSID Rev.—For. Inv. L.J. 47 (1994). For a discussion of the national foreign direct investment codes of several nations, *see* Michael A. Geist, *Toward a General Agreement on the Regulation of Foreign Direct Investment*, 26 L. & Pol'y. Int'l Bus. 673, 686–706 (1995); Antonio Parra, *Principles Governing*

to foreign enterprises, such as Anglo-American methods of contract interpretation.[20] Many developing States have also passed legislation guaranteeing compensation in the event of expropriation,[21] and have entered into bilateral investment treaties with capital-exporting countries, which normally establish a range of baseline guarantees to qualifying investors.

Also, in a reversal of the previously dominant doctrine that investment disputes should be resolved under the laws and within the judicial system of the host state,[22] many developing States have enacted investment laws allowing for settlement of disputes in a neutral forum, using the facilities and procedural rules of arbitral institutions such as the International Chamber of Commerce and International Centre for the Settlement of Investment Disputes.[23] Likewise, regional and bilateral investment treaties have multiplied around the globe, often providing foreign investors both substantive protections and mandatory arbitration of disputes.[24] Finally, there have been a number of incentives offered by developing States to attract foreign direct investment, including tax breaks, inexpensive financing, and land at reduced prices.[25]

Foreign Investment as Reflected in National Investment Codes, 7 ICSID Rev.—For. Inv. L.J. 428 (1992). International organizations have also shifted their emphasis from the regulation of foreign direct investment to the liberalization of government policies toward such investment. *See* Brewer, *supra* note 2, at 639; *see also* OECD, *Checklist for Foreign Direct Investment Incentives* (2003), available at www.oecd.org/dataoecd/45/21/2506900.pdf (providing a guide for policy makers on the liberalization of their home economy in order to attract further investment). However, several countries have recently started introducing various investment restrictions and controls. *See e.g.*: Karl P. Sauvant, *The Regulatory Framework for Investment: Where Are We Headed?*, 15 Research in Global Strategic Management 407–33 (2011).

20 For a discussion of such practices in Central and Eastern Europe, *see* Gray & Jarosz, *supra* note 2, at 32.

21 For examples of such legislation in Central and Eastern Europe, *see id.* at 29; Geist, *supra* note 19.

22 On this so-called "Calvo Doctrine," *see* Donald Shea, The Calvo Clause: A Problem of Inter-American and International Law and Diplomacy (1955).

23 Adeoye Akinsanya, *International Protection of Direct Foreign Investments in the Third World*, 36 Int'l & Comp. LQ 58, 70–75 (1987). Despite the benefits of introducing investor–State dispute resolution mechanisms, it is still unclear whether such a regime has helped host States attract foreign investments. *See e.g.* Jason Webb Yackee, *Do Bilateral Investment Treaties Promote Foreign Direct Investment? Some Hints from Alternative Evidence*, 51 Va. J. Int'l L. 397 (2010); U.N. Conference on Trade and Development, The Impact of International Investment Agreements on Foreign Direct Investment: An Overview of Empirical Studies 1998–2004, Working Draft (2014).

24 On the wider implication of such investment treaties, *see* Marian Nash (Leich), *U.S. Practice: Bilateral Investment Treaties*, 87 AJIL 433 (1993). *See also* Tillman Rudolf Braun, *Globalization: The Driving Force in International Investment Law*, in The Backlash Against Investment Arbitration (Michael Waibel et al. eds. 2010); Stephen M. Schwebel, *The Overwhelming Merits of Bilateral Investment Treaties*, 32 Suffolk Transnat'l L. Rev. 263 (2009); J.X. Zhan, *The Spread of BITs and Their Changing Face*, 24 ICSID Rev.—For. Inv. L.J. 339 (2009); However, according to UNCTAD, the number of effective treaty terminations outpaced the number of new IIAs signed in 2017.

25 Geist, *supra* note 19, at 679.

To some degree, these changes were probably brought about as a result of competition among developing states for FDI. As developing States' demand for foreign direct investment increased in the late 1970s and early 1980s, the supply of available capital was decreasing significantly.[26] While FDI to developing countries reached a peak of US$17.24 billion in 1981, it fell to US$11.86 billion in 1982 and US$7.8 billion in 1983.[27] This was due in part to rising interest rates and falling commodity prices, causing many developing States to default on their debts to Western banks in the 1980s.[28] This series of defaults caused some international banks and investors to tighten the supply of capital flowing to these States. Many multinationals took to borrowing funds from their foreign subsidiaries, rather than injecting capital into them.[29] One way States found to attract an ever-smaller pool of foreign funds was to liberalize the local regulatory regime, and to provide other guarantees that reduce the political risk that would otherwise make investing expensive.[30]

As a consequence of the market liberalization and developing States' apparent embrace of FDI, one could assume that foreign investors would look forward to ever-decreasing political risk in the twenty-first century.[31] But despite new laws and treaties, as well as a new culture of mutual benefit between capital exporters and capital importers, the potential for a trend reversal remains real, and political risk concerns persist.[32] Such a trend is more likely to occur during financial crises, such as the 2001–02 Argentinian crisis or the global financial disruption

[26] In 1993 and 1994, it is estimated that half of all foreign direct investment flowing to developing countries went to East Asia and to the Pacific, while lower income countries, excluding China and India, received only about US$3 billion. MIGA, Annual Report 1995, available at http://www.miga.org.

[27] Organisation for Economic Cooperation and Development (OECD), Development Cooperation—1984 Review 64, Table IV-1 (1984).

[28] The total debt of developing countries exceeded $950 billion in 1985, causing the international capital flow to developing countries to slow and interest rates to rise. Shihata, *supra* note 10, at 672.

[29] *Id.* at 674.

[30] "Political risk" can be broadly defined as the risk that the laws of a country will change to the investor's detriment after it has invested capital in the country, reducing the value of its investment. Put simply, it is the risk of adverse government intervention. *See* Philipp Harms, International Investment, Political Risk, and Growth (2000); David A. Jodice, Political Risk Assessment: An Annotated Bibliography (1985); *see also* Thomas Nektarios Papanastasiou, The Legal Protection of Foreign Investments against Political Risk: Japanese Business in the Asian Energy Sector (2015).

[31] Expropriations appear to have peaked in 1975, with eighty-three expropriations in twenty-eight different countries, but declined by 50 percent the following year. Between 1980 and 1985, the rate of expropriation averaged three per year. U.N. Centre on Transnational Corporations, *The New Environment,* UNTC Current Studies, Series A, No. 16 (New York: United Nations, 1990), at 18.

[32] *See generally* Peter B. Kenen, The International Financial Architecture (2001); Andreas Lowenfeld, International Economic Law 565–616 (2002); Grant Nulle, *IMF Ignores Causes of Crisis*, Financial Times, Aug. 18, 2003, at 10; Adam Thomson, *Argentina Defiant towards Private Creditors*, Financial Times, Mar. 11, 2004, at 11.

that resulted from the 2008 sub-prime loan debacle. The current global instability has affected developed and developing countries alike, and resulted in a decrease in global cross-border capital flows (exacerbated by difficulties in the Eurozone)[33] and an increase in the regulation of foreign investments and limits on the entry of foreign investments (a trend described as "investment protectionism").[34] Moreover, UNCTAD highlights that in 2017 the number of treaty terminations for the first time outpaced the number of new IIAs signed, and that many countries have agreed to replace their existing investment treaties with those exhibiting a "sustainable development orientation, preservation of regulatory space and improvements to or omissions of ISDS."[35]

Today, host States can interfere with private property and foreign investment more subtly than through direct confiscation and transfer of title. Over the last few decades, the risk of indirect, *de facto* or regulatory expropriation, or of other, less extreme interference, has come to the forefront of business consciousness in the developing world.[36] Moreover, there is an ongoing discussion about how non-investment concerns such as human rights affect a host State's liability to compensate investors for expropriation. This discussion follows a general debate regarding the integration of human rights law into international investment law.[37] Thus,

[33] Susan Lund et al., *The New Dynamics of Financial Globalization*, McKinsey Global Institute Report (2017), available at https://www.mckinsey.com/industries/financial-services/our-insights/the-new-dynamics-of-financial-globalization

[34] Since the global financial crisis that began in 2008, several States have banned inward FDI for national security reasons; *see* M. Sornarajah, The International Law on Foreign Investment 168–69 (3d ed. 2010); *see also* Alvaro Cuervo-Cazurra, *Host Country Concerns and Policies toward State-Owned MNEs*, Columbia FDI Perspectives on Topical Foreign Direct Investment Issues, No. 237 (Oct. 22, 2018), available at http://ccsi.columbia.edu/files/2016/10/No-237-Cuervo-Cazurra-FINAL.pdf. The Committee on Foreign Investment in the United States (CFIUS) increasingly undertakes national security reviews of cross-border transactions involving Chinese State-owned enterprises, based on the concern that Chinese enterprises or sovereign wealth funds could gain access to natural resources, technology, or other vital sectors of the American economy through mergers with U.S. companies, compromising U.S. national security. *See e.g.* Zhang Monan, *Investment Protectionism in the Name of National Security*, China–US Focus (Sept. 6. 2017), available at https://www.chinausfocus.com/finance-economy/investment-protectionism-in-the-name-of-national-security

[35] UNCTAD—Issues Note 2018, *Recent Developments in the International Investment Regime* (2018). Furthermore, the Court of Justice of the European Union, in its much anticipated opinion, ruled that ISDS clauses included in intra-EU BITs are incompatible with the provisions of EU law and, as such, inapplicable; See Case C-284/16 *Slowakische Republic v Achmea BV* [2018] ECLI:EU:C:2018:158.

[36] It is not straightforward to distinguish host-State measures that constitute indirect expropriation (which requires adequate compensation) from regulatory measures that do not constitute expropriation and therefore do not require compensation. *See* Vera Korzun, *The Right to Regulate in Investor–State Arbitration: Slicing and Dicing Regulatory Carve-Outs*, 50(2) Vand. J. Transnat'l L. 375 (2017); *see also* Katia Yannaca-Small, *Indirect Expropriation and the Right to Regulate: How to Draw the Line?*, in Arbitration under International Investment Agreements: A Guide to the Key Issues 445–77 (Katia Yannaca-Small ed. 2010).

[37] *See* Vivian Kube & Ernst-Ulrich Petersmann, *Human Rights Law in International Investment Arbitration*, 11(1) AJWH 99 (2016); *See also* Moshe Hirsch, *Investment Tribunals and Human Rights: Divergent Paths*, in Human Rights in International Investment Law and Arbitration

even when an investor remains in full control of his assets, he may find their value evaporated no less effectively than in an outright taking.[38]

Nevertheless, the political risks described in this book are not restricted only to developing and transition economies. Indeed, recent cases before several arbitration tribunals and the European Court of Human Rights demonstrate that overzealous regulators and the demands of local interest groups at times can make even the most "advanced" country a risky place for the foreign investor.[39]

Whether an investor brings capital to a developed or developing country, how can he assess and manage the incumbent political risk before deciding whether to invest? What can an investor do to deter manifestations of political risk once the investment has been made? How can international law be brought to bear as protection against political risk? Finally, what remedies are available if political risk materializes to the investor's detriment? This book is an attempt to suggest some answers to these questions.

In the first part of the text, we offer guidance on the assessment and pre-investment management of political risk. In Chapter 1, we discuss the types of political risk that foreign investors are likely to encounter, and suggest some practical steps that might be taken to measure such risk in a particular State before investing capital. We then turn to the actions that the investor can take to reduce exposure to political risk prior to investing. Chapter 2 analyzes the types of investment projects most often undertaken in developing States, and provides an analysis of the structures that can be implemented to reduce exposure to political risk. Chapter 3 deals with the modalities of political risk insurance, which typically provides coverage against non-commercial risks such as currency inconvertibility, expropriation, and war, and is available from nationally sponsored insurance agencies, private insurance companies, and the World Bank's Multilateral Investment Guarantee Agency.

In the second part of the book, we turn to the international law framework of investment protection and political risk. Chapter 4 covers the general background international law pertaining to State responsibility, in particular State responsibility incurred in relation to foreign investment, as well as the general nature and

107–13 (Pierre-Marie Dupuy et al. eds. 2009); José E. Alvarez, *The Use (and Misuse) of European Human Rights Law in Investor–State Dispute Settlement*, in The Impact of EU Law on International Commercial Arbitration 72 (Franco Ferrari ed. 2017), available at SSRN: https://papers.ssrn.com/sol3/papers.cfm?abstract_id=2875089.

[38] *See Metalclad Corp. v. Mexico*, ICSID Case No. ARB(AF)/97/1, Award of Mar. 9, 1998, 40 I.L.M. 36 (2001), at para. 103 (the host State's regulatory action can have the effect of an outright taking).

[39] *See e.g. Loewen Group Int'l v. U.S.A.*, ICSID Case No. ARB(AF)/98/3, 42 I.L.M. 811 (2003), Award of June 26, 2003 (a U.S. trial court's conduct toward a Canadian investor was "a disgrace by any standard" and violated international standards of fair and equitable treatment).

types of remedies available to investors when a State expropriates an investor's property or interferes with its investment. In Chapter 5, we discuss the principles of customary international law related to expropriation. This chapter includes an overview of the historical development of the international law of expropriation, as developed in international arbitration decisions, commentators, treaties, and State practice. The current state of the customary international law of expropriation is also discussed, including the various substantive protections established in customary and conventional international law, such as the "full compensation" standard for expropriation, the public purpose requirement, and the prohibition against discrimination.

Investors look not only to customary international law principles, however: they increasingly rely on the substantive protections provided in a growing number of investment treaties. The modern international law of investment protection as embodied in multilateral and bilateral investment treaties, including principles such as fair and equitable treatment, and full protection and security, is covered in Chapter 6. Also included is a detailed discussion of methods of valuation of damaged or expropriated property.

Finally, in a third section, we provide practical guidance on the procedural recourse available to investors who face political risks that have materialized. Chapter 7 concerns the jurisdictional requirements for invoking investment treaty protections—who has standing to maintain a claim, what assets qualify as protected "investments," and the effect of related contractual forum selection clauses. In Chapter 8, we provide an overview of international arbitration procedure—both under arbitration treaties and contractual arrangements—particularly under the auspices of the World Bank's International Centre for the Settlement of Investment Disputes (ICSID) and arbitration rules of the United Nations Commission on International Trade Law (UNCITRAL). Next, Chapter 9 addresses the possibility of mediation, conciliation, and other non-litigious forms of alternative dispute resolution, methods which have drawn significant attention in recent years. Finally, in Chapter 10, we discuss the actions that an investor's home government may take to protect the investor in response to unreasonable host-State interference with investment. Every author must ultimately end his research and choose his field of battle, even so broad a field as the one we attempt to cover here. This book is limited in scope to the topics just described, and does not address the related and vitally important topics of commercial risk involved in direct foreign investment;[40] business, financial, or tax strategies for

[40] Commercial risks are the types of risks inherent in any business venture, such as the risk of low consumer demand, higher than expected manufacturing costs, insolvency of purchasers, and cost overruns in production. Commercial risk is thus the business risk that remains even in the most stable political climate. While commercial risks affect any business, whether operating in its home country or abroad, these risks are often greater in a developing country due to lack of a developed infrastructure, primitive telecommunications systems, and an unskilled, uneducated, and

FDI;[41] or political risks connected with import/export transactions and portfolio investment.[42] Nor do we discuss the political risks of any particular country in detail. Because such risks necessarily evolve over time, such a discussion would be of limited value. There are, however, several services that provide up-to-date political risk assessment on a country-by-country basis.[43]

Cross-border investment has become a central driving force in local economies around the world. Indeed, more than ever private investment and trade, as much as national politics, shape the development of global commerce.[44] In part through the management of political risk, private parties—and their counsel—are today called upon to help draw the contours of international law alongside national legislatures and executives.[45]

This unconscious collaboration may at first seem an odd result of the historical clash between capital importers and capital exporters. But on further reflection, it is only natural that private investors and the States where they seek their fortune should find common ground, even if by way of occasional collisions. The increased flow of investment means new opportunities for those businesses willing and able to assess and address political risk, and at the same time offers the surest path to sustainable growth for countries too small or impecunious to rely on domestic capital. Furthermore, the tables began to turn on the traditional capital exporting States: formerly less-developed countries now invest heavily abroad, including projects in Western Europe and North America. Some of the world's most developed countries are therefore softening their previously uncompromising pro-investor approach in anticipation of conflicts where roles are reversed and they are compelled to defend their own regulatory actions.[46]

---

relatively impoverished consumer base. As a practical matter, however, it may sometimes be difficult to distinguish between political and commercial risks. For example, the failure of a government-operated utility to deliver services to an investor's facility may be either commercial or political in nature. On commercial risk and commercial risk management, *see* Tim Boyce, Commercial Risk Management (2003).

[41] Raymond Rody, International Business Negotiations: Strategies, Tactics and Practices (2002); Peter Buckley, The Strategy and Organization of International Business (1993).

[42] Yen Yee Chong, Investment Risk Management (2004).

[43] *See* The Economist Intelligence Unit, *Country Reports*, available at http://www.eiu.com; *see also* The Economist Intelligence Unit, *Country Risk Service*, available at http://www.eiu.com.

[44] *See* Susan Strange, The Retreat of the State: The Diffusion of Power in the World Economy (1996); Susan Strange, Mad Money: When Markets Outgrow Governments (1998).

[45] *See e.g.* Tamara Lothien & Katharina Pistor, *Local Institutions, Foreign Investment and Alternative Strategies of Development: Some Views from Practice*, 42 Colum. J. Transnat'l L. 101, 106.

[46] *See* Noah Rubins, *Loewen v. United States: The Burial of an Investor–State Claim*, 21 Arb. Int'l 1, 32–36 (2005); Guillermo Aguilar Alvarez & William W. Park, *The New Face of Investment Arbitration: NAFTA Chapter 11*, Mealey's Int'l Arb. Rep. (January 2004), at 39, 41. There is a growing trend of foreign investments flowing from emerging markets' firms to developed States. Investments by developing country firms in other developing counties (known as "South-South" investment) are also at a higher level; *see* Rudolf Dolzer & Christoph Schreuer, Principles of International

Therefore, most foreign investment participants understand the delicate balance between international law constraints and the legitimate interests of development and sovereignty.[47] The increased control over political risk that private investors now enjoy, in part as a result of the investment treaties that States themselves conclude, is mutually beneficial. States have insulated themselves from external political pressure and lowered the cost of foreign investment by demonstrating their resolve to provide a predictable investment climate. At the same time, private investors must properly appreciate the extent of their new rights if they are to lower political risk and the accompanying financial burden.

INVESTMENT LAW 7–8 (2d ed. 2012); *see also* Anabel Gonzalez et al., *South-South Investment: Development Opportunities and Policy Agenda*, The World Bank (Mar. 28, 2015), available at http://blogs.worldbank.org/trade/south-south-investment-development-opportunities-and-policy-agenda

[47] The maze of bilateral and multilateral investment treaties bears witness to this development. *See e.g.* K.V.S.K. NATHAN, THE ICSID CONVENTION: THE LAW OF THE INTERNATIONAL CENTRE FOR SETTLEMENT OF INVESTMENT DISPUTES (2000).

PART I

ASSESSMENT AND PRE-INVESTMENT MANAGEMENT OF POLITICAL RISK

1

POLITICAL RISK

In this chapter, we discuss the general nature of political risk: the various types or manifestations of political risk, factors that contribute to political risk, and ways that investors can assess the political risks inherent in particular investment regimes or with respect to certain investments. **1.01**

A. Risk and Investment

"Risk" is a concept explored at length in the economic, political science, and legal literature.[1] Here we will not delve into theoretical detail about the nature of risk, but a brief discussion of the relationship between risk and investment is in order. As a general matter, human action is aimed at achieving a goal or result at some time in the future. Because the future is uncertain, every human action involves a "risky speculation."[2] If the future is as predicted by the actor, the action is successful and he earns a "psychic profit." But if the future does not unfold as expected, the result sought may not be achieved. In this case, the actor does not achieve his goal; he suffers a loss. **1.02**

[1] For general background on the theory of risk and human behavior, *see* Ludwig von Mises, Human Action (4th ed. 1996), esp. ch. VI, available at http://www.mises.org; Frank H. Knight, Risk, Uncertainty and Profit (1971 [1921]), esp. ch. 7, available at http://www.econlib.org; Richard von Mises, Probability, Statistics, and Truth (1957), esp. chs. 1 and 3; also Tim Bedford & Roger Cooke, Probabilistic Risk Analysis: Foundations and Methods (2001); Peter Bernstein, Against the Gods: The Remarkable Story of Risk (1998).

[2] Mises, Human Action, *supra* note 1, at 106.

1.03 Investment, including foreign direct investment (FDI), is one type of human action in which the profit sought is economic or monetary in nature. The investor seeks to earn a monetary profit at some future time—a future time at which the investor forecasts that revenues from products or services sold will exceed the previous costs of the investment plus interest.[3] For the investor, and for our purposes, risk should therefore be understood as the possibility that future conditions will be less favorable than forecast—that future events will yield less revenue than expected.

1.04 Obviously, investors face a variety of "risks" in this sense, in that any number of events may unfold that lead to economic loss. In hindsight there can be no risks, only history. The future is uncertain because neither natural events nor human action can be predicted with certainty.[4] Demand for a given product may not develop as the investor predicts; a competitor might undercut the business in which he has invested; or there may be an unanticipated natural disaster that affects consumer demand or costs. All investors must face such risks.

1.05 But investors also face risks due to the actions of the State that controls the territory hosting the investment. States engage in a variety of actions that can cause loss for foreign investors. They can unexpectedly raise taxes, seize the investor's assets, outlaw the investment activity, or impose new and unexpected regulatory conditions. This type of risk is the result of the exercise of political power,[5] and is naturally referred to as *political* risk.[6]

1.06 Several prominent commentators agree that "political risk" implies "threats to the profitability of a project that derive from some sort of governmental action or

---

[3] *Id.* at 637.

[4] *See also* Hans-Hermann Hoppe, *On Certainty and Uncertainty, Or: How Rational Can Our Expectations Be?*, 10(1) R. Austrian Econ. 49–78 (1997), available at http://www.mises.org.

[5] As Hoppe notes:

> One can acquire and increase wealth either through homesteading, production and contractual exchange, or by expropriating and exploiting homesteaders, producers, or contractual exchangers. There are no other ways. Both methods are natural to mankind. Alongside an interest in producing and contracting there has always been an interest in non-productive and non-contractual property and wealth acquisitions. And in the course of economic development, just as the former interest can lead to the formation of productive enterprises, firms and corporations, so can the latter lead to large-scale enterprises and bring about governments or states.

Hans-Hermann Hoppe, *Banking, Nation States and International Politics: A Sociological Reconstruction of the Present Economic Order*, 4(1) R. Austrian Econ. 55, 60–61 (1990), available at http://www.mises.org.

See the German sociologist, Franz Oppenheimer's view on the two mutually exclusive ways of acquiring wealth; Franz Oppenheimer, The State 24–27 (1926). *See also* Albert Jay Nock, Our Enemy, The State 3 (1973).

[6] For a holistic approach toward political risk management, *see generally* Thomas Nektarios Papanastasiou, The Legal Protection of Foreign Investments against Political Risk: Japanese Business in the Asian Energy Sector 33–37 (2015).

inaction rather than from changes in economic conditions in the marketplace."[7] Political risk is the probability that a host government will, by act or omission, reduce the investor's ability to realize an expected return on his investment. Most commonly, political risk manifests itself by the host State directly or indirectly *confiscating, interfering with, or destroying all or a portion of an investor's property rights.*[8]

For purposes of investors concerned with political risk, the primary distinction to be made is between detriment (loss) proximately caused by the host State or its agents, and that caused by the commercial realities of supply and demand or by natural disaster. This line is far harder to draw in practice than in theory: the scenarios investors face in carrying out a long-term business project on foreign soil are complex and affected by a range of factors both within and outside government control.[9] **1.07**

B. Political Risk and Property Rights

Since political risk involves State interference with investors' property rights, an understanding of "property" and "property rights" is an important part of any analysis of political risk.[10] "Property" is a broad concept that includes, in common-law terminology, realty and personalty, and tangibles and intangibles such as rights under contracts. In civil-law terminology, property consists of **1.08**

[7] Theodore H. Moran, *Political and Regulatory Risk in Infrastructure Investment in Developing Countries: Introduction and Overview*, 5(6) CEPMLP J. 3 (1999) (citing Harvard Professor Louis Wells, Jr.); political risk is defined as "the host government's unwarranted interference with the foreign investment which should be political in nature and should adversely affect the investment's operation or damage its economic interests"; *see* Papanastasiou, *supra* note 6, at 24.

[8] In various contexts, including within the discourse of investment arbitration, political risk is sometimes referred to as "regulatory risk." *See e.g.* S. Linn Williams, *Political and Other Risk Insurance: OPIC, MIGA, Eximbank and Other Providers*, 5 Pace Int'l L. Rev. 59 (1993); *Técnicas Medioambientales Tecmed S.A. v. Mexico*, ICSID Case No. ARB(AF)/00/2, Award of May 29, 2003, paras. 117–23, 43 I.L.M. 133, 163–66 (2004). One type of political risk not often recognized as such is the innate ability of legislatures to enact new laws, to change the "rules of the game" from day to day. As Italian legal theorist Bruno Leoni pointed out, even if a given statute is written clearly, "we are *never certain* that tomorrow we shall still have the rules we have today." Bruno Leoni, Freedom and the Law 75 (3d ed. 1991) (emphasis in the original). *See also* N. Stephan Kinsella, *Legislation and the Discovery of Law in a Free Society*, 11 J. Libertarian Stud. 132 (1995), available at http://www.mises.org. On the impact of judicial corruption on political risk analysis as it pertains to investments, *see* Luis Enrique Cuervo & Vernon Valentine Palmer, *Judicial Protection of Foreign Investors in Latin America: Exposé des Motifs*, 77 Tul. L. Rev. 1053, 1054 (2003).

[9] Georgio Sacerdoti, *The Source and Evolution of International Legal Protection for Infrastructure Investments Confronting Political and Regulatory Risks*, 5(7) CEPMLP J. 4–5 (2008).

[10] The conceptual aspects of property under international law remain relatively unexplored. Rosalyn Higgins, *The Taking of Property by the State: Recent Developments in International Law*, 176 Recueil des Cours 259, 268 (1982) (complaining that "it is as if we international lawyers say: property has been defined for us by our municipal legal system; and in any event, we *know* property when we see it" (emphasis in the original)).

"things," which may be divided into the corresponding categories of immovables and movables, and corporeal and incorporeal.[11] The term "property rights," as used in this text and as commonly understood, refers to ownership of property, which comprises three elements or ingredients: *usus* (the right to use), *fructus* (the right to the fruits of property, such as interest or rentals), and *abusus* (the right to dispose of or sell the property). The common law regards property rights as a similarly divided "bundle" of rights, the major components of which are the rights to control, possess, use, exclude, profit, and dispose of property.

1.09 For example, for an investor who owns a manufacturing plant, property rights include: (1) ownership of the land, the factory on the land, and the inventory and equipment located in the factory; (2) the right to use the factory to manufacture the goods that the investor deems profitable; (3) the right to manage its business as it deems proper; (4) the right to sell goods and capital assets; and (5) the right to repatriate those proceeds. Each of these elements may be vital to the investor's ability to obtain a reasonably expected rate of return on investment. A wide range of government actions and non-actions can alter or diminish any of these rights, and therefore should form part of any comprehensive political risk analysis. Examples of State interference with the investor's private property rights include:

- confiscation of the investor's real and personal property;
- refusal to allow the investor to remove equipment from the host State;
- imposition of regulation or taxes to such a degree that the investment becomes practically worthless or economically unfeasible;
- legislation compelling transfer of technology or permitting violations of the investor's intellectual property rights;
- repudiation or forced renegotiation of a contract between a State-owned entity and the investor;
- non-payment of debt owed to the investor;
- imposition of unexpected controls on the conversion or export of local currency;
- unfair calling of performance on a bond or letter of credit by the host government; and
- loss of assets or contract rights due to war, civil war, insurrection, terrorism, or other unrest.

Political risk comprises scenarios such as these, where the host government undermines the enjoyment of the investment more drastically than was anticipated at the time the investment was made.[12]

---

[11] *See* N. Stephan Kinsella, *A Civil Law to Common Law Dictionary*, 54 La. L. Rev. 1265 (1994), available at http://www.KinsellaLaw.com. In *Libyan American Oil Co. v. Libyan Arab Republic*, Sole Arbitrator Mahmassani discussed concession rights as forming part of the incorporeal (*i.e.* intangible) property of the investor. *Libyan American Oil Co. (LIAMCO) v. Government of the Libyan Arab Republic* (1977), 62 I.L.R. 140, 189 (1980), 20 I.L.M. 1, 53 (1981).

[12] *Metalclad Corp. v. Mexico*, ICSID Case No. ARB(AF)/97/1, Award of Mar. 9, 1998, para. 103, 40 I.L.M. 36 (2001) (expropriation occurs whenever government interference with property has the

Why is political risk so prevalent, such a real and necessary part of business planning? One widely accepted explanation, known as the "obsolescing bargain" theory, suggests that the very nature of investment and the effect of risk drives governments to increase interference or decrease support over time vis-à-vis foreign investment.[13] At the outset of a project, foreign investors tend to demand additional concessions or higher returns as a result of the perceived risks of entry and the intensive exposure of the start-up phase. Once the investment is underway, however, the host government is less prepared to maintain the start-up conditions, since the risk often will have declined, along with the cost of financing. Where a project is long-term with heavy capital investment (sunk costs) at the start, and uses assets that are not easily sold or converted to other purposes, the government has a great deal of leverage over the foreign investor, who cannot credibly threaten to abandon his investment plans if conditions deteriorate. This imbalance creates an almost irresistible temptation for local officials to extract short-term political advantage by shifting foreign investment profits to constituents either within the government or the public at large.[14] **1.10**

The societal pressure that can lead to unpredictable intervention in foreign-owned investment by host States is often intensified by domestic perceptions about the way the benefits of investment are distributed between the foreigner and the local population. Depending on the type of project, benefits in terms of poverty alleviation in developing countries can be diffuse and indirect. As a result, local populations may question the equity of favorable conditions offered to the foreign investor. This problem can be particularly acute in oil and gas exploitation, which greatly benefits direct participants, but sometimes has little effect on employment, services, and other activity in other sectors of the economy.[15] We will address this problem in detail below. **1.11**

C. Types of Political Risk

For analytical purposes, we identify several types of political risk. Other observers have categorized these risks differently, and often certain potential outcomes or government acts straddle two or more parts of the typology.[16] The main categories **1.12**

effect of depriving the owner, in whole or in significant part, of the use or reasonably-to-be-expected economic benefit of property).

[13] Raymond Vernon, In the Hurricane's Eye: The Troubled Prospects of Multinational Enterprises 32–59 (1998).

[14] About the "obsolescing bargain" theory in the power sector, *see* Papanastasiou, *supra* note 6, at 19–20.

[15] Jonathan Walters, *Caspian Oil and Gas: Mitigating Political Risks for Private Participation*, 7(5) CEPMLP J. 2–3 (2001), available at http://documents.worldbank.org/curated/en/152381468032950270/pdf/353700rev0Caspian0oil0prague2000a.pdf.

[16] Political risks are very "heterogeneous" in nature; *see* Claire A. Hill, *How Investors React to Political Risk*, 8(2) Duke J. Comp. & Int'l L. 288–313 (1998).

of risk include: (1) outright expropriation (including confiscation and nationalization); (2) regulatory interference (including indirect and creeping expropriation); (3) currency risk; (4) civil unrest; (5) breach of State contracts; (6) corruption; and (7) trade restrictions. While these distinctions are useful in understanding the nature of political risk and its various manifestations, the distinction between types is often blurred in actual situations, which may involve elements from more than one of these seven groups. There is also an increase in new types of political risk, particularly in the infrastructure industry, as "ongoing sources of threat."[17] In addition, the role of political risk insurance agencies in covering risks such as devaluation that "do not readily fall under the established political risk categories" has given rise to additional difficulty in defining the notion of political risk with precision.[18]

1. Expropriation, nationalization, and confiscation

1.13 "Expropriation" is the taking by a host State of property owned by a foreign investor and located in the host State. In a classic expropriation, the State accomplishes the "taking" by acting under local law to annul the investor's title to or beneficial ownership of the property in question. The taking can, if necessary, be implemented through the use of force against the investor. Professor Wortley elaborates upon the definition of expropriation:

> When, by the action of State E, O, an owner, is expropriated, the legal bond between O and the thing claimed by him is severed by the law of State E, and, *by that law*, O is no longer regarded as having an enforceable claim to the thing expropriated; State E thenceforward accords to itself, or to its nominee, the protection of an owner in respect of the thing taken.[19]

1.14 As Professor Brownlie has explained, "the essence of the matter is the deprivation by state organs of a right of property either as such, or by permanent transfer of the power of management in control."[20]

1.15 Examples of expropriation of movable property abound in the context of the Iran–U.S. Claims Tribunal,[21] including the *Pereira* case,[22] where Iranian Revolutionary

---

[17] Moran, *supra* note 7, at 7.

[18] Tomoko Matsukawa & Odo Habeck, *Review of Risk Mitigation Instruments for Infrastructure Financing and Recent Trends and Developments*, Trends and Policy Options Paper No. 4, PPIAF, World Bank 7 (2007).

[19] B.A. Wortley, Expropriation in Public International Law 1 (1959) (emphasis in the original).

[20] Ian Brownlie, Principles of Public International Law 508–09 (2003).

[21] The Iran–U.S. Claims Tribunal was established on Jan. 19, 1981 under the Algiers Accords to resolve disputes between nationals of the United States and Iran and the opposite government arising out of allegations of interference with property rights. Declaration of the Government of the Democratic and Popular Republic of Algeria Concerning the Settlement of Claims by the Government of the United States of America and the Government of the Islamic Republic of Iran (Claims Settlement Declaration), 1 Iran–US C.T.R. 9, 15 (1981–82).

[22] *William L. Pereira Associates, Iran (Pereira) v. Iran*, Award No. 116-1-3, 5 Iran–U.S. C.T.R. 198 (1984).

Guards confiscated the contents of the claimant's office and a company car, and in which case the State was ordered to pay damages in the amount of the value of the property. In *Leonard and Mavis Daley*,[23] Iranian Revolutionary Guards confiscated a car and a Rolex watch, and Iran was ordered to pay compensation. Later examples of classic expropriation of ongoing enterprises can be found in the *AGIP*,[24] *Benvenuti*,[25] and *Amco Asia*[26] arbitral decisions, all of which involved joint ventures between foreign investors and States or State agencies that were forcibly taken over by military action of the host State. In *AGIP*, an oil distribution business was nationalized by legislation, then the company's headquarters were occupied by Congolese army troops. In *Benvenuti*, the Congolese army seized and occupied a plastic bottle factory and water bottling plant. In *Amco Asia*, the Indonesian army seized a hotel complex belonging to U.S. investors. In each of these cases, a tribunal found that the State's actions violated internationally recognized ownership rights and ordered that damages be paid to the aggrieved investors.

A once-common form of expropriation applied to ongoing enterprises was to confiscate a controlling share of equity in a holding company that owned the enterprise. Examples of expropriation by taking shares of foreign investors can be found in *American Int'l Group*[27] and *INA Corp. v. Iran*.[28] In both of these cases, the Iranian government seized claimants' shares of Iranian insurance companies pursuant to the 1979 law of nationalization of insurance and credit enterprises.[29] **1.16**

It is important to note at the outset that at customary international law, States bear no international liability toward *domestic* investors for the expropriation of their property.[30] Thus, the international law of expropriation deals only with **1.17**

[23] *Leonard and Mavis Daley v. Iran*, Award No. 360-10514-1, 19 IRAN–U.S. C.T.R. 232 (1988).

[24] *AGIP S.p.A. v. Government of the People's Republic of the Congo*, ICSID Case No. ARB/77/1, Award of Nov. 30, 1979, 21 I.L.M. 726 (1982).

[25] *S.A.R.L. Benvenuti & Bonfant v. Government of the People's Republic of the Congo*, ICSID Case No. ARB/77/2, Award of Aug. 8, 1980, 67 I.L.R. 345 (1984).

[26] *Amco Asia Corp. v. Indonesia*, ICSID Case No. ARB/81/1, Award of Nov. 20, 1984, 24 I.L.M. 1022 (1984).

[27] *American Int'l Group Inc. et al. (AIG) v. Iran*, Award No. 93-2-3, 4 IRAN–U.S. C.T.R. 96 (1983).

[28] *INA Corp. v. Government of Iran*, Award No. 184-161-1, 8 IRAN–U.S. C.T.R. 373 (1985).

[29] The Government of the Islamic Republic of Iran nationalized banks on June 7, 1979, insurance companies on June 25, 1979, and certain heavy industries beginning on July 5, 1979. Thus, the two cases mentioned are not only examples of direct expropriation, but also of nationalization, discussed in Section C.1 *infra*.

[30] *See* Chapter 4, Section F; also *Banco Nacional de Cuba v. Farr*, 383 F.2d at 185; *Banco Nacional de Cuba v. Sabbatino*, 307 F.2d 845, 861 (2d Cir. 1962), *rev'd. on other grounds*, 376 U.S. 398 (1964). This fundamental premise has been altered in the case of the first Protocol to the European Convention on Human Rights, which requires member States to respect the sanctity of individual property rights of locals and foreigners alike. For a useful overview of the law of expropriation under the Convention, *see* Elyse M. Freeman, *Regulatory Expropriation under NAFTA Chapter 11: Some Lessons from the European Court of Human Rights*, 42 COLUM. J. TRANSNAT'L L. 177 (2003); Helen Mountfield, *Regulatory Expropriations in Europe: The Approach of the European*

expropriation of property of an investor with a nationality other than that of the host State. Where the investor is a physical person with potentially more than one nationality, the "effective nationality" rule traditionally determines which citizenship is controlling for purposes of diplomatic protection. According to this rule, a person is considered a national of the State with which he has the closest factual connection.[31] In the case of a corporate investor, the place of incorporation and other formal indicia of citizenship generally supply the relevant nationality under international law.[32]

1.18 Some expropriations are considered "legal" and some "illegal" under international law.[33] Expropriation is considered "legal" only if it is: (1) non-discriminatory; (2) carried out for a public purpose; and (3) accompanied by full compensation.[34] Although the distinction between "legal" and "illegal" expropriations is of limited significance as a factor influencing the amount of compensation due to an investor following expropriation,[35] whether an expropriation is "illegal" can be relevant for certain other reasons. First, many States will be reluctant to undertake actions that are considered to be illegal under international law. Also, some national laws concerning expropriation, such as the act of State doctrine in the United States, provide for different results depending upon whether the expropriation is "legal" or "illegal" under international law.[36] Further, according to a traditional view, illegality may offer the investor the right to demand restitution of property, rather than only damages in compensation.[37] Finally, some political risk

---

Court of Human Rights, 11 NYU Environ. L.J. 136 (2003); Hélène Ruiz Fabri, *The Approach Taken by the European Court of Human Rights to the Assessment of Compensation for "Regulatory Expropriations" of the Property of Foreign Investors*, 11 NYU Environ. L.J. 148 (2003); *see also* José E. Alvarez, *The Use (and Misuse) of European Human Rights Law in Investor–State Dispute Settlement*, in The Impact of EU Law on International Commercial Arbitration 72 (Franco Ferrari ed. 2017), available at SSRN: https://papers.ssrn.com/sol3/papers.cfm?abstract_id=2875089.

[31] *Nottebohm Case (Lichtenstein v. Guatemala)*, 1955 I.C.J. 4, 23 (1955); *Merge Claim*, 22 I.L.R. 443, 455, Ital.–U.S. Concil. Comm'n. (1955). *See also* Chapter 4, Section F.1.

[32] *Barcelona Traction Case (Belgium v. Spain)*, 1970 I.C.J. 5, 46 I.L.R. 178, available at http://www.icj-cij.org. The *Barcelona Traction* rule allows for four exceptions where formal criteria can be ignored for purposes of corporate nationality: (1) equitable concerns; (2) where the State under whose protection the corporation would naturally fall is unable to act; (3) where the State of incorporation itself is the tortfeasor, the State in which a large shareholder resides may be able to exercise diplomatic protection; and (4) where the corporation has since gone out of business. *See also Tokios Tekelés v. Ukraine*, ICSID Case No. ARB/02/18, Decision on Jurisdiction of Apr. 29, 2004, available at http://www.worldbank.org/icsid (absent fraud, the place of incorporation of the corporate claimant should be respected for purposes of nationality), Chapter 4, Section F.

[33] This topic is discussed in detail in Chapter 5.

[34] *See* Chapter 5, Section B.

[35] *Id.*

[36] *See* Chapter 4, Sections G.2.c and G.3; also UNCTAD, *Taking of Property*, UNCTAD/ITE/IIT/15 (2000), available at http://www.unctad.org/en/docs/psiteiitd15.en.pdf, at 24 *et seq.*

[37] *See* Chapter 10, Section E.

insurance contracts require that an expropriation be "illegal" under international law before a claim may be made on the policy.[38]

The risk of expropriation is typically greater in high-profile, capital-intensive infrastructure or natural resources projects, such as oil projects, mining projects, and power projects.[39] As explained, these projects are most vulnerable to the "obsolescing bargain" problem. Furthermore, governments stand to gain a great deal politically from taking over investments such as these, which are widely seen as providing essential services or based on "national patrimony." Expropriation is also more prone to occur in times of political instability, such as prevailed following the systemic changes in Cuba in 1959[40] and Iran in 1979. Additionally, because expropriation involves the annulment of property rights, it is also more likely to occur in States lacking an extensive tradition of broad-based private property ownership. An analysis of the history, legal and political institutions, and prevailing philosophy and culture of the host State can shed some light on the State's ability to withstand the socio-political pressure to expropriate. **1.19**

Before turning to the next category of political risk, some comment is in order regarding terminology in the area of expropriation. The word "nationalization" is often used interchangeably with "expropriation." Technically speaking, however, the terms can be seen to differ: nationalization is a specific form or manifestation of expropriation. Nationalization generally refers to a sweeping government policy to take over *all* foreign investment, or all foreign investment within a particular industry, for the purpose of social or economic reform.[41] Professor Renato Ribeiro explains that an "expropriation" takes place when the State "takes possession of personal, individually-held assets and rights of foreigners and usually makes prompt and fair payment for them," while a "nationalization" is a "general, impersonal form of expropriation which the state uses in the larger interests of **1.20**

---

[38] *See* Chapter 3.

[39] *See e.g.* Chapter 5, Section A.2.b for a discussion of Libya's nationalization of its oil industry in the 1970s.

[40] *See* Eric N. Baklanoff, Expropriation of U.S. Investment in Cuba, Mexico, and Chile (1975).

[41] Richard M. Mosk, *Expropriation: What to Do About It?*, 5 Cal. Int'l Pract. 11 (1993–94). For a further discussion of the distinction between expropriation and nationalization, see Wortley, *supra* note 19, at 93 ("The word 'nationalization' is not a term of art, but it usually signifies expropriation in pursuance of some national political programme intended to create out of existing enterprises, or to strengthen, a nationally controlled industry. Nationalization differs in its scope and extent, rather than in its juridical nature from other types of expropriation"); Brownlie, *supra* note 20, at 509 ("Expropriation of one or more major national resources as part of a general programme of social and economic reform is now generally referred to as nationalization . . ."); Isi Foighel, Nationalization: A Study in The Protection of Alien Property in International Law 19 (1957) ("nationalization" is "the compulsory transfer to the state of private property dictated by economic motives and having as its purpose the continued and essentially unaltered exploitation of the particular property").

society to advance a program of economic and social reform." Its purpose is "to have the ownership of wealth and natural resources, as well as the means to production, perform a social function."[42] Examples of nationalizations include the takeover of the banking and insurance industries by Iran in June of 1979 following the Islamic Revolution[43] and Chile's appropriation of American copper interests in 1971.[44] Widespread nationalization also occurred in Peru in 1968, when the government seized the International Petroleum Company's holdings, as well as a range of mining companies, sugar producers, and banks.[45] A more recent example of nationalizations occurred in Venezuela, where President Hugo Chavez promoted a nationalization program in a range of sectors, including oil and gas, mining, and agriculture.[46]

1.21 Finally, the term "confiscation," when used to differentiate from other forms of expropriation, refers to the State seizure of property without compensation, usually to punish the owner for who he is or for what he has done.[47] J.E.S. Fawcett defined confiscation as "the taking of private property by the state without payment or compensation[48] to the divested owner."[49] Beginning in 2002, confiscation shook the social and economic structure of Zimbabwe. There, the Mugabe government initiated a "land reform" program to transfer agricultural land to the

---

[42] Renato Ribeiro, Nationalization of Foreign Property in International Law i (1977).

[43] *See generally INA Corp., supra* note 28, and *AIG, supra* note 27.

[44] Following the election of Salvadore Allende in Chile in 1971, the Chilean Congress expropriated copper mines owned by two American companies, Kennecott Copper Corporation and Anaconda Copper Company. Evrett W. Benton, *The Libyan Expropriations: Further Developments on the Remedy of Invalidation of Title*, 11 Hous. L. Rev. 924, 935 (1974). *See also* Baklanoff, *supra* note 40.

[45] Amy L. Chua, *The Privatization-Nationalization Cycle: The Link between Markets and Ethnicity in Developing Countries*, 95 Col. L. Rev. 223, 239 (1995).

[46] Papanastasiou, *supra* note 6, at 53. See also, *Rusoro Mining Ltd. v. Venezuela*, ICSID Case No. ARB(AF)/12/5, Award of Aug. 22, 2016, available at: https://www.italaw.com/sites/default/files/case-documents/italaw7507.pdf; *Venezuela Holdings B.V. and others (formerly Mobil Corporation and others) v. Venezuela*, ICSID Case No. ARB/07/27, Award of Oct. 9, 2014, available at: https://www.italaw.com/sites/default/files/case-documents/italaw4011.pdf; *Vestey Group Ltd v. Venezuela*, ICSID Case No. ARB/06/4, Award Apr. 15, 2016, available at: https://www.italaw.com/sites/default/files/case-documents/italaw7230.pdf.

[47] Matias F. Travieso-Diaz, *Some Legal and Practical Issues in the Resolution of Cuban Nationals' Expropriation Claims against Cuba*, 16 U. Pa. J. Int'l Bus. L. 217, 229–30 (1995). Brownlie, *supra* note 20, at 509 ("if compensation is not provided, or the taking is regarded as unlawful, the taking is sometimes described as confiscation"); Black's Law Dictionary (6th ed. 1990) defines "confiscation" as "the seizure of private property by the government without compensation to the owner, often as a consequence of conviction for crime, or because possession or use of the property was contrary to law." *See also Am. Ins. Ass'n v. Garamendi*, 539 U.S. 396 (2003) (U.S. Supreme Court referred to Nazi Germany's seizure of private assets as "confiscation").

[48] *British Petroleum Exploration Co. (Libya) Ltd. v. Government of Libya*, 53 I.L.R. 297, 329 (1973) ("the fact that no offer or compensation has been made indicates that the taking was also confiscatory").

[49] J.E.S. Fawcett, *Some Foreign Effects of Nationalisation of Property*, 27 Brit. Yb. Int'l L. 355 (1950).

"native" population, in part by encouraging paramilitary groups to take the land from farmers of European origin.[50]

Regardless of the terminology or the precise form of State action, the result of expropriation is uniform. The assets that the foreign investor has brought to the host country, or those he has acquired there to undertake a business enterprise, are transferred to the local government or its designee, or simply dissipated or destroyed. It is important to recognize the sea change that has transpired over the past decades to reduce this particular political risk to a shadow of its former self. As Rudolph Dolzer explains: **1.22**

> In this period of globalization, decreased official development aid and increased privatization and liberalization, formal expropriation has become anathema for developing states. The former concepts of economic decolonization and permanent sovereignty over natural resources have—in theory and, in many corners, in practice—been replaced by structural adjustment, good governance, export-led growth and vivid competition for foreign investment.[51]

This is not to say that governments no longer engage in outright seizure of foreign property. In 1994, for example, Boris Yeltsin issued a decree allocating certain buildings in a particularly picturesque part of St. Petersburg to be used as accommodations for visiting dignitaries. The facilities, however, were owned by a Russian–German joint venture that provided private security services and sold police equipment. After extended judicial and administrative battles, the local authorities entered the property in 1996, sealing the premises and forcing employees of the joint venture to leave with only their personal belongings. The German investor left Russia on a ferry shortly thereafter, leaving behind even his car and personal computer. An arbitration tribunal formed under the aegis of the Germany–Russian bilateral investment treaty later found that Russia had directly expropriated buildings, automobiles, and other property in violation of international law obligations.[52] **1.23**

But if in the 1960s and 1970s outright expropriation was one of the most prominent political risks that foreign investors feared and sought to mitigate, today it has receded to the remote horizon. Instead, developing States have adopted from the industrialized world more subtle means of wealth redistribution **1.24**

---

[50] The Press Association, *Zimbabwe: Attempted Farm Eviction*, NY Times, Aug. 15, 2002, at A13; Human Rights Watch, *Fast Track Land Reform in Zimbabwe* (Mar. 2002), http://www.hrw.org/reports/2002/zimbabwe.

[51] Rudolph Dolzer, *Indirect Expropriations: New Developments?*, 11 NYU Environ. L.J. 64, 65 (2003).

[52] *Sedelmayer v. Russian Federation*, ad hoc tribunal, Award of July 7, 1998. Another direct expropriation took place in Latvia in 1996. In *Swembalt S.A. v. Latvia*, a Swedish company brought a ship to Riga as a floating Swedish commercial center. The port authorities, claiming that municipal officials had not been authorized under local law to issue the necessary permits, towed it from its mooring and eventually sold it at auction for scrap. *Swembalt S.A. v. Latvia*, UNCITRAL Award of Oct. 23, 2000, 2004(2) Stockholm Arb. Rep. 97.

and economic control, giving rise to a very real modern-day risk of "de facto" expropriation by regulation.[53]

2. Regulatory interference

1.25 Thus, the greater contemporary risk to foreign investors is government interference that does not formally transfer title away from the investor, but damages or destroys his ability to control or benefit from the investment he has made. Government measures that eliminate substantially all of an investment's value may constitute regulatory expropriation, including creeping or indirect expropriation—where a series of State acts accumulates to deprive an investment of its value.[54] Such State actions can deprive the investor of the productive use and benefit of its assets, making ownership practically worthless, even though the investor may retain formal attributes of ownership.[55] In the *Starrett* decision, the Iran–U.S. Claims Tribunal explained:

> Measures taken by a state can interfere with property rights to such an extent that these rights are rendered so useless that they must be deemed to have been expropriated, even though the state does not purport to have expropriated them and the legal title to the property formally remains with the original owner.[56]

1.26 Some define "creeping expropriation" as government measures that impose incremental restrictions and controls (such as excessive or repetitive regulatory measures) to make it difficult for the investor to continue in business at the profit level that justified the project in the first place.[57] Such government measures may lead

---

[53] *See* C. Yannaca-Small, *"Indirect Expropriation" and the "Right to Regulate" in International Investment Law*, OECD Working Paper on International Investment No. 2004/4 (2004).

[54] While the phrase "de facto expropriation" is perhaps a better description than "creeping expropriation" or "indirect expropriation" (Robert B. Shanks, *Insuring Investment and Loans against Currency Inconvertibility, Expropriation, and Political Violence*, 9 Hastings Int'l & Comp. L. Rev. 417, 424 (1986)), the latter terms have received widespread acceptance and will be used more frequently in this book. "Creeping expropriation" stresses that the State has taken a series of measures with a cumulative expropriatory effect, while "indirect" emphasizes the fact that the investor's formal or nominal title to the asset was not actually affected. In practice, much *de facto* expropriation is both "creeping" and "indirect." On regulatory expropriation generally, *see* Jack Coe, Jr. & Noah Rubins, *Regulatory Expropriation and the Tecmed Case: Context and Contributions*, in International Investment Law and Arbitration 597 (Todd Weiler ed. 2005); Sean D. Murphy, *Contemporary Practice of the United States relating to International Law*, 95 AJIL 873, 881–85 (2001); UNCTAD, *Taking of Property, supra* note 36, at 11–12. *See also Methanex Corp. v. United States*, Final Award on Jurisdiction and Merits of Aug. 3, 2005 (NAFTA Chapter 11), available at http://www.state.gov/documents/organization/51052.pdf, at Part IV-Chapter D, paras. 6–7 (non-discriminatory regulations for a public purpose, such as environmental laws, not considered expropriation).

[55] Noah Rubins, *Must the Victorious Claimant Relinquish Title to Expropriated Property?*, 4 J. World Inv. 481 (2003).

[56] In other decisions, such as *Golpira v. Iran*, Award No. 32-211-2, 2 Iran–U.S. C.T.R. 171, 177 (1983) and *Int'l Technical Products Corp. v. Iran*, Award No. 196-302-3, 9 Iran–U.S. C.T.R. 206 (1985), the Iran–U.S. Claims Tribunal found expropriation based on an unreasonable interference with the use and control of property of U.S. nationals.

[57] Robert B. Shanks, *Insuring Investment and Loans against Currency Inconvertibility, Expropriation, and Political Violence*, 9 Hastings Int'l & Comp. L. Rev. 417, 424 (1986).

to the sale or abandonment of the project to the government or to local private investors,[58] but the government may obtain no obvious direct benefit. Although each measure in isolation may not be enough to damage the investor's rights in any fundamental way, the cumulative effect of the measures can nevertheless be confiscatory, depriving the investor of control or a substantial portion of the benefits of his enterprise.[59]

As we will see later, whether a host government's measures result in "expropriation" within the definition of customary international law is largely a function of the depth of the harm to the foreign investor. The legal analysis is complicated, however, by the recognition of commentators and arbitrators that regulation is central to any State's responsibility to its populace. Only by exercising their "police power" can governments protect health and safety, maintain order, and try to increase prosperity, although all of these actions may also have a deleterious impact on foreign investment. According to some, customary international law will not impose liability where a State has enacted generally applicable regulation for a "legitimate" purpose.[60] The ad hoc tribunal in *CME v. Czech Republic* emphasized the possibility of non-compensable harm from regulation in an award finding that the Czech government's failure to preserve a Dutch investor's broadcast license constituted expropriation: **1.27**

> Of course, deprivation of property and/or rights must be distinguished from ordinary measures of the State and its agencies in proper execution of the law. Regulatory measures are common in all types of legal and economic systems in order to avoid use of private property contrary to the general welfare of the (host) State.[61]

The U.S. Restatement on Foreign Relations Law likewise summarizes this view of customary law: **1.28**

> A state is not responsible for loss of property or for other economic disadvantage resulting from *bona fide* general taxation, regulation, forfeiture for crime, or other action of the kind that is commonly accepted as within the police power of states, if it is not discriminatory.[62]

---

[58] *CME Czech Republic B.V. v. Czech Republic* (UNCITRAL), Final Award of Mar. 13, 2003, available at https://www.italaw.com/sites/default/files/case-documents/ita0180.pdf.

[59] Gloria L. Sandrino, *The NAFTA Investment Chapter and Foreign Direct Investment in Mexico: A Third World Prospective*, 27 Vand. J. Transnat'l L. 259 n.276 (1994). *See also* Rudolf Dolzer, *Indirect Expropriation of Alien Property*, 1 ICSID Rev.—For. Inv. L.J. 41 (1986) and Detlev F. Vagts, *Coercion and Foreign Investment Rearrangements*, 72 AJIL 17 (1978); Yves Fortier, *Caveat Investor: The Meaning of "Expropriation" and the Protection Afforded Investors under NAFTA*, News from ICSID, Summer 2003, at 1, 10. *See also* Chapter 3, Section A.2.b (discussing OPIC's definition of creeping expropriation).

[60] Brownlie, *supra* note 20, at 508–09.

[61] *CME Czech Republic, B.V. v. Czech Republic*, UNCITRAL Partial Award of Sept. 13, 2001, para. 603, available at https://www.italaw.com/sites/default/files/case-documents/ita0178.pdf.

[62] United States Restatement (Third) of Foreign Relations Law § 712.

As a result of this approach, some early arbitral decisions focused upon the intent of the State in adopting the measure in question.[63]

1.29 However, later decisions, beginning with those of the Iran–U.S. Claims Tribunal, have downplayed the question of government "intent" in determining the legal effect of regulatory measures. In *Tippets*, for example, the tribunal concluded that:

> The intent of the government is less important than the effects of the measures on the owner, and the form of the measures of control or interference is less important than the reality of their impact.[64]

1.30 The role of intent has further diminished since then. In arbitration under bilateral and multilateral investment treaties, tribunals have repeatedly discounted the purpose of a regulatory measure as a consideration for expropriation analysis.[65] One of the strongest statements of this position came in the *Santa Elena* case, where the Costa Rican government had effectively ejected the foreign investor from his land by designating the property as part of a nature preserve:

> Expropriatory environmental measures—no matter how laudable and beneficial to society as a whole—are, in this respect, similar to any other expropriatory measure that a state may take in order to implement its policies: where property is expropriated, even for environmental purposes, whether domestic or international, the state's obligation to pay compensation remains.[66]

1.31 Clearly, this trend is the result of a practical recognition that regulation is rarely enacted for only one purpose, or even for a single dominant purpose. Furthermore, the evidentiary burden on the claimant and the tribunal in establishing requisite intent makes such a criterion counterproductive in many instances. Nevertheless, the exclusion of purpose and intent from expropriation analysis is currently the subject of much debate in the academic community: many suggest that a view of indirect expropriation that focuses exclusively upon effects will deter host

---

[63] *The Oscar Chinn Case (U.K. v. Belgium)*, P.C.I.J. Ser. A/B, No. 63 (1934); *Sea-Land Service Inc. v. Iran*, 6 Iran–U.S. C.T.R. 149, 166 (1984). *See also* Brownlie, *supra* note 20, at 509; Burns H. Weston, *"Constructive Takings" under International Law: A Modest Foray into the Problem of Creeping Expropriation*, 16 Va. J. Int'l L. 103, 170 (1975) ("deference should be given to the original intent of the administrating government and, thus, to the broad 'regulatory' competence that States traditionally have enjoyed under international law"). *But cf.* Brownlie, *supra* note 20, at 509 (taxation designed to confiscate may be considered expropriation at international law); British Practice in International Law 202–06 (Eli Lauterpacht ed. 1964) (same).

[64] *Tippets, Abbett, McCarthy, Stratton (Tippets) v. TAMS-AFFA Consulting Engineers of Iran*, Award No. 141-7-2, 6 Iran–U.S. C.T.R. 219, 225–26 (1984). *See also Phelps Dodge Corp. and Overseas Private Investment Corp. v. Iran*, Award No. 217-99-2, 10 Iran–U.S. C.T.R. 121 (1986).

[65] *Metalclad, supra* note 12, para. 111.

[66] *Compañia del Desarrollo de Santa Elena S.A. v. Costa Rica*, ICSID Case No. ARB/96/1, Final Award of Feb. 17, 2000, paras. 71–72. *See also Antoine Goetz et al. v. Burundi*, ICSID Case No. ARB/95/3, Decision of Feb. 10, 1999, para. 124, 15 ICSID Rev.—For. Inv. L.J. 457, 513 (2000); *but cf. Methanex, supra* note 54. It should be noted that the intent of the State may remain relevant in determining whether an expropriation is "legal" or "illegal" under international law, once it has been determined that a taking has occurred. *See* Chapter 5, Section B.1.

governments from undertaking necessary regulatory action, especially in the field of environmental law.[67] We will return to this contentious issue later in the book, when we present the substantive international law of investment protection.

There is a practically limitless range of regulatory measures that can potentially harm or even destroy foreign investment. One of the simplest and most common is the withholding of promised operation permits. In many instances, sunk costs cannot be recovered in large-scale investment projects, because they are invested in single-purpose equipment or facilities. In several cases, host governments have encouraged foreign investors to establish operations within their territory, only to withdraw their support for the project later. In *Metalclad*, Mexican federal authorities assured the foreign investor that all necessary permits for a landfill enterprise had been granted, but allowed municipal authorities to thwart the opening of the facility.[68] The *Tecmed* case involved similar circumstances, where a privatized landfill was deprived of its license soon after it came into foreign hands.[69] In *Santa Elena*, meanwhile, U.S. investors obtained permission to build a tourist complex in Costa Rica, but the government later changed its mind and designated the site as part of a nature preserve.[70] **1.32**

Another form of indirect expropriation occurs when the State effectively takes control of the foreign-owned investment vehicle by enacting legislation restricting control over corporate management. Iran imposed regulatory measures widely after 1979 replacing the management of foreign corporations with government-appointed managers and directors.[71] While such action is not a direct expropriation of assets, in several cases it was held to have the same effect as expropriation, depriving the owners of the right to use their property. This may be distinguished from the direct seizure of a controlling share of the entity that holds the investor's assets, which is perhaps more correctly classified as direct expropriation.[72] **1.33**

[67] *See* Howard Mann, *NAFTA and the Environment: Lessons for the Future*, 13 Tul. Envt'l L.J. 387, 405–06 (2000); Daniel R. Loritz, *Comment: Corporate Predators Attack Environmental Regulations: It's Time to Arbitrate Claims Filed under NAFTA Chapter 11*, 22 Loy. LA Int'l & Comp. L. Rev. 533, 546–47 (2000) (stating that while environmental regulations should remain legal under NAFTA, the mere threat of suit for multimillion-dollar damages chills regulatory activity); Joel C. Beauvais, *Student Article: Regulatory Expropriations under NAFTA: Emerging Principles and Lingering Doubts*, 10 NYU Envt'l L.J. 245 (2002).

[68] *Metalclad, supra* note 12.

[69] *Técnicas Medioambientales Tecmed, supra* note 8.

[70] *Compañia del Desarrollo, supra* note 66.

[71] *Starrett Housing Corp. v. Government of Iran*, Award No. ITL 32-24-1, 4 Iran–U.S. C.T.R. 122 (1983); for further discussion, see Charles N. Brower, *Current Developments in the Law of Expropriation and Compensation: A Preliminary Survey of Awards of the Iran–United States Claims Tribunal*, 21 Int'l Law. 643 (1987).

[72] Indirect expropriation may also take the form of a forced sale disguised as a voluntary private sale. In this regard, the effects of the threat of expropriation, if sufficiently severe, may be indistinguishable from the effects of actual expropriation. This form of expropriation was commonly employed by the Nazi regime in Germany. Wortley, *supra* note 19, at 1.

1.34 Although the point at which the host State's regulatory actions constitute expropriation under international law may not always be clear, the investor can mitigate the effects of certain potential regulatory measures by including "stabilization clauses" in State contracts. This sort of agreement provides that the law of the host State in effect on the date of the contract will govern the parties' relationship, regardless of future changes made to the law.[73] The investor may also negotiate more specific assurances from the host State that particular regulations will not be imposed. If the investor is able to obtain such assurances, then regulations later imposed in violation of the stabilization clause would be subject to the dispute resolution provisions of the investment contract—normally international arbitration.[74] Investors may also consider obtaining insurance against the imposition of particular taxes and regulations.[75] These topics and strategies are discussed in further detail in this text.

1.35 The variety of regulatory interference is well demonstrated in the following hypothetical case based on an actual situation, where U.S. investors owned just under half of the shares in a fishing joint venture in a host State.[76] Following a coup in the host country, the new government became hostile to both the foreign and the local investors. The expatriate manager and his family were threatened with physical harm, and they soon left the country. Next, a foreign refrigeration expert whose services were vital to the joint venture's operations was denied the right to extend his visa; he also was forced to leave. Government authorities then interfered with the joint venture's fishing permits. Harbor authorities refused to allow ships dealing with the joint venture to use port facilities, and it became very difficult for the company to export its catch. Finally, when the investor had been reduced to flying out a single load of seafood per day on a small company plane, the government refused to permit the joint venture to fly its plane unless it was accompanied by a government-approved pilot and "seafood inspector." This extra passenger had the effect of displacing his weight in seafood—a serious problem, given that the "inspector" weighed nearly 200 kilograms, having been selected because he was the heaviest member of the armed forces.

---

[73] Such clauses are discussed in detail in Chapter 2, Section D.3. The case of *Occidental Petroleum v. Ecuador* centered around just such a stabilization clause, which specifically froze the Ecuadorean tax regime as of the date of the signing of the investment contract. *Occidental Petroleum Exploration Co. v. Ecuador*, LCIA Case No. UN3467, Final Award of July 1, 2004. *See also Government of Kuwait v. American Independent Oil Co. (AMINOIL)*, 66 I.L.R. 518 (1982), 21 I.L.M. 976 (1982).

[74] *See* discussions in Chapter 5, Section C, Chapter 4, Sections B and C, and Section C.5, *infra*, regarding breach of contract as a political risk, and the international law consequences of such a breach of contract.

[75] Political risk insurance is discussed in Chapter 3.

[76] Example supplied in Shanks, *supra* note 57, at 426. This investment was insured by the Overseas Private Investment Corporation (discussed in Chapter 3), which paid on a claim by the investor arising out of the underlying events.

1.36 While this example may well demonstrate sufficient regulatory interference in the investor's operations to constitute expropriation, many situations are not as obvious. Whether interference by a host State rises to the level of expropriation is a fact-intensive inquiry that must be considered on a case-by-case basis.[77] But the risk to the foreign investor remains, even if State measures do not entirely destroy investment value. Customary international law has little to say about non-expropriatory regulatory measures, particularly if foreign investors can challenge their fairness in the host State's courts. As we will see later, however, States have recognized the importance of this category of political risk for FDI, and investment treaties include a number of substantive protections designed to compensate foreign investors where such measures are unreasonable, unfair, or discriminatory.[78]

3. Currency risk

1.37 Investors who invest directly in a foreign country are particularly vulnerable to a range of alterations in the currency regime. The decision to invest, normally based upon the considered expectation of a reasonable rate of return from foreign-based operations, is closely linked in many ways to interactions between local and international money.[79] Governments frequently implement measures that change the nature of that interaction, measures that can have an important impact on the foreign investor's ability to realize the expected return. Foreign-owned businesses also face the risk that the host State will either prohibit the conversion of local currency revenues into "hard" currency, or otherwise increase controls over the exchange of currency.[80]

1.38 In addition, foreign investors also face the risk of the prohibition of the transfer of funds. For this reason, most investment treaties add a provision for the right to transfer funds in a freely usable currency and at the market rate.[81] However, even if treaties tend to include "absolute statements" related to the protection

[77] A more detailed analysis of the law of expropriation is provided in Chapter 5, and in the context of investment treaties, in Chapter 6.

[78] The substantive protections of fair and equitable treatment, full protection and security, national treatment, and most-favored nation treatment are explained in Chapter 6.

[79] *CMS Gas Transmission Company v. Argentina*, ICSID Case No. ARB/01/8, Award of May 12, 2005, paras. 136–38, 275, available at: https://www.italaw.com/sites/default/files/case-documents/ita0184.pdf.

[80] Currency risk cannot be discounted even in the natural resources and commodities sectors, where output is sold in for export and generates foreign currency directly. Jonathan J. Green, *Managing Risks in International Power Projects*, 672 PLI/Comm. L. & Prac. Course Handbook Series 669 (1993).

[81] For example, art. 83(2) of the Japan–Malaysia Economic Partnership Agreement (EPA) (entry into force July 13, 2006) recognizes that "[e]ach Country shall allow transfers to be made in freely usable currency at the market rate of exchange prevailing on the date of the transfer"; *see* Papanastasiou, *supra* note 6, at 116.

of the right to transfer funds, it is argued that the inclusion of such statements is unrealistic and "cannot bind a state in times of financial crisis" or when a contracting party has exchange shortfalls necessitating currency controls.[82]

1.39 A host country may block conversion either passively, by accepting the investor's application for hard currency at the central bank but blocking the foreign exchange necessary to effect the remittance, or actively, through the imposition of exchange controls or the declaration of a moratorium on exchange.[83] One political risk investment insurance provider, the U.S. Overseas Private Investment Corporation (OPIC), deems currency to be "inconvertible" if the investor is unable to legally convert its earnings from the host country's currency into U.S. dollars for a period of ninety days. But other, less restrictive controls on currency exchange can also present serious pitfalls for foreign investors,[84] particularly those involved in large projects involving intensive, dollar-denominated financing and high volumes of income in local currency, as in electrical generation or highway concessions.

1.40 Investors may also face the risk of currency devaluation brought about by government policies. Thus, upon conversion, such currency may be worth less than expected. Even where inflation and the devaluation of currency are the direct result of government action,[85] such conditions have often been classified as commercial rather than political risk. After the crises in Latin America and Asia, however, this classification has been seriously questioned. Most observers agree that the loss in value of the currencies in those economies was primarily the result of government choices in fiscal and trade policy. In many cases, foreign investors made their decision to invest based in part on such political criteria as government expenditures and tax collection efficiency, the trade balance level, and the existence of infrastructure for sustainable development. During the Mexican crisis of 1996, it was the government's publicly announced cooperation with the International Monetary Fund (IMF) that stopped the exodus of foreign peso holdings. The IMF's purported goal was to ensure the implementation of political reform necessary to stabilize the Mexican economy. Thus, many investors

---

[82] M. Sornarajah, International Law of Foreign Investment 207 (3d ed. 2010).

[83] Peter F. Fitzgerald, *Overview of Risks in International Financing*, 707 PLI/Comm. L. & Prac. Course Handbook Series 7 (1995).

[84] *See e.g.* G.H. Yu, *China's Foreign Exchange Regulations and Direct Foreign Investment*, 28(6) J. World Trade 99 (1994); S. Paksoy, *Foreign Investment and Exchange Regulations in Turkey*, 18 Comp. L. Yb. Int'l Bus. 241 (1996).

[85] On the link between money inflation (inflation of the supply of money and credit by central government policy) and price inflation (which is typically what is meant today by the expression "inflation," but which is caused by, merely a symptom of, money supply inflation), *see* Murray N. Rothbard, What Has Government Done to Our Money? (4th ed. 1990), available at http://www.mises.org; Murray N. Rothbard, Man, Economy, and State: A Treatise on Economic Principles (1962), at ch. 12, § 11 (pp. 850–78), available at http://www.mises.org; and Mises, Human Action, *supra* note 1, at ch. XXXI *et passim*.

have taken the view that currency risk is a political rather than purely commercial concern.[86]

Financial crises such as those experienced in Latin America, Russia, and Southeast Asia in the mid- to late 1990s compound currency risks and increase the possibility that the host State will impose new regulations shifting the burden of recovery onto foreign investors. This threat is particularly acute in the public services sector: as the local currency drops in value, enterprises with foreign-denominated costs (particularly debt service obligations) must raise more revenue to maintain previous rates of return. Since public services prices are normally regulated by the State, but based upon formulae that take costs into account, a government faced with sharply devaluated currency may seek to alter the original formula to prevent the foreign operator from "passing through" increased costs to consumers, and to avoid absorbing the cost of devaluation itself. This is precisely what occurred in Argentina in 2001–02, when the government "floated" the peso (once pegged in value at one dollar), which could no longer support an artificial exchange rate. In concert with this move, the Argentine government froze most utility rates, which had been periodically modified according to foreign price indexes. More radically, the government "pesified" contracts, converting dollar obligations into pesos at the previous rate of one-to-one. Meanwhile, the peso lost two-thirds of its value. For foreign investors in public utility providers, this combination was devastating.[87] **1.41**

Currency crises, and the resulting imposition of currency restrictions, often occur in developing economies after intense short-term economic expansion. Paradoxically, therefore, foreign investors should pay particular attention to fiscal practices before investing in a booming economy. In particular, currency pressure tends to be cyclical, and a careful examination of the history of government fiscal policies and responses to crisis can give potential investors a reasonable view of possible future outcomes.[88] **1.42**

4. Civil disturbance

In some parts of the world, the risk that civil disturbance will affect foreign-owned commercial operations cannot be ignored. Such a risk subsumes a range of different levels of disorder and violence, from widespread strikes and sabotage to **1.43**

---

[86] Any doubt that currency devaluation is a political risk dissipates when currency devaluation is combined with price controls, which prevent businesses from passing through the cost of devaluation to consumers.

[87] *CMS Gas Transmission Co. v. Argentina*, ICSID Case No. ARB/01/8, Award of May 12, 2005, available at http://ita.law.uvic.ca/documents/CMS_FinalAward_000.pdf.

[88] Peter B. Kenen, The International Financial Architecture (2001). *See also* William A. Lovett, *Lessons from the Recent Peso Crisis in Mexico*, 4 Tul. J. Int'l & Comp. L. 143 (1996) (identifying as causes of the Mexican financial crisis investor overconfidence and large capital inflows after the signing of NAFTA).

terrorism, riots, revolution, and civil or external war. If the host State proves unable to insulate business interests from the direct and indirect effects of civil strife, investors may find their property damaged or destroyed, or they may be unable to carry on day-to-day operations due to workforce shortages, the threat of violence, or the disruption of connections to supplies or markets. Situations of war also sometimes lead to the commandeering of buildings and factories by government or rebel military forces.

1.44 Unlike many other risks analyzed here, this type of political risk may not be within the control of the host State. Under customary international law, unless it can be demonstrated that the host State has assumed the risk of loss to the investor, it is not obliged to compensate for damage caused by the non-governmental actors such as rioters, rebels, or looters.[89] The tribunal in *Sea-Land Service Inc. v. Iran*[90] upheld this principle, stating that "a finding of expropriation would require, at the very least, that the tribunal be satisfied that there was deliberate governmental interference with the conduct of Sea-Land's operation, the effect of which was to deprive Sea-Land of the use and benefit of the investment."[91] In the absence of a specific treaty, contract, or local law providing otherwise, therefore, civil disturbance carries few legal consequences for the host State.[92] However, such risk is usually insurable.[93]

1.45 Furthermore, investment treaties have added a new tool for controlling foreign investors' civil disturbance risk. As we will explain in more detail in Chapter 5, most investment treaties require the host State to provide "full protection and security" to qualifying foreign investors and their assets. While the extent of this obligation is not entirely clear, some tribunals have imposed a "negligence" standard, requiring the State to take all reasonable actions to prevent harm

[89] Brower, *supra* note 71, at 652. For a more complete discussion of the international law of State responsibility, see Chapter 4. For examples of cases in which a State was held responsible for political violence, *see American Manufacturing and Trading Co. v. Zaire*, ICSID Case No. ARB/93/01, Award of Feb. 21, 1997 (under BIT, Zaire held responsible for damage caused to foreign-owned assets by rebel forces); *Computer Science Corp. v. Government of Iran*, Award No. 221-65-1, 10 Iran–U.S. C.T.R. 269 (1986) (government of Iran held responsible for actions of Iranian Revolutionary Committee because committee was a legitimate organ of government) and *Pereira, supra* note 22 (government of Iran responsible for expropriatory action where notice of confiscation issued by Revolutionary Guards).

[90] *Sea-Land Service, supra* note 63.

[91] *Id.* at 166. Although this claim did not arise from political violence, the principle would be applicable to such a situation.

[92] *Asian Agricultural Products Ltd. (AAPL) v. Sri Lanka*, ICSID Case No. ARB/87/3, *reprinted at* 30 I.L.M. 577 (1991) (holding that the destruction of a plant in the fight against an insurgent guerrilla warranted compensation under the "full protection and security" provision of the applicable investment treaty, but not under customary international law). Recovery may be possible under the customary international law of State responsibility if the insurgents who destroyed or confiscated the property in question manage to become the government. In this case, acts the insurgents carried out to gain power may be considered acts of State.

[93] *See* Chapter 3.

from befalling foreign businesses.[94] Some recent investment treaties explicitly require the host State to provide adequate police protection from civil disturbances.[95]

With the inclusion of a specific guarantee, such as a protection and security clause, in modern bilateral investment treaties, the host State reaffirms its obligation to protect foreign investments in case of damage suffered due to wars or civil disturbance and it recognizes the right to compensation "effectively realizable, freely convertible and freely transferrable in a freely usable currency."[96] **1.46**

5. Breach of State contracts

An investor who has acquired rights in the host country through a concession, license, or other contract concluded directly with the local government or its instrumentality must remain alert to the possibility that the State will either annul the contract or compel a change in its terms. Repudiation may take the form of a breach of contractual obligations, enactment of laws undermining the purpose or effectiveness of the contract, or passing legislation annulling the contract altogether.[97] State contracts are more susceptible to alteration or breach than private agreements, because under the law of most jurisdictions, they are subject to a separate body of jurisprudence (administrative law) which gives significant weight to public interest concerns in assessing liability for the State's violation of obligations.[98] Many governments require that their own law govern any contracts that they sign with foreign entities, so that their administrative law will be given full effect, and some national laws grant exclusive jurisdiction over administrative law disputes to a specialized court, often known as a Council of State.[99] **1.47**

Nevertheless, in many circumstances State contracts can be subject to neutral dispute resolution procedures, and States have been held to standards of contract implementation similar to those applicable in commercial transactions. In the *LETCO* arbitration,[100] Liberia revoked a twenty-year agreement it had signed **1.48**

---

[94] *Asian Agricultural Products, supra* note 92, para. 85(B); *CME Czech Republic B.V.*, Partial Award, *supra* note 61, para. 613, available at https://www.italaw.com/sites/default/files/case-documents/ita0178.pdf.

[95] *See e.g.* U.S.–Chile Free Trade Agreement, art. 10(4)(2)(6), available at http://www.ustr.gov.

[96] *See* art. 103(2) of the Japan–Thailand EPA (entry into force Nov. 1, 2007); *see also* Papanastasiou, *supra* note 6, at 120–21.

[97] Brownlie, *supra* note 20, at 522–26.

[98] *See* Jody Freeman, *The Contracting State*, 28 Fla. St. U.L. Rev. 155 (2000); Thomas W. Wälde & George N'Di, *Stabilizing International Investment Commitments: International Law versus Contract Interpretation*, 31 Tex. Int'l L.J. 216, 236 n.83 (1996), version available at http://www.dundee.ac.uk/cepmlp.

[99] *See e.g.* Le Conseil d'État in France or in Greece.

[100] *Liberian Eastern Timber Corp. (LETCO) v. Government of Liberia*, ICSID Case No. ARB/83/2, Award of Mar. 31, 1986, and Rectification of June 17, 1986, 26 I.L.M. 647 (1987). *See also* *Técnicas Medioambientales Tecmed*, *supra* note 8 (regulatory action by Mexico effectively ending the

with a French company, which provided the foreign investor the exclusive right to conduct certain timber operations. An International Centre for Settlement of Investment Disputes (ICSID) tribunal ordered Liberia to pay damages for breach of the contract. In the *Himpurna* arbitration, Indonesia attempted to suspend a power plant project involving a foreign investor and the State-owned electric company, PLN. Indonesia insisted that the resulting breach of contract was excused due to the country's financial crisis and by operation of the *force majeure* clause of the applicable contract. The tribunal awarded damages to Himpurna, the foreign investor, as the *force majeure* clause was not triggered by a financial crisis and PLN could not be excused from liability because of its nature as a State-owned corporation.[101]

1.49 Contract rights are normally recognized as assets or "investments" within the definition provided in investment treaties. These rights themselves may therefore be subject to international law requirements of compensation for expropriation. For example, in the *Phillips* case, Iran nullified a joint venture agreement between Iran's State oil company and an American firm. The Iran–U.S. Claims Tribunal there held the government's actions to constitute expropriation.[102]

1.50 In any event, the terms of the State contract itself have a significant impact upon the risk that the State party is likely to breach it, and on the private party's ability to obtain compensation for harm caused by such a breach. In particular, attention should be paid to the governing law and arbitration or forum selection clauses in State contracts, as well as to waivers of State immunity.[103]

1.51 Nevertheless, the repudiation of a State contract does not necessarily constitute a violation of international law.[104] But with the inclusion of "umbrella" or (*pacta sunt servanda*) clauses in investment protection treaties, the violation of State contracts (and other State commitments in relation to foreign investments) may be more readily elevated to the level of international law, result in international responsibility.[105]

economic use of Tecmed's investment was an expropriatory breach of contract, as the affected asset was purely contractual in nature).

[101] *See Himpurna California Energy Ltd. (Bermuda) v. PT. (Persero) Perusahan Listruik Negara (Indonesia)*, Mealey's Int'l Arb. Rep., Dec. 1999 at A-26.

[102] *Phillips Petroleum Co. Iran v. Iran, The Nat'l Iranian Oil Co.*, Award No. 425-39-2, 21 Iran–U.S. C.T.R. 79 (1989). *See also* Chapter 5, Section C (discussing breached contract and expropriation); also Chapter 4, Sections B and C; UNCTAD, *Taking of Property, supra* note 36, at 37.

[103] *See* Chapter 2, Section E.

[104] Especially, when the host State acts not in its sovereign capacity, but merely as a party to the contract. *See* Jeswald Salacuse, The Law of Investment Treaties 273 (2010); *see also Noble Ventures Inc. v. Romania*, ICSID Case No. ARB/01/11, Award of Oct. 12, 2005; *Compagnie Generale des Eaux v. Argentina*, ICSID Case No ARB/97/3, Decision on Annulment of July 3, 2002, para. 95.

[105] Papanastasiou, *supra* note 6, at 122.

6. Corruption

The problem of corruption, which has received a great deal of attention in recent years, is an often-ignored segment of political risk. In fact, corruption in the political apparatus of a host State can have a significant impact on the establishment, operation, expansion, and disposal of foreign-owned assets, and should form an important part of political risk analysis. Corruption is generally understood to occur when government officials demand some personal benefit as a condition to fulfilling official functions. **1.52**

Most frequently, corruption affects the establishment of investment. Government officials may require payment of a bribe before signing investment agreements, concession contracts, licenses, or permits. It is also relatively common practice in some developing countries for foreign investors to pay fees to private or semi-private intermediaries for "access" to important officials, with some portion of these funds finding its way into the officials' personal accounts.[106] Other forms of corruption affect the ongoing operations of foreign businesses. For example, unofficial payments may be required in order to participate in tenders for lucrative State contracts, or to gain access to certain internal markets. Commercial disputes may be impossible to resolve favorably in the courts without the liberal application of "incentive money" to judges. The variety of corrupt practices is nearly limitless, and in some places makes fair competition with other market players difficult to achieve. **1.53**

The risk created by this sort of systemic corruption is multiplied for investors from countries that have implemented strict anti-corruption laws. These laws impose heavy sanctions, including jail sentences, upon corporate officers who authorize payments of this sort anywhere in the world.[107] Foreign investors must therefore identify with precision not only the risk that their business competitiveness will be adversely affected by corruption, but also the risk that their local representatives will engage in corrupt practices without their knowledge. It is essential in this regard to establish clear internal guidelines and transparent corporate governance structures to reduce the possibility of liability for the company and its owners. **1.54**

7. Trade restrictions

In this book, we deal primarily with risks directly related to investment rather than to trade. As explained earlier, FDI is subject to a far wider range of serious political **1.55**

[106] For an analysis of the corruption impact in infrastructure projects of developing countries, *see* Thomas-Nektarios Papanastasiou, Corruption in the Infrastructure Provision: The Role of Accountability Mechanisms in the Community Driven Development Projects of Indonesia (2016).

[107] *See e.g.* Lucinda A. Low, *Coping with the Foreign Corrupt Practices Act: A Primer for Energy and Natural Resource Sectors*, 2(2) CEPMLP Internet J. (1997).

risks than either portfolio investment or trade, since most profit-making activities take place within the territorial jurisdiction of the host State. Nevertheless, unexpected new trade restrictions can have a negative impact upon investors, as well as upon those who directly trade in the affected goods and services.

1.56 A pertinent example can be found in a dispute which arose as a result of France's ban on the import of British beef. The restriction was put in place as a response to the "mad cow disease" epidemic in the United Kingdom.[108] The dispute arose when beef that had been cleared for import from Britain into France was denied entry because of the newly-imposed French embargo. The parties to a certain supply contract agreed to ship the beef back to the United Kingdom, where it was destroyed by the British authorities. The France-based buyer brought arbitration against the U.K. seller for sums it had already paid for the meat. The tribunal ultimately found against the buyer, largely on the premise that an embargo formed part of the political risk related to the parties' contract. The arbitrators reasoned that because political risk passed to the buyer under the FOB Incoterm applicable to the transaction, the buyer was to bear the consequences of France's decision to impose unforeseen trade barriers.

1.57 We find the inverse fact situation in the North American Free Trade Agreement (NAFTA) case of *S.D. Myers v. Canada*. In *Myers*, a U.S. company established an enterprise in Canada to process locally produced PCB, a form of toxic waste, in its Michigan processing facility. In part to support a domestic PCB-processing industry, the Canadian government banned the export of these waste products to the United States. This measure did significant harm to Myers' Canadian business, although it was still able to engage in other waste-processing activities in Canada. While the NAFTA tribunal declined to find that Canada had expropriated Myers' investment, it nevertheless held the State liable for discriminatory and unfair and inequitable conduct toward the American investor, since the trade barrier was disproportionate to any legitimate ecological goal, and was designed in part to shut foreign businesses out of the local market.[109]

1.58 These two awards remind foreign investors that even if the host State provides a stable domestic regulatory framework for the production of goods, the investment may still be vulnerable to trade barriers, if the enterprise depends upon imported components or exported final products. Furthermore, the risk of trade barriers is less predictable than some other political risks, because trade is a two-way street: an embargo can be imposed either by the host State or by some other government. Investors may therefore be obliged to undertake political risk analysis encompassing certain important countries other than the host country, States upon which the investment will rely for inputs or end markets.

[108] Yearbook of Commercial Arbitration, vol. XXVI 18–23 (A.J. van den Berg ed. 2001).
[109] *S.D. Myers Inc. v. Canada*, Partial Award of Nov. 13, 2000, 40 I.L.M. 1408 (2001).

The international legal system does provide important tools for assessing the risk of trade restrictions. A great number of States are members of the World Trade Organization (WTO), which evolved out of the Bretton Woods/GATT structures of the post-World War II period.[110] WTO members are subject to uniform and stabilized trade practices, negotiated on a multilateral basis.[111] States that violate WTO standards may be subject to inter-governmental arbitration and retaliatory sanctions. Within certain free-trade areas, such as NAFTA and the European Union, trade barriers are completely eliminated, and structures are in place to compel payment of compensation directly.[112] Under the WTO/GATT, some trade restrictions are permissible under treaty exceptions, however. In particular, measures with discriminatory impact are allowed to stand if they are necessary to protect national security[113] or the health and safety of humans and animals.[114] **1.59**

There are therefore at least three conditions that make the risk of trade restrictions rather difficult for foreign investors to assess and control. First, in most circumstances trade remains outside the scope of most investment treaties, and therefore investors cannot normally invoke dispute resolution provisions directly to obtain redress against an offending State for unfair or excessive trade barriers. Rather, they must petition their home governments for "espousal" of their claims, either on a diplomatic level or before State-to-State dispute resolution bodies such as the WTO. Espousal of claims often depends as much upon the political influence of the petitioner as upon the legal merits of his case. Second, as noted, any legal claim against a State for compensation may be blocked because most free trade agreements permit a range of "necessary" measures. Finally, trade by its nature involves more than one country, and therefore the investor who relies upon either import or export must simultaneously take into account trade conditions in a range of States. **1.60**

D. Measuring Political Risk

In this section, we discuss factors that investors should consider when measuring political risk in a particular State prior to investing. As already noted, we do not address in detail the investment climate of any particular State, **1.61**

---

[110] For an overview of WTO jurisprudence, *see* Andreas Lowenfeld, International Economic Law 21–297 (2003).

[111] The WTO has 164 members as of Aug. 20, 2018. *Understanding the WTO: The Organization: Members and Observers*, http://www.wto.org/english/thewto_e/whatis_e/tif_e/org6_e.htm.

[112] For a thorough account of NAFTA and E.U. trade law in the context of global commerce, *see* The EU, The WTO and the NAFTA: Towards a Common Law of International Trade? (Joseph H.H. Weiler ed. 2000).

[113] General Agreement on Tariffs and Trade (GATT), available at http://www.wto.org, art. XXI.

[114] *Id.*, art. XX.

as any such attempt would inevitably fall short of the advice of experienced local counsel and specialized political risk services familiar with a particular country.[115] In any event, investment environments and their accompanying political risk often change very quickly. Here we provide some overarching guidelines that an investor may follow when analyzing political risk in a developing country.[116]

1.62 Prior to investing in a foreign country, an investor should carefully assess all the risks associated with the investment, including political risks.[117] A complete analysis of political risk requires consideration of a number of factors.

1.63 First, investors should consider the legal structure of the host State. The investor should look for "a well-developed legal and regulatory framework, including favorable tax and labor codes, investment laws, property laws, the protection of intellectual property rights, and competition policy, as well as relative industrial deregulation."[118] Lacunae in important areas provide an opportunity for special interests within the host society to change or interpret existing rules in their favor. An independent judiciary that has developed substantial jurisprudence in administrative, procurement, and State contracts law can provide a very effective damper on political risk.

1.64 Also in this context, the investor should carefully examine local laws governing foreign investment.[119] Many recent investment codes enacted in developing and transition economies provide important assurances covering FDI. Azerbaijan's

---

[115] For a useful overview of political risk measurement services and techniques, see Claude B. Erb et al., *Political Risk, Financial Risk and Economic Risk*, 52(6) Financial Analysts J. 28 (Nov./Dec. 1996), available at http://www.duke.edu/~charvey/Country_risk/pol/pol.htm

[116] On investors' tendency to cyclically overestimate and underestimate political risk, *see* Claire A. Hill, *How Investors React to Political Risk*, 8 Duke J. Comp. & Int'l L. 283, 306 (1998).

[117] While the apprehension of political risk in many parts of the world is certainly justified, investors may in fact overestimate dangers somewhat, in an abundance of caution. In a study in which executives were asked whether they had removed assets from foreign countries on the basis of a corporate decision (due to poor performance, weak management, or lack of resources) or due to coercive State action, the latter accounted for 5.4 percent of divestment from 1951 to 1975, and 3.7 percent from 1967 to 1971. F.N. Burton & Hisashi Inoue, *Expropriations of Foreign-Owned Firms in Developing Countries: A Cross-National Analysis*, 18 J. World Trade L. 396, 397 (1984). The direct expropriation of the property of U.S. nationals in developing countries from 1964 to 1974 has been estimated at a mere 1.6 percent of the total value of U.S. FDI. *Id.* at 397–98.

[118] Malcolm D. Rowat, *Multilateral Approaches to Improving the Investment Climate in Developing Countries: The Cases of ICSID and MIGA*, 33 Harv. Int'l L.J. 104 (1992); *see also* Michael A. Geist, *Toward a General Agreement on the Regulation of Foreign Direct Investment*, 26 Law & Pol'y. Int'l Bus. 673, 686–706 (1995) (discussing the foreign investment codes of several nations). On structural risk in Argentina, which is responsible for the country's cyclical economic history, *see* Peter B. Kenen, The International Financial Architecture 13–19 (2001) (explaining the need for evaluating whether capital inflows in an economy are sustainable or temporary). *See also* Grant Nulle, *IMF Ignores Causes of Crisis*, Financial Times, Aug. 18, 2003, at 10.

[119] *See* Jeswald W. Salacuse, The Three Laws of International Investment: National, Contractual, and International Frameworks for Foreign Capital, ch. 6, sec. 8.2(a) (2013).

foreign investment law permits the free establishment of foreign joint ventures and subsidiaries and provides tax incentives and unrestricted repatriation of profits for foreign businesses.[120] Tanzania's investment code likewise provides for full compensation in the event of expropriation, and establishes mandatory settlement of investment disputes through international arbitration.[121]

However, foreign investors should be wary of taking such liberal investment codes at face value. It is equally important to know how such codes have been interpreted and implemented by host States. Further, if these local guarantees lack direct investor-State arbitration provisions, in practice they retain the status of local law, since they can only be enforced in local courts. The host State may therefore avoid application of the law's substantive protections, either by pressuring the courts or by changing the law.[122] In addition, it is observed that several countries have recently started taking a protectionist approach, introducing various investment restrictions and controls.[123] **1.65**

The investor should next consider economic, cultural, political, historical, and legal aspects of the host country that may affect political risk. Relevant economic issues include short-term economic stability, including an analysis of inflation rates, price stability, and exchange rates.[124] This exercise may also involve scrutiny of balance of payments and sovereign debt problems. A weak or unstable economy, in combination with other factors, may increase political risk, as a State in a weakened economic condition may be more likely to resort to expropriation of foreign investment to alleviate political pressures. The investor should also consider the political stability of the host State.[125] This exercise demands not only an understanding of local political structures, such as how officials are elected and appointed and the relative power of the various branches of government, but also familiarity with current political leaders and their policies and philosophies, especially in relation to investment protection, transparency, and sustainable fiscal policy. An analysis of the State's history regarding respect for the property of foreign investors is useful as well. An investor considering a power project in Iran **1.66**

[120] *See generally* Commerce, The Official Newsletter of the C.I.S.-American Chamber of Commerce (Fall 1995).

[121] Tanzania's investment law of 1997, (Act No. 26 of 1997, Official Gazette No. 40 Vol. 78) provides for full compensation (Article 22) and includes arbitration (Article 23), available at: https://investmentpolicy.unctad.org/investment-laws/laws/60/tanzania-united-republic-of-investment-act.

[122] *See* Chapter 4. But *see Tradex Hellas S.A. v. Albania*, ICSID Case No. ARB/94/2, Decision on Jurisdiction of Dec. 24, 1996, 14 ICSID Rev.—For. Inv. L.J. 161 (1999) (internationalizing domestic law under the ICSID rules).

[123] Karl P. Sauvant, *The Regulatory Framework for Investment: Where Are We Headed?*, 15 Research in Global Strategic Management 407–33 (2011).

[124] Rowat, *supra* note 118, at 104.

[125] Investment trends indicate that investors are more likely to invest in States in which there are assurances that the legal and political systems are unlikely to undergo radical changes. Geist, *supra* note 118, at 686.

or Mexico has reason to be cautious, considering the history of economic interference of these States.[126] States that have a history of protecting property rights, on the other hand, are generally less likely, other things being equal, to confiscate foreign investments in the future.

1.67 Finally, treaties on the protection and promotion of foreign investment between the host State and the investor's home State can be very important for an accurate political risk analysis. The most widespread investment treaties, discussed in detail in Chapters 6 and 7, are bilateral investment treaties, known as BITs. These international instruments spread quickly in the 1990s and 2000s, and today there are over 3,000 treaties worldwide.[127] This network is complemented by regional agreements such as the NAFTA, the Association of Southeast Asian Nations (ASEAN) Treaty, and the Energy Charter Treaty. These investment treaties represent an undertaking by signatory States that they will provide predictable conditions and an even playing field to qualifying foreign investors and investments, including repatriation of profits, compensation for expropriation, fair and equitable treatment, and full protection and security. The violation of these standards of treatment normally triggers the private investor's direct right of international arbitration against the host State.[128] Where a potential investment locale is subject to an applicable investment treaty, the foreign investor can enjoy greater confidence that unreasonable government interference with his activities will be minimized. States are less likely to engage in unpredictable and detrimental conduct if their actions could violate the specific terms of a treaty, rather than the rather amorphous dictates of customary international law.

1.68 But the existence of an applicable investment treaty cannot eliminate political risk.[129] Ultimately, States are sovereign within their territory, and are free to take whatever action they deem necessary.[130] Investment treaties may compel governments to pay compensation to foreign investors as a consequence of regulatory or other action, but there is no international police force or global government that can restrict the State's freedom to act. Nor is full compensation a "sure thing." As will become clear in Chapter 6, treaty-based investment protection is

[126] Regarding Mexico, *see generally* Baklanoff, *supra* note 40.

[127] UNCTAD, *World Investment Report: Investment and the Digital Economy* (2017), at 111, available at http://unctad.org/en/PublicationsLibrary/wir2017_en.pdf.

[128] *See generally* Andreas Lowenfeld, *Investment Agreements and International Law*, 42 Colum. J. Transnat'l L. 123 (2003); Chapters 6 and 7.

[129] Indeed, a World Bank report suggests that investors take for granted the limited power of investment treaties to deter State action detrimental to their interests. *See* M. Hallward-Driemeier, *Do Bilateral Investment Treaties Attract Foreign Direct Investment? Only a Bit—and They Could Bite*, World Bank Policy Research Working Paper No. 3121 (2003), available at http://documents.worldbank.org/curated/en/113541468761706209/pdf/multi0page.pdf.

[130] Legislative or parliamentary sovereignty is discussed in further detail in Chapter 4, Section B.1.

still novel, and the outcome of any particular arbitration proceeding can be difficult to predict. As a result, while investors should take into account the applicability of international agreements, their primary concerns should be to assess the gravity of political risk in a given jurisdiction, and to avoid investment disputes whenever possible.[131]

An investor should normally seek advice on various aspects of political risk from competent local legal counsel and economic consultants who have first-hand experience in the State in which investment is being considered. Many multinational companies also retain in-house political risk managers.[132] **1.69**

In addition to such advice, the investor may consider using a political risk service. Political risk service-providers are organizations that specialize in providing investors with up-to-date information regarding political (and other) risk, primarily in developing countries. One such service is the Economist Intelligence Unit's Country Risk Service.[133] This service provides risk analysis, including political risk, for over 100 countries. They produce a report for each country quarterly.[134] **1.70**

The Economist Intelligence Unit also produces a quarterly comparison of the countries covered by the Country Risk Service, assigning each State an overall grade of A through E and a more detailed rating of 1 through 100. There are also other significant political risk and related services.[135] **1.71**

In addition, the economic and political sections of many countries' foreign missions prepare periodic reports on local investment climate in countries where their nationals are economically active. These assessments can be particularly useful to foreign investors, since the diplomats who provide them are often **1.72**

---

[131] For a discussion of practical steps that an investor can take to reduce the impact of expropriation on its assets, *see* Philip Stansbury, *Planning against Expropriation*, 24 Int'l Law. 677 (1990).

[132] S. Linn Williams, *Political and Other Risk Insurance: OPIC, MIGA, Eximbank and Other Providers*, 5 Pace Int'l L. Rev. 59, 63 (1993).

[133] The Economist Intelligence Unit, Country Reports, available at http://www.eiu.com; *see also* The Economist Intelligence Unit, Country Risk Service, available at http://www.eiu.com.

[134] Each report typically includes: credit risk ratings reflecting a country's short-term foreign exchange risks, medium-term lending risks, and political and policy risks; analysis and forecasts of the state of government finances, economic growth, and domestic financial indicators (money supply, interest rates, inflation, and exchange rates); two-year projections of the country's external finances, including the current account, external borrowings, and debt-service payments; an analysis of the form and sources of international finance flows (FDI, bond issues, portfolio investment, and commercial and official lending); and short-term trade risk analysis based on the evaluation of the overall financial position of the country, as well as foreign exchange reserves.

[135] Such services include those offered by: The PRS Group, https://www.prsgroup.com/; Control Risks Group, http://www.crg.com; GRM Inc., Global Risk Management, http://www.grminc.com/ ; and Business Environment Risk Intelligence, http://www.beri.com.

well-connected in the host country and enjoy a kind of access to decision-makers that is denied to most private business people.

1.73 While political risk services are a valuable source of information in measuring political risk, these services are best used in conjunction with other methods of determining political risk, such as the advice of experienced local counsel and other counsel familiar with political risk issues.

2

STRUCTURING TRANSACTIONS TO MINIMIZE POLITICAL RISK

2.01 Once an investor has decided to invest in a country where political risk is a significant consideration, he or she should begin reviewing methods to minimize that risk. This chapter and the next focus on affirmative steps that the investor can take to reduce exposure to political risk. While in Chapter 3 we will turn to *investment insurance*, the present chapter concentrates upon business structures and provisions in *investor–State contracts* that can be used to reduce the risks described in Chapter 1.

A. Project Types

2.02 Two of the major categories of foreign direct investment (FDI) that involve agreements between investors and host States are *petroleum extraction arrangements* and *infrastructure projects*. Each is briefly discussed in this section to provide some context for the business structures and contractual terms and provisions explained later in this chapter.

1. Petroleum arrangements

2.03 Almost all developing States with substantial hydrocarbon resources have created State-owned oil companies. Developing States explore for, develop, and produce petroleum through these State oil companies, through direct arrangements with foreign investors, or through indirect arrangements between the State oil companies and foreign or multinational corporations.[1]

2.04 Where foreign investors are involved, there are four basic models that are used today for the exploitation of petroleum resources in developing States: the *concession agreement*,[2] the *production sharing agreement*,[3] the *participation agreement*, and the *service contract*.[4] While each of these agreements share certain basic features, they differ in many respects, including the level of control granted to the investor and the system for determining the private party's compensation. Hybrids of these arrangements are also often used, which can make precise categorization of a particular arrangement difficult.[5]

---

[1] Ernest E. Smith & John S. Dzienkowski, *A Fifty-Year Perspective on World Petroleum Arrangements*, 24 Tex. J. Int'l L. 13, 35 (1989).

[2] "Concession" is the name sometimes given to a contract between a State (or subdivision or agency of a State) and a national of another State.

[3] *See* various articles in "Special Feature: Production Sharing Contracts," in 3(1) Oil, Gas & Energy Law Intelligence (OGEL), available at http://www.gasandoil.com/ogel, including Philip R. Weems, *An Introduction to Upstream Government Petroleum Contracts: Their Evolution and Current Use*; Frank C. Alexander, Jr., *Production Sharing Contracts and Other Host Government Contracts* (46 Rocky Mt. Min. L. Inst. 20–1 (2000)), 3(1) OGEL (Mar. 2005); M. Bunter, *Indonesia: From Concession to Contract*; Giuditta Cordero Moss, *Contract or License? Regulation of Petroleum Investment in Russia and the Role of Foreign Legal Advice* (version also reprinted in 3(11) CEPMLP J.); Bede O.N. Nwete, *To What Extent Can Stabilisation Clauses Mitigate the Investor's Risks in a Production Sharing Contract?* 3(1) OGEL (Mar. 2005); A.F.M. Maniruzzaman, *Understanding Stabilization Techniques in Production Sharing Agreements: Some Remarks. See also* Christopher Clement-Davies, *Public/Private Partnerships in Central and Eastern Europe: Structuring the Concession Agreement*, 2001(1) Bus. L. Int'l 17 (2001), version available at https://heinonline.org/HOL/Page?collection=journals&handle=hein.journals/blawintnl2001&id=21&men_tab=srchresults; Frank C. Alexander, Jr., *The Three Pillars of Security of Investment under PSCs and other HGCs*, Fifty-Fourth Annual Institute on Oil and Gas Law (Institute for Energy Law of the Center for American and International Law, Publication 640, Release 54, 2003); Peter D. Cameron, International Energy Investment Law: The Pursuit of Stability, paras 1.73–1.113 (2010); for an overview of production sharing agreements, *see* Jonathan Hines & Aset A. Shyngyssov, *Kazakhstan Enacts PSA Law: Summary Analysis of Its Terms*, 3 OGEL (2005); *see also* Republic of Cyprus (Ministry of Energy, Commerce, Industry and Tourism), "Model Exploration and Production Sharing Contract," Nicosia, 2016, available at: http://www.mcit.gov.cy/mcit/hydrocarbon.nsf/All/EFCD315C63D1D2B2C2257FA2002794F4/$file/%CE%9A%CE%B1%CE%B8%CE%BF%CE%B4%CE%B7%CE%B3%CE%B7%CF%84%CE%B9%CE%BA%CF%8C%20%CE%A3%CE%B7%CE%BC%CE%B5%CE%AF%CF%89%CE%BC%CE%B1.pdf.

[4] *See* Weems, *supra* note 3, at Sec. III.A (grouping Upstream Government Petroleum Contracts (UGPCs) into four types: (1) concessions or licenses; (2) PSCs (production sharing contracts); (3) risk service contracts; and (4) hybrid or association type contracts).

[5] Smith & Dzienkowski, *supra* note 1, at 35–36.

a. Concession agreement

A typical concession agreement "grants 'the exclusive right to explore, search, and drill for, produce, store, transport, and sell Petroleum' within the designated concession acreage for a specified number of years."[6] Modern concession agreements are usually for a shorter period of time than concession agreements negotiated during the first half of the twentieth century, and typically impose upon the investor obligations to develop certain levels of petroleum production and to provide a work program (usually setting forth the time and manner of such development). The investor normally undertakes to make a number of periodic payments to the State, including rent, a royalty (either in kind or in cash, usually at the option of the State), and taxes on income earned in the State.[7] **2.05**

b. Production sharing agreement

In a production sharing agreement, a State-owned oil company, in return for a share of hydrocarbons produced, grants the investor the right to explore and develop petroleum in a specified area, and to recover its costs and an agreed-upon level of profit.[8] The investor is often required to abide by certain development obligations and a work program imposed by the State-owned oil company. As with the concession agreement, the investor is usually required to pay taxes on income earned in the State.[9] **2.06**

c. Participation agreement

In a participation agreement, a joint operating company is formed between the State and the investor to explore for and develop petroleum. The State contributes the land or exploration rights, and the investor contributes the technology and expertise and usually funds the project. The company is then operated by a **2.07**

---

[6] *Id.* at 36, *quoting* Abu Dhabi Specimen Draft Oil Concession Agreement, art. 2, reprinted in Keith W. Blinn et al., International Petroleum Exploration and Exploitation Agreements: Legal, Economic, and Policy Aspects (1986).

[7] Smith & Dzienkowski, *supra* note 1, at 36–37; Patrick Blanchard, *Electric and Gas Concessions and BOTs in the Ivory Coast: Innovating Attempts During the Nineties*, 7 Int'l Bus. L.J. 829 (2000). For typical types of terms in concession agreements, *see* Clement-Davies, *supra* note 3. Changes to the taxation regime for hydrocarbons enterprises in 2005 suggest that the future will be quite different. Myrna Robinson-Waters & Christopher Hamel-Smith, *The New Oil Tax Regime: Taxation or Expropriation?*, Business Guardian, July 21, 2005, available at http://library2.nalis.gov.tt/gsdl/collect/news3/index/assoc/HASHb346/9a743359.dir/4290.jpg.

[8] Smith & Dzienkowski, *supra* note 1, at 36–37. Venezuela, for example, has in the past considered allowing foreign producers to take more than 90 percent of the oil pumped under leases granted to the producers, at least initially, to allow the companies to recover their investment costs. Wall Street Journal, Mar. 9, 1995. See also *ConocoPhillips Petrozuata B.V., ConocoPhillips Hamaca B.V. and ConocoPhillips Gulf of Paria B.V. v. Bolivarian Republic of Venezuela*, ICSID Case No. ARB/07/30, Award of March 8, 2019, available at https://www.italaw.com/sites/default/files/case-documents/italaw10402.pdf. Subsequently the State sought to reclaim most of that value, first by imposing successively more burdensome taxes and royalties, and then taking over many hydrocarbon projects altogether.

[9] Smith & Dzienkowski, *supra* note 1, at 37–39.

management team that includes representatives of the State and the investor. In some cases, ownership and management are shared equally; in other cases, the State owns 51 percent and the investor 49 percent. Many participation arrangements are the result of renegotiations of long-term concession agreements.[10]

d. Service contract

2.08 In a service contract, the investor agrees, either for a fee or a share of production, to provide the State with services or information so that it can develop its own hydrocarbon resources. One type of service contract, the "risk service contract," is a hybrid of a service contract and a participation agreement. In this arrangement, the investor explores for petroleum using its own funds, with no right to repayment unless it discovers exploitable resources. If it makes such a discovery, the investor is obliged to develop the site, and is paid in cash or in production.[11]

2. Infrastructure projects

2.09 Infrastructure projects in developing States, such as power plants, telecommunication facilities, airports, and roads, have experienced enormous growth.[12] Instead of borrowing money and building and operating such projects themselves, developing States have increasingly turned to consortia of foreign investors. One reason for this is that in such an arrangement developing States are able to avoid carrying large amounts of debt on their books that would prohibit the borrowing of capital for other purposes. Additionally, developing States often do not have the expertise to build and operate such projects themselves.

2.10 States and private contracting parties can choose from an array of different arrangements when developing infrastructure projects, each of which has a particular way of allocating responsibilities and risks between the parties. Many of these commonly used contract types are known by their acronyms: BOT (build, operate, and transfer),[13] BOOT (build, own, operate, and transfer), ROT (refurbish,

[10] *Id.* at 39–40.

[11] *Id.* at 40–41.

[12] Nina N. Hoque & J. Michael Robinson, *An Examination of the Build, Operate and Transfer Model for International Projects in Emerging Markets*, International Infrastructure Projects X–1 (1995). *See also* Jonathan J. Green, *Managing Risks in International Power Projects*, 672 PLI/Comm. Prac. Law Handbook Series 669 (1993); *see also* J. Gomez-Ibanez, *Private Infrastructure in Developing Countries: Lessons from Recent Experience*, paper presented to the Commission on Growth and Development at the Workshop "Global Trends and Challenges," New Haven, CT, Sept. 28–29, 2007.

[13] Emmanuel Fontaine, *Unforeseeability in BOT Contracts for Public Infrastructure*, 15 Int'l Construction L. Rev. 504 (1998); V.U. Nguyen, *Foreign Investment in Vietnam by Build Operate and Transfer Projects: An Update*, 9 Butterworth's J. Int'l Banking Fin. L. 482 (1994). For a description of a coal-fired electric plant BOT project that ended in arbitration, *see PSEG Global Inc. et al v. Turkey*, ICSID Case No. ARB/02/5, Decision on Jurisdiction of June 4, 2004.

operate, and transfer), BLT (build, lease, and transfer), and BOO (build, own, and operate, with no requirement to transfer).[14]

The Infrastructure Development Enabling Act of the Indian state of Andhra Pradesh provides useful descriptions of these and other types of concession agreements:[15] **2.11**

(i) **Build-and-Transfer (BT)**—A contractual arrangement whereby the Developer undertakes the financing and construction of a given infrastructure or development facility and after its completion hands it over to the Government, Government Agency or the Local Authority. The Government, Government Agency or the Local Authority would reimburse the total Project investment, on the basis of an agreed schedule. This arrangement may be employed in the construction of any infrastructure or development Projects, including critical facilities, which for security or strategic reasons, must be operated directly by the Government or Government Agency or the Local Authority.

(ii) **Build-Lease-and-Transfer (BLT)**—A contractual arrangement whereby a Developer undertakes to finance and construct Infrastructure Project and upon its completion hands it over to the Government or Government Agency or the Local Authority concerned on a lease arrangement for a fixed period, after which ownership of the facility is automatically transferred to the Government or Government Agency or the Local Authority concerned.

(iii) **Build-Operate-and-Transfer (BOT)**—A contractual arrangement whereby the Developer undertakes the construction, including financing, of a given infrastructure facility, and the operation and maintenance thereof. The Developer operates the facility over a fixed term during which he is allowed to a charge facility users appropriate tolls, fees, rentals and charges not exceeding those proposed in the bid or as negotiated and incorporated in the Contract to enable the recovery of investment in the Project. The Developer transfers the facility to the Government or Government Agency or the Local Authority concerned at the end of the fixed term that shall be specified in the Concession Agreement. This shall include a supply-and-operate situation which is a Contractual arrangement whereby the supplier of equipment and machinery for a given infrastructure facility, if the interest of the Government, Government Agency or the Local Authority so requires, operates the facility providing in the process technology transfer and training to Government, Government Agency or the Local Authority nominated individuals.

(iv) **Build-Own-and-Operate (BOO)**—A contractual arrangement whereby a Developer is authorized to finance, construct, own, operate and maintain an Infrastructure or Development facility from which the Developer is allowed to recover this total investment by collecting user levies from facility users. Under his Project, the Developer owns the assets of the facility and may choose to

---

[14] Hoque & Robinson, *supra* note 12, at X–2. For further discussion of the BOT model, *see* J. Michael Robinson, *The Build, Own, and Transfer Model for International Projects in Emerging Markets*, 8 Int'l LQ 126 (1996); *see also* Louis T. Wells & Rafiq Ahmed, Making Foreign Investment Safe: Property Rights and National Sovereignty (2007).

[15] *See* Andhra Pradesh Infrastructure Development Enabling Act, 2001 (Act No. 36 of 2001, of the state of Andhra Pradesh of the Republic of India), esp. Sch. I and Ch. I, sec. 2(h) (defining "Concession Agreement"), https://www.italaw.com/sites/default/files/case-documents/ita0694.pdf.

assign its operation and maintenance to a facility operator. The Transfer of the facility to the Government, Government Agency or the Local Authority is not envisaged in this structure; however, the Government, Government Agency or Local Authority may terminate its obligations after specified time period.

(v) **Build-Own-Operate-Transfer (BOOT)**—A contractual arrangement whereby a Developer is authorized to finance, construct, maintain and operate a Project and whereby such Project is to vest in the Developer for a specified period. During the operation period, the Developer will be permitted to charge user levies specified in the Concession Agreement, to recover the investment made in the Project. The Developer is liable to transfer the Project to the Government, Government Agency or the Local Authority after the expiry of the specified period of operation.

(vi) **Build-Transfer-and-Operate (BTO)**—A contractual arrangement whereby the Government or Government Agency or the Local Authority contracts out an infrastructure facility to a Developer to construct the facility on a turn-key basis, assuming cost overruns, delays and specified performance risks. Once the facility is commissioned satisfactorily, the Developer is given the right to operate the facility and collect user levies under a Concession Agreement. The title of the facilities always vests with the Government, Government Agency or the Local Authority in this arrangement.

(vii) **Contract-Add-and-Operate (CAO)**—A contractual arrangement whereby the Developer adds to an existing infrastructure facility which it rents from the Government, Government Agency or the Local Authority and operates the expanded Project and collects user levies, to recover the investment over an agreed franchise period. There may or may not be a transfer arrangement with regard to the added facility provided by the Developer.

(viii) **Develop-Operate-and-Transfer (DOT)**—A contractual arrangement whereby favorable conditions external to a new Infrastructure Project which is to be built by a Developer are integrated into the BOT arrangement by giving that entity the right to develop adjoining property and thus, enjoy some of the benefits the investment creates such as higher property or rent values.

(ix) **Rehabilitate-Operate-and-Transfer (ROT)**—A contractual arrangement whereby and existing facility is handed over to the private sector to refurbish, operate (collect user levies in operation period to recover the Investment) and maintain for a franchise period, at the expiry of which the facility is turned over to the Government or Government Agency or the Local Authority. The term is also used to describe the purchase of an existing facility from abroad, importing, refurbishing, erecting and consuming it within the host country.

(x) **Rehabilitate-Own-and-Operate (ROO)**—A contractual arrangement whereby an existing facility is handed over to the Operator to refurbish and operate with no time limitation imposed on ownership. As long as the operator is not in violation of its franchise, it can continue to operate the facility and collect user levies in perpetuity.

2.12 Perhaps the most common of these project structures is the BOOT model. Under this arrangement, an investor or consortium of investors constructs a facility (such as an airport or a power plant), owns and operates it for a limited period of time (usually twenty to twenty-five years), and then transfers the project to the host State. While they own the infrastructure, operators usually receive payment through a take-or-pay arrangement with the State agency or ministry that will purchase the project's output (such as electricity).[16] This usually requires payments to the investors sufficient to cover costs of construction and operation of the project and to provide for a reasonable rate of return.[17]

In a BOOT project, the primary documents binding the private parties and the State and State agencies are a State concession agreement, a take-or-pay contract with the State agency that is to purchase project output, a "State support" agreement, and a performance guarantee from the State. The concession agreement is the document by which the State grants investors permission to build, own, and operate the infrastructure project. The take-or-pay agreement, as mentioned previously, reduces or eliminates commercial risk to the foreign party by ensuring that a certain amount of output will be sold regardless of the level of market demand.[18] In a State support agreement, the host government undertakes that investors will be paid in some relatively stable and convertible currency (normally U.S. dollars or Euros).[19] Institutional lenders (without whom very few large-scale infrastructure projects would be possible) frequently require that the central government of the host State provide a performance guarantee, backing up the State agency's obligations to purchase project output under the take-or-pay contract.[20] Another important document is the contract for construction of the project, which is usually a turnkey, fixed-price contract backed by payment and performance bonds.[21] **2.13**

All project types involving an operation phase (most commonly BOT and BOOT) suffer from a particular acuity of political risk, in that the foreign contracting party remains exposed to host State action over an extended period of time before the project is transferred back to government control. Indeed, the feasibility and rate of return of the BOT or BOOT project for financing purposes are established based in large part on profits the investor will glean over time from operations throughout the fixed license period. If the private party is prevented from operating the project for part of the agreed period, of if unexpected regulations or other administrative actions significantly reduce profitability, then the construction **2.14**

[16] For a discussion of "take-or-pay" type arrangements, *see e.g.* T.N. Leach, *Frey v. Amoco Production Co.: Payment of Mineral Royalties on Take-or-Pay Settlements in Louisiana*, 67 Tul. L. Rev. 840 (1993); J. Michael Medina, *The Take-or-Pay Wars: A Cautionary Analysis for the Future*, 27 Tulsa L.J. 283 (1991); A.F. Brooke II, *Great Expectations: Assessing the Contract Damages of the Take-or-Pay Producer*, 70 Tex. L. Rev. 1469 (1992); Scott E. Masten & Keith J. Crocker, *Efficient Adaptation in Long-Term Contracts: Take-or-Pay Provisions for Natural Gas*, 75 Am. Econ. Rev. 1083 (1985).

[17] Hoque & Robinson, *supra* note 12, at X–2, 4.

[18] Take-or-pay contracts may not insulate the seller from credit risk, however. *See CMS Gas Transmission Co. v. Argentina*, ICSID Case No. ARB/01/8, Final Award of Apr. 25, 2005, para. 445 (under severe economic conditions, sellers must assume that there will be an increase in "delinquent accounts" in relation to take-or-pay contracts).

[19] Hoque & Robinson, *supra* note 12, at X–6.

[20] *Id.*; Green, *supra* note 12.

[21] Bruno de Cazalet, *Construction Contracts in the Framework of BOT Projects*, 1998 Int'l Bus. L.J. 405 (1998).

costs will not be recouped—or will be recouped at a rate of return lower than that which investors expected to obtain at the bidding stage.

2.15 This is what occurred in 2004 in Iran, when a Turkish–Austrian company completed the construction of Teheran's new international airport terminal. The BOT contract provided that the foreign enterprise would operate the terminal for several years before handing it back to the Iranian Ministry of Transport. But on the day the facility was to open, the military ejected company personnel from the airport and demanded cancellation of the contract, on grounds that foreign operation of the terminal constituted a threat to national security.[22] Had the airport been built on a BT, or build and transfer (turnkey) basis (presumably at a far higher contract price), the foreign contractor would have been more insulated from government intervention: presuming that payment is staggered, the company could to some degree hold the project hostage, refusing to complete work if the "rules of the game" were changed.

3. Other arrangements between investors and States

2.16 In addition to the types of investment contracts discussed, there are many other types of direct investment that an investor can make in a developing State where provisions that protect against political risk would be useful. Examples include concessions for the exploration and production of natural resources other than petroleum, agreements allowing production and distribution of products in the host State, and agreements allowing the investor to manufacture products in the host State to be distributed abroad.

B. Transaction Structures

1. Structures prior to investing

2.17 Careful planning of investment structures can play an important role in reducing exposure to political risk. Such decisions should be made after consulting with local counsel familiar with local legislation and regulations concerning business organizations, export controls, and insolvency, among others. Some general considerations that may contribute to controlling political risk are discussed later in this section.

2.18 A great deal of attention has been given in recent years to the benefits of owning and operating investments through a parent company of a carefully selected nationality. As will be explained in detail later,[23] investors may be able to invoke the

[22] Nazila Fathi, *Conservatives in Iran Battle the Spread of Foreign Investment*, NY Times, Oct. 10, 2004, at 20.

[23] *See* Chapter 7.

protections of investment protection treaties in addition to those in force between their home State and the host State, by investing through a company incorporated in a third State. For example, an investment made directly in the Russian Federation by an American corporation would not benefit from the guarantees of any investment treaty, since the Russian Federation never ratified the Russia–U.S. bilateral investment treaty (BIT).[24] But if the same company has a wholly-owned Belgian subsidiary, which in turn signs a concession agreement in Russia, the same investment probably would fall under the protection of the Belgium–Russia BIT.[25] Therefore, before deciding where to incorporate the primary operating companies or holding companies for a project, investors should carefully consider the existence and text of the host State's treaty partners, just as businesses routinely examine the tax consequences of corporate nationality.[26]

As a general rule, exposure to political risk is dependent to a large degree on the magnitude of assets that the foreign investor maintains within the territory of the host State.[27] One way to reduce exposure to adverse regulation, therefore, is to conduct operations in the host State through a local subsidiary of a foreign parent company. Intellectual property, technology, management skills, and other intangible assets can then be owned by the parent, and leased or otherwise put at the disposal of the local operating company. This approach makes it more difficult for the host State to interfere in the project through unexpected regulation.[28] **2.19**

The investor may also wish to diversify operations into several affiliated companies located in the host State.[29] A nationalization program aimed at banking, for example, may not affect a foreign-owned financial institution's real estate holdings if they are held by separate legal entities. **2.20**

---

[24] Source: U.S. State Department, available at: https://www.state.gov/e/eb/ifd/bit/117402.htm.

[25] *See CME Czech Republic B.V. v. Czech Republic*, UNCITRAL Partial Award of Sept. 13, 2001, https://www.italaw.com/sites/default/files/case-documents/ita0178.pdf, para. 412 (U.S. citizen permitted to initiate investment arbitration against host State not only based upon the U.S.–Czech BIT, but also on the Dutch–Czech BIT, since he controlled his investment through a shareholding in a Dutch Antilles company). But there may be limits to the structural arrangements investors may use in order to gain the benefit of investment treaties. *See Tokios Tekeles v. Ukraine*, ICSID Case No. ARB/02/18, Decision on Jurisdiction of Apr. 29, 2004 (tribunal recognized corporate nationality of Lithuanian company despite 99 percent Ukrainian shareholding, but suggested in *dicta* that the result might be different had the company been formed "manifestly for the purpose of gaining access to ICSID arbitration"); *see also Philip Morris Asia Ltd. v. Australia*, UNCITRAL, PCA Case No. 2012-12, Award on Jurisdiction and Admissibility of Dec. 17, 2015, available at: https://www.italaw.com/sites/default/files/case-documents/italaw7303_0.pdf (rejecting claim as inadmissible based on finding that Philip Morris Asia acquired a Hong Kong subsidiary only in order to bring its claim under the Hong Kong–Australia BIT).

[26] *See* Chapter 6.

[27] Philip R. Stansbury, *Planning against Expropriation*, 24 Int'l L. 677 (1990).

[28] Richard M. Mosk, *Expropriation: What to Do About It?*, 5 Calif. Int'l Practitioner 11, 14 (1993–94).

[29] *Id.*

2.21 Structuring the financing of a project to include borrowing from international, governmental, or quasi-governmental agencies, such as the U.S. Overseas Private Investment Corporation, the European Bank for Reconstruction and Development, or the International Finance Corporation can also reduce political risk. Developing countries generally prefer to maintain good relationships with such entities so as not to impede their own borrowing for future capital needs. A host State may therefore be less likely to interfere in property rights of a project funded by such an entity.[30]

2.22 Another technique used to minimize political risk is sometimes called "hostage taking."[31] A foreign investor sometimes has a relationship calling for various duties or performances by both the investor and the host State or an agent thereof in the course of the investment relationship. To reduce risks, the foreign investor tries always to have some payment to withhold or a service that can be postponed until the State or affiliated entity performs.[32]

2.23 In many cases, foreign investors can gain a good deal of protection from host State interference by structuring business in such a manner that the local population has a stake in the project's success. Just as local unions, non-governmental organizations, and citizens' groups can induce governments to take measures adverse to foreign business interests,[33] civil society can place pressure on political elites to ensure a stable investment environment, if local and foreign interests are sufficiently aligned. For example, the investor could consider using an increased proportion of local suppliers and contractors, and incorporating a substantial local component in the mid- and high-level management of the operating entity. Another suggestion is to leverage assets by leasing or financing assets with local creditors.[34] In addition, even when not required by the local law of the host State, attracting local private sector ownership participation in the core business may offer some measure of political protection from government interference.[35]

2. Modification of structures when interference is threatened

2.24 Before the host State adopts measures detrimental to foreign business, investors will usually have indications that something is about to happen. Signs may

[30] *See* Chapter 3; Joseph P. Hadley, *Use of Political Risk Insurance in Connection with Project Financings*, in International Infrastructure Projects VIII-3 (1995).

[31] Thomas O. Schelling, *An Essay on Bargaining*, 46 Am. Econ. Rev. 281, 300 (1956) (originating the term "hostage taking" in negotiation theory).

[32] John N. Hazard, *Risks in Investing in the USSR: Can There Be Protection against Them?*, 11 NYL Sch. J. Int'l & Comp. L. 457, 458 (1990).

[33] *See e.g. Tecnicas Medioambientales Tecmed S.A. v. Mexico*, ICSID Case No. ARB (AF)/00/2, Award of May 29, 2004, 43 I.L.M. 133 (2004) (local population's protests induced Mexican government to expropriate waste storage facility).

[34] *Id.*

[35] Stansbury, *supra* note 27, at 682.

include parliamentary debates favoring unexpected regulation, increasing tension between the State and a particular investor or the foreign business community as a whole, or a change in government. As former Iran–U.S. Claims Tribunal judge Richard Mosk has observed, "it is unusual for an investor to be surprised by a published expropriation decree or the appearance of government officials to take possession."[36] Thus, as signs begin to mount that the regulatory regime may change for the worse, some foreign investors may seriously consider reducing operations and transferring inventory, equipment, and currency out of the host State. The host State may respond by tightening export control laws to block attempts to shift assets abroad.[37] In addition, an investor's attempt to pull out of a country may cause the State to seize the project altogether, particularly where the enterprise is engaged in supplying a public service or vital good.[38] As a result, the advisability of such actions must be decided on a case-by-case basis.

The investor would be wise, however, to reduce or eliminate new flows of capital into the host State where the capital would be subject to seizure. If the local subsidiary has borrowed funds from the host State and loans are secured by standby letters of credit from foreign banks, and it appears that there may be improper demands for payment, the investor should notify the banks not to pay, and seek injunctive relief if necessary.[39] In addition, the investor should divert any goods or inventory en route to the host State, if possible.[40] **2.25**

To prepare for the contingency of expropriation or other detrimental State intervention, the investor should maintain detailed records of all financial and other transactions. Duplicates of all records should be kept at a location outside of the host State. This has become a far less burdensome task in recent years with the increasing use of paperless and computer records and backup. Key paper documents can be scanned and easily transmitted electronically, along with other records and communications, to backup servers outside the host country. **2.26**

[36] Mosk, *supra* note 28, at 16.

[37] As an example, during the Argentine financial crisis of 2001–02, a collapse of confidence in Argentina's banking system resulted in massive deposit withdrawals. In response to the run on the banks Argentina suspended payments on its external debt and restricted deposit withdrawals (a step that became known as the "*corralito*"). *See The Argentine Crisis: A Chronology of Events after the Sovereign Default*, Standard & Poor's, Apr. 12, 2002, available at http://www.standardandpoors.com/europe/francais/Fr_news/Argentine-Chronology-of-Events_12-04-02.html; *Learning from Argentina's Crisis*, FRBSF Economic Letter 2002–31, Oct. 18, 2002, available at http://www.frbsf.org/publications/economics/letter/2002/el2002-31.html.

[38] Mosk, *supra* note 28, at 16.

[39] *Id.* at 17.

[40] It is possible to structure import transactions such that goods on the high seas not yet paid for may be diverted from the host State. "[A] straight non-negotiable bill of lading from the company to itself (i.e. the company is both consignor and consignee) may be subject to diversion upon order of the corporation." Stansbury, *supra* note 27, at 680.

2.27 Philip Stansbury explains that:

> [a]n expropriation case is not just an argument about the proper public international law standard. An expropriation case is a highly detailed factual case in which the company must prove income, cash flow, assets, and values, in addition to defending against counterclaim. Once the expropriation has occurred, documents and records within the host country will be in the control of the entity with the responsibility to minimize the company's affirmative recovery and to maximize the host country government's counterclaims.[41]

The same advice applies equally to cases involving other, non-expropriatory State measures.

2.28 As soon as possible, the investor should also notify his home government of a threatened expropriation or other interference with property rights.[42] Early diplomatic action by influential foreign States may help to prevent the adoption of detrimental measures in the first place.[43]

C. Investor–State Contracts in General

2.29 The subject of investor–State contracts is vast, and many commentators have provided extensive analysis of various aspects of the contracting process from a myriad of business, legal, and other perspectives. This chapter focuses specifically on considerations of the political risk that foreign businesses face in contracting with sovereign States or their instrumentalities.[44]

2.30 While FDI does not always involve a contractual document or set of documents binding the foreign enterprise and the host government, such agreements can have a beneficial effect on regulatory stability in a number of ways. For example, the very

---

[41] *Id.* at 683.

[42] *Id.* at 686.

[43] Further discussion of the possibility of diplomatic protection and State-to-State dispute resolution can be found in Chapter 10.

[44] A number of useful works provide more general information on State contracts. *See e.g.* Detlev F. Vagts, *Dispute-Resolution Mechanisms in International Business*, 3 Recueil Des Cours 9 (1987) and the bibliography contained therein; A.Z. El Chiati, *Protection of Investment in the Context of Petroleum Agreements*, 4 Recueil des Cours 9 (1988) and the bibliography contained therein; Ernest E. Smith et al., International Petroleum Transactions (1993); Blinn et al., *supra* note 6; Georges R. Delaume, Transnational Contracts: Applicable Law and Settlement of Disputes (1982); Ralph H. Folsom et al., International Business Transactions (1992); A.F. Lowenfeld, International Private Investment (2d ed. 1982); Raymond F. Mikesell, Petroleum Company Operations and Agreements in the Developing Countries (1984); James Barrows, *International Trends and Latest Changes in Oil Laws, Concession, and Production-Sharing Agreements Worldwide*, Inst. Int'l Oil & Gas L. A–1 (1983); Bertrand Montembault, *The Stabilisation of State Contracts Using the Example of Oil Contracts: A Return of the Gods of Olympia?*, 6 Int'l Bus. L.J. 593 (2003). For research on State contracts and political risk, *see* Thomas Nektarios Papanastasiou, The Legal Protection of Foreign Investments against Political Risk: Japanese Business in the Asian Energy Sector, ch. 7 (2015).

existence of a contract between the investor and the host State may reduce political risk by compelling all signatories to contemplate potential areas of disagreement before they arise. Also, such a contract may establish dispute resolution procedures that will ensure the adjudication of disagreements outside the local judicial system.[45]

However, not all investment activity involves a State contract or license, and moreover, foreign businesses will not always have enough influence to induce the host State to enter into a special contractual arrangement. Even if the State agrees to negotiate a contract, it may be reluctant to agree to provisions tending to stabilize the commercial and regulatory regime. The State may insist that some of the clauses the investor requests are unnecessary or inconsistent with the State's investment code or other legislation, or with international law. For instance, a State may object to a clause entitling the investor to receive revenues in U.S. dollars, if local currency regulations prohibit foreign-denominated transactions. **2.31**

A variety of contractual provisions and clauses can change the dynamics of political risk associated with a given project, and should be considered in the course of negotiations with a host State or its agency or instrumentality. The first three provisions discussed (the *arbitration clause*, the *governing law clause*, and the *stabilization clause*) are extremely important to both dispute avoidance and resolution, and should be included, if possible, in any State contract. As will be explained in this chapter, these provisions complement one another: the arbitration clause allows disputes between the parties to be heard before a neutral tribunal, the choice-of-law clause establishes the rules that the tribunal will apply to settle the dispute, and the stabilization clause prevents the host State from unilaterally changing those rules. **2.32**

A second set of clauses discussed are designed to give guidance to judges or arbitrators once disputes arise. A *damages* clause can define the basis on which damages should be calculated if State liability is established. An *interest rate* clause designates the interest that will accrue upon an arbitral award from the time the award is rendered until paid. And the phrasing of a *force majeure* clause can be vital to properly allocating the risk of adverse and unexpected governmental measures.[46] **2.33**

Other clauses discussed include a *conversion of currency* clause, which obligates the host State to allow a private party to remit earnings abroad in foreign currency; a clause obviating the need to *exhaust local remedies* before requesting international arbitration (or limiting the scope of obligatory local remedies); and a *waiver of* **2.34**

[45] Georges R. Delaume, *How to Draft an ICSID Arbitration Clause*, 7 ICSID Rev.—For. Inv. L.J. 168 (1992). More on the drafting of investor–State arbitration clauses can be found in Section D.1.

[46] For a discussion of forum selection, choice of law, and other clauses in transnational contracts, *see* The Law of Transnational Business Transactions, chs. 4 and 8 (Ved P. Nanda ed. 1994).

sovereign immunity, which is designed to facilitate enforcement of a court judgment or arbitral award against the host State.

D. Core State Contract Clauses Affecting Political Risk

1. Arbitration clause

2.35 Arbitration clauses have become nearly ubiquitous in international contracts, including those concluded with State parties. The advantages of arbitration over litigation for both private and public parties are well documented and widely accepted.[47] Nevertheless, some governments remain hesitant to agree to the adjudication of disputes abroad before an international tribunal, particularly in relation to public infrastructure and natural resources extraction projects, which are seen as close to the core of State sovereignty.[48] Foreign private parties are nevertheless generally well-advised to seek the inclusion of an arbitration clause in State contracts. In the absence of such a clause, disputes that arise in relation to the investment contract may be subject to the jurisdiction of the host State's courts, perhaps exclusively. As a result, the investor may be left without any neutral forum to obtain effective recourse against the State. Even if he is able to obtain a favorable judgment through litigation, he may find it difficult to enforce abroad.

2.36 Too often, contracting parties view arbitration clauses as unimportant in comparison with the substantive elements of a contract under negotiation. During the planning of a project and the negotiation of contracts, many parties (both private and public) consider serious disputes to be only a remote possibility. Indeed, in some cultures, insisting on an arbitration clause with specific procedural provisions can be seen as disrespectful, overly pessimistic, and suspicious. In fact, drafting a clear, complete, and consistent dispute resolution clause can contribute to the avoidance of irreconcilable conflict as much as to resolving such differences. Parties are more likely to observe their commitments under a contract if they are convinced that a neutral tribunal will take them to task for their failings based upon predictable and objective criteria. The most important features of a well-drafted arbitration clause are described in detail in Chapter 8 of this book.[49]

---

[47] *See e.g.* William H. Knull, III & Noah Rubins, *Betting the Farm on International Commercial Arbitration: Is It Time to Offer an Appeals Option?*, 11 Am. Rev. Int'l Arb. 531, 538–41 (2000); Gary Born, International Commercial Arbitration in the United States 5–8 (1994); Robert D. Fischer & Roger S. Haydock, *International Commercial Disputes: Drafting an Enforceable Arbitration Agreement*, 21 Wm. Mitchell L. Rev. 941, 947–48 (1996). *See also* Chapter 8, *infra*.

[48] *See Compañía de Aguas del Aconquija S.A. and Vivendi Universal S.A. v. Argentina*, ICSID Case No. ARB/97/3, Decision on Application for Annulment of July 3, 2002, 41 I.L.M. 1135 (2002); *SGS Société Générale de Surveillance S.A. v. Philippines*, ICSID Case No. ARB/02/6, Award of July 7, 2004 (State contracts included clauses relegating disputes to local courts in the host State).

[49] For an analysis of various arbitration clauses included in actual contracts that were concluded between State agencies and foreign investors, *see* Papanastasiou, *supra* note 44, at 177–84.

If an investor is unable to include an arbitration clause in project contracts, or is compelled to assent to arbitration in a forum he fears is less than neutral, he may nevertheless have access to international arbitration of investment disputes. Chapter 7 describes how investors can initiate arbitration without the benefit of any direct arbitration agreement at all, if they benefit from the protections of bilateral or multinational investment treaties binding the investor's home State and the host State.[50] As will be explained later in this book, these treaties also provide foreign businesses with a range of guarantees separate from their contractual rights, which can be vindicated directly against the host State through arbitration, as long as certain jurisdictional requirements are met.[51] **2.37**

2. Choice-of-law clause

Whether or not the investment contract contains an arbitration clause, a choice-of-law provision can increase predictability and stability over the life of a long-term project. In the absence of a choice-of-law clause, a judge or arbitral panel adjudicating a dispute between the parties over the interpretation or implementation of the project contracts is likely to apply the law of the host State as the governing law of the agreement, since in most judicial systems the place of contractual performance is considered to be the jurisdiction most closely related to the dispute.[52] While there can be no sweeping assumption that the law of the host State is inappropriate or undesirable for a foreign contracting party, there can be little doubt that in some cases allowing local law to govern an investor–State contract increases political risk. Most importantly, local law may be subject to alteration or manipulation to advance the economic interests of the State contracting party in the investment transaction.[53] Furthermore, the foreign contracting party may find the intricacies of local law unfamiliar and unpredictable, while the State party will have the advantage in any dispute that arises of conducting battle on familiar ground. **2.38**

However, it is generally accepted that parties to a contract, even where one of those parties is a State or government instrumentality, are free to choose the law **2.39**

---

[50] Jan Paulsson, *Arbitration without Privity*, 10 ICSID Rev.—For. Inv. L.J. 232 (1995); *see also* Chapter 7, *infra*.

[51] *See* Chapter 6.

[52] Tang An, *The Law Applicable to a Transnational Economic Development Contract*, 21 J. World Trade 95 (1987); Virtus C. Igbokwe, *Developing Countries and the Law Applicable to International Arbitration of Oil Investment Disputes*, 14 J. Int'l Arb. 99 (1997); Brice M. Clagett, *Present State of the International Law of Compensation for Expropriated Property and Repudiated State Contracts*, in Private Investors Abroad § 12.05[2][a] (Southwestern Legal Foundation ed. 1989); Junji Nakagawa, Nationalization, Natural Resources and International Investment Law: Contractual Relationship as a Dynamic Bargaining Process 75–97 (2018).

[53] This risk can also be addressed by including a "stabilization clause" in the project agreement. *See* Section D.3, *infra*.

that will govern their relationship.[54] Most decision-makers will therefore give full effect to a choice-of-law clause, even if the legal system chosen is unrelated to the parties or the subject of their agreement.[55] Party autonomy in the selection of the law applicable to their contracts is particularly well-established in arbitration proceedings, and most modern arbitration statutes guarantee the sanctity of this choice.[56] Nevertheless, contracting parties should be aware that the enforceability of a choice-of-law clause will be subject to mandatory laws at the place of arbitration (or litigation), which may limit the freedom of the parties to select a legal system unrelated to their transaction.[57]

2.40 Assuming that a choice-of-law clause will be enforced, the issue arises as to which law to designate in the contract. For the reasons elaborated, the foreign party is likely to prefer a governing law different from that of the host State. Where investors are in a position to influence the choice of law, many push for the

[54] *Texaco Overseas Petroleum Co. and California Asiatic Oil Co. (TOPCO) v. Government of Libya*, 53 I.L.R. 389 (1979), 17 I.L.M. 1 (1978), para. 25; *Libyan American Oil Co. (LIAMCO) v. Government of Libya* (1977), 62 I.L.R. 140 (1980), 170 (1980), 20 I.L.M. 1, 32–34 (1981); *see also* Robert von Mehren & P. Nicholas Kourides, *International Arbitrations between States and Foreign Private Parties: The Libyan Nationalization Cases*, 75 AJIL 476, 510 (1981). For a discussion of how the Iran–U.S. Claims Tribunal has interpreted choice-of-law clauses, *see* John R. Crook, *Applicable Law in International Arbitration: The Iran–U.S. Claims Tribunal Experience*, 83 AJIL 278 (1989). But for a contrary view, *see* M. Sornarajah, The International Law on Foreign Investment 284–86, 296 (3d ed. 2010) (opining that the governing law in a contract between a host State and a foreign private entity should be the State's municipal law). For a discussion of choice-of-law clauses generally in transnational contracts, *see* Georges R. Delaume, Law and Practice of Transnational Contracts 4–30 (1988); Jeswald Salacuse, The Three Laws of International Investment: National, Contractual, and International Frameworks for Foreign Capital, ch. 6, sec. 8.2(a) (2013).

[55] The trend in the U.S. courts, for example, is to recognize validly concluded choice-of-law clauses, as long as the parties' choice is not "unreasonable." *The Bremen v. Zapata Off-Shore Co.*, 407 U.S. 1 (1972); *General Eng'g. Corp. v. Martin Marietta Alumina Inc.*, 783 F.2d 352 (3d Cir. 1986). *See generally* Kristine M. Paden, *Choice of Law, Choice of Forum and Arbitration Clauses Override U.S. Security Rights*, 6 Transnat'l L. 431 (1993).

[56] Tibor Várady et al., International Commercial Arbitration 532 (1999). *See also* UNCITRAL Model Law on International Commercial Arbitration, art. 28(1) ("The arbitral tribunal shall decide the dispute in accordance with such rules of law as are chosen by the parties as applicable to the substance of the dispute. Any designation of the law or legal system of a given State shall be construed, unless otherwise expressed, as directly referring to the substantive law of that State and not to its conflict of laws rules").

[57] *See e.g.* Yayan Mulyana & Jan K. Schaefer, *Indonesia's New Framework for International Arbitration: A Critical Assessment of the Law and Its Application by the Courts*, 17 Mealey's Int'l Arb. Rep. 39, 57 (2002) (under Indonesian law, it is unclear whether arbitrators should honor the parties' choice of law if the selected law lacks a substantial connection to the contract). Even in U.S. courts, not all choice-of-law provisions will be enforced. Restatement (Second) of Conflict of Laws § 187(2) ("The law of the state chosen by the parties to govern their contractual rights and duties will be applied, even if the particular issue is one which the parties could not have resolved by an explicit provision in their agreement directed to that issue, unless ... (a) the chosen state has no substantial relationship to the parties or the transaction and there is no other reasonable basis for the parties' choice"). *See also Shamil Bank of Bahrain v Beximco Pharmaceuticals Ltd*, [2004] 1 W.L.R. 1784 (the English Court of Appeal refused to enforce a contractual clause calling for the application of Sharia law, since it did not refer to the legal system of a single country).

application of a commercially sophisticated and well-developed body of law from a neutral jurisdiction, such as English law or New York law. A choice of New York law to govern an investment agreement might be achieved with the following language:

> This Agreement and all documents executed in connection with this Agreement, and their validity, enforcement, and interpretation, and all disputes arising under any such document, shall be governed by the substantive laws of the State of New York (without regard to any conflict of laws principles).

In selecting the applicable law, there is no "ideal" system that will maximize stability in all circumstances and all areas of activity. While New York and English law are possibly the most developed in the world in the areas of banking and the interpretation of commercial contracts, they may have rather less to say about other sectors, such as hydrocarbons, high technology, or agriculture. The parties to a contract should carefully consider which legal system is most likely to offer clear solutions to the disagreements that are likely to arise in connection with the particular subject matter of the project at hand. Experienced international corporate counsel are accustomed to making this sort of determination in a flexible and open-minded way, and should be consulted when negotiating a choice-of-law clause.[58] **2.41**

It is not uncommon that host States and their agencies strongly resist the adoption of foreign choice-of-law clauses. As a matter of sovereignty, many governments find it difficult to accept subjecting themselves to the law of another sovereign State.[59] **2.42**

An alternative solution is to designate the agreement itself as the governing law, supplemented either by the laws of the host State, "international law," or rules common to both the host State and international law. In *MINE v. Guinea*,[60] for example, the parties had selected the law of Guinea as the governing law, fixed at the date of the agreement, but only regarding issues as to which the contract was silent or incomplete. **2.43**

The parties to a State contract may also agree to "international law" as the governing law.[61] But however attractive "international law" might appear at first blush **2.44**

[58] On many occasions, counsels of the parties may agree to choose more than one municipal law as the governing law, a process known in French as *dépeçage*, meaning that different parts of the contract shall be governed by different laws. *See* Margaret L. Moses, The Principles and Practice of International Commercial Arbitration 72–73 (2008).

[59] *See* Daniel E. Vielleville & Baiju Simal Vasani, *Sovereignty over Natural Resources Versus Rights under Investment Contracts: Which One Prevails?*, 5(2) TDM 21 (2008).

[60] *Maritime Int'l Nominees Establishment v. Government of Guinea*, ICSID Case No. ARB/84/4, ad hoc Committee Decision of Dec. 22, 1989, 5 ICSID Rev.— For. Inv. L.J. 95, 111–12 (1990).

[61] *See* David J. Branson & Richard E. Wallace, Jr., *Choosing the Substantive Law to Apply in International Commercial Arbitration*, 27 Va. J. Int'l L. 39 (1986); Chiati, *supra* note 44, at 121 *et seq.*; and Leo J. Bouchez, *The Prospects for International Arbitration: Disputes between States and Private Enterprises*, 8 J. Int'l Arb. 81, 100 (1991); Von Mehren & Kourides, *supra* note 54, at 511

to foreign contracting parties, many commentators recognize the drawbacks of such a designation. Most importantly, international law may be poorly adapted to complex commercial or financial arrangements. Even where international law precedent exists in a certain area, the rules of customary international law are often only vaguely defined, and with significant lacunae. Furthermore, international law rules (formed in relations between States) can only be applied to private parties by rough analogy. Professor Bowett concludes in this regard that:

> at present there are no international law rules of contract law. This is not to doubt the capacity of international law to develop such rules, but simply to state that at present it is difficult to identify any such body of rules.[62]

2.45 Professor Vagts points out that international law does not address issues such as

> what is a workmanlike way of financing and operating a hotel in Djakarta, or what are the rights of Saudi Arabia, in shipping oil out of the country, to choose a contractor other than Aramco, the party with whom the state contracted as to exploring for and extracting the minerals.[63]

2.46 He opines that a contractual designation of international law will lead arbitrators to "examine the civil/commercial law systems of the leading jurisdictions and deduce from them those commercial law concepts that are common to all."[64] This is similar to "general principles of law common to civilized nations," which constitute one of the primary sources of customary international law.[65] Since the function of a choice-of-law clause is to increase predictability and lower political risk, the practical utility of "international law" or "general principles of law" as governing a high-stakes State contract is open to serious doubt.

2.47 In some State contracts, a compromise is reached between the interests of private and public parties, resulting in a designation of the host State's laws as governing, but only to the extent that they are consistent with international law. For example, in *Kaiser Bauxite v. Jamaica*,[66] the governing law provision provided that "the Arbitral Tribunal shall apply the law of Jamaica and such rules of international law as may be applicable." In this and other cases, tribunals have ruled that such a

("Because the parties are not required to choose the law of their own nationality or, indeed, the law of any nationality, there is no compelling reason why they should not elect to have their contractual relations governed by principles and concepts that are not attached to any sovereign").

62 Derek William Bowett, *State Contracts with Aliens: Contemporary Developments on Compensation for Termination or Breach*, 59 Brit. Yb. Int'l L. 49, 54 (1988).

63 Detlev F. Vagts, *Protecting Foreign Investment: An International Law Perspective*, in Foreign Direct Investment in the 1990s: A New Climate in the Third World 109 (Cynthia Day Wallace ed. 1990).

64 *Id.*

65 Statute of the International Court of Justice (1945), art. 38(1)(c), available at http://www.icj-cij.org.

66 *Kaiser Bauxite Co. v. Government of Jamaica*, ICSID Case No. ARB/74/3, Decision on Jurisdiction and Competence of July 5, 1975, 1 ICSID Rep. 296, 301 (1993).

formulation calls for the application of local law, but only within the confines of internationally accepted norms.[67]

A similar approach was taken in a concession agreement between Texaco Overseas Petroleum Company (TOPCO) and the Libyan Arab Republic. The choice-of-law clause in that agreement established the governing law as: **2.48**

> the principles of law of Libya common to the principles of international law and in the absence of such common principles then by and in accordance with the general principles of law, including such of those principles as may have been applied by international tribunals.[68]

The problem that arose in the interpretation of this clause was that, as previously discussed, international law does not cover private contractual relations. As a result, one could argue that there are no relevant principles of Libyan law that are "common to international law." **2.49**

There are two other constructions of this sort of provision which better preserve the intent of the parties. First, international law principles, while created in the context of State-to-State interaction, can be analogized to identify principles that usefully apply to private parties or investor–State relations.[69] **2.50**

Second, a judge or arbitrator can find limiting principles in internationally accepted commercial guidelines, most notably the UNIDROIT Principles of International Commercial Contracts[70] and the Convention on the International Sale of Goods (CISG).[71] These documents, while drafted with the participation of States and with regard to the wide variety of legal practices around the world, are purely commercial in character, designed to govern private or semi-private transactions. Indeed, the UNIDROIT Principles, CISG, and other international agreements and guidelines on commercial contracts are often used independently as a choice of law in both purely private and investor–State contracts. **2.51**

---

67 This is also the language used in the choice-of-law provision of the Convention on the Settlement of Investment Disputes Between States and Nationals of Other States, of Mar. 18, 1965, art. 54(1), 17 U.S.T. 1270 (the Washington Convention), available at http://www.worldbank.org/icsid ("In the absence of [agreement to the contrary], the Tribunal shall apply the law of the Contracting State party to the dispute (including its rules on the conflict of laws) and such rules of international law as may be applicable"). While there is disagreement as to the precise application of art. 42(1), the majority opinion appears to be that domestic law of the host State governs the investment, as long as it does not conflict with principles of international law. Emmanuel Gaillard & Yas Banifatemi, *The Meaning of "and" in Article 42(1), Second Sentence, of the Washington Convention: The Role of International Law in the ICSID Choice of Law Process*, 18 ICSID Rev.—For. Inv. L.J. 375 (2003).

68 *TOPCO, supra* note 54, Preliminary Award, 53 I.L.R. 389, 404 (1979).

69 For example, the sanctity of State contracts can be derived by analogy to the public international law principle of *pacta sunt servanda*.

70 The UNIDROIT Principles were re-drafted in 2004 and later in https://www.unidroit.org/publications/513-unidroit-principles-of-international-commercial-contracts.

71 United Nations Convention on Contracts for the International Sale of Goods (1980), available at http://www.cisg.law.pace.edu/cisg/text/cisg-toc.html.

2.52 In many cases, the parties to an investment contract will also specifically address the kinds of relief they want to include or exclude from the judge's or arbitrator's authority. For example, it may be advisable for the parties to specify that an arbitral tribunal is empowered to issue injunctive relief as well as a monetary award, or that the costs of arbitration may be shifted to the losing party regardless of the provisions of the applicable law. Where U.S. law applies, many non-U.S. parties require an exclusion of punitive damages, which are all but unknown in civil law systems. To ensure that the judge or arbitrator calculates damages rigorously, the parties occasionally expressly require that damages be assessed according to the applicable law, rather than according to equity or general principles.[72]

3. Stabilization clause

a. Types of stabilization clauses

2.53 Developing State governments' desire to maintain an image as an attractive destination for FDI[73] appear to have reduced the frequency of the large-scale expropriations and nationalizations that took place in many oil-producing countries during the twentieth century. But investors still face the risk that the host State might change fiscal and regulatory terms that reduce the investor's profits or otherwise detrimentally affect the investor. Even where the parties to a State contract have used a choice-of-law clause to exclude application of local law to interpret the agreement itself, the private investor remains exposed to the risk of such changes to the regulatory regime.

---

[72] This situation arose in *CMI Int'l Inc. v. Ministry of Roads and Transportation, Iran*, 4 Iran–US C.T.R. 263, Award No. 245 (99-245-2) of Dec. 27, 1983, in which the tribunal, refusing to measure damages in accordance with the terms of Idaho law as specified in the parties' purchase order, stated that it was not "rigorously tied to the law of the contract, at least insofar as the assessment of damages is concerned." The tribunal calculated damages based on "general principles of law." *Id.* at 319.

[73] *See* Alexander, *Production Sharing Contracts, supra* note 3, at sec. 20.02, which lists the following factors driving "[t]he high degree of competition among host governments for foreign investment by IOCs [international oil companies]":

1. nationalization of national oil companies (NOCs);
2. the low price "scare" of 1998 and early 1999, which resulted in:
   (a) "merger-mania" among IOCs—resulting in fewer IOCs; and
   (b) IOCs using lower price assumptions (in spite of the current high international crude oil and gas prices) upon which to run economics in order to assess E&P opportunities, thereby requiring generally greater financial concessions on the part of host governments in order to attract foreign investment;
3. the fact that there is more exploration acreage available today than ever before in the history of the international petroleum industry (including more countries as well as more areas—such as deep water environments); and
4. (4) the perception that we may begin to see a world of fewer, and larger, foreign investor energy companies investing the bulk of their capital in a few Middle Eastern countries (such as: Iran, Iraq, Kuwait, and Saudi Arabia).

So-called "stabilization" clauses are meant to insulate the foreign private party from alterations in local mandatory laws that make doing business more costly or difficult. Stabilization clauses often provide that the private party and the investment project itself will be subject to the host State's laws only to the extent that they are in force on a given date (typically the date that the agreement takes effect). The clause is thus designed to freeze the law of the host State as it was on that date, or at least its economic effect.[74] Legislation, decrees, and regulations the host State issues subsequently are to have no effect on the agreement, the investor, or his investment. In practice, these provisions can "preclude the application to an agreement of any subsequent legislative (statutory) or administrative (regulatory) act issued by the government ... that modifies the legal situation of the investor."[75] 2.54

There are other types of stabilization clauses in addition to the traditional formulation described.[76] A "consistency clause" requires that any subsequently enacted law must be consistent with terms of the already concluded agreement. Another version requires that the agreement be performed in good faith. While this does not limit the host State's right to change its laws, it implicitly "preclud[es] the unilateral modification or termination of the agreement by either party."[77] Stabilization clauses are often distinguished from "intangibility" clauses, which require mutual consent to change the terms of a concession.[78] 2.55

Another tool often used to insulate private contracting parties from regulatory risk is the "balancing clause," which does not prevent a change in the law, but envisages "automatic adjustments or renegotiation of contract terms in the event of specified circumstances."[79] Such provisions allow local law to evolve and apply 2.56

---

[74] The State's municipal law, as it stands on a given date, is often chosen as the law to govern certain local matters, with the possible adjunction of extra-State laws or norms, such as international law or "general principles of law." *See generally* Chiati, *supra* note 44, at 121 *et seq*. For discussion of international law principles underlying the validity of stabilization clauses, *see* Chapter 4, Section B.2.a.

[75] *Id.* at 115. For further examples and discussion of stabilization clauses, *see Id.* at 115–21; Amaechi David Nwokolo, *Is There a Legal and Functional Value for the Stabilization Clause in International Petroleum Agreements?*, 2003–04(8) CEPMLP Ann. Rev. 8 (2004), http://www.dundee.ac.uk/media/dundeewebsite/cepmlp-nh/car/CAR%2008_17072017.pdf; Alexander, *The Three Pillars*, *supra* note 3, § 7.03; Nwete, *supra* note 3; Maniruzzaman, *supra* note 3; Montembault, *supra* note 44; Thomas W. Wälde & George N'Di, *Stabilizing International Investment Commitments: International Law versus Contract Interpretation*, 1 CEPMLP J. (Professional Paper PP13) (1994), available at http://www.dundee.ac.uk/cepmlp; Margarita T.B. Coale, *Stabilization Clauses in International Petroleum Transactions*, 30 Denv. J. Int'l L. & Pol'y. 217 (2002); *see also* Cameron, *supra* note 3, ch. 2, sec. C; Papanastasiou, *supra* note 44, at 188–95; Lorenzo Cotula, *Reconciling Regulatory Stability and Evolution of Environmental Standards in Investment Contracts: Towards a Rethink of Stabilization Clauses*, 1 J. World Energy L. 158–79 (2008).

[76] Nwokolo, *supra* note 75, at sec. 3.

[77] *Id.*

[78] *See* note 82, *infra*, and accompanying text.

[79] *See* Cameron, *supra* note 3, para. 2.37.

to the project at the government's discretion, while maintaining the economic equilibrium of contractual relations (normally between a private party and State entity).

b. Examples of stabilization clauses

2.57 Stabilization clauses are particularly useful in large-scale, capital-intensive natural resource extraction projects, where changes in taxes or State royalties can completely alter economic feasibility for the investor and its creditors.[80] The concession contract between the parties in *LIAMCO v. Libya* provides an example of the type of stabilization clause often included in oil and gas agreements:

> (1) The Government of Libya, the Commission and the appropriate provincial authorities will take all steps necessary to ensure that the Company enjoys all the rights conferred by this Concession. The contractual rights expressly created by this Concession shall not be altered except by mutual consent of the parties.
> (2) This Concession shall throughout the period of its validity be construed in accordance with the Petroleum Law and the Regulations in force on the date of execution of the Agreement of Amendment by which this [paragraph] (2) was incorporated into this Concession Agreement. Any amendment to or repeal of such Regulations shall not affect the contractual rights of the Company without its consent.[81]

2.58 The first paragraph makes clear that the contractual rights secured by the concession cannot be altered without the mutual consent of the parties. The second part establishes that the municipal law by which the concession is to be interpreted is fixed as of a certain date, so that later government legislation or actions will not undermine the company's economic expectations.[82]

2.59 Another example of a stabilization and intangibility clause is as follows:[83]

> This agreement shall be construed in accordance with the Petroleum and Tax Laws and related regulations in force on the date of execution. Any amendment to, or

[80] *See Occidental Petroleum Exploration Co. v. Ecuador*, LCIA Case No. UN3467, Final Award of July 1, 2004, 43 I.L.M. 1248 (2004), available at https://www.italaw.com/sites/default/files/case-documents/ita0571.pdf, at paras 103–04 ("Economic Stability" clause operated to prevent alteration of value added tax regime as applied to foreign investor's petroleum project).

[81] *LIAMCO, supra* note 54, 62 I.L.R. at 170.

[82] The first paragraph, which requires mutual consent to change the concession contract, is sometimes referred to as an "intangibility clause" or prohibition on unilateral changes clause, to distinguish it from a stabilization clause, which freezes the law as of a certain date. *See e.g.* Bouchez, *supra* note 61, at 86 *et seq.* Most such clauses, however, combine both elements, which are complementary. Chiati, *supra* note 44, at 115–16. Here, the term "stabilization clause" broadly refers to both intangibility and stabilization provisions. According to one commentator: "An intangibility clause is aimed at achieving a compromise in the event that a change of law affects the terms of an already concluded agreement. Unlike the traditional stabilization clauses an intangibility clause contemplates that a host state may have the requirement to change the terms of an already concluded agreement but such alteration must not be done unilaterally." Nwokolo, *supra* note 75, at sec. 3.

[83] This and the following two examples are taken from Nwokolo, *supra* note 75, at sec. 3.1.

> repeal of such laws or regulations, shall not affect the contract rights or obligations of the contractor without its consent.

The stabilization clause portion limits the application of laws and regulations to the agreement to those in force at a specified date. The intangibility clause requires the contractor-investor's consent to any changes in law affecting contractual rights or obligations. **2.60**

A more modern example of a stabilization clause for use in a production sharing, participation, or service agreement provides: **2.61**

> After the effective date of this agreement, if there is a change in the domestic law that results in a material adverse impact on the economic value derived from operations by the contractor, the [State-owned company] will ensure that the contractor will derive the same economic benefits as it would have derived if the change in law had not been affected.

This clause has an effect similar to that of a consistency clause, but instead of specifying that law inconsistent with the terms of the agreement does not apply, it requires that the State take steps to place the investor in the same position it would have occupied had the law remained unchanged. **2.62**

The following is an example of a modern consistency clause: **2.63**

> Nothing in this clause shall be read or construed as imposing any limitation or constraint on the scope, or due and proper enforcement, of legislation of general application that does not discriminate, or have the effect of discriminating against the Contractor, and provides in the interest of safety, health, welfare or protection of the environment ... provided, however that the state will ensure that such measures are in accordance with the current international petroleum industry standards and are not unreasonable.

Such a clause gives the host State more discretion, and the investor less protection, than the preceding example, since the host State retains the right to enact legislation with full effect on the parties' contractual relations, as long as this is done in a non-discriminatory fashion and meets other basic requirements. **2.64**

c. *Validity of stabilization clauses*

International law and practice generally uphold the validity of stabilization clauses and the State's right to bind itself through the adoption of such clauses.[84] The tribunal in *TOPCO* stated that "[n]othing can prevent a State, in the exercise of its sovereignty, from binding itself irrevocably by the provisions of a concession and **2.65**

[84] *See* Nwokolo, *supra* note 75, at sec. 4.2 (discussing various main views about the legal validity and effect of stabilization clauses under international law, including the view that the State is free to revoke a stabilization clause, and concluding that "[t]here is still an element of confusion surrounding the legal character and effect of stabilization clauses, especially under international law"); also Alexander, *The Three Pillars*, *supra* note 3, § 7.03[2].

from granting to the concessionaire irretractable rights."[85] Some commentators have objected that State sovereignty cannot be fettered by an agreement with a private party, particularly to the extent that the State is barred from carrying out its legislative authority.[86] As the *TOPCO* tribunal explained, however, "in entering into concession contracts with the plaintiffs, the Libyan State did not *alienate* but *exercised* its sovereignty."[87] More importantly, a stabilization clause does not prevent the State from enacting legislation as it sees fit, but only from *enforcing* new regulations against the concessionaire or licensee.

2.66 While judges and tribunals generally affirm the validity of stabilization clauses, there is a lack of consensus as to the consequences of the State's violation of such a provision.[88] In particular, some arbitrators have refused to order specific performance of concession agreements, even those containing a stabilization clause. This reluctance arises out of respect for State sovereignty and recognition that an award of specific performance may be unenforceable.[89] More commonly, the violation of a stabilization clause will have an effect on the amount of damages awarded or on the certainty that damages will be awarded.[90]

2.67 The decisions from a few key historic international arbitrations illustrate the generally accepted international practice concerning the interpretation and application of stabilization clauses.

2.68 In *TOPCO*, Libya nullified the property rights of several oil companies in violation of the terms of a concession agreement.[91] The agreement contained a stabilization clause very similar to the clause at issue in *LIAMCO v Libya*, set out in subsection (b) above. The tribunal recognized the validity of a stabilization clause in a concession agreement. The clause was one factor in the tribunal's decision to declare an illegal expropriation, and to award the claimant the very uncommon

---

[85] *TOPCO, supra* note 54, 53 I.L.R. at 474, *quoting Saudi Arabia v. Arabian American Oil Co. (ARAMCO)* (1958), 27 I.L.R. 117, 168 (1963); *see also* Chiati, *supra* note 44, at 161 ("[s]tabilization clauses, validly entered into, are valid and binding"), and Bouchez, *supra* note 61, at 86.

[86] *See* Ian Brownlie, Principles of Public International Law 526 (6th ed. 2003), discussing the view that stabilization clauses are invalid because of the modern concept of permanent sovereignty over natural resources.

[87] *TOPCO, supra* note 54, 53 I.L.R. at 482 (emphasis added). *See also* Chapter 7, quote at text accompanying note 14.

[88] As stated in *LIAMCO, supra* note 54, 62 I.L.R. at 205, international law does not provide a full set of clear rules on assessing the quantum of damages for breach of obligations. *See* M.N. Shaw, International Law 743 *et. seq.* (5th ed. 2003).

[89] Troy Elder, *The Case against Awards of Specific Performance in Transnational Commercial Disputes*, 13(1) Arb. Int'l 1 (1997).

[90] *See* Chiati, *supra* note 44, at 165, stating that "the extent of the indemnity due to the investor... may vary from compensation for the value of the property taken to the financial equivalent of restitution and may even include, at least theoretically, punitive damages" (footnote omitted). *See also* Nwokolo, *supra* note 75, at sec. 5 (discussing the "functional value" of stabilization clauses); and Shaw, *supra* note 88, at 743 *et seq.*; F.V. García-Amador, *State Responsibility in Case of "Stabilization" Clauses*, 2 J. Transnat'l L. & Pol'y. 23, 50 (1993).

[91] *TOPCO, supra* note 54, 53 I.L.R. at 422 *et seq.*

relief of restitution (*i.e.* a return of the property).[92] Although the award was atypical with respect to remedies, the tribunal stated that this was "the normal sanction for non-performance of contractual obligations."[93] The tribunal held that where the contract has been stabilized on a certain date by specific clauses, "the decision of a State to take nationalizing measures ... carries international consequences ..."[94] This conclusion demonstrates the potential significance of a stabilization clause to help convince an arbitrator to grant a remedy to an aggrieved investor.

In *LIAMCO v. Libya*, discussed briefly earlier in this chapter, Libya had awarded concessions to LIAMCO in 1955, and then nationalized those concession rights in 1973.[95] The tribunal held this to be a breach of the concession, and awarded the claimant approximately US$80 million in damages.[96] The contractual stabilization clause stipulated that "contractual rights expressly created by this Concession shall not be altered except by mutual consent of the parties."[97] Largely on the basis of this language, the tribunal held that a "nationalization of concession rights ... constitutes ... a source of liability to compensate the concessionaire for said premature termination of the concession agreement."[98] The court declined to award lost profits, but the stabilization clause in the concession was one factor that led the arbitrators to award substantial "equitable compensation."[99] **2.69**

The tribunal in *Aminoil* dedicated significant space to a discussion of stabilization clauses.[100] In 1948, Kuwait granted the Aminoil company a concession for the exploration and exploitation of petroleum and natural gas in what was then called the Kuwait "Neutral Zone."[101] In 1961, Kuwait became fully independent, and the concession was modified by a supplemental agreement. In December 1974, the Organization of Petroleum Exporting Countries (OPEC) countries adopted the "Abu Dhabi formula," which effectively raised taxes on the oil that Aminoil was producing. Aminoil objected to the change in tax levies.[102] **2.70**

[92] *Id.* at 507. The award of restitution against a State is rare in concession cases; usually tribunals will award damages only. F.A. Mann, Further Studies in International Law 126 (1990); Marjorie M. Whiteman, 2 Damages in International Law 827 (1937); B.A. Wortley, Expropriation in Public International Law 76 (1959). For a discussion of the remedy of *restitutio in integrum, see* Rosalyn Higgins, Problems and Process: International Law and How We Use It 298 *et seq.* (1994).

[93] *TOPCO, supra* note 54, 53 I.L.R. at 507.

[94] *Id.* at 471.

[95] *LIAMCO, supra* note 54, 62 I.L.R. at 160 *et seq.*

[96] *Id.* at 218.

[97] *Id.* at 191.

[98] *Id.* at 217.

[99] *Id.* at 217–18.

[100] *Government of Kuwait v. American Independent Oil Co. (AMINOIL)*, 66 I.L.R. 518 (1982), 21 I.L.M. 976 (1982).

[101] *Id.*, 21 I.L.M. at 989.

[102] *Id.*, 21 I.L.M. at 995 *et seq.*

Negotiations between the parties were unsuccessful, and Kuwait seized Aminoil's assets in 1977.[103] In the ensuing arbitration, Aminoil claimed that both the initial regulatory change and the eventual taking violated the stabilization clause contained in the concession agreement. The stabilization clause read:

> The Sheikh shall not by general or special legislation or by administrative measures or by any other act whatever annul this Agreement except as provided in Article 11. No alteration shall be made in the terms of this Agreement by either the Sheikh or the Company except in the event of the Sheikh and the Company jointly agreeing that it is desirable in the interest of both parties to make certain alterations, deletions or additions to this Agreement.[104]

2.71 The tribunal affirmed the validity of stabilization clauses in general, although it reasoned that this particular clause could not accomplish what it appeared to contemplate on its face. First, the tribunal held that the stabilization clause did not prohibit nationalization, because it contained no express prohibition on such takings.[105] The arbitrator stated that a "contractual limitation on the state's right to nationalize . . . would be a particularly serious undertaking which would have to be expressly stipulated for . . ."[106] He reasoned further that "[t]he case of nationalization is certainly not expressly provided against by the stabilization clauses of the Concession."[107] Thus, this particular clause was found to imply no contractual responsibility for the seizure, although the tribunal did recognize that where language is clearer, stabilization clauses can have such an effect. Second, the tribunal held that during protracted negotiations Aminoil had consented to allow changes to the agreement, and that this "brought about a metamorphosis in the whole character of the Concession."[108] The tribunal concluded that by compromising with the State, the investor had implicitly agreed to dilute the stabilization clause. Under this weakened stabilization clause, nationalization did not violate the concession agreement, as long as compensation was paid.[109]

2.72 The *Aminoil* tribunal held that the stabilization clause justified only an award of damages, and not injunctive relief to reinstate the previous regulatory regime. Nevertheless, the existence of the stabilization clause—even weakened—was an important element in the tribunal's award of damages.[110]

---

[103] *Id.*, 21 I.L.M. at 996–98. *See also* the discussions of the *AMINOIL* case in Fernando R. Tesón, *State Contracts and Oil Expropriations: The AMINOIL–Kuwait Arbitration*, 24 VA. J. INT'L L. 323 (1984); and Geoffrey Marston, *The Aminoil–Kuwait Arbitration*, 17 J. WORLD TRADE L. 177 (1983).

[104] *AMINOIL, supra* note 100, 21 I.L.M. at 990–91.

[105] *Id.* at 1023.

[106] *Id.*

[107] *Id.*

[108] *Id.*

[109] *Id.* at 1024.

[110] *Id.* at 1032.

The investor negotiating a stabilization clause can draw two valuable lessons from the *Aminoil* decision. The first is that a stabilization clause should be very explicit in what it is meant to prohibit. The second is that a stabilization clause should provide that, absent express written agreement to the contrary, its terms are binding regardless of subsequent compromise, negotiation, or amendment of the contract. This should allow the parties to modify the concession terms by mutual agreement if circumstances change, without jeopardizing the overall stability of project terms and regulatory conditions.[111] **2.73**

Negotiating parties might consider the following stabilization clause text, which takes into account the case law discussed: **2.74**

> All laws, decrees, and regulations of [the Host State], whether legislative, judicial, or administrative, applicable to this Agreement or the relationship between the parties and in effect as of the date of this Agreement in accordance with [the governing law clause], including, without limitation, [cite investment laws of the Host State prohibiting expropriation without compensation, currency transfer laws, and any other laws of critical interest to the investor] shall be the only laws, decrees, and regulations governing this Agreement and the parties in relation thereto. This provision may be modified only with the express consent of both parties, as evidenced by a written agreement between the parties specifically referring to this clause, and shall not otherwise be considered modified by subsequent compromise or negotiation between the parties or amendments or modifications to this Agreement.

It is possible that the host State will implement new regulations or repeal existing ones despite the inclusion of such a clause in a State contract. But there can be little doubt that, properly drafted, language such as that proposed can serve as an important tool for the aggrieved investor in obtaining compensation for any harm such changes may cause.[112] **2.75**

4. *Force majeure* clause

A *force majeure* clause excuses a party from carrying out its obligations under a contract when events outside the control of that party make performance impractical or impossible.[113] The most traditional *force majeure* situation involves natural disasters, but the parties are free to define the circumstances that trigger *force majeure*. In particular, contracts between private parties and State agencies or subdivisions often include rather elaborate *force majeure* clauses designed to **2.76**

---

[111] In a separate opinion, Sir G. Fitzmaurice reasoned that stabilization clauses do not need to be absolutely precise to be effective, and that the character of the concession and the stabilization clause remained the same despite subsequent negotiations and amendments. *Id.* at 1051–53.

[112] *See e.g. Occidental Petroleum, supra* note 80 (finding of unfair and inequitable treatment under BIT and compensation based largely on presence of tax stabilization clause in concession contract); *CMS Gas Transmission Co., supra* note 18 (finding of unfair and inequitable treatment under BIT and compensation based in part on presence of stabilization clause in gas transmission license).

[113] Jennifer M. Bund, Note and Comment, *Force Majeure Clauses: Drafting Advice for the CISG Practitioner*, 17 JL & Com. 381, 399–401 (1998).

shift the risk of adverse government action onto the State party. This is done by describing unexpected regulations, legislation, and denial of licenses or permits as instances of *force majeure*, but only for the private party. This prevents the host State from extracting additional benefit from contractual relations by threatening or implementing new conditions that effectively change the terms of the parties' agreement without negotiation.[114]

2.77 *Force majeure* clauses played an important role in the resolution of disputes in the wake of the Indonesian financial crisis of 1998. Over several years before that time, the Indonesian government had taken steps to expand energy production by granting licenses to foreign companies to build power stations and other facilities in cooperation with the State-owned electricity company, PLN, and the government-run oil giant Pertamina. The American-controlled enterprise Karaha Bodas Company (KBC) signed such a contract to build a geothermal power plant in Indonesia. When the local economy collapsed in 1998, demand for electricity evaporated. Under the contract, PLN was obligated to purchase all the energy generated by Karaha Bodas's plant. Instead, President Suharto issued a decree canceling the project. Arbitration ensued, and the tribunal focused on the contractual allocation of the risk that the government would take this kind of action.[115]

2.78 The Karaha Bodas contract's *force majeure* clause was central to this analysis. It read: "Events of *force majeure* shall include, but [are] not limited to ... (e) with respect to [Karaha Bodas Company] only, any Government Related Event."[116] "Government Related Event," in turn, was defined in the contract to include the cancellation of the contract by government decree. Ultimately, the tribunal held the Indonesian parties liable for breach of contract, ruling that:

> The Presidential Decrees were Force Majeure Events for KBC, but not for Pertamina and PLN. The legal consequence is that, while KBC was entitled to invoke the Presidential Decrees as a legitimate excuse not to perform its obligations, Pertamina and PLN were not entitled to do so as far as the performance of their own obligations is concerned.[117]

2.79 Political *force majeure* language can be tailored to the preferences of the parties, allocating the risk of certain types of government action to the State party (*e.g.* annulment of contract, interference from army or police, *etc.*) and others to the investor (*e.g.* changes in tax treatment, legitimate environmental penalties or

---

[114] *See generally* DELAUME, *supra* note 54, at 50–57. For a review of contractual structure in relation to the allocation of *force majeure* risk between public and private parties, as well as the resulting degree of exposure for foreign investors, see PAPANASTASIOU, *supra* note 44, at 195–99.

[115] *Karaha Bodas Co. v. Perusahaan Pertambangan Minyak Dan Gas Bumi Negara*, 190 F. Supp. 2d 936 (S.D. Tex. 2001).

[116] *Karaha Bodas Co. LLC v. Perusahaan Pertambangan Minyak Dan Gas Bumi Negara et al. [Pertamina]*, UNCITRAL Final Award of Sept. 30, 1999, MEALEY'S INT'L ARB. REP. (Mar. 2001), para. 54.

[117] *Id.*

injunctions, *etc.*). In the most general terms, the parties to a State contract might consider adding some variation of the following language to the end of a more universal *force majeure* clause (dealing with natural disasters and other unforeseeable events):

> In no event shall any act of [the State], including any change in the laws or regulations of [the State], excuse [the State agency or subdivision]'s duty to perform its obligations under this Agreement.

E. Clauses for Guidance of Courts and Tribunals

1. Damages clause

As discussed, by including a stabilization clause in a State contract, a private contracting party may be able to obtain a wider range of remedies in a resulting dispute resolution procedure.[118] Incorporating a "damages clause" in the State contract is perhaps a more predictable way of ensuring that the investor is awarded the full value of his rights should a breach of contract occur.[119] **2.80**

Damages clauses frequently provide that if the State seizes the investor's property or violates its contractual rights, the State is obliged to provide compensation equal to the full value of the investment. An example of this type of clause is found in a prominent Ghanaian concession contract, which contained an arbitration clause with the following paragraph: **2.81**

> If any Contractor's rights, interests or property provided for herein are expropriated, nationalized or otherwise taken by reason of any act of the State or any central or local governmental authority of Ghana, then the arbitrators shall apply the principle of full and fair compensation for loss of profits determined on the basis of a going concern.[120]

Such a clause may also make a State more reluctant to expropriate in the first place, since much of the temptation to take property is removed if the expropriating party is certain that it will have to pay for the property seized. For this reason, the terms "full and fair" and "lost profits", which may be subject to conflicting **2.82**

[118] *See* Garcia-Amador, *supra* note 90.

[119] For an extensive discussion of the awards of damages granted by international tribunals and the drafting of damages clauses, *see generally* Markham Ball, *Assessing Damages in Claims by Investors against States*, 16 ICSID Rev.—For. Inv. L.J. 408 (2001); Paul Friedland & E. Wong, *Measuring Damages for the Deprivation of Income-Producing Property*, 6 ICSID Rev.—For. Inv. L.J. 400 (1991); Felix Praendl, *Measure of Damages in International Commercial Arbitration*, 23 Stan. J. Int'l L. 263 (1987). Irmgard Marboe, Calculation of Compensation and Damages in International Investment Law 5.288 *et seq* (2nd ed. 2017); Antonias Dimolitsa, *Contractual Remedies: Clauses Penales and Liquidated Damages Clauses* in Interest, Auxiliary and Alternative Remedies in International Arbitration 15, (Filip J.M. De Ly and Laurent Levy eds. 2008).

[120] Chiati, *supra* note 44, at 166.

interpretation, may be better replaced by a specific method to determine asset values,[121] to avoid disputes over the appropriate valuation method.

2.83 Perhaps the most common form of damages provision in State contracts provides for "liquidated damages." This kind of clause "constitute[s] an amount agreed between the Parties that is due without any obligation on the injured party to quantify its loss or damage."[122] By agreeing to liquidated damages for breach of contract, the parties can significantly reduce political risk, by eliminating the uncertainty involved in any tribunal's quantification of harm and the mustering of evidence on quantum of damages. The parties should, however, pay close attention to the compatibility of liquidated damages with the law applicable to the merits of the dispute. In *Nat'l Oil Co. v. Libyan Sun Oil*, for example, a U.S. corporation contracted with a Libyan State-owned company to explore for oil. The parties' contract included a liquidated damages provision calling for an award to the Libyan side of US$100 million if the U.S. company failed to undertake exploration on the terms agreed. The tribunal upheld the Libyan respondent's claim based on this clause, but found strict application of liquidated damages conflicted with Libyan law:

> The Arbitral Tribunal is of the opinion that the amount of money that would be payable by Sun Oil as "liquidated damages" under [the contract] would be "grossly exaggerated" and should therefore be reduced in accordance with the mandatory provision of Art. 227(2) [of the Libyan Civil Code].[123]

The tribunal then reduced the damages amount to US$20 million.[124]

2.84 Nor should parties assume that liquidated damages clauses will be sacrosanct if governed by a developed country's legal system. On at least one occasion, an arbitral tribunal applying U.S. law disregarded a liquidated damages clause, having found strict adherence to be contrary to public policy.[125] English law will disregard any damages clause that a court or tribunal finds is punitive in nature, regardless of the way in which the parties have described the imposition in their contract.[126]

---

[121] *See* discussion of valuation in Chapter 6, Section E.

[122] *Component Builders Inc., et al. v. Iran et al.*, Iran–U.S. Claims Tribunal Case No. 395, Award 431-395-3 of Aug. 10, 1989, para. 14.1.

[123] *Nat'l Oil Co. v. Libyan Sun Oil Co.*, ICC Case No. 4462, Final Award of Feb. 23, 1987, 29 I.L.M. 565 (1990), para. 89.

[124] *Id.* The tribunal took into account three factors when assessing the proper level of damages: (1) the general circumstances of the case; (2) the actual losses suffered by the claimant; and (3) the claimant's failure to mitigate its losses. *Id.* at para. 92.

[125] *Dole Ocean Liner Express v. Georgia Vegetable Co.*, 84 F.3d 772 (5th Cir. 1996) (arbitral tribunal awarded damages in excess of that mandated by contractual liquidated damages provision, finding limitation to be contrary to public policy).

[126] *Cavendish Square Holding BV v Talal El Makdessi and ParkingEye Limited v Beavis*, [2015] UKSC 67, 2015 WL 6655167.

In the alternative or in addition, the parties may choose to incorporate a damages clause defining methods of valuation for lost or destroyed assets. In this way, the parties reduce the risk that mandatory rules of applicable law will invalidate the damages provision.[127] A damages clause of this type might provide as follows: **2.85**

> If any court or arbitral tribunal, constituted pursuant to [arbitration clause] or otherwise ("Tribunal"), determines that any portion of the Investor's assets (including contractual rights) has been expropriated, nationalized, or confiscated, or that any of the rights or interests of the Investor (including those provided under this Agreement) have been altered, modified, or taken, and if such Tribunal determines that compensation is due to the Investor, then the Tribunal shall award the Investor full compensation for any resulting loss, including both *damnum emergens* and *lucrum cessans*.
>
> If the [describe investment] was a going concern as of the date of the taking, damages shall be computed using the discounted cash flow method of valuation in accordance with generally accepted accounting principles of the United States; otherwise, damages shall be computed by estimating the fair market value of the property or interest taken, in accordance with generally accepted accounting principles of the United States.

2. Interest rate clause

The parties to a State contract may also wish to include a clause setting forth the rate at which interest will accrue on any arbitral award, and establishing the date from which interest will be determined. These are often hotly disputed issues, and how they are resolved can have a significant impact on the amount ultimately awarded in arbitration.[128] In the vast majority of cases, arbitrators and judges will follow the parties' express agreement on the interest rate and the way it should be applied.[129] Nevertheless, Islamic law does place limitations on the imposition of interest, and therefore contracting parties should carefully examine the compatibility of any interest rate clause and the law applicable to the contract.[130] **2.86**

An interest rate clause might provide as follows: **2.87**

> Any [award/judgment] rendered in accordance with Article [dispute resolution clause] of this Agreement shall include:

[127] For a discussion of limitation of liquidated damages clauses in international arbitration, *see* Praendl, *supra* note 119, at 293–95.

[128] *Wena Hotels Ltd. v. Egypt*, ICSID Case No. ARB/98/4, Award of Dec. 8, 2000, 41 I.L.M. 896, 918–19 (2002) (over US$11 million in interest award, in excess of principal amount); *Maffezini v. Spain*, ICSID Case No. ARB/97/7, Award of Nov. 13, 2000, 16 ICSID Rev—For. Inv. L.J. 1 (2001), paras. 95–96 (30 million pesetas awarded in interest on a 27 million peseta principal award).

[129] *See e.g. R.J. Reynolds Tobacco Co. v. Iran (Iranian Tobacco Co.)*, Award No. 143-35-3, 8 Iran–U.S. C.T.R. 55 (1985).

[130] Mahmoud A. El-Gamal, *Interest and the Paradox of Contemporary Islamic Law and Finance*, 26 Fordham Int'l L.J. 108, 126 (2003).

1. (a) pre-judgment interest at a rate of [stipulate rate], accruing from the date of breach until judgment is rendered; and
2. (b) post-judgment interest at a rate of [stipulate rate], accruing on all outstanding amounts of the [award/judgment] (including pre-judgment interest) from the date of the [award/judgment is rendered] until payment is made.

3. Local remedies clause

2.88 Under customary international law, an investor's home State is not entitled to take up its citizen's claim against the host State unless the private party has first "exhausted" all reasonably available remedies within the local legal system.[131] Generally speaking, however, private parties to State contracts are not required to petition local judicial or administrative bodies in the host State before invoking a contractual dispute resolution clause.[132] In *Elf Aquitaine Iran v. Nat'l Iranian Oil Co.*, the sole arbitrator considered the respondent's contention that Elf could not have recourse to arbitration, since a "Special Committee" had been established under Iranian law to review the oil production agreement at issue, and that Elf had the opportunity to make its case in that forum. The arbitrator dismissed this jurisdictional objection:

> The International Court of Justice has declared that "The rule that local remedies must be exhausted before international proceedings may be instituted is a well-established rule of customary international law ... This rule of local remedies or redress that would require ELF to present its claims to the Special Committee before turning to an international remedy does, however, govern only complaints made by a State in the exercise of its right of diplomatic protection of its nationals ... and not ... to a request from a party to an agreement on arbitration to initiate arbitral proceedings under that agreement. The parties have by choosing arbitration established a procedure for settlement of disputes which excludes the national legal

[131] *See* Chapter 4, section E. On the exhaustion of local remedies at customary international law, *see generally* Steven Schwebel, *Arbitration and the Exhaustion of Local Remedies*, in Justice in International Law 171 (1994); Andrea Bjorklund, *Waiver and the Exhaustion of the Local Remedies Rule in NAFTA Jurisprudence*, in NAFTA Investment Law and Arbitration 253 (2004); P. Peters, *Exhaustion of Local Remedies: Ignored in Most Bilateral Investment Treaties*, 44(2) Netherlands Int'l L. Rev. 233 (1997); A.A. Cancado Trindade, The Application of the Rule of Exhaustion of Local Remedies in International Law: Its Rationale in the International Protection of Individual Rights (1983)

[132] *See e.g.* Institute of International Law, Resolution on Arbitration between States, State Enterprises or State Entities, and Foreign Enterprises, 16 Yb. Comm. Arb. 236 (1991), art. 8 ("The requirement of exhaustion of local remedies as a condition of implementation of an obligation to arbitrate is not admissible unless the arbitration agreement provides otherwise"); Manual of Public International Law 582 (Max Sørensen ed. 1958); *see also* art. 26 of the ICSID Convention, according to which the requirement to exhaust local remedies is excluded "unless otherwise stated". Arbitration tribunals constituted under investment protection treaties have unanimously accepted claimants' right to initiate investor–State arbitration without first exhausting local remedies, absent a contrary treaty provision. *See e.g.: AES Corp. v. Argentina*, ICSID Case No. ARB/02/17, Decision on Jurisdiction of Apr. 26, 2005, paras 69, 70; *Saipem S.p.A. v. Bangladesh*, ICSID Case No. ARB/05/07, Award of June 30, 2009, paras 174–84; *CME Czech Republic B.V. v. Czech Republic*, UNCITRAL Final Award of Mar. 14, 2003, para. 412.

> remedies provided for in national legislations. The established procedure also implies that each party is entitled to have disputes settled by arbitration without evoking diplomatic protection and thus without fulfilling conditions to be met in order for their government to exercise diplomatic protection.[133]

Nevertheless, certain domestic legal systems, which retain some historical hostility toward private dispute resolution, may prevent a claimant from hauling the government or State-owned entities before an arbitral tribunal when it has not first exhausted local remedies. **2.89**

There are also some clauses in BITs that require the exhaustion of local remedies, although such clauses are relatively uncommon.[134] According to certain other investment protection treaties, the claimant must submit the dispute to domestic courts before having recourse to international arbitration, but litigation need only be pursued only for a limited period of time (usually no more than eighteen months). If there is no resolution of the dispute through domestic proceedings by then, the investor can gain access to international arbitration.[135] **2.90**

Furthermore, the *Elf Aquitaine* limitation of the local remedies rule, while generally beneficial to the foreign investor who has chosen not to seek diplomatic protection from his home State, may create complications if local remedies *are* useful for strategic or practical purposes. In particular, local administrative remedies may be the surest way to preserve important rights, to obtain provisional relief, or to engage the host government in meaningful negotiations. **2.91**

For these reasons, the private party to a State contract may be well-advised to include explicit language separating contractual dispute resolution from remedies the private party may seek in local courts. This would entail both a waiver of the local remedies rule by the State and consent of both sides to proceedings outside the arbitration process. At the same time, the parties should carefully craft such an agreement to prevent frivolous or redundant litigation, which can defeat the purpose of arbitration. This can be achieved by requiring that local proceedings be terminated before arbitration begins. Such a clause might provide: **2.92**

1. The Parties are not required to exhaust any local remedies before invoking dispute resolution under [arbitration clause].
2. Notwithstanding [arbitration clause] of this Agreement, the Parties may, *but are not required to*, pursue any administrative, judicial, or other remedies available under the laws of the Host State. Such recourse shall not be considered incompatible with the [arbitration clause].

---

[133] *Elf Aquitaine Iran v. Nat'l Iranian Oil Co.*, Preliminary Award of Jan. 14, 1982, 1984 Revue de l'Arbitrage 401, para. 28.

[134] *See* Rudolf Dolzer & Christoph Schreuer, Principles of International Investment Law (2d ed. 2012) at 265.

[135] *Id.* at 266.

3. Any Party who has initiated local remedies must terminate such proceedings before invoking the [arbitration clause]. Pending local proceedings shall not prevent a Party who did not initiate such proceedings from initiating dispute resolution procedures in accordance with the [arbitration clause].

4. Waiver of sovereign immunity

2.93 Sovereign immunity, described in detail later in this book,[136] declined in importance over the course of the twentieth century for purposes of dispute resolution. The "restrictive" view of sovereign immunity has been codified in most legal systems around the world, limiting States' ability to defeat the jurisdiction of national and international tribunals in connection with commercial matters.[137] Furthermore, it has been widely recognized that States are free to explicitly or implicitly waive immunity irrevocably—a vital power if governments are to engage in economic activity with private parties. Therefore, as a general rule, sovereign immunity will not prevent an arbitration tribunal or court from assuming jurisdiction over a State or its instrumentality if the parties have signed a valid agreement to resolve disputes in the given forum.[138]

2.94 However, the enforcement of judgments and arbitral awards present a very different problem. Most legal systems bestow a higher level of sovereign immunity on State assets, in order to reduce the disruption of international relations and diplomacy that can result from the seizure of government property to satisfy an award or judgment.[139] This is true even for awards covered by the Washington (ICSID) Convention, which obligates member States to recognize ICSID awards as local judgments, but preserves each State's law on sovereign immunity for the attachment of assets.[140] There is some authority in the United States and elsewhere for the proposition that a State's consent to arbitration constitutes a waiver of immunity from execution of an award that results from that process.[141] But the dominant approach in most legal systems is that even if the agreement to arbitrate is explicit, sovereign immunity over *property* will not be deemed waived unless there is clear evidence that this was the State's intent.[142] Consequently, a private investor who enters into a State contract should not assume that an arbitration clause will be sufficient evidence of the State's waiver of immunity from execution on its assets.

---

[136] *See* Chapter 4, Section G.

[137] Georges R. Delaume, *Sovereign Immunity and Transnational Arbitration*, 3 Int'l Arb. 28 (1987).

[138] *See e.g.* 28 U.S.C. § 1605(a)(1) (1988); Chapter 4, Section G.

[139] *See* Chapter 4, Section G.2.

[140] Washington Convention, *supra* note 67, at art. 55. *See also* Chapter 8, Section B.2.b.

[141] *Ipitrade Int'l S.A. v. Nigeria*, 465 F. Supp. 824 (D.C. 1978); *Libyan American Oil Co. v. Socialist Peoples' Libyan Arab Jamahiriya*, 482 F. Supp. 1175 (D.C. 1980).

[142] *Ohntrup v. Firearms Centre Inc.*, 516 F.Supp. 1281 (1981); *Socialist Libyan Arab Popular Jamahiriya v. Libyan American Oil Co.*, 162 I.L.R. 228 (1980).

While many States may be reluctant to provide a sweeping waiver of sovereign immunity, limited waiver of immunity clauses are a standard element of State contracts. Such a provision is normally linked clearly to the arbitration clause and limits the waiver of sovereignty to enforcement of an award rendered under the contract in question.[143] The waiver may also be limited to particular assets or areas of activity. ICSID provides a sample waiver of immunity clause: **2.95**

> The Host State hereby waives any right of sovereign immunity as to it and its property in respect of the enforcement and execution of any award rendered by an Arbitral Tribunal constituted pursuant to this agreement.[144]

Some sovereign immunity clauses explicitly stipulate that the waiver is "irrevocable" and "unconditional". If such terms are omitted, there may be an increased risk that the host State will withdraw the waiver of immunity clause by a later sovereign act.[145] **2.96**

The waiver of immunity clause was of vital assistance to the foreign investor in *Karaha Bodas v. Pertamina*. As noted, KBC contracted with Indonesia's State-owned national oil company, Pertamina. In the project agreements, Pertamina expressly waived: **2.97**

> "any ... right of immunity (sovereign or otherwise) which it or its assets now has or may acquire in the future ..." and "consent[ed] in respect of the enforcement of any judgment against it ... "[146]

After an award of US$261 million was rendered in KBC's favor, the company sought enforcement in a number of jurisdictions, including Canada and Hong Kong, and Texas and New York in the United States. The courts involved took particular notice of the waiver of immunity clause, allowing KBC to seize any assets within their jurisdiction shown to belong to Pertamina.[147] **2.98**

Private parties often encounter sovereign immunity issues in so-called "hot products" cases, where the host State has expropriated private property and then exported the assets to a third country for sale. To limit the State's right to claim immunity in such circumstances, the private investor should seek to include a provision waiving immunity from suit in any State to which property has been exported following seizure by the host State. **2.99**

---

[143] There is also a distinction between sovereign–public acts (*iure imperii*) and commercial–private acts (*iure gestionis*). According to the restrictive theory of sovereign immunity, States are immune only in relation to sovereign conduct. *See* SALACUSE, *supra* note 54, at 152–53; PAPANASTASIOU, *supra* note 44, at 185.

[144] Available at http://icsidfiles.worldbank.org/icsid/icsid/staticfiles/model-clauses-en/15.htm.

[145] For more examples of sovereign immunity waiver clauses, *see* PAPANASTASIOU, *supra* note 44, at 184–88.

[146] *Karaha Bodas Co., L.L.C. v Perusahaan pertambangan Minyak Dan Gas Bumi Negara, Ministry of Finance of Indonesia*, 313 F.3d 70, 76 (2nd Cir. 2002).

[147] *See e.g. id.*

F. Other Useful Contractual Provisions

1. Conversion of currency clause

2.100 In many contracts, the private contracting party will require assurance that proceeds from the project received in local currency can be converted into other currencies without restriction. This can be important where the foreign company has borrowed funds on the international capital markets in dollars or euros to finance a project that will yield a stream of income in local currency. If after the project begins the host State passes a law limiting the conversion of its currency, the foreign company may find itself flush with local cash, but nevertheless unable to pay its debts.

2.101 Many developing countries have adopted investment codes securing the right to free conversion of currency.[148] International investment treaties routinely provide the same guarantee.[149] Particularly if the project contract includes a stabilization clause, the foreign investor may therefore be protected against currency inconvertibility without a specific clause on the subject. The investor may gain additional protection, and remove all doubt as to the allocation of the risk of currency inconvertibility, by including a specific provision covering the point. A convertibility clause might read:

> The State shall permit the Investor to convert all earnings from or returns on [describe investment] from [local currency] into any other currency within five business days of a written request from the Investor. The State shall not permit any agency, instrumentality or subdivision of the State to impair or delay any such conversion.

2. Payment of currency to offshore account (service and technical assistance contracts)

2.102 It is relatively common practice, particularly in the context of State contracts for services and technical assistance, that payment to the foreign private party is made in hard currency directly to an account located outside the host State. Such an arrangement reduces political risk by limiting the value of the investor's assets that are subject to the host State's direct territorial control. Otherwise put, a host government will have a far more difficulty interfering with an investor's money if it is held in U.S. dollars located in a London bank, than if held in local currency in the host State's capital.

---

148 *See* discussion in Chapter 1, Section C. For further discussion of repatriation of earnings and capital investment and repatriation, *see* Paul H. Vishny, Guide To International Commercial Law §§ 5.23, 11.09 (1994).

149 *See* Chapter 6, Section C.6.

3. Binding the State as a party to the contract

Where the investor engages in a project with a State agency or subdivision, the State itself also executes the contract. Without the State's signature, some of the clauses discussed in this chapter may not be effective. For example, if a State agency purports to waive sovereign immunity on behalf of the State, the State may later challenge the authority of the agency to have made such a waiver. Furthermore, enforcement of judgments and awards against State agencies and instrumentalities can prove problematic, since most maintain few assets abroad. By implicating the State directly, the foreign investor does not eliminate the difficulties of enforcement, but at the very least diversifies the options available to achieve satisfaction of an award. **2.103**

In the *Turkmenneft* case,[150] Bridas, an Argentine corporation, signed a series of contracts with Turkmenistan's national gas company to explore and develop natural gas reserves in the Turkmen desert. At the time the project was negotiated, the government in Ashkhabad lent its support in a variety of ways, and many of the clauses in the contract suggested that there would be particular government action or inaction. Disputes later arose, with Turkmenneft accusing Bridas of cost overruns and delays, and the government ultimately ejected the company from the project sites. The foreign investor initiated arbitration proceedings in Houston, Texas, asserting that both the gas company and the Turkmenistan government itself were parties to the contract and subject to the jurisdiction of the arbitrators. The tribunal agreed, finding that although Turkmenistan had not signed the contract, it had implicitly acceded to its terms through a comfort letter and other actions. The arbitrators issued an award in Bridas's favor. **2.104**

Ultimately, however, the Turkmen government moved to set aside the award in the U.S. federal court. After an initial loss at the district court level, it prevailed in the Fifth Circuit Court of Appeals. The Fifth Circuit noted that Turkmenneft was entitled to a "presumption of independent status" and that Bridas had failed to satisfy the burden of proving that Turkmenneft's signature was on behalf of Turkmenistan. The Fifth Circuit also concluded that "a signatory may not estop a non-signatory from avoiding arbitration regardless of how closely affiliated that non-signatory is with another signing party."[151] **2.105**

---

150 *Bridas S.A.P.I.C. v. Government of Turkmenistan [Turkmenneft]*, 345 F.3d 347 (5th Cir. 2003). *See also* Chapter 7, Section B.2 (discussing the *Turkmenneft* case in the context of binding States as parties to investment contracts).

151 *Id.* at 358–60. The arbitration award in SCC Case No. 38-39/1997 ("The Y Contract" and "The X Contract," respectively) (Jurisdictional Award reported at https://sccinstitute.com/media/56056/government_guarantee_case.pdf) provides a contrary example. There, a company owned by the government of Kazakhstan entered into a supply contract with a foreign corporation. The contract included an arbitration clause referring disputes to arbitration under the Stockholm Chamber of Commerce Rules. The government of Kazakhstan issued the foreign party a guarantee. When the State-owned company breached the contract, the foreign company initiated arbitration against it and Kazakhstan. The sole arbitrator held that the government's undertaking was

2.106 The *Bridas* case serves as a useful lesson to both States and investors. To reduce uncertainties and disputes, the parties to a quasi-State contract (*i.e.* one involving a State-owned agency or enterprise) should clearly define the role of the State in the project. If the government as a whole is to answer for the actions of independent agencies, its signature should appear on the contract, provided by a duly authorized representative. If the State is not to be bound by any obligations in the context of the project, then any comfort letters or other expressions of support should set forth the extent of government involvement.

an integral part of the disputed project, and that the government was therefore subject to the arbitration agreement. *See* Christer Söderlund, *The State as a Party in Arbitration and Issues of Sovereign Immunity* at 5, presented on Sept. 17, 2004 in Almaty, Kazakhstan, (discussing SCC Case No. 38-39/1997); 2003(1) Stockholm Arb. Rep. 251 (reviewing the case).

3

INVESTMENT INSURANCE

The purchase of political risk insurance is one of the most direct and simplest steps that an investor can take to reduce exposure to political risk. Political risk insurance is similar in many respects to ordinary business risk insurance. It typically provides coverage against political risks such as currency inconvertibility, expropriation, and political violence.[1] Such insurance is available from a number of sources, including State-sponsored insurance agencies such as the United States' Overseas Private Investment Corporation (OPIC);[2] private insurers such **3.01**

---

[1] Malcolm D. Rowat, *Multilateral Approaches to Improving the Investment Climate of Developing Countries: The Cases of ICSID and MIGA*, 33 Harv. Int'l L.J. 103, 122 (1992).

[2] For an analysis of the various insurance mechanisms provided by political risk insurance State agencies and multilateral organizations, *see* Thomas Nektarios Papanastasiou, The Legal Protection of Foreign Investments against Political Risk: Japanese Business in the Asian Energy Sector, ch. 6 (2015): Political Risk Insurance, the Role of NEXI, and Comparison with MIGA (2015); Jeswald Salacuse, The Three Laws of International Investment: National, Contractual, and International Frameworks for Foreign Capital, 246–73 (2013); Andreas R. Ziegler and Louis-Philippe Gratton, *Investment Insurance*, in The Oxford Handbook of International Investment Law 524–48 (Peter Muchlinski et al. eds. 2008); Other helpful sources include: Gary W. Orloff, *Private Political Risk Insurance for Energy Investors*, in Maclean International Energy Network, Going International Seminar (Dallas, Texas, July 28, 1993); B. Thomas Mansbach, *Financing and Political Risk: Risk Sharing and Project Finance: The Programs of the Overseas Private Investment Corporation, State Bar of Texas Advanced International Law Institute, Investment and Trade with Emerging Economies*, B-1 (Houston, Texas, May 14, 1993); Rowat, *supra* note 1; Klaus P. Berger, *The New Multilateral Investment Guarantee Agency*

as Lloyds of London; and the World Bank's Multilateral Investment Guarantee Agency (MIGA).[3] Almost all major capital-exporting States sponsor political risk insurance agencies, most of which are members of the International Union of Credit and Investment Insurers, otherwise known as the Berne Union.[4] The largest State-sponsored insurance agencies are OPIC, Germany's PwC Deutsche Revision, and Japan's Nippon Export and Investment Insurance (NEXI). Together these agencies represent over 80 percent of all outstanding national political risk coverage.[5]

3.02 This chapter focuses primarily on the MIGA and OPIC insurance schemes. In addition, we discuss other national insurance programs and private insurers that offer political risk insurance.

A. OPIC[6]

1. Background

3.03 OPIC is a self-sustaining U.S. government agency[7] that sells political risk insurance for foreign direct investment (FDI),[8] finances projects directly through

Globalizing the Investment Insurance Approach towards Development, 15 Syr. J. Int'l L. & Com. 13 (1988); Ibrahim F.I. Shihata, *Factors Influencing the Flow of Foreign Investment and the Relevance of a Multilateral Investment Guarantee Scheme*, 21 Int'l L. 671 (1987) [hereinafter, Shihata, *Factors*]; Adeoye Akinsanya, *International Protection of Direct Foreign Investment in the Third World*, 36 ICLQ 58 (1987); Pratap Chatterjee, *The Convention Establishing the Multilateral Guarantee Agency*, 36 ICLQ 76 (1987). H. Zakariye, *Insurance against Political Risks in Oil Development*, 4 J. Energy Nat. Resources & Envt'l L. 217 (1986); Ibrahim F.I. Shihata, *Towards a Greater Depolitization of Investment Disputes: The Role of ICSID and MIGA*, 1 ICSID Rev.—For. Inv. L.J. 1 (1986) [hereinafter, Shihata, *Depolitization*].

[3] For a list of various sources of investment insurance and the role of investment insurance in the Monterey framework, *see* Inaamul Haque & Ruxandra Burdescu, *Monterey Consensus on Financing for Development: Response Sought from International Economic Law*, 27 BC ICLQ 219, 254 (2004).

[4] *See* Shihata, *Depolitization, supra* note 2, at 95; Theodor Meron, Investment Insurance in International Law 47 (1976). The Berne Union was established in 1934, and was originally concerned only with commercial risks in export transactions. After World War II, both State and private political risk insurance companies began to join the Berne Union. For more information on the Berne Union and its history, *see* http://www.berneunion.org.uk and https://www.berneunion.org/Stub/Display/41; a list of political risk insurers that are members of the Berne Union is provided on the Berne Union official web-page: http://www.berneunion.org/Members.

[5] Rowat, *supra* note 1, at 119.

[6] *See* Overseas Private Investment Corporation Act, 22 U.S.C. §§ 2191–2200b (2010). For further discussion of OPIC and investment insurance, *see* Paul H. Vishny, Guide to International Commercial Law §§ 13.13, 13.14 (1994).

[7] Records show that OPIC recorded a net positive income since it commenced operations until at least 2016. Opic Program Handbook 1, available at https://www.opic.gov/who-we-are/faqs (as of Aug. 2018). Between 1971 and 1981, OPIC issued US$8.6 billion of insurance coverage for political risks; between 1981 and 1984, it issued US$12.8 billion of coverage. Akinsanya, *supra* note 2, at 68 (1987).

[8] 22 U.S.C. § 2194(a). In 2011, OPIC had net income in the amount of US$269 million. Since then, it has been reported that OPIC operates "at no net cost to tax-payers"; *see* https://

loans,[9] assists in project financing through loan guarantees,[10] and furnishes a variety of other investor services to U.S. investors. OPIC complements the U.S. Agency for International Development (USAID), which finances projects primarily on a government-to-government basis.[11]

OPIC was established under the Foreign Assistance Act of 1969[12] to take over political risk insurance functions from USAID, due to the latter agency's inability to cope with the volume of requests for political risk insurance, which increased sharply during the 1960s. Pursuant to the terms of its charter, OPIC inherited USAID's insurance portfolio. **3.04**

In the early 1970s, Chile nationalized properties of U.S. investors that had been insured by USAID, and subsequently by OPIC, leading to insurance claims against OPIC in excess of US$360 million. This led to congressional battles regarding the feasibility of government-sponsored political risk insurance, which OPIC barely survived. In the mid-1970s, OPIC settled the Chilean claims, and attempted to transfer its insurance portfolio to private companies. The private sector, however, was unwilling to insure against political risk on the terms offered by OPIC. OPIC was subsequently reauthorized by Congress in 1978, 1981, and 1985.[13] OPIC was nearly eradicated in 1996, when Congress almost failed to reauthorize it. The proponents of OPIC managed to rescue the organization through a tentative compromise that would authorize the agency temporarily, until 1997.[14] Most recently, **3.05**

www.opic.gov/press-releases/2012/opic-records-net-income-269-million-fy2011-helping-reduce-us-budget-deficit-34th.

9 22 U.S.C. §§ 2194(c) and 2195(b). OPIC makes direct loans for new and expanding enterprises, typically ranging from US$2 million to US$30 million. Such loans are usually project-financed loans made on a limited recourse basis, but OPIC also considers more conventional lending techniques. Such loans are made only for projects either sponsored by U.S. small businesses or involving their substantial participation. OPIC also guarantees loans in a slightly larger amount. Furthermore, OPIC is authorized to provide permanent capital through equity investments by purchasing stock. Due to the greater risk of such activity, OPIC is very selective in this program. It should be mentioned that a loan from OPIC or a similar governmental organization may reduce political risk, because many developing States seek to maintain constructive relationships with such entities to preserve opportunities to obtain capital in the future.

10 22 U.S.C. § 2194(b).

11 *See* USAID, USAID History, available at http://www.usaid.gov; Mansbach, *supra* note 2.

12 Foreign Assistance Act of 1969, Pub. L. 91-175, Dec. 30, 1969, 83 Stat. 805; *see also* John S. Diaconis, *Political Risk Insurance: OPIC's Use of a "Fiduciary Agent" to Facilitate Resolution of Subrogation Claims*, 23 Int'l L. 271 (1989).

13 Robert B. Shanks, *Insuring Investment and Loans against Currency Inconvertibility, Expropriation, and Political Violence*, 9 Hastings Int'l & Comp. L. Rev. 417, 421 (1986). *See also* Steven Franklin & Gerald T. West, *The Overseas Private Investment Corporation Amendments Act of 1978: A Reaffirmation of the Developmental Role of Investment Insurance*, 14 Tex. Int'l L.J. 1 (1979) (providing a complete discussion of the origins and background of OPIC).

14 For a discussion of OPIC's historical troubles, *see* Maura B. Perry, *A Model for Efficient Foreign Aid: The Case for Political Risk Insurance Activities of the Overseas Private Investment Corporation*, 36 Va. J. Int'l L. 511 (1996).

in 2003 Congress reauthorized OPIC through September 30, 2007,[15] and since that time, OPIC has been subject to periodic reauthorizations by the Congress. OPIC is an integral part of the political risk insurance market for U.S. businesses.

3.06 OPIC's stated goal is to encourage American overseas private investment in sound business projects, which are seen to improve U.S. global competitiveness, create jobs for U.S. citizens, and increase U.S. exports.[16] OPIC's insurance is backed by the full faith and credit of the U.S. government,[17] as well as by OPIC's own reserves. Its services are available for U.S. investments in over 160 countries and territories.[18] It is managed by a board of fifteen directors, appointed by the President of the United States.[19] OPIC's political risk insurance often operates in conjunction with other programs, such as those of the U.S. Trade Development Agency and the U.S. Export-Import Bank,[20] as well as the World Bank.[21] OPIC may also share insurance risks with private political risk insurers.[22]

3.07 Examples of past OPIC risk insurance contracts include over US$300 million of coverage in connection with power generation plants in the Philippines, US$100 million in insurance in connection with the construction and operation of a 350-mile natural gas pipeline in Colombia, and US$100 million in connection with the development of offshore oil-producing properties off the coast of the Republic of Congo.[23] More recently, OPIC committed to multiple projects to improve infrastructure in many regions around the globe. For example, in 2017, OPIC committed $611.7 million to Sub-Saharan Africa across twenty-two projects.[24] In Asia, OPIC committed a $20 million loan to Water Credit Investment Fund, a social impact investment fund that lends to microfinance institutions and small and medium businesses that enable low-income families

[15] *OPIC Annual Report 2004* (Nov. 2003), at 3, available at https://www.opic.gov/sites/default/files/docs/04_AnnualReport.pdf.

[16] Peter Watson, *Private Sector Investment in Development*, Aspen Institute (July 31, 2004), available at http://www.opic.gov; *see also* Pat K. Chew, *Political Risk in U.S. Investments in China: Chimera of Protection and Predictability?*, 34 Va. J. Int'l L. 615, 669 (1994) (stating that OPIC's purpose is "to promote social and economic growth and friendly developing states, without harming the economic interest of the United States").

[17] 22 U.S.C. §§ 2191, 2197(c).

[18] OPIC Insurance Department homepage, available at https://www.opic.gov/what-we-offer/political-risk-insurance.

[19] 22 U.S.C. § 2193(b).

[20] The Eximbank Export Credit Insurance Program, which is a division of the Export–Import Bank of the United States, provides political and commercial risk insurance for export of goods through its Export Credit Insurance Program. Political risks covered include expropriation, inconvertibility of currency, and political violence. Commercial risks covered include buyer's insolvency or protracted default. *See generally* 12 U.S.C. § 635(a) (2000) *et seq.*

[21] 22 U.S.C. § 2194(a)(2); Mansbach, *supra* note 2, at B-1.

[22] 22 U.S.C. § 2194b(a).

[23] OPIC Annual Report 15 (1994).

[24] OPIC Annual Report 10 (2017), available at: https://www.opic.gov/sites/default/files/files/OPIC-Annual_Report-2017_1.pdf.

(about 4.6 million people) to obtain affordable water and sanitation products and services.[25]

OPIC has committed large sums to the energy sector. For example, in 2017, it extended $2.4 billion through political risk insurance to support projects in the power sector of Africa.[26] Another recent example is the support of Noble Energy (an American company) in developing "Leviathan," an offshore oil and natural gas field about 80 miles off the coast of Israel, by providing $500 million in political risk insurance.[27] **3.08**

According to OPIC, its political risk insurance and financing help U.S. businesses of all sizes invest in scores of emerging markets and developing countries worldwide. Only until 2005, it is estimated that OPIC had supported US$164 billion worth of investments, which in turn helped developing countries to generate more than 732,000 host-country jobs and US$13 billion in government revenues. OPIC projects have also generated US$69 billion in U.S. exports and created more than 264,000 American jobs.[28] **3.09**

2. Risks covered by OPIC insurance

OPIC insures both new projects and expansions of existing enterprises, and can cover equity investments, loans, technical assistance agreements, leases, and any other investment structures that subject the investor to long-term exposure to political risk.[29] **3.10**

The investor may purchase insurance coverage for one or more of the following three types of risks: (1) *currency inconvertibility*, which is the inability to convert profits and other remittances into U.S. dollars; (2) *expropriation*, which is the confiscation of the investor's property by the host State without adequate compensation; (3) *political violence*, which includes war, revolution, insurrection, and civil strife; and (4) loss due to business interruption caused by any of the above risks.[30] In addition, OPIC offers specialized insurance coverage for certain specific types of investments. While an investor may elect one or more of these types of coverage, such election usually must be made when the insurance contract is issued.[31] **3.11**

---

[25] *Id.* at 11.
[26] *Id.* at 14.
[27] *Id.*
[28] OPIC Press Release, Mar. 1, 2005.
[29] For a better understanding of OPIC scope of coverage, *see* Appendix I: OPIC Contact of Insurance. Contract of Guarantee for Equity Investments (October 2018) https://www.miga.org/sites/default/files/2018-10/MIGA%20Equity%20Investments%20Template%20October%202018%20FINAL.pdf.
[30] 22 U.S.C. § 2194(a)(1).
[31] Mansbach, *supra* note 2, at B-4.

3.12 OPIC may refuse to insure claims that it believes to be too risky, or may require the investor to alter various terms of the transaction to control such risks before OPIC will offer insurance.[32]

a. Currency inconvertibility

3.13 Currency inconvertibility insurance coverage compensates investors if they cannot convert currency from the local currency into U.S. dollars and transfer those remittances outside of the host country.[33] Covered transfers include earnings, returns on capital investments, loan principal and interest payments, technical assistance fees, and other amounts received in relation to investment projects. This coverage also extends to losses the investor suffers as a result of discriminatory exchange rates[34] and exchange control authorities' failure to act upon an application to obtain foreign currency.[35] To obtain OPIC insurance for currency convertibility, the investor must first demonstrate to OPIC that it has a legal right under host-country law as it stands to convert local currency into U.S. currency. OPIC will then insure the investor against the abrogation of this right. If a claim is made by an investor for currency inconvertibility, OPIC will not pay until the investor has waited for a certain period of time, usually sixty days, to permit the host State to comply with the applicant's request to obtain foreign currency.

3.14 If an investor makes a valid claim to OPIC for currency inconvertibility, OPIC pays the claim by "buying" the local currency from the affected business at prevailing exchange rates and "selling" the currency to the U.S. Embassy in the country for use in covering local operating expenses. The embassy then credits OPIC's account for the amount provided.[36] This ability to recoup payouts to beneficiaries of currency inconvertibility policies gives OPIC a major advantage over private insurers.[37]

3.15 It should be noted that OPIC currency inconvertibility coverage does not extend to losses suffered as a result of devaluation of a country's currency.[38] In addition, as noted, the beneficiary may only collect benefits under a currency inconvertibility

---

[32] OPIC makes investors aware of this in its program handbook, OPIC PROGRAM HANDBOOK, *supra* note 7; *see also* OPIC Country List, available at https://www.opic.gov/doing-business-us/OPIC-policies/where-we-operate; Shanks, *supra* note 13, at 428.

[33] 22 U.S.C. § 2194(a)(1)(A); OPIC PROGRAM HANDBOOK, *supra* note 7, at 18.

[34] Diaconis, *supra* note 12, at Part II.

[35] OPIC PROGRAM HANDBOOK, *supra* note 7, at 18.

[36] Shanks, *supra* note 13, at 426–28. This arrangement allows OPIC to circumvent the local country's central banking system. OPIC's risk is that the currency will devaluate before it can be used by the appropriate U.S. government entity. In cases where this risk is high, OPIC is authorized to enter into swap agreements on commercial terms (*id.*); Mark R. Yzaguire, *Project Finance and Privatization: The Bolivian Experience*, 20 HOUS. J. INT'L L. 597, 616–19 (1998); Perry, *supra* note 14, at 554; Ana-Mita Betancourt, *OPIC Political Risk Insurance for Infrastructure Projects in Emerging Markets*, in PROJECT FINANCING IN EMERGING MARKETS 179, 183–84 (1996).

[37] Shanks, *supra* note 13, at 426–28.

[38] OPIC PROGRAM HANDBOOK, *supra* note 7, at 18.

insurance policy if the currency was convertible into U.S. dollars at the time the insurance was issued.[39]

Investors should keep in mind that OPIC does not automatically approve claims for coverage of currency inconvertibility based upon the implementation of regulations that have the effect of restricting convertibility. This is illustrated by the *First Trust of New York* coverage claim, brought in connection with the restrictions imposed in 2002 on convertibility of the Argentine peso.[40] There, the claimant was denied coverage, because it was unable to prove that it had made a sufficient effort to actually convert the Argentine peso into U.S. dollars. Nor had First Trust in fact deposited the pesos into an Inconvertibility Account. Thus, a claim for inconvertibility cannot merely rely on the generally known facts surrounding a currency crisis. In the words of the arbitral award denying coverage: 3.16

> [t]he OPIC insurance contract provides that local currency is deemed inconvertible if the foreign enterprise ... is unable to legally convert Local Currency into U.S. dollars or to transfer U.S. dollars to the U.S. Further, the OPIC insurance contract provides that no compensation is payable if the Insured has not made all reasonable efforts to convert Local Currency and transfer to the United States U.S. dollars or cause the Foreign Enterprise to do so. Accordingly, in order for the Argentine Peso to be deemed inconvertible, the Insured ... using reasonable efforts, must not have been able convert Local Currency into U.S. dollars or to transfer U.S. dollars out of Argentina to the United States between January 25, 2002 and July 25, 2002. OPIC would only be obligated to pay compensation under the OPIC Insurance Contract if such reasonable efforts failed.[41]

b. Expropriation

Expropriation insurance protects against the nationalization, confiscation, or expropriation of an enterprise,[42] as well as against creeping expropriation,[43] which OPIC defines as a series of illegal government actions that cumulatively deprive an investor of the financial benefit of his investment.[44] With limited exceptions, however, OPIC's standard contract does not permit claims from investors to recover only part of the value of their investment due to creeping or indirect expropriation. As a result, an investor must be willing to surrender whatever is left of its ownership (and residual value) of the investment.[45] 3.17

---

[39] *Id.*

[40] *OPIC Memorandum of Determination in the Inconvertibility Claim of First Trust of New York, National Association*, Argentina—Contract of Ins. No. F181, available at https://www.opic.gov/sites/default/files/docs/TGNclaim2002.pdf.

[41] *Id.* at 5.

[42] 22 U.S.C. § 2194(a)(1)(B).

[43] For further discussion, *see* Chapter 1, Section C and Chapter 5, Section B.3.

[44] For OPIC's definition of expropriation, see arts. 4(01) and 4(02) of OPIC's Contract of Insurance, Form 234 KGT 12-85 (revised R/2003) NS, reprinted in Appendix I.

[45] Shanks, *supra* note 13, at 422–26; *see also* David A. Gantz, *Symposium: Global Trade Issues in the New Millennium: Potential Conflicts between Investor Rights and Environmental Regulation under*

3.18 An investor may also obtain coverage against the failure of the host State to perform specific obligations which the parties identify at the outset of the project as vital to the project's success. Such coverage is offered on a case-by-case basis.[46]

3.19 For equity investments, the amount of compensation to which the equity holder is entitled under OPIC expropriation insurance is based on the book value of the investment as of the date of expropriation. Where the asset expropriated is a loan, payment is based on outstanding principal and accrued interest.[47] In order to receive payment from OPIC, the expropriation must continue for at least six months, and must violate international law or constitute a material breach of local laws.[48]

3.20 OPIC expropriation insurance does not normally cover losses due to generally applicable regulation or taxation by host governments or actions provoked or instigated by the investor.[49]

3.21 Most of OPIC's coverage determinations have concerned questions of expropriation. The *Marine Insurance Corporation* claim for coverage in the wake of the confiscation of MIC's property by the Egyptian government is an illustrative example of a case in which coverage was denied.[50] To obtain compensation from OPIC, MIC had to prove that (1) the activity was attributable to a foreign government, (2) there was a breach of international law, or material breaches of municipal law, and (3) the acts on which the claim is based had the effect of confiscation by directly depriving MIC of the right to use, control, or dispose of covered property. OPIC denied MIC's claim, finding the last two elements to be lacking.

3.22 MIC argued first that harassment by local government-employed stevedores constituted expropriation. OPIC quickly rejected this position:

> Nothing [MIC] has submitted demonstrates that these entities acted in bad faith or in violation of their contractual commitments to [MIC]. Even assuming that this had occurred, a state does not commit a violation of international law by engaging in commercial actions of this character. That is especially true when the state affords the foreign national a dispute settlement procedure … [MIC] filed actions, and later at least one appeal, in Egyptian courts regarding some of these matters, and it appears that judgments were found in favor of the GOE entities. There has been no claim that [MIC] suffered a denial of justice in the proceedings in Egyptians courts.

NAFTA's Chapter 11, 33 Geo. Wash. Int'l L. Rev. 651, 721–23 (2001) (discussing *In Re. Revere Copper and Brass Inc. and Overseas Private Investment Corp.*, 17 I.L.M. 1321 (1978)).

46 OPIC Program Handbook, *supra* note 7, at 18–19.

47 *Id.*

48 OPIC Contract of Insurance, *supra* note 44, art. 4(1) (second revision).

49 OPIC Program Handbook *supra* note 7, at 18–19.

50 *OPIC Memorandum of Determination in the Confiscation Claim of Marine Shipping Corp., Egypt—Contract of Ins. No. C015*, available at https://www.opic.gov/sites/default/files/docs/claim_marine_shipping.pdf.

> Accordingly, there is no basis for concluding that the alleged instances of harassment constituted violations of international or local law.[51]

Alternatively, MIC presented a creeping expropriation claim. According to MIC, the port authority had demanded excess rent of US$88,000, and had otherwise made it impossible for MIC to conduct its business.[52] The adjudicator noted that the investment treaty between the United States and Egypt probably protected MIC against the kind of fees the port authority had imposed.[53] Moreover, it continued, there was a neutral arbitral tribunal available to which MIC could have presented its claim.[54] As MIC had not initiated arbitration under the treaty, it had not properly exhausted available remedies, and international law had not been violated. Other problems that would have prevented MIC from recovering on its expropriation policy in any event included a lack of evidence of the compensation amount claimed, MIC's contribution to the loss by failing to pay Egyptian taxes, and the company's insufficient record keeping.[55] **3.23**

The OPIC determination in the *Citibank N.A.* case, concerning investments in Sudan, was more favorable to the insured.[56] Citibank sought coverage in relation to Sudan's banking regulations.[57] Citibank had complied with Sudan's banking statutes, which were based on Islamic law. After the United States imposed political sanctions on Sudan, the Sudanese Central Bank approved Citibank's request to transfer certain proceeds to the United States, but imposed a fine of 1.5 times the repatriated amount for allegedly illegal transactions under Islamic law.[58] The Central Bank then seized the amount of the fine. **3.24**

Here, in contrast to the *MIC* decision, OPIC found that Citibank had exhausted local remedies in Sudan before filing its insurance claim.[59] Furthermore, the Central Bank's explicit reasoning for its seizure of Citibank assets left no doubt that Sudan had taken action against Citibank in political retaliation against the United States, in contravention of international law. The Sudanese action was also found to be in violation of international law because of its arbitrary nature: the Sudanese government had not taken similar steps in previous years,[60] court decisions were inconsistent,[61] the grounds for the seizure were not found in **3.25**

[51] *Id.*
[52] *Id.*
[53] *Id.*
[54] *Id.*
[55] *Id.*
[56] *OPIC Memorandum of Determination in the Expropriation Claim of Citibank N.A., Sudan—Contract of Ins. No. X002 and Annex XC796*, available at https://www.opic.gov/sites/default/files/docs/citibankclaim2000.pdf.
[57] *Id.*
[58] *Id.*
[59] *Id.* at 10.
[60] *Id.* at 11.
[61] *Id.*

any previous legal documents relating to the Central Bank,[62] and Citibank was not granted access to any appellate body to plead its case.[63]

c. Political violence

3.26 Political violence insurance offers compensation for damage to property or lost income caused by various forms of unrest and aggression.[64] Types of violence covered include declared war, undeclared war, hostile actions by national or international forces, civil war, revolution, insurrection, and civil strife. Civil strife may be included or excluded from coverage, at the investor's option. Actions undertaken primarily to achieve labor or student rights objectives are not normally covered under OPIC policies.[65] When deciding whether to insure an investor against political violence, OPIC examines both the conditions in the host country and the specific conditions affecting the project in particular.[66] Robert B. Shanks, then-Vice President and General Counsel of OPIC, provided an example of how this works:

> For example, if OPIC were asked to insure an oil pipeline, its staff would begin by examining the country in which the pipeline was to be built. More specifically, OPIC would look at the region of the country, the level of political violence that had taken place there historically, and the potential for friction among various political, religious, and socio-economic groups. It would look to such variables as the existence in the area of active guerilla groups, the government's ability to control violence, and the level of police or military presence. OPIC might also examine the topography around the project to determine whether troop movement or guerilla attacks would be relatively easy or relatively more difficult to negotiate. OPIC would also study the characteristics of the project itself. For example, would the pipeline be buried or built on the surface and, if buried, how deep? OPIC would then consider the pumping stations and assess the redundancy of capacity among the stations. In other words, if one station were damaged, OPIC would want to know the economic effect on the project in terms of reduced oil flow. Finally, OPIC would want to know what provisions the company has made for repair. It might well require as a condition of insurance, that the company maintain a spare parts inventory at a certain level, or even maintain an entire pumping station in parts that could be transported quickly by helicopter to replace a damaged station and avoid costly down time.[67]

3.27 After examining such factors, OPIC makes a determination of whether or not to offer political violence insurance for a project, and at what rate.

3.28 OPIC political violence insurance will pay for two types of losses: business income loss or asset damage. The investor may purchase insurance for either one or

62 *Id.* at 12.
63 *Id.*
64 22 U.S.C. § 2194(a)(1)(C).
65 OPIC Program Handbook, *supra* note 7, at 19.
66 Shanks, *supra* note 13, at 428–29.
67 *Id.*

both. With regard to business income loss, compensation is based on expected net income plus continuing normal operating expenses that must be paid during the time the damage is being repaired. OPIC will also pay for expenses that reduce the business income loss, such as renting a temporary facility. Compensation is paid until productive capacity is restored, for a period up to one year. With the addition of an "off-site" rider, OPIC will compensate for income losses that result from damage to specific sites outside the investor's facility.[68] Asset coverage compensates for loss of or damage to tangible property caused by political violence. Compensation is based on the adjusted cost of the property or replacement cost. Adjusted cost is defined as the least of (1) the original cost of the item, (2) the fair market value of the item at the time of loss, or (3) the cost to repair the item. OPIC will pay replacement cost up to twice the equipment's original cost, provided the item is actually replaced within three years.[69]

A pertinent example is the political violence claim of *Tea Importers Inc. and C.W. Trading Co. Inc., Rwanda*.[70] There, OPIC determined that the claimant had suffered a loss due to political violence covered by the insurance policy. The determination is particularly important, as it recognizes a state of civil strife as sufficiently violent to trigger coverage under the insurance policy. The OPIC adjudicator concluded: "Political violence continued at the time of the Loss, if not at the level of an active civil war, then at the level of civil strife in the form of reprisals for earlier acts of violence and intimidation of Hutus by Tutsis."[71] **3.29**

The *Tea Importers* case further demonstrates that OPIC may take a rather permissive view of causation in political violence cases. The memorandum describes well the somewhat attenuated connection between the Rwandan civil war and the loss of the investor's property: **3.30**

> OPIC finds that direct causation is established. As discussed, the fighting between the RPF and the government constitutes at least civil strife. The Rwandan government did not requisition the … car [in question] independently of the civil strife. According to the investor, the manager heard that he was going to be accused of participating in the ethnic killings. Like others threatened with arrest in the prevailing conditions, he had little prospect of a fair trial or humane pretrial detention and fled the country. The Rwandan authorities confiscated the vehicle because it had been used to enable a person accused of a political violence-related act to escape the

---

68 OPIC Program Handbook, *supra* note 7, at 19.

69 *Id.*

70 *OPIC Memorandum of Determination in the Political Violence Claim of Tea Importers Inc. and C.W. Trading Co. Inc., Rwanda—Contract of Ins. Nos. 9890, 9891, and 9969*, available at https://www.opic.gov/sites/default/files/docs/teaimporters.pdf. Another interesting case involving this type of coverage deals with the problem of political violence in Afghanistan. *OPIC Memorandum of Determinations in the Political Violence Claim of Shelter for Life Int'l Inc., Afghanistan—Contract of Ins. No. F.377*, available at https://www.opic.gov/sites/default/files/docs/Shelter-for-Life-March_5_2004.pdf.

71 *Id., Contract of Ins. Nos. 9890, 9891, and* 9969, at 4.

Country. Clearly the Loss would not have occurred but for the conditions of political violence that existed.[72]

d. Stand-alone terrorism insurance

3.31 Since 2003, OPIC has offered stand-alone terrorism insurance to protect U.S. businesses overseas.[73] This type of policy is available for equity or property investments, and covers losses sustained as a result of politically motivated violence, so long as the perpetrators are not national or international armed forces. It is reflective of the twenty-first-century perception of risk that the policy also compensates for losses arising out of the use of weapons of mass destruction (chemical, biological, radiological, or other similar weapons).[74] This is an area in which the original political role of OPIC again comes to the fore. The terrorism coverage was a direct result of the September 11, 2001 terrorist attacks in the United States and responds to the need to offer U.S. companies a means for insuring against the new and potentially hostile work environment that the heightened terror threat level entails.[75]

e. Arbitration award default coverage

3.32 As explained in detail elsewhere in this book, international arbitration is the most common form of dispute resolution used by investors to mitigate the effects of certain kinds of political risk, including the breach of State contracts, expropriation, and other host-State measures. International treaties facilitate the enforcement of international arbitration awards across borders, allowing judgment creditors to seek out and ultimately seize the losing side's assets in most corners of the world. As a result, most international arbitration awards are satisfied voluntarily.[76] Nevertheless, there is some risk that an aggrieved investor will prevail in arbitration only to face recalcitrance on the part of the respondent, and will have difficulty locating attachable assets out of which the award can be forcibly satisfied. This risk is particularly acute in cases involving State parties, which often

---

[72] *Id.*

[73] OPIC Press Release, July 31, 2003.

[74] *Id.* at 10 ("Coverage includes protection against the use of chemical, biological, radiological or other weapons of mass destruction"). Strangely enough, this formulation could lead to coverage problems in the event of a loss due to nuclear attack. While it might be covered by the catch-all provision "other weapons of mass destruction," it is problematic that such an obvious weapon is not listed expressly. This might be due to the reluctance of a government agency to admit that a non-governmental faction may get a hold of such a weapon. While a *contra proferentem* reading of the contract should mandate coverage for a nuclear attack, this reading is not the only reasonable interpretation.

[75] For a more thorough discussion of trade policy after the Sept. 11, 2001 terrorist attacks, including a short discussion of OPIC's role in counter-terrorism strategies, *see* Elizabeth Pietanza, *Comment: Winning the Risky Global Business Game: Parrying the Thrusts from Terrorism with an International Insurance Coalition*, 34 Cal. W. Int'l L.J. 85 (2003).

[76] Alan Redfern & Martin Hunter, Law and Practice of International Commercial Arbitration 443 (3d ed. 1999) (statistics imply that most awards are carried out voluntarily).

have relatively few assets outside their borders, and may in any event enjoy substantial sovereign immunity from attachment.

Arbitration Award Default (AAD) insurance is a relatively recent form of political risk coverage designed to address this rather narrow aspect of political risk, which has been offered by OPIC and a number of private insurers since the late 1990s. In the *Patuha* and *Himpurna* arbitrations against Indonesia, for example, the projects in question benefited from OPIC political risk insurance that included the risk of default on an eventual arbitration award.[77] Under such a policy, the insurer will pay the beneficiary all or part of an arbitration award obtained in relation to a qualifying investment project, if it becomes clear that the respondent will not voluntarily comply with its terms. **3.33**

It should be noted that even without specific AAD coverage, a State's refusal to honor a validly rendered international arbitration award may constitute a violation of international law, triggering OPIC's more general expropriation policy.[78] **3.34**

f. Specialized insurance

OPIC has also developed specialized forms of insurance coverage for a range of industries and investment types, including financial institutions, leasing, oil and gas, natural resources, and contractors and exporters. **3.35**

OPIC offers coverage to financial institutions for project loans, gold loans, commercial paper transactions, or floating rate notes purchased by certain institutions, cross border leases, debt-for-equity investments, and commodity price swaps.[79] With regard to loans, currency inconvertibility insurance covers defaults in scheduled payments resulting from the debtor's inability to convert the payments into U.S. dollars or the inability to transfer the payments outside the host country. Expropriation and political violence insurance covers defaults in payment directly related to these events.[80] **3.36**

OPIC's insurance of leases is similar to its insurance for loans. OPIC can insure both capital and operating leases. Currency inconvertibility insurance covers defaults in lease payments resulting from the debtor's inability to convert the **3.37**

---

77 *See* Mark Kantor, *International Project Finance and Arbitration with Public Sector Entities: When Is Arbitrability a Fiction?*, 24 Fordham Int'l L.J. 1122, 1132 n.30 (2001).

78 *See* U.S. Restatement (Third) of Foreign Relations Law, § 712 cmt. h ("a state may be responsible ... if, having committed itself to a special forum for dispute resolution, such as arbitration, it fails to honor such commitment; or if it fails to carry out a judgment or award rendered by ... such special forum"). *See also* Kantor, *supra* note 77, at 1132 n.30 (OPIC referred to the violation of international law under an expropriation policy as foundation for the *Himpurna* insurance claims in addition to AAD coverage).

79 OPIC Program Handbook, *supra* note 7, at 21–22.

80 *Id.*

payments into U.S. dollars, or the inability to transfer the payments outside the host country. Expropriation and political violence insurance cover defaults directly related to these events.[81]

3.38 Governmental political risk insurers such as OPIC also offer specialized oil and gas policies to encourage hydrocarbon exploration, development, and production in developing countries. An investor may choose between two types of coverage: exploration coverage and interference with operations coverage.

3.39 Exploration coverage expands expropriation coverage to insure against losses due to material changes that the host State unilaterally imposes upon project agreements. This includes the abrogation, impairment, repudiation, or breach of concession agreements, production sharing agreements, service contracts, risk contracts, and other agreements between the U.S. company and the host State. To trigger coverage under an exploration policy, such actions must last for at least six months, and prevent the insured from effectively exercising its fundamental rights with respect to the project agreement, such as the right to take and export petroleum or to be paid for it. Coverage also provides compensation for confiscated tangible assets and bank accounts.[82]

3.40 Interference with operations coverage expands political violence coverage to insure against the cessation of operations for six months or more as a result of political violence. Compensation for this sort of business interruption is based on the amount of investment made, less return of capital. Compensation must be repaid to OPIC, without interest, if within five years the political violence has abated and the insured can resume operations.[83]

3.41 In addition, OPIC offers insurance tailored to the energy investor's form of business. For example, if the investor has a service contract with the State, OPIC can insure against seizure of the insured's equipment and bank accounts, or against the State's refusal to allow the repatriation of equipment that the investor has brought into the country to perform the service contract.[84]

3.42 OPIC also offers specialized insurance for natural resources projects outside the oil and gas sector. In addition to insurance for confiscation and political violence, the investor can insure against breach by the host State of mineral exploration contracts and development rights, as well as against the deprivation of other rights vital to the success of the project.[85]

---

81 *Id.* at 22.
82 *Id.* at 23.
83 *Id.*
84 *Id.*; Mansbach, *supra* note 2, at B-5.
85 OPIC Program Handbook, *supra* note 7, at 23.

g. Contractors and exporters

For contractors and exporters, OPIC offers insurance covering the wrongful calling of bid, performance, or advance payment guarantees, custom bonds, or other guarantees; the loss of physical assets and bank accounts due to confiscation or political violence, and inconvertibility of proceeds from the sale of equipment used at the site; and losses due to unresolved contractual disputes with a foreign buyer. This coverage protects contractors in international construction, sales, and service contracts, as well as the exporters of goods.[86] **3.43**

3. Eligibility for OPIC insurance

OPIC political risk insurance may only be issued if the investor, the country that is the situs of the investment, and the investment itself meet OPIC's requirements. In addition, OPIC will take certain political criteria into account when deciding whether to offer insurance coverage. **3.44**

a. Eligible investors

To be eligible for OPIC insurance, an investor must be either a U.S. citizen; a corporation, partnership, or other association organized under the laws of the United States, its States, or territories, which is beneficially owned by U.S. citizens; or a foreign business at least 95 percent owned by U.S. citizens, by associations owned by U.S. citizens, or other foreign entities that are 100 percent U.S.-owned.[87] **3.45**

With regard to the beneficial ownership of corporations, OPIC considers a corporation organized under the laws of the United States or its States or territories to be beneficially owned by U.S. citizens if more than 50 percent of each class of its issued and outstanding stock is owned either directly or beneficially by U.S. citizens. Where shares of stock in a corporation with widely dispersed public ownership are held in the names of trustees or nominees (including stock brokerage firms) with addresses in the United States, such shares may be deemed to be owned by U.S. citizens, unless the investor has knowledge to the contrary. OPIC also permits the determination of U.S. beneficial ownership by tracing shareholdings through foreign corporate holders to the ultimate beneficial owners.[88] **3.46**

---

[86] *Id.* at 24.

[87] 22 U.S.C. § 2198(c); OPIC PROGRAM HANDBOOK, *supra* note 7, at 17. The maximum contingent insurance liability that OPIC may have outstanding to any one investor is 15 percent. 22 U.S.C. § 2194(a).

[88] OPIC PROGRAM HANDBOOK, *supra* note 7, at 17.

b. Eligible projects

3.47 Investments take many forms, including conventional equity investments and loans, construction and service contracts, production sharing agreements, leases, and various contractual arrangements such as consigned inventory, licensing, and franchising, and technical assistance agreements.[89] However, an investment project will qualify for OPIC insurance coverage only if the investment is (1) a new investment, (2) the result of a privatization process, or (3) an expansion or modernization of an existing plant or investment.[90] Acquisitions of existing operations will be eligible for coverage only if the investor contributes additional capital for modernization or expansion.

3.48 There is no requirement that a foreign enterprise targeted by the investor be itself owned or controlled by U.S. investors. Insurance is normally not available, however, for investments in enterprises that are majority-owned and controlled by a foreign government.[91] In addition, in the case of a project with foreign ownership, OPIC will insure only the portion of the investment made by U.S. investors.[92] Thus, investment vehicles owned by nationals of more than one State will not be able to rely on OPIC insurance to insure the full value of their investment. Such investors should consider MIGA or private insurance, or co-insurance.

3.49 Finally, for an investment project to be eligible for OPIC insurance, the investor must submit a Request for Registration for Political Risk Investment Insurance before the investment is made or irrevocably committed.[93]

c. Eligible countries

3.50 OPIC may not offer insurance for a project that is located in a country with which the United States has not entered into an OPIC bilateral investment agreement.[94] These treaties provide, among other things, that the host State must approve OPIC-insured projects, that OPIC will be subrogated to the rights of the insured in the event it pays out on a claim, that OPIC can dispose of local currency through U.S. government channels in the host country, and that disputes between OPIC and the host State, if not resolved through negotiation, will be subject to international arbitration.

3.51 As of August 2018, OPIC programs are available in more than 160 developing and post-conflict countries.[95] Investors should contact OPIC to determine the

[89] *Id.* at 5.
[90] 22 U.S.C. § 2191.
[91] OPIC Program Handbook, *supra* note 7, at 4.
[92] 22 U.S.C. § 2194(a)(2).
[93] *See* Applying for Insurance, available at https://www.opic.gov/what-we-offer/financial-products/apply, for specific instructions on registration and downloads of requisite forms.
[94] 22 U.S.C. § 2197(a).
[95] For a list of eligible states, *see*: https://www.opic.gov/doing-business-us/OPIC-policies/where-we-operate.

status of OPIC assistance in a particular country, or to obtain a current list of countries for which insurance is available.

d. Political considerations

OPIC, like most political risk insurers, is somewhat selective in its offer of coverage. OPIC is required by U.S. law to support projects that contribute to the developmental needs and improve the environmental conditions of the host country, as well as those that foster private initiative and competition on a local level.[96] Factors OPIC examines when deciding whether to provide coverage include whether the project will lead to an increased availability of goods and services at reduced cost in the host country; whether the project will lead to technology transfer or the development of local workers' skills; and whether the project will stimulate other local enterprises.[97] In particular, OPIC must give preferential treatment to investments in countries with a per capita income of less than $984 per annum in 1986 U.S. dollars.[98] OPIC discourages monopolistic practices and projects involving anticompetitive advantages, and may require additional scrutiny and special justification before becoming involved.[99] **3.52**

OPIC also examines the potential adverse effects projects may have on the local environment. In particular, OPIC looks to the effects on tropical forests, national parks, endangered species, and the health and safety of the public.[100] OPIC encourages investors to submit environmental assessments as early in the insurance application process as possible so as not to delay OPIC's coverage decision.[101] **3.53**

Nor may OPIC support projects that undermine internationally recognized "workers rights."[102] In fact, OPIC contracts require investors to respect worker's rights, including collective bargaining.[103] **3.54**

OPIC will also closely examine the effect a proposed foreign investment will have on the U.S. economy. Coverage will be denied to projects that are likely to have a "negative impact" on U.S. employment or trade.[104] For example, OPIC will not support what it refers to as a "runaway plant," which refers to the substitution of an existing U.S. facility with a foreign one to produce the same goods for the same markets.[105] OPIC may also decline coverage to projects that are likely to have an **3.55**

[96] OPIC PROGRAM HANDBOOK, *supra* note 7, at 5–6; OPIC DEVELOPMENT UPDATE: EXPANDING OPIC's DEVELOPMENT IMPACT ASSESSMENT (2003), available at http://www.opic.gov.
[97] 22 U.S.C. § 2191; OPIC DEVELOPMENT UPDATE, *supra* note 96, at 14–15.
[98] 22 U.S.C. § 2191(2).
[99] OPIC PROGRAM HANDBOOK, *supra* note 7, at 6.
[100] 22 U.S.C. § 2191(n); OPIC PROGRAM HANDBOOK, *supra* note 7, at 7.
[101] *Id.*
[102] 22 U.S.C. § 2191a(a)(1); OPIC PROGRAM HANDBOOK, *supra* note 7, at 8.
[103] *Id.*
[104] 22 U.S.C. § 2191(m); OPIC PROGRAM HANDBOOK, *supra* note 7, at 7.
[105] 22 U.S.C. §§ 2191(k), 2191(l); OPIC PROGRAM HANDBOOK, *supra* note 7, at 7.

adverse effect on the U.S. balance of payments.[106] It should be noted that private insurers typically do not qualify or limit insurance coverage availability based on this sort of political considerations.[107]

4. Terms

a. Duration

3.56 The term of an OPIC insurance policy may extend a maximum of twenty years.[108] For loans, leases, and transactions covered by the contractors and exporters program, the coverage term is generally equal to the duration of the underlying contract. While the insured may terminate the insurance contract at will, OPIC may only terminate the contract for very limited reasons, which are specified in the contract.[109]

b. Cost

3.57 OPIC insurance premiums are based on rate schedules[110] determined by reference to the type of investment and the types of coverage sought.[111] Premiums may vary based on the risk profile of the particular project, but usually not by more than one-third.

3.58 Coverage elections for most equity and shareholder debt investments are based on what OPIC designates "coverage ceilings" and "active amounts." A "coverage ceiling" is the maximum amount of insurance available for a project during the life of the project, while the "active amount" is the amount of insurance currently in force during a particular contract period. There is no charge for the difference between the "coverage ceiling" and the "active amount."[112]

3.59 Coverage elections for other investment types, such as technical assistance contracts, are based on a "maximum insured amount," a "current insured amount," and a "standby amount." The "maximum insured amount" and "current insured amount" are similar to the "coverage ceiling" and "active amount." The difference between the two is the "standby amount," for which there is a charge.[113]

3.60 Investors interested in OPIC insurance should contact OPIC for current rates. The OPIC Handbook provides examples of tables showing the standard insurance

---

106 *Id.*

107 *See* Section D, *infra.*

108 22 U.S.C. § 2197(E); terrorism coverage extends for a maximum of only ten years. OPIC Program Handbook, *supra* note 7, at 20.

109 Mansbach, *supra* note 2, at B-4.

110 22 U.S.C. § 2197(d).

111 Orloff, *supra* note 2, at 7.

112 *See* OPIC's product description of its available insurances at https://www.opic.gov/what-we-offer/political-risk-insurance/details-cost.

113 *Id.*

premiums for manufacturing services, institutional loans and leases, oil and gas, infrastructure/natural resources, contractors and exporters, and capital markets.[114]

c. Insurance limits

OPIC will only insure and pay claims covering 90 percent of a loss, and requires that investors bear the risk of loss for the remaining 10 percent.[115] The only exception to this requirement is for loans and leases from financial institutions to unrelated third parties, which may be insured for 100 percent of principal and interest.[116] **3.61**

d. Coverage multiples and amount of insurance

OPIC typically issues insurance commitments equal to 270 percent of the initial investment—90 percent representing the original investment and 180 percent to cover future earnings. The maximum amount of coverage available for any one project is US$100 million. Coverage amounts may be limited for investments in countries where OPIC has a high portfolio concentration and for highly sensitive projects.[117] **3.62**

e. Application

The OPIC insurance program has a two-step application process. As noted, investors are first required to register projects with OPIC, and this before the investment has been made or irrevocably committed.[118] Registration is free of charge and is treated as privileged business information by OPIC. Registration does not commit the registrant to make any investment, nor does it obligate OPIC to sell any insurance to the registrant.[119] Upon receipt of the Request for Registration, OPIC will send a confirmation letter and application forms. Registration, once granted, is valid for two years. **3.63**

Once the final form of an investment is determined, the investor must submit an Application for Political Risk Investment Insurance. This application provides OPIC with the detailed information necessary to determine a project's eligibility and underwriting risks. **3.64**

Investors should be careful to avoid omissions and misstatements during the application process. The law of most jurisdictions requires that prospective insured persons and entities accurately and completely disclose all information material to the insurance contract; failure to do so can render an insurance contract void *ab* **3.65**

[114] *See* OPIC Program Handbook, *supra* note 7, at 29–30.
[115] 22 U.S.C. § 2197(f).
[116] OPIC Program Handbook, *supra* note 7, at 28.
[117] *Id.*
[118] *See* Applying for Insurance, available at https://www.opic.gov/what-we-offer/political-risk-insurance/register, for specific instructions on registration and downloads of requisite forms.
[119] *See id.*; Mansbach, *supra* note 2, at B-4.

initio.[120] Although materiality is often defined by statute, under the common law, a material fact is one that induces the insurer to take an action that it might not otherwise have taken.[121] It is advisable for an investor to seek advice from experienced counsel when completing an OPIC application for insurance.

B. Other National Insurance Programs

3.66 Most capital-exporting State governments, and some in the developing world, have established national investment insurance agencies similar to OPIC.[122] All national programs require that the investor have a relationship with the sponsoring country to obtain coverage.[123] Most programs are limited to new investments, although some are not restricted to private sector projects.[124] Most programs offered by industrialized countries also require that the project fulfill certain policy objectives of the sponsoring State.[125]

3.67 Most national programs also offer long-term coverage, usually at least fifteen to twenty years,[126] and, with the exception of OPIC, concentrate coverage in regions where they have special interests. For example, in 1989, "Asia accounted for over 80% of the Japanese [investment insurance] program."[127]

1. Japan: NEXI

3.68 The Japanese trade and investment insurance system was established in 1950 to support Japanese foreign trade by reducing risks inherent in overseas transactions, such as war and currency controls. The system was managed from 1950 to 2001 by the Export-Import Insurance Division (EID) of Japan's Ministry of Economy, Trade and Industry (METI), formerly the Ministry of International Trade and Industry. In April 2001, Nippon Export and Investment Insurance (NEXI) was established as an independent administrative institution to manage Japan's trade and investment insurance system, with METI as its "competent minister." The Japanese government, through METI, provides NEXI's capital and reinsures insurance agreements underwritten by NEXI.[128] In 2017 NEXI was restructured

[120] S. Linn Williams, *Political and Other Risk Insurance: OPIC, MIGA, EximBank and Other Providers*, 5 Pace Int'l LR 59, 103–05 (1993).
[121] *Id.*
[122] *Id.* at 94; *see also* Akinsanya, *supra* note 2.
[123] Rowat, *supra* note 1, at 120.
[124] Williams, *supra* note 120, at 95.
[125] *Id.* at 96.
[126] *Id.*
[127] *Id.*
[128] The discussion in this section is based on information supplied by NEXI, available at http://www.nexi.go.jp; for an analysis of NEXI-specific insurance instruments provided for Japanese overseas power investments, *see also* Papanastasiou, *supra* note 2, at 145–62.

as a government-owned special stock company.[129] NEXI often operates in parallel with the lending and guarantee facilities of the Japan Bank for International Cooperation (JBIC) and with the development programmes of the Japan Investment and Cooperation Agency (JICA).[130]

NEXI's stated mission is to help to promote Japanese trade and investment by mitigating the risks in exports and overseas investments that cannot be covered by ordinary insurance. NEXI offers overseas investment insurance, as well as other insurance products, including: export credit insurance; short-term trade insurance for manufacturers; overseas untied loan insurance; export bill insurance; and prepayment import insurance.[131] **3.69**

Over the past decades, the total insured amount and amount of claims paid covers about 20 percent of total Japanese exports. **3.70**

a. Overseas investment insurance

NEXI's Overseas Investment Insurance is offered as a hedge against both political and commercial risks.[132] Political risks covered include expropriation, war or civil disturbance that make business activities impossible, as well as restrictions on the repatriation of dividends or foreign exchange controls.[133] NEXI does not cover losses resulting from host government actions that are in accordance with domestic and international law.[134] **3.71**

Insurance for Equity Investments is available to Japanese companies carrying out FDI abroad, either by establishing a subsidiary outside Japan or through a partnership with an existing foreign company. Such companies can also obtain insurance for new investment in existing companies outside Japan. Losses may be recoverable when the relevant subsidiary or the joint venture is forced to discontinue its business due to war, terrorism, or *force majeure*, such as a natural disaster. The insurance also covers losses incurred where the investor is unable to remit dividends to Japan due to imposition of currency conversion controls, or suspension of remittance.[135] **3.72**

[129] The Special Account for Trade Reinsurance held by the government was abolished, and all assets and liabilities from the account were assumed by the "new" NEXI; *see* NEXI Annual Report 7 (FY 2016), available at https://www.nexi.go.jp/corporate/booklet/pdf/annual2016-e.pdf.

[130] JBIC also provides certain risk mitigation mechanisms, although its main function is financing Japanese investments abroad with NEXI being the main insurance provider. For an overview of JBIC's function, *see* Papanastasiou, *supra* note 2, at 148–50.

[131] *See* NEXI Annual Report, *supra* note 129.

[132] NEXI insures through the Overseas Investment Insurance tool and pays claims covering 97.5 percent of losses due to political risks and 95 percent due to commercial risks. *See* Papanastasiou, *supra* note 2, at 161.

[133] NEXI Annual Report, *supra* note 129, at 21.

[134] *See* Papanastasiou, *supra* note 2, at 153.

[135] NEXI Annual Report, *supra* note 129, at 21.

3.73 Insurance for Rights and Acquired Profits is also available to cover real estate and mining rights outside Japan, as well as equipment that Japanese companies bring directly into a country outside Japan without establishing a local subsidiary. Losses may be compensable when the covered asset becomes useless due to *force majeure*, or when the company is unable to remit proceeds from the sale of business property due to currency controls or other restrictions.[136]

b. Export credit insurance

3.74 Export and intermediary trade insurance covers losses suffered by a Japanese company that exports goods to a foreign country or undertakes intermediary trade. Losses may be compensable when the company is unable to ship goods due to (1) war, revolution, import restriction/prohibition, or *force majeure* such as natural disaster, or (2) the importer's bankruptcy. This insurance also covers losses suffered when the company is unable to collect the export or service proceeds after shipping goods for the same reasons as previously mentioned.[137]

c. Overseas loan insurance

3.75 NEXI also provides insurance covering long-term loans provided by Japanese companies: (1) to enable a foreign partner in a joint venture to acquire equity in the business; (2) to provide funds to a foreign company for its business; or (3) to provide funds to a foreign company to help it develop natural resources that the Japanese company plans to import into Japan on a long-term basis.[138]

3.76 Insurance for Loans and Bonds, for example, covers losses suffered by a Japanese company or commercial bank that provided a foreign government or company with long-term business funds unrelated to exports from Japan, or which purchased bonds issued by a foreign government or company for the purpose of long-term business financing. The losses may be incurred when the Japanese company or bank is unable to redeem the principal and interest on the loan due to war, revolution, controls on foreign currency conversion, suspension of remittance, *force majeure*, or bankruptcy/default of the borrower or bond issuer.[139]

3.77 Insurance for Debt Guarantee is also available to Japanese businesses that assume surety obligations for overseas subsidiaries' or foreign partners' long-term loans

[136] *Id.*

[137] *Id.* at 16; there is also a specified export credit insurance for supporting exports conducted by Japanese SMEs and those engaged in the business of agriculture, forestry, and fishery; *see also*, NEXI Annual Report, *supra* note 129, at 18.

[138] Additionally, NEXI provides specified insurance covering the risks of non-repayment of loans made by Japanese commercial banks to projects that are related to Japan's supply of natural resources and energy, or to projects with significant Japanese interests in natural resources; *see* NEXI Annual Report, *supra* note 129, at 20.

[139] *Id.* at 19.

obtained in connection with overseas joint ventures or mineral resource development financing agreements. This insurance covers losses suffered by a Japanese company or a commercial bank that guarantees loans taken out by a foreign government or company. The losses may be incurred when the guarantor is called upon to fulfill its guarantee obligation because the primary obligor fails to repay borrowings due to war, revolution, currency conversion controls, suspension of remittance, *force majeure*, or the bankruptcy of the borrower.[140]

d. Export bill insurance

Export Bill Insurance covers losses suffered by a Japanese commercial bank that purchases documentary bills of exchange drawn without a letter of credit in order to collect export proceeds. **3.78**

Covered losses may be incurred if the bank is unable to collect due to non-payment caused by (1) war, revolution, foreign currency control, suspension of remittance, or *force majeure*, or (2) bankruptcy of a foreign importer. This insurance mitigates concerns that the bank may have when purchasing bills without a letter of credit. **3.79**

Export Bond Insurance covers losses suffered by a Japanese commercial bank or other company that issues letters of guarantee (bid bonds and performance bonds) for a Japanese exporter. Covered losses may be incurred if the insured is compelled to pay on a surety based on a foreign importer's unjustified call.[141] **3.80**

e. Prepayment import insurance

Prepayment Import Insurance covers losses suffered by a Japanese importer that purchases goods from a foreign country by advance payment and does not receive the goods on time. Covered losses are incurred when the importer cannot collect a prepayment despite a request for reimbursement, due to (1) war, revolution, foreign currency conversion controls, suspension of remittance, or *force majeure*; or (2) bankruptcy or default of the counterparty.[142] **3.81**

f. Other insurance products

Other insurance products cover export contracts; export proceeds, losses from technology supply contracts or contracts for the export of plants, ships, rolling stock, and other merchandise and equipment. **3.82**

Short-Term Trade Insurance for Manufacturers, for example, covers losses suffered by Japanese manufacturers that export goods or undertake intermediary trade to a foreign country. Coverage is similar to Export Credit Insurance.[143] Insurance Covering Loans (Buyer Credit) covers losses suffered by a Japanese commercial **3.83**

[140] *Id.*
[141] *Id.* at 18.
[142] *Id.*
[143] *Id.* at 16.

bank that provides loans to a foreign importer to purchase goods and services from a Japanese company.[144]

3.84 Intellectual Property License Insurance is also available, covering losses from an inability to collect royalties on Japanese technology, know-how, or intellectual property rights due to political risks (such as war or bankruptcy).[145]

2. Germany: Deutsche Revision

3.85 Until relatively recently, the German federal government administered its investment insurance program through Treuarbeit AG, an agency headquartered in Hamburg.[146] Germany offered insurance for investments and loans with equity features, as well as guarantees for service contracts in the petroleum sector. Treuarbeit's stated objective was to promote investment by German enterprises in foreign countries through the transfer of capital, technology, and entrepreneurial experience.

3.86 Treuarbeit insurance covered risks associated with nationalization, expropriation, measures equivalent to expropriation, wrongful failure to act by public authorities, war, other armed conflicts, revolution and insurrection, blockage of payment, moratorium on payment, and bans on currency convertibility or transfer. Investors domiciled in the Federal Republic of Germany were eligible for Treuarbeit insurance.

3.87 Before offering investment insurance for a given project, Treuarbeit preferred that investment promotion and protection agreements between Germany and the potential host country be in place. In the absence of such a treaty, Treuarbeit would look to the legal system of the proposed host State to see that it offered adequate legal protection against political risk. Investors were also required to have obtained all necessary permits for planned investments, and to have complied with all other legal requirements in force in the country concerned. The investor was required to bear at least 5 percent of any loss sustained. Coverage of returns on investment was limited to 10 percent per year, up to 50 percent of the maximum capital guaranteed during the whole period of the guarantee.

3.88 Insurance was granted for periods of up to fifteen years, with terms of up to twenty years in exceptional cases. Insurance contracts could be extended for up to five additional years. The investor had to pay a processing fee of 1 percent of the guaranteed amount up to DM10 million, and 0.5 percent for amounts exceeding DM10 million, but this fee did not exceed DM20,000 for any single transaction.

---

[144] *Id.* at 19.

[145] *Id.* at 16.

[146] *See* Bundeshaushaltgesetz 1959, art. 18, para. 1; Bundesgesetzblatt II, 793 (1959) for Treuarbeit's initial statutory basis. *See also* http://www.agaportal.de.

For the coverage of capital and earnings, the premium was 0.5 percent per year of the maximum amount of coverage applicable at the beginning of the respective year of guarantee.

Today, the German federal government offers political risk coverage for German citizens through its agents, PwC Deutsche Revision and Euler Hermes Kreditversicherungs AG.[147] Many of the parameters for insurance issued by Treuarbeit remain in force under this new arrangement. Germany provides insurance for direct investments, expenditures for the establishment of manufacturing plants or corporate offices, loans with equity features, and other valuable investment rights.[148] Its objective is first and foremost to promote the German export economy by providing State-sponsored investment guarantees.[149] An additional purpose is the further implementation of German foreign policy toward developing nations.[150] **3.89**

Specifically, German investment guarantees cover expropriation, breach of contract, war or other armed conflict or terror, and currency inconvertibility.[151] The German government continues to view insurance as a secondary mechanism to mitigate political risk.[152] Bilateral investment treaties are the fundamental means by which the German government seeks to protect its citizens' investments in developing and transition countries.[153] The subsidiary nature of investment insurance in German law stems from the historical evolution of State investment guarantees from the federal appropriations power, which was meant to be used to provide support to treaties that the executive branch negotiated for the benefit of its citizens.[154] Nevertheless, investment guarantees underwritten by the German government remain substantial. Germany's gross exposure amounted to €1.1 billion euros in 2017, down from previous years due to the difficult geopolitical situation.[155] The government has sought to further catalyze FDI from small and **3.90**

---

[147] *See* PRICEWATERHOUSECOOPERS, JAHRESBERICHT 2003. INVESTITIONSGARANTIEN DER BUNDESREPUBLIK DEUTSCHLAND: DIREKTINVESTITIONEN AUSLAND 13 (2004). PwC and EHK manage the coverage of political risks. See https://www.agaportal.de/en and https://www.pwc.de/en/offentliche-unternehmen/investitionsgarantien-des-bundes.html.

[148] Available at https://www.investitionsgarantien.de/en/main-navigation/investitionen-investitionsgarantien/grundlagen-investitionsgarantien/grundzuege-investitionsgarantien.

[149] PwC, *Jahresbericht 2003, supra* note 147, at 12.

[150] Bundesministerium der Justiz, *Richtlinien für die Übernahme von Garantien für Direktinvestitionen im Ausland. Neufassung vom 19. August 2004*, BUNDESANZEIGER, no. 163 (Aug. 31, 2004). There is a discussion of the practical changes introduced by this amendment in PwC, JAHRESBERICHT 2004. INVESTITIONSGARANTIEN DER BUNDESREPUBLIK DEUTSCHLAND: DIREKTINV ESTITIONEN AUSLAND 21–25 (2005); PwC, *Jahresbericht 2003, supra* note 147, at 10–11.

[151] PwC, *Jahresbericht 2003, supra* note 147; Bundesministerium der Justiz, *supra* note 150.

[152] PwC, *Jahresbericht 2003, supra* note 147, at 9.

[153] *Id.* Germany's BITs often envisage subrogation of the insured's rights to Germany (as the insurer country), transforming commercial/investment disputes into diplomatic disputes with the host country; *see* SALACUSE, *supra* note 2, at 248–49.

[154] PwC, *Jahresbericht 2003, supra* note 147, at 9; *see also* Haushaltsgesetz 2004, § 3.1.1.2, (b).

[155] PwC, *Investment Guarantees of the Federal Rep. of Germany, Annual Report 2017*, available at: https://www.investitionsgarantien.de/_Resources/Persistent/16465bb69967d6464c653d8d0f8

medium enterprise by eliminating application fees for investments of less than €5 million.[156] In 2017, 31 percent of applications came from small and medium-sized enterprises (SMEs).[157]

3.91 In order to qualify for PwC Deutsche Revision coverage, the investor must be a German citizen or have its headquarters in Germany.[158] The investor is obligated to absorb minor losses, and is always expected to carry at least 5 percent of any loss.[159] Insurance is granted for periods of up to fifteen years, with twenty-year terms granted in exceptional cases. Terms may be extended up to five additional years.[160] The investor must pay a processing fee to be determined as a function of the total insurance amount sought.[161] As noted, there is no fee for investments of less than €5 million.[162]

3. Australia: Export Finance and Insurance Corporation[163]

3.92 Political risk insurance is available in Australia through the Export Finance Insurance Corporation (EFIC). Policies cover up to 90 percent of insured losses incurred as a result of political risk.[164] Policies are normally issued for terms from five to fifteen years for equity investments, or eight years for loans and loan guarantees.[165]

3.93 Risks covered include expropriation, defined by EFIC as the situation when "the host government through arbitrary or discriminatory action confiscates or denies access to … investment or condones actions by others which have a similar effect." EFIC also insures against exchange transfer or blockage, occurring when "the host government prevents [the investor] from either converting local currency and/or transferring foreign exchange from … investment earnings, or … returning capital, or imposes a discriminatory rate of exchange," and war damage, which includes "war, riot or other civil commotion that damages or removes the physical assets of … investment."[166]

3.94 The EFIC offers insurance only to investors who can demonstrate that the investment project in question will significantly benefit Australia. Premiums vary

---

8a20fb9ad18fd/Annual%20Report%202017.%20Investment%20Guarantees%20of%20the%20Federal%20Republic%20of%20Germany.pdf.

156 PwC, *Jahresbericht 2003, supra* note 147, at 5.

157 PwC, *Annual Report 2017, supra* note 155, at 28.

158 Bundesgarantien Für Direktinvestitionen Im Ausland Richtlinien 3 (2004).

159 *Id.* at 5 (2004).

160 *Id.* at 5 (2004).

161 *Id.* at 6 (2004).

162 Investitionsgarantien Der Bundesrepublik Deutschland, Direktinvestionen Ausland, Jahresbericht 2003 5 (2003).

163 Much of the following discussion draws on information supplied by the Export Finance Insurance Corporation of Australia at http://www.efic.gov.au.

164 *See* http://www.efic.gov.au/attachments/db/efi/60.pdf.

165 *Id.*

166 *Id.*

depending on the project host country, the nature of the investment, and the type of risk. Investors are required to have notified the EFIC of their intention to invest prior to making the investment.

4. Other countries

In the United Kingdom, political risk insurance is provided through the Export Credits Guarantee Department (ECGD). The ECGD offers insurance against expropriation, political violence, and currency inconvertibility.[167] **3.95**

In Denmark, the Danish International Development Agency provides political risk insurance in connection with Danish investments in developing countries. Risks covered include expropriation, currency inconvertibility, and political violence. To qualify for insurance, investments must be beneficial to economic development in the host State, and the host government must approve such investments.[168] **3.96**

In Norway, the Norwegian Agency for Development Aid provides political risk insurance for Norwegian investment abroad.[169] Again, risks covered include expropriation, currency inconvertibility, and political violence, as well as natural disasters, breach of contract, and boycotts.[170] **3.97**

The Swiss Investment Risk Guarantee Agency (IRG) provides political risk guarantees to Swiss natural and juridical persons that invest in developing countries. IRG's guarantees cover nationalization and other forms of expropriation, war and civil disturbance, inability to transfer compensation for war damage or transaction proceeds resulting from a forced sale. IRG's guarantees may cover up to 70 percent of the investment capital or the loan amount.[171] **3.98**

Political risk insurance is available in Canada through the Foreign Investment Insurance program of the Export Development Corporation (EDC), established by the Export Development Act of 1969. These policies cover up to 90 percent of losses due to three types of political risk: "transfer of funds," expropriation, and political violence. "Transfer of Funds" insurance covers conversion of local currency into hard currency, as well as repatriation of currency. Insurance is provided for up to fifteen years. This insurance is available for a variety of business **3.99**

---

[167] For more information, *see* http://www.ecgd.gov.uk.

[168] Akinsanya, *supra* note 2, at 68–69; http://www.ekf.dk. Danida's mission is first and foremost to assist developing countries with economic development and overcome the huge poverty problems faced by a majority of the population of these countries. *See* Om Danida, available at http://um.dk/en/danida-en/.

[169] Available at https://www.giek.no/buy-from-norway/.

[170] *See* Garanti Institutet for Eksportkredit, Alminnelige Garantivilkår for investeringer, art. 2, available at http://www.giek.no/print.asp?page=84&msgpage=0&msgpost=0&type=.

[171] *See* Loi fédérale sur la garantie contre les risques de l'investissement, Mar. 20, 1970, RO 1970 1130, RS 977.0, cited in Ziegler and Gratton, *supra* note 2, at 533–34.

structures, including equity investments, loans, loan guarantees, insurance for assets or equipment, service contracts, and petroleum exploration and development contracts. Premiums vary based on the host country and the industry. The EDC also offers export credit insurance.[172]

C. MIGA

1. Background

3.100 The World Bank, a multilateral lending agency and MIGA's parent company, was formed over seventy years ago. It consists of the International Bank for Reconstruction and Development (IBRD),[173] the International Development Association (IDA), the International Centre for the Settlement of Investment Disputes (ICSID), and the International Finance Corporation (IFC),[174] as well as MIGA.[175]

3.101 MIGA was formed in 1988 by forty-two World Bank member countries,[176] modeled on OPIC and offering similar political risk insurance.[177] MIGA is both

[172] *Foreign Investment Insurance* brochure from Export Development Corporation (05-95), http://www.edc.ca. On political risk insurance offered by the Austrian government, *see* http://www.oekb.at; also Heins Rindler, *The Insurance of Austrian Investment Abroad against Political Risk: A Comparative Approach with Special Regard to Developmental Aspects*, 47 ÖSTERREICHISCHE ZEITSCHRIFT FÜR ÖFFENTLICHES RECHT UND VÖLKERRECHT 17 (1994).

[173] The International Bank for Reconstruction and Development provides funding for developing countries with relatively high per capita income. The money used for this activity is raised through the sale of AAA-rated bonds in international capital markets. Repayment of IBRD loans is usually over a period of twelve to fifteen years, and such loans are extended only to governments or to agencies that can obtain a government guarantee; for IBRD information, *see* https://www.worldbank.org/en/who-we-are/ibrd.

[174] The International Finance Corporation (IFC) was created in 1956. On the IFC generally, *see* Thomas L. Brewer, *International Investment Dispute Settlement Procedures: The Evolving Regime for Foreign Direct Investment*, 26 L. & POL'Y. INT'L BUS. 633, 655 (1995). The IFC provides direct project financing for private investment in developing countries. It invests in commercial enterprises in various sectors through loans and equity financing in collaboration with other investors. The IFC does not require government repayment guarantees. It should be noted that if a project is financed in part by a loan from the IFC or a similar international organization, political risk may be reduced, due to developing States' desire to maintain positive relationships with such entities in order to maintain available sources of capital.

[175] For an analysis of the internal organization and operations of MIGA, *see* PANAYIOTIS M. PROTOPSALTIS, *MULTILATERAL INVESTMENT GUARANTEE AGENCY (MIGA)* (2014); for a comparison between MIGA insurance and IBRD/IFC guarantees, *see also* PAPANASTASIOU, *supra* note 2, at 162–67.

[176] *MIGA Investment Guarantee Guide* (2015), https://www.miga.org/guide/investment-guarantee-guide [hereinafter, *MIGA Guide*]. MIGA was created by the Convention Establishing the Multilateral Investment Guarantee Agency, opened for signature Oct. 11, 1985 (entered into force Apr. 12, 1988), 24 I.L.M. 1598 [hereinafter, the MIGA Convention]; U.S. laws relating to MIGA can be found at 22 U.S.C. §§ 290k–290k-11; for further discussion, *see* IBRAHIM F.I. SHIHATA, MIGA AND FOREIGN INVESTMENT—ORIGINS, OPERATIONS, POLICIES AND BASIC DOCUMENTS OF THE MULTILATERAL INVESTMENT GUARANTEE AGENCY (1988).

[177] Mansbach, *supra* note 2, at B-6.

legally and financially independent. It is composed of a Council of Governors, which comprises one representative of each member country. This Council elects a Board of Directors that is responsible for the general operation of MIGA and the election of the President.[178]

MIGA's primary purpose is to encourage the flow of investment to and among developing States.[179] It pursues this objective by providing insurance or "guarantees"[180] (including coinsurance and reinsurance) to mitigate political risk in relation to investments carried out in member countries using resources originating in other member countries.[181] MIGA has adopted the objective to support SMEs investing in member countries, mirroring similar developments at OPIC.[182] It is this group of investors that traditionally faced the greatest difficulty in gaining insurance coverage for projects from national or private sources.[183] **3.102**

MIGA's insurance program helps to fill gaps often left by national insurance programs which, due to their respective national objectives, often impose strict eligibility requirements that exclude many investors and investments.[184] MIGA may co-guarantee investments with national agencies through parallel or joint **3.103**

---

[178] MIGA Convention, *supra* note 176, arts. 30–34.

[179] *Id.*, art. 2, at 1608; *see also* MIGA, *Annual Report 2017* (2017), http://www.miga.org/sites/default/files/archive/Documents/Annual-Report-2017.pdf; Gerald T. West, Investment Insurance and Developmental Impact 13 (2001).

[180] In this book, the terms "insurance" and "guarantees" are used interchangeably. However, the term "guarantees" was selected by MIGA instead of the term "insurance." As a legal concept, the term "guarantees" was considered as being more adaptable to diverse national jurisdictions, in both common law and continental legal systems. Arghyris Fatouros was among the first legal scholars to use the term guarantees; see Arghyris A. Fatouros, *Government Guarantees to Foreign Investors* (1962).

[181] MIGA Convention, *supra* note 176, art. 2; *see also* MIGA, *Annual Report 2017, supra* note 179; West, *supra* note 179, at 17, 36. *See generally* Chris M. Peter, *MIGA and GRIP: Two International Investment Insurance Programmes*, 12 World Competition: L. & Economics Rev. 95 (1989).

[182] One of MIGA's projects was Raffeisen Bank of Romania, which was created by the well-known Austrian bank of the same name. MIGA provided guarantees in the amount of €80 million for the project against currency transfer restrictions and expropriation. *See* MIGA, *Annual Report 2004* (2004), https://www.miga.org/report/2004-annual-report, *Development Impact* section; for a discussion of OPIC, *see* Section A, *supra.*

[183] Motomichi Ikawa, *Introduction*, in International Political Risk Management: Exploring New Frontiers 2 (Theodor H. Moran ed. 2001).

[184] Shihata, *Factors, supra* note 2, at 690. Ikawa, *supra* note 183, at 2. This mission became more important after the internet boom of the late 1990s and the ensuing stagnation in FDI. Private investment insurance became increasingly unavailable for valuable projects. It became MIGA's mission to mitigate this problem: in fiscal year 2004, it contributed US$1.1 billion in insurance coverage for some thirty-five new projects. MIGA, *Annual Report 2004, supra* note 182, *Operational Overview* section; MIGA, *Operational Policies of the MIGA* (2015), http://www.miga.org/sites/default/files/archive/Documents/Operations-Regulations.pdf (MIGA's Operational Policies became effective on Jan. 6, 2015 and replaced MIGA's Operational Regulations) [hereinafter, MIGA, *Operational Policies*].

underwriting, provide reinsurance for these agencies,[185] or insure investments that fail eligibility tests for national insurance schemes such as OPIC.[186] MIGA attempts to diversify its contingent liabilities both by country[187] and by economic sector.[188]

3.104 MIGA also guarantees investments made by investors from developing countries that do not have their own national insurance programs.[189] For example, MIGA offered US$13.3 million of coverage to EFES Sinai Yatirim ve Ticaret, a Turkish beverage company, for its equity investment in Coca Cola Almaty Bottlers in Kazakhstan.[190]

3.105 MIGA has rapidly expanded since its formation in 1988. As of August 2018, MIGA country membership rose to 181 members (156 developing countries and 25 industrialized countries).[191] Since its inception in 1988, MIGA has issued more than $45 billion in guarantees, supporting over 800 projects in 110 member countries.[192] MIGA's $4.8 billion in coverage for fiscal year 2017 is expected to support $16 billion in public and private co-investment.[193] Since the turn of the twenty-first century, the trend in coverage has remained generally positive, despite the global economic slowdown and financial crisis that followed the U.S. sub-prime mortgage crisis in 2008.

2. Risks covered by MIGA insurance

3.106 Like OPIC, MIGA insurance covers risks of currency inconvertibility, expropriation, and political violence. MIGA also covers breach of contract loss as a separate class of risk coverage.[194]

---

185 MIGA Convention, *supra* note 176, art. 2. MIGA issued US$45 million in reinsurance coverage to the Export Development Corporation of Canada for CAMECO Corporation's investment in the Kumtor gold mine in Kyrgyzstan. MIGA press release, Oct. 25, 1995; MIGA, *Annual Report 2017, supra* note 179.

186 Berger, *supra* note 2, at 41.

187 MIGA continues to make progress in its diversification efforts. In 2004, in terms of net exposure of MIGA per region, sub-Saharan Africa represents 13 percent, Asia and the Pacific 15 percent, Europe and Central Asia 37 percent, Latin America and the Caribbean 30 percent, and the Middle East and North Africa 7 percent of MIGA's total portfolio. MIGA, *Annual Report 2004, supra* note 182, *Operational Overview* section, Table 4.

188 Sectoral diversification fluctuates with the market. MIGA, *Annual Report 2004, supra* note 182, *Operational Overview* section, Table 6.

189 Berger, *supra* note 2, at 41.

190 MIGA press release, Oct. 25, 1995.

191 *See* MIGA Country List, at https://www.miga.org/member-countries.

192 MIGA, *Annual Report 2017, supra* note 179, at 13.

193 *Id.* at 16.

194 MIGA Convention, *supra* note 176, art. 11.

a. Currency inconvertibility

Currency inconvertibility insurance covers currency transfer restrictions that prevent the investor from transferring profits or liquidation proceeds out of the host country. Excessive delays in acquiring foreign exchange caused by host government action or inaction, adverse changes in exchange control laws or regulations, or deterioration in conditions governing the conversion and transfer of local currency are also covered by currency inconvertibility insurance.[195] **3.107**

On receipt of the blocked local currency from the investor, MIGA pays compensation in the currency of its guarantee. As under OPIC insurance, risks of devaluation and depreciation of currency are excluded, because they are considered "normal business risks."[196] **3.108**

b. Expropriation

MIGA expropriation coverage protects against acts that deprive the investor of ownership or control of its investments.[197] Creeping expropriation is also covered.[198] **3.109**

However, MIGA differs from OPIC, in that MIGA excludes from expropriation coverage of "non-discriminatory measures of general application which governments normally take for the purpose of regulating economic activity in their territories."[199] This means that investors may not receive insurance compensation for a wide range of regulations that cause substantial damage to their business.[200] **3.110**

Where the owner demonstrates that equity investments have been expropriated, MIGA pays the net book value of the insured investment.[201] While most national insurance schemes cover only "total" expropriation,[202] MIGA may, in certain circumstances, cover partial losses. For partial expropriation of funds or assets, MIGA pays the insured portion of the funds or the net book value of the expropriated assets. For loans and loan guarantees, MIGA insures the outstanding **3.111**

---

[195] *Id.*, art. 11(a)(i); MIGA, *Commentary on the Convention Establishing the MIGA*, § 13, https://www.miga.org/sites/default/files/archive/Documents/commentary_convention_november_2010.pdf [hereinafter, MIGA, *Commentary*]; *see also MIGA Guide, supra* note 176; MIGA, *Operational Policies, supra* note 185, at 11, §§ 1.25–1.28.

[196] Berger, *supra* note 2, at 30; *MIGA Guide, supra* note 176; MIGA, *Operational Policies, supra* note 185, at 17, § 1.57; *see also* discussion of currency inconvertibility as a political risk in Chapter 1, Section C.3.

[197] MIGA Convention, *supra* note 176, art. 11(a)(ii); MIGA, *Commentary, supra* note 195, § 14; MIGA, *Operational Policies, supra* note 185, at 12–14, §§ 1.31–1.42.

[198] MIGA Convention, *supra* note 176, art. 11(a)(ii); *MIGA Guide, supra* note 176.

[199] MIGA Convention, *supra* note 176, art. 11(a)(ii), at 1611; *MIGA Guide, supra* note 176.

[200] MIGA, *Operational Policies, supra* note 184, at 13, § 1.37. *See* discussion of de facto expropriation, Chapter 1, Section C.2.

[201] MIGA Convention, *supra* note 176, art. 11(a)(ii); *MIGA Guide, supra* note 176.

[202] Berger, *supra* note 2, at 31.

principal and any accrued and unpaid interest. MIGA will pay compensation only upon assignment of the investor's remaining interest in the expropriated investment to MIGA.[203]

c. Political violence

3.112 MIGA war and civil disturbance coverage insures against losses arising from politically motivated acts of war or civil disturbance, including revolution, insurrection, *coups d'état*, sabotage, and terrorism.[204]

3.113 For equity investments affected by these circumstances, MIGA pays the investor's share of the least of the book value of the assets, replacement cost of the assets, or, for damaged assets, the cost of repair. For loans and loan guarantees, MIGA pays the insured portion of the principal and interest payments in default as a direct result of damage to the assets of the project caused by war or civil disturbance.[205]

3.114 War and civil disturbance coverage also extends to events which result in an interruption of project operations essential to overall financial viability for at least one year. This feature is effective when the investment is considered a total loss; MIGA will pay the book value of the total insured equity investment. For loans and loan guarantees, MIGA pays the insured portion of the principal and interest payments in default as a result of business interruption caused by insured events.[206]

d. Breach of contract

3.115 Breach of contract coverage compensates investors for any breach or repudiation by the host government of a contract with the holder of a guarantee, in cases where the holder does not have recourse to another forum, or where a decision of the available forum is not forthcoming within a reasonable period of time, where such a decision cannot be enforced.[207]

e. Other coverage

3.116 MIGA may also cover certain other non-commercial risks. It may provide coverage against losses resulting from the failure of:

- the Host Government to make a payment when due under an unconditional financial payment obligation or guarantee (Non-Honoring of Sovereign Financial Obligations risk);

[203] MIGA Convention, *supra* note 176, art. 11(a)(ii); *MIGA Guide, supra* note 176.

[204] MIGA Convention, *supra* note 176, art. 11(a)(iv); MIGA, *Commentary, supra* note 195, § 16; *MIGA Guide, supra* note 176; MIGA, *Operational Policies, supra* note 184, at 15–16, §§ 1.46–1.52.

[205] *MIGA Guide, supra* note 176; MIGA, *Operational Policies, supra* note 184, at 15–16, §§ 1.46–1.52.

[206] *Id.*

[207] MIGA Convention, *supra* note 176, art. 11(a)(iii); MIGA, *Commentary, supra* note 195, § 15; MIGA, *Operational Policies, supra* note 184, at 14, § 1.43; Theodor H. Moran, International Political Risk Management: Exploring New Frontiers 41–73 (2001).

- a State-owned enterprise or public authority to make a payment when due under an unconditional financial payment obligation or guarantee (Non-Honoring of Financial Obligations by a State-Owned Enterprise risk); and
- the Host Government to enforce a final arbitral award for a specified monetary amount rendered against the Host Government pursuant to the dispute resolution mechanism set forth in a bilateral investment treaty (Non-Enforcement of Arbitral Award Rendered pursuant to Bilateral Investment Treaty risk).[208]

Thus, investors with special needs or unique situations should contact MIGA directly to determine whether MIGA will insure against such events.

3. Eligibility for MIGA insurance[209]

a. Eligible investors

As noted, MIGA requires that the investor seeking insurance be a national of a member country other than the host country. A corporation will be eligible for coverage if it is either incorporated in a member country and has its principal place of business there, or if it is majority-owned by nationals of member countries. State-owned corporations are eligible if they operate on a commercial basis.[210] **3.117**

b. Eligible projects

Insurance may be obtained for new investments that are "economically sound," are owned by investors of any member country, and are destined to be implemented in any developing member country. New investments also include expansion, modernization, and refinancing of existing projects, reinvestment of earnings, and acquisitions that involve the privatization of State enterprises. MIGA also considers the environmental impact of the project.[211] Eligible investments have to be new, and medium- or long-term in nature. They may encompass equity investments, shareholder loans, and loan guarantees issued by equity holders, provided the loans have a minimum average maturity of three years. Loans to unrelated borrowers can be insured, provided that equity in the project is being insured concurrently.[212] **3.118**

[208] *Id.*, art. 11(b); MIGA, *Commentary, supra* note 195, § 17; MIGA, *Operational Policies, supra* note 184, at 16–17, §§ 1.53–1.55.

[209] *See also* Rowat, *supra* note 1, at 128–30 and 140–44; Berger, *supra* note 2, at 29–37.

[210] MIGA Convention, *supra* note 176, art. 13, at 1613; *MIGA Guide, supra* note 176; MIGA, *Operational Policies, supra* note 184, at 8–10, §§ 1.16–1.21.

[211] MIGA Convention, *supra* note 176, art. 12; MIGA, *Commentary, supra* note 195, § 21; *MIGA Guide, supra* note 176.

[212] MIGA Convention, *supra* note 176, art. 12; MIGA, *Commentary, supra* note 195, §§ 19–20; *MIGA Guide, supra* note 176; MIGA, *Operational Policies, supra* note 184, at 3–6, §§ 1.02–1.12.

3.119 The host government must approve an investment before MIGA will offer political risk insurance.[213] Unlike OPIC, however, which requires the host State's specific approval, MIGA will consider the investment to be approved if the host government does not respond within a reasonable period of time.[214]

3.120 Before insuring a project, MIGA must examine the economic soundness of the investment, consistency with the host country's declared development objectives, and compliance with the host country's laws.[215] While these regulations require a complex analysis by MIGA, which may cause delays in the decision to insure a project, the organization's Operational Regulations recommend that a decision should be made within 120 days of receipt of an application for insurance.[216]

3.121 Other forms of investment are also eligible for MIGA insurance, including, for instance, technical assistance and management contracts, and franchising and licensing agreements, provided the arrangement to be covered has a duration of at least three years, and the investor's remuneration is tied to the project's operating results.[217]

c. Eligible countries

3.122 To be eligible for MIGA insurance, an investment must be made in the territory of a "developing member country,"[218] defined as a State listed as such on Schedule A to the MIGA Convention.[219] As mentioned before, MIGA currently has 181 member countries.[220]

3.123 As noted, the host government must approve the project before MIGA will issue insurance coverage.[221] In most cases, MIGA will submit a request for approval on

[213] MIGA Convention, *supra* note 176, art. 15; MIGA, *Commentary, supra* note 195, §§ 25–27; *MIGA Guide, supra* note 176.

[214] MIGA Convention, *supra* note 176, art. 38(b); MIGA, *Commentary, supra* note 195, § 25; *see MIGA Guide, supra* note 176. Another important aspect of MIGA's decision-making process is an environmental impact analysis. For more information, *see id.*

[215] MIGA Convention, *supra* note 176, art. 12. *See generally* West, *supra* note 179; G.I. Malumfashi, *Environmental and Social Due Diligence Vis-à-Vis Political Risk Insurance: An Assessment of the Role of the Multilateral Investment Guarantee Agency (MIGA)*, 2(1) Oil & Gas L. Intelligence (2004).

[216] Berger, *supra* note 2, at 33.

[217] One such project is the multilevel cooperation between MIGA and other multinational organizations, States, and private organizations to bring much needed technical assistance and FDI to Afghanistan. MIGA, *Annual Report 2004, supra* note 182, *Regional Activities: Asia and the Pacific: Technical Assistance* section.

[218] MIGA Convention, *supra* note 176, art. 14; MIGA, *Commentary, supra* note 195, § 24; *MIGA Guide, supra* note 176.

[219] MIGA Convention, *supra* note 176, art. 3(c).

[220] MIGA Country List, *supra* note 191.

[221] MIGA Convention, *supra* note 176, art. 15; *MIGA Guide, supra* note 176; MIGA, *Operational Policies, supra* note 184, at 26–27, §§ 3.22–3.26.

the investor's behalf. For some countries, a copy of the standard government investment approval, normally issued by the local agency or ministry responsible for foreign investment, will be acceptable for MIGA to initiate coverage.

d. Political considerations

Political considerations are not as important in obtaining insurance coverage from MIGA as is the case for some national agencies.[222] For example, MIGA does not require that the host State meet any "human rights" standard, as does OPIC. Nevertheless, MIGA will not provide guarantees if a project violates international law. It therefore arguably is not allowed to provide funding for projects that would facilitate the breach of any of the core human rights norms.[223] **3.124**

4. Terms

a. Amount of insurance

MIGA's guarantee authority is limited to a total at any one time of 150 percent of its unimpaired subscribed capital and reserves.[224] Underwriting authority for individual investment projects is limited to 5 percent of MIGA's total capacity to issue guarantees. Regardless of the nature of the project to be insured, MIGA can currently issue up to US$200 million per project.[225] **3.125**

Insurance can be obtained for up to 90 percent of the amount invested, plus up to an additional 450 percent covering earnings attributable to the investment. For loans and loan guarantees, MIGA will provide up to an additional 135 percent for interest accruing to increased principal.[226] **3.126**

For technical assistance and similar contracts, MIGA can insure up to 90 percent of the total value of payments under the agreement. Therefore, regardless of the nature of the project, the investor is required to remain at risk for at least 10 percent of any loss.[227] **3.127**

b. Cost

MIGA's Operational Policies authorize the agency to set insurance premiums on a case-by-case basis at annual levels between 0.3 and 1.5 percent of the guaranteed amount for each individual type of risk covered.[228] MIGA is a self-sustaining **3.128**

---

[222] Shihata, *Factors, supra* note 2, at 690.

[223] MIGA's *Environmental and Social Review Procedures, Exclusions* § 15, available at https://www.miga.org/guide/understanding-migas-environmental-and-social-due-diligence-process.

[224] MIGA, *Operational Policies, supra* note 184, at 31, §§ 3.47; MIGA Convention, *supra* note 176, art. 22.

[225] *MIGA Guide, supra* note 176.

[226] *Id.*

[227] *Id.*

[228] MIGA, *Operational Policies, supra* note 184, at 30, § 3.43.

Table 3.1 MIGA Base Rates

I. Manufacturing/Services		
Type of Guarantee	*Current*	*Standby*
a. Currency Transfer	0.50%	0.25%
b. Expropriation	0.60%	0.30%
c. Breach of Contract	0.80%	0.40%
d. War and Civil Disturbance **	0.45%	0.20%
II. Natural Resources *		
Type of Guarantee	*Current*	*Standby*
a. Currency Transfer	0.50%	0.25%
b. Expropriation	0.90%	0.45%
c. Breach of Contract	1.00%	0.50%
d. War and Civil Disturbance **	0.45%	0.20%
III. Oil and Gas		
Type of Guarantee	*Current*	*Standby*
a. Currency Transfer	0.50%	0.25%
b. Expropriation	1.25%	0.50%
c. Breach of Contract	1.25%	0.50%
d. War and Civil Disturbance**	0.60%	0.25%

* Includes agribusiness and forestry projects involving land ownership or concessions, or other types of projects where large landholdings are involved.
** Add 0.10 percent for Current and 0.05 percent for Standby for Sabotage and Terrorism coverage.

organization, and its premiums are generally commensurate with those of national investment insurance agencies. MIGA has abandoned publicly available guidelines on insurance premium levels,[229] Table 3.1 provides a list of rates published by MIGA in the 1990s. Even when published, these rates were subject to adjustment based on project risk profile. For more precise information on premiums, investors should contact MIGA directly.

3.129 The amounts of insurance described in the previous subsection represent the maximum amount of guarantee available for any insured investment. The "current" column in Table 3.1 is the amount of coverage in force for the portion of the investment at risk during the contract period. The standby amount represents the difference between the current amount and the maximum amount. This is a reserve of insurance coverage that the investor may put into effect at each annual election of coverage, to take into account changes in the value or amount of investment that is at risk.[230]

[229] MIGA, *Commentary, supra* note 195, § 54; Moran, *supra* note 207, at 165–97.
[230] *MIGA Guide, supra* note 176.

c. Duration

The term of MIGA insurance is more than one year and not more than fifteen years. The standard duration of coverage is fifteen years, but for non-equity investments (such as loan agreements), policies will typically mimic the term of the agreement to be insured. The term can be extended to twenty years if MIGA finds that the nature of the project "justifies" such an extended contract.[231] **3.130**

Once provided, MIGA may not terminate coverage unless the insured investor defaults on its contractual obligations, or if one of the situations described under MIGA's Operational Policies occurs.[232] **3.131**

d. Co-insurance

MIGA will cooperate with both public and private political risk insurers by entering into coinsurance and reinsurance arrangements for joint coverage of eligible investment projects.[233] In 1995, for example, MIGA concluded its first reinsurance agreement with the export credit guarantee department of the United Kingdom for a project in Tunisia, and also co-insured its first project with Sezione Speciale per L'Assicurazione del Credito All'Esportazione of Italy, covering a project in Argentina.[234] **3.132**

e. Disputes

Disputes between MIGA and an investor arising under an insurance contract are settled through arbitration in accordance with the terms of the particular Insurance Contract.[235] **3.133**

The MIGA Convention provides for subrogation to MIGA of the rights that the investor has acquired against the host country as a result of the events giving rise to the claim, and requires that disputes arising between MIGA and the host State be submitted to ICSID arbitration if negotiations and conciliation fail.[236] **3.134**

f. Applying for MIGA insurance

Before an investment is made or irrevocably committed, an investor seeking MIGA coverage must submit a Preliminary Application for Guarantee to MIGA. Business information of the applicant for MIGA insurance is kept confidential.[237] **3.135**

---

231 MIGA, *Operational Policies, supra* note 184, at 19, § 2.04(a).

232 *Id.* at 19–20, §§ 2.05–2.07.

233 MIGA Convention, *supra* note 176, art. 20, at 1614; MIGA, *Commentary, supra* note 195, § 50; *MIGA Guide, supra* note 176.

234 MIGA, *Annual Report 1995*, available at http://documents.worldbank.org/curated/en/736251468764686048/Multilateral-Investment-Guarantee-Agency-MIGA-annual-report-1995.

235 MIGA Convention, *supra* note 176, art. 57, §§ 76–78; *see also* Rowat, *supra* note 1, at 131.

236 MIGA Convention, *supra* note 176, arts. 18, 57; *see also* Rowat, *supra* note 1, at 131. ICSID is discussed in Chapter 8.

237 *MIGA Guide, supra* note 176; MIGA, *Operational Policies, supra* note 184, at 27, § 3.28.

3.136 If MIGA determines that the investment and investor are eligible for coverage, it will send to the investor a Notice of Registration, along with a Definitive Application for Guarantee. There is no fee for filing either a Preliminary Application or a Definitive Application, and there is no obligation on the part of the investor to accept a Contract of Guarantee if one is offered.

D. Private Insurance

1. Background

3.137 Private insurers offer political risk insurance that both complements and competes with the government-sponsored insurance programs described.[238] As Malcolm Rowat explains:

> The U.S. Private Sector's entry into the modern political risk insurance market dates from the early 1970s when Congress ordered the privatization of OPIC's underlying activities so that the organization would eventually confine itself to a reinsurance role. Congress deemed the experiment, which lasted until 1978, a failure and concluded that the commercial rather than developmental orientation of the program undermined some of OPIC's basic objectives.[239]

3.138 This rapidly growing sector of the private insurance market[240] is concentrated mainly in three insurance centers—London, New York, and Bermuda.

3.139 Private insurance companies, which were recorded offering political risk insurance, include the Chubb Group (New Jersey), Lloyd's of London, Citicorp International Trade Indemnity (CITI), Zurich, Sovereign, Professional Indemnity Association (PIA, New York), Pan Financial (London and New York), American International Group (AIG), and Pool d'Assurance des Risques Internationaux et Speciaux (PARIS).[241]

2. Risks covered by private insurance

3.140 Private political risk insurance is generally divided into two categories: asset coverage and contract coverage. Asset coverage may include political risks such as confiscation, nationalization, expropriation (including creeping expropriation), and repossession of equipment. Contract coverage may include loss from contract repudiation, currency inconvertibility, and contract cancellation due to political violence.[242] Thus, the risks covered are similar to the risks covered by State-sponsored insurance.

---

[238] Orloff, *supra* note 2, at 1.
[239] Rowat, *supra* note 1, at 125 (internal citations omitted).
[240] *Id.*
[241] *Id.* at n.84.
[242] Orloff, *supra* note 2, at 4.

Private political violence insurance usually excludes war between the world's major powers or between the country of the investor and the host State.[243] Also, private political risk insurance is generally not available to cover risks of war losses to land-based assets.[244] 3.141

While, as noted earlier, commercial insurance providers often provide AAD coverage, such companies may refuse to issue AAD policies for particular countries. A range of considerations can lead private providers to such a decision, including credit ratings, banking standards, and recent events affecting one or more industries in the country. According to one observer, for example, several insurance firms were declining to provide AAD cover for China in 1999. This attitude was apparently prompted by a perception that China was experiencing a surplus of electricity, and that therefore State-owned power purchasers would default on long-term fixed price commitments, leading to a proliferation of arbitration claims.[245] 3.142

As with government-sponsored insurance, compensation under private policies is usually based upon book value. Asset coverage insurance policies can usually be expanded to cover license cancellations, trade embargoes, strikes, riots, loss of income following expropriation, and other types of political risk.[246] In addition, each insurer will have further limitations and qualifications as to the amounts and types of insurance it can offer. 3.143

3. Terms

The terms offered by the private insurers are between one and three years, significantly less extensive than those offered by OPIC and MIGA.[247] Indeed, one criticism of private insurance is that it is too short-term to be very effective against political risk.[248] Because of the prevailing short duration periods, private insurers are also less able to offer reinsurance for coverage provided by national programs.[249] 3.144

Underwriting limits range from US$5 million to US$300 million per risk, depending on the insurer and the country in which the investment is located.[250] These limits are in the same range as those of OPIC (US$100 million per project) and MIGA (US$50 million per project). 3.145

---

[243] Rowat, *supra* note 1, at 125.
[244] Williams, *supra* note 120, at 96.
[245] Mark Kantor, posting on OGEMID investment law list server of Apr. 20, 2005.
[246] Orloff, *supra* note 2, at 5.
[247] Chew, *supra* note 16, at 674.
[248] Peter F. Fitzgerald, *Overview of Risks in International Financing*, 707 PLI COMM. L. & PRAC. COURSE HANDBOOK SERIES 7 (1995).
[249] Rowat, *supra* note 1, at 126.
[250] Orloff, *supra* note 2, at 3.

3.146 Private market fees are substantially higher than those of government insurance programs, and in some cases can be as much as 7 percent of the amount invested for coverage in high-risk countries.[251] For example, Lloyd used to offer a rate for insuring investments in the former Soviet republics of between 2 and 3 percent of the value of the investment.[252] Premiums are based on a number of factors, including the size of the investment, the nationality of the investor, risks associated with the host country, risks covered by the insurance, and the structure of the investment.[253] Despite relatively higher rates, however, private insurance remains attractive to certain investors, particularly those who fall outside the eligibility requirements of programs such as OPIC and MIGA. Unlike many nationally sponsored insurance programs, private political risk insurance is often quoted for a single amount for the duration of the coverage, rather than on an annual basis.[254]

E. General Considerations

3.147 Whether OPIC, MIGA, other government-subsidized, or private insurance is best suited for any particular investment can only be determined on a case-by-case basis. On the one hand, private insurance is more flexible, can be customized to meet the needs of a particular investment, and can often be negotiated in days rather than months. Because private insurers are not bound by the same public policy constraints as State-sponsored insurers, they may be more flexible in negotiating the terms of policies. In addition, private insurance policies can (and usually must) be kept in strict confidence. Many private insurers prefer that the host country remain unaware of the insurance to avoid moral hazard, "the same reasons that defense lawyers do not want a jury apprised of the existence of insurance in liability cases."[255] Also, because private insurance companies offer insurance based on their own business judgment rather than on political considerations, they have much greater freedom than national programs to choose what projects they will insure.[256]

3.148 Yet, while private insurance is more flexible, its provision in the least-developing countries and fragile States remains limited, if not restricted. It is reported that private insurance is concentrated in resource-rich countries.[257] On the other

[251] Rowat, *supra* note 1, at 126.
[252] Orloff, *supra* note 2, at 6.
[253] *Id.* at 6–7.
[254] Williams, *supra* note 120, at 97.
[255] *Id.* at 101.
[256] Rowat, *supra* note 1, at 125.
[257] MIGA, *World Investment and Political Risk Report 2010* (2011), available at http://documents.worldbank.org/curated/en/273261468332370710/World-investment-and-political-risk-2010.

hand, the coverage of multilaterals and ECAs plays an important role, especially in assuming more political risk in developing countries and in politically unstable States. In particular, multilateral providers such as MIGA are not driven by purely commercial concerns. Therefore, they can insure projects in a politically risky environment and assume more risk than private insurers.[258] In addition, government-subsidized insurance is generally less expensive, and can also be issued for much longer terms. Also, OPIC and MIGA have better facilities for covering currency inconvertibility risks than do private insurers.[259]

As between OPIC, MIGA, or other government-subsidized insurance, selection of a policy will often be based upon price and eligibility requirements. Some investors are attracted to government-sponsored political risk insurance for reasons other than insurance coverage. OPIC, for example, carries the full faith and credit of the U.S. government, and has experience resolving disputes between investors and States, which increases the chance of an acceptable settlement in the event of expropriation.[260] By the same token, MIGA's participation in a project may reduce political risk, because developing States seek to maintain a productive relationship with MIGA's parent, the World Bank. **3.149**

[258] Hannah Mayer, *Political Risk Insurance and Its Effectiveness in Supporting Private Sector Investment in Fragile States*, Report of The LSE-Oxford Commission on State Fragility, Growth and Development (2018), at 10–11, available at https://www.theigc.org/wp-content/uploads/2018/05/Political-risk-insurance.pdf.

[259] Orloff, *supra* note 2, at 7.

[260] Chew, *supra* note 16, at 670; Mansbach, *supra* note 2, at B-3.

PART II

THE INTERNATIONAL LAW FRAMEWORK OF INVESTMENT PROTECTION AND POLITICAL RISK

4

STATE RESPONSIBILITY AND REMEDIES UNDER CUSTOMARY INTERNATIONAL LAW

A private international business transaction—that is, a transaction between nationals of different countries—will often involve questions concerning conflicts of laws. For example, in a contract for the sale of goods between a German national and a French national, does German or French law apply? If the contract is to be performed in London, does English law have a role to play? Such a transaction may even involve international law to an extent—for example, in the interpretation of international trade agreements between the home States of the contracting parties. But aspects of public international law, the law governing relationships among States, would be irrelevant in such private contracts. **4.01**

When a transaction binds a national of one State and another sovereign State, however, international law may have a range of applications and raise a number of challenging questions: Can the sovereign State bind itself by means of a contract with an individual or corporation? May the State later breach that contract if necessary for the "public good"? Does the investor then have remedies that it can **4.02** pursue against the State, or must remedies be pursued by the investor's home State? If the investor is a corporation, which State is its "home State" under international law?

4.03 The norms of international law therefore can have a significant impact on international economic transactions. Although there is no global mechanism or body authorized to enforce principles of international law or coerce recalcitrant States to comply with principles of international law, States nevertheless tend to abide by these principles. As Detlev Vagts notes:

> [e]ventually, after considerable commotion and maneuvering in foreign courts and in the petroleum markets, Libya's Quadaffi did pay the oil companies whose contracts he had flamboyantly canceled. Other oil states in the Middle East have likewise done what arbitrators ordered. Only a few scattered episodes of persistent failure to honor an award to a private party mar this record.[1]

4.04 One reason that States comply with international law, despite the absence of any effective enforcing agency, is that States that defy international law nevertheless suffer undesirable consequences.[2] For example, even if a State as a practical or political-legal matter will not face military action in response to an unlawful expropriation, it may not wish to be seen as a lawbreaker or to face other measures, such as boycotts or seizures of the State's property located in other jurisdictions. States hoping to court foreign investment will also be reluctant to develop a reputation for having little respect for contractual obligations or the principles of law upon which investors rely.

4.05 It therefore stands to reason that States will at least hesitate before taking action that is clearly contrary to international law, such as the expropriation of a foreign investor's property without paying compensation, especially if the State has reinforced its obligations by entering into a treaty or "internationalized" investor–State contract.[3] As a result, knowledge of customary international law can

---

[1] Detlev F. Vagts, *Protecting Foreign Investment: An International Law Perspective*, in Foreign Direct Investment in the 1990s: A New Climate in the Third World 110 (Cynthia Day Wallace ed. 1990).

[2] On State compliance with international law, *see* Louis Henkin, How Nations Behave 9–98 (2d ed. 1969); Peter M. Haas, *Why Comply, or Some Hypotheses in Search of an Analyst*, in International Compliance with Non-Binding Accords 21 (Edith Brown Weiss ed. 1997); Christopher C. Joyner, *The Reality and Relevance of International Law in the Post-Cold War Era*, in The Global Agenda 211 (C.W. Kegley & E.R. Wittkopf eds. 1995); Markus Burgstaller, Theories of Compliance with International Law (2004). In the words of Professor Kirgis, "The enforcement tools of international law are … imperfect. Not only are they applied unevenly in some cases, but they frequently work slowly if at all … Despite all this, there are international enforcement mechanisms that do work in ways that may not always be obvious. In particular, the international community, no less than domestic society within any nation-state, conducts much of its daily business on the basis of self-enforcing norms that never make the headlines. Enlightened self-interest makes those norms effective." *See* Frederic L. Kirgis, *Enforcing International Law*, ASIL Insights, Jan. 1996, available at http://www.asil.org/insights/insight1.htm.

[3] For a discussion of the "internationalization" of contracts, *see* Chapter 2, Section D; Section B.2.a, *infra*.

aid the investor in obtaining a remedy for unlawful interference with property rights, for example by convincing its home government to engage in diplomatic negotiations with the host State; by seizing the property of the host State through a third State's courts; or by invalidation of title to expropriated property.

Thus, although customary international law offers few absolute guarantees, it can nevertheless moderate the conduct of host States. This chapter discusses the nature of State responsibility and the obligations of States with respect to foreign investment and investors, primarily under customary international law. Also covered are the remedies generally available to investors when a State incurs responsibility under customary international law, and the limitations placed upon such remedies. Chapter 5 will describe the history and development of the particular customary international law rules pertaining to investment protection, followed by Chapters 6 and 7, which will explore the modern law of investment protection as expressed in investment treaties and national investment laws and jurisdictional requirements for invoking such protections through international arbitration. **4.06**

In the present chapter, Section A provides a short overview of the nature and sources of customary international law, while the next section addresses whether international law permits a sovereign State to bind itself to a contract with a national of another State. "State responsibility" for acts that are considered illegal under international law is covered in Section C. **4.07**

Section D summarizes the remedies generally available to the investor or its home State following a taking of the investor's property, and the subsequent section covers the customary law requirement that local remedies be exhausted. Another pre-condition to recovery under customary international law, that the affected investor be a "national" of the State pursuing remedies against the host State for expropriation, is discussed in Section F. Finally, Section G discusses host State immunity from the jurisdiction of the national courts of other States in connection with investment claims. **4.08**

A. International Law in General

International law has been defined as "the body of rules governing the mutual relations of states."[4] International law is founded on certain underlying principles. **4.09**

The first of these principles is that all States are sovereign within their own territory. The corollary to this basic rule is "*pari parim non habet imperium*, which **4.10**

[4] Isi Foighel, Nationalization: A Study in the Protection of Alien Property in International Law 41 (1957); *see also* Hugh Thirlway, The Sources of International Law 1–25 (2014).

means that no state could be expected to submit to the laws of another."[5] The concept of absolute sovereignty is, however, counterbalanced by various rules and norms derived from the mutual consent of sovereign States, and which are said to bind all States.

4.11 The principles of international law are primarily drawn from:

- *international conventions*, such as treaties between States;
- *international custom*, as evidence of a widespread and representative practice accepted as law;
- *general principles of law recognized by civilized nations*; and
- as subsidiary sources, judicial decisions, and the teachings of *qualified publicists* around the world.[6]

---

[5] Rosalyn Higgins, Problems and Process: International Law and How We Use It 78–79 (1994).

[6] Statute of the International Court of Justice, art. 38(1) (1945), available at http://www.icj-cij.org. Customary law and conventional law are the primary sources of international law, although, as noted, there are other, secondary sources. Accordingly, in this book, unless the context indicates otherwise, we use the term "customary international law" to refer to principles of international law, as distinct from the rules established in treaties. The customary international law related to treaty interpretation is codified in the Vienna Convention on the Law of Treaties, 1969, 1155 U.N.T.S. 331, available at https://www.icj-cij.org/en/statute. Public international law is widely viewed as positivistic, as its principles derive from particular identifiable "sources." The degree to which natural law or other norms, such as those pertaining to "human rights," play a role in international law is much debated. *Jus cogens*, for example, comprises those norms of international law that are so fundamental that they override all other sources of international law; the prohibition against torture may be an example of this. *See e.g.* arts. 53 and 64 of the 1969 Vienna Convention on the Law of Treaties (treaties that conflict with a "peremptory norm of general international law" are void). Such a peremptory norm is defined in art. 53 as "a norm accepted and recognized by the international community of States as a whole as a norm from which no derogation is permitted and which can be modified only by a subsequent norm of general international law having the same character." The U.S. Restatement of the Foreign Relations Law coincides with this standard, providing that a norm of *jus cogens* is established where there is acceptance and recognition by a "large majority" of States, even if "a very small number of states" dissents. Restatement (Third) of the Foreign Relations Law of the United States [hereinafter, the Restatement] § 102, and reporter's note 6 (1986), citing Report of the Proceedings of the Committee of the Whole, May 21, 1968, U.N. Doc. A/Conf. 39/11 at 471–72. As one commentator explains:

> The idea of international jus cogens as a body of "higher law" of overriding importance for the international community is steadily gaining ground. First embodied in the 1969 Vienna Convention on the Law of Treaties, it was recently confirmed by the 1986 Vienna Convention on the Law of Treaties. In its judgment in the Nicaragua Case the International Court of Justice (ICJ) clearly affirmed jus cogens as an accepted doctrine in international law. The ICJ relied on the prohibition on the use of force as being "a conspicuous example of a rule of international law having the character of jus cogens." The importance of the concept for the international legal order is further confirmed by the trend to apply it beyond the law of treaties, in particular in the law of state responsibility. By relying on ideas closely linked to jus cogens the International Law Commission (ILC) proposed the notion of international crimes resulting from the breach by a state of an international obligation "essential for the protection of fundamental interests of the international community".

Gennady M. Danilenko, *International Jus Cogens: Issues of Law-Making*, 2(1) Eur. J. Int'l L. 42 (1991), available at http://www.ejil.org/journal/Vol2/No1/art3.html (internal citations omitted).

One significant rule of international law requires that a State pay compensation to a foreign investor following expropriation. As will be discussed, this rule nevertheless takes account of the fundamental concept of sovereignty, in that a State is not prevented *per se* from expropriating property in its territory, as long as it observes certain conditions imposed by international law. To a large degree, international law principles related to foreign investment are shaped by the tension between the concept of absolute sovereignty and the international rules and norms that restrict the freedom of States to act. **4.12**

B. Can a Sovereign Restrict Its Future Actions?

1. In general

A core question of customary international law in the context of international investment is whether a State is internationally bound by the promises it makes to a national of another State. Otherwise put, is it a violation of international law for a State that enters into an agreement with a national of another State to breach the terms of that agreement, for instance by changing its laws in a way contrary to the terms of the agreement. Or—absent contrary international treaty—does the State enjoy absolute sovereignty and discretion over changes of its laws within its own territory, such that changes in the State's municipal law, even if contrary to the terms of an investor–State contract, are not sanctioned by international law? **4.13**

The argument that States cannot be bound by a prior agreement derives from the notion that States are absolutely sovereign within their own borders.[7] In the municipal law context, the doctrine of legislative or parliamentary supremacy recognizes that the acts of one legislature or parliament cannot bind a later legislature or parliament.[8] In the United States, for example, the U.S. Supreme Court has held: **4.14**

> The taking of private property for public use upon just compensation is so often necessary for the proper performance of governmental functions that the power is

For a summary of the normative reach and foundations of international human rights law, *see* Thomas Burgenthal et al., International Human Rights in a Nutshell (3d ed. 2002). About the normative and institutional evolution of human rights and their impact on various doctrines of general international law, see The Oxford Handbook of International Human Rights Law (Dinah Shelton ed. 2013).

[7] Some commentators have also posited economic sovereignty of States, based on the principles of economic self-determination and permanent sovereignty over natural resources; *see* M. Sornarajah, The International Law on Foreign Investment 119 (3d ed. 2010).

[8] Moreover, as a matter of constitutional theory, a contract with a private party cannot restrict the legislative power of a State, and a commitment to the contrary must be given by the parliament and not by the executive branch. *See* Peter Cameron, International Energy Investment Law: The Pursuit of Stability 91 (2010).

deemed essential to the life of the State. It cannot be surrendered, and, if attempted to be contracted away, it may be resumed at will.[9]

As Bowett has noted, the law of England is very similar in this regard:

> Where the Crown acts in an executive capacity to vary or terminate a contract, its action is deemed to be lawful, and no breach of contract . . . "[A] government cannot fetter its duty to act for the public good. It cannot bind itself—by an implication in the contract—not to perform its public duties."[10]

4.15 Despite the universally recognized sovereignty of independent States, governmental powers are not limitless under customary international law.[11] A State will be bound in certain circumstances to certain promises it makes to another State or a national of another State. Thus, although international law does not require a State to permit the entry of foreign direct investment (FDI) into its territory (unless such permission is dictated by treaty),[12] once a State has entered into certain international agreements, they must generally be observed.[13] In the oft-repeated formulation of the *Sapphire* case:

> It is a fundamental principle of law, which is constantly being proclaimed by international Courts, that contractual undertakings must be respected. The rule "pacta sunt servanda" is the basis of every contractual relationship.[14]

---

[9] *Georgia v. City of Chattanooga*, 264 U.S. 472, 480 (1924).

[10] Derek William Bowett, *State Contracts with Aliens: Contemporary Developments on Compensation for Termination or Breach*, 59 Brit. Yb. Int'l L. 49, 57–58 (1988), *quoting Czarnikow v. Rolimpex*, [1977] 3 W.L.R. 686 *per* Lord Denning MR, following *The Amphitrite*, [1921] 3 K.B. 500. *See also* H.L.A. Hart, The Concept of Law (1961); and A.V. Dicey, Introduction to the Study of the Law of the Constitution (8th ed. 1982) at ch. I, esp. pp. 18 *et seq.* (discussing parliamentary sovereignty).

[11] In general, the State's sovereignty is circumscribed by customary principles and standards that are related to State responsibility for injury to aliens such as the *international minimum standard. See* Rudolf Dolzer & Christoph Schreuer, Principles of International Investment Law 3, 17–18 (2d ed. 2012). For one view on the extent to which a State may discriminate against foreign investors under international law, *see* A.F.M. Maniruzzaman, *Expropriation of Alien Property and the Principle of Non-Discrimination in International Law of Foreign Investment: An Overview*, 8 J. Transnat'l L. & Pol'y. 57 (1998).

[12] Ibrahim F.I. Shihata, *Recent Trends Relating to Entry of Foreign Direct Investment*, 9 ICSID Rev.—For. Inv. L.J. 47 (1994). This principle of international law was also set forth in the Havana Charter for an International Trade Organization (U.S. Department of State Pub. 3206 (1947)), which, although never ratified, represented a codification of then-accepted international law principles. Michael A. Geist, *Toward a General Agreement on the Regulation of Foreign Direct Investment*, 26 L. & Pol'y. Int'l Bus. 673, 680 (1995). An example of a treaty establishing binding rules on the establishment of foreign investment is the North American Free Trade Agreement (NAFTA), Dec. 17, 1992, U.S.–Can.–Mex. (entered into force Jan. 1, 1994), 32 I.L.M. 605, which requires each member State to allow the entry of investment originating in other member States on the most favorable terms granted to investors from any member State or to investors from third countries. Certain sectors of the economy of each member State are excluded from this requirement. For more on NAFTA, *see* Chapter 6; also http://www.nafta-sec-alena.org and http://www.naftaclaims.com. Most bilateral investment treaties (BITs) concluded by the United States include similar rights of entry and establishment. *See* Chapter 6 for a discussion of such treaties.

[13] Adeoye Akinsanya, *International Protection of Direct Foreign Investments in the Third World*, 36 ICLQ 58, 59 (1987).

[14] *Sapphire Int'l Petroleum Ltd. (Sapphire) v. Nat'l Iranian Oil Co.*, 35 I.L.R. 136, 181 (1953).

Pacta sunt servanda means that contracts are to be observed.[15] In the *Texaco Overseas Petroleum Co. and California Asiatic Oil Co.* (*TOPCO*) case,[16] Sole Arbitrator Dupuy confirmed this principle, referring to the *Sapphire* decision: "the maxim *pacta sunt servanda* should be viewed as a fundamental principle of international law."[17]

While this principle of international law is of benefit to the investor wishing to hold a State to its promises, it also benefits the State making the promise. Without the ability to enter into binding agreements, the State would be unable to obtain the benefits obtained by such agreements. As the tribunal in *Revere Copper & Brass Inc. v. Overseas Private Investment Corp.* explained: **4.16**

> The situation in Jamaica with respect to the aluminum companies ... was the almost classic one of a government seeking to obtain substantial long term commitments from foreign investors for the economic development of its natural resources and for that purpose providing substantial inducements in the way of tax and other assurances for limited periods of time. *If the sovereign power of a State cannot be fettered in this manner by entering into binding contracts, the State would be deprived of the power by contracts to meet essential needs.* Inevitably, in order to meet the aspirations of its peoples, the Government may for certain periods of time impose limits on the sovereign powers of the State ... Under international law the commitments made in favor of foreign nationals are binding notwithstanding the power of Parliament and other governmental organs under the domestic Constitution to override or nullify such commitments. Any other position would mean in this case that Jamaica could not in the exercise of its sovereign powers obtain foreign private capital to develop its resources or attract foreign industries. To suggest that for the purpose of obtaining

---

[15] *Daimler Financial Services A.G. v. Argentina*, ICSID Case No. ARB/05/1, Award of Aug. 22, 2012, para. 146: "The rule pacta sunt servanda is the basis of every contractual relationship"; *see also* Thomas Wälde, *The "Umbrella" (or Sanctity of Contract/Pacta Sunt Servanda) Clause in Investment Arbitration: A Comment on Original Intentions and Recent Cases*, 1(4) TDM (2004). In *Amco Asia Corp. v. Indonesia*, ICSID Case No. ARB/81/1, Decision on Jurisdiction of Sept. 25, 1983, para. 14(i), the tribunal acknowledged that the fundamental principle *pacta sunt servanda* is "a principle common to ... all systems of internal law and to international law." In *Daimler Financial Services A.G. v. Argentina*, ICSID Case No. ARB/05/1, Decision on Annulment of Jan. 7, 2015, the ad hoc Annulment Committee rejected the claimant's argument that the rule *pacta sunt servanda* was of a peremptory nature (*see* paras. 177 and 205).

[16] *Texaco Overseas Petroleum Co. and California Asiatic Oil Co. (TOPCO) v. Government of Libya*, 53 I.L.R. 389 (1979), 17 I.L.M. 1 (1978).

[17] *Id.* at para. 51. The origin of the *pacta sunt servanda* principle remains controversial. It was undoubtedly one of the most important elements of classical Roman legal thought, perhaps best epitomized by the legend of Consul Marcus Atilius Regulus, who was captured during the First Punic War. The consul was sent as a hostage to Rome, having sworn to his captors to return to face torture and death in Carthage if he did not secure a peace treaty in Rome. Once in Rome, he eloquently made the case for continued war with Carthage, and winning a renewed commitment by the Roman Senate to continue the war he returned to Carthage in fulfillment of his oath to die at the hands of the Carthaginians. *See* Appian, Roman History 409 (1912). In a more contemporary context, the principle of *pacta sunt servanda* appears to have become part of modern arbitration arbitration jurisprudence. *See* Stanimir A. Alexandrov, *Introductory Note* to *SGS Societe Generale de Surveillance S.A. v. Pakistan*, ICSID Case No. ARB/01/13, 42 I.L.M. 1285, 1287 (2003).

> foreign capital the Government could only issue contracts that were non-binding would be meaningless.[18]

And as Professor Dupuy recognized in *TOPCO*:

> [n]othing can prevent a State, in the exercise of its sovereignty, from binding itself irrevocably by the provisions of a concession and from granting to the concessionaire irretractable rights ... [I]n entering into concession contracts with the plaintiffs, the Libyan State did not *alienate* but *exercised* its sovereignty.[19]

Thus, it is a well-established principle of international law that a State can enter into a commitment that will later bind it. Entering into a binding agreement is an *exercise* of sovereignty, rather than a limitation on the State's freedom to act.[20]

4.17 It is important to recognize, however, that the binding force of State contracts does not actually *prevent* the State from breaching the agreement. As discussed, State sovereignty implies the power to breach agreements. It does mean, however, that the State may bear liability for the violation of a binding agreement. In other words, the act of breach may entail certain international consequences, as discussed in further detail in Section C, *infra*.

2. State promises in investor–State contracts

a. Internationalization of investor–State contracts

4.18 Although a State can bind itself by contract to nationals of another State,[21] it is generally accepted that a State is not automatically liable under international law for breach of a private contract.[22] Many investor–State contracts, in fact, are

---

[18] *Revere Copper & Brass Inc. (Revere) v. Overseas Private Investment Corp.*, American Arbitration Association Award Case No. 16 10 0137 76, *reproduced at* 17 I.L.M. 1321, 1342–43 (1978) (emphasis added).

[19] *TOPCO, supra* note 16, at 482 (citing *Saudi Arabia v. Arabian American Oil Co. (ARAMCO)* (1958), 27 I.L.R. 117, 168 (1963) (emphasis added)). *See also* Chapter 7, quote at text accompanying note 14.

[20] This was affirmed as early as 1923 in *The SS "Wimbledon", U.K. et al. v. Germany*, Judgment, P.C.I.J. Ser. A, No. 1 (1923), I.C.G.J. 235 (P.C.I.J. 1923), Aug. 17, 1923, Permanent Court of International Justice, at 25:

> The Court declines to see in the conclusion of any Treaty by which a State undertakes to perform or refrain from performing a particular act an abandonment of its sovereignty. No doubt any convention creating an obligation of this kind places a restriction upon the exercise of the sovereign rights of the State, in the sense that it requires them to be exercised in a certain way. But the right of entering into international engagements is an attribute of State sovereignty.

[21] *See e.g.* Robert Jennings, *State Contracts in International Law*, 27 Brit. Yb. Int'l L. 156 (1961) (arguing that there are no basic objections to the existence of an international law of contract); *see also* C.F. Amerasinghe, *State Breaches of Contracts with Aliens in International Law*, 58 AJIL 881 (1964); Irmgard Marboe & August Reinisch, *Contracts between States and Foreign Private Law Persons*, in Max Planck Encyclopedia of Public International Law (2011). *See also* Chapter 7, quote at text accompanying note 14.

[22] Oppenheim's International Law 927 (Sir Robert Jennings & Sir Arthur Watts eds. 1992). *See also* Chapter 6, Section C.5.a.

governed solely by the law of the host State,[23] and thus (unless an international treaty provides otherwise) may be unilaterally modified by the host State to the detriment of the investor. Mann points out that:

> [t]here is no general principle of law which would preclude a State from enacting legislation which interferes with or even abrogates contracts governed by its laws and covers contracts made by itself; such legislation occurs everywhere and extremely frequently without objection.[24]

An alien investor who opens a restaurant and whose permit is later revoked by the State for alleged health violations, for example, may be unable to claim that the revocation of the permit was a breach of customary international law, unless accompanied by other State misconduct, such as a denial of justice.[25]

Generally, a contract between a host State and a national of another State binds **4.19**
the State under international law only when it is "internationalized." Once a contract is "internationalized," a State can be held responsible under international law for a breach of the contract.[26] "Internationalization" of a contract occurs when the contract is made subject to international law (or international law in combination with domestic law), and/or the parties incorporate a "stabilization clause" providing that, to the extent that the law of the host State governs the contract, it will not be unilaterally modified by the State.[27]

---

[23] In the *Case concerning the Payment of Various Serbian Loans issued in France (France v. Kingdom of the Serbs, Croats and Slovenes)*, Judgment, P.C.I.J. Ser. A, No. 20, the P.C.I.J. held that "[a]ny contract which is not a contract between States in their capacity as subjects of international law is based on the municipal law of some country." In the *Case concerning the Payment in Gold of the Brazilian Federal Loans issued in France (France v. United States of Brazil)*, Judgment, P.C.I.J. Ser. A, No. 21, the P.C.I.J. reiterated its approach taken in the *Serbian Loans Case* and ruled that the law applicable to a contract between a State and a foreign private entity is a question of private international law to be decided "by reference to the actual nature of the obligations in question and to the circumstances attendant upon their creation, [as well as] the expressed or presumed intention of the Parties." However, the P.C.I.J. attached weight to the law of the State which is party to the contract (in this case, Brazil). This approach was later rejected in favor of a more general rule that, in the absence of any choice of law by the parties, a contract between a State and a foreign private entity shall be subject "to the rules of law with which the contract has the closest link"; *see* arts. 1 and 5 of the Resolution of the Institut de Droit International, "*The Proper Law of the Contract in Agreements between a State and a Foreign Private Person*," Sept. 11, 1979, [1979] 58-II AnnIDI 193.

[24] F.A. Mann, *The Consequences of an International Wrong in International and National Law*, 48 Brit. Yb. Int'l L. 1, 60 n.1 (1977).

[25] Nevertheless, where an investment treaty provides additional rights, an investor may be able to challenge the refusal or revocation of a regulatory permit. *See e.g. Tecnicas Medioambientales Tecmed S.A. v. Mexico*, ICSID Case No. ARB(AF)/00/2, Award of May 29, 2003, 43 I.L.M. 133, paras. 117–23 (2004), http://www.worldbank.org/icsid; *Metalclad Corp. v. Mexico*, ICSID Case No. ARB(AF)/97/1, Award of Aug. 30, 2000, 40 I.L.M. 36 (2001), para. 103, http://www.worldbank.org/icsid. For further discussion on the relation between contract and property rights in the context of an expropriation, see Chapter 5, Section C.

[26] For a historic account of the legal foundations of the internationalization of investment contracts, *see* Julien Cantegreil, *The Audacity of the Texaco/Calasiatic Award: René-Jean Dupuy and the Internationalization of Foreign Investment Law*, 22(2) EJIL 441, 444–48 (2011).

[27] Bowett, *supra* note 10, at 51–52. Stabilization clauses are most commonly found in contracts in the energy and mining sector; *see* Cameron, *supra* note 8, at 68. For a brief but thorough

A typical international choice-of-law clause defines the governing law of the agreement as follows:

> [T]he principles of law of Libya common to the principles of international law and in the absence of such common principles then by and in accordance with the general principles of law, including such of those principles as may have been applied by international tribunals.[28]

4.20 Professor Bowett concludes that the primary purpose of such a clause is to invoke the international law concept of *pacta sunt servanda*.[29] In the previous example, if Libya were to attempt unilaterally to alter such an agreement, its action would be contrary to the *pacta sunt servanda* principle, and would be inconsistent with principles of Libyan law common to international law. General principles of law, which include the principle of *pacta sunt servanda*, would therefore prevent Libya from terminating the agreement outside the framework of the contract itself.[30]

4.21 Professor García-Amador has provided a helpful explanation of the role of stabilization and choice-of-law clauses in "internationalizing" a contract. He maintains that the choice of international law in itself can "internationalize" a contract.[31] By contrast, a stabilization clause in a contract governed by the law of the host State would be of little effect, he argues, and the State could change the applicable law at will. However, if the stabilization clause is contained in a contract governed by international law, then a State that infringes rights included in that contract should incur international responsibility. García-Amador's conclusions are worth repeating:

> The choice-of-law clauses ... are also "stabilization" devices. Actually, both the [choice of international law clause and stabilization clause] and the [modern concession] agreements as a whole aim to create a legal situation which precludes changes in the municipal law of the contracting State in violation of the stipulations of the agreement ... Stabilization clauses incorporate in concession agreements not only express, but the specific concrete commitment on the part of the contracting State not to change the terms of the contractual relationship without the consent of the other contracting party. This commitment may make a difference from the point of view of international responsibility. The breach of the obligations contained in

---

discussion of internationalization of contracts in the context of oil concessions, *see* Margarita T.B. Coale, *Stabilization Clauses in International Petroleum Transactions*, 30 Denv. J. Int'l L. & Pol'y. 217 (2002). *See also* Chapter 2, Sections D.2 and D.3. While some observers maintain that both choice of international law and a stabilization clause are necessary to internationalize a contract, others contend that a stabilization clause standing alone can also fulfill this function, if properly drafted. *See* Michael Dickstein, *Revitalizing International Law Governing Concession Agreements*, 6 Int'l Tax & Bus. Law. 54 (1988).

[28] *TOPCO, supra* note 16, at 404.

[29] Bowett, *supra* note 10, at 54.

[30] *Id.* at 54.

[31] F.V. García-Amador, *State Responsibility in Case of "Stabilization" Clauses*, 2 J. Transnat'l L. & Pol'y. 23, 49–50 (1993). On internationalization, *see also* Ian Brownlie, Principles of Public International Law 527 *et seq.* (6th ed. 2003).

> a stabilization clause may well be viewed as a circumstance aggravating the responsibility of the contracting State. The breach of any of the obligations emanating from the contractual relationship entails responsibility, but when there is a breach of an obligation involving an explicit State's promise to respect the agreement, the breach logically becomes a more serious act or omission, entailing a higher degree of responsibility. It is also logical to think that the higher degree of responsibility will affect the measure of reparation.[32]

A number of international tribunals have affirmed the significance of contract "internationalization."[33] In *TOPCO*, Sole Arbitrator Dupuy found that one effect of the internationalization of a contract is that individuals acquire and can enforce certain international law rights against the State.[34] **4.22**

b. Arguments that investor–State contracts cannot be internationalized

Although arbitral tribunals have generally attributed binding effect to internationalized investor–State contracts, arguments persist that the internationalization of private contracts is contrary to the very nature of international law. Many of these arguments appear to confuse the issue of whether a State can be "bound" by its promises to investors by contract, and the consequences of the breach of such contracts. **4.23**

The arbitrator in the *Khemco* case, for example, concluded that to hold sovereign States bound by contracts with private parties would allow "private interests to prevail over duly established public interest, making impossible actions required for the public good."[35] In the *Aminoil* arbitration, the tribunal ruled that a stabilization clause in an oil concession contract should not be presumed to imply that a State has lost the right to expropriate a contract running for a period of sixty years. The tribunal found that a contractual limitation of the State's right to nationalize would be a "particularly serious undertaking which would have to be expressly stipulated for" and that it was "to be expected that it should cover only a limited period" of time. Nevertheless, it held that the stabilization clause would reinforce the necessity of indemnification in case of nationalization.[36] **4.24**

---

32 *Id.* Of course, it is also useful to allocate jurisdiction to an international arbitrator via an arbitration clause. *See* Chapter 8 for further discussion of international arbitration.

33 International tribunals generally affirm States' practice of binding themselves (especially in energy contracts) through the inclusion of stabilization clauses. *See* A.D. Nwokolo, *Is There a legal and Functional Value for the Stabilization Clause in International Petroleum Agreements?*, 8 CEPMLP Ann. Rev. (2004). For a review of "classic" international arbitration cases in the international petroleum industry, *see* Cameron, *supra* note 8, at 103–43.

34 *TOPCO, supra* note 16, para. 48.

35 *Amco Asia Corp. (Khemco) v. Indonesia*, 27 I.L.M. 1314, para. 178 (1988). The advent of modern investment treaties has significantly altered this analysis. As explained in Chapter 7, many investment treaties expressly include contractual rights within the scope of protected investments, and may also include a specific "umbrella" clause requiring the observance of contractual undertakings. On the effect of "umbrella clauses" upon private contractual rights, *see* Chapter 6, Section C.5.

36 *Government of the State of Kuwait v American Independent Oil Co. (AMINOIL)*, Award of Mar. 24, 1982, (1982) 21 I.L.M. 976, 1022–23. This reasoning was sharply criticized by arbitrator Fitzmaurice in his separate opinion, where he took the position that the purpose of the

4.25 Likewise, Professor Brownlie argues that there is little evidence that breach of contract, even one subject to international choice-of-law and stabilization clauses, constitutes a violation of international law.[37] Under international law, he maintains, some element beyond mere breach of contract, such as a confiscatory taking or a denial of justice,[38] is required before the sovereign will incur public international law liability. Brownlie concludes that breach of contract by a State is regulated only by the principles that govern the treatment of aliens.[39]

4.26 According to the contrary view, however, the breach of a contract can be considered a "confiscatory taking" of the investor's contract rights, and should be compensated in the same manner as any other taking.[40] The State's *non-material* breach of an internationalized contract may not give rise to State responsibility, just as regulatory interference with tangible property that does not rise to the level of expropriation may not entail responsibility at customary international law.[41]

4.27 While a State is normally "bound" under international law in relation to its promises made to investors in an internationalized contract, this does not mean that the State cannot breach the contract—it simply means that the State is obligated to pay compensation for the value of any contractual rights the investor has lost.[42] Just as a State is free to expropriate tangible property located within its territory upon the payment of full compensation,[43] so a State may breach

stabilization clause was not to prevent confiscatory nationalizations, but rather to prevent "any measure terminating the concession before its time"; *see also* André von Walter, *Oil Concession Disputes, Arbitration on*, in Max Planck Encyclopedia of Public International Law, paras. 11 and 43 (2008).

[37] Brownlie, *supra* note 31, at 522–23.

[38] A denial of justice is "any defect in the organization of courts or in the exercise of justice which entails a violation of the international legal duties of States with respect to the judicial protection of alien." 10 Encyclopedia of Public International Law 96 (Rudolf Dolzer et al. eds. 1987). *See generally* Jan Paulsson, Denial of Justice under International Law (2005).

[39] Brownlie, *supra* note 31, at 522–23.

[40] For example, in *ADC Affiliate Ltd. and ADC & ADMC Management Ltd. v. Hungary*, ICSID Case No. ARB/03/16, Award of Oct. 2, 2006, 15 ICSID Rep. 539, at paras. 304, 439, and 476, the claimant argued that the legislative evisceration of the contractual agreements underlying an airport project constituted an unlawful expropriation in breach of the Cyprus–Hungary BIT. The respondent argued that the claims were purely contractual in nature and therefore inadmissible. The tribunal concluded that an act of a State that brings about the end of an investment agreement without compensation constitutes the "clearest possible case of expropriation," and found that the change in law had been an unlawful expropriation.

[41] *But see Metalclad, supra* note 25, para. 103 (holding that where there is an applicable investment treaty, government action substantially interfering with the reasonable investment-backed expectations of the investor may constitute expropriation).

[42] The requirement of compensation for breach of contract is discussed in Chapter 5, Section C. *See also* Chapter 1, Section C.5, discussing the relationship between political risk and the breach of State contracts.

[43] *See* Chapter 5.

an internationalized contract, but must pay compensation.[44] Judge Higgins has underlined this point, stating that:

> a state may still engage in what it sees as actions in the public good that violate contracts; but there is no reason why the foreign investor should underwrite this exercise in state sovereignty.[45]

Professor Bowett has also expressed doubt that a State can bind itself by signing an "internationalized" contract. Arguing against the analogy between internationalized contracts and international treaties, he reasons that: **4.28**

> The investment contract between a State and a private entity not only is not a treaty but cannot even be regarded as analogous to a treaty. For there is a world of difference between an agreement under international law between two equal, sovereign States and a contract between a State and a private party governed prima facie by the State's own law. Obviously, with a treaty one state cannot use its own municipal law to vary its treaty obligations towards another State. But is by no means obvious why, with a private law contract, the State party should not assert that right.[46]

C. State Responsibility

1. In general

The law of State responsibility concerns the accountability of States for violation of international law, and the requirement that States make reparation for such violations.[47] Thus, the law of State responsibility is not concerned with the content of international law (*i.e.* the particular rules that States should not breach), but rather with the consequences of a violation of international law by a State.[48] In other words, once it has been determined that a State has committed a wrong **4.29**

---

[44] Rudolf Dolzer & Christoph Schreuer, Principles of International Investment Law 84 (2d ed. 2012).

[45] Higgins, *supra* note 5, at 143.

[46] Bowett, *supra* note 10, at 54. Similarly, Sornarajah asserts that it cannot be accepted that investor–State contracts "are akin to treaties and their violation is unlawful"; Sornarajah, *supra* note 7, at 402, 406–10.

[47] U.N. Doc. A/CN.4/L.602/Rev.1 (2001) [hereinafter, Draft Articles], available at https://documents-dds-ny.un.org/doc/UNDOC/LTD/G01/638/25/pdf/G0163825.pdf?OpenElement. While not yet opened for signature as an international treaty, the Draft Articles were adopted by resolution of the U.N. International Law Commission in 2001. Since it codifies existing law for the most part, this document is generally recognized to reflect customary international law. On the development of the law of State responsibility, *see generally* Higgins, *supra* note 5, at 146–68. "The *consequence* of state responsibility is the liability to make reparation." *Id.* at 162 (emphasis in the original). *See also* Brownlie, *supra* note 31, at 420 *et seq.*; Restatement, *supra* note 6, § 901 ("[u]nder international law, a state that has violated a legal obligation to another state is required to terminate the violation and, ordinarily, to make reparations, including in appropriate circumstances restitution or compensation for loss or injury").

[48] M.N. Shaw, International Law 694 (5th ed. 2003). For a detailed treatment of the topic of State responsibility, *see* Brownlie, *supra* note 31, at 420 *et seq.*

under international law (the subject of the remainder of this chapter and of Chapter 5), it is the doctrine of State responsibility that dictates whether reparation should be forthcoming.[49]

4.30 State responsibility arises when a State acts (or fails to act) in violation of an obligation it owes to another State, and the action results in loss or damage to the non-breaching State.[50] In the *Spanish Zone of Morocco Case*,[51] Judge Huber stated that:

> [r]esponsibility is the necessary corollary of a right. All rights of an international character involve international responsibility. If the obligation in question is not met, responsibility entails the duty to make reparation.[52]

4.31 The law of State responsibility is implicated, for example, following a State's breach of treaty obligations.[53] The arbitrator in *Rainbow Warrior* stated that:

> The legal consequences of a breach of a treaty, including the determination of the circumstances that may exclude wrongfulness (and render the breach only apparent) and the appropriate remedies for breach, are subjects that belong to the customary law of state responsibility.[54]

4.32 The law of State responsibility has been codified in the Draft Articles on State Responsibility for Internationally Wrongful Acts.[55] Investment tribunals have broadly accepted that the Draft Articles reflect customary international law and articulate the general principles of State responsibility in investment arbitration.[56]

2. Acts of State agencies

4.33 The Draft Articles codify the rules of customary international law with respect to the attribution of conduct to a State in Chapter II. Although these Articles expressly cover the obligations a responsible State may owe to another *State*, to

---

49 *See, in general,* The Law of International Responsibility (James Crawford et al. eds. 2010).

50 Draft Articles, supra note 47, art. 2; *United States Diplomatic and Consular Staff in Tehran*, Judgment, 1980 I.C.J. Rep. 3, 29, para. 56. *Cf.* page 41, para. 90; *Military and Paramilitary Activities in and against Nicaragua (Nicaragua v. United States of America)*, Merits, Judgment, I.C.J. Reports 1986, at 14, 117–18, para. 226; *The Gabcíkovo-Nagymaros Project (Hungary v. Slovakia)*, Merits, Judgment, I.C.J. Reports 1997, at 54, para. 78; *see also* Shaw, *supra* note 48, at 696–97.

51 *British Properties in Spanish Zone of Morocco (Spain v. U.K.)*, 2 R.I.A.A. 615 (1925).

52 *Id.* at 641.

53 Mann, *supra* note 24, at 8 (breach of a treaty, "at any rate if it is substantial, constitutes an international wrong and cannot simply be likened to a breach of contract").

54 *The Rainbow Warrior Arbitration*, 82 I.L.R. 519 (1990).

55 Draft Articles, *supra* note 47.

56 *See F.-W. Oil Interests Inc. v. Trinidad & Tobago*, ICSID Case No. ARB/01/14, Award of Mar. 3, 2006, para. 202; *Bayindir Insaat Turizm Ticaret Ve Sanayi A.S. v. Pakistan*, ICSID Case No. ARB/03/29, Award of Aug. 27, 2009, n.19; *Mohammad Ammar Al-Bahloul v. Tajikistan*, SCC Case No. 064/2008, Partial Award on Jurisdiction and Liability of Sept. 2 2009, para. 165; *Tulip Real Estate and Development Netherlands B.V. v. Turkey*, ICSID Case No. ARB/11/28, Award of Mar. 10, 2014, para. 281.

several *States*, or to the *international community* as a whole, this "is without prejudice to any right arising from the international responsibility of a State, which may accrue directly to any person or entity other than a State."[57] Investment treaty tribunals have had no difficulty in relying on State responsibility principles to decide issues of attribution. Therefore, as the tribunal observed in *Flemingo Duty Free*, the Draft Articles have been systematically applied to decide whether acts of corporations or other agencies impacting a foreign investor or its investment should be attributed to the host State, potentially giving rise to that State's responsibility.[58] The tribunal in *Jan de Nul* concluded that the customary law of attribution applies by analogy to the responsibility of States toward private investors.[59]

State responsibility can cover not only the unlawful acts or omissions of the State itself,[60] but also certain acts or omissions of agencies and instrumentalities of the State, or of individuals with close connections to State functions or structures.[61] Whether State responsibility is incurred depends upon the relationship between the State and the agency or individual that commits the act. The act of a State agency will normally be imputed to the State itself under international law where the agency acts in a public capacity or pursuant to the State's authorization. For example, in *Vivendi I*, the ad hoc annulment committee relied on Article 4 of the Draft Articles to establish that "[a]ll international claims against a state are based on attribution, whether the conduct in question is that of a central or provincial government or other subdivision."[62] **4.34**

[57] Draft Articles, *supra* note 47, art. 33.

[58] *Flemingo Duty Free Shop Private Ltd. v. Poland*, UNCITRAL, PCA (Permanent Court of Arbitration), Award of Aug. 12, 2016, para. 420.

[59] *Jan de Nul N.V. and Dredging Int'l N.V. v. Egypt*, ICSID Case No. ARB/04/13, Award of Nov. 6, 2008, para. 156.

[60] Investment tribunals have routinely attributed international responsibility for the conduct of different organs and State entities, including the executive branch (*Eureko B.V. v. Poland*, Ad Hoc, Partial Award and Dissenting Opinion of Aug. 19, 2005, para. 129); the judiciary (*Robert Azinian et al. v. Mexico*, ICSID Case No. ARB(AF)/97/2, Award of Nov. 1, 1999, para. 98), the legislature (*Sergei Paushok, CJSC Golden East Co. and CJSC Vostokneftegaz Co. v. Government of Mongolia*, Award on Jurisdiction and Liability of April 28, 2011, para. 298); sub-national, municipal, or provincial governments (*Parkerings-Compagniet AS v. Lithuania*, ICSID Case No. ARB/05/8, Award of Sept. 11, 2007, para. 258); central banks (*Invesmart, B.V. v. Czech Republic*, UNCITRAL, Award (Redacted) of June 26, 2009, para. 363) and miscellaneous State-related bodies (*see e.g. European Media Ventures S.A. v. Czech Republic*, UNCITRAL, Partial Award on Liability of July 8, 2009, para. 60, for the Media Council).

[61] Draft Articles, *supra* note 47, art. 4. Art. 4(2) of the ILC Draft Articles defines the organ of a State as any person who has such a status in accordance with internal law. This is a rare case where the internal law of a state is dispositive factor for purposes of international law.

[62] *Compañía de Aguas del Aconquija S.A. and Vivendi Universal S.A. (formerly Compagnie Générale des Eaux) v. Argentina*, ICSID Case No. ARB/97/3, Decision on Annulment of July 3, 2002, n.17.

4.35 Even if the State agency is not technically part of the State's internal structure, if it exercises governmental functions, its conduct may be attributable to the State.[63] As the tribunal held in *Bosh International*, article 5 of the Draft Articles also applies to autonomous institutions which exercise legislative or administrative functions.[64] In the *Pereira* and *Leonard and Mavis Daley* cases, Iran was ordered to pay compensation for the seizure of foreign nationals' property by the paramilitary Revolutionary Guards.[65] In *Salini v. Morocco*, the tribunal declared the Kingdom of Morocco liable for the actions of an independent State-owned commercial company. The arbitrators concluded that:

> it is clear that [the company's] main object is to accomplish tasks that are under State control (building, managing and operating of assets falling under the province of the public utilities responding to the structural needs of the Kingdom of Morocco with regard to infrastructure and efficient communication networks) . . .
>
> Thus, since [the company] is an entity, from a structural as well as a functional point of view, which is distinguishable from the State solely on account of its legal personality, the Tribunal . . . concludes that . . . [the company] is a State company, acting in the name of the Kingdom of Morocco.[66]

4.36 By contrast, *Lauder v Czech Republic*, the tribunal concluded that a contract with the claimant's investment vehicle had been terminated as the result of acts by a private company independent from the State. The result therefore could not be expropriation.[67] In *Al Tamimi*, the tribunal found that the actions of an Omani State-owned enterprise were not attributable to Oman, because it did not exercise regulatory, administrative, or governmental authority, and did not meet the test for attribution under the US–Oman Free Trade Agreement.[68]

4.37 The acts of a State agency or instrumentality may be imputable to the State even if the act was beyond the legal capacity of the agency involved, so long as the bodies in question "have acted at least to all appearances as competent officials or organs or they must have used powers or methods appropriate to their official capacity."[69]

---

63 Draft Articles, *supra* note 47, art. 5. *See generally* Shaw, *supra* note 48, at 700 *et seq.*

64 *Bosh Int'l Inc. and B&P Ltd. Foreign Investments Enterprise v. Ukraine*, ICSID Case No. ARB/08/11, Award of Oct. 25, 2012, para. 176.

65 *See* discussion in Chapter 1, Section C.1.

66 *Salini Costruttori S.p.A. v. Morocco*, ICSID Case No. ARB/00/4, Decision on Jurisdiction of July 23, 2001, paras. 33 and 35, published at 129 J. de Droit Int'l (J.D.I.) 196 (2002). But *cf. Maffezini v. Spain*, ICSID Case No. ARB/97/7, Award of Nov. 13, 2000, 16 ICSID Rev—For. Inv. L.J. 1 (2001), para. 62 (actions of State-owned company not imputable to the State where the company was not exercising public functions in providing faulty investment advice). *See generally* Abby Cohen Smutny, *State Responsibility and Attribution: When Is a State Responsible for the Acts of State Enterprises?*, in International Investment Law and Arbitration 17 (Todd Weiler ed. 2005).

67 *Ronald S. Lauder v. Czech Republic*, UNCITRAL, Final Award of Sept. 3, 2001, paras. 202 and 274.

68 *Adel A Hamadi Al Tamimi v. Sultanate of Oman*, ICSID Case No. ARB/11/33, Award of Oct. 27, 2015, para. 316.

69 Draft Articles, *supra* note 47, art. 7. *See also Jean Baptista Caire v. Mexico*, 5 R.I.A.A. 516 (1929); Shaw, *supra* note 48, at 704.

For example, in *Kardassopoulos v. Georgia*, the tribunal found that where an entity empowered to exercise governmental authority acts *ultra vires*, its conduct is nevertheless attributable to the State.[70]

The State will not normally be responsible under customary international law for political violence, such as the actions of rioters or rebels, absent bad faith or negligence.[71] Subsequent to overthrow or other fundamental regime change, a State may be held responsible for harm caused to foreign investors by the new government in furtherance of the coup prior to assuming authority.[72] The acts of the private supporters of a revolution, however, cannot normally be attributed to the State following regime change.[73] Neither can the violent acts of an organized criminal organization be attributed to the State, unless the State acts at the bidding of such private actors.[74] **4.38**

With the expansion of the European Union's intervention in the field of FDI, the international responsibility of E.U. Member States for national measures taken in compliance with their obligations under E.U. law is an issue that has begun to arise with increasing frequency.[75] In *Electrabel*, the claimant argued that Hungary's termination of a power purchase agreement, in order to comply with a decision of the European Commission on illegal State-aid under E.U. law, breached the Energy Charter Treaty's provisions on expropriation and fair and equitable treatment.[76] The tribunal found that in principle, Hungary was not legally responsible for acts by the European Commission under the ECT or under international law. Given that the European Union, as a Regional Economic Integration Organization, is a contracting party to the ECT with authority to take decisions binding on certain **4.39**

---

[70] *Ioannis Kardassopoulos v. Georgia*, ICSID Case No. ARB/05/18, Decision on Jurisdiction of July 6, 2007, para. 190; *see also Noble Ventures Inc. v. Romania*, ICSID Case No. ARB/01/11, Award of Oct. 12, 2005, para. 81.

[71] Shaw, *supra* note 48, at 705–06. *See also Home Frontier and Foreign Missionary Society (U.S. v. Gr. Br.)* case, 6 R.I.A.A. 42 (1920); *Youmans Claim (U.S. v. Mex.)*, 4 R.I.A.A. 110 (1926). As explained in Chapter 6, the situation may be very different if the investor benefits from the protections of an investment treaty. *See American Manufacturing & Trading Inc. v. Zaire*, ICSID Case No. ARB/93/01, Award of Feb. 21, 1997 (State held liable for destruction of foreign property by rebel forces due to application of "full protection and security" provision of the BIT).

[72] Draft Articles, *supra* note 47, art. 10.

[73] *United States Diplomatic and Consular Staff in Tehran (United States v. Iran)*, 1980 I.C.J. Rep. 3, 29.

[74] *Jan Oostergetel and Theodora Laurentius v. Slovakia*, UNCITRAL, Final Award of Apr. 23, 2012, para. 163.

[75] Angelos Dimopoulos, EU Foreign Investment Law 259 *et seq.* (2011); *see also* F. Hoffmeister, *Litigating against the European Union and Its Member States—Who Responds under the ILC's Draft Articles on International Responsibility of International Organizations?*, 21 EJIL 723 (2010).

[76] *Electrabel S.A. v. Hungary*, ICSID Case No. ARB/07/19, Decision on Jurisdiction, Applicable Law and Liability of Nov. 30, 2012; *see also* Andreas Kulick, *Case Comments, Electrabel S.A. v. The Republic of Hungary, ICSID Case No. ARB/07/19, Decision on Jurisdiction, Applicable Law and Liability, 30 November 2012 (Gabrielle Kaufmann-Kohler, Brigitte Stern, V.V. Veeder)*, 15 J. World Investment & Trade 273–84 (2014).

other contracting parties with respect to matters covered by the ECT, the tribunal concluded that:

> As regards protection under the ECT, investors can have had no legitimate expectations in regard to the consequences of the implementation by an EU Member State of any such decision by the European Commission. In other words, the possible interference with a foreign investment through the implementation by an EU Member State of a legally binding decision of the European Commission was and remains inherent in the framework of the ECT itself.[77]

4.40 Consequently, the tribunal held that "it would be absurd if Hungary could be liable under the ECT for doing precisely that which it was ordered to do by a *supra*national authority whose decisions the ECT itself recognizes as legally binding on Hungary."[78] As a doctrinal gateway for this finding, the tribunal relied on Article 6 of the Draft Articles, which provides that the conduct of an organ placed at the disposal of a State by another State shall be considered an act of the former State under international law if the organ is acting in the exercise of elements of the governmental authority of the State at whose disposal it is placed. In the tribunal's view, while the European Union is not a State under international law, it can nevertheless be so regarded for the purposes of the case at hand, since it is a contracting party to the ECT.[79] Accordingly, the ECT did not protect the claimant from the respondent's implementation of a binding decision of the European Commission under E.U. law.[80]

3. For injury to investors

4.41 Under customary international law, State responsibility may arise when a State injures a national of another State.[81] The traditional view under customary international law is that injury to an individual accrues directly to his home State, rather than to the individual himself. According to this view, following an expropriation, the expropriating State has harmed the investor's home State rather than the investor,[82] and the individual may be left with no effective remedy.[83] As stated by Mann:

---

[77] *Electrabel, supra* note 76, para. 4.142.

[78] *Id.* at para. 6.72.

[79] *Id.* at para. 6.74.

[80] *Id.* at para. 4.169.

[81] SHAW, *supra* note 48, at 701.

[82] HIGGINS, *supra* note 5, at 51 ("individuals are extremely handicapped in international law from the procedural point of view. They have little access to international arenas; and are dependent upon the nationality-of-claims rule, whereby an individual must, generally speaking, pursue a claim at the international level by giving his government to take it up on his behalf").

[83] Some scholars nevertheless maintain that individuals have certain rights under international law. *See e.g.* HIGGINS, *supra* note 5, at 53. This perspective has gained ground as a result of the direct right of action provided to individual and corporate investors under modern investment treaties. *See* Zachary Douglas, *The Hybrid Foundations of Investment Treaty Arbitration*, 74 BRIT. YB. INT'L L. 151, 282 (2003) ("Investment treaties create a sub-system of state responsibility for investor/state disputes. The host state's breach of an investment treaty creates new secondary rights and obligations

> [a]s a matter of public international law it is free from doubt that, except in very special circumstances, the rights accruing from an international wrong are vested in the victim State and lie against the wrongdoing State.[84]

Thus, under customary international law, if a State incurs liability by causing injury to a foreign investor, liability runs to the home State of the injured investor, rather than to the investor himself, and the home State thus "owns" any remedies under international law.[85] **4.42**

According to international treaty law, however, bilateral investment treaties (BITs) and free trade agreements (FTAs) have transformed investors into empowered third-party beneficiaries of treaties, who may disregard the domestic jurisdiction of the courts in which they operate their investments, and assert their rights independently of their home States.[86] Some commentators have gone as far as to suggest that investment claims vindicate the investor's *own* rights rather than those of the home State, and that investors are "elevated" to the level of international law.[87] **4.43**

In any event, individuals may enjoy some remedies for economic injury by States that can be pursued under customary international law or domestic law. These remedies are discussed in Section D.2. **4.44**

D. Remedies under International Law for State Actions against Investors

1. Remedies available to the State

When a State acts in violation of international law and incurs responsibility toward another State, the injured State may pursue remedies available to it under international law. These include both remedies available under customary international law and those set forth in international agreements between the parties. **4.45**

as between the investor and the host state. The national state of the investor has no residual interest in these new rights and obligations").

[84] Mann, *supra* note 24, at 14 (footnote omitted).

[85] *Mavrommatis Palestine Concessions (Greece v. Great Britain)*, P.C.I.J. Ser. A, No. 2 (1924), at 12.

[86] *See generally* Zachary Douglas, *The Hybrid Foundations of Investment Treaty Arbitration*, 74 Yb. Int'l L. 151 (2003); *see also* José E. Alvarez, *Are Corporations Subjects of International Law?* 9 Santa Clara J. Int'l L. 1, 13 (2011).

[87] Tillman Rudolf Braun, *Globalization: The Driving Force in International Investment Law*, in The Backlash against Investment Arbitration 491–506 (Michael Waibel et al. eds. 2010) ("insofar as modern bilateral investment treaties assure investors substantive rights along with associated formal enforcement procedures, they contribute to a fundamental change in international law—the individual or legal person in private law is assigned individual rights through a treaty in international law and this is upgraded to the status of a partial subject of international law"); *see also* Thomas Wälde, *Investment Arbitration under the Energy Charter Treaty: An Overview of Key Issues*, 1 TDM (2004).

One of the most cited pronouncements on remedies comes from the Permanent Court of International Justice in *Chorzów Factory*:[88]

> The essential principle contained in the notion of an illegal act—a principle which seems to be established by international practice and in particular by the decisions of arbitral tribunals—is that reparation must, as far as possible, wipe out all the consequences of the illegal act and re-establish the situation which would, in all probability, have existed if that act had not been committed. Restitution in kind or, if this is not possible, payment of a sum corresponding to the value which a restitution in kind would bear; the award, if need be, of damages for loss sustained which would not be covered by restitution in kind or payment in place of it—such are the principles which should serve to determine the amount of compensation due for an act contrary to international law.[89]

4.46 This passage describes two remedies that a State may invoke in response to a violation of international law: reparation in kind or the payment of compensation. Regarding restitution in kind, Mann has stated that "as a rule public international law has for long recognized restitution in kind as a right, probably as the principal right, against the wrongdoing State."[90] The remedy of restitution in kind for the taking of property of an alien, however, is usually not available.[91]

4.47 Other remedies include suspension of diplomatic relations with the offending State, suspension or termination of treaty obligations, freezing of the offending State's assets, and the imposition of economic sanctions.[92] These and other remedies are discussed in detail in Chapter 10.

4.48 The response to the violation, however, must be in proportion to the harm done.[93] In particular, in response to purely economic injury to its national, a State may not apply force against the offending State.[94]

2. Remedies available to the investor

4.49 As discussed, the customary view of State responsibility is that claims can accrue only to sovereign States. As a practical matter, however, this view of international law has been overshadowed to some degree in modern practice. Brand notes: "One of the most striking developments of international law in the twentieth century is the extent to which the private party (*i.e.*, the non-sovereign) has

[88] *Factory at Chorzów (Germany v. Poland)*, P.C.I.J. Ser. A, No. 17 (1928).
[89] *Id.* at 47.
[90] Draft Articles, *supra* note 47, art. 35 (restitution), art. 36 (damages). *See also* Mann, *supra* note 24, at 3.
[91] *See* Chapter 10, Section F.
[92] Restatement, *supra* note 6, § 905, com. (b), at 381.
[93] *Id.*
[94] *See* Chapter 10, Section F.

become the subject of rules of international law."[95] In many cases, the investor may in fact pursue remedies independently of its home State.[96]

4.50 This was also stressed in the related cases of *Hulley Enterprises v. Russia, Yukos v. Russia*, and *Veteran Petroleum v. Russia*. The awards acknowledge, with identical wording, that Part II of the Draft Articles, setting out the consequences of internationally wrongful acts, is concerned with claims between States and may not directly apply to cases involving persons or entities other than States. But the tribunals were mindful that the Draft Articles reflect customary international law, and to the extent that a matter is not covered by an applicable investment treaty they can provide guidance by analogy.[97]

4.51 The general categories of remedies that are available to an investor following State action against its investment are summarized below. The U.S. Restatement of Foreign Relations Law (which codifies at least one view of customary international law) provides that following expropriation of the investor's property or breach of a contract between the State and the investor:

> (2) A person of foreign nationality injured by a [taking of property or breach of contract in violation of international law] may pursue any remedy provided by
> (a) international agreement between the person's state of nationality and the state responsible for the injury;
> (b) the law of the state responsible for the injury,
> (c) the law of another state, or
> (d) agreement between the person injured and the state responsible for the injury.[98]

4.52 Besides the widespread practice of investor–State claims under investment treaties, described in detail in Chapters 6 and 7, a well-known example of a remedy under section 2(a) is the filing of a claim by a U.S. national with the Iran–U.S. Claims Tribunal.[99] The Iran–U.S. Claims Tribunal was established pursuant to

[95] Ronald A. Brand, *External Sovereignty and International Law*, 18 Fordham Int'l L.J. 1685, 1692 (1995). *See also* Higgins, *supra* note 5, at 48–55 (criticizing the traditional subject-object distinction under international law and discussing the applicability of international law to individuals).

[96] The laws of a State may, of course, prohibit a national of that State from pursuing its remedies against an expropriating sovereign if the State itself is pursuing remedies. *See e.g.* Chapter 10, Section B.3.

[97] *Veteran Petroleum Ltd. (Cyprus) v. Russian Federation*, PCA Case No. AA 228, Final Award of July 18, 2014, n.10; *Yukos Universal Ltd. (Isle of Man) v. Russian Federation*, PCA Case No. AA 227, Final Award of July 18, 2014, n.10; *Hulley Enterprises Limited (Cyprus) v. Russian Federation*, PCA Case No. AA 226, Final Award of July 18, 2014, n.10.

[98] Restatement, *supra* note 6, § 713.

[99] The Iran–U.S. Claims Tribunal was established on Jan. 19, 1981, to resolve, among other things, disputes between U.S. nationals and the government of Iran arising from expropriation. Declaration of the Government of the Democratic and Popular Republic of Algeria Concerning the Settlement of Claims by the Government of the United States of America and the Government of the Islamic Republic of Iran (Claims Settlement Declaration), 1 Iran–US C.T.R. 9 (1983). The Iran–U.S. Claims Tribunal has jurisdiction over disputes between U.S. nationals, including citizens of the United States and corporations at least 50 percent owned by U.S. citizens and formed under

an agreement between Iran and the United States for the express purpose of providing U.S. nationals with remedies for the taking of their property by the Iranian government.

4.53 Investors may also pursue remedies under the laws of the State responsible for the injury.[100] The effectiveness of such an action will depend both upon the provisions of local law (including any municipal foreign investment code) and the independence of the judiciary from political interference.

4.54 Investors may pursue remedies against the offending State in the courts of their home State or a third State. Often, however, the private plaintiff will encounter the barriers of sovereign immunity (which may shield the expropriating State from jurisdiction in the courts of another State) or the so-called "act of State" doctrine (which prevents national courts from sitting in judgment over the actions of a foreign State).[101] Both of these obstacles are described in Section G.

4.55 Finally, the investor can seek redress under the terms of an agreement between the investor and the State. Such agreements may contain a choice of international law or some neutral national legal system to govern the relationship between parties;[102] an international arbitration clause or forum selection clause requiring that disagreements between the parties be settled before a neutral tribunal, rather than by the courts of the contracting State; and a stabilization clause. As explained above, contracts with such provisions are often said to be "internationalized," such that States executing such contracts are normally held to have agreed that by violating such a contract, they may incur international responsibility.[103] As stated by Judge Higgins:

> Arbitral clauses which refer to international law as the applicable law effectively remove the alleged inability of individuals to be the bearer of rights under international law. This is being done by mutual consent, of course—but the point is that there is *no inherent reason* why the individual should not be able directly to invoke international law and to be the beneficiary of international law.[104]

---

the laws of the United States, and the government of Iran, which includes any agency, political subdivision, instrumentality, or controlled entity thereof. The dispute must have been outstanding as of Jan. 19, 1981. Claims Settlement Declaration, art. VII, 1 Iran–US C.T.R. at 11–12.

[100] For analysis of the national foreign investment codes of several countries, *see* Geist, *supra* note 12, at 686–706; Antonio Parra, *Principles Governing Foreign Investment as Reflected in National Investment Codes*, 7 ICSID Rev.—For. Inv. L.J. 428 (1992); *see also* Markus Burgstaller & Michael Waibel, "Investment Codes," in VI Max Planck Encyclopedia of Public International Law 300–09 (Rudiger Wolfrum ed. 2012).

[101] *See* discussion in Section G, *infra*.

[102] *See* Chapter 2, Section D.2.

[103] A useful discussion of the use of stabilization and choice-of-law clauses in "internationalizing" an investor–State agreement is found in F.V. García-Amador, *State Responsibility in Case of "Stabilization" Clauses*, 2 J. Transnat'l L. & Pol'y. 23 (1993). *See also* M. Sornarajah, The Settlement of Foreign Investment Disputes 223–78 (2000); Section B.2.a, *supra*.

[104] Higgins, *supra* note 5, at 54 (emphasis in the original).

The investor's remedies may be limited by prior resolution of the dispute by the investor's home State. As the Permanent Court of International Justice ruled in 1924, "[o]nce a State has taken up a case on behalf of one of its subjects before an international tribunal, in the eyes of the latter the State is the sole claimant."[105] **4.56**

E. Exhaustion of Local Remedies

Unless the host State has waived the defense, before an an investor's home State can advance an international law claim against another State, the investor is usually required to pursue any judicial or administrative remedies reasonably available under the law of the host State.[106] The International Court of Justice has affirmed that "[t]he rule that local remedies must be exhausted before international proceedings may be instituted is a well-established rule of customary international law."[107] The Court continued: **4.57**

> Before resort may be had to an international court in such a situation, it has been considered necessary that the State where the violation occurred should have an opportunity to redress it by its own means, within the framework of its own domestic legal system.[108]

This rule is echoed in the International Law Commission's Draft Articles on State Responsibility: **4.58**

> When the conduct of a State has created a situation not in conformity with the result required of it by an international obligation concerning the treatment to be accorded to aliens, whether natural or juridical persons, but the obligation allows that this or an equivalent result may nevertheless be achieved by subsequent conduct of the State, there is a breach of the obligation only if the aliens concerned have exhausted the effective local remedies available to them without obtaining the treatment called for by the obligation or, where that is not possible, an equivalent treatment.[109]

The purpose of this rule is to give the State the opportunity to address within its own legal framework the alleged wrong and thus reduce the number of international claims that might otherwise be brought. Another reason for this rule is to **4.59**

---

[105] *Mavrommatis Palestine Concessions, supra* note 85, at 12.

[106] Shaw, *supra* note 48, at 730–32. The Iran–U.S. Claims Tribunal has applied public international law without requiring exhaustion of remedies. It has been argued that exhaustion of remedies is not required by claimants before the tribunal because it is itself the product of diplomatic protection. John R. Crook, *Applicable Law in International Arbitration: The Iran–U.S. Claims Tribunal Experience*, 83 AJIL 278, 300 (1989); *see also* dissenting opinion of member Mahmoud M. Kashani Regarding Order of Dec. 15, 1982, 1 Iran-U.S. C.T.R. 455, 463, 465 (1981–82) and *Amoco Int'l Finance Corp. v. Government of Iran*, Award No. 310-56-3, 15 Iran–U.S. C.T.R. 189, 197 (1987).

[107] *Interhandel Case (Switzerland v. United States)*, 1959 I.C.J. Rep. 6, 26–27.

[108] *Id.*

[109] Draft Articles, *supra* note 47.

respect the sovereignty and jurisdiction of the host State by not pre-empting its legal system.[110]

4.60 It is important to emphasize that the local remedies rule is normally inapplicable to claims initiated by investors under modern investment treaties.[111] As will be explained in more detail in Chapter 7, the Washington (ICSID) Convention, which governs many such disputes, expressly excludes the application of the local remedies rule.[112]

4.61 Even where international treaty arbitration takes place outside the ICSID system, many bilateral and multilateral investment treaties expressly or impliedly excuse claimants from taking claims first to domestic tribunals for adjudication.[113] Other treaties, however, expressly incorporate a requirement that local remedies be exhausted before access to international arbitration will be granted.[114]

4.62 The phrase "local remedies" is interpreted broadly under customary international law. According to the panel in the *Ambatielos Case*, "local remedies" means "the whole system of legal protection, as provided by municipal law," including "the use of procedural facilities which municipal law makes available to litigants."[115] Generally, the claimant must take up all appeals available under local law,[116]

[110] SHAW, *supra* note 48, at 730.

[111] On the exhaustion of local remedies in the context of investment treaties, *see generally* Steven Schwebel, *Arbitration and the Exhaustion of Local Remedies*, in JUSTICE IN INTERNATIONAL LAW 171 (1994); Andrea Bjorklund, *Waiver and the Exhaustion of the Local Remedies Rule in NAFTA Jurisprudence*, in NAFTA INVESTMENT LAW AND ARBITRATION 253 (Todd Weiler ed. 2004); P. Peters, *Exhaustion of Local Remedies: Ignored in Most Bilateral Investment Treaties*, 44(2) NETHERLANDS INT'L L. REV. 233 (1997).

[112] Convention on the Settlement of Investment Disputes between States and Nationals of Other States, of Mar. 18, 1965, art. 54(1), 17 U.S.T. 1270 (the "Washington Convention"), available at http://www.worldbank.org/icsid. *See also* C.F. Amerasinghe, *Whither the Local Remedies Rule?*, 5 ICSID REV.—FOR. INV. L.J. 292, 293–95 (1990); *Franck Charles Arif v. Moldova*, ICSID Case No. ARB/11/23, Award of Apr. 8, 2013, para. 334; *Abengoa S.A. y COFIDES S.A. v. Mexico*, ICSID Case No. ARB(AF)/09/2, Award of Apr. 18, 2013, para. 626; *AES Corp. and Tau Power B.V. v. Kazakhstan*, ICSID Case No. ARB/10/16, Award of Nov. 1, 2013, para. 233.

[113] *See e.g.* Australia–Hungary BIT (1991); *Nykomb Synergetics Technology Holding A.B. v. Latvia*, Arbitral Award of Dec. 16, 2003, para. 2.4.b.2; *ECE Projektmanagement Int'l GmbH and Kommanditgesellschaft PANTA Achtundsechzigste Grundstücksgesellschaft mbH & Co. v. Czech Republic*, PCA Case No. 2010-5, Award of Sept. 19, 2013, para. 4.745 ("where recourse to the local courts has been held to be relevant to the question of breach, that does not make it into a mandatory precondition for the admissibility of the claim before an investment tribunal, nor into a constitutive requirement for the claim").

[114] *See e.g.* Belgium–Romania BIT (1978). In the context of the NAFTA, tribunals have ruled that the local remedies rule has been modified under the NAFTA by virtue of art. 1121 (and for Mexico, Annex 1120(1)), which establishes a "qualified and special rule on the relationship between domestic and international judicial proceedings, and a departure from the general rule of customary international law on the exhaustion of local remedies"; *see Marvin Roy Feldman Karpa v. Mexico*, ICSID Case No. ARB(AF)/99/1, Award of Dec. 16, 2002, para. 73.

[115] *Ambatielos Case (Greece v. U.K.)*, 12 R.I.A.A. 91 (1951).

[116] *Finnish Ships Case (Finland v. U.K.)*, 3 R.I.A.A. 1479, 1498 (1934).

although recourse will not normally be required if it can be shown that taking such action would be futile.[117]

In addition, remedies need only be exhausted if they are available[118] and *effective*.[119] In particular, the local remedies rule does not apply if the alien can demonstrate that remedies are inadequate, either because of lack of due process or lack of the substantive right of just compensation.[120] Furthermore, the local remedies rule is inapplicable where one State has directly breached international law causing immediate injury to another State, such as when diplomatic agents are assaulted.[121] In this regard, Judge Higgins has stated: **4.63**

> What then of the local-remedies rule? Is not the traditional stipulation correct—namely, that no international wrong (and thus no responsibility [therefor]) arises until local remedies have been exhausted? This received wisdom follows only if one accepts the starting-point—that the assault, or the breach of contract, or the fraudulent trading are not themselves international laws, being of interest only at the level of municipal law.[122]

Nevertheless, absent explicit or implied waiver,[123] the rule of exhaustion of local remedies normally applies where a State complains of injury to its nationals.[124] **4.64**

---

[117] *Panevezys-Saldutiskis Railway Case (Estonia v. Lithuania)*, P.C.I.J. Ser. A/B, No. 76 (1939), at 18 ("There can be no need to resort to the municipal courts if those courts have no jurisdiction to afford relief; nor is it necessary again to resort to those courts if the result must be a repetition of a decision already given").

[118] *The Loewen Group Inc. and Raymond L. Loewen v. U.S.A.*, ICSID Case No. ARB(AF)/98/3, Award of June 26, 2003, paras. 167–69.

[119] *ST-AD GmbH v. Bulgaria*, PCA Case No. 2011-06 (ST-BG), Award on Jurisdiction of July 18, 2013, para. 365 ("This rule is interpreted to mean that applicants are only required to exhaust domestic remedies that are available and effective. In determining whether any particular remedy meets the criteria of availability and effectiveness, regard must be had to the particular circumstances of the individual case"). *See also* Shaw, *supra* note 48, at 730–31. *Cf. Loewen supra* note 119 at paras. 209–11 (suggesting that discretionary appeal to the U.S. Supreme Court and applying for bankruptcy protection were reasonably available remedies that the claimant should have tried before turning to treaty arbitration).

[120] Brice M. Clagett, *Present State of the International Law of Compensation for Expropriated Property and Repudiated State Contracts*, in Private Investors Abroad § 12.05[1][a] (Southwestern Legal Foundation ed. 1989).

[121] *Ambiente Ufficio S.P.A. et al. (formerly Giordano Alpi et al.) v. Argentina*, ICSID Case No. ARB/08/9, Decision on Jurisdiction and Admissibility of Feb. 8, 2013, paras. 607–08 (holding that the futility exception limits the application of treaty provisions requiring recourse to domestic courts, by analogy to the futility exception to the local remedies rule in diplomatic protection).

[122] Higgins, *supra* note 5, at 153. On the apparent decline of the local remedies rule, *see* Amerasinghe, *supra* note 112.

[123] For example, the local remedies rule will not apply if a State and a private investor have agreed in writing to waive the requirement. Indeed, under one view, a State's consent to arbitration in a private contract constitutes an implied waiver of the local remedies rule. Stephen Schwebel & J. Gillis Wetter, *Arbitration and the Exhaustion of Local Remedies*, 60 AJIL 484, 486 (1966).

[124] Shaw, *supra* note 48, at 731.

F. Nationality of Claims

4.65 Under customary international law, a State acquires rights in relation to the injury to an investor by another State only if there is a requisite link of nationality between the potential claimant State and the injured person.[125] International law does not generally regulate the relationship between a State and its own nationals,[126] and therefore the customary international law of expropriation does not apply to property taken from nationals of the expropriating State.[127]

4.66 Customary international law provides very different rules for determining nationality depending upon whether the injured investor is a physical person or a corporate entity. The rules applicable to these categories of persons may also vary substantially according to the terms of an applicable investment treaty.[128]

1. Individuals

4.67 Under customary international law, a State may intervene only on behalf of individuals who are nationals of that State.[129] A somewhat controversial issue is the moment in time as of which citizenship is to be determined for this purpose. Indeed, there has been a great deal of dispute as to whether there is any uniform rule at all requiring "continuous nationality" after the date of injury.[130]

---

[125] For a more detailed analysis of customary international law on nationality, *see* Francisco Orrego Vicuna, *Changing Approaches to the Nationality of Claims in the Context of Diplomatic Protection and International Dispute Settlement*, in Liber Amicorum Ibrahim F.I. Shihata: International Finance And Development Law 503 (S. Schlemmer-Schulte & K.-Y. Tung eds. 2001); Pia Acconci, *Determining the Internationally Relevant Link between a State and a Corporate Investor*, 5 J. World Inv. & Trade 139 (2004); Ian Sinclair, *Nationality of Claims: British Practice*, 27 Brit. Yb. Int'l L. 125 (1950). *See also* the discussion in Chapter 10, Section B.1.a.

[126] *Hussein Nuaman Soufraki v. United Arab Emirates*, ICSID Case No. ARB/02/7, Award of July 7, 2004, para. 55 ("It is accepted in international law that nationality is within the domestic jurisdiction of the State, which settles, by its own legislation, the rules relating to the acquisition (and loss) of its nationality)".

[127] Foighel, *supra* note 4, at 104; *see also* sources cited in Chapter 1, Section C.1. However, certain international human rights instruments have changed this traditional paradigm within the scope of their application. In particular, Protocol 1 of the European Convention on Human Rights provides, at Article 1: "Every natural or legal person is entitled to the peaceful enjoyment of his possessions. No one shall be deprived of his possessions except in the public interest and subject to the conditions provided for by law and by the general principles of international law." On the basis of this provision, citizens of States party to this protocol may initiate claims for expropriation against their own State of nationality before the European Court of Human Rights. *See e.g. Croitoru v. Moldova*, ECHR Application No. 18882/02, Judgment of July 20, 2004 (Moldovan national obtained redress under Protocol 1 in connection with bank deposits for Moldova's failure to enforce a Parliament decision to revalue the savings of citizens in the Savings Bank in compensation for losses caused by inflation).

[128] *See* Chapter 7, Sections B.3.b and D.

[129] Shaw, *supra* note 48, at 721 *et seq.*

[130] *See e.g.* D.P. O'Connell, International Law 1035 (2d ed. 1970) (continuous nationality rule is "discretionary practice" rather than "substantive rule of law"); Ian Sinclair, *Nationality of Claims: British Practice*, 27 Brit. Yb. Int'l L. 125, 130 (1950) (same); B. Weston, International

In *Loewen v. United States*, the tribunal found that it lacked jurisdiction on the basis that the investor had failed to maintain Canadian nationality until the end of the case, because a crossborder bankruptcy proceeding had forced it to reorganize as a U.S. company.[131] This approach has been much criticized.[132] **4.68**

In 2000, the International Law Commission's rapporteur on diplomatic protection, Professor Dugard, concluded that there was no rule of customary international law with respect to continuous nationality because opinions and practice as to the dates on which a claimant must have the requisite nationality had varied so widely.[133] According to the Commission: **4.69**

> The [*Loewen* decision]—on this aspect of the case—is seriously flawed. While most of the decision is carefully reasoned and researched ... the crucial issue before the tribunal, that of the *dies ad quem*, is disposed of in a manner which gives no indication that the tribunal applied its mind to the matter at all. It simply asserts, without any examination whatsoever of authority (despite the fact that counsel referred the tribunal to the relevant authorities), that under customary international law "there must be continuous national identity from the date of the events giving rise to the claim ... through to the date of the resolution of the claim."[134]

The tribunals in *Hulley, Yukos*, and *Veteran Petroleum* disagreed with the continuous nationality rule applied in *Loewen*, holding that nationality is to be adjudged as of the date of the filing of the claim.[135] In *Serafin Garcia v Venezuela*, **4.70**

Claims: Postwar French Practice 83 (1971) (same); Administrative Decision No. V: Decisions and Opinions (U.S.A. v. Germany), 7 R.I.A.A. 199 (1924) ("it may well be doubted whether the alleged rule [of continuous nationality] has received such universal recognition as to justify the broad statement that it is an established rule of international law"); U.N. Doc. A/CN.4/506/Add. 1, draft art. 9 (there is too much variety in State practice to posit any customary international law rule at all on continuous nationality); Bruno Simma, *The Work of the International Law Commission at its 52nd Session, Report of the Ad Hoc Committee of Legal Advisers to the Council of Europe on International Law*, Sept. 4, 2000, at 24, published at https://www.coe.int/en/web/cahdi/20th-meeting-meeting-documents?p_p_id=101&p_p_lifecycle=0&p_p_state=maximized&p_p_col_id=column-1&p_p_col_count=1&_101_struts_action=%2Fasset_publisher%2Fview_content&_101_assetEntryId=2785827&_101_type=content.

131 Loewen, *supra* note 119, at paras. 225–38.

132 *See e.g.* Emmanuel Gaillard, La Jurisprudence du Cirdi 788 (2004).

133 Andrea K. Bjorkland, *The Emerging Civilization of Investment Arbitration*, 113 Penn. State L. Rev. 169, 1280 (2009), citing International Law Commission, Report to the International Law Commission on Diplomatic Protection, A/CN.4/506/Add.1 (Apr. 20, 2000). Dugard identifies the following alternatives: (1) date of espousal of claim; (2) date of initial negotiations; (3) date of filing the claim; (4) date of the signature of the applicable treaty creating the adjudicative forum; (5) date of ratification of the applicable treaty; (6) date of entry into force of the applicable treaty; (7) date of "presentation" of the claim; (8) date oral hearings conclude; (9) date of judgment; (10) date of payment or settlement of the claim. U.N. Doc. A/CN.4/506/Add. 1 at 11. For a critique of this aspect of the *Loewen v. United States* NAFTA award, *see* Jan Paulsson, *Continuous Nationality in Loewen*, 20 Arb. Int'l 213 (2004); Noah Rubins, *Loewen v. United States: The Burial of an Investor–State Claim*, 21 Arb. Int'l 1, 23–28 (2005).

134 ILC, Fifty-Eighth Session, Seventh report on diplomatic protection by John Dugard, Special Rapporteur, U.N. Doc. A/CN.4/567, Mar. 7, 2006, para. 41.

135 *Veteran Petroleum, supra* note 97, paras. 562–63; *Yukos, supra* note 97, paras. 551–52; *Hulley, supra* note 97, paras. 550–51.

the majority of the tribunal concluded that the claimants' nationality when they invested was irrelevant to determining whether they have standing under the treaty. According to the majority, the relevant dates were the date of the alleged violation and the date when the arbitral proceeding commences.[136]

4.71 In the framework of Article 25 of ICSID, it is generally recognized that the determination of standing to institute proceedings, including nationality, is made as of the date when proceedings are instituted.[137] In *Pey Casado*, the tribunal held that the moment for evaluating the claimant's nationality is the date when the parties agreed to submit the dispute to arbitration, as well as the date of ICSID registration.[138] In *Siag*, the tribunal found that the ICSID Convention does not require a claimant to maintain its nationality continuously until an award is rendered.[139]

4.72 Overall, as Professor Mendelson explains:

> [t]here is substantial support for a rule requiring the claimant State to have been the State of nationality at the time of the injury ... There is less, but still significant, support for a requirement that the victim should possess the same nationality up to the point of the formal presentation of the claim.[140]

4.73 In addition, and in particular where the person concerned holds more than one nationality, under general international law the State must have a reasonable connection, a "genuine link," to the individual before it can extend diplomatic protection or interpose a claim on her behalf.

4.74 The best-known source of this "genuine link" rule is the *Nottebohm Case*,[141] in which the International Court of Justice was asked to decide whether Liechtenstein could exercise diplomatic protection to maintain a claim against Guatemala on behalf of Friedreich Nottebohm. Mr Nottebohm had been granted Liechtenstein citizenship during World War II, but had practically no other ties to that State, and had lived in Guatemala for most of his life. The Court held that Liechtenstein was "not entitled to extend its protection to Nottebohm vis-à-vis Guatemala,"

---

[136] *Serafin Garcia Armas and Karina Garcia Gruber v. Venezuela*, PCA Case No. 2013-3, Decision on Jurisdiction of Dec. 15, 2014, paras. 214–18; *see also* Dissenting Opinion of Rodrigo Oreamuno Blanco, arguing that to enjoy the protection afforded by the BIT, a claimant must have the nationality of one of the contracting parties when investing.

[137] Christoph H. Schreuer, The ICSID Convention: A Commentary 92 (2009). *Ceskoslovenska obchodní banka, A.S. v. Slovakia*, ICSID Case No. ARB/97/4, Decision of the Tribunal on Objections to Jurisdiction of May 24, 1999, para. 31. *See* Chapter 7, Section B.3.b and D.

[138] *Víctor Pey Casado and President Allende Foundation v. Chile*, ICSID Case No. ARB/98/2, Award of May 8, 2008, para. 238; *see also Ioan Micula, Viorel Micula et al. v. Romania*, ICSID Case No. ARB/05/20, Decision on Jurisdiction and Admissibility of Sept. 24, 2008, para. 111.

[139] *Waguih Elie George Siag & Clorinda Vecchi v. Egypt*, ICSID Case No. ARB/05/15, Award of June 1, 2009, paras. 497–99.

[140] Maurice Mendelson, *The Runaway Train: The "Continuous Nationality Rule" from the Panevezys-Saldutsikis Railway Case to Loewen*, in International Investment Law and Arbitration 97, 123 (Todd Weiler ed. 2005).

[141] *Nottebohm Case (Liechtenstein v. Guatemala)*, 1953 I.C.J. 111, 20 I.L.R. 567 (1953).

since his "effective nationality" was Guatemalan.[142] Under this rule, then, if an individual has only nominal nationality in a State, that State may not be entitled to compensation for a wrong occasioned upon him.[143]

It is generally accepted that the "genuine link" test does not apply in the framework of ICSID.[144] In *Siag*, the tribunal ruled that the regime established under Article 25 of the ICSID Convention does not leave room for a test of dominant or effective nationality.[145] In *Micula*, the claimants were two brothers who had renounced Romanian nationality and become Swedish nationals. The respondent argued that the Swedish nationality was not effective, and that the claimants maintained dominant links with Romania. The tribunal rejected this position, finding that the *Nottebohm* test does not apply in the context of ICSID or the relevant investment treaty.[146] **4.75**

2. Corporations

As with individuals, for a State to make a claim on behalf of a corporation, there must be some tangible link between it and the State seeking to espouse its claim. Generally speaking, a corporation has the nationality of the State under the laws of which it was created.[147] Some tribunals have confirmed that the place of incorporation constitutes a sufficient connection, while others have referred to the location of the company's administrative center or the nationality of shareholders.[148] **4.76**

The leading case on the subject is *Barcelona Traction*, which concerned a Spanish electric plant owned by a Canadian company. The majority of the company's shareholders were Belgian.[149] Spain suspended payment on the company's bonds in 1936 as a result of the Spanish Civil War. Although payments resumed in 1940, the government blocked the repatriation of the funds, preventing the company from paying its creditors.[150] Spain declared the company bankrupt in 1948, and **4.77**

---

[142] *Id.*, 22 I.L.R. at 359.

[143] Brownlie, *supra* note 31, at 465.

[144] According to Aaron Broches, *The Convention on the Settlement of Investment Disputes between States and Nationals of Other States*, 136 Recueil des Cours 358 (1972): "It is necessary to realize, however, that the Legal Committee abstained from defining 'nationality' and that there was a general recognition that in the course of ruling on their competence Commissions and Tribunals might have to decide whether a nationality of convenience [referring to the *Nottebohm* case] or a nationality acquired involuntarily by an investor could or should be disregarded."

[145] *Waguih Elie George Siag and Clorinda Vecchi v. Egypt*, ICSID Case No. ARB/05/15, Decision on Jurisdiction of Apr. 11, 2007, para. 198.

[146] *Ioan Micula, supra* note 138, paras. 100–06.

[147] *Case Concerning Barcelona Traction, Light & Power Co. (Belg. v. Spain)*, 1970 I.C.J. 4, 42 (Second Phase), 46 I.L.R. 178.

[148] Shaw, *supra* note 48, at 727; Brownlie, *supra* note 31, at 464 *et seq.*

[149] 87 percent of the company was owned by Belgian nationals. *Barcelona Traction, supra* note 147, 1970 I.C.J. at 12.

[150] *Id.* at 8.

sold new shares in the company's subsidiaries at public auction, cancelling the existing, foreign-owned shares.[151]

4.78 Belgium sued Spain before the International Court of Justice. Spain challenged Belgium's standing, arguing that because the company was incorporated in Canada, only Canada could seek compensation. The Court ruled that only the company (and not its shareholders) could have a cognizable claim, and therefore only Canada could bring an action against Spain.[152] The Court reasoned that a decision to contrary would result in multiple claims concerning the same dispute from minority shareholders' home States.[153] The Court thus confirmed the customary rule of international law that gives the right of diplomatic protection of a company to the State of incorporation. But it left shareholders without any remedy, particularly where the State of incorporation chooses not to pursue remedies under international law.

4.79 Many observers have opined on this basis that under international law a State whose nationals control a company cannot maintain a claim against an expropriating State. What if the company is incorporated in the host State? The *Barcelona Traction* court recognized this issue, but did not address it:

> It is quite true that is has been maintained that, for reasons of equity, a State should be able, in certain cases, to take up the protection of its nationals, shareholders in a company which has been the victim of a violation of international law. Thus a theory has been developed to the effect that the State of shareholders has a right of diplomatic protection when the State whose responsibility is invoked is the national State of the company. Whatever the validity of this theory may be, it is certainly not applicable to the present case, since Spain is not the national state of Barcelona Traction.[154]

4.80 Although the ICJ did not answer the question in *Barcelona Traction*, it is generally accepted that a shareholder's home State may pursue a claim on its behalf if the injured corporation is locally incorporated (and therefore no State can espouse its claim).[155] This exception prevents a State from evading international law by requiring all FDI to be maintained in locally incorporated subsidiaries.[156]

---

151 *Id.* at 9.

152 *Id.* at 36–49. The court stated that there are two situations where a shareholder's home State may have standing: first, if a shareholder is injured directly, such as by the impairment of dividend or voting rights; and second, if a treaty varies the general rule. *Id.* at 36.

153 *Id.* at 49.

154 *Barcelona Traction, supra* note 147, 1970 I.C.J. at 48.

155 Restatement, *supra* note 6, § 713, com. e (1987). A recent trend seems to indicate a solidifying independent right for injured shareholders and their States at customary international law. *See Elettronica Sicula S.p.A. (ELSI) (United States v. Italy)*, Judgment of July 20, 1989, 1989 I.C.J. Rep. 15; *U.N. Compensation Comm., Decision of Governing Council on Business Losses of Individuals*, S/AC.26/1191/4, at Dec. 123 (2001); *International Law Association, Committee on Diplomatic Protection of Persons and Property*, First Report of 69th Conference (2001).

156 Clagett, *supra* note 120, at § 12.01[1].

In addition, investors should be aware that the *Barcelona Traction* rule has been all but eliminated in the context of investment treaties, since shareholders are almost always qualifying "investors" with an independent right to arbitration under treaty terms.[157] The more particular aspects of corporate nationality under treaty-based rules will be discussed in Chapter 7. **4.81**

3. Partnerships

Many investments in developing States are structured as either joint ventures or partnerships between the foreign investor and the host State or other local participant. A question often arises as to whether, following interference with the property rights of the partnership or venture, the home country of the foreign investors has standing to bring a claim on behalf of the partnership under international law. A similar question is raised in the case of a partnership consisting of individuals or corporations with different home States. Which State has standing to bring a claim? **4.82**

Professor Ohly has summarized the customary rule of international law as follows: **4.83**

> Under customary international law ... "both partners and partnerships are eligible claimants if they meet the nationality requirements," but partnerships are entitled to protection as entities only when all of their members are nationals of the claimant State. Hence, under the customary rule, if a single partner is a non-national of the claimant State, the claim of the partnership will not be entertained. Owing, however, to "the conception of the severability of the interests of partners in partnership property," international tribunals have had little difficulty in disaggregating the interests of partners and in permitting "citizen partners in a firm consisting partly of nationals and partly of aliens ... to recover their pro rata share of partnership claims."[158]

The decisions of international tribunals have generally followed this rule—where a partnership consists of partners from different States, "international tribunals consistently have rendered awards to claimant state partners based upon their pro rata interests in the firm."[159] **4.84**

Thus, for a State to espouse a claim on behalf of a partnership itself, it would appear that all partners should be nationals of the claimant State. Where partners are nationals of different claimant States, which includes the situation of a joint **4.85**

---

[157] *See e.g. CMS Gas Transmission Co. v. Argentina*, ICSID Case No. ARB/01/8, Decision on Objections to Jurisdiction of July 17, 2003, available at http://www.asil.org/ilib/cms-argentina.pdf; *American Manufacturing & Trading Co. v. Zaire*, ICSID Case No. ARB/93/1, Award of Feb. 21, 1997; *Genin v. Estonia*, ICSID Case No. ARB/99/2, Award of June 25, 2001, para. 324.

[158] D. Christopher Ohly, *A Functional Analysis of Claimant Eligibility*, in International Law of State Responsibility for Injuries to Aliens 281, 291 (Richard B. Lillich ed. 1983). *See also* Richard B. Lillich, *Joint Ventures and the Law of International Claims*, 10 Mich. J. Int'l L. 430 n.28 (1989).

[159] Lillich, *supra* note 158, n.64.

venture between a foreign investor and the host government, a State may bring a claim on behalf of partners of the partnership for their pro-rata share of a claim in accordance with the rules described for individuals and corporations.[160]

G. Immunity of States from Jurisdiction

1. The doctrine of restrictive sovereign immunity

4.86 Sovereign immunity is a doctrine that prohibits the courts of one State from exercising jurisdiction over another State, or over its agents or instrumentalities.[161] Judge Higgins has explained that:

> [u]nder classical international law, states, including governments thereof, were granted immunity from the territorial jurisdiction of other states. Various reasons of policy have been suggested, all interrelated. First, the reason may be found in the doctrine of sovereign equality: pari parim non habet imperium, which means that no state could be expected to submit to the laws of another. Secondly, it has been said that it would offend the dignity of a state to submit to the jurisdiction of another.[162]

4.87 Before the twentieth century, the shield of sovereign immunity was often absolute—that is, a State would not subject another State to jurisdiction in its courts for any private dispute.[163]

4.88 As States became increasingly involved in commercial activities during the late nineteenth century, they began to question the expediency of such an unbending doctrine of absolute immunity. Judge Higgins has summarized the reasons for the resulting shift:

> As states began to engage in functions not wholly reserved to the states, this doctrine of absolute immunity began to be questioned. It began to be asked why, if two identical contracts were made, one with a private person and another with his government, the former could be sued in his contract and the latter could not … absolute immunity increasingly seemed an inappropriate phenomena in the face of the requirements of the contemporary commercial world and of notions of stability, fairness, and equity in the market place.[164]

4.89 European courts began to develop a policy of "restrictive immunity," according to which a State would not be immune from court jurisdiction in connection

---

[160] *See generally id.*

[161] Troland S. Link, *Foreign Sovereign Immunity, Expropriation, Act of State, and Comity*, 703 PLI/Comm. L. & Prac. Handbook Series 183 (1994).

[162] Higgins, *supra* note 5, at 78–79. Isi Foighel wrote that "a state is competent, and solely competent, to do within its territory those acts which actually or potentially are done in the exercise of the governmental power of the state." Foighel, *supra* note 4, at 42.

[163] *See e.g. The Schooner Exchange v. McFadden*, 11 U.S. 116 (1812).

[164] Higgins, *supra* note 5, at 79.

with disputes arising primarily out of its commercial activities.[165] Under this limited version of the doctrine, a distinction is drawn between *acta jure imperii*, which refers to acts of public authority for which immunity persists, and *acta jure gestionis*, which refers to commercial acts for which States are deprived of any special protection.[166] This position is reflected in the European Convention on State Immunity, which, although it has not gained widespread acceptance, represents the views of some European States:

> A Contracting State may not claim immunity from the jurisdiction of a court of another Contracting State if it has on the territory of the State of the forum an office, agency, or other establishment through which it engages, in the same manner as a private person, in an industrial, commercial, or financial activity, and the proceedings relate to that activity of the office, agency or establishment.[167]

In 2004, the General Assembly adopted the U.N. Convention on Jurisdictional Immunities of States and Their Property,[168] which embraced the policy of restrictive immunity. Although the Convention is not yet in force, it has been signed by many States, and the restrictive theory is widely accepted in national courts.[169] **4.90**

In 1945, the United States recognized the doctrine of restrictive sovereign immunity, announcing that it would recognize State immunity "with regard to sovereign or public acts (*jure imperii*) of a state, but not with respect to private acts (*jure gestionis*)."[170] Before 1976, sovereign immunity was largely a matter of discretion by the executive branch; courts typically followed its recommendations in deciding whether a claim should be heard, in accordance with the doctrine of restrictive sovereign immunity. This recognition was ultimately codified in the Foreign Sovereign Immunities Act of 1976 (the "FSIA"),[171] which sets forth criteria for determining whether a U.S. court may assume jurisdiction over a sovereign State or an agency of a sovereign State, and provides procedures for service of process, execution of judgments, and attachment of government-owned assets.[172] **4.91**

Statutes similar to the FSIA have been adopted by a number of capital-exporting States. These include the State Immunity Act of 1978 in the United Kingdom, **4.92**

---

[165] Link, *supra* note 161, at 183.

[166] Higgins, *supra* note 5, at 79.

[167] European Convention on State Immunity (May 16, 1972), art. 7(1).

[168] G.A. Res. 59/38, Annex, Dec. 2, 2004.

[169] *See,* James Crawford, Brownlie's Principles of Public International Law 489–90 (8th ed. 2012).

[170] Letter of Jack B. Tate, *Acting Legal Advisor, to Acting Attorney General,* 26 Dep't. St. Bull. 984 (1952).

[171] 28 U.S.C. §§ 1602–11 (as amended 1997).

[172] For in-depth discussion of the FSIA, *see* Joseph W. Dellapenna, Suing Foreign Governments and Their Corporations (2001); Sarah Schano, *The Scattered Remains of Sovereign Immunity for Foreign States after* Republic of Argentina v. Weltover, Inc.*—Due Process Protection or Nothing,* 27 Vanderbilt J. Transnat'l L. 673 (1994).

the State Immunity Act of 1981 in Canada, the Foreign State Immunities Act of 1981 in South Africa, and the Australian Foreign State Immunities Act of 1985.[173] In most civil law jurisdictions in Europe, however, the doctrine of sovereign immunity generally takes the form of "a judicial construct discoverable only from the study of the jurisprudence of the relevant courts."[174] And while industrialized States have generally accepted the doctrine of restrictive immunity, many countries in the developing world retain an absolute view of sovereign immunity.

4.93 There are two approaches that can be taken in determining whether a State should be immune from jurisdiction. The first is the "nature" test—is the act of the State one that only a sovereign can perform? The other is the purpose test—does the act further a sovereign interest, or the State's private or mercantile concerns? In applying the restrictive immunity doctrine, many national laws look to the nature, rather than the purpose, of the State act.[175] However, there is little agreement as to which acts are by their nature public, and which are private.

4.94 The U.S. FSIA and the related act of State doctrine, are discussed in detail below. A brief discussion of an analogous statute in the United Kingdom follows.[176]

2. Sovereign immunity in the United States: the Foreign Sovereign Immunities Act

4.95 Before a claim against a foreign State can be adjudicated in a U.S. court, the court must first determine whether it has jurisdiction over the foreign State.[177] As noted, the FSIA, enacted in 1976, specifies criteria for determining whether a U.S. court may assume jurisdiction over a sovereign State or its agency, and provides procedures for service of process, execution of judgments, and attachment of government-owned assets.[178]

---

[173] *See* HIGGINS, *supra* note 5, at 80.

[174] Joseph W. Dellapenna, *Foreign State Immunity in Europe*, 5 NY INT'L L. REV. 51 (1992).

[175] In the United States, *see* Foreign Sovereign Immunities Act, § 1603(d); in Great Britain, *see Trendtex Trading Corp. v. Central Bank of Nigeria*, 1 Q.B. 529 (1977); and in Germany, *see Claims Against the Empire of Iran*, 45 I.L.R. 57 (1963) ("as a means of determining the distinction between *actus jure imperii* and *jure gestionis* one should rather refer to the nature of the state transaction or the resulting legal relationship, and not to the motive or purpose of the state activity"). France has historically looked to the purpose of an act, but more recent decisions have relied upon the "nature" test. Dellapenna, *supra* note 174, at n.108.

[176] For further discussion of sovereign immunity and the act of State doctrine, *see* VED P. NANDA & DAVID K. PANSIUS, LITIGATION OF INTERNATIONAL DISPUTES IN U.S. COURTS, chs. 8, 10 (1995); PAUL H. VISHNY, GUIDE TO INTERNATIONAL COMMERCIAL LAW §§ 12.03–12.10, 12.26 (1994); Peter M. McGowan, *Arbitration Clauses as Waivers of Immunity from Jurisdiction and Execution under the Foreign Sovereign Immunities Act of 1976*, 5 NYL SCH. J. INT'L & COMP. L. 409, 417–19 (1984).

[177] *Siderman de Blake v. Argentina*, 965 F.2d 699, 713 (9th Cir. 1992), *cert. den.*, 113 S.Ct. 1812 (1993). A U.S. court may only exercise jurisdiction over a foreign sovereign pursuant to the FSIA. *Argentina v. Amerada Hess Shipping Corp.*, 488 U.S. 428 (1989).

[178] *See* references cited in note 175, *supra*.

The FSIA provides that all "foreign States" are entitled to immunity from the jurisdiction of the courts of the United States,[179] and then sets forth a number of exceptions to this rule.[180] For the most part, these exceptions deny immunity to sovereign States in connection with their commercial activities. For the purposes of the FSIA, a "State" includes government agencies and instrumentalities, such as State-owned corporations.[181] For most aspects of the FSIA, there is no distinction drawn between States and their instrumentalities, but States themselves enjoy substantially more protection from execution on assets than do their instrumentalities.[182] This is typical of the sovereign immunity provisions of most legal systems, which provide a higher level of sovereign immunity to State assets, in order to reduce the disruption of international relations and diplomacy that can result from the seizure of government property to satisfy an award or judgment. **4.96**

The exceptions to immunity set forth in the FSIA are exclusive.[183] In general, the FSIA distinguishes between different types of State activities. Exceptions relevant to the current discussion are as follows: (1) the sovereign expressly or impliedly waives its immunity;[184] (2) the sovereign has carried on a commercial activity having adequate contact with the United States;[185] (3) the sovereign has, in violation of international law, expropriated property located in the United States, or if a foreign State that is engaged in commercial activity in the United States owns or operates the expropriated property, even if the property is located outside the United States;[186] and (4) an arbitral award is being enforced against the sovereign.[187] **4.97**

It should be noted that the U.S. Supreme Court has recently ruled that the FSIA applies retroactively. Accordingly, the FSIA's standards for immunity and exceptions apply even to conduct that took place before 1976.[188] **4.98**

---

[179] 28 U.S.C. §§ 1604, 1330(a), (b).

[180] 28 U.S.C. § 1605.

[181] 28 U.S.C. § 1603. However, the U.S. Supreme Court has limited the definition of "State" for FSIA purposes: the majority of a foreign corporation's shares must be directly owned by a foreign sovereign in order for the corporation to qualify as a foreign government "instrumentality," and therefore benefit from "State" status under the FSIA. *Dole Food Co. v. Patrickson*, 538 U.S. 468, 123 S.Ct. 1655, 1663 (2003).

[182] *See* 28 U.S.C. § 1610. Service of process also differs somewhat, with less onerous requirements for serving instrumentalities. 28 U.S.C. § 1608.

[183] 28 U.S.C. § 1602.

[184] 28 U.S.C. § 1605(a)(1).

[185] 28 U.S.C. § 1605(a)(2).

[186] 28 U.S.C. § 1605(a)(3).

[187] 28 U.S.C. § 1610(a)(6). Nor will the act of State doctrine offer an effective defense to the enforcement of an arbitral award against a foreign sovereign. 9 U.S.C. § 15. For a discussion of the enforcement of foreign arbitral awards pursuant to the New York Convention, see Chapter 8, Section L. It should also be noted that although the FSIA codified the prevailing view of restrictive sovereign immunity in 1976, exceptions for torture and terrorism were added in 1996, to make it easier for American citizens to bring private suits in U.S. courts for acts committed outside the United States by States designated as "sponsors of terrorism." *See* 28 U.S.C. § 1605(a)(7).

[188] *Austria v. Altmann*, 541 U.S. 677, 124 S.Ct. 2240 (2004).

a. The waiver of immunity exception

4.99 The most direct and effective way for an investor to ensure that a foreign sovereign will be subject to the jurisdiction of U.S. courts is to negotiate a contractual waiver of sovereign immunity.[189] A State is subject to the jurisdiction of U.S. courts if it explicitly waives sovereign immunity, either in an investment protection treaty or in a contract between the investor and the State.[190] A waiver of immunity to prejudgment attachment must be explicit.[191]

4.100 Significantly, U.S. courts will not give effect to a subsequent withdrawal of a waiver of sovereign immunity, unless such withdrawal is pursuant to the terms of the waiver.[192] Thus, a State may by waiver "irrevocably" alienate its right to later plead sovereign immunity.

b. The commercial activity exception

4.101 To the extent that a State engages in "commercial activity," it will not be entitled to sovereign immunity. By contrast, when a State engages in "non-commercial activities," it is entitled to exercise sovereign immunity, unless the action against it sounds in tort. The FSIA defines "commercial activity" as "either a regular course of commercial conduct or a particular commercial transaction or act."[193] U.S. courts have interpreted commercial activity to be any activity in which a private person could engage.[194] The U.S. Supreme Court has held, more specifically, that commercial activity is "the type of actions by which a private party engages in 'trade and traffic or commerce.' "[195]

4.102 To fall within the "commercial activities" exception to the FSIA, the activities of the foreign State must meet one of the following three requirements: the State undertakes commercial activity in the United States; the State performs an act in the United States in connection with its commercial activity elsewhere; or the State performs an act outside the United States in connection with a commercial activity elsewhere, and that act causes a direct effect in the United States.[196] With regard to the final, "direct effect" requirement, the U.S. Supreme Court held in

---

[189] *See* Chapter 2, Section E.4 for a discussion of such clauses.

[190] 28 U.S.C. § 1605(a); *see also* Clagett, *supra* note 120, § 12.05[1][b].

[191] *S. & S. Machinery Co. v. Mashinexportimport*, 706 F.2d 411, 17 (2d Cir. 1983) ("waivers of immunity from suit or from execution of judgment have no bearing upon the question of immunity from prejudgment attachment"), *cert den.*, 464 U.S. 850 (1983).

[192] 28 U.S.C. § 1605(a)(1).

[193] 28 U.S.C. § 1603(d).

[194] *Texas Trading and Milling Corp. v. Nigeria*, 647 F.2d 300, 309 (2d Cir. 1981), *cert. den.*, 454 U.S. 1148 (1982).

[195] *Argentina v. Weltover Inc.*, 504 U.S. 607, 112 S.Ct. 2160, 2166 (1992). For further interpretations of what is meant by commercial and non-commercial activity, *see e.g. SEDCO Inc. v. Petroleos Mexicanos Mexican Nat'l Oil Co.*, 767 F.2d 1140 (5th Cir. 1985); *M.O.L. v. Bangladesh*, 736 F.2d 1326 (9th Cir. 1984); *Practical Concepts Inc. v. Bolivia*, 613 F. Supp. 863 (D.D.C. 1985).

[196] 28 U.S.C. § 1605(a)(2).

Weltover that an "effect is 'direct' if it 'follows as an immediate consequence of the defendant's . . . activity.' "[197]

4.103 Another case interpreting the "commercial activities" exception was *Siderman de Blake v. Argentina*.[198] In that case, the night before the military overthrow of the Argentine government in 1976, an Argentine citizen was tortured, and he, his wife, and his son were expelled from Argentina. A year later, Argentina expropriated an Argentine corporation owned by the family through a dubious "judicial intervention." Among the corporation's assets was the hotel Gran Corona in Buenos Aires. The Sidermans brought suit in a U.S. District Court, which dismissed the expropriation claims on grounds of sovereign immunity under the FSIA. The plaintiffs appealed to the Ninth Circuit Court of Appeals, which held that the actions of the Argentine government fell within the "commercial activities" exception to the FSIA. In particular, the court held that the Sidermans' claim was "based upon a commercial activity carried on in the United States by the foreign state."[199]

4.104 The mere existence of a contract between the State and the investor may also help mitigate sovereign immunity issues. This is because courts may be more willing to exercise jurisdiction over a contract-based issue than over a suit based solely upon expropriation: expropriation is more likely to be viewed by a court as a "sovereign" act.[200]

c. The expropriation exception

4.105 The expropriation exception to the FSIA provides that a State is not immune from jurisdiction in a U.S. court if property is taken in violation of international law,[201] and either (1) the property or proceeds of the property is present in the United States in connection with the commercial activity carried on in the United States by the foreign State, or (2) the property or proceeds of the property is owned or

[197] *Weltover, supra* note 195, 112 S.Ct. at 2168. For a discussion of the commercial activity test under the FSIA and a criticism of the *Weltover* case, see Sharon D. Ruccolo, *The Foreign Sovereign Immunities Act: Encouraging Foreign Plaintiffs to Sue Foreign Sovereigns in American Courts*, 25 Rutgers L.J. 517 (1994).

[198] *Siderman, supra* note 177.

[199] 28 U.S.C. § 1605(a)(2). First, Argentina's continuing management and operation of the hotel, and receipt of profits from the hotel, were considered to be commercial activities, because they were the kind of activities in which a private party might engage. Second, the Court ruled that these activities were being carried on "in the United States," due to the advertising of the hotel in the United States and the solicitation of U.S. guests through the national airline of Argentina, which was its agent. It was noted that the hotel also accepted U.S. credit cards. *Siderman, supra* note 177, at 712.

[200] Clagett, *supra* note 120, § 12.05[3][a].

[201] *West v. Multibanco Comermex S.A.*, 807 F.2d 820, 826 (9th Circuit), *cert. den*, 482 U.S. 906 (1987). For an explanation of the characteristics of expropriation in violation of international law, *see* Chapter 5.

operated by an agency or instrumentality of the foreign State, and that agency or instrumentality is engaged in commercial activity in the United States.[202]

4.106 In *Siderman*, the court sought to determine whether the government's seizure of the plaintiff's hotel violated international law. First, it was found that the hotel had been taken for the personal profit of government officials, and therefore not for any public purpose. Further, the expropriation was discriminatory, because it was based on the fact that the Sidermans were Jewish. Finally, no compensation had been paid.[203] Therefore, the court held that the expropriation was illegal under international law, and that the sovereign immunity defense was not effective for this reason, in addition to the "commercial activities" exception.[204]

4.107 Because it is not a violation of customary international law for a State to expropriate the property of its own citizens without payment of full compensation,[205] a court may not assert jurisdiction over a foreign State under the expropriation exception of the FSIA in relation to a claim brought by a national of the expropriating State. In *Chuidian v. Philippine Nat'l Bank*,[206] the Ninth Circuit refused to apply the expropriation exception of the FSIA where the plaintiff was a citizen of the defendant State at the time of the expropriation.[207] However, nationals of the defendant State may still be able to rely on the FSIA's commercial activities exception to bypass sovereign immunity constraints.[208]

4.108 In connection with suits connected to expropriations of property, the Cuban Liberty and Democratic Solidarity (LIBERTAD) Act of 1996[209] also bears mention. The LIBERTAD Act (also known as the Helms-Burton Act, after its principal sponsors) was enacted to prevent the Cuban government from selling property that was confiscated from U.S. nationals. The Act establishes a federal cause of action whereby a U.S. national whose property was illegally confiscated by the Cuban government may file a suit against any person or entity who collaborates with Cuba by trafficking in the confiscated property. Title IV of the Act also requires the denial of visas to and exclusion from the United States of persons who, after March 12, 1996, confiscate or "traffic" in confiscated property in Cuba claimed by U.S. nationals. The Act is designed to protect the status of confiscated U.S. property by exposing purchasers of such property to the possibility of

202 28 U.S.C. § 1605(a)(3).

203 *Siderman, supra* note 177, at 712.

204 *See also West v. Multibanco Comermex S.A.*, 807 F.2d 820 (9th Cir. 1987), *cert. den.* 482 U.S. 906 (1987).

205 *See* Section F, *infra*; also Chapter 5, Section B.4 (regarding national treatment and the international minimum standard); Higgins, *supra* note 5, at ch. 6.

206 *Chuidian v. Philippine Nat'l Bank*, 912 F.2d 1095 (9th Cir. 1990).

207 *See also De Sanchez v. Banco Central de Nicaragua*, 770 F.2d 1385 (5th Cir. 1985).

208 *Siderman, supra* note 177, at 711–13.

209 Cuban Liberty and Democratic Solidarity (LIBERTAD) Act of 1996, Pub. L. No. 104-114, 110 Stat. 785 (Mar. 12, 1996).

lawsuits in U.S. courts, hampering Cuba's ability to sell the property at attractive prices.[210]

3. The act of State doctrine

The act of State doctrine is a judicial creation in the United States which provides that a court should not pass judgment over the acts of a foreign State carried out in its own territory, because such inquiry may interfere with the foreign policy prerogative of the executive branch.[211] The doctrine was originally based on principles of comity and sovereign immunity. In 1897, the U.S. Supreme Court in *Underhill v. Hernandez*[212] provided one of the earliest formulations of act of State doctrine, in connection with the detention of a U.S. citizen by the Government of Venezuela. The Court stated that: **4.109**

> Every sovereign state is bound to respect the independence of every other sovereign state, and the courts of one country will not sit in judgment on the acts of the government of another done within its own territory. Redress of grievances by reason of such acts must be obtained through the means open to be availed of by sovereign powers as between themselves.[213]

More than half a century later, in the seminal act of State case, *Banco Nacional de Cuba v. Sabbatino*,[214] the Supreme Court de-emphasized the "sovereign immunity" rationale for the rule, instead underlining the doctrine's foundation on the Constitutional separation of powers. The Court held that the judiciary is not permitted to interfere in matters that are primarily the responsibility of the executive or legislative branches of the government, declaring that: **4.110**

> the judicial branch will not examine the validity of a taking of property within its own territory by a foreign sovereign government, extant and recognized by this country at the time of suit, in the absence of a treaty or other unambiguous agreement regarding controlling legal principles, even if the complaint alleges that the taking violates customary international law.[215]

In *Sabbatino*, Cuba nationalized sugar belonging to the plaintiff after he had arranged to sell it to a New York buyer. Cuba then sold the sugar to the same buyer, on the same terms. The U.S. Supreme Court declined to invalidate the Cuban government's title to the sugar, holding that the expropriation was an **4.111**

---

210 *But see* 28 U.S.C. § 1611(c) (specifying that notwithstanding certain exceptions to immunity, "the property of a foreign state shall be immune from attachment and from execution in an action brought under section 302 of the Cuban Liberty and Democratic Solidarity (LIBERTAD) Act of 1996 to the extent that the property is a facility or installation used by an accredited diplomatic mission for official purposes").

211 Danny Abir, *Suing a Foreign Government: A Note on Siderman v. Republic of Argentina*, 15 Whittier L. Rev. 575, 580 (1994).

212 *Underhill v. Hernandez*, 168 U.S. 250 (1897).

213 *Id.* at 252.

214 *Banco Nacional de Cuba v. Sabbatino*, 376 U.S. 398 (1964).

215 *Id.* at 428.

"act of State."[216] It was this case that prompted Congress to enact the Second Hickenlooper Amendment,[217] an exception to the act of State doctrine.

4.112 The view of the act of State doctrine as based on the separation of powers was echoed by the Ninth Circuit Court of Appeals, which held that the rule

> reflects the prudential concern that the courts, if they question the validity of sovereign acts taken by foreign states, may be interfering with the conduct of American foreign policy by the Executive and Congress.[218]

4.113 It should be noted that while sovereign immunity under the FSIA may only be raised by the State seeking the benefit of protection, the act of State doctrine may be invoked by a third party. Thus, in a "hot products" case such as *Sabbatino*, where a third party is in possession of property claimed by the investor,[219] the third party may seek to intervene, relying upon the act of State doctrine.

4.114 The act of State doctrine is a significant barrier to investors attempting to recover expropriated property that has been imported into the United States. Nevertheless, several exceptions to the act of State doctrine as crafted by *Sabbatino* have since developed.

4.115 The first of these is the so-called "Bernstein exception," according to which a court need not apply the act of State doctrine where the executive branch has advised that it is unnecessary to do so. In *Bernstein v. N.V. Nederlandsche-Amerikaansche Stoomvaart-Maatschappij*,[220] a Jewish businessman brought a claim in a U.S. District Court to recover property seized by the Nazi regime during World War II. After the Court of Appeals dismissed the claim based on the act of State doctrine, the Department of State submitted a letter to the court stating that the judiciary was relieved of any restraint on the exercise of jurisdiction to adjudicate the validity of the German government acts. The court relied on this letter to reverse its decision, holding that the act of State doctrine was inapplicable in such circumstances.

4.116 Another limitation placed upon the act of State doctrine is the "commercial activity exception." This exception derives from the same reasoning as that used for the commercial activities exception of the FSIA: a State may not engage in commercial activities, only to rely upon sovereign status to protect it from related litigation in U.S. courts.[221]

---

[216] *Id.* at 439.

[217] 22 U.S.C. § 2370(e)(2) (1970).

[218] *Siderman, supra* note 177, at 707 (*quoting Liu v. China*, 892 F.2d 1419, 1431 (9th Cir. 1989)).

[219] *See* Chapter 10, Section E for a discussion of the "hot products" cases.

[220] *Bernstein v. N.V. Nederlandsche-Amerikaansche Stoomvaart-Maatschappij*, 210 F.2d 375 (2d Cir. 1954).

[221] This exception has been derived from Justice White's plurality opinion in *Alfred Dunhill Inc. v. Cuba*, 425 U.S. 682 (1976). Although the decision was divided 5–4, Justice Stevens did not join in the portion of the opinion stating that the act of State doctrine should not be applied to

The act of State doctrine is also inapplicable if the government action in question violates a treaty between the United States and the defendant State. In such case, a U.S. court may accept jurisdiction and grant relief.[222] **4.117**

Yet another exception was created by the Hickenlooper Amendment,[223] a statute enacted by Congress in reaction to *Sabbatino*. The Amendment directs U.S. courts to adjudicate claims against States that are based on certain types of expropriation, if the foreign State has not provided compensation for the property taken. The Hickenlooper Amendment provides, in relevant part: **4.118**

> [N]o court in the United States shall decline on the ground of the federal act of state doctrine to make a determination on the merits giving effect to the principles of international law in a case in which a claim of title or other right to property is asserted by any party including a foreign state ... based upon (or traced through) a confiscation or other taking ... by an act of that state in violation of the principles of international law.

However, U.S. courts have read this exception narrowly, such that it applies only in cases where the expropriated property has been brought into the United States.[224] In the *Hunt* case,[225] for example, the plaintiff, whose oil interests in Libya were nationalized, brought an action for conversion against the purchaser of oil to which he once had a right. The plaintiff argued that the act of State doctrine was not applicable by operation of the Hickenlooper Amendment, because the taking had been illegal. The court responded that the Hickenlooper Amendment only concerned the taking of "title or other right in property," and that in the present case, the State had only expropriated contractual rights. In *French v. Banco Nacional de Cuba*,[226] the New York Court of Appeals further narrowed the scope of the exception, holding that the amendment was limited to specific, identifiable, and traceable property. **4.119**

commercial transactions of States. Abir provides a somewhat more compelling argument in favor of the commercial activities exception to the act of State doctrine: since act of State is a court-made rule, it should be subordinated to the will of Congress. In the FSIA, Congress provided court jurisdiction over claims involving the commercial activities of foreign States. Thus, a plaintiff who meets the requirements set forth in the commercial activities section of the FSIA should be entitled to maintain a suit, notwithstanding the act of State doctrine. Abir, *supra* note 211. For an argument that the *Dunhill* case did not establish a commercial exception to the act of State doctrine, see Ifeanyi Achebe, *The Legal Problems of Indigenization in Nigeria: A Lesson for Developing Countries*, 12 Hastings Int'l & Comp. LR 637, 659–62 (1989).

[222] *Kalamazoo Spice Ext. Co. v. Provisional Military Government of Socialist Ethiopia*, 729 F.2d 422 (6th Cir. 1984).

[223] 22 U.S.C. § 2370(e)(2).

[224] *Empresa Cubana Exportadora Inc. v. Lamborn & Co.*, 652 F.2d 231 (2d. Cir. 1981).

[225] *Hunt v. Coastal States Gas Producing Co.*, 583 S.W. 2d 322 (Tex. Civ. App. 1979).

[226] *French v. Banco Nacional de Cuba*, 23 N.Y.2d 46, 242 N.E.2d 704 (1968).

4.120 Finally, a State cannot raise the act of State doctrine as a defense to a counterclaim in a suit that the State originally initiated, except to the extent that the value of the counterclaim exceeds the value of the foreign State's claim.[227]

4. Sovereign immunity in the United Kingdom

a. The State Immunity Act

4.121 In the United Kingdom, the restrictive theory of sovereign immunity is codified in the State Immunity Act of 1978.[228] Under the State Immunity Act, sovereign States are "immune from the jurisdiction of the courts of the United Kingdom" except as otherwise provided for in the State Immunity Act. Exceptions to immunity relevant to this discussion are as follows: (1) voluntary submission to the jurisdiction of British courts;[229] (2) commercial transactions of the foreign State;[230] and (3) certain claims relating to the ownership, possession, or use of property located in the United Kingdom.[231]

4.122 The State Immunities Act defines "commercial transactions" as any contract for the supply of goods or services; any loan or other transaction for the provision of finance, or a guaranty or indemnity of any such loan; or any other transaction or activity (whether of a commercial, industrial, financial, professional, or other similar character) into which a State enters or in which it engages other than in the exercise of its sovereign authority.[232]

4.123 Service of process is made on the foreign State through the Foreign and Commonwealth Office of the United Kingdom, or in any other manner to which the foreign State has agreed.[233] A court may not order injunctions, specific performance, or execution against any non-commercial property of a foreign State without the defendant's consent.[234]

b. Doctrine of judicial restraint and abstention

4.124 English law recognizes a doctrine similar to that of the U.S. act of State doctrine. The 1921 case *Luthor v. Sagor*[235] involved property nationalized by the Soviet Union, which was sold to the defendant and brought into the United Kingdom. Regarding the Soviet nationalization decree, the court stated in dicta that "courts

---

[227] *First Nat'l City Bank v. Banco Nacional de Cuba*, 406 U.S. 759 (1972).

[228] State Immunity Act (1978), *reprinted in* 17 I.L.M. 1123 (1978). The State Immunity Act applies only to events that occurred after the Act took effect. *Hispano Americana Mercantil S.A. v. Central Bank of Nigeria*, 2 Lloyd's Rep. 277, 279 (C.A. 1978).

[229] State Immunity Act, *supra* note 228, § 2.

[230] *Id.* at § 3.

[231] *Id.* at § 6.

[232] *Id.* at § 3(3).

[233] *Id.* at § 12.

[234] *Id.* at § 13.

[235] *Luthor v. Sagor*, 3 K.B. 532 (1921).

of one country will not sit in judgment on the acts of the government of another done within its own territory."[236]

A more recent case, *Buttres Gas and Oil Co. v. Hammer*,[237] confirmed that English law recognizes a concept similar to that of the act of State doctrine, separate and apart from sovereign immunity issues addressed by the State Immunities Act. In that case, the court stated that a foreign decree that applied to the territory of another State could not be challenged in U.K. courts. The court concluded that this principle is not "a variety of 'act of state' but one of judicial restraint or abstention."[238] **4.125**

[236] *Id.* at 548.
[237] *Buttress Gas and Oil Co. v. Hammer*, 3 W.L.R. 787 (1978).
[238] *Id.* at 804.

5

HISTORY AND DEVELOPMENT OF THE CUSTOMARY INTERNATIONAL LAW OF EXPROPRIATION AND INVESTMENT PROTECTION

The international law of expropriation was for many decades the subject of fierce divisions between the developed and developing world. As the U.S. Supreme Court has noted: "There are few issues in international law today on which opinion seems to be so divided as the limitations on a state's power to expropriate the property of aliens."[1] **5.01**

Historically, viewpoints on expropriation have at times appeared to be politically motivated. Capital-exporting States tended to insist that host States respect the property and contractual rights of their nationals investing abroad. Capital-importing States, on the other hand, have often demanded the right to self-determination and control over their natural resources, arguing that the collective interests of society outweigh the interests of individuals such as private investors. Today, the picture is not nearly so clear. the development of investment treaties—and in particular of the North American Free Trade Agreement (NAFTA)—have **5.02**

[1] *Banco Nacional de Cuba v. Sabbatino*, 376 U.S. 398, 424 (1964).

placed traditional capital exporters like the United States and Canada on the receiving end of investment-related international law.[2] Meanwhile, investors from the "developing world" are venturing further afield, leading their home States to rethink the benefits that stable investment rules can bring.

5.03 This chapter discusses the customary international law of expropriation and investor protection. The first part covers the history of the international law of expropriation, including the traditional standard, the challenges to that standard by capital-importing countries in the 1960s, and the interpretation of the law by judicial and arbitral bodies. The role that treaties and State practice have had in shaping the law of expropriation is also addressed.

5.04 The current state of relevant principles of international law is also discussed, including a discussion of the "full compensation" standard. (The modern conventional international law of investment protection as embodied in investment treaties is covered in Chapter 6, along with a detailed discussion of methods of valuation of expropriated property.)

5.05 This chapter also briefly touches upon the related topic of the breach of contract by States. As will become clear, the breach of an investment contract by a host State may give rise to a cause of action under international law, separate from but related to the cause of action arising from the taking of property.

5.06 The conclusions reached in this chapter may be summarized as follows: a State may expropriate the property of aliens within its borders,[3] but must compensate the foreigner for the full value of the property taken. If the international law of

[2] As one of the authors has elsewhere observed, constantly envisioning itself as the condemned party in each new arbitral award issued far away, Washington appears to have lost sight of the unquestionable benefits that modern investment treaties have bestowed upon American business and the American economy in general. International law cannot be a one-way street, and as capital-exporting States more frequently become respondents in investment arbitration, they will be forced to adopt a long-term view of development and their own self-interest to preserve the hard-won gains they have achieved. Noah Rubins, *Loewen v. United States: The Burial of an Investor–State Claim*, 21 Arb. Int'l 1, 36 (2005).

[3] Regarding expropriation by a State of property outside of its borders, F.A. Mann stated that "there is no doubt that a State lacks international jurisdiction to take property situated outside its territory and such takings are, therefore, necessarily ineffective." F.A. Mann, *The Consequences of an International Wrong in International and National Law*, 48 Brit. Yb. Int'l L. 1, 46 (1977). In the aftermath of the attacks of Sept. 11, 2001, however, this debate was re-opened. The Proliferation Security Initiative, announced in 2003 by the United States, is an international effort or alliance between the United States and many European and other States. *See* the entry "Proliferation Security Initiative" in Wikipedia, at http://en.wikipedia.org/wiki/Proliferation_Security_Initiative. The PSI's professed goal is to combat the proliferation of weapons of mass destruction. One professed goal is to police the high seas and to assert enforcement jurisdiction, as well as prescriptive jurisdiction with regard to ships carrying or being believed to carry weapons of mass destruction. Since 2003, the PSI has evolved considerably, including a much broader scope of proliferation security issues, such as customs enforcement, export controls, proliferation finance, and intangible transfers of technology. Thus, an expropriation by a member State of the initiative beyond its borders may well occur. To what extent such an act would be legal under international norms remains to be seen.

expropriation has changed since the nineteenth century, the change is primarily that one State may no longer use force against another to rectify or prevent a taking of property by the host State.

A. History and Sources of the Law of Expropriation

1. Expropriation and standards of compensation prior to World War II

Because expropriation was relatively rare prior to the twentieth century,[4] legal standards of compensation evoked relatively little discussion or debate.[5] International arbitral decisions that did address expropriation routinely held, however, that States have the right to "appropriate private property for public use,"[6] but upon such expropriation, the State had an obligation to pay full compensation.[7] In fact, this principle was so well settled that in treaties among European countries, compensation for expropriated property was rarely mentioned—it was taken for granted.[8] 5.07

The seminal pre-World War II case regarding the international law of expropriation, the *Chorzów Factory* case,[9] arose from Poland's expropriation of a nitrate factory in Upper Silesia that had been owned by German nationals. After Germany brought a claim before the Permanent Court of International Justice, the court 5.08

[4] J.E.S. Fawcett, *Some Foreign Effects of Nationalisation of Property*, 27 Brit. Yb. Int'l L. 355, 356 (1950). Fawcett cites a series of nineteenth-century instances of expropriation, and states that they were "for the most part settled by the application of standards based on freedom of contract, the sanctity of private property, and the duty of the state to compensate the owners of property taken for the public use." *Id.* at 357. For a discussion of the development of the law of expropriation, *see also* Andreas Lowenfeld, International Economic Law 397–403 (2002). (suggesting that the formula of full, prompt, and adequate compensation, known today as the Hull formula, and the rival perspective that a foreigner is no safer from expropriation than the local citizen—known today as the Calvo doctrine—emerged from the discourse and practice of the nineteenth century. Lowenfeld points out that while during the nineteenth century the legal doctrine of compensation seems to have been well settled in theory, constant challenges threatened its practical relevance as a legal doctrine).

[5] Halliburton Fales, *A Comparison of Compensation for Nationalization of Alien Property with Standards of Compensation under United States Domestic Law*, 5 Northwestern J. Int'l L. & Bus. 871, 876 (1983).

[6] *Uptan Case (U.S. v. Venez.)*, 9 R.I.A.A. 234, 236 (1905).

[7] *See* Chapter 4 (discussing State responsibility for expropriation or other actions that have international consequences). For a discussion of the early law of expropriation, *see* Isi Foighel, Nationalization: A Study in the Protection of Alien Property in International Law 115–16 (1957) ("compensation must be adequate or just, i.e., corresponding to the loss that results from the dispossession"); Alexander P. Fachiri, *Expropriation in International Law*, 6 Brit. Yb. Int'l L. 159, 169–70 (1925)("expropriation is only permissible for public purposes and then only on payment of full compensation by the state"); Frederick S. Dunn, *The Protection of Nationals* (1932). For a contrary view, *see* John Fischer Williams, *International Law and the Property of Aliens*, 9 Brit. Yb. Int'l L. 1 (1928).

[8] *See* Fales, *supra* note 5, at 872.

[9] *Factory at Chorzów (Germany v. Poland)* (Indemnity), P.C.I.J. Ser. A, No. 17 (1928).

ruled that the expropriation was in violation of the German–Polish Convention Concerning Upper Silesia.[10] Regarding the compensation owing for an illegal expropriation, the Court stated:

> The essential principle contained in the actual notion of an illegal act—a principle which seems to be established by international practice and in particular by the decisions of arbitral tribunals—is that reparation must, as far as possible, wipe out all consequences of the illegal act and reestablish the situation which would, in all probability, have existed if that act had not been committed. Restitution in kind, or, if that is not possible, payment of a sum corresponding to the value which a restitution in kind would bear [must be made].[11]

5.09 The Court went on to state in *dicta* that a lawful expropriation does not require actual restitution (*i.e.* return of the property taken), but only payment of "the just price of what was appropriated" measured as "the value of the undertaking at the moment of dispossession, plus interest to the day of payment."[12] This was, essentially, an affirmation of the principle that even in the case of a "lawful" expropriation, the proper level of compensation is the value of the property taken—that is, full compensation is owing for both legal and illegal expropriations. For illegal takings, the host State was also obligated to make restitution in kind, if possible.

5.10 International arbitrations both prior to and following the *Chorzów Factory* case support the proposition that the proper level of compensation following an expropriation is the full value of the property taken. Early twentieth-century cases in which full compensation was ordered include the *Delagoa Bay* arbitration,[13] the *Spanish Zone of Morocco* arbitration,[14] the *Goldenberg Case*,[15] the *De Salba Claim*,[16] the *Selwyn Case*,[17] the *Norwegian Shipowners' Claim*,[18] and the *Lena Goldfields* arbitration.[19]

---

[10] *Certain German Interests in Polish Upper Silesia and the Factory at Chorzów (Germany v. Poland)* (Judgment No. 7) (Merits), P.C.I.J. Ser. A, No. 7 (1926).

[11] *Chorzów Factory, supra* note 9, at 47.

[12] *Id.* Judge Higgins has criticized this statement of the P.C.I.J:

> I do not believe that a central element in the law of compensation should be resolved by making deductions from an *obiter dictum* over the Permanent Court 40–5 years previously, when it was addressing only (and was only *thinking* about) a different situation—an unlawful taking.

Rosalyn Higgins, Problems and Process: International Law and How We Use It 144 (1994) (emphasis in the original).

[13] *Delagoa Bay and East African Railway Co. (U.S.A. and Great Britain v. Portugal), reprinted in* Marjorie M. Whiteman, 3 Damages in International Law 1694–703 (1943).

[14] *British Properties in Spanish Zone of Morocco (Spain v. U.K.)*, 2 R.I.A.A. 615 (1925).

[15] *Goldenberg Case (Germany v. Romania)*, 2 R.I.A.A. 901 (1928).

[16] *De Salba v. Panama (U.S.A. v. Panama)*, 6 R.I.A.A. 358 (1933).

[17] *Selwyn Case (G.B. v. Venezuela)*, 9 R.I.A.A. 380 (1903).

[18] *Norwegian Shipowners' Claims (Norway v. U.S.A.)*, 1 R.I.A.A. 307 (1922).

[19] *Lena Goldfields Arbitration* (1930), *reprinted in* 56 Cornell L.Q. 42, 51–52 (1950). For a fascinating historical analysis of one of the lesser-known investment disputes arising out of the Soviet Union's cancellation of concessions, *see* V.V. Veeder, *Lloyd George, Lenin and Cannibals: The Harriman Arbitration*, 16 Arb. Int'l 115 (2000).

In *Delagoa Bay*, for example, Portugal cancelled a thirty-five-year railway concession that had been granted to a British company. In a subsequent arbitral proceeding, the tribunal stated: 5.11

> Even if the present case should be regarded as one of legal expropriation, the fact remains that the effect was to dispossess private persons from their rights and privileges of a private nature conferred upon them by the concession, and that ... the State, which is the author of such dispossession, is bound to make full reparation for the injuries done by it.[20]

In the *Norwegian Shipowners' Claim*, a number of Norwegian nationals entered into contracts with U.S. shipyards to build vessels for use by Norway during World War I. Following its declaration of war on Germany, the United States seized these ships for its own use. Norway brought suit before the Permanent Court of International Justice, which, in its ruling, noted that it was not bound by U.S. law "in so far as these provisions restricted the right of the claimants to receive immediate and full compensation, with interest from the day on which the compensation should have been fully paid"[21] in accordance with principles of equity. The tribunal then awarded to the claimants the fair market value of the ships that had been seized. 5.12

The principle of full compensation for expropriation has long been established as a fundamental rule of customary international law. In one study of sixty international claims tribunals set up between 1840 and 1940 to deal with disputes arising from injury to aliens,[22] *none* of the arbitral panels "held that the appropriate measure of compensation was less than the full value of the property taken, and many specifically affirmed the need for full compensation."[23] 5.13

The United States first precisely articulated the principle of full compensation in 1938, when Secretary of State Cordell Hull, in a letter to the Mexican government regarding the nationalization of certain agricultural and oil-related properties, insisted that expropriation of foreign-owned property must be accompanied by "prompt, adequate, and effective" compensation.[24] This phrasing has now come to be known as the "Hull formula," and it has been interpreted to require 5.14

---

[20] *Delagoa Bay, supra* note 13, at 1698.

[21] *Norwegian Shipowners' Claims, supra* note 18, at 340.

[22] On injury to aliens by expropriation of their property and the requisite compensation, *see* Ian Brownlie, Principles of Public International Law 508–09 *et pass.* (6th ed. 2003).

[23] Patrick M. Norton, *A Law of the Future or a Law of the Past? Modern Tribunals and the International Law of Expropriation*, 85 AJIL 474, 477 (1991). *But see* C.F. Amerasinghe, *Issues of Compensation for the Taking of Alien Property in the Light of Recent Cases and Practice*, 41 ICLQ 22, 23 (1992) ("it may be noted that at the time the rule of full compensation is alleged to have come into existence and later in the nineteenth century the expropriations that took place were almost entirely of an individual nature. There were no complications emanating from, e.g., the nature of state economies, which were at that time all based on *laissez-faire* principles").

[24] Norton, *supra* note 23, at 476; Green H. Hackworth, Digest of International Law 658 (1942).

compensation in the amount of the full fair market value of an investment as a going concern.[25]

5.15 During this early period in the development of international law on expropriation, capital-exporting States occasionally applied military force when full compensation was not forthcoming to their investors.[26] Professor Wortley points out that in the mid-nineteenth century,

> British and many European and American investors [following expropriation of their property,] could expect their Governments to make use, if need be, of such measures as embargo, or pacific blockade, or naval demonstrations, and generally to use the same means as from time to time were used to obtain specific restitution.[27]

5.16 An example of the use of force to protect the property of nationals abroad can be seen in Britain's threat of naval intervention with respect to claims of its citizens against the government of Sicily in 1836.[28] Thus, not only did traditional international law require that an alien be fully compensated for the taking of its property, but it also permitted the use of force by the alien's home State to protect such rights.[29]

2. Challenges to the traditional standard

a. Latin American States

5.17 As early as the nineteenth century, a number of Latin American States challenged the international law standards discussed,[30] arguing that (1) aliens whose property was expropriated were entitled only to treatment equivalent to that granted by the expropriating State to its own nationals, and no more (and that the national treatment might well be that no compensation is required at all);[31] and (2) States were not obligated to recognize any international claims in relation to expropriation.[32] This view of expropriation was consistent with these States' general economic policy, which was in many ways hostile to foreign investment,[33] although

[25] Pat K. Chew, *Political Risk and U.S. Investments in China: Chimera of Protection and Predictability?*, 34 Va. J. Int'l L. 615, 641 (1994).

[26] Ian Brownlie, International Law and the Use of Force by States 289 (1963).

[27] B.A. Wortley, Expropriation in Public International Law 58 (1959).

[28] Fawcett, *supra* note 4, at n.2 ("British naval guns were brought to bear in the *Sicilian Sulphur Monopoly* case").

[29] For further discussion of the use of force under international law, *see* Chapter 10, Section F.

[30] Jeswald W. Salacuse, The Three Laws of International Investment: National, Contractual, and International Frameworks for Foreign Capital 322–24 (2013).

[31] *See* Chapter 4, Section F (international law does not generally regulate a State's seizure of its own nationals' property); and Section B.4, *infra* (regarding national treatment and the international minimum standard under current international law).

[32] *See* Francisco Orrego Vicuna, *The International Regulation of Valuation Standards and Processes: A Reexamination of Third World Perspectives*, in 3 The Valuation of Nationalized Property in International Law 131–48 (Richard B. Lillich ed. 1975).

[33] Some of the constitutions of Latin American States, for instance, have prohibited ownership of real property by foreign entities. Robert B. Shanks, *Insuring Investment and Loans against*

according to another view, it was a reaction to the economic and political intervention of the United States in Latin America.[34]

As an expression of their view of international law, many of these countries insisted upon the inclusion a so-called "Calvo clause" in investment contracts,[35] by which the investor agreed to renounce the right to diplomatic protection, and to submit all disputes to the jurisdiction of the host State's courts.[36] 5.18

While several decisions have been rendered on this issue, particularly by the US–Mexican General Claims Commission during the 1920s and the 1930s, no clear solution has emerged from these decisions. As the General Claims Commission held in the *North American Dredging Co.* case: 5.19

> The Commission does not feel impressed by arguments either in favor or in opposition to the Calvo clause, insofar as these arguments go to extremes. The Calvo clause is neither upheld by all outstanding international authorities and by the soundest among international awards, nor is it universally rejected.[37]

The Calvo Doctrine and accompanying Calvo clauses have declined in prominence in recent decades,[38] as Latin American States increasingly accept the standard of full compensation following expropriation and the settlement of investment disputes through international arbitration.[39] 5.20

Currency Inconvertibility, Expropriation, and Political Violence, 9 HASTINGS INT'L & COMP. L. REV. 417, 432 (1986).

[34] According to Sornarajah, the rationale of treating aliens equivalently to the host State's nationals was a matter of risk allocation. As the alien voluntarily takes the risk of investing in the host State, he deserves the same treatment as those nationals who suffer the same fate as him. Moreover, the idea of recognizing foreign investors' international claims (outside the domestic legal systems of the host States) was seen by Latin Americans as the vehicle which provided the United States with influence and presence in Latin America through foreign investments. M. SORNARAJAH, THE INTERNATIONAL LAW ON FOREIGN INVESTMENT 124, 126 (3d ed. 2010).

[35] Several Latin American countries incorporated the Calvo doctrine into their constitution and legislation as well. *See* SALACUSE, *supra* note 30, at 322.

[36] Brice M. Clagett, *Present State of the International Law of Compensation for Expropriated Property and Repudiated State Contracts*, in PRIVATE INVESTORS ABROAD § 12.02 (Southwestern Legal Foundation ed. 1989). The validity of such clauses is questionable, since according to the dominant view a private person cannot deprive a State of its right to exercise diplomatic protection. BROWNLIE, *supra* note 22, at 521. While the United States has refused to recognize Calvo clauses, Clagett opines that such clauses may be effective in stopping a proceeding to which the alien, rather than its home State, is a party. For a discussion of the Calvo doctrine, *see* HACKWORTH, *supra* note 24, at 530, 635 (1943), and Stanley D. Metzger, *Property in International Law*, 50 VA. L. REV. 594, 598–600 (1964).

[37] U.S. Department of State, Digest of International Law [U.S. Gov. Print. Off. 1967] vol. 8, 19.

[38] At the same time, a new kind of "Calvo doctrine" has been revived by the United States and Canada, which now insist that foreigners should receive no better treatment than their own citizens. This idea is now codified in many new U.S. and Canadian investment treaties. *See e.g.* D. Manning-Cabrol, *The Imminent Death of the Calvo Clause and the Rebirth of the Calvo Principle: Equality of Foreign and National Investors*, 26 L. POL'Y. INT'L BUS. 1169 (1995).

[39] *See e.g.* Chapter 6, Section B.2, discussing the standards of compensation for expropriation provided in the North American Free Trade Agreement (NAFTA) and other investment treaties. For more on NAFTA, see http://www.nafta-sec-alena.org and http://www.naftaclaims.com. The

5.21 As the International Law Commission commented in the context of the Draft Articles on Diplomatic Protection, "[t]he Calvo clause is difficult to reconcile with international law if it is to be interpreted as a complete waiver of recourse to international protection in respect of an action by the host State constituting an internationally wrongful act (such as a denial of justice) or where the injury to the alien was of direct concern to the State of nationality of the alien."[40]

b. Nationalization in the twentieth century

5.22 Many States nationalized the property of both their own citizens and foreign investors without compensation in the early twentieth century, often following revolutions that wrought radical changes in political and economic structures.[41] The new governments that arose out of these transformations often had little respect for private property, particularly in foreign hands.[42] Some argued that international standards requiring full compensation following expropriation were a "tool used by 'imperialist' powers,"[43] and that such standards are created by, and to serve the interests of, industrialized States in exploiting less developed countries.[44]

5.23 Such sudden transitions occurred in the Soviet Union in 1917,[45] Mexico in 1938,[46] Bulgaria, Czechoslovakia, Hungary, and Poland between 1945 and 1948,

development of BITs and the explicit protections they provide to investors have contributed to the decline of the Calvo doctrine, and strengthened general acceptance of strict international standards for the treatment of aliens. *See* Andreas F. Lowenfeld, *Investment Agreements and International Law*, 42 Colum. J. Transnat'l L. 123 (2003) (arguing that the law of expropriation found in BITs and the Washington Convention entered customary international law binding non-signatories). *See also CMS Gas Transmission Co. v. Argentina*, ICSID Case No. ARB/01/8, 2003, 42 I.L.M. 788 (2003) (holding that in the area of investment law, BIT provisions giving rise to claims for minority shareholders have become a general international custom, a rule to be followed unless disproved). *But cf.* Bernard Kishoiyian, *The Utility of Bilateral Investment Treaties in the Formulation of Customary International Law*, 14 J. Int'l L. & Bus. 327 (1994) (outlining the resistance of many developing countries to the pressure to internationalize investment contracts).

[40] Draft Articles on Diplomatic Protection adopted by the Drafting Committee on second reading in 2006 (International Law Commission), U.N. Doc. A/CN.4/L.684, U.N. Doc. A/61/10, 16, GAOR 61st Session Supp. 10, 83, Commentary to art. 14.

[41] F.N. Burton & Hisashi Inoue, *Expropriations of Foreign-Owned Firms in Developing Countries: A Cross-National Analysis*, 18 J. World Trade L. 396, 396–97 (1984) (between 1960 and 1977, seven countries accounted for 72.5 percent of the total number of expropriations. These countries were Algeria, Chile, Cuba, Ethiopia, Sri Lanka, Uganda, and Venezuela.) *Id.* at 413. For further discussion, *see* Edith Penrose et al., *Nationalization of Foreign-Owned Property for a Public Purpose: An Economic Perspective on Appropriate Compensation*, 55 Mod. L. Rev. 351 (1992).

[42] This fact in part explains the high percentage of expropriation directed against the perceived leaders of both democracy and capitalism, the United States and the United Kingdom. In their 1984 study, Burton and Inoue examined 1,857 cases of expropriation, intervention, forced sales, and forced contract renegotiation between the years 1960 and 1977. The study showed that United States and British firms accounted for 90 percent of all expropriated properties. Burton & Inoue, *supra* note 41, at 402.

[43] James C. Hsiung, Law and Policy in China's Foreign Relations 141 (1972).

[44] Chew, *supra* note 25, at 642.

[45] *See* Fawcett, *supra* note 4, at 357–63.

[46] For further discussions of expropriations by the government of Mexico following the revolution of 1910–20, *see* Tali Levy, *NAFTA's Provision for Compensation in the Event of Expropriation: A*

China in the 1950s,[47] Bolivia in 1952, and Egypt in 1956,[48] among others. Both the Soviet Union and Cuba, for example, after their respective revolutions of 1917 and 1959,[49] attempted to abolish the institution of private property, and refused to pay any compensation to foreign businesses that had suffered the confiscation of their assets.[50] Ultimately, Cuba alone seized the property of approximately 450 U.S. companies, with assets estimated at over US$2 billion.[51]

Expropriations triggered by political change continued into the 1970s.[52] Uganda, for instance, nationalized the property of foreign investors beginning in 1970, when the Obote government moved to acquire 60 percent ownership in all companies in the banking, manufacturing, mining, agriculture, and transport sectors. Although this percentage was reduced to 49 percent following General Amin's military coup in 1971, 500 U.K. firms were subject to expropriation in 1973. In 1974, Ethiopia began to expropriate on a massive scale, when the provisional military government took power. Although compensation was promised, none was voluntarily paid. In Algeria, asset seizures focused on the petroleum and mining industries. In Venezuela, a range of takings took place in the petroleum industry, but adequate compensation was generally paid for the expropriated property.[53] **5.24**

During the 1950s, 1960s, and 1970s, nationalization programs were also implemented by the newly independent and prosperous States of the Middle East, Asia, and Africa,[54] usually involving the expropriation of petroleum rights **5.25**

Reassessment of the "Prompt, Adequate and Affective" Standard, 31 Stan. J. Int'l L. 423 (1995); Amy L. Chua, *The Privatization-Nationalization Cycle: The Link between Markets and Ethnicity in Developing Countries*, 95 Col. L. Rev. 223 (1995); Eric N. Baklanoff, Expropriation of U.S. Investment in Cuba, Mexico, and Chile (1975).

[47] For further discussion, *see* Chew, *supra* note 25, at 625. Nationalization in China was a slow process, but by 1957, there was virtually no foreign direct investment left there.

[48] Most prominently, the Suez Maritime Canal Company was nationalized on July 26, 1956. *See* Foighel, *supra* note 7, at 25.

[49] Cuba began expropriating foreign-owned property in 1959, but most of the expropriations occurred in the second half of 1960. Matias F. Travieso-Diaz, *Some Legal and Practical Issues in the Resolution of Cuban Nationals' Expropriation Claims against Cuba*, 16 U. Pa. J. Int'l Bus. L. 217, 219–24 (1995); for further discussion, *see* Michael W. Gordon, The Cuban Nationalizations: The Demise of Foreign Private Property 69–108 (1976) and Baklanoff, *supra* note 46. *See also* Chapter 10, Section D.3 and Chapter 4, Section G, discussing the Cuban Liberty and Democratic Solidarity Act.

[50] Clagett, *supra* note 36, § 12.02. Following a series of expropriations by the Soviet Union of foreign-owned private property, a number of countries, including the United States, withheld diplomatic recognition of the Soviet government. After the expropriation of American property in Cuba, the United States terminated diplomatic and consular relations with Cuba. Adeoye Akinsanya, *International Protection of Direct Foreign Investments in the Third World*, 36 ICLQ 58, 61 (1987).

[51] Burton & Inoue, *supra* note 41, at 413.

[52] A comprehensive analysis of nationalization and resulting disputes can be found in Junji Nakagawa, Nationalization, Natural Resources and International Investment Law: Contractual Relationship as a Dynamic Bargaining Process (2018).

[53] Burton & Inoue, *supra* note 41, at 413–14.

[54] Many of these States were transformed practically overnight from beggars to barons, due to the sudden discovery and exploitation of oil resources. For example, when Libya gained independence

from multinational corporations operating under the auspices of concession agreements. These takings often resulted not so much from socialist ideological inspiration as from the desire of these States to enjoy a greater share in the profits derived from their petroleum reserves or in other cases, from their challenge to end "colonial" terms of contracts with foreign corporations, effecting post-colonial nationalizations.[55]

5.26 While some expropriations were driven by ideological revolution, as discussed, some were motivated, at least in part, by specific political events. For example, the expropriations by Libya that gave rise to the *British Petroleum*,[56] *TOPCO*,[57] and *LIAMCO*[58] arbitrations were triggered in part by the United Kingdom's refusal to react to Iran's occupation of three islands in the Persian Gulf, which were then nominally under British protection.[59] Another politically motivated expropriation occurred in 1973, when the Libyan government nationalized the interests of the Nelson Bunker Hunt Oil Company in Benghazi in response to U.S. support for Israel during the Yom Kippur War.[60]

c. *Justifications for expropriation and the U.N. resolutions on permanent sovereignty*

5.27 Following many of these expropriations, the States concerned publicly defended the right to expropriate without being subject to the customary international law requirement to pay full compensation.[61] In the post-colonial era, the newly independent States argued that customary international law regarding traditional principles such as the States' international responsibility for injuries to aliens (and consequently, the expropriation and the requirement for full compensation principle), was shaped by Western countries at a time "when the international community was restricted to only a few states."[62] Some, especially in the Middle East and Africa, argued that they were tied to long-term contracts that had been concluded

---

in 1951, it was an exceedingly poor country with a sparse and under-educated population. After its entry into the "club" of oil producers, Libya's annual income from oil exports was estimated to exceed US$16 billion by 1979. Libya's per capita income rose from US$40 in 1951 to US$6,500 in 1977. Robert B. von Mehren & P. Nicholas Kourides, *International Arbitrations between States and Foreign Private Parties: The Libyan Nationalization Cases*, 75 AJIL 476, 477 (1981). *See also* Clagett, *supra* note 36, § 12.02.

[55] *See* Salacuse, *supra* note 30, at 324–29.

[56] *British Petroleum Exploration Co. (Libya) Ltd. (BP) v. Government of Libya*, 53 I.L.R. 297 (1973).

[57] *Texaco Overseas Petroleum Co. and California Asiatic Oil Co. (TOPCO) v. Government of Libya* (1977), 53 I.L.R. 389 (1979), 17 I.L.M. 1 (1978).

[58] *Libyan American Oil Co. (LIAMCO) v. Government of Libya* (1977), 62 I.L.R. 140 (1980), 20 I.L.M. 1 (1981).

[59] Von Mehren & Kourides, *supra* note 54, at 483.

[60] *New York Times*, July 8, 1973, Section 4 at 2, col. 4.

[61] For further discussions of de-colonialization and self-determination, *see* Higgins, *supra* note 12, at ch. 7.

[62] S.N. Guha Roy, *Is the Law of Responsibility of States for Injuries to Aliens a Part of Universal International Law?*, 55 AJIL 863 (1961).

between foreign investors and former colonial authorities, and that the continuation of these arrangements despite de-colonialization deprived them of essential control over their ostensibly independent economies.[63] These States argued that such contracts, which they had not negotiated, were even more repugnant as they gave foreign interests the power to dispose of their natural resources.[64] This position eventually developed into the claim that the right of sovereign States to "economic self-determination" was *inalienable*, and that therefore the requirement of full compensation following expropriation should be inapplicable, as it would render any major economic restructuring impossible.[65]

These views are reflected in a series of U.N. General Assembly Resolutions endorsed, for the most part, by developing States.[66] The first of these resolutions,[67] and the only one that received broad support from States in both the developed and developing world, was General Assembly Resolution 1803 (XVII) of 1962, the Declaration on Permanent Sovereignty Over Natural Resources.[68] This resolution stated: **5.28**

> Nationalization, expropriation or requisitioning shall be based on grounds or reasons of public utility, security or the national interest which are recognized as overriding purely individual or private interests, both domestic and foreign. In such cases the

[63] Norton, *supra* note 23, at 496.

[64] Penrose et al., *supra* note 41, at 353.

[65] Brownlie, *supra* note 22, at 515 *et pass.; see also* Frank Dawson & Burns Weston, *"Prompt Adequate and Effective": A Universal Standard of Compensation?*, 30 Fordham L. Rev. 727, 738 (1962), who state:

> To assert, as do some, that states lacking sufficient gold reserves, foreign exchange or other financial resources should not undertake social and economic reforms, which may necessitate enacting extensive deprivation laws is both unrealistic and patronizing ... extensive deprivations may be of such absolute and relative magnitude as to render "full" compensation truly impossible.

[66] Although U.N. General Assembly resolutions do not have the force of law, they are often cited as evidence of international custom. Chew, *supra* note 25, at 642; Gaetano Arangio-Ruiz, *The Normative Role of the General Assembly of the United Nations and the Declaration of Principles of Friendly Relations*, 137 Recueil Des Cours 419, 434–518 (1972 III). *See also* Erik Suy, *Innovations in International Law-Making Processes*, in The International Law and Policy of Human Welfare 187, 190 (1978); F. Blaine Sloan, *The Binding Force of a "Recommendation" of the General Assembly of the United Nations*, 25 Brit. Yb. Int'l L. 1 (1948); D.H.N. Johnson, *The Effect of Resolutions of the General Assembly of the U.N.*, 32 Brit. Yb. Int'l L. 97 (1955); Rosalyn Higgins, The Development of International Law through the Political Organs of the United Nations (1963).

[67] Foreshadowing these Resolutions was a draft article adopted by the Third Committee of the General Assembly of the United Nations, which states:

> The people may, for their own ends, freely dispose of their natural wealth and resources without prejudice to any obligations arising out of international economic co-operation, based upon the principle of mutual benefit, and international law. In no case may the people be deprived of its own means of subsistence.

G.A. Res. 626 (VII), U.N. GAOR, 7th Sess. (1952).

[68] G.A. Res. 1803 (XVII), U.N. GAOR, 17th Sess., Agenda Item 39, para. 4, U.N. Doc. A/RES/1803 (XVII) (1962), *reprinted in* 2 I.L.M. 223 (1963).

> owner shall be paid appropriate compensation, in accordance with the rules enforced in the State taking such measure in the exercise of its sovereignty and in accordance with international law. In any case where the question of compensation gives rise to a controversy, the national jurisdiction of the state taking such measures shall be exhausted. However, upon agreement by sovereign States and other parties concerned, settlement of the dispute should be made through arbitration or international adjudication.

5.29 Eighty-seven States supported General Assembly Resolution 1803, two opposed it, and twelve abstained. Ten of the abstaining States were from the Socialist bloc.[69] While this resolution affirmed the requirements that States act "in accordance with international law" and that compensation be paid following expropriation, it sparked widespread debate over the meaning of the phrase "appropriate compensation." The United States voted in favor of Resolution 1803 because, in its view, the term "appropriate" compensation was equivalent to "prompt, adequate, and effective" compensation.[70] Many developing States disagreed, arguing that the "appropriate compensation" standard allowed them to pay less than full compensation following an expropriation. Subsequent arbitral decisions almost unanimously affirm the interpretation of the United States.[71]

5.30 In 1973, the General Assembly, without the support of capital-exporting States, adopted Resolution 3171, which purported to further erode international law standards of full compensation following expropriation. This resolution provided that, in the event of an expropriation,

> each State is entitled to determine the amount of possible compensation and the mode of payment, and that any disputes which may arise should be settled in accordance with the national legislation of each State carrying out such measures.[72]

5.31 According to this resolution, the foreign investor is not guaranteed compensation, but only "possible compensation". No reference is made to the appropriate level of compensation (except that the matter should be settled in accordance with the legislation of the host State), and no reference is made to international law. Thus, according to Resolution 3171, the host State has wide discretion in determining the amount of compensation due, if any, and is not bound by any external, objective principles such as those provided by customary international law.

---

[69] Chew, *supra* note 25, at 643; *see also* Stephen M. Schwebel, *The Story of the U.N.'s Declaration on Permanent Sovereignty over Natural Resources*, 49 ABAJ 463 (1963).

[70] Schwebel, *supra* note 69.

[71] But *see CME Czech Republic B.V. v. Czech Republic*, Dissenting Opinion of Ian Brownlie of Mar. 14, 2003, available at http://ita.law.uvic.ca/documents/CME-2001Dissent.pdf (asserting that "just compensation" provides less compensation for expropriation than the "Hull" formula of "prompt, adequate and effective" compensation).

[72] G.A. Res. 3171 (XXVIII), U.N. GAOR, 28th Sess. para. 3, U.N. doc. A/9030 (XVIII) (1973) G.A. Res. 1803 (XVII), U.N. GAOR, 17th Sess., Agenda Item 39, para. 4, U.N. Doc. A/RES/1803 (XVII) (1962), *reprinted in* 2 I.L.M. 223 (1963).

The following year, the U.N. General Assembly passed Resolution 3201, "The Declaration on the Establishment of a New International Economic Order," again without the support of most industrialized countries. This resolution declared the right of each State to exercise control over and exploit its natural resources, "including the right to nationalization or transfer of ownership to its nationals."[73] **5.32**

In 1974, the General Assembly passed the Charter of Economic Rights and Duties of States (Resolution 3281), which asserted that States have "permanent sovereignty over their natural wealth and resources," and that the definition of compensation was the prerogative of each State alone.[74] The resolution provided that a State has the right to **5.33**

> nationalize, expropriate or transfer ownership of private property, in which case appropriate compensation should be paid by the State adopting such measures, taking into account relevant laws and regulations and all circumstances that the State considers pertinent. In any case where the question of compensation gives rise to a controversy, it shall be settled under the domestic law of the nationalizing State and by its tribunals, unless it is freely and mutually agreed by all States concerned that other peaceful means be sought on the basis of this operand equality of States and in accordance with the principle of free choice of meanings.

Again, there was no reference in the document to international law, although it did require States to pay "appropriate compensation." One hundred and twenty States voted in favor of Resolution 3281, six States opposed it, and ten abstained.[75] Negative votes came from Belgium, Denmark, West Germany, Luxembourg, the United Kingdom, and the United States. **5.34**

Based in part on these resolutions, some developing countries have since argued that the expropriating State has the authority to determine its own rules governing compensation, rather than applying some objective international standard.[76] However, even at the time, it is doubtful that the founding documents of the "New International Economic Order" reflected the condition of customary international law with regard to compensation following expropriation.[77] The Charter of Economic Rights and Duties of States has, according to Brownlie, "a **5.35**

---

[73] G.A. Res. 3201 (S-VI), U.N. GAOR, Sixth Special Sess., agenda item 7, para. 6, U.N. doc. A/RES/3201 (S-VI) (1974), *reprinted in* 13 I.L.M. 715 (1974).

[74] Charter of Economic Rights and Duties of States, G.A. Res. 3281 (XXIX), U.N. GAOR, 29th Sess., Agenda Item 48, U.N. Doc. A/RES/3281 (XXIX) (1974), reprinted in 14 I.L.M. 251 (1975). *See also* Andres Rozental, *The Charter of Economic Rights and Duties of States and the New International Economic Order*, 16 Va. J. Int'l L. 309 (1976); F.V. García Amador, *The Proposed New International Economic Order: A New Approach to the Law Governing Nationalization and Compensation*, 12 Law. Americas—U. Miami J. Int'l L. 1 (1980).

[75] Chew, *supra* note 25, at 644.

[76] *Id.* at 645.

[77] Gillian White, *A New International Economic Order?*, 16 Va. J. Int'l L. 323, 330 (1976); Edward McWhinney, *The International Law-Making Process and the New International Economic Order*, 14 Can. Yb. Int'l L. 57, 67 (1976).

strong political and programmatic flavour and does not purport to be a declaration of pre-existing principles."[78]

5.36 By contrast, General Assembly Resolution 1803 does reflect to some degree the state of current international law regarding expropriation. As sole Arbitrator Dupuy concluded in the *TOPCO* arbitration,

> Resolution 1803 (XVII) seems to this Tribunal to reflect the state of customary law existing in this field. Indeed, on the occasion of the vote on a resolution finding the existence of a customary rule, the States concerned clearly expressed their views.[79]

5.37 Furthermore, the ICJ held in the case of *Armed Activities on the Territory of Congo* that the principle of permanent sovereignty over natural resources,

> as expressed in General Assembly resolution 1803 (XVII) of 14 December 1962 and further elaborated in the Declaration on the Establishment of a New International Economic Order (General Assembly resolution 3201 (S.VI) of 1 May 1974) and the Charter of Economic Rights and Duties of States (General Assembly resolution 3281 (XXIX) of 12 December 1974) ... is a principle of customary international law.[80]

5.38 The traditional rule of international law that following an expropriation an alien must be paid the full value of the property taken has also been attacked by some international law scholars. Some of these commentators have suggested that in the modern era, private property rights must be balanced against the rights of the public, especially in the case of large-scale nationalizations with the stated purpose of "reform."[81] According to this view, "balancing" should sometimes allow the State to take private property or repudiate contracts with aliens without the obligation to pay full compensation.[82]

5.39 Early drafts of the Restatement of Foreign Relations Law of the United States, in sections regarding expropriation, also appeared to support a more relaxed standard of compensation for expropriation.[83] These preliminary versions provided that "just compensation" would *ordinarily* be equal to the value of the investment, implying some circumstances would support compensation less than the asset value. In addition, comments to these drafts suggested that one criterion characterizing "creeping expropriation" was the State's *intent* to expropriate the property in question, rather than simply to regulate its economy for the "common good."[84]

---

[78] Brownlie, *supra* note 22, at 518.

[79] *TOPCO, supra* note 57, 17 I.L.M. at para. 87.

[80] *Armed Activities on the Territory of the Congo (Democratic Republic of the Congo v. Uganda)*, Judgment of Dec. 19, 2005, ICJ Rep. 168, para. 244.

[81] Brownlie, *supra* note 22, at 515 et pass.

[82] Norton, *supra* note 23, at 493. But *cf. Clagett, supra* note 36, § 12.04[2] ("If a man steals $10 from me and gives me back $4, he has still stolen $6. I am not able to understand why similar conduct by governments should be viewed any differently").

[83] Clagett, *supra* note 36, § 12.02.

[84] Such a "subjective" criterion would raise serious evidentiary concerns. Shanks, *supra* note 33, at 424.

The final version, as discussed in Section B, firmly adopts the traditional statement of the law.[85]

3. Arbitral awards after World War II

Despite the contrary assertions of some developing States and commentators, judicial and arbitral decisions following World War II tend to support the proposition that international law requires an expropriating State to compensate fully the alien for the value of property taken. Examples of early arbitrations in which full compensation was awarded are the *ARAMCO*,[86] *Sapphire*,[87] *Abu Dhabi*,[88] *Qatar*,[89] and *Lighthouses*[90] cases. In each of these proceedings, "the tribunal held the concessionaire state to the terms of its concession, or to damages for its breach, largely on the basis of this body of international precedent."[91] All of these awards support the proposition that international law requires that an expropriating State pay to an alien the full value of the property taken.[92] **5.40**

A series of arbitrations arising out of the Libyan oil nationalizations of the 1970s also support an uncompromising standard of full compensation for expropriation.[93] In *BP*, Arbitrator Lagergren referred to reparation as a vehicle for establishing the amount of compensation, implying that full compensation is the appropriate standard following an expropriation.[94] In *TOPCO*, Arbitrator Dupuy ordered restitution from Libya.[95] It can be inferred that had he ordered damages, Dupuy would have quantified the compensation according to the full market value of the concession. The *LIAMCO* case, by contrast, relied upon a lesser "equitable compensation" standard.[96] Even in the *LIAMCO* case, however, Sole Arbitrator Mahmassani awarded the claimants the "reasonable value" of the property taken.[97] **5.41**

A subsequent case, *AMINOIL*,[98] concerned Kuwait's 1977 expropriation of a petroleum concession held by the American Independent Oil Company. Kuwait **5.42**

---

[85] Clagett, *supra* note 36, § 12.03[5].
[86] *Saudi Arabia v. Arabian American Oil Co. (ARAMCO)* (1958), 27 I.L.R. 117 (1963).
[87] *Sapphire Int'l Petroleum Ltd. v. Nat'l Iranian Oil Co.*, 35 I.L.R. 136 (1953).
[88] *Petroleum Development Ltd. v. Sheikh of Abu Dhabi*, 18 I.L.R. 144 (1951).
[89] *Ruhr of Quatar v. Int'l Marine Oil Co.*, 20 I.L.R. 534 (1953).
[90] *Lighthouses Arbitration (France v. Greece)*, 23 I.L.R. 299 (1956).
[91] Norton, *supra* note 23, at 477.
[92] *Id.* at 478.
[93] Peter Cameron describes these 1970s arbitral awards as the "classic tests." States in the Middle East unilaterally changed the terms of petroleum contracts, destroying foreign investors' interests. For more details, *see*: Peter Cameron, International Energy Investment Law: The Pursuit of Stability 103 (2010).
[94] *BP, supra* note 56, 53 I.L.R. at 347.
[95] *TOPCO, supra* note 57, 17 I.L.M. at 32.
[96] *LIAMCO, supra* note 58, 62 I.L.R. at 210.
[97] *Id.* at 211–15.
[98] *Government of Kuwait v. American Independent Oil Co. (AMINOIL)*, 21 I.L.M. 976 (1982).

admitted that it owed compensation to the claimant company, but sought to value the property using a "book value" method. The claimant, meanwhile, insisted upon a method of valuation based upon the present value of the company's future cash flow. The parties agreed to submit the issue to arbitration.[99] The tribunal applied international law, according to the parties' submission, to resolve the dispute.[100] The tribunal found that the appropriate level of compensation was "appropriate compensation" for a "lawful expropriation," which was to be determined by an inquiry into all the circumstances surrounding the case.[101] This value was determined by the tribunal to be the depreciated replacement value of the fixed assets and the going concern value of the enterprise, adjusted to take account of interest and inflation.[102]

5.43 Some of the decisions of the Iran–U.S. Claims Tribunal are also evidence of the state of international law on expropriation.[103] Many of the opinions concerning expropriation were based on the application of the following passage from Article 4 of the U.S.–Iran Treaty of Amity:

> [Property of investors] shall not be taken except for a public purpose, nor shall it be taken without the prompt payment of just compensation. Such compensation shall be in an effectively revisable form and shall represent the full equivalent of the property taken.[104]

5.44 While many of the Claims Tribunal's decisions turn on the wording of this paragraph of the treaty, many also consider the dictates of customary international law. In practically all of the decisions that considered international law, the tribunal required the payment of full compensation.[105]

---

[99] *Id.* at 1031–36.

[100] *Id.* at 1032.

[101] *Id.*

[102] *Id.* at 1040–42.

[103] Certain commentators question the utility of Iran–U.S. Claims Tribunal decisions as authority establishing rules of international law on expropriation, largely because of the unique circumstances surrounding the establishment of the tribunal and the wording of the Algiers Accords, which circumscribed the tribunal's work. Katherarina A. Byrne, *Regulatory Expropriation and State Intent*, Can. Yb. Int'l L. 89, 93 (2000); Peter T. Muchlinski, Multinational Enterprises and the Law 508 (1995). Nevertheless, most observers agree that "the decisions of the Tribunal do constitute a very significant source of jurisprudential development of public international law." Charles N. Brower & Jason Brueschke, The Iran–U.S. Claims Tribunal 644 (1998); *see also* Jack Coe, Jr. & Noah Rubins, *Regulatory Expropriation and the Tecmed Case: Context and Contributions*, in International Investment Law and Arbitration 597, 609–10 (2005).

[104] Treaty of Amity, Economic Relations, and Consular Rights between the United States of America and Iran, signed Aug. 15, 1955, entered into force June 16, 1957, 284 U.N.T.S. 93, T.I.A.S. No. 3853, 8 U.S.T. 899 [hereinafter, Treaty of Amity], available at http://www.parstimes.com/law/iran_us_treaty.html.

[105] *Shahin Shane Ebrahimi (Shahin) v. Government of Iran*, Award No. 560-44/46/47-3 (1994), 30 Iran–U.S. C.T.R. 170, 177.

In two early expropriation cases argued before the Iran–U.S. Claims Tribunal, the panels applied customary international law. In these decisions, *Tippets*[106] and *American Int'l Group (AIG)*,[107] the tribunal found that international law requires that full value be paid for expropriated property. In *Tippets*, the tribunal determined the market value of the expropriated company, and awarded the U.S. claimant the full value of its 50 percent interest.[108] In *American Int'l Group*, the tribunal stated that **5.45**

> it is a general principle of public international law that even in a case of lawful nationalization the former owner of the nationalized property is normally entitled to compensation for the value of the property taken.[109]

The court concluded that the proper method of valuation is the "fair market value … at the date of nationalization," or, if that is not available, **5.46**

> The appropriate method is to value the company as a going concern, taking into account not only the net book value of its assets but also such elements as good will and likely future profitability, and the company been allowed to continue its business under its former management.[110]

AIG concerned an insurance company that was 35 percent owned by U.S. nationals. The tribunal did not discuss any particular standard of compensation, but did use the going concern method of valuation to assess the investor's interests, which corresponds to the full value of the enterprise.[111] **5.47**

In another case, *INA Corp.*,[112] the court applied the Treaty of Amity, which, as noted, required full compensation equal to the fair market value of the expropriated property. In *dicta*, however, the tribunal suggested that **5.48**

> at least as far as "large scale nationalizations of a lawful character [are concerned], international law has undergone a gradual reappraisal, the effect of which may be to undermine the doctrinal value of any 'full' or 'adequate' … compensation standard."[113]

Judge Lagergren echoed this sentiment in a separate opinion,[114] which Judge Holtzman separately downplayed as Lagergren's personal view. Holtzman **5.49**

[106] *Tippets, Abbett, McCarthy, Stratton (Tippets) v. TAMS-AFFA Consulting Engineers of Iran*, Award No. 141-7-2, 6 Iran–U.S. C.T.R. 219 (1984).

[107] *American Int'l Group Inc. et al. (AIG) v. Iran*, Award No. 92-2-3, 4 Iran–U.S. C.T.R. 96 (1983).

[108] *Tippets, supra* note 106, at 225–28.

[109] *AIG, supra* note 107, at 107, 6.

[110] *Id.*

[111] *See* Chapter 6, Section E (discussing methods of valuation).

[112] *INA Corp. v. Government of Iran*, Award No. 184-161-1, 8 Iran–U.S. C.T.R. 373 (1985).

[113] *Id.* at 378. *See also AGIP S.p.A. v. Government of the People's Republic of the Congo*, ICSID Case No. ARB/77/1, Award of Nov. 30, 1979, 8 Yb. Comm. Arb. 133 (1983) (stating in *dicta* that the "principle of full compensation for losses is limited in certain circumstances").

[114] *INA, supra* note 112, at 390.

emphasized that while a few arbitral tribunals had stated that they were using an "appropriate compensation" standard, they had actually awarded full compensation.[115]

5.50 Thus, in nearly every case where the claims tribunal ruled on the issue of compensation for expropriation under customary international law, it affirmed that full compensation is the appropriate standard.[116] Judge Allison, in a separate opinion in the *Shahin* case, summarized the claims tribunal's jurisprudence regarding the customary international law of expropriation:

> In sum, there is virtual total uniformity in the Tribunal's rulings on the standard of compensation under international law. Every decision rendered by this Tribunal, whether based upon the Treaty of Amity or customary international law, or both of them, has concluded that compensation must equal the full value of the expropriated property as it stood on the date of taking. Moreover, every award rendered by this Tribunal, including the Award in the instant Cases, has provided claimants what the Tribunal determined to be the *full value* of their interest in the property taken, *regardless of whether the taking was lawful or unlawful* or whether the parties relied on the Treaty of Amity or customary international law.[117]

5.51 Finally, in several contract-based arbitrations conducted under the auspices of ICSID,[118] tribunals also considered the international law of expropriation.[119] Two of these cases involve the expropriation of investments in Congo.[120] In *AGIP*, the Congolese government nationalized the interests of a corporation 90 percent owned by Italian nationals. The contract specified the law of Congo as applicable, supplemented by international law.[121] *Benvenuti* involved the expropriation of a Congolese company in which Italian nationals held a 40 percent equity interest. Various actions of the Congolese State, culminating in the occupation of the company's plant by the army, precipitated the arbitral proceedings. Because the agreement between the investors and the State did not contain an express choice-of-law clause, the arbitrators relied on Article 42(1) of the Washington Convention[122] to select Congolese law as governing, supplemented by principles

---

[115] *Id.* at 393, 401.

[116] *See e.g. BP, supra* note 56; *TOPCO, supra* note 57; *Amoco Int'l Finance Corp. (Khemco) v. Government of Iran*, Award. No. 310-56-3, 15 Iran–U.S. C.T.R. 189, 266 (1987); *Sola Tiles Inc. v. Government of Iran*, Award No. 298-317-1, 14 Iran–U.S. C.T.R. 223 (1987); and *SEDCO Inc. v. Nat'l Iranian Oil Co. et al.*, Award No. 309-129-3, 15 Iran–U.S. C.T.R. 23 (1987).

[117] *Shahin, supra* note 105, Separate Opinion of Richard C. Allison, at para. 36 (emphasis added).

[118] *See* Chapter 8.

[119] ICSID cases considering expropriation according to the terms of BITs are discussed in Chapter 6, Section C.1.

[120] *S.A.R.L. Benvenuti et Bonfant v. People's Republic of Congo*, ICSID Case No. ARB/77/2, Award of Aug. 8, 1980, 21 I.L.M. 740 (1982); *AGIP, supra* note 113.

[121] *AGIP, supra* note 113, at 727.

[122] *See* Chapter 8, Section B.2.b.

of international law.[123] In both cases, the arbitrators awarded full compensation for the assets taken.

5.52 In the *LETCO v. Liberia* arbitration,[124] the tribunal applied Liberian law, but stated that Liberian law was consonant with international law, and that "according to international law ... LETCO is entitled to compensation for damages for both its lost investments and its foregone future profits."[125]

5.53 Thus, with the exception of *LIAMCO*, arbitral awards considering the issue have consistently affirmed that the customary international law requires a State expropriating the property of a foreign national to pay the full value of that property, measured where possible by the market price. Although no tribunal has expressly invoked the Hull formula, the result has been the same.[126]

4. Treaties as evidence of customary international law

5.54 One of the sources of customary international law is State practice as evidenced in the treaties they conclude. As one commentator explains:

> A series of recurrence of treaties laying down a similar rule may produce a principle of customary international law to the same effect. Such treaties are thus a step in the process whereby a rule of international custom emerges.[127]

5.55 Most bilateral investment treaties (BITs) in effect today provide that full compensation should be paid following an expropriation. For example, the United States–Kazakhstan BIT provides that investments shall not be expropriated, directly or indirectly, unless the expropriation is for a public purpose, is performed in a non-discriminatory manner, and upon payment of prompt, adequate, and effective compensation.[128] The same is true with respect to the majority of BITs around the world.[129] Regional treaties also confirm these principles, some providing for

---

[123] *Benvenuti, supra* note 120, at 752.

[124] *Liberian Eastern Timber Corp. (LETCO) v. Government of Liberia*, ICSID Case No. ARB/83/2, Award of Mar. 31, 1986, 26 I.L.M. 647 (1987).

[125] *Id.* at 658, 670.

[126] Norton, *supra* note 23, at 488. For further discussion of full compensation, *see* Chapter 6, Section E.

[127] J.G. Starke, *Treaties as a "Source" of International Law*, 23 BRIT. YB. INT'L L. 341, 344 (1946). "[T]reaties ... *can* provide evidence of a general conception of international customary law" (emphasis in the original). FOIGHEL, *supra* note 7, at 41. *See also* Lazare Kopelmanas, *Custom as a Means of the Creation of International Law*, 18 BRIT. YB. INT'L L. 127 (1937).

[128] United States–Kazakhstan BIT (1992), art. III(1). For further discussion of BITs, *see* Chapter 6. *See also* Andreas F. Lowenfeld, *Investment Agreements and International Law*, 42 COLUM. J. TRANSNAT'L L. 123 (2003) (arguing that the law of expropriation found in the BIT and the ICSID Convention has become part of customary international law).

[129] *See e.g.* Australia–Vietnam BIT (1991), 30 I.L.M. 1064 (1991); Germany–Poland BIT (1989), 29 I.L.M. 333 (1990); U.K.–Panama BIT (1983), 23 I.L.M. 708 (1984); China–Japan BIT (1988), 28 I.L.M. 575 (1989).

an additional requirement of "due process of law."[130] The expropriation provisions in these treaties are described in detail in Chapter 6.

5.56 Some have argued that these treaties, and the protections that they offer to foreign investment, are evidence of customary international law. Professor Brownlie opines that:

> It is a fact that a very considerable number of hosts to foreign capital are willing to conclude treaties for the protection of investments which contain a provision for the payment of "prompt, adequate, and effective" compensation in cases of expropriation or, more frequently, "just compensation". While these are negotiated deals, the pattern of agreements surely constitutes evidence of an international standard based upon the principle of compensation.[131]

5.57 F.A. Mann also believed that "these treaties establish and accept and thus enlarge the force of traditional conceptions of the law of state responsibility for foreign investment."[132] Mann argued that States cannot credibly insist on the one hand that customary international law allows them to set the level of compensation following expropriation, and on the other hand accept the principle of full compensation in the treaties that they sign.[133]

5.58 This has also been confirmed in the practice of investment tribunals. As the tribunal held in *Mondev*, the vast number of bilateral and regional investment treaties that run between North and South, and East and West, form a body of concordant practice which has necessarily influenced the content of rules governing the treatment of foreign investment in current international law.[134] The tribunal in *Cargill* confirmed that "extensive adoption of identical treaty language by many States may in and of itself serve—again with care—as evidence of customary international law."[135]

5.59 In *CME v Czech Republic*, the tribunal noted that the fact that the possibility of payment of compensation determined by the law of the host State "has disappeared from contemporary international law as it is expressed in investment treaties in such extraordinary numbers, and with such concordant provisions, as to have reshaped the body of customary international law itself."[136] In the same

---

[130] *See e.g.* NAFTA, art. 1110(1)(c); Comprehensive Economic and Trade Agreement (CETA) between Canada, and the European Union and its Member States, art. 8(12) para. 1; EU–Singapore Free Trade Agreement (authentic text as of May 2015), Investment Chapter, art. 9(6)(1)(b).

[131] Brownlie, *supra* note 22, at 520 (citations omitted).

[132] F.A. Mann, *British Treaties for the Promotion and Protection of Investment*, 52 Brit. Yb. Int'l L. 241, 249 (1981).

[133] *Id.* For a contrary opinion, *see* Bernard Kishoiyian, *The Utility of Bilateral Investment Treaties in the Formulation of Customary International Law*, 14 NWJ Int'l L. & Bus. 327 (1994).

[134] *Mondev Int'l Ltd. v. U.S.A.*, ICSID Case No. ARB (AF)99/2, Award of Oct. 11, 2002 (NAFTA), paras. 117 and 125.

[135] *Cargill Inc. v. Mexico*, ICSID Case No. ARB (AF)/05/2, Award of Sept. 18, 2009, para. 276.

[136] *CME Czech Republic B.V. v. Czech Republic,* UNCITRAL, Final Award of Mar. 14, 2003, para. 498.

direction, the ICSID tribunal in *Siag* observed that several requirements for the legality of an expropriation "are also included to varying degrees in most treaties" and therefore "have become part of customary international law."[137] Conversely, other investment tribunals have held that the BIT provisions on expropriation codify or refer to the customary rules of international law on the requirements of lawful expropriation.[138]

The tribunal in *Accession Mezzanine* addressed the relationship between customary law on expropriation and traditional systems of diplomatic protection, on the one hand, and treaty provisions on expropriation and investor–State arbitration, on the other: **5.60**

> Expropriation has been and is now part of international law, and the change from dispute resolution under the system of diplomatic protection to investor–state arbitration has not modified that. It is true that BITs have become the most reliable source of law in this area, as have the awards of ICSID, other investor–state tribunals acting under the UNCITRAL Arbitration Rules, and other modern-day tribunals, such as the Iran–U.S. Claims Tribunal, state practice, and writings of scholars. But that is not inconsistent with the continuing relevance of customary and general principles of international law, at least as to BIT obligations that are silent as to scope and content, as well as any other sources of international law with respect to expropriation.[139]

5. Negotiated settlements

Many twentieth-century expropriation claims were settled by lump-sum payments from the expropriating State to the home State of the foreign individuals and corporations whose property was taken. In these cases, the two governments negotiated to arrive at a total compensation amount for all outstanding claims, and then the receiving State distributed payments to individual investors (normally on a pro-rata basis).[140] In many of these settlements, the States involved agreed to an amount less than full compensation for the property expropriated.[141] **5.61**

One example of a lump-sum settlement for less than full value compensation was concluded between the United States and China in 1979. Within the framework of efforts to normalize relations with China, the United States agreed to settle **5.62**

[137] *Waguih Elie George Siag & Clorinda Vecchi v. Egypt*, ICSID Case No. ARB/05/15, Award of June 1, 2009, para. 428.

[138] *Generation Ukraine Inc. v. Ukraine*, ICSID Case No. ARB/00/9, Final Award of Sept. 16, 2003, para. 11(3); *Glamis Gold Ltd. v. U.S.A.*, UNCITRAL, Final Award of June 8, 2009, para. 354.

[139] *Accession Mezzanine Capital L.P. and Danubius Kereskedohaz Vagyonkezelo v. Hungary*, ICSID Case No. ARB/12/3, Decision on Respondents' Objection under Arbitration Rule 41(5) of Jan. 16, 2013, para. 68.

[140] *See* discussion of the United States Foreign Claims Settlement Commission in Chapter 10, Section G.

[141] *See e.g.* Chew, *supra* note 25, at 648.

outstanding claims for a lump sum of US$80.5 million,[142] which was substantially less than the estimated value of the total claims of American investors.[143] U.S. businesses ultimately received approximately 14 percent of the estimated value of their investments, on a principal-plus-interest basis.[144] A more recent lump-sum settlement was negotiated in 1992 between the United States and Germany regarding the expropriation of assets of U.S. nationals by East Germany. Although such settlements usually do not include accrued interest, in this case the settlement included the payment of simple interest from the time that the U.S. properties were taken.[145]

5.63 Some commentators have argued that the results of these lump-sum settlement negotiations between States (*i.e.* the payment of less than full compensation) create international custom, which constitutes one source of international law,[146] and should therefore be viewed as evidence of a corresponding customary international law norm.

5.64 The *Khemco* tribunal[147] took issue with this position, concluding that the existence of lump-sum settlements for less than full value of property taken cannot be seen as evidence of any underlying legal principle.

> as a rule, a State practice as reflected in settlement agreements cannot be considered as giving birth to customary rules of international law, unless it presents specific features which demonstrate the conviction of the State's parties that they were acting in application of what they consider to be settled law. The provisions of such an agreement, indeed, are the outcome of negotiations in which many motivations other than legal ones may have prevailed. This is especially true here, where certain commercial advantages given to companies (even if they were not expressly detailed in the agreements) produced the concessions that they accepted on the standard of compensation.

5.65 U.S. courts have taken the same approach.[148] The Second Circuit Court of Appeals has stated that

> the notion that, merely because a negotiated settlement will not result in full payment, a victim of expropriation has no right to more than partial compensation

---

[142] Agreement Concerning the Settlement of Claims, May 11, 1979, U.S.-P.R.C., 30 U.S.T. 1958, *reprinted* in 18 I.L.M. 551 (1979).

[143] Chew, *supra* note 25, at 629.

[144] Clagett, *supra* note 36, § 12.05[3][a].

[145] Agreement between the Government of the United States of America and the Government of the Federal Republic of Germany Concerning the Settlement of Certain Property Claims, May 13, 1992, T.I.A.S. 11959; Matias F. Travieso-Diaz, *Alternative Recommendations for Dealing with Expropriated U.S. Property in Post-Castro Cuba*, 12 Cuba in Transition 101, 107 (ASCE 2002), available at https://ascecuba.org//c/wp-content/uploads/2014/09/v12-travieso2.pdf; Travieso-Diaz, *supra* note 49, at 226.

[146] Statute of the International Court of Justice, art. 38(1) (1945), available at http://www.icj-cij.org.

[147] *Khemco, supra* note 116, at 266.

[148] *See e.g. Banco Nacional de Cuba v. Chase Manhattan Bank*, 658 F.2d 875 (2d Cir. 1981).

> simply confuses adjudication with compromise ... we should no more look to the outcome of such a process to determine the rights and duties of the parties in expropriation matters than we would look to the results of settlements in ordinary tort or contract cases to determine the rules of damages to be applied.[149]

Thus, for the purposes of international law formation, there may be an important distinction between negotiations that were clearly based upon perceptions of customary law and those based primarily upon economic and political considerations.[150] Since almost all lump-sum settlement agreements have been concluded on the basis of a variety of interests, it is difficult to draw any general conclusions about the extent to which such negotiations reflect customary international law.[151] **5.66**

B. Current State of the Law of Expropriation

Currently, investment treaties play a dominant role in developing international law on expropriation, leaving less space for customary international law.[152] Nevertheless, many commentators have expressed the view that the wide propagation of BITs has influenced the evolution of customary law, particularly regarding expropriation and compensation.[153] Relying on the history and sources of law previously discussed, some scholars have posited a "modern" formulation of the international law of expropriation: A State may always expropriate property of investors within its borders; however, for such an expropriation to be legal, it must not be discriminatory, it must be for a public purpose, and it must be accompanied by full compensation, which must be prompt, adequate, and effective.[154] Thus, an expropriation that is non-discriminatory and for a public **5.67**

---

[149] *Id.* at 892.

[150] *Khemco, supra* note 116, at 266.

[151] It should be noted, however, that some commentators suggest that lump-sum settlements do form part of the foundation of the international law of expropriation. *See e.g.* Burns H. Weston et al., International Claims: Their Settlement by Lump Sum Agreement 1975–95 (1999), which complements the earlier version of the same book examining settlement concluded before 1975, namely Richard B. Lillich & Burns H. Weston, International Claims: Their Settlement by Lump Sum Agreement (1975) (arguing that while international lump-sum settlements are *lex specialis*, with every settlement reflecting the special underlying circumstances and motivation of each negotiation, there are principles which unite all the different agreements, especially with regards to the principle of the sanctity of private property).

[152] Thomas W. Walde & Borzu Sabahi, *Compensation, Damages, and Valuation*, in The Oxford Handbook of International Investment Law 1069–70 (Peter Muchlinski et al. eds. 2008).

[153] S. Schwebel, *The Reshaping of the International Law of Foreign Investment by Concordant Bilateral Investment Treaties*, in Law in the Service of Human Dignity—Essays in Honour of Florentino Feliciano 241 (S. Charnovitz et al. eds. 2005). Whether investment treaties contribute to the creation of customary law is still controversial. *See* Sornarajah, *supra* note 34, at 129.

[154] Expropriation in violation of a treaty is also illegal. Foighel, *supra* note 7, at 49. In such a case, however, the illegality will arise from the treaty breach (in addition to possible illegality arising from failure to comply with customary international law norms).

purpose is legal, but the requirement of compensation makes this legality conditional.[155] Some arbitrators have opined that "due process of law" constitutes an additional requirement for the legality of the expropriation.[156] According to this view, an expropriation that does not meet all of these requirements is "illegal."[157] Expropriation that is discriminatory or not for a public purpose is considered illegal *per se*, whether or not compensation is paid.[158] This view of the law of expropriation has received considerable support in State practice and the decisions of international tribunals.[159]

5.68 As noted, under customary international law, a State is sovereign within its territory, and is at liberty to take control of alien property. This sovereignty, however, exists within the framework of international law, which requires that the taking be non-discriminatory and carried out for a public purpose and obliges the State to pay compensation in the full amount of the value of the property taken.[160] Professor Wortley explains:

> Because a sovereign State may control and expropriate property in its territory, this does not mean that it can, at will, disregard the claims made, by virtue of public international law, to restitution or to just compensation, or that it may always insist on its own conception of private property.[161]

5.69 The state of customary international law discussed is reflected in the *Restatement (Third) of the Foreign Relations Law of the United States*, Section 712, which provides in part:

> A state is responsible under international law for injury resulting from:
>
> (1) A taking by the state of the property of a national of another state that
>
> (a) is not for a public purpose, or

---

[155] BROWNLIE, *supra* note 22, at 514. Brownlie also discusses "[t]he practical distinctions between expropriation unlawful *sub modo*, i.e. only if no provision is made for compensation, and expropriation unlawful *per se* ..." *Id.* at 538–39.

[156] RUDOLF DOLZER & CHRISTOPH SCHREUER, PRINCIPLES OF INTERNATIONAL INVESTMENT LAW 100 (2d ed. 2012).

[157] BROWNLIE, *supra* note 22, at 514–15, 519–20 (citing other conditions that may make an expropriation "unlawful").

[158] BROWNLIE, *supra* note 22, at 514–15 (contending that expropriation is also illegal if "it includes seizures which are a part of crimes against humanity or genocide, involve breaches of international agreements, are measures of unlawful retaliation or reprisal against another state ... or concern property owned by a foreign state and dedicated to official state purposes").

[159] *See* the sources discussed in Section A, *supra*. *See also* BROWNLIE, *supra* note 22, at 514.

[160] WORTLEY, *supra* note 27, at 12. *See also* von Mehren & Kourides, *supra* note 54, at 516, 517; *TOPCO*, *supra* note 57, at paras. 59–62; L.T. Kissam & E.K. Leach, *Sovereign Expropriation of Property and Abrogation of Concession Contracts*, 28 FORDHAM L. REV. 177, 224 (1959); Abdel-Wahab, *Economic Development Agreements and Nationalization*, 30 U. CINCINNATI L. REV. 418, 440 (1961).

[161] WORTLEY, *supra* note 27, at 12 ("What, indeed, does the state acquire by its act of expropriation? Simply a title by its own *national* law that other States may not recognize if they think that the title has been acquired in a manner not recognized by *international* law"). *Id.* at 16 (emphasis in the original). *See* the discussion of invalidation of title in Chapter 10, Section E.

(b) is discriminatory, or
(c) not accompanied by provision for just compensation.[162]

The Restatement provides that for compensation to be "just," it must, **5.70**

> in the absence of exceptional circumstances, be in an amount equivalent to the value of the property taken, or within a reasonable time thereafter with interest from the date of taking, and in a form economically usable by the foreign national.

Customary international law is also reflected in the Guidelines on the Treatment of Foreign Direct Investment[163] promulgated by the World Bank in 1992, which are based on a broad survey of existing legal instruments.[164] As pointed out in the Introductory Note,[165] the Guidelines were the result of an attempt to "establish legal—or quasi-legal—guidelines or standards for the treatment of foreign direct investment." The Guidelines were "based upon consideration of other pronouncements in the field, such as bilateral investment treaties," but do not have any force of law. At the same time, many observers agree that the rules codified in the Guidelines "have considerable credibility," as a result of the broad-based methodology and sources used to compile them. According to its drafters, at least, the Guidelines "would seem to approach more closely the status of an international agreement."[166] **5.71**

Regarding expropriation, the Guidelines provide that: **5.72**

> [A] State may not expropriate or otherwise take in whole or in part a foreign private investment in its territory, or take measures which have similar effects, except ... against the payment of appropriate compensation ... Compensation for a specific investment taken by the State will, according to the details provided below, be deemed "appropriate" if it is adequate, effective, and prompt.[167]

---

[162] Restatement (Third) of the Foreign Relations Law of the United States § 712 [hereinafter, the Restatement]. *See also Marvin Roy Feldman Karpa v. Mexico*, ICSID Case No. ARB(AF)/99/1, Award of Dec. 16, 2002, 42 I.L.M. 625 (2003), para. 99 (stating that the "public purpose" test has little importance in most situations, since the test is so easily satisfied). *See also* UNCTAD, *Taking of Property*, Paper No. UNCTAD/ITE/IIT/15 (2000), available at http://www.unctad.org/en/docs/psiteiitd15.en.pdf.

[163] World Bank, Guidelines on the Treatment of Foreign Direct Investment (1992), 31 I.L.M. 1379 (1992), available at: https://www.italaw.com/documents/WorldBank.pdf [hereinafter, the Guidelines].

[164] The events leading to the drafting of the Guidelines are briefly discussed in Ibrahim Shihata & Antonio R. Parra, *Applicable Substantive Law in Disputes between States and Private Foreign Parties: The Case of Arbitration under the ICSID Convention*, 9 ICSID Rev.—For. Inv. L.J. 191 (1994). Some ICSID tribunals have looked to the Guidelines for support in matters of investment protection law, including expropriation. *See e.g. Compañia del Desarrollo de Santa Elena S.A. v. Costa Rica*, ICSID Case No. ARB/96/1, Award of Feb. 17, 2000, para. 78.

[165] Seymour J. Rubin, *Introductory Note [to the World Bank: Report to the Development Committee and Guidelines on the Treatment of Foreign Direct Investment]*, 31 ILM 1363 (1992).

[166] *Id.*

[167] Guidelines, *supra* note 163, at Guideline IV, §§ 1–2.

5.73 The specific requirements of customary international law for an expropriation to be "legal" will be discussed in further detail in Chapter 6.[168]

1. Public purpose and non-discrimination

5.74 As mentioned earlier, expropriation must be carried out for a "public purpose" to be considered "legal" under international law.[169] "Public purpose" has been defined as "reasons of public utility, judicial liquidation and similar measures."[170] General Assembly Resolution 1803 (on permanent sovereignty over natural resources) mentions the public purpose requirement, while the 1974 Charter of Economic Rights and Duties of States does not.[171] Exceedingly few decisions turned on whether an expropriation was carried out for a "public purpose."[172] This may be because it is very easy for an expropriating State to couch any taking in terms of some "public purpose."[173]

5.75 An expropriation must also be "non-discriminatory" to be considered "legal" under international law. A discriminatory taking is one that singles out a particular person or group of people without a reasonable basis. The arbitrator in *LIAMCO* reaffirmed the principle that a discriminatory expropriation would be *per se* unlawful.[174] Like the "public purpose" requirement, the "non-discrimination" requirement is not extensively discussed in the literature or by international tribunals. As in the case of the "public purpose" requirement, this may be because proving discrimination can be extremely difficult.[175] The Restatement

[168] In the investment treaty context, *see Marvin Roy Feldman Karpa v. Mexico, supra* note 162, at paras. 137–141, 42 I.L.M. at 654–55 (examining the public purpose and non-discrimination tests, and noting the difficulty in establishing by sufficient evidence that an expropriation is illegal *per se*). The public purpose requirement is also arguably problematic on the grounds that the concept is not objective. *See e.g.* Hans-Hermann Hoppe, *Fallacies of the Public Goods Theory and the Production of Security*, 9 J. LIBERTARIAN STUD. 27 (1989), available at http://www.mises.org, arguing that there is no objective way to distinguish "public" goods from private ones. Similarly, it could be argued that public purpose is difficult, if not impossible, to objectively and rigorously define and identify in practice.

[169] *But see LIAMCO, supra* note 58, 62 I.L.R. at 194 ("it is the general opinion in international theory that the public utility principle is not a necessary requisite for the legality of a nationalization").

[170] *Chorzów Factory, supra* note 9, at 22.

[171] *See* discussion, *supra*, Section A.2.c.

[172] *See also* Clagett, *supra* note 36, § 12.01[1].

[173] As noted by Newcombe and Paradell, "in practice, the public purpose requirement has rarely arisen in international expropriation cases and states have been afforded a wide margin of appreciation in determining whether an expropriation serves a public purpose." *See* ANDREW NEWCOMBE & LUIS PARADELL, LAW AND PRACTICE OF INVESTMENT TREATIES: STANDARDS OF TREATMENT 371 (2009). An obvious case where an expropriation could be challenged as illegal based on a lack of public purpose would be where a public official has seized property for his personal use. Restatement, *supra* note 162, § 712, com. (f), at 200.

[174] *LIAMCO, supra* note 58, 62 I.L.R. at 194.

[175] M.N. SHAW, INTERNATIONAL LAW 751 (5th ed. 2003).

emphasizes that discrimination renders expropriation illegal only if unreasonable, and provides that:

> classifications, even if based on nationality, that are rationally related to the state's security or economic policies might not be unreasonable.[176]

This position is echoed by Professor Brownlie: **5.76**

> The test of discrimination is the intention of the government: the fact that only aliens are affected may be incidental, and, if the taking is based on economic and social policies, it is not directed against particular groups simply because they own the property involved.[177]

2. Compensation

a. Full compensation as standard under international law

As Professor Brownlie notes, "it is significant that the right to compensation, on whatever basis, is recognized in principle."[178] It is practically undisputed that payment of compensation in *some* amount is required following an expropriation, whether the taking is legal or illegal. As mentioned in the discussion of the history and sources of the international expropriation law, international law is generally considered to require that a State that expropriates the property of an investor pay to the investor the full value of the property taken.[179] In a case involving a concession or other State contract, compensation should cover not only the loss of tangible property, but also the loss of contractual rights.[180] Evidence of this maxim can be found in the decisions of international tribunals,[181] the provisions of many investment treaties,[182] and in the writings of commentators.[183] As Professor Norton has observed: **5.77**

---

[176] Restatement, *supra* note 162, § 712, com. (f), at 200.

[177] Brownlie, *supra* note 22, at 515 n.95 (citations omitted).

[178] *Id.* at 519.

[179] Some commentators assert that, in light of the General Assembly resolutions discussed in Section A.2, some States continue reject full as a requirement of international law. *See* Sornarajah, *supra* note 34, at 445.

[180] Amerasinghe, *supra* note 23, at 37.

[181] *See* Section A.3, *supra*. *See also Tecnicas Medioambientales Tecmed S.A. v. Mexico*, ICSID Case No. ARB(AF)/00/2, Award of May 29, 2003, 43 I.L.M. 133, paras. 183, 188; *Wena Hotels Ltd. v. Egypt* (Merits), ICSID Case No. ARB/98/4, Award of Dec. 8, 2000, at para. 96, reprinted in 41 I.L.M. 896 (2002); *S.D. Myers Inc. v. Canada*, Partial Award of Nov. 13, 2000, paras. 301–17 *et pass., reprinted in* 40 I.L.M. 1408, 1490 (2001), and Second Partial Award (Damages) of Oct. 21, 2002, paras. 122, 300, both available at https://www.italaw.com/cases/969 (holding that full compensation for all economic losses proved by the claimant must be paid); *Metalclad Corp. v. Mexico*, Case No. ARB(AF)/97/1, Award of Aug. 30, 2000, 40 I.L.M. 36 (2001), para. 103 (discussing the problem of assessing the fair market value of an ongoing enterprise lacking a profit history); *Santa Elena, supra* note 164, para. 78, 39 I.L.M. 1317, 1330.

[182] *See* Section A.4, *supra*, and Chapter 6.

[183] *See e.g.* Charles Hyde, 3 International Law 710–27 (1949); Alexander P. Fachiri, *International Law and the Property of Aliens*, 10 Brit. Yb. Int'l L. 32 (1929); Chandler P. Anderson, *Title to Foreign Confiscated Property*, 20 AJIL 528 (1926); Fawcett, *supra* note 4. But *see* Penrose et al., *supra* note 41, at 352:

Recent international tribunals have consistently affirmed a requirement under international law that full compensation be paid for expropriations of foreign property. A theoretical debate persists over the scope of possible exceptions to that standard, but the recent decisions suggest that only truly extraordinary circumstances would be likely to support such exceptions.[184]

5.78 The "full compensation" requirement may also be stated as a requirement that compensation for expropriation must be "prompt, adequate, and effective."[185] In this context, "prompt" means that at or before the time of the taking, either compensation has been paid or provision has been made for a determination of the amount of compensation to be paid, with interest from the time of the taking.[186] The term "effective" indicates that compensation must be made in a freely convertible currency. This precludes forms of payment such as soft currency, unmarketable bonds, or I.O.U.s.[187]

5.79 "Adequate" compensation, as discussed, means that the investor is paid the full value of the property taken, which in the case of an ongoing business will normally correspond to the going-concern value.[188] Value should be assessed as of the time of the taking, but the investor should be indemnified by the State for any depression in value caused by the threat of expropriation prior to the time of the actual expropriation.[189] Pre-expropriation reduction in value resulting from background conditions or generally applicable government measures, however, cannot generally be taken into account.[190]

5.80 As mentioned earlier, the Restatement suggests that "exceptional circumstances" may justify less than full compensation in the event of expropriation.[191] The Restatement offers two examples of such exceptional circumstances: national agricultural land reform and war.[192] In the case of land reforms, however, the

---

> That the state should pay compensation for the takeover of private assets is not questioned, and, in general, both international and domestic law hold that in most circumstances the government is obliged to pay to the owner of property it nationalized a compensation that is fair/just/full/adequate/appropriate/effective. These terms are imprecise, can easily have different ethical, economic and legal implications, and are clearly not interchangeable.

See also Williams, *supra* note 7, at 162. For further discussion, *see e.g.* SHAW, supra note 175, at 743 *et seq.*; BROWNLIE, *supra* note 22, at 514, 519, 522 *et pass.*; HIGGINS, *supra* note 12, at 142; Derek William Bowett, *State Contracts with Aliens: Contemporary Developments on Compensation for Termination or Breach*, 59 BRIT. YB. INT'L L. 49, 59 (1988). For arguments that international law requires the payment of "appropriate" compensation rather than full compensation in some circumstances, see Amerasinghe, *supra* note 23.

184 *Norton, supra* note 23, at 503.

185 *See id.* at 476.

186 Clagett, *supra* note 36, § 12.01[1].

187 *Id.*

188 *Id.*

189 *Id.* at § 12.01[2].

190 *Id.*

191 Restatement, *supra* note 162, § 712, com. (d), at 199.

192 *Id. See also* BROWNLIE, *supra* note 22, at 511–14.

Restatement exception to full compensation is limited: a less stringent standard would not be justified if the property taken is used in a business enterprise authorized or encouraged by the State, if the property was a going concern taken over and operated by the State, if the taking discriminated against aliens, or if the taking otherwise violated international law.[193]

Commentators have suggested other exceptions to the "full compensation" rule. **5.81**
Professor Brownlie lists the most widely advanced exceptions:

> under treaty provisions; as a legitimate exercise of police power, including measures of defense against external threats; confiscation as a penalty for crimes; seizure by way of taxation or other fiscal measures; loss caused indirectly by healthy and planning legislation and the concomitant restrictions on the use of property; the destruction of property of neutrals as a consequence of military operations, and a taking of enemy property as part payment of reparation for the consequences of an illegal war.[194]

Brownlie also suggests that expropriation is not illegal if carried out in connection **5.82**
with the nationalization of a major industry, as long as compensation is paid "on a basis compatible with the economic objectives of the nationalization, and the viability of the economy as a whole."[195]

Finally, arbitrators in several cases have suggested in *dicta* that less than full com- **5.83**
pensation would be payable following expropriation in certain circumstances. In *INA*, for example, Judge Lagergren opined that full compensation may not be payable in the context of large-scale nationalizations.[196]

Thus, the circumstances in which, according to some observers, a State may be **5.84**
excused from paying full compensation for expropriated property can be divided into three categories: where there are treaty provisions to the contrary; where the taking is within the exercises of legitimate "police power,"[197] both internal and external (including taxation, certain types of regulation, confiscation for crimes, or where the taking is the result of war); and in cases of large-scale nationalization for the purpose of reform.[198]

---

193 *Id.*

194 *Id.* at 511–12. *See also id.* at 447 ("There is some debate as to the possibility of penal damages in international law").

195 *Id.* at 514.

196 *See* text accompanying note 104, *supra.*

197 According to the *police power* doctrine, there are certain conditions under which host States may not be liable to pay compensation. *See e.g. Saluka Investments B.V. v. Czech Republic* (UNCITRAL), Partial Award of Mar. 17, 2006, para. 255: "It is now established in international law that States are not liable to pay compensation to a foreign investor when, in the normal exercise of their regulatory powers, they adopt in a non-discriminatory manner *bona fide* regulations that are aimed at the general welfare."

198 According to UNCTAD, nationalization is explained as "outright takings in all economic sectors or on an industry-specific basis" where on the other hand, expropriation is called the "firm specific takings." *See* UNCTAD, *Taking of Property*, UNCTAD Series on Issues in International Investment Agreements (2000), at 4.

b. Justifications for the full compensation standard

5.85 It is obvious that an investor is harmed to the extent that his property is taken, and that he can only be made whole if he receives in compensation the actual value—or the "full" value—of the property. The State presumably benefits by taking the investor's property, and should therefore pay its value to the investor.[199] It makes little difference to an investor *why* his property has been taken. Brice Clagett argues cogently that the measure of compensation should not depend upon the motivation for the taking:

> [T]here remains a significant body of opinion, even including some Western scholars, arguing that when a particular expropriation is part of a broad-scale nationalization of an entire industry or segment of the economy, something less than full compensation—partial compensation—is all that is required … I call [this theory] the "partial confiscation" theory. If a man steals $10 from me and gives me back $4, he has still stolen $6. I am not able to understand why similar conduct by governments should be viewed any differently. And I have never seen any suggestion of a principled—or even an unprincipled—basis on which "partial" compensation might be measured or calculated.[200]

5.86 The argument for a customary law standard of compensation independent of State intent is supported by the consideration that even fully "legal" expropriation must be accompanied by compensation of some kind. It stands to reason that, if the government's admirable intentions do not exempt the State from paying compensation, such considerations should also be irrelevant in determining the *quantum* of compensation due. According to this view, the investor suffers no worse harm where the taking is motivated by malice, as compared to a "benevolent" expropriation.[201]

c. Compensation for illegal and legal expropriation

5.87 Some commentators suggest that the standard of compensation for expropriation depends upon whether the act is legal or illegal. Professor Bowett notes that:

> There would seem to be little value in making the distinction between a lawful and an unlawful taking unless consequences flowed from it: and it would be extraordinary if the distinction was of no consequence.[202]

5.88 Bowett maintains that there may in fact be three different standards of compensation, for (1) an unlawful taking, (2) a lawful ad hoc taking, and (3) a lawful,

---

[199] *See* Richard A. Epstein, Takings: Private Property and the Power of Eminent Domain (1985) (discussing the legitimate purposes of certain State takings).

[200] Clagett, *supra* note 36, § 12.04[2], pp. 12–15 to 12–16, citing Judge Lagergren's concurrence propounding this theory in *INA Corp. v. Government of Iran*, Award No. 184-161-1, 8 Iran–U.S. C.T.R. 373 (1985).

[201] *See also* Brownlie's discussion of the relevance of intent and motive in connection with State responsibility, at Brownlie, *supra* note 22, at 426 *et pass.; LIAMCO, supra* note 58, 62 I.L.R. at 194 (discussing the relevance of State intent).

[202] Bowett, *supra* note 183, at 59.

general act of nationalization.[203] Even if, as some commentators argue,[204] full compensation need not be paid in cases of large-scale nationalization carried out for the purpose of reform, Bowett's view appears to have been rejected by most tribunals.[205]

Professor Brownlie notes: **5.89**

> The practical distinctions between expropriation unlawful sub modo, i.e. only if no provision is made for compensation, and expropriation unlawful per se, would seem to be these: the former involves a duty to pay compensation only for direct losses, i.e. the value of the property, the latter involves liability for consequential loss (lucrum cessans); the former confers a title which is recognized in foreign courts (and international tribunals), the latter produces no valid title.[206]

Here, Brownlie implies that a lawful expropriation requires compensation only for direct losses. However, to the extent that such payment constitutes less than "full" compensation, such an assertion would appear unjustified.[207] **5.90**

It has also been argued that where an expropriation is illegal (*e.g.* a taking that is discriminatory or not carried out for a public purpose), the host State is in the first instance obligated to make restitution in kind, if possible. Section 901 of the Restatement provides, for example: **5.91**

> [u]nder international law, a state that has violated a legal obligation to another state is required to terminate the violation and, ordinarily, to make reparations, including in appropriate circumstances restitution or compensation for loss or injury.[208]

Even if a host State carries the obligation to make restitution, however, a court or arbitral ruling to this effect is practically unenforceable.[209] **5.92**

d. Valuation

While it is well settled under international law that "full" compensation is required following expropriation, the method to be used in determining the precise magnitude of that compensation is far more controversial. For example, should full compensation be based upon the book value of the investor's expropriated assets? Should modern assessment systems, such as the "discounted cash flow" method, be used? Are "future profits" part of the value of the investor's property? How are **5.93**

---

203 *Id.* at 73.

204 Section B.2.a, *supra*.

205 *See e.g.* notes 11–12 and 109 and accompanying text.

206 Brownlie, *supra* note 22, at 515 (footnotes omitted).

207 More widely accepted is Professor Brownlie's assertion that a *per se unlawful* expropriation does not shift valid title, as might be recognized in national courts and international tribunals. *See* Chapter 10, Section E (discussing invalidation of title and exceptions to foreign sovereign immunity).

208 Restatement, *supra* note 162, § 901. *See also, e.g.*, notes 11–12 and 109 and accompanying text.

209 *See* Chapter 10, Section F (nations do not have the right to use force against host States in response to unlawful expropriations).

intangibles, such as goodwill, to be measured? Various valuation methods and their application by international arbitral tribunals are discussed in Chapter 6.

3. Indirect and creeping expropriation

5.94 As noted in Chapter 1, direct expropriation, such as confiscation and nationalization, involves the physical seizure of assets or the formal transfer of title to them under local law.[210] Under customary international law, a range of other, subtler State measures may also constitute expropriation.[211] As the OECD explains:

> Expropriation or deprivation of property could also occur through interference by a state in the use of that property or with the enjoyment of the benefits even where the property is not seized and the legal title to the property is not affected. The measures taken by the State have a similar effect to expropriation or nationalisation and are generally termed "indirect", "creeping", or "de facto" expropriation, or measures "tantamount" to expropriation.[212]

5.95 Indirect expropriation—regulatory interference that has an effect equivalent to expropriation—can be difficult to define or identify. In part, this is because customary international law also recognizes States' need to engage in regulation in the normal exercise of police powers, to advance the welfare and safety of their populations.[213] Some commentators have therefore suggested that generally applicable regulations designed to achieve a "legitimate" purpose do not give rise to State liability and the concomitant obligation to compensate for the harm caused to foreign investors. Others insist that State measures should be considered expropriatory to the extent that their effect is to eliminate all (or nearly all) of an investment's value.[214] It is well accepted, however, that expropriation need not be carried out through a single measure. Rather, "creeping" expropriation may occur where a series of State acts have the cumulative effect of depriving an asset of its value.

5.96 A number of international legal instruments include indirect takings within the definition of expropriation. As explained in Chapter 6, the North American Free

---

210 *See* Chapter 1, Section C.

211 Today, it is very rare for a State to undertake an outright direct taking of foreign property due to the "negative publicity and ... the lasting damage to the State's reputation as a venue for foreign investments." *See* Dolzer & Schreuer, *supra* note 156, at 101.

212 OECD Directorate for Financial and Enterprise Affairs, *"Indirect Expropriation" and the "Right to Regulate" in International Investment Law*, Working Papers on International Investment, No. 2004/4 (September 2004), available at https://www.oecd.org/daf/inv/investment-policy/WP-2004_4.pdf.

213 Regarding the police power doctrine, the tribunal in *Saluka Investments v. Czech Republic* noted that a State is "not liable to pay compensation to a dispossessed alien investor when it adopts general regulations that are 'commonly accepted as within the police power of States' forms part of customary international law today." *See Saluka Investments v. Czech Republic, supra* note 197, para. 262.

214 Cameron cites a number of writers who have addressed the issue of police powers to regulate and the obligation to compensate. *See* Cameron, *supra* note 93, at 221 n.144.

Trade Agreement is typical of hundreds of investment protection treaties around the world, in that it provides that:

> No Party may directly or indirectly nationalize or expropriate an investment of an investor of another Party in its territory *or take a measure tantamount to nationalization or expropriation* of such an investment ("expropriation"), [except on payment of compensation].[215]

OPIC's Standard Contract defines "expropriation" to include "an act or series of acts of the foreign governing authority" where: **5.97**

> the act(s) (i) constitute an outright taking of the Investor's property or (ii) *have the effect of taking the Investor's insured investment in that the acts (A) prevent, unreasonably interfere with, deprive, or unduly delay effective enjoyment of the Investor's fundamental rights in the insured investment* (rights are "fundamental" if without them the Investor is substantially deprived of the benefits of the investment) . . .[216]

Similarly, expropriation insurance policies issued by the World Bank's Multilateral International Guaranty Agency (MIGA) cover both "creeping" and indirect expropriation, providing compensation for losses: **5.98**

> due to any direct or indirect action or inaction, in one or a series of events, attributable to the Host Government which directly:
> (a) deprives or prevents the Guarantee Holder from exercising its ownership rights or effective control of, or in all or a portion of the Guaranteed Investment; or
> (b) deprives the Guarantee Holder or the Project Enterprise, as applicable, of the use and control of any funds constituting dividends, profits or other monetary benefits derived from the Guaranteed Investment . . .[217]

At the same time, however, the MIGA contract provides support for a limitation on indirect expropriation in relation to "legitimate" regulations:[218] **5.99**

[215] North American Free Trade Agreement, art. 1110(1) (emphasis added). *Cf. Methanex Corp. v. United States*, Final Award on Jurisdiction and Merits of Aug. 3, 2005 (NAFTA Chapter 11), available at http://www.state.gov/documents/organization/51052.pdf, at part IV, ch. D, paras. 6–7 (non-discriminatory regulations for a public purpose, such as environmental laws, not considered expropriation).

[216] OPIC Contract of Insurance, § 4.01 (emphasis added), *reprinted* in Appendix I. *See* Chapter 3 for further discussion of OPIC.

[217] MIGA Contract of Guarantee for Equity Investments, §§ 4.1–4.2 (2004) [hereinafter, MIGA Contract]. See also MIGA Contract of Guarantee for Equity Investments (October 2018), available at https://www.miga.org/sites/default/files/2018-10/MIGA%20Equity%20Investments%20Template%20October%202018%20FINAL.pdf. *See* Chapter 3 for further discussion of MIGA.

[218] For further discussion of regulation as expropriation, see the discussion in Chapter 1, Section C and Chapter 6, Section C.1; also Shaw, *supra* note 175, at 740–42, *et pass.*; OECD Directorate, *supra* note 212 (surveying standards defining indirect and creeping expropriation by a variety of commentators and legal instruments); Burns H. Weston, *Constructive Taking under International Law: A Modest Foray into the Problem of "Creeping Expropriation,"* 16 Va. J. Int'l L. 103 (1975); Rudolph Dolzer, *Indirect Expropriation of Alien Property*, 1 ICSID Rev.—For. Inv. L.J. 41 (1986); Thomas Waelde & Abba Kolo, *Multilateral Investment Treaties and Environmental Expropriation of Foreign Investment*, Alexander's Gas and Oil Connection—Speeches, available at https://www.ogel.org/article.asp?key=801; Patrick J. Donovan, *Creeping Expropriation and*

No measure shall constitute an Expropriation under [the] above [Section], if it constitutes a bona fide, non-discriminatory measure of general application that governments normally take for the purpose of regulating economic activity, ensuring public safety, raising revenues or protecting the environment, unless the measure is designed by the Host Government to have a confiscatory effect.[219]

5.100 Nevertheless, in some recent decisions by ICSID, tribunals have preferred to establish a breach of fairness rather than finding indirect expropriation.[220] International investment tribunals distinguish regulatory measures from expropriatory takings using four methods: the sole effect test, the investor's legitimate expectations, the purpose test, and the proportionality test.[221]

4. Other investment-related norms: national treatment and the international minimum standard

a. National treatment

5.101 Some twentieth-century commentators maintained that a State was required under customary international law to treat aliens at least as well as it treats its own citizens.[222] In 1957, Isi Foighel surmised that

states are bound to give to the foreigner the same protection as is accorded to the country's own nationals in respect of his person or property. A lower degree of

---

MIGA: The Need for Tighter Regulation in the Political Risk Insurance Market, 7 Gonz. J. Int'l L. 10 (2003–04), available at http://blogs.law.gonzaga.edu/gjil/2006/03/creeping-expropriation-and-miga-the-need-for-tighter-regulation-in-the-political-risk-insurance-mar/; Robert Volterra, *Mitigating Expropriation Risk for Oil & Gas Investment in the Caspian Region*, IEA Roundtable on Caspian Oil & Gas Scenarios (Apr. 15, 2003).

[219] MIGA Contract, *supra* note 217, § 4.2. There is current discussion among commentators about whether the host State should be liable to compensate in light of human rights violations by the investor. This discussion follows a general debate regarding the integration of human rights law into international investment law. *See also* Fabrizio Marrella, *On the Changing Structure of International Investment Law: The Human Right to Water and ICSID Arbitration*, 12 Int'l Community Law Rev. 359 (2010): "The test of this decade for international investment law is when a decision needs to be made between ensuring the profits of a private investor and protecting human or environmental rights. The answer is certainly difficult, since a balance has to be made by arbitrators outside the specific context of human rights courts or international bodies. The unity of international law and not its fragmentation can provide the basis to reconcile conflicting rules."

[220] *See e.g.* Dolzer & Schreuer, *supra* note 156, at 117 *et. seq.*

[221] For a detailed analysis, *see* Cameron, *supra* note 93, at 223–29.

[222] *See e.g.* John Fischer Williams, *International Law and the Property of Aliens*, 9 Brit. Yb. Int'l L. 1, 28 (1928). It is generally accepted that with regard to certain matters, aliens will inevitably receive less favorable treatment compared to that received by locals. Professor Brownlie remarks that

it is not contended that the alien should have political rights in the host state as of right. Moreover, the alien must take the local law as he finds it in regard to regulation of the economy and restriction on employment of aliens in particular types of employment ... More general variations may of course be created by treaty.

Brownlie, supra note 22, at 502.

protection for the foreigner in this respect will be taken as a breach of the international law of aliens and will incur liability for the state of residence.[223]

Many observers take the position that, at least in commercial matters, no obligation exists at customary international law to offer "national treatment" to aliens.[224] The absence of such a duty was affirmed in the *Oscar Chinn* case. There, a British citizen was engaged in short-haul shipping in Congo, then a Belgian colony. Mr. Chinn was driven out of business when the government of Belgium began to heavily subsidize a State-owned competitor. The United Kingdom espoused his claim against Belgium before the Permanent Court of International Justice, which found that Belgium was not responsible for the discrimination that Mr. Chinn had suffered: **5.102**

> Freedom of trade does not mean the abolition of commercial competition; it presupposes the existence of such competition. Every undertaking freely carrying on its commercial activities may find itself confronted with obstacles placed in its way by rival concerns which are perhaps its superiors in capital or organization. It may also find itself in competition with concerns in which States participate . . .[225]

Thus, States may not incur international liability for providing special treatment to their own citizens, unless a treaty imposes a contrary duty.[226] **5.103**

b. The international minimum standard of treatment

As explained earlier, many developing countries took the position in the nineteenth and early twentieth centuries that no absolute standards of treatment existed at international law, and that therefore foreigners could expect no better treatment than that meted out to local citizens.[227] **5.104**

This position was contested vehemently by capital-exporting States. They posited the existence of an "international minimum standard" of treatment, as described by the U.S. State Department in a 1953 letter to Guatemala, issued following government interference with property owned by the United Fruit Company, a U.S. corporation: **5.105**

---

[223] FOIGHEL, *supra* note 7, at 46. *See also id.* at 47 ("the rules of international law against discrimination can be considered to be satisfied when foreigners are given formal equality with the nationals of the country in question in respect of protection in similar situations").

[224] A.F.M. Maniruzzaman, *Expropriation of Alien Property and the Principle of Non-Discrimination in International Law of Foreign Investment: An Overview*, 8 J. TRANSNAT'L L. & POL'Y. 57 (1998); *see also* MUCHLINSKI, *supra* note 103, at 626–27; Georg Schwarzenberger, *Equality and Discrimination in International Economic Law*, in THE YEARBOOK OF WORLD AFFAIRS 164 (1971).

[225] *The Oscar Chinn Case (U.K. v. Belgium)*, Decision of Dec. 12, 1934, P.C.I.J. Ser. A/B, No. 63 (1934), at 84. For extended commentary and critique, *see* Todd Weiler, *Saving Oscar Chin* [sic]: *Non-Discrimination in International Investment Law*, in INTERNATIONAL INVESTMENT LAW AND ARBITRATION 557 (Todd Weiler ed. 2005).

[226] Indeed, the obligation to provide "national treatment" to qualifying foreign investors is one of the fundamental substantive protections contained in nearly every investment treaty. *See* Chapter 6, Sections B and C.4.

[227] On the "Calvo" doctrine, *see* Section A.2.a, *supra*.

> The Government of the United States is warranted in expecting not only that the law of Guatemala shall be applied fairly as to American nationals without discrimination, but also that both the law itself and its application shall conform at least to minimum standards required by international law.[228]

5.106 Despite opposition from developing countries, it appears that "international law has firmly come down on the side of required minimum standards of treatment."[229] The 1930 Hague Codification Conference, for example, accepted an absolute baseline of treatment of aliens, "a moral standard for civilized states."[230] The content of the customary law on international minimum standards has been the subject of much debate, however. It was long recognized to impose a relatively high threshold for State liability.[231] The extent of this customary law norm was set forth in the *Neer Claim*, where a U.S.–Mexico Mixed Claims Commission ruled that:

> the propriety of governmental acts should be put to the test of international standards … the treatment of alien, in order to constitute an internal delinquency should amount to an outrage, to bad faith, to willful neglect of duty, or to an insufficiency of government action so far short of international standards that every reasonable and impartial man would readily recognize its insufficiency.[232]

5.107 Until very recently, most commentators and tribunals have supported the notion that, absent contrary treaty provisions, a State need do no more for foreign investors than prevent the extreme conduct described in the *Neer* decision. But with the spread of investment protection treaties, some observers believe that the customary law standard has become more demanding. According to this view, States are required to treat foreign investors fairly and equitably according to modern sensibilities, rather than those prevailing at the beginning of the twentieth century.[233] While NAFTA tribunals have been reluctant to accept evolution of the customary law standard,[234] some other tribunals have attributed it "contemporary" content.[235]

---

[228] Department of State Bull., vol. 29 (1953), p. 358, *quoted in* Foighel, *supra* note 7, at 49.

[229] Higgins, *supra* note 12, at 159.

[230] *See* Brownlie, *supra* note 22, at 502–03.

[231] Foighel, *supra* note 7, at 54.

[232] *Neer Claim* (*L.F.H. Neer and Pauline Neer (U.S.A.) v. Mexico) (U.S. v. Mexico)*, U.S.–Mexico General Claims Commission, Decision of Oct. 15, 1926, 4 R.I.A.A. 60, 61–62 (1926), available at http://law.dal.ca/kindred.intllaw/NEER.htm.

[233] *Mondev v. U.S.A., supra* note 134, at paras. 116 and 123 ("To the modern eye, what is unfair or inequitable need not equate with the outrageous or the egregious. In particular, a State may treat a foreign investment unfairly and inequitably without necessarily acting in bad faith … the content of the minimum standard today cannot be limited to the content of customary international law as recognised in arbitral decisions in the 1920s"). *See also Merril & Ring Forestry v. Canada*, Ad hoc—UNCITRAL Arbitration Rules, Award of Mar. 31, 2010, para. 213.

[234] Dolzer & Schreuer, *supra* note 156, at 139.

[235] *Id. See* also R. Dolzer and A. von Walter, *Fair and Equitable Treatment and Customary Law: Lines of Jurisprudence*, in Investment Treaty Law: Current Issues 99 (F. Ortino et al. eds. 2007).

However, there has been little opportunity so far for international tribunals to test this proposition directly.[236] 5.108

C. Breach of Contract and Expropriation

Expropriation not only affects tangible assets. Expropriation may be accompanied by breach of a State contract pursuant to which the investor operates its enterprise or owns assets in the host State.[237] Indeed, when a State repudiates an investment contract, the purpose is often to take effective control of foreign-owned assets or enterprises.[238] More specifically, many of the foreign investor's rights, such as the right to operate for a period of years, may be contained in a State contract. Thus, expropriation and repudiation of State contracts are frequently intertwined.[239] 5.109

As explained earlier, the remedy for the host State's expropriation of the investor's property is payment to the investor of the full value of the property taken. It is generally accepted under international law that contract rights are property rights.[240] Accordingly, where expropriation is accompanied by breach of State contracts, compensation to the investor should normally include the value of any lost contract rights: it would make little sense for compensation to include only the value of tangible assets, but to exclude contract rights. For example, when valuing an ongoing enterprise using the discounted cash flow (DCF) method (discussed in Chapter 6), the future cash flows of the enterprise must be calculated, and future cash flows depend in part upon the contract rights associated with the enterprise. However, a simple breach of a contract by the host State cannot normally constitute expropriation.[241] Some have argued that the breach of 5.110

[236] *But see Elettronica Sicula S.p.A. (ELSI) (U.S. v. Italy)*, Judgment of July 20, 1989, 1989 I.C.J. Rep. 15, 76 (apparently setting a minimum standard slightly more demanding than that established in *Neer*: judicial action fails to satisfy the standard if it reflects "a wilful disregard of due process of law ... which shocks, *or at least surprises*, a sense of judicial propriety" (emphasis added)).

[237] In many cases, the investor–State contract has been "internationalized" in the manner discussed in Chapter 4, Section B.2, so that the relationship between the parties is subject to international law and the State cannot unilaterally terminate the agreement.

[238] *See e.g. BP, supra* note 56; *Texaco, supra* note 57; *LIAMCO, supra* note 58.

[239] *See* Section B.3, *supra*, discussing indirect or *de facto* expropriation as other types of expropriation.

[240] *See* HIGGINS, *supra* note 12, at 140. *See also Chorzów Factory, supra* note 9, and *Norwegian Shipowners' Claims, supra* note 18.

[241] *See, e.g. Siemens A.G. v. Argentina*, ICSID Case No. ARB/02/8, Award of Feb. 6, 2007, para. 253 ("The actions of the State have to be based on its 'superior governmental power.' It is not a matter of being disappointed in the performance of the State in the execution of a contract but rather of interference in the contract execution through governmental action").

an internationalized contract by a State constitutes a wrong under international law, apart from any accompanying violation caused by expropriation without the payment of full compensation.[242] Judge Higgins concludes that "the distinction between mere breach of contract and a taking of property will have relevance for the determination of any compensation."[243]

[242] Brownlie, *supra* note 22, at 512–27 *et pass*. As noted elsewhere, absent an "internationalization" clause of some sort, the breach of a contract alone does not normally violate customary international law. Oppenheim's International Law 927 (Sir Robert Jennings & Sir Arthur Watts eds. 1992). *See also* Chapter 6, Section C.5.a and Chapter 4, Section B.2.a.

[243] Higgins, *supra* note 12, at 140.

6

THE SUBSTANTIVE LAW OF CONTEMPORARY INTERNATIONAL INVESTMENT PROTECTION

A. Introduction

So far, we have focused primarily on identifying elements of political risk and reducing the chance that these risks will materialize. Clearly the ideal solution for both investor and host State would be that this book end there. But it is an unavoidable fact that political risk does at times cease to be risk, and investors find themselves facing government measures that harm them and their investments. Therefore, we turn now to the investor's international law rights in such a situation. In this chapter we will deal with the "substance" of international investment protection law, the rights and obligations that investors can invoke to find their way back to the condition they enjoyed before political risk became economic reality. The procedures by which investors can invoke these rights in practice are complex enough to warrant separate chapters.[1] **6.01**

[1] *See* Chapter 7 (on the right of investors to invoke arbitration against the host State under investment treaties); and Chapter 8 (on arbitration procedure).

6.02 An important distinction is in order at the outset with regard to the sources of international law rights. In the preceding chapter, we discussed "customary" international law, the norms created over the years through the accumulation of State practice and the opinions of learned commentators. This body of law must be contrasted to treaty or conventional law, which derives from the actual texts of specific agreements between governments, establishing rules of conduct applicable only to the signatory States. Treaty law may simply codify or clarify customary international law, or it may supplement or even override custom in a particular area.[2] The rather complex interaction of custom and treaty is particularly acute in the field of investment protection. As we have already explained, the customary law of expropriation provides a baseline of rights for foreign investors, even when no treaty exists between the host State and the investor's State of origin. Likewise, such customary norms as sovereign immunity and the act of State doctrine, incorporated and adapted in national legislation around the world, form part of the default regime governing the legal relations between States and private parties. But with over 2,000 bilateral investment treaties (BITs) and several important regional instruments in force today, some investors enjoy a wider range of rights and remedies than was the case when custom was the only applicable legal source. Even when an investor invokes an investment treaty, however, customary international law does not lose its relevance: most investment treaties leave the interpretation of key concepts to customary law. By the same token, some contend that the contours of customary international law have evolved through the enactment and application of investment treaties, and through the decisions that tribunals have rendered pursuant to their dispute resolution provisions. We will therefore strive to be as clear as possible with regard to the source of rights and obligations described in this chapter. The symbiotic relationship between treaty and custom, however, makes absolute clarity practically impossible.[3]

6.03 The substantive protections of investment treaties described in this chapter, which form the backbone of modern international law on foreign investment,

[2] U.N. Conference on Trade and Development (UNCTAD), Trends in International Investment Agreements: An Overview, UNCTAD/ITE/IIT/13, at 39 (1999), available at http://www.unctad.org/en/docs/iteiit13_en.pdf ("[d]epending on their form and substance international instruments may give effect to, specify or supplement customary law, they may replace or derogate from it, and they may create new rules").

[3] On the interaction between investment treaties and customary law, *see* Stephen Schwebel, *The Influence of Bilateral Investment Treaties on Customary International Law*, Proceedings of the 98th Annual Meeting of the American Society of International Law (Mar. 31–Apr. 3, 2004); Abdullah Al Faruque, *Creating Customary International Law through Bilateral Investment Treaties: a Critical Appraisal*, 44(2) Indian J. Int'l L. 292 (2004); Steffen Hindelang, *Bilateral Investment Treaties, Custom and a Healthy Investment Climate: The Question of Whether BITs Influence Customary International Law Revisited*, 5 J. World Inv. 789–809 (2004); Tarcisio Gazzini, *The Role of Customary International Law in the Field of Foreign Investment*, 8(5) J. World Inv. 691–715 (2007); Patrick Dumberry, *Are BITs Representing the "New" Customary International Law in International Investment Law?*, 28(4) Penn. State Int'l L. Rev. 676–701 (2010). *See also* Martins Paparinskis, The International Minimum Standard and Fair and Equitable Treatment 142–53 (2013).

are often echoed in the national investment laws of developing and transition-economy countries.[4] In particular, many national investment codes place limitations on the State's authority to expropriate foreign assets, sometimes granting rights superior to those provided at customary international law.[5] Some such laws also guarantee fair and equitable treatment,[6] proper application of domestic law by governmental authorities,[7] national treatment,[8] repatriation of profits, and other standards of treatment.[9] Domestic legislation can therefore form an important part of foreign investors' legal protection, and should be carefully analyzed along with any investment treaties to which the host State and the investor's home State are parties.

B. Investment Protection Treaties

1. Bilateral investment treaties

A BIT is an international agreement concluded between two States in which **6.04**
each offers certain protections to investors and foreign investment originating in the other State party.[10] Since the first BIT was concluded in 1959 between

---

[4] *See generally* Antonio Parra, *Principles Governing Foreign Investment as Reflected in National Investment Codes*, 7 ICSID Rev.—For. Inv. L.J. 428 (1992). *See also* Jeswald W. Salacuse, The Three Laws of International Investment: National, Contractual, and International Frameworks for Foreign Capital 51–74 (2013).

[5] *See e.g.* Democratic Republic of Congo, Law No. 004/2002 of Feb. 21, 2002 on the Investment Code 6 Official Journal of the Democratic Republic of Congo (2002), art. 26(1) ("The rights to individual or collective property acquired by an investor are guaranteed by the constitution of the DRC. An investor cannot be directly or in part, nationalized or expropriated by a new law, and/or a decision by a local authority, which has the same effect, except for motives of public use and subject to the payment of a fair and equitable compensatory indemnity"), available at https://www.investindrc.cd/en/info-center/laws?task=document.viewdoc&id=161.

[6] *See e.g.* Republic of Algeria, Loi No. 16-09 du 29 Chaoual 1437 correspondant au 3 aout 2016 relative à la promotion de l'investissement, 46 Journal Officiel de la République Algérienne 16, art. 21, available at http://www.andi.dz/PDF/legislation/develop_inv/1609%20fr.pdf.

[7] Law on Foreign Investment of Armenia, art. 9, available at http://www.parliament.am/legislation.php?sel=show&ID=1552&lang=eng.

[8] Law on Foreign Investment of Ukraine (1996), art. 7, available at https://www.wipo.int/edocs/lexdocs/laws/en/ua/ua019en.pdf.

[9] A minority of domestic investment codes also provide investors the right to direct arbitration against the State should disputes arise in connection with their investments. *See e.g.* Law on Investment of Lithuania, art. 6.3 ("In the event of disputes, foreign investor (investors) shall have the right to apply directly to the International Centre for the Settlement of Investment Disputes"), available at https://www.wto.org/english/thewto_e/acc_e/ltu_e/WTACCLTU45_LEG_3.pdf.

[10] For further discussion of BITs, *see generally* Kenneth J. Vandevelde, United States Investment Treaties: Policy and Practice (1992); Jeswald W. Salacuse, *BIT by BIT: The Growth of Bilateral Investment Treaties and Their Impact on Foreign Investment in Developing Countries*, 24 Int'l Law. 655 (1990); Michael R. Reading, *The Bilateral Investment Treaty in ASEAN: A Comparative Analysis*, 42 Duke L.J. 679 (1992); Athena J. Pappas, *References on Bilateral Investment Treaties*, 4 ICSID Rev.—For. Inv. L.J. 189 (1989); Mohamed I. Khalil, *Treatment of Foreign Investment in Bilateral Investment Treaties*, 7 ICSID Rev.—For. Inv. L.J. 339 (1992); Eileen D. Denza & Shelagh B. Brooks, *International Protection of Investment Treaties*, 36 ICLQ 909 (1987);

Germany and Pakistan, over 3,324 treaties (bilateral and multilateral) with provisions on investment protection have been signed or ratified.[11] Over 80 percent of BITs have been concluded since 1987, reflecting intensive growth over recent decades.[12] Many of the recently concluded BITs link developing countries with other developing countries, or transition economies of the former Soviet bloc to the developing world.[13] Most recently, large economic blocs have envisaged reforming the system of international investment protection by adopting comprehensive agreements with substantive rules for the promotion of cross-border investments.[14]

6.05 BITs were designed to encourage the flow of foreign direct investment, primarily from capital-exporting States to capital-importing countries. By concluding such a treaty, host States present their territory as an attractive venue for investment, helping them to compete with other States for limited international capital.[15]

T. Modybo Ocran, Bilateral Investment Protection Treaties: A *Comparative Study*, 8 NYU J. Int'l & Comp. L. 401 (1987); Valerie H. Ruttenberg, *The United States Bilateral Investment Treaty Program: Variations on the Model*, 9 U. Pa. J. Int'l Bus. L. 121 (1987); Glenn Gallins, *Bilateral Investment Protection Treaties*, 2 J. Energy Nat. Resources & Envt'l L. 77 (1984); Stephen M. Schwebel, *The Overwhelming Merits of Bilateral Investment Treaties*, 32 Suffolk Transnat'l L. Rev. 263 (2009); J.X. Zhan, *The Spread of BITs and Their Changing Face*, 24 ICSID Rev.—For. Inv. L.J. 339 (2009); T. Büthe & H. Milner, *Bilateral Investment Treaties and Foreign Direct Investment: A Political Analysis*, in The Effect of Treaties on Foreign Direct Investment—Bilateral Investment Treaties, Double Taxation Treaties, and Investment Flows 171 *et seq.* (Karl P. Sauvant & Lisa E. Sachs eds. 2009).

[11] UNCTAD, World Investment Report—Investment and the Digital Economy, 111 (2017), available at http://unctad.org/en/PublicationsLibrary/wir2017_en.pdf.

[12] The rapid growth in the number of investment treaties has been decelerating since 2002. *See* UNCTAD, World Investment Report, 6–7 (2004), available at https://unctad.org/en/Docs/wir2004overview_en.pdf. Nevertheless, thirty-seven international investment agreements were signed in 2016 (including thirty new BITs and seven treaties with investment provisions), bringing the total number of international investment agreements to 3,324. *See supra* note 11, at 111.

[13] UNCTAD, Bilateral Investment Treaties 1959–1999, 3–4 (2000), available at http:\\www.unctad.org/en/docs/poiteiiad2.en.pdf ("By the end of 1999, out of the total 1,857 BITs ... 476 (26%) were between developing countries (compared with 40—or 10%—at the end of 1989)").

[14] Rudolf Dolzer & Christoph Schreuer, Principles of International Investment Law 13–14 (2d ed. 2012). These agreements are most often negotiated in the context of free trade agreements (FTAs) that address trade issues as well. With the Lisbon Treaty, the European Commission acquired exclusive competence to negotiate and conclude FTAs on behalf of member States. Some recent examples are the E.U.–Canada Comprehensive Economic and Trade Agreement (CETA) and the EU–Japan Economic Partnership Agreement (EJEPA), the E.U.–New Zealand Trade Agreement, the E.U.–Australia Trade Agreement, the E.U.–Singapore FTA, the E.U.–Mexico Trade Agreement, and the E.U.–Mercosur regional trade Agreement, which address a wide scope of trade and investment issues. *See* E.U. Commission Trade Policy—Negotiations & Agreements, available at http://ec.europa.eu/trade/policy/countries-and-regions/negotiations-and-agreements/.

[15] Jose Luis Siqueiros, *Bilateral Treaties on the Reciprocal Protection of Foreign Investment*, 24 Cal. W. Int'l L.J. 255, 257 (1994); Z. Elkins et al., *Competing for Capital: The Diffusion of Bilateral Investment Treaties, 1960–2000*, in The Backlash against Investment Arbitration: Perceptions and Reality 369–406 (Michael Waibel et al. eds. 2010).

Another purpose of BITs was to counter the challenge to the customary international law of investor protection mounted by developing States as part of the New International Economic Order (NIEO) during the 1960s and 1970s.[16] Many of the early BITs were negotiated on the foundation of the OECD's draft Convention on the Protection of Foreign Property, prepared in 1967.[17]

The provisions and structure of most BITs are broadly similar.[18] A first section of this chapter deals with the scope of the treaty's application, in particular the criteria that qualify investors and investments for BIT benefits.[19] The second part of most BITs sets forth the substantive protections of the treaty (described later in detail), including national and most-favored nation (MFN) treatment, compensation for expropriation, and fair and equitable treatment. While treaties signed before 1970 normally provided for State-to-State dispute resolution before the International Court of Justice or an ad hoc tribunal, modern BITs include provisions giving qualifying investors the ability to submit disputes regarding treaty violations directly to international arbitration.[20] **6.06**

[16] Kenneth J. Vandevelde, *U.S. Bilateral Investment Treaties: The Second Wave*, 14 MICH. J. INT'L L. 621 n.19 (1993); Eileen Denza & Shelagh Brooks, *Investment Protection Treaties: United Kingdom Experience*, 36 ICLQ 908, 909–10 (1987); M. SORNARAJAH, INTERNATIONAL LAW OF FOREIGN INVESTMENT 232–33 (3d ed. 2010); Andrew T. Guzman, *Why LDCs Sign Treaties that Hurt Them: Explaining the Popularity of Bilateral Investment Treaties*, 38 VA. J. INT'L L. 639, 669 (1998). On the NIEO, see Introduction, text at n.10 *et seq.*; Chapter 5, Section A.2.c.

[17] The OECD (Organisation for Economic Cooperation and Development) Draft Convention influenced many BITs, but never came into force. INTERNATIONAL CHAMBER OF COMMERCE, BILATERAL TREATIES FOR INTERNATIONAL INVESTMENT 7–8 (1977). The OECD Draft Convention was in turn inspired in part by the so-called Abs-Shawcross Convention of 1959. *See* Hermann Abs & Lord Hartley Shawcross, *A Proposed Convention to Protect Private Foreign Investment*, 9 J. PUB. L. 115, 120 (1960). On the collapse of negotiations to ratify the OECD Convention, see Peter Muchlinski, *The Rise and Fall of the Multilateral Agreement on Investment*, in FOUNDATIONS AND PERSPECTIVES ON INTERNATIONAL TRADE LAW 114 (Ian Fletcher ed. 2001).

[18] Jennifer Tobin & Susan Rose-Ackerman, *Foreign Direct Investment and the Business Environment in Developing Countries: The Impact of Bilateral Investment Treaties*, Yale Law & Economics Research Paper No. 293 (2004), available at http://papers.ssrn.com/sol3/papers.cfm?abstract_id=557121. For sources suggesting the need for a unified global treaty regulating foreign investment, *see* Michael A. Geist, *Toward a General Agreement on the Regulation of Foreign Direct Investment*, 26 LAW & POL'Y. INT'L BUS. 673 (1995); C.F. Bergsten & E.M. Graham, *Needed: New International Rules for Foreign Direct Investment*, 7 INT'L TRADE J. 15 (1992); Jeswald W. Salacuse, *Towards a New Treaty Framework for Direct Foreign Investment*, 50 J. AIR L. & COMM. 969 (1985); Edward M.A. Kwaw, *Trade Related Investment Measures in the Uruguay Round: Towards a GATT for Investment?*, 16 NCJ INT'L COMM. & REG. L. 309 (1991).

[19] The scope of investment treaty coverage is addressed in Chapter 7.

[20] Investor–State dispute resolution provisions most commonly provide for arbitration under the auspices of the International Centre for the Settlement of Investment Disputes (ICSID), but many also offer options such as *ad hoc* arbitration under the UNCITRAL rules, or institutional commercial arbitration under the Stockholm Chamber of Commerce or International Chamber of Commerce rules. Arbitration procedure is covered in detail in Chapter 8.

2. The North American Free Trade Agreement

6.07 The North American Free Trade Agreement (NAFTA)[21] was signed in 1992 by the United States, Canada, and Mexico.[22] NAFTA entered into force at the beginning of 1994. The objectives of the treaty, set forth in article 102, include:

> (c) increasing substantially investment opportunities in the territories of the Parties . . .
> (e) creating effective procedures for the implementation and application of the Agreement . . . and for the resolution of disputes.

NAFTA covers a wide range of international commercial issues, most prominently the elimination of trade barriers. Chapter 11 of NAFTA is dedicated to investment protection, and is based upon the U.S. Model BIT of the time (with an array of significant modifications). Charles Brower and Lee Steven explain the structure of NAFTA's investment chapter thus:

> Section A of Chapter 11 establishes the substantive investment protections that each NAFTA Party is required to honor, including the better of national treatment or most favored nation treatment, the minimum international standard of treatment, elimination of performance requirements, free transfer of funds, and expropriation protection. The point of these protections is to establish a rule-based investment regime in which foreign direct investment can thrive. Specific barriers to and restrictions on investment are eliminated and positive guarantees are extended. Moreover, all of this is done at the international level so as to place all three NAFTA countries and their investors, so far as possible, on an equal footing.
>
> Section B of Chapter 11 is intended to reinforce that regime and make it work by giving foreign investors standing to bring claims in arbitration against the NAFTA Parties for breach of the substantive investment protections found in Section A.[23]

6.08 Article 1120 provides for direct investor–State arbitration. Qualified investors are given a choice of dispute-resolution alternatives under various arbitration rules.[24] Notably, an investor may advance claims in arbitration under the ICSID Rules. However, ICSID arbitration cannot be brought against Mexico (and until recently against Canada) since it has not ratified the ICSID Convention.[25]

---

[21] North American Free Trade Agreement (NAFTA), Dec. 12, 1992, U.S.–Mex.–Can., 32 I.L.M. 605 (1993), available at http://www.nafta-sec-alena.org.

[22] *See generally* NAFTA Investment Law and Arbitration: Past Issues, Current Practice, Future Prospects (Todd Weiler ed. 2004). Guillermo Aguilar Alvarez & William Park, *The New Face of Investment Arbitration: NAFTA Chapter 11*, 28 Yale J. Int'l L. 365 (2003); Charles N. Brower, *Investor–State Disputes Under NAFTA: The Empire Strikes Back*, 40 Colum. J. Transnat'l L. 43 (2001); Jack Coe, Jr., *Taking Stock of NAFTA Chapter 11 in Its Tenth Year: An Interim Sketch of Selected Themes, Issues, and Methods*, 36 Vand. J. Transnat'l L 1381 (2003); Bart Legum, *The Innovation of Investor–State Arbitration under NAFTA*, 43 Harv. Int'l L.J. 531 (2002). Meg Kinnear et al., Investment Disputes under NAFTA (2006).

[23] Charles N. Brower & Lee A. Steven, *NAFTA Chapter 11: Who Then Should Judge? Developing the International Rule of Law under NAFTA Chapter 11*, 2 Chi. J. Int'l L. 193 (2001).

[24] NAFTA, *supra* note 21, art. 1120.

[25] The United States has been a party to the ICSID Convention since it joined NAFTA, but the Convention only entered into force for Canada at the end of 2013. Mexico signed the ICSID Convention on Jan. 11, 2018, but it has yet to ratify it.

In such circumstances Article 1120 allows an investor to bring claims under the ICSID Additional Facility Rules, which do not require both implicated States to be parties to the ICSID Convention, or under the UNCITRAL Arbitration Rules.[26]

Like most BITs, NAFTA provides qualifying investors and investments protection from expropriation, and establishes an absolute "minimum standard" of treatment consonant with international law and "including fair and inequitable treatment and full protection and security."[27] NAFTA also provides that each member State must treat investors from other member States in the same manner as domestic investors with respect to "acquisition, expansion, management, conduct, operation, and sale ... of investments." In light of the federal structure of all three member States, the treaty provides that subdivisions of the member nations (such as states or provinces) are bound by these obligations as well.[28] Article 1103 also provides that each State must treat investors and investments at least as well as it treats the investors and investments from other States. **6.09**

Investors should note, however, that these provisions are subject to a number of qualifications and exceptions. For instance, the requirements of articles 1102 and 1103 (national treatment and MFN treatment), along with other requirements, do not apply to any *existing* non-conforming measures that were maintained at the time NAFTA entered into force.[29] Annexes to the treaty establish further exemptions in each member State for particular economic sectors. **6.10**

Also of note is the role of the NAFTA Free Trade Commission (FTC), a body composed of the three member States' trade ministers, granted authority under NAFTA to issue binding "interpretations" of treaty provisions. Although the FTC has rarely exercised this power, its occasional intervention in ongoing disputes, issuing potentially far-reaching determinations, has provoked sharp criticism from various quarters.[30] **6.11**

---

[26] See Dolzer & Schreuer, *supra* note 14, at 16–17.

[27] NAFTA, *supra* note 21, art. 1105. But see the award in *Methanex Corp. v. United States*, Final Award on Jurisdiction and Merits of Aug. 3, 2005 (NAFTA Chapter 11), available at https://www.italaw.com/cases/683, at part IV, chs. C–E (environmental regulations did not violate obligations to provide national treatment and minimum standards of treatment under international law).

[28] *Id.*, art. 1102(3).

[29] *Id.*, art. 1108(1)(a)(ii)–(iii).

[30] Todd Weiler, *NAFTA Article 1105 and the Free Trade Commission: Just Sour Grapes, Or Something More Serious?*, 29 Int'l Bus. Law. 491 (2001); Stefan Matiation, *Arbitration with Two Twists: Loewen v. United States and Free Trade Commission Intervention in NAFTA Chapter 11 Disputes*, 24 U. Penn. J. Int'l Econ. L. 451 (2003). Gabrielle Kaufmann-Kohler, *Interpretive Powers of the Free Trade Commission and the Rule of Law*, in Fifteen Years of NAFTA Chapter 11 Arbitration 174–94 (E. Gaillard ed. 2011); Eleni Methymaki & Antonios Tzanakopoulos, *Masters of Puppets? Reassertion of Control through Joint Investment Treaty Interpretation*, in Reassertion of Control over the Investment Treaty Regime 155–81 (Andreas Kulick ed. 2017).

3. The Energy Charter Treaty

6.12 The Energy Charter Treaty (ECT) is dedicated to the promotion of investment in the energy sector,[31] and is today one of the most widely ratified investment protection instruments in the world.[32] The ECT is a sectoral agreement (meaning that it applies to investments in the energy sector), and this characteristic makes it unique compared to other international investment agreements which apply to geographic regions.[33] The ECT was concluded on December 17, 1994 and has since been ratified by over fifty countries in Europe, the former USSR, and Asia, as well as Australia.

6.13 In the words of Professor Wälde, the ECT

> constitutes the so far most ambitious project to set up an international investment (plus trade) regime. Different from previous attempts ... it has succeeded in achieving the status of a legally binding multilateral convention ... The Energy Charter Treaty followed the non-binding 1991 "European Energy Charter." It was originally meant by the Western countries to be a multilateral version of the by now familiar bilateral investment treaties (BITs), mainly to protect Western foreign investment in the volatile, but very strategic CIS oil & gas industries. The quid pro quo ... [for] protection of Western investment (BIT-style) ... [was] access of Eastern

[31] Energy Charter Treaty (ECT), art. 2 (Purpose of Treaty), 34 I.L.M. 360, 385 (1995), available at http://www.encharter.org ("This Treaty establishes a legal framework in order to promote long-term cooperation in the energy field, based on complementarities and mutual benefits, in accordance with the objectives and principles of the Charter"); Energy Charter, Preamble ("Wishing to implement the basic concept of the European Energy Charter initiative which is to catalyze economic growth by means of measures to liberalize investment and trade in energy; Affirming that Contracting Parties attach the utmost importance to the effective implementation of full national treatment and most favored nation treatment, and that these commitments will be applied to the Making of Investments pursuant to a supplementary treaty; Having regard to the objective of progressive liberalization of international trade and to the principle of avoidance of discrimination in international trade as enunciated in the General Agreement on Tariffs and Trade and its Related Instruments and as otherwise provided for in this Treaty; Determined progressively to remove technical, administrative and other barriers to trade in Energy Materials and Products and related equipment, technologies and services ...").

[32] ECT, *supra* note 31, 34 I.L.M. 360 (1995). For further discussion of the background of the ECT, *see* Peter Cameron, *Creating a Legal Framework for Investment in the Commonwealth of Independent States Energy Sector: Lessons from the Energy Charter Experiment*, 1 TULSA J. COMP. & INT'L L. 233 (1994); Kaj Hober, *The Energy Charter Treaty—An Overview*, 8 J. WORLD INV. & TRADE 321 (2007). More generally on the ECT, *see* THE ENERGY CHARTER TREATY: AN EAST–WEST GATEWAY FOR INVESTMENT AND TRADE (Thomas W. Wälde ed. 1996); Richard Happ, *Dispute Settlement under the Energy Charter Treaty*, 45 GERMAN YB. INT'L L. 331 (2003); Thomas W. Wälde, *Energy Charter Treaty-based Investment Arbitration: Controversial Issues*, 6 J. WORLD INV. & TRADE 373 (2004). The United States is not a party to the ECT, having stated that, although it remains committed to both the overall goals of the ECT and to the treaty process, the current text of treaty is incompatible with U.S. BIT standards. U.S. Statement on the European Energy Charter Treaty, 34 I.L.M. 556 (1995). On May 20, 2015, the United States signed the 2015 International Energy Charter, which is a declaration of political intention aiming at strengthening energy cooperation between the signatory States, but does not carry any legally binding obligation or financial commitment.

[33] SALACUSE, *supra* note 4, at 349–50.

> energy trade to Western markets (GATT-style). As a consequence of bargaining dynamics, it has now become as well a multilateral treaty affecting West-West (and East/East) investment. In consequence, it is not only influenced by BIT-type obligations and procedures, but also characterised by a diluted version of Western (mainly European, but also NAFTA [style]) economic integration law.[34]

The ECT provides substantive protections similar to those found in BITs and NAFTA. These guarantees apply only to investments within the energy sector, however.[35] Qualifying investments enjoy guarantees of fair and equitable treatment, constant protection and security, freedom from unreasonable or discriminatory measures, MFN treatment, national treatment, and treatment according to international law, whichever is most favorable, limitations on and compensation for expropriation and losses caused by war and civil disturbance, freedom of transfer of capital and returns in relation to investments within its area of operation, and good faith consideration of requests for entry and temporary employment of key personnel.[36] **6.14**

Article 26 of the ECT provides for direct investor–State arbitration similar to the provisions of European BITs.[37] Qualifying investors are given a wide choice of dispute-resolution alternatives for the adjudication of any dispute related to the provisions of the treaty. These options include the host State's courts, ICSID, the ICSID Additional Facility, the Stockholm Chamber of Commerce, or ad hoc arbitration under the UNCITRAL rules. It is important to note that article 26 will apply exclusively to disputes arising out of obligations contained in Part III of the ECT (on investment protection).[38] Other obligations, such as those concerning trade, transit, technology transfer, and other aspects of energy activity, are excluded from its scope. Furthermore, unlike some BITs and NAFTA, the commitments that signatory States make in the ECT in the pre-investment phase require only that "best efforts" be made to avoid discrimination.[39] Thus, while **6.15**

[34] Thomas W. Wälde, *Investment Arbitration under Energy Charter Treaty: From Dispute Settlement to Treaty Implementation*, 12 Arb. Int'l 429, 430 (1996).

[35] *See* ECT, *supra* note 31, art. 1(5) ("energy sector" defined as "the exploration, extraction, refining, production, storage, land transport, transmission, distribution, trade, marketing, or sale of Energy Materials and Products . . . or concerning the distribution of heat to multiple premises").

[36] ECT, *supra* note 31, art. 10(1) (providing fair and equitable treatment; constant protection and security, freedom from unreasonable or discriminatory measures, MFN treatment, national treatment, and treatment according to international law, whichever is most favorable); art. 11 (on movement of key personnel); art. 12 (on compensation of losses); art. 13 (on expropriation); art. 14 (on capital transfers).

[37] *See* in general Investment Protection and the Energy Charter Treaty (Graham Coop & Clarisse Ribeiro eds. 2008); Thomas Roe et al., Settlement of Investment Disputes under the Energy Charter Treaty (2015).

[38] *See Plama Consortium Ltd. v. Bulgaria*, ICSID Case No. ARB/03/24, Decision on Jurisdiction of Feb. 8, 2005, at para. 121.

[39] Wälde, *supra* note 34, at 437. *See also* Gillian Turner, *Investment Protection through Arbitration: The Dispute Resolution Provisions of the Energy Charter Treaty*, 1 Int'l Arb. L. Rev. 166, 167 (1998).

breach of treatment obligations related to established investments are subject to arbitration, violations of provisions related to investment access do not appear to give investors any such right.[40]

4. Other regional investment treaties

a. The Lomé Conventions and the Cotonou Agreements

6.16 The first significant multilateral instrument to embody the principles and establish the dispute resolution system codified in BITs was the series of treaties known collectively as the Lomé Conventions.[41] These agreements have evolved since 1975 to govern economic relations between the European Union and the African, Caribbean, and Pacific (ACP) Group of States.[42] The relevant provisions, however, differ somewhat from other investment treaties. The EU's European Development Fund (EDF) (which finances infrastructure projects in the ACP countries) and EU governments were eager to provide protection for Western contractors involved in these projects. The Third Lomé Convention[43] therefore incorporated arbitration clauses similar to those found in BITs, although more limited in scope.[44] These treaties did not provide for the same general investor protections as found in BITs, instead focusing upon contractual disputes. In 1989, a fourth Lomé Convention was concluded,[45] which—due to political considerations—further complicated the treaty's dispute resolution clause.[46] As a result, very few cases were initiated under the Lomé conventions.[47]

6.17 Following an extensive public debate, the European Union and the ACP countries concluded the Cotonou Agreement in February 2000, which was revised in 2010. Even though the Cotonou Agreement already includes several references to investment promotion and protection, it does not spell out any concrete legal obligations or dispute-settlement mechanisms, but rather sets the framework for further negotiations with a view to concluding bilateral or multilateral investment agreements.[48]

---

[40] Turner, *supra* note 39, at 168.

[41] Austin Amissah, *The ACP/EEC Conciliation and Arbitration Rules*, 8 Arb. Int'l 167 (1992); Ramesh F. Ramsaran, Negotiating the Lomé IV Convention (1990); Gianluca Brusco, *Eurocentrism and Political Conditionality: The Case of the Lomé Convention*, in Europe, Diplomacy and Development 103 (Carol Cosgrove-Sacks ed. & Carla Santos assist. ed. 2001).

[42] Jan Paulsson, *Arbitration without Privity*, 10 ICSID Rev.—For. Inv. L.J. 232, 241 (1995).

[43] Third ACP-EEC Convention of Dec. 8, 1984 (Lomé III), 24 I.L.M. 574 (1985).

[44] *Id.*, art. 238(1) ("Any dispute arising between the authorities of an ACP State and a contractor, supplier or provider of services, candidate or tenderer, on the occasion of the placing or performance of a contract financed by the Fund [EDF] shall be settled by arbitration in accordance with procedural rules adopted by the Council of Ministers").

[45] Fourth ACP-EEC Convention of Dec. 15, 1989 (Lomé IV), 29 I.L.M. 783 (1991).

[46] Amissah, *supra* note 41, at 170.

[47] For an extended analysis of the dispute settlement mechanism of Lomé Convention *see* Paulsson, *supra* note 42, at 241–46; Amissah, *supra* note 41.

[48] *See* Kim Talus, EU Energy Law and Policy: A Critical Account 228–30 (2013).

b. Mercosur

Four nations are currently party to the southern cone free trade zone known as Mercosur: Brazil, Argentina, Paraguay, and Uruguay.[49] Venezuela formally acceded to Mercosur on July 31, 2012, and its membership is currently under dispute due to alleged violations of key membership requirements.[50] **6.18**

The Mercosur agreement itself deals exclusively with issues of trade and tariffs. But in 1994, the Mercosur Council[51] adopted two important investment protection protocols.[52] The Colonia Protocol[53] provides the investments of the nationals of Mercosur countries with national treatment and treatment at least as favorable as that provided to investors from non-Mercosur States.[54] Further, the document establishes obligations of fair and equitable treatment and a prohibition on "unjustified or discriminatory measures,"[55] limits the imposition of performance requirements,[56] and ensures the free transfer of profits and capital out of member countries.[57] The treaty also provides qualified investors the right to initiate arbitration against the host State under the ICSID or UNCITRAL rules to vindicate these rights.[58] The Buenos Aires Protocol[59] provides similar substantive protection **6.19**

---

[49] Treaty of Asuncion, Mar. 26, 1991, 30 I.L.M. 1041 (1991). Chile, Bolivia, Colombia, Guyana, Suriname, Ecuador, and Peru are associate members, which means that they lack voting rights and full trading privileges. For more on the investment aspects of Mercosur, *see* Noah Rubins, *Investment Arbitration in Brazil*, 4 J. World Inv. 1071 (2003).

[50] Protocolo de Adhesión del Estado Plurinacional de Bolivia al MERCOSUR, available at http://www.mercosur.int/innovaportal/v/4054/1/innova.front/textos-fundacionales.

[51] Article 3 of Additional Protocol to the Treaty of Asuncion on the Institutional Structure of Mercosur (Protocol of Ouro Preto) provides that "[t]he Council of the Common Market [Mercosur Council] is the highest organ of Mercosur, with responsibility for the political leadership of the integration process and for making the decisions necessary to ensure the achievement of the objectives defined by the Treaty of Asuncion and the final establishment of the common market." 31 I.L.M. 1244 (1995).

[52] Article 38 of the Protocol of Ouro Preto provides that "[t]he States Parties undertake to take all the measures necessary to ensure, in their respective territories, compliance with the decisions adopted by the Mercosur organs..." Chapter V of the protocol, entitled "Legal Sources of Mercosur," clarifies the normative value of the decisions of the Council in arts. 41 and 42. Article 41 of the protocol provides that "[t]he Decisions of the Council ... adopted since the entry into force of the Treaty of Asuncion" constitute legal sources of Mercosur. Article 42 provides that "[t]he decisions adopted by the Mercosur organs ... shall be binding and, when necessary, must be incorporated in the domestic legal systems in accordance with the procedures provided for in each country's legislation."

[53] Protocol for the Reciprocal Promotion and Protection of MERCOSUR Investments (Colonial Protocol), approved by Common Market Council Decision No. 11/93 of Jan. 17, 1994. An unofficial English translation of this protocol is available at http://www.cvm.gov.br/ingl/inter/mercosul/coloni-e.asp.

[54] *Id.*, art. 3(2).

[55] *Id.*, art. 3(1).

[56] *Id.*, art. 3(4).

[57] *Id.*, art. 5.

[58] *Id.*, art. 9.

[59] Protocol for the Promotion and Protection of Investments in Mercosur from Non-Member Countries (Buenos Aires Protocol), approved by Common Market Council Decision No. 11/94 of Aug. 5, 1994. Under the Buenos Aires Protocol, host States enjoy discretion as to whether to accord

and access to arbitration, but bestows these rights upon investors from any non-member country. Thus, the Buenos Aires Protocol appears to operate as a forceful foreign investment code for the entire Mercosur region.[60] The Mercosur investment protocols are for now not in force. Protocols within the Mercosur rule-making framework are ineffective until thirty days after all four member States have converted the protocol into domestic law. As of 2019, only Argentina had incorporated the Colonia Protocol into domestic law, and only Argentina and Paraguay had adopted the Buenos Aires Protocol.[61]

6.20 After failing to adopt the Colonia and the Buenos Aires Protocols, the four parties of the Mercosur Agreement made a second attempt to implement an investment protection agreement, signing the Protocol on Investment Cooperation and Facilitation (the "Mercosur Facilitation Protocol") in April 2017.[62] The Mercosur Facilitation Protocol is based on the Brazilian model BIT, the Agreement on Cooperation and Facilitation of Investments (ACFI). Commentators have suggested that the "regionalization of the Brazilian model" using the ACFI ignores the realities of four countries facing very different political, economic, and investment policy needs.[63] The Mercosur Facilitation Protocol maintains the

national treatment and MFN treatment to established investments of third-country investors. Also, the Buenos Aires Protocol contains no provisions on performance requirements.

[60] Rubins, *supra* note 49, at 1088–89. At least one experienced commentator holds the opinion that the Buenos Aires protocol is not a self-executing investment protection agreement at all, but only an attempt to harmonize future protections granted to foreign investors. According to this interpretation, the Protocol "only provides a ceiling on the scope of protection to non-Mercosur country investors that may be granted, for example under the discrete investment treaties each Member country may conclude with non-Mercosur countries and does not give rise to any specific rights from non-Mercosur country investors to claim rights directly arising from this Protocol." Horacio Grigera Naòn, *The Settlement of Investment Disputes between States and Private Parties*, 1 J. World Inv. 59, 63 (2000); Horacio Grigera Naòn, *Foreign Investment Arbitration in Latin America: The New Environment*, American Bar Assn. Section of Int'l Law and Practice Newsletter (Winter 1995), at 14–23. But *see* Maryse Robert et al., *Negotiating Investment Rules*, in An Integrated Approach to the European Union–Mercosur Association 265, 270–79 (Paolo Giordano ed. 2002) (suggesting that the Buenos Aires and Colonia Protocols provide direct protections to covered investors); U.S. Dept. of State, *Investment Climate Brazil 2000* (describing Buenos Aires protocol as an "investment protection treaty" like a BIT); *see also* Peter Malanczuk, *State-to-State and Investor-to-State Dispute Settlement in the OECD Draft Multilateral Investment Agreement*, in Multilateral Regulation of Investment 137 (E.C. Nieuwenhuys & Marcel M.T.A. Brus eds. 2001); Sistema Economico Latinamericano, International Negotiations on Foreign Investment: Elements for the Latin American and Caribbean Position.

[61] Sept. 29, 2002 Communication with Manuel Olarreaga, Mercosur Secretariat. *See* Argentina Law No. 24891 of May 11, 1997 (incorporating Colonia Protocol); Argentina Law No. 24554 of Sept. 13, 1995 (incorporating Buenos Aires Protocol); Paraguay Law No. 593/95 of June 15, 1995 (incorporating Buenos Aires Protocol). There is no indication when the remaining Mercosur states will ratify these documents, and because the governments themselves did not participate directly in their drafting, they may never enter into force.

[62] *See* the Mercosur Protocol, available at http://www.mre.gov.py/tratados/public_web/DetallesTratado.aspx?id=6E8bE7i%2FWyKPb1VlfV2uLw%3D%3D&em=lc4aLYHVB0dF+kNrtEvsmZ96BovjLlz0mcrZruYPcn8%3D.

[63] Facundo Pérez-Aznar & Henrique Choer Moraes, *The Mercosur Protocol on Investment and Facilitation: Regionalizing an Innovative Approach to Investment Agreements*, EJIL Talk!, Eur.

existing Mercosur dispute settlement system, which employs a permanent court, confirming a preference for institutionalized dispute settlement. Another characteristic of the Mercosur Protocol is its rejection of protection standards found in traditional BITs, following the Brazilian ACFI.[64] As of 2019, the Mercosur Facilitation Protocol has not yet entered into force.

c. The ASEAN Investment Agreement

The Association of South East Asian Nations (ASEAN) concluded the Agreement for the Promotion and Protection of Investments in December 1987.[65] The ASEAN Investment Agreement covers investments made within ASEAN members States by nationals and companies of other ASEAN members.[66] The agreement establishes various host State obligations to create favorable conditions for qualifying investments, including simplification of investment procedures and approval processes;[67] to ensure transparency and predictability by providing up-to-date public information on laws and regulations;[68] to accord fair and equitable treatment and full protection and security;[69] compensation for expropriation;[70] and to observe "any obligation arising from a particular commitment" made with regard to a specific investment of investors of another contracting party.[71] Article IV protects investments against unjustified and discriminatory measures with regard to management, maintenance, use, enjoyment, extension, disposition, or liquidation of investments, and MFN treatment has been accorded in respect of a limited range of benefits.[72] The ASEAN Investment Agreement contains no national treatment provision. Further, tax measures are expressly excluded from the agreement's scope of protection.[73] Article IX, as amended by a 2004 protocol, provides for investor–State dispute resolution under a variety of auspices, including the Kuala Lumpur arbitration center.[74] The first case filed under the 6.21

J. Int'l L. (Sept. 2017), available at https://www.ejiltalk.org/the-mercosur-protocol-on-investment-cooperation-and-facilitation-regionalizing-an-innovative-approach-to-investment-agreements/.

64 *Id.*

65 Agreement among the Governments of Brunei Darussalam, the Republic of Indonesia, Malaysia, the Republic of the Philippines, the Republic of Singapore, and the Kingdom of Thailand for the Promotion and Protection of Investments of Dec. 15, 1987, 27 I.L.M. 612 (1988) [hereinafter, ASEAN Investment Agreement].

66 *Id.*, Preamble and art. II.

67 Protocol to amend the ASEAN Investment Agreement of Sept. 12, 1996, art. III(A).

68 *Id.*, art. III(B).

69 ASEAN Investment Agreement, *supra* note 65, arts. IV(2), III(2).

70 *Id.*, art. VI.

71 *Id.*, art. III(3).

72 *Id.*, art. IV (MFN treatment limited to fair and equitable treatment and restitution, compensation or other remedies).

73 *Id.*, art. V.

74 If the disputing parties cannot agree on the applicable procedural rules within three months, then the agreement provides as a default a purely *ad hoc* three-member tribunal. The chairman in such cases must be a national of a third ASEAN State. In such cases, the International Court of Justice acts as the appointing authority. ASEAN Investment Agreement, *supra* note 65, art. X(3)–(4).

ASEAN Investment Agreement was *Yaung Chi Oo v. Myanmar*.[75] That arbitration was dismissed on jurisdictional grounds because the investment in question had not been "approved in writing" by Myanmar, as required for retroactive application of the agreement.

6.22 In an effort to facilitate investment flows and improve the protection level, the ASEAN nations (which have expanded to ten)[76] adopted a new investment treaty in 2009, the Comprehensive Investment Agreement (ACIA), which entered into force on March 29, 2012 and replaced the 1987 ASEAN Agreement for the Promotion and Protection of Investments.[77] ACIA contains several investment treatment provisions (including national treatment), similar to the protections provided in most BITs. However, ACIA establishes exceptions related to public morals, public order, human rights, animal or plant life and health, compliance with specific domestic laws and regulations,[78] as well as security exceptions.[79]

6.23 In addition to the investor–State dispute resolution choices established in the earlier ASEAN treaty, ACIA allows investors to submit their claims before any regional center for arbitration in the ASEAN region, in an effort to support the development of these dispute resolution facilities.

Finally, ASEAN adopted an economic agreement with Australia and New Zealand, which includes investment provisions similar to ACIA (Chapter 11), the ASEAN–Australia–New Zealand Free Trade Agreement.[80]

d. The Trans-Pacific Partnership Agreement

6.24 The Trans-Pacific Partnership Agreement (TPP) started as an as an expansion of the Trans-Pacific Strategic Economic Partnership Agreement (TPSEP or P4), signed by Brunei, Chile, New Zealand, and Singapore in 2005.[81] TPP thereafter

---

[75] *Yaung Chi Oo Trading PTE Ltd. v. Myanmar*, Award of Mar. 31, 2003, 42 I.L.M. 540 (2003). *See also* Emmanuel Gaillard, *The First Association of South East Asian Nations Award*, NYLJ (Aug. 7, 2003), at 3.

[76] The nations that are currently parties to the ASEAN treaty are Brunei, Cambodia, Indonesia, Malaysia, Myanmar, the Philippines, Singapore, Thailand, Laos, and Vietnam. The list is available at http://asean.org/asean/asean-member-states/.

[77] The 2009 ASEAN Comprehensive Investment Agreement (ACIA), available at http://www.asean.org/storage/images/2013/economic/aia/ACIA_Final_Text_26%20Feb%202009.pdf.

[78] *Id.*, art. 17.

[79] *Id.*, art. 18.

[80] The ASEAN-Australia-New Zealand Agreement entered into force on Jan. 1, 2010 and is available at http://www.asean.org/storage/images/2013/economic/afta/AANZFTA/Agreement%20Establishing%20the%20AANZFTA.pdf.

[81] The Trans-Pacific Strategic Economic Partnership Agreement (TPSEP or P4) is available at https://www.mfat.govt.nz/assets/FTAs-agreements-in-force/P4/Full-text-of-P4-agreement.pdf.

evolved as a proposed FTA between twelve countries: Australia, Brunei, Canada, Chile, Japan, Malaysia, Mexico, New Zealand, Peru, Singapore, Vietnam, and the United States.[82]

TPP was signed in 2016, but has not yet entered into force due to political and economic resistance from several countries. Although the United States was among the first countries to promote the TPP, advocating the benefits of free trade and open markets across the trans-Pacific region, the Trump administration withdrew the United States from the agreement in January 2017.[83] The remaining eleven TPP countries agreed to revive the agreement. In March 2018, the eleven remaining parties signed a revised version of the TPP, the Comprehensive and Progressive Agreement for Trans-Pacific Partnership. The revived agreement entered into force at the end of 2018.[84] 6.25

TPP contains thirty chapters on a broad variety of subjects such as eliminating tariffs and non-trade barriers in financial services, textiles, telecommunications, and manufacturing; provisions on intellectual property, environmental protection, good governance, labor standards, and human rights.[85] Chapter 9 deals with the investment protection. 6.26

Article 9(19) provides that investors may bring arbitration under the ICSID Convention (if applicable), the UNCITRAL Arbitration Rules, or any other institutional rules by agreement.[86] The tribunal can only award monetary damages or restitution of property, but not injunctive relief.[87] If the respondent fails to comply with a final award, the claimant can call for the establishment of a panel to declare the host State's default.[88] 6.27

[82] The Trans-Pacific Partnership Agreement (TPP) is available at https://ustr.gov/trade-agreements/free-trade-agreements/trans-pacific-partnership/tpp-full-text.

[83] White House Presidential Memorandum Regarding Withdrawal of the United States from the Trans-Pacific Partnership Negotiations and Agreement (Jan. 23, 2017), available at https://www.whitehouse.gov/presidential-actions/presidential-memorandum-regarding-withdrawal-united-states-trans-pacific-partnership-negotiations-agreement/ (directing the State Department to "withdraw the United States as a signatory to the Trans-Pacific Partnership (TPP), to permanently withdraw the United States from TPP negotiations, and to begin pursuing, wherever possible, bilateral trade negotiations to promote American industry, protect American workers, and raise American wages").

[84] The Comprehensive and Progressive Agreement for Trans-Pacific Partnership contains all provisions of the original TPP, but suspended a range of terms for which the United States had militated over the objection of the other TPP signatories.

[85] TPP, *supra* note 82.

[86] *Id.*, art. 9(19).

[87] *Id.*, art. 9(29) at para. 1.

[88] *Id.*, art. 9(29) at para. 11.

C. The Substantive Protections of Investment Protection Instruments

1. No expropriation without compensation

a. The standard

6.28 The customary international law rules governing expropriation, which were discussed at length in Chapter 5, were codified as a core guarantee of modern investment treaties.[89] Indeed, the very first BIT, signed by Germany and Pakistan in 1959, contained language reminiscent of the customary law rules on expropriation that were articulated during the first half of the twentieth century:

> Nationals or companies of either party shall not be subjected to expropriation of their investments in the territory of the other party except for public benefit against compensation, which shall represent the equivalent of the investments affected. Such compensation shall be actually realizable and freely transferable in the currency of the other party without delay. Adequate provision shall be made at or prior to the time of expropriation for the determination and the grant of such compensation.[90]

6.29 Investment protection instruments do not prevent the host State from expropriating foreign investors' property. Rather, these texts dictate the conditions under which States must carry out measures of expropriation. In particular, investment treaties invariably require that the State provide compensation. If the State adheres to the conditions stipulated in applicable treaties, foreign property owners are unlikely to be in a position to invoke international law to reverse the taking or to conserve obtain additional compensation.

6.30 Treaty texts are clear that even where the State carries out a taking on the basis of public welfare and refrains from discrimination, it is legally obligated to

[89] *See e.g. Generation Ukraine Inc. v. Ukraine*, ICSID Case No. ARB/00/9, Final Award of Sept. 16, 2003, para. 11(3), where the tribunal concluded that the BIT standard on expropriation is "simply a conventional codification of standards that have long existed in customary international law." For analysis of the expropriation standard under investment treaties, see *generally* Thomas Nektarios Papanastasiou, The Legal Protection of Foreign Investments against Political Risk: Japanese Business in the Asian Energy Sector 51–87 (2015); Jack Coe, Jr. & Noah Rubins, *Regulatory Expropriation and the Tecmed Case: Context and Contributions*, in International Investment Law and Arbitration: Leading Cases from the ICSID, NAFTA, Bilateral Treaties and Customary International Law 597, 613–19 (Todd Weiler ed. 2005); Rudolph Dolzer, *Indirect Expropriation: New Developments?*, 11 NYU Environ. L.J. 64 (2003); P.M. Norton, *Back to the Future: Expropriation and the Energy Charter Treaty*, in The Energy Charter Treaty, *supra* note 32; Tali Levy, *NAFTA's Provision for Compensation in the Event of Expropriation: A Reassessment of the "Prompt, Adequate and Affective" Standard*, 31 Stan. J. Int'l L. 423 (1995); Bjorn Kunoy, *Developments in Indirect Expropriation Case Law in ICSID Transnational Arbitration*, 6 J. World Inv. & Trade 467 (2005).

[90] Germany–Pakistan BIT (1959), art. 3(2).

compensate affected investors for the loss of their property. Therefore, it is widely accepted that any expropriation that is not accompanied by appropriate compensation constitutes a treaty violation. The *Santa Elena* tribunal reaffirmed this principle in the context of environmental regulations that had effectively expropriated the claimants' property:

> While an expropriation or taking for environmental reasons may be classified as a taking for a public purpose, and thus may be legitimate, the fact that the Property was taken for this reason does not affect either the nature or the measure of the compensation to be paid for the taking. That is, the purpose of protecting the environment for which the Property was taken does not alter the legal character of the taking for which adequate compensation must be paid. The international source of the obligation to protect the environment makes no difference. Expropriatory environmental measures—no matter how laudable and beneficial to society as a whole—are, in this respect, similar to any other expropriatory measures that a state may take in order to implement its policies: where property is expropriated, even for environmental purposes, whether domestic or international, the state's obligation to pay compensation remains.[91]

As a result, authorities dealing with public purpose and discrimination in the context of expropriation provisions are scarce. Tribunals have focused instead on the compensation requirement, the basis for liability in nearly all successful expropriation cases in recent years. **6.31**

As noted in Chapter 5, customary international law recognized a right to the restitution of expropriated property where the taking was "illegal *per se*," at least in theory. Investment treaty practice has little to say about the return of expropriated property. Under the ILC Draft Articles on State Responsibility, restitution is available as a remedy only if is not "materially impossible" and "does not involve a burden out of all proportion to the benefit derived from restitution instead of compensation."[92] Under NAFTA Chapter 11, host States are always entitled to "pay monetary damages and any applicable interest in lieu of restitution."[93] **6.32**

---

[91] *Compañía de Desarrollo de Santa Elena S.A. v. Costa Rica*, ICSID Case No. ARB/96/1, Final Award of Feb. 17, 2000, 15 ICSID Rev.—For. Inv. L.J. 169 (2000), paras. 71–72. Likewise, in *Phelps Dodge Corp. and Overseas Private Investment Corp. v. Iran*, the Iran–United States Claims Tribunal held that the claimant was entitled to compensation for Iran's seizure of its factory, although the taking had been motivated by a legitimate public purpose. *Phelps Dodge Corp. and Overseas Private Investment Corp. v. Iran*, Case No. 99, Award No. 217-99-2 of Mar. 19, 1986, 10 Iran–U.S. C.T.R., 121, 130.

[92] International Law Commission (ILC), Draft Articles on Responsibility of States for Internationally Wrongful Acts, in Report of the International Law Commission on the Work of its Fifty-Third Session, U.N. GAOR, 56th sess., Supp. No. 10, at 43, U.N. Doc. A/56/10 (2001), available at http://www.un.org/documents/resga.htm and http://www.un.org/law/ilc [hereinafter, the ILC Draft Articles on State Responsibility]; *see also* Robert Rosenstock, *The ILC and State Responsibility*, 96 AJIL 792 (2002), available at https://documents-dds-ny.un.org/doc/UNDOC/GEN/N01/557/81/img/N0155781.pdf?OpenElement.

[93] NAFTA, *supra* note 21, art. 1135(1).

The Washington Convention (which governs ICSID arbitration) also appears to favor monetary relief over restitution.[94] Indeed, since the *Chorzow Factory* judgment, international tribunals have only very rarely awarded restitution.[95]

6.33 Investment instruments generally define expropriation broadly to include both direct and indirect takings. Even where an investment protection instrument speaks only of "expropriation" in general terms, arbitral decisions have recognized that the very concept of expropriation includes measures equivalent in effect to a taking.[96] The ICSID tribunal in *Santa Elena* held:

> There is ample authority for the proposition that a property has been expropriated when the effect of the measures taken by the state has been to deprive the owner of title, possession or access to the benefit and economic use of his property.[97]

6.34 As a result, the distinctions between direct, indirect, and "creeping" expropriation, and between these forms of taking and measures "tantamount to" expropriation has faded in recent investment treaty practice[98] when compared to customary international law.[99] As will become clear, instances of "direct" expropriation have become relatively uncommon, with new and more subtle patterns of administrative and regulatory interference emerging to achieve the same result. The expropriation provisions of modern investment protection instruments are therefore designed precisely to offer protection in a wide range of factual circumstances.[100]

---

[94] Convention on the Settlement of Investment Disputes between States and Nationals of Other States ("Washington Convention"), of Mar. 18, 1965, art. 54(1), 17 U.S.T. 1270, available at https://treaties.un.org/doc/Publication/UNTS/Volume%20575/volume-575-I-8359-English.pdf. Article 54(1) requires contracting States to recognize a Convention award "as binding and enforce the *pecuniary* obligations imposed by that award" (emphasis added).

[95] The *Chorzow Factory Case, Germany v. Poland* (Merits), P.C.I.J. Collection of Judgements, Ser. A, No. 17, Award of Sept. 13, 1928; *see* PAPANASTASIOU, *supra* note 90, at 61.

[96] *See*, e.g. *El Paso Energy Int'l Co. v. Argentina*, ICSID Case No. ARB/03/15, Award of Oct. 31, 2011, paras. 233–56; *Biwater Gauff (Tanzania) Ltd. v. Tanzania*, ICSID Case No. ARB/05/22, Award of July 24, 2008, para. 452; *Generation Ukraine Inc. v. Ukraine*, ICSID Case No. ARB/00/9, Final Award of Sept. 16, 2003, para. 20(22); *Ronald S. Lauder v. Czech Republic*, UNCITRAL Final Award of Sept. 3, 2001, para. 200; *PSEG Global Inc. et al. v. Turkey*, ICSID Case No. ARB/02/5, Award of Jan. 19, 2007, para. 278.

[97] *Santa Elena, supra* note 92, at para. 77. *See also Metalclad Corp. v. Mexico*, Case No. ARB(AF)/97/1, Award of Aug. 30, 2000, 40 I.L.M. 36 (2001), para. 103.

[98] UNCTAD, 1 INTERNATIONAL INVESTMENT AGREEMENTS: KEY ISSUES 240–41 (2000).

[99] G.C. Christie, *What Constitutes a Taking of Property under International Law*, 38 BRIT. YB. INT'L LAW 307, 310–11 (1964); Burns H. Weston, "*Constructive Takings" under International Law: A Modest Foray Into the Problem of "Creeping Expropriation*," VA. J. INT'L L. 103 (1975); Rudolph Dolzer, *Indirect Expropriation of Alien Property*, 1 ICSID REV.— FOR. INV. L.J. 41 (1986); Rosalyn Higgins, *The Taking of Property by the State: Recent Developments in International Law*, RECUEIL DES COURS 261 (1982-III).

[100] *See* L. Yves Fortier & Stephen L. Drymer, *Indirect Expropriation in the Law of International Investment: I Know It When I See It, or Caveat Investor*, 19 ICSID REV.— FOR. INV. L.J. 293 (2004).

b. Applicable provisions

i. "Standard" text Treaty texts requiring compensation for expropriation have evolved somewhat since 1959, and today there is a substantial variety in the wording.[101] The Sweden–Russian Federation BIT offers a typical example: 6.35

> No Contracting Party shall expropriate or nationalise capital investments made by investors of the other Contracting Party or take other measures tantamount in their consequences to the expropriation or nationalization ... except for the cases when the expropriation is made: (a) in the public interest; (b) on a nondiscriminatory basis; (c) in a legally established manner and (d) with quick and adequate and effective compensation.[102]

ii. What constitutes expropriation As noted, investment instruments are relatively uniform in their scope, covering expropriation, nationalization, and all measures having equivalent effect. Some treaties offer a pithier definition of expropriation, such as the Netherlands–Ukraine BIT: 6.36

> Neither Contracting Party shall take any measures depriving, directly or indirectly, nationals of the other Contracting Party of their investments, unless the following conditions are complied with ...[103]

Because customary international law, which informs the interpretation of investment treaties, includes in the definition of expropriation those measures that have equivalent effect, it is unclear whether the absence of express language on this point affects the scope of investment protection. 6.37

Some treaties list certain types of regulations which are not to constitute indirect expropriation, regardless of the effect on foreign investors. Such exemptions are most often in the areas of technology licensing, taxation, and financial services. For example, a protocol to the Canada–Venezuela BIT establishes several carve-outs of this type: 6.38

> The provisions of Article VII [on expropriation] do not apply to the issuance of compulsory licenses granted in relation to intellectual property rights, or to the revocation, limitation or creation of intellectual property rights, to the extent that such revocation, limitation or creation is consistent with the Agreement Establishing the World Trade Organization done at Marrakech, April 1994.[104]

---

[101] *See e.g.* NAFTA, *supra* note 21, art. 1110; ECT, *supra* note 31, art. 13; ASEAN Investment Agreement, *supra* note 65, art. 6; U.S. Model BIT (2012), art. 6. For an overview of treaty provisions on expropriation, *see* UNCTAD, *supra* note 13, at 235–56.

[102] Sweden–Russian Federation BIT (1995), art. 4(1).

[103] Netherlands–Ukraine BIT (1994), art. 6.

[104] Canada–Venezuela BIT (1996), Annex, art. 6(b). *See also* NAFTA, *supra* note 21, art. 1110(7). *See generally* Carlos M. Correa, *Investment Protection in Bilateral and Free Trade Agreements: Implications for the Granting of Compulsory Licences*, 26 Mich. J. Int'l L. 331 (2004).

6.39 The most prominent limitations on expropriation relate to public safety and police powers, as codified in a small but growing number of BITs.[105] The culmination of this trend can be found in the U.S. Model BIT of 2012, which provides:

> Except in rare circumstances, nondiscriminatory regulatory actions by a Party that are designed and applied to protect legitimate public welfare objectives, such as public health, safety, and the environment, do not constitute indirect expropriations.[106]

6.40 Analogous provisions can be found in certain other treaties, including NAFTA.[107] As UNCTAD observed in its 2015 World Investment Report, fourteen of the eighteen investment treaties concluded in 2014 contained a clause recognizing that the parties need not relax public health standards to attract foreign capital.[108] CETA, the comprehensive FTA between Canada and the European Union, provides that:

> except in the rare circumstance when the impact of a measure or series of measures is so severe in light of its purpose that it appears manifestly excessive, non-discriminatory measures of a Party that are designed and applied to protect legitimate public welfare objectives, such as health, safety and the environment, do not constitute indirect expropriations.[109]

6.41 iii. **Compensation** Many States have introduced changes into recent investment protection treaties reflecting concerns that earlier texts leave gaps in investor protection. One obvious example is the replacement of the once-common "Hull Formula" ("prompt, adequate, and effective" compensation) by a requirement that compensation for expropriation be "full".

6.42 There remains substantial variety in the wording of provisions describing the requisite level of compensation for expropriation.[110] The most important distinction is between treaties calling for application of the Hull Formula and those offering a less specific description of the compensation required.[111] Some treaties give no guidance at all as to the requisite payment level. The most common alternative formulation, however, is "appropriate compensation," commonly found in treaties signed by China.[112] There is some authority for the

[105] *See* Eva Nanopoulos & Rumiana Yotova, *"Repackaging" Plain Packaging in Europe: Strategic Litigation and Public Interest Considerations*, 19(1) J. Int'l Economic L. 175–210 (2016).

[106] U.S. Model BIT, *supra* note 102, at Annex B, art. 4(b). *See also* India Model BIT, 2015, art. 5(4), (5), available at http://investmentpolicyhub.unctad.org/Download/TreatyFile/3560.

[107] NAFTA, *supra* note 21, art. 1114 (possibly limiting claims related to environmental measures not otherwise contrary to international law), art. 1110(8) (exempting from expropriation coverage measures of general application imposing costs on the debtor that cause it to default on its debt); India–Singapore Comprehensive Economic Cooperation Agreement (2005), art. 6(10).

[108] UNCTAD, *World Investment Report 2015: Reforming International Investment Governance*, 112 (2015), available at http://unctad.org/en/PublicationsLibrary/wir2015_en.pdf.

[109] The EU–Canada Comprehensive Economic and Trade Agreement (CETA), Annex 8-A(3), available at http://ec.europa.eu/trade/policy/in-focus/ceta/ceta-chapter-by-chapter/.

[110] UNCTAD, *supra* note 13, at 243.

[111] Papanastasiou, *supra* note 90, at 62–65.

[112] UNCTAD, *supra* note 12, at 244.

proposition that "appropriate" compensation may be less than the full value of the assets taken, in part determined by equitable considerations such as the host State's economic situation and the State's motivation for taking the expropriatory measure.[113] However, it is not clear that "appropriate" compensation will differ in most cases from payment assessed according to the Hull Standard. The China–Brunei BIT, for example, calls for "appropriate compensation or compensations" for expropriated property, but then defines such payment as "equivalent to the genuine value of the expropriated investment immediately before the expropriated action was taken or became publicly known, whichever is the earlier."[114]

A minority of treaties offer a basic methodology for determining the quantum of compensation for expropriation. For example, the ECT provides: **6.43**

> compensation shall amount to the fair market value of the Investment expropriated at the time immediately before the Expropriation or impending Expropriation became known in such a way as to affect the value of the Investment (hereinafter referred to as the "Valuation Date"). Such fair market value shall at the request of the Investor be expressed in a Freely Convertible Currency on the basis of the market rate of exchange existing for that currency on the Valuation Date. Compensation shall also include interest at a commercial rate established on a market basis from the date of Expropriation until the date of payment.[115]

c. *Application*

i. Direct expropriation As a general rule, direct expropriation occurs when an investor has been deprived of some essential component of its property rights, which has been destroyed or transferred to another, most commonly (but not necessarily) the State.[116] Some tribunals have held that a direct transfer of ownership also requires State intent to take, as well as a causal nexus between the measure in question and the loss of title to property.[117] **6.44**

As noted, direct expropriation has become relatively rare since the advent of modern investment treaties. Instead, host State interference has tended to affect the investor's property rights indirectly, either through regulations that prevent the investment activity from going forward (revocation or refusal of licenses, for **6.45**

[113] Campbell McLachlan et al., International Investment Arbitration: Substantive Principles 416 (2d ed. 2017); *See also* M. Sornarajah, The International Law on Foreign Investment 209–10 (3d ed. 2010).

[114] China–Brunei BIT (2000), art. 4(2). *See also* Comoros–Mauritius BIT, art. 7(1).

[115] ECT, *supra* note 31, art. 13(1). *See also* China–Djibouti BIT (2003), art. 4(2); Comoros–Mauritius BIT, art. 7(1).

[116] *See Enron Creditors Recovery Corp. (formerly Enron Corp.) and Ponderosa Assets, L.P. v. Argentina*, ICSID Case No. ARB/01/3, Award of May 22, 2007, para. 243; *Nat'l Grid Plc. v. Argentina*, UNCITRAL, Award of Nov. 3 2008, para. 145.

[117] *See Sempra Energy Int'l v. Argentina*, ICSID Case No. ARB/02/16, Award of Sept. 28, 2007, para. 282.

example) or by imposing conditions on operations that eliminate the value of the investor's interest in his enterprise.[118]

6.46 In the relatively few cases of direct expropriation, tribunals have had little difficulty in determining that compensation was due under investment treaty provisions. In *Swembalt v. Latvia*,[119] for example, a Swedish company brought a vessel to the port of Riga for use as a floating commercial center. A few months later, claiming that the investor had not procured necessary licenses, Riga city officials ordered the ship towed, and ultimately sold it at auction for scrap. The owner received none of the (rather meager) proceeds. The tribunal applied the expropriation provision in a single sentence, stating:

> the Republic of Latvia, by taking the ship away, preventing SwemBalt from using it and, finally, by auctioning it and permitting that it be scrapped without any compensation to SwemBalt, has breached its obligations under the Investment Agreement and general international law.[120]

6.47 In *Sedelmayer v. Russian Federation*,[121] a German investor had a business selling security equipment in St. Petersburg. The enterprise's headquarters were located on Kammeny Ostrov, a leafy island in the Neva River delta. Some time later, President Yeltsin issued a decree allocating the building for use as an official guest residence. Police forces ejected staff, sealed the premises, and confiscated personal property inside. The tribunal appears to have applied the expropriation provisions of the Germany–Russian Federation BIT, but took as given that the circumstances entitled the claimant to compensation for the assets lost.[122]

6.48 **ii. Indirect expropriation: the dominant view** Despite the growing body of arbitral decisions addressing claims of indirect expropriation, the precise contours of the law still remain unclear. It is generally accepted that certain types of measures affecting private property will constitute expropriation requiring compensation, even though the owner retains formal ownership.[123] The difficulty lies in drawing

---

[118] *See* Thomas Nektarios Papanastasiou, *Protecting Foreign Investments against Expropriation: A Comparative Study of Japan's EPAs*, 1(2) Int'l J. Pub. L. & Pol'y. 171–201 (2011).

[119] *Swembalt A.B. v. Latvia*, UNCITRAL Award of Oct. 23, 2000, 2004(2) Stockholm Arb. Rep. 97. For commentary on *Swembalt, see* Noah Rubins, *Swembalt: An Introduction and the Dilemma of Default*, 2004(2) Stockholm Arb. Rep. 119; Farouk Yala, *Swembalt: The Notion of Investment and Attribution of State Responsibility under a BIT*, 2004(2) Stockholm Arb. Rep. 128; Dany Khayat, *Swembalt: When Less Is Not More—Expropriation and Compensation*, 2004(2) Stockholm Arb. Rep. 141.

[120] *Swembalt, supra* note 121, at para. 38.

[121] *Sedelmayer v. Russian Federation*, Award of July 7, 1998, available at https://www.italaw.com/cases/982.

[122] *See e.g. id.* at 92.

[123] *See Revere Copper v. OPIC*, American Arbitration Association Award Case No. 16 10 0137 76, Award of Aug. 24, 1978, 228 *et seq.*, *reproduced at* 17 I.L.M. 1321 (1978). As for the jurisprudence of the European Court of Human Rights, *see Sporrong & Lönnroth v. Sweden*, Judgment of Sept. 23, 1982, Series A, 52, paras 63–69 ("[i]n the absence of formal expropriation, that is to say a transfer of ownership, the Court considers that it must look behind the appearances and investigate the realities of the situation complained of").

the line between non-compensable other governmental activity and measures amounting to indirect, compensable expropriation.[124]

Where State action does not result in the direct seizure of investments, most arbitral tribunals seeking to determine whether expropriation has occurred have followed the "effects" doctrine.[125] According to this approach, the most significant criterion for determining whether disputed State action constitutes indirect expropriation is the impact of the measure on the property in question.[126] The determinative factors are the intensity and duration of the economic deprivation suffered by the investor as the result of the impugned measures.[127] **6.49**

The "effects" doctrine has been established in a line of cases tracing back to the *Phillips* case, where the Iran–U.S. Claims Tribunal ruled that "liability to compensate for the expropriation of alien property does not depend on proof that the expropriation was intentional."[128] According to this view, the single most important criterion in establishing State liability for expropriation is the extent of the negative effect of government measures on the investor's property rights. Other considerations, in particular the host State's intent or justification for its actions, have almost no role to play in the analysis.[129] As the tribunal held in *Siemens v. Argentina*: **6.50**

> The Treaty refers to measures that have the effect of an expropriation; it does not refer to the intent of the State to expropriate. The quotation of the finding of the PCA in *Norwegian Shipowners* refers to "whatever the intentions" of the US were

[124] Dolzer & Schreuer, *supra* note 14, at 102; Papanastasiou, *supra* note 90, at 65–67; *see also* Catherine Yannaca-Small, "Indirect Expropriation" and the "Right to Regulate" in International Investment Law, OECD Working Papers on International Investment 2004/4 (Sept. 2004), at 6–7 and 9–10.

[125] *See e.g. Nat'l Grid, supra* note 118, para. 147; *SAUR Int'l S.A. v. Argentina*, ICSID Case No. ARB/04/4, Decision on Jurisdiction and Liability of June 6, 2012, paras. 366 and 441.

[126] *Saipem S.p.A. v. Bangladesh*, ICSID Case No. ARB/05/07, Award of June 30, 2009, para. 133.

[127] *Telenor Mobile Communications A.S. v. Hungary*, ICSID Case No. ARB/04/15, Award of Sept. 13, 2006, para. 70; *see also* Christoph Schreuer, *The Concept of Expropriation under the ETC and other Investment Protection Treaties*, 3 TDM (2005), at para. 82.

[128] *Phillips Petroleum Co. Iran v. Iran, The Nat'l Iranian Oil Co.*, Award No. 425-39-2, 21 Iran–U.S. C.T.R. 79, 115 (1989). *See also Tippets, Abbett, McCarthy, Stratton (Tippets) v. TAMS-AFFA Consulting Engineers of Iran*, Award No. 141-7-2, 6 Iran–U.S. C.T.R. 219 (1984), 225–26 (declaring intent less important than effects, and form less important than reality of impact); George Aldrich, The Jurisprudence of the Iran–U.S. Claims Tribunal 603–04 (1996).

[129] *See Biloune v. Ghana Invs. Centre*, Award of June 30, 1990, 95 Int'l L. Rep. 183, 209 (1993) (although there was evidence that the host State's actions toward the foreign investor were in part politically motivated, the tribunal noted that such circumstances were irrelevant to its conclusion that Ghana's measures constituted expropriation). *See also Compañía de Aguas del Aconquija S.A. and Vivendi Universal S.A. v. Argentina*, ICSID Case No. ARB/97/3, Award of Aug. 20, 2007, para. 7(5)(20) ("[t]here is extensive authority for the proposition that the state's intent, or its subjective motives are at most a secondary consideration"). On the emergence of an "effects" doctrine, *see* Todd Weiler, *A First Look at the Interim Merits Award in S.D. Myers v. Canada*, 24 Hastings Int'l & Comp. L. Rev. 87 (2001); Dominique Carreau & Patrick Juillard, Droit International Économique 501 (2003).

when the US took the contracts. A different matter is the purpose of the expropriation, but that is one of the requirements for determining whether the expropriation is in accordance with the terms of the Treaty and not for determining whether an expropriation has occurred.[130]

6.51 One of the primary issues raised by an "effects" analysis is the threshold level of interference that will trigger State liability for expropriation. It is clear that government measures resulting in total destruction of investment value are tantamount to expropriation. By the same token, an investor will have difficulty maintaining a treaty claim for expropriation where most of the value of his investment remains. As the tribunal held in *Tokios Tokelés v. Ukraine*:

> Although neither the relevant treaty text nor existing jurisprudence have clarified the precise degree of deprivation that will qualify as "substantial", one can reasonably infer that a diminution of 5% of the investment's value will not be enough for a finding of expropriation, while a diminution of 95% would likely be sufficient.[131]

6.52 Where the threshold lies within this range is a controversial question with no clear answers, and will depend on the circumstances surrounding each case. According to the tribunal in *Saluka v. Czech Republic*:

> It thus inevitably falls to the adjudicator to determine whether particular conduct by a state "crosses the line" that separates valid regulatory activity from expropriation. Faced with the question of when, how and at what point an otherwise valid regulation becomes, in fact and effect, an unlawful expropriation, international tribunals must consider the circumstances in which the question arises. The context within which an impugned measure is adopted and applied is critical to the determination of its validity.[132]

6.53 Recent tribunals applying the effects doctrine have most frequently relied upon the *Metalclad* panel's statement that expropriation

> includes ... interference with property which has the effect of depriving the owner, in whole *or significant part*, of the use or reasonably-to-be-expected economic benefit of property ...[133]

6.54 In that case, the U.S. investor had acquired land in Mexico for use as a landfill. Although the company had received assurances from the federal government that all necessary permits had been issued, the local authorities refused to grant permission to begin construction. The tribunal found that the host State's actions had deprived Metalclad of the ability to use its property for its intended purpose, and that this was sufficient harm to constitute expropriation. However, the

---

[130] *Siemens A.G. v. Argentina*, ICSID Case No. ARB/02/8, Award of Feb. 6, 2007, para. 270, with reference to *Norwegian Shipowners' Claims (Norway v. U.S.)*, 1 R.I.A.A. 307 (1922), 325.

[131] *Tokios Tokelés v. Ukraine*, ICSID Case No. ARB/02/18, Award of July 26, 2007, para. 120.

[132] *Saluka Investments B.V. v. Czech Republic* (UNCITRAL), Partial Award of Mar. 17, 2006, paras. 263–64.

[133] *Metalclad, supra* note 98, at para. 103 (emphasis added).

oft-cited threshold of destruction in "significant part" was mere *dicta* in *Metalclad*. The investor's landfill enterprise was completely prevented from operating, and therefore determined to have lost all its value. Subsequent tribunals have therefore employed the *Metalclad* formula, but struggled to identify the level of damage to investment that is "substantial."[134]

In *Feldman*, the claimant sought compensation for tax rebates denied to his products. The tribunal ultimately found that no expropriation had occurred, because several lines of the claimant's activity remained unaffected by the practices in question.[135] **6.55**

In *Occidental v. Ecuador*, the claimant argued that the host State's refusal to refund VAT payments constituted an expropriation of its asset, said to be the company's claim to receive a VAT reimbursement. While the tribunal ultimately found that Ecuador's conduct violated its duty to accord Occidental fair and equitable treatment, it refused to hold that an expropriation had occurred. Relying on *Metalclad*, the tribunal noted that "there must be a deprivation, [and] this deprivation must affect at least a *significant* part of the investment."[136] **6.56**

Moreover, in a subsidiary line of cases, tribunals have departed from the "effects" doctrine, requiring that the claimant demonstrate more than just a substantial decline in the value of investments as a result of government measures. In *Pope & Talbot*, the NAFTA tribunal provided a more demanding interpretation of the treaty term "tantamount to expropriation." It found that, even accepting the investor's evidence that the profits of its enterprise had been significantly reduced by a change in Canadian lumber export quotas, more tangible forms of interference in business operations would be required before expropriation could occur: **6.57**

> The Investor remains in control of the Investment, it directs the day-to-day operations of the Investment, and no officers or employees of the Investment have been detained by virtue of the Regime. Canada does not supervise the work of the officers or employees of the Investment, does not take any of the proceeds of company sales (apart from taxation), does not interfere with management or shareholders' activities, does not prevent the Investment from paying dividends with its shareholders, does not interfere with the appointment of directors or management and does not

[134] The denial or non-renewal of permits or licenses has become one of the most common fact patterns underlying successful expropriation cases in international arbitration under investment treaties. *See e.g. Middle East Cement Shipping & Handling Co. S.A. v. Egypt*, ICSID Case No. ARB/99/6, Award of Apr. 12, 2002, 18 ICSID Rev.—For. Inv. L.J. 602, 628 (2003) (withdrawal of permit to export cement held to constitute indirect expropriation); *Antoine Goetz et al. v. Burundi*, ICSID Case No. ARB/95/3, Award of Feb. 10, 1999, 15 ICSID Rev.—For. Inv. L.J. 457 (2000), para. 124 (revocation of company's "free zone" certification constituted indirect expropriation).

[135] *See Feldman v. Mexico*, ICSID Case No. ARB (AF)/99/1, Award of Dec. 16, 2002, 42 I.L.M. 625 (2003), at para. 152.

[136] *Occidental Petroleum Exploration Co. v. Ecuador*, LCIA Case No. UN3467, Final Award of July 1, 2004, 43 I.L.M. 1248 (2004), at para. 88 (emphasis added), available at http://www.italaw.com/sites/default/files/case-documents/ita0571.pdf.

take any other actions ousting the Investor from full ownership and control of the Investment.[137]

6.58 This strict view of indirect expropriation, which appears to be inconsistent with the reasoning in the majority of decisions rendered under modern investment protection instruments, nevertheless finds some continuing resonance.[138] In *CMS v. Argentina*, the claimant demonstrated that the Argentine government's freeze of gas transportation tariffs and forced conversion of private service contracts from dollars to devaluated pesos at a one-to-one rate resulted in massive reduction of the local investment vehicle's profitability. Indeed, according to the tribunal's own calculations, the investment had lost approximately 98.5 percent of its value.[139] While finding that Argentina's actions violated other standards of protection contained in the applicable Argentina–U.S. BIT, the arbitrators declined to hold Argentina liable for expropriation of the investment:

> Substantial deprivation was addressed in detail by the tribunal in the *Pope & Talbot* case. The Government of Argentina has convincingly argued that the list of issues to be taken into account for reaching a determination on substantial deprivation, as discussed in that case, is not present in the instant dispute. In fact, the Respondent has explained, the investor is in control of the investment; the Government does not manage the day-to-day operations of the company; and the investor has full ownership and control of the investment.[140]

6.59 Indeed, despite the apparent dominance of the "effects doctrine," there have been few arbitral awards finding expropriation where the investment in question retained any of its value. One of the only such awards came in *CME v. Czech Republic*, where the Czech government had deprived a local media company, in which the Dutch claimant corporation owned a share, of the ability to broadcast according to the initial conditions of its license. While the tribunal implied that this exclusion of the broadcast company from its sphere of activity constituted a complete destruction of its value,[141] the final damages award revealed that the company had lost only about 87 percent of its value.[142] Nevertheless, the tribunal

---

[137] *Pope & Talbot Inc. v. Canada*, Interim Award of June 26, 2000, 40 I.L.M. 258 (2001), para. 100. For a criticism of this award, *see* Zachary Douglas, *Property, Investment and the Scope of Investment Protection Obligations*, in The Foundations of International Investment Law: Bringing Theory into Practice 377–78 (Zachary Douglas et al. eds. 2014).

[138] Indeed, the *Pope & Talbot* standard appears to enjoy greater authority in the context of NAFTA's art. 1110, upon which that statement was based. *See e.g. Waste Management Inc. v. Mexico*, ICSID Case No. ARB(AF)/00/3, Award of Apr. 30, 2004, paras. 159–61 (no expropriation found where the investor "at all times had control and use of its property. It was able to service its customers and to collect fees from them").

[139] *CMS Gas Transmission Co. v. Argentina*, ICSID Case No. ARB/01/8, Award of May 12, 2005, paras. 468–69.

[140] *Id.* at para. 263.

[141] *CME Czech Republic B.V. v. Czech Republic*, UNCITRAL Partial Award of Sept. 13, 2001, para. 607, available at https://www.italaw.com/sites/default/files/case-documents/ita0178.pdf.

[142] *CME Czech Rep. B.V. v. Czech Republic*, Final Award of Mar. 14, 2003, para. 620, available at https://www.italaw.com/sites/default/files/case-documents/ita0180.pdf.

followed the example of *Metalclad* and *Tippets* to establish indirect expropriation of the claimant's investment.[143]

iii. Indirect expropriation: the minority view As noted, the dominant body of authority in modern investment protection law, expressed in the "effects doctrine," places relatively little importance on the justifications for host State action otherwise considered to be equivalent to expropriation. This is not surprising, given that the vast majority of investment treaties and codes contain no explicit exception from liability for measures aimed at protecting human health, the environment, national security, or other public goals.[144] Nevertheless, a subsidiary line of case law has drawn inspiration from the U.S.–Iran Claims tribunal's decision in *Sea-Land* to look beyond the effects of State action to the legitimacy of its motivations.[145] **6.60**

In *Técnicas Medioambientales Tecmed S.A. v. Mexico*,[146] the Spanish investor had obtained a license to operate a hazardous waste disposal site in Mexico. Local public protest led the environmental authorities to refuse to renew the license when it expired. More importantly, however, subsequent to the non-renewal of the landfill license, Mexico implemented regulations prohibiting the disposal of hazardous waste within 25 kilometers of any town with more than 100,000 inhabitants.[147] Since the property was only eight kilometers from the city of Hermosillo, this made the landfill site unusable for waste disposal. The tribunal analyzed the facts of the case and held that the Mexican authorities' decision, incorporated into a government resolution cancelling the permit and shutting down the landfill, had "negative effects on the Claimant's investment and its rights to obtain the benefits arising therefrom."[148] More specifically, the operating company's **6.61**

[143] *CME*, Partial Award, *supra* note 143, at para. 591.

[144] There is a trend towards revising international investment agreements with the purpose of protecting the State's right to regulate and reducing regulatory disputes. As Vera Korzun comments, host States are increasingly willing to "incorporate into the treaty text a reference to the *right to regulate* as a rationale for various exceptions and exclusions, non-precluded measures, and deviations from investor protection obligations" (emphasis in the original); *see* Vera Korzun, *The Right to Regulate in Investor–State Arbitration: Slicing and Dicing Regulatory Carve-Outs*, 50 VAND. J. TRANSNAT'L L. 2, 355–414, 362–63, 365 (2017), available at http://ssrn.com/abstract=2950939.

[145] *See Sea Land Service Inc. v. Iran*, 6 IRAN–U.S. C.T.R. 149, 166 (1984) (noting that under the circumstances recovery would require "deliberate governmental interference" with the claimant's operations); Katharina A. Byrne, *Regulatory Expropriation and State Intent*, 38 CAN. YB. INT'L L. 89, 91–92 (2001). *But cf.* CHARLES BROWER & JASON BRUESCHKE, THE IRAN–U.S. CLAIMS TRIBUNAL 429, 461 (1998) (stating that the language in *Sea Land* relates to attribution in the context of failures to act due to general deterioration in the management of port services).

[146] *Tecnicas Medioambientales Tecmed S.A. v. Mexico*, ICSID Case No. ARB(AF)/00/2, Award of May 29, 2003, 43 I.L.M. 133 (2004). For an overview and analysis of the *Tecmed* award, *see* Coe & Rubins, *supra* note 90, at 644–66.

[147] *Tecmed*, *supra* note 148, at para. 106.

[148] *Id.* at para. 117.

> economic and commercial operations in the Landfill after such denial have been fully and irrevocably destroyed, just as the benefits and profits expected or projected by the Claimant [Tecmed] as a result of the operation of the Landfill.[149]

6.62 However, the tribunal's analysis did not end there. This appears to have shifted the burden of proof to Mexico, to show that the expropriation was *justified* as falling within the State's police power. The tribunal sought to determine

> whether such actions or measures are proportional to the public interest presumably protected thereby and the protection legally granted to investments, taking into account the significance of such impact plays a key role in deciding the proportionality.[150]

6.63 The arbitrators suggested that "a serious urgent situation, crisis, need or social emergency" could be "weighed against the deprivation or neutralization of the economic or commercial value of the Claimant's investment" to lead to the conclusion that an otherwise expropriatory regulation "[does] not amount to an expropriation under the Agreement and international law."[151] Ultimately, however, it was found that neither environmental concerns nor the threat of civil disturbance due to public protests could justify the Mexican government's effective taking of the claimant's investment.[152]

6.64 **iv. Indirect expropriation and the permanence requirement** It is generally accepted that under modern investment protection treaties (as was the case under customary international law) State interference with property must be "non-ephemeral" to be considered expropriation.[153] In *S.D. Myers v. Canada*, for

---

[149] *Id.*

[150] *Id.* at para. 122. Cited in support of this approach was the decision of the European Court of Human Rights in *Matos e Silva, Lda., et al. v. Portugal*, 37 Eur. Ct. H.R., para. 85 (1996), available at https://www.bailii.org/eu/cases/ECHR/1995/47.html. In that case, a company engaged in raising fish and extracting salt from Portuguese land under a century-old royal concession was deprived of its license when the government decided to establish a nature preserve on the property. The claimant prevailed, demonstrating that Portugal had substantially interfered with its property rights, and that the unreasonably long process and discriminatory application of the measures outweighed the recognized public benefit served. *See also Mellacher et al. v. Austria*, [1989] Eur. Ct. H.R. 25, para. 48 (10522/83), available at http://www.worldlii.org/eu/cases/ECHR/1989/25.html; *Pressos Compañia Naviera S.A. et al. v. Belgium*, [1997] Eur. Ct. H.R. 44, para. 38 (17849/91), available at http://www.worldlii.org/eu/cases/ECHR/1997/44.html.

[151] *Tecmed, supra* note 148, at para. 139.

[152] However, arbitral tribunals increasingly consider host States' regulatory interests alongside the rights of foreign investors, particularly in relation to human rights protection. *See* Vivian Kube & Ernst-Ulrich Petersmann, *Human Rights Law in International Investment Arbitration*, 11(1) AJWH 99 (2016); *See also* Moshe Hirsch, *Investment Tribunals and Human Rights: Divergent Paths*, in Human Rights in International Investment Law and Arbitration 107–13 (Pierre-Marie Dupuy et al. eds. 2009); José E. Alvarez, *The Use (and Misuse) of European Human Rights Law in Investor–State Dispute Settlement*, in The Impact of EU Law on International Commercial Arbitration 72 (Franco Ferrari ed. 2017), available at SSRN: https://papers.ssrn.com/sol3/papers.cfm?abstract_id=2875089.

[153] J.M. Wagner, *International Investment, Expropriation and Environmental Protection*, 29 Golden Gate UL Rev. 465 (1999). *See also Tecmed, supra* note 148, at para. 116.

example, the tribunal declined to hold Canada liable for expropriation, because the export ban that had caused harm to the U.S. claimant ended after sixteen months.[154] At the same time, the tribunal noted that "in some contexts and circumstances it would be appropriate to view a deprivation as amounting to an expropriation even if it were partial and temporary."[155]

The NAFTA tribunal in *Glamis Gold* rejected an expropriation claim because the alleged delays and governmental stonewalling were only temporary in duration.[156] In *Cargill*, the tribunal found that NAFTA did not contemplate claims for "temporary" taking.[157] In the same vein, several other tribunals have found that expropriatory measures must not be of a temporary or "ephemeral" nature.[158] By contrast, the UNCITRAL tribunal in *Servier* held that the terms of the France–Poland BIT did not require dispossession to be permanent in the sense of continuing *ad infinitum*, although deprivation be more than transitory.[159] The NAFTA tribunal in *Archer Daniels* opted for an intermediate approach. Relying on *LG&E v Argentina*, it found that **6.65**

> generally, expropriation must be permanent, that is to say, it cannot have a temporary nature, unless the investment's successful development depends on the realization of certain activities at specific moments that may not endure variations.[160]

In this regard, tribunals have not tended to defer to formal labels or host State characterizations as to the duration of offending measures. In *CMS*, for example, Argentina relied upon the explicitly temporary nature of the "Emergency Measures" that had caused harm to the claimant's investments. The subsequent renegotiation of foreign investors' licenses, it insisted, would eliminate any offending State actions in the near future. The tribunal ruled that those negotiations had been ongoing for over five years, and that "if delays exceed a reasonable period of **6.66**

[154] *S.D. Myers Inc. v. Canada*, Partial Award of Nov. 13, 2000, 40 I.L.M. 1408 (2001), at paras. 286–88. *See also* the European Court of Human Rights case of *Hauer v. Land Rheinland-Pfalz*, 1979 E.C.R. 3727 (German winegrower's claim of interference with property rights denied where European Commission order prohibiting the planting of certain vines applied only for a transitory period of three years).

[155] *Id.*

[156] *Glamis Gold Ltd. v. U.S.A.*, UNCITRAL, Final Award of June 8, 2009, para. 360.

[157] *Cargill Inc. v. Mexico*, ICSID Case No. ARB(AF)/05/2, Award of Sept. 18, 2009, para. 348.

[158] *See*, among various authorities, *Tza Yap Shum v. Peru*, ICSID Case No. ARB/07/6, Award of July 7, 2011, para. 163; *Abengoa S.A. y COFIDES S.A. v. Mexico*, ICSID Case No. ARB(AF)/09/2, Award of Apr. 18, 2013, paras. 584–87 and 610; *Bernhard von Pezold et al. v. Zimbabwe*, ICSID Case No. ARB/10/15, Award of July 28, 2015, para. 516.

[159] *Les Laboratoires Servier S.A.S., Biofarma S.A.S., Arts et Techniques du Progres S.A.S. v. Poland*, UNCITRAL, Award (Redacted) of Feb. 14, 2012, para. 577.

[160] *Archer Daniels Midland Co. and Tate & Lyle Ingredients Americas Inc. v. Mexico*, ICSID Case No. ARB(AF)/04/5, Award of Nov. 21, 2007, at para. 243, citing *LG&E Energy Corp., LG&E Capital Corp., and LG&E Int'l Inc. v. Argentina*, ICSID Case No. ARB/02/1, Award of Oct. 3, 2006, para. 193.

time the assumption that they might become permanent features of the governing regime gains in likelihood."[161]

6.67 In *Achmea v Slovakia*, the tribunal had to assess a profit ban, which had subsequently been ruled unconstitutional by the Slovak Constitutional Court. The tribunal drew a distinction between (1) a "deprivation" for what is from the outset intended to be a limited (and relatively short) period, and (2) a "deprivation" that is intended at the time of its adoption to be permanent but which, in the event, is reversed after a relatively short period of time. In the tribunal's analysis, deprivations of the former kind would not ordinarily constitute expropriation, although they could breach of other BIT provisions, such as non-discrimination or fair and equitable treatment.[162] In the present case, although the ban on profits was reversed only after the intervention of the Constitutional Court, the tribunal could not disregard the domestic court's judgment. Accordingly, the tribunal found that the measure that the domestic court had overturned had effected only a temporary deprivation, which did not constitute expropriation.[163]

6.68 Some tribunals have also drawn a distinction between a single expropriatory measure and "creeping expropriation," multiple measures that together cause expropriation. In *Azurix*, for example, the tribunal explained that:

> The parties hold also different views on the time needed for a set of measures to have an expropriatory effect. There is no specific time set under international law for measures constituting creeping expropriation to produce that effect. It will depend on the specific circumstances of the case. Arbitral tribunals have considered that a measure is not ephemeral if the property was out of the control of the investor for a year (*Wena*) or an export license was suspended for four months (*Middle East Cement*), or that the measure was ephemeral if it lasted for three months (*S.D. Myers*). These cases involved a single measure. When considering multiple measures, it will depend on the duration of their cumulative effect. Unfortunately, there is no mathematical formula to reach a mechanical result. How much time is needed must be judged by the specific circumstances of each case.[164]

2. Fair and equitable treatment

a. The standard

6.69 Besides expropriation, the "fair and equitable treatment" standard is perhaps the most-discussed and debated in modern foreign investment law.[165] Like

---

[161] *CMS, supra* note 141, at para. 107.

[162] *Achmea B.V. (formerly Eureko B.V.) v. Slovakia* [I], PCA Case No. 2008-13, Final Award of Dec. 7, 2012, paras. 289–91.

[163] *Id.* at paras. 292–93.

[164] *Azurix Corp. v. Argentina*, ICSID Case No. ARB/01/12, Award of July 14, 2006, para. 313.

[165] For analysis of the fair and equitable treatment standard in investment protection treaties, *see* Christoph Schreuer, *Fair and Equitable Treatment in Arbitral Practice*, 6 J. World Trade & Inv. 357 (2005); Stephen Vasciannie, *The Fair and Equitable Treatment Standard in International Investment Law and Practice*, 70 Brit. Yb. Int'l L. 99 (2000); J.C. Thomas, *Reflections on Article*

compensation for expropriation, the requirement that host States treat qualifying foreign investors fairly and equitably is part of the substantive protection included in nearly every contemporary investment treaty.[166] This standard is designed to create an objective baseline of treatment for qualifying foreigners, which the host State must provide regardless of how it treats its own investors.[167]

It can be challenging for both investors and States to understand the precise contours of this broad and versatile guarantee. Writing in the context of NAFTA, Judge Brower has said that the standard gives arbitral tribunals the authority to "articulate a variety of rules necessary to achieve [a given treaty's] object and purpose in particular disputes."[168] Likewise, F.A. Mann's view is that the standard requires a tribunal "to decide whether in all the circumstances the conduct in issue is fair and equitable or unfair and inequitable."[169] Or, as Stephen Vasciannie opines: **6.70**

> [T]he standard serves the useful purpose of giving foreign investors the opportunity to question administrative and other actions without actually embarking upon deliberations on the requirements of either municipal law or customary law. Investors are thus able to approach host States with the abstract question whether a particular form of treatment is unfair or inequitable in the context of investment relations . . . [170]

1105 of NAFTA: History, State Practice and the Influence of Commentators, 17 ICSID Rev.—For. Inv. L.J. 21 (2002); Barnali Choudhury, *Evolution or Devolution? Defining Fair and Equitable Treatment in International Investment Law*, 6 J. World Inv. & Trade 297 (2005); Courtney Kirkma, *Fair and Equitable Treatment: Methanex v. United States and the Narrowing Scope of NAFTA Article 1105*, 34 L. & Pol'y. Int'l Bus. 343 (2002); Patrick Dumberry, *The Quest to Define "Fair and Equitable Treatment" for Investors under International Law: The Case of the NAFTA Chapter 11 Pope & Talbot Awards*, 3 J. World Inv. 657 (2002); *Methanex, supra* note 27, at part IV, chs. C–E. *See also* Martins Paparinskis, The International Minimum Standard and Fair and Equitable Treatment 90 (2013); Jonathan Bonnitcha, Substantive Protection under Investment Treaties: A Legal and Economic Analysis 143 *et seq.* (2014); Andrew Newcombe & Lluis Paradell, Law and Practice of Investment Treaties: Standards of Treatment 255 (2009); Roland Klager, "Fair and Equitable Treatment" in International Investment Law 117 *et seq.* (2011).

[166] *See* Lucy Reed & Daina Bray, *Fair and Equitable Treatment: Fairly and Equitably Applied in Lieu of Unlawful Indirect Expropriation?*, in Contemporary Issues in International Arbitration and Mediation: The Fordham Papers *2007* (Arthur W. Rovine ed. 2008); *See also* Thomas Nektarios Papanastasiou, *The Role of Economic Partnership Agreements in Protecting Foreign Investments against Political Risk: An Analysis of Japan's EPAs*, 21(4) J. Graduate School Asia-Pacific Studies 95–124, 109–14 (2011).

[167] Schreuer, *supra* note 167, at 361–62; *United Parcel Service Inc. v. Canada*, Award of Nov. 22, 2002, 7 ICSID Rep. 288, para. 97 (emphasizing that the fair and equitable treatment standard may be violated even if the treatment accorded the foreign investor is no different than that meted out to locals).

[168] Brower, *supra* note 22, at 56.

[169] F.A. Mann, *British Treaties for the Promotion and Protection of Investments*, 52 Brit. Yb. Int'l L. 241, 244 (1981).

[170] Vasciannie, *supra* note 167, at 163.

b. Applicable provisions

6.71 "Fair and equitable treatment" is one of the most common guarantees contained in modern investment treaties,[171] and the provisions establishing the obligation of fair and equitable treatment are relatively uniform.[172] Many BITs contain a text similar to that found in the Germany–Bulgaria treaty:

> Each Contracting Party shall in any case accord investments by investors of the other Contracting Party fair and equitable treatment.[173]

6.72 While most such provisions call for "fair and equitable treatment," some guarantee "just and equitable" or simply "equitable" treatment.[174] A large number of treaties combine fair and equitable treatment with other standards in a single provision, most frequently with full protection and security, but also with national and MFN treatment.[175] There is no evidence that these textual variations alter the scope or content of the provision.[176]

6.73 The term "treatment" is sometimes limited to the treatment of foreign "investors" or the treatment of "investments" made by such investors. In the absence of textual limitations, the standard is sufficiently broad to encompass a number of components. The tribunal in *Rompetrol v. Romania* interpreted the fair and equitable treatment standard in article 3(1) of the Netherlands–Romania BIT to prohibit a range of State behavior: (1) conduct directed against the investor itself or its investment; (2) conduct directed against individuals who were not themselves investors, for their activity on behalf of and in the interest of the investor or its investment; and (3) conduct directed against individuals in their personal capacity, for the purpose of harming the investor or its investment.[177]

6.74 Certain recent treaties include adjustments to the fair and equitable standard that appear focused on instances where the investor has been denied due process. Such innovations are in large part a response by capital-exporting States to claims brought against the United States under the NAFTA.[178] The new Central

---

[171] *See e.g.* NAFTA, *supra* note 21, art. 1105(1); ECT, *supra* note 31, art. 10(1); U.S. Model BIT, *supra* note 102, art. 5. Nevertheless, some BITs do not expressly guarantee fair and equitable treatment. *See e.g.* Egypt–Japan BIT (1978); Italy–Romania BIT (1990); India–Singapore Comprehensive Economic Cooperation Agreement, *supra* note 108.

[172] UNCTAD, *supra* note 13, at 219–24.

[173] Germany–Bulgaria BIT (1986), art. 2(4).

[174] UNCTAD, *supra* note 13, at 214.

[175] Mohammed I. Khalil, *Treatment of Foreign Investment in Bilateral Investment Treaties*, 7 ICSID Rev.—For. Inv. L.J. 339, 355 (1992).

[176] UNCTAD, *supra* note 13, at 216.

[177] *The Rompetrol Group N.V. v. Romania*, ICSID Case No. ARB/06/3, Award of May 6, 2013, para. 200.

[178] *See e.g.* United States–Singapore Free Trade Agreement, Jan. 15, 2003, U.S.–Sing., art. 15(5), 42 I.L.M. 1026 (2003), available at https://ustr.gov/sites/default/files/uploads/agreements/fta/singapore/asset_upload_file708_4036.pdf . *See generally* Noah Rubins, *The Arbitral Innovations of Recent U.S. Free Trade Agreements: Two Steps Forward, One Step Back*, 8 Int'l Bus. L.J. 865 (2003);

American Free Trade Agreement (CAFTA), for example, provides that fair and equitable treatment "prescribes the customary international law minimum standard of treatment of aliens," and further clarifies that

> "fair and equitable treatment" includes the obligation not to deny justice in criminal, civil, or administrative adjudicatory proceedings in accordance with the principle of due process embodied in the principal legal systems of the world.[179]

The concept of the denial of justice had been developed in four categories: **6.75**

(1) denial of access to court;
(2) delay;
(3) due process; and
(4) substantive fairness of decisions.[180]

Even in the absence of any explicit reference to due process, investment treaty tribunals have interpreted the fair and equitable treatment standard as encompassing a requirement of due process and transparency.[181] In a number of cases, arbitrators have concluded that fair procedures is an important element of fair and equitable treatment.[182] For example, in *Metalclad v. Mexico*, a lack of procedural propriety (a failure to hear the investor) was considered in the tribunal's ruling that the fair and equitable treatment guaranteed in the NAFTA had been breached.[183] **6.76**

c. Application

i. The dominant view Most tribunals deciding whether a government action violates the fair and equitable treatment standard have adopted a straightforward interpretative approach consonant with the general object and purpose of investment treaties.[184] Considering that these treaties' primary goal is to create **6.77**

David Gantz, *The Evolution of FTA Investment Provisions: From NAFTA to the United States–Chile Free Trade Agreement*, 19 Am. U. Int'l L. Rev. 679, 740–46 (2004).

179 Dominican Republic–Central American Free Trade Agreement, art. 10(5)(2), available at https://ustr.gov/trade-agreements/free-trade-agreements/cafta-dr-dominican-republic-central-america-fta/final-text.

180 *Robert Azinian et al. v. Mexico*, ICSID Case No. ARB(AF)/97/2, Award of Nov. 1, 1999, paras. 102–03, available at https://www.italaw.com/sites/default/files/case-documents/ita0057.pdf.

181 *See e.g.: Bayindir Insaat Turizm Ticaret Ve Sanayi A.S. v. Pakistan*, ICSID Case No. ARB/03/29, Award of Aug. 27, 2009, para. 178; *Rusoro Mining v. Venezuela*, ICSID Case No. ARB(AF)/12/5, Award of Aug. 22, 2016, para. 524; *Jan de Nul N.V. and Dredging Int'l N.V. v. Egypt*, ICSID Case No. ARB/04/13, Award of Nov. 6, 2008, para. 187.

182 *See e.g. Frontier Petroleum Services Ltd. v. Czech Republic* (UNCITRAL), Final Award of Nov. 12, 2010, paras. 289 and 398. *See also Deutsche Bank A.G. v. Sri Lanka*, ICSID Case No. ARB/09/2, Award of Oct. 31, 2012, para. 478.

183 *Metalclad, supra* note 98, at paras 91 and 97–101.

184 Art. 31(1), Vienna Convention on the Law of Treaties, in Basic Documents of International Law 349 (Ian Brownlie ed. 1983), available at http://www.un.org/law/ilc (treaties should be interpreted "in good faith in accordance with the ordinary meaning to be given to the terms of the treaty in their context and in the light of its object and purpose"). See also *Pope & Talbot Inc. v. Canada*, Award on the Merits of Apr. 10, 2001, available at https://www.italaw.com/cases/

favorable conditions for foreign investments and to reduce political risk,[185] many tribunals have ruled that "fair and equitable treatment" is a standard intended to accord broad protections to qualifying investors, including a stable and predictable investment environment, in order to maximize the flow of foreign direct investments. The tribunal in *MTD v. Chile* succinctly summarized this trend:

> fair and equitable treatment should be understood to be treatment in an even-handed and just manner, conducive to fostering the promotion of foreign investment. [The BIT's] terms are framed as a pro-active statement—"to promote," "to create," "to stimulate"—rather than prescriptions for a passive behavior of the State or avoidance of prejudicial conduct to the investors.[186]

6.78 According to this view, a State may violate its obligation to accord investments fair and equitable treatment should it substantially alter the legal or regulatory framework pursuant to which those investments were made. In particular, State measures that are contrary to express assurances made to investors as an inducement to invest and upon which investors relied may constitute a breach of the fair and equitable treatment standard. Such is the case, according to Vasciannie, because:

> if a host country provides an assurance of fair and equitable treatment, it presumably wishes to indicate to the international community that investments within its jurisdiction will be subject to treatment compatible with some of the many expectations of foreign investors.[187]

6.79 As a result, tribunals assess whether State measures violate the fair and equitable treatment standard may need to examine "the impact of the measure on the reasonable investment-backed expectations of the investor; and whether the state is attempting to avoid investment-backed expectations that the state created or reinforced through its own acts."[188]

6.80 As previously described, *CME v. Czech Republic* involved the claimant's investment in a joint venture to operate a local television station. The arbitral tribunal, applying the Netherlands–Czech Republic BIT, found that the Czech Republic's legislative and regulatory changes had unlawfully harmed CME's investment by ignoring the rules governing the investor's business:

863, at para. 115 (applying a "plain meaning" interpretation to give content to the fair and equitable treatment standard).

[185] *See e.g.* Belgium–Luxembourg–Soviet Union BIT (1989), preamble (the parties, "DESIRING to create favorable conditions for investments by investors of one Contracting Party in the territory of the other Contracting Party, and CONCSIOUS of the positive effect that the present Treaty can have on fostering business contacts and strengthening trust in the area of investments, have agreed as follows ..."); *Tecmed, supra* note 148, at para. 155 (basing broad interpretation on treaty purpose).

[186] *MTD Equity Sdn. Bhd. and MTD Chile S.A. v. Chile*, ICSID Case No. ARB/01/7, Award of May 25, 2004, para. 113, available at https://www.italaw.com/cases/717.

[187] Vasciannie, *supra* note 167, at 99.

[188] Jan Paulsson, *Investment Protection Provisions in Treaties*, in Investment Protection/La Protection de L'Investissement 19, 22 n.8 (2000).

> [The Government] breached its obligation of fair and equitable treatment by evisceration of the arrangements in reliance upon [which] the foreign investor was induced to invest.[189]

This obligation to safeguard "pre-existing decisions that were relied upon by the investor to assume its commitments as well as to plan and launch its commercial and business activities"[190] appears central to the concept of fairness and equity within the meaning of modern investment treaties.[191] This concept of investment stability was emphasized in the *CMS* award, in which the tribunal found that Argentina's alteration of the gas transportation regulatory regime was unfair and inequitable: **6.81**

> One principle objective of the protection envisaged is that fair and equitable treatment is desirable "to maintain a stable framework for investments and maximum effective use of economic resources." There can be no doubt, therefore, that a stable legal and business environment is an essential element of fair and equitable treatment.[192]

While many investment treaties contain specific provisions ensuring the State's observance of contracts and other undertakings,[193] the fair and equitable treatment standard has also been found to add force to the internationalization of State contracts and their breach by host governments. As the NAFTA tribunal in *Mondev* noted, **6.82**

> [a] governmental prerogative to violate investment contracts would appear to be inconsistent with the principles [e.g. fair and equitable treatment] embodied in Article 1105.[194]

The linkage between fairness and equity and the *pacta sunt servanda* principle finds resonance in international law. The rule of sanctity of contracts is a fundamental part of nearly all modern legal systems,[195] and is codified in article 26 of the Vienna Convention on the Law of Treaties.[196] **6.83**

Most tribunals have viewed the fair and equitable treatment standard as an objective one. Thus, consonant with the dominant approach to expropriation, the State may incur liability regardless of its motivation for taking the offending measures.[197] In *Occidental v. Ecuador*, the tribunal reaffirmed this principle: **6.84**

---

189 *CME*, Partial Award, *supra* note 143, at para. 611.

190 *Tecmed*, *supra* note 148, at para. 154.

191 *See* Coe & Rubins, *supra* note 90, at 656–57.

192 *CMS*, *supra* note 141, at para. 274. *See also Metalclad*, *supra* note 98, at para. 99.

193 On so-called "umbrella clauses," *see* Section C.5.

194 *Mondev Int'l Ltd. v. United States of America*, ICSID Case No. ARB(AF)/99/2, Award of Oct. 11, 2002, 42 I.L.M. 85 (2003), para. 134. NAFTA art. 1105(1) reads: "Each Party shall accord to investments of investors of another Party treatment in accordance with international law, including fair and equitable treatment and full protection and security."

195 Bing Cheng, General Principles of Law as Applied by International Courts and Tribunals 112–14 (1993).

196 ILC Draft Articles on State Responsibility, *supra* note 93, art. 26.

197 *CMS*, *supra* note 141, at para. 280.

> The stability of the legal and business framework is ... an essential element of fair and equitable treatment ... Moreover, this is an objective requirement that does not depend on whether the Respondent has proceeded in good faith or not.[198]

6.85 **ii. The minority view** One of the issues most frequently arising in connection with the "fair and equitable" treaty standard is the extent to which the protection should be interpreted and applied in light of the customary international law principles from which it arguably arises. In particular, many host States have taken the position that they should bear responsibility only for actions sufficiently offensive as to cross the high threshold established in the *Neer* arbitration of 1926.[199] There, examining a claim arising out of the unpunished murder of a U.S. citizen in Mexico, the Mexican Claims Commission declared that host State treatment of foreign citizens violates international law if it amounts "to an outrage, to bad faith, to wilful neglect of duty, or to an insufficiency of governmental action so far short of international standards that every reasonable and impartial man would readily recognize its insufficiency."[200] Several tribunals have noted the relevance of customary international law to the determination of whether State action is unfair and inequitable, particularly in applying treaties (such as NAFTA) that expressly dictate reference to international law. At the same time, it is commented that the fair and equitable treatment standard and its relation to the minimum standard of treatment under customary international law has provoked the discussion "on whether these standards provide only as much protection as foreign investors receive in their capacity as aliens under the customary international law minimum standard of protection of aliens, or whether they offer a higher level of protection."[201] Many observers agree that the law has evolved a good deal since the days of *Neer*, and that the modern treaty prohibition against unfair treatment is substantially more robust than the customary norms of the 1920s. As the *Mondev* tribunal explained:

> To the modern eye, what is unfair or inequitable need not equate with the outrageous or the egregious. In particular, a State may treat a foreign investment unfairly and inequitably without necessarily acting in bad faith ... the content of the minimum standard today cannot be limited to the content of customary international law as recognised in arbitral decisions in the 1920s.[202]

6.86 The modern concept of fair and equitable treatment has undoubtedly broadened beyond the minimum standard, encompassing elements beyond the scope

---

[198] *Occidental Petroleum, supra* note 138, at para. 183, 186.

[199] *Neer Claim (L.F.H. Neer and Pauline Neer (U.S.A.) v. Mexico) (U.S. v. Mexico)*, U.S.–Mexico General Claims Commission, Decision of Oct. 15, 1926, 4 R.I.A.A. 60, 61–62 (1926), available at http://law.dal.ca/kindred.intllaw/NEER.htm.

For a detailed analysis of the "additive" law debate in connection with the fair and equitable standard, *see* Schreuer, *supra* note 167, at 361–64. *See also CMS, supra* note 141, at paras. 282–84.

[200] *Neer, supra* note 201, at 61–62.

[201] *See* Christopher Dugan et al., Investor–State Arbitration 491 (2012).

[202] *Mondev, supra* note 196, at paras. 116 and 123.

of customary international law. One of these elements is the investor's legitimate expectations, which is at the core of the fairness requirement.[203] The tribunal in *Parkerings v. Lithuania* determined that

> [t]he expectation is legitimate if the investor received an explicit promise or guarantee from the host State, or if implicitly, the host State made assurances or representation, that the investor took into account in making the investment. Finally, in the situation where the host State made no assurances or representation, the circumstances surrounding the conclusion of the agreement are decisive to determine if the expectation of the investor was legitimate. In order to determine the legitimate expectation of an investor, it is also necessary to analyze the conduct of the State at the time of the investment.[204]

3. Full protection and security

a. The standard

The host State's obligation to protect and secure qualifying foreign investments **6.87**
is codified in nearly all investment treaties.[205] Commentators have suggested that the full protection and security standard should be interpreted as a complement to fair and equitable treatment.[206] According to a number of tribunal decisions and commentators, while the fairness obligation protects investors from the State's affirmative conduct, the undertaking to protect enjoins the State from *failing to act* as reasonably necessary to safeguard covered investments from private actors (such as demonstrators, employees, business partners, competitors) or from elements of the host State itself, such as the military, police, *etc.*[207]

---

[203] Papanastasiou, *supra* note 90, at 99–100.

[204] *Parkerings-Compagniet A.S. v. Lithuania*, ICSID Case No. ARB/05/8, Award of Sept. 11, 2007, para. 331, available at https://www.italaw.com/sites/default/files/case-documents/ita0619.pdf.

[205] For an analysis of jurisprudential developments on the protection and security standard, *see* Staminir Alexandrov, *The Evolution of the Full Protection and Security Standard*, in Building International Investment Law: The First 50 Years of ICSID (Meg Kinnear et al. eds. 2016); Paul Friedland, *AAPL v. Sri Lanka: Rethinking Protection and Security for 21st Century Claims (Arbitration Academy 2016, The Berthold Goldman Lecture)*, 3 Les Cahiers de l'Arbitrage/Paris J. Int'l Arb. 605–29 (2016); Christoph Schreuer, *Full Protection and Security*, 1(2) J. Int'l Dispute Settlement 353–69 (2010); G. Cordero Moss, *Full Protection and Security*, in Standards of Investment Protection 133–36 (August Reinisch ed. 2008); For an analysis of the FPS standard and its connection to several types of political risk (*e.g.* civil disturbance, disorder, and physical violence), *see* Papanastasiou, *supra* note 90, at 103–08.

[206] Thomas, *supra* note 167, at 22–39. *See also Asian Agricultural Products Ltd. (AAPL) v. Sri Lanka*, ICSID Case No. ARB/87/3, Award of June 21, 1990, Separate Opinion of Samuel Asante, 30 I.L.M. 577, 639 (1991).

[207] ILC, Commentaries to the ILC Draft Articles on Responsibility of States for Internationally Wrongful Acts, 70 (2001), available at http://legal.un.org/ilc/texts/instruments/english/commentaries/9_6_2001.pdf ("conduct attributable to the State can consist of actions or omissions. Cases in which the international responsibility of a State has been invoked on the basis of an omission are at least as numerous as those based on positive acts, and no difference in principle exists between the two").

6.88 "Full protection and security" has appeared in treaties concerning the treatment of aliens and their property for over a century, and today is a very common standard in modern BITs and multilateral treaties. Treaties of Friendship, Commerce and Navigation (FCN Treaties), developed by capital-exporting countries in the nineteenth century, envisaged the protection by host States of alien individuals and their property. This provision, initially far less common in treaty texts than language governing tariffs and other trade barriers, grew in currency in the inter-war period.[208] By the mid-twentieth century, FCN treaties almost invariably contained a protection and security clause.[209] In this regard, both conventional and customary law before the last quarter of the twentieth century were focused on *physical* security of foreigners and access to justice.[210] This emphasis arose out of the fear of xenophobic violence and the inadequacy of local police forces in some capital-importing countries, including the defeated powers after World War I. After World War II, the number of the FCN treaties increased. Most frequently, the post-war treaties provided for "full protection and security" and the submission of disputes over the implementation of treaty obligations to State-to-State resolution at the International Court of Justice. The OECD's 1967 Draft Convention on the Protection of Foreign Property, the first major (but failed) attempt to create a multilateral instrument on the topic, continued the line of protection provisions from FCN treaties, guaranteeing "the most constant protection and security" to alien-owned property.[211] On that basis, investment treaty tribunals have most frequently applied the standard in the context of threats or damage to people and facilities connected with protected investments,[212] often as a result of civil strife.[213]

6.89 Several more recent cases have raised the question whether full protection and security covers not only to cases of *physical* attacks, but also threats to the *legal* security of foreign investors and investments. Only a few treaties contain specific language providing for "full legal protection and security."[214] Faced with wording

---

[208] *See e.g.* Treaty of Friendship, Commerce and Navigation Between Argentina and the United States of July 27, 1853, art. 8, available at http://avalon.law.yale.edu/19th_century/argen02.asp.

[209] United States–Germany FCN Treaty (1923) (according to foreign nationals "the most constant protection for their persons and property"); Thomas, *supra* note 167, at 39.

[210] Robert R. Wilson, The International Law Standard in Treaties of the United States 103–04 (1953). *See also Saluka Investments, supra* note 134, paras. 483 and 484 ("The 'full protection and security' standard applies essentially when the foreign investment has been affected by civil strife and physical violence ... the 'full security and protection' clause is not meant to cover just any kind of impairment of an investor's investment, but to protect more specifically the physical integrity of an investment against interference by use of force"); *Rumeli v Kazakhstan*, Award of July 29, 2008, para. 668; *see further* art 8.10(5) of CETA ("For greater certainty, 'full protection and security' refers to the Party's obligations relating to the physical security of investors and covered investments").

[211] OECD, Draft Convention on the Protection of Foreign Property, OECD Publication No. 23081 (1967), reproduced in 7 I.L.M. 117 (1968), art. 1(a).

[212] *See e.g. PSEG Global, supra* note 97, at para. 258.

[213] *See e.g. Saluka Investments, supra* note 134, 2006, para. 483.

[214] *See e.g.* art. 3(1) of the Croatia–San Marino BIT.

like this in the Argentina–Germany BIT (which included the words "legal security"), the tribunal in *Siemens v. Argentina* held:

> In the instant case, "security" is qualified by "legal". In its ordinary meaning "legal security" has been defined as "the quality of the legal system which implies certainty in its norms and, consequently, their foreseeable application." It is clear that in the context of this meaning the Treaty refers to security that it is not physical. In fact, one may question given the qualification of the term "security", whether the Treaty covers physical security at all. Arguably it could be considered to be included under "full protection", but that is not an issue in these proceedings.[215]

Where the BIT lacks clear reference to legal protection, the outcome is less certain. Some tribunals have rejected the proposition that full protection and security extends to situations of legal insecurity or, noting the traditional context of the obligation—to protect the investor from third parties, such as "mobs, insurgents, rented thugs and others engaged in physical violence against the investor in violation of the state monopoly of physical force."[216] Other tribunals have extended the scope of required protection to circumstances beyond physical safety, such as access to justice,[217] due process,[218] legal protection in civil disputes,[219] and proper sanction of wrongdoers.[220] In *CME v. Czech Republic*, the majority found that under the full protection and security standard: **6.90**

> The host State is obligated to ensure that neither by amendment of its laws nor by actions of its administrative bodies is the agreed and approved security and protection of the foreign investor's investment withdrawn or devalued.[221]

This interpretation was met with opposition in a dissenting opinion.[222] **6.91**

b. Applicable provisions

As previously noted, practically all modern investment treaties require the protection of investments.[223] BITs vary in the precise formulation of the standard. Some **6.92**

215 *See Siemens, supra* note 132, Award of Jan. 17, 2007, para. 303.

216 *See Eureko B.V. v. Poland*, Partial Award of Aug. 19, 2005, paras. 240, 248, 250–53; *Eastern Sugar B.V. (Netherlands) v. Czech Republic*, SCC Case No. 088/2004, Award of Mar. 27, 2007, para. 203; *B.G. Group Plc. v. Argentina* (UNCITRAL), Final Award of Dec. 24, 2007, para. 324.

217 *See Tecmed, supra* note 148, at para. 177; *Ronald S. Lauder, supra* note 97, at para. 314.

218 *See Saluka Investments, supra* note 134, paras 496, 493.

219 *See Ceskoslovenska Obchodni Banka, A.S. v. Slovakia*, ICSID Case No. ARB/97/4, Award of Dec. 29, 2004, para. 170.

220 *See Wena Hotels Ltd. v. Egypt*, ICSID Case No. ARB/98/4, Award of Dec. 8, 2000, paras. 82, 84, 94–95.

221 *See CME, supra* note 143, para. 613.

222 *See id.*, Dissenting Opinion of the Arbitrator Jaroslav Hándl against the Partial Arbitration Award of Sept. 13, 2001, at pp. 16–17.

223 In some BITs, the fair and equitable treatment standard is not accompanied by a protection provision, but none of the prominent national models adopts this approach; nor do the most important multilateral treaties, such as NAFTA and the ECT. *But see* India–Singapore Comprehensive Economic Cooperation Agreement, *supra* note 108 (no guarantee of full protection and security of investments).

provide for "full" protection,[224] others "most constant" protection and security.[225] It is generally accepted, however, that such variations make no significant difference in the level of protection that the host State must provide to qualifying foreign investors and their property.[226]

6.93 A minority of treaties links protection with customary international law.[227] Such a combination is somewhat less common than in the case of fair and equitable treatment.[228] The effect of requiring full protection and security "in accordance with international law" is unclear. Views vary as to whether full protection and security reflects a general rule of customary international law, or represents a specific standard of treatment available only through treaty stipulation.[229] In its 2001 interpretive note, the NAFTA Free Trade Commission interpreted article 1105(1) of the NAFTA to the effect that the obligation to provide full security and protection in the NAFTA imposes no obligation beyond treatment required by the customary international law minimum standard of treatment of aliens.[230] NAFTA tribunals have subsequently adopted this interpretation.[231]

6.94 By contrast, in *Azurix v. Argentina*, the tribunal held that under article II.2(a) of the Argentina–U.S. BIT, which provided that investors "shall in no case be accorded treatment less than that required by international law," international law sets "a floor, not a ceiling, in order to avoid a possible interpretation of these standards below what is required by international law."[232] The tribunal added that

---

[224] NAFTA, *supra* note 21, art. 1105(1); U.S–Trinidad & Tobago BIT (1994), art. II(3)(a); U.S.–Argentina BIT (1991), art. II(2)(a).

[225] *See* Wilson, *supra* note 212, at 92–93.

[226] *AAPL, supra* note 208, at para. 50. Christoph Schreuer, *Full Protection and Security*, 1(2) J. Int'l Dispute Settlement 353 (2010); August Reinisch, Standards of Investment Protection 135 (2008), ("[i]t may thus be concluded that arbitral practice does not deem the wording of the treaty as decisive for the scope of application of the standard of full protection and security—not even when the analysis of the question starts from the formulation of the treaty"). In one potentially significant textual variation, the protection obligation appears to extend only to ensuring the normal functioning of the legal system. *See e.g.* Argentina–Cuba BIT, art. 3(1) ("Each Contracting Party shall at all times ensure fair and equitable treatment to the investments and investors of the other Contracting Party, and shall accord them full *legal* protection, and shall not interfere in their management, maintenance, use, sale, or disposition by unjustified or discriminatory means" (emphasis added)); *see also* Colonia Protocol, *supra* note 61, art. 3(2); Ecuador–El Salvador BIT (1994), art. IV(2) (providing for "legal" protection).

[227] *See* NAFTA, *supra* note 21, art. 1105(1); U.S.–Albania BIT (1995), art. II(3)(a).

[228] Scott K. Gudgeon, *United States Bilateral Investment Treaties: Comments on their Origin, Purposes and General Treatment Standards*, 4 Int'l Tax & Bus. Law. 105, 124 (1986). *See e.g.* Canada–Armenia BIT (1997), art. 2(2) (providing for "fair and equitable treatment in accordance with principles of international law," as well as "full protection and security" without any reference to international law).

[229] *See* Reinisch, *supra* note 228, at 136.

[230] NAFTA Free Trade Commission on July 31, 2001.

[231] *See e.g. Mondev, supra* note 196, paras. 121–25.

[232] *See Azurix, supra* note 166, para. 361.

the relationship between customary law and the full protection and security standard was immaterial, because:

> [T]he minimum requirement to satisfy this standard has evolved and the Tribunal considers that its content is substantially similar whether the terms are interpreted in their ordinary meaning, as required by the Vienna Convention, or in accordance with customary international law.[233]

Other tribunals have taken an intermediate approach, whereby a treaty provision requiring full protection and security should be interpreted in a manner consistent with the customary standard,[234] although the terms "full protection" may entail a more onerous responsibility than customary law.[235] **6.95**

In certain treaties, some States have explicitly restricted the scope of required protection to circumstances related to physical security.[236] Trade agreements signed by the United States, for example, the U.S.–Chile Free Trade Agreement, the U.S.–Singapore Free Trade Agreement, and the Dominican Republic–Central American Free Trade Agreement, refer specifically to customary international law as the relevant liability threshold. Thus, the U.S.–Chile Free Trade Agreement establishes that: **6.96**

> The obligation … to provide "full protection and security" requires each Party to provide the level of *police protection* required under customary international law.[237]

Many recent U.S. treaties include an additional explanatory note that further clarifies the intent of the parties to adopt a limited guarantee of security: **6.97**

> For greater certainty, [the provision on full protection and security and fair and equitable treatment] prescribes the customary international law minimum standard of treatment of aliens as the minimum standard of treatment to be afforded to covered investments. The concepts of "fair and equitable treatment" and "full protection and security" do not require treatment in addition to or beyond that which is required by that standard, and do not create additional substantive rights.[238]

---

[233] *Id.*

[234] *See American Manufacturing & Trading Inc. (AMT) v. Zaire*, ICSID Case No. ARB/93/1, Award of Feb. 21, 1997, paras. 6.06 and 6.07. *See also The Channel Tunnel Group Ltd., France-Manche S.A. v. U.K. and France (Eurotunnel)*, Partial Award of Jan. 30, 2007, para. 275 (noting that the application of the standard under general international law would not add much to the protection accorded by the applicable treaty).

[235] *AAPL, supra* note 208, paras. 67–69.

[236] *See* Helge Elisabeth Zeitler, *The Guarantee of "Full Protection and Security" in Investment Treaties Regarding Harm Caused by Private Actors*, 1 Stockholm Int'l Arb. Rev. (2005).

[237] U.S.–Chile Free Trade Agreement, art. 10(4)(2)(b) (emphasis added); U.S.–Singapore Free Trade Agreement, art. 15(5)(2)(b).

[238] *See* U.S. Free Trade Agreements (FTAs) with Morocco (2004), art. 10(5), and Australia (2005), art. 11(5); *see also* U.S. Model BIT, *supra* note 102, at art. 5(2)(b). *See generally* Noah Rubins, *The Arbitral Innovations of Recent U.S. Free Trade Agreements: Two Steps Forward, One Step Back*, 8 Int'l Bus. L.J. 865, 876–80 (2003); David Gantz, *The Evolution of FTA Investment Provisions: From NAFTA to the United States—Chile Free Trade Agreement*, 19 Am. U. Int'l L. Rev. 679 (2004).

6.98 As a result of this treaty language, the diversity of treaty texts in the area of protection has increased significantly. Future arbitral decisions may therefore depend as much on the precise wording of the clause as on the factual circumstances. But the recent trend towards referring to customary international law in relation to these clauses does not appear to be stifling the application of the "full protection and security" guarantee.[239]

c. Application

6.99 The tribunal in *Asian Agricultural Products Ltd. (AAPL) v. Sri Lanka* was the first to apply the full protection and security clause of an investment treaty.[240] In that case, a U.K. company that operated a shrimp farm in Sri Lanka sought compensation after its facility had been destroyed by Sri Lankan security forces during an operation against Tamil rebels. The claimant argued that "full protection and security" should be interpreted as imposing strict liability upon the host State, such that any harm that befalls an investor or his property is the responsibility of the State. The respondent contended that only basic "due diligence" was required of the State, and since the claimant had been injured as a result of a rebellion outside the government's control, no liability could follow. The tribunal found that the BIT guarantee of "full protection" did not impose strict liability, but does impose upon the host State a "standard of due diligence" with regard to qualifying foreign investors and their assets.[241] Sri Lanka had not taken reasonable steps to control its forces when responding to the insurgency, and the resulting lack of care resulted in damage to the foreign investor's property. The State was therefore liable to compensate.

---

239 Gudgeon, *supra* note 230. Article 1105(1) of NAFTA obliges the parties to provide investors and investments "full security and protection" in accordance with international law. NAFTA, *supra* note 21, art. 1105(1). The meaning of this provision was debated in *Pope & Talbot, supra* note 186. The tribunal there held that the obligation was not necessarily restricted to the international law minimum standard of treatment. In *ADF Group Inc. v. U.S.A.*, ICSID Case No. ARB(AF)/00/1, Award of Jan. 9, 2003, the tribunal concluded that reference to international law did not limit "full protection and security" to mere police protection, since "both customary international law and the minimum standard of treatment of aliens it incorporates are constantly in a process of development." *Id.* at para. 179. *See also Methanex, supra* note 27, at Part IV, chs. C–E.

240 *AAPL, supra* note 208. *See also* Stephen Vasciannie, *Bilateral Investment Treaties and Civil-Strife: The AAPL–Sri Lanka Arbitration*, 39 Netherlands Int'l L. Rev. 332–54 (1992); John Boloro, *Aspects of the Law on the Responsibility of a Host State for Injuries Caused to Foreign Investment During Internal Armed Conflcits: The ICSID Award in Asian Agricultural Products Limited (AAPL) v. Republic of Sri Lanka*, 18 S. African Yb. Int'l L. 105–26 (1992).

241 *AAPL, supra* note 208, at para. 85(B). *See also Janes Case*, 4 R.I.A.A. 82, 86 (1925); *Sambiaggio*, 10 R.I.A.A. 499, 524 (1904); M. Bedjaoui, *Responsibility of States: Fault and Strict Liability*, 10 Encyclopaedia of Public International Law 359 (1987); Ian Brownlie, System of the Law of the Nations 452 (1986) (stating that "substantial negligence" in taking reasonable precautionary and preventive action would entail liability. *But cf.* C.F. Amerasinghe, State Responsibility for Injuries to Aliens 281–82 (1967) ("mere lack or want of diligence" suffices to establish State liability, and there is no need to prove malice or negligence); in the context of protection of the individual, *see Velasquez-Rodriguez Case*, Inter-Am. C.H.R. (ser. C) No. 4 (1988), para. 79.

In *AMT v. Zaire*, the tribunal again considered the content of a BIT's "full protection and security" guarantee in the context of a rebel insurgency.[242] Damage to the claimant's property was caused by off-duty Zairian soldiers on a looting spree. Zaire argued that it could not be held responsible under the applicable U.S.–Zaire treaty for the actions of individuals who were not under its control. The tribunal disagreed, and finding that the State was obligated to protect the investor from the acts of third parties: 6.100

> [t]he obligation incumbent on Zaire is an obligation of vigilance, in the sense that Zaire as the receiving State of investments made by AMT, an American company, shall take all measures necessary to ensure the full enjoyment of protection and security of its investment and should not be permitted to invoke its own legislation to detract from any such obligation. Zaire must show that it has taken all measure [sic] of precaution to protect the investments of AMT on its territory.[243]

At the same time, the *AMT* tribunal was mindful to reaffirm the *AAPL* conclusion that States are not subject to strict liability. Rather, the tribunal noted, the applicable level of protection is one of "due diligence," which prohibits unreasonable "inaction" or "omission" that allows injury or property destruction to occur.[244] 6.101

The tribunal in *CME v. Czech Republic* adopted the same position, and further articulated the level of due diligence required of the host State. In that case, the actions and omissions of a quasi-governmental media regulatory body, along with the machinations of a local businessman, resulted in the exclusion of a Dutch company from a television broadcasting joint venture. The foreign company initiated arbitration in Stockholm pursuant to the Netherlands–Czech Republic BIT, alleging that the Czech Republic had violated the treaty, in part by failing to protect the investment from the local businessman's scheme. The arbitrators held that the Czech Republic had breached its obligation to ensure protection and security: 6.102

> The host State is obligated to ensure that neither by amendment of its laws nor by actions of its administrative bodies is the agreed and approved security and protection of the foreign investor's investment withdrawn or devalued.[245]

The same set of facts, however, led a separate tribunal to a contrary conclusion. In *Lauder v. Czech Republic*, CME's main shareholder invoked the U.S.–Czech Republic BIT to advance an identical claim in *ad hoc* arbitration. The *Lauder* tribunal rejected the claim, finding no causal relationship between the harm suffered and the Czech Republic's actions.[246] 6.103

[242] *AMT, supra* note 236. *See also* Charles Chatterjee, *The Arbitration between American Manufacturing & Trading Inc. and the Republic of Zaire: When Challenges to Jurisdiction of an ICSID Tribunal Are Not Valid*, 16 J. Int'l Arb. 37 (1999).

[243] *AMT, supra* note 236, at para. 6.05.

[244] *AAPL, supra* note 208, at para. 85(B).

[245] *CME, supra* note 143, at para. 613.

[246] *Ronald S. Lauder, supra* note 97, at para. 274, available at https://www.italaw.com/cases/documents/611. For a variety of perspectives on the conflicting results in the *CME* and *Lauder*

6.104 In *Tecmed v. Mexico*,[247] the claimant had invested in a waste disposal facility in Mexico. The Mexican government refused to renew a necessary license, in part due to public protests in the local community. Ultimately, the facility had to be shut down. The claimant contended that Mexico had breached the "full protection and security" provision (among others) of the Spain–Mexico BIT, alleging that Mexican municipal and State authorities had encouraged the local community's opposition to the landfill. Tecmed also insisted that Mexican authorities, including the police and courts, "did not act as quickly, efficiently and thoroughly as they should have to avoid, prevent or put an end to the adverse social demonstrations expressed through disturbances in the operation of the Landfill or access thereto, or the personal security or freedom to move about of the members of [the investor's] staff related to the Landfill."[248] According to the *Tecmed* arbitrators, there was no causal link between the public protests and the Mexican government's inaction. As a result, they declined to find a breach of the full protection and security obligation, echoing the *Lauder* tribunal's reasoning:

> The Arbitral Tribunal agrees with the Respondent, and with the case law quoted by it, in that the guarantee of full protection and security is not absolute and does not impose strict liability upon the State that grants it.[249]

6.105 Thus, the triggering point of host State liability for failure to protect remains somewhat difficult to pinpoint. However, the arbitral decisions described, viewed in conjunction with the particular investment protection text and relevant commentary, suggest patterns of conduct that are more or less likely to violate the State's duty to protect and secure investments.

6.106 It seems relatively clear that States are obliged under the full security provision of investment treaties to ensure police protection sufficient to allow the foreign investor to go about his business. As noted, both the *AAPL* and *AMT* tribunals suggested that the protection and security obligation imposes a duty of reasonable diligence. But does this duty extend beyond the area of police protection to oblige the State to prevent the illegal or unfair actions of private commercial parties in the marketplace?[250] Or obstruction by disgruntled employees or neighbors? The

awards, *see* the commentary of Hans Bagner, *Jeremy Carver, Bohuslav Klein & Wolfgang Kühn, How to Avoid Conflicting Awards: The Lauder and CME Cases*, 5 J. World Inv. & Trade 7–35 (2004).

[247] *TECMED, supra* note 148.

[248] *Id.* at para. 175.

[249] *Id.* at para. 177. *See also Case Concerning Elettronica Sicula S.p.A. (ELSI) (U.S.–Italy)*, Judgment of July 20, 1989, 1989 I.C.J. Rep. 15, at para. 108 ("the provision of constant protection and security cannot be construed as the giving of a warranty that property shall never in any circumstances be occupied or disturbed").

[250] *See e.g. Ceskoslovenska Obchodni Banka, supra* note 221, para. 170. The World Bank takes an expansive view on this point, suggesting that investment treaties should be applied such that "full protection and security will be accorded to the investor's rights regarding ownership, control and substantial benefits over his property, including intellectual property." World Bank, Guidelines on the Treatment of Foreign Direct Investment (1992), 31 I.L.M. 1379 (1992), art. III(3)(a), available at https://www.italaw.com/documents/WorldBank.pdf [hereinafter, the Guidelines].

CME decision suggests so, but that tribunal's reasoning is directly contradicted by the *Lauder* panel, which found that the State bore no responsibility for the acts of private parties, regardless of whether it *could* have stepped in to help the foreign investor. The more restrictive approach of *Lauder* would appear to be more in line with customary international law, which normally imposes State liability for third-party action only if the State "acknowledges and adopts the conduct in question as its own."[251]

Since *Lauder* and *CME*, some tribunals have followed the *CME* approach (with significant clarifications), as in *Azurix*,[252] and others have adopted the *Lauder* approach, as in *Saluka*.[253] Arbitrators generally do appear to consider the standard to be a broad guarantee against negligent State omissions.[254] But because the standard is one of negligence rather than strict liability, whether there is a breach depends on the tribunal's view as to the State's conduct was reasonable in light of all the circumstances.[255] This objective approach is reflected in the 1961 Harvard Draft Convention on the International Responsibility of States for Injuries to Aliens: **6.107**

> What degree of protection is required varies with the circumstances ... Among the factors to be taken into account in determining whether the duty of due diligence has been discharged is that of the *foreseeability* of the risk ... The means which a State has available to protect an alien must also be taken into account ... [I]nquiry must also be made into the question whether effective use was made of all available measures ...[256]

[251] ILC Draft Articles on State Responsibility, *supra* note 93, at art. 11 ("Conduct which is not attributable to a State under the preceding articles shall nevertheless be considered an act of that State under international law if and to the extent that the State acknowledges and adopts the conduct in question as its own"); *Case Concerning United States Diplomatic and Consular Staff in Tehran*, Judgment of May 24, 1980, 1980 I.C.J. Rep. 3.

[252] *See e.g. Azurix, supra* note 166. The *Azurix* tribunal concluded that the protection standard covers legal security, unless the word "full" is absent. In such case, then protection is limited to physical integrity. However, the *Azurix* reasoning was rejected by the tribunal in *Parkerings v. Lithuania*, which found that variations in the wording of security clauses (such as "full protection" or "just protection") have no effect on the requisite level of protection. *Parkerings-Compagniet, supra* note 206, Award of Sept. 11, 2007. *See also* Papanastasiou, *supra* note 90, at 107.

[253] *Saluka Investments, supra* note 134, at para. 291.

[254] *See* Coe & Rubins, *supra* note 90, at 613–19. *See also Wena Hotels, supra* note 222, at paras. 88–94 (on omissions as a basis for State liability); *Antoine Goetz, supra* note 136 (government's withdrawal of authorization held to violate full protection and security obligation).

[255] *See Tecmed, supra* note 148, at para. 177; *Tellini Case* (League of Nations, 1924), *cited in* Kalliopi K. Koufa, Specific Human Rights Issues: New Priorities, U.N. Doc. E/CN.4/Sub.2/2004/40 (2004) (a State is responsible for political crimes committed in their territory only if "the State has neglected to take all reasonable measures for the prevention of the crime and the pursuit, arrest and bringing to justice of the criminal"); *Home Insurance Co. Case* (1927), cited in 3 Green H. Hackworth, Digest of International Law 630 (1942); *Too v. Greater Modesto Insurance Associates and the U.S.A.*, 23 Iran–U.S. C.T.R. 378 (1991), at para. 22; Restatement (Third) of Foreign Relations Law of the United States, § 711, lit. e. (1987); Tom Hickman, *The Reasonableness Principle: Reassessing Its Place in the Public Atmosphere*, 63 Cambr. L.J. 166 (2004).

[256] Explanatory Note to art. 13(1) of the 1961 Harvard Draft Convention on the International Responsibility of States for Injuries to Aliens, *cited in* 8 Marjorie M. Whiteman, Digest of

4. Prohibition against discrimination

a. The standard

6.108 The principle of non-discrimination is at the core of investment protection, and can be found in nearly all modern investment treaties.[257] The prohibition of discriminatory treatment is embodied in three different provisions. The "national treatment" clause obligates host States to offer qualifying foreign investors the same privileges as they provide to their own citizens or corporations. The "most-favored nation" clause ensures that nationals of signatory States will enjoy any advantages extended to nationals of third-party States.[258] Finally, a less common clause prohibits "arbitrary and discriminatory measures," suggesting that States may incur treaty liability as a result of disparate treatment of investors and investments accorded on a basis other than nationality.

6.109 The "national treatment" and MFN standards are closely related:

> MFN treatment is an effective legal basis for extending national treatment to third parties. If one host country grants another country national treatment, the host country must extend national treatment to all countries that have an MFN clause within it.[259]

6.110 These treaty provisions are understood to require "equal" treatment.[260] In the context of international trade, from whence the obligation emerged, "non-discrimination is often translated operationally in commercial treaties to mean effective equality

INTERNATIONAL LAW 739–40 (1967) (emphasis added). *See also* Commentaries, *supra* note 209, at 145 ("obligations of prevention are usually construed as best efforts obligations, requiring States to take all reasonable or necessary measures to prevent a given event from occurring").

[257] Todd J. Grierson-Weiler & Ian A. Laird, *Standards of Treatment*, in THE OXFORD HANDBOOK OF INTERNATIONAL INVESTMENT LAW 261–304 (Peter Muchlinski et al. eds. 2008); *see also* Todd Weiler, *Saving Oscar Chin [sic]: Non-Discrimination in International Investment Law*, in INTERNATIONAL LAW, INVESTMENT LAW AND ARBITRATION 557, 558 (Todd Weiler ed. 2005). On non-discrimination in investment treaties generally, *see* Todd Weiler, *Prohibitions against Discrimination in NAFTA Chapter 11*, in NAFTA INVESTMENT LAW AND ARBITRATION 27 (Todd Weiler ed. 2004); A.F.M. Maniruzzaman, *Expropriation of Alien Property and the Principle of Non-Discrimination in International Law of Foreign Investment: An Overview*, 8(2) J. TRANSNAT'L L. & POL'Y. 57, 58 (1998). As noted elsewhere in this book (see Chapter 5, Section B), anti-discrimination treaty provisions are ubiquitous in part because customary international law does not require national treatment of aliens. Gudgeon, *supra* note 230, at 117.

[258] An MFN clause was employed in the 1778 Treaty of Amity and Commerce between the United States and France, available at http://avalon.law.yale.edu/18th_century/fr1788-1.asp. *See also* U.S.–Argentina FCN Treaty, *supra* note 210, art. IV; Kenneth Vandevelde, *The Bilateral Treaty Program of the United States*, 21 CORNELL INT'L L.J. 21, 201 (1988). Nearly all investment treaties contain MFN provisions, but *see* India–Singapore Free Trade Agreement (2005) (no MFN clause in investment protection chapter).

[259] Jian Zhou, *National Treatment in Foreign Investment Law: A Comparative Study from a Chinese Perspective*, 10 TOURO INT'L L. REV. 39, 90 (2000).

[260] On the relationship between MFN and national treatment standards, *see Parkerings-Compagniet, supra* note 206, paras. 366–71.

of opportunity to compete on equivalent terms and conditions."[261] Essential to the determination of discriminatory State action is that there be disparate treatment, that treatment of the protected investor be inferior, and that the favored and protected investors be comparable, *i.e.* in similar circumstances.[262] It is generally accepted that State measures may violate non-discrimination provisions whether intentional or well-meaning, so long as the effect is discriminatory.[263]

b. Applicable provisions

The first BIT, between Germany and Pakistan, incorporated the non-discrimination principle in particularly broad and explicit terms: **6.111**

> Capital investments by nationals or companies of either Party in the territory of the other Party shall not be subjected to any discriminatory treatment on the ground that ownership of or influence upon it is vested in nationals or companies of the former Party, unless legislation and rules and regulations framed thereunder existing at the time of coming into force of this Treaty provide otherwise.
>
> . . .
>
> Neither Party shall subject to discriminatory treatment any activities carried on in connection with investments including the effective management, use or enjoyment of such investments by the nationals or companies of either Party in the territory of the other Party unless specific stipulations are made in the documents of admission of an investment.[264]

Subsequent investment treaties have tended more clearly to separate the three types of non-discrimination previously described.

i. National treatment While nearly every investment protection instrument includes a national treatment clause, a few BITs do lack such a provision.[265] Modern investment treaties most frequently define national treatment as that **6.112**

[261] Non-Discrimination, Most-Favored-Nation Treatment and National Treatment, World Trade Organization Secretariat, Doc. WT/CTE/EDB/1 (2002). *See also Advisory Opinion on Minority Schools in Albania*, P.C.I.J. Ser. A/B, No. 64 (1935), at 19 ("Equality in law precludes discrimination of any kind; whereas equality in fact may involve the necessity of different treatment in order to obtain a result which establishes an equilibrium between different situations").

[262] This "like circumstances" requirement was at the core of the P.C.I.J.'s dismissal of a discrimination claim in *The Oscar Chinn Case (U.K. v. Belgium)*, P.C.I.J. Ser. A/B, No. 63 (1934) ("The inequality of treatment could only have amounted to a discrimination forbidden by the Convention if it had applied to concerns in the same position as [the favored entity], and this was not the case"). *See also* Hirsch Lauterpacht, The Development of International Law by the International Court 265 (1982).

[263] *Feldman, supra* note 137, at paras. 183–84 ("If [national treatment] violations are limited to those where there is explicit (presumably de jure) discrimination against foreigners, e.g., through a law that treats foreign investors and domestic investors differently, it would greatly limit the effectiveness of the national treatment concept in protecting foreign investors"); *Pope & Talbot, supra* note 186, at paras. 78–79; Vandevelde, *supra* note 10, at 77. *See also* Burns H. Weston, *The Charter of Economic Rights and Duties of States and the Deprivation of Foreign-owned Wealth*, 75 AJIL 437, 445 (1981).

[264] Germany–Pakistan BIT (1959), arts. 1–2.

[265] *See e.g.* Sweden–China BIT (1982), art. 2; Norway–China BIT (1984), art. 4(3).

which is "no less favorable than" treatment afforded to local businesses.[266] Only a few instruments provide illustrations of the sort of measures that would run afoul of the national treatment obligation.[267]

6.113 Investment treaties vary as to whether they require national treatment to qualifying foreign investments only after an investment is established in the host State, or in the pre-establishment phase as well. The majority of BITs extend such protection only to established investments. The ECT, for example, obliges each member State to provide national treatment to "investments in its Area," and primarily in the domains of "management, maintenance, use, enjoyment or disposal" of such investments.[268] Other treaties, particularly most of those concluded by the United States and Canada, ensure equal market access as well.[269] NAFTA, for example, grants national treatment to investors and investments with respect to "*the establishment, acquisition*, expansion, management, conduct, operation, and sale or other disposition of investments."[270]

6.114 A number of investment protection instruments provide expressly that national treatment need only be ensured with respect to investors or investments that are in "like" or "similar" circumstances.[271] As noted, some tribunals have considered "like circumstances" as part of the national treatment obligation even where not expressly included in the applicable treaty text.[272]

6.115 Many national treatment provisions in investment treaties are subject to specific limitations and exceptions. Such exclusions may relate to particular economic

---

266 UNCTAD, *supra* note 99, at 174–75.

267 *See e.g.* Protocol to Germany–Pakistan BIT (1959) (discriminatory treatment includes "[r]estricting the purchase of raw or auxiliary materials, of power or fuel, or of means of production or operation of any kind, impeding the marketing of products within or outside the country, as well as any other measures not applied to the same extent ... to persons residing within the country ... or to investments of such persons").

268 *See e.g.* ECT, *supra* note 31, art. 10(7). *See also* Jamaica–U.K. BIT (1987), art. 3.

269 *See e.g.* U.S. Model BIT, *supra* note 102, art. 3 ("1. Each Party shall accord to investors of the other Party treatment no less favorable than that it accords, in like circumstances, to its own investors with respect to the establishment, acquisition, expansion, management, conduct, operation, and sale or other disposition of investments in its territory. [] 2. Each Party shall accord to covered investments treatment no less favorable than that it accords, in like circumstances, to investments in its territory of its own investors with respect to the establishment, acquisition, expansion, management, conduct, operation, and sale or other disposition of investments").

270 NAFTA, *supra* note 21, art. 1102(1) (emphasis added).

271 *See e.g.* U.S. Model BIT, *supra* note 102, art. 3; NAFTA, *supra* note 21, art. 1102(1)–(2); Canada–Chile Free Trade Agreement (1997), art. G-02(1)–(2); U.K.–Belize BIT (1982), art. 3(1) ("Neither Contracting Party shall ... subject investments or returns of nationals or companies of the other Contracting Party to treatment less favorable than that which it accords in the same circumstances to investments or returns of its own nationals").

272 *ECE Projektmanagement Int'l GmbH and Kommanditgesellschaft PANTA Achtundsechzigste Grundstücksgesellschaft mbH & Co. v. Czech Republic*, PCA Case No. 2010-5, Award of Sept. 19, 2013, paras. 4.832–4.839 (examining whether the claimants' project and a competitor's project were sufficiently similar so as to require equal treatment although the applicable BIT did not mention that requirement).

sectors, subject matters, or more general exceptions. The exceptions to national treatment in the U.S.–Argentina BIT, for example, include:

> air transportation; ocean and coastal shipping; banking; insurance; energy and power production; custom house brokers; ownership and operation of broadcast or common carrier radio and television stations; ownership of real property; ownership of shares in the Communications Satellite Corporation; the provision of common carrier telephone and telegraph services; the provision of submarine cable services; use of land and natural resources.[273]

Other common exceptions relate to taxation, intellectual property rights, financial incentives, and public procurement.[274] Express general exceptions may include measures aimed at protecting public health, order and morals, and national security.[275] 6.116

Some of Japan's investment treaties permit member States to impose particular investment-related formalities on foreign investors without running afoul of national treatment.[276] For example, both the Japan–Indonesia EPA and the Japan–Malaysia EPA provide that: 6.117

> Notwithstanding paragraph 1, each Party may prescribe *special formalities* in connection with investment activities of investors of the other Party in its Area, provided that such formalities do not materially impair the protection afforded by the former Party to investors of the other Party and to their investments pursuant to this Chapter.[277]

ii. Most-favored nation treatment MFN clauses, like national treatment obligations, are relatively uniform, with variations similar to those already described with regard to national treatment. Indeed, MFN and national treatment are frequently included in a single treaty clause.[278] A typical "stand alone" MFN clause is found in the New Zealand–Singapore BIT: 6.118

> Except as otherwise provided for in this Agreement, each Party shall accord to investors and investments of the other Party, in relation to the establishment,

---

[273] Protocol to US–Argentina BIT (1991). Pursuant to NAFTA's Annex II, each contracting party is permitted to make reservations with respect to industries in restrictive measures are permissible. Existing exceptions include, *inter alia*, Mexico's primary energy sector and railroads, U.S. airlines and radio communications, and Canada's cultural industries.

[274] *See e.g.* South Korea–Mongolia BIT (1991), art. 7(b); U.S. Model BIT, *supra* note 102; U.K.–Jamaica BIT, art. 3; NAFTA, *supra* note 21, art. 1108(7)(a)–(b). *See also* Peter Muchlinski, Multinational Enterprises and the Law 241, 269 (1995).

[275] *See* Protocol to Germany–Pakistan BIT (1959) ("Measures taken for reasons of public security and order, public health or morality shall not be deemed as discrimination").

[276] Papanastasiou, *supra* note 90, at 91.

[277] Agreement between Japan and the Republic of Indonesia for an Economic Partnership (2008), art. 59(2) (emphasis added), available at https://www.mofa.go.jp/region/asia-paci/indonesia/epa0708/agreement.pdf; *see also* the Agreement between Japan and the Government of Malaysia for an Economic Partnership (2006), art. 75(3), available at https://www.mofa.go.jp/region/asia-paci/malaysia/epa/content.pdf.

[278] For an analysis of MFN clauses, *see* McLachlan et al., *supra* note 115, at 343.

acquisition, expansion, management, conduct, operation, liquidation, sale, transfer (or other disposition), protection and expropriation (including any compensation) of investments, treatment that is no less favorable than that it accords in like situations to investors and investments from any other State or separate customs territory which is not party to this Agreement.[279]

6.119 Variations in the stated scope of MFN clause application are significant, because investors can only acquire by way of an MFN provision rights "which fall within the subject-matter of the clause."[280] Many treaties (such as the New Zealand–Singapore BIT reproduced at para. 6.118) provide a list of investment activities for which MFN treatment is guaranteed.[281] Others simply declare broadly that MFN treatment is due with regard to "all matters covered" by the treaty.[282]

6.120 As with national treatment clauses, MFN provisions vary with respect to coverage of investments before they are admitted or established.[283]

6.121 Most investment treaties exclude some areas of activity from most-favored-nation treatment, for example measures necessary to maintain public order and national security. Exceptions may be based on reciprocity, such as matters relating to taxation, treatment accorded under regional integration treaties, and labor issues. Other exceptions may include government procurement, subsidy to a specific economic sector, intellectual property rights, and atomic energy.[284]

6.122 **iii. Arbitrary and discriminatory measures** Some investment treaties include a provision prohibiting arbitrary and discriminatory measures, in addition to the nearly ubiquitous national treatment and MFN clauses. Where they appear, such clauses are relatively uniform in wording, as in the U.S.–Argentina BIT:

> Neither Party shall in any way impair by arbitrary or discriminatory measures the management, operation, maintenance, use, enjoyment, acquisition, expansion, or disposal of investments.[285]

6.123 Investment treaties do not generally provide guidance as to what measures should be considered "arbitrary" or "discriminatory," although in light of the coverage already offered by the national treatment provision, prohibited discrimination

---

[279] New Zealand–Singapore BIT (2000), art. 28.

[280] International Law Commission, Draft Rules on Most-Favored-Nation Clauses (1978), art. 9, available at http://legal.un.org/ilc/texts/instruments/english/commentaries/1_3_1978.pdf.

[281] *See also* U.K.–Czech Republic BIT (1993), art. 3(2).

[282] *See e.g.* Belgium–Russian Federation BIT (1989) ("Each Contracting Party guarantees that the most favored nation clause shall be applied to investors of the other Contracting Party in all areas covered by the present Treaty"). Some U.K. investment treaties include an additional provision specifying that MFN treatment extends to all operative clauses in the treaty, referring to them by article number. *See e.g.* U.K.–Peru BIT (1994), art. 3(3).

[283] McLachlan et al., *supra* note 115, at 343–54; Pia Acconci, *Most-Favored Nation Treatment*, in The Oxford Handbook of International Investment Law 363–406 (Peter Muchlinski et al. eds. 2008); *see also* Papanastasiou, *supra* note 90, at 95–98.

[284] UNCTAD, *supra* note 99, at 197–200.

[285] U.S.–Argentina BIT (1991), art. II(2)(b).

could be on the basis of criteria other than nationality, such as race, ethnicity, sex, age, or perhaps sector of economic activity.

c. Application

i. National treatment In invoking the national treatment standard of investment protection instruments, very few investors have complained that host State regulations on their face targeted them on account of nationality. Most tribunals have instead been faced with situations of alleged *de facto* differential treatment. In *R.F.C.C. v. Morocco*, for example, the Italian claimant consortium had participated in a public tender to build highways in Morocco. Although its bid was the most competitive in price, Morocco's highway authority (ADM) awarded the tender to a local consortium. R.F.C.C. brought action under the Italy–Morocco BIT on grounds that this constituted a violation of national treatment. The tribunal first noted that the claimant did not need to demonstrate intent to discriminate: **6.124**

> Even if there has been no conduct that is discriminatory *per se*, there can nevertheless be a violation of the obligation to accord to foreign investors treatment no less favorable than that accorded to national investors. This could be the case if the difference in treatment between national and foreign investors is based upon criteria that are arbitrary or devoid of any objective foundation.[286]

Nevertheless, the arbitrators examined the basis for the highway authority's tender decision, and held that no violation had occurred in light of the circumstances: **6.125**

> [I]t has been established that ADM attributed decisive importance to the financial risk connected to the Consortium's offer, which was denominated partially in dirhams and partially in foreign currency. It is undeniable that such an offer implies for the employer an exchange risk that affects the price of the work. This is an objective difference between the Italian and Moroccan offers. One cannot blame ADM for basing its decision to award [the contract] to the Moroccan group on this difference ... Since the Moroccan and Italian offers were objectively different ... we do not see how the non-discrimination obligation contained in the BIT could have been violated.[287]

Also contentious in the area of national treatment has been determining when foreign and local investors are in "like circumstances,"[288] and therefore comparable for discrimination purposes.[289] In *Loewen v. United States*, the Canadian **6.126**

[286] *Consortium R.F.C.C. v. Morocco*, ICSID Case No. ARB/00/6, Award of Dec. 22, 2003, at para. 74.

[287] *Id.* at para. 75.

[288] *See*, in particular, Jürgen Kurtz, *The Use and Abuse of WTO Law in Investor—State Arbitration: Competition and Its Discontents*, 20 EJIL 749 (2010); Robert Howse & Efraim Chalamish, *The Use and Abuse of WTO Law in Investor—State Arbitration: A Reply to Jürgen Kurtz*, 20 EJIL 1087 (2010), debating the question of "likeness" and a "competitive relationship" in the framework of the WTO and investor–State arbitration.

[289] Professor Weiler explains that "once a *prima facie* breach of a non-discrimination provision has been established, the burden shifts to the respondent government to explain why the difference in treatment is justified." Weiler, *Saving Oscar Chin*, *supra* note 259, at 573; *Pope & Talbot*, *supra* note 139, at paras. 35–36.

claimant (LGI) argued, *inter alia*, that Mississippi courts had not provided "national treatment" as required by article 1102 of NAFTA. LGI insisted that the local plaintiff's use of anti-Canadian argumentation before the jury, and the jury members' expressed antipathy toward LGI as a foreign company, contributed to an arbitrary verdict against it.[290] The tribunal declined to find a breach of the national treatment standard. The arbitrators reasoned that such a holding would require LGI first to identify a local investor in "like circumstances" whose treatment by the government could be compared to that which LGI received.[291] The tribunal rejected O'Keefe, the plaintiff in the Mississippi trial, as a proper comparator. The fact that LGI and O'Keefe were litigants in the same case, the tribunal held, was insufficient to make up for the range of distinct circumstances that characterized the positions of the two parties.[292]

6.127 Other tribunals have taken a more liberal view. The arbitrators in *Occidental v. Ecuador* applied a broad conception of "like circumstances," comparing the U.S. claimant, an oil producer, to Ecuadorian export enterprises operating in sectors other than hydrocarbons.[293] In *Feldman v. Mexico*, the claimant was a U.S. distributor of cigarettes operating in Mexico. There, the tribunal had no difficulty in identifying the proper comparator for determining whether there was differential treatment violating NAFTA:

> In the Tribunal's view, the "universe" of firms in like circumstances are those foreign-owned and domestic-owned firms that are in the business of reselling/exporting cigarettes. Other Mexican firms that may also export cigarettes, such as Mexican cigarette producers, are not in like circumstances.[294]

6.128 The "like circumstances" analysis used in *S.D. Myers v. Canada* was slightly more complex. In that case, the claimant was a U.S.-owned company that sought to move chemical waste products out of Canada for processing in Michigan. The Canadian government put an end to this business plan by banning any export of the waste products in question. As in *Feldman*, the tribunal focused exclusively on the claimant's sector of activity, and found that Myers was in "like circumstances" with all of its Canadian competitors:

> The concept of "like circumstances" invites an examination of whether a non-national investor complaining of less favorable treatment is in the same "sector" [of business activity] as the national investor.[295]

[290] *The Loewen Group Inc. and Raymond L. Loewen v. U.S.A.*, ICSID Case No. ARB(AF)/98/3, Memorial of Loewen Group Inc. of Oct. 18, 1999, at para. 171.

[291] *Id.* at para. 140. Art. 1102(1) provides: "Each Party shall accord to investors of another Party treatment no less favorable than that it accords, in like circumstances, to its own investors with respect to the establishment, acquisition, expansion, management, conduct, operation, and sale or other disposition of investments."

[292] *Loewen, supra* note 292, at para. 140.

[293] *Occidental Petroleum, supra* note 138, at paras. 174–76.

[294] *Feldman, supra* note 137, at para. 171.

[295] *S.D. Myers, supra* note 156, at para. 251. *See also Methanex, supra* note 27, at Part IV, chs. C–E.

In *Apotex*, the tribunal identified specific elements that may play an important role in determining a suitable comparator for purposes of discrimination claims: 6.129

> The Parties also accept that it is appropriate in the identification of comparators which are in "like circumstances" to look at, inter alia, whether those which are said to be comparators: (i) are in the same economic of business sector; (ii) have invested in, or are businesses that compete with the investor or its investments in terms of goods or services; or (iii) are subject to a comparable legal regime or regulatory requirements, as the Claimants and their investments.[296]

ii. Most-favored nation treatment Arbitrators' primary consideration in applying MFN clauses is whether the subject matter of the third-party right in question falls within the scope of the particular MFN clause. In the words of the *Ambatielos* panel, "the most-favored-nation clause can only attract matters belonging to the same category of subject as that to which the clause itself relates."[297] This principle is known as *esjudem generis*.[298] Arbitration tribunals have historically tended to construe MFN clauses broadly, since "[l]iterally and historically, the m.f.n. standard means what it says: the treatment of a nation, that is the other contracting party, as the most favored nation, that is as the nation more favored than any other. In other words, it means preferential treatment."[299] For example, in the *Morocco Case*, the United States benefited from MFN clauses in a treaty of commerce. The International Court of Justice determined that these MFN clauses imported the provisions of a treaty exempting British citizens in Morocco from local law, and granting jurisdiction over them to the British government: "the United States acquired by virtue of the most-favored-nation clauses, civil and criminal consular jurisdiction in all cases in which United States nationals were defendants."[300] 6.130

In investment arbitration practice, this approach has led arbitrators routinely to accept the "importation" of substantive rights into an applicable investment treaty 6.131

[296] *Apotex Holdings Inc. and Apotex Inc. v. United States of America*, ICSID Case No. ARB/(AF)/12/1, Award of Aug. 25, 2014, para. 8.15, available at https://www.italaw.com/sites/default/files/case-documents/italaw3324.pdf; *see also* McLachlan et al., *supra* note 115, at 339.

[297] *Ambatielos Claim (Greece v. U.K.)*, 12 R.I.A.A. 91, 107 (1956).

[298] Lord McNair, The Law of Treaties 272–305 (1961). McNair illustrates the rule with the example of a State A, which benefits from MFN status under a commercial treaty with State B. Under the *ejusdem generis* rule, State A could not demand extradition of a criminal in State B under preferential extradition conditions State B grants State C. Likewise, in commenting on the Draft Articles on Most Favored Nation Clauses, the United Nations International Law Commission provides the example that "if the most-favoured nation clause promises most-favored nation treatment solely for fish, such treatment cannot be claimed under the same clause for meat." International Law Commission, *Report of the Int'l Law Comm'n. on the Work of Its Thirtieth Session*, U.N. Doc. No. A/CN.4/SER.A/1978/Add.1, Part 2, at 30 (1978).

[299] Georg Schwarzenberger, *Principles and Standards of International Economic Law*, 117 Recueil des Cours 1, 71 (1966).

[300] *Case Concerning Rights of Nationals of the United States of America in Morocco (France v. United States)*, 1952 I.C.J. Rep. 176, 190. But *cf. Ambatielos Claim, supra* note 299; *Anglo-Iranian Oil Co. Case (U.K. v. Iran)*, 1952 I.C.J. Rep. 116.

from treaties that the host State has ratified with other countries. In *MTD v. Chile*, for example, the Malaysian claimant sought to import a number of more favorable provisions into the Malaysia–Chile BIT from other Chilean treaties. These provisions included an "umbrella clause," which the applicable treaty lacked. Neither the tribunal nor the respondent in that case seemed troubled with such application of the MFN clause.[301]

6.132 With regard to more favorable *procedural* rights, the seminal decision came in *Maffezini v. Spain*.[302] There, investors were required under the Argentina–Spain BIT to pursue their claims in the courts of the host country for eighteen months before they would be allowed to initiate arbitration against the host State. The Chile–Spain BIT, meanwhile, imposed no such condition. It provided that the investor could opt for arbitration after the six-month negotiation period had expired. While Spain argued that only *substantive* protections could be "imported" by operation of the MFN clause, the tribunal disagreed, formulating a simple rule to determine the scope of an MFN clause: "If ... matters are more favorably treated in a third-party treaty then, by operation of the clause, that treatment is extended to the beneficiary under the basic treaty. If the third-party treaty refers to a matter not dealt with in the basic treaty, that matter is *res inter alios acta* in respect of the beneficiary of the clause."[303] The tribunal went on to find that procedural provisions on dispute settlement were sufficiently related to the subject matter of the Argentina–Spain BIT to fall within the MFN clause. "[T]oday dispute settlement arrangements are inextricably related to the protection of foreign investors ... as arrangements designed to better protect the rights of such persons abroad."[304]

6.133 More recently, the arbitrators in *Gas Natural* reasoned that "the most crucial element" of BIT protection "has been the provision for independent international arbitration of disputes between investors and host states," and that therefore:

> Unless it appears clearly that the state parties to a BIT or the parties to a particular investment agreement settled on a different method for resolution of disputes that may arise, most-favored-nation provisions in BITs should be understood to be applicable to dispute settlement.[305]

---

[301] *See MTD, supra* note 188, at paras. 100, 187.

[302] *Emilio Augustín Maffezini v. Spain*, ICSID Case No. ARB/97/7, Decision on Jurisdiction, 16 ICSID Rev.—For. Inv. L.J. 212 (2001).

[303] *Id.* at 227–28.

[304] *See also* Francisco Orrego Vicuña, *Bilateral Investment Treaties and the Most-Favored-Nation Clause: Implications for Arbitration in the Light of a Recent ICSID Case*, Presentation to Swiss Arbitration Association Conference, Zurich, Jan. 25, 2002, at 2. For an analysis of the possible application of MFN clauses to expand the definition of "investment" under investment treaties, *see* Noah Rubins, *The Notion of Investment in International Investment Arbitration*, in Arbitrating Investment Disputes 283, 320–23 (Norbert Horn ed. 2004).

[305] *Gas Natural SDG S.A. v. Argentina*, ICSID Case No. ARB/03/10, Decision on Jurisdiction of June 17, 2005, paras. 29 and 49, available at http://www.investmentclaims.com/decisions/Gas%20Natural%20SDG%20-%20Jurisdiction.pdf. *See also Siemens, supra* note 132, Decision on Jurisdiction of Aug. 3, 2004 (MFN clause extended to procedural rights); but *cf. Plama Consortium,*

A stricter approach toward the relation of MFN clauses to dispute settlement mechanisms was taken by the tribunal in *Plama v Bulgaria*.[306] That tribunal rejected the reasoning in *Maffezini*, arguing that even if investor–State arbitration is a "generally accepted avenue for resolving disputes," the agreement of the parties to arbitrate is yet a basic prerequisite (based in the host State's consent to arbitration), and that "such an agreement should be clear and unambiguous."[307] The tribunal also stated that a contrary conclusion could provoke a "chaotic situation," where a host State could "be confronted with a large number of permutations of dispute settlement provisions from the various BITs which it has concluded."[308] Consequently, it concluded that "an MFN provision in a basic treaty does not incorporate by reference dispute settlement provisions in whole or in part set forth in another treaty, unless the MFN provision in the basic treaty leaves no doubt that the Contracting Parties intended to incorporate them."[309] **6.134**

As a result of the ambiguity caused by different arbitral decisions regarding the operation of the MFN clause, some FTAs no indicate specifically that the dispute settlement clause they contain cannot be replaced by operation of most-favored-nation treatment. For example, article 139(2) of the China–New Zealand Free Trade Agreement indicates that "[f]or greater certainty, the obligation in this article does not encompass a requirement to extend to investors of the other Party dispute resolution procedures other than those set out in this chapter."[310] **6.135**

iii. Prohibition on arbitrary and discriminatory measures Very few tribunals have directly applied "arbitrary and discriminatory measures" clauses to particular facts. It is therefore difficult to assess the extent to which such a provision serves to complement national and MFN treatment to prohibit discrimination on bases other than nationality. One of the only decisions to address the matter came in *CMS*. There, the claimant argued that the Argentine government's suppression and freeze of gas transportation tariffs through "pesification" was *de facto* discriminatory, in violation of a provision in the U.S.–Argentina BIT that read: **6.136**

> Neither Party shall in any way impair by arbitrary and discriminatory measures the management, operation, maintenance, use, enjoyment, acquisition, expansion, or disposal of investments.[311]

supra note 38, at para. 119, available at https://www.italaw.com/cases/857. For an overview of the debate over the scope of MFN clauses, *see* Ruth Teitelbaum, *Recent Developments in the Interpretation of Most Favored Nation Clauses*, 22(3) J. Int'l Arb. 225 (2005).

306 *Plama Consortium, supra* note 38.

307 *Id.* at para. 198.

308 *Id.* at para. 219.

309 *Id.* at para. 223.

310 The New Zealand–China Free Trade Agreement (2008), available at https://www.mfat.govt.nz/en/trade/free-trade-agreements/free-trade-agreements-in-force/nz-china-free-trade-agreement/text-of-the-new-zealand-china-fta-agreement/; Similar provisions are found in other FTAs, such as in TPPA (art. 9.3), CETA (art. X.7.4); *See also* McLachlan et al., *supra* note 115, at 350.

311 U.S.–Argentina BIT (1991), art. II(2)(b).

6.137 In particular, the claimant demonstrated that the measure in question affected only gas transporters, while other public services had not suffered similar treatment. Moreover, export-oriented manufacturing businesses, dominated by local interests, reaped huge benefits from artificially low gas prices. The tribunal found that, although the measures in question were unfair and inequitable, they could not be deemed discriminatory, since businesses in other sectors could not be proven to be in "similar circumstances" to gas transporters.[312]

5. *Pacta sunt servanda* and the "umbrella" clause

a. The standard

6.138 Many investment treaties include some form of an "observance of undertakings" clause (also known as an "umbrella clause" or a "*pacta sunt servanda* clause").[313] As explained elsewhere in this book, a State's breach, modification or even annulment of a contract, particularly one created and governed by its own municipal law, does not necessarily constitute a breach of customary international law.[314] As a result, a number of treaties drafted during the mid-twentieth century included clauses designed to elevate a State's violation of private, municipal-law rights to the level of international law.[315]

6.139 The purpose of umbrella clauses is "to ensure that each Party to the treaty will respect specific undertakings towards nationals of the other Party."[316] Such clauses

---

312 *CMS, supra* note 141, at paras. 293–95.

313 On umbrella clauses, *see generally* Christoph Schreuer, *Travelling the BIT Route: of Waiting Periods, Umbrella Clauses and Forks in the Road*, 5(2) J. World Inv. & Trade 231 (2004); Thomas W. Wälde, *The "Umbrella" Clause in Investment Arbitration—A Comment on Original Intentions and Recent Cases*, 6 J. World Inv. & Trade 184 (2005); Anthony Sinclair, *The Origins of the Umbrella Clause in the International Law of Investment Protection*, 20 Arb. Int'l 411 (2004); UNCTAD, International Investment Agreements: Key Issues (2004), at 6–8. *See also* James Crawford, *Treaty and Contract in Investment Arbitration*, 24(3) Arb. Int'l 351 (2008); McLachlan et al., *supra* note 115, at 128–39; Salacuse, *supra* note 4, at 389–91; Papanastasiou, *supra* note 90, at 121–23.

314 Oppenheim's International Law 927 (Sir Robert Jennings & Sir Arthur Watts eds. 1992); Stephen Schwebel, *On Whether the Breach by a State of a Contract with an Alien Is a Breach of International Law*, in International Law at the Time of Its Codification 401 (1987); Restatement, *supra* note 257, § 712, cmt. h ("not every repudiation or breach by a state of a contract with a foreign national constitutes a violation of international law"); ILC Articles on Responsibility of States for Internationally Wrongful Acts, GA Res. 56/83, Dec. 14, 2001, Commentary to art. 4 at para. 6 ("The breach by a State of a contract clearly does not as such entail a breach of international law"), reprinted in James Crawford, The International Law Commission's Articles on State Responsibility: Introduction, Text and Commentaries 96 (2002); Schreuer, *supra* note 167, at 250; *SGS Société Générale de Surveillance S.A. v. Pakistan*, ICSID Case No. ARB/01/13, Decision on Jurisdiction of Aug. 6, 2003, para. 167 ("under general international law, a violation of a contract entered into by a State with an investor of another State, is not, by itself, a violation of international law").

315 For an exhaustive historical analysis of early umbrella treaties and clauses, *see* Sinclair, *supra* note 316, at 413–27. *See also Eureko B.V. v. Poland*, Ad Hoc, Partial Award and Dissenting Opinion of Aug. 19, 2005, para. 251.

316 Rudolf Dolzer & Margrete Stevens, Bilateral Investment Treaties 81 (1995). *See also* Lucy Reed et al., *Guide to ICSID Arbitration* 52 (2004) (umbrella clauses are "meant

are widespread in investment treaty practice, but a number of important questions about their application and interpretation remain open.[317]

b. Applicable provisions

Umbrella clauses require the host State to honor investment-related obligations. The Turkey–Russian Federation BIT contains a typical clause of this sort: 6.140

> Each Contracting Party shall observe any obligation it may enter into with regard to investments of investors of the other Contracting Party.[318]

The breadth of coverage of such clauses varies, both in terms of the type of undertaking guaranteed and the relationship of that commitment to investors and investments. Some umbrella clauses appear exceedingly broad, and are therefore likely to be given broad interpretation, while others impose limitations on the undertakings the State is obligated to observe under the treaty. Investors should be cautious before making general assumptions about the sanctity of contracts, simply because an applicable treaty contains some form of *pacta sunt servanda* provision. The most salient variations include: 6.141

- coverage of "any" obligation undertaken by the State, or only of "specific" or "particular" obligations.[319]
- coverage of "agreements" and "obligations" only, or "commitments" and "undertakings" more generally.[320]
- coverage of obligations assumed in connection with investors *and* investments, or only in relation to "investments" or "investors."
- the location of the clause among the other substantive standards of investment protection, in a separate section dealing with "non-derogation," or in more general provisions of the treaty dealing with miscellaneous issues.[321]

---

to cover every conceivable commitment with respect to investments flowing between the two States").

[317] The umbrella clause now forms part of the main elements of the European Union's comprehensive international investment policy; *see* European Commission, *Towards a comprehensive European international investment policy*, COM(2010)343 final, at p. 8, (Dec. 13, 2013), available at https://www.eesc.europa.eu/en/our-work/opinions-information-reports/opinions/towards-comprehensive-european-international-investment-policy. *See also* art. 9(5)(5) of Chapter 9 of the E.U.–Singapore Free Trade Agreement, available at http://trade.ec.europa.eu/doclib/press/index.cfm?id=961.

[318] Turkey–Russian Federation BIT (1997), art. 2(2).

[319] *Cf. e.g.* U.K. Model BIT (1987) ("Each Contracting Party shall observe *any* obligation it may have entered into with regard to investments of nationals or companies of the other Contracting Party") (emphasis added); and ASEAN Investment Treaty, art. III ("Each Contracting Party shall observe *any* obligation arising from a particular commitment it may have entered into Title with regard to a specific investment of nationals or companies of the other Contracting Parties") (emphasis added).

[320] *Cf. e.g.* Israel–Ukraine BIT (1994), art. 2(3) (referring to "specific agreements") and France–Ukraine BIT (1994), art. 10 (referring to "specific undertakings").

[321] *See e.g.* France–Ukraine BIT (1994), art. 10. As noted, one tribunal viewed the position of the umbrella clause in the Switzerland–Pakistan BIT after the main investment protection provisions as

- further conditions, such as the deliberate frustration or undermining of "clearly spelt out" commitments, which "substantially alters the balance of rights and obligation in the contractual written obligation" without reasonable compensation.[322]
- Some other more rare variations contain an ambiguous reference to the host State's obligation to maintain the level of treatment accorded to investors of the other party "in accordance with its laws and regulations."[323]

6.142 One of the broadest umbrella clauses can be found in the ECT:

> Each Contracting Party shall observe any obligations it has entered into with an Investor or an Investment of an Investor of any other Contracting Party.[324]

6.143 This language ensures that undertakings extended to either the foreigner himself or his investment vehicle (in the form of a concession or license) will be covered by the observance guarantee. The tribunal in *Plama v. Bulgaria* suggested a broad interpretation of article 10(1) of the ECT, in that the term refers to "any obligation regardless of its nature, i.e., whether it be contractual or statutory."[325] By contrast, an ICSID *ad hoc* committee took a narrower view of a similar text, concluding that the words "entered into" suggest that the obligation must be consensual (and therefore not statutory).[326] The tribunal in *Al-Bahloul v. Tajikistan* reached a similar result specifically in relation to the ECT.[327]

6.144 It should be noted that a number of significant bilateral and multilateral investment treaties lack umbrella clauses altogether.[328] Furthermore, relatively few

a factor depriving the text of direct "internationalizing" effect on State contracts. *SGS v. Pakistan, supra* note 317, at para. 169.

[322] *See e.g.* E.U.–Singapore FTA, *supra* note 320, Chapter 9, art. 9(5)(5): "Where a Party, itself or through any entity mentioned in paragraph 5 of Article 9.1 (Definitions), had given a specific and clearly spelt out commitment in a contractual written obligation towards a covered investor of the other Party with respect to the covered investor's investment or towards such covered investment, that Party shall not frustrate or undermine the said commitment through the exercise of its governmental authority either: (a) deliberately; or (b) in a way which substantially alters the balance of rights and obligation in the contractual written obligation unless the Party provides reasonable compensation to restore the covered investor or investment to a position which it would have been in had the frustration or undermining not occurred."

[323] *See e.g.* Japan–Thailand EPA (2007), art. 100: "Each Party shall maintain, in accordance with its laws and regulations, the level of treatment which has been accorded to investors of the other Party and their investments with respect to investment activities," reprinted in Papanastasiou, *supra* note 90, at 133–34.

[324] ECT, *supra* note 31, art. 10(1), last sentence.

[325] *Plama Consortium, supra* note 38, Award of Aug. 27, 2008, para. 186, available at https://www.italaw.com/sites/default/files/case-documents/ita0671.pdf.

[326] *CMS Gas Transmission Co. v. Argentina*, Annulment Decision of Sept. 25, 2007, para. 95(a).

[327] *Mohammad Ammar Al-Bahloul v. Tajikistan*, SCC Case No. 064/2008, Partial Award on Jurisdiction and Liability of Sept. 2, 2009, para. 257, available at https://www.italaw.com/sites/default/files/case-documents/ita0023_0.pdf.

[328] Most notably, NAFTA and most treaties based upon U.S. Model BITs. See also Unified Agreement for the Investment of Arab Capital in the Arab States (1980); Russian Federation

national investment codes include these provisions. A few such laws incorporate a "non-interference" clause that may operate in similar fashion, although such clauses have rarely been tested in arbitration. The investment law of Kyrgyzstan, for example, provides:

> The Kyrgyz Republic through its authorized governmental bodies shall abstain from interference in the economic activity, rights and legally recognized interests of foreign investors.[329]

The absence of an umbrella clause in a particular applicable investment protection instrument may not be irremediable. As explained earlier, the most-favored-nation clause contained in nearly every investment protection treaty and national investment code will normally ensure that a qualifying investor receives all benefits offered to a national of a third-party State. Therefore, to the extent that the host State has entered into at least one investment treaty that provides *pacta sunt servanda* coverage, the investor should be able to "import" the third-party clause into the applicable instrument.[330] 6.145

c. *The effect of an umbrella clause*

Despite the clear language of most umbrella clauses, there has been debate as to whether such a clause elevates *every* State contract to an international level. According to the broadest approach, most umbrella clauses internationalize *all* State municipal-law obligations,[331] and breaches of those obligations (no matter how insignificant) can constitute treaty violations as well. The more restrictive approach is based on the view that the umbrella clause was created to prevent States from abusing their dual status as legislator and contracting party. 6.146

i. The dominant view According to the now-dominant broader approach, a broadly-worded umbrella clauses imposes treaty liability upon the host State for the violation of any undertaking, including contractual obligations in direct agreements between States and investors (such as concession contracts), representations made by government officials to attract investment, or broader 6.147

Model BIT (2002); Canada Model BIT (2004), available at https://www.italaw.com/documents/Canadian2004-FIPA-model-en.pdf.

329 Law of the Kyrgyz Republic on Foreign Investment (1997), art. 3(1), available at http://www.libertas-institut.com/de/Mittel-Osteuropa/Law%20on%20Foreign%20Investments%20-%20new%20version.pdf.

330 *See* Section C.4.c.ii, *supra; MTD, supra* note 188, at para. 187 (in a dispute arising under the Malaysia–Chile BIT, which contained no umbrella clause, the tribunal applied the umbrella clause of the Denmark–Chile BIT by operation of the applicable treaty's MFN clause).

331 *See SGS Société Générale de Surveillance S.A. v. Philippines*, ICSID Case No. ARB/02/6, Decision on Jurisdiction of Jan. 29, 2004, at para. 117 ('Whether collateral guarantees, warranties or letters of comfort given by a host State to induce the entry of foreign investments are binding or not, i.e. whether they constitute genuine obligations or mere advertisements, will be a matter for determination under the applicable law').

undertakings contained in the State's national legislation.[332] In the words of Professor Mann, these clauses "render wrongful"

> [t]he variation of the terms of a contract or license by legislative measures, the termination of the contract or the failure to perform any of its terms, for instance, by non-payment . . .[333]

6.148 Certain other commentators, examining early drafts of umbrella treaties, compared them to stabilization clauses (discussed at length in Chapter 2) and expressed little doubt that they should apply at least to all contract obligations between signatory States and the citizens of other signatory States.[334] In particular, Prosper Weil opined in 1969 that while breach of State contracts may not constitute a violation of international law absent some additional element of illegality (such as denial of justice or expropriation), an umbrella treaty "turns the obligation to perform the contract into an international obligation . . . any failure to perform the contract, even if legal under the national law of the contracting State, gives rise to its international liability . . ."[335]

6.149 One of the first investment arbitration cases to examine the umbrella clause was *SGS v. Philippines*.[336] There, the claimant initiated arbitration under the Switzerland–Philippines BIT in relation to the respondent State's breach of contracts for the provision of pre-shipment customs inspection services. The claimant invoked the BIT's umbrella clause, which provided:

---

[332] *See*, for example, *Eureko B.V. v. Poland*, Ad Hoc Partial Award of Aug. 19, 2005; *Noble Ventures Inc. v. Romania*, ICSID Case No. ARB/01/11, Award of Oct. 12, 2005, para. 53 ('[a]n umbrella clause is usually seen as transforming municipal law obligations into obligations directly cognizable in international law').

[333] F.A. Mann, *British Treaties for the Promotion and Protection of Investments*, 52 Brit. Yb. Int'l L. 241, 246 (1981). *See also* Vandevelde, *supra* note 10, at 78 ("Under this clause, a party's breach of an investment agreement with an investor becomes a breach of the BIT, for which the investor . . . may seek a remedy under the investor-to-state . . . disputes procedures. In effect, this clause authorizes use of the BITs' disputes procedures to enforce investment agreements between the investor and the host state").

[334] Oppenheim's International Law, *supra* note 317, at 927. The question remains, however, whether the contractual obligations of State-owned corporations or agencies can be attributed to the State, such that they are 'obligations entered into' by the State. *See Impreglio S.p.A. v. Pakistan*, ICSID Case No. ARB/03/3, Decision on Jurisdiction of April 22, 2005, at para. 223 (declining to apply umbrella clause to contracts entered into by the Pakistan Water and Power Development Authority).

[335] Prosper Weil, *Problèmes relatifs aux contrats passés entre un Etat et un particulier*, 128 Recueil des Cours 94, 130 (1969).

[336] *SGS v. Philippines, supra* note 334. For analysis of this decision, particularly in contrast to the conflicting decision in *SGS v. Pakistan, see* Emmanuel Gaillard, *Investment Treaty Arbitration and Jurisdiction Over Contract Claims: the SGS Cases Considered*, in International Investment Law and Arbitration 325 (2005); Stanimir Alexandrov, *Breaches of Contract and Breaches of Treaty: the Jurisdiction of Treaty-based Arbitration Tribunals to Decide Breach of Contract Claims in SGS v. Pakistan and SGS v. Philippines*, 5 J. World Inv. 555 (2004); Judith Gill & M. Gearing, *Contractual Claims and Bilateral Investment Treaties: a Comparative Review of the SGS Cases*, J. Int'l Arb. 397 (2004).

> Each Contracting Party shall observe any obligation it has assumed with regard to specific investments in its territory by investors of the other Contracting Party.[337]

The claimant insisted that this text elevated the contract breaches in question to the level of international law, subject to adjudication before the ICSID tribunal. The Philippines argued (in part based on the previously decided *SGS v. Pakistan* case) that the clause was aspirational, and that contract breaches must be litigated in the contractual forum. The tribunal took the view that the clause means what it says: **6.150**

> if commitments made by the State towards specific investments do involve binding obligations or commitments under the applicable law, it seems entirely consistent with the object and purpose of the BIT that they are brought within the framework of the BIT by the [umbrella clause].[338]

The *MTD* tribunal appeared to adopt this same approach, rejecting Chile's assertion that not every violation of a contractual obligation would contravene the umbrella clause. The tribunal noted the higher standard of conduct required under the BIT in comparison to customary international law: **6.151**

> the Tribunal notes the statement of the Respondent that under international law the breach of a contractual obligation is not ipso facto a breach of a treaty. Under the BIT ... this is what the parties had agreed. The Tribunal has to apply the BIT.[339]

Likewise, in *Fedax*, the respondent State was compelled by the applicable BIT to pay a promissory note exactly according to its terms. While the tribunal mentioned the umbrella clause only in passing, it concluded that: **6.152**

> the Republic of Venezuela is under the obligation to honor precisely the terms and conditions governing such investment ... as well as to honor the specific payments established in the promissory notes issued.[340]

The tribunal reached the same conclusion in *Noble Ventures v. Romania*, where it was held that international treaties may include clauses by virtue of which the **6.153**

---

[337] Switzerland-Philippines BIT (1997), art. X(2).

[338] *SGS v. Philippines, supra* note 334, at para. 117–119. The *SGS v. Philippines* tribunal nevertheless dismissed the case for want of jurisdiction. In reaching this result, the arbitrators relied upon the relevant contract's dispute resolution clause, which called for adjudication exclusively in the courts of the Philippines. The tribunal held that overriding this provision would amount to a violation of the contract, and that in any event the umbrella clause could have no effect without a determination that the Philippines had breached the contract under municipal law—a factual issue better decided in the parties' initially-chosen forum. *Id.* at paras. 135–36.

[339] *MTD, supra* note 188, at para. 187. *See also Joseph C. Lemire v. Ukraine*, ICSID Case No. ARB/06/18, Decision on Jurisdiction and Liability of Jan. 21, 2010, para. 498 ("any violation of the private law agreement becomes ipso iure a violation of the international law BIT").

[340] *Fedax N.V. v. Venezuela*, ICSID Case No. ARB/96/3, Award of March 9, 1998, 37 I.L.M. 1391 (1998), at para. 29.

host State is obligated to comply with its contractual obligations with qualifying investors. Any contractual violation is thereby internationalized as a breach of the treaty:

> [T]wo States may include in a bilateral investment treaty a provision to the effect that, in the interest of achieving the objects and goals of the treaty, the host State may incur international responsibility by reason of a breach of its contractual obligations towards the private investor of the other Party, the breach of contract being thus "internationalized," i.e. assimilated to a breach of the treaty . . .[341]

6.154 In *CMS v. Argentina*,[342] the U.S. investor had purchased an interest in the Argentine gas pipeline company, TGN. This investment was based in part on its understanding of the gas transportation tariff structure, embodied in the local gas law and the company's license. These conditions provided that TGN would be entitled to a reasonable rate of return, through such mechanisms as dollar-denominated tariffs and annual adjustments based upon the U.S. Producer Price Index. During Argentina's financial crisis in 2000–02, the government first eliminated the PPI adjustments, then forcibly converted tariffs into devaluated pesos (destroying about 70 percent of their value), and refused to allow the newly pesified gas tariffs to rise. The tribunal appears to have had little doubt that these changes in the regulatory and contractual regime surrounding the claimant's investment violated the umbrella clause of the U.S.–Argentina BIT:

> The Tribunal must therefore conclude that the obligation under the umbrella clause of . . . the Treaty has not been observed by the Respondent to the extent that legal and contractual obligations pertinent to the investment have been breached and have resulted in the violation of the standards of protection under the Treaty.[343]

6.155 The tribunal in *SGS v. Paraguay* upheld the broad interpretation of the umbrella clause adopted in *SGS v. Philippines*. The dispute concerned not only the breach of a contractual agreement, but also the evisceration of alleged subsequent oral and written promises to make good on debts to the claimant. The tribunal asserted jurisdiction over the claim, finding that the umbrella clause:

> creates an obligation for the State to constantly guarantee observance of its commitments entered into with respect to investments of investors of the other Party. The obligation has no limitations on its face—it apparently applies to all such commitments, whether established by contract or by law, unilaterally or bilaterally, etc. Not all of Claimant's Article 11 claims are predicated on breach of the Contract itself: Claimant has also alleged that Paraguayan officials subsequently made various oral and written commitments to respect the Contract and to make payment of amounts owed to SGS, which commitments were allegedly breached.

[341] *Noble Ventures Inc. v. Romania*, ICSID Case No. ARB/01/11, Award of Oct. 12, 2005, at para. 54. *See also Bureau Veritas, Inspection, Valuation, Assessment and Control, BIVAC B.V. v. Paraguay*, ICSID Case No. ARB/07/9, Decision on Jurisdiction, of May 29, 2009, paras. 141–42.

[342] *CMS, supra* note 141.

[343] *Id.* at para. 303.

> But even as to the Article 11 claims that are predicated directly on Paraguay's alleged breach of the Contract, we have no hesitation in treating the Contract's obligations as "commitments" within the meaning of Article 11.[344]

The *SGS v. Paraguay* tribunal also rejected the distinction between *acta jure imperii* and *acta jure gestionis* emphasized by the *El Paso v. Argentina* tribunal: **6.156**

> Given the unqualified text of Article 11 of the Treaty, and its ordinary meaning, we see no basis to import into Article 11 the non-textual limitations that Respondent proposed in its Reply. Article 11 does not exclude commercial contracts of the State from its scope. Likewise, Article 11 does not state that its constant guarantee of observance of such commitments may be breached only through actions that a commercial counterparty cannot take, through abuses of state power, or through exertions of undue government influence.[345]

ii. The restrictive view The "plain meaning" approach to observance of undertakings clauses has not been universally accepted. Most prominent in this regard is the decision in *SGS v. Pakistan*,[346] which was one of the first to address the effect of umbrella clauses, and involved the same claimant and contracts very similar to those that later gave rise to the *SGS v. Philippines* dispute. The tribunal was particularly concerned by the possible consequences of adopting a broad interpretation of the clause, which it feared **6.157**

> would amount to incorporating by reference an unlimited number of State contracts, as well as other municipal law instruments setting out State commitments including unilateral commitments to an investor of the other Contracting Party ... Secondly, the Claimant's view of [the umbrella clause] tends to make [the other protections] of the BIT substantially superfluous. There would be no real need to demonstrate a violation of those substantive treaty standards if a simple breach of contract, or of municipal statute or regulation, by itself, would suffice to constitute a treaty violation on the part of a Contracting Party and engage the international responsibility of the Party. A third consequence would be that an investor may, at will, nullify any freely negotiated dispute settlement clause in a State contract ... [the] investor could always defeat the State's invocation of the contractually specified forum, and render any mutually agreed procedure of dispute settlement, other than BIT-specified ICSID arbitration, a dead-letter, at the investor's choice.[347]

344 *SGS Société Générale de Surveillance S.A. v. Paraguay*, ICSID Case No. ARB/07/29, Decision on Jurisdiction of Feb. 12, 2010, para. 167.

345 *Id.* at para. 168.

346 *SGS v. Pakistan, supra* note 317. For a critique of the decision, see Thomas W. Wälde, *The Treatment of the "Umbrella" or "Pacta Sunt Servanda" Clause in the SGS v. Pakistan Jurisdictional Decision (2003): Correct?*, 1(5) Oil, Gas & Energy Law Intelligence (December 2003) ("The tribunal, in its jurisdictional decision, was in my mind wrong to treat the umbrella clause in such a dismissive way it did").

347 *SGS v. Pakistan, supra* note 317, at para. 168. The tribunal in *Pan American Energy LLC and BP Argentina Exploration Co. v. Argentina and BP America Production Co., Pan American Sur S.R.L., Pan American Fueguina, S.R.L. and Pan American Continental S.R.L. v. Argentina*, ICSID Case Nos. ARB/03/13 & ARB/04/8, Decision on Preliminary Objections of July 27, 2006, paras. 100–05 and 110–13 reiterated this argumentation holding that it is "more than conclusive." In the same direction, *see El Paso Energy Int'l Co. v. Argentina*, ICSID Case No. ARB/03/15, Decision on Jurisdiction of Apr. 27, 2006, paras. 71–74.

6.158 Ultimately, the tribunal's decision not to adjudicate Pakistan's breaches of the SGS contracts was largely driven by its view of the particular clause in the Switzerland–Pakistan BIT. It reasoned that the provision was weakly phrased, and inserted at the end of the treaty, rather than alongside other substantive protections such as fair and equitable treatment.[348] The "observance of undertakings," therefore, was not among the treaty's "first order" obligations, and "was *not* meant to project a substantive obligation" at all.[349]

6.159 Similarly, in *Salini v. Jordan*, the tribunal rejected the "elevation" of contract claims to the international sphere, underlining the generality of the language in the applicable umbrella clause.[350]

6.160 The tribunal in *El Paso v. Argentina* further qualified the scope of the umbrella clause by reference to the nature of the impugned State act. The tribunal distinguished between the State acting as a sovereign and the State acting as merchant, especially through instrumentalities. In the tribunal's view, the object and purpose of the umbrella clause was not to protect investors from breaches of ordinary contracts, but to "cover additional investment protections contractually agreed by the State as a sovereign—such as a stabilization clause—inserted in an investment agreement." Accordingly,

> [A]n umbrella clause cannot transform any contract claim into a treaty claim, as this would necessarily imply that any commitments of the State in respect to investments, even the most minor ones, would be transformed into treaty claims. These far-reaching consequences of a broad interpretation of the so-called umbrella clauses, quite destructive of the distinction between national legal orders and the international legal order, have been well understood and clearly explained by the first Tribunal which dealt with the issue of the so-called "umbrella clause" in the *SGS v. Pakistan* case and which insisted on the theoretical problems faced. It would be strange indeed if the acceptance of a BIT entailed an international liability of the State going far beyond the obligation to respect the standards of protection of foreign investments embodied in the Treaty and rendered it liable for any violation of any commitment in national or international law "with regard to investments".[351]

6.161 The same approach was taken by the *ad hoc* Committee in *Vivendi*, where the distinction between contract claims and treaty claims was clarified:

> whether there has been a breach of the BIT and whether there has been a breach of contract are different questions. Each of these claims will be determined by reference

[348] *Id.* at paras. 166, 169.

[349] *Id.* at para. 170 (emphasis in the original).

[350] *Salini Costruttori S.p.A. & Italstrade S.p.A. v. Jordan*, ICSID Case No. ARB/02/13, Decision on Jurisdiction of Nov. 9, 2004 (art. 2(4) of the BIT stated that "[e]ach Contracting Party shall create and maintain in its territory a legal framework apt to guarantee the investors the continuity of legal treatment, including the compliance, in good faith, of all undertakings assumed with regard to each specific investor").

[351] *El Paso Energy Int'l Co. v. Argentina*, ICSID Case No. ARB/03/15, Decision on Jurisdiction of Apr. 27, 2006, paras. 71–74.

to its own proper or applicable law—in the case of the BIT, by international law in the case of the Concession Contract, by the proper law of the contract, in other words, the law of Tucumán. For example, in the case of a claim based on a treaty, international law rules of attribution apply, with the result that the state of Argentina is internationally responsible for the acts of its provincial authorities. By contrast, the state of Argentina is not liable for the performance of contracts entered into by Tucumán, which possesses separate legal personality under its own law and is responsible for the performance of its own contracts.[352]

In *dicta*, the tribunal in *Joy Mining v. Egypt* appears to have adopted a more moderate stance.[353] The dispute in *Joy Mining* arose out of a transaction between the British claimant corporation and an Egyptian State-owned company in relation to phosphate extraction. Under the terms of the primary contract, the Egyptian company was to purchase mining equipment from the claimant, which provided bank guarantees that the buyer could hold until satisfied with the quality of the equipment supplied. Not long after delivery, the Egyptian company experienced problems with the equipment, and refused to release the guarantee it had received under the contract. Ultimately, Joy Mining brought a claim against Egypt under the U.K.–Egypt BIT, alleging breach of the treaty's "umbrella clause." The tribunal dismissed the claim on grounds that there was no covered investment, but noted that even had such an investment existed, **6.162**

> it could not be held that an umbrella clause inserted in the Treaty, and not very prominently, could have the effect of transforming all contract disputes into investment disputes under the Treaty, unless of course there would be a clear violation of the Treaty rights and obligations or a violation of contract rights of such a magnitude as to trigger the Treaty protection, which is not the case. The connection between the Contract and the Treaty is the missing link that prevents any such effect. This might be perfectly different in other cases where that link is found to exist, but certainly it is not the case here.[354]

Thus, the *Joy Mining* tribunal suggested that while umbrella clauses are not merely adhortatory, as the *SGS v. Pakistan* arbitrators had concluded, the particular clause at issue would be triggered only by a contractual breach of significant magnitude.[355] **6.163**

---

[352] *Compañia de Aguas del Aconquija S.A. and Vivendi Universal (formerly Compagnie Générale des Eaux) v. Argentina*, ICSID Case No. ARB/97/3, Decision on Annulment of July 3, 2002, para. 96.

[353] *Joy Mining Machinery Ltd. v. Egypt*, ICSID Case No. ARB/03/11, Decision of Aug. 6, 2004. For an overview and commentary on the case, *see* Nick Gallus, *No Joy for British Mining Company at ICSID*, 2(4) Oil, Gas & Energy Law Intelligence (2004); Farouk Yala, *La notion d'investissement*, 2004(2) Les Cahiers de L'Arbitrage 15, 17–19; Richard Happ & Noah Rubins, *Awards and Decisions of ICSID Tribunals in 2004*, 47 Germ. Yb. Int'l L. 878, 913 (2004). It should be noted that the President of the *Joy Mining* tribunal, Francisco Orrego Vicuna, would shortly thereafter issue the final award in *CMS v. Argentina*, which adopted a broader application of umbrella clauses.

[354] *Joy Mining, supra* note 356, at para. 81.

[355] *See also Garanti Koza LLP v. Turkmenistan*, ICSID Case No. ARB/11/20, Award of Dec. 19, 2016, para. 330 ("A failure by a government agency to pay for a box of pencils delivered pursuant to an agreement to provide office supplies, for example, would not come within the reach of Article 2(2), because it would have nothing to do with an investment").

6.164 Similarly, according to some scholars, a broad interpretation of the umbrella clause

> would turn a breach of any one of those obligations, however minor, into the breach of an international obligation engaging the international responsibility of the State. Such an approach would distort the synallagmatic nature of the contract, in which both parties assume mutually interdependent rights and duties. It would transform the obligations of the State, whilst leaving the obligations of the investor governed by municipal law. The result would be to distort the parties' bargain rather than ensure its observance.[356]

6.165 In the words of Professor Crawford:

> there is the view that an umbrella clause is operative and may form the basis for a substantive treaty claim, but that it does not convert a contractual claim into a treaty claim. On the one hand it provides, or at least may provide, a basis for a treaty claim even if the BIT in question contains not generic claims clause; on the other hand, the umbrella clause does not change the proper law of the contract or its legal incidents, including provisions for dispute settlement.[357]

6.166 Following this same theme, the *Toto v. Lebanon* tribunal concluded that contractual claims are distinct from treaty claims, and are properly governed by domestic contract law. In the event that the contract contains an exclusive forum clause (such as the domestic courts of the host State or commercial arbitration), the contractual claims have to be submitted to that forum for settlement. However, the breach of contract may form the basis for a separate treaty claim, which falls within the jurisdiction of an investment treaty tribunal.[358] Therefore, in the tribunal's view, "[t]he contractual jurisdiction clause and the Treaty jurisdiction clause are not mutually exclusive clauses." Rather, much will depend on the cause of action of the claim and whether the State acts as an ordinary commercial agent or as a *puissance publique*:

> The contractual jurisdiction clause provided for in the Contract applies to actions and matters that are violations of the Contract; the Treaty jurisdiction clause applies to actions and matters that constitute violations of the substantive Treaty provisions even if the same actions and matters may give rise to breach of contract. It must also be noted that contractual claims founded on the investment contract do not have the same cause of action as the Treaty claims. When the State acts in the context of the performance of the contract as a "puissance publique," a violation of the Contract would also constitute a violation of the Treaty, and the Tribunal will have jurisdiction for disputes arising from such violations. When the State acts as an ordinary employer, the contractual jurisdiction clause will be fully operative, and the Tribunal will have no jurisdiction ... Based on the foregoing, it can be said that the Contract's jurisdiction clause does not affect the Tribunal's jurisdiction over Treaty claims since the Contracts jurisdiction clause covers only contractual matters

---

356 McLachlan et al., *supra* note 115, at 136.

357 James Crawford, *Treaty and Contract in Investment Arbitration*, 24(3) Arb. Int'l 351–74 (2008).

358 *Toto Costruzioni Generali S.p.A. v. Lebanon*, ICSID Case No. ARB/07/12, Decision on Jurisdiction of Sept. 11, 2009, paras. 200–13.

> and does not extend to Treaty matters contractual jurisdiction clause, the Tribunal will not have jurisdiction with respect to claims for actions that are only contract violations and are not at the same time Treaty violations. However, when such actions are breaches of the contract and also violations of the Treaty, the Tribunal will have jurisdiction notwithstanding the Contract's jurisdiction clause.[359]

6. Repatriation of investment-related funds

One of the most common investor protections included in treaties and national investment codes is the guarantee of repatriation of profits.[360] As explained earlier in this book, host States have not infrequently sought to protect their balance of payments by altering currency exchange and export controls.[361] Such actions can have a devastating effect on investments that are funded through foreign debt or equity participation, where financing must be repaid out of venture profits converted into foreign currency on a regular basis in order to avoid default and insolvency, or loss of investor confidence and decline in value.[362] As a result, nearly all investment protection instruments contain a provision limiting the host State's ability to restrict the repatriation abroad of investment proceeds. A qualifying foreign investor who suffers harm as a result of the host State's breach of such a provision is entitled to compensation. Some treaties also specifically provide for the payment of interest to investors on any payments abroad that have been delayed as a result of exchange or other controls in violation of the repatriation provision. **6.167**

The scope of payments subject to the repatriation guarantee is generally extremely broad, but depends upon the particular treaty or legislative text in question. Treaties for the most part take either an *exhaustive* or *illustrative* approach to the issue, and a single host State may have signed bilateral treaties falling into each of the two categories.[363] The Finland–Kazakhstan treaty, for example, guarantees the transfer of all payments relating to investments, and sets forth an illustrative, but non-exhaustive list of payment types enjoying such protection: **6.168**

> Each Contracting Party shall guarantee to investors of the other Contracting Party the return of movable property relating to investments without undue delay, and in

---

[359] *Id.* at paras. 214–17.

[360] *See* Chapter 1, Section C.

[361] Samuel Asante, *The Concept of the Good Corporate Citizen in International Business*, 4 ICSID Rev.—For. Inv. L.J. 1, 18–19 (1989); Andrew Walter, British Investment Treaties in South Asia: Current Status and Future Trends, 14 (2000), available at http://personal.lse.ac.uk/wyattwal/images/British.pdf (noting that both Bangladesh and Sri Lanka have included in their investment treaties the possibility of restrictions on free transfer of investment profits to protect balance of payments).

[362] UNCTAD, Bilateral Investment Treaties in the Mid-1990s 75 (1998).

[363] For a detailed analysis of transfer of capital provisions in investment treaties, *see* Dolzer & Stevens, *supra* note 319, at 85–95; *see* also Abba Kolo, *Transfer of Funds: The Interaction between the IMF Articles of Agreement and Modern Investment Treaties: a Comparative Law Perspective*, in International Investment Law and Comparative Public Law 357 (Stephan W. Schill ed. 2010).

any case within three months, and without restriction and the transfer in freely convertible currency of payments relating to investments and in particular of:

(1) Profits, dividends, interest, royalties, licensing fees, commissions, fees for technical assistance and services and other income derived from investments made by an investor of the other Contracting Party;
(2) Loans or sums of money paid to liquidate corresponding debts;
(3) Amounts due to an investor as a result of the sale or partial or full liquidation of investments;
(4) Salaries and other earnings accruing to nationals of the country of the investor for work in the territory of the receiving country relating to investments.[364]

6.169 Under such a provision, even a payment not covered by this very broad clause would arguably by subject to the repatriation guarantee, as long as "related to an investment." Kazakhstan's BIT with Egypt, meanwhile, establishes an exhaustive list of payment types covered by the guarantee:

Both of the two contracting parties shall guarantee, in accordance with its national laws for the investors of the other party and after fulfilling all its taxes obligations, and to transfer the following payments related to investments:

(a) The incomes [defined as profits, interest, capital gains, dividends, royalties and other fees];
(b) Proceeds of sale or liquidation of the whole of any part of the investment;
(c) Funds in repayment of loans related to investments;
(d) Payments of royalties, and other fees;
(e) Wages and other remunerations earned by citizens of the other party against labor and services which are related to investments established in the territory of the former party in accordance with its laws.[365]

6.170 A number of investment treaties (most of which were signed before 2000) provide certain exceptions to the free repatriation of investment-related funds. Most commonly, currency export can be restricted if the host State faces a serious balance-of-payments problem.[366] The Netherlands–Philippines BIT, for example, makes the repatriation guarantee subject to the broad "good faith" discretion of the host State:

Each Contracting Party shall in respect of investments permit nationals of the other Contracting Party the unrestricted transfer in freely convertible currency of their investments and of the earnings from it to the country designated by those nationals, subject to the right of the former Contracting Party to impose equitably and in good faith such measures as may be necessary to safeguard the integrity and independence of its currency, its external financial position and balance of payments, consistent with its rights and obligations as a member of the International Monetary Fund.[367]

---

[364] Finland–Kazakhstan BIT (1992), art. 6.

[365] Egypt–Kazakhstan BIT (1993), art. 5.

[366] Reed et al., *supra* note 319, at 52. *See e.g.* El Salvador–Peru BIT (1996), art. 8(4); Colombia–Peru BIT (2001), art. 6(4); Canada–Russian Federation BIT (1989), art. VII(2) (excusing exchange controls "in cases where exceptional balance of payments difficulties exist, and then for a period not exceeding eighteen months").

[367] Netherlands–Philippines BIT (1985), art. 7(1).

Investors should also be mindful of any other limitations on the right to repatriation of capital. In particular, some treaties and investment codes prevent the export of "equity capital" until "one year after it has entered the territory of the Contracting Party unless its legislation provides for a more favourable treatment."[368] **6.171**

Transfer of funds provisions have gained attention with respect to countries facing financial difficulties. For example, in *Continental Casualty v. Argentina*,[369] the host State had prevented the claimant's local subsidiary from withdrawing and transferring US$19 million to the United States. The claimant argued that this amounted to a violation of its right under the BIT to effect "all transfers related to an investment." Argentina defended its sovereign right to enact "specific regulations for balance-of-payment difficulties," in accordance with the standards established in multilateral agreements such as the General Agreement on Tariffs and Trade, the General Agreement on Trade in Services, and the International Monetary Fund.[370] Argentina also claimed that its regulation of monetary transfers conformed with international customary law, as a manifestation of the exercise of monetary sovereignty by States.[371] The tribunal ultimately found no breach of the "transfer of funds" provision. The tribunal found that although the provision was broadly drafted, not every trans-border movement of funds by the investor's subsidiary would be "related to an investment" and therefore subject to protection.[372] The transfer in question was a short-term deposit unrelated to the claimant's investment, and the State's restriction therefore did not breach the BIT.[373] **6.172**

Other arbitral tribunals, however, have found a breach of "transfer of funds" provisions in respect of a ban on profits,[374] forced exchanges of currency and a refusal to release foreign currency to allow a loan repayment,[375] and a "tariff in exchange of investment" policy.[376] Other arbitral tribunals have declined to find a breach in the case of foreign exchange controls,[377] procedures requiring **6.173**

[368] Norway–Chile BIT (1993), Art. 5(4).

[369] *Continental Casualty Co. v. Argentina*, ICSID Case No. ARB/03/9, Award of Sept. 5, 2008, available at https://www.italaw.com/sites/default/files/case-documents/ita0228.pdf.

[370] *See* arts. VIII and XIV of the Amended Articles of Agreement of the International Monetary Fund (1992) 31 I.L.M. 1309; arts. XII and XVIII(B) of the GATT and the Marrakesh Understanding on the Balance-of-Payment Provisions of the GATT 1994; art. XII of the GATS. On the relationship between the IMF system and BITs' protection for the transfer of funds, *see* Andrew Paul Newcombe & Lluis Paradell, Law and Practice of Investment Treaties: Standards of Treatment 401–03 (2009).

[371] *Continental Casualty Co., supra* note 373, para. 238.

[372] *Id.* at para. 242.

[373] *Id.* at para. 244.

[374] *Achmea, supra* note 164, para. 286.

[375] *Bernhard von Pezold, supra* note 160, paras. 608–09.

[376] *AES Corp. and Tau Power B.V. v. Kazakhstan*, ICSID Case No. ARB/10/16, Award of Nov. 1, 2013, paras. 423–27 (in that case, the tribunal found that the breach of the provision on the repatriation of funds was already covered and absorbed by the FET standard).

[377] *OI European Group B.V. v. Venezuela*, ICSID Case No. ARB/11/25, Award of Mar. 10, 2015, para. 624.

the acquisition of foreign currency at the official exchange rate,[378] and where the claimant had failed to comply with established procedures when requesting a transfer of funds abroad.[379]

6.174 More recently, the question has arisen whether "transfer of funds" provisions are compatible with EU law where they restrict States' ability to stabilize balance of payments,[380] both in BITs signed between EU member States[381] and in treaties with third countries.[382]

D. Combination of Substantive Violations

6.175 The description of the substantive protections of investment treaties and of the fact patterns that have led investors to invoke them demonstrates that a single State measure or series of measures can violate more than one treaty obligation. The requirement contained in most investment treaties that any expropriation be undertaken on a "non-discriminatory basis," for example, to some extent reinforces the "national treatment" obligation. In *Metalclad*, Mexico refused to grant a promised permit to a foreign investor, without which a planned waste disposal facility could not operate. The NAFTA tribunal found that Mexico had violated treaty provisions requiring compensation for expropriation *and* had denied the investor fair and equitable treatment.[383] In *CME*, the Czech Republic was found to have breached provisions prohibiting expropriation without compensation, requiring fair and equitable treatment, and calling for full protection and security of investments.[384]

6.176 While the investor can only recover compensation once, where the State's action violates more than one provision of a treaty, tribunals appear more comfortable declaring the State liable for a violation of international law. In *Middle*

[378] *Rusoro Mining Ltd. v. Venezuela*, ICSID Case No. ARB(AF)/12/5, Award of Aug. 22, 2016, para. 577.

[379] *Metalpar S.A. and Buen Aire S.A. v. Argentina*, ICSID Case No. ARB/03/5, Award of June 6, 2008, para. 179.

[380] *See* art. 56 of the EC Treaty (prohibiting "all restrictions on the movement of capital" and "all restrictions on payments between Member States").

[381] *See e.g. Achmea, supra* note 164, Award on Jurisdiction, Arbitrability and Suspension of Oct. 26, 2010, paras. 247–49.

[382] *See also* Case C-205/06, *Commission v. Austria*, Judgment of Mar. 3, 2009, [2009] E.C.R. I-01303; Case C-249/06, *Commission v. Sweden*, Judgment of Mar. 3, 2009; Case C-118/07, *Commission v. Finland*, Judgment of Nov. 19, 2009.

[383] *See Metalclad, supra* note 98. The *Metalclad* panel's decision on fair and equitable treatment was ultimately annulled in a controversial ruling by the Supreme Court of British Columbia. *See* Jack Coe, Jr., *Metalclad—A Retrospective*, in NAFTA Arbitration Reports 65 (Chris Thomas & Cameron Mowatt eds. 2002); William Dodge, *International Decision: Metalclad Corp. v. Mexico*, 95 AJIL 910 (2001); Chapter 8, Section L.2.a.ii.

[384] *See CME*, Partial Award, *supra* note 143, at paras. 586–614.

East Shipping,[385] the Greek claimant sought compensation for the seizure and sale of its vessel. The claimant had not been notified of the sale. The tribunal linked the BIT's expropriation, due process, and fair and equitable treatment provisions: "[T]hough, normally, a seizure and auction ordered by the national courts do not qualify as a taking, they can be a 'measure the effects of which would be tantamount to expropriation' if they are not taken 'under due process of law.' "[386] The tribunal continued:

[T]he BIT requires that "Investments by investors of a Contracting Party shall, at all times, be accorded fair and equitable treatment ... in the territory of the other Contracting Party." This ... provision must be given particular relevance in view of the special protection granted ... against measures tantamount to expropriation and the requirement for due process of law ... [A] matter as important as the seizure and auctioning of a ship ... should have been notified by a direct communication [to the claimant].[387]

E. Compensation for Breach

6.177 It is well settled under international law and in the practice of international tribunals applying investment treaties that the proper level of compensation for expropriation is the "full" value of the assets taken.[388] This formulation has been interpreted to mean "fair market value."[389] Indeed, many investment treaties explicitly define the proper level of compensation in such terms, as does the BIT between Argentina and the United States:

> Compensation shall be equivalent to the fair market value of the expropriated investment immediately before the expropriatory action was taken or became known, whichever is earlier.[390]

6.178 Likewise, the damages due from the State to an investor for violation of any other breach of international law, including violation of an investment treaty,[391] is the full amount by which the value of the affected investment has declined as a direct

---

[385] *E.g. Middle East Cement Shipping & Handling Co. S.A. v. Egypt*, ICSID Case No. ARB/99/6, Final Award of Apr. 12, 2002, available at http://ita.law.uvic.ca/documents/MECement-award.pdf.

[386] *Middle East Cement Shipping & Handling*, *supra* note 136, at para. 139.

[387] *Id.* at para. 143. *See also S.D. Myers*, *supra* note 156 (breach of national treatment also worked a breach of fair and equitable treatment clause).

[388] *See* Chapter 5, Section B.2; *see also* Papanastasiou, *supra* note 90, at 62–65.

[389] *Phillips*, *supra* note 130, at para. 106; *Tecmed*, *supra* note 148, at para. 189; *CME*, Partial Award, *supra* note 143, at para. 508.

[390] Argentina–U.S. BIT (1991), art. IV(1).

[391] On the magnitude of monetary compensation for discrimination and fair and equitable treatment, *see* Thomas Wälde & Borzu Sabahi, *Compensation, Damages, and Valuation*, in The Oxford Handbook of International Investment Law 1082–89 (Peter Muchlinski et al. eds. 2008); *see also* McLachlan et al., *supra* note 115, at 9.95–9.200.

result of the wrongful acts in question.[392] This principle finds its foundation in the ruling of the Permanent Court of International Justice in the *Chorzów* case:

> reparation [for violation of international law] must, as far as possible, wipe out all the consequences of the illegal act and re-establish the situation which would, in all probability, have existed if that [illegal] act had not been committed.[393]

6.179 While full compensation is generally accepted both under treaty and customary law, some observers continue to take a somewhat less stringent approach. In a dissenting opinion in *CME v. Czech Republic*, Professor Ian Brownlie wrote that "just compensation" mandated by the applicable BIT should be interpreted to provide substantially less remuneration to the claimant than would the Hull formula of "prompt, adequate and effective" compensation.[394] He pointed to U.N. General Assembly resolutions such as the Charter of Economic Rights and Duties of States,[395] opining that "just compensation" should be the same as "appropriate compensation," a standard offered in the 1970s by developing countries that requires consideration of the investor's "reasonable expectations" and the hardship an award will cause to the host government.[396] In particular, Professor Brownlie insisted that damages should have been limited to the amount that CME actually invested.

6.180 The optimal method of determining the quantum of compensation is particularly controversial.[397] The proper method generally depends upon the nature of the

[392] *CMS, supra* note 141, at para. 401; *Metalclad, supra* note 98, at para. 122; *S.D. Myers, supra* note 156, at para. 322; *Emilio Augustín Maffezini v. Spain*, ICSID Case No. ARB/97/7, Award of Nov. 13, 2000, 16 ICSID Rev.—For. Inv. L.J. 248 (2001), paras. 95–97.

[393] *Factory at Chorzów* (Claim for Indemnity) *(Germany v. Poland)*, P.C.I.J. Ser. A, No. 17 (1928), at 47. *See also Lusitania Claim*, 7 R.I.A.A. 32, 39 (1923) ("the fundamental concept of 'damages' is ... reparation for a loss suffered; a judicially ascertained *compensation* for wrong. The remedy should be commensurate with the loss, so that the injured party may be made whole"); *see also* Wälde & Sabahi, *supra* note 395, at 1056–61.

[394] *CME*, Dissenting Opinion, *supra* note 224, at paras. 20–21. Professor Brownlie appears to have ignored the language of the applicable treaty, which provided that "just compensation" "shall represent the genuine value of the investments affected." Netherlands–Czech Republic BIT, art. 5(c).

[395] Charter of Economic Rights and Duties of States, G.A. Res. 3281, 29 U.N. GAOR Supp. (No. 31) at 50, 51–55, U.N. Doc. A/9631 (1974), 14 I.L.M. 251, 252–60 (1975) ("Every State has and shall freely exercise full permanent sovereignty, including possession, use and disposal, over all its wealth, natural resources and economic activities").

[396] *CME*, Dissenting Opinion, *supra* note 224, at paras. 26, 32, 34, 75 ("Is it reasonable to suppose that, when a State like the Czech Republic, with a deregulated sector of its economy, accepts foreign investment, it is accepting the risk of national economic disaster?").

[397] *See generally* Manuel Abdala & Pablo Spiller, *Damage Valuation of Indirect Expropriation in International Arbitration Cases*, 14 Am. Rev. Int'l Arb. 447 (2003); Charles Chatterjee, *The Use of the Discounted Cash Flow Method in the Assessment of Compensation*, 10(4) J. Int'l Arb. 19 (1993); Maurice Mendelson, *What Price Expropriation?: Compensation for Expropriation: The Case Law*, 79 AJIL 414 (1985); Markham Ball, *Assessing Damages in Claims by Investors against States*, 16 ICSID Rev.—For. Inv. L.J. 408 (2001); *See also* Charles N. Brower & Jarrod Wong, *General Principles of Valuation: The Case of Santa Elena*, in International Investment Law and Arbitration: Leading Cases from the ICSID, NAFTA, Bilateral Treaties and Customary International Law 747–76 (Todd Weiler ed. 2005); Irmgard Marboe, *Compensation and Damages*

asset harmed. For tangible assets for which there is a well-developed market, such as drilling equipment or a plot of land, the most appropriate basis for determining quantum of compensation is the market value of the assets in question. "Market value" refers to a property's value as determined in a transaction between willing buyers and sellers, each with adequate information about the asset.[398] According to the Iran–United States Claims Tribunal, the fair market value of an asset is equivalent to

> the price that a willing buyer would pay to a willing seller in circumstances in which each had good information, each desired to maximize his financial gain, and neither was under duress or threat.[399]

Even where there is no ready market by which to determine value directly, the market value of an asset can be assessed in terms of the reasonable perceptions of hypothetical buyers and sellers. As defined by the American Society of Appraisers, market value is equivalent to **6.181**

> the price, expressed in terms of cash equivalents, at which property would change hands between a hypothetical willing and able buyer and a hypothetical willing and able seller, acting at arms length in an open and unrestricted market, when neither is under compulsion to buy or sell and when both have reasonable knowledge of the relevant facts.[400]

1. Discounted cash flow

Where the damaged or expropriated asset is a working enterprise, or a "going concern," it is generally accepted that the most accurate method of assessing market value is the "discounted cash flow method," commonly known as DCF.[401] This method of valuation is "almost universally used and accepted by both the business **6.182**

in International Law—The Limits of "Fair Market Value," 7(5) JWIT 723, 725 (2006); for a detailed analysis on this topic, *see* Sergey Ripinsky & Kevin Williams, Damages in International Investment Law (2008).

[398] William C. Lieblich, *Determining the Economic Value of Expropriated Income-Producing Property in International Expropriations*, 8 J. Int'l Arb. 37, 63 (1991). U.S. courts have held that fair market value is "the price which would be agreed upon by a willing seller and a willing buyer under usual and ordinary circumstances, after consideration of all available uses and purposes, without any compulsion upon the seller to sell or the buyer to buy." *Poole v. N.V. Deli Maatschappij*, 243 A.2d 67, 70 (Del. 1968).

[399] *Starrett Housing Corp. v. Government of Iran*, Award No. ITL 32-34-1, 4 Iran–U.S. C.T.R. 122, para. 277 (1983).

[400] American Society of Appraisers, International Glossary of Business Valuation Terms, 4 (2001), available at http://www.bvappraisers.org/glossary/glossary.pdf. *See also* Jerome Ortscheidt, La Réparation du Dommage dans L'Arbitrage Commercial International 199 (2001).

[401] *Biloune, supra* note 131, 95 Int'l Law Rep. 184, 228 (1994) ("Normally, in cases of expropriation of a going concern, the most accurate measure of the value of the expropriated property is its fair market value, which in its nature takes into account future profits. The discounted cash flow method of valuation is often used to calculate the worth of the enterprise at the time of the taking"); *Amco Asia Corp. v. Indonesia*, ICSID Case No. ARB/81/1, Award of Nov. 20, 1984 (*Amco I*), 24 I.L.M. 1022 (1985); Paul Friedland & E. Wong, *Measuring Damages for the Deprivation of Income-Producing Assets: ICSID Case Studies*, 6 ICSID Rev.—For. Inv. L.J. 400, 426 (1991) ("Generally, where ICSID tribunals have been satisfied that the asset taken was a 'going concern,' they have

and academic communities in valuing capital assets."[402] The following is a brief explanation of the DCF method:

> [T]he DCF method involves first calculating the cash receipts expected in each future year, and then subtracting that year's expected cash expenditure. The result is the net cash flow for the year. Because cash to be received in the future is worth less than the same amount of cash received today, the net cash flow for each future year is then discounted (i.e., reduced) to determine its value on the valuation date, which is usually referred to as its "present value" as of that date. This discounting is accomplished through the application of a discount factor derived from a discount rate that reflects the time value of money, expected inflation, and any risks attached to the cash flows ... the sum of the present values of the net cash flows for all future years is the value of an asset or enterprise as determined by the DCF method.[403]

6.183 This method of valuation reflects the reality that the economic value of an enterprise to its owner is equal to its ability to generate a cash flow.[404] Lieblich has noted that, "if future profits (or, more correctly, future cash flows) may not be taken into consideration in determining the value of expropriated property, it is not possible to determine its value at all."[405] As Lieblich further explains:

> [C]ash is the proper focus of any method that is used to measure economic value. Profits, in contrast, are an accounting construct that is designed to provide information concerning the allocation of the business' cash receipt and outlays over time ...... but profits do not necessarily accurately reflect a firm's actual net cash flows in a specific period, and therefore are not the appropriate object of an inquiry into the firm's economic value.[406]

6.184 Professor Lauterpacht has concurred with this conclusion, since "[a]n asset is worth only so much as it can earn; and it is in terms of its earning capacity that its economic value must be measured ... [T]he correct way of reflecting the relationship between earning capacity and value [is through] the concept of discounted cash flow (DCF)."[407]

6.185 Some commentators have objected that the DCF method is too "speculative," or may generate controversy, because it is impossible to know future economic conditions or to select a discount rate that accurately reflects future risk.[408] Any

applied, whether explicitly or not, the DCF method"); Guidelines, *supra* note 252, 31 I.L.M. at 1383; Lieblich, *supra* note 402, at 70.

402 Lieblich, *supra* note 402, at 70.

403 *Id.* at 38–39.

404 *See id.* at 61 ("That the economic value of an asset is determined by the asset's expected capacity to generate revenues is by no means a recent insight").

405 *Id.* at 76.

406 *Id.* at 62.

407 Elihu Lauterpacht, *Issues of Compensation and Nationality in the Taking of Energy Investments*, 8 J. Energy & Nat. Res. L. 241, 245–46 (1990).

408 For example, the tribunal in *Occidental v. Ecuador* case looked to the DCF method to calculate the compensation owed to the claimant after the cancellation of its rights in a hydrocarbon block. It awarded US$1,769,625,000, stating that "[t]hese net cash flows are appropriately determined by calculating the flow of benefits ('cash flows') that the Claimants would have reasonably

sensible determination of value, however, must inquire into the future. "The only way to escape uncertainty in awarding compensation is to employ methods—such as book value—that are irrelevant to economic value because they focus on the past and not the future."[409]

Another argument against discounted cash flow calculation is that such an approach amounts to an award of "future profits," according to some inappropriate under international law and practice. Many tribunals and commentators draw a distinction between the value of "hard" assets (net book value) and the "profits" that the assets will produce. Just as the arguments for "partial" compensation are difficult to understand, this reasoning is also problematic: "the value of income-producing assets depends entirely on the cash that they are expected to generate in the future."[410] **6.186**

2. Net book value

Some commentators and tribunals have suggested that "net book value" should determine the quantum of compensation for damage to assets.[411] The term "book value" or "net book value" represents the difference between the investment's assets and liabilities as shown on a balance sheet and determined in accordance with generally accepted accounting principles.[412] "Book value" and "net book value" are accounting terms, however, and are not generally considered to be the most accurate methods of assessing the value of particular assets on an open market.[413] **6.187**

---

been expected to earn in the 'but for' state of the world in which the termination of the Participation Contract hypothetically did not occur relative to the actual cash flow that the Claimants will derive subsequent to the termination. The difference between these two cash flow streams (the 'but for' state of the world with no termination less the actual state of the world with contract termination), discounted to the date of the actual contract termination, is the economically appropriate and reliable measure of the cumulative economic harm suffered by the Claimants as a consequence of the contract termination." *See Occidental Petroleum and Occidental Exploration and Production v. Ecuador*, ICSID Case No. ARB/06/11, Award of Oct. 5, 2012, para. 708, available at https://www.italaw.com/sites/default/files/case-documents/italaw1094.pdf.

409 Lieblich, *supra* note 402, at 77.

410 *Id.* at 67. It is generally recognized that in calculating the value of expropriated property, a tribunal must exclude diminution in value caused by the fact of the taking. *INA Corp. v. Iran*, Award No. 184-161-1, 8 Iran–U.S. C.T.R. 373, 380 (1985) ("'Fair market value' may be stated as the amount which a willing buyer would have paid a willing seller for the shares of a going concern, disregarding any diminution of value due to the nationalization itself or the anticipation thereof, and excluding consideration of events thereafter that might have increased or decreased the value of the shares"). *See also* Charles N. Brower, *Current Developments in the Law of Expropriation and Compensation: A Preliminary Survey of Awards of the Iran–United States Claims Tribunal*, 21 Int'l Law. 639, 665 (1987).

411 For a review of net book value method, *see* Thomas R. Stauffer, *Valuation of Assets in International Takings*, 17 Energy L.J. 459–88 (1996); *see also* Todd Weiler & Luis Miguel Diaz, *Causation and Damages in NAFTA Investor–State Arbitration*, in NAFTA Investment Law and Arbitration: Past Issues, Current Practice, Future Prospects 199 (Todd Weiler ed. 2004).

412 Lieblich, *supra* note 402, at 64.

413 Lauterpacht, *supra* note 264, at 245–46.

Book value does not reflect the right to receive a portion of the revenues of a business. Rather, book value assumes that there is a "real" value to property, to which "profits" are added. But, as Judge Higgins has pointed out, "[t]here is no 'real' value of property, to which the estimate of profits is then added."[414]

3. Comparable transactions

6.188 Whether a particular asset is directly tradeable or not, there may be identifiable transactions for the sale of other, similar assets that can be used as a benchmark for determining fair market value. For example, even if a plot of land has remained in the same hands for decades before expropriation, its value may be estimated by examining the price for which nearby tracts of similar size and quality were purchased at about the time of the taking. Most important in this exercise is that the asset examined be "comparable," that the transaction was carried out at "arm's length," *i.e.* between unrelated buyer and seller, and that it have occurred reasonably near in time to the valuation date. These criteria can make suitable transactions difficult to find. But where they are identified, such sales of comparable assets can be a powerful indicator of fair market value.

4. Arbitral decisions

6.189 Despite widespread support in the business and academic communities for "market value" as the proper measure of compensation and the DCF valuation method as the most reliable way to quantify damages,[415] arbitral tribunals have been somewhat inconsistent in their application of these standards.

a. Tangible property

6.190 Where the expropriated or damaged investment is in the form of movable or immovable assets, but not a going concern, many tribunals employ the "market value" approach to valuation. For example, in the *SEDCO*[416] case, the Iran–U.S. Claims Tribunal found that Iran had expropriated oil rigs belonging to the claimant. The tribunal stated that the claimant should be compensated for

> the fair market value of the properties, i.e., what a willing buyer and a willing seller would reasonably have agreed on as a fair price at the time of the taking in the absence of coercion on either party.[417]

6.191 The oil rigs were valued at "liquidation value," the price they would fetch on the open market. The tribunal also assessed the market value of an expropriated parcel

---

[414] Higgins, *supra* note 100, at 144.
[415] Lieblich, *supra* note 402, at 70.
[416] *SEDCO Inc. v. Nat'l Iranian Oil Co. et al.*, Award No. 309-129-3, 15 Iran–U.S. C.T.R. 23 (1987).
[417] *Id.* at 35.

of land, using as its basis a comparable arm's length transaction. Compensation was based on the price paid for a similar parcel of land one year earlier. Another parcel of land was valued using "current cost accounting", by which the book value of the land was increased using a price index.

b. Business enterprises—going concern

Where a business enterprise that is a going concern has been expropriated, a number of tribunals have applied the DCF method of valuation.[418] The DCF method has been explicitly applied in several published decisions of the Iran–U.S. Claims Tribunal, and in numerous ICSID decisions.[419] 6.192

In the *Phillips* case, U.S. nationals sought compensation for the expropriation of their interests in an Iranian joint venture for the operation of oil fields in the Persian Gulf. The tribunal stated that the valuation of a going concern must be based upon its ability to generate revenues, and adopted the DCF method to make this determination. The tribunal also engaged an expert to evaluate the assets using a so-called "underlying asset valuation" method, assessing the depreciated value of the tangible assets and adding an "intangible asset" value, based on historic income. The DCF approach yielded a value of about US$55 million, while the alternative method amounted to US$60 million. The award was ultimately based upon the DCF valuation.[420] 6.193

In *Starrett*, the tribunal used the discounted cash flow method in valuing the claimant's right to participate in a venture for the construction of an apartment complex. The tribunal required payment of fair market value, which was determined to be the going-concern value, determined by the tribunal-appointed expert's DCF valuation. However, the tribunal then reduced the award by over 90 percent from the expert's result, adjusting the DCF method in light of concepts of "equity."[421] 6.194

In *AIG*, which involved the nationalization of an insurance company, the award indicated that the claimant should receive the full market value of its 35 percent interest in the enterprise, and that any effects of nationalization should not be considered in arriving at the value. The tribunal stated that it was constrained to 6.195

[418] *See generally* Charles Chaterjee, *The Use of the Discounted Cash Flow Method in the Assessment of Compensation: Comments on the Recent World Bank Guidelines on the Treatment of Foreign Direct Investment*, 10(4) J. Int'l Arb. 19 (1993).

[419] *See Phillips, supra* note 130; *Starrett, supra* note 403; *Amco I, supra* note 405; *Amco Asia Corp. v. Indonesia*, ICSID Case No. ARB/81/1, Award of June 5, 1990, 5 Int'l Arb. Rep. D-5 (1990); *CMS, supra* note 141; *Nat'l Grid Plc. v. Argentina*, UNCITRAL Award of Nov. 3, 2008, paras. 275–77; *Enron Creditors Recovery Corp. (formerly Enron Corp.) and Ponderosa Assets, L.P. v. Argentina*, ICSID Case No. ARB/01/3, Award of May 22, 2007, para. 385; *Occidental Petroleum, supra* note 412, para. 690.

[420] *Phillips, supra* note 130.

[421] *Starrett, supra* note 403, at paras. 138–77.

value the company as a going concern, taking into account not only the net book value of its assets, but also such elements as goodwill and likely future profitability, had the company been allowed to continue its business under its former management.[422]

6.196 The parties each submitted estimates of the enterprise's value, which were widely disparate. The tribunal chose a figure that was approximately 25 percent of what the claimant had requested, but several times greater than the value proposed by the respondent State.

6.197 In the two *Amco Asia* ICSID arbitrations, both tribunals adopted the DCF valuation method. These cases involved the seizure by the Indonesian army of a hotel complex belonging to American investors. The first tribunal stated:

> Now, while there are several methods of valuation of going concerns, the most appropriate one in the present case is to establish the net present value of the business, based on a reasonable projection of the foreseeable net case flow during the period to be considered, said net cash flow being then discounted in order to take into account the assessment of the damages at the date of the prejudice.[423]

6.198 The DCF method was also accepted in the *LIAMCO* arbitration,[424] but only as a method to value the "future profits" portion of an award.[425] This case arose out of Libya's nationalization of the LIAMCO's oil concessions in 1973–74. After determining that the company was owed "appropriate" compensation, the arbitrator concluded that LIAMCO should receive the "*damnum emergens*," or the value of the tangible nationalized property, but that

> the controversial question in this connection is the scope of compensation and the manner of its determination as regards the incorporeal property of the concession rights per se and whether or not that determination should include the loss of profits (*lucrum cessans*).[426]

6.199 The arbitrator thus divided LIAMCO's enterprise into its tangible assets and its capacity to generate revenue. The arbitrator then valued seventy oil wells on the basis of the cost to construct them, adjusted for depletion, amortization, and depreciation. Regarding the nationalized concession, the claimant submitted two analyses, both apparently using the DCF method. One valued the property prior to the nationalization decrees at approximately US$186 million, while the other took into account the higher taxes and royalty rates that Libya imposed following

---

422 *American Int'l Group Inc. et al. (AIG) v. Iran*, Award No. 93-2-3, 4 Iran–U.S. C.T.R. 96, 109 (1983).

423 *Amco I, supra* note 405, at 1037.

424 *Libyan American Oil Co. (LIAMCO) v. Government of Libya* (1977), 62 I.L.R. 140 (1980), 20 I.L.M. 1 (1981).

425 As discussed, many commentators consider a distinction between "value of assets" and "future profits" to be of questionable utility.

426 *LIAMCO, supra* note 428, 20 I.L.M. at 132.

the expropriation, and valued the property at approximately US$56 million. Based on the "measure of equitable compensation,"[427] the arbitrator awarded US$66 million without further explanation.[428]

Thus, the DCF method has been embraced by some tribunals as the proper method to value a going concern. It is important to note, however, that there is also lingering resistance to application of the DCF method. In *Metalclad*, for instance, the claimant sought US$90 million in compensation, supporting its valuation with a DCF analysis. The tribunal's final award of substantially less (approximately US$17 million) reflected sunk costs rather than future cash flows, largely because the arbitrators recognized that the landfill in question had never in fact begun operations.[429] The *Khemco* case also deserves special mention for its reasoning in this regard. This case arose from Iran's expropriation of the claimant's interest in an oil venture. The tribunal rejected the DCF method, stating that: 6.200

> [The DCF method] is instead a projection into the future to assess the amount of the revenues which would possibly be earned by the undertaking year after year, up to 18 years later in this Case. These forecasted revenues are actualized at the time by way of a discounting calculation, and capitalized as the measure of the compensation to be paid, as well as the alleged market value of the enterprise. With such a method, *lucrum cessans* becomes the sole element of compensation.[430]

The tribunal also rejected the "book value" approach suggested by the respondent State, and instead adopted what it termed the "going concern" value. It asked the parties to submit statements relating to various tangible and intangible components of the enterprise, from which it would derive the value of the enterprise as a whole. 6.201

Likewise, in *Tecmed v. Mexico,* the tribunal rejected the DCF approach, due to the "non-relevance of the brief history of the operation," the "difficulties in obtaining objective data allowing for application of the discounted cash flow method on the basis of estimates for a protracted future," "together with the fact that such future cash flow also depends upon investments to be made."[431] 6.202

The tribunal in *Vivendi v. Argentina* award also pointed out that "many international tribunals have stated that an award based on future profits is not appropriate unless the relevant enterprise is profitable and has operated for a sufficient period to establish its performance record."[432] 6.203

---

427 *Id.* at 159–60.

428 The arbitrator did not award compensation for a second, less profitable concession. *Id.* at 162.

429 *Metalclad, supra* note 98. The tribunal was not swayed by the claimant's counter-argument that the landfill had no established track record only because of the host State's interference.

430 *Amoco Int'l Finance Corp. v. Iran (Khemco)*, 15 Iran–U.S. C.T.R. 189, 258–59 (1987).

431 *Tecmed, supra* note 148, at para. 186.

432 *Vivendi, supra* note 131, at para. 8.3.3.

c. Business enterprises—not a going concern

6.204 When it is not clear whether an enterprise is a going concern, tribunals are often reluctant to use the DCF method of valuation (or any other method of valuation that takes future revenues or profits into account). Several cases decided under the auspices of ICSID have taken this approach. In *Benvenuti v. Congo*,[433] the tribunal refused to apply the DCF method because it did not believe that the expropriated water bottling plant was a going concern. Instead, it awarded the amount originally invested into the project by the investors. In *AAPL*,[434] the tribunal likewise declined to apply the DCF method to assess the compensation for the destruction of a shrimp farm, holding that the facility was not a going concern. The tribunal awarded net book value of the assets instead.[435]

6.205 Certain cases decided by the Iran–U.S. Claims Tribunal have also taken this approach. In *Phelps Dodge*,[436] a case involving a copper tubing factory that was still under construction when it was expropriated, the tribunal refused include elements of "lost profits" and "goodwill" in its award. It reasoned that because the enterprise had not become a going concern when it was expropriated, "any conclusions [regarding lost profits and goodwill] would be highly speculative."[437] In *Sola Tiles*,[438] although the enterprise was a going concern, the tribunal did not award compensation for "goodwill" or "lost profits" because the tribunal was not convinced that the company, which sold luxury tiles, would have been able to continue in business after the revolution, due to the subsequent changes in Iranian society. The tribunal instead awarded book value. Similar reasoning was applied and a similar result reached in *Thomas Earl Payne*,[439] which involved a motion picture film distribution company.

6.206 In the *INA Corp.* case,[440] involving the expropriation of an insurance company, the tribunal awarded the amount that the claimant had invested in the enterprise approximately one year before the expropriation took place. In *Tippets*,[441] the tribunal, at the request of the claimant, determined the value of the business based on the "dissolution value," which was described as the value of the enterprise after the collection of all assets and the discharge of all obligations.

---

433 *Benvenuti & Bonfant v. Government of the People's Republic of the Congo*, ICSID Case No. ARB/77/2, Award of Aug. 8, 1980, 67 I.L.R. 345 (1984).

434 *AAPL, supra* note 208, at 567.

435 *Id.* at 567. *See also Southern Pacific Properties (Middle East) Ltd. v. Egypt*, ICSID Case No. ARB/84/3, Award of May 20, 1992, paras. 184–91; *Rumeli, supra* note 212, at para. 726; *LG&E, supra* note 162, at paras. 89–90.

436 *Phelps Dodge, supra* note 92.

437 *Id.* at 132–33.

438 *Sola Tiles Inc. v. Iran*, Award No. 298-317-1, 14 Iran–U.S. C.T.R. 223 (1987).

439 *Thomas Earl Payne v. Iran*, Award No. 245-335-2, 12 Iran–U.S. C.T.R. 3 (1986).

440 *INA, supra* note 414.

441 *Tippets, supra* note 130, at 219.

d. Comparing the menu of options: CME v. Czech Republic

The damages award in *CME v. Czech Republic* is illustrative of the analysis that arbitrators undertake when considering complex compensation issues.[442] There, the tribunal was faced with a number of competing damage quantification methods in setting the amount of compensation for the investor's share in a Czech television company according to a measure of "fair market value," established in the applicable Netherlands–Czech Republic BIT. To arrive at fair market value, the tribunal selected a primary and secondary valuation method from among five alternative formulae proposed by the claimant. 6.207

First, the claimant suggested using the price offered for the company by a Swedish media company in a contract to acquire the investor's parent company. This acquisition contract was signed several months before the expropriation, but was never consummated. This figure, CME argued, most closely corresponded to the international law definition of "fair market value," which is "the price that a willing buyer would pay a willing seller in circumstances in which each had good information, each desired to maximize his financial gain, and neither was under duress or threat." According the claimant, the Swedish company had been willing to pay US$600 million for the Czech investment.[443] The Czech Republic opposed this method of valuation, arguing that the offer in question was for a range of assets in addition to the expropriated investment, and that in any event the offer had dropped significantly from US$600 million over the time leading up to the taking, leaving less than half of the amount "on the table" as of the relevant valuation date. Other objections included the value of specific synergies that the Swedish company had included in its assessment, that the offer was not made in cash, but in stock (which was subject to market fluctuations), and uncertainty that the transaction would ever have been consummated.[444] The tribunal agreed with the claimant that the Swedish transaction "gives an objective view of the fair market value" of the investment, and adopted the purchase price as a base for its award. However, the tribunal made several downward adjustments to the offer price, mainly as a result of what it viewed as the claimant's inaccurate interpretation of the offer, resulting in a value of US$328 million.[445] 6.208

The claimant also engaged an expert to apply the DCF method to its investment vehicle's earnings. CME argued that such a method was well established in international arbitration practice, particularly where compensation is to be awarded for "the destruction or taking of going concerns where no active market for the asset exists."[446] The Czech Republic agreed that DCF analysis would be an 6.209

---

[442] Noah Rubins, *The Final Damages Award in CME v. Czech Republic, B.V. v. Czech Republic: An Overview*, Mealey's Int'l Arb. Rep., September 2003, at 35.
[443] *CME*, Final Award, *supra* note 144, at paras. 98–100.
[444] *Id.* at paras. 352–56.
[445] *Id.* at paras. 526–53.
[446] *Id.* at para. 161.

appropriate method to use, but took issue with several of the assumptions upon which the Claimant's DCF valuation had been made. The respondent challenged the end point of the relevant cash flow period, as well as CME's projections of growth in the television advertising market. Given the agreement of the parties, the tribunal accepted that a DCF analysis should be used to supplement or confirm the "arm's length buyer" figure that emerged from the Swedish transaction. Unusually, both parties' experts concurred as to the proper discount rate to be applied. The tribunal dismissed most of the Czech Republic's objections to CME's methodology, and noted that the remaining gap between the DCF results offered by the parties' experts, which amounted to about US$210 million, was primarily the result of differing estimates of six variables. After analyzing the parties' assumptions as to each of the disputed variables, the tribunal ruled that CME's expert had been overly optimistic as to the Czech company's continuing market dominance in the future, adjusted CME's figure downward, and found that the result confirmed the result of the proposed arm's-length transaction. However, the arbitrators refused to rely specifically on the DCF valuation in their award, primarily because the projections involved "a rather high element of uncertainty and speculation."[447]

6.210 As confirmation of other methods, CME offered the tribunal a "trading multiple" analysis, which entailed a review of the market capitalization of "comparable companies" within the broadcasting market. A "trading multiple" was derived by dividing the market value of each of twenty-nine publicly traded media companies around the world by their earnings before interest, tax, depreciation, and amortization (EBITDA) for a given year, and then determining the average resulting ratio for all the companies analyzed. CME argued that this procedure was "a common method by which buyers and sellers value companies that are going concerns."[448] The Czech Republic objected to this approach, arguing that it provides only a backward-looking "snapshot" of a company's performance, and that the companies examined were not comparable to the Czech entity in question.[449] Ultimately, the tribunal did not address the trading multiple method in its analysis, instead relying primarily upon the arm's-length purchase offer and DCF calculations to arrive at the quantum of compensation.[450]

---

447 *Id.* at para. 604.

448 *Id.* at para. 166.

449 *Id.* at paras. 366–67.

450 In *CMS v. Argentina*, Argentina argued that the damage to the claimant's investment (shares in TGN, a local gas pipeline company whose stock was not publicly traded) should be determined according to the ratio between the net assets and market capitalization of certain "comparable" companies trading on the Buenos Aires stock exchange. The tribunal refused to apply this method, because "there were significant differences between TGN and those companies regarding asset levels, business segments, financing policy, and other issues," and instead applied a DCF analysis). *CMS, supra* note 141, at para. 404.

CME also proposed adopting the contemporaneous views of independent market analysts, who assessed the company's prospects periodically throughout the relevant period. The Czech Republic opposed the use of analyst reports as prone to inflating the company's earnings potential.[451] While the tribunal declined to repeat the Czech Republic's doubts about the veracity of market analysts' reports in general, it also refused to consider these reports in its evaluation of the fair market value of CME's investment. The fact that several analysts had evaluated CME's Czech broadcasting operations at over US$600 million "[could] not change the Tribunal's view" that the lower results yielded by the DCF and arm's length offer marked the proper level of compensation. The tribunal reasoned that "[a]nalysts, as a matter of principle, can only value a company on the basis of the underlying facts and financial data of the corporation." The tribunal "cannot determine what level and what quality of financial data was given to the analysts."[452] **6.211**

As another possible method of assessing the value of its investment, the claimant suggested using the amount that the company paid to its onetime director for his 5.8 percent stake in the investment two years before the expropriation took place. The claimant argued that this figure could be extrapolated to derive a purchase price for 100 percent of the investment vehicle in 1997, and then divided by the company's EBITDA for that year to derive a multiplier. Applying this factor to the company's EBITDA the year before the expropriation, the claimant asserted that the company had a fair market value of US$542 million. The tribunal rejected this limited sale of shares as an appropriate benchmark for the valuation of the entire investment enterprise. The sale took place two years before the investment was destroyed, the shareholding constituted a minority stake, and furthermore the seller's position as a former director of the company influenced the price paid.[453] **6.212**

e. Equitable considerations

Although international tribunals have generally upheld the traditional international law principle of full compensation for breaches of international law, and despite the increasing willingness of tribunals to apply modern methods of valuation, some tribunals continue to invoke equitable principles to modify awards of compensation. **6.213**

In *LIAMCO*, the claimant submitted two calculations of the value of "future profits" of an oil concession. The ultimately arbitrator awarded an amount **6.214**

[451] *CME*, Final Award, *supra* note 144, at para. 369 ("Recent scandals surrounding the conflicts of interest between analysts and investment bankers working in the same firms demonstrates unequivocally that the analyst valuations cannot and should not be relied upon uncritically for an objective valuation of [the investment]").

[452] *Id.* at paras. 608–09.

[453] *Id.* at paras. 610–11.

between the two alternatives, as a "measure of equitable compensation."[454] In *Khemco*, the tribunal stated:

> The choice between all the available methods must rather be made in view of the purpose to be attained, in order to avoid arbitrary results and to arrive at an equitable compensation in conformity with the applicable legal standards.[455]

6.215 The *Phillips* award also refers to "equity." There, the Iran–U.S. Claims Tribunal stated that "the need for some adjustments is understandable, as the determination of value by a tribunal must take into account all relevant circumstances, including equitable considerations."[456]

6.216 Norton observes that in many arbitrations, tribunals, "after elaborate analysis of the law, seemingly pluck the amount of an award out of thin air."[457] He then offers several examples:

> The AMINOIL award, for example, indicates no basis whatsoever for its calculations … Similarly, in LIAMCO, Mahmassani chose a figure between those offered by the parties and gave no explanation at all … Much the same can be said of many of the decisions of the Iran–U.S. Claims Tribunal.[458]

6.217 Today, investment arbitration tribunals appear to have increasing experience and confidence in determining the appropriate magnitude of compensation. Nevertheless, the quantum of damages remains one of the least understood and most unpredictable areas of international investment law.[459]

F. Conclusion

6.218 Even where investment treaties do not explicitly so provide, tribunals have normally found that a State is responsible for paying full compensation for all harm caused by its breaches of an applicable treaty's substantive protections. At the same time, there is little agreement regarding the optimal method of valuing property to arrive at the most accurate estimation of "full" compensation. In the words of Professor Amerasinghe:

> Full compensation has been arrived at by a variety of methods, depending on a variety of factors, including the nature of the property or interests taken and other circumstances relating to the property taken. No preference has been shown for a particular method, such as the discounted cash flow method … It would seem that

[454] *LIAMCO, supra* note 428, 20 I.L.M. at 159–60.
[455] *Khemco, supra* note 434, at 256.
[456] *Phillips, supra* note 130, at para. 112.
[457] Patrick M. Norton, *A Law of the Future or a Law of the Past? Modern Tribunals and the International Law of Expropriation*, 85 AJIL 474, 495 (1991).
[458] *Id.*
[459] *See generally* Stauffer, *supra* note 415, at 459.

> the assessment of full compensation is at the present time filled with variables and is certainly not a very scientific process.[460]

Nevertheless, the DCF approach is considered to be the best method for valuing lost profits, and despite the critics that it promotes excessive levels of compensation and speculative results, if the DCF method is properly applied, and assisted with the appropriate use of experts' valuation-reports, then tribunals can be in the position to assess correctly the DCF claims.[461] **6.219**

[460] C.F. Amerasinghe, *Issues of Compensation for the Taking of Alien Property in the Light of Recent Cases and Practice*, 41 ICLQ 22, 64 (1992).
[461] *See* MCLACHLAN et al., *supra* note 115, at 9.89–9.94.

PART III

INVESTMENT DISPUTES AND POLITICAL RISK

7

ESTABLISHING ARBITRAL JURISDICTION

A. Introduction

Should the host State fail to carry out its obligations to a foreign investor under a contract, its own national investment code, or a treaty with the investor's home State, the investor may be able to vindicate its rights through international arbitration. As explained elsewhere, in many cases arbitration offers the parties the only neutral forum in which to resolve disputes, and the only means to obtain a remedy that is enforceable across borders.[1] Such a right is hardly automatic, however. As in arbitration between private parties, the State must expressly consent to such extra-judicial dispute resolution,[2] consent which must **7.01**

[1] Chapter 8, Section A. *See also* Nigel Rawding, *Protecting Investments under State Contracts: Some Legal and Ethical Issues*, 11 Arb. Int'l 341, 342–46 (1995).

[2] *See* generally, Christoph Schreuer, *Consent to Arbitration*, in The Oxford Handbook of International Investment Law, ch. 21, 830–67 (Peter Muchlinski et al. eds. 2008).

be contained in the relevant contract,[3] investment code,[4] or investment protection treaty.[5]

7.02 In the context of contracts, the consent to arbitrate is contained in a single document, either signed before the dispute arises (an arbitration clause) or afterwards (a voluntary submission). Consent to arbitration pursuant to investment protection instruments comes in two parts, sometimes referred to as consent "without privity":

> First, the host State consents by including a standing offer to submit to [investment arbitration] jurisdiction in its national legislation or in a bilateral or multilateral investment treaty. Second, the investor—which may not have been an investor at the time of the State's offer—consents by accepting that offer later, either in writing to the host State at any time or by filing a request to arbitrate . . .[6]

7.03 For all of the differences between contractual arbitration and dispute resolution under the auspices of national laws and investment protection treaties, the central importance of consent remains the same. Learned commentators have only figuratively referred to the treaty-based dispute resolution process as "without privity";[7] it is no small matter for a private party to compel a State to arbitrate, and tribunals tend to scrutinize the extent of their own authority to adjudicate investor–State disputes.[8]

7.04 In addition to establishing consent through a contract or investment protection instrument, if the investor seeks to initiate arbitration under the auspices of the International Centre for the Settlement of Investment Disputes (ICSID), he must satisfy a range of additional jurisdictional requirements. While some of these limitations are similar to those codified in investment treaties and other consent documents, the criteria applied are not necessarily identical, and therefore are given particular attention in the next section.

---

[3] *See* Christopher F. Dugan et al., Investor–State Arbitration, ch. X (2012).

[4] *See* Michele Potestà, *The Interpretation of Consent to ICSID Arbitration Contained in Domestic Investment Laws*, 27(2) Arb. Int'l 149–70 (2011).

[5] *See generally* Christoph Schreuer, *Consent to Arbitration*, in The Oxford Handbook of International Investment Law (Peter Muchlinski et al. eds. 2008).

[6] Lucy Reed et al., Guide to ICSID Arbitration 35 (2004). *See also Tradex Hellas S.A. v. Albania*, ICSID Case No. ARB/94/2, Decision on Jurisdiction of Dec. 24, 1996, 14 ICSID Rev.—For. Inv. L.J. 161, 187 (1999) ("consent can also be effected unilaterally by a Contracting State in its national laws the consent becoming effective at the latest if and when the foreign investor files its claim with ICSID making use of the respective national law").

[7] Jan Paulsson, *Arbitration without Privity*, 10 ICSID Rev.—For. Inv. L.J. 232 (1995); Andrea Bjorklund, *Contract without Privity: Sovereign Offer and Investor Acceptance*, 2 Chi. J. Int'l L. 183 (2001).

[8] William Park, *The Arbitrability Dicta in First Options v. Kaplan: What Sort of Kompetenz-Kompetenz Has Crossed the Atlantic?*, 12 Arb. Int'l 137, 138–39 (1996); Mahir Jalili, *Kompetenz-Kompetenz: Recent U.S. and U.K. Developments*, 13(4) J. Int'l Arb. 169, 170 (1996).

B. Contractual Arbitration

1. The validity and effect of an arbitration clause

A contractual arbitration clause compels the parties, whether private or sovereign, to submit disputes related to their agreement to a private tribunal for resolution, normally to the exclusion of national courts.[9] Since arbitration is a creature of contract, a tribunal derives its authority to hear the parties' dispute entirely from the consent of the parties, as expressed in the arbitration clause. The particular contours of this delegation are found in the parties' agreement to arbitrate. As a result, nearly all national arbitration laws recognize that tribunals only have jurisdiction to decide issues that the parties have agreed to submit to them, and according to the parameters that the parties specify.[10] **7.05**

National arbitration statutes and case law in most countries, as well as prominent arbitration rules, confirm that an arbitral tribunal has the authority in the first instance to decide whether or not the submission to arbitration gives it jurisdiction to hear the matters presented.[11] However, national courts normally retain the power to review the tribunal's jurisdictional decision, and to refuse enforcement of—or even annul—an arbitral award rendered on the basis of an inadequate submission to arbitration.[12] **7.06**

States have at times opposed arbitration despite the existence of a valid arbitration clause on grounds that the binding nature of arbitration is contrary to State sovereignty. However, it is generally accepted that a State's acceptance of dispute **7.07**

---

[9] *See generally* Paul H. Vishny, Guide to International Commercial Law §§ 12.37–12.40 (1994); Chapter 2, Section D.1; Chapter 8, Section C.

[10] *See e.g.* UNCITRAL Model Law, art. 34(2)(iii); Bulgaria Law on International Commercial Arbitration, art. 47(5); Estonia Arbitration Act, art. 7(4); Mexico Civil Code, art. 1457(1)(c).

[11] *See e.g.* Convention on the Settlement of Investment Disputes between States and Nationals of Other States [hereinafter, Washington Convention], 4 I.L.M. 532 (1965), arts. 15, 41(1) ("[t]he Tribunal shall be the judge of its own competence") and ICSID Arbitration Rules, Rule 41(2); UNCITRAL Arbitration Rules, art. 21(1) ("[t]he arbitral tribunal shall have the power to rule on objections that it has no jurisdiction"). In some cases, express reference to issues of jurisdiction within the arbitration clause have bolstered tribunals' enforcement of the submission to arbitrate. The arbitration clause in the *TOPCO* concession, for example, provided that "[t]he Arbitrators ... shall determine the applicability of this Clause and the procedure to be followed in the Arbitration." *Texaco Overseas Petroleum Co. and California Asiatic Oil Co. (TOPCO) v. Government of Libya* (1977), 53 I.L.R. 389, 403–04, 17 I.L.M. 1 (1978). On the "internationalization" of contracts, see Chapter 2, Section D.1 and Chapter 4, Section B.2.a.

[12] Alan Redfern & Martin Hunter, Law and Practice of International Commercial Arbitration 5–8 (4th ed. 2004); *Waste Management Inc. v. Mexico*, ICSID Case No. ARB(AF)/98/2, Award of June 2, 2000, at para. 16; Judgment of the High Court of Singapore of Aug. 14, 2017 in *Swissbourgh Diamond Mines (Pty.) Ltd. et al. v. Lesotho*, PCA Case No. 2013-29 (setting aside an arbitral award which dealt with a dispute falling outside the scope of the parties' submission to arbitrate.

resolution by arbitration constitutes an exercise, not a derogation, of its sovereignty.[13] As one ICC sole arbitrator reasoned in 1974:

> I must admit that I have found some difficulties to follow a line of reasoning that a State, just because of its supreme position and qualities, should be unable to give a binding promise. The principle *pacta sunt servanda* is generally acknowledged in international law ... A sovereign State must be sovereign enough to make a binding promise both under international law and municipal law ... To require or assume then that a promise of a State to submit to arbitration in order to be binding, has to be confirmed in the face of the arbitrator, would probably impair the sovereignty of a State and its dignity more than the arbitrator's performance of his task, conferred upon him in accordance with what the parties have agreed upon.[14]

7.08 Sole Arbitrator Mahmassani confirmed this principle in the *LIAMCO* arbitration:

> It is widely accepted in international law and practice that an arbitration clause survives the unilateral termination by the State of the contract in which it is inserted and continues in force even after its termination. This is a logical consequence of the interpretation of the intention of the contracting parties, and appears to be one of the basic conditions for creating a favorable climate for foreign investment.[15]

7.09 In the *British Petroleum* case, the arbitrator relied on the following portion of the arbitration clause (which also establishes the scope of the submission to arbitration and the method for choosing the arbitrators) to establish the consent of the parties to arbitrate:

> If at any time during or after the currency of this Concession any difference or dispute shall arise between the Government and the Company concerning the interpretation or performance hereof, or anything herein contained or in connection herewith, or the rights and liabilities of either of such parties hereunder and if such parties should fail to settle such difference or dispute by agreement, the same shall, failing any agreement to settle it any other way, be referred to two Arbitrators, one of whom shall be appointed by each such party, and an Umpire who shall be appointed by the Arbitrators immediately after they are themselves appointed.[16]

---

[13] *See TOPCO, supra* note 11, 53 I.L.R., at 482, para. 78 ("[V]erification should be made as to whether the act considered [the contract] does in fact alienate the sovereignty of the State over such resources. The moment the examination of the legal relationship established between the parties shows that the State retains not only the enjoyment of its sovereignty, but also a significant part of its exercise, the conclusion should be that the contractual act creating it within the international legal order is valid, because this was done by virtue of an act *which itself* expresses the sovereignty of the State ... [I]n entering into concession contracts with the plaintiffs, the Libyan State did not *alienate* but *exercised* its sovereignty and ensured that it would not be affected in principle, the limitations accepted by it in respect of the exercise of certain of its prerogatives having been accepted only in particular areas and for a specific period of time" (emphasis added)).

[14] ICC Case No. 2321, Preliminary Award (1974), in Collection of ICC Arbitral Awards 1974–1985 8–9 (Sigvard Jarvin & Yves Derains eds. 1990). *See also* discussion of *pacta sunt servanda* at Chapter 2, Section D.3.c and Chapter 4, Section B.1.

[15] *Libyan American Oil Co. (LIAMCO) v. Government of Libya* (1977), 62 I.L.R. 140 (1980), 20 I.L.M. 1, 40 (1981).

[16] *British Petroleum Exploration Co. (Libya) Ltd. v. Government of Libya* (1973/1974), 53 I.L.R. 297, 302 (1979).

Where the parties have signed a valid agreement to arbitrate, the State may not unilaterally revoke its consent,[17] such as by changing its internal law.[18] Nor may a State, according to most applicable laws, avoid its obligations under an arbitration clause by cancelling the contract in which the arbitration clause is found. According to the "separability" doctrine, an arbitration clause is severable from the remainder of the contract, and thus remains in force even if the agreement of which it is a part is nullified or invalid.[19] "It is well-established in case law that the unilateral cancellation of a contract can have no effect on the arbitration clause, which continues to be operative."[20] This basic rule is codified in a number of international arbitration rules, including the UNCITRAL Rules, which specifically provide: **7.10**

> The arbitral tribunal shall have the power to rule on its own jurisdiction, including any objections with respect to the existence or validity of the arbitration agreement. For that purpose, an arbitration clause that forms part of a contract shall be treated as an agreement independent of the other terms of the contract. A decision by the arbitral tribunal that the contract is null shall not entail automatically the invalidity of the arbitration clause.[21]

2. Binding the sovereign—who must sign?

In many investment transactions, the private investor signs the governing agreements not with the sovereign State as such, but with an agency, government-controlled corporation, or some other subsidiary entity. At the same time, the investor may wish to involve the State itself in a dispute resolution procedure arising **7.11**

[17] *See* ICSID Report of the Executive Directors on the Convention on the Settlement of Investment Disputes Between States and Nationals of other States (2003) (in effect from Jan. 1, 2003 until Apr. 9, 2006) at para. 23 ("Consent to jurisdiction must be in writing and once given cannot be withdrawn unilaterally"). For a case concerning the withdrawal of consent to the jurisdiction of the International Court of Justice, see *Nicaragua v. United States*, 1986 I.C.J. Rep. 14, at paras. 176–79 (despite the United States' withdrawal of its submission to the compulsory jurisdiction of the Court, the ICJ could decide the claim of Nicaragua against the United States).

[18] Jiménez de Aréchega, *L'Arbitrage entre les Etats et les Sociétés Privées Etrangères*, in Melanges En L'Honneur De Gilbert Gidel 367, 375 (1961), cited in *TOPCO, supra* note 11. *See also IBM World Trade Corp. v. Ecuador*, ICSID Case No. ARB/02/10, Decision on Jurisdiction of Dec. 22, 2003, at paras. 71–72, where the tribunal rejected Ecuador's objection that it lacked jurisdiction under Ecuadorian law.

[19] The doctrine of separability was addressed by the English courts in *Fiona Trust & Holding Corp. et al. v. Privalov et al.* [2007] U.K.H.L. 40, at para. 17. The House of Lords there confirmed that the principle of separability means that the invalidity or rescission of the main contract does not necessarily entail the invalidity or rescission of the arbitration agreement. Accordingly, the arbitration agreement must be treated as a "distinct agreement," which may be void or voidable only on grounds which relate directly to the arbitration agreement.

[20] *TOPCO, supra* note 11, at 409. On the doctrine of separability of arbitration clauses from contracts more generally, *see* Nigel Blackaby et al., Redfern and Hunter on International Arbitration, paras. 5.100–5.111 (6th ed. 2015).

[21] UNCITRAL Arbitration Rules (as adopted in 2013), art. 23(1). *See also* ICC Rules, art. 6(9); LCIA Rules, art. 23; ICDR Rules, art. 19; Model Law, art. 16(1); English Arbitration Act 1996, s. 7.

out of the contract, since the measures adversely affecting the private party's contractual rights may emanate from some other part of the government. Moreover, the special-purpose public entity may own few assets outside the host State's territory against which an award could be enforced.

7.12 Given the importance of consent in establishing arbitral jurisdiction over a State, the identity of the State party to an investment contract and the circumstances surrounding the signature can determine whether the private party is able to invoke an arbitration clause against the State itself.[22] The parallel *Yashlar* and *Keimir* arbitrations are illustrative in this regard.[23]

7.13 In October 1991, Turkmenistan solicited bids to attract capital and technology to explore and develop its hydrocarbon resources. Bridas, an Argentine corporation, was the successful bidder on the Yashlar concession in eastern Turkmenistan, and signed an agreement with the State-owned enterprise Turkmengeologia, creating Joint Venture Yashlar. Two years later, before any substantial work had begun on the Yashlar concession, Bridas prevailed in a second tender, this time for the Keimir Block. In 1993, Bridas signed the Keimir joint venture agreement with Turkmenneft, the State oil company. Both agreements provided that any disputes would be submitted to ICC arbitration, and both were governed by the laws of England. The Government of Turkmenistan, although actively involved in the bidding process, was not a party to either joint venture agreement, nor did Bridas seek to make it one. Bridas did insist on adding to both agreements a clause conditioning the effectiveness of the agreement on receipt of written confirmation from the government that all of the rights granted to the joint venture were effective without further licenses or other actions. Having expended some US$150 million without locating oil, Bridas suspended operations at Yashlar in December 1995. Meanwhile, Bridas encountered difficulties at Keimir as well, and disagreements developed in relation to budget overruns. In November 1995, exports from Keimir ceased.

[22] One of the most controversial issues in international commercial arbitration is the effect of arbitration agreements on non-signatories: *see e.g.*: Bernard Hanotiau, *Non-Signatories in International Arbitration: Lessons from Thirty Years of Case Law*, in International Arbitration 2006: Back to Basics? 341 (Albert Jan van den Berg ed. 2007); William W. Park, *Non-signatories and International Contracts: An Arbitrator's Dilemma*, in Multiple Party Actions in International Arbitration 1 (Belinda Macmahon ed. 2009). The issue has frequently arisen in the context of a State-owned entity with separate legal personality that appears as the signatory to an investment contract, while the foreign investor seeks to bind the State to the arbitration agreement. This issue arose, for example, in *Arab Republic of Egypt v. Southern Pacific Properties Ltd.*, Paris Cour d'appel, July 12, 1984 (1985) 10 Yb. Comm. Arb. 113; Cour de cassation, Jan. 6, 1987 (1987) 26 I.L.M. 1004. *See*, however, *Southern Pacific Properties (Middle East) Ltd. v. Egypt*, ICSID Case No. ARB/84/3, 3 ICSID Rep. 131, 189 (1995).

[23] *See generally* George Rosenberg, *State as Party to Arbitration*, 20 Arb. Int'l 387, 393–403 (2004).

7.14 In April 1996, Bridas initiated the first of two arbitrations, arising out of Joint Venture Keimir.[24] An arbitration related to Yashlar followed in June of the same year.[25] Pursuant to the respective arbitration clauses, the *Yashlar* proceeding was sited in Stockholm; the *Keimir* arbitration took place in Houston, Texas. In the *Yashlar* arbitration, Bridas filed its claim against the Turkmenistan Ministry of Oil & Gas, which had acceded to the contract, and the Government of Turkmenistan, which had not signed the agreement. Likewise, in Keimir, Bridas brought claims against the government, as well as against Turkmenneft. Turkmenistan objected in both cases to jurisdiction on grounds that it had not agreed to arbitrate any claims with Bridas.

7.15 The two panels reached opposite conclusions as to whether the government was subject to arbitral jurisdiction. The panels agreed on the starting point: both concluded that the government had not been a party to the joint venture agreements or their respective arbitration clauses. The *Yashlar* panel found that it had no jurisdiction to hear claims against the government:

> The Government of Turkmenistan obviously chose not to become a party to the JV Agreement, but rather to authorise an agreement to be entered into by a body which was a legal entity in its own right having its own separate funds. Nor can it have escaped the notice of Bridas that the Government itself did not appear in the JV Agreement as their contracting partner. Whatever was said at the bidding round about the role of the Government, the Government did not become a signatory to the agreement and obviously must have made a deliberate decision not to do so. Nor is this surprising. The activities of the Turkmenian Party in the Joint Venture are commercial rather than sovereign activities. It need hardly be added that the Government's acts of authorisation and approval and its acts of control, however far reaching, do not of themselves make it a party to the JV Agreement.[26]

7.16 In the *Keimir* award, meanwhile, the tribunal found that multiple references in the project contracts to necessary government decrees[27] created a legitimate expectation for the foreign investor that Turkmenistan itself would be bound to arbitrate should it fail to take the actions described in the contract. The tribunal held that:

> Taken in isolation, none of these provisions would be conclusive support for the proposition that it was the intention of the parties for the Government to be bound by the provisions of the contract, but cumulatively they constitute a significant involvement of government powers and interests in the contractual relationship.
>
> . . .

---

[24] *Bridas SAPIC, Bridas Energy Int'l Ltd. and Intercontinental Oil and Gas Ventures Ltd. v. Government of Turkmenistan and Concern Balkannebitgazsenagat (Keimir)*, ICC Case No. 9058, First Partial Award of June 25, 1999, available from Mealey's Int'l Arb. Rep. for a fee.

[25] *Joint Venture Yashlar and Bridas SAPIC v. Government of Turkmenistan (Yashlar)*, ICC Case No. 9151, Interim Award of June 8, 1999, available from Mealey's Int'l Arb. Rep. for a fee.

[26] *Id.* at para. 569.

[27] These decrees included tax rebates, customs benefits, and the right to use government-owned land.

> The legitimate expectation of a party can translate into intention. That is, the legitimacy of the expectation reflects the intention of the representor for the representee to have an expectation. The expectation reflects the intention of the representee. The Claimants were entitled to have a legitimate expectation that what was represented and guaranteed to them in the JV Agreement would be fulfilled. Only the Government could fulfil those requirements. It saw fit to have them included in the JV Agreement, by Presidential Decree it confirmed that the requisite approvals and consent were in place to conduct operations "based on the conditions established in the [JV Agreement]" and it saw fit to have the most important of them guaranteed with its consent. It cannot now resile from these facts or from the conclusion to which they lead: the Government is bound by the contractual commitments that only it could perform.[28]

7.17 Ultimately, Turkmenistan sought set aside the *Keimir* award in U.S. federal court. While the Texas federal district court declined Turkmenistan's motion, this decision was overturned by the Court of Appeals for the Fifth Circuit. The appeals court held that the *Keimir* panel had exceeded its powers by extending the arbitration clause to the government of Turkmenistan:

> we are simply unable to conclude that the parties, one, a multinational corporation who has negotiated joint venture agreements in the past, and the other, a sovereign nation, both represented by able Counsel, intended Turkmenneft to sign the JVA as an agent of the Government in the absence of clearer language to that effect.[29]

7.18 Another ICC arbitral award gave rise to two conflicting judgments in *Dallah Real Estate and Tourism Holding Co. v. Government of Pakistan*. In that case, a Saudi Arabian company signed a contract for the construction of houses at pilgrimage sites in 1996 with Awami Hajj Trust, a body that had been established by an ordinance promulgated by the President of Pakistan. Following a change of government, the trust ceased to exist as a legal entity and the housing project came to a halt. Although the government was not a signatory to the contract, Dallah commenced ICC arbitration against Pakistan, arguing that the State was the "true party" to the contract.

7.19 In a first Partial Award dated June 26, 2001, the tribunal concluded that Pakistan was indeed a party to the agreement, and therefore bound by the arbitration

---

[28] *Keimir, supra* note 24, at 19.

[29] *Bridas S.A.P.I.C. v. Government of Turkmenistan [Turkmenneft]*, 345 F.3d 347, 358 (5th Cir. 2003). Although the Fifth Circuit reversed the federal district court's findings of jurisdiction, which relied on principles of agency and estoppel, it remanded for further findings under the alter ego doctrine. *Turkmenneft*, 345 F.3d at 359–60. On remand, the district court held that the government was not the alter ego of Turkmenneft and therefore vacated the awards as to the government. Bridas appealed, and in 2006 the Fifth Circuit reversed the district court's finding and endorsed the enforcement of the award against Turkmenistan. Central to the Fifth Circuit's decision was the finding that the government had "exercised its power as a parent entity to deprive Bridas of a contractual remedy", by "[i]ntentionally bleeding" Turkmenneft of funds to avoid judgment. 447 F.3d 411, 419–20 (5th Cir. 2006). *See also* Chapter 2, Section F.3 (discussing the *Turkmenneft* case and the issue of binding the State as a party to an investment contract).

clause, founding the tribunal's jurisdiction to adjudicate Dallah's claim. Given Pakistan's involvement in the negotiation and performance of the contract, the tribunal concluded that the trust was a "part and a division of the Defendant to which it is fully assimilated ... having been no more than the *alter ego* of the Defendant which appears, in substance, as the real party in interest, and therefore as the proper party to the Agreement and to the Arbitration with the Claimant."[30] The tribunal issued a second Partial Award in January 2004, awarding damages to Dallah for breach of contract.[31]

Dallah sought leave to enforce the award in England.[32] Pakistan resisted enforcement, arguing that there had been no valid arbitration agreement with Pakistan on the basis of the English Arbitration Act 1996 and article V(1)(a) of the New York Convention. The U.K. Supreme Court (applying French law) held that there had been no common intention between the signatories that the State should be bound by the arbitration agreement.[33] In the Supreme Court's view, the contract (including its arbitration clauser) had been between Dallah and the trust, with the government cited only in its capacity as loan guarantor, not as a party that could be bound to arbitrate. The Supreme Court criticized the ICC tribunal's findings and concluded that "there was no material sufficient to justify the tribunal's conclusion" that the government was a party. On this basis, it refused to enforce the award in the U.K.[34] **7.20**

Meanwhile, Dallah applied to the French courts to enforce the final award. Pakistan applied there in parallel to set aside the awards. A few months after the U.K. Supreme Court's decision, the Paris Court of Appeal delivered its judgment. The French court rejected Pakistan's position, applying the same law to the same facts as were before the U.K. Supreme Court. The Paris Court of Appeal ruled that the ICC tribunal had correctly asserted jurisdiction over Pakistan, although it was not a signatory to the agreement.[35] The French court focused in particular on the fact that Pakistan had been directly involved in negotiating, implementing, **7.21**

---

30 *Dallah Real Estate and Tourism Holding Co. v. Ministry of Religious Affairs, Government of Pakistan*, ICC Case No. 9987, Partial Award of June 26, 2001, Int.l J. Arab Arb., at 364.

31 *Dallah Real Estate and Tourism Holding Co. v. Ministry of Religious Affairs, Government of Pakistan*, ICC Case No. 9987, Second Partial Award of Jan. 19, 2004, Int.l. J. Arab Arb., at 371.

32 *See Dallah Real Estate and Tourism Holding Co. v. Ministry of Religious Affairs, Government of Pakistan* [2010] U.K.S.C. 46 (Nov. 3, 2010); *Dallah Estate and Tourism Holding Co. v. Ministry of Religious Affairs, Government of Pakistan* [2009] EWCA Civ. 755 (July 20, 2009). For a critical approach, *see* Gary Born & Michal Jorek, *Dallah and the New York Convention*, Apr. 7, 2011, Kluwer Arbitration Blog; Gary B. Born, International Arbitration: Cases and Materials 246 (2d ed. 2015) *et seq.*; Ali Malek & Christopher Harris, *A Pilgrimage to Paris: Dallah v. Pakistan*, 2(4) Int'l J. Arab Arb. 23–55 (2010).

33 *Dallah Real Estate and Tourism Holding Co. v. Ministry of Religious Affairs, Government of Pakistan* [2010] U.K. Supreme Court, at paras. 132 *et seq.*

34 *Id.* at para. 145.

35 *Gouvernement du Pakistan, Ministère des Affaires Religieuses v. Société Dallah Real Estate & Tourism Holding Co.*, Paris Court of Appeal, No. 09-28533 of Feb. 17, 2011.

and terminating the agreement. On the basis of the pre-contractual conduct of the parties, the French court concluded that Pakistan behaved as if "the contract was its own," whereas the creation of the trust was purely formal. Thus, the government was the "true party".

7.22 Notwithstanding these judgments, the dominant view appears to be that the State will not be bound to arbitrate if it has not clearly expressed its consent by signing a contract containing an arbitration clause.[36] While arbitrators have shown some flexibility in this regard where a State-controlled agency or corporation has presented itself as representing the State, courts have readily annulled such awards in the absence of clear evidence that the State consented to submit to arbitration.[37]

3. ICSID arbitration clauses: special concerns

7.23 As previously noted, certain important jurisdictional limitations apply where the parties have designated the ICSID Arbitration Rules to govern the adjudication of their dispute.

7.24 **a. Disputes subject to ICSID jurisdiction** The jurisdiction of ICSID is expressly limited by the terms of the Washington Convention to "any legal dispute arising directly out of an investment."[38] Therefore, even if the parties have agreed that they will submit their disputes to ICSID arbitration, no such proceeding will go forward unless the dispute submitted is legal in nature and arises out of an investment.[39]

7.25 The first of these two requirements has so far posed few problems for claimants invoking ICSID arbitration clauses.[40] A number of tribunals have viewed the phrase "any legal dispute" broadly, finding that almost any difference of position

[36] *Westland Helicopters Ltd. v. Arab Organisation for Industrialisation et al.*, Award of Apr. 19, 1994, 28 I.L.M. 688 (1989); *SPP (Middle East) Ltd., Southern Pacific Properties Ltd. v. Egypt and General Co. for Tourism and Hotels*, ICC Case No. 3493, Award of Feb. 16, 1983. *See also Egiazaryan v. OJSC OEK Finance* [2015] EWHC 3532 (Comm) (Burton J.); and *Svenska Petroleum Exploration A.B. v. Government of Lithuania* (No. 2) [2006] EWCA Civ. 1529, [2007] QB 886, at paras. 81 *et seq.*, where the English Court of Appeal confirmed, as a matter of general principle, that a government is not to be taken to be a party to an agreement or to have submitted to arbitration simply because it has put forward a State organization to contract with a foreign investor.

[37] *Southern Pacific Properties Ltd. v. Egypt* (France Cour de Cassation), Decision of Jan. 6, 1987, 13 Yb. Comm. Arb. 152 (1988); *Westland Helicopters v. Egypt et al.* (Switz. Sup. Ct.), Decision of July 19, 1988, 16 Yb. Comm. Arb. 174 (1991).

[38] Washington Convention, *supra* note 11, at art. 25(1).

[39] *See* Christoph H. Schreuer et al., The ICSID Convention: A Commentary 83 and 106, paras. 3, 6–7, and 85 (2d ed. 2010). *See also ICSID Executive Directors' Report* at 1 ICSID Rep. 28 ("consent alone will not suffice to bring a dispute within [ICSID's] jurisdiction. In keeping with the purpose of the Convention, the jurisdiction of the Centre is further limited by reference to the nature of the dispute and the parties thereto").

[40] In *Consortium Groupement L.E.S.I.—Dipenta v. Algeria*, ICSID Case No. ARB/03/8, Award of Jan. 10, 2005, Part 2, para. 19, the tribunal found that the fact that an action is being brought against a State is sufficient for the existence of the dispute within the meaning of art. 25(1) of the ICSID Convention.

between the parties on issues of law constitutes a legal dispute within ICSID's jurisdiction.[41] In the *CSOB* case, the respondent State argued that the investment dispute between the parties was politically sensitive, and therefore had ceased to be a "legal" dispute. The tribunal disagreed, holding that:

> While it is true that investment disputes to which a State is a party frequently have political elements or involve governmental actions, such disputes do not lose their legal character as long as they concern legal rights or obligations or the consequences of their breach.[42]

The second of these two requirements has proven to be more controversial, with particular emphasis on the question of when a dispute arises "directly out of" an "investment." It must be noted that article 25(1) of the ICSID Convention offers no definition of "investment," although several proposals were advanced during the negotiation process.[43] Indeed, the definition of the "investment" proved to be the most contentious issue during negotiations between capital-exporting and capital-importing countries, and eventually resulted in a compromise: while article 25(1) contains an open-ended reference to an "investment," contracting States maintain the right "to notify the Centre of the class or classes of disputes which it would or would not consider submitting to the jurisdiction of the Centre" pursuant to article 25(4).[44] **7.26**

In any event, where consent to ICSID arbitration is contained in a specific agreement between the investor and host State, the question whether the underlying transaction or property is an investment is relatively uncontroversial.[45] **7.27**

---

[41] *See e.g. Jan de Nul N.V. and Dredging Int'l N.V. v. Egypt*, ICSID Case No. ARB/04/13, Decision on Jurisdiction of June 16, 2006, at para. 74; *Abaclat et al. (formerly Giovanna a Beccara et al.) v. Argentina*, ICSID Case No. ARB/07/5, Decision on Jurisdiction and Admissibility of Aug. 4, 2011, at para. 255. *See also* International Bank for Reconstruction and Development, Report of the Executive Directors on the Convention on the Settlement of Investment Disputes Between States and Nationals of Other States (1965), available at https://icsid.worldbank.org/en/Pages/icsiddocs/REPORT-OF-THE-EXECUTIVE-DIRECTORS-ON-THE-ICSID-CONVENTION.aspx, at para. 26 ("[t]he expression 'legal dispute' has been used to make clear that while conflict of rights are within the jurisdiction of the Centre, mere conflict of interests are not. The dispute must concern the existence or scope of a legal right or obligation, or the nature or extent of the reparation to be made for breach of a legal obligation").

[42] *Ceskoslovenska Obchodni Banka, A.S. (CSOB) v. Slovakia*, ICSID Case No ARB/97/4, Decision on Jurisdiction of May 24, 1999, 14 ICSID Rev.—For. Inv. L.J. 251, 272 (1999), at para. 61.

[43] *See* the analysis of the tribunal in *Ambiente Ufficio S.P.A. et al. (formerly Giordano Alpi et al.) v. Argentina*, ICSID Case No. ARB/08/9, Decision on Jurisdiction and Admissibility of Feb. 8, 2013, paras. 448–54.

[44] *Philip Morris Brand Sàrl (Switzerland), Philip Morris Products S.A. (Switzerland) and Abal Hermanos S.A. (Uruguay) v. Oriental Republic of Uruguay*, ICSID Case No. ARB/10/7, Decision on Jurisdiction of July 2, 2013, at paras. 197–98.

[45] The same would be asserted according to UNCITRAL arbitration. *See e.g. Biloune and Marine Drive Complex Ltd. v. Ghana Investments Centre and the Government of Ghana* (UNCITRAL), Award on Jurisdiction and Liability of Oct. 27, 1989, 95 I.L.R. 184 (1990) (claims of denial of justice and violation of human rights rejected on jurisdictional grounds, since they were not related to the "approved project" as required by the contractual submission to arbitration).

This is either because the parties refer to the operation in question as an "investment," or because the definition of investment in the agreement is closely tailored to the parties' relationship.[46] Logically speaking, the inclusion of an ICSID dispute resolution clause in a State contract would make little sense unless both parties understood the subject of their dealings to be within the basic jurisdiction of ICSID.[47] As a result, ICSID tribunals have yet to dismiss a case for want of "investment" where the host State's consent was contained in an express arbitration clause in a contract with the claimant.[48]

7.28 Nevertheless, most commentators agree that the limits on ICSID's jurisdiction are objective and absolute, and therefore cannot be circumvented by the parties' agreement.[49] The parties to an investor–State contract should therefore carefully consider whether their transaction could be considered "investment-related" for ICSID purposes before including an ICSID clause. The meaning of "investment" in this sense is discussed at length in Section E.

b. Nationality and article 25(2)(b)

7.29 In addition to the subject-matter limitations just explained, ICSID arbitration can only be invoked to resolve disputes between member States and investors of other member States.[50] Therefore, including an ICSID clause in a contract will do little good if the two States concerned have not ratified the Washington Convention by the time a dispute is brought before the Centre.[51]

---

[46] ICSID has published a set of model arbitration clauses, including Clause 3, which provides an express statement that the transaction underlying the agreement constitutes an investment: "It is hereby stipulated that the transaction to which this agreement relates is an investment." 4 ICSID Rep. 360 (1997).

[47] Heribert Golsong, *A Guide to Procedural Issues in International Arbitration*, 18 Int'l Law. 633, 634–35 (1984); C.F. Amerasinghe, *Submissions to the Jurisdiction of the International Centre for Settlement of Investment Disputes*, 5 J. Mar. L. & Comm. 211, 223 (1974).

[48] *See e.g. Liberian Eastern Timber Corp. (LETCO). v. Liberia*, ICSID Case No. ARB/83/2, Decision on Jurisdiction of Oct. 24, 1984, 2 ICSID Rep. 349, 350 (1994).

[49] Noah Rubins, *The Notion of Investment in International Investment Arbitration*, in Arbitrating Foreign Investment Disputes 283, 289–90 (Norbert Horn ed. 2004); Schreuer et al., *supra* note 39, at 25; Moshe Hirsch, The Arbitration Mechanism of the International Centre for the Settlement of Investment Disputes 59 (1993); Aron Broches, *Bilateral Investment Protection Treaties and Arbitration of Investment Disputes*, in Selected Essays: World Bank, ICSID, and Other Subjects of Public and Private International Law 447, 455 (1995).

[50] Washington Convention, *supra* note 11, art. 25(1); Schreuer et al., *supra* note 39, at 141–44, 162–64.

[51] The States in question need not have been members of the Washington Convention at the time the contract is signed, provided that they have become members by the date the Request for Arbitration is submitted to ICSID. *See* Washington Convention, *supra* note 11, art. 25(1); *also Cable Television of Nevis Ltd. and Cable Television of Nevis Holdings Ltd. v. Federation of St. Kitts and Nevis*, ICSID Case No. ARB/95/2, Award of Jan. 13, 1997, 13 ICSID Rev.—For. Inv. L.J. 328, 357 (1998). Emmanuel Gaillard, *Some Notes on the Drafting of ICSID Arbitration Clauses*, 477 PLI/Comm. Law & Prac. Course Handbook Series 33 (1988); Chapter 8, Section B.2.b.

The issue of the claimant's nationality, whether a corporation or an individual, is determined largely as a function of the home State's local law on the subject.[52] The rules applied in determining citizenship for these purposes are described in detail in Section D. 7.30

A great deal of attention has been paid in the jurisprudence to the ICSID Convention's provisions on foreign-controlled local corporations, which investors often create or employ as investment vehicles to sign contracts with the host State and its agencies. The Washington Convention expressly recognizes that in some cases a company organized under the law of the host State may still be considered "foreign" for purposes of arbitration. After all, many countries require that certain investment activities be carried out exclusively by local corporations.[53] Article 25(2)(b) of the Washington Convention provides that "nationals of another Contracting State" include: 7.31

> any juridical person which had the nationality of the Contracting State party to the dispute ... and which, because of foreign control, the parties have agreed should be treated as a national of another Contracting State for the purposes of this Convention.[54]

Thus, even where the private contracting party is a national of the host State, it may invoke an ICSID arbitration clause if it has been agreed that the company will be treated as foreign for purposes of the Convention, and it is actually controlled by foreigners.[55] 7.32

Generally, the ownership of a majority of shares is the primary criterion that parties have in mind when they agree to consider a local business to be foreign-controlled within the meaning of article 25(2)(b). If a local operating company is more than 50 percent owned by an entity of qualifying nationality, the host State company is normally deemed to be a citizen of another State for purposes of 7.33

---

52 *See* Aron Broches, *The Convention on the Settlement of Investment Disputes between States and Nationals of Other States*, 136 Recueil Des Cours 331, 359–60 (1972-II). *See also Hussein Nuaman Soufraki v. United Arab Emirates*, ICSID Case No. ARB/02/7, Decision of the Ad Hoc Committee on the Application for Annulment of Mr Soufraki of June 5, 2007, at para. 60.

53 Amazu Asouzu, *A Review and Critique of Arbitral Awards on Article 25(2)(b) of the ICSID Convention*, 3 J. World Inv. 397, 398 (2002).

54 *See* Mary L. Moreland, *"Foreign Control" and "Agreement" under ICSID Article 25(2)(b): Standards for Claims Brought by Locally Organized Subsidiaries against Host States*, 9 Currents Int'l Trade L.J. 18 (2000); Schreuer et al., *supra* note 39, at 294–334; Reed et al., *supra* note 6, at 17–19; Asouzu, *supra* note 53. *See also* David A.R. Williams QC, *Jurisdiction and Admissibility*, in The Oxford Handbook of International Investment Law 893–97 (Peter Muchlinski et al. eds. 2008).

55 It is generally understood that art. 25(2)(b) sets "foreign control" as an "outer limit," an objective requirement that cannot be replaced by an agreement of the contracting States. *See Caratube Int'l Oil Co. LLP v. Kazakhstan*, ICSID Case No. ARB/08/12, Award of June 5, 2012, para. 336. *See also* Schreuer et al., *supra* note 39, at 312, para. 813.

arbitral jurisdiction.[56] In *Klöckner v. Cameroon*, for example, the tribunal affirmed jurisdiction where qualifying investors owned 51 percent of a local entity's shares.[57]

7.34 Also relevant to the determination of nationality is effective control in day-to-day management of the local operating company. In *Vacuum Salt v. Ghana*, Greek investors held only 20 percent of the local operating company's shares, while the remaining stake was in the hands of Ghanaian interests.[58] The tribunal dismissed the case for lack of jurisdiction, because it did "not find here indications of foreign control of Vacuum Salt such as to justify regarding it as a national of an ICSID Contracting State other than Ghana." However, the tribunal did not exclude the possibility that, in certain circumstances, minority foreign shareholders could still be viewed as controlling the local entity, if they can demonstrate that effective control nevertheless remained in their hands. The effectiveness of foreign control, once established, is not normally diminished because qualifying investors exercise control indirectly[59] or jointly.[60]

7.35 Some tribunals have found that the very existence of an ICSID clause in a contract between the foreign-controlled local entity and the host State indicates the State's consent to treat the local company as foreign for purposes of the Washington Convention.[61] As the *LETCO* tribunal reasoned:

> When a Contracting State signs an investment agreement, containing an ICSID arbitration clause, with a foreign controlled juridical person with the same nationality as the Contracting State and it does so with the knowledge that it will only be subject to ICSID jurisdiction if it has agreed to treat that company as a juridical person of another Contracting State, the Contracting State should be deemed to have agreed to such treatment by having agreed to the ICSID arbitration clause. This is especially the case when the Contracting State's laws require the foreign investor to establish itself locally as a juridical person in order to carry out an investment.[62]

---

[56] Paul Szasz, *A Practical Guide to the Convention on the Settlement of Investment Disputes*, 1 Cornell Int'l L.J. 1, 20 (1968).

[57] *Klöckner Industrie-Anlagen GmbH et al. v. Cameroon and Société Camerounaise des Engrais*, ICSID Case No. ARB/81/2, Award of Oct. 21, 1983, 2 ICSID Rep. 9 (1994).

[58] *Vacuum Salt Products Ltd. v. Ghana*, ICSID Case No. ARB/92/1, Award of Feb. 16, 1994, 9 ICSID Rev.—For. Inv. L.J. 72 (1994), at para. 38.

[59] *Société Ouest Africaine des Bétons Industriels v. Senegal*, ICSID Case No. ARB/82/1, Decision on Jurisdiction of Aug. 1, 1984, 2 ICSID Rep. 175, 182–83, 204 (1994).

[60] *Camuzzi Int'l S.A. v. Argentina*, ICSID Case No. ARB/03/7, Decision on Jurisdiction of June 10, 2005, at paras. 31 and 41; *Sempra Energy Int'l v. Argentina*, ICSID Case No. ARB/02/16, Decision on Jurisdiction of June 10, 2005, paras. 51 and 54.

[61] *Amco Asia Corp. v. Indonesia*, ICSID Case No. ARB/81/1, Decision on Jurisdiction of Sept. 25, 1983, 1 ICSID Rep. 389, 392–93 (1993); *LETCO, supra* note 48, at paras. 9–10. *But cf. Holiday Inns S.A. et al. v. Morocco*, ICSID Case No. ARB/72/1, Decision on Jurisdiction of July 1, 1973, *described in* Pierre Lalive, *The First "World Bank" Arbitration: Some Legal Problems*, 51 Brit. Yb. Int'l L. 123 (1980) (implied agreement to treat local company as "foreign" for purposes of Washington Convention should be found only "in the event that the specific circumstances would exclude any other interpretation of the intention of the parties").

[62] *LETCO, supra* note 48, at 352. In *Caratube v. Kazakhstan*, an ICSID tribunal noted that when the offer of arbitration is contained in an investment contract, the acceptance of the offer would

Nevertheless, it is advisable for contracting parties to ensure that the State's consent is clearly expressed in this regard, for example by incorporating into their contract the model "control" language proposed by ICSID: 7.36

> It is hereby agreed that, although the Investor is a national of the Host State, it is controlled by nationals of [name(s) of other Contracting States] and shall be treated as a national of [that]/[those] State[s] for the purposes of the Convention.[63]

C. Preliminary Treaty Concerns

1. Exhaustion of local remedies

Under customary international law, a claim cannot be interposed by an investor's home State unless and until the foreign investor had "exhausted" local remedies.[64] The basic customary international law rule is that 7.37

> the respondent State must first have an opportunity to redress by its own means within the framework of its own domestic legal system the wrong alleged to have been done to the individual.[65]

In the realm of diplomatic protection, therefore, no international claim can be advanced until local remedies have been exhausted, to the extent that they are not illusory or futile.[66]

It is generally accepted that modern investment treaties have largely done away with the local remedies requirement of customary international law.[67] Instead, most of these treaties permit the investor to resort directly to international 7.38

"create an assumption that the claimant fulfils the conditions of that offer." *See Caratube, supra* note 55, at para. 331.

[63] ICSID Model Clause 7, available at http://icsidfiles.worldbank.org/icsid/icsid/staticfiles/model-clauses-en/9.htm#c.

[64] *See generally* Chapter 10, Section B.1.b, and Chapter 4, Section E. On the exhaustion of local remedies, *see generally* Stephen M. Schwebel & J. Gillis Wetter, *Arbitration and the Exhaustion of Local Remedies*, in Justice in International Law 171 (Stephen M. Schwebel ed. 1994); Andrea Bjorklund, *Waiver and the Exhaustion of the Local Remedies Rule in NAFTA Jurisprudence*, in NAFTA Investment Law and Arbitration 253 (Todd Weiler ed. 2004); Paul Peters, *Exhaustion of Local Remedies: Ignored in Most Bilateral Investment Treaties*, 44(2) Netherlands Int'l L. Rev. 233 (1997); A.A. Cancado Trindade, The Application of the Rule of Exhaustion of Local Remedies in International Law: Its Rationale in the International Protection Of Individual Rights (1983).

[65] *Interhandel Case (Switzerland v. U.S.A.)*, 1959 I.C.J. Rep. 6, 27 ("the rule that local remedies must be exhausted before international proceedings may be instituted is a well-established rule of customary international law").

[66] *Finnish Ships Case (Finland v. U.K.)*, Award of May 9, 1934, 3 R.I.A.A. 1479 (1934); *Panavesyz-Saldaiskis Railway Case (Estonia v. Lithuania)*, P.C.I.J. Ser. A/B, No. 76 (1939), at 18.

[67] On the issue of exhaustion of local remedies and international investment protection, *see* Christoph Schreuer, *Calvo's Grandchildren: The Return of Local Remedies in Investment Arbitration*, in The Law and Practice of International Courts and Tribunals 1–17 (2005); R.B. Love, *The Local Remedies Issue in Venezuelan Investment Treaty Disputes*, 5 TDM (2008).

arbitration against the State in search of remedies for violation of an applicable treaty's substantive provisions, without prior recourse to domestic courts or other local avenues of recourse, as long as all other jurisdictional requirements are satisfied.[68] Although Article 26 of the ICSID Convention provides for consent to arbitration "to the exclusion of any other remedy," a State may nonetheless condition its consent to "the exhaustion of local administrative or judicial remedies."[69]

7.39 Where the host State has carried out measures through its *judicial system*, however, remnants of the exhaustion of remedies rule appear to remain.[70] In such cases, the issue of local remedies ceases to be one of *jurisdiction*, and becomes one of *admissibility*.[71] As the *Maffezini* tribunal explained this difference:

> the requirements of the exhaustion of domestic remedies differs depending on whether the appeal to an international tribunal contends that the domestic tribunal was guilty of a denial of justice, or whether the claim seeks the vindication of rights guaranteed in a treaty, for example, which empowers the tribunal to interpret and apply the treaty. In the former case, the right to appeal to an international tribunal, if it exists at all, can only be based on a denial of justice by the domestic courts. In such a case, if there was no denial of justice, the case will have to be rejected, whether or not the domestic court committed errors of law or fact in rendering its judgement. This is not true in a case where, as here, the parties have a treaty right to obtain a final determination from the international tribunal

---

[68] *See* Martin Dietrich Brauch, *Exhaustion of Local Remedies in International Investment Law*, IISD Best Practices Series, 7–10 (2017). A minority of investment treaties and national investment laws expressly maintain the requirement of exhaustion of local remedies. *See e.g.* Malaysia–Netherlands BIT (1971), art. 12; Ghana–Romania BIT (1989), art. 4(3); Albania–Lithuania BIT (2007), art. 8(2). *See also* art. 28(4) of the model BIT adopted by the Southern African Development Community in 2012. Other investment treaties create an "exhaustion period" of litigation in local courts. *See e.g.* Germany–Argentina BIT (1991), art. 10(2), (3)(a); Netherlands–Jamaica BIT (1991), art. 9; Malta–Serbia BIT (2010, not yet in force), art. 9(2). Generally speaking, international arbitration becomes available under such provisions a certain number of months after the court litigation is commenced, regardless of whether a judgment has been rendered. The Washington Convention permits State parties to condition their consent to arbitration on the exhaustion of local remedies, but such a condition must be stated expressly. Washington Convention, *supra* note 11, at art. 26.

[69] *Compañía de Aguas del Aconquija S.A. and Vivendi Universal (formerly Compagnie Générale des Eaux) v. Argentina*, ICSID Case No. ARB/97/3, Decision on Annulment of July 3, 2002, at para. 52.

[70] *See e.g. Mr. Franck Charles Arif v. Moldova*, ICSID Case No. ARB/11/23, Award of Apr. 8, 2013, at paras. 334 and 345; *Abengoa S.A. y COFIDES S.A. v. Mexico*, ICSID Case No. ARB(AF)/09/2, Award of Apr. 18, 2013, at para. 626.

[71] *Loewen Group, Inc. and Raymond L. Loewen v. United States of America*, ICSID Case No. ARB(AF)/98/3, Award of June 26, 2003, 42 I.L.M. 811 (2003), at para. 207. For an explanation of the difference between substance, admissibility, and jurisdiction in the application of the local remedies rule under international law, *see* Christopher Greenwood, *State Responsibility for the Decisions of National Courts*, in Issues of State Responsibility Before International Judicial Institutions 55, 61–68 (2004); Ian Brownlie, Principles of Public International Law 472–73 (6th ed. 2003). *See also* Williams, *supra* note 54, ch. 22 at 870 *et seq.*

on the scope of their rights under the treaty, provided they have first exhausted all available domestic remedies.[72]

7.40 In the North American Free Trade Agreement (NAFTA) arbitration *Loewen v. United States*,[73] the claimant was subjected to arbitrary and discriminatory treatment during a lawsuit in the state courts of Mississippi. It complained that the excessive verdict could not be appealed, because execution of the judgment would begin unless a massive bond was posted. The United States insisted that the claimant corporation had failed to exhaust additional remedies within the U.S. judicial system before filing an international claim under NAFTA. The tribunal ultimately ruled that the claimant had not demonstrated the futility of (1) pursuing bankruptcy protection under the laws of the United States, or (2) seeking discretionary review and stay of execution from the U.S. Supreme Court.[74] In part because the claimant had not exhausted these remedies, nor demonstrated that they were futile, the tribunal dismissed the case.[75]

7.41 More recent jurisprudence of investment treaty tribunals confirms that the futility exception applies to the exhaustion of local remedies (when the latter is applicable), in cases where there are no reasonably available local remedies to provide effective redress, or the local remedies provide no reasonable possibility of remedy.[76]

7.42 The approach of the European Court of Human Rights (ECtHR), while obviously inspired by a treaty very different in purpose and wording from NAFTA, is equally illuminating. In applying the provisions of the European Convention on Human Rights dealing with the sanctity of private property, the Court has

[72] *Emilio Augustín Maffezini v. Spain*, ICSID Case No. ARB/97/7, Decision on Jurisdiction of Jan. 25, 2000, at para. 30. As Professor James Crawford, Rapporteur to the International Law Commission, explained, "an aberrant decision by an official lower in the hierarchy, which is capable of being reconsidered, does not of itself amount to an unlawful act." UN Doc. A/CN 4/498 at para. 75. Or, as Professor Alfred Rubin has noted: "Justice cannot be presumed to have been denied until it has been sought, and thus there must be an 'exhaustion of local remedies.'" Alfred Rubin, *Book Review—Application of the Rule of Exhaustion of Local Remedies in International Law*, 25 Harv. Int'l L.J. 517, 518 (1984).

[73] *Loewen, supra* note 71; Noah Rubins, *Loewen v. United States: The Burial of an Investor-State Claim*, 21 Arb. Int'l 1, 15–23 (2005).

[74] *Loewen, supra* note 71, at para. 207. In fact, there was a third possible remedy, namely "collateral review" before a U.S. federal district court. While this potential avenue of recourse was debated during the merits hearing, the tribunal did not appear concerned with LGI's failure to opt for it. This could be due to the U.S. Supreme Court's decision in *Pennzoil v. Texaco*, 481 U.S. 1 (1987), which would have made a collateral review petition potentially frivolous and sanctionable under U.S. civil procedure rules.

[75] *Loewen, supra* note 71, at paras. 209 ("No doubt there are some situations in which it would be reasonable to expect an impecunious claimant to file [for protection] under (U.S. bankruptcy law) in order to exercise an available right of appeal") and 211 (insufficient evidence to determine whether Supreme Court review was futile).

[76] *Ambiente Ufficio S.P.A. et al. (formerly Giordano Alpi et al.) v. Argentina*, ICSID Case No. ARB/08/9, Decision on Jurisdiction and Admissibility of Feb. 8, 2013, at paras. 607–08, citing 15(a) of the 2006 ILC Draft Articles on Diplomatic Protection.

refused to allow the local remedies rule to become a formalistic or technical bar to relief for claimants who would otherwise have recourse for treaty violations. In *Sovtransavto Holding v. Ukraine*,[77] a Russian company sought judicial redress in Ukraine against local minority shareholders in a joint venture who had diluted the Russian shareholding to gain control of the enterprise. After losing in the court of first instance, Sovtransavto appealed to the Ukrainian Supreme Economic Court. The appeal was dismissed without prejudice for late payment of court fees, but was time-barred by the time Sovtransavto resubmitted its case. While recognizing that the claimant had not necessarily exhausted all available local remedies, the Court found Ukraine had violated the Convention:

> [T]he rule on the exhaustion of domestic remedies must be applied with some degree of flexibility and without excessive formalism and is neither absolute nor capable of being applied automatically.[78]

7.43 This flexible view of local remedies draws support from the fact that, unlike cases of diplomatic espousal, complaints before the ECtHR (and tribunals formed pursuant to investment treaties) are decided "in the context of machinery for the protection of ... rights that the Contracting States have agreed to set up."[79]

7.44 Other tribunals have approached exhaustion of local remedies not as a requirement for jurisdiction or admissibility, but as a necessary element of the violation of a substantive treaty standard.[80] However, in academic writings today the rule is largely viewed as procedural rather than substantive.[81]

2. "Fork in the road"

7.45 While most investment treaties do away with the investor's need to exhaust local remedies (at least in connection with non-judicial measures), some investment treaties require that the investor choose definitively between litigating the dispute

---

[77] *Sovtransavto Holding v. Ukraine*, (2003) ECHR 476.

[78] *Id.* at para. 81.

[79] *Ilhan v. Turkey*, (2000) ECHR 353, at para. 59. The Court's refusal to require exhaustion in all cases is despite an express provision in the Convention preserving the local remedies rule. European Convention on Human Rights, art. 35 ("The Court may only deal with the matter after all domestic remedies have been exhausted, according to the generally recognized rules of international law"). By contrast, NAFTA makes no direct mention of local remedies, other than to require that they be *abandoned*. North American Free Trade Agreement (NAFTA), Dec. 17, 1992, U.S.–Can.–Mex., 32 I.L.M. 605 (1992), available at http://www.nafta-sec-alena.org and http://www.naftaclaims.com, art. 1121.

[80] *See* Ursula Kriebaum, *Local Remedies and the Standards for the Protection of Foreign Investment*, in International Investment Law for the 21st Century: Essays in Honour of Christoph Schreuer 418 *et seq.* (C. Binder et al. eds. 2009). *Cf. Compañía de Aguas del Aconquija S.A. and Vivendi Universal v. Argentina (Vivendi II)*, Award of Aug. 20, 2007, at paras 7.4.10 and 7.4.11.

[81] *Id.* at 423. *See also* ILC, Draft Articles on State Responsibility, Commentary to Article 44(4), citing *Elettronica Sicula S.p.A. (ELSI) (U.S.A. v. Italy)*, Judgment, 1989 I.C.J. Rep. 48, at para. 63, referring to the exhaustion of local remedies rule "as being distinct, in principle, from 'the merits of the case.'"

in local courts or before an international tribunal. This treaty requirement, popularly known as a "fork in the road" clause, is designed to prevent the re-opening on an international plane of disputes already adjudicated in national court systems.[82]

The wording of fork-in-the-road clauses varies somewhat. One of the more straightforward variations can be found in the France–Argentina BIT: **7.46**

> Once an investor has submitted the dispute either to the jurisdictions of the Contracting Party involved or to international arbitration, the choice of one or the other of these procedures shall be final.[83]

A more complex formulation is found in many U.S. investment treaties: **7.47**

> 2. If [an investment] dispute cannot be settled amicably, the national or company concerned may choose to submit the dispute for resolution:
>   (a) to the courts or administrative tribunals of the Party that is a party to the dispute; or
>   (b) in accordance with any applicable, previously agreed dispute-settlement procedures; or
>   (c) in accordance with the terms of paragraph 3(a).
> 3. (a) Provided that the national or company concerned has not submitted the dispute for resolution under paragraph 2(a) or (b) and that six months have elapsed from the date on which the dispute arose, the national or company concerned may choose to consent in writing to the submission of the dispute for settlement by binding arbitration.[84]

It is no easy matter to assess whether a particular court action related to an investment constitutes a choice of forum triggering a fork-in-the-road provision. Tribunals have recognized that investors are often required under local law defensively to invoke local remedies of various kinds in order to avoid waiver or otherwise to comply with domestic legislation.[85] **7.48**

Moreover, arbitrators have often refused to find that a choice has been made where local proceedings did not entail the same cause of action as that later advanced under the treaty.[86] Professor Schreuer explains: **7.49**

---

[82] Michael Polkinghorne, *Investor–State Dispute Resolution under the Energy Charter Treaty: Which Fork? Which Road?*, Mealey's Int'l Arb. Rep., April 2004, at 13; Christoph Schreuer, *Travelling the BIT Route: Of Waiting Periods, Umbrella Clauses and Forks in the Road*, 5 J. World Inv. & Trade 231, 239–49 (2004); Reed et al., *supra* note 6, at 58–59.

[83] France–Argentina BIT (1991), art. 2.

[84] U.S.–Romania BIT (1992), art. VI(2)–(3).

[85] *CMS Gas Transmission Co. v. Argentina*, ICSID Case No. ARB/01/8, Decision on Jurisdiction of July 17, 2003, 42 I.L.M. 788 (2003), at para. 78; *Alex Genin et al. v. Estonia*, ICSID Case No. ARB/99/2, Award of June 25, 2001, 17 ICSID Rev.—For. Inv. L.J. 395 (2002), at para. 333. *See also Enron Creditors Recovery Corp. (formerly Enron Corp.) and Ponderosa Assets, L.P. v. Argentina*, ICSID Case No. ARB/01/3, Decision on Jurisdiction of Jan. 14, 2004, at para. 98.

[86] *See e.g.* in *Desert Line Projects LLC v. Yemen*, ICSID Case No. ARB/05/17, Award of Feb. 6, 2008, at paras. 135–38, the tribunal rejected an objection of fork in the road, because the local arbitration under the contract was premised on a different cause of action from the investment treaty arbitration.

The fork in the road provision and the consequent loss of access to international arbitration applies only if the same dispute between the same parties has been submitted to domestic courts or administrative tribunals of the host State before the resort to international arbitration.[87]

7.50 As a result, a number of decisions have narrowed the preclusive effect of a fork-in-the-road clause to cases where (1) the local action was begun before the initiation of international arbitration;[88] (2) the subject matter of the dispute in the local forum is the same as that submitted to arbitration;[89] and (3) the parties in both domestic and international proceedings are identical.[90] Furthermore, investment treaty tribunals have drawn a distinction between a forum selection clause in an investment contract (providing for the jurisdiction of local courts or contractual arbitration) and an arbitration clause in a BIT.[91] Other tribunals have adopted a different standard in deciding whether to apply a fork-in-the-road clause, assessing claims to be brought before them share the same "fundamental basis" as the claims brought before domestic courts.[92]

7.51 In any event, investors should examine the provisions of applicable investment protection instruments carefully to determine whether recourse to local courts or administrative tribunals by them or their local enterprise may impact their ability to initiate international arbitration later.[93]

7.52 NAFTA and a limited number of other investment treaties contain a variation of the "fork in the road," which might be termed a "no U-turn" provision. Article

[87] Schreuer et al., *supra* note 39, at 247–48.

[88] *Azurix Corp. v. Argentina*, ICSID Case No. ARB/01/12, Decision on Jurisdiction of Dec. 8, 2003, 43 I.L.M. 262 (2004), at para. 91. In *M.C.I. Power Group, L.C. and New Turbine, Inc. v. Ecuador*, ICSID Case No. ARB/03/6, Award of July 31, 2007, at para. 186, the tribunal found that the claimant could not have exercised the fork-in-the-road provision, given that the treaty was not in force at the time of submission to domestic courts.

[89] *Ronald S. Lauder v. Czech Republic*, UNCITRAL, Final Award of Sept. 3, 2001, at para. 162; *Middle East Cement Shipping and Handling Co. S.A. v. Egypt*, ICSID Case No. ARB/99/6, Award of Apr. 12, 2002, 18 ICSID Rev.—For. Inv. L.J. 602 (2003), at para. 71; *Eudoro A. Olguin v. Paraguay*, ICSID Case No. ARB/98/5, Decision on Jurisdiction of Aug. 8, 2000, 6 ICSID Rep. 156 (2004), at para. 30.

[90] *CMS, supra* note 85, at para. 80; *Azurix, supra* note 88, at para. 87; *Genin, supra* note 85, at para. 333; *Pan American Energy LLC and BP Argentina Exploration Co. v. Argentina and BP America Production Co., Pan American Sur SRL, Pan American Fueguina, SRL and Pan American Continental SRL v. Argentina*, ICSID Case Nos. ARB/03/13 & ARB/04/8, Decision on Preliminary Objections of July 27, 2006, at paras. 154–57.

[91] *See e.g. AES Corp. v. Argentina*, ICSID Case No. ARB/02/17, Decision on Jurisdiction of Apr. 26, 2005, at paras. 92–97, with further references to previous cases against Argentina. *See also Aguas del Tunari S.A. v. Bolivia*, ICSID Case No. ARB/02/3, Decision on Respondent's Objections to Jurisdiction of Oct. 21, 2005.

[92] *See Pantechniki S.A. Contractors & Engineers v. Albania*, ICSID Case No. ARB/07/21, Award of Jul. 30, 2009, at paras. 61 and 67, referring to the *Woodruff Case* (1903–05), R.I.A.A. Vol. IX 213–23, at 223. *See also Yuri Bogdanov and Yulia Bogdanov v. Moldova*, SCC Case No. V091/2012, Final Award of Apr. 16 2013, at paras. 173–74; *AES Corp. and Tau Power B.V. v. Kazakhstan*, ICSID Case No. ARB/10/16, Award of Nov. 1, 2013, at para. 227; *H&H Enterprises Investments Inc. v. Egypt*, ICSID Case No. ARB/09/15, Award of May 6, 2014, at paras. 369–70.

[93] Reed et al., *supra* note 6, at 59.

1121 of NAFTA provides that a disputing investor may submit a NAFTA claim to arbitration only if

> the investor ... waive[s its] right to initiate or continue before any administrative tribunal or court under the law of any Party, or other dispute settlement procedures, any proceedings with respect to the measure of the disputing Party that is alleged to be a breach ... before an administrative tribunal or court under the law of the disputing Party.[94]

Thus, while a claimant may litigate his dispute domestically at home or in the host State before bringing a NAFTA claim, once he begins arbitration, he is barred from returning to the courts, regardless of the outcome of the arbitration proceedings.[95]

3. Waiting periods

Many modern investment treaties require that an investor provide notice of a dispute and wait a certain amount of time (ostensibly to engage in negotiation with the host State) before invoking investor–State arbitration. The most common duration of the resulting "waiting period" is six months, but some treaties impose lengthier negotiation requirements,[96] while others impose only a three-month period.[97] **7.53**

The nature of such a waiting period requirement, and the procedure to be followed in satisfying these provisions through issue of a "trigger letter," is covered in detail in Chapter 8.[98] **7.54**

D. Who May Initiate Arbitration under Investment Protection Instruments

It is an important jurisdictional requirement for treaty-based arbitration that the claimant investor have the proper nationality to benefit from the host State's **7.55**

---

[94] NAFTA, *supra* note 79, art. 1121.

[95] *Waste Management Inc. v. Mexico*, ICSID Case No. ARB(AF)/98/2, Award of June 2, 2000, 40 I.L.M. 56 (2001), at paras. 26–28 (dismissing claim on jurisdictional grounds where claimant had not effectively waived and ceased all court proceedings prior to initiating claim). *See also* William S. Dodge, *Waste Management, Inc. v. Mexico: Arbitral Award on Jurisdiction under NAFTA Where Requisite Waiver of Other Remedies Reserves, and Applicant Pursues, Municipal Law Claims in Other Fora*, 95 AJIL 186 (2001).

[96] Belgium/Luxembourg–Gabon BIT (2005), art. 10(2) (twelve-month waiting period).

[97] France–Chile BIT (1992), art. 8(1)–(2) (requiring amicable negotiation, but "[I]f the dispute has not been resolved within six months of the date it arose, it shall be submitted, at the investor's request," to arbitration); U.S.–Argentina BIT (1991), art. VII(3)(a) ("Provided that ... six months have elapsed from the date on which the dispute arose, the national or company concerned may choose to consent in writing to the submission of the dispute for settlement by binding arbitration"); U.S.–Azerbaijan BIT, art. IX(3)(a) (three-month waiting period from time dispute arises).

[98] *See* Chapter 8, Section D. *See also* Schreuer, *supra* note 82, at 232–39.

submission to arbitration.[99] Since States expect concessions in exchange for investment protections, they are unwilling to extend such guarantees to private entities whose country of origin has not gone through the negotiation process to arrive at the conclusion of an investment treaty. Furthermore, host governments do not normally want their own citizens to have access to investment arbitration; local citizens have access to a broader range of domestic remedies, and are much less likely to find bias, discrimination, or unfamiliar procedures in their own judicial system.[100]

7.56 The criteria that qualify a foreign entity as an "investor" and therefore as a potential claimant under an investment protection instrument depend in the first instance upon the wording of the treaty or national law in question. As explained earlier, additional requirements may apply in accordance with the Washington Convention if the claimant seeks to initiate arbitration under ICSID auspices.[101] While the customary international law rules on individual and corporate nationality described elsewhere in this book may be relevant to a tribunal's decision whether a particular investor possesses the requisite citizenship for treaty protection, the specific applicable treaty or investment code provisions normally take precedence, and should therefore be given particular attention.[102]

7.57 As is the case under customary international law, treaty texts and arbitration practice draw a distinction between physical and legal persons, establishing separate rules for each type of investor.

1. Individuals

a. Treaty provisions

7.58 Most investment treaties and codes establish a straightforward definition of an individual "investor" or "national of a Party," entitled to invoke substantive protections and international arbitration. The U.S.–Egypt BIT, for example, provides:

---

[99] On citizenship and investment arbitration, *see generally* Francisco Orrego Vicuna, *Changing Approaches to the Nationality of Claims in the Context of Diplomatic Protection and International Dispute Settlement*, in LIBER AMICORUM IBRAHIM F.I. SHIHATA 503 (S. Schlemmer-Schulte & K.-Y. Tung eds. 2001); Robert Wisner & Nick Gallus, *Nationality Requirements in Investor–State Arbitration*, 5 J. WORLD INV. & TRADE 927 (2004).

[100] For a justification, *see Joseph C. Lemire v. Ukraine*, ICSID Case No. ARB/06/18, Award of Mar. 28, 2011, at para. 57 ("Foreigners, who lack political rights, are more exposed than domestic investors to arbitrary actions of the host State and may thus, as a matter of legitimate policy, be granted a wider scope of protection").

[101] On the distinction between the nationality requirements of the BIT and of the ICSID Convention, *see Ioan Micula et al. v. Romania*, ICSID Case No. ARB/05/20, Decision on Jurisdiction and Admissibility of Sept. 24, 2008, at para. 85.

[102] *Eudoro A. Olguín v. Paraguay*, ICSID Case No. ARB/98/5, Award of July 26, 2001, 6 ICSID REP. 156 (2004) (rejecting application of customary law "effective nationality" rule in light of specific treaty provisions on citizenship); *Champion Trading Co. et al v. Egypt*, ICSID Case No. ARB/02/9, Decision on Jurisdiction of Oct. 21, 2003 (same). *See also* HIRSCH, *supra* note 49, at 76–77; SCHREUER et al., *supra* note 39, at 267. *See also* Chapter 4, Section F (on nationality of claims); Chapter 10, Section B.1.a (same).

"national" of a Party means a natural person who is a national of a party under its applicable law.[103]

A large proportion of investment treaties offer no indication of the rules governing citizenship of individuals. The Austria–Croatia BIT is typical in this regard, providing: 7.59

> the term "investor" means in respect of either Contracting Party ... nationals of a Contracting Party who make an investment in the other Contracting Party's territory.[104]

Most commentators agree that tribunals will normally give substantial deference to the law of the alleged State of nationality,[105] even where the applicable treaty does not specifically designate home State law as governing the question of nationality.[106] In *Champion Trading v. Egypt*, for example, several of the claimants were U.S. citizens whose father, also a U.S. citizen, had been born in Egypt as an Egyptian citizen. The Egyptian law on nationality was based upon *jus sanguinis*, such that any person born of an Egyptian father would also be considered Egyptian under local law. Although the claimants were born and had spent most of their lives in the United States, and had only cursory connections to Egypt, the tribunal deferred to Egyptian law, found them to be Egyptian citizens, and dismissed their claims.[107] 7.60

While tribunals generally turn to the home State's law in determining the nationality of physical persons, it is less clear to what extent they will defer to the host State's interpretation or application of that law. In *Soufraki v. United Arab Emirates*, the claimant initiated arbitration under the Italy–UAE BIT.[108] 7.61

---

[103] U.S.–Egypt BIT (1982), art. I(1)(e). *See also* ASEAN Investment Agreement, art. I(1); Energy Charter Treaty, art. 1(7), 34 I.L.M. 360 (1995), available at http://www.encharter.org. *See also* Comprehensive and Economic Trade Agreement between Canada, of the one part, and the European Union and its Member States, of the other part (CETA), Chapter 8, Section A, art. 8(1) ("natural person means: ... (b) in the case of the European Union, a natural person having the nationality of one of the Member States of the European Union according to their respective laws ...").

[104] Austria–Croatia BIT (1997), art. 1(2)(a).

[105] *See e.g. Waguih Elie George Siag & Clorinda Vecchi v. Egypt*, ICSID Case No. ARB/05/15, Decision on Jurisdiction of Apr. 11, 2007, at para. 146 (referring to an "international law rule that the municipal law of the state determines nationality"). *See also Mr. Franck Charles Arif v. Moldova*, ICSID Case No. ARB/11/23, Award of Apr. 8, 2013, at para. 354.

[106] Schreuer, *supra* note 82, at 267; Wisner & Gallus, *supra* note 99, at 928.

[107] *Champion Trading*, *supra* note 102, at 17; Wisner & Gallus, *supra* note 99, at 928–29. While the U.S.–Egypt BIT allowed dual nationals to initiate arbitration, the treaty provided for ICSID arbitration as the only dispute resolution option. The arbitrators dismissed the claims brought by individual U.S. citizens who also had Egyptian citizenship in accordance with the rule prohibiting dual nationals contained in art. 25(2)(a) of the Washington Convention, explained in Section D.1.b.

[108] *Hussein Nuaman Soufraki v. United Arab Emirates*, ICSID Case No. ARB/02/7, Award of July 7, 2004. *See* Richard Happ & Noah Rubins, *Awards and Decisions of ICSID Tribunals in 2004*, 47 GERM. YB. INT'L L. 878, 904–05 (2004); Wisner & Gallus, *supra* note 99, at 930. Farouk Yala, *Soufraki v. United Arab Emirates (Observations)*, 2004 LES CAHIERS DE L'ARBITRAGE/GAZETTE DU PALAIS 22.

The respondent State objected to jurisdiction on grounds that the claimant was not a national of Italy under Italian law. While Soufraki had unquestionably been Italian for a period of time prior to the dispute, he had acquired Canadian citizenship, and lost his Italian nationality automatically by operation of Italian law. The claimant argued that he had reacquired Italian citizenship before the case began, and submitted a Certificate of Nationality issued by the Italian authorities, as well as an Italian passport and a letter from the Italian foreign ministry confirming his citizenship. The tribunal held that it was not bound to accept these documents as conclusive, and that it could undertake its own investigation to determine whether Soufraki was a national of Italy. Ultimately, the tribunal dismissed the case, finding that there was no evidence that the Italian officials in question knew that Soufraki had lost his Italian citizenship when they issued the confirmation documents.[109]

7.62 It is a reality of modern international commerce that businesspeople not infrequently possess two or more nationalities at the same time. Investment treaties rarely address the issue of dual nationality. Rather, subject to the limitations of the Washington Convention a physical person can generally bring an investment claim if he possesses the nationality of a contracting State other than the State party to the dispute, even if he or she holds other passports as well.[110] Certain recent investment accords have sought to eliminate the possible conflicts between individuals' multiple citizenships. The Dominican Republic–Central American Free Trade Agreement (DR–CAFTA) provides:

> investor of a Party means … a national … of a Party, that attempts to make, is making, or has made an investment in the territory of another Party; *provided, however, that a natural person who is a dual national shall be deemed to be exclusively a national of the State of his or her dominant and effective nationality.*[111]

7.63 Pursuant to such a provision, a tribunal is required to apply the "effective nationality" doctrine drawn from customary international law, described in Chapter 10. As a result, individuals who lack close connections to the State of which they claim nationality may be prevented from initiating arbitration, even if they qualify as "nationals" under the relevant State's domestic citizenship law.[112]

---

[109] *Id.* at paras. 53–68, 81.

[110] *See*, in this regard, *Serafin Garcia Armas and Karina Garcia Gruber v. Venezuela*, PCA Case No. 2013-3, Decision on Jurisdiction of Dec. 15, 2014, at paras. 180–81.

[111] Dominican Republic–Central American Free Trade Agreement (2004), art. 10(28) (emphasis added). *See also* U.S. Model BIT (2012), art. 1 ("a natural person who is a dual national shall be deemed to be exclusively a national of the State of his/her dominant and effective nationality").

[112] The tribunal in *Michael Ballantine and Lisa Ballantine v. Dominican Republic*, PCA Case No. 2016-17, Procedural Order No. 2 of Apr. 21, 2017 at paras. 24 *et seq.*, was the first to examine the meaning of "dominant and effective nationality" under art. 10(28) of the Dominican Republic–Central America Free Trade Agreement in the context of an investor who has dual nationality,

b. The Washington Convention

The Washington Convention does not provide any additional guidance as to when an individual should be considered a "national" of a contracting State. However, the Convention imposes one important and express jurisdictional limitation: dual nationals who possess the nationality of the host State are excluded from ICSID arbitration.[113] **7.64**

Notably, Professor Schreuer suggests that a dual national might be able to circumvent the prohibition of article 25(2)(a) by renouncing the nationality of the host State before initiating arbitration. He notes: **7.65**

> Obviously, the benefits from such a step would have to be weighed against any costs arising from the surrender of the host State's nationality. Also, the investor would have to ensure that the renunciation of the nationality is valid under the host State's law. A written affirmation to this effect is advisable.[114]

An ICSID tribunal confirmed Professor Schreuer's opinion in *Víctor Pey Casado v. Chile*. There, Mr Pey Casado, a Spanish/Chilean dual national, renounced his Chilean citizenship before initiating ICSID arbitration against Chile in 1998. Chile argued that the tribunal lacked jurisdiction *ratione personae* and that the renunciation of nationality was invalid as a matter of Chilean law. Citing Professor Schreuer's commentary, the tribunal held that a foreign investor with dual nationality may have access to ICSID arbitration against a contracting State, so long as she has renounced host State nationality prior to her consent to arbitration, and provided that the renunciation is valid under domestic law.[115] Having found that Mr. Pey Casado had effectively relinquished Chilean nationality, the tribunal dismissed the respondent State's preliminary objection. The tribunal's decision with in this respect was upheld by a subsequent *ad hoc* annulment committee.[116] **7.66**

---

including that of the host State. In its decision on bifurcation, the tribunal noted that the analysis of "dominant and effective nationality" will include a number of elements, including the State of habitual residence, the circumstances in which the second nationality was acquired, the individual's personal attachment to a particular country, and the center of the person's economic, social and family life.

[113] Washington Convention, *supra* note 11, art. 25(2)(a); Rudolf Dolzer & Margrete Stevens, *Bilateral Investment Treaties* 141 (1995); Zachary Douglas, The International Law of Investment Claims 321 (4th ed. 2009) (Rule 37). *See*, more generally, Michael Waibel, *Investment Arbitration: Jurisdiction and Admissibility* (2014), University of Cambridge Faculty of Law Research Paper No. 9/2014, at 34–38.

[114] Schreuer et al., *supra* note 39, at 272.

[115] *Víctor Pey Casado and President Allende Foundation v. Chile*, ICSID Case No. ARB/98/2, Award of May 8, 2008, at paras. 301–23.

[116] *Víctor Pey Casado and President Allende Foundation v. Chile*, ICSID Case No. ARB/98/2, Decision on the Application for Annulment of the Republic of Chile of Dec. 18, 2012, at paras. 102, 117, 121.

7.67 Less certain is the case of involuntary acquisition or conservation of host State nationality.[117] In *Champion Trading*, the arbitrators suggested that in certain circumstances dual nationals who hold host State nationality against their will should not be barred from ICSID arbitration:

> The Tribunal does not rule out that situations might arise where the exclusion of dual nationals could lead to a result which was manifestly absurd or unreasonable.... One could envisage a situation where a country continues to apply the *jus sanguinis* over many generations. It might for instance be questionable if the third or fourth foreign born generation, which has no ties whatsoever with the country of its forefathers, could still be considered to have, for the purposes of the Convention, the nationality of this State.[118]

2. Corporations

7.68 Investment protection instruments vary widely in the way they define nationality for the purpose of identifying corporate "investors."[119] Most commonly, investment treaties provide that a company is considered a national of the State where it is created.[120] The U.S.–Moldova BIT, for example, provides:

> "company" of a Party means any kind of corporation, company, association, enterprise, partnership, or other organization, *legally constituted under the laws and regulations of a Party* or a political subdivision thereof whether or not organized for pecuniary gain, or privately or governmentally owned or controlled.[121]

7.69 Some treaties, including many of those signed by Germany, establish the corporate seat (*siège social*) as the main indicator of company citizenship, regardless of where or under which law the legal entity was created.[122] Still other instruments

---

[117] Commentators agree that a host State cannot abusively impose its nationality upon a foreign investor with the purpose of evading arbitral jurisdiction. *See* Schreuer et al., *supra* note 39, at 272, para. 447.

[118] *Champion Trading, supra* note 102, at 16–17. *See also* Farouk Yala, *Champion Trading, et al. v. Egypt (Observations)*, 2004 Les Cahiers de l'Arbitrage/Gazette du Palais 19 (criticizing the tribunal's formalistic approach, particularly when faced with "authentic" foreign investment).

[119] *See generally* Markus Burgstaller, *Nationality of Corporate Investors and International Claims against the Investor's Own State*, 7 JWI 857–82 (2006); Pia Acconci, *Determining the Internationally Relevant Link between a State and a Corporate Investor: Recent Trends Concerning the Application of the Genuine Link Test*, 5 J. World Inv. & Trade 139 (2004); Okan Beygo, *Nationality of Corporations in International Claims Arising Out of Foreign Investment Disputes*, 46 Revue Hellénique De Droit International 33 (1993); Reed et al., *supra* note 6, at 41–42.

[120] *See e.g. ADC Affiliate Ltd. and ADC & ADMC Management Ltd. v. Hungary*, ICSID Case No. ARB/03/16, Award of Oct. 2, 2006, at para. 359 (rejecting a "genuine link" requirement).

[121] U.S.–Moldova BIT (1994), art. 1(b) (emphasis added).

[122] *See e.g.* Germany–Bangladesh BIT (1981), art. 8(4)(a) (a qualifying German "company" is "any juridical person as well as any commercial or other company or association with or without legal personality *having its seat in the German area of application* of the present Agreement and lawfully existing consistent with legal provisions, irrespective of whether the liability of its partners. associates or members is limited or unlimited and whether or not its activities are directed at profit" (emphasis added)).

provide that a company's nationality is determined "based upon the nationality of dominant shareholders."[123]

Yet another category of treaties narrows the definition of corporate investor, requiring a combination of both incorporation under the given State's law and some criterion of real involvement there, such as the corporate seat or substantial business activity. The Switzerland–Botswana BIT, for example, defines a corporate investor of a contracting party as: **7.70**

> juridical entities, including corporations ... that were constituted or otherwise organized in accordance with the legislation of such Contracting Party, and which maintain their seat, as well as real economic activities, in the territory of that same Contracting Party.[124]

Finally, some treaties offer a more flexible standard of corporate nationality, granting investor status not only to companies incorporated in the home State, but also to those created in the host State and controlled by nationals of the other treaty signatory.[125] **7.71**

As a general rule, however, States apply either the head office or the place of incorporation criterion in order to determine nationality of legal entities.[126] **7.72**

One controversial issue arising out of these varying definitions of corporate nationality is whether a company that otherwise qualifies as an "investor" for purposes of an investment treaty should be barred from bringing an arbitration claim against the host State if its ultimate beneficial owners are of non-qualifying nationality. As explained in Chapter 2, the seminal *Barcelona Traction* case established a customary rule respecting the corporate form, but nevertheless allowing **7.73**

[123] Reed et al., *supra* note 6, at 42.

[124] Switzerland–Botswana BIT (1998), art. 1(1)(b).

[125] *See e.g.* Netherlands–Argentina BIT (1992), art. 1(b)(3). Such provisions appear to echo at least one view of customary international law on the subject. 1 Oppenheim's International Law 859–60 (Sir Robert Jennings & Sir Arthur Watts eds. 1996) ("It is usual to attribute a corporation to the state under the laws of which it has been incorporated and to which it owes its legal existence; to this initial condition is often added the need for the corporation's head office, registered office, or its siège social to be in the same state"). *See also Venezuela Holdings B.V. et al. (formerly Mobil Corp. et al.) v. Venezuela*, ICSID Case No. ARB/07/27, Decision on Jurisdiction of June 10, 2010, at paras. 150–60 (holding that the claimant's subsidiaries incorporated under U.S. and Bahamian law were "Dutch investors" for the purposes of the BIT, because they were 100 percent owned and controlled by a "legal person constituted under the law" of the Netherlands). *See further Swisslion DOO Skopje v. Former Yugoslav Republic of Macedonia*, ICSID Case No. ARB/09/16, Award of July 6, 2012, at para. 132, holding that a company incorporated in Skopje was "Swiss" for the purposes of the BIT, because more than 50 percent of its equity interest was owned by a Swiss company.

[126] *Víctor Pey Casado and President Allende Foundation v. Chile*, ICSID Case No. ARB/98/2, Award of May 8, 2008, at para. 549.

"veil piercing" in "exceptional" circumstances to ascertain the nationality of the true interests at stake in an international claim.[127]

7.74 Modern investment arbitration tribunals have generally demonstrated reluctance to consider the nationality of a claimant corporation's shareholders, absent contrary provisions in the relevant investment protection instrument.[128] In *Tokios Tokelés v. Ukraine*, the claimant was a Lithuanian publishing company doing business in Ukraine through a local subsidiary.[129] When Tokios invoked the arbitration provisions of the Lithuania–Ukraine BIT, Ukraine objected that the Lithuanian company was a mere shell, and that it should be considered a Ukrainian corporation and ineligible for treaty protection, since 99 percent of its shares were held by Ukrainian nationals. The majority of the arbitrators noted that the treaty in question contained no express requirement that a company do business in its home State or be controlled by interests there to qualify for protection, and that therefore an additional "control" or "substantial business activity" test would be inappropriate.[130] They acknowledged that the "veil piercing" doctrine formed part of customary international law, but concluded that in any event the respondent State had not satisfied the strict requirements for looking behind the corporate form.[131]

3. Continuous nationality

7.75 With regard to both individuals and corporations, nationality is not always eternal. Physical persons move from country to country, and corporations are

[127] *Case Concerning Barcelona Traction Case (Belgium v. Spain)*, 1970 I.C.J. 4 (Second Phase), 46 I.L.R. 178. *See also* Chapter 2, Section F.2 and Chapter 10, Section B.1.a.ii.

[128] Wisner & Gallus, *supra* note 99, at 939–44.

[129] *Tokios Tokelés v. Ukraine*, ICSID Case No.ARB/02/18, Decision on Jurisdiction of Apt. 29, 2004. *See also* Happ & Rubins, *supra* note 108, at 892–95. *See also Rompetrol Group N.V. v. Romania*, ICSID Case No. ARB/06/3, Decision on Respondent's Preliminary Objectionson Jurisdiction and Admissibility of Apr. 18, 2008, at paras. 85 and 92–93; *H&H Enterprises, supra* note 92, Decision on Respondent's Objections to Jurisdiction of Jun. 5, 2012, at para. 68, where the tribunal rejected the respondent's request to pierce the corporate veil of the corporate claimant (a company incorporated under the laws of California) reject jurisdiction under art. 25(2)(a) of the ICSID Convention, on grounds that the claimant's shareholder had the dual nationality of both contracting parties to the U.S.–Egypt BIT.

[130] *Tokios Tokelés, supra* note 129, at para. 38.

[131] *Id.* at paras. 53–56 ("there is no evidence in the record that the Claimant used its formal legal nationality for any improper purpose"). But *cf. Loewen, supra* note 71, at para. 237 (refusing to recognize Canadian corporation as Canadian where "[a]ll of the benefits of any award would clearly inure to the American corporation"); *Banro American Resources Inc. and Société Aurifère du Kivu et du Maniema S.A.R.L. v. Democratic Republic of the Congo*, Case No. ARB/98/7, Award of Sept. 1, 2000, 17 ICSID Rev—For. Inv. L.J. 382 (2003) (stating in *dicta* that "in general, ICSID tribunals do not accept the view that their competence is limited by formalities, and rather they rule on their competence based on a review of the circumstances surrounding the case, and, in particular, the actual relationship among the companies involved. This jurisprudence reveals the willingness of ICSID tribunals to refrain from making decisions on their competence based on formal appearances, and to base their decisions on a realistic assessment of the situation before them").

bought, sold, and reorganized. In cases where claimants possess the necessary citizenship to advance a treaty claim, but subsequently assume a different nationality, it remains for tribunals to determine whether the individual or company maintained the necessary citizenship long enough to pursue the claim to conclusion.[132] Very few investment treaties address this issue directly, nor (at least with regard to corporations) does the Washington Convention.[133]

There has been a great deal of dispute as to the relevant moment in time for assessing nationality, and no clear rule of customary international law appears to have emerged.[134] Professor Dugard has identified at least *ten* possibilities for the date until which requisite citizenship must be maintained, adopted by various commentators and tribunals, ranging from the date on which a government espouses a national's claim, through the date of filing the claim, until the date of judgment or the date of settlement.[135] Investment treaty practice is also somewhat inconsistent. **7.76**

In *Klöckner v. Cameroon*,[136] the government of Cameroon signed two investment agreements with Klöckner, a German company, each of which included an ICSID arbitration clause. Both Cameroon and Germany were ICSID contracting States. At the same time, the Cameroon government signed a third **7.77**

---

[132] Maurice Mendelson, *Runaway Train: The "Continuous Nationality" Rule from the Panavezys-Saldutiskis Railway case to Loewen*, in INTERNATIONAL INVESTMENT LAW AND ARBITRATION 97 (Todd Weiler ed. 2005); Rubins, *supra* note 73, at 23–26; Matthew Duchesne, *The Continuous-Nationality-of-Claims Principle: Its Historical Development and Current Relevance to Investor–State Investment Disputes*, 36 GW INT'L L. REV. 783 (2004).

[133] For an overview of treaty provisions dealing with the necessary duration of nationality, *see* Mendelson, *supra* note 132, at 126–34.

[134] *See e.g.* D. O'CONNELL, INTERNATIONAL LAW 1035 (1970) (continuous nationality rule is "discretionary practice" rather than "substantive rule of law"); Ian Sinclair, *Nationality of Claims: British Practice*, 27 BRIT. YB. INT'L L. 125, 130 (1950) (same); B. WESTON, INTERNATIONAL CLAIMS: POSTWAR FRENCH PRACTICE 83 (1971) (same); *Administrative Decision No. V: Decisions and Opinions (U.S.A. v. Germany)*, 7 R.I.A.A. 199 (1924) ("it may well be doubted whether the alleged rule [of continuous nationality] has received such universal recognitöon as to justify the broad statement that it is an established rule of international law"). Professor John Dugard, the U.N. International Law Commission's special rapporteur on diplomatic protection, concluded in a 2000 report that there was too much variety in State practice to posit any customary international law rule at all on continuous nationality. U.N. Doc. A/CN.4/506/Add. 1, draft Article 9; Bruno Simma, *The Work of the International Law Commission at its 52nd Session*, Report of the Ad Hoc Committee of Legal Advisers to the Council of Europe on International Law, Sept. 4, 2000, at 24, available at https://documents-dds-ny.un.org/doc/UNDOC/GEN/N00/400/06/pdf/N0040006.pdf?OpenElement.

[135] Dugard identifies the following alternatives: (1) date of espousal of claim; (2) date of initial negotiations; (3) date of filing the claim; (4) date of the signature of the applicable treaty creating the adjudicative forum; (5) the date of ratification of the applicable treaty; (6) the date of entry into force of the applicable treaty; (7) the date of "presentation" of the claim; (8) the date oral hearings conclude; (9) the date of judgment; (10) the date of payment or settlement of the claim. U.N. Doc. A/CN.4/506/Add. 1 at 11. For a critique of this aspect of the *Loewen* award, *see* Jan Paulsson, *Continuous Nationality in Loewen*, 20 ARB. INT'L 213 (2004).

[136] *Klöckner, supra* note 57.

agreement, called the Establishment Agreement of 1973, with a local company called SOCAME, in connection with Klöckner's investments. The Establishment Agreement also contained an ICSID arbitration clause. When the Establishment Agreement was signed, the local company was 51 percent owned by Klöckner and 49 percent by the government of Cameroon. Afterward, Klöckner failed to subscribe to a required capital increase, and its 51 percent share in SOCAME reverted to Cameroon by contract. At the time the arbitration was filed, therefore, SOCAME was wholly owned by the contracting State, Cameroon. Klöckner nevertheless filed for arbitration, and Cameroon counterclaimed, arguing that as majority shareholders of SOCAME at the time ICSID jurisdiction attached, Klöckner should be substituted for SOCAME as a party to the dispute. The tribunal ruled that it had jurisdiction over the counterclaim and disputes under the Establishment Agreement.[137] The arbitrators summarized the state of thinking at the time on change of claimant nationality:

> Knowledgeable writers are divided on the issue of the effects on the ICSID arbitration clause of a subsequent change of nationality or control. On the one hand, Mr. Amerasinghe has maintained that this change affects neither the validity nor the effect of the forum clause because, in his view, "the ICSID Convention implies that the relevant time for the fulfillment of the nationality requirement is that date when the consent to jurisdiction is effective for both parties. It also means that any change in the nationality of the juridical person after that date is immaterial for purposes of ICSID's jurisdiction." On the other hand, Mr. Delaume seems to be of a different view; in analyzing the hypothesis of an assignment to a third party of the investment agreement during its performance, he maintains that if the assignee is a "national of the State party to the agreement or of a non-contracting State," the Centre's jurisdiction would disappear.[138]

7.78 The *Loewen* tribunal adopted a strict approach to continuous nationality. In that case, the Canadian claimant corporation was forced into bankruptcy proceedings after the start of NAFTA arbitration against the United States. The reorganization that followed resulted in most of its assets being transferred to a U.S. company. The tribunal ruled that NAFTA is silent on the issue of continuous nationality,[139] and that therefore customary international law was the rule of decision. Here, the arbitrators were very succinct:

> In international law parlance, there must be continuous national identity from the date of the events giving rise to the claim … through the date of the resolution of the claim.[140]

---

[137] *Id.* at 17.

[138] *Id.* at 16 (internal cites omitted, *citing* C.F. Amerasinghe, *The International Centre for the Settlement of Investment Disputes and Development through the Multinational Corporation*, 9 Vand. J. Transnat'l L. 793, 809–10 (1976); Georges R. Delaume, *Le Centre International pour le Réglement des Différends Relatifs aux Investissements (CIRDI)*, 109 J. de Droit Int'l 775, 797 (1982).

[139] *Loewen, supra* note 71, at para. 228.

[140] *Id.* at para. 225.

The tribunal therefore dismissed the claim for lack of requisite nationality. **7.79**

Nevertheless, there is support for the view that as long as a claimant possesses the necessary nationality on the date its claim is submitted, subsequent change of citizenship should not divest a tribunal of jurisdiction.[141] In the case of *El Paso v. Argentina*, the Argentine Republic raised the preliminary objection that the claimant had lost its investor status following the commencement of the arbitration proceedings, due to the fact that the investments in question had been sold. The tribunal dismissed this objection, noting that "no rule prescribing continuous ownership of the investment could be deduced from the ICSID Convention and the BIT or from the relevant case-law."[142] **7.80**

As Professor Mendelson concludes: **7.81**

> To summarise the position regarding [investment treaties], in some cases there is a continuous nationality rule, and in other cases not. But even where continuous nationality is required, in no case is there any basis in the treaty for holding that it needs to continue beyond the date of instituting proceedings.[143]

4. Shareholders as investors

The question frequently arises whether the shareholders and parent corporations of corporate entities are able to bring claims in their own right with regard to State measures affecting the subsidiary.[144] **7.82**

In most instances, shareholders and parent corporations may initiate arbitration under applicable investment treaties in relation to harm that befalls the companies in which they hold shares, regardless of whether the company owned has standing to do so. Whether a shareholder has standing in a particular case depends entirely on the circumstances surrounding the dispute, particularly the text of the treaty applicable to the entity that wishes to sue. Potential claimants must therefore examine applicable treaties closely: any generalization is ultimately unreliable. **7.83**

---

[141] Similarly, Douglas suggests that there is no rationale for insisting on holding the relevant nationality after the arbitral proceedings have commenced; Douglas, *supra* note 113, at 291 (Rule 31).

[142] *See El Paso Energy Int'l Co. v. Argentina*, ICSID Case No. ARB/03/15, Award of Oct. 31, 2011, at para. 146 (noting that all that is required is ownership of the claim at the time of consent to arbitration as well as at the time of the registration of the claim).

[143] Mendelson, *supra* note 132, at 134. *See also* Rubins, *supra* note 73, at 24–26.

[144] *See* on this point, Patrick Dumberry, *The Legal Standing of Shareholders before Arbitral Tribunals: Has Any Rule of Customary International Law Crystallized?* 18(3) Mich. J. Int'l L. 353 *et seq.* (2010); Stanimir A. Alexandrov, *The "Baby Boom" of Treaty-Based Arbitrations and the Jurisdiction of ICSID Tribunals: Shareholders as Investors and Jurisdiction Ratione Temporis*, 4 L. & Pract. Int'l Cts. & Tribunals 19 (2005); Ian A. Laird, *A Community of Destiny: The Barcelona Traction Case and the Development of Shareholder Rights to Bring Investment Claims*, in International Investment Law and Arbitration, *supra* note 132, at 77.

7.84 Like all jurisdictional questions in investment arbitration, the legal analysis must be undertaken in two steps.[145] First, the arbitral tribunal must determine whether the respondent has consented to arbitrate with the entity in question. As explained earlier, in investment arbitration, consent is expressed in the text of the applicable bilateral or multilateral investment treaty. If the treaty provides consent to arbitrate with the shareholder in question, and if the claimant seeks ICSID arbitration (rather than arbitration under the UNCITRAL rules or some other commercial arbitration rules), then the tribunal must determine if the claimant has standing to invoke ICSID arbitration under the Washington Convention. If the answer to the first question is positive, but the second is negative, then only non-ICSID arbitration is possible.

7.85 Most treaties define "investor" very broadly, focusing exclusively on the nationality of the potential claimant, rather than its relationship to the entity directly involved in the investment dispute. One common formulation can be found, for instance, in the BIT between Finland and Albania:

> The term "investor" means: any natural person who is (a) a national of either Contracting Party in accordance with its laws and regulations; and (b) any legal person such as a company or other organization constituted in accordance with the laws and regulations of the Contracting Party and having its seat in the territory of the same Contracting Party.[146]

7.86 The investor–State dispute resolution provisions of many BITs are extremely broad as well, and require only that an "investor" or "national" be party to a dispute in relation to an "investment." It is not necessary according to the text of such clauses that the claimant own the investment directly:

> Disputes with regard to an investment which arise within the terms of this Agreement between an investor of one Contracting Party and the other Contracting Party, which have not been amicably settled shall be [subject, *inter alia*, to international arbitration].[147]

7.87 Where the applicable treaty contains provisions such as these, it appears that *any* entity that has the appropriate nationality can bring a claim against a host State, as long as the dispute is connected to an "investment" within the meaning of the treaty.[148]

7.88 Other definitions of "investor" are narrower, however, and may limit the ability of shareholders or parent corporations to bring claims against host States in response to actions detrimental to their investments. Most commonly, narrowed definitions

---

[145] For more on the two-step jurisdictional analysis, *see* Rubins, *supra* note 49, at 289–90.
[146] Finland–Albania BIT (1997), art. 1.
[147] U.K.–Argentina BIT (1990), art. 8(1).
[148] On the meaning of "investment," *see* Section E, *infra*.

of "investor" in BITs require that the claimant "have control over" the company actually making the investment.[149] Such a provision may prevent holding companies or minority shareholders from bringing a claim. Similarly, some investment treaties only consider a company to be an "investor" of a contracting State if it carries on "real economic activities" there. The North Korea–Thailand BIT, for example, provides:

> the term "investor" shall mean ... legal entities ... which are constituted or otherwise duly organized under the law of [a] Contracting Party and have their seat, together with real economic activities, in the territory of that same Contracting Party.[150]

The "economic activities" requirement can prevent holding companies from initiating arbitration based on a treaty of the State of their incorporation, even if they directly own 100 percent of the investment in question. Once again, the vast majority of investment treaties define "investor" broadly, and link standing to sue exclusively to the ownership or control of an "investment" as defined by the treaty. In most cases, therefore, the question of standing rests largely upon the definition of "investment." **7.89**

In *CMS v. Argentina*,[151] the claimant company owned 29.42 percent of TGN, an Argentine corporation and concession holder for the transmission of natural gas. CMS claimed that Argentina's actions violated the substantive provisions of the Argentina–U.S. BIT. Argentina objected that CMS was not an "investor," because it "does not hold the rights upon which it bases its claim—to wit, TGN being the licensee, and CMS only a minority shareholder in this company, only TGN could claim for any damage suffered."[152] The tribunal assessed the BIT definition of "investment," which included "shares of stock ... in a company."[153] Argentina argued that such language only allows claims in relation to measures affecting the shares as such (*e.g.* the seizure of shares or interference with dividend or voting rights).[154] The tribunal rejected this narrow approach, adopting instead the claimant's position that "shareholders have a protected right of their own arising from their investment."[155] The tribunal found "no bar in current **7.90**

149 U.S.–Canada Free Trade Agreement, art. 1611 (1992) (requiring "control" of enterprise); Jeswald Salacuse, *Towards a Global Treaty on Foreign Investment: The Search for a Grand Bargain*, in Arbitrating Foreign Investment Disputes 51, 63 (Norbert Horn ed. 2004).

150 North Korea–Thailand BIT (2002), art. 1(2)(b). *See also* Latvia–Poland BIT (1993), art. 1(1)(b).

151 *CMS, supra* note 85.

152 *Id.* at para. 36.

153 Argentina–United States BIT (1991), art. I(1).

154 *CMS, supra* note 85, at para. 59.

155 *Id.* at para. 62. This conclusion appears also to comport with customary international law, which has evolved significantly since the contrary holding in *Barcelona Traction, supra* note 127. *See Elettronica Sicula S.p.A. (ELSI) (U.S. v. Italy)*, Judgment of July 20, 1989, 1989 ICJ Rep. 15; U.N. Compensation Comm., Decision of Governing Council on Business Losses of Individuals,

international law to the concept of allowing claims by shareholders independently from those of the corporation concerned."[156]

7.91 In the *Lauder* case, the U.S. claimant owned a minority (but controlling) share in a Dutch company, *CME*, which controlled the Czech operating company that was the subject of the dispute. The Czech Republic opposed jurisdiction on grounds that the claimant had "failed to prove that he owns or controls an investment in the Czech Republic."[157] The Czech Republic ultimately withdrew this objection, and jurisdiction was upheld with the arbitrators making no mention of the indirect nature of Lauder's investment. It is unlikely that the Czech Republic could have prevailed on this point: Lauder's claim was based on the U.S.–Czech BIT, which expressly extends protection to indirect investments.[158]

7.92 However, this does not necessarily mean that the assets owned by the local company constitute protected "investments" upon which shareholders may rely for the purposes of establishing a treaty violation.

7.93 In *BG Group v. Argentina*, the claimant, a British corporation, had a direct and indirect ownership interest in two natural gas distribution companies incorporated in Argentina (MetroGAS and GASA). The claimant argued that the amendments in Argentina's tariff regime constituted a violation of the Argentina–U.K. BIT, with respect to two types of "investments": (1) B.G.'s indirect equity in MetroGAS and GASA under article 1(a)(ii) of the BIT;[159] and (2) BG's rights under article 1(a)(iii) and (v) of the BIT.[160] Argentina objected to the tribunal's jurisdiction, on the basis that BG was advancing "derivative" claims that it had

S/AC.26/1191/4, of Dec. 123 (2001); International Law Association, Committee on Diplomatic Protection of Persons and Property, First Report of 69th Conference (2001). By contrast, many systems of municipal law prohibit the claims of shareholders in relation of damage done to the company in which they own shares, a principle known in English law as the "rule against reflective loss." *Johnson v Gore Wood & Co* [2002] 2 AC 1. In the investment treaty context, this has given rise to recent debate and modification of new model treaties to limit reflective loss claims. David Gaukrodger, *Investment Treaties and Shareholder Claims, Analysis of Treaty Practice*, OECD Working Papers on International Investment 2014/03 (2014).

156 *CMS, supra* note 85, at para. 48.

157 *Lauder, supra* note 89, at paras. 77, 153–55.

158 United States–Czech Republic BIT, art. I(1)(a) ("'investment' means every kind of investment in the territory of one Party owned or controlled directly or indirectly by nationals or companies of the other Party, such as equity, debt, and service and investment contracts"). A similar objection was made and then withdrawn by the respondent in *Wena v. Egypt*. There, Egypt initially argued that the tribunal lacked jurisdiction on grounds that "the Claimant has made no investment in Egypt," apparently believing that the funds used to develop the Egyptian facilities had not been provided by the claimant, but instead by some third party. *Wena Hotels Ltd. v. Arab Egypt*, ICSID Case No. ARB/98/4, Decision of June 29, 1999, *reprinted at* 41 I.L.M. 881, 885 (2002).

159 Article 1(a)(ii) of the Argentina–UK BIT defines "investments" as "shares in and stock and debentures of a company and any other form of participation in a company, established in the territory of either of the Contracting Parties."

160 Article 1(a)(iii) and (v) of the Argentina–U.K. BIT defines "investments" as "claims to money" and "business concessions" respectively.

not consented to arbitrate. The tribunal noted that BG's claims were properly before it "only to the extent that BG has standing to bring them."[161] With respect to the first type of investment, the tribunal had no difficulty finding that BG's derivative claim of compensation for damage to the value of its shares (caused by measures having a direct impact on the activities of MetroGAS and GASA) fell within the scope of Argentina's consent, relying on previous ICSID jurisdiction.[162] However, the tribunal did not agree that BG had standing to bring a claim on behalf of MetroGAS and GASA for damages to "claims to money and performance *under contracts entered into by MetroGAS*" and "benefits from the *Licence granted by the Government to MetroGAS*" (emphasis in the original).[163] Given that BG was not a party to the contracts or the license, it did not "own" such rights under article 1(a)(iii) and (v) of the BIT, such that it could directly assert them before the tribunal.[164] Furthermore, contrary to article 1117 of NAFTA or article 25(2)(b) of the ICSID Convention, the U.K.–Argentina BIT did not include a mechanism for foreign investors to bring claims "on behalf of an entity in the territory of the host State which they own or control ... directly or indirectly."[165] Accordingly, the tribunal found that BG was not entitled to assert—directly or indirectly—rights to money or performance that it did not own. In the tribunal's view, *CMS* was not sufficient authority to depart from the language of the BIT.[166]

Similarly, in *Impregilo v. Argentina*, the tribunal noted that the *CMS* tribunal had accepted jurisdiction "not on the basis of any rights of the Argentine company TGN or any rights relating to the License, which were not protected investments, but on account of the existence of the shareholding of CMS in the Argentine company."[167] Accordingly, the *Impregilo* tribunal did not accept jurisdiction over the contractual claims of the locally-incorporated company in which the claimant had a 42.58 percent equity stake,[168] because the local company did not qualify as an "investor" under the BIT.[169] The tribunal in *El Paso v. Argentina* similarly held that El Paso could not assert the contractual rights and licenses held by Argentinian companies which did not qualify as "investors" under the BIT and the ICSID Convention.[170] **7.94**

---

161 *B.G. Group Plc. v. Argentina*, UNCITRAL, Final Award of Dec. 24, 2007, at para. 184.
162 *Id.* at paras. 203–05.
163 *Id.* at para. 207.
164 *Id.* at para. 210.
165 *Id.* at para. 211.
166 *Id.* at para. 214.
167 *Impregilo S.p.A. v. Argentina*, ICSID Case No. ARB/07/17, Award of June 21, 2011, at para. 244.
168 *Id.* at para. 238.
169 *Id.* at paras. 243–46.
170 *El Paso, supra* note 142, at paras. 178–89. *See also Poštová banka, A.S. and ISTROKAPITAL S.E. v. Hellenic Republic*, ICSID Case No. ARB/13/8, Award of Apr. 9, 2015, at paras. 245–47.

7.95 As previously noted, the limits of jurisdiction under the Washington Convention are not necessarily the same as the scope of the investment treaty that provides consent to arbitration. However, there is little evidence that ICSID imposes any significant additional jurisdictional requirements with regard to shareholders, whether direct or indirect. Article 25 of the Washington Convention establishes the scope of ICSID jurisdiction. While article 25(2)(a) normally excludes physical persons of dual nationality from ICSID arbitration, it has nothing to say about corporate entities that own part of an investment through shareholdings, directly or indirectly.

7.96 Notably, in *CMS*, Argentina sought to annul the arbitral award on the basis that the tribunal had manifestly exceeded the "outer limits" of the ICSID Convention, because CMS had no *jus standi* under article 25(2)(b) of the ICSID Convention (regardless of the wording of the applicable BIT) insofar as its claim was concerned "not with its rights as shareholder, but with the alleged 'dismantling' of a tariff regime that granted rights to TGN, not to CMS."[171] The *ad hoc* annulment committee rejected these arguments, noting that article 25 of the ICSID Convention does not define the term "investment," which is left largely to the terms of applicable BIT. Given that article I(1) of the Argentina–U.S. BIT covered minority shareholders and did not require that the investor obtain a majority stake or otherwise control the company, this remained "compatible with the object and purpose of the ICSID Convention."[172] The fact that the locally incorporated company may itself claim for the violation of its rights under contracts, licenses, or other instruments under article 25(2)(b) of the ICSID Convention does not affect the right of action of foreign shareholders under the BIT to protect their own interests in a qualifying investment.[173]

7.97 Indeed, in a string of cases, ICSID tribunals have found little reason to restrict ICSID jurisdiction in relation to shareholders or parent corporations. The tribunals in *AMT v. Zaire*,[174] *Genin v. Estonia*,[175] and *Goetz v. Burundi*,[176] among others, held that "ICSID jurisprudence does not limit standing only to individuals directly targeted by disputed measures, but extends also to shareholders."[177] After

---

[171] *CMS Gas Transmission Co. v. Argentina*, ICSID Case No. ARB/01/8, Decision of the Ad Hoc Committee on the Application for Annulment of the Argentine Republic of Sept. 25, 2007, at para. 65.

[172] *Id.* at paras. 72–73.

[173] *Id.* at para. 74, referring to *Continental Casualty Co. v. Argentina*, ICSID Case No. ARB/03/9, Decision on Jurisdiction of Feb. 22, 2006, at para. 86; and *Enron Creditors Recovery, supra* note 85, Decision on Jurisdiction (Ancillary Claim) of Aug. 2, 2004, at para. 49.

[174] *American Manufacturing & Trading v. Zaire*, ICSID Case No. ARB/93/1, Award of Feb. 21, 1997 (American company's "investment" was its shares in a Zairian company).

[175] *Genin, supra* note 85, at para. 324 (U.S. citizen's equity in Estonian company qualified as "investment").

[176] *Antoine Goetz et al. v. Burundi*, ICSID Case No. ARB/95/3, Award of Feb. 10, 1999, at para. 89.

[177] *Id.*

finding that shares constituted an investment under the applicable BIT, the *CMS* tribunal surveyed ICSID case law and held that the "trend" indicated that the essence of "investment" under the Washington Convention lay "not with the question of majority or control."[178] Thus, the tribunal found, minority shareholders as well as parent companies and controlling equity holders satisfy the *ratione personae* requirements of the Washington Convention's article 25.

E. What Is Protected by Investment Protection Instruments

1. Overview

As a rule, investment protection instruments extend protection only to assets that qualify as "investments" according to their terms. Similarly, the foreign private party's right to initiate dispute resolution against the host State under a treaty or investment law extends only to disputes arising out of that party's investments.[179] **7.98**

The reason for this limitation is the perception among both less-developed and industrialized States that private "investment" is a catalyst for development and prosperity.[180] Nevertheless, considering the impact of FDI on host States' economic development, various economic theories have been formulated.[181] Investment protection treaties, including the Washington Convention and BITs, constitute a **7.99**

[178] *CMS, supra* note 85, at para. 55.

[179] As explained later, investment treaties view investment as a kind of asset. Draft OECD Multilateral Agreement on Investment, art. II(2), available at http://www1.oecd.org/daf/mai/pdf/ng/ng987r1e.pdf (investment is "every kind of asset owned or controlled, directly or indirectly, by an investor"). Economists and legal commentators more often describe investment is a phenomenon, a process, or an action. M. Sornarajah, The International Law on Foreign Investment 8 (3d ed. 2010) ("Foreign investment involves the transfer of tangible or intangible assets from one country into another for the purpose of use in that country to generate wealth under the total or partial control of the owner of the assets"); Rudolf Bernhardt, 8 Encyclopedia of Public International Law 246 (1990) (investment is "a transfer of funds or materials from one country ... to another country ... for a direct or indirect participation in the earnings of that enterprise").

[180] On the importance of foreign investment to industrialized countries, *see* Wesley Sholz, *International Regulation of Foreign Direct Investment*, 31 Cornell Int'l L.J. 485, 486 (1998). On the role of investment in Third World development, *see* World Bank, *The Role of Foreign Direct Investment in Development*, Presentations to the 41st Meeting of the Development Committee, at 39 (1991); Ibrahim Shihata, Legal Treatment of Foreign Investment: The World Bank Guidelines 11 (1993); Thomas W. Wälde, *Investment Arbitration under the Energy Charter Treaty*, 12 Arb. Int'l 429, 430–31 (1996). The ostensible benefits of FDI include wage increases, reduced unemployment, increased demand for local goods, inflow of foreign capital, opening of markets, improved balance of payments, transfer of industrial skills and knowledge, transfer of management skills, increased tax revenues, and improved infrastructure. Ted G. Telford & Heather A. Ures, *The Role of Incentives in Foreign Direct Investment*, 23 Loy. Int'l & Comp. LR 605, 615–16 (2001).

[181] For a comprehensive review of the conflicting economic theories on foreign investment, *see* Sornarajah, *supra* note 179, at 47–60.

conscious, and potentially politically costly, derogation of State sovereignty.[182] The State's sacrifice of freedom of action is done for a particular purpose, and that purpose closely defines the scope of operation of investment protection instruments. The primary motivation for both developing and developed States in concluding these agreements is, in the words of the Washington Convention preamble, "the role of private international investment" in "international cooperation for economic development."[183] Thus, there is a recognition that a certain category of cross-border economic activity, called "investment," helps expand welfare around the globe.[184] The corollary is that other kinds of operations are not considered to have the same effect: short-term capital flows, particularly those involving speculation in debt or currency, are widely seen by host States as sources of monetary or economic instability, rather than stability and prosperity.[185] The derogation of State sovereignty necessary for a direct investor–State dispute resolution system is therefore generally viewed to be worth undertaking to the extent it helps a developing country compete to attract "good" asset flows, designated as "investment."[186]

7.100 Ian Brownlie, in a dissenting opinion in the *CME v. Czech Republic* final award, was adamant on this point. "Investment," he insisted, does not include all kinds of property, and it is essential that arbitrators confer the benefits of investment protection treaties only upon property rights that qualify as investment. To do otherwise would betray the intent—and consent—of the sovereign contracting parties to arbitrate their disputes with aliens operating in their territory.[187]

---

[182] *See* Barton Legum, *Federalism, NAFTA Chapter Eleven and the Jay Treaty of 1794*, News from ICSID, Spring 2001 (for the United States, investor–State arbitration "requires the federal government's liability to be decided not by judges appointed by the President with the advice and consent of the Senate, but by a panel of international arbitrators"). For a Mexican point of view on the extent of derogation from State sovereignty as a result of investment treaties and the consequent political cost, *see* Bernardo Sepulveda Amor, *The NAFTA and the Claims of Mexican Jurisdiction*, 19 Hous. J. Int'l L. 565, 586–91 (1997).

[183] Washington Convention, *supra* note 11, Preamble. For an illuminating and convincing economic analysis of developing countries' motivation in signing BITs, *see* Andrew T. Guzman, *Why LDCs Sign Treaties That Hurt Them: Explaining the Popularity of Bilateral Investment Treaties*, 38 Va. J. Int'l L. 639 (1998).

[184] Thomas W. Wälde & Todd Weiler, *Investment Arbitration under the Energy Charter Treaty in the Light of New NAFTA Precedents: Towards a Global Code of Conduct for Economic Regulation?*, in Investment Treaties and Arbitration 159, 160–62 (Gabrielle Kaufmann-Kohler & Blaise Stucki eds. 2002).

[185] Axelle Lemaire, *Le nouveau visage de l'arbitrage entre État et investisseur étranger: le chapitre 11 de l'ALENA*, janv.–mars Revue de L'Arbitrage 43, 59 (2001).

[186] Despite the overall benefits introducing the Investor–State dispute resolution regime, it is still unclear whether such a regime has helped host States to attract foreign investments. *See e.g.* Jason Webb Yackee, *Do Bilateral Investment Treaties Promote Foreign Direct Investment? Some Hints from Alternative Evidence*, 51 Va. J. Int'l L. 397 (2010); U.N. Conference on Trade and Development, *The Impact of International Investment Agreements on Foreign Direct Investment: An Overview of Empirical Studies 1998–2004* (Working Draft 2014).

[187] *CME Czech Republic B.V. v. Czech Republic*, Final Award of Mar. 13, 2003, Separate Opinion of Ian Brownlie, at para. 33, available at https://www.italaw.com/sites/default/files/case-documents/ita0180.pdf.

2. "Investment" as defined in treaties and investment laws

Treaties signed before the 1990s often provided a relatively restricted definition of "investment," sometimes expressly linking the concept to "capital" or requiring that a local business enterprise be established to qualify for protection.[188] This was also the approach taken in the 1972 International Chamber of Commerce Guidelines for International Investments. The ICC paper is "quite clearly directed at foreign nationals who wish to establish businesses and investments in the ordinary sense of the word, bringing capital into the host State and having a management role and a clear financial stake in the business enterprise."[189] **7.101**

Subsequent BITs, including those based on U.S. and Organisation for Economic Cooperation and Development (OECD) models, have adopted a broad, descriptive approach to the scope of covered investment.[190] While these definitions differ, most provide an extremely general statement of coverage.[191] Possibly the broadest such general definition is contained in the ASEAN Agreement for the Promotion and Protection of Investments, which describes investment as "every kind of asset."[192] This is distinct, and marginally more useful, than the circular approach of some U.S. BITs, which inform us that investment is "every kind of investment owned or controlled directly or indirectly."[193] Treaties of this sort normally illustrate the subject-matter scope of their application by providing a non-exhaustive list of asset categories that fall within the definition of "investment."[194] Typical categories found in most investment treaties include real estate and other direct property rights, shareholdings and other forms of participation in companies, **7.102**

---

[188] World Bank, Legal Framework for the Treatment of Foreign Investment: Survey of Existing Instruments, Progress Report and Background Studies 24 (1992). The evolution of the notion of investment in early bilateral treaties was at times driven by the negotiation process, where asset types that capital-importing States did not recognize as significant or worthy of protection were nevertheless included in BITs at the insistence of capital-exporting States. During the negotiation of the 1986 U.K.–China BIT, for example, the Chinese initially refused to include "goodwill" as part of the definition of investment, but ceded to U.K. insistence that such intangibles should be covered. Eileen Denza & Shelagh Brooks, *Investment Protection Treaties: United Kingdom Experience*, 36 ICLQ 908, 917 (1987).

[189] N.V.S.K. Nathan, *Submissions to the International Centre for Settlement of Investment Disputes in Breach of the Convention*, 12 J. Int'l Arb. 27, 29 (1995); ICC Publication No. 272 (1973).

[190] UNCTAD, International Investment Agreements: Flexibility for Development 70 (2000); UNCTAD, Trends in International Investment Agreements 45 (1999) (in most BITs "[t]he definition of investment is broad and open-ended so that it can accommodate new forms of foreign investment"); Rubins, *supra* note 49, at 292.

[191] Rudolph Dolzer & Margrete Stevens, Bilateral Investment Treaties 25–31 (1995).

[192] Agreement among the Government of Brunei Darussalam, Republic of Indonesia, Malaysia, Republic of the Philippines, Republic of Singapore, and the Kingdom of Thailand for the Promotion and Protection of Investments, signed Dec. 15, 1987 (ASEAN Investment Agreement), art. I(3).

[193] U.S.–Trinidad and Tobago BIT (1994), art. I(d).

[194] Such a list would seem somewhat redundant where the treaty definition is "every kind of asset," although disputes could theoretically arise as to the meaning of "asset."

claims to payment or performance, intellectual property and other intangibles, and concession agreements.[195]

7.103 The NAFTA provides a somewhat different approach to defining investment, setting forth a broad but *exhaustive* list of covered economic activities.[196] Investments under NAFTA include both foreign direct investment (FDI) (an enterprise),[197] portfolio investment (equity securities), partnership and other interests that give the owner a right to share in profits or liquidated assets,[198] and tangible and intangible property "acquired in the expectation … of economic benefit."[199] Loan financing, meanwhile, is only protected where funds flow within a business group, or where debt is issued on a relatively long-term basis.[200] Contract rights that do not fall under other categories of investment are covered only if they involve a "commitment of capital or other resources in the territory of a Party … to economic activity in such territory."[201] NAFTA complements its exhaustive list of investment categories with a negative definition, establishing certain kinds of property that are *not* to be considered investments under the treaty.

> investment does not mean,
>
> (i) claims to money that arise solely from
>
> 1. commercial contracts for the sale of goods or services by a national or enterprise in the territory of a Party to an enterprise in the territory of another Party, or
> 2. the extension of credit in connection with a commercial transaction, such as trade financing, other than a loan covered by subparagraph (d); or
>
> (j) any other claims to money that do not involve the kinds of interests set out in subparagraphs (a) through (h) …[202]

7.104 Another innovative approach to subject-matter scope in investment treaties can be found in the definition from the investment chapter of the U.S.–Singapore Free

[195] SCHREUER et al., *supra* note 39, at 129.

[196] For instance, in *Grand River Enterprises v. United States*, the tribunal found that the list of art. 1139 of NAFTA is "exclusive and not illustrative" and therefore inventory loans were a qualifying "investment"; *see Grand River Enterprises Six Nations Ltd. et al. v. United States of America*, UNCITRAL, Award of Jan. 12, 2011, at paras. 82 and 109–11.

[197] NAFTA, *supra* note 79, art. 1139(a).

[198] *Id.*, art. 1139(e)–(f).

[199] *Id.*, art. 1139(g).

[200] *Id.*, art. 1139(d); Jürgen Kurtz, *A General Investment Agreement in the WTO? Lessons from Chapter 11 of NAFTA and the OECD Multilateral Agreement on Investment*, 23 U. PA. J. INT'L ECON. L. 713, 734 (2002).

[201] NAFTA, *supra* note 79, art. 1139(h) (such contracts include those "involving the presence of an investor's property in the territory of the Party, including turnkey or construction contracts, or concessions," and "contracts where remuneration depends substantially on the production, revenues or profits of an enterprise").

[202] *Id.* Certain post-NAFTA bilateral accords have followed the NAFTA exhaustive-list model for defining "investment," including the Canada–Chile Free Trade Agreement. Canada–Chile Free Trade Agreement (1997), art. G(40), 36 I.L.M. 1067 (1997).

Trade Agreement, which was signed in May 2003.[203] Like the U.S. Model BIT, the USSFTA defines investment broadly as "every asset owned or controlled, directly or indirectly, by an investor, that has the characteristics of an investment,"[204] and includes a non-exhaustive list of "forms" such investment may take. Besides the typical "core" investment types, such as enterprises, shares, intellectual property rights, and moveable or immovable property,[205] the USSFTA also covers various debt instruments,[206] "futures, options, and other derivatives,"[207] and "turnkey, construction, management, production, concession, revenue-sharing, and other similar contracts."[208] The pact is also innovative in that it includes explanatory notes, designed to clarify and narrow the apparently sweeping definition. For example, the drafters point out that not only is the list of investment types not exhaustive, but certain activities or assets that are included in the list may *not* qualify as investment, depending on their economic nature:

> Where an asset lacks the characteristics of an investment, that asset is not an investment regardless of the form it may take. The characteristics of an investment include the commitment of capital, the expectation of gain or profit, or the assumption of risk.[209]

Similarly, the notes specify with regard to debt instruments that: **7.105**

> Some forms of debt, such as bonds, debentures, and long-term notes, are more likely to have the characteristics of an investment, while other forms of debt, such as claims to payment that are immediately due and result from the sale of goods or services, are less likely to have such characteristics.[210]

A number of recent investment agreements have attempted to refine the definition of "investments" in a way that reflects the economic priorities and social expectations of the host State, by requiring specific characteristics or linking the concept of "investment" to a contribution to sustainable development.[211] For example, article 1 of the Morocco–Nigeria BIT (2016) defines "investment" as: **7.106**

> an enterprise in the territory of one State established, acquired, expanded or operated, in good faith, by an investor of the other State in accordance with law of the Party in whose territory the investment is made taken together with the asset of the enterprise which contribute sustainable development of that Party and has the

[203] Alexa Olesen, *Singapore to Ink Landmark Free Trade Pact with the United States*, Associated Press, May 4, 2003.
[204] United States–Singapore Free Trade Agreement (USSFTA) (2003), art. 15(1)(13).
[205] *Id.*, art. 15(1)(13)(a), (b), (f), (h).
[206] *Id.*, art. 15(1)(13)(c).
[207] *Id.*, art. 15(1)(13)(d).
[208] *Id.*, art. 15(1)(13)(e).
[209] *Id.* at Note 15-1.
[210] USSFTA, *supra* note 204, at Note 15-2.
[211] Hamed El-Kady, *Towards a New Conceptualization of International Investment Agreements*, BCDR Int'l Arb. Rev. 331 (2016).

characteristics of an investment involving a commitment of capital or other similar resources, pending profit, risk-taking and certain duration.[212]

7.107 More recent BITs have gone as far as requiring "a significant physical presence of the investment in the territory of Host State" and "an effective contribution to the Host State's economy,"[213] whereas the ASEAN–India Investment Agreement enables reservations with a view to excluding "admission, establishment, acquisition, expansion, management, conduct, operation, liquidation, sale, transfer or other disposition of portfolio investments from the benefits" of the agreement.[214]

7.108 An additional requirement is that only investments made in accordance with host country law could be given protection. Thus, investments that fail to comply with the legislation of the host State upon their entry and establishment cannot enjoy the protection of the investment agreement, as they do not qualify as protected investments due to their original illegality.[215] Thus, article 8(1) of Chapter Eight of CETA defines covered investments with respect to a Party as an investment:

(a) in its territory;
(b) made in accordance with the applicable law at the time the investment is made . . .[216]

7.109 Investment laws containing consent to international arbitration often provide a definition of investment that is narrower than that found in investment treaties.[217] Common limitations include the requirement of State approval of the underlying project and a focus on traditional capital contributions. The 1997 foreign investment law of Tanzania, for example, defines investment as "the creation or acquisition of new business assets, and includes the expansion, restructuring, or rehabilitation of an existing business enterprise."[218] Other investment laws

[212] *See* Tarcisio Gazzini, *Nigeria and Morocco Move Towards a "New Generation" of Bilateral Investment Treaties, EJIL:Talk!,* May 8, 2017, available at https://www.ejiltalk.org/nigeria-and-morocco-move-towards-a-new-generation-of-bilateral-investment-treaties/. *See also* art. 1(1) of the Egypt–Mauritius BIT (2014) ("every kind of asset ... that has ... the commitment of capital or other resources, the expectation of gain or profit, the assumption of risk, the contribution to sustainable development, and established or acquired ... in accordance with the laws and regulations of the latter Contracting Party").

[213] *See* Iran–Slovakia BIT (2016), art. 1(2).

[214] *See* ASEAN–India BIT (2014), art.4(6).

[215] *See* UNCTAD, *Scope and Definition,* UNCTAD Series on Issues in International Investment Agreements II (2011), at 10–11. *See also* A. Newcombe, *Investor Misconduct: Jurisdiction, Admissibility or Merits?,* in Evolution in Investment Treaty Law and Arbitration 187 (C. Brown and K. Miles eds. 2011).

[216] EU–Canada Comprehensive Economic and Trade Agreement, available at https://eur-lex.europa.eu/legal-content/EN/TXT/PDF/?uri=CELEX:22017A0114(01)&from=EN.

[217] N.V.S.K. Nathan, *Submissions to the International Centre for Settlement of Investment Disputes in Breach of the Convention,* 12 J. Int'l Arb. 27, 29 (1995). *See also e.g.* Egypt Investment Law (1977), art. 2.

[218] Tanzania Inv. Act (1997), art. 3, available at http://tanzania.eregulations.org/media/INVESTMENT%20ACT.pdf.

adopted in capital-importing countries track the broad BIT language on the definition of "investment."[219]

3. "Investment" in ICSID arbitration

The Washington Convention offers no definition of "investment." It simply provides in article 25(1) that "[t]he jurisdiction of the Centre shall extend to any legal dispute arising directly out of an investment ...".[220] As Delaume explained shortly after the Convention was adopted: **7.110**

> The term "investment" is not defined in the Convention. This omission is intentional. To give a comprehensive definition ... would have been of limited interest since any such definition would have been too broad to serve a useful purpose [or] might have arbitrarily limited the scope of the Convention by making it impossible for the parties to refer to the Centre a dispute which would be considered by the parties as a genuine "investment" dispute though such dispute would not be one of those included in the definition in the Convention.[221]

Commentators have long debated whether there is an objective boundary to the definition of investment for purposes of ICSID jurisdiction.[222] To the extent that such a boundary comes to be adopted as a general rule, the definition of "investment" contained in an investment treaty or national investment code may permit arbitration of disputes that are non-arbitrable within the ICSID **7.111**

[219] Madagascar Investment Code (1989), art. 3; Kyrgyzstan Law on Foreign Investment (1992), art. 1. At least one national investment code appears to have taken the exhaustive approach of NAFTA Chapter 11. Albania Law on Foreign Investments (1993), art. 1(3). Some examination of the definition of investment contained in the Albanian investment code was undertaken by the tribunal in *Tradex, supra* note 6. For a general overview of the protections provided in national investment legislation, *see* Antonio Parra, *The Scope of New Investment Laws and International Instruments*, in 4 Economic Development, Foreign Investment and the Law 27 (Robert Pritchard ed. 1996).

[220] Washington Convention, *supra* note 11, at art. 25(1). The lack of a precise definition is not for want of trying; during the drafting of the Convention, various proposals were tabled by delegates who sought to provide more explicit guidance as to the scope of the Centre's jurisdiction. The First Draft of the Convention set forth a very general definition, "any contribution of money or other assets of economic value for an indefinite period, or ... not less than five years." Washington Convention, First Draft, art. 30, 1 Analysis of Documents Concerning the Origin and Formulation of the Convention 116 (1970). Ultimately, the definition-less version of the Convention prevailed. W.M. Tupman, *Case Studies in the Jurisdiction of the International Centre for Investment Disputes*, 35 ICLQ 813, 816 (1986).

[221] Georges R. Delaume, *Convention on the Settlement of Investment Disputes between States and Nationals of Other States*, 1 Int'l Law. 64, 70 (1966).

[222] *See* Washington Convention, *supra* note 11, at art. 25(1); Institution Rules, art. 2(1) (requiring potential Claimants to submit to the Secretariat not only details concerning the parties' consent, but also evidence that the dispute arises directly out of an investment); Schreuer et al., *supra* note 39, at 125; Hirsch, *supra* note 49, at 59; Carolyn Lamm & Abby Cohen-Smutny, 12(11) *The International Centre for Settlement of Investment Disputes: Responses to Problems and Changing Requirements*, Mealey's Int'l Arb. Rep. 20 (1997); Aron Broches also recognized that "[a]n investment protection treaty could not effectively establish jurisdiction of the Centre beyond [the Article 25(1)] limitation *ratione materiae* ..." Broches, *supra* note 49, at 447, 455; Rubins, *supra* note 49, at 289 et seq. Douglas, *supra* note 113, at 189–202 (Rule 23).

system, and therefore subject to arbitration only under some other agreed-upon dispute resolution system, such as UNCITRAL or the International Chamber of Commerce (which make no particular reference to the notion of investment).[223] In a recent series of ICSID decisions, tribunals have appeared to confirm the existence of such an objective boundary to the notion of investment.[224]

7.112 Professor Schreuer suggests that "investments" exhibit certain common characteristics.[225] First, investment projects tend to have an extended duration. Thus, one-time sales or purchases of goods or short-term commercial credits would normally not be investments.[226] At the same time, "[I]t is entirely clear from [the] negotiating history that the term 'investment' in article 25(1) of the [Washington] [C]onvention does not exclude from its scope an investment simply because it is a short-term investment."[227] Second, investments normally display a certain regularity of profit and return.[228] According to this position, infusions of capital made without any reasonable, substantiated belief that profit will result could be

[223] Most prominently, this situation could occur with regard to entry of investment or certain contractual rights. The opposite outcome, where an activity or asset qualifies as an "investment" for purposes of the Washington Convention but not under the parties' consent instrument, could result where a treaty or investment law covers only investments made within the territory of the host state. *See Philippe Gruslin v. Malaysia*, ICSID Case No. ARB/99/3, Award of Nov. 27, 2000, at para. 13.7 (assets qualified as investment only if within territory of host State, but Washington Convention definition held to contain no such territorial limitation).

[224] *Salini Costruttori S.p.A. v. Morocco*, ICSID Case No. ARB/00/4, Decision on Jurisdiction of July 23, 2001, at para. 44, reprinted in 129 J.D.I. 196 (2002). *See also Fedax N.V. v. Venezuela*, ICSID Case No. ARB/96/3, Decision Objects to Jurisdiction of July 11, 1997, reprinted in 37 I.L.M. 1378 (1998); *Joy Mining Machinery Ltd. v. Egypt*, ICSID Case No. ARB/03/11, Decision on Jurisdiction of Aug. 6, 2004; *Dipenta v. Algeria*, ICSID Case No. ARB/03/8, Award of Jan. 10, 2005. Despite the recent support for a separation of "investment" for purposes of consent and for purposes of ICSID jurisdiction, some tribunals continue to examine only the definition of investment contained in the consent to arbitration. In *Middle East Cement*, for example, an expropriated ship that was allegedly owned by the claimant's parent company and leased to the claimant was deemed an investment, primarily because the applicable Greece–Egypt BIT included leased property in its definition. No consideration was given to whether this arrangement would satisfy the "investment" requirement of Washington Convention, art. 25(1). *Middle East Cement, supra* note 89, at 136.

[225] Schreuer et al., *supra* note 39, at 140.

[226] Presumably, this criterion refers to the host State's desire to encourage commitments of capital from abroad upon which it can rely for economic development. Operations of limited duration, in the host State's view, are unpredictable and prone to withdrawal or non-renewal when conditions deteriorate, worsening financial volatility in the country rather than mitigating it.

[227] U.S. Senate, 89th Congress, 2d Session, Executive Report No. 2, at 15. But *see* Emmanuel Gaillard, *Chronique des sentences arbitrales*, 126 J.D.I. 273, 292 (1999) (naming extended duration as one of three elements of investment); Farouk Yala, *Salini v. Morocco (Observations)*, 2003 Cahiers de L'Arbitrage/Gazette du Palais 9.

[228] Even where no profits are eventually realized, the expectation of return is a typical aspect of investment. In his concurring opinion in *CME*, Professor Brownlie suggested that this was an indispensable feature of any true investment, "as a form of expenditure or transfer of funds for the precise purpose of obtaining a return." *CME*, Separate Opinion of Ian Brownlie, *supra* note 187, at para. 34.

excluded from the definition of "investment."[229] Third, in part due to extended duration and the expectation of profit, investment normally entails the assumption of some form of risk by both parties.[230] Transactions where the risk is primarily or entirely placed on the host State by contract (in particular the prepaid sale of goods) may fall outside the realm of protected investments. The element of risk, however, is more complex than it first appears. Even absent the obvious risk of a failed or unprofitable enterprise connected with a long-term infrastructure or resource exploitation project, some tribunals have suggested that the credit risk involved in bond purchases,[231] or the risk of default that attaches to any contractual arrangement[232] could also support the conclusion that an investment exists. A fourth feature is that the commitment be substantial. While there is reason to doubt that a small investment is less an "investment,"[233] some tribunals have examined the magnitude of the claimant's total expenditures in determining whether an investment has been made.[234] The final factor is the operation's significance for the host State's development.[235] Particularly where consent is achieved by way of a unilateral State offer to arbitrate, contained in a domestic law or international investment treaty, the intended scope of that offer should logically

[229] *Id.* at para. 20; *see also Metalclad Corp. v. Mexico*, ICSID Case No. ARB(AF)/97/1, Award of Sept. 2, 2000, at para. 122.

[230] For a discussion of the risk criterion in ICSID arbitration, *see* Farouk Yala, *The Notion of Investment in ICSID Case Law—Some Un-conventional Thoughts on Salini, SGS &Mihaly*, 22(2) J. INT'L ARB. 105 (2005).

[231] *Fedax, supra* note 224, at para. 40.

[232] *Salini, supra* note 224.

[233] What is "substantial" depends upon the position of the parties. A commitment of $100,000 may be a major dedication of resources for a start-up company, but a mere incidental expense for a multinational corporation. Likewise, an insignificant amount for the United States could be a substantial influx for a small Latin American country. Moreover, the drafters of the Washington Convention considered and rejected a minimum amount in dispute as a jurisdictional requirement for ICSID. 2 ANALYSIS OF DOCUMENTS CONCERNING THE ORIGIN AND THE FORMULATION OF THE ICSID CONVENTION 34, 257–58, 260, 497–99 (1970). At the same time, certain investment protection instruments do expressly limit the definition of investment to commitments of a certain minimum magnitude. *See e.g.* Community Investment Code of the Economic Community of the Great Lakes Countries (1987), art. 15 (US$1 million minimum "investment"); ASEAN Investment Agreement (1987), art. I(1) (defining "investor" to exclude owners of *de minimis* stakes); TANZANIA INVESTMENT ACT (1997), art. 2(2)(a) (setting minimum capital contribution for protected foreign investment at US$300,000).

[234] *LETCO, supra* note 48, at 350 (in determining that claimant had made an investment, particular emphasis placed on size of expenditure). *But cf. Mihaly Int'l Corp. v. Sri Lanka*, ICSID Case No. ARB/00/2, Award of Mar. 15, 2002, reprinted in 16 ICSID REV.—FOR. INV. L.J. 142, 151–56 (2001) ("the question whether an expenditure constitutes an investment is hardly to be governed by whether or not the expenditure is large or small").

[235] Noah Rubins, *The Notion of "Investment" in International Investment Arbitration*, ARBITRATING FOREIGN INVESTMENT DISPUTES 299 (Norbert Horn ed. 2004) ("While duration, risk, expectation of profit, and commitment of resources are primarily characteristics of the investor's participation, here we look exclusively at the State's motivation to accept and protect the operation in question"). Delaume has suggested that the State's viewpoint should in fact be dominant for purposes of defining investment in many cases. Delaume, *supra* note 221, at 70. But *cf. Dipenta, supra* note 224, at para. 13(iv) (rejecting project's contribution to development as a useful criterion).

derive primarily from the host State's *ex ante* preferences, not the behavior of the investor.[236] Therefore, some observers conclude that States would be more likely to accept as "investment" (*i.e.* economic activity subject to international legal protection) projects that contribute significantly to their development, including some that are largely "commercial," "contractual," or "trade-related" in nature.

4. Problem areas

7.113 The notion of investment and its definition has yet to become a serious barrier to jurisdiction in investor–State arbitration.[237] Nevertheless, respondent States have raised the issue as a jurisdictional objection in a large number of ICSID cases. Tribunals have tended to approach each such objection largely on its own merits and with regard to the circumstances of the case at hand.[238]

7.114 The assets at the core of the classical notion of investment, such as land,[239] factories and other production facilities,[240] and concessions for the exploitation of minerals and hydrocarbons[241] have been repeatedly accepted without comment or objection as within ICSID's subject-matter jurisdiction, and within the scope of most arbitral consents in BITS and investment laws.[242] More problematic areas that have yet to be fully explored by arbitral tribunals, and which the OECD has described as "issues requir[ing] further work to determine their appropriate treatment" in future investment agreements,[243] include intellectual property,[244] public

---

[236] However, a range of capital exporting States that provide political risk insurance to their investors through agencies analogous to the United States' Overseas Private Insurance Corporation (OPIC) require that the project to be insured contribute to the socio-economic development of the host State in order to receive coverage. This is the case in Australia, Denmark, Netherlands, Canada, and other countries. *See* Adeoye Akinsanya, *International Protection of Direct Foreign Investments in the Third World*, 36 ICLQ 68–69 (1987). On OPIC and MIGA, *see* Chapter 3, Sections A and C.

[237] Georges R. Delaume, *Consent to ICSID Arbitration*, in The Changing World of International Law in the Twenty-First Century 155, 174 (1998).

[238] Generally, tribunals interpret "investment" liberally. *Fedax, supra* note 224 ("investment" should be liberally interpreted). *But cf. Amco Asia, supra* note 61 (requirements *ratione materiae* should be construed conservatively, "to find out and to respect the common will of the parties").

[239] *Compañia del Desarrollo de Santa Elena v. Costa Rica*, ICSID Case No. ARB/96/1. *But see* Draft OECD Multilateral Agreement on Investment at 11 n.1, found at http://www1.oecd.org/daf/mai/pdf/ng/ng987r1e.pdf (noting that further discussion is needed to determine the appropriate treatment of real estate).

[240] *Asian Agricultural Products Ltd. v. Sri Lanka*, ICSID Case No. ARB/87/3, 30 I.L.M. 577, 594–97 (1991).

[241] *Antoine Goetz v. Burundi, supra* note 176.

[242] Alejandro Escobar, *Requirements Ratione Materiae*, in Course on Dispute Settlement in International Trade, Investment and Intellectual Property 19 (2003).

[243] Draft OECD Multilateral Agreement on Investment, at 11 no. 2, available at http://www1.oecd.org/daf/mai/pdf/ng/ng987r1e.pdf.

[244] *See* on recent bibliography, Douglas, *supra* note 113, at 186–87; Gabriel M. Lentner, *Litigating Patents in Investment Arbitration: Eli Lilly v. Canada*, 12(10) J. Intel. Prop. L. & Pract. 815–16 (2017); Henning Grosse Ruse-Khan, *The Protection of Intellectual Property and International Investment Law*, 19(1) J. Int'l Econ. L. 87–90 (2016); Carlos Correa & Jorge E. Viñuales, *Intellectual Property Rights as Protected Investments: How Open are the Gates?* 19(1) J. Int'l Econ. L. 91–120 (2016); Eva Nanopoulos & Rumiana Yotova, *"Repackaging" Plain*

debt,[245] and indirect investments.[246] Several of these themes are covered in the following sections.

a. Pre-investment expenditures

The majority of investment treaties, including bilateral agreements based on the OECD model, extend protection only to investments (however defined) once established, leaving host states free to promulgate whatever rules they deem appropriate with regard to the admission of foreign capital.[247] "Pre-investment," or "investment-making" activity is most commonly protected only by a loose best-efforts obligation (*e.g.* Energy Charter Treaty), or a requirement of non-discriminatory access, often with sectoral limitations (*e.g.* the pre-2004 U.S. BIT model).[248] Under most arbitral consent documents, therefore, a mere intention to invest, no matter how clearly stated, does not normally entitle a foreign national to the full panoply of legal protection, or access to arbitration.[249] **7.115**

Furthermore, according to certain commentators, the ICSID Convention's jurisdiction likewise will not extend to the establishment phase, even if a particular **7.116**

Packaging in Europe: Strategic Litigation and Public Interest Considerations, 19(1) J. Int'l Econ. L. 175–210 (2016).

245 *See* on this issue Michael Waibel, *Opening Pandora's Box: Sovereign Bonds in International Arbitration*, 101 AJIL 711–59 (2007); Pietro Ortolani, *Are Bondholders Investors? Sovereign Debt and Investment Arbitration after* Poštová, 30(2) LJIL 383–404 (2017); Daniella Strik, *Investment Protection of Sovereign Debt and Its Implications on the Future of Investment Law in the EU*, 29(2) J. Int'l Arb. 183–204 (2012).

246 *See e.g.* Michail Dekastros, *Portfolio Investment: Reconceptualising the Notion of Investment under the ICSID Convention*, 14(2) JWIT 286–319 (2013).

247 Some treaties are explicit in reserving the host State's right to screen investments. *See e.g.* ASEAN Investment Agreement (1987), art. II(1) ("This Agreement shall apply only to investments brought into, derived from or directly connected with investments brought into the territory of any Contracting Party by nationals or companies of any other Contracting Party and which are specifically approved in writing and registered by the host country and upon such conditions as it deems fit for the purposes of this Agreement"); China Model BIT, art. 1(1) ("The term 'investment' means every kind of asset invested by investors of one Contracting Party in accordance with the laws and regulations of the other Contracting Party in the territory of the latter"). There are some important exceptions to this tendency, most notably the U.S. model BIT and NAFTA. However, the lack of treaties covering the pre-investment phase reflects the widely held opinion that customary international law has little to say about the admission of new investment from abroad. *See* Akinsanya, *supra* note 236, at 58–59.

248 Patricia McKinstry Robin, *The BIT Won't Bite: The American Bilateral Investment Treaty Program*, 33 Am. UL Rev. 931, 947–48 (1984). On the issue of pre-establishment protection and admission, *see* Joseph E. Stiglitz, *Is there a Post-Washington Consensus?*, in The Washington Consensus Reconsidered: Towards a New Global Governance (Narcís Serra & Joseph E. Stiglitz eds. 2008); Eric Neumayer et al., *Are Stricter Investment Rules Contagious? Host Country Competition for Foreign Direct Investment through International Agreements*, 152(1) Review of World Economics 177–213 (2015).

249 Zachary Douglas argues that "the notion of a 'pre-investment' ... is conceptually on par with new parents insisting that their child should be deemed to have been born at the start of their antenatal classes." *See* Douglas, *supra* note 114, at 187.

consent document extends to entry of investments.[250] As the tribunal observed *in obiter* in *Joseph Lemire v. Ukraine*, it is debatable whether pre-investment activities merit treaty protection.[251] The tribunal in *Nordzucker v. Poland* further explained that if pre-investment relations with those participating in privatization tenders were subject to arbitration, "the State would be exposed to many international arbitration proceedings commenced by unsuccessful bidders."[252] For example, the question of when a commitment of capital to a project becomes an "investment" for jurisdictional purposes led to the dismissal on jurisdictional grounds of the claimant's case in *Mihaly v. Sri Lanka*.

7.117 In *Mihaly*,[253] the American claimant corporation signed a "letter of intent" with the government of Sri Lanka, outlining the framework for negotiations that were to lead to the build, operate and transfer (BOT) construction of a 300-megawatt power plant.[254] Mihaly had been selected by the government out of twenty-five candidates, and it held the exclusive right to enter into the letter of intent, which established benchmarks that the company had to meet to obtain final approval to begin work on the plant.[255] On the basis of the letter, Mihaly spent several million dollars obtaining financing, negotiating project documents, and engaging consultants for feasibility studies. After these expenditures had been made, the Sri Lankan government refused to sign the project agreement, and Mihaly filed a claim with ICSID. The tribunal held that business development expenditures did not rise to the level of "investment" under the U.S.–Sri Lanka BIT and the Washington Convention, even though those costs constituted 2 to 4 percent of the total projected investment value. The tribunal relied largely on the fact that the letter of intent created no binding obligation for Sri Lanka to conclude a project contract with Mihaly.

7.118 Subsequent tribunals have also been reluctant to find pre-investment expenditures to constitute "investment," particularly where not expressly included in the scope

---

[250] Schreuer et al., *supra* note 39, at 130 ("clauses in BITs that cover disputes concerning the admission or establishment of investments cannot create a basis for ICSID's jurisdiction since there is no investment"); Antonio Parra, *Provisions on the Settlement of Investment Disputes in Modern Investment Laws, BITs, and Multilateral Instruments on Investment*, 12 ICSID Rev.—For. Inv. L.J. 287, 325 (1997) ("where the dispute is over the denial of admission, it might be argued that, since there is in fact no investment, the dispute could not be said to arise out of one, and hence would fall outside the scope of the ICSID Convention").

[251] *Joseph C. Lemire v. Ukraine*, ICSID Case No. ARB/06/18, Decision on Jurisdiction and Liability of Jan. 21, 2010, at para. 89.

[252] *Nordzucker A.G. v. Poland*, UNCITRAL, Partial Award (Jurisdiction) of Dec. 10, 2008, at 189.

[253] *Mihaly, supra* note 234, at 151–56.

[254] Robert Hornick, *The Mihaly Arbitration: Pre-Investment Expenditure as a Basis for ICSID Jurisdiction*, 20 J. Int'l Arb. 189, 189–90 (2003); Walid Ben Hamida, *The Mihaly v. Sri Lanka Case: Some Thoughts Relating to the Status of Pre-Investment Expenditures*, in International Investment Law and Arbitration, *supra* note 132, at 47; Farouk Yala, *Mihaly v. Sri Lanka (Observations)*, 2003 Cahiers de l'Arbitrage/Gazette du Palais 15.

[255] *Mihaly, supra* note 234, at para. 40.

of the applicable investment protection instrument. In *Nagel v. Czech Republic*,[256] the claimant entered into an agreement with a Czech State-owned enterprise to "jointly seek to obtain the necessary licenses and other permits to establish, own and operate a business" in the Czech Republic. Ultimately, the project that the joint "business" was intended to undertake was awarded to a different company by the Czech government through an open tender. The tribunal's decision turned upon whether the claimant's rights under the Cooperation Agreement were an "asset" having financial value, the primary definition of "investment" under the applicable U.K.–Czech Republic BIT. It found that the Czech party was not obligated to guarantee obtaining the project, that the parties' agreement "was only of a preparatory nature," and that the rights derived from it had no financial value.[257] The tribunal therefore concluded that Nagel's contractual rights "were not such as to constitute an 'asset' and an 'investment' within the meaning of Article 1 of the Investment Treaty."[258]

The determination whether a particular transaction classifies as an "investment" or a "pre-investment expenditure" is primarily fact-specific. For example, the tribunal in *Houben v. Burundi* distinguished the case before it from *Mihaly*, ruling that a real estate project requiring the acquisition of a parcel of land and various other activities in advance of the project constituted an "investment" for the purposes of article 25 of the ICSID Convention.[259] The tribunal in *PSEG v. Turkey* awarded out-of-pocket expenses for the period of preparation and negotiation of the investment.[260] **7.119**

b. Contingent rights

In *Joy Mining v. Egypt*,[261] a tribunal dealt with the question of whether contingent rights to shareholding qualify as an investment. The dispute in *Joy Mining* arose out of a transaction between the British claimant corporation and an Egyptian State-owned company, IMC, related to the exploitation of phosphate resources in the Egyptian desert.[262] Under the terms of the primary contract, IMC was to purchase mining equipment from Joy Mining, which in turn provided bank **7.120**

256 *William Nagel v. Czech Republic*, SCC Case No. 049/2002, Award of Sept. 9, 2003, 2004(1) Stockholm Arb. Rep. 141. For commentary on *Nagel*, *see* Sarah François-Poncet & Caline Mouawad, *Observations on Nagel v. Czech Republic*, 2004(1) Stockholm Arb. Rep. 168; Farouk Yala, *Nagel v. Czech Republic (Observations)*, 2004 Cahiers de l'Arbitrage/Gazette du Palais 15.

257 *Nagel*, *supra* note 256, at 164.

258 *Id.* at 165.

259 *Joseph Houben v. Burundi*, ICSID Case No. ARB/13/7, Award of Jan. 12, 2016, at para. 129.

260 *PSEG Global Inc. et al. v. Turkey*, ICSID Case No. ARB/02/5, Award of Jan. 19, 2007, at paras. 316–17.

261 *Joy Mining*, *supra* note 224.

262 Commentary on *Joy Mining* can be found in: Nick Gallus, *No Joy for British Mining Company at ICSID*, 2(4) Oil, Gas & Energy L. Intelligence (2004); Farouk Yala, *Joy Mining v. Egypt (Observations)*, 2004 Les Cahiers de L'Arbitrage/Gazette du Palais 17; Happ & Rubins, *supra* note 108, at 913–16.

guarantees that the buyer could hold until satisfied with the quality of the equipment supplied. Not long after delivery, IMC experienced problems with the equipment. Joy Mining insisted that any failings were due to geological conditions at the site, as well as the buyer's substandard maintenance. Because of this dispute, IMC refused to release the guarantee that it had received under the contract. Ultimately, Joy Mining brought a claim against Egypt under the U.K.–Egypt BIT.

7.121 Addressing Egypt's jurisdictional objection, the tribunal analyzed whether Joy Mining owned an investment within the meaning of the BIT and the Washington Convention. The Egypt–U.K. BIT contained a broad and non-exhaustive list of assets considered to be "investments."[263] The arbitrators considered whether a bank guarantee such as that which Joy Mining had given to IMC fell within the scope of this definition. Without a great deal of explanation, the tribunal concluded that a "contingent liability" such as a bank guarantee cannot be seen as an "asset," and that to find otherwise would "go far beyond the concept of investment, even if broadly defined."[264] The tribunal then considered whether the guarantee could be considered a "pledge" or a "claim to money or to any performance under contract having a financial value," two other investment types specified in the BIT. The answer was negative: "[e]ven if a claim to return of performance and related guarantees has a financial value it cannot amount to recharacterizing as an investment dispute a dispute which in essence concerns a contingent liability."[265]

7.122 Although it had already determined that Joy Mining's guarantee letters did not fall within the scope of BIT protection, it examined the scope of ICSID jurisdiction as well. The tribunal reaffirmed the objective nature of ICSID jurisdiction, insisting that "[t]he parties to a dispute cannot by contract or treaty define as investment, for the purpose of ICSID jurisdiction, something which does not satisfy the objective requirements of Article 25 of the Convention."[266] The arbitrators listed these objective criteria as duration, regularity of profit and return, an element of risk, a substantial commitment, and contribution to the host State's development.[267] The tribunal found the Joy Mining transaction lacking in several of these areas: the duration of the commitment was short, with the purchase price paid at an early stage; there was no regularity of return; and the risk involved was purely commercial in nature.[268] The transaction was therefore found to fall outside the scope of ICSID jurisdiction, because it did not constitute an "investment" for purposes of article 25 of the Washington Convention.[269]

---

263 Egypt–U.K. BIT (1975), art. 1(a).

264 *Joy Mining, supra* note 224, at para. 45.

265 *Id.* at para. 47 (distinguishing *Fedax, supra* note 224).

266 *Joy Mining, supra* note 224, at para. 50.

267 *Id.* at para. 53; Schreuer et al., *supra* note 39, at 140; Rubins, *supra* note 49, at 297–300.

268 *Joy Mining, supra* note 224, at para. 57.

269 *See also PSEG Global, supra* note 260, at para. 193 (option to acquire equity "contingent" and cannot constitute basis for "investment" or "investor" status).

c. *Contract rights*

Tribunals have at times struggled to classify various forms of purely contractual rights, which some observers suggest fall outside the notion of investment as conceived by the drafters of the Washington Convention.[270] The tribunal in *Azinian v. Mexico* described the dilemma in the context of NAFTA's scope: **7.123**

> The problem is that the Claimants' fundamental complaint is that they are the victims of a breach of the Concession Contract. NAFTA does not, however, allow investors to seek international arbitration for mere contractual breaches. Indeed, NAFTA cannot possibly be read to create such a regime, which would have elevated a multitude of ordinary transactions with public authorities into potential international disputes. The Claimants simply could not prevail merely by persuading the Arbitral Tribunal that the [Mexican state authority] breached the Concession Contract.[271]

As previously noted, however, many modern investment treaties specifically state that rights to performance or payment obtained by contract are a form of investment.[272] Furthermore, the line between breach of contract and expropriation of protected assets can blur, particularly where contracts are related to a concession other infrastructure project. As the *Azinian* tribunal framed the problem: **7.124**

> Labelling is ... no substitute for analysis. The words "confiscatory," "destroy contractual rights as an asset," or "repudiation" may serve as a way to describe breaches which are to be treated as extraordinary, and therefore as acts of expropriation, but they certainly do not indicate on what basis the critical distinction between expropriation and an ordinary breach of contract is to be made. The egregiousness of any breach is in the eye of the beholder ...[273]

Accordingly, a host State's breach of a contract entered into with a foreign investor may also breach the State's treaty obligations under a BIT, depending on the nature of the State's conduct.[274] **7.125**

In general, tribunals have considered construction, management, and other contracts to be "investments" where they are part of an overall project that meets the basic criteria of investment. **7.126**

---

[270] *See* Douglas, *supra* note 113, at 202–32 (highlighting the distinction between rights *in rem* and rights *in personam*, according to which the latter "do not generally qualify as an investment independently of the rights *in rem*"; James Crawford, *Treaty and Contract in Investment Arbitration*, 24(3) Arb. Int'l 351 (2008); Stanimir Alexandrov, *Breach of Treaty Claims and Breach of Contract Claims: Is It Still Unknown Territory?*, in Arbitration under International Investment Agreements: A Guide to the Key Issues 323 (Katia Yannaca-Small ed. 2010).

[271] *Azinian v. Mexico*, ICSID Case No. ARB(AF)/97/2, Award of Nov. 1, 1999 at para. 87, *reprinted at* 39 I.L.M. 537 (2000).

[272] *See* Energy Charter Treaty, *supra* note 103, art. 1(6)(c) ("claims to money and claims to performance pursuant to contract having an economic value and associated with an investment").

[273] *Azinian, supra* note 271, at para. 90.

[274] Stanimir A. Alexandrov & James Mendenhall, *Breach of Treaty Claims and Breach of Contract Claims: Simplification of International Jurisprudence*, in Contemporary Issues in International Arbitration and Mediation: The Fordham Papers 2014 24–44 (2015).

7.127 In the case of *Klöckner v. Cameroon*,[275] for example, the claimant entered into a suite of contracts, designed to govern the establishment and operation of a fertilizer plant. The package included a framework agreement, a supply and construction contract, an agreement on tax and customs privileges, and a management agreement, all but the last of which included an ICSID arbitration clause. The Klöckner Group contributed cash and equipment in exchange for equity participation in the enterprise. The tribunal accepted jurisdiction over all but the management contract. Likewise, in *CSOB v. Slovakia*, the arbitrators noted that "a dispute that is brought before the Centre must be deemed to arise directly out of an investment even when it is based on a transaction which, standing alone, would not qualify as an investment under the Convention, provided that the particular transaction forms an integral part of an overall operation that qualifies as an investment."[276]

7.128 One area of frequent dispute is whether construction contracts constitute an investment for jurisdictional purposes. In *Autopista Concesionada de Venezuela v. Venezuela*,[277] the claim arose out of a project to build and operate a highway in Venezuela. The respondent did not dispute that the project qualified as an investment for purposes of the Washington Convention, but the tribunal, *sua sponte*, examined the transaction in light of Article 25(1) of the Convention. Besides the parties' express contractual statement that the road works constituted an investment, the tribunal noted in particular the size of the resource commitment and the extended time period over which the project was to be executed, and ruled that there was no doubt that the dispute arose out of an "investment":

> [A]ccording to the Agreement, Aucoven was to design, construct, operate, exploit, conserve, and maintain the Caracas-La Guaira Highway and the Caracas-La Guaira old road . . . [T]he parties expressly agreed to consider these works as an investment, which seems reasonable. Indeed, the performance of the Agreement, which implies substantial resources during significant periods of time, clearly qualifies as an investment in the sense of Article 25 of the ICSID Convention.[278]

7.129 The arbitrators in *Salini v. Morocco*[279] faced a construction agreement similar in some respects to the one in *Autopista*. Morocco objected to the jurisdiction of the ICSID tribunal on a number of grounds, one of which was that the transaction in question was actually a subcontract for the provision of construction services, and that it therefore could not be an "investment," whether for purposes of the BIT or the Washington Convention.[280]

---

275 *Klöckner, supra* note 57.

276 *CSOB, supra* note 42, at para. 72.

277 *Autopista Concesionada de Venezuela, C.A. v. Venezuela*, ICSID Case No. ARB/00/5, Award on Jurisdiction of Sept. 27, 2001, reprinted in 16 ICSID Rev.—For. Inv. L.J. 469 (2001).

278 *Id.* at para. 101. *But cf. Société Ouest Africaine des Bétons Industriels, supra* note 59.

279 *Salini, supra* note 224.

280 *See generally* Eloïse Obadia, *ICSID, Investment Treaties and Arbitration: Current and Emerging Issues*, Investment Treaties and Arbitration, at 67, 70–71 (2002).

The Italy–Morocco BIT was even broader in its scope of application than most such treaties, and explicitly covered almost all manner of contractual rights. "Investments" under the BIT included: **7.130**

c) ... rights to any contractual performance having economic value; ... [and]
e) any economic right conferred by law or contract ...

It therefore posed no great difficulty for the arbitrators to find that the construction agreement fell within the bilateral treaty's scope. A more significant challenge lay in deciding whether the same agreement also constituted an investment for purposes of ICSID jurisdiction. Relying on the preamble of the Washington Convention, the tribunal arrived at three central factors that it felt would indicate the presence of investment for purposes of the Convention: a contribution, a certain duration over which a deal is implemented, and the existence of risk.[281] As to the first criterion, the tribunal found that the Italian claimants had provided the equipment and personnel necessary to carry out the project, used their know-how in the construction activity, and procured the necessary financing by furnishing bank guarantees. In the eyes of the arbitrators, therefore, Salini and its co-claimants had "contributed in cash, in kind, and in labor."[282] With regard to the duration of the enterprise, the tribunal opined that the minimum length of time for an investment "according to doctrine" is two to five years.[283] Finally, the tribunal turned to the risks undertaken by the Italian companies, finding that the construction contract in question allocated responsibility in such a way that the claimants stood a significant chance of unpredictable loss. The Moroccan State agency had the right to terminate the contract prematurely, and to alter certain terms without changing the contract price. The claimants also bore such risks as the increased cost of labor as a result of changes in Moroccan legislation, accidents or harm caused to the property, increased work volume (up to 20 percent of the planned project), and *force majeure*.[284] **7.131**

More recent tribunals have found that various types of contracts also qualify as "investments". In *Sanum Investments v. Laos*, for example, the tribunal found that loans are undoubtedly "claims to money" that qualify as investments within the meaning of the PRC–Laos BIT, "as long as they are invested."[285] By the same **7.132**

[281] *Salini, supra* note 224, at para. 52.

[282] *Id.* at para. 53.

[283] *Id.* at para. 54 (*citing* D. Carreau et al., Droit International Economique 558–78 (3d ed. 1990); Christoph Schreuer, *Commentary on the ICSID Convention*, 11 ICSID Rev.—For. Inv. L.J. 318 *et seq.* (1996).

[284] *Salini, supra* note 158, at para. 55. As to these risks, the tribunal commented: "It matters little in this regard that the risks were freely agreed upon. It also matters little that the entrepreneur's compensation was not linked to the operation of the constructed facility. A construction project that takes several years, the cost of which cannot be established with any certitude ex ante creates a manifest risk for the entrepreneur." *Id.* at para. 56. *See also Dipenta, supra* note 254, at para. 14.

[285] *Sanum Investments Ltd. v. Laos*, PCA Case No. 2013-13, Award on Jurisdiction of Dec. 13, 2013, at para. 320.

token, the tribunal in *Anglia Auto Accessories v. Czech Republic* found that a final and binding arbitral award granting damages qualifies as an "asset belonging to an investor," and therefore an investment per treaty definition.[286] In *Inmaris Perestroika v. Ukraine*, the tribunal found that a "bareboat" charter contract (pursuant to which a State-owned vessel would be refurbished) formed the basis for a "claim to performance" and therefore constituted an "investment" within the meaning of the Germany–Ukraine BIT.[287] In *SGS v. Paraguay*, the tribunal concluded that a pre-shipment inspection and import-certification contract between the claimant and the Ministry of Finance of Paraguay had an economic value for SGS, and therefore although it was "intangible" constituted a qualifying investment within the meaning of the BIT.[288] In the tribunal's view:

> The Tribunal is not persuaded, as Paraguay argued, that the characterization of something as an "asset" for purposes of the BIT's "investment" definition should turn on the Claimant's accounting treatment of the claimed investment—i.e., whether the Contract is recorded on SGS's books as an asset. Rather, the question of what constitutes an asset (whether tangible or intangible) must be viewed more broadly, in terms of the item's economic value, rather than limited to the potentially artificial confines of accounting treatment.[289]

7.133 The tribunal in *Mytilineos Holdings v. Serbia* also adopted a "holistic" approach to defining investment in relation to contractual rights.[290] In that case, the Greek claimant argued that the Republic of Serbia had breached the Greece–Yugoslavia BIT by undermining its interest in seven contracts it had entered into with a "socially-owned" company in Yugoslavia, providing for cooperation in the mineral extraction and metallurgy business. The transaction comprised several sale and purchase contracts, two bank guarantees (provided by a State-owned bank) and a framework cooperation agreement.[291] Under the contracts, Mytilineos would provide financing and spare parts in exchange for the sale of copper and the right to acquire equity in the socially owned company, if it were to be privatized.[292] Eventually, the Serbian Agency for Privatization restructured and privatized the company in contravention of the contractual arrangement.

---

286 *Anglia Auto Accessories Ltd. v. Czech Republic*, SCC Case No. V2014/181, Final Award of Mar. 10, 2017, at para. 151.

287 *Inmaris Perestroika Sailing Maritime Services GmbH et al. v. Ukraine*, ICSID Case No. ARB/08/8, Decision on Jurisdiction of Mar. 8, 2010, at para. 84.

288 *SGS Société Générale de Surveillance S.A. v. Paraguay*, ICSID Case No. ARB/07/29, Decision on Jurisdiction of Feb. 12, 2010, at paras. 83–90. On the same basis, the tribunal in *SGS Société Générale de Surveillance S.A. v. Pakistan*, ICSID Case No. ARB/01/13, Decision on Jurisdiction of Aug. 6, 2003, at para. 135, found that a pre-shipment inspection services contract and the resulting rights constituted investments within the definition of the Switzerland–Pakistan BIT.

289 *SGS v. Paraguay, id.* at para. 83.

290 *Mytilineos Holdings S.A. v. The State Union of Serbia & Montenegro and Republic of Serbia*, UNCITRAL, Partial Award on Jurisdiction of Sept. 8, 2006.

291 *Id.* at paras. 24–29.

292 *Id.* at para. 37.

The claimant initiated proceedings against Serbia, alleging that the respondent had harmed commercial interests acquired under the agreements and bank guarantees. Serbia argued that it could not carry responsibility based on the alleged breach of contractual obligations by a commercial entity independent of the State.[293] The majority of the tribunal noted that article 1(1)(c) of the BIT defined "investment" as "every kind of asset invested by an investor of one Contracting Party" including "claims to money or any other claim under contract having an economic value." In the majority's view, this "broad asset-based definition of investment" suggested that the term embraces "everything of economic value" and was left deliberately very broad.[294] Ultimately, the majority opted for a "holistic view" of the claimant's business: **7.134**

> Taken together the Agreements not only provided for sales, services and loans transactions between two commercial partners but they also provided for the establishment of a long-term business relationship which included the provision of credit, spare parts and machinery to the local partner of [the claimant] in Serbia and Montenegro, RTB-BOR, for the purpose of modernizing the latter's production facility ... During the intended seven years duration of all of the Agreements Claimant expected various returns and profits. This engagement, which was made with a view to eventual equity participation after privatization, was substantial in monetary terms and also not without risks. Therefore, the combined effect of the Agreements is clearly more than an ordinary commercial transaction.[295]

One of the arbitrators dissented, arguing that the seven contracts in question "by their form and by their substance" constituted "regular commercial contracts" and did not fall within the definition of "investment" of the BIT.[296] **7.135**

The tribunal in *Amto v. Ukraine* adopted a more nuanced approach to the definition of "investment" in the context of the Energy Charter Treaty.[297] Under article 1(6) of the ECT, an "investment" refers to "any investment associated with an Economic Activity in the Energy Sector." The claimant, an energy company engaged in an electricity project in Ukraine, argued that its shareholding in a company that provided technical services to its nuclear power plant also constituted an investment for the purposes of the ECT. The tribunal made clear that the interpretation of the words "associated with" involves a question of degree, and refers primarily to the factual rather than legal association between the alleged investment and an energy-related project. Accordingly, "a mere contractual **7.136**

[293] *Id.* at paras. 45 *et seq.*

[294] *Id.* at paras. 103–05, referring to Noah Rubins, *The Notion of "Investment" in International Investment Arbitration*, in Arbitrating Foreign Investment Disputes 283 and 291 (Norbert Horn ed. 2004).

[295] *Id.* at paras. 124–25.

[296] *Mytilineos, supra* note 290, Dissenting Opinion from the Arbitral Award on Jurisdiction of Sept. 6, 2006, at para. 2.

[297] *Ltd. Liability Co. Amto v. Ukraine*, SCC Case No. 080/2005, Final Award of Mar. 26, 2008, at paras. 42 *et seq.*

relationship with an energy producer is insufficient to attract ECT protection where the subject matter of the contract has no functional relationship with the energy sector." On the facts of the case, however, the tribunal found that the technical services were sufficiently close to the production of electrical energy through multiple contracts over a substantial period of time to attract ECT protection.[298]

d. Indirect equity investments

7.137 In the context of the definition of "investor," foreign corporations frequently establish local ventures as indirect subsidiaries, incorporated in the host State and held in a multi-tier arrangement. For example, a U.K. company may establish a Dutch Antilles holding company, which in turn owns half of the shares in an Argentine oil refinery. The British parent corporation owns the other half of the shares in the Argentine enterprise directly. If a dispute arises in connection with the operation of the local operating company, the British company would clearly have an "investment" subject to arbitration under the U.K.–Argentina BIT. But would that "investment," and consequently the recovery due for treaty breach, be limited to the 50 percent direct ownership interest, or could the investor pursue a claim for the entire local concern? As previously mentioned in the context of "investors," some BITs, particularly those based on the U.S. model agreement, include both "direct and indirect" equity holdings and other asset infusions as "investments."[299] NAFTA also covers all investments possessed or controlled, directly or indirectly, by an investor.[300] Most of the investment treaties of Latin America, however, are silent on the criterion of "directness."

7.138 In the *Lauder* case, the Czech Republic opposed jurisdiction on a number of grounds, one of which was that the claimant had "failed to prove that he owns or controls an investment in the Czech Republic."[301] Presumably, this argument arose specifically out of the U.S. claimant's indirect investment in the Czech operating company—he personally owned no equity at all in assets located in the Czech Republic, all of which were held by a Dutch company, CME. In its final brief, however, the Czech Republic withdrew this objection. Jurisdiction was upheld, with the arbitrators making no mention of the indirect nature of Lauder's investment. However, Lauder's claim was based upon the U.S.–Czech BIT, which (like nearly all U.S. BITs) includes in the definition investments that are only indirectly controlled by the claimant.[302] Furthermore, because *Lauder v. Czech Republic* was

[298] *Id.* at para. 43.
[299] *See e.g.* U.S.–Azerbaijan BIT, art. 1(d) (2000); Argentina–El Salvador BIT, art. 1(1)(c) (1996).
[300] Lemaire, *supra* note 185, at 58.
[301] *Lauder, supra* note 89, at paras. 77, 153–55.
[302] U.S.–Czech Republic BIT (1991), art. I(1)(a) ("'investment' means every kind of investment in the territory of one Party owned or controlled directly or indirectly by nationals or companies of the other Party, such as equity, debt, and service and investment contracts").

conducted under the UNCITRAL Rules, the tribunal was not obliged to consider whether, independent from the BIT's definition of "investment," Lauder's indirect shareholding constituted an investment for purposes of article 25(1) of the Washington Convention.[303]

In *Fedax N.V. v. Venezuela*, the tribunal considered the respondent's jurisdictional objection that the claimant had made no investment in Venezuela, because it was merely the assignee of a promissory note, transferred to it from a Venezuelan company.[304] The respondent argued that an investment must be "direct" to fall within the competence of ICSID under article 25(1) of the Convention. The tribunal disagreed: **7.139**

> [J]urisdiction can exist even in respect of investments that are not direct, so long as the dispute arises directly from such transaction. This interpretation is also consistent with the broad reach that the term "investment" must be given in light of the negotiating history of the Convention.[305]

Notably, the governing Netherlands–Venezuela BIT defined "investment" broadly: **7.140**

> [T]he term "Investment" shall comprise every kind of asset and more particularly though not exclusively: ... (ii) rights derived from shares, bonds, and other kinds of interests in companies and joint ventures ...[306]

The tribunal noted that this phrasing "evidences that the Contracting Parties to the Agreement intended an expansive meaning for the term 'investment.' "[307] Although no mention is made in the Dutch–Venezuela BIT of indirect investments, the tribunal referred to a range of multilateral investment protection and promotion agreements that include indirect investment within their express scope. From this the arbitrators deduced a general global trend recognizing the validity of indirect investment and the importance of such transactions to international development.[308] The tribunal also pointed out that a review of Venezuelan practice in drafting investment treaties revealed that "every time the Republic of Venezuela has wished to exclude investments that are not manifestly direct, [it] has done so in unequivocal terms."[309] **7.141**

---

303 See also *Wena, supra* note 158, at 885–86; *Genin, supra* note 85, at para. 324 (U.S. citizen's equity in Estonian company, nominally owned by three holding companies, including one formed in the Isle of Man, qualified as "investment" under the U.S.–Estonia BIT).

304 *Fedax, supra* note 224.

305 *Id.* at para. 24.

306 Netherlands–Venezuela BIT (1991), art. 1(a).

307 *Fedax, supra* note 224, at para. 32.

308 *Id.* at paras. 34–35; Parra, *supra* note 219, at 40. One text of particular interest in this regard is the World Bank Guidelines on the Treatment of Foreign Direct Investment, which are not restricted to "direct" investments. World Bank, Guidelines on the Treatment of Foreign Direct Investment (1992), 31 I.L.M. 1379 (1992), available at: https://www.italaw.com/documents/WorldBank.pdf.

309 *Fedax, supra* note 224, at para. 36.

7.142 In *CSOB*, the respondent argued that the loan transaction underlying the claimant's case did not constitute an "investment" for purposes of the Washington Convention or the applicable BIT.[310] Slovakia based this argument on the fact that the loan in question "did not involve a transfer of resources in the territory of the Slovak Republic." The tribunal disagreed, upholding jurisdiction and stating generally that "investment as a concept should be interpreted broadly ... [A]n international transaction which contributes to cooperation designed to promote the economic development of a Contracting State may be deemed to be an investment."[311]

7.143 The "distance" of a claimant from his investment may have certain limits.[312] However, in *Gruslin v. Malaysia*, the claimant, a national of Belgium, invested US$2.3 million in Malaysian securities, using a Luxembourg mutual fund.[313] Subsequent exchange controls imposed by Malaysia allegedly destroyed the entire value of the Malaysian securities that Gruslin had purchased.[314] The BIT between Malaysia and Belgium defined investment broadly, including "shares and other types of holding." However, the definition provided that such assets would constitute investments *only* "provided that such assets when invested ... are invested in a project classified as an 'approved project' by the appropriate Ministry in Malaysia ..."[315] Malaysia argued that it intended this language "to limit the encouragement and protection of foreign investment made in its territory to investment made in projects that contributed to the manufacturing and industrial capacity of the country. Portfolio and stock market investment, the kind of investment involved in the case at hand, does not fall within the definition [of investment]."[316] The tribunal ultimately agreed, and dismissed the case.

---

310 *CSOB, supra* note 42, at para. 76.

311 *Id.*

312 *See also Enron Creditors Recovery Corp. (formerly Enron Corp.) and Ponderosa Assets, L.P. v. Argentina*, ICSID Case No. ARB/01/3, Decision on Jurisdiction of Jan. 14, 2004, at para. 52 ("The Tribunal notes that while investors can claim in their own right under the provisions of the treaty, there is indeed a need to establish a cut-off point beyond which claims would not be permissible as they would have only a remote connection to the affected company").

313 *Gruslin, supra* note 223, at para. 8.1.

314 *Id.* at para. 8.3.

315 Malaysia–Belgium–Luxembourg BIT (1979), art. 1(i).

316 *Gruslin, supra* note 223, at para. 17.1.

8

ARBITRATION PROCEDURE

A. Introduction

Much has been written in the context of commercial disputes concerning the advantages of international arbitration over litigation in national courts.[1] Private dispute resolution procedures offer the parties control over the skills and experience of the decision-maker, a notable advantage in technically complex cases.[2] **8.01**

[1] *See* Nigel Blackaby et al., Redfern and Hunter on International Arbitration (6th ed. 2015); Gary Born, International Commercial Arbitration in the United States 5–8 (1994); Margaret Wang, *Are Alternative Dispute Resolution Methods Superior to Litigation in Resolving Disputes in International Commerce?*, 16 Arb. Int'l 189 (2000); Robert D. Fischer & Roger S. Haydock, *International Commercial Disputes: Drafting an Enforceable Arbitration Agreement*, 21 Wm. Mitchell L. Rev. 941, 947–48 (1996); Earl McLaren, *Effective Use of International Commercial Arbitration: A Primer for In-house Counsel*, 19 J. Int'l Arb. 473, 473–76 (2002); William H. Knull, III & Noah Rubins, *Betting the Farm on International Arbitration: Is It Time to Offer an Appeal Option?*, 11 Am. Rev. Int'l Arb. 531, 536–43 (2000)

[2] *See* Ramona Martinez, *Recognition and Enforcement of International Arbitral Awards under the United Nations Convention of 1958: The "Refusal" Provisions*, 24 Int'l Law. 487, 488 (1990).

In some instances, arbitration may be less expensive and less time-consuming than court litigation, although in large disputes the savings in cost and time can be marginal. Unlike litigation in most jurisdictions, arbitration can be made subject to strict confidentiality by agreement of the parties.[3]

8.02 In the context of disputes arising out of the manifestations of political risk, the advantage of arbitration is clear: it can provide a reliable, neutral forum for a foreign investor to obtain remedies against the State or its instrumentalities, with the possibility of enforcement across borders.[4] The outcome of lawsuits in a host State's own courts can be influenced through political pressure. Litigation against government entities in the courts of other States face other barriers, as States may enjoy sovereign immunity in judicial settings.[5] Moreover, in the absence of any global convention on the enforcement of court judgments, a judicial victory may be pyrrhic for the investor, left without the means to obtain satisfaction of the court's judgment by seeking out and attaching the State's commercial assets in other countries.[6]

8.03 In the last chapter, we described how investors can gain access to international arbitration mechanisms to vindicate rights vis-à-vis host States by means of contracts, investment protection treaties, and national statutes on investment. Here, we turn to arbitration procedure. First, the chapter will describe the most prominent

---

[3] Parties should be aware, however, that the extent of confidentiality absent specific agreement will depend upon the applicable arbitration rules and the law at the place of arbitration. In many jurisdictions, there is no implied duty of confidentiality in agreements to arbitrate. *See Bulgarian Foreign Trade Bank Ltd. v. A.I. Trade Finance Inc.*, Case T-1881-99 (Swedish Supreme Court, 2000), 15(11) Int'l Arb. Rep. at B-1 (2000); *Esso Australia Resources Ltd. v. Plowman*, [1995] 183 C.L.R. 10. *See also* Hans Smit, *Confidentiality*, 9 Am. Rev. Int'l Arb. 233 (1988); Michael Collins, *Privacy and Confidentiality in Arbitration Proceedings*, 11 Arb. Int'l 321 (1995); Yves Fortier, *The Occasionally Unwarranted Assumption of Confidentiality*, 15 Arb. Int'l 131 (1999). *See also* Ileana M. Smeureanu, Confidentiality in International Arbitration (2011).

[4] Blackaby et al., *supra* note 1, at paras 1.99–1.102; Knull & Rubins, *supra* note 1, at 538–39; Peter Sherwin et al., *Ch. 19. The Decision to Arbitrate*, in Proskauer on International Litigation and Arbitration: Managing, Resolving, and Avoiding Cross-Border Business or Regulatory Disputes (2007).

[5] On sovereign immunity, *see* Chapter 4, Section G. On litigation to invalidate title of expropriated property, *see* Chapter 10, Section E.

[6] International arbitration awards, if properly rendered, are far easier to enforce internationally than court judgments. The Convention on the Recognition and Enforcement of Foreign Arbitral Awards (1958), 21 U.S.T. 2517, 330 U.N.T.S. 38, available at http://www.uncitral.org/uncitral/en/uncitral_texts/arbitration/NYConvention.html, compels courts in most countries to enforce arbitration awards as if they were local court judgments, with only limited grounds for blocking such enforcement. No such broad-based convention exists with regard to court judgments, although there are some bilateral judicial recognition treaties (for example, between Cyprus and the Russian Federation). Blackaby et al., *supra* note 1, at paras. 1.87–1.91, 11.04. The Convention on the Recognition and Enforcement of Foreign Judgments in Civil and Commercial Matters, The Hague [the Hague Convention], Feb. 1, 1971, 1144 U.N.T.S. 249, available at https://www.hcch.net/en/instruments/conventions/full-text/?cid=78, has only five contracting parties: Albania, Cyprus, Kuwait, the Netherlands, and Portugal (as of May 27, 2018).

international arbitration rules. Next, we will cover the pre-dispute drafting of an arbitration clause. Finally, we offer a guide through a "typical" arbitration, whether initiated pursuant to contract or treaty, from the lodging of a claim and the arbitrator selection process, through written and oral argument, to the issuance and challenge of awards. While throughout this chapter reference is made to a number of different arbitration rules, two systems are described in detail, as they are of particular relevance to investor–State disputes: ad hoc arbitration under the rules of the United Nations Commission on International Trade Law, as revised in 2010 and supplemented in 2013 (the 2013 UNCITRAL Rules)[7] and arbitration under the aegis of the International Centre for the Settlement of Investment Disputes (ICSID).[8]

B. A Brief Overview of Prominent Arbitration Rules[9]

1. Ad hoc arbitration: the United Nations Commission on International Trade Law (UNCITRAL)

The UNCITRAL Rules constitute the most commonly-used *ad hoc* arbitration procedure. Arbitration under *ad hoc* rules means that the procedure is not administered by any arbitral institution.[10] While UNCITRAL arbitration is unadministered absent contrary agreement of the parties, many arbitral **8.04**

---

[7] United Nations Commission on International Trade Law (UNCITRAL) Arbitration Rules, G.A.R. 98, U.N. GAOR, 31st Session, Supplement No. 39 at 182, U.N. Doc. A/31/39 (1976).

[8] Convention on the Settlement of Investment Disputes Between States and Nationals of Other States [hereinafter, the Washington Convention], Mar. 18, 1965, 17 U.S.T. 1270, 575 U.N.T.S. 159, 60 A.J.I.L. 829 (1966), 4 I.L.M. 532 (1965), available at https://icsid.worldbank.org/en/Pages/icsiddocs/ICSID-Convention.aspx. *See also* the ICSID Rules of Procedure for Arbitration Proceedings (1968), as amended in 2006, available at https://icsid.worldbank.org/en/Pages/icsiddocs/ICSID-Convention-Arbitration-Rules.aspx. *See further* Aurélia Antonietti, *The 2006 Amendments to the ICSID Rules and Regulations and the Additional Facility Rules*, 21(2) ICSID Rev.—For. Inv. L.J. 427–48 (2006).

[9] For a detailed comparison of various arbitration rules systems, *see* Robert H. Smit et al., Comparison of International Arbitration Rules (4th ed. 2013); Jan Paulsson et al., The Freshfields Guide to Arbitration and ADR 49–66 (2d ed. 1999); *Comparison of the NAFTA, ICSID, Additional Facility and UNCITRAL Rules*, 11(4) J. Int'l Arb. 159 (1994).

[10] Truly *ad hoc* proceedings, where the parties agree to arbitration without specifying *any* recognized procedural rules, are relatively rare. In relation to the danger of such improvised dispute resolution, it is argued that:

> The principal disadvantage of *ad hoc* arbitration is that it depends for its full effectiveness on co-operation between the parties and their lawyers, supported by an adequate legal system in the place of arbitration. It is not difficult to delay proceedings, for example by refusing at the outset to appoint an arbitrator, so that there is no arbitral tribunal in existence and no agreed book of rules to say what is to be done ... It will then be necessary to rely on such provisions of law as may be available to offer the necessary support.

Blackaby et al., *supra* note 1, at para. 1.145.

institutions, including the International Chamber of Commerce (ICC), the American Arbitration Association (AAA), the LCIA, and the Arbitration Institute of the Stockholm Chamber of Commerce (SCC), routinely provide administrative support to proceedings conducted pursuant to the UNCITRAL Rules, if the parties so agree.[11]

8.05 The UNCITRAL Rules were adopted by the United Nations in 1976, and have found broad acceptance among both private companies and States, in the developed and developing world.[12] The UNCITRAL Rules are used, in modified form, in proceedings before the Iran–U.S. Claims Tribunal.[13] In 2006, the UNCITRAL Commission decided that the 1976 UNCITRAL Rules had to be revised to reflect recent developments in arbitral practice. The revision aimed to enhance the efficiency of arbitration under the Rules without altering the original structure of the text, its spirit or drafting style. The 1976 Rules were revised in 2010 and further supplemented in 2013 by a new article 1 paragraph 4, which incorporates the UNCITRAL Rules on Transparency.[14] The new UNCITRAL Rules, effective as of August 15, 2010, include a number of innovative features to enhance procedural efficiency, such as provisions on multiple-party arbitration and joinder, liability, procedures for the replacement of an arbitrator and objections to experts appointed by the arbitral tribunal, and detailed provisions on interim measures. The 2010 UNCITRAL Rules also respond to concerns related to costs, introducing the requirement for reasonableness and a review mechanism regarding the costs of arbitration.

8.06 The absence of an administering institution may offer some advantage in terms of cost, since the parties incur no direct administrative expenses.[15] However, the fees charged by the arbitrators are rather difficult to predict in UNCITRAL

---

[11] John P. Karalis, International Joint Ventures: A Practical Guide 207 (1992); David J. Branson & W.M. Tupman, *Selecting an Arbitral Forum: A Guide to Cost-Effective International Arbitration*, 24 Va. J. Int'l L. 4 (1984).

[12] Nicholas C. Ulmer, *Drafting the International Arbitration Clause*, 20 Int'l Law. 1335, 1339 (1986); Karalis, *supra* note 11, at 214.

[13] J.J. van Hof, Commentary on the UNCITRAL Arbitration Rules: The Application by the Iran–U.S. Claims Tribunal (1991). For a critique of the UNCITRAL Rules as used by the Iran–U.S. Claims Tribunal, *see* Stewart A. Baker & Mark D. Davis, *Establishment of an Arbitral Tribunal under the UNCITRAL Rules: The Experience of the Iran–United States Claims Tribunal*, 23 Int'l Law. 81 (1989).

[14] 1976 UNCITRAL Rules, 31 U.N. GAOR Supp. (no. 17) at 35, U.N. Doc. A/31/17 (1976), available at http://www.uncitral.org/pdf/english/texts/arbitration/arb-rules/arb-rules.pdf; 2010 UNCITRAL Rules, available at http://www.uncitral.org/pdf/english/texts/arbitration/arb-rules-revised/arb-rules-revised-2010-e.pdf].

[15] On the advantages and disadvantages of *ad hoc* arbitration vis-à-vis institutional arbitration, *see* Edlira Aliaj, *Dispute Resolution through Ad Hoc and Institutional Arbitration*, 2(2) Ac. J. Bus. 241–50 (2016); Won-Suk Oh & Yongil Kim, *A Comparative Study on the Institutional Arbitration and* Ad Hoc *Arbitration*, 19(1) J. Arb. Stud. 25–44 (2009); Gordon Blanke, *Institutional versus* Ad Hoc *Arbitration: A European Perspective*, 9(2) ERA Forum 275–82 (2008).

arbitration, as they must be negotiated directly between the parties and the tribunal—a negotiation in which the parties have relatively little bargaining leverage, or incentive to use it.[16] Administered arbitration, by contrast, is subject to standardized fee schedules.

Ad hoc arbitration under the UNCITRAL Rules may provide the parties (and the arbitral tribunal) superior control over the arbitral process than would be the case in administered proceedings, and therefore "may offer more flexibility and may be useful for large, complex, or unconventional disputes."[17] At the same time, it is important to consider the possibility that a party will be forced to solicit the assistance of the local courts at the place of arbitration to ensure the smooth progress of the proceedings, in the absence of any arbitral institution empowered to deal with issues such as arbitrator disqualification, payment of advances, and discovery.[18] **8.07**

2. Institutional arbitration

The majority of international arbitration, both commercial and investment-related, is conducted under the auspices of one of several prominent arbitration "institutions" around the world.[19] Professor Larsen explains well the role of the arbitral institution, already discussed to some extent in the context of *ad hoc* arbitration: **8.08**

> These institutions do not themselves "decide" arbitration cases. The arbitrations often take place not in the home city of the institution, but at a location designated by the parties or arbitrators. Rather, for a fee, arbitral institutions administer arbitrations including receiving and distributing pleadings, and perhaps appointing arbitrators or reviewing an award for technical accuracy usually in connection with a decision by the parties to use the arbitration rules of the institution. These rules regulate such issues as the choice of arbitrators, the process of replacing an ill or deceased arbitrator, challenges to arbitrators for lack of independence, how and when parties file their pleadings, provisional remedies, the power of the arbitrators to hear witnesses, language(s) of the proceeding, evidentiary issues, and the drafting and signing of the arbitral award.[20]

---

[16] Blackaby et al., *supra* note 1, at para. 4.210 ("The problem is that each party is reluctant to upset the arbitrators by appearing to criticize their fees, because each party has it clearly in mind that the same arbitrators will be sitting in judgment on its case. It may seem foolish to bargain over a few hundred dollars a day if, by doing so, a claim worth many millions of dollars may be put in jeopardy"); Pierre Karrer, *Arbitration Saves! Costs: Poker and Hide-and-Seek*, 3(1) J. Int'l Arb. 35, 39 (1986).

[17] McLaren, *supra* note 1, at 479–80.

[18] *See* Karl-Heinz Böckstiegel, *The Relevance of National Arbitration Law for Arbitrations under the UNCITRAL Rules*, 1(3) J. Int'l Arb. 223, 232–36 (1984).

[19] On the function of these institutions, *see* Gerbay Rémy, The Functions of Arbitral Institutions (2016).

[20] Clifford Larsen, *International Commercial Arbitration*, ASIL Insights, 2 (April 1997), available at http://www.asil.org/insights/insight97041.pdf.

The extent of institutional involvement in arbitration proceedings varies, and depends upon the provisions of the particular set of rules and the practices of each institution.

a. International Chamber of Commerce (ICC)

8.09 The International Court of Arbitration of the International Chamber of Commerce (ICC), established over ninety years ago and headquartered in Paris, is perhaps the best-known institution administering the arbitration of international commercial disputes.[21] Indeed, a substantial proportion of international arbitrations are conducted under ICC auspices,[22] and the institution handles about 800 cases per year. Since 1923, the ICC has administered approximately 23,000 cases from all over the world. In 2017, a total of 810 new cases were filed, involving 2,316 parties from 142 countries, representing an aggregate value of over US$30.85 billion.[23] Although the ICC is dedicated mostly to commercial disputes, it has also administered thirty-nine cases based on bilateral investment treaties (BITs).[24] A significant proportion of arbitrations conducted under the ICC rules (ICC Rules) involve States or agencies or subdivisions of States.[25] 15.4 percent of the cases filed in 2017 involved a State, a public entity or a State-owned company.[26] The reputation of the ICC and its institutional expertise, as well as the truly international nature of its cases and staff, make it a particularly attractive option for significant and complex disputes.[27]

8.10 In 1998, the ICC promulgated new procedural rules after extensive worldwide consultations. These new rules modified a number of aspects of ICC procedure that had given rise to uncertainty and disputes since the previous rules were put in place in 1988.[28] In 2012, the ICC again issued revised arbitration rules in an

[21] Hans Smit, *The Future of International Arbitration: A Single Transnational Institution?*, 25 Colum. J. Transnat'l L. 9 (1986); Robert H. Smit, *An Inside View of the ICC Court*, 10 Arb. Int'l 53 (1994).

[22] Stephen R. Bond, *How to Draft an ICC Arbitration Clause*, 7 ICSID Rev.—For. Inv. L.J. 153, 157 (1992); Ulmer, *supra* note 12, at 1336.

[23] *See* 2017 ICC Court Statistics, available at https://www.flickr.com/photos/international-chamber-of-commerce/sets/72157694229086035.

[24] *Id. See also* Rocío Digón & Marek Krasula, *The ICC's Role in Administering Investment Arbitration Disputes*, in Contemporary Issues in International Arbitration and Mediation: The Fordham Papers (8) 2014 58 *et seq.* (Arthur W. Rovine ed. 2015).

[25] Blackaby et al., *supra* note 1, at para. 1.185 n.195; *see also* ICC, *Arbitration Involving States and State Entities under the ICC Rules of Arbitration—Report of the ICC Commission on Arbitration and ADR* (2017), available at https://iccwbo.org/publication/arbitration-involving-states-state-entities-icc-rules-arbitration-report-icc-commission-arbitration-adr/.

[26] *See* ICC, ICC Announces 2017 Figures Confirming Global Reach and Leading Position for Complex, High-Value Disputes (2018), available at https://iccwbo.org/media-wall/news-speeches/icc-announces-2017-figures-confirming-global-reach-leading-position-complex-high-value-disputes/.

[27] Karalis, *supra* note 11, at 206.

[28] Rules of Arbitration of the International Chamber of Commerce (1998), available at https://www.trans-lex.org/750200/_/icc-arbitration-rules-1998/ [hereinafter, the 1998 ICC Rules]. *See also* W. Laurence Craig et al., Annotated Guide to the 1998 ICC Arbitration Rules 3–18

attempt to respond to the needs of the international business community and to address the growing complexity of international disputes, such as multiparty arbitration,[29] more efficient case management techniques and the possibility of emergency arbitrators for urgent measures.[30] In 2017, the ICC further revised its 2012 Arbitration Rules to increase efficiency and transparency.[31] The most recent Rules include simplified "Expedited Procedure Provisions" for disputes under US$2 million,[32] a streamlined initial procedural phase[33] and enhanced rules on transparency, enabling the ICC Court (the main administrative body) to communicate reasons for its decisions.[34] In parallel, the ICC also issued a "Note to Parties and Arbitral Tribunals on the Conduct of Arbitration," providing clarity and practical guidance to the parties and tribunals on the application and interpretation of the rules.[35]

While the ICC Rules are broadly similar to many other institutional procedures **8.11** as well as to the UNCITRAL Rules, there are at least two aspects that set ICC arbitration apart. First, the ICC Court plays an important role in each arbitration case, although it does not actually resolve disputes.[36] In discharging its duties, the ICC Court is assisted by the Secretariat, which closely monitors the progress of the proceedings and assists the parties and the tribunals in relation to the arbitration.[37] The ICC Court's duties include the confirmation, replacement, or appointment of arbitrators (in the absence of agreement) and the consideration of challenges to arbitrators.[38] Furthermore, if a respondent party does not submit an answer, or if a party a jurisdictional objection or questions whether all of the claims may be determined together in a single arbitration, the ICC Court may conduct a *prima facie* review of the request for arbitration, dismissing the case if

(1998). Prior to the reform of the ICC Rules, they were occasionally criticized as vague, and the procedure as expensive. Karalis, *supra* note 11, at 206.

[29] *See* ICC, Effective Management of Arbitration—A Guide for In-House Counsel and Other Party Representatives, Commission on Arbitration and ADR, (2018), at 19, available at https://cdn.iccwbo.org/content/uploads/sites/3/2017/05/effective-management-of-arbitration-icc-guide-english-version.pdf.

[30] Rules of Arbitration of the International Chamber of Commerce (2012), available at http://internationalarbitrationlaw.com/about-arbitration/international-arbitration-rules/2012-icc-arbitration-rules, App. IV ("Case Management Techniques"), art. 29 and App. V ("Emergency Arbitrator Rules").

[31] Rules of Arbitration of the International Chamber of Commerce (2017), available at https://cdn.iccwbo.org/content/uploads/sites/3/2017/01/ICC-2017-Arbitration-and-2014-Mediation-Rules-english-version.pdf.pdf.

[32] *See* 2017 ICC Rules, *supra* note 31, art. 30 and App. VI.

[33] *Id.*, art. 23(2).

[34] *Id.*, art. 11(4).

[35] *See* ICC, Note to Parties and Arbitral Tribunals on the Conduct of the Arbitration (2017), available at https://iccwbo.org/publication/note-parties-arbitral-tribunals-conduct-arbitration/ [hereinafter, ICC Note].

[36] *See* 2017 ICC Rules, *supra* note 31, art. 1(2).

[37] *See* ICC Note, *supra* note 35, Section I.A, para. 3.

[38] *See* 2017 ICC Rules, *supra* note 31, arts. 12(2), 12(8), 14(3), 15(1).

agreement to ICC arbitration is manifestly absent under the law of the arbitration agreement.[39] Such review is designed to filter out frivolous claims, and in some instances prevents the use of ICC procedures for purely tactical advantage. In certain circumstances, the Court may also decide to consolidate two or more arbitrations pending under the ICC Rules.[40]

8.12 Further, all ICC awards are submitted to the ICC Court, which reviews and may modify the award as to its form and may also draw the tribunal's attention to points of substance, without prejudice to the tribunal's liberty of decision.[41] Typographical or computational corrections or award interpretations must also be approved by the Court.[42] The ICC Court is not a court of appeal; its substantive comments constitute drafting advice and are not mandatory.[43] But many observers agree that the Court's involvement make ICC awards "coherent in substance and consistent in form."[44] Since 2010 the ICC Court has provided tribunals with an "award checklist" to ensure compliance with the formal requirements of the ICC Rules.[45]

8.13 The second unique feature of ICC arbitration is the "Terms of Reference," a foundation document drafted jointly by the parties and the tribunal at the outset of each case, which serves to frame the issues in dispute and lay the ground rules for further proceedings.[46] The Terms of Reference include, *inter alia*, details of the parties' identities, a summary of their respective claims, defences and requested

---

[39] *Id.*, art. 6(3)–(9); *see also* Thomas H. Webster & Dr. Michael Buhler, Handbook of ICC Arbitration: Commentary, Precedents, Materials 111–21 (2014); Katia Yannaca-Small, *Indirect Expropriation and the Right to Regulate: How to Draw the Line?* in Arbitration under International Investment Agreements: A Guide to the Key Issues 445–77 (Katia Yannaca-Small ed. 2010) . On the standard of *prima facie* review applied by the ICC Court, *see* Sandra Synková, Courts' Inquiry into Arbitral Jurisdiction at the Pre-Award Stage: A Comparative Analysis of the English, German and Swiss Legal Order 93–95 (2013). For an analysis of the previous ICC Rules (which contained a similar *prima facie* test), *see* Laurence Craig et al., International Chamber of Commerce Arbitration 155–60 (3d ed. 2000); Yves Derains & Eric A. Schwartz, A Guide to ICC Arbitration 76–109 (2d ed. 2005). *See further* Section F, *infra*.

[40] *See* 2017 ICC Rules, *supra* note 31, art. 10.

[41] *Id.*, arts. 1(2), 34. *See also* Jason Fry et al., The Secretariat's Guide to ICC Arbitration, paras. 3-32 and 3-120 (No. 729E, 2012); Webster & Buhler, *supra* note 39, at 497–503; Simon Greenberg, *Arbitral Award Scrutiny under Scrutiny: An Assessment*, in Arbitral Institutions under scrutiny: ASA Special Series No. 40, 89 (Philipp Habegger et al. eds. 2013); Hossein Abedian, *Judicial Review of Arbitral Awards in International Arbitration—A Case for an Efficient System of Judicial Review*, 28(6) J. Int'l Arb. 553 (2011). *See also* Ulmer, *supra* note 12, at 1337; Craig et al., *supra* note 28, at 375–84.

[42] *See* 2017 ICC Rules, *supra* note 31, art. 36.

[43] *See* Webster & Buhler, *supra* note 39, at 504.

[44] Ulmer, *supra* note 12, at 1337.

[45] *See* ICC Award Checklist (1998, 2012 and 2017 ICC Arbitration Rules), available at https://cdn.iccwbo.org/content/uploads/sites/3/2016/04/ICC-Award-Checklist-English.pdf.

[46] *See* 2017 ICC Rules, *supra* note 31, art. 23. Jean-Claude Goldsmith, *How to Draft Terms of Reference*, 3 Arb. Int'l 298 (1987); Michael E. Schneider, *The Terms of Reference*, ICC Bull. Supp. 26 (1997); Craig et al., *supra* note 28, at 273–83.

relief, and to the extent possible, an estimate of the monetary value of claims.[47] The Terms of Reference are signed by the parties and the tribunal, and are transmitted to the Court for approval.[48] After the Terms of Reference have been signed or approved by the Court, no party can advance additional claims without prior leave from the arbitral tribunal.

While some have criticized the Terms of Reference as an unnecessary and time-consuming exercise,[49] most practitioners agree that there are important benefits to this ICC innovation.[50] In particular, the Terms of Reference "may be useful as a protection of awards against attack, as a tool for organizing the future path of the arbitral proceedings, and sometimes as a means to *rapprochement* of the parties."[51] **8.14**

Also important to note is that the administrative costs and arbitrator fees associated with ICC arbitration are determined according to a regressive scale, based upon the amount in dispute.[52] This system offers predictability for the parties, who can estimate the range of costs based on the value claimed. The ICC costs include a non-refundable filing fee of US$5,000, a provisional advance fixed by the Secretary-General (intended to cover the costs of arbitration until the "Terms of Reference" are completed or until the case management conference when the Expedited Procedure Provisions apply) and the advance on costs fixed by the Court at a later stage.[53] At the end of an arbitration, parties may make costs claims in respect of arbitrators' fees and ICC administrative expenses and in respect of the cost of legal representation and disbursements. The arbitral tribunal may then award costs in favor of one or more parties. Some observers have suggested that ICC arbitration is too expensive, and that its system for determining fees lacks transparency.[54] In practice, however, ICC arbitration is roughly comparable to arbitration under other prominent administered rules.[55] Furthermore, the ICC Court has the power to fix the arbitrators' fees at a figure higher or lower than the scale reflects, as necessary in light of exceptional circumstances.[56] **8.15**

---

47 *See* 2017 ICC Rules, *supra* note 31, art. 23(1)(c).

48 *Id.*, art. 23(2).

49 Gillis Wetter, *The Present Status of the International Court of Arbitration of the ICC: An Appraisal*, 1 Am. Rev. Int'l Arb. 91 (1990); Hans Smit, *supra* note 21, at 26–27. The time limit for establishing the Terms of Reference has been reduced from two months to one month, and there are no Terms of Reference in expedited procedures.

50 Stephen Bond, *ICC Terms of Reference Rules Saves Time and Money While Promoting Common Understanding*, Mealey's Int'l Arb. Rep., Aug. 1991, at 33.

51 Craig et al., *supra* note 28, at 275.

52 ICC online cost calculator, available at https://iccwbo.org/dispute-resolution-services/arbitration/costs-and-payments/cost-calculator/. The Stockholm Chamber of Commerce calculates costs on a similar basis.

53 *See* 2017 ICC Rules, *supra* note 31, arts. 37, 38 and App. III.

54 *See e.g.* Karrer, *supra* note 16, at 40–43.

55 For further justification of ICC pricing, *see* Craig et al., *supra* note 28, at 29–32.

56 *See* 2017 ICC Rules, *supra* note 31, art. 38(2).

8.16 Parties seeking to incorporate ICC arbitration into their contract may wish to adopt the model clause recommended by the ICC:

> All disputes arising out of or in connection with the present contract shall be finally settled under the Rules of Arbitration of the International Chamber of Commerce by one or more arbitrators appointed in accordance with the said Rules.[57]

8.17 As with all standard arbitration clauses, the parties should carefully consider modifications concerning the place of arbitration, language of arbitration, number of arbitrators, and the method for selecting arbitrators, as well as other matters discussed in this chapter. Furthermore, if the parties wish to exclude recourse to the Emergency Arbitrator Provisions, they must expressly opt out by adding wording to that effect, such as "the Emergency Arbitrator Provisions shall not apply."[58] In addition, for disputes of a monetary value below US$2 million, the parties are free to opt out of the application of the Expedited Procedure Provisions by expressly stipulating this in the arbitration clause. They can also raise the claim threshold for applying Expedited Procedure.[59] As explained in the subsequent chapter, the parties might also choose to introduce a multi-tiered dispute resolution clause, which requires the parties to submit their dispute to ICC mediation—or any other alternative dispute resolution method—prior to the initiation of ICC arbitration.[60]

b. The International Centre for the Settlement of Investment Disputes (ICSID)

8.18 The International Centre for the Settlement of Investment Disputes was established in 1965 as an arm of the World Bank,[61] "to provide facilities for conciliation and arbitration of investment disputes between Contracting States and nationals of other Contracting States."[62] ICSID was created by a multilateral treaty, known as the Washington Convention, to satisfy the need for a de-politicized mechanism for the resolution of investment disputes between developing States and foreign investors.[63] As has been discussed in elsewhere in this book in

---

57 Paulsson et al., *supra* note 9, at 130–31.

58 *See* 2017 ICC Arbitration and Mediation Rules 76 (2017), available at https://cdn.iccwbo.org/content/uploads/sites/3/2017/01/ICC-2017-Arbitration-and-2014-Mediation-Rules-english-version.pdf.pdf.

59 *Id.* at 76.

60 Figueres Jiménes Dyalá, *Multi-Tiered Dispute Resolution Clauses in ICC Arbitration*, 14(1) ICC Int'l Ct. Arb. Bull. 71 (2003).

61 Christoph Schreuer et al., The ICSID Convention: A Commentary (2009).

62 Washington Convention, *supra* note 8, art. 1, at 532. *See generally* Paul H. Vishny, Guide to International Commercial Law §§ 12.37–12.40 (1994); Aron Broches, *The Convention on the Settlement of Investment Disputes Between States and Nationals of Other States*, 136 Recueil des Cours 331 (1972).

63 Washington Convention, *supra* note 8; Kenneth S. Jacobs, *Reinvigorating ICSID with a New Mission and with Renewed Respect for Party Autonomy*, 33 Va. J. Int'l L. 123 (1992); Antonio R. Parra, The History of ICSID (2d ed. 2017); Building International Investment Law: The First 50 Years of ICSID (Meg Kinnear et al. eds. 2015).

the context of investment protection treaties, ICSID offers investors and States a neutral forum in which to arbitrate disputes, while precluding investors' home States from becoming directly involved in investment disputes.[64] In addition, in part due to the involvement of the World Bank, many developing states view ICSID as a more neutral institution than commercial arbitral institutions such as the ICC.[65] In recent years, however, ICSID has attracted criticism from various interest groups,[66] especially after three contracting States decided to withdraw from the ICSID Convention.[67]

Before the creation of ICSID, the World Bank assisted in the settlement of disputes between States and foreign investors, including disputes arising out of the nationalization of Anglo–Iranian Oil Company's assets in Iran in 1951 and 1952 and the nationalization of the Suez Canal by Egypt in 1956.[68] The Washington Convention was an outgrowth of these requests to assist.[69] Assisted by a committee of legal experts from various member countries, The World Bank drafted the Washington Convention and submitted it for signature and ratification to its members.[70] ICSID is located at the principal office of the World Bank in Washington, DC.[71] The institution is governed by an Administrative Council, composed of one representative of each member State.[72] The President of the International Bank for Reconstruction and Development acts as Chairman of the Administrative Council.[73] **8.19**

[64] Washington Convention, *supra* note 8, art. 28(1). *See also* Jacobs, *supra* note 63, at 127; Ibrahim Shihata, *The Settlement of Disputes Regarding Foreign Investment: The Role of the World Bank, With Particular Reference to ICSID and MIGA*, 1 Am. UJ Int'l L. & Pol'y. 97, 102–03 (1986). On the limits of the depoliticization of investment disputes through international arbitration, *see* Martins Paparinskis, *The Limits of Depoliticization in Contemporary Investor–State Arbitration*, 3 Select Proceedings of the European Society of International Law (2010).

[65] Malcolm D. Rowat, *Multilateral Approaches to Improving the Investment Climate of Developing Country: The Case of ICSID and MIGA*, 33 Harv. Int'l L.J. 103, 107 (1992). *See*, however, Julien Fouret, *The World Bank and ICSID: Family or Incestuous Ties?* 4(1) Int'l Org. L. Rev. 121 (2007), highlighting the possible conflicts of interest between ICSID and the World Bank.

[66] *See* Leon E. Trakman, *The ICSID under Siege*, 45 Cornell Int'l L.J. 603 (2012); Susan D. Franck, *The Legitimacy Crisis in Investment Treaty Arbitration: Privatizing Public International Law through Inconsistent Decisions*, 73(4) Fordham L. Rev. 1521 (2005); *ICSID in Crisis: Straight-Jacket or Investment Protection?*, Bretton Woods Project (2009), available at http://www.brettonwoodsproject.org/art-564878; Kendall Grant, *The ICSID under Siege: UNASUR and the Rise of a Hybrid Regime for International Investment Arbitration*, Osgoode Legal Studies Research Paper Series, Paper 108 (2015); Ibironke T. Odumosu, *The Antinomies of the (Continued) Relevance of ICSID to the Third World*, 8(2) San Diego Int'l L.J. 345–85 (2007).

[67] The withdrawing countries were Bolivia (2007), Ecuador (2008), and Venezuela (2012).

[68] Rowat, *supra* note 63, at 106.

[69] Jacobs, *supra* note 36, at 123–24.

[70] Shihata, *supra* note 64, at 101.

[71] Washington Convention, *supra* note 8, art. 2.

[72] *Id.*, art. 4(1).

[73] *Id.*, art. 5.

8.20 While the parties to a dispute may appoint any independent and impartial individual to serve as arbitrator, ICSID draws the candidates that it appoints from a Panel of Arbitrators that it maintains. Each contracting State may submit up to four names to be included on the panel.[74] The Washington Convention requires that panel members "be persons of high moral character and recognized competence in the fields of law, commerce, industry or finance."[75]

8.21 As of mid-2018, 153 States had ratified the Washington Convention and nine more have signed it but not yet ratified.[76] ICSID arbitration clauses have also become widespread in BITs, national investment laws and codes, and State contracts.[77] Indeed, a large proportion of BITs in force and all major multilateral investment protection treaties (including the North American Free Trade Agreement and the Energy Charter Treaty) provide for the submission of disputes to ICSID arbitration.[78] As a result, the case load at ICSID has increased dramatically since the late 1990s and mid-2000s and today the Centre handles about forty to fifty new cases each year.[79]

8.22 Unlike most forms of international commercial arbitration, ICSID arbitration operates within a "completely autonomous jurisdictional system."[80] "An ICSID tribunal exercises full control over a dispute subject only to the Convention, the ICSID Rules, and the parties' choice of substantive law and procedure."[81] Thus, national courts have no jurisdiction to support or intervene directly in ICSID proceedings.[82] One commentator has noted that while the UNCITRAL Rules and the rules of the International Chamber of Commerce allow the parties to choose "the law" to be applied to an arbitration, neither of these sets of rules is as flexible as the Washington Convention, which allows parties to choose the "rules of law" to be applied. This broad language allows the parties to submit different issues to rules from different legal systems, to apply rules common to more than one legal system, to combine national and international legal systems, and—most importantly—to apply the rules of international law, alone or in conjunction with

---

74 *Id*, art. 13.

75 *Id.*, art. 14(1).

76 *See* Database of ICSID Member States, available at https://icsid.worldbank.org/en/Pages/about/Database-of-Member-States.aspx (as of May 2018).

77 Rowat, *supra* note 65, at 118.

78 *Id.*

79 *See* ICSID, *The ICSID Caseload—Statistics* (Issue 2017-1), at 8–9, available at https://icsid.worldbank.org/en/Documents/resources/ICSID%20Web%20Stats%202017-1%20(English)%20Final.pdf.

80 David A. Soley, *ICSID Implementation: An Effective Alternative to International Conflict*, 19 Int'l Law. 521, 524 (1985).

81 Jacobs, *supra* note 63, at 131.

82 *See* Christoph Schreuer, *Interaction of International Tribunals and Domestic Courts in Investment Law*, in Contemporary Issues in International Arbitration and Mediation: The Fordham Papers, (4) 2010 at 71 (Arthur W. Rovine ed. 2011); Edward Baldwin et al., *Limits to Enforcement of ICSID Awards*, 23(1) J. Int'l Arb. 1 (2006).

national legal systems.[83] If the parties do not choose the governing law, the tribunal will apply "the law of the Contracting State party to the dispute (including its rules on conflict of laws) and such rules of international law as may be applicable."[84] Commentators have suggested that this provision may allow arbitrators to apply international law not only to fill gaps left by local law, but also to use international law in place of local law where the two are in conflict.[85] The *ad hoc* committee in *Amco v. Indonesia* agreed:

> Article 42(1) of the Convention authorizes an ICSID tribunal to apply rules of international law only to fill up lacunae in the applicable domestic law and to ensure precedence of international law norms where the rules of the applicable domestic law are in collision with such norms.[86]

As explained in more detail in Chapter 7, the scope of ICSID's jurisdiction is limited by the terms of the Washington Convention. As a result, a claimant must satisfy three basic conditions before ICSID will register a Request for Arbitration. **8.23**

First, ICSID will only register disputes that arise "between a Contracting State (or any constituent subdivision or agency of a Contracting State designated to the Centre by that State) and a national of another Contracting State."[87] Therefore, both the investor's home State and the respondent State must have signed and ratified the Washington Convention.[88] **8.24**

The rules regarding determining the claimant's nationality for these purposes are described in Chapter 7. It should be noted that where an investment contract is signed by a foreign-controlled local corporation, ICSID may nevertheless accept jurisdiction if the parties have agreed that the entity "should be treated as a **8.25**

[83] Shihata, supra note 64, at 189; Emmanuel Gaillard & Yas Banifatemi, *The Meaning of "and" in Article 42(1), Second Sentence of the Washington Convention: The Role of International Law in the ICSID Choice of Law Process*, 18(2) ICSID Rev.—For. Inv. L.J. 375 (2003).

[84] Washington Convention, *supra* note 8, art. 42(1), at 539. *See also* Aron Broches, *A Guide for Users of the ICSID Convention*, News from ICSID, 7 (Winter 1991).

[85] Shihata, *supra* note 64, at 192.

[86] *Amco Asia Corp. v. Indonesia* (1985), ICSID Case No. ARB/81/1, Committee Decision of May 16, 1986, 25 I.L.M. 1439 (1986). *See also Amco Asia Corp. v. Indonesia*, ICSID Case No. ARB/81/1 (Resubmitted Case), Award of June 5, 1990, 17 Yb. Comm. Arb. 73, 76 (1992) ("If there are no relevant host-State laws on a particular matter, a search must be made for the relevant international laws. And, where there are applicable host-State laws, they must be checked against international laws, which will prevail in case of a conflict"); Shihata, *supra* note 64, at 193; *Liberian Eastern Timber Corp. (LETCO) v. Government of Liberia*, 26 I.L.M. 647, 658 (1987) (suggesting that international law may have applicability even if the parties expressly choose the law of the contracting state as the governing law).

[87] Washington Convention, *supra* note 8, art. 25(1).

[88] *Id.* Parties wishing to include an ICSID arbitration clause in a contract prior to the ratification of the Washington Convention by one of the States concerned may do so; in such a case, ICSID jurisdiction becomes effective when the non-member State signs and ratifies the Convention. Emmanuel Gaillard, *Some Notes on the Drafting of ICSID Arbitration Clauses*, 477 PLI/Comm. Law & Prac. Course Handbook Series 33 (1988); Chapter 7, Section B.3.b.

national or another Contracting State for the purpose of the Convention."[89] It is also essential to keep in mind that ICSID arbitration may only be initiated directly against a Washington Convention member State itself. The only exception to this rule is where the host State in question has expressly notified ICSID that the particular constituent subdivision (province or municipality) or agency (State-owned company) may be a respondent in ICSID arbitration.[90]

8.26 Second, both the host State and the investor must consent to submit their dispute to ICSID for adjudication.[91] Today, most consent to ICSID arbitration occurs through the operation of investment protection treaties or national investment codes, with the State's open offer of consent incorporated in the treaty, perfected through the claimant's submission of a Request for Arbitration. Consent may also be evidenced more traditionally, by including an ICSID arbitration clause in an investment agreement.[92] The model clause for adopting ICSID arbitration reads as follows:

> The [Government]/[name of constituent subdivision or agency] of name of Contracting State (hereinafter the "Host State") and name of investor (hereinafter the "Investor") hereby consent to submit to the International Centre for Settlement of Investment Disputes (hereinafter the "Centre") any dispute arising out of or relating to this agreement for settlement by [conciliation]/ [arbitration]/ [conciliation followed, if the dispute remains unresolved within time limit of the communication of the report of the Conciliation Commission to the parties, by arbitration] pursuant to the Convention on the Settlement of Investment Disputes between States and Nationals of Other States(hereinafter the "Convention").[93]

---

[89] Washington Convention, *supra* note 8, art. 25(2)(b). ICSID Model Clause 7 addresses this issue: "It is hereby agreed that, although the Investor is a national of the Host State, it is controlled by nationals of name(s) of other Contracting State(s) and shall be treated as a national of [that]/ [those] State[s] for the purposes of the Convention." ICSID Model Clauses, Doc. ICSID/5/Rev. 2 (1993), available at http://icsidfiles.worldbank.org/icsid/icsid/staticfiles/model-clauses-en/main-eng.htm. Even absent such explicit agreement, tribunals have at times found an implied agreement to treat a foreign-controlled local corporation as a foreign company for purposes of the Washington Convention. *Liberian Eastern Timber Corp. v. Liberia*, ICSID Case No. ARB/83/2, Decision on Jurisdiction of Oct. 24, 1984, 2 ICSID Rep. 346, 352 (1994).

[90] Washington Convention, *supra* note 8, art. 25(1), (3). *See Cable Television of Nevis Ltd. and Cable Television of Nevis Holdings Ltd. v. St. Kitts and Nevis*, ICSID Case No. ARB/95/2, Award of Jan. 13, 1997, 13 ICSID Rev—For. Inv. L.J. 328 (1998), at paras. 345–52 (in the absence of a designation to ICSID of a province of the respondent State, jurisdiction did not exist with regard to disputes arising out of a contract with that province). Only ten States have designated their subdivisions or agencies as potential ICSID respondents. *See* ICSID, Designations by Contracting States Regarding Constituent Subdivisions or Agencies (2005).

[91] Washington Convention, *supra* note 8, art. 25(1); Chapter 7, Section A *et pass.*

[92] Jacobs, *supra* note 63, at 128.

[93] The parties should modify the model clause as necessary in accordance with the particular circumstances of their contract. For example, the jurisdiction of ICSID may be limited to certain disputes, as illustrated by ICSID Model Clause 4: "The consent to the jurisdiction of the Centre recorded in citation of basic clause above shall [only]/[not] extend to disputes related to the following matters: ... " ICSID Model Clauses, *supra* note 89.

Ratification of the Washington Convention alone, however, does not constitute consent to ICSID jurisdiction.[94] Moreover, each Washington Convention member State may notify ICSID of any class of disputes that it expressly excludes from ICSID jurisdiction.[95] **8.27**

The third main jurisdictional requirement, that the dispute "arise directly out of an investment," has given rise to extensive discussion and jurisprudence.[96] The Washington Convention does not define the term "investment," but the concept has been broadly interpreted.[97] Disputes determined to arise out of an "investment" have been related to a range of economic sectors, including industrial production, natural resource exploitation, construction, management contracts, technical assistance contracts, and licensing agreements.[98] **8.28**

It is important to note that the procedure for the challenge and enforcement of ICSID awards is entirely distinct from that applicable to commercial arbitration awards. While ICSID awards may qualify as "foreign awards" for purposes of the New York Convention, they receive additional, preferential treatment under the Washington Convention itself. Most significantly, the losing party to ICSID arbitration may only challenge the award before a second ICSID panel, called an "*ad hoc* committee," on the basis of the limited grounds listed in the Washington Convention. Second, enforcement of a valid ICSID award need not be "confirmed" in the national courts of any Washington Convention member State: any such award is to be enforced *directly*, "as if it were a final judgment of a court in that State."[99] This added element of enforceability does not affect the enforcing State's law on sovereign immunity in relation to execution against State-owned assets.[100] **8.29**

---

[94] Georges R. Delaume, *The Convention for Settlement of Investment Disputes between States and Nationals of Other States*, in 2 Transnational Contracts, booklet 17 at 5 (1990).

[95] Washington Convention, *supra* note 8, art. 25(4). Only five States have announced the exclusion of certain classes of disputes from ICSID arbitration.

[96] *See e.g.* Noah Rubins, *The Notion of "Investment" in International Investment Arbitration*, in Arbitrating Foreign Investment Disputes 283 (Norbert Horn ed. 2004); Farouk Yala, *The Notion of "Investment" in ICSID Case Law: A Drifting Jurisdictional Requirement?*, 22(2) J. Int'l Arb. 105 (2005); discussion at Chapter 7, Sections B.3.a, E.3 and E.4.c.

[97] William Rant et al., *ICSID's Emerging Jurisprudence: The Scope of ICSID's Jurisdiction*, 19 NYUJ Int'l L. & Pol. 33, 36 (1986) (the "related to investment" requirement serves mainly to exclude disputes arising out of ordinary sales contracts).

[98] Jacobs, *supra* note 63, at 129. One version of ICSID's Model Clause addresses the issue of "investment" for purposes of ICSID jurisdiction, providing: "It is hereby stipulated that the transaction to which this agreement relates is an investment." ICSID Model Clauses, *supra* note 89 (Model Clause 3). Such an agreement is not dispositive of the issue, however, since "[I]t is not enough to call a sale of goods an 'investment' . . . in order to satisfy the requirements of the Washington Convention." Gaillard, *supra* note 88, n.26.

[99] Washington Convention, *supra* note 8, art. 54(1).

[100] *Id.*, art. 55.

8.30 In 1978, ICSID created the Additional Facility for the Administration of Conciliation, Arbitration, and Fact Finding Proceedings, to extend the use of ICSID's services to certain disputes falling outside the scope of ICSID jurisdiction. In particular, the Additional Facility is available for disputes in which one of the States involved (either the host State or the investor's home State) is not a party to the Washington Convention.[101] The Additional Facility Arbitration Rules are based on the ICSID Rules. One key difference is that Additional Facility awards are not enforceable under the Convention, but require an independent basis for enforcement, such as the New York Convention.[102]

8.31 ICSID has frequently updated its procedural framework. There have been four rounds of changes following the adoption of the rules, the last of which entered into force in April 2006. Those amendments incorporated important improvements: a strengthened disclosure requirement for arbitrators;[103] a provision on the possibility to hold open hearings;[104] expanded transparency provisions to publish arbitral awards;[105] the opportunity for *amicus curiae* briefs;[106] and the possibility of early dismissal of claims for "manifest lack of legal merit."[107] ICSID launched the latest amendment process in October 2016, and invited member States to suggest topics for consideration.[108] In January 2017, ICSID issued a similar invitation to the public. In August 2018, the ICSID Secretariat proposed comprehensive changes to modernize its rules.[109] The ICSID member States met in September 2018 in Washington, DC, to discuss the proposed amendments. A series of working papers culminated in a rule revision published in August 2019, which the ICSID Secretariat expected to present for a vote in early 2020.[110]

c. Stockholm Chamber of Commerce (SCC)

8.32 The Arbitration Institute of the Stockholm Chamber of Commerce (SCC) has emerged as one of the world's leading arbitration institutions for the settlement of disputes between investors and States. The SCC has administered about 100 investment treaty arbitrations since 1993, most prominently involving claims based

101 ICSID Additional Facility Arbitration Rules (2003), available at http://www.worldbank.org/icsid.

102 *Id.*, art. 19.

103 *See* Arbitration Rule 6(2), art. 13(2) of the Arbitration (Additional Facility) Rules.

104 *See* Arbitration Rule 32(2), art. 39(2) of the Arbitration (Additional Facility) Rules.

105 *See* Arbitration Rule 48(4), art. 53(3) of the Arbitration (Additional Facility) Rules.

106 *See* Arbitration Rule 37(2), art. 41(3) of the Arbitration (Additional Facility) Rules.

107 *See* Arbitration Rule 41(5), art. 45(6) of the Arbitration (Additional Facility) Rules.

108 The potential areas for amendment are discussed here: https://icsid.worldbank.org/en/Documents/about/List%20of%20Topics%20for%20Potential%20ICSID%20Rule%20Amendment-ENG.pdf.

109 *See* Tom Jones, *ICSID Unveils Draft of New Rules,* Global Arbitration Review (Aug. 3, 2018) available at https://globalarbitrationreview.com/article/1172618/icsid-unveils-draft-of-new-rules.

110 *Proposals for Amendment of the ICSID Rules*, ICSID Working Paper 3, August 2019.

on the Energy Charter Treaty (ECT).[111] According to the SCC, at least sixty-one investment treaties stipulate that the SCC Arbitration Rules are to be used to settle disputes, and sixty more designate the SCC as the appointing authority for UNCITRAL arbitration.[112]

The SCC is one of three possible arbitration systems for use in investment disputes under the ECT.[113] Out of the 114 known ECT cases since 2001, 22 were brought to arbitration at the SCC.[114] 8.33

The SCC revised its arbitration rules at the beginning of 2017.[115] The new Arbitration Rules incorporate a number of changes designed to modernize the system and make it more flexible. This includes a new "summary procedure" (by which factual or legal issues can be adjudicated on a preliminary and simplified basis),[116] new provisions on the joinder of additional parties and multiple contracts,[117] broadened authority to consolidate arbitrations,[118] new rules on an early case management conference,[119] security for costs guidelines,[120] and standards for procedural efficiency.[121] The new SCC Arbitration Rules also introduced significant amendments to the Rules for Expedited Arbitrations, which govern quick procedures in smaller disputes.[122] The SCC Rules also envisage the possibility of emergency arbitration, by which a claimant can obtain interim measures in a matter of days from a specially-appointed arbitrator before the commencement of a full arbitration procedure.[123] 8.34

The new SCC Arbitration Rules also introduced specific rules in relation to investment treaty disputes. In contrast with ordinary commercial arbitration, 8.35

---

[111] Stockholm Chamber of Commerce Arbitration Institute, *A Great Year for Investment Treaty Disputes*, available at http://www.sccinstitute.com/statistics/investment-disputes-2017/.

[112] Stockholm Chamber of Commerce Arbitration Institute, *The Administration of Investment Disputes*, available at http://www.sccinstitute.com/dispute-resolution/investment-disputes/.

[113] Energy Charter Treaty, art. 26(4)(c).

[114] ECT Secretariat, *Changing Dynamics of Investment Cases under the Energy Charter Treaty (ECT)* (May 18, 2018), available at https://energycharter.org/what-we-do/dispute-settlement/cases-up-to-18-may-2018/.

[115] Rules of the Arbitration Institute of the Stockholm Chamber of Commerce (2017), available at http://www.sccinstitute.com/dispute-resolution/rules/.

[116] *Id.*, art. 39.

[117] *Id.*, arts. 13, 14.

[118] *Id.*, arts. 11(iv), 15.

[119] *Id.*, art. 28.

[120] *Id.*, art. 38.

[121] *Id.*, arts. 2(1), 49(3), 50.

[122] For an overview of these amendments, *see* Stockholm Chamber of Commerce Arbitration Institute, *2017 SCC Rules—Key changes*, available at http://sccinstitute.com/media/164883/main_changes_new_rules_2017.pdf.

[123] *See* Stockholm Chamber of Commerce Arbitration Institute, *SCC Practice Note on Emergency Arbitrator Decisions Rendered 2015–2016*, available at http://www.sccinstitute.com/media/194250/ea-practice-note-emergency-arbitrator-decisions-rendered-2015-2016.pdf. *See also* Kaj Hobér, *Emergency Arbitration: A lasting trend?*, Funding in Focus (July 2016), available at https://www.vannin.com/downloads/funding-in-focus-three.pdf.

where absent party agreement a sole arbitrator is normally selected, in investment disputes the default is three arbitrators, unless the SCC Board decides otherwise.[124] The SCC also recognizes that investment arbitrations may involve the interests of non-disputing parties, who may bring an important perspective to the tribunal's decision-making process. Appendix III enables third parties to make a submissions, subject to qualification criteria.[125] This includes either a true third party intervening on a "material factual or legal issue," or a non-participating State party to the relevant international treaty for issues of treaty interpretation.[126]

8.36 Arbitration costs are fixed by the SCC based on the amount in dispute. The SCC also offers an online fee calculator that can provide a reasonably accurate estimate of these costs.[127]

8.37 The SCC proposes a model arbitration clause for inclusion in contracts:

> Any dispute, controversy or claim arising out of or in connection with this contract, or the breach, termination or invalidity thereof, shall be finally settled by arbitration in accordance with the Arbitration Rules of the Arbitration Institute of the Stockholm Chamber of Commerce.
>
> *Recommended additions:*
>
> The arbitral tribunal shall be composed of three arbitrators/a sole arbitrator.
>
> The seat of arbitration shall be [...].
>
> The language to be used in the arbitral proceedings shall be [...].
>
> This contract shall be governed by the substantive law of [...].

d. London Court of International Arbitration (LCIA)

8.38 The LCIA, formerly known as the London Court of International Arbitration, was created in 1892 and today administers international disputes under its new International Arbitration Rules, adopted in 2014.[128] The new LCIA Arbitration

[124] *Cf.* SCC Arbitration Rules, *supra* note115, art. 16 (abandoning the presumption of three arbitrators and enables the Board to appoint a sole arbitrator, depending on "the complexity of the case, the amount in dispute and any other relevant circumstances") and App. III, art. 2(2).

[125] *Id.*, App. III, arts. 3, 4.

[126] *Id.*, App. III, art. 4(1).

[127] Stockholm Chamber of Commerce Arbitration Institute, *Calculator*, available at http://www.sccinstitute.com/dispute-resolution/calculator/.

[128] LCIA Arbitration Rules (2014), available at http://www.lcia.org/dispute_resolution_services/lcia-arbitration-rules-2014.aspx; Shai Wade et al., A Commentary on the LCIA Arbitration Rules 2014 (2015); Khaled Moyeed & Clare Montgomery, *Key Changes in the LCIA's new Arbitration Rules*, Kluwer Arbitration Blog (2014), available at http://arbitrationblog.kluwerarbitration.com/2014/08/29/key-changes-in-the-lcias-new-arbitration-rules/. For the LCIA Arbitration Rules (1998), available at http://www.lcia.org/Dispute_Resolution_Services/LCIA_Arbitration_Rules.aspx, *see* V.V. Veeder, *London Court of International Arbitration: The New 1998 LCIA Rules*, 23 Yb. Comm. Arb. 366 (1998); Sarah Scofield, *A Report on The London Court of International Arbitration (LCIA): History, Practices, Past Procedures, and the New Rules*, World Arb. & Med. Rep., Oct. 1998, at 269.

Rules were adopted with a view to ensuring an effective, efficient, and fair process. The 2014 LCIA Rules introduced several novelties, such as emergency arbitrators,[129] enhanced powers of the tribunal for the conduct of the proceedings,[130] new provisions related to costs, and general guidelines for the parties' legal representatives.[131]

The primary administering institution of the LCIA is the LCIA Court of Arbitration, which fulfills some of the same functions carried out by the ICC's International Court of Arbitration. The LCIA Court is made up of up to thirty-five members from around the world, including a President (a post occupied by Paula Hodges QC as of 2019) and seven Vice Presidents.[132] The LCIA's caseload is somewhat smaller than that of the ICC, with an average of about 300 new arbitration referrals each year.[133] The LCIA has seen a steady increase in referrals over recent years, from 128 in 2007 to 326 in 2015.[134] **8.39**

Unlike the ICC Court, the LCIA Court does not screen arbitration requests on a *prima facie* basis, nor does it review awards for form or quality.[135] Nevertheless, the LCIA Court plays an active role in the arbitral process, particularly in the appointment of arbitrators. Indeed, only the LCIA Court can actually "appoint" an arbitrator, and therefore retains the final say as to an arbitrator candidate's suitability, particularly with regard to impartiality and independence.[136] The LCIA Rules also give the Court authority to determine arbitrators' fees, and require any newly-appointed arbitrator to agree in writing to fee rates conforming to the LCIA Schedule of Arbitration Fees and Costs.[137] It should be noted that the Schedule of Costs establishes arbitrator fees on the basis of the number of hours of work actually performed, rather than on a per-case basis. As of May 2018, the hourly rate for administrative activities of the LCIA was between £150 and £250, in addition to the registration fee of £1,750. The tribunal's fees are calculated by reference to work done by its members in connection with the arbitration at rates appropriate to the particular circumstances of the case, including the complexity **8.40**

---

129 2014 LCIA Rules, *supra* note 128, art. 9(B).

130 *Id.*, art. 14.

131 *Id.*, Annex.

132 Paulsson et al., *supra* note 9, at 55–56. *See also* Constitution of the LCIA Arbitration Court (adopted 1990, amended 1998, 2002, 2008, 2009, 2010, 2011, 2015, and 2017), available at http://www.lcia.org/LCIA/constitution-of-the-lcia-court.aspx.

133 *See* LCIA, Facts and Figures 2017 Casework Report, at 4, available at http://www.lcia.org/LCIA/reports.aspx.

134 *Id.*

135 Veeder, *supra* note 69, at 366–67.

136 2014 LCIA Rules, *supra* note 128, art. 5. According to art. 5(7), "[n]o party or third person may appoint any arbitrator under the Arbitration Agreement: the LCIA Court alone is empowered to appoint arbitrators (albeit taking into account any written agreement or joint nomination by the parties)."

137 *Id.*, art. 5(4).

and special qualifications of the arbitrators. Each arbitrator's hourly rate cannot exceed £450 except in "exceptional cases."[138]

8.41 The model arbitration clause proposed by the LCIA is as follows:

> Any dispute arising out of or in connection with this contract, including any question regarding its existence, validity or termination, shall be referred to and finally resolved by arbitration under the LCIA Rules, which Rules are deemed to be incorporated by reference into this clause.
>
> The number of arbitrators shall be [one/three].
>
> The seat, or legal place, of arbitration shall be [City and/or Country].
>
> The language to be used in the arbitral proceedings shall be [ ].
>
> The governing law of the contract shall be the substantive law of [ ].[139]

Again, parties should consider possible modifications to this basic clause as necessary to conform to the particular circumstances of their transaction.

C. Drafting the Arbitration Clause

8.42 Most international arbitration occurs as a result of a provision in the parties' contract, whereby they agree to submit all disputes (or some category of disputes) to an arbitral tribunal, forgoing their right to litigate in court the issues that they have so submitted. As already explained in detail in Chapters 6 and 7, the direct investor–State provisions contained in investment treaties mean that contractual arbitration clauses are no longer the only route to effective, non-judicial dispute resolution. Nevertheless, where investment involves a contract with a State or State-controlled entity, including a carefully-drafted agreement to arbitrate is the most predictable way for the parties to ensure that any disputes are adjudicated in a neutral forum, with enforceable results.

8.43 Each of the established arbitration rules systems provides sample clauses that can be inserted into contracts, in some cases with minimal adjustment.[140] Nevertheless, as already noted, the parties to an international contract should carefully consider a range of possible modifications to "boilerplate" clauses, which can ensure a more predictable result, better suited to the disputes likely to arise from particular contractual relations. In this regard, the parties to an international agreement enjoy broad freedom in most jurisdictions around the world.[141]

---

[138] LCIA Schedule of Costs, available at http://www.lcia.org/Dispute_Resolution_Services/schedule-of-costs.aspx.

[139] *See* LCIA, *Recommended Clauses*, available at http://www.lcia.org/dispute_resolution_services/lcia_recommended_clauses.aspx. *See further* PAULSSON et al., *supra* note 9, at 132–33.

[140] PAULSSON et al., *supra* note 9, at 127–41.

[141] *See* Michael F. Hoellering, *How to Draft an AAA Arbitration Clause*, 7 ICSID REV.—FOR. INV. L.J. 141 (1992).

When drafting an arbitration clause, the parties should consider the following issues, among others.[142] 8.44

1. The scope of the arbitral clause

In order to avoid jurisdictional arguments at the outset of an arbitration, it is normally best to draft the arbitration clause in maximally broad fashion.[143] Absent a particular need to do so, selecting some issues for submission to arbitration and leaving others to the local judiciary in the host State can tempt courts (particularly if subject to outside influence) to disregard the arbitration clause altogether. One common formulation provides for the submission to arbitration of all disputes "arising under" the relevant contract, or "related to the performance" of the contract. However, certain national courts have interpreted these clauses rather strictly.[144] In order to establish a strong foundation for application of the arbitration clause to ancillary action by a State contracting party (such as regulation), the private contracting party might consider language similar to that contained in the UNCITRAL model clause, which covers "any dispute, controversy or claim arising out of or relating to this contract, or the breach, termination or invalidity thereof."[145] 8.45

2. Pre-arbitration procedures

It should be considered whether any particular dispute resolution procedures should be required before the initiation of arbitration. In particular, the parties can establish a requirement that the putative claimant submit a notice of dispute 8.46

[142] For further discussion of these issues, *see id.* at 141 *et seq.*; IBA Guidelines for Drafting International Arbitration Clauses (2010), adopted by a resolution of the IBA Council, Oct. 7, 2010; Blackaby et al., *supra* note 1, ch. 2: Agreement to Arbitrate; Aldo Frignani, *Drafting Arbitration Agreements*, 24(4) Arb. Int'l 561–70 (2008); Bond, *supra* note 19; Georges R. Delaume, *How to Draft an ICSID Arbitration Clause*, 7 ICSID Rev.—For. Inv. L.J. 168 (1992); Stephen R. Bond, *How to Draft an Arbitration Clause*, 6 J. Int'l Arb. 65 (1989); Ulmer, *supra* note 12; William W. Park, *Arbitration of International Contract Disputes*, 39 Bus. Law. 1783 (1984).

[143] Irene Welser & Susanne Molitoris, *The Scope of Arbitration Clauses—Or "All Disputes Arising out of or in Connection with this Contract,"* in Austrian Yearbook of International Arbitration 18 (Christian Klausegger et al. eds. 2012). On pathological arbitration clauses, *see* Frederick E. Sherman & Steven C. Bennett, *Avoiding "Pathological" Arbitration Clauses*, The Practical Lawyer 43 (Aug. 2006); Marie-Hélène Maleville, *Pathologies des Clauses Compromissoires*, 1 RDAI/IBLJ 61 (2000); Frédéric Eisemann, *La clause d'arbitrage pathologique*, in Arbitrage Commercial-Essais in Memoriam Eugenio Minolo 129 (1974).

[144] A U.S. court has held that the phrase "arising under" in an arbitration clause should be read narrowly to cover "disputes and controversies relating to the interpretation of the contract and matters of performance." *Mediterranean Enterprises Inc. v. Sangyong Corp.*, 708 F.2d 1958 (9th Cir. 1983). *See also* Bond, *supra* note 22, at 159. For a broader interpretation followed in Germany and Switzerland, *see* Christian Koller, *Die Schiedsvereinbarung*, in Schiedsverfahrensrecht, para. 3/259, 7 (Christoph Liebscher et al. eds. 2012); Stefan Kröll, *Die schiedsrechtliche Rechtsprechung 2004*, SchiedsVZ 139, 141 (2005); Karl Heinz Schwab & Gerhard Walter, Schiedsgerichtsbarkeit 25–26 (7th ed. 2005).

[145] 1976 UNCITRAL Rules, *supra* note 7, art. 1(1).

to the respondent, and that arbitration may begin only after a certain period of time has elapsed following such notice. This type of provision, if drafted tightly and with only a limited period of time (one or three months, for example), can encourage settlement of the dispute through amicable negotiations.[146] While mediation and conciliation are by definition consensual mechanisms that cannot be forced upon an unwilling party, an arbitration clause can require a good-faith attempt to engage in alternative dispute resolution before having recourse to arbitration.[147] Again, such provisions should set a relatively short time period for any such mandatory pre-arbitration ADR, to prevent a recalcitrant party from delaying adjudication of the dispute indefinitely. Furthermore, such a clause should preserve the parties' right to seek interim relief from courts during the course of ADR, to avoid irreparable harm to the parties.

3. Applicable rules

8.47 As is clear from the brief discussion in Section B, the choice of arbitration rules can have a significant impact on the conduct of arbitral proceedings. Most importantly, the parties must decide whether their dispute should be resolved on an *ad hoc* basis, or under the auspices of an arbitral institution. As previously noted, the choice of purely *ad hoc* arbitration, without referring to any set of procedural rules such as the UNCITRAL Rules, entails significant risks of delay and obstruction, and should be avoided except in exceptional circumstances. The possible benefits and drawbacks of UNCITRAL arbitration are described in Section B.1.

8.48 There is a great number of arbitral institutions around the world.[148] In broad terms, the rules of these institutions are similar, but should be examined carefully to determine whether they are suitable for a particular transaction. The reputation, caseload, experience and expertise of staff, and extent of support and intervention in proceedings are also factors that should be considered when selecting an administrating body and arbitral rules.[149] In disputes of limited size, the differing

146 *See e.g. Multi-Tiered Dispute Resolution Clauses*, International Bar Association Litigation Committee (2015).

147 *See* Chapter 9, Section C.

148 The most well-known arbitral institutions, besides ICSID, the ICC, the SCC, and LCIA, include the American Arbitration Association's International Centre for Dispute Resolution, the Arbitration Centre of the Federal Economic Chamber in Vienna, the Singapore International Arbitration Centre, the Hong Kong International Arbitration Centre, the Australian Centre for International Commercial Arbitration in Melbourne, the British Columbia International Commercial Arbitration Centre in Vancouver, the Chamber of National and International Arbitration of Milan, the Japan Commercial Arbitration Association in Tokyo, the Netherlands Arbitration Institute in Rotterdam, the International Centre for Arbitration in Kuala Lumpur, and the Saudi Centre for Commercial Arbitration in Riyadh. *See* Hoellering, *supra* note 141, at 143.

149 Blackaby et al., *supra* note 1, at paras. 1.159–1.164 (listing permanency, modern arbitration rules, qualified staff, and reasonable charges as primary concerns when choosing an arbitral institution). *See further* Jie Zheng, *Competition between Arbitral Institutions in China—Fighting for a Better System?*, Kluwer Arbitration Blog (2015), available at http://arbitrationblog.

administrative and arbitrator fees for various arbitral institutions may also be a factor to consider, although such expenses are normally only a small fraction of the amount paid to counsel in international arbitration proceedings.[150]

4. Composition of the tribunal

Constituting an arbitral tribunal is one of the central aspects of most international arbitration rules. Therefore, to the extent that the parties have incorporated rules by reference in their contract, many basic questions about the tribunal's composition will already be answered—unless the parties supplement or override these default procedures. **8.49**

The most fundamental question is the number of arbitrators who will form the tribunal. While in some forms of commodity arbitration panels may be composed of five[151] or even more individuals, in the realm of international commercial arbitration and investment disputes, one or three arbitrators decide practically all cases.[152] Some of the prominent arbitration rules provide for a three-member tribunal if the parties fail to agree otherwise,[153] while others establish a sole arbitrator as the default result. The ICC and LCIA Rules call for a sole arbitrator in the absence of party agreement, but leave significant discretion to the arbitral institution to mandate a three-member panel in appropriate circumstances.[154] **8.50**

The primary advantage of a sole arbitrator over a three-member panel is in speed and economy. A sole arbitrator can act more expeditiously to resolve procedural disputes, without having to consult with colleagues, and may be able to draft an award more quickly, since there is no need to coordinate the busy schedules of three arbitrators to arrange deliberations. A three-member tribunal, naturally, is **8.51**

kluwerarbitration.com/2015/10/16/competition-between-arbitral-institutions-in-china-fighting-for-a-better-system/.

[150] On expedited procedures for smaller disputes, *see* 2017 ICC Rules, *supra* note 31, art. 30 and App. VI.

[151] One of the first ICC tribunals to comprise five arbitrators was constituted in the case of *PT Ventures v. Unitel* (ICC Case 21404/ASM), dealing with a US$2.8 billion claim of four shareholders in an Angolan telecoms company over unpaid dividends and other alleged breaches of their shareholders' agreement. *See* Tom Jones, *Five-Member ICC Panel Hears Multibillion-Dollar Case*, Global Arb. Rev. (May 30, 2018).

[152] Derains & Schwartz, *supra* note 39, at 144–45 (more than three arbitrators appointed in only one case in the past twenty years, to the authors' knowledge).

[153] 2013 UNCITRAL Rules, *supra* note 7, art. 7(1).

[154] The ICC Court is authorized to establish a three-member tribunal even absent agreement of the parties, where "it appears to the Court that the dispute is such as to warrant the appointment of three arbitrators." 2017 ICC Rules, *supra* note 31, art. 12(2). As a rule of thumb, the ICC Court tends to order a three-person tribunal when the amount in dispute exceeds US$1.5 million. Paulsson et al., *supra* note 9, at 67. Like the ICC Rules, the LCIA Rules provide for a sole arbitrator absent contrary agreement of the parties, "unless the parties have agreed in writing otherwise or if the LCIA Court determines that in the circumstances a three-member tribunal is appropriate (or, exceptionally, more than three)." 2014 LCIA Rules, *supra* note 128, art. 5(8).

more costly, since fees must be paid to each of the arbitrators. On the other hand, a three-member panel can offer significant benefits. A wider range of cultural, linguistic, technical, and legal skills can be incorporated into a three-member panel. Moreover, the parties enjoy greater control over the composition of the tribunal in such cases, since they can each choose one arbitrator, and perhaps influence the selection of the chairman by direct negotiation or through their appointee. Finally, many observers believe that the presence of three decision-makers instead of one results in a more thoroughly reasoned (and perhaps more accurate) award.

8.52 Some arbitration clauses also specify particular qualifications that arbitrators must possess in order to serve on the tribunal. It is relatively common for parties to agree, for example, that a sole arbitrator or the chairman of a tribunal not be of the same nationality as any of the parties. In contracts involving particularly complicated subject matter additional experience, language skills, or education can also be required. In this regard, however, the parties should be careful not to restrict the pool of eligible candidates too much. After a dispute arises, such qualifications may seem less important than the ability to select precisely the arbitrator that each party prefers.[155]

5. Arbitral situs

8.53 For a number of reasons, selecting the place where the arbitration will take place is an extremely important part of the drafting of an arbitration clause.[156] In particular, the municipal laws of the forum of the arbitration may have a significant effect on the way the arbitration is conducted.[157] The local arbitration statute will normally determine the procedural law to be applied by the arbitrators in instances where the chosen arbitration rules are silent.[158] Other important issues related to local law include the scope of questions capable of submission to arbitration ("arbitrability"), the extent to which courts will support the arbitral process through interim measures of protection, and the rules governing the recognition, enforcement, and annulment of arbitration awards.[159] Indeed, it is only

---

[155] Paulsson et al., *supra* note 9, at 74 (advising restrictions on arbitrator qualifications "only if they are fundamental to the efficient operation of the proceedings").

[156] A useful, if somewhat dated discussion of the advantages and disadvantages of various arbitration sites is provided in Survey of International Arbitration Sites (J. Stewart McClendon ed. 1993). *See also* Loukas A. Mistelis, *Arbitral Seats: Choices and Competition*, in International Arbitration and International Commercial Law: Synergy Convergence and Evolution 367 *et seq.* (Stefan Kröll et al. eds. 2011); Michael L. Morkin, *How to Choose Arbitration*, in International Arbitration Checklists 209, 212–14 (Lawrence W. Newman & Grant Hanessian eds. 2004).

[157] *See* Loukas A. Mistelis, *Reality Test: Current State of Affairs in Theory and Practice Relating to "Lex Arbitri"*, 17(2) Am. Rev. Int'l Arb. 155 *et seq.* (2006).

[158] Hoellering, *supra* note 78, at 144. The influence of local law upon the arbitral process is far less in the case of ICSID arbitration. *See* Section L.2.b, *infra*.

[159] For an argument that problems associated with the "localization" of arbitration have decreased due to the increasing number of States that have enacted laws strictly limiting interference with a review of arbitral proceedings conducted within their territories, *see* Patrick Thieffry,

in the courts at the place of arbitration that a dissatisfied party may seek to nullify the award. Parties should therefore choose a jurisdiction with a modern and comprehensive statute on international commercial arbitration, and a judicial system accustomed to handling such cases.[160] It is naturally difficult to estimate the suitability of courts and domestic laws for all circumstances, but surveys suggest that parties feel particularly comfortable designating France,[161] Switzerland,[162] Belgium,[163] the United States, and the United Kingdom.[164]

8.54 In most countries, the parties are free to use the procedural rules of an international arbitral institution, of another jurisdiction, or draft their own rules.[165] Belgium has gone even further in "delocalizing" arbitrations held in its territory (*i.e.* ensuring that arbitral awards are not subject to undue interference from procedural rules of the forum), enacting a statute that blocks any application to set aside an award where neither side is Belgian and the parties have expressly excluded judicial review.[166] Nevertheless, local arbitration law may influence arbitration procedure where the rules chosen are silent on a particular issue.[167]

8.55 The problem of whether disputes are arbitrable has declined in importance in recent years, as the trend in many countries is to allow arbitration of a range of matters that were formerly beyond the scope of arbitration.[168] U.S. courts,

Negotiating Settlement of Disputes Provisions in International Business Contracts: Recent Developments in Arbitration and Other Processes, 45 Bus. Law 577 (1990). *But cf.* Noah Rubins, *The Arbitral Seat is No Fiction*, Mealey's Int'l Arb. Rep. (Jan. 2001).

[160] Ulmer, *supra* note 12, at 1343.

[161] In a non-exhaustive survey of ICC arbitration for the period 1992–98, parties designated France as the arbitral situs more often than any European country. In France, recourse against an award is limited to the following procedural grounds: absence of an arbitration agreement, improper composition of the arbitral tribunal, violation of the arbitral tribunal of its duties, disregard of the principles of adversarial defense, and violation of international public policy by the recognition or enforcement of the award. Thieffry, *supra* note 159, at 601–02, *citing* Nouveau Code de Procedure Civile, art. 1502, Annex 1-9-10.

[162] Thieffry, *supra* note 159, at 602.

[163] *Id.* at 602–03.

[164] Parties designating arbitration in England should bear in mind that the English Arbitration Act 1996 may envisage court review of the merits of an arbitrated dispute. This rather unusual situation can be rectified with an "exclusion agreement" in the arbitration clause, waiving the right of appeal to the English courts for review of the substance of the award. Ulmer, *supra* note 12, at 1344.

[165] *Id.*

[166] *See* William W. Park, *The Specificity of International Arbitration: The Case for FAA Reform*, 36 Vand. J. Transnat'l L. 1241, 1258 n.69 (2003).

[167] Noah Rubins, *In God We Trust, All Others Pay Cash: Security for Costs in International Commercial Arbitration*, 11 Am. Rev. Int'l Arb. 307, 314–15 (2000) ("If the arbitration rules are silent, judges and arbitrators may fill in gaps in those rules using the *lex arbitri* chosen by the parties or determined by appropriate choice-of-law rules").

[168] Eric A. Schwartz, *The Domain of Arbitration and Issues of Arbitrability: The View from the ICC*, 9 ICSID Rev—For. Inv. L.J. 17, 19 (1994) ("[A]s a practical matter, today the issue of arbitrability is not an obstacle to the arbitration of most international commercial disputes. It is, moreover, now much more widely accepted than previously that a dispute should not be considered to be non-arbitrable simply because it concerns matters of public policy"). *See also* Bernard Hanotiau, *The Law*

for example, have demonstrated a willingness to enforce international arbitral awards even if the issues that are the subject of the award would not be arbitrable under domestic law. In *Mitsubishi Motors*,[169] for example, the U.S. Supreme Court found that claims arising under the Sherman Antitrust Act, usually beyond the scope of arbitration, are arbitrable in international distribution agreements.[170]

8.56 The place of arbitration will also impact the prevailing party's ability to enforce an eventual award.[171] First, the situs of the arbitration becomes significant when a party seeks to annul an arbitral award. As discussed later in this chapter, such actions to set aside are governed by local law at the place of arbitration. While a large number of States have adopted or adapted the UNCITRAL Model Law on International Commercial Arbitration, there remains a great deal of variation among domestic laws in this regard, and courts' consistency in implementing such laws.[172] Further, the New York Convention requires courts in signatory States to recognize arbitral awards as binding and enforce them, but many signatories have submitted a reservation limiting the Convention's effect to awards rendered in States that are also party to the Convention. Thus, the parties should be sure to designate a situs within a New York Convention signatory State.[173]

Applicable to Arbitrability, 26 Singapore Academy L.J. 874–85 (2014); Loukas A. Mistelis & Stavros Brekoulakis, Arbitrability: International and Comparative Perspectives (2009).

[169] *Mitsubishi Motors Corp. v. Soler Chrysler Plymouth Inc.*, 473 U.S. 614 (1985).

[170] The issue of arbitrability may arise in connection with the U.S. act of State doctrine. In *Libyan American Oil Co. v. Socialist People's Libyan Arab Jamahirya*, 482 F. Supp. 1175 (D.C. 1980), *vacated without op.* 684 F.2d 1032 (D.C. Cir. 1981), following Libya's nationalization of LIAMCO's oil concession, an arbitration award was rendered in LIAMCO's favor in Geneva. LIAMCO attempted to enforce the award in New York under the auspices of the New York Convention, and one of Libya's defenses was that the issue of nationalization was not arbitrable. The court agreed, finding that it could not compel arbitration, because this would have required a review of the nationalization itself, which was an act of State of Libya. *Id.* at 1178–79. LIAMCO appealed, but the parties settled before the appeal could be heard. The promulgation of the Hickenlooper Amendment in the U.S. (discussed in Chapter 4, Section G.3) reduces the likelihood that such a defense would be accepted today.

[171] For a comprehensive country-by-country analysis of specific issues in the area of enforcement, *see* Enforcement of Investment Treaty Arbitration Awards: A Global Guide 121 *et seq.* (Julien Fouret ed. 2015).

[172] UNCITRAL Model Law on International Commercial Arbitration 1985, with amendments as adopted in 2006, available at http://www.uncitral.org/pdf/english/texts/arbitration/ml-arb/07-86998_Ebook.pdf. In the United States, for instance, even international arbitration awards may be subject to annulment based upon "manifest disregard of law," not a ground contained in the UNCITRAL Model Law. *See* Noah Rubins, *Manifest Disregard of the Law and Vacatur of Arbitral Awards in the United States*, 12 Am. Rev. Int'l Arb. 363, 364–67 (2001). On the risk of annulment under Indonesian law, *see* Noah Rubins, *The Enforcement and Annulment of International Arbitration Awards in Indonesia*, 20 Am. U. Int'l L. Rev. 359 (2005).

[173] This does not apply with respect to ICSID arbitration. *See* Section L.2 in the first edition of this book.

6. Rules of evidence and document production

The parties should give consideration to the extent to which they wish to establish specific rules on the production and presentation of documentary and witness evidence. While the revised versions of the most prominent institutional rules such as those previously described contain basic procedures in this area,[174] some others lack specific instructions, and give wide discretion to the tribunal to set the scope of the parties' obligation to produce documents and witnesses.[175] Particularly where the parties come from different legal traditions, establishing some supplemental ground rules for evidentiary matters may increase predictability and avoid unnecessary disputes early in the proceedings. **8.57**

While the parties may incorporate rules of evidence or document production imported from a particular national legal system, they may consider referring in their arbitration clause to the International Bar Association's Rules on the Taking of Evidence in International Arbitration (the 2010 IBA Rules).[176] **8.58**

The Rules[177] were "designed to fill the void intentionally left in most institutional and ad hoc rules between the submission of initial pleadings and the issuance of the award," and were considered to be a fusion of civil law and common law traditions, particularly adapted to the context of international dispute resolution proceedings.[178] Since their issuance in 1999, these Rules progressively gained wide acceptance within the international arbitration community and were used in various contexts. They were revised in 2010. Unlike the prior version, the new Rules were drawn up with a view to application in investment arbitration as well as commercial disputes.[179] **8.59**

---

[174] *See e.g.* 2013 UNCITRAL Rules, *supra* note 7, arts. 17(1), 20(4), 21(2), 27, 29(3), 30(3); SCC Arbitration Rules, *supra* note115, arts. 23(1), 28(3), 31; LCIA Rules, *supra* note 128, arts. 15(2)–15(6), 21(3), 22(1)(iv)–(vi), 25(1)(ii); 2017 ICC Rules, *supra* note 31, arts. 19, 22(2)–(5), 25(1) and App. IV(d)(i)–(v). *See further* ICC, *ICC Arbitration Commission Report on Managing E-Document Production* (2012), available at https://iccwbo.org/publication/icc-arbitration-commission-report-on-managing-e-document-production/.

[175] *See generally* Reto Marghitola, Document production in international arbitration (2015); Derains & Schwartz, *supra* note 39, at 281–83; Martin Hunter, *Modern Trends in the Presentation of Evidence in International Commercial Arbitration*, 3 Am. Rev. Int'l Arb. 204 (1992).

[176] International Bar Association, *Rules on the Taking of Evidence in International Arbitration* (the 2010 IBA Rules on the Taking of Evidence), available at https://www.ibanet.org/ENews_Archive/IBA_30June_2010_Enews_Taking_of_Evidence_new_rules.aspx.

[177] International Bar Association, Rules on the Taking of Evidence in International Commercial Arbitration. These Rules replaced the IBA Supplementary Rules Governing the Presentation and Reception of Evidence in International Commercial Arbitration, issued in 1983. For examples of previous ICSID tribunals relying on the 1999 IBA Rules, *see Caratube Int'l. Oil Co. LLP v. Kazakhstan*, ICSID Case No. ARB/08/12, Procedural Order No. 2 of Apr. 26, 2010, at para. 1.2; *EDF (Services) Ltd. v. Romania*, ICSID Case No. ARB/05/13, Procedural Order No. 3 of Aug. 29, 2008, at paras. 19, 29, 47.

[178] David Rivkin, *IBA Rules on the Taking of Evidence in International Commercial Arbitration*, 24a Yb. Comm. Arb. 408, 409 (1999).

[179] Examples of tribunals relying on the 2010 IBA Rules include *Poštová banka, A.S. and ISTROKAPITAL SE v. Hellenic Republic*, ICSID Case No. ARB/13/8, Procedural Order No. 6 of

8.60 The 2010 IBA Rules "are intended to provide an efficient, economical and fair process for the taking of evidence in international arbitrations, particularly those between Parties from different legal traditions. They are designed to supplement the legal provisions and the institutional, ad hoc or other rules that apply to the conduct of the arbitration."[180] The 2010 IBA Rules maintain the basic procedural framework of the previous version, but update them in multiple respects.[181] Among the most significant revisions is the requirement that the tribunal consult with the parties at the earliest appropriate time to agree on an efficient, economical and fair process for taking evidence[182] and to provide guidance on "e-discovery."[183] The revised Rules also contain additional provisions on confidentiality[184] legal privilege, including the need to maintain equality particularly if the parties are subject to different legal or ethical rules.[185] The new rules expressly state that it is not improper for the parties to discuss prospective testimony with witnesses and experts. Finally, the 2010 IBA Rules incorporate an express requirement of good faith when taking and producing evidence, and authorize the tribunal to consider bad faith conduct when awarding arbitration costs.[186]

8.61 If the parties wish to adopt the IBA Rules in their arbitration clause, the IBA recommends the following language:

> [In addition to the institutional, *ad hoc* or other rules chosen by the parties,] [t]he parties agree that the arbitration shall be conducted according to the IBA Rules on the Taking of Evidence in International Arbitration as current on the date of [this agreement/the commencement of the arbitration].[187]

July 20, 2014, at 4–5; *Churchill Mining Plc. and Planet Mining Pty. Ltd. v. Indonesia*, ICSID Case No. ARB/12/14 and 12/40, Procedural Order No. 5 of Mar. 19, 2013, at paras. 4 and 7. For an overview of NAFTA tribunals' practice, *see* Christina L. Beharry, *Objections to Requests for Documents in International Arbitration: Emerging Practices from NAFTA Chapter 11*, 27(1) ICSID Rev.—For. Inv. L.J. 33–64 (2012).

[180] 2010 IBA Rules, *supra* note 176, Preamble.

[181] *See generally* Peter Ashford, The IBA Rules on the Taking of Evidence in International Arbitration: A Guide (2013); Georg von Segesser, *The IBA Rules on the Taking of Evidence in International Arbitration*, 28(4) ASA Bull. 735–52 (2010).

[182] 2010 IBA Rules, *supra* note 176, art. 2(1).

[183] *Id.*, arts. 3(3)(a)(ii), 3(12)(b), 9(2). *See further* Richard D. Hill, *The New Reality of Electronic Document Production in International Arbitration: A Catalyst for Convergence?*, 25(1) Arb. Int'l. 87–102 (2009).

[184] *Id.*, arts. 2(2)(d), 3(8), 3(13), 9(3)(a)–(b), 9(4).

[185] *Id.*, art. 9(2)(b), (3).

[186] *Id.*, Preamble, recital 3 and art. 9(7). For a critique of the concept of "good faith" in the 2010 IBA Rules, *see* Pedro J. Martinez-Fraga, *In Good Faith, Bad Faith, But Not Losing Faith: A Commentary on the 2010 IBA Rules on the Taking of Evidence in International Arbitration*, 43 Georgetown J. Int'l L. 411 (2012); Margaret Moses, *Is Good Faith in the IBA Evidence Rules Good?*, Kluwer Arbitration Blog (Nov. 15, 2012), available at http://arbitrationblog.kluwerarbitration.com/2012/11/15/is-good-faith-in-the-iba-evidence-rules-good/.

[187] For other recommended options, see the ICCA Drafting Sourcebook for Organizing International Arbitrations, Draft of Mar. 1, 2014, available at https://www.arbitration-icca.org/media/2/13963492574410/27032014_icca_draft_01_drafting_sourcebook_for_organising_international_arbitrations.pdf.

7. Applicable substantive law

One of the central aspects of any dispute resolution proceeding is the system of law according to which the decision-maker will adjudicate the dispute.[188] The freedom of the parties to designate this system of law was covered previously.[189] As several noted practitioners advise, **8.62**

> the parties should strive to select one body of national law as the applicable law and set it out plainly in a separate clause in the agreement. This is the single greatest assurance of certainty in the resolution of legal disputes that arise.[190]

The problems related to selecting an applicable law, and combining national, international, and general principles of law in a contractual choice of law are also addressed more fully in Chapter 2.[191] **8.63**

8. Consistency among arbitration clauses

Many projects will involve multiple contracts and multiple parties, including participants other than a single investor and the host State, each with its own concerns regarding dispute resolution. For example, most project lenders prefer that loan agreements be interpreted literally in the event of a dispute.[192] Lenders will therefore usually prefer litigation under developed common-law systems with which they are familiar, such as the substantive laws of New York or England.[193] Project finance also involves contractors, subcontractors, architects, and engineers, **8.64**

---

[188] On the controversial issue of "applicable law clauses" in investment treaty arbitration, *see* Jorge E. Viñuales, *Sources of International Investment Law: Conceptual Foundations of Unruly Practices*, in THE OXFORD HANDBOOK ON THE SOURCES OF INTERNATIONAL LAW 1069 (Jean d'Aspremont & Samantha Besson eds. 2017); Ole Spiermann, *Investment Arbitration: Applicable Law*, in INTERNATIONAL INVESTMENT LAW 1373 (Marc Bungenberg et al. eds. 2015); Christoph Schreuer, *Jurisdiction and Applicable Law in Investment Treaty Arbitration*, 1(1) MCGILL J. DISP. RES. 1 (2014); Jürgen Kurtz, *Building Legitimacy through Interpretation in Investor–State Arbitration: On Consistency, Coherence and the Identification of Applicable Law*, in THE FOUNDATIONS OF INTERNATIONAL INVESTMENT LAW 157 *et seq.* (Zachary Douglas et al. eds. 2014); HEGE ELISABETH KJOS, APPLICABLE LAW IN INVESTOR–STATE ARBITRATION 61 (2013); Lorand Bartels, *Jurisdictions and Applicable Law Clauses: Where Does a Tribunal Find the Principal Norms Applicable to the Case before It?*, in MULTI-SOURCED EQUIVALENT NORMS IN INTERNATIONAL LAW 115 *et seq.* (Tomer Broude & Yuval Shany eds. 2011); Yas Banifatemi, *The Law Applicable in Investment Treaty Arbitration*, in ARBITRATION UNDER INTERNATIONAL INVESTMENT AGREEMENTS: A GUIDE TO THE KEY ISSUES 191 *et seq.* (Katia Yannaca-Small ed. 2010); ZACHARY DOUGLAS, THE INTERNATIONAL LAW OF INVESTMENT CLAIMS 39 *et seq.* (2009); SCHREUER, *supra* note 61, at 545 *et seq.; see further* Matina Papadaki, *Compromissory Clauses as the Gatekeepers of the Law to Be "Used" in the ICJ and the PCIJ*, 5(3) J. INT'L. DISPUTE SETTLEMENT 560–604 (2014).

[189] *See* Chapter 2, Section D.2. On some of the difficulties that can arise where the parties have not clearly designated the applicable law, *see* Ole Lando, *The Law Applicable to the Merits of the Dispute*, 2 ARB. INT'L 104 (1986).

[190] PAULSON et al., *supra* note 9, at 30.

[191] Chapter 2, Section D.2 *et pass.*; PAULSSON et al., *supra* note 9, at 11–24.

[192] *See generally* RAVI C. TENNEKOON, THE LAW AND REGULATION OF INTERNATIONAL FINANCE (1991).

[193] *Id.*

each of whom may have their own preferences regarding the parameters of dispute settlement. In addition, political and commercial insurance contracts normally contain separate dispute settlement mechanisms.

8.65 A detailed discussion of the problems that can arise in a complex dispute involving a multitude of contracts with different dispute mechanisms, such as duplicate litigation and arbitration concerning the same issues, is beyond the scope of this book. The investor should be aware, however, that an arbitration clause negotiated with the host State must co-exist with the dispute settlement mechanisms binding other entities involved in the project. Whenever possible, the investor should strive to harmonize the provisions in other contracts concerning the project, such as contracts with contractors and suppliers, and in particular seek to have compatible substantive and procedural rules apply to all aspects of a dispute to avoid conflicting results.

D. Pre-Arbitration Procedures

8.66 Many contractual arbitration clauses, and nearly all modern investment treaties, require that prior to commencing formal arbitration proceedings, the claimant provide the respondent written notice of the existence and nature of a dispute.[194] This so-called "trigger letter" sets in motion any contractually agreed pre-arbitration period for negotiation toward an amicable settlement of the dispute.[195] A few investment treaties also contain an "exhaustion" requirement, whereby aggrieved investors must first file local court proceedings in the host State before they may bring a claim in international arbitration.[196]

8.67 Where an applicable investment treaty or national investment law contains such a waiting or exhaustion provision, and a treaty signed by the host State with another country provides for less onerous pre-arbitration procedures, or none at all, the investor may be able to "import" the more advantageous treaty provisions under

---

[194] On pre-arbitration procedural requirements, *see generally* Gary Born & Marija Scekic, *Pre-Arbitration Procedural Requirements: "A Dismal Swamp,"* in Practising Virtue Inside International Arbitration 234 *et seq.* (David D. Caron et al. eds. 2015).

[195] France–Chile BIT (1992), art. 8(1)–(2) (requiring amicable negotiation, but "[I]f the dispute has not been resolved within six months of the date it arose, it shall be submitted, at the investor's request," to arbitration); U.S.–Argentina BIT (1991), art. VII(3)(a) ("Provided that ... six months have elapsed from the date on which the dispute arose, the national or company concerned may choose to consent in writing to the submission of the dispute for settlement by binding arbitration"); U.S.–Azerbaijan BIT (1997), art. IX(3)(a) (three-month waiting period from time dispute arises).

[196] *See e.g.* Germany–Argentina BIT (1991), art. 10(2), (3)(a) (establishing eighteen-month "exhaustion period" of litigation in local courts). Generally speaking, international arbitration becomes available under such provisions a certain number of months after the court litigation is commenced, regardless of whether a judgment has been rendered.

a most-favored-nation provision of the applicable investment protection instrument. This was the holding of the arbitral tribunal in *Maffezini v. Spain*,[197] where the MFN provision of a BIT entitled an Argentine investor to the more relaxed procedural requirements of another BIT ratified by respondent Spain. Under the Argentina–Spain BIT, investors were required to pursue their claims in the courts of the host country for eighteen months before initiating arbitration against the host state. The Chile–Spain BIT imposed no such condition. A majority of subsequent tribunals have confirmed this broad utility of MFN clauses.[198]

By contrast, other tribunals have reached different conclusions on the possibility of relying on the MFN clause to import provisions containing more favorable pre-arbitration requirements (or no requirements at all). For instance, in *ICS v. Argentina*, the claimant relied on the MFN clause in article 3 of the Argentina–UK BIT to import more favorable pre-arbitration requirements from other BITs and sidestep the eighteen-month litigation requirement in article 8 of the Argentina–U.K. BIT.[199] The *ICS* tribunal rejected the claimant's argument and concluded that the eighteen-month litigation requirement was a prerequisite to Argentina's acceptance of a claim being brought before the arbitral tribunal and that "failure to respect the pre-condition to the Respondent's consent to arbitrate cannot but lead to the conclusion that the Tribunal lacks jurisdiction over the present dispute."[200] The tribunal concluded that on the basis of the circumstances prevailing when the BIT in question was concluded the parties understood the term "treatment" to refer only to substantive obligations and not to procedural requirements.[201] In reaching this conclusion, the tribunal also relied in part on the ICJ's reasoning in *Democratic Republic of Congo v. Rwanda*, whereby **8.68**

[197] *Emilio Agustín Maffezini v. Spain*, ICSID Case No. ARB/97/7. The origins of the use of MFN in respect of access to procedural matters is often traced back to the 1956 arbitral award in the *Ambatielos claim*, where it was held that the "administration of justice" was an important part of the rights of traders and therefore should be treated as included within the phrase "all matters relating to commerce and navigation" by virtue of the MFN clause; *see The Ambatielios Claim (Greece v. U.K.)*, U.N. R.I.A.A., vol. XII, 83, at 107.

[198] *See Austrian Airlines v. Slovakia*, UNCITRAL, Final Award of Oct. 9, 2009, at para. 124; *Quasar de Valors SICAV S.A. et al. v. Russia*, SCC No. 24/2007, Award on Preliminary Objections of Mar. 20, 2009, at para. 100; *RosInvestCo. U.K. Ltd. v. Russia*, SCC Case No. V079/2005, Award on Jurisdiction of Oct. 1, 2007, at paras. 131–32; *Nat'l. Grid Plc. v. Argentina*, UNCITRAL, Decision on Jurisdiction of June 20, 2006, at para. 89; *Gas Natural SDG S.A. v. Argentina*, ICSID Case No. ARB/03/10, Decision on Jurisdiction of June 17, 2005, at paras. 29 and 49; *AWG Group Ltd. v. Argentina*, UNCITRAL, Decision on Jurisdiction of Aug. 3, 2006, at para. 59. *See also* Chapter 6, Section C.4.b.ii for an overview of the case law on the application of MFN clauses in investment treaties. *See further* ILC, *Study Group on the Most-Favored-Nation Clause*, Final report, A/CN.4/L.852, Sixty-seventh session, Geneva (2015), at paras. 104 *et seq.* for a comprehensive overview of the interpretation by investment tribunals of MFN clauses in relation to procedural matters.

[199] *ICS Inspection and Control Services Ltd. (U.K.) v. Argentina*, PCA Case No. 2010-9 (UNCITRAL), Award on Jurisdiction of Feb. 10, 2012, at paras. 113 *et seq.*

[200] *Id.* at para. 362.

[201] *Id.* at paras. 289–96, 326–27.

consent is expressed in a compromissory clause in an international agreement, any conditions to which such consent is subject must be regarded as constituting the limits thereon. The Court accordingly considers that the examination of such conditions relates to its jurisdiction and not to the admissibility of the application.[202]

8.69 The approach taken in *ICS v. Argentina* was reiterated by other investment treaty tribunals,[203]although not without dissent.[204]

8.70 Some tribunals have held that pre-arbitration negotiation provisions are purely procedural in nature, and that an international tribunal "cannot allow itself to be hampered by a mere defect of form."[205] In the *Military and Paramilitary Activities* case before the ICJ, for example,[206] the United States alleged that Nicaragua had not satisfied the pre-arbitral negotiation period contained in the applicable Treaty of Friendship, Commerce and Navigation Treaty, because during negotiations Nicaragua had not specifically raised any alleged violations of the Treaty. The ICJ rejected the U.S. objection to jurisdiction, since Nicaragua could theoretically remedy the defect and begin its case again, but that this would be a futile exercise:

In the view of the Court, it does not necessarily follow that, because a State has not expressly referred in negotiations with another State to a particular treaty as having been violated by conduct of that other State, it is debarred from invoking a compromissory clause in that treaty . . . It would make no sense to require Nicaragua

---

[202] *Id.* at para. 258; *Case Concerning the Armed Activities on the Territory of the Congo (New Application: 2002) (Democratic Republic of the Congo v. Rwanda)*, Judgment of Feb. 3, 2006, I.C.J. Rep. 2006, p. 6 at para. 88.

[203] *See Daimler Financial Services A.G. v. Argentina*, ICSID Case No. ARB/05/1, Award of Aug. 22, 2012; *Kılıç İnşaat İthalat İhracat Sanayi ve Ticaret Anonim Şirketi v. Turkmenistan*, ICSID Case No. ARB/10/1, Decision on Article VII.2 of the Turkey–Turkmenistan Bilateral Investment Treaty of May 7, 2002; *ST-AD GmbH v. Bulgaria*, UNCITRAL PCA Case No. 2011-06, Award on Jurisdiction of July 18, 2013.

[204] *See Daimler Financial Services A.G. v. Argentina*, ICSID Case No. ARB/05/1, Dissenting Opinion of Judge Charles N. Brower of Aug. 15, 2012, available at https://www.italaw.com/cases/documents/1522. *See also* Decision on Annulment of Jan. 7, 2015, at paras. 121 *et seq.* (rejecting an application on annulment on grounds of "internal inconsistencies" of the award in its findings concerning the BIT's eighteen-month clause and the scope of the BIT's MFN clauses). *See further Hochtief A.G. v. Argentina*, ICSID Case No. ARB/07/31, Decision on Jurisdiction of Oct. 24, 2011, at paras. 95–96 (taking the view that an eighteen-month domestic litigation requirement was not a matter of jurisdiction but a matter of admissibility that could be waived or cured by acquiescence) and the Separate and Dissenting Opinion of J. Christopher Thomas, Q.C., at para. 2.

[205] *Certain German Interests in Polish Upper Silesia*, Decision on Jurisdiction, P.C.I.J. Ser. A, No. 6 (1925), at 14. *See also* Lucy Reed et al., Guide to ICSID Arbitration 57 (2004); *SGS Société de Surveillance Générale S.A. v. Pakistan*, ICSID Case No. ARB/01/13, Decision on Jurisdiction of Aug. 6, 2003. *See also* ICC Case No. 11490, Final Award (2012) XXXVII YB Comm. Arb. 32 (the provision in the arbitration clause that disputes be settled amicably constituted "no condition precedent to referral to arbitration"). For a different approach, *see Wintershall Aktiengesellschaft v. Argentina*, ICSID Case No. ARB/04/14, Award of Dec. 8, 2008, at para. 139 (finding that art. 10(2) of the Argentina–Germany BIT imposed an "obligation" to submit a dispute to local courts for eighteen months, which could not be considered as a "mere defect of form"). *See further* Douglas, *supra* note 188, at 160.

[206] *Military and Paramilitary Activities in and Against Nicaragua (Nicaragua v. U.S.A.)*, Judgment on Jurisdiction and Admissibility of Nov. 26, 1984, 1984 I.C.J. Rep. 427.

now to institute fresh proceedings based on the Treaty, which it would be fully entitled to do.[207]

In *Lauder v. Czech Republic*, the tribunal rejected the respondent State's objection based on the claimant's failure to observe the six-month negotiation period under the applicable U.S.–Czech Republic BIT: **8.71**

> the Arbitral Tribunal considers that this requirement of a six-month waiting period of [the BIT] is not a jurisdictional provision, i.e. a limit set out to the authority of the Arbitral Tribunal to decide on the merits of the dispute, but a procedural rule that must be satisfied by the Claimant . . . As stated above, the purpose of this rule is to allow the parties to engage in good-faith negotiations before initiating the arbitration.[208]

In most cases, the notice of dispute is a very simple document that can be prepared with relatively little expenditure of time or money.[209] Submitting a notice letter, even if not required by the relevant contract or treaty, can result in some material advantages for investors who seek to safeguard assets, reverse regulations or contractual breaches, or generally obtain more advantageous treatment from the host State during a crisis period. Such a letter of intent to arbitrate puts the government on notice that its continued refusal to abide by its obligations (under contract or international law) will have significant legal, political, and economic consequences for the country. The letter may also induce the host government to keep contracts and treaty texts in mind when implementing further measures in response to political pressure or financial crisis. **8.72**

Under normal circumstances, a notice of dispute in investor–State arbitration is not served upon the respondent government through diplomatic channels or pursuant to separate treaties on service of process.[210] In contract arbitration, the agreement itself will normally indicate where notices are to be sent. In arbitration pursuant to investment treaties, the claimant generally delivers a copy of the notice to the ministry or official mostly directly responsible for the investment within the respondent State, as well as to the head of government. It is normally practice to send a number of copies of the notice of dispute to other government **8.73**

---

[207] *Id.* at 428.

[208] *Ronald S. Lauder v. Czech Republic*, UNCITRAL, Final Award of Sept. 3, 2001, at para. 187. *See also Consorzio Groupement L.E.S.I.—Dipenta v. Algeria*, ICSID Case No. ARB/08/8, Decision of Jan. 10, 2005, at para. 32(iv) (pre-arbitration procedures "are not absolute, and it should be possible to dispense with them in the case where it appears from the evidence that a settlement attempt would be destined to fail, due to the clearly demonstrated attitude of the other party").

[209] Note, however, that some investment treaties require a more substantial document, sometimes referred to as a "detailed memorandum." *See* Belgium–Russian Federation BIT (1989), art. 10(1).

[210] Indeed, diplomatic representation and espousal are normally prohibited in the context of investor–State arbitration under investment treaties, as part of the goal of depoliticizing investment disputes. Article 8(3) of the Italy–Morocco BIT (1990), for example, provides expressly that "the two Contracting Parties shall refrain from handling, through diplomatic channels, all questions pertaining to an arbitration or to pending legal proceedings . . ."

offices, such as the head of State and the Ministry of Foreign Affairs. However, as with other pre-arbitration requirements, service of process is generally construed liberally in international arbitration proceedings, as long as the respondent actually has notice of the dispute, and unless the parties have agreed to some specific arrangement.[211]

E. Request for Arbitration

8.74 Once any pre-arbitration procedures have been satisfied, the claimant may formally initiate arbitration through a launching submission, which is most frequently referred to as a "Request for Arbitration."[212] The UNCITRAL Rules designate this first submission as a "Notice of Arbitration", not to be confused with the "notice of dispute" (otherwise known as a "trigger letter"), described in Section D.[213]

8.75 ICSID establishes a rather elaborate procedure to be followed to initiate arbitration. ICSID's Rules of Procedure for the Institution of Conciliation and Arbitration Proceedings (the ICSID Institution Rules) stipulate that the claimant must send a Request for Arbitration to the Secretary-General of ICSID, containing a range of obligatory information.[214] Most importantly, the claimant must "designate precisely each party to the dispute and state the address of each"; indicate the claimant's nationality and, if the claimant is an individual, certify that he is not a national of the Respondent State as well; and provide information concerning the issues in dispute, confirming that the dispute is of a legal nature and arises directly out of an investment.[215] Certain other information must also be included in the Request for Arbitration in particular circumstances, and potential claimants should read the Institution Rules carefully before sending a Request. Key factual statements to be included in the Request (particularly those dealing with nationality) must be substantiated with supporting documentation.[216] In many cases, the claimant takes the initial steps towards forming an arbitral tribunal in the Request for Arbitration, although the ICSID Rules and Convention allow the parties to agree later on the method of appointment. This normally means indicating a preference for three arbitrators and naming one individual who will

---

[211] *Certain German Interests in Polish Upper Silesia*, Decision on Jurisdiction, P.C.I.J. Ser. A, No. 6 (1925), at 14.

[212] *See* 2017 ICC Rules, *supra* note 31, art. 4; 2014 LCIA Rules, *supra* note 128, art. 1; 2017 SCC Rules, *supra* note122, art 6.

[213] 2010 UNCITRAL Rules, *supra* note 7, art. 3.

[214] ICSID Institution Rules, arts. 1–2.

[215] *Id.*, art. 2(1). *See* Chapter 7 for a description of the jurisdictional requirements of ICSID arbitration under art. 25 of the Washington Convention.

[216] ICSID Institution Rules, art. 2(2).

serve on the tribunal. At the same time, the claimant may propose a candidate for President of the tribunal.

After receiving the non-refundable registration fee from the claimant, the ICSID Secretary-General will expedite a copy of the Request to the respondent State.[217] The Secretary-General will then review the request to determine whether it is manifestly outside the scope of ICSID jurisdiction, and if it is not, she will register the arbitration request at the Centre.[218] Once the request has been registered, the arbitration is deemed to have commenced.[219] At that point, the respondent State cannot avoid the proceedings by refusing to respond to the Request for Arbitration, since the ICSID Rules mandate moving ahead in the face of such a default.[220] **8.76**

The 2010 UNCITRAL Rules provide for the method of service of process for all notices, including the Notice of Arbitration. They establish that "[a] notice, including a notification, communication or proposal, may be transmitted by any means of communication that provides or allows for a record of its transmission."[221] If an address has been designated by a party specifically for this purpose or authorized by the arbitral tribunal, any notice shall be delivered to that party at that address, and if so delivered shall be deemed to have been received. Delivery by electronic means such as facsimile or e-mail may only be made to an address so designated or authorized.[222] In the absence of such designation or authorization, a notice is: "(a) Received if it is physically delivered to the addressee; or (b) Deemed to have been received if it is delivered at the place of business, habitual residence or mailing address of the addressee."[223] If after reasonable efforts delivery cannot be effected, "a notice is deemed to have been received if it is sent to the addressee's last-known place of business, habitual residence or mailing address by registered letter or any other means that provides a record of delivery or of attempted delivery."[224] The 2010 UNCITRAL Rules also specify that a notice sent in hard copy **8.77**

---

[217] *Id.*, art. 5.

[218] On review of Requests for Arbitration by the ICSID Secretariat, *see* Section F, *infra. See also* Christopher Dugan et al., Investor–State Arbitration 122 (2011); Sergio Puig & Chester Brown, *The Secretary-General's Power to Refuse to Register a Request for Arbitration under the ICSID Convention*, 27(1) ICSID Rev.—For. Inv. L.J. 172–91 (2012).

[219] ICSID Institution Rules, art. 6. *See e.g. Vacuum Salt Products Ltd. v. Ghana*, ICSID No. ARB/92/1, Award of Feb. 16, 1994 ("On 28 May 1992, ICSID received the Request for Arbitration in this case submitted by [claimant] ... Pursuant to Rule 5 of the Rules of Procedure for the Institution of Conciliation Arbitration Proceedings, the Secretary-General of ICSID by letters dated 29 May 1992 ... transmitted a copy of the Request and of the accompanying documentation to Ghana").

[220] *See e.g. Tradex Hellas S.A. (Greece) v. Albania*, ICSID No. ARB/94/2, Award on Jurisdiction of Dec. 24, 1996 (Albania's failure to respond to Request led to Secretary-General's appointment of its arbitrator). On default of a party to arbitration, *see* Section G, *infra.*

[221] 2010 UNCITRAL Rules, *supra* note 7, art. 2(1).

[222] *Id.*, art. 2(2).

[223] *Id.*, art. 2(3).

[224] *Id.*, art. 2(4).

is "deemed to have been received on the day it is delivered,"[225] while "[a] notice transmitted by electronic means is deemed to have been received on the day it is sent, except that a notice of arbitration so transmitted is only deemed to have been received on the day when it reaches the addressee's electronic address."[226] Meanwhile, "Arbitral proceedings shall be deemed to commence on the date on which the notice of arbitration is received by the respondent."[227] Although the UNCITRAL rules were not originally designed for arbitration against a sovereign State, these notice provisions have been followed in practice with regard to notice in investment arbitration.[228]

8.78 While the Request for Arbitration normally includes the basic factual and legal allegations underlying the claim, the leading arbitration rules do not require that it treat such issues in any detail. Nevertheless, some claimants have used the Request for Arbitration to provide a full analysis of both facts and law in a lengthy document.[229] A detailed Request for Arbitration naturally entails greater expense and longer preparation time than the summary notice envisaged in most arbitration rules, the fuller approach can provide important advantages to claimants.

8.79 First, the Request for Arbitration is the only substantive document the arbitral tribunal initially reviews, and for a significant period of time it will face no rebuttal by the respondent. This is particularly the case under the ICSID Rules, which do not contemplate an answer to the Request for Arbitration before the tribunal is formed. By presenting its position persuasively and comprehensively at the outset, a claimant may be able to establish a lasting, favorable impression of the case in the arbitrators' minds. A strongly-formulated Request for Arbitration may be advantageous in the adjudication of jurisdictional challenges. If the arbitrators are familiar with the details of the claim first from the claimant's perspective, and are convinced that it has a legitimate basis, the tribunal could be reluctant to dismiss the case on "technical" grounds. Second, a thorough Request for Arbitration can strengthen a private claimant's position in negotiations with the government respondent, regardless of whether the arbitration progresses to conclusion. By taking the opportunity in the Request for Arbitration to describe the factual and legal basis for the claim and to provide comprehensive analysis in support of its claim

---

225 *Id.*, art. 2(5).

226 *Id.*, art. 2(5).

227 *Id.*, art. 3(2).

228 *See e.g. Lauder, supra* note 208 ("On 19 August, 1999, Ronald S. Lauder initiated these arbitration proceedings by giving notice of arbitration to the Czech Republic"); *Adams v. Mexico*, Notice of Claim, Feb. 16, 2001 (UNCITRAL claim served directly upon the Secretary of Economy at the Foreign Investment Directorate of Mexico). Respondent States are bound by all provisions of the UNCITRAL Arbitration Rules by operation of their consent to arbitrate in the relevant investment treaty.

229 The Notice of Claim in *Loewen Group Inc. v. U.S.A.*, ICSID Case No. ARB(AF)/98/3, which served as the Request for Arbitration in that case, was sixty-seven pages long, and included nearly 120 pages of supporting affidavits and other materials.

of compensation, claimants may be able to gain valuable leverage in negotiations, having demonstrated a reasonable probability of success, as well as the approximate amount of an eventual award. Third, in exceptional circumstances, where a claimant is seeking provisional measures together with the filing of an arbitration request, a well-formulated Request for Arbitration may provide the tribunal with a sufficient basis to assert *prima facie* jurisdiction and issue interim relief where the respondent's conduct may inflict irreparable harm that cannot be otherwise remedied.[230]

On the other hand, many practitioners insist that a relatively short request for arbitration is preferable in most cases.[231] On this view, presenting the full panoply of legal arguments at the earliest stage of the arbitration provides the respondent additional time in which to craft a response. Furthermore, by building a detailed argument before taking the time to fully explore the evidentiary basis, the claimant creates the risk that it will have to change its position later in the proceedings in light of newly-discovered information. Instead, the claimant may prefer to include only a basic description of the background facts of the case and overarching legal theory, withholding the details of legal argument for its full memorial, to be filed after the tribunal is formed. **8.80**

Most arbitration rules call for a formal Answer to the Request for Arbitration. Where envisaged, the respondent provides its Answer to the arbitral institution before the formation of the arbitration tribunal.[232] Other systems, like UNCITRAL prior to 2010 and ICSID,[233] provide for no further written submissions until the arbitrators have been selected. **8.81**

F. Approval by Arbitral Institution

Under many institutional arbitration systems, the arbitral institution is charged with screening requests for arbitration to ensure that there is credible evidence of a valid agreement to arbitrate the dispute.[234] **8.82**

---

[230] *See generally* Cameron A. Miles, Provisional Measures before International Courts and Tribunals 159 *et seq.* (2017).

[231] *E.g.* Lucy Reed & John Beechey, panel discussion at "International Dispute Resolution by the Rules," Conference sponsored by the American Bar Association, Washington, D.C., Sept. 12, 2003.

[232] 2017 ICC Rules, *supra* note 31, art. 5 ("Within 30 days from the receipt of the Request from the Secretariat, the respondent shall submit an Answer (the 'Answer')"); 2017 SCC Rules, *supra* note 122, art. 9 ("The Secretariat shall set a time period within which the Respondent shall submit an Answer to the SCC").

[233] ICSID Arbitration Rule 41(5), introduced in 2006, allows a respondent to seek early dismissal of claims that are manifestly without legal merit, *see* Section F.

[234] *See e.g.* 2017 ICC Rules, *supra* note 31, art. 6; 2017 SCC Rules, *supra* note 122, art. 7. On *prima facie* review under the SCC Rules, see Annette Magnusson & Hanna Larsson, *Recent Practice of the Arbitration Institute of the Stockholm Chamber of Commerce Prima Facie Decisions on Jurisdiction and Challenges of Arbitrators*, 2004(2) Stockholm. Arb. Rep. 47.

8.83 Within the ICSID system, the ICSID Secretary-General reviews the request for arbitration to establish that the claimant has presented a case that is *prima facie* within the jurisdiction of the Centre.[235] While occasionally cases are rejected at this stage,[236] the ICSID Secretary-General is not authorized to engage in an in-depth analysis of the merits. The Secretariat's duty is to block cases that are manifestly outside the scope of a valid submission to arbitration before either side invests substantial resources in the prosecution of the case.[237] This oversight protects claimants from using ICSID arbitration as a means to exert unreasonable pressure upon host States.[238] As previously noted, the decision to register or reject a claim is based largely upon the materials submitted by the claimant in its request; the respondent has no opportunity to oppose registration. The Secretary-General is not permitted to consider opposing arguments, although she may solicit additional information from the claimant to assist in making the decision.[239]

8.84 Pursuant to ICSID Arbitration Rule 41(5) and article 45(6) of the Additional Facility Rules, a respondent can object at a very early stage to a claim that is "manifestly without merit."[240] The tribunal is empowered to dismiss the claim without further proceedings if it upholds the objection. However, this "summary judgment" procedure is not an institutional screening mechanism, but rather a

[235] Washington Convention, *supra* note 8, art. 36(3). *See also* art. 28(3) in relation to requests for conciliation. *See further* Report of the Executive Directors on the Convention, para. 20 ("the Secretary-General is given the power to refuse registration of a request for conciliation proceedings or arbitration proceedings, and thereby to prevent the institution of such proceedings, if on the basis of the information furnished by the applicant he finds that the dispute is manifestly outside the jurisdiction of the Centre"). *See also Int'l. Co. for Railway Systems (ICRS) v. Jordan*, ICSID Case No. ARB/09/13, Procedural Order No. 2 Concerning the Respondent's Request to Stay the Proceedings of July 9, 2010, at paras. 23, 28, 29.

[236] As of 1991, only three cases had been refused registration. ICSID, Report of the Secretary-General to the Administrative Council 2 (1991).

[237] Antonio Parra, *The Screening Power of the ICSID Secretary*, 2(1) News from ICSID 10 (1985). *See further* Eloïse Obadia & Frauke Nitschke, *Chapter 4: The Role of the Secretariat, Litigating International Investment Disputes*, in Litigating International Investment Arbitration Disputes: A Practitioner's Guide 80 (Chiara Giorgetti ed. 2014); Martina Polasek, *The Threshold for Registration of a Request for Arbitration under the ICSID Convention*, 5(2) Disp. Res. Int'l. 177 (2011); Schreuer et al., *supra* note 61, at 455.

[238] ICSID Report, *supra* note 258, at 10; Moshe Hirch, The Arbitration Mechanism of the International Centre for the Settlement of Investment Disputes 43 (1993).

[239] Parra, *supra* note 237, at 12. In *Commerce Group Corp. and San Sebastian Gold Mine Inc. v. El Salvador*, ICSID Case No. ARB/09/17, the Secretary-General of ICSID requested that the claimants submit additional information for purposes of determining whether their Request was "manifestly outside the jurisdiction of the Centre" pursuant to art. 36(3) of the ICSID Convention. El Salvador filed a letter contending that the dispute was "manifestly outside ICSID's jurisdiction" because the claimants had not stopped court proceedings in El Salvador in breach of the mandatory waiver provision of CAFTA. Following clarifications and documentation provided by the claimants, the Secretary-General registered the claimants' request.

[240] See ICSID Arbitration Rules, *supra* note 8, art. 41(6).

tool by which the arbitral tribunal can decide swiftly on the merits of claims that are obviously unfit to proceed.[241]

Under the ICC Rules, a respondent can advance early jurisdictional objections soon after the request for arbitration has been submitted. The ICC Secretary General may refer such matters to the ICC Court for decision. The ICC Court can dismiss the claims if it is convinced that there is no valid agreement to arbitrate, even on a *prima facie* basis.[242] The ICC Court's rejection of a jurisdictional challenge does not bind the tribunal once formed, which may freely adjudicate the extent of its own jurisdiction.[243] Under the ICSID Rules as well, once the tribunal has been constituted, the respondent is free to challenge the competence of the arbitral tribunal on any grounds.[244] **8.85**

The UNCITRAL Rules do not provide for any *prima facie* review of requests for arbitration, even if the *ad hoc* arbitration is administered by an institution such as the ICC, which normally carries out initial screening. Instead, the respondent must raise all jurisdictional arguments before the arbitral tribunal after it is formed. The absence of any registration process may in fact make UNCITRAL arbitration quicker in the early stages than institutional arbitration. **8.86**

G. Default of a Party

It is possible, and not uncommon, that the respondent will refuse to participate in arbitration proceedings.[245] A party may never participate, or may stop responding **8.87**

---

[241] *See* Aïssatou Diop, *Objection under Rule 41(5) of the ICSID Arbitration Rules*, 25(2) ICSID Rev.—For. Inv. L.J. 312–36 (2010); Inna Uchkunova, *Rule 41(5) of the ICSID Arbitration Rules: The Sleeping Beauty of the ICSID system*, Kluwer Arbitration Blog (2014), available at http://arbitrationblog.kluwerarbitration.com/2014/06/27/rule-415-of-the-icsid-arbitration-rules-the-sleeping-beauty-of-the-icsid-system/. *See also Trans-Global Petroleum Inc. v. Jordan*, ICSID Case No. ARB/07/25, Decision on the Respondent's Objection under Rule 41(5) of the ICSID Arbitration Rules of May 12, 2008; *Brandes Investment Partners, L.P. v. Venezuela*, ICSID Case No. ARB/08/3, Decision on the Respondent's Objection under Rule 41(5) of the ICSID Arbitration Rules of Feb. 2, 2009; *see further Elsamex S.A. v. Honduras*, ICSID Case No. ARB/09/4 (on the use of art. 41(5) in ICSID annulment proceedings).

[242] 2017 ICC Rules, *supra* note 31, art. 6(3), (4).

[243] 2017 ICC Rules, *supra* note 31, art. 6(5), (6); *see also* Blackaby et al., *supra* note 1, at paras. 5.105–5.109; Derains & Schwartz, *supra* note 39, at 103–09; Webster & Buhler, *supra* note 39, at 134 *et seq.*; Andrea Carlevaris, *Preliminary Matters: Bi-furcation, Request for Provisional Measures*, in Litigating International Investment Arbitration Disputes: A Practitioner's Guide 180 (Chiara Giorgetti ed. 2014).

[244] Washington Convention, *supra* note 8, art. 41(1) ("The Tribunal shall be the judge of its own competence"); art. 41(2) (directing the tribunal to consider "any objection by a party to the dispute that that dispute is not within the jurisdiction of the Centre, or for other reasons is not within the competence of the Tribunal").

[245] On party default in international arbitration, *see* Chartered Institute of Arbitrators, Party Non-Participation—International Arbitration Practice Guideline (2016), available at https://www.ciarb.org/media/1311/2011partynonparticipation.pdf. *See also* Eric de Brabandere, Investment Treaty Arbitration as Public International Law 115–16 (2014).

or appearing at some later stage in the proceedings.[246] Generally, a submission to arbitrate is binding and irrevocable, regardless of whether it is included in a contract or a treaty. Indeed, it is central to the efficient working of any private dispute resolution system that one side's obstructive behavior should not frustrate the process or prevent the claimant from obtaining relief.[247] Despite concerns for due process[248] and the risk of annulment,[249] default judgments are well-grounded in international law, including explicit incorporation into the procedures of the International Court of Justice.[250] Therefore, under normal circumstances, the arbitration will proceed to a "default" ruling, despite the fact that only one side presented its case.[251]

8.88 The Washington Convention provides in considerable detail the procedure to be followed in case of default:

> (1) Failure of a party to appear or to present his case shall not be deemed an admission of the other party's assertions.

---

[246] For example, the occupation of Crimea by the Russian Federation in 2014, several investors advanced claims against Russia in connection with their Crimean investments under the 1998 Russia–Ukraine BIT. In a letter to the Permanent Court of Arbitration, the Russian Federation refused to participate in the proceedings or appoint legal representatives, and declared that it "does not recognize the jurisdiction of an international arbitral tribunal" to resolve Crimea-related claims. *See Aeroport Belbek LLC and Mr. Igor Valerievich Kolomoisky v. Russia*, PCA Case number 2015-07, Press Release dated Jan. 6, 2016, available at https://pcacases.com/web/sendAttach/1553; *see also Everest Estate LLC et al. v. Russia*, PCA Case number 2015-36, Press Release dated Aug. 9, 2016, available at https://pcacases.com/web/sendAttach/1856.

[247] *See* Schreuer, *supra* note 61, at 694; ICC Rules, *supra* note 31, art. 21(2); UNCITRAL Rules, *supra* note 7, art. 28.

[248] In *Interprods Ltd. v De La Rue Int'l. Ltd.* [2014] EWHC 68 (Comm), the English High Court dismissed an application to annul an arbitral award on the basis that it was rendered in the face of the respondent's default. Although the case pertained to commercial arbitration, it provides useful guidance in the investor–State context.

[249] In the ICSID context, see Washington Convention, art. 45 (on rules of procedure and evidence in situations of default) and art. 52(1)(d) (annulment possible for a serious departure from a fundamental rule of procedure (art. 52(1)(d)). *See* Schreuer et al., *supra* note 61, at 710.

[250] Statute of the International Court of Justice (1945), art. 53 [hereinafter, the ICJ Statute], available at http://www.icj-cij.org. *See also* Stanimir Alexandrov, *Non-Appearance before the International Court of Justice*, 33 Colum. J. Transnat'l L. 41 (1995); Ken Highet, *Nonappearance and Disappearance before the ICJ*, 81 AJIL 237 (1987). In the context of investor–State arbitration, *see* Noah Rubins, Swembalt v. Latvia: An Overview and the Dilemma of Default, 2 Stock. Int'l Arb. Rep. 119 (2004). For a recent analysis, *see* Alexander Wentker, *Venezuela's Non-Participation before the ICJ in the Dispute over the Essequibo Region*, EJIL:Talk! (June 29, 2018), available at https://www.ejiltalk.org/venezuelas-non-participation-before-the-icj-in-the-dispute-over-the-essequibo-region/. Outside the context of the ICJ, *see also* China's Note Verbale dated Aug. 1, 2013 in *The South China Sea Arbitration (Philippines v. People's Republic of China)*, PCA Case No. 2013-19.

[251] *See generally* Aron Broches, *The Convention on the Settlement of Investment Disputes between States and Nationals of Other States: Applicable Law and Default Procedure*, in International Arbitration Liber Amicorum for Martin Domke 12 (1967); Arshad Masood, *Default Procedure in Arbitration under the World Bank Convention*, 22 L. Rev. 1 (1970); William Northcote, *Default, ex parte and Want of Prosecution Proceedings in International Commercial Arbitration*, 14 Advocate's Q. 319 (1992); Gerald Fitzmaurice, *The Problem of the Non-Appearing Defendant Government*, 51 Brit. Yb. Int'l L. 89 (1980); Rubins, *supra* note 250.

(2) If a party fails to appear or to present his case at any stage of the proceedings the other party may request the Tribunal to deal with the questions submitted to it and to render an award. Before rendering an award, the Tribunal shall notify, and grant a period of grace to, the party failing to appear or to present its case, unless it is satisfied that that party does not intend to do so.[252]

Other rules systems deal with default in other ways. The ICC Rules allow the ICC Secretary General to refer to the ICC Court of Arbitration the question of whether an arbitration should proceed to default if a respondent fails to submit an Answer.[253] In such cases, the Court may decide that the arbitration should proceed if it is *prima facie* satisfied that an arbitration agreement under the Rules exists. Otherwise, the ICC will dismiss the case. All parties then retain the right to ask a court of competent jurisdiction if there is a binding arbitration agreement. It is important to recall that the Court's discretion is only on a *prima facie* basis: the ICC Rules elsewhere state simply that "[I]f any of the parties refuses or fails to take part in the arbitration or any stage thereof, the arbitration shall proceed notwithstanding such refusal or failure."[254] **8.89**

Once an ICC tribunal receives a case file from the ICC Court, it is empowered (but not obliged) to "fill in" an absent respondent's side of the story.[255] At the same time, nearly all international arbitration rules grant arbitrators the authority to request documentation from a party. Tribunals sometimes bring this power to bear to mitigate the effects of a one-sided presentation of the facts.[256] **8.90**

---

252 Washington Convention, *supra* note 8, art. 45. *See also* SCHREUER et al., *supra* note 61, at 708 *et seq.* For cases of non-appearance before ICSID tribunals, *see Kaiser Bauxite Co. v. Government of Jamaica*, ICSID Case No. ARB/74/3, Decision on Jurisdiction of July 6, 1975, at paras. 3–10; *Antoine Goetz et al. v. Burundi*, ICSID Case No. ARB/95/3, Award of Feb. 10, 1999, at para. 24.

253 2017 ICC Rules, *supra* note 31, art. 6(3)–(4) ("[i]f any party against which a claim has been made does not submit an Answer ... the arbitration shall proceed and any question of jurisdiction or of whether the claims may be determined together in that arbitration shall be decided directly by the arbitral tribunal, unless the Secretary General refers the matter to the Court for its decision pursuant to Article 6(4)").

254 *Id.*, art. 6(8).

255 *Id.*, art. 25. By contrast, the 2014 Rules of the International Centre for Dispute Resolution (a division of the American Arbitration Association), available at https://www.adr.org/sites/default/files/ICDR_Rules.pdf, could be seen to preclude *ex officio* review of jurisdictional objections, which must be raised by a party no later than the filing of the statement of defense. AAA International Rules, art. 19(3). *See also* art. 26 on default ("If a party fails to submit an Answer in accordance with Article 3, the arbitral tribunal may proceed with the arbitration").

256 Generally in commercial arbitration, where one party has raised a fact, and provided sufficient evidence to prove that fact, *prima facie*, the burden of proof shifts to the opposing side. If the fact remains uncontroverted by the opposing party, it is accepted by the decision-maker as established. But some commentators have posited a duty on the part of an arbitral tribunal to investigate and to rule *ex officio* to prevent illegality or injustice. In particular, where there are signs of fraud, money laundering, or bribery, some have opined that arbitrators should seek evidence from independent sources. *See e.g.* Bernardo Cremades & David Cairns, *Transnational Policy in International Arbitral Decision-Making: the Cases of Bribery, Money Laundering and Fraud*, in DOSSIERS OF THE ICC INSTITUTE OF WORLD BUSINESS LAW—MONEY LAUNDERING, CORRUPTION AND FRAUD 65 (2003); Domitille Baizeau & Tessa Hayes, *The Arbitral Tribunal's Duty and Power to Address Corruption Sua Sponte*, in INTERNATIONAL ARBITRATION AND THE RULE OF LAW: CONTRIBUTION AND CONFORMITY, ICCA Congress Series Vol. 19, 225–65 (Andrea Menaker ed. 2017); Vladimir Khvalei, *Using Red*

8.91 An ICSID tribunal's obligation to act *ex officio* appears strongest with regard to jurisdiction, where the ICSID Rules suggest that the tribunal should build a defence in the absent respondent's stead.[257] As Professor Schreuer explains:

> As a consequence of default, the procedure is no longer adversarial. The initiative is shifted to the tribunal, which must examine the cooperating party's submissions on its own motion. This puts an extra burden on the tribunal but also on the cooperating party. The latter may be called upon to prove assertions which might otherwise be accepted as uncontested.[258]

8.92 The default provisions of the ICSID rules were analyzed and applied in *Goetz v. Burundi*,[259] where the Respondent selected an arbitrator, but did not appear at an initial hearing—ostensibly because an embargo prevented its lawyers from making the trip to Paris. Later, Burundi failed to submit any written pleadings or to appear at the merits hearing, despite extensions of time granted by the tribunal.[260] At the hearing, the tribunal took a proactive approach to the establishment of fact, posing a range of questions to claimant's counsel and witnesses and requesting additional evidence.[261] In rendering its decision, the tribunal presented the dilemma of default, drawing guidance from the ICJ decision in the *Nicaragua* case:

> The Tribunal deeply regrets that the Respondent, while it has not defaulted in the proper sense of the term, has declined to present its case. As the International Court of Justice has stated, this kind of situation "obviously has a negative impact on the sound administration of justice." By not submitting a Counter-Memorial, by not appearing at the hearing, by not submitting to the Tribunal any comments other than requests for extensions of time or suspension of the case, the Republic of Burundi has deprived the Tribunal of the assistance that the presentation of argument or submission of at least some evidence would have provided ... The Tribunal, like the

---

Flags to Prevent Arbitration from Becoming a Safe Harbor for Contracts that Disguise Corruption, 24 ICC Int'l. Court Arb. Bull., Special Supplement 15 *et seq.* (2013); Yas Banifatemi, *The Impact of Corruption on "Gateway Issues" of Arbitrability, Jurisdiction, Admissibility and Procedural Issues*, in Addressing Issues of Corruption in Commercial and Investment Arbitration, Dossiers of the ICC Institute of World Business Law 16 *et seq.* (Domitille Baizeau & Richard H. Kreindler eds. 2015); Teresa Giovannini, *Ex Officio Powers to Investigate: When Do Arbitrators Cross the Line?*, in Stories from The Hearing Room: Experience from Arbitral Practice (Essays in Honour of Michael E. Schneider) 60 (Domitille Baizeau & Bernd Ehle eds. 2015).

[257] ICSID Rules, *supra* note 8, art. 42(3)–(4). The ICSID approach to the problem is directly inspired by the ICJ Statute, *supra* note 250, art. 53, which provides:

1. Whenever one of the parties does not appear before the Court, or fails to defend its case, the other party may call upon the Court to decide in favor of its claim.
2. The Court must, before doing so, satisfy itself, not only that it has jurisdiction ... but also that the claim is well founded in fact and law.

[258] Schreuer et al., *supra* note 61, at 712. *See also* Note E to Arbitration Rule 42 of 1968, 1 ICSID Rep. 104.

[259] *Antoine Goetz et al. v. Burundi*, ICSID Case No. ARB/95/3, Award of 10 Feb. 1999, 15 ICSID Rev.—For. Inv. L.J. 457 (2000).

[260] *Id.* at paras. 35–46.

[261] *Id.* at para. 46.

> [International Court of Justice], certainly bears the duty to verify the arguments of the appearing Party, but nevertheless it would be impossible for us to confirm their exactitude in every detail—a task which, in certain cases and due to the absence of any contradiction, could prove practically impossible.[262]

H. Appointment of Arbitrators

The appointment of arbitrators is one of the most important phases of the arbitration process. It is therefore unsurprising that there is a massive literature on the science and art of selecting members of an arbitral tribunal.[263] **8.93**

The majority of international arbitration tribunals in disputes of significant size are appointed in a similar way. Under all the major international arbitration rules, the parties may agree to a sole arbitrator (or any odd number of arbitrators, for that matter), but absent such agreement, a panel of three individuals will decide their dispute. As noted earlier, many practitioners consider that the increased expertise, breadth of knowledge, and consultation that results from a three-member tribunal makes such a panel less likely to err in its deliberations, and therefore the **8.94**

[262] *Id.* at paras. 53–56 (internal cites omitted). The *Goetz* case raises echoes of the venerable Libyan oil concession cases, where several arbitrators were disturbed by Libya's absence and resolved to fill in for the respondent State in critically reviewing the claimant's case. One of the best known of the resulting awards came in the *BP v. Libya* case, based upon the breach of a concession agreement. There, the arbitrator, Judge Gunnar Lagergren, clearly struggled with these issues in assessing the claims before him, concluding: "With respect to the analysis of facts and their legal implications the Tribunal has had the benefit of argument presented by the Claimant alone. However, the Tribunal has felt both entitled and compelled to undertake an independent examination of the legal issues deemed relevant by it, and to engage in considerable legal research going beyond the confines of the materials relied upon by the Claimant. The conclusions in the Award therefore are based on a broader consideration of the issues than that permitted by the format of the Claimant's argument in support of its claims. Thus, the Tribunal to the greatest extent possible has endeavored to eliminate any inherent adverse effects for the Respondent of its decision not to appear as a party in the proceedings." *British Petroleum Exploration Co. (Libya) Ltd. v. Libya*, Award on the Merits of Dec. 10, 1973, 53 I.L.R. 297 (1979).

[263] *See generally* Gavin Griffith, *Constitution of Arbitral Tribunals: The Duty of Impartiality in Tribunals or Choose your Arbitrator Wisely*, 16 The Arbitrator: J. of the Institute of Arbitrators Australia 229 (1998); Wendy Miles, *Practical Issues for Appointment of Arbitrators*, 20 J. Int'l Arb. 219 (2003); Douglas E. McLaren, *Party-Appointed vs. List-Appointed Arbitrators*, 20 J. Int'l Arb. 233 (2003); Chiara Giorgetti, *The Arbitral Tribunal: Selection and Replacement of Arbitrators*, in Litigating International Investment Disputes: A Practitioner's Guide 143–72 (2014); Michael Waibel & Yanhui Wu, *Are Arbitrators Political?*, ASIL Research Forum 13 (Nov. 5, 2011) (noting that "the parties to investment arbitration cases and especially their counsel spend a great deal of time and effort to scrutinize the backgrounds of arbitrators, their relationship with the parties, published works and prior appointments. The time spent on choosing the right arbitrators suggests that the personality and background of the arbitrators matters substantially for arbitration outcomes"); Wendy Miles, *International Arbitrator Appointment*, 57 Disp. Res. J. 36 (2002). *See further* George H. Aldrich, *The Selection of Arbitrators*, in The Iran-United States Claims Tribunal and the Process of International Claims Resolution (David Caron & John Crook eds. 2000) (discussing in some detail the process for choosing the third-country arbitrators at the Iran–US Claims Tribunal).

additional cost and time involved, when compared to a sole arbitrator is, in most cases, considered to be justified.[264] As a result, a tribunal of three is generally advisable in any case where arbitration costs are not a primary concern.

8.95 In cases adjudicated by a three-person tribunal, each party first names one arbitrator (as previously mentioned, the claimant often names an arbitrator as part of its Request for Arbitration).[265] The President (or Chairman, as the third arbitrator is sometimes called) is then jointly selected, either by the parties (under the ICSID Rules),[266] by the two party-appointed arbitrators (under the UNCITRAL Rules),[267] or by the arbitral institution.[268]

8.96 If the parties fail to appoint arbitrators by the stipulated deadline, or if the party-appointed arbitrators cannot agree upon a chairman, then this task falls to the appointing authority.[269] In ICSID arbitration, this role is fulfilled by the ICSID Secretariat,[270] while under the UNCITRAL Rules the Permanent Court of Arbitration in The Hague selects a person or institution to serve as appointing authority.[271] When acting as the appointing authority and requested to appoint a sole or presiding arbitrator, the PCA Secretary-General will generally follow the list-procedure envisaged in the UNCITRAL Arbitration Rules.[272] In accordance with the UNCITRAL Rules, the Secretary-General will exercise his discretion when requested to appoint an arbitrator for a defaulting party. The Secretary-General's choice of arbitrators is not limited to any particular pool of candidates, and can therefore choose the most appropriate person for the matter at hand.

---

264 Nevertheless, some investment disputes have been presided by sole arbitrators. *See e.g. Misima Mines Pty. Ltd. v. Papua New Guinea*, ICSID Case No. ARB/96/2; *Gruslin v. Malaysia*, ICSID Case No. ARB/94/1; *Pantechniki S.A. Contractors & Engineers v. Albania*, ICSID Case No. ARB/07/21; *Malaysian Historical Salvors, SDN, BHD v. Malaysia*, ICSID Case No. ARB/05/10.

265 2017 ICC Rules, *supra* note 31, art. 12(4); SCC Rules, *supra* note 105, art. 6; 2010 UNCITRAL Rules, *supra* note 7, art. 9(1). Note, however, that according to 2017 ICC Rules art. 12(2), where the parties have not agreed upon the number of arbitrators, the Court will appoint a sole arbitrator, unless the Court finds the dispute to warrant the appointment of three.

266 Washington Convention, *supra* note 8, art. 37(2)(b).

267 2010 UNCITRAL Rules, *supra* note 7, art. 9(1). Another common method of forming the arbitration tribunal is known as the "list method," whereby the appointing institution provides list from which each party strikes names. The parties then rank remaining candidates, and the appointing institution appoints the highest-ranked remaining candidates as a panel. This method is also not infrequently used to select the chairman of a panel.

268 2017 ICC Rules, *supra* note 31, art. 12(3).

269 On the institutional process of selecting arbitrators, *see* Eva Muller, *How Do International Institutions Select Arbitrators?*, 17 J. Int'l Arb. 157 (2000). *See also* David Gaukrodger, *Appointing Authorities and the Selection of Arbitrators in Investor–State Dispute Settlement: An Overview*, OECD Consultation Paper (March 2018).

270 A.A. de Fina, *Different Strokes for Different Folks: Institutional Appointment of Arbitrators*, Arb. & Disp. Res. L.J. 31–35 (2000).

271 UNCITRAL Rules, *supra* note 7, art. 7(2). Frequently, the PCA designates the ICSID Secretariat as the appointing authority in investor–State arbitration.

272 1976 UNCITRAL Rules, *supra* note 7, art. 6(3); 2010 UNCITRAL Rules, *supra* note 7, art. 8(2).

Much has been written about the task of choosing the optimal candidate for party-appointed arbitrator.[273] Basic qualifications include a nationality other than that of the opposing party, a command of the language of the proceeding (and, possibly, the primary language of the underlying documents), technical and legal knowledge appropriate to the dispute, organizational skills, and availability.[274] However, other less tangible attributes may be equally important in the selection of an arbitrator, making the appointment process more of an art than a science. Some of these characteristics include decisiveness, procedural competence, sound judgment, and—perhaps most importantly—persuasiveness. The ability to persuade is essential, because while all three arbitrators must be unbiased and independent of the parties, in practice each party-appointed arbitrator may find himself in the position of explaining the positions of the party that appointed him to the chairman, who is effectively the final decision-maker in the arbitration. **8.97**

One requirement in all the major arbitration rules and most national laws is that arbitrators be impartial and independent.[275] Under the UNCITRAL arbitration **8.98**

[273] *See e.g.* Andreas Lowenfeld, *The Party-Appointed Arbitrator in International Controversies*, 30 Tex. Int'l L.J. 59 (1995); Claudia T. Salomon, *Selecting an International Arbitrator: Five Factors to Consider*, 17 Mealey's Int'l Arb. Rep. 25 (Oct. 2002); Constantine Partasides, *The Art of Selecting the Right Arbitrator*, lecture, London School of Economics, London (Nov. 9, 2011).

[274] David Hacking, comments at meeting of Chicago International Dispute Resolution Association, Chicago, IL, Oct. 15, 1999.

[275] On the challenge of arbitrators for lack of impartiality or independence, *see generally* Maria Nicole Cleis, The Independence and Impartiality of ICSID Arbitrators Current Case Law, Alternative Approaches, and Improvement Suggestions (2017); Charles N. Brower, *The Ethics of Arbitration: Perspectives from a Practicing International Arbitrator*, 5 Berkeley J. Int'l L. Publicist 1, 3 (2010); Chiara Giorgetti, *Challenges of International Investment Arbitrators : How Does it Work, and Does it Work?*, 7 World Arb. & Mediation Rev. 303 (2013); Audley Sheppard, *Arbitrator Independence in ICSID Arbitration*, in International Investment Law for the 21st Century: Essays in Honour of Christoph Schreuer 131, 133–36 (Christina Binder et al. eds. 2009); Noah Rubins & Bernhard Lauterburg, *Independence, Impartiality and Duty of Disclosure in Investment Arbitration*, in Investment and Commercial Arbitration: Similarites and Divergences 153 (Christina Knahr et al. eds. 2010); Nathalie Bernasconi-Osterwalder et al., *Arbitrator Independence and Impartiality: Examining the Dual Role of Arbitrator and Counsel*, IV Annual Forum for Developing Country Investment Negotiators, Background Papers, 8–16 (2010); Stavros Brekoulakis, *Systemic Bias and the Institution of International Arbitration: A New Approach to Arbitral Decision-Making*, 4 J. Int'l Disp. Settlement 553 (2013); Judith Levine, *Dealing with Arbitrator "Issue Conflicts" in International Arbitration*, 61 Disp. Resol. J. 60 (2006); Markham Ball, *Probity Deconstructed: How Helpful, Really, are the New International Bar Association Guidelines on Conflicts of Interest in International Arbitration?*, 21 Arb. Int'l 323, 326 (2005); Marie Öhrström, *Decisions by the SCC Institute Regarding Challenge of Arbitrators*, 1 Stockholm Arb. Rep. 35 (2002); Dominique Hascher, *ICC Practice in Relation to the Appointment, Confirmation, Challenge and Replacement of Arbitrators*, 6(2) ICC Int'l Ct. Arb. Bull. 4, 6 (November 1995). *See also* Doak Bishop & Lucy Reed, *Practical Guidelines for Interviewing, Selecting, and Challenging Party-Appointed Arbitrators in International Commercial Arbitration*, 14 Arb. Int'l 395, 408–09 (1998); W. Michael Tupman, *Challenge and Disqualification of Arbitrators in International Commercial Arbitration*, 38 Int'l & Comp. LQ 26, 50 (1989); Craig et al., *supra* note 28, at 203–36; Martin Hunter & Jan Paulsson, *A Code of Ethics for Arbitrators in International Commercial Arbitration*, 13 Int'l Bus.

rules, for example, an arbitrator can be disqualified for any fact that could be seen as giving rise to justifiable doubts as to the arbitrator's impartiality and independence.[276] By the same token, an arbitrator, from the time of his or her appointment and throughout the arbitral proceedings, must without delay disclose any such circumstances to the parties and the other arbitrators. In the investment arbitration context, this basic rule can complicate the composition of the tribunal, since certain connections with one of the States party to the dispute could be considered compromising.[277] Generally speaking, while arbitrators are frequently challenged on grounds of lack of impartiality and independence, such challenges are rarely successful.[278] One of the best-known instances of repeated arbitrator challenges came in *ConocoPhillips v. Venezuela*, where the respondent advanced six separate challenges against various members of the tribunal, all of which were unsuccessful.[279] However, in *Blue Bank v. Venezuela*, the Chairman of the ICSID Administrative Council upheld a challenge by Venezuela against the arbitrator appointed by the claimant, based on the arbitrator's partnership in a law firm whose New York and Caracas offices were acting as claimant's counsel in another ICSID case against Venezuela.[280] In *Burlington v. Ecuador*, the Chairman of the ICSID Administrative Council removed the claimant's party-appointed arbitrator for having been appointed multiple times by the claimant's law firm, a circumstance that he concluded "manifestly evidences an appearance of lack of impartiality . . . ."[281] In *Caratube v. Kazakhstan*, the respondent's party-appointed arbitrator was removed due to his prior appointment by the respondent in another, very similar dispute, leading to "an objective circumstance demonstrating

Law. 153, 155 (1985); and H.L. Yu & Lawrence Shore, *Independence, Impartiality and Immunity of Arbitrators—US and English Perspectives*, 52 Int'l & Comp. LQ 935, 963 (2003).

276 2013 UNCITRAL Rules, *supra* note 7, arts. 11–13; *see also* 2017 ICC Rules, *supra* note 31, art. 7(1); 2014 LCIA Rules, *supra* note 128, art. 5(2).

277 The International Bar Association has promulgated Guidelines meant to assist arbitrators and counsel in determining when circumstances exist that might give rise to justifiable doubts as an arbitrator's impartiality and independence. IBA Guidelines on Conflicts of Interest in International Arbitration, available at https://www.ibanet.org/ENews_Archive/IBA_July_2008_ENews_ArbitrationMultipleLang.aspx. *See generally* Nathalie Voser & Neomi Rao, *Background Information on the IBA Guidelines on Conflicts of Interest in International Arbitration*, 5 Bus. L. Int'l 433, 442 (2004).

278 *See* Baiju S. Vasani & Shaun A. Palmer, *Challenge and Disqualification of Arbitrators at ICSID: A New Dawn?*, 30(1) ICSID Rev.—For. Inv. L.J. 1–23 (2014) (noting that prior to the *Blue Bank* decision, "there had been over 40 challenges to arbitrators appointed in ICSID arbitrations. In several instances, the arbitrator resigned voluntarily, but, in the remaining cases (where the challenge was adjudicated), only one challenge had been upheld and 35 rejected").

279 For an overview, *see ConocoPhillips Petrozuata B.V., ConocoPhillips Hamaca B.V. and ConocoPhillips Gulf of Paria B.V. v. Venezuela*, Decision on the Proposal to Disqualify L. Yves Fortier, Q.C., Arbitrator of Dec. 15, 2015.

280 *See Blue Bank Int'l. & Trust (Barbados) Ltd. v. Venezuela*, ICSID Case No. ARB/12/20, Decision on the Parties' Proposals to Disqualify a Majority of the Tribunal of Nov. 12, 2013.

281 *See Burlington Resources Inc. v. Ecuador*, ICSID Case No. ARB/08/5, Decision on the Proposal for Disqualification of Professor Francisco Orrego Vicuña of Dec. 13, 2013.

his inability to exercise independent and impartial judgment in the present arbitration."[282]

8.99 In order to determine proper qualifications, many counsel to arbitrating parties conduct an interview of arbitrator candidates, carefully limited to avoid tainting the candidate with any appearance of bias.[283] As prominent arbitrator A.A. de Fina explains:

> Whilst interview for a sole arbitrator may properly be conducted by both parties to an arbitration, the nature of a party appointment will mean in most instances that only the appointing party through their lawyers will conduct the interview. Nothing can be done or said at such an interview which may prejudice the prospective appointee if ultimately appointed, or which might give rise to challenge and disqualification. An interview must therefore be limited to such matters as availability, conflict, experience, training, qualification, specialist expertise and the like. Under no circumstances can aspects going to the nature of the dispute or its merits be raised or canvassed even indirectly. In any event, the interview should be carried out only by counsel for a party and in the absence of that party.

8.100 In addition to the possibility of an interview (a practice more widely accepted in North America than in Europe and Asia), counsel often scour the candidate's published writings and other professional activities, seeking to ascertain whether the individual would be naturally disposed to the appointing party's positions. A claimant in investment arbitration, for example, will often look for an arbitrator who has represented clients against governments or State-owned enterprises, or who has opined positively about expanded protection standards for investors.[284] In the words of one practitioner:

> rational disputants with so much at stake want to retain some measure of control over who decides the dispute. They want to choose their own arbitrator and to constitute a panel of arbitrators who can truly appreciate, from personal experience or involvement, the points each makes and *particularly* the point of view of the selecting party. Thus, a rational party will start with a field including only disinterested candidates, whose integrity is unimpeachable ... but he will then choose those who will give him the greatest confidence that he will prevail.[285]

8.101 Therefore, additional criteria often play a role in arbitrator selection. For example, an individual with an established reputation within the industry in which the dispute arose or with regard to the legal issues in dispute may have a disproportionate influence upon his tribunal colleagues and upon the final result. Likewise,

[282] *See Caratube Int'l. Oil Co. LLP and Devincci Salah Hourani v. Kazakhstan*, ICSID Case No. ARB/13/13, Decision on the Proposal for Disqualification of Bruno Boesch of Mar. 20, 2014.

[283] A.A. de Fina, *The Party Appointed Arbitrator in International Arbitrations: Role and Selection*, 15 Arb. Int'l 381, 392 (1999).

[284] On the selection of arbitrators on the basis of their ideological inclinations, see Chiara Giorgetti, *Who Decides Who Decides in International Investment Arbitration?*, 35 U. Pa. J. Int'l. L. 431, 446 (2013).

[285] James D. Wangelin, *Effective Selection of Arbitrators in International Arbitration* (1999).

a forceful personality (assuming that the arbitrator agrees with the appointing party's position) will allow the candidate to make his voice heard over that of the other party-appointed arbitrator.[286]

8.102 The participation of State parties has an important effect on the appointment of arbitrators. The claimant may seek a candidate with a great deal of experience and recognition, since it is widely perceived that only well-established jurists have the resolve to render large awards against governments, which may have serious economic consequences for the country involved. From the opposite perspective, respondent governments may want to be sure that their party-appointed arbitrator is familiar with conditions in their country, including humanitarian and development concerns that they may feel justify their conduct vis-à-vis foreign investors.[287]

8.103 Despite the importance of selecting arbitrators, it is difficult to collect information about arbitrators' "decision history" and "management skills," due to the confidential treatment of arbitration awards. Some observers believe that this lack of information undermines transparency decreases arbitrator diversity.[288]

I. Initial Session of the Tribunal

8.104 Once the tribunal has been formed, it will usually call upon the parties to attend, either in person or telephonically, an initial conference or hearing to discuss preliminary matters and to confirm the agreement of the parties or the decision of the tribunal on issues of situs, language, arbitral rules and modifications thereto, and the like.[289] The tribunal usually circulates a draft agenda, inviting the parties' comments well in advance of the first session. ICSID has developed a template draft agenda which takes into account standard procedural items, such as the procedural calendar. The draft agenda is often accompanied by a draft procedural order which guides the parties in reaching agreements on specific issues.[290]

---

[286] For more on suggested criteria for choosing arbitrators, *see* Claudia T. Salomon, *Selecting an International Arbitrator: Five Factors to Consider*, Mealey's Int'l Arb. Rep., Oct. 2002, at 25.

[287] At least one practitioner has opined that some developing governments select arbitrators from a very short list, such that in one case a nominee had served fifteen times in various proceedings as the government's party-appointed arbitrator. C. Mark Baker, *Fulbright & Jaworski Conference on Arbitration*, Washington, DC, Sept. 26, 2002.

[288] There are fewer opportunities for selecting women or arbitrators from outside North America and Europe, *see* Catherine A. Rogers & José María de la Jara, *Generating Needed Information about Arbitrators, One Arbitration at a Time*, Kluwer Arbitration Blog (Sept. 15, 2018), available at http://arbitrationblog.kluwerarbitration.com/2018/09/15/generating-needed-information-about-arbitrators-one-arbitration-at-a-time/.

[289] For a brief analysis of the first session of the tribunal, *see* Interview with Albert Jan van den Berg on the First Session (video), available at https://livestream.com/ICSID/events/3915475/videos/81480656.

[290] *See* International Council for Commercial Arbitration and Permanent Court of Arbitration, *ICCA Drafting Sourcebook for Logistical Matters in Procedural Orders*, ICCA Reports, No. 2 (2015);

Most frequently, the initial session will also be used to establish the initial briefing schedule, which often begins with a Statement of Claim and Statement of Defense from the claimant and respondent, respectively.[291] Under the ICC Rules, the "Terms of Reference" are often negotiated, drafted, and/or signed during the initial session. As previously explained, this document, unique to the ICC system, is used to frame the issues in dispute between the parties, to encapsulate their respective views of the facts, and to set forth basic procedural aspects of the case for the future reference of the parties and the tribunal.[292] **8.105**

Under all major arbitration rules, including ICC, ICSID, and UNCITRAL, the parties are free to agree upon any legal place of the arbitration (the "*arbitral situs*"), and to jointly designate one or more languages in which the proceedings will be conducted. However, the ICSID Rules and Washington Convention provide that where there is no contrary agreement of the parties, hearings will take place at the World Bank in Washington, DC.[293] The UNCITRAL Rules require the arbitral tribunal to determine the place of arbitration if the parties cannot agree.[294] Under other arbitration regimes as well, the arbitrators (or the arbitral institution, in the case of the ICC) retain wide discretion in choosing the arbitral situs that best suits the needs of the parties to the dispute.[295] **8.106**

The decision to designate a particular country as the place of arbitration almost always brings with it a choice of *lex arbitri*, importing to a large degree the mandatory rules of the forum with regard to the conduct of arbitration, ethical standards for counsel and arbitrators, and interim measures.[296] Perhaps most importantly, if arbitration is not conducted within the ICSID system, the arbitral situs will be the proper place to challenge any eventual award in national courts.[297] The tribunal in *UPS v. Canada* provided a thorough analysis of the **8.107**

Veijo Heiskanen, *Key to Efficiency in International Arbitration*, 30(3) ICSID Rev.—For. Inv. L.J. 481–85 (2015); Albert Jan van den Berg, *Time and Costs: Issues and Initiatives from an Arbitrator's Perspective*, 28(1) ICSID Rev.—For. Inv. L.J. 218–22 (2013); Nassib G. Ziadé, *Achieving Efficiency in Arbitration: The Role of the Institutions*, 25(1) News from ICSID (2008); Jan Paulsson, *The Timely Arbitrator: Reflections on the Böckstiegel Method*, 22(1) Arb. Int'l. 19–26 (2006).

[291] *ADF Group Inc. v. U.S.A.*, ICSID Case No. ARB(AF)/00/1, NAFTA, Minutes of the First Session of the Tribunal, Feb. 3, 2001.

[292] 2017 ICC Rules, *supra* note 31, art. 23. *See* Section B.2.a.

[293] ICSID Rules, *supra* note 8, art. 13(1); Washington Convention, *supra* note 8, art. 63. It is important to bear in mind that the place of arbitration is practically irrelevant in ICSID arbitration, since the ICSID Convention insulates the proceedings from all court intervention, including for the set-aside of awards. Since there is no legal "seat" of an ICSID arbitration, the venue for hearings is purely a matter of logistics and convenience.

[294] 2010 UNCITRAL Rules, *supra* note 7, art. 18.

[295] 2017 ICC Rules, *supra* note 31, art. 18(1); 2017 SCC Rules, *supra* note 122, art. 25. Herman Verbist, *The Practice of the ICC International Court of Arbitration with Regard to the Fixing of the Place of Arbitration*, 12 Arb. Int'l 347 (1996). UNCITRAL, Notes on Organizing Arbitral Proceedings, U.N. Doc. A/CN.9/410, arts. 21–23, available at https://www.uncitral.org/pdf/english/texts/arbitration/arb-notes/arb-notes-e.pdf.

[296] *See e.g.* Rubins, *supra* note 159, at 23.

[297] New York Convention, *supra* note 6, art. V(1)(e).

considerations relevant to the arbitrators' determination of the arbitral situs. In that case, the U.S. claimant requested that the UNCITRAL arbitration take place in Washington, DC., Boston, or New York, while the respondent sought the designation of a Canadian city as the arbitral situs. The tribunal considered a range of factors, including: (1) the suitability of the local arbitration law; (2) whether the situs country had signed the New York Convention; (3) the convenience of the parties and arbitrators, including travel distances; (4) the availability and cost of support services; and (5) the proximity of the subject matter in dispute and the location of relevant evidence.[298] After assessing all of these factors, the tribunal ruled that the arbitration would take place in Washington.[299]

8.108 Generally speaking, each arbitration will have one, or possibly two, "working languages." Where a single language is designated, all pleadings (oral and written) must be made in that language, and in some cases supporting documentary evidence must be translated into the working language. In bilingual arbitration (relatively rare in contractual cases),[300] each party may choose which of the working languages it will use to make its submissions. In contractual arbitration, the working language of the arbitration is normally designated in the arbitration clause itself. Investment treaties, however, almost never indicate any particular working language for dispute resolution. The UNCITRAL Rules provide no default language either, leaving full discretion in this matter to the arbitral tribunal in the absence of party agreement.[301] The ICC and LCIA Rules attribute particular importance to the prevailing language of an underlying contract (if one exists) in the arbitrators' determination of the language of the proceedings.[302] The ICSID Rules, meanwhile, specify that French, English, and Spanish are the

[298] *United Parcel Service Inc. v. Canada*, Decision of the Tribunal on the Place of Arbitration of Oct. 17, 2001, available at http://www.state.gov/documents/organization/6032.pdf.

[299] *Id.* at paras. 16–19. While the factors considered were nearly evenly balanced between a U.S. and Canadian situs, the decision of a Canadian court to partially set aside a NAFTA award in *Metalclad*, described in Section L.2.a.ii, *infra*, proved decisive.

[300] UNCITRAL Notes, *supra* note 295, at art. 19; Frank-Bernd Weigan, Practitioner's Handbook on International Commercial Arbitration, paras. 14.393 *et seq.* (2009). For authorities suggesting that one language is normally appropriate, and that increasingly the language chosen is English, *see* Bond, *supra* note 142, at 65 ("simultaneous interpretation at hearings and translation of all documents into two or more languages are enormously expensive and time-consuming"); Markham Ball, *Just Do It—Drafting the Arbitration Clause in an International Agreement*, 10(4) J. Int'l Arb. 29 (1993) ("Normally, parties from most countries will agree to English. Proceedings in two languages with simultaneous or sequential translations are possible, if expensive and somewhat awkward"); Serge Lazareff, *The Language of Institutional Arbitration*, 8(1) ICC Bull. 18 (1997) (suggesting that English is the most common medium of communication in the international business community, and a *lingua franca* for foreign investment). *But cf.* Paulsson et al., *supra* note 9, at 46 (multiple languages "ensures that the tribunal has the power to recognize and deal with the difficulties that one party might have in properly presenting its case in a foreign language").

[301] 2010 UNCITRAL Rules, *supra* note 7, art. 19(1). *See also* 2017 SCC Rules, *supra* note 122, art. 26.

[302] 2017 ICC Rules, *supra* note 31, art. 20; 2014 LCIA Rules, *supra* note 128, art. 17.

official languages, and that another language can be selected only with the approval of the tribunal.[303] As previously noted, two languages can be selected under these rules, and if the parties cannot reach agreement, each side may select one of the three official languages, and both languages will be used in the proceeding.

J. Written Submissions

1. Statement of Claim and Statement of Defense

Generally, the first written submissions to the arbitral tribunal are the Statement of Claim and Statement of Defense. In the first of these submissions, the claimant lays out the legal theories upon which he will rely, and states the factual basis that will underlie each argument. The respondent's Statement of Defense likewise presents each counter-argument, and responds to the factual allegations of the Statement of Claim. Under most arbitration rules, any jurisdictional objections must be raised no later than the Statement of Defense. It is also at this point that the respondent should present any counterclaims it wishes to interpose against the claimant.[304] **8.109**

2. Splitting the case into phases

If the claimant raises objections to the jurisdiction of the tribunal or other discrete issues of law or fact, the tribunal may divide the arbitral procedure into two or more parts, where the tribunal's analysis is focused only on a limited range of issues in each phase.[305] Frequently, bifurcation or trifurcation[306] is at the request of one of the parties (most often the respondent), but this is not universally so. Some arbitration rules, including the ICSID Additional Facility Rules, explicitly provide for separating briefing and oral hearings on competence (jurisdiction) and liability into component parts.[307] Such a division is **8.110**

---

[303] ICSID Rules, *supra* note 8, art. 22(1).

[304] 2014 LCIA Rules, *supra* note 128, art.15(3); UNCITRAL Rules, *supra* note 7, art. 21(3) ("or at a later stage in the arbitral proceedings if the arbitral tribunal decides that the delay was justified under the circumstances"); 2017 SCC Rules, *supra* note 122, art. 29(2)(iv). In ICC arbitration, counterclaims are normally to be presented in the Answer to the Request for Arbitration, but may be presented even after the signing of the Terms of Reference, with leave of the tribunal. 2017 ICC Rules, *supra* note 31, arts. 5(5), 19; Derains & Schwartz, *supra* note 39, at 73. Note that under most procedural rules, the Statement of Claim and Statement of Defense may be amended later in the proceeding, with the leave of the tribunal.

[305] Blackaby et al., *supra* note 1, at paras. 5.115–5.116; Massimo V. Benedettelli, *To Bifurcate or Not To Bifurcate? That is the (Ambiguous) Question*, 29(3) Arb. Int'l. 493–506 (2013).

[306] Splitting an arbitration case into phases is normally referred to as "bifurcation," regardless of the number of stages of the proceedings. Thomas J. Tallerico & J. Adam Behrendt, *The Use of Bifurcation and Direct Testimony Witness Statements in International Commercial Arbitration Proceedings*, 20(3) J. Int'l Arb. 295, 295–96 (2003).

[307] ICSID Additional Facility Arbitration Rules, *supra* note 101, art. 46(2), (4); *ADF Inc., supra* note 291.

designed to reduce the cost incurred by respondent States in connection with claims that are ultimately determined to fall outside the competence of an arbitral tribunal. Bifurcation also permits the parties and the arbitrators to focus discussions and deliberation on a limited universe of issues and evidence, and more clearly to analyze the questions posed during each phase. The issuance of partial awards on different aspects of a dispute may also provide the parties an opportunity to negotiate a solution to the dispute after the *bona fides* of the case are established.

8.111 One prominent arbitrator opines that separation of jurisdictional objections from the merits of a dispute is almost always preferable, unless "the facts on which the challenge to jurisdiction are based are so closely connected to the facts of the dispute as to be virtually inseparable."[308] He continues:

> It is a waste of time and money for an arbitral tribunal to have conducted an arbitration from beginning to end if its award then proves to be invalid for lack of jurisdiction ... it should hear arguments on the issue of jurisdiction as a preliminary matter and render an interim award on the point. This enables the parties to know where they stand at a relatively early stage.[309]

8.112 For similar reasons, some investment arbitration tribunals have divided cases into three phases, with a final round of pleadings on the quantum of damages, should liability of the respondent State be established.[310]

---

[308] Sigvard Jarvin, *Objections to Jurisdiction*, in THE LEADING ARBITRATORS' GUIDE TO INTERNATIONAL ARBITRATION 83, 88 (Lawrence W. Newman & Richard Hill eds. 2004). *See also Mesa Power Group, LLC v. Canada*, PCA Case No. 2012-17, Procedural Order No. 2 of Jan. 18, 2013, at para. 16 ("[I]t is good ... to let the parties 'know where they stand' ... at an early stage and not to impose the burden of fully fledged proceedings on a party that disputes being subject to arbitration"); Lucy Greenwood, *Does Bifurcation Really Promote Efficiency?*, 28(2) J. INT'L ARB. 105–11, 107 (2011).

[309] Jarvin, *id.*; Sigvard Jarvin, *La loi-type CNUDCI sur l'arbitrage commercial international*, in REVUE DE L'ARBITRAGE 518 (1996).

[310] *See e.g.* Tallerico & Behrendt, *supra* note 306, and sources cited therein. For example, *see Apotex Holdings Inc. and Apotex Inc. v. U.S.A.*, ICSID ARB(AF)/12/1, Procedural Order deciding bifurcation of Jan. 25, 2013. Tribunals have not always been successful in untangling issues of jurisdiction and liability. Indeed, despite its clear framing of the difference between jurisdiction and the merits, the *UPS* tribunal appears to have determined jurisdiction over the claim partly based on the strength of the claimant's substantive allegations of unfair and inequitable treatment. *United Parcel Service of America Inc. v. Canada*, Award on Jurisdiction of Nov. 22, 2002, at paras. 30–37, available at https://www.italaw.com/sites/default/files/case-documents/ita0884.pdf. Similarly, the tribunal in *Methanex v. U.S.A.* appeared to struggle with the division between preliminary and merits issues. In that case, the tribunal found that pursuant to NAFTA art. 1101, claimants must first demonstrate a "legally significant connection" between the disputed government measures and the harm caused. Because the claimant's merits case included allegations that the Governor of California had implemented measures to favor an American company at the expense of a Canadian competitor, Methanex was ultimately required to present evidence on the merits during the jurisdictional phase. *Methanex Corp. v. U.S.A.*, Preliminary Award on Jurisdiction and Admissibility of Aug. 7, 2002, at paras. 110–61.

3. Written submissions and documentary evidence

At both the jurisdictional phase (if any) and during proceedings on the merits of the case, the bulk of international arbitration is conducted through the parties' exchange of written memorials and supporting written evidence, which serve as the primary basis of decision for the arbitral tribunal.[311] The claimant submits a memorial, followed by the respondent's counter-memorial, the claimant's reply, and the respondent's rejoinder. While the parties may request further exchanges of pleadings, more than two exchanges during a single phase (jurisdiction, merits, damages, *etc.*) is relatively uncommon. **8.113**

The practice of evidence collection in international arbitration proceedings is something of a hybrid of civil law and common law traditions, and has been codified by the International Bar Association in its Rules on the Taking of Evidence in International Arbitration.[312] While these rules are not automatically binding on parties or arbitrators absent agreement, they are frequently adopted, either expressly or implicitly, by tribunals as guidelines for the conduct of the evidentiary portion of arbitral proceedings. As the IBA Rules indicate, international arbitration procedure differs from litigation practice in many countries, in that most direct witness testimony, both for fact and expert witnesses, is submitted in written, rather than oral, form. Witness statements therefore often make up a substantial portion of the parties' submissions.[313] Furthermore, the production of documents (known as "discovery" in U.S. court practice) is often limited.[314] According to the IBA Rules, each party is initially required to produce only the documents upon which it will rely. Additional documents can be obtained from the opposing side only by order of the tribunal, on the basis of a specific request: **8.114**

> Within the time ordered by the Arbitral Tribunal, any Party may submit to the Arbitral Tribunal a Request to Produce. A Request to Produce shall contain:
> (a) (i) a description of each requested Document sufficient to identify it, or
> (ii) a description in sufficient detail (including subject matter) of a narrow and specific requested category of Documents that are reasonably believed to exist; in the case of Documents maintained in electronic form, the requesting Party may, or the Arbitral Tribunal may order that it shall be required to, identify specific files, search terms, individuals or other means of searching for such Documents in an efficient and economical manner;

---

[311] *See generally* J. Gillis Wetter, *The Conduct of the Arbitration*, 2(2) J. Int'l Arb. 20–23 (1985).

[312] International Bar Association, Rules on the Taking of Evidence in International Arbitration, available at https://www.ibanet.org/ENews_Archive/IBA_30June_2010_Enews_Taking_of_Evidence_new_rules.aspx.

[313] George M. von Mehren & Claudia T. Salomon, *Submitting Evidence in International Arbitration: A Common Lawyer's Guide*, 20(3) J. Int'l Arb. 285 (2003); Tallerico & Behrendt, *supra* note 306.

[314] 2010 IBA Rules, *supra* note 176, art. 3. *See generally* Reto Marghitola, Document Production in International Arbitration (2015).

(b) a statement as to how the Documents requested are relevant to the case and material to its outcome; and
(c) (i) a statement that the Documents requested are not in the possession, custody or control of the requesting Party or a statement of the reasons why it would be unreasonably burdensome for the requesting Party to produce such Documents, and
(ii) statement of the reasons why the requesting Party assumes the Documents requested are in the possession, custody or control of another Party. [315]

K. Oral Argument

8.115 Under most international arbitration rules, the parties are free to forego oral hearings on any or all issues, but such hearings must generally take place if one of the parties so requests. Some arbitration rules leave ultimate discretion on the issue to the arbitration tribunal. The law of the place of arbitration may also contain provisions requiring oral hearings in certain circumstances.[316] Where it is up to the arbitrators to decide whether oral hearings should take place, the decision is likely to be influenced by a range of factors, including:

> on the one hand, that it is usually quicker and easier to clarify points at issue pursuant to a direct confrontation of arguments than on the basis of correspondence and, on the other hand, the travel and other cost of holding hearings, and that the need of finding acceptable dates for the hearings might delay the proceedings. The arbitral tribunal may wish to consult the parties on this matter.[317]

8.116 During hearings, some arbitrators consider it useful to limit the aggregate amount of time each party has to present oral statements and examine witnesses. In general, it is considered appropriate to allocate the available time equally to each side, unless the arbitral tribunal decides that a different allocation is justified. Before

---

[315] *Id.*, art. 3(2)–(3). Obtaining evidence from non-parties can be extremely difficult in arbitration proceedings. In the United States, parties to arbitration can obtain documents from third parties in two ways. First, the Federal Arbitration Act allows tribunals, but not parties independently, to obtain evidence from persons not party to the dispute (9 U.S.C. § 7). Another statute allows any interested party to request a discovery order from a U.S. district court (28 U.S.C. § 1782). For more on the applicability and limitations of these statutes in the collection of third-party evidence in international arbitration, *see* Hans Smit, *American Assistance to Litigation in Foreign and International Tribunals: Section 1782 of Title 28 of the U.S.C. Revisited*, 25 Syr. J. Int'l L. & Com. 1, 5–8 (1998); Johnson Schwartz, *Court-Assisted Discovery in Aid of International Commercial Arbitrations: Two Recent U.S. Cases Regarding the Applicability of 28 U.S.C. § 1782*, 15(9) J. Int'l Arb. 53 (1998); Brian Eric Bomstein & Julie M. Levitt, *Much Ado About 1782: A Look At Recent Problems With Discovery in the United States for Use in Foreign Litigation under 28 § 1782*, 20 U. Miami Inter-Am. L. Rev. 429 (1989); Jonathan Clark Green, *Are International Institutions Doing Their Job?*, 90 Am. Soc'y. Int'l L. Proc. 62, 70 (1996); Peter F. Schlosser, *Coordinated Transnational Interaction in Civil Litigation and Arbitration*, 12 Mich. J. Int'l L. 150, 170 n.84 (1990).

[316] UNCITRAL Notes, *supra* note 295, art. 74.

[317] *Id.*, art. 75.

deciding, the arbitral tribunal may wish to consult the parties as to how much time they think they will need.[318]

Arbitration rules typically give broad latitude to the arbitral tribunal to determine the order of presentations at the hearings. Within that latitude, practices differ, for example, as to whether opening or closing statements are heard and their level of detail; the sequence in which the claimant and the respondent present their opening statements, arguments, witnesses, and other evidence; and whether the respondent or the claimant has the last word. In view of such differences, or when no arbitration rules apply, it may foster efficiency of the proceedings if the arbitral tribunal clarifies to the parties, in advance of the hearings, the manner in which it will conduct the hearings, at least in broad terms.[319] **8.117**

The length of a hearing depends primarily on the complexity of the issues to be argued and the amount of witness evidence to be presented. The length also depends upon the procedural style used in the arbitration. Some arbitrators prefer to have evidence and arguments presented in writing before the hearings, with the oral phase focused on issues that have not been sufficiently clarified. Such arbitrators generally tend to plan shorter hearings than those who prefer that most of the evidence and arguments be presented to the arbitral tribunal orally in full detail.[320] A typical arbitration hearing will take five working days, and it is relatively uncommon for hearings to last more than ten working days. **8.118**

L. Award

1. Drafting and issuing the award

At each stage of the proceedings, oral argument is frequently followed by post-hearing briefs, after which the arbitrators deliberate and draft the award. It is difficult to generalize about the amount of time that normally elapses between the parties' final submissions and the release of the arbitrators' decision. While some arbitration rules establish a time limit for the issue of an award,[321] tribunals will not hesitate to ask the parties or the arbitral institution for additional time, and such an extension is unlikely to be refused. Rarely in investment arbitration does the tribunal return an award in less than four months, and delays of up to a year **8.119**

---

318 *Id.*, art. 78. Different allocations of time may be necessary if one party is presenting a large number of witnesses for cross-examination, while the other party is not.

319 *Id.*, art. 80.

320 *Id.*, art. 81.

321 2017 ICC Rules, *supra* note 31, art. 31(1) (setting six-month time limit for issue of award after signing of Terms of Reference). The Court may extend the time limit pursuant to a reasoned request from the arbitral tribunal or on its own initiative if it decides it is necessary to do so.

are relatively common.[322] The most common period between the end of hearings and the release of a decision appears to be six to eight months. In contract cases of limited size or complexity, the amount of time may be less.

8.120 The award drafting process usually begins with a meeting of the arbitrators, without the presence of the parties. While this deliberation session sometimes takes place immediately after the close of oral hearings, it may take more time for the arbitrators to gather, particularly if the schedule calls for an additional round of post-hearing briefing. During the closed discussion session, the arbitrators will discuss the merits of each side's presentation, attempting to come to a consensus on the proper outcome of the case. After deliberations are complete, the chairman is normally charged with writing the first draft of the award, attempting to incorporate the concerns and comments of his co-arbitrators in order to achieve a unanimous decision, if possible. The chairman then circulates the draft to the other members of the tribunal for comment. The process of comments and redrafting may repeat several times, leading finally to the issue of the award. If one of the arbitrators does not agree with the conclusions of the majority, he may issue a separate or dissenting opinion, which will be delivered to the parties along with the award. A separate or dissenting opinion has no legal force, and normally will not affect the binding nature of the majority decision on the parties.[323]

2. Challenge of awards

8.121 One of the primary attractions of the arbitral system is that the vast majority of awards are voluntarily implemented, either with the respondent's payment of amounts ordered by the tribunal, or the abandonment of the dispute (should the claimant be defeated). This widespread compliance with arbitration awards is due in large part to the enforcement provisions of international treaties, which ensure that in most circumstances a losing respondent will be unable to avoid execution on assets in scores of national court jurisdictions around the world. Nevertheless, it is not uncommon that losing parties seek to alter or overturn arbitration awards, where they are dissatisfied with the result or perceive defects in the process that led to the award.

[322] Global Arbitration Review, *How Long Is Too Long to Wait for an Award?* (Feb. 18, 2016), available at https://vannin.com/press/pdfs/18-2-16_How_long_is_too_long_to_wait_for_an_award_.pdf.

[323] Alan Redfern, *Dissenting Opinions in International Commercial Arbitration: The Good, the Bad, and the Ugly*, 20 Arb. Int'l 223 (2004); Jacques Werner, *Dissenting Opinions: Beyond Fears*, 9(4) J. Int'l Arb. 23 (1992); Laurence Shore & Kenneth Juan Figueroa, *Dissents, Concurrences and a Necessary Divide between Investment and Commercial Arbitration*, 3 Global Arb. Rev. 18, 20 (2008); Albert Jan van den Berg, *Dissenting Opinions by Party-Appointed Arbitrators*, in Investment Arbitration in Looking to the Future: Essays on International Law in Honor of W. Michael Reisman 821–43 (Mahnoush Arsanjani et al. eds. 2011).

a. Enforcement and challenge in national courts

i. Enforcement of awards The vast majority of arbitration awards, including those against State parties, are satisfied voluntarily.[324] Part of the reason for this widespread compliance is the powerful transnational effect of such awards under the terms of the New York Convention of 1958.[325] The New York Convention requires courts in signatory States to recognize the binding nature of foreign arbitral awards, and to enforce such awards according to local rules of procedure.[326] The judgment debtor has only limited grounds upon which it may block enforcement of the award through the courts.[327] **8.122**

When the New York Convention was drafted, many States were hesitant to become parties, fearing that its provisions would conflict with national laws.[328] It was for this reason that the United States did not accede to the New York Convention until 1970, when Congress harmonized the Federal Arbitration Act.[329] By that time, the New York Convention had already been widely ratified, and U.S. businesses faced difficulties enforcing awards in States that offered its benefits only to awards rendered in other member States.[330] **8.123**

[324] Martinez, *supra* note 2, at 493.

[325] New York Convention, *supra* note 6. *See also* Martinez, *supra* note 2; Matthew Saunders & Claudia Salomon, *Enforcement of Arbitral Awards against States and State Entities*, 23(3) Arb. Int'l. 467–76 (2007); recognition by a court of an arbitral award bars re-litigation of the same issues; enforcement of an award, on the other hand, "means applying judicial remedies to assure that an award is carried out." James H. Carter, *Dispute Resolution and International Agreements*, 703 PLI/Comm. Law & Prac. Course Handbook Series 405 (1994), at Part IV.A.2. Although recognition necessarily precedes enforcement (a court must recognize an award before it can enforce it), not all recognition leads to enforcement. Richard J. Graving, *Status of the New York Arbitration Convention: Some Gaps in Coverage by New Acceptances Confirm its Vitality*, 10 ICSID Rev.—For. Inv. L.J. 1, 8 (1995).

[326] Karalis, *supra* note 11, at 201. The State enforcing the award may not impose "substantially more onerous conditions or higher fees or charges" than it would charge to recognize domestic awards. New York Convention, *supra* note 6, art. III.

[327] On the enforcement of arbitral awards, *see generally* Blackaby et al., *supra* note 1, ch. 11; Ved P. Nanda & David K. Pansius, Litigation of International Disputes in U.S. Courts, chs. 10–12 (1995); Vishny, *supra* note 62, § 12.40; Ian F.G. Baxter, *International Business Disputes*, 39 Int'l & Comp. LQ 288 (1990); Leo J. Bouchez, *The Prospects of International Arbitration*, 8 J. Int'l Arb. 81 (1991); Peter M. McGowan, *Arbitration Clauses as Waivers of Immunity from Jurisdiction and Execution under the Foreign Sovereign Immunities Act of 1976*, 5 NYL Sch. J. Int'l & Comp L. 409 (1984); Note, *Enforcing International Commercial Arbitration Agreements and Awards Not Subject to the New York Convention*, 23 Va. J. Int'l L. 784 (1981); J. Stewart McClendon, *Enforcement of Foreign Arbitral Awards in the United States*, 4 Nw. J. Int'l L. & Bus. 58 (1982).

[328] Kristin T. Roy, *The New York Convention and Saudi Arabia: Can a Country Use the Public Policy Defense to Refuse Enforcement of Non-Domestic Arbitral Awards?*, 18 Fordham Int'l L.J. 925 (1995).

[329] 9 U.S.C. § 201–8; *see also* Roy, *supra* note 328, at 930. The United Kingdom acceded in September, 1975. Graving, *supra* note 325, at 16.

[330] Martinez, *supra* note 2, at 492. Until 1970, the United States enforced international arbitral awards through friendship, commerce, and navigation treaties. Karalis, *supra* note 11, at 200. While the Convention requires that states recognize awards made in *any* other State, a number of signatories (including the United States) have entered a reservation permitted by the Convention

8.124 Today, the New York Convention is one of the most- widely ratified commercial treaties in the world. As of mid-2018, 159 States were parties,[331] through ratification, accession, or succession,[332] representing developed, developing, and transition States, including almost all of the major trading countries in the world. In addition, the European Union has established a specific treaty for the recognition and enforcement of judgments issued by courts in E.U. member States and Switzerland.[333]

8.125 The New York Convention provides that the courts of a contracting State may refuse enforcement of a foreign arbitral award only in seven specific circumstances.[334] Five of these defenses to enforcement relate to procedural matters.[335] The first ground for non-enforcement is the absence of a valid arbitration agreement, for instance if one of the parties did not have capacity to execute the arbitration agreement, or if the agreement was induced by fraud or executed under duress.[336] Second, the New York Convention permits non-enforcement if the respondent did not receive proper notice of the arbitration proceedings, or was denied the opportunity to present its case.[337] Most courts applying this exception to recognition will seek to determine whether the complaining party was offered the chance to be heard, rather than whether the party availed itself of that opportunity.[338] A party that boycotts arbitration proceedings will rarely be successful in raising the "due process" defense to enforcement of the resulting arbitral award. Third, a court may refuse to enforce an award if it falls outside the terms of the submission

indicating that they need only apply the Convention to awards made in States that are also party to the New York Convention. New York Convention, *supra* note 6, art. I(3).

331 *See* list of ratifying States at http://www.newyorkconvention.org/countries, last visited Sept. 10, 2018.

332 "Ratification" is the formal consent by a state to be bound by a treaty that its representative has signed. "Accession," which is only possible if a treaty provides for it, is adherence to a treaty without having taken part in the negotiations that produced the treaty. It has the same effect as signature and ratification. "Succession" takes place when one State succeeds another and assumes its obligations under a treaty. Depending upon the circumstances, succession may be mandatory or optional. Richard J. Graving, *Mini-Glossary of Treaty Terms* (1992), available from the Institute for Transnational Arbitration at http://www.cailaw.org/ita.

333 Council Regulation (EC) No. 44/2001 of Dec. 22, 2000 on jurisdiction, recognition, and enforcement of judgment in civil and commercial matters, OJ L 12/1, Jan. 16, 2001 (previously known as the "Brussels and Lugano Conventions").

334 New York Convention, *supra* note 6, art. V.

335 *Id.*, art. V(1).

336 *Id.*, art. V(1)(a). *See also* Martinez, *supra* note 2, at 497. Because of the availability of this defense, it is important that the investor who is executing an investment agreement with a State agency satisfy itself that the State agency has authority to enter into the arbitration agreement under the host State's laws. Vincent Sama, *Problems in Enforcement of Foreign Arbitral Awards* (transcript of seminar), 6 World Arb. & Med. Rep. 77, 79 (1995).

337 New York Convention, *supra* note 6, art. V(1)(b). It is unclear whether this defense will be adjudicated according to the law of the enforcing State or the law at the place of arbitration. Martinez, *supra* note 2, at 499.

338 Sama, *supra* note 336, at 79.

to arbitration.[339] Enforcement may also be refused on grounds that the tribunal was improperly constituted,[340] or that the award has been set aside or suspended by courts at the place of arbitration.[341]

Two other grounds for non-recognition of a foreign arbitral award may be raised by the reviewing court on its own motion: that the subject matter of the dispute is not subject to adjudication by arbitration,[342] or that enforcement of the award would be contrary to the public policy of the State in which enforcement is sought.[343] Courts in most countries have construed this last "public policy" exception narrowly, preventing excessive judicial interference in foreign arbitral awards.[344] In the United States, for example, one court ruled that the public policy defense should be accepted only where enforcement of the award would be contrary to "the most basic notions of morality and justice."[345] **8.126**

The New York Convention's defenses to enforcement of international arbitration awards have been widely translated into analogous grounds for *annulling* arbitral awards in the courts at the place of arbitration. The scope and application of the most relevant of these grounds are therefore reviewed in greater detail in the following section, dealing with the setting aside of awards. **8.127**

ii. Challenge of awards Where an arbitration proceeding takes place outside the boundaries of the ICSID system, the national law at the place of arbitration—and the courts of that jurisdiction—control the losing party's quest to annul the award. There are no international treaties restricting a State's approach to the review of arbitration awards rendered within their territory.[346] There is a great deal of variation between national legislation on arbitration around the world, although harmonization is increasing. Most modern arbitration statutes provide a very short list of grounds for annulling international arbitration awards. Most of these grounds are similar to the exceptions to recognition and enforcement of awards contained in article V of the New York Convention.[347] **8.128**

339 New York Convention, *supra* note 6, art. V(1)(c).

340 *Id.*, art. V(1)(d).

341 *Id.*, art. V(1)(e).

342 *Id.*, art. V(2)(a).

343 *Id.*, art. V(2)(b).

344 Saul Perloff, *The Ties that Bind: The Limits of Autonomy and Uniformity in International Commercial Arbitration*, 13 U. Pa. J. Int'l Bus. L. 323, 333 (1987).

345 *Fotochrome Inc. v. Copal Co.*, 517 F.2d 512, 516 (2d Cir. 1975).

346 William Craig, *Uses and Abuses of Appeal from Awards*, 4 Arb. Int'l 174 (1988); Hamid Gharavi, The International Effectiveness of the Annulment of an Arbitration Award 29 (2002). *See also* Albert Jan van den Berg, *Should the Setting Aside of the Arbitral Award Be Abolished?* 29(2) ICSID Rev.—For. Inv. L.J. 1–26 (2014).

347 The English Arbitration Act 1996 provides a wide range of grounds for setting aside domestic arbitration awards, even allowing appeal as to questions of law, but requires that awards covered by the New York Convention be recognized and enforced unless one of the narrow exceptions to enforcement under that treaty is demonstrated. English Arbitration Act 1996, arts. 67–69, 103.

8.129 The UNCITRAL Model Law on International Commercial Arbitration,[348] while adopted verbatim in only a few countries,[349] has served as a guidepost for many jurisdictions seeking to modernize and harmonize legislation on arbitration. The UNCITRAL Model Law establishes six bases for setting aside awards at the arbitral situs: (1) invalidity of the agreement to arbitrate; (2) lack of notice to a party or other inability to present the case; (3) inclusion in the award of matters outside the scope of submission; (4) irregularity in the composition of the tribunal; (5) non-arbitrability of the subject matter; and (6) violation of domestic public policy.[350] In the United States, the international provisions of the Federal Arbitration Act allow the refusal of confirmation on the same grounds as those established in the New York Convention, as long as the award in question was rendered outside the United States.[351] Where the arbitral situs is within the United States, both the domestic and international sections of the Federal Arbitration Act (FAA) apply, including extra-statutory grounds for vacatur such as manifest disregard of law.[352]

8.130 Of the UNCITRAL Model Law annulment grounds, the first defect is difficult to make out in arbitration initiated under investment treaties, since the agreement to arbitrate is composed of an international agreement between sovereign States and

---

348 UNCITRAL Model Law, *supra* note 172.

349 The UNCITRAL website, http://www.uncitral.org/uncitral/en/uncitral_texts/arbitration/1985Model_arbitration_status.html, provides a list of "enactments" of the UNCITRAL Model Law, but this list is deceptive. Many of the countries noted there introduced legislation based on the UNCITRAL Model Law, but with substantial modifications.

350 UNCITRAL Model Law, *supra* note 172, art. 34(2). In some jurisdictions, the parties to an arbitration clause may to some extent narrow the grounds upon which national courts may set aside an arbitral award. Fischer & Haydock, *supra* note 1, at 973. However, in some countries, parties are unable to waive their right to all judicial review of arbitration awards. In New York, for instance, the right to cross-examination has been deemed a fundamental element of due process, and is therefore probably unwaivable. Steven J. Stein & Daniel R. Wotman, International Commercial Arbitration in New York 87–96 (1986). Professor Park suggests that at least in three areas, judicial review should be impossible to waive, in the interests of fairness and integrity of the arbitral system: (1) arbitrability; (2) the right to be heard; and (3) international public policy. William Park, *Safeguarding Procedural Integrity in International Arbitration*, 63 Tul. L. Rev. 647, 707 (1989). Nevertheless, the choice of certain arbitration rules may effect such a waiver. In particular, the LCIA Rules provide that in choosing arbitration under that system "the parties also waive irrevocably their right to any form of appeal, review or recourse to any state court or other judicial authority, insofar as such waiver may be validly made." 2014 LCIA Rules, *supra* note 128, art. 26(9). Even where arbitral rules are silent, many legal systems recognize the validity of "exclusion agreements," by which the parties voluntarily restrict judicial review or eliminate it altogether. *See e.g.* Swiss federal law on arbitration, the Loi Fédéral de Droit International Privé (LDIP), which allows express waiver of all judicial review where all parties are non-Swiss, in art. 192. The most extreme expression of limited judicial review was under the Belgian arbitration law in force until 2000, which *as a default rule* allowed no action for annulment of arbitral awards rendered in Belgium in disputes between foreign parties. Law of Mar. 27, 1985 (Belg.) enacting Code Judiciaire, art. 1717.

351 9 U.S.C. §§ 201 *et seq.*

352 *Yusuf Ahmed Alghanim & Sons, W.L.L. v. Toys "R" Us Inc.*, 126 F.3d 15, 24–25 (2d Cir. 1997); *Industrial Risk Insurers v. M.A.N. Guttehoffnungshutte GmbH*, 141 F.3d 1434, 1441 (11th Cir. 1998); *Spector v. Torenberg*, 852 F.Supp. 201, 205–06 (S.D.N.Y. 1994).

the Claimant's request for arbitration. Nor do the bases for invalidity common in the commercial arbitration context, such as coercion, fraud, lack of identity of the parties, and so forth, normally apply where arbitration is "without privity," as investment arbitration has been described.[353] In practice, the most common of the Model Law grounds that losing parties use to challenge arbitration awards are that the arbitrators decided issues outside the scope of their authority, and that the award violates public policy.

The range of issues that losing parties may bring to court under the "excess of powers" rubric is extremely broad, and therefore difficult to characterize generally. The subjects complained of fall most commonly into one of two categories. First, the defeated party may assert that the arbitrators' departure from the agreed-upon rules of procedure is so serious that the parties' agreement to arbitrate has been subverted. The most frequently cited defect of this kind is consolidation, where disputes between a single party on one side and multiple parties on the other are merged into one proceeding. In *Oxford Shipping Co. Ltd. v. Nippon Yusen Kaisha*,[354] an English court ruled that arbitrators may not consolidate without the consent of the parties involved. Many commentators agree that consolidation can amount to a rewriting of the arbitration agreement, since the parties agreed to arbitrate disputes between themselves, not between themselves and several other parties.[355] Nevertheless, courts have refused to annul on this ground where the complaining party could be deemed to have accepted the procedure.[356] The second class of "excess of mandate" challenges are those dealing with the subject matter of issues the arbitral tribunal has decided, and whether they fall within the scope of the agreement to arbitrate. In the investment context, this kind of challenge could be mounted where the tribunal has accepted jurisdiction over issues beyond the scope of consent—for example, tort claims or purely commercial disputes unrelated to an "investment" as required by most investment treaties. Frequently, losing parties try to open the merits of the dispute to judicial review by asserting that the arbitrators were mistaken in 8.131

353 Jan Paulsson, *Arbitration without Privity*, 10 ICSID Rev.—For. Inv. L.J. 232 (1995).

354 [1984] 2 Lloyd's Rep. 374.

355 Thomas E. Carbonneau, Cases and Materials on the Law and Practice of Arbitration 27 (2000).

356 *OIAETI v. SOFIDIF*, Court of Cassation, Decision of Mar. 8, 1988, *reprinted at* 1987 Revue de l'Arbitrage 339 (reversing lower court decision annulling an award against several Iranian public companies where the arbitrators had consolidated various disputes); *see also Karaha Bodas Co. LLC v. Perusahaan Pertambangan Minyak Dan Gas Bumi Negara et al. [Pertamina]*, UNCITRAL Final Award of Sept. 30, 1999, Mealey's Int'l Arb. Rep. (Mar. 2001), at C-2 *et seq.* (UNCITRAL tribunal consolidated claims that claimant had brought against Pertamina and PLN, two Indonesian State-owned entities, under closely related project agreements. Pertamina eventually opposed enforcement of the award, in part on grounds that this consolidation was in excess of the arbitrators' mandate. The court rejected the challenge, finding that the two parties were closely related and suffered no detriment from consolidation). The arbitral tribunal's decision in the *Karaha Bodas* arbitration is summarized in pertinent part in *Karaha Bodas Co. v. Perusahaan Pertambangan Minyak Das Gas Bumi Negara [Pertamina]*, 364 F.3d 274, 282–85 (5th Cir. 2004).

their choice of law or incorrectly applied the law to the facts at hand.[357] In *Bridas S.A.P.I.C. et al. v. Turkmenistan et al.*, the ICC arbitral tribunal awarded compensation to the claimant for lost profits in breach of contract, with damages determined by the discounted cash flow method at a discount rate of about 10 percent.[358] Turkmenistan moved to set aside the award in U.S. court (the situs of the arbitration had been Houston, Texas), contending that neither party had argued for that particular rate, and that the arbitrators had in fact "split the baby," setting the discount rate between the parties' estimates without any basis in law. The Court rejected this challenge, finding that the arbitrators had provided sufficient reasoning to conclude that they applied the law in their deliberations. "It is not th[e] Court's role," it concluded, "to sit as the panel did and reexamine the evidence under the guise of determining whether the arbitrators exceeded their powers."[359]

8.132 In most jurisdictions, awards that violate public policy can be subject to court annulment. Some arbitration statutes specify that an award can be set aside where international public policy is offended,[360] while others make domestic public policy the relevant set of norms.[361] Still other national statutes are unclear whether local or international public policy should serve as the basis for challenge, leading to confusion and debate.[362] In the E.U. context, according to the Court of Justice of the European Union (CJEU), E.U. member States must take into consideration, when reviewing arbitral awards, both their own public policy and E.U. public policy.[363] Within the international commercial arbitration context, courts in developed countries around the world have been hesitant to set aside awards on this basis, given the vagueness of the standard and the potential for its abuse. In the words of England's Court of Appeal, public policy

[357] Under most legal systems, arbitrators must decide according to the law chosen by the parties. Unless the parties expressly agree otherwise, the arbitrators arguably exceed their powers when they rule as *amiable compositeurs*, according to general principles of justice and equity. *Inter-Arab Investment Guarantee Corp. v. Banque Arabe d'Investissements*, Paris Cour d'Appel, decision of Oct. 23, 1997 ("the arbitrators had to decide in law and to give reasons for their decision"). In other jurisdictions, *amiable composition* is permitted as long as the parties do not prohibit it. This is the case in the United States, where arbitrators need not even provide written reasons for their award unless the parties expressly require it.

[358] *Bridas S.A.P.I.C., Bridas Energy Int'l, Intercontinental Oil & Gas Ventures, and Bridas Corp. v. Turkmenistan, Balkannebitgazsenagat and Turkmenneft*, Civil Action No. H-99-2171 (S.D. Tex. Oct. 1, 2001).

[359] *Id.* at 27 (*citing Nat'l. Oil Corp. v. Libyan Sun Oil Co.*, 733 F. Supp. 800, 819 (D. Del.)).

[360] French Civil Code, art. 1504.

[361] UNCITRAL Model Law, *supra* note 172, art. 36(1). No such statutory ground exists under the U.S. Federal Arbitration Act, but has been ruled by courts to be "specific application of the more general doctrine, rooted in the common law, that a court may refuse to enforce contracts that violate law or public policy." *United Paperworkers Int'l Union v. Misco Inc.*, 484 U.S. 29, 42 (1987).

[362] Swiss Law on Private International Law, art. 190(2).

[363] George A. Bermann, *Navigating EU law and the Law of International Arbitration*, 28 Arb. Int'l 397 (2012).

> is never argued at all but when other points fail. It has to be shown that there is some element of illegality or that the enforcement of the award would be clearly injurious to the public good or, possibly, that enforcement would be wholly offensive to the ordinarily reasonable and fully informed member of the public . . .[364]

Most frequently cited as possible cognizable violations of public policy include contracts or concessions obtained by bribery, illegal or immoral agreements, or denial of due process in the conduct of arbitration. In some cases, an award could be subject to public policy challenge if the award or underlying transaction creates a monopoly or overly dominant market position for the winning party.[365] According to the law in most jurisdictions, the mere violation of local law by the arbitrators[366] or minor defects in the arbitral process[367] will not be enough to set aside the resulting award. Instead, it must be fundamentally unconscionable for the national court to give effect to the arbitration award—a test that is rarely met.[368] Nevertheless, in less developed countries that have a less favorable attitude toward arbitration in general, broader concepts of public policy could find application. Like "excess of powers," the public policy challenge is frequently used by losing respondents, particularly States, to draw courts closer to the merits of their dispute. By arguing that the arbitrators have made a substantive decision that leads to an unjust or morally unconscionable result, respondents hope national courts at the place of arbitration will be reluctant to place their imprimatur on the resulting award, and will effectively act as a court of appeal on the merits.[369] **8.133**

Losing parties have so far been largely unsuccessful in seeking to annul awards rendered under investment treaties subject to the New York Convention.[370] In **8.134**

[364] *Deutsche Schachtbau- und Tiefbohrgesellschaft GmbH v. Ras Al Khaimah Nat'l. Oil Co.*, [1987] 2 All E.R. 769, 779 (Ct. App. 1987).

[365] *DO Zdravilisce Radenska v. Kajo-Erzeugnisse Essenzen GmbH*, Supreme Court of Slovenia, decision of Oct. 20, 1993, *reprinted at* 24 YB. COMM. ARB. 920 (1999) (annulling arbitration award rendered in Yugoslavia on grounds that the contract in dispute violated competition law and therefore Slovenian public policy).

[366] *General Electric Co. v. Renusagar Power Co. Ltd.*, [1994] 81 Company Cases 171 (India S.C.).

[367] *See e.g.* Moscow City Court, Decision of Nov. 10, 1994, Model Arb. Law Case No. 146.

[368] *Parsons and Whittemore Overseas Co. v. Société Générale de l'Industrie du Papier*, 508 F. 2d 969, 974 (2d Cir. 1974) (losing party sought relief from an award rendered against it for failing to complete a project in Egypt as a result of U.S. government actions against Egypt during the Six Day War. The Second Circuit found that despite the U.S. policy supporting the losing party's position, this was not enough to avoid the award. Public policy could only be invoked "where enforcement would violate the forum State's most basic notions of morality and justice," since the exception was "not meant to enshrine the vagaries of international politics"; German Bundesgerichtshof Judgment of May 15, 1986, *published in* N.J.W., Nov. 26, 1986, at 3027 (non-recognition or vacatur of international arbitration awards is appropriate only when "the arbitral procedure suffered from a serious deficiency affecting the bases of civil and economic life").

[369] Most courts in developed countries, however, have refused to take the bait. In one such action to set aside an award, the Swiss Supreme Court rebuffed the respondent, refusing to "decide as an appellate instance; the merits of an award cannot be reviewed under the cover of public policy." Swiss Federal Tribunal, Judgment of Jan. 8, 1995, *reprinted at* 22 YB. COMM. ARB. 789 (1997).

[370] *See generally* Noah Rubins, *Judicial Review of Investment Arbitration Awards*, in NAFTA: INVESTMENT LAW AND ARBITRATION 359 (Todd Weiler ed. 2004).

CME v. Czech Republic, the respondent State faced an award of US$269 million plus 10 percent interest per annum.[371] The UNCITRAL tribunal had its seat in Stockholm, and the Czech Republic sought to annul the award in the courts there.[372] In 2003, the Swedish Court issued its opinion, rejecting the Czech Republic's motion to set aside the award.[373] The Czech Republic had put forward a number of arguments under the Swedish Arbitration Act, most notably under the "excess of powers" and "public policy" rubrics. Perhaps the central argument presented was that the tribunal had exceeded its powers by ignoring the proper system of applicable law. The choice-of-law clause of the Netherlands–Czech BIT called for application of the terms of the BIT, Czech law, and international law, with no indication which body of law, if any, should take precedence. The Czech Republic asserted that the arbitrators had completely disregarded Czech law, and had invoked rules not part of international law. The Swedish Court disagreed, noting that the arbitrators had spent a great deal of time discussing whether the BIT required them to apply Czech law, and had ultimately decided that the clause provided a "menu" of options from which they had full discretion to choose. Under the Swedish Arbitration Act, it stated, "an excess of mandate may be involved only where the arbitrators' interpretation of the choice of law clause proves to be baseless such that their assessment may be equated with ... having ignored a provision regarding applicable law."[374] The Czech Republic also argued that the *CME* award violated Swedish public policy, or, in the words of the Swedish arbitration statute, that the Stockholm award and the manner in which it came about were "manifestly incompatible with the principles on which the legal system of Sweden is based."[375] The Court rejected this submission with minimal discussion, simply stating that the Czech Republic had "no shown ample reason for why the arbitration award or the manner in which it came about should be in violation of *ordre public* and thereby invalid based on the grounds asserted."[376]

8.135 Subsequent challenges of awards, primarily by respondent States but also by claimants, have met with similar caution on the part of national courts.[377] In *S.D.*

[371] *CME Czech Rep. B.V. v. Czech Republic* (UNCITRAL), Final Award of Mar. 13, 2003, available at https://www.italaw.com/sites/default/files/case-documents/ita0180.pdf.

[372] As part of the filing of that action, the Czech government posted a bond for the full amount of the award, such that CME would promptly receive payment on its claim should the Czech challenge fail. *Czech Republic Will Pay Immediately If Stockholm Court Upholds Award*, PRNews Wire-First Call (Mar. 31, 2003), available at http://www.finanznachrichten.de/nachrichten/artikel-1931445.asp.

[373] *Czech Republic v. CME Czech Republic B.V.*, Svea Court of Appeal, Case No. T 8735-01, decision of May 15, 2003 (the Stockholm Court Decision), available at https://www.italaw.com/sites/default/files/case-documents/ita0182.pdf.

[374] *Id.* at 91.

[375] Sweden Arbitration Act, art. 33.

[376] Stockholm Court Decision, *supra* note 373, at 105.

[377] One exception appears to be the Paris Court of Appeal, which has been the relevant jurisdiction for challenging the awards of all investment treaty tribunals seated in France. Since the early 2010s, the Court of Appeal has annulled a disproportionate number of awards against States,

Myers, Canada challenged a NAFTA award against it, arguing that courts should give less deference to investment arbitration awards than commercial awards, in light of the public interest concerns at stake.[378] The Ontario court rejected this position and upheld the challenged award,[379] as did the Canadian federal court in *Feldman.*[380]

The most prominent exception to this record of judicial deference is the *Metalclad* case.[381] There, Mexico sued Metalclad in the Supreme Court of British Columbia (the trial-level court at the place of arbitration), asking it to set aside a US$20 million award rendered under NAFTA. After receiving extensive briefings and oral argument, Justice Tysoe rendered an opinion on May 2, 2001.[382] Mexico's challenge rested largely on the argument that the *Metalclad* tribunal had exceeded its authority in a variety of ways. In particular, Mexico argued that the arbitrators had created a new basis for liability under NAFTA's "fair and equitable treatment" provision (article 1105), namely the violation of a "transparency" requirement found elsewhere in the treaty.[383] After receiving these arguments, Judge Tysoe explained: **8.136**

> the Tribunal ... set out its understanding of transparency and it then reviewed the relevant facts. After discussing the facts and concluding that the Municipality's denial of the construction permit was improper, the Tribunal stated its conclusion which formed the basis of its finding of a breach of Article 1105; namely, Mexico had failed to ensure a transparent and predictable framework for Metalclad's business planning and investment. Hence, the Tribunal made its decision on the basis of transparency. This was a matter beyond the scope of the submission arbitration because there are no transparency obligations contained in Chapter 11.[384]

despite the generally pro-arbitration posture of the French courts and French law. *See e.g., Venezuela v. Rusoro Mining Limited*, Case No 16/20822, Decision of January 29, 2019 (annulling most of a $1.2 billion investment treaty award on grounds that the damages had been calculated on the basis of facts pre-dating an applicable three-year limitation period).

[378] *Attorney General of Canada v. S.D. Myers Inc.*, Court File No. T-81-03 (Memorandum of Fact and Law of the Applicant Attorney General of Canada) (undated), at paras. 137–38.

[379] *Attorney General of Canada v. S.D. Myers Inc.*, Judgment of Jan. 13, 2004 (Can. Fed. Ct.), 29 Yb. Comm. Arb. 183 (2004), available at https://www.italaw.com/sites/default/files/case-documents/ita0756.pdf ("While Art. 34 provides that a Court may set aside an award where 'it is in conflict with the public policy of Canada', public policy does not refer to a political position, it refers to 'fundamental notions and principles of justice.' In this case the Tribunal's decision does not breach fundamental notions and principles of justice so that the decision is not in conflict with the public policy of Canada").

[380] *Mexico v. Marvin Roy Feldman Karpa*, Judgment of Dec. 3, 2003 (Superior Court of Justice of Ontario), 29 Yb. Comm. Arb. 167 (2004), available at https://www.italaw.com/sites/default/files/case-documents/ita0327.pdf ("I accept the proposition that judicial deference should be accorded to arbitral awards generally and to international commercial arbitrations in particular").

[381] *See* Henri C. Alvarez, *Setting Aside Additional Facility Awards: The Metalclad Case*, in Annulment of ICSID Awards 267 (Emmanuel Gaillard & Yas Banifatemi eds. 2004).

[382] *Mexico v. Metalclad Corp.*, 2001 B.C.S.C. 664 (2001). *See also* Yelena Faynblyum, *The Metalclad Appeal: A Pyrrhic Victory*, http://www.cba.org/cba/newsletters/environmental-06-2001/eco3.asp.

[383] *Metalclad, supra* note 382, at para. 66.

[384] *Id.* at para. 68.

8.137 In so doing, Judge Tysoe stressed that he did not view the arbitrators' decision as merely giving content to article 1105:

> In the present case . . . the Tribunal did not simply interpret the wording of Article 1105. Rather, it misstated the applicable law to include transparency obligations and it then made its decision on the basis of the concept of transparency.[385]

Because the arbitrators had decided that Mexico's actions constituted a violation of the NAFTA due to a lack of transparency, Judge Tysoe set aside that portion of the award.[386]

8.138 Finally, in a number of investment treaty arbitrations, tribunals consider whether respondent States should be held responsible under a BIT because their local courts had annulled commercial arbitration awards. In *Saipem v. Bangladesh*,[387] the ICSID tribunal concluded that the annulment of an ICC award by the Bangladeshi courts constituted an illegal judiciary expropriation of the claimant's investment. Similarly, the tribunal in *White Industries v. India*[388] decided that the State's challenge against an ICC award, which dragged through appeals for many years, constituted a violation of India's obligation to provide investor an "effective means" to assert its claims and enforce its rights.

b. Challenge by ad hoc annulment (ICSID awards)

8.139 As noted previously, the Washington Convention is unique in that it completely bars challenge in national courts, since "each contracting State shall recognize an award rendered pursuant to this Convention as binding and enforce the pecuniary obligations imposed by that award within its territories as if it were a final judgment of a court in that State."[389]

8.140 Chapter VII of the ICSID Arbitration Rules contains the provisions for recourse against arbitral awards.[390] Under these rules, a losing party may request that the Chairman of ICSID's Administrative Council designate a three-member panel to review an award, known as an "ad hoc Committee". The scope of review is limited, and the procedural rules used are identical to those used in the main case.[391] The Washington Convention further provides for complete waiver of judicial recourse,

---

[385] *Id.* at para. 70.

[386] This decision engendered a great deal of controversy. *See e.g.* Todd Weiler, *Metalclad and the Government of Mexico: A Play in Three Parts*, 2 J. World Invest. 685 (2001); Ian A. Laird, *The Weakening of the International Rule of Law in the NAFTA Zone*, presentation prepared for May 3, 2002, CD Howe/Munk Centre Conference on NAFTA Chapter 11, at 12–14.

[387] *Saipem S.p.A. v. Bangladesh*, ICSID Case No. ARB/05/07, Award of June 30, 2009.

[388] *White Industries Australia Ltd. v. India*, UNCITRAL, Final Award of Nov. 30, 2011.

[389] Washington Convention, *supra* note 8, art. 54.

[390] ICSID Rules, *supra* note 8, arts. 50–55. *See generally* Annulment of ICSID Awards, *supra* note 381; *see also* R. Doak Bishop & Silvia M. Marchilli, Annulment under the ICSID Convention (2012).

[391] ICSID Rules, *supra* note 8, art. 53.

providing in article 53 that "[t]he award shall be binding on the parties and shall not be subject to any appeal or to any other remedy except those provided for in this Convention."[392] This bar against appeal in national courts is far more reliable than private contractual waivers, because the Washington Convention binds all member States to ensure that their courts recognize and enforce ICSID awards on the mere presentation of a certified copy.[393]

The grounds for overturning an ICSID award are listed in the Washington Convention, and appear relatively narrow: **8.141**

> Either party may request annulment of the award by an application in writing addressed to the Secretary-General on one or more of the following grounds:
> (a) that the Tribunal was not properly constituted;
> (b) that the Tribunal has manifestly exceeded its powers;
> (c) that there was corruption on the part of a member of the Tribunal;
> (d) that there has been a serious departure from a fundamental rule of procedure; or
> (e) that the award has failed to state the reasons on which it is based.[394]

Thus, the ICSID grounds for annulment are roughly equivalent to the narrow grounds for non-recognition provided in the New York Convention, except that they do not provide for any "public policy" justification for annulment.[395] Furthermore, these grounds may be *permissive* rather than *mandatory, i.e.* an ad hoc committee may not be constrained to annul an ICSID award in every case where it finds grounds as enumerated in article 52(1). Article 52(3) merely states that in such cases the ad hoc committee "shall have the authority" to annul the award. The *Klöckner* Committee found that despite this apparently permissive language, finding of grounds for annulment "must in principle lead to total or partial annulment of the award, without the Committee having any discretion."[396] The *MINE* ad hoc Committee disagreed, stating that "[a]n ad hoc Committee retains a measure of discretion in ruling on applications for annulment ... It may ... refuse to exercise its authority to annul an award where annulment is clearly not required to remedy procedural injustice and annulment would unjustifiably erode the binding force and finality of ICSID awards."[397] **8.142**

---

392 Washington Convention, *supra* note 8, art. 53.

393 *Id.*, arts. 53–54.

394 Washington Convention, *supra* note 8, art. 52.

395 Indeed, the ICSID grounds are narrower than those in the New York Convention, as there is no provision for annulment based upon any violation of public policy.

396 *Klöckner Industrie-Anlagen GmbH et al. v. Cameroon and Société Camerounaise des Engrais*, ICSID Case No. ARB/81/2, Committee Decision of May 3, 1985, 114 I.L.R. 243 (1999), at para. 179.

397 *Maritime Int'l. Nominees Establishment (MINE) v. Government Guinea*, ICSID Case No. ARB/84/4, ad hoc Committee Decision of Dec. 22, 1989, 5 ICSID Rev.—For. Inv. L.J. 95 (1990), at para. 4.10. *See also* Eric A. Schwartz, *Finality at What Cost?*, in Annulment of ICSID Awards, *supra* note 381, at 43, 48.

8.143 Despite the apparent restriction of grounds for annulment to procedural matters, the first three awards referred to appeals panels were set aside.[398] This result raised some concerns in the arbitration community as to the finality and legitimacy of ICSID awards.[399] In particular, critics charged that the *Klöckner* and *Amco* ad hoc annulment committees had exceeded their mandate, which should ostensibly have encompassed only the safeguard of procedural regularity, and penetrated to the merits of the disputes they examined.[400]

8.144 However, on closer analysis of the annulment panels' reasoning, there is reason to conclude that the relatively high incidence of annulment in those early years was not due to any inevitable expansion of appellate scope or systemic weakness. Rather, there appears to have been some "breaking-in" period of inexperience among both arbitrators and ad hoc committee members with the recently adopted ICSID rules, or, in the words of the *Klöckner* committee, an "absence of any previous interpretation of the Washington Convention and the lack of sufficiently clear or consistent indications from prior international practice."[401] The intent of the drafters, meanwhile, was clearly to allow annulment only in extremely rare circumstances. This goal is evidenced repeatedly in the *travaux préparatoires* of the Washington Convention; for instance, drafting committees rejected "manifestly incorrect application of the law" as a ground for annulment, and also consciously decided not to remove the word "manifestly" from the excess of powers ground in article 52(1)(b).[402]

8.145 More recent ad hoc panels have taken a rather strict approach to the grounds for annulment. In *Wena Hotels v. Egypt*,[403] the petitioning State sought annulment

---

[398] *See MINE, supra* note 397; *Klöckner, supra* note 396; *Amco Asia Corp. v. Indonesia*, ICSID Case No. ARB/81/1, Committee Decision of May 16, 1986, 25 I.L.M. 1439 (1986).

[399] Michael Reisman, *The Breakdown of the Control Mechanism in ICSID Arbitration*, 4 Duke L.J. 739 (1989); Mark Feldman, *The Annulment Proceedings and the Finality of ICSID Arbitral Awards*, 2 ICSID Rev.—For. Inv. L.J. 85 (1987); Alan Redfern, *ICSID: Losing Its Appeal?*, 3 Arb. Int'l 98 (1987).

[400] This criticism does not take issue with the existence of internal avenues of recourse in the ICSID system, but rather suggests that ad hoc committees implementing the agreed-upon procedure have not carried out the limited scope of appeal contemplated by parties to the Washington Convention and contracts incorporating the ICSID Rules. Aron Broches, *Observations on the Finality of ICSID Awards*, 6 ICSID Rev.—For. Inv. L.J. 321, 358 (1992).

[401] *Klöckner, supra* note 396, at para. 118. *See also* Emmanuel Gaillard, *CIRDI Chronique des sentences arbitrales*, 114 J. de Droit Int'l 135, 191 (1987).

[402] ICSID, Convention on the Settlement of Investment Disputes between States and Nationals of Other States: Analysis of Documents Concerning the Origin and the Formulation of the Convention (1970), at 851–54. More recent cases demonstrate that annulment panels may be becoming more circumspect about award challenges, and that ICSID's internal appeal system has become stricter with time. *Wena Hotels Ltd. v. Egypt*, ICSID Case No. ARB/98/4, Committee Decision of Feb. 5, 2002, 41 I.L.M. 933 (2002); *see also* Daniel Q. Posin, *Recent Developments in ICSID Annulment Procedures*, 13 World Arb. & Med. Rep. 170, 171 (2002) (describing the *Wena Hotels* case).

[403] *Wena Hotels, supra* note 402.

based upon a number of grounds, including the failure to state reasons, errors in the allocation of the burden of proof, that it had not been given the opportunity to be heard on the issue of interest, and excess of powers. In each instance, the ad hoc panel rejected these arguments, emphasizing that only the violation of "fundamental" rules of procedure can justify annulment.[404] In *Vivendi v. Argentina* as well, the committee took a narrow view of most of the article 52 grounds for annulment, but nevertheless held that the tribunal had exceeded its powers by failing to address fundamental issues.[405]

However, several recent ad hoc committees have annulled ICSID awards. These decisions resulted in controversy about the scope of annulment under article 52 of the ICSID Convention.[406] For example, in 2010, the award in *Fraport v. Philippines* was annulled due to a "serious departure from a fundamental rule of procedure."[407] In two other ICSID cases, ad hoc committees annulled awards based on a manifest excess of powers. In *Sempra Energy Int'l v. Argentina*,[408] the ad hoc committee decided that the tribunal had incorrectly interpreted a provision in the relevant BIT, and similarly, in the *Enron Creditors Recovery Corp. v. Argentina*,[409] it concluded that the tribunal had failed to apply the proper law. **8.146**

ICSID's narrow scope of appellate review, combined with the total waiver of judicial recourse, is unique. Because of the difficulties in arbitrating and enforcing an award against a sovereign, the drafters of the ICSID rules sought increased finality and neutrality through this arrangement, rather than more rigorous scrutiny of arbitrators' rulings.[410] According to Professor Schreuer: **8.147**

404 *Id.* at para. 73.

405 *Compañía de Aguas del Aconquija S.A. and Vivendi Universal v. Argentina*, ICSID Case No. ARB/97/3, Committee Decision of July 3, 2002, 41 I.L.M. 1135 (2002). For a critique of this decision, *see* Carlos Ignacio Suarez Anzorena, *Vivendi v. Argentina: on the Admissibility of Requests for Partial Annulment and the Ground of a Manifest Excess of Powers*, in Annulment of ICSID Awards, *supra* note 381.

406 *See* Blackaby et al., *supra* note 1, at para. 10.15. At the request of the Philippines, the ICSID Secretariat issued a report on annulment: ICSID, Background Paper on Annulment for the Administrative Council of ICSID, *Provided to State Parties* (Aug. 12, 2012), available at https://icsid.worldbank.org/en/Documents/resources/Background%20Report%20on%20Annulment_English.pdf.

407 The ad hoc committee considered that the tribunal's decision to allow admission of evidence after the close of proceedings only for the Respondent, while not offering such an opportunity to the Claimant, consisted of a "serious departure from a fundamental rule of procedure"; *see Fraport A.G. Frankfurt Airport Services Worldwide v. Philippines*, ICSID Case No. ARB/03/25, Decision on Annulment of Dec. 23, 2010.

408 *Sempra Energy Int'l. v. Argentina*, ICSID Case No. ARB/02/16, Decision on Annulment of June 29, 2010.

409 *Enron Creditors Recovery Corp. (formerly Enron Corp.) and Ponderosa Assets v. Argentina*, ICSID Case No. ARB/01/3, Decision on Annulment of July 30, 2010.

410 *See generally* David D. Caron, *Reputation and Reality in the ICSID Annulment Process*, 7 ICSID Rev.—For. Inv. L.J. 21 (1992).

The two decisions in *Wena* and *Vivendi* rendered in 2002 demonstrate that ICSID's review mechanism has found its proper place. It has abandoned the early activism of the *Klockner* case and now presents itself as what it was designed for: an unusual remedy for unusual situations. The recent cases have helped to dispel the fears about frequent attacks on awards for trivial reasons leading to protracted and expensive litigations.[411]

[411] Christoph Schreuer, *Three Generations of ICSID Annulment Proceedings*, in ANNULMENT OF ICSID AWARDS, *supra* note 381, 17, 42.

9

MEDIATION AND CONCILIATION OF INVESTMENT DISPUTES

Litigation and arbitration are arguably the most widely known and commonly publicized forms of dispute resolution.[1] However, not all investment-related disputes are resolved through fully adversarial processes.[2] Increasingly, both private businesses and governments turn to various forms of mediation and **9.01**

[1] *See* Anna Spain, *Integration Matters: Rethinking the Architecture of International Dispute Resolution* 32(1) U. Pa. J. Int'l L. 19 (2010).

[2] Richard Hill, *Non-Adversarial Mediation*, 12(4) J. Int'l Arb. 135 (1995); Vincent Fischer-Zernin et al., *Arbitration and Mediation: Synthesis or Antithesis?* 5(1) J. Int'l Arb. 21 (1988); Richard Hill, *The Theoretical Basis of Mediation and Other Forms of ADR: Why They Work*, 14 Arb. Int'l 173 (1998); Klaus Peter Berger, *Integration of Mediation Elements into Arbitration "Hybrid" Procedures and "Intuitive" Mediation by International Arbitrators*, 19 Arb. Int'l 387 (2003).

conciliation in the face of serious disagreements, rather than resorting immediately to international arbitration.[3] Indeed, some investment contracts require not only a pre-arbitration period of good faith negotiation, but refer the parties to alternative dispute resolution (ADR) as a prerequisite to filing a formal claim. Further, a number of investment treaties specifically mention the possibility of ADR procedures, although such provisions are rarely mandatory.[4] This chapter will address these alternatives to arbitration and litigation. We will also discuss the different methods by which mediation and conciliation may be imposed as a mandatory step preceding arbitration or litigation, with particular attention to investment contracts.

A. Mediation and Conciliation Defined

9.02 Neither mediation nor conciliation is strictly defined in a legal sense. Both represent forms of dispute resolution somewhere at the center of a continuum of third-party intervention in disputes.[5] At one end of the spectrum, a facilitator may simply help to coax the parties to the negotiation table. More intensive intermediary activity may include assisting with the negotiation process (such as providing "good offices"), providing a neutral assessment of the relative merits of the parties' respective positions, or devising settlement proposals.[6] The most "invasive" form of dispute resolution is arbitration, which calls for the third party to render a decision that is binding on all participants.

[3] Klaus Lionnet, *Arbitration and Mediation—Alternatives or Opposites*, 4(1) J. Int. Arb. 69 (1987); Fischer-Zernin, *supra* note 2, at 21; Anthony Connerty, *The Role of ADR in the Resolution of International Disputes*, 12 Arb. Int'l 47 (1996); Guy Block et al., *A Remarkable Example of Promotion of Arbitration and ADR: The Resolution of Disputes in the Belgian Newly Liberalized Energy Sector*, 18 Arb. Int'l 401 (2002). In 2008, the European Union adopted the Mediation Directive to encourage the use of mediation procedures in civil and commercial law disputes. *See* Directive 2008/52/EC of the European Parliament and of the Council of May 21, 2008 on certain aspects of mediation in civil and commercial matters, O.J. L136 (24.05.2008).

[4] On recent developments in the framework of investor-State mediation under international treaties, *see* Anna Joubin-Bret, *Investor–State Mediation (ISM): A Comparison of Recent Treaties and Rules*, in Contemporary Issues in International Arbitration and Mediation: The Fordham Papers 2014, 152–56 (Arthur W. Rovine ed. 2015); Susan D. Franck, *Using Investor-State Mediation Rules to Promote Conflict Management: An Introductory Guide*, 29(1) ICSID Rev.—For. Inv. L.J. 66–89 (2014).

[5] Mediation and conciliation form part (along with arbitration) of the alternative dispute resolution system (abbreviated as ADR), which comprises any method of resolving disputes without litigation. There is no agreed definition on the term "ADR." According to a general approach to define this term, "ADR is used to cover the full range of alternatives to litigation potentially available to resolve a civil dispute." *See* Susan Blake et al., The Jackson ADR Handbook 1–2 (2013). For a combined legal and economic approach to ADR, *see* Talia Fisher, *Law and Economics of Alternative Dispute Resolution*, in 3 The Oxford Handbook of Law & Economics, ch. 14 (Francesco Parisi ed. 2017).

[6] *See* Jeswald W. Salacuse, The Global Negotiator: Making, Managing, and Mending Deals around the World in the Twenty-First Century 229–55 (2003).

While "conciliation" is a term frequently used synonymously with "mediation,"[7] certain authors draw a distinction.[8] For some, conciliation is less invasive than mediation, and is limited to facilitating the parties' efforts to negotiate.[9] Others assert to the contrary, that the term "conciliation" suggests that a neutral third party will provide a specific settlement proposal, while a mediator will convey information between the parties, but will not offer any concrete solution.[10] Still others view conciliation and mediation as a form of arbitral procedure that is binding on the parties, but unfettered by any particular rules of law.[11] Here, both the terms "conciliation" and "mediation" are used broadly, referring to non-binding proceedings in which a person or a panel assists the parties in an independent manner in their attempt to reach an amicable settlement of their dispute. **9.03**

Specific permutations of third-party dispute management are described in this section without attempting to attach any particular definition.[12] **9.04**

As already noted, conciliation differs from mere negotiation in that the former involves the independent assistance of an outsider in resolving the dispute, whereas in settlement negotiations the parties do not solicit third-party assistance.[13] **9.05**

The difference between conciliation and arbitration is that conciliation ends either in the settlement of the dispute agreed by the parties, or it ends unsuccessfully;[14] whereas in arbitration, the presiding tribunal imposes a binding decision **9.06**

[7] Christian Bühring-Uhle, Arbitration and Mediation in International Business 273 (1996); James F. Smith, *Mediation and the Principles of UNIDROIT*, in Contratación Internacional: Comentarios A Los Principios Sobre Los Contratos Comerciales Internacionales Del UNIDROIT 237 (1998).

[8] Vincent Fischer-Zernin et al., *Arbitration and Meditation: Synthesis or Antithesis?*, 5(1) J. Int'l Arb. 21 (1988); Frank E.A. Sander, *Varieties of Dispute Processing*, 70 FRD 79, 114 (1976).

[9] *Id. See also* Bernard Mayer, The Dynamics of Conflict Resolution: A Practitioners Guide (1st ed. 2000).

[10] *See* Bernardo Cremades, *Global Mediation*, Israel Bar Ass'n. Newsletter (May 3, 2003), available at http://www.israelbar.org.il/article_inner.asp?catID=179&pgID=3559 (further noting that "mediation" is a term most often used in common-law jurisdictions, while "conciliation" is more widespread in civil-law countries).

[11] In the international context, this sort of procedure is often referred to as "arbitration *ex aequo et bono*" or "*amiable composition*." For more on the terminology of mediation (and its application in North America, Australia, Britain, and Canada), *see* Linda R. Singer, Settling Disputes 24–25 (1990); Richard J. Graving, *The International Commercial Arbitration Institutions: How Good A Job Are They Doing?*, 4 Am. UJ Int'l L. & Pol'y. 319, 323 n.12 (1989).

[12] For definitions of mediation and conciliation, *see* Henry Brown & Arthur Marriott, ADR Principles and Practice 108 (1993).

[13] *See* Jean-Pierre Cot, *Conciliation*, in Max Planck Encyclopedia of Public International Law, para. 3 (2006); J.G. Merrills, International Dispute Settlement 64–90 (4th ed. 2005). *See also* United Nations General Assembly Resolution 50/50 United Nations Model Rules for the Conciliation of Disputes between States, UN Doc. A/RES/50/50 (Dec. 11, 1995).

[14] Lionnet, *supra* note 3; Fischer-Zernin, *supra* note 2, at 30 ("Sometimes 'conciliation' denotes a less formal procedure than mediation or one in which the neutral party is less active. Most often, however, it seems that the terms 'conciliation' and 'mediation' are used interchangeably . . ."). *See generally* Kenji Tashiro, *Conciliation or Mediation during the Arbitral Process: A Japanese View*, 12(2) J. Int'l Arb. 119 (1995).

upon the parties, unless they have settled the dispute before the award is made.[15] Most simply put,

> In conciliation or similar forms of dispute settlement, a person chosen by the parties to a dispute assists them in finding agreement on the solution for their dispute. In arbitration, the person whom the parties have chosen decides for them how the dispute must be resolved.[16]

9.07 In practice, such conciliation proceedings are referred to by various terms, including "mediation." Nevertheless, in the legal tradition of some countries, a distinction is drawn between conciliation and mediation to emphasize the fact that in conciliation a third party seeks to bring together the disputing parties to help them find their own settlement, while a mediator suggests terms for the resolution of the dispute.[17] Notably, the European Union has defined the term "mediation" as a structured process, however named or referred to, whereby two or more parties to a dispute attempt by themselves, on a voluntary basis, to reach an agreement on the settlement of their dispute with the assistance of a mediator. This process may be initiated by the parties or suggested or ordered by a court or prescribed by the national law.[18]

9.08 As will become clear, the precise procedures that conciliators apply vary widely. Indeed, the primary asset of conciliation is precisely this broad freedom to fashion a form of interaction best suited to bring the parties to an agreement, in light of their interests and backgrounds and the dispute at hand. The broad purposes of conciliation were ably summarized in a 1925 treaty between France and Switzerland, which established a commission to resolve inter-State disputes. The commission's function was:

> to elucidate the questions in dispute, to collect with that object all useful information by inquiry or otherwise, and to endeavour to bring the Parties to an agreement. It may, after examining the case, intimate to the Parties the terms of settlement which seem to it suitable, and lay down a time-limit within which they are to reach their decision.[19]

---

[15] Ricky H. Diwan, *Problems Associated with the Enforcement of Arbitral Awards Revisited*, 19 Arb. Int'l 55 (2003); Bruno Leurent, *Reflections on the International Effectiveness of Arbitration Awards*, 12 Arb. Int'l 269 (1996). *See also* Gunther Horvath, *The Duty of the Tribunal to Render an Enforceable Award*, 18(2) J. Int'l Arb. 135 (2001). For a general comparison, *see* Nicholas Butler, *Arbitration and Conciliation Treaties*, in Max Planck Encyclopedia of Public International Law (2006).

[16] Michael E. Schneider, *Combining Arbitration with Conciliation*, 2(1) Oil, Gas & Energy Law Intelligence 1 (Mar. 2003).

[17] *See e.g.* Edna Sussman, *The Advantages of Mediation and the Special Challenges to Its Utilization in Investor State Disputes* (Feb. 5, 2011), available at SSRN: https://ssrn.com/abstract=2372313, describing mediation as a "more formal and structured process, in which the neutral delivers a non-binding opinion of the merits to the parties and makes a recommendation."

[18] 2008 Mediation Directive, *supra* note 3, art. 3(a).

[19] Max Habicht, Post War Treaties for the Pacific Settlement of International Disputes 226 (1931). *See also* J.G. Merrills, International Dispute Settlement 64–90 (4th ed. 2005).

This basic approach has changed relatively little since then, and is widely applied in the commercial and investment contexts, as well as in disputes between States. Richard Hill provides an illustrative example of the goals of mediation, based on interests, rather than legal entitlements: **9.09**

> Two people both have a legitimate claim to an orange and neither is willing to accept half the orange. If the claim is resolved in accordance with a judicial paradigm, one person will get some portion (possibly none) of the orange, and the other will get the remaining portion. But the people decide to call a mediator, who asks each person what they intend to do with the orange. The first person answers that she intends to use the rind to make perfume, while the second answers that she intends to use the pulp to make orange juice. The mediation process yields a solution that is fair and that better satisfies the interests of each party than could any solution based on an adversarial process.[20]

Conciliators seek to achieve amicable settlements of this sort using techniques that fall into three broad types, any or all of which may be applied to a particular dispute.[21] **9.10**

1. Information gathering

Traditionally, State-to-State conciliation was to a large degree a process of information gathering, allowing a neutral third party to assess the fact situation on the ground within the framework of the issues presented by the parties.[22] In modern commercial and investor–State conciliation, the evidence collection process is normally carried out according to the model of arbitration, but on a far more limited scale.[23] The mediator will normally solicit basic evidentiary submissions from the parties, and may question the parties or solicit comments in order to assess the reliability of the evidence submitted.[24] Only rarely will conciliators **9.11**

---

[20] Hill, *Theoretical Basis, supra* note 2, at 180.

[21] For more on conciliator techniques, *see* Stephen B. Goldberg, *The Dynamic of Mediation: Is Creative Genius the Key to Successful Mediation?*, paper given at the WIPO Conference on Mediation in Geneva (Mar. 29, 1996), available at http://www.arbiter.wipo.int/events/conferences/1996/goldberg.html. *See also* Jacob Bercovitch & Scott Sigmund Gartner, International Conflict Mediation: New Approaches and Findings 41 (2009).

[22] *See e.g.* S. Bastid, *La Commission de conciliation franco-siamoise*, 1 Etudes en l'Honneur de Georges Scelle 1 (1950) (border dispute between Siam and France resolved by conciliation after the investigation by a commission of ethnic, geographical, and economic evidence).

[23] Johannes Trappe, *Conciliation in the Far East*, 5 Arb. Int'l 183 (1989) ("Conciliation proceedings are similar to arbitration. The parties submit their views in writing and in most cases also at a hearing. With their written pleadings, they submit the available evidence, *i.e.* documents, survey reports, expert's evidence, and the like. The conciliators are authorised to order the parties to provide complementary evidence and to put questions in order to gain a complete picture of the relevant facts").

[24] *See e.g.* art. 8(6) of the IBA Rules for Investor–State Mediation (Oct. 4, 2012), according to which "[t]he mediator may at any time during the mediation suggest or request that a party provide such additional information or material as the mediator sees fit," available at https://icsid.worldbank.org/en/Documents/process/IBA%20Rules%20for%20Investor-State%20Mediation%20(Approved%20by%20IBA%20Council%204%20Oct%202012).pdf.

seek written or oral witness evidence. Nevertheless, it is not uncommon for the parties to empower the conciliator to undertake an independent inquiry into the circumstances of the dispute.

9.12 The investigation normally undertaken by conciliators is limited not only in the interest of economy and expeditiousness. In some disputes, excessive exploration of the facts can actually undermine the parties' efforts to reach an amicable settlement. This counterintuitive principle was underlined by the conciliation commission formed in 1958 to resolve a dispute between Morocco and France involving the former State's diversion of an airplane carrying Algerian revolutionaries.[25] Morocco requested that the commission interview the diverted plane's passengers, but this request was denied:

> [T]o have taken this evidence would, in the opinion of the Commission, have been likely to embitter Franco-Moroccan relations and thus defeat the purpose of the mission with which the Commission had been entrusted by the two governments.[26]

9.13 Likewise, in investor–State disputes, too much investigation can lead to a hardening of positions and the collapse of conciliation. Both investors and States may react defensively to newly discovered facts which are only tangentially related to the dispute at hand (compliance with tax laws or human rights norms, for example), and this may make it more difficult for them to compromise. Moreover, to the extent that a proliferation of facts are perceived to support one party's legal position, that party may lose interest in conciliation, believing that its case can be won swiftly through arbitration or litigation.[27] Since the goal of the conciliation process is settlement on terms acceptable to the parties, rather than the determination of entitlements through application of law to facts, a focus on ascertaining the "truth" may be extraneous and counter-productive.[28]

2. Assessment of positions

9.14 As in arbitration, conciliation/mediation is concerned to a large degree with assessing the positions of the parties, both in terms of the economic circumstances and the law applicable to the dispute. However, the approach of many mediators

---

[25] C. Rousseau, *Echec de la procédure d'enquête det de conciliation dans l'affaire du déroutement de l'avion transportant de Rabat à Tunis les chefs nationalistes algériens le 22 octobre 1956*, 62 RGDIP 691 (1958).

[26] Jean-Pierre Cot, International Conciliation 193 (1972). *See also* Merrills, *supra* note 13, at 71.

[27] Smith, *supra* note 7, at 241 ("Mediation is less likely to be successful if … the facts and the law leave no doubt which party would prevail"); George Coombs, Jr., *International Dispute Resolution*, in Transnational Litigation 7–12 to 7–14 (1992).

[28] On the contrast between "rights-based" dispute resolution (such as arbitration) and "interest based" techniques (such as conciliation), *see* William L. Ury et al., Getting Disputes Resolved: Designing Systems to Cut the Costs of Conflict 3–19 (1988); Hill, *Theoretical Basis*, *supra* note 2, at 173–75.

in this regard differs markedly from that of arbitrators, in that the assessment of the validity of the parties' claims, and the disclosure of this information to the parties before the close of proceedings, can play an important role in the settlement of the dispute.

Individuals and bureaucratic entities alike tend to form overly optimistic views of their likelihood of success in an adversarial proceeding to resolve their disputes.[29] In an investment dispute, therefore, both the investor and host State may hold inflated opinions of the merits of their respective legal positions. This phenomenon can distort the calculation of the risks of defeat in arbitration or litigation, pushing the parties to brave the adversarial process and shun early settlement. **9.15**

Conciliation/mediation provides the opportunity for the parties to receive a "reality check" that (if properly administered) can correct their assessment of litigation risk and prepare them for the prospect of settlement with some of their claims (or defenses) unsatisfied. The informal character of the mediation process is particularly well-suited to the assessment of positions, since the mediator will often spend time with each of the parties separately, eliciting more candid information and also providing ongoing feedback as to the weaker and stronger aspects of each party's legal case. **9.16**

3. Determining interests and solution building

One of the most important functions of a mediator is to identify each party's interests in the dispute. Again, because the conciliation/mediation process is not bound by the constraints of any legal system, it can facilitate the parties' exit from the "zero-sum game" of entitlements (as it is sometimes perceived) and the achievement of a solution that better satisfies all sides' preferences.[30] Parties to a dispute often have difficulty sharing accurate information about their interests directly with one another, as one mediation practitioner explains: **9.17**

> If you tell the other party how you prioritize your interests, and what you regard as most important, there is always the risk that the other party will take advantage of your openness to make you pay dearly for something that you care about very much and that it cares about very little. Suppose, for example, that we have one bowl of chocolate ice cream and two bowls of vanilla ice cream to share, and disagree about how to share them. In a spirit of openness, I tell you honestly that I much prefer chocolate to vanilla. You are indifferent to flavor, but you take advantage of my openness, and tell me that you, too, much prefer chocolate, and will only let me have the one bowl of chocolate in exchange for both bowls of vanilla. My openness has cost me dearly.[31]

---

[29] *See* Section G.3.

[30] *See* Nancy A. Welsh & Andrea K. Schneider, *Becoming "Investor–State Mediation,"* 1(1) Penn. St. JL & Int'l Af. 86–88 (2012); Jeswald W. Salacuse, *Is There A Better Way? Alternative Methods of Treaty Based Investor–State Dispute Resolution*, 31(1) Fordham Int'l. L.J. 155 (2007).

[31] Goldberg, *supra* note 21.

9.18 A skilled conciliator, meanwhile, can overcome this barrier by building trust with each of the parties and acting as a neutral repository for the information about their preferences, thereby reducing the risk of strategic behavior by one of the parties. The conciliator is then able to explore various ways of combining these interests in a settlement that provides each party what it values most, perhaps depriving it only of that which it values least.[32] In the context of investment disputes, solution-building may lead to a renewal of investment activity on modified terms, ensuring a flow of capital to the host State and continued return on that capital to the investor.

9.19 All of these conciliation/mediation techniques are interrelated and supported by a combination of "plenary" meetings, where each side is given the opportunity to express its grievances or provide information in the presence of the conciliator and the opposing party, and "caucusing," where the conciliator elicits the parties' views separately and in private.[33]

B. Potential Advantages of Mediation/Conciliation

9.20 In many situations, conciliation (as well as mediation) may offer certain advantages over adversarial dispute settlement systems such as arbitration or litigation.[34] As will be explained in more detail later, the informal procedures normally used in conciliation entail lower costs and speedier settlement—if settlement is reached at all. Confidentiality is more easily conserved, as are ongoing relations between investor and State, than in the no-holds-barred struggle of arbitration.[35] Former ICC Secretary-General Eric Schwartz has summarized the advantages of ADR methods, including conciliation and mediation, in the context of commercial disputes between private parties:

> There are powerful forces that militate in favour of ADR. The conduct of formal litigation or even arbitration, may, in addition to being costly and possibly time-consuming, entail considerable disruption and distraction for the parties involved. Ultimate victory may therefore be obtained at what, in retrospect, appears to the winning party to be a disproportionately high cost.[36]

---

[32] Roger Fisher et al., Getting to Yes 42–55 (1991).

[33] Lord Donaldson, *Alternative Dispute Resolution*, 58 Arb. 102 (1992) (the Chinese word for "conciliator" translates as "a go-between who wears out a thousand sandals").

[34] Thomas W. Wälde, *Investment Arbitration Under the Energy Charter Treaty—from Dispute Settlement to Treaty Implementation*, 12 Arb. Int'l 429 (1996).

[35] On advantages of mediation and conciliation over arbitration, *see* Michael Clancy & Thomas W. Wälde, *Efficiency in Mediation: Solving a Complex Cross-Border Energy Infrastructure Dispute in the Shadow of Three Moving Regulatory Regimes*, 5 J. World Inv. & Trade 257 (2004); Thomas W. Wälde, *Mediation/Alternative Dispute Resolution in Oil, Gas and Energy Transactions: Superior to Arbitration/Litigation from a Commercial and Management Perspective*, 13(8) CEPMLP J. (2003).

[36] Eric Schwartz, *International Conciliation and the ICC*, 5(2) ICC Int'l Court Arb. Bull. 5 (1994).

These same considerations apply equally where conflicts arise between foreign investors and host States. In particular, the informality of conciliation, and the reduced financial commitment the process entails, may facilitate the settlement of disputes involving governments, which otherwise may be forced to occupy entrenched positions as a result of psychological, bureaucratic, or political pressures. **9.21**

1. Costs

The arbitration or litigation of investment disputes can be an extremely costly undertaking.[37] While reliable generalizations are problematic, administrative costs and arbitrator fees alone routinely exceed US$250,000, with attorneys' fees several times greater.[38] According to the Organisation for Eonomic Cooperation and Development (OECD), the average cost of investor–State arbitration has "skyrocketed" in the last decade, from around US$1 or $2 million in 2005 to around US$8 million in 2012, in some cases ballooning to US$30 million.[39] On average, the largest cost component is legal counsel and experts (approximately 82 percent of the total) and arbitrator fees (about 16 percent of the overall cost).[40] Notably, a number of claims brought by foreign investors have been discontinued because the claimants were unable to pay the cost of the arbitral proceedings.[41] **9.22**

Because the conciliation process is relatively informal, entails little supervision by administrating institutions, and most often involves only one decision-maker rather than three, these costs can be far lower in a conciliation setting.[42] Anecdotal **9.23**

[37] For a recent discussion of costs issues, *see* Susan Franck, *Rationalizing Costs in Investment Arbitration*, 88(4) Wash. Univ. L. Rev. 769 (2011); David Riesenberg, *Fee Shifting in Investor–State Arbitration: Doctrine and Policy Justifying Application of the English Rule*, 60(4) Duke L.J. 990 (2011); David Smith, *Shifting Sands: Cost-and-Fee Allocation in International Investment Arbitration*, 51 Va. J. Int'l. L. 749 (2011); Lucy Reed, *More on Corporate Criticism of International Arbitration*, Kluwer Arbitration Blog (July 16, 2010); Nicolas Ulmer, *The Cost Conundrum*, 26(2) Arb. Int'l. 221–51 (2010). *See also* UNCTAD, Investor–State Disputes: Prevention and Alternatives to Arbitration (2010), at 16–18, with further examples.

[38] According to the European Parliament, "[a]verage legal and arbitration costs of a case are US$8 million, with the main part being the cost of legal representation and experts (80% of the total). Law firms charge as much as US$1,000 per hour, per lawyer, with several on each case. The arbitrators' fees are also high, at an average of US$3,000 a day, plus travel and subsistence" (internal references omitted); *see* European Parliament Briefing Paper (Jan. 2015), at 5, available at http://www.europarl.europa.eu/RegData/etudes/BRIE/2015/545736/EPRS_BRI(2015)545736_EN.pdf.

[39] *See* D. Gaukrodger & K. Gordon, *Investor–State Dispute Settlement: A Scoping Paper for the Investment Policy Community*, OECD Working Papers on International Investment, at 19, 2012/03, available at http://dx.doi.org/10.1787/5k46b1r85j6f-en.

[40] *Id.*

[41] *See e.g. Quadrant Pacific Growth Fund L.P. and Canasco Holdings Inc. v. Costa Rica*, ICSID (AF), Oct. 27, 2010, at paras. 69 and 71 (noting that "it is plausible to question whether Claimants had thoughtfully considered the costs involved in this arbitration and whether they had been adequately advised on the matter before filing their claim").

[42] Kent Wilson, *Savings Costs in International Arbitration*, 6 Arb. Int'l 151 (1990); Pierre Karrer, *Arbitration Saves! Costs: Poker and Hide-and-Seek*, 3(1) J. Int'l Arb. 35 (1986); Catherine Li, *Evaluating the Various Non-Litigation Processes for Resolving Disputes: The Cost-Effectiveness Approach*, 18(4) J. Int'l Arb. 435 (2001).

evidence suggests that even large disputes can be mediated for relatively modest sums.[43] Most frequently, the conciliator's fees are a matter for the conciliator and the parties to negotiate, although some ADR rules systems specify hourly rates for conciliators somewhat lower than the pay level for an arbitrator in a comparable dispute.[44] Because mediation is considered an "amicable" process, the parties normally share the costs and fees equally, and bear their own legal fees,[45] subject to the terms of any settlement that is reached.[46] Therefore, neither party bears the risk of having to pay double the costs or more.

9.24 More importantly, regardless of the hourly rates agreed, the total time that the parties spend preparing and presenting their positions, and the hours the mediator spends adjudicating, should be significantly less than in an arbitration or litigation of the same dispute.[47] Moreover, the conspicuous absence of document production (discovery) and multiple pleading exchanges in most ADR proceedings plays a major role in the reduced expense. Since any settlement will be executed voluntarily and will not be subject to judicial challenge or appeal as would an arbitral award or court judgment, mediators feel less pressure to "leave no stone unturned" in the fact-finding process, as long as a solution acceptable to both sides can be found.[48]

9.25 Where conciliation/mediation is handled under the auspices of an institution, administrative fees are normally also significantly lower than in more adversarial proceedings, since the management functions of ADR are rather minimal. Moreover, the flexibility of the conciliation process allows the parties a greater degree of control over the amounts spent on the dispute settlement process.[49]

---

[43] The *Tesoro Petroleum Corp.* dispute reportedly cost less than US$11,000 in administrative and conciliator fees (not including lawyers' fees). *See* Lester Nurick & Stephen Schnably, *The First ICSID Conciliation: Tesoro Petroleum Corp. v. Trinidad & Tobago*, 1 ICSID Rev.—For. Inv. L.J. 340, 343 (1986). A further example is the *Enel Green Power S.p.A. v. El Salvador* dispute, which concerned an eight-year controversy over control of a geothermal power venture in El Salvador. Having won an ICC arbitration and launched ICSID proceedings, the parties negotiated a settlement.

[44] *See e.g.* ICC Mediation Rules (2014), art. 3, Appendix, available at https://iccwbo.org/dispute-resolution-services/mediation/mediation-rules/#Appendix.

[45] *See e.g.* IBA Rules for Investor–State Mediation, *supra* note 24, art. 12(1).

[46] ICC Mediation Guidance Notes (2013), at para. 39, available at https://cms.iccwbo.org/content/uploads/sites/3/2014/12/icc-mediation-guidance-notes-english.pdf.

[47] Linda C. Reif, *Conciliation as a Mechanism for the Resolution of International Economic and Business Disputes*, 14 Fordham Int'l L.J. 578 (1991).

[48] Thomas W. Wälde, *Pro-Active Mediation of International Business and Investment Disputes Involving Long-Term Contracts: From Zero-Sum Litigation to Efficient Dispute Management*, 1 Oil, Gas & Energy Law Intelligence 2 (Sept. 2003).

[49] Erik Langeland, *The Viability of Conciliation in International Dispute Resolution*, 50 Disp. Resol. J. 34 (1995). The reduced cost of conciliation may eliminate some of the power imbalance that can distort the dispute resolution process and its results in the investor–State context. Both developing States and small- to mid-sized investors can at times be unable to fully protect their interests in arbitration or litigation as a result of limited resources.

It is important to keep in mind, however, that conciliation/mediation will save the parties money only if it is successful. While litigation and arbitration end in a more or less final resolution of the parties' dispute, conciliation/mediation may be only the first step on the road to a later adversarial process. If no settlement is reached, or if the agreement concluded during the conciliation/mediation process proves insufficiently durable, the parties may find themselves in precisely the same situation as if they had never tried ADR—except for having spent time and money in the failed attempt to find compromise. Because of conciliation's relatively modest cost, and due to the potentially significant savings should litigious conflict be avoided, in most cases this risk will be acceptable to parties who are otherwise disposed to resort to a mediated solution. **9.26**

2. Speed of resolution

Closely related to the economy of conciliation/mediation is its relative speed.[50] One of the main drawbacks of litigation, and even arbitration, as a means of dispute resolution is that can be a lengthy process. Arbitration under investment treaties, for example, rarely takes less than two years from the appointment of a tribunal to a final award (assuming that the case is not dismissed on jurisdictional grounds).[51] Recent statistical data reveals that the average length of investor–State arbitration is approximately 3.6 years from the filing of the request for arbitration to the date of the final award.[52] UNCTAD notes that it takes three to four years for a case to be heard and decided. Delays in arbitrator appointment, sequential phases on jurisdiction and the merits, and lengthy periods between written submissions have caused some ICSID arbitrations to drag out over several years.[53] **9.27**

[50] Ronald D. Rotunda, *Cautionary Lessons from American Securities Arbitration: Litigation v. Arbitration*, 5 Arb. Int'l 199 (1989); Margaret Wang, *Are Alternative Dispute Resolution Methods Superior to Litigation in Resolving Disputes in International Commerce?*, 16 Arb. Int'l 189 (2000); V.S. Deshpande, *How International Arbitration Can Always Prevail over Litigation*, 4(4) J. Int'l Arb. 9 (1987).

[51] *See e.g. Robert Azinian et al. v. Mexico*, ICSID Case No. ARB(AF)/97/2 (twenty-nine months); *Asian Agricultural Products Ltd. v. Sri Lanka*, ICSID Case No. ARB/87/3 (thirty months); *Tradex Hellas S.A. (Greece) v. Albania*, ICSID Case No. ARB/94/2 (forty months); *American Manufacturing & Trading Inc. v. Democratic Republic of the Congo*, ICSID Case No. ARB/93/1 (forty-two months); *Ceskoslovenska obchodni banka, A.S. v. Slovakia*, ICSID Case No. ARB/97/4 (eighty-eight months).

[52] Anthony Sinclair, *ICSID Arbitration: How Long Does It Take?*, 4(5) Global Arb. Rev. J. (2009).

[53] *Amco Asia Corp. v. Indonesia*, ICSID Case No. ARB/81/1 (129 months from constitution of tribunal to final disposition of the case). Nor is commercial arbitration immune from criticism for a lack of expediency. Andrew I. Okekeifere, *The UNCITRAL Model Law and the Problem of Delay in International Commercial Arbitration*, 14(1) J. Int'l Arb. 125 (1997); Cedric Harris, *Abuse of the Arbitration Process-Delaying Tactics and Disruptions: A Respondent's Guide*, 9(2) J. Int'l Arb. 87 (1992); Lord Justice Bingham, *The Problem of Delay in Arbitration*, 5(4) Arb. Int'l 333 (1989).

9.28 By contrast, conciliation (whether successful or not) rarely takes more than a few months.[54] Because both sides to the dispute are more or less committed to the process (since either party is free to abandon conciliation altogether at any time), the selection of the conciliator, presentation of positions, and other procedural events are normally free from the delay tactics that can slow arbitration and litigation.[55] The period of time between written and oral presentations can be very short, since the focus is on the expression of interests, rather than the formal presentation of legal rights. Conciliation is also accelerated by the absence of witness evidence, which is one of the more time-consuming aspects of adversarial proceedings.

9.29 As with the question of economy, conciliation will provide benefits in speed only if it ends in a durable settlement. Otherwise, any time spent in the ADR process, even if only a few months, is added to the time occupied by subsequent binding dispute resolution, such as arbitration or litigation.

3. Confidentiality

9.30 All forms of ADR, including negotiation, conciliation, mediation, and arbitration, are conducted privately, in contrast to the general publicity of litigation proceedings in national courts.[56] However, the assumption of complete and automatic confidentiality in arbitration is questionable. Court cases in a number of jurisdictions[57] indicate that under most international arbitration rules,[58] the parties are under no automatic, absolute obligation to refrain from disclosing various aspects of the dispute, including a final award.[59] Adversarial

---

[54] R. Collins, *Alternative Dispute Resolution: Choosing the Best Option*, 2(3) Australian Construction Law Newsletter 3 (1989) (estimating that arbitration takes about three times longer than mediation, and litigation three times longer than arbitration).

[55] On tactical delays and various others abuses of process in international arbitration, *see* Guerrilla Tactics in International Arbitration (Günther J. Horvath & Stephan Wilske eds. 2013).

[56] Leon E. Trakman, *Confidentiality in International Commercial Arbitration*, 18(1) Arb. Int'l 1–18 (2002); Klaus Reichert, *Confidentiality in International Mediation*, 59 Disp. Resol. J. 60 (2005).

[57] *See*, in particular, *AI Trade Finance Inc. v. Bulgarian Foreign Trade Bank Ltd*, Stockholm City Court, Case No. T-111-98 (1998) ("a party to arbitration proceedings cannot be deemed to be bound by a duty of confidentiality, unless the parties have concluded an agreement concerning this").

[58] Examples of arbitration rules that impose confidentiality include: Singapore International Arbitration Centre Rules, Rule 39.1, available at http://siac.org.sg/our-rules/rules/siac-rules-2016; World Intellectual Property Organization, arts. 75–78, available at http://www.arbiter.wipo.int/arbitration/rules/index.html. Examples of confidentiality provisions in mediation include: Hong Kong International Arbitration Centre Mediation Rules, art. 12, available at http://www.hkiac.org/mediation/rules/hkiac-mediation-rules; WIPO Mediation Rules, arts. 15–18, available at http://www.arbiter.wipo.int/mediation/rules/index.html.

[59] L. Yves Fortier, *The Occasionally Unwarranted Assumption of Confidentiality*, 15 Arb. Int'l 131 (1999); Jan Paulsson & Nigel Rawding, *The Trouble with Confidentiality*, 11(3) ICC Int'l Court Arb. Bull. 303–20 (1994); Jean R. Haynes, *International Arbitration May Not Be as Confidential as You Think—or Want*, in Conflicting Legal Cultures in Commercial Arbitration 99 (Stefan M. Frommel & Barry Alexander Rider eds. 1999).

proceedings can be particularly vulnerable to disclosure where issues of "public interest" are concerned, as is frequently the case in investment disputes.[60] Indeed, an increasing body of investment arbitration decisions suggests that the public policy implications of investor–State disputes necessitate the wholesale disclosure of decisions and even submissions from the parties,[61] in part to facilitate *amicus curiae* intervention from non-disputing parties that have a legitimate interest in the proceedings.[62] Several investment arbitration proceedings have now been opened to the public, part of an increasing trend of openness.[63] In this direction, new arbitration rules on investor–State arbitration reflect the growing impetus for more transparency and openness of disputes involving

[60] *See e.g. Philip Morris Asia Ltd. v. Australia*, UNCITRAL, PCA Case No. 2012-12, available at https://www.italaw.com/cases/851; *Vattenfall A.B. et al. v. Germany*, ICSID Case No. ARB/12/12, available at https://icsid.worldbank.org/en/Pages/cases/casedetail.aspx?CaseNo=ARB/12/12; *Esso Australia Resources Ltd. v. Plowman*, [1995] 183 C.L.R. 10. *See also* João Ribeiro & Michael Douglas, *Transparency in Investor–State Arbitration: The Way Forward*, 11 Asian Int'l. Arb. J. 49–67 (2015).

[61] *See e.g.* James D. Fry & Odysseas G. Repousis, *Towards a New World for Investor–State Arbitration Through Transparency*, 48 NYU J. Int'l L. & Pol. 795 (2016). Stephan W. Schill, *Transparency as a Global Norm in International Investment Law*, Kluwer Arbitration Blog (Sept. 15, 2014); Christian J. Tams & Alessandra Asteriti, *Transparency and Representation of the Public Interest in Investment Treaty Arbitration*, in International Investment Law and Comparative Public Law (Stephan W. Schill ed. 2010).

[62] *See e.g. Philip Morris Brand Sàrl (Switzerland), Philip Morris Products S.A. (Switzerland) and Abal Hermanos S.A. (Uruguay) v. Uruguay*, ICSID Case No. ARB/10/7, Procedural Order No. 4 of Mar. 24, 2015; *Bernhard von Pezold et al. v. Zimbabwe*, ICSID Case No. ARB/10/15, Procedural Order No. 2 of June 26, 2012; *Apotex Holdings Inc. and Apotex Inc. v. U.S.A.*, ICSID Case No. ARB(AF)/12/1, Procedural Order on the Participation of the Applicant, Mr Barry Appleton, as a Non-Disputing Party, Mar. 4, 2013, at paras. 19 and 27; *Eli Lilly and Co. v. Government of Canada*, ICSID Case No. UNCT/14/2, Procedural Order No. 4 of Feb. 23, 2016, at para. B; *Glamis Gold Ltd. v. U.S.A.*, UNCITRAL, Final Award of June 8, 2009, at para. 286.

[63] *See Methanex v U.S.A.*, Decision of the Tribunal on Petitions from Third Persons to intervene as "Amici Curiae," Jan. 15, 2001, available at https://www.italaw.com/cases/683; *United Parcel Service of America Inc. v. Government of Canada*, Award on Jurisdiction of Nov. 22, 2002, available at http://www.state.gov/s/l/c3749.htm; *Aguas Argentinas S.A., Suez, Sociedad General de Aguas de Barcelona S.A. and Vivendi Universal S.A. v. Argentina*, ICSID Case No. ARB/03/19, Order in Response to a Petition for Transparency and Participation as *Amicus Curiae* of May 19, 2005, available at https://www.italaw.com/cases/1057. Recent bilateral investment treaties signed by the United States, Canada, and other countries require the publication of all legal submissions and awards, as well as the opening of hearings to the public. *See e.g.* US–Uruguay BIT (2004), art. 10(1):

> Each Party shall ensure that its:
>
> (a) laws, regulations, procedures, and administrative rulings of general application; and
> (b) adjudicatory decisions respecting any matter covered by this Treaty are promptly published or otherwise made publicly available.

The Canada–El Salvador BIT (1999) provides at art. XIV(1): "Each Contracting Party shall, to the extent practicable, ensure that its laws, regulations, procedures, and administrative rulings of general application respecting any matter covered by this Agreement are promptly published or otherwise made available in such a manner as to enable interested persons and the other Contracting Party to become acquainted with them."

significant public interests of the host State vis-à-vis the private interests of foreign investors.[64] Naturally, the parties to arbitration can sign an express confidentiality agreement, but such matters are often neglected until after arbitration begins, when agreement on anything can be exceedingly difficult.

9.31 Conciliation proceedings, like negotiations, are almost universally conducted confidentially and on a without-prejudice basis.[65] Since the parties are free to enter into a conciliation agreement after their dispute arises, and relations between them are generally sufficiently amicable to modify any existing agreement, express confidentiality obligations can be put in place before the process begins. Indeed, it is only through firm assurances as to the privacy and confidentiality of the process at the outset that mediators can elicit frank disclosures about interests, positions, facts, and preferences that provide the foundation for amicable settlement. Nearly all conciliation rules prevent the parties from introducing information gleaned through the conciliation process in any subsequent litigation or arbitration.

9.32 Many countries have implemented laws further safeguarding the confidentiality of the mediation process.[66] By choosing a mediation venue that has such a statute, the parties can ensure a court-ordered remedy (injunctive or monetary) to any unauthorized disclosure of confidential information, and also gain support in preventing such information from being used in parallel or subsequent adversarial proceedings.[67]

---

[64] *See e.g.* 2010 UNCITRAL Arbitration Rules, art. 7 and the UNCITRAL Rules on Transparency in Treaty-based Investor–State Arbitration, available at http://www.uncitral.org/pdf/english/texts/arbitration/arb-rules-2013/UNCITRAL-Arbitration-Rules-2013-e.pdf; United Nations Convention on Transparency in Treaty-based Investor–State Arbitration (2014) (the "Mauritius Convention").

[65] See, e.g., IBA Rules for Investor–State Mediation, art. 10, available at https://www.ibanet.org/Publications/publications_IBA_guides_and_free_materials.aspx#collapse5; ICC Mediation Rules, art. 9, available at https://iccwbo.org/dispute-resolution-services/mediation/mediation-rules/; LCIA Mediation Rules, art. 10, available at http://www.lcia.org/Dispute_Resolution_Services/LCIA_Mediation_Rules.aspx#Anchor-Article-33869. Corporate users of ADR may not be aware of the confidentiality distinction between arbitration and conciliation. In a recent study of U.S. corporate counsel, 43.2 percent of respondents said they chose arbitration in part because it is confidential, while 44.9 percent said the same about mediation. David B. Lipsky & Ronald L. Seeber, The Appropriate Resolution of Corporate Disputes 17 (1996).

[66] *See e.g.* E.U. Mediation Directive, *supra* note 3, art. 7(1).

[67] *See e.g.* U.S. Uniform Mediation Act (2001). *See also Farm Assist Ltd. (In Liquidation) v. Secretary of State for the Environment, Food and Rural Affairs (No. 2)* [2009] EWHC 1102 (TCC) at para. 43, where the English High Court ruled that mediation proceedings are confidential both as between the parties and as between the parties and the mediator. Even if the parties agree that matters can be disclosed outside the mediation, the mediator can enforce the confidentiality provision and the court will generally uphold that confidentiality, unless disclosure is necessary in the interest of justice. *See further Cumbria Waste Management v. Baines Wilson* [2008] EWHC 786; *Brown v. Rice and Patel* [2007] EWHC 625 (Ch.); *Aird v Prime Meridian* [2006] EWCA Civ. 1866 at para. 5.

4. Flexibility

Mediation, like negotiation, also offers a high level of flexibility to the parties. Even where the parties have chosen a set of "procedural" rules, such systems provide only the most general framework for the parties' work with the conciliator.[68] Parties are free to discuss the relative merits of their respective positions free from rigid rules on the exchange of information, and the procedures can be tailored to meet their respective needs, the nature of the disputants, and the particular circumstances of the dispute.[69] In particular, unlike adversarial dispute resolution systems, conciliation allows the neutral third party to communicate informally and separately with each of the parties. The conciliator can thereby offer sympathy and critique equally to both sides without undermining their credibility, and can choose the proper stage of the process to create and propose solutions to the parties' dispute. **9.33**

The flexibility of conciliation/mediation may be a particularly important asset in investor–State disputes. While corporate investors—particularly those from industrialized countries—will likely feel relatively comfortable with the formal structure of arbitration and litigation, government officials (especially those outside the justice ministry and public prosecutor's office) will almost inevitably be out of their element. More accustomed to international negotiation or internal inter-agency talks, host State representatives may be reluctant to compromise in the context of arbitration, where they perceive themselves to be at a disadvantage. The benefits of informality may be further accentuated where one or both of the parties are from East Asia, where adversarial dispute resolution is contrary to widely-held cultural expectations, and compromise through informal exchanges is generally preferred.[70] **9.34**

---

[68] Linda C. Reif, *Conciliation as a Mechanism for the Resolution of International Economic and Business Disputes*, 14 Fordham Int'l L.J. 578, 585 (1991); Steven J. Burton, *Combining Conciliation with Arbitration of International Commercial Disputes*, 18 Hastings Int'l Comp. L. Rev. 637, 639 (1995).

[69] Indeed, this flexibility may be the primary source of participants' satisfaction with conciliation. Lipsky & Seeber, *supra* note 65, at 17 (81.1 percent of U.S. corporate counsel surveyed said they had used mediation because it provided a "more satisfactory process").

[70] Trappe, *supra* note 23, at 179–83; J.D. Fine, *Continuum or Chasm? Can West Meet East? Commercial Arbitration and Alternative Dispute Resolution Techniques in the Western Nations of the LAWASIA Region*, 6(4) J. Int'l Arb. 27, 31–33 (1989); Pheng Low Sui, *The Influence of Chinese Philosophies on Mediation and Conciliation in the Far East*, 62(1) Arb. 16 (1996). For a humorous illustration of the Japanese preference for conciliation, *see* Charles R. Stevens & Kazunobu Takahashi, *The East Asian Preference for Conciliation: An Example in a Kabuki Play*, 5 Arb. Int'l 43 (1989). *See also* Thomas-Nektarios Papanastasiou, *Mediation in Japan (in Greek)*, 5–6 Epitheorisi Politikis Dikonomias J. 522–34 (2016).

5. Impact on continuing business relations

9.35 For many parties, conciliation and mediation offer a superior means of dispute resolution because they offer greater potential to preserve long-term business relationships between the disputants than do litigation or arbitration.[71] As Professor Wälde explains:

> All litigation methods tend to undermine, and mostly destroy, an existing commercial relationship and thus significant asset value: Building international commercial and investment relationships is a high-risk, expensive and therefore, if successful, very valuable asset building activity in itself.[72]

9.36 Arbitration and litigation have a detrimental effect on business relationships for a number of reasons. Most importantly, such adversarial systems are based upon entitlements, rewarding participants who insist upon the full range of their rights under the applicable rules. Parties therefore frequently occupy relatively extreme positions at the outset of a dispute, hoping to coerce a settlement by convincing the other side that its entitlement is great.[73] Such strategic behavior can lead to accusations and emotional escalation among the parties, with each side becoming convinced of its own exclusive entitlement.[74] As a result, even though a solution is imposed by the judge or arbitrator, one or both sides may remain dissatisfied and unwilling to cooperate in the future.

9.37 By contrast,

> The mediator's skill is not in deciding what is right under applicable law and proven evidence, but rather what kind of renegotiated deal the parties can accept, and prefer to the always present option to go to litigation. The consequence of this radically different approach is that a proper mediator will pro-actively seek to identify the causes for the dispute, the blockages hindering the parties from settling by direct negotiations and possibilities for a new deal.[75]

9.38 In many investor–State disputes, the parties share an economic interest in the continuation of the investor's activity in the host country in one form or another.

---

[71] *See e.g.* Susan D. Franck, *Using Investor–State Mediation Rules to Promote Conflict Management: An Introductory Guide*, 29(1) ICSID Rev.—For. Inv. L.J. 77–78 (2014). *See also* Roberto Echandi & P. Kher, *Can International Investor–State Disputes Be Prevented? Empirical Evidence from Settlements in ICSID Arbitration*, 29(1) ICSID Rev.—For. Inv. L.J. 41 *et seq.* (2014); Roberto Echandi, *Complementing Investor–State Dispute Resolution: A Conceptual Framework for Investor–State Conflict Management*, in Prospects in International Investment Law and Policy 270 (Roberto Echandi & Pierre Suave eds. 2013).

[72] Wälde, *supra* note 48, at 1. *See also* Thomas Wälde, *Efficient Management of Transnational Disputes: Mutual Gain by Mediation or Joint Loss in Litigation*, 22 Arb. Int'l. 205–33 (2006).

[73] Fisher, *supra* note 32, at 6, 21, 139–40.

[74] Wälde, *supra* note 35, at 2 ("facts presented in arbitration will be very selective and aim at showing the other party's conduct in the darkest light possible. Legal theories will equally be sought which revile the conduct of the other party as much as possible … the logic of litigation intensifies mutual antagonism").

[75] Wälde, *supra* note 48, at 3.

Many such disputes arise out of long-term concessions or infrastructure projects, which offer both a substantial long-term benefit for the host State and its population, but also a reliable source of profit, prestige and experience for the investor.[76] As a result, it is the very goal of mediation—to build rather than to deconstruct—that makes it a promising dispute resolution avenue for conflicts between host States and foreign investors.[77]

C. Contracting to Mediate and Conciliate in Investment Disputes

Because conciliation/mediation can only proceed if both sides remain willing to explore settlement options, it is not necessary that the parties have entered into a mediation agreement before their dispute arose in order to engage in such proceedings. The parties may generally agree to enter into conciliation/mediation at any point in their dispute. Most often, consent to mediation will occur before formal arbitration or litigation proceedings commence, but not infrequently the parties will agree to suspend ongoing arbitration if they believe that conciliation offers the opportunity of a durable settlement.[78] Nevertheless, the presence of an ADR clause in an investment contract or treaty may encourage the parties to accede to conciliation/mediation and participate fully in the process, and will certainly remove unnecessary initial points of discussion regarding the structure and conduct of the conciliation process. Contractual provisions on conciliation can "help a party to propose an amicable settlement to the other(s) without 'losing face.'"[79] **9.39**

The parties need not conduct conciliation according to any pre-established rule system. Rather, if they are able to agree upon a conciliator or a method for appointing one (or more, as the case may be), they can leave the organization of conciliation proceedings to the discretion of the neutral, or make specific **9.40**

[76] In the commercial context, it would appear that this consideration leads to the use of mediation over arbitration more often in the natural resources extraction and construction sectors than in some other areas of activity. Lipsky & Seeber, *supra* note 65, at 12–13.

[77] Both investors and governmental representatives from many Asian societies may have a cultural disposition to find the conflict of litigation inherently distasteful, preferring the consensus-building and relationship-preserving approach of conciliation. Leonard L. Riskin, *Mediation and Lawyers*, 43 Ohio St. L.J. 29 (1982); *see also* Papanastasiou, *supra* note 70.

[78] In theory, conciliation can proceed in parallel with arbitration or litigation, but the rancor of adversarial proceedings, and the fixed positions they force the parties to occupy, make the combination an inauspicious one. For this reason, some conciliation rules suggest or require the suspension of other dispute resolution proceedings until the conclusion of the conciliation process. *See e.g.* UNCITRAL Conciliation Rules (1980), 20 I.L.M. 300 (1981), art. 16, available at http://www.uncitral.org/uncitral/en/uncitral_texts/arbitration.html.

[79] Dyalá Jiménez-Figueres, *Amicable Means to Resolve Disputes: How the ICC ADR Rules Work*, 21(1) J. Int'l Arb. 91, 92 (2004).

provision for particular procedures. In order to avoid the possible delay and disagreement this initial negotiation may cause, the parties may also choose one of several available rules systems to govern their conciliation/mediation process.

9.41 Each of the main institutions that offer ADR rules also provide model conciliation clauses for inclusion in contracts, which can also be adapted for use as stand-alone conciliation agreements after a dispute has arisen.[80] The parties should modify the relevant model clause according to the circumstances of their transaction and their preferences, in particular considering:

- whether the parties should be "obliged" to undertake conciliation/mediation for a certain period of time before they may abandon the process (regardless of the difficulty of compelling participation);[81]
- whether the conciliation/mediation should be conducted by a single person, or by a panel of two or three;
- the institution (if any) that will serve as "appointing authority" should the parties be unable to select one or more conciliators on their own;
- qualifications or limitations (nationality, for example) to be placed on conciliator candidates;[82]
- the extent of confidentiality during the proceedings and the penalties for breach of confidentiality obligations;
- whether conciliation/mediation should stand alone as the sole agreed dispute resolution mechanism, or as part of an escalating chain of procedures, from negotiation to arbitration or litigation.[83]

9.42 In the next section we examine some of the most prominent conciliation and mediation rules systems, with particular application in the context of investment disputes.

---

[80] Further information on ICSID's Conciliation Rules, *see* ICISD Convention, Regulations and Rules (2006), available at https://icsid.worldbank.org/en/Documents/icsiddocs/ICSID%20Convention%20English.pdf [hereinafter, the ICSID Conciliation Rules]; 17 (1996) on the ICC Mediation Rules at *supra* note 44; on the UNCITRAL Conciliation Rules at *supra* note 78.

[81] On the idea of mandatory mediation for investment disputes, *see* Nancy A. Welsh, *Mandatory Mediation and Its Variations*, in Investor–State Disputes: Prevention and Alternatives to Arbitration II, 108 *et seq.* (Susan D. Franck & Anna Joubin-Bret eds. 2011). *See also* Thomas W. Wälde, *Chapter 12—Improving the Mechanisms for Treaty Negotiation and Investment Disputes, Competition and Choice as the Path to Quality and Legitimacy*, in Yearbook on International Investment Law & Policy 2008–2009 535–36 (Karl Sauvant ed. 2009), suggesting a cost sanction for parties refusing to mediate as per *Dunnett v. Railtrack* [2002] EWCA Civ. 302.

[82] *See e.g.* the "Competency Criteria for Investor–State Mediators," issued by the International Mediation Institute in 2016 to facilitate the selection of mediators for disputes involving private sector entities and States, available at https://www.imimediation.org/download/104/investor–State-mediation-task-force/1472/investor–State-mediation-competency-criteria.pdf.

[83] Henry Brown & Arthur Marriott, ADR Principles and Practice 416–20 (2d ed. 2002); Jiménez-Figueres, *supra* note 79.

1. UNCITRAL Conciliation Rules

a. Overview

9.43 UNCITRAL (the United Nations Commission on International Trade Law) adopted its Conciliation Rules in 1980, after considering the comments submitted by member States and interested non-governmental organizations.[84] These Rules were then promulgated by the U.N. General Assembly.[85] The UNCITRAL Conciliation Rules, like most other systems, are quite simple, consisting of only twenty Articles.[86] They describe the means of appointing a conciliator and his role in the proceedings, default procedures to be followed, confidentiality, and the means of embodying the parties' settlement in an agreement. Any of the UNCITRAL Rules can be varied by agreement of the parties, as long as such agreement does not conflict with mandatory rules of law to which the parties are subject.[87]

b. Initiating conciliation

9.44 A party to a dispute can initiate conciliation under the UNCITRAL Rules by inviting the other party or parties in writing to participate.[88] This invitation should briefly describe the nature of the dispute, but need not provide any details concerning the amount at stake, legal or factual positions, or relief sought.[89] Indeed, it is advisable for the requesting party to draft the invitation as pithily as possible, to avoid the appearance of pre-judgment and to encourage the other side to accept the conciliation proposal. Conciliation can begin if the other side responds positively to the invitation within thirty days.[90] This confirmation need not be in writing, but formal evidence of consent is preferable.[91] Unlike institutional conciliation rules, the UNCITRAL Rules allow the inviting party to "keep the door open" longer than thirty days, either by extending the deadline for response contained in the invitation, or by simply accepting a late response when it arrives.[92]

9.45 Where the parties have not otherwise agreed, UNCITRAL conciliation is carried out by a sole conciliator.[93] In such a situation, the conciliator is normally appointed jointly by both sides.[94] A panel of three conciliators is constituted through

[84] UNCITRAL Conciliation Rules, *supra* note 78. *See* Vinod Agarwal, *Alternative Dispute Resolution Methods*, DFM Doc. No. 14 (March 2001), available at https://www.unitar.org/pft/sites/unitar.org.pft/files/DocSeries14.pdf.

[85] U.N.G.A. Res. 35/52 of Dec. 4, 1980.

[86] *See* note 80, *supra*, for online resources.

[87] UNCITRAL Conciliation Rules, *supra* note 78, art. 1(2), (3).

[88] *Id.*, art. 2(1).

[89] Gerold Hermann, *Commentary on the UNCITRAL Conciliation Rules*, 6 Yb. Comm. Arb. 170, 174 (1981).

[90] UNCITRAL Conciliation Rules, *supra* note 78, art. 2(2)–(3).

[91] Hermann, *supra* note 89, at 174.

[92] *Id.* at 175.

[93] UNCITRAL Conciliation Rules, *supra* note 78, art. 3.

[94] *Id.*, art. 4(1)(a).

appointment by each party of one member, with the presiding conciliator selected by consensus.[95] Where assistance is required either in finding a candidate with appropriate qualifications or one acceptable to both sides to serve as sole or presiding conciliator, the UNCITRAL Rules permit the parties to seek assistance from an "appropriate institution or person."[96] Many organizations maintain mediator lists, and some will provide advice on selecting conciliators in light of the facts and issues related to a particular dispute. Unless the parties so agree, however, such an institution may only *recommend* a candidate, and cannot impose a conciliator upon the parties.[97] Since in most instances such agreement will not have been reached before the dispute arises, the UNCITRAL Rules direct the assisting institution as follows:

> In recommending or appointing individuals to act as conciliator, the institution or person shall have regard to such considerations as are likely to secure the appointment of an independent and impartial conciliator and, with respect to a sole or third conciliator, shall take into account the advisability of appointing a conciliator of a nationality other than the nationalities of the parties.[98]

9.46 Once the parties or institution have appointed the conciliator(s), the conciliation proceeding has begun. Since no institution oversees the ad hoc procedure, no set initial payment of fees is necessary to commence. The conciliator, however, *may* request that each party pay an advance upon the estimated costs of mediation before beginning work.[99]

c. Managing the process

9.47 As the first step in an UNCITRAL conciliation proceeding, the panel asks each side to submit a short written summary of its view of the dispute and the primary issues separating the parties.[100] Because not all of the parties may be fully aware of the constitution of the conciliation panel, this initial request should include contact details for each mediator, the mode of his appointment, and the procedure for making any deposit against procedural costs.[101] The parties must deliver this summary statement to the other parties to the conciliation, as well as to the panel. If necessary, the panel may then request an additional, more detailed statement of position from the parties, which (unlike the initial statement) may be accompanied by documentary or written witness evidence.[102]

---

[95] *Id.*, art. 4(1)(c).

[96] *Id.*, art. 4(2).

[97] *Id.*, art. 4(2)(a)–(b); Hermann, *supra* note 89, at 177.

[98] UNCITRAL Conciliation Rules, *supra* note 78, art. 4, final para.

[99] *Id.*, art. 18(1).

[100] *Id.*, art. 5(1). *See also* Gavan Griffith & Andrew D. Mitchell, *Contractual Dispute Resolution in International Trade: The UNCITRAL Arbitration Rules (1976) and the UNCITRAL Conciliation Rules (1980)*, 3(1) Melbourne J. Int'l. L. 197 *et seq*. (2002).

[101] Hermann, *supra* note 89, at 178.

[102] UNCITRAL Conciliation Rules, *supra* note 78, art. 5(2).

The panel is authorized to request any other information from the parties at any time.[103]

9.48 The remainder of the conciliation procedure is left largely within the discretion of the conciliation panel,[104] framed by a number of broad guidelines for the conduct of parties and conciliators. Conciliators are to act impartially and independently in assisting the parties to reach a negotiated settlement of their dispute. The UNCITRAL Rules underline the overriding role of equity in the ADR process, with law relegated to a subsidiary position in the panel's deliberations:

The conciliator will be guided by principles of objectivity, fairness and justice, giving consideration to, among other things, the rights and obligations of the parties, the usages of the trade concerned and the circumstances surrounding the dispute, including any previous business practices between the parties.[105]

9.49 UNCITRAL conciliation panels may, at a party's request, call witnesses to give evidence, but this authority is far more limited than in arbitration cases. In particular, the requesting party must bear the cost associated with the witness's testimony, unless the witness has been called jointly by both sides.[106] Furthermore, the panel "is not empowered to appoint an expert or hear a witness on his own initiative."[107]

9.50 Parties may be assisted by counsel or by some other third party, but the identity of such representatives must be notified to the other party in advance. Such notice must also indicate whether counsel acts "for purposes of representation or assistance," presumably to allow the panel and the other side to understand the scope of third parties' authority to accept settlement proposals.[108] The UNCITRAL Rules require that all parties cooperate with the conciliation panel in good faith, and comply with any requests to "submit written materials, provide evidence and attend hearings."[109] The UNCITRAL Rules discourage the parties from pursuing arbitration, litigation, or other forms dispute resolution while the conciliation process is ongoing.[110] Nevertheless, in recognition of the legitimate purposes of parallel litigation, in particular to avoid running afoul of statutory time limitations,

[103] *Id.*, arts. 5(3), 11; Hermann, *supra* note 89, at 179.

[104] UNCITRAL Conciliation Rules, *supra* note 78, art. 7(3) ("The conciliator may conduct the conciliation proceedings in such a manner as he considers appropriate, taking into account the circumstances of the case, the wishes the parties may express, including any request by a party that the conciliator hear oral statements, and the need for a speedy settlement of the dispute").

[105] *Id.*, art. 7(2).

[106] UNCITRAL Conciliation Rules, *supra* note 78, art. 17(1)(c); Hermann, *supra* note 89, at 180.

[107] Hermann, *supra* note 89, at 180.

[108] UNCITRAL Conciliation Rules, *supra* note 78, art. 6; Hermann, *supra* note 89, at 179.

[109] *Id.*, art. 11.

[110] *Id.*, art. 16.

the UNCITRAL Rules allow a party to undertake such actions "where, in his opinion, such proceedings are necessary for preserving his rights."[111]

9.51 The UNCITRAL system provides more specific parameters for the conciliator or panel to make settlement proposals to the parties. At any point in the proceeding when the conciliator believes that he has identified the necessary elements of a successful agreement, he submits a draft outlining his proposal to both sides, soliciting their comments. If necessary, the draft can be revised to reflect the parties' reactions.[112] This document then becomes the basis of a settlement agreement, drawn up with or without the conciliator's assistance, to which the parties formally accede by signature to end their dispute.[113]

9.52 It is important to note that the UNCITRAL Rules specifically prohibit a party from using any information received through conciliation in order to gain strategic advantage in later adversarial proceedings. The Rules are comprehensive in this regard, designed to encourage an atmosphere of informality and compromise during the conciliation process:

> The parties undertake not to rely on or introduce as evidence in arbitral or judicial proceedings, whether or not such proceedings relate to the dispute that is the subject of the conciliation proceedings:
> (a) Views expressed or suggestions made by the other party in respect of a possible settlement of the dispute;
> (b) Admission made by the other party in the course of the conciliation proceedings;
> (c) Proposals made by the conciliator;
> (d) The fact that the other party had indicated his willingness to accept a proposal for settlement made by the conciliator.

2. The ICC Mediation Rules

a. Background

9.53 The International Chamber of Commerce, based in Paris, has offered conciliation services since its founding in 1919. Indeed, the very first dispute resolved under the auspices of the ICC's Court of Arbitration was the result of conciliation.[114] During the interwar period, more ICC disputes were resolved by conciliation than by arbitration.[115] In recent years, however, the use of the ICC's conciliation

---

[111] *Id.*

[112] *Id.*, art. 13(1).

[113] UNCITRAL Conciliation Rules, *supra* note 78, art. 13(2).

[114] George L. Ridgeway, Merchants of Peace 325–26 (1938) ("after an hour's discussion, the parties came to a common understanding and agreed to accept a compromise which was made into a formal agreement and signed by them").

[115] Schwartz, *supra* note 36, at 5; Pierre Michel Eisemann, *The Court of Arbitration: Outline of its Changes from Inception to the Present Day*, in International Chamber of Commerce: 60 Years of ICC Arbitration 391, 397 (1984); *Outgoing Secretary General Bond Sees Greater Role for ICC Court*, 2 World Arbitration and Mediation Rep. 164, 165 (June 1991) (80 percent of cases submitted to the ICC before 1939 were settled by conciliation). *See also* Peter M. Wolrich,

procedures has declined markedly. In the six years following the ICC's update of its Optional Conciliation Rules in 1988, there were on average only ten conciliation requests submitted annually, compared to over 300 ICC arbitration cases filed each year during the same period.[116]

In July 2001, the ICC replaced the Optional Conciliation Rules with its 2001 ADR Rules (the ICC ADR Rules).[117] While these rules were designed to be applicable to any of a range of dispute resolution mechanisms, where the parties have not expressly made a choice in this regard mediation is the default ADR method that will be applied. While the scope of the ADR Rules was limited to "business disputes,"[118] such limitation was not intended to exclude the mediation of investment-related disputes involving a State or governmental entity. Rather, this provision was designed to prevent the application of the ADR Rules to labor or family disputes, which may be subject to conflicting mandatory dispute resolution regimes in certain legal systems.[119] **9.54**

As of January 1, 2014, the ICC Mediation Rules replaced the 2001 ADR Rules to reflect contemporary practices. These rules provide users with clear parameters for the conduct of proceedings while recognizing and maintaining the need for flexibility. These new rules integrated the practices developed by the ICC in the application of the 2001 ADR Rules and reinforced the powers of the ICC International Centre for ADR in its administration of procedures aimed at an amicable settlement.[120] The goal of the 2014 revision was to facilitate the use of ADR and enhance the effectiveness of mediation administered by the ICC, making the Rules more user-friendly. Notably, the ICC Mediation Rules are no longer applicable solely to "business disputes," but cover any kind of "dispute,"[121] including investment disputes.[122] **9.55**

ICC ADR Rules: The Latest Addition to ICC's Dispute Resolution Services, ICC INT'L COURT ARB. BULL. 7, 8–9 (2001).

[116] Schwartz, *supra* note 36, at 6.

[117] Wolrich, *supra* note 115, at 7, 9; Douglas Earl McLaren, *The New ICC ADR Rules*, MEALEY'S INT'L ARB. REP. (Mar. 2002), at 21. *See also* note 44, *supra*.

[118] ICC ADR Rules, 2001, available at https://arbitrationlaw.com/sites/default/files/free_pdfs/ICC%20ADR%20Guide.pdf.

[119] ICC MEDIATION GUIDANCE NOTES, *supra* note 46, at 6. Nor may the Rules be used to adjudicate personal injury claims. Wolrich, *supra* note 115, at 13.

[120] *See* Alexandra Munoz, *The New ICC Mediation Rules of 2014: Evolution not Revolution*, 2 CAHIERS DE L'ARBITRAGE 325 (2014); H. Tümpel & C. Sudborough, *ICC's ADR Rules 2001–2010: Current Practices, Case Examples and Lessons Learned*, in II ADR IN BUSINESS, PRACTICE AND ISSUES ACROSS COUNTRIES AND CULTURES (A. Ingenhousz ed. 2011).

[121] ICC Mediation Rules, *supra* note 44, art. 1(2).

[122] *See* Energy Charter Secretariat, Guide on Investment Mediation (2016), available at https://energycharter.org/fileadmin/DocumentsMedia/CCDECS/2016/CCDEC201612.pdf.

b. Initiating the process

9.56 The parties may jointly or independently initiate ICC mediation by submitting a Request for Mediation to the ICC.[123] This document should be brief, outlining the nature of the dispute and, if possible, an assessment of its value, to allow the mediator (and the other party, if the Request is submitted unilaterally) to understand the basic positions and prepare for the first meeting with the parties.[124] The Request for Mediation must also be accompanied by a non-refundable registration fee, which was set at US$3,000 at the time of publication.[125] If the Request is submitted unilaterally, the ICC will inform all other parties of the proposal and may even assist the parties in considering the proposal.[126] If the response is negative or not received within fifteen days (or within such additional time as may be reasonably determined by the Centre), proceedings will not be initiated.[127]

9.57 The ICC mediation process is conducted by a "Mediator" (under the previous ADR Rules, a "Neutral") selected in the first instance jointly by the parties.[128] Where the parties are unable to agree on a Mediator, the ICC secretariat may, after consulting with the parties, either propose a list of Mediators to the parties or designate one for them, subject (to the extent possible) to any particular qualifications or attributes upon which the parties may agree, taking into account nationality, language skills, training, qualifications and experience, and availability and ability to conduct the mediation.[129] Where the Centre appoints a Mediator, it will often do so on the basis of a proposal by an ICC National Committee or Group. If within fifteen days a party objects to the Mediator appointed by the Centre and notifies the Centre and all other parties in writing, stating the reasons for the objection, the Centre will appoint another Mediator.[130]

9.58 Regardless of whether the parties or the ICC designates the Mediator, the ICC will request that the prospective Mediator sign a statement of acceptance, availability, impartiality, and independence and disclose in writing "any facts or circumstances which might be of such nature as to call into question the Mediator's independence in the eyes of the parties, as well as any circumstances that could give rise to reasonable doubts as to the Mediator's impartiality."[131] In the case of ICC-designated Mediator, any disclosure will normally disqualify the individual and lead to

[123] ICC Mediation Rules, *supra* note 44, arts. 2(1), 3(1).

[124] ICC Mediation Rules, *supra* note 44, art. 2(1)(a)–(h). ICC Mediation Guidance Notes *supra* note 46, at 6; Wolrich, *supra* note 115, at 14–15.

[125] ICC Mediation Rules, *supra* note 44, arts. 2(2), 3(2) and Appendix, art. 1.

[126] ICC Mediation Rules, *supra* note 44, art. 3(2).

[127] ICC Mediation Rules, *supra* note 44, art. 3(4); Jiménez-Figueres, *supra* note 79, at 95; Wolrich, *supra* note 115, at 15; McLaren, *supra* note 117, at 21–22.

[128] ICC Mediation Rules, *supra* note 44, art. 5(1).

[129] *Id.*, art. 5(4).

[130] *Id.*, art. 5(5).

[131] *Id.*, art. 5(3).

a different appointment.[132] Where the parties have chosen the Mediator, the ICC sends any disclosed information to the parties, allowing them the opportunity to reject the candidate and choose another.[133]

c. Managing the process

The ICC Mediation Rules are somewhat unique, in that where the parties have agreed to participate in dispute resolution under ICC auspices, they are obligated to participate in the process, at least until after the first meeting with the Mediator.[134] This requirement is designed to give some meaning to the parties' submission to mediation, and to leave open the possibility that the initial meeting with the Mediator will convince an otherwise recalcitrant party that advantageous settlement is possible through ADR and that the process should continue.[135] **9.59**

The first meeting between the parties and the mediator is to occur as soon as possible after registration of the dispute, and can occur either in person or by telephone or video conference.[136] It is at this session that the procedure to be followed is established, by consensus or by the Mediator if no agreement can be reached.[137] The ICC Mediation Rules provide almost no guidelines in this regard, directing only that: **9.60**

> In establishing and conducting the mediation, the Mediator shall be guided by the wishes of the parties and shall treat them with fairness and impartiality.[138]

However, the ICC Mediation Guidance Notes provide some further elucidation: **9.61**

> During all meetings (both joint and private) the mediator will seek to create an environment conducive to constructive negotiations, but the purpose of the meetings may vary. Some may be used for the parties and/or their lawyers to make presentations to each other. Others may be used for the mediator to explore the background to the dispute, identify the interests and needs of each of the parties for their mutual benefit, and consider any alternative options for settlement. Later in the process, meetings may be used for bargaining, with offers and counter-offers being exchanged either directly or via the mediator. If agreement is reached, then the meetings may be used to draft and agree upon the terms of a written settlement agreement.[139]

At the core of mediation will be one or more "mediation sessions," which are attended by all parties, their advisers (if any) and the mediator. The number of **9.62**

---

[132] Jiménez-Figueres, *supra* note 79, at 95.

[133] *Id.*

[134] ICC Mediation Rules, *supra* note 44, art. 7(2); Wolrich, *supra* note 115, at 12, 19.

[135] *See* on the previous regime (with similar rules), Guide to ICC ADR, at 7.

[136] *Id.*, ICC Mediation Guidance Notes *supra* note 46, at 11; Wolrich, *supra* note 115, at 19–20.

[137] ICC Mediation Rules, *supra* note 44, art. 7.

[138] *Id.*, art. 7(3).

[139] *See* ICC Mediation Guidance Notes, *supra* note 46, at para. 14.

these sessions and their duration will vary depending on the requirements of the case and the approach favored by the mediator and the parties.[140] The mediator can hold meetings or conference calls with all of the parties present (a joint meeting) and may also meet with each of the parties separately.[141] Where this happens, the Mediator will confirm that new information discussed in private 'caucus' will not be disclosed without permission.[142]

9.63 In the course of the mediation, the parties can exchange settlement proposals, which may lead to a negotiated agreement. Such proposals can be made directly between the parties or through the mediator. Since control over the decision to settle and the terms of any agreement remains with the parties, the mediator has no power to impose a settlement.[143] However, if all parties so request, the mediator may recommend settlement terms for their consideration.[144]

9.64 Like the UNCITRAL Conciliation Rules, the ICC Mediation Rules prohibit the use in subsequent or parallel proceedings of information procured as part of the mediation process, including proposals made by the Mediator or expressions by a party of willingness to accept such a proposal.[145] However, the ICC Mediation Rules expressly provide that the fact that mediation is taking place is not in itself confidential.[146]

9.65 Because ICC mediation is subject to oversight by the ICC, the parties incur administrative costs as well as fees paid to the mediator or mediators. In addition to the registration fee, the ICC sets the administrative fee it is to receive on a case-by-case basis, in light of the institution's involvement in the proceedings (*i.e.* providing mediator CVs, appointing mediators, facilitating correspondence, offering space for mediation sessions, *etc.*). This fee is currently capped at US$30,000.[147]

9.66 Unless otherwise agreed, the fees of the Mediator are to be calculated on an hourly basis for the time "reasonably spent by the Mediator in the proceedings," at a rate commensurate with the complexity of the case and other relevant factors.[148] This rate is established by the ICC, in conjunction with the Mediator and the parties.[149] If agreed by the parties and the Mediator, the Centre may fix the Mediator's fees on the basis of a single fixed fee for the whole proceedings, rather than an hourly rate.[150] The Mediator's fees and expenses

140 *Id.* at para. 11.
141 *Id.* at para. 4.
142 *Id.* at para. 13.
143 *Id.* at para. 6.
144 *Id.* at para. 40.
145 ICC Mediation Rules, *supra* note 44, art. 9(2); Wolrich, *supra* note 115, at 21–22.
146 *Id.*, art. 9(1)(a).
147 *Id.*, App., art. 2.
148 *Id.*, App., art. 3(1).
149 *Id.*
150 *Id.*

are fixed exclusively by the Centre, and fee arrangements between the parties and the Mediator are prohibited. While no further guidance is provided in the Mediation Rules, it is likely that the ICC will normally set the hourly rate at or slightly below the mediator's standard hourly rate for services (assuming he is a lawyer or consultant).[151]

3. The ICSID Conciliation Rules

a. *Overview*

The Washington (ICSID) Convention, described in detail elsewhere in this book,[152] establishes a conciliation system alongside the ICSID Arbitration Rules.[153] The Conciliation Rules are supported by the provisions of Chapter III of the Washington Convention.[154] The ICSID Conciliation Rules form the ADR system most commonly mentioned in investment treaties. The interconnection of these Rules to the Washington Convention endows them with a certain additional weight in the context of investor–State disputes, despite the consensual nature of the process. For example, the State is under an international obligation to accord "serious consideration" to the final report of ICSID conciliators.[155] **9.67**

The ICSID conciliation system is subject to the same objective jurisdictional requirements as arbitration under ICSID auspices.[156] The dispute must be legal in nature, arise directly out of an investment, and involve a Washington Convention signatory State and a national of another member State.[157] Since the ICSID conciliation process is consensual, there is unlikely to be any disagreement between the parties as to the Centre's authority to administer the proceedings. Nevertheless, the ICSID Secretariat will make a *prima facie* review of the **9.68**

[151] For a comparison of the (previous) ICC ADR Rules and the American Arbitration Association Mediation Rules, *see* McLaren, *supra* note 117, at 23–24.

[152] Convention on the Settlement of Investment Disputes Between States and Nationals of Other States, March 18, 1965, 17 U.S.T. 1270, 575 U.N.T.S. 159, 60 A.J.I.L. 829 (1966), 4 I.L.M. 532 (1965), available at https://icsid.worldbank.org/en/documents/icsiddocs/icsid%20convention%20english.pdf [hereinafter, the Washington Convention]; discussed in further detail in Chapters 7 and 8.

[153] *See* note 80, *supra*, for online resources.

[154] The original Conciliation Rules were adopted on Sept. 25, 1967 and published with non-binding explanatory notes. The Conciliation Rules have been amended three times. The first amendment took effect in 1984, the second in 2003, and the most recent version came into effect rom April 2006. The newest rules were adopted after two years of public consultation. *See* ICSID Convention Conciliation Rules, available at https://icsid.worldbank.org/en/Pages/icsiddocs/ICSID-Convention-Conciliation-Rules.aspx. *See further* Aurélia Antonietti, *The 2006 Amendments to the ICSID Rules and Regulations and the Additional Facility Rules*, 21(2) ICSID Rev.—For. Inv. L.J. 427–48 (2006).

[155] Washington Convention, *supra* note 152, art. 34(1).

[156] Christoph Schreuer, The ICSID Convention: A Commentary 95–96 (1st ed., 2001).

[157] Washington Convention, *supra* note 152, art. 25(1).

dispute to verify that it falls within the scope of its jurisdiction under article 25 of the Washington Convention.[158]

b. Initiating the process

9.69 For ICSID conciliation to begin, a party to the dispute (or both jointly) must submit a request for conciliation pursuant to the ICSID Institution Rules.[159] These rules establish the same system for registering disputes for both arbitration and conciliation. The Request must be submitted in six copies[160] to the Secretary-General of ICSID in English, Spanish, or French,[161] and shall:

(a) designate precisely each party to the dispute and state the address of each;
(b) state, if one of the parties is a constituent subdivision or agency of a Contracting State, that it has been designated to the Centre by that State pursuant to Article 25(1) of the Convention;
(c) indicate the date of consent and the instruments in which it is recorded, including, if one party is a constituent subdivision or agency of a Contracting State, similar data on the approval of such consent by that State unless it had notified the Centre that no such approval is required;
(d) indicate with respect to the party that is a national of a Contracting State:
  i. its nationality on the date of consent; and
  ii. if the party is a natural person:
    A. his nationality on the date of the request; and
    B. that he did not have the nationality of the Contracting State party to the dispute either on the date of consent or on the date of the request; or
  iii. if the party is a juridical person which on the date of consent had the nationality of the Contracting State party to the dispute, the agreement of the parties that it should be treated as a national of another Contracting State for the purposes of the Convention;
(e) contain information concerning the issues in dispute indicating that there is, between the parties, a legal dispute arising directly out of an investment; and
(f) state, if the requesting party is a juridical person, that it has taken all necessary internal actions to authorize the request.[162]

---

[158] For more on ICSID jurisdiction and the requirements and legal nature of "investment," *see* Chapter 7, Sections B.3.a, E.3, E.4.c, and Chapter 8, Section B.2.b. *See also* Lucy Reed et al., Guide to ICSID Arbitration 15–16, 44–46 (2004).

[159] ICISD Convention, Regulations and Rules (2006), available at https://icsid.worldbank.org/en/Documents/icsiddocs/ICSID%20Convention%20English.pdf. The Washington Convention drafters intended that requests for conciliation would be submitted jointly by both parties to the dispute, although this is not specified in the Institution Rules. 2 Documents Concerning the Origin and the Formulation of the ICSID Convention 771 (1968). Indeed, art. 28(1) of the Washington Convention, *supra* note 152, suggests that joint filing is not necessary, since a party requesting conciliation must "send a copy of the request to the other party," a superfluous step if the request is filed jointly.

[160] ICSID Institution Rules, *supra* note 159, art. 4.

[161] *Id.*, art. 1(1); ICSID Administrative and Financial Regulations (2006), reg. 34(1), available at https://icsid.worldbank.org/en/Documents/resources/2006%20CRR_English-final.pdf.

[162] ICSID Institution Rules, *supra* note 159, art. 2.

The requesting party or parties should attach all documents necessary to corroborate this information. A Request for Conciliation should also be accompanied by the appropriate non-refundable registration fee, which at the time of publication was US$25,000.[163] An administrative charge of US$42,000 is levied by the Centre upon the registration of a request for conciliation and annually thereafter. For cases registered before July 1, 2016, the annual administrative charge is levied by the Centre on the date of the constitution of the Conciliation Commission.[164] **9.70**

Once the Secretary-General has received the Request and the registration fee, he or she will decide whether or not to register the dispute with ICSID. As previously noted, registration will be forthcoming unless one of the jurisdictional requirements of Washington Convention article 25(1) is clearly not met.[165] If the Secretary-General finds that the dispute is manifestly outside the jurisdiction of the Centre, she will notify the parties that registration has been denied and provide reasons.[166] If the dispute is registered, the Secretary-General will inform the parties of this decision and invite them to constitute a Conciliation Commission.[167] **9.71**

The request may in addition set forth any provisions agreed by the parties regarding the number of conciliators or arbitrators and the method of their appointment, as well as any other provisions agreed concerning the settlement of the dispute.[168] Following registration, and assuming that the parties have not agreed ahead of time on any specific procedure for forming a panel, the requesting party proposes an uneven number of panel members (normally one or three) and the method for their appointment.[169] Within twenty days, the other party must either accept the proposal or suggest an alternative composition method, in which case the requesting party shall notify the other party of whether it rejects or accepts such proposal within twenty days after receipt of the reply.[170] If no agreement has been reached sixty days after the Request for Conciliation was registered, either party may inform the Secretary-General that it opts for the default composition system established in article 29(2)(b) of the ICSID Convention.[171] **9.72**

---

163 ICSID Schedule of Fees, effective July 1, 2017, available at https://icsid.worldbank.org/en/Pages/icsiddocs/Schedule-of-Fees.aspx.

164 *Id.*

165 ICSID Institution Rules, *supra* note 159, art. 6.

166 ICSID Institution Rules, *supra* note 159, art. 6(1)(b). According to Polasek, the ICSID Secretary-General had refused by 2011 the registration of thirteen requests under art. 36(3) of the ICSID Convention; *see* Martina Polasek, *The Threshold for Registration of a Request for Arbitration under the ICSID Convention*, 5 Disp. Res. Int'l 187–88 (2011).

167 *Id.*, art. 7.

168 ICSID Conciliation Rules, *supra* note80, art. 3.

169 ICSID Conciliation Rules, *supra* note80, art. 2(1)(a).

170 *Id.*, art. 2(1)(b), (c).

171 *Id.*, art. 2(3).

9.73 Unlike most other conciliation rules, the ICSID Rules call for a Conciliation Commission of three members, where the parties have not otherwise agreed.[172] Under the default mechanism, each party appoints one Commission member, and the President is chosen by mutual agreement.[173] Any vacancies on the Commission remaining after ninety days from the notice of registration are filled by the President of the World Bank.[174]

c. Managing the process

9.74 ICSID establishes a somewhat more structured procedural system for conciliation than do most other ADR rules. While the parties can derogate from the rules if they choose, default provisions are included regarding the place of Commission sessions, the fixing of session dates, procedural languages, and the conduct of hearings, among other details. Nevertheless, the core of the conciliation procedure remains flexible, framed by articles 22 and 23, which define the duties of the Commission and the parties. The Commission is to "clarify the issues in dispute" by "hear[ing] the parties," and then "may … recommend that the parties accept specific terms of settlement" and that they "refrain … from specific acts that might aggravate the dispute" while it seeks to facilitate agreement between them.[175] In discharging these functions, the Commission is authorized at any time during the conciliation to request information in oral or written form, request evidence from third parties, or conduct independent inquiries at a place connected with the dispute (but this only with the consent and participation of the parties).[176] The parties, meanwhile, must "cooperate in good faith with the Commission," provide all requested information and documentation, and obey the Commission's procedural directions.[177]

9.75 Within sixty days after the Commission is constituted (or later if the parties agree), it holds its first session. At this meeting, the conciliator or President of the Commission will attempt to obtain agreement of the parties on a range of procedural matters, including record of hearings, the language of the proceedings, and the sequence and schedule of oral and written submissions.[178] Where no agreement is reached, the Commission has the authority to arrange the proceedings as it sees fit.

---

172 Washington Convention, *supra* note 152, art. 29(2)(b).

173 ICSID Conciliation Rules, *supra* note80, art. 3(1) (one party writes to the other naming two persons, identifying one of them as the conciliator he appoints and the other as a proposed President of the Commission. The other party then replies, naming a conciliator and indicating either consent with the proposed President or suggesting an alternative).

174 Washington Convention, *supra* note 152, arts. 5, 30; ICSID Conciliation Rules, *supra* note80, art. 4.

175 ICSID Conciliation Rules, *supra* note80, art. 22(2).

176 *Id.*, art. 22(3).

177 *Id.*, art. 23.

178 *Id.*, arts. 13(1), 20(1).

In all ICSID conciliation proceedings, however, the head of the Commission invites each party to file a written statement of its position. The standard deadline for the submission of this statement is thirty days after the constitution of the Commission (even before the first session is held).[179] 9.76

The ICSID system includes a specific provision on the testimony of witnesses and experts. Any party may request that such testimony be heard, although the Commission retains discretion in this regard. Where witness evidence is to be provided, the Rules further adopt litigation-style examination, providing that witnesses and experts "shall, as a rule, be examined before the Commission by the parties under the control of its President."[180] 9.77

Another unique feature of ICSID conciliation is the Commission Report, which must be filed by the conciliators in each proceeding, whether or not the parties reach agreement on a settlement.[181] The Report must be drawn up and signed within sixty days after the conciliation is closed and must contain detailed information about the parties, the nature of the dispute and the course of the proceeding.[182] While the Report must indicate whether the parties reached an agreement, it does not include the terms and conditions of such agreement unless the parties jointly request that such information form part of the Report.[183] 9.78

The ICSID conciliation system establishes a significant level of confidentiality, which can be further augmented by agreement of the parties. Hearings "shall take place in private and, except as the parties otherwise agree, shall remain secret." Furthermore, as under the UNCITRAL conciliation rules, parties to ICSID conciliation may not "invoke or rely on any views expressed or statements or admissions or offers of settlement made by the other party in the conciliation proceedings, or the report or any recommendations made by the Commission" in any subsequent proceeding before a court or arbitral tribunal.[184] 9.79

The fees to be paid to ICSID conciliators are set forth in the ICSID fee schedule, and is the same as that for ICSID arbitrators. This rate, US$3,000 per day at the time of publication,[185] is likely to be higher than in most other forms of ADR, particularly where the Commission is composed according to default procedures, with three members. 9.80

179 *Id.*, art. 25(1).
180 *Id.*, art. 28(2).
181 *Id.*, arts. 30–32.
182 *Id.*, art. 32.
183 *Id.*, art. 30(1).
184 Washington Convention, *supra* note 152, arts. 35–36.
185 ICSID Schedule of Fees, *supra* note 163, at para. 3.

d. Experience with the ICSID Conciliation Rules

9.81 Perhaps for some of the reasons explored elsewhere in this chapter, the ICSID Conciliation Rules were invoked only nine times in the first fifty years of their existence.[186] A report was issued in five of these proceedings,[187] and the parties settled prior to the constitution of the commission on two further occasions.[188] The remaining two cases are currently pending.[189] An additional two disputes were brought to conciliation under the ICSID Additional Facility Rules, and in one these cases the sole conciliator issued a report[190] and one is currently pending.[191]

9.82 The first conciliation case, registered in 1982, ended in settlement before a conciliation commission was formed.[192] The same parties initiated conciliation again over a decade later. In that case, the three-member conciliation commission rendered a report, but it is unclear whether the parties followed the panel's recommendations.[193] Another conciliation, *TG World Petroleum Ltd. v. Niger*, was registered in December 2003.[194] The dispute arose out of Niger's alleged wrongful termination of a concession contract for the exploration of an oilfield. After termination, the government had reassigned the contract to a Chinese oil company. TG World Petroleum's concession contained a dispute resolution clause calling for ICSID conciliation proceedings and, if those were unsuccessful, ICSID arbitration.[195] While the parties opted for conciliation, a commission was never constituted: the case was settled in April 2005 without the assistance of ICSID conciliators. The most recent ICSID conciliation, arising out of a water services and electricity concession in Gabon, was registered in 30 March 2018, and is still underway as of this writing.[196]

9.83 In at least one instance, *Tesoro Petroleum v. Trinidad & Tobago*,[197] the ICSID conciliation procedure led to an amicable settlement in a relatively short time and

[186] *See* Cases under the ICSID Conciliation and Additional Facility Conciliation Rules at the ICSID Search Cases Database, available at https://icsid.worldbank.org/en/Pages/cases/AdvancedSearch.aspx#.

[187] *See RSM Production Corp. v. Cameroon*, ICSID Case No. CONC/11/1; *Togo Electricité v. Togo*, ICSID Case No. CONC/05/1; *T.G. World Petroleum Ltd. v. Niger*, ICSID Case No. CONC/03/1; *SEDITEX Engineering Beratungsgesellschaft für die Textilindustrie m.b.H. v. Madagascar*, ICSID Case No. CONC/94/1; *Tesoro Petroleum Corp. v. Trinidad and Tobago*, ICSID Case No. CONC/83/1.

[188] *See T.G. World Petroleum, supra* note 187.

[189] *See Xenofon Karagiannis v. Albania*, ICSID Case No. CONC/16/1; *Société d'Energie et d'Eau du Gabon v. Gabon*, ICSID Case No. CONC/18/1.

[190] *See Equatorial Guinea v. CMS Energy Corp. et al.*, ICSID Case No. CONC(AF)/12/2.

[191] *See Hess Equatorial Guinea Inc. and Tullow Equatorial Guinea Ltd. v. Equatorial Guinea*, ICSID Case No. CONC(AF)/12/1.

[192] *SEDITEX Engineering Beratungsgesellschaft für die Textilindustrie m.b.H. v. Madagascar*, ICSID Case No. CONC/82/1.

[193] *SEDITEX, supra* note 187.

[194] *Supra* note 187.

[195] Herbert Smith, Arbitration Update 1 (Jan. 2004).

[196] *Société d'Energie et d'Eau du Gabon, supra* note 189.

[197] *Tesoro Petroleum, supra* note 187.

with limited cost to the parties.[198] There, Tesoro and the Republic of Trinidad & Tobago entered into a joint venture for hydrocarbon exploration. The dispute focused upon dividend payments. According to the agreement, the dividends were not to be paid for the first five years. After such time, on approval of the board of directors (which consisted equally of representatives from Tesoro and the Republic of Trinidad and Tobago) and while respecting a general policy of re-investment, dividends were to be paid out. When economic conditions and oil prices changed, the Trinidad government changed the tax regime governing the joint venture. When the government refused to allow dividends for 1981 and 1982, Tesoro declared that it wanted to sell its shares, which were subject to the government's right of first refusal.

The parties agreed upon a sole conciliator, Lord Wilberforce, and the Commission was constituted four months after the request was registered. A preliminary procedural meeting was held on March 9, 1984, and proceedings concluded on November 27, 1985. Lord Wilberforce presented the parties with a Report containing a settlement proposal, and the parties continued to negotiate for another eight months before ending their dispute. **9.84**

4. The IBA Rules for investor–State mediation

a. Background

The most recent development in the context of investor–State mediation was the creation of special rules for the mediation of investor–State disputes by the International Bar Association Council ("the IBA Rules").[199] The IBA Rules were designed for the mediation of investment-related differences or disputes involving States and State entities.[200] They were published in 2012 and have already been used for the mediation of an investment dispute between a French-owned construction company and the Philippines under the France–Philippines BIT, which is administered by the ICC International Centre for ADR.[201] **9.85**

[198] *See* Nurick & Schnably, *supra* note 43, at 340.

[199] For an extensive analysis, *see* Anna Joubin-Bret & Barton Legum, *A Set of Rules Dedicated to Investor–State Mediation: The IBA Investor–State Mediation Rules*, 29(1) ICSID Rev.—For. Inv. L.J. 17–24 (2014).

[200] IBA Rules for Investor–State Mediation, *supra* note 24, art. 1(1).

[201] *See* "In an apparent first, investor and host-State agree to try mediation under IBA Rules to resolve an investment treaty dispute," IAReporter (Apr. 14, 2016), available at https://www.iareporter.com/articles/in-an-apparent-first-investor-and-host-state-agree-to-try-mediation-under-iba-rules-to-resolve-an-investment-treaty-dispute/. The France–Philippines BIT does not expressly provide for mandatory conciliation, but art. 11(1) provides that disputes relating to the interpretation or the application of the agreement must be settled, if possible, by diplomatic means.

b. Initiating the process

9.86 As in the ICSID Conciliation Rules, the parties may jointly or unilaterally initiate IBA mediation. The mediation is deemed to commence either on the date when the disputing parties agree to mediate (if the parties had not agreed before the dispute arose), or when one of the parties sends a written request to mediate, if the parties agreed to the IBA Mediation Rules in advance.[202] The written request shall contain: (1) a summary of the dispute sufficient to identify the subject matter; (2) identification of the legal instrument to which the differences or disputes relate; (3) the names and contact details of the requesting party and its representative(s); and (4) either a reference to the agreement to mediate or an invitation to the other party or parties to mediate under these rules.

9.87 As in the ICC Mediation Rules, the IBA mediation process is conducted by a sole "Mediator" (unless the parties designated two co-mediators[203]), to be selected within twenty-one days from the commencement of the mediation.[204] Where the parties are unable to agree on a Mediator within twenty-one days, they are to agree on an institution or person who will assist them in choosing a mediator (the "Designating Authority") within fourteen days.[205] If the parties do not agree on a Designating Authority within fourteen days, then the Secretary-General of the Permanent Court of Arbitration will select a Designating Authority for them.[206]

9.88 A Mediator under the IBA Rules is subject to certain prerequisites. According to article 3(1), "[t]he mediator shall be impartial and independent." Prior to accepting an appointment, a potential mediator must provide to the parties or the Designating Authority a signed and dated Statement of Independence and Availability, disclosing "any facts or circumstances that might call into question the mediator's independence or impartiality in the eyes of the parties," "the mediator's availability and willingness to conduct the mediation expeditiously and efficiently" and the mediator's proposed fee basis.[207] In the course of the mediation process, any party may object to a particular mediator "for any reason" (preferably stating the reason), following which the mediator may either resign or discuss the objection with the parties. If the objecting party maintains its objection, the mediator must resign and a new mediator will be designated.[208]

202 *See* IBA Rules for Investor–State Mediation, *supra* note 24, art. 2.
203 *Id.*, arts. 4(1), 6.
204 *Id.*, art. 4(5).
205 *Id.*, art. 4(6) and App. C ("Choice of Mediator through Designating Authority").
206 *Id.*, art. 4(7).
207 *Id*, art. 3.
208 *Id.*, art. 5.

c. Managing the process

The mediator has broad discretion in the conduct of the mediation. The mediator may communicate with one or all of the parties, request further information from the parties and, subject to the parties' agreement, consult one or more experts.[209] The mediator must always take into account "the wishes of the parties, the circumstances of the case and the overall goal of a cost-efficient and timely settlement of the differences or disputes."[210] Further, the mediator shall be guided by the principles of fairness, objectivity, independence, and impartiality.[211] **9.89**

The key function of the mediator is to assist the parties to reach a settlement voluntarily, making free and informed choices about the process and the outcome as expeditiously and efficiently as possible.[212] Although a mediator may make recommendations concerning an appropriate resolution of the dispute, the IBA Rules do not provide the authority to impose a settlement on the parties.[213] **9.90**

Although the IBA Mediation Rules contain the standard clauses found in most mediation rules, with certain novel features they differ from the ICSID Conciliation Rules.[214] For example, article 9 of the IBA Mediation Rules provides for a "Mediation Management Conference" as soon as practicable after the designation of the mediator, where the disputing parties are to discuss with the mediator: **9.91**

(a) any outstanding procedural issues, such as the languages and the location of the mediation sessions;
(b) a provisional timetable for the conduct of the mediation;
(c) confidentiality and privacy arrangements;
(d) any prescription or limitation periods and whether the parties wish to address such periods by agreement;
(e) whether the parties wish to agree in writing not to commence or not to continue any arbitral or judicial proceedings relating to the differences or disputes that are the subject of the mediation while the mediation is pending;
(f) whether special arrangements for the approval of a settlement agreement need to be made; and
(g) financial arrangements, such as the calculation and payment of the mediator's fees and expenses.

During the mediation management conference, the parties may also identify a representative who is authorized to settle the dispute as well as any third party whose participation is necessary or useful to settle the dispute.[215] **9.92**

---

209 *Id.*, arts. 7(3), 8(3), 8(6).
210 *Id.*, arts. 7(4), 8(1).
211 *Id.*, art. 7(1).
212 *Id.*, art. 8(2).
213 *Id.*, arts. 7(2), 8(6).
214 On the differences and possible synergies between the IBA Mediation Rules and the ICSID Conciliation Rules, *see* Frauke Nitschke, *The IBA's Investor–State Mediation Rules and the ICSID Dispute Settlement Framework*, 29(1) ICSID Rev.—For. Inv. L.J. 112–32 (2014).
215 *See* IBA Rules for Investor–State Mediation, *supra* note 24, art. 9(2).

9.93 The IBA Mediation Rules also provide new rules on confidentiality and transparency. Transparency has become more and more relevant to investor–State disputes, given the public interests at stake.[216] IBA mediation is normally private, and all documents prepared and communications made are confidential, and not to be used "for any other purpose, including, in particular, in legal proceedings."[217] Every person participating in the mediation (including experts) is bound by the duty of confidentiality.[218] However, confidentiality does not extend to the fact that mediation is taking place under the IBA Mediation Rules or the outcome of such proceedings, unless the parties specifically agree to keep it confidential.[219]

D. ADR and Investment Treaties

9.94 As explained in the previous chapter, investment treaties have become an essential part of investment-related dispute resolution since the first arbitration based on such a treaty was initiated in 1987.[220] On the whole, BITs and regional treaties concentrate on arbitration as the primary means to resolve investment disputes. There is no uniform treatment of conciliation or other forms of ADR in investment treaties.[221]

9.95 The majority of investment treaty texts concluded prior to 2006 contain no reference at all to any dispute resolution besides negotiation and arbitration (both investor-to-State and State-to-State).[222] Naturally, silence on this point does not mean that the parties to an investment dispute falling within the scope of the dispute resolution clause of a BIT are barred from conciliation or other forms of ADR. Since conciliation is by definition the result of mutual consent, it matters little whether this consensus to attempt conciliation is achieved before or after the dispute arises. Furthermore, most BITs do call for the "amicable settlement" of disputes, where possible, a phrase widely seen as encouraging the use of ADR

216 *See* Joubin-Bret & Legum, *supra* note 199, at 23.

217 *See* IBA Rules for Investor–State Mediation, *supra* note 24, art. 10(1)–(2).

218 *Id.*, art. 10(5).

219 *Id.*, art. 10(3).

220 The *AAPL* case, *supra* note 51, Award of June 27, 1990, 6 ICSID Rev.—For. Inv. L.J. 526 (1991) represents the first time in ICSID where "arbitration proceedings were brought not on the basis of an arbitration clause or a compromise but on the basis of an undertaking made in the treaty protecting investments between the states issuing and accepting the investment." Charles Leben, *Hans Kelsen and the Advancement of International Law*, 9 Eur. J. Int'l L. 287 (1998), available at http://www.ejil.org. *See also* Thomas L. Brewer, *International Investment Dispute Settlement Procedures: The Evolving Regime for Foreign Direct Investment*, 26 L. & Pol'y. Int'l Bus. 633 (1995); Chapter 7.

221 For an extensive analysis of the integration of mediation in the BIT context, *see* Nancy A. Welsh & Andrea Kupfer Schneider, *The Thoughtful Integration of Mediation into Bilateral Investment Treaty Arbitration*, 18 Harv. Neg. L. Rev. 71–142 (2003).

222 *See e.g.* Czech Republic–Venezuela BIT (1995).

techniques such as conciliation.[223] A number of treaties, while they do not designate any particular form of non-adversarial dispute resolution, suggest the possibility of conciliation by expressly sanctioning "the resolution of disputes by way of an amicable agreement,"[224] or "in accordance with ... previously agreed dispute-settlement procedures."[225]

Certain countries—in particular Germany, the United Kingdom, Sweden, and India—have made particular efforts to encourage conciliation by including reference to ADR in the BITs they negotiate.[226] In the context of the European Union, the European Commission has recently proposed the development of a system of "prevention and amicable resolution" of investment disputes within the E.U. area, in order to supplant the current network of intra-E.U. BITs.[227] It also appears that India, in its negotiation of investment protection agreements, has sought on a number of occasions to include such a provision. The result in at least one instance – the Sweden-India BIT – was a three-step dispute resolution procedure, beginning with negotiation, followed by mandatory conciliation under the UNCITRAL rules, and finally leading to arbitration if this process does not lead to settlement: **9.96**

> (2) If [an investment] dispute has not been settled within a period of six months the investor that is a party to the dispute may submit the dispute to resolution according to the following options:
> (a) to the courts or administrative tribunals of the [State] that is party to the dispute;
> (b) in accordance with any applicable, previously agreed dispute settlement procedure; or
> (c) to international conciliation under the Rules of [UNCITRAL].
> (3) Should the investor fail to exercise the options in paragraph 2(a) and 2(b) of this Article or where the conciliation proceedings under Article 2(c) of this paragraph [sic] are terminated other than by the signing of a settlement agreement, the dispute shall be referred to international arbitration ... .[228]

An increasing number of investment agreements provide for the use of ADR prior to the submission of the investment dispute to arbitration.[229] Indeed, **9.97**

[223] *See* ICSID, History of the ICSID Convention: Documents Concerning the Origin and the Formulation of the Convention 3 (1968); Ole Spiermann, *Individual Rights, State Interests and the Power to Waive ICSID Jurisdiction under Bilateral Investment Treaties*, 20 Arb. Int'l 179 (2004).

[224] Colombia–Spain BIT (1995), art. 11.

[225] United States–Estonia BIT (1994), art. 6(b).

[226] *See e.g.* Czech Republic–Singapore BIT (1995), art. 13(a)–(b); Denmark–India BIT (1995), art. 9 ("the investor shall be entitled to submit the case ... to international conciliation under the rules of United Nations Commission on International Trade Law").

[227] *See* European Commission, Inception Impact Assessment—Prevention and Amicable Resolution of Investment Disputes within the Single Market (2017), available at https://ec.europa.eu/info/law/better-regulation/initiatives/ares-2017-3735364_en.

[228] Sweden–India BIT (2000), art. 9. *See also* 2016 India Model BIT, art. 31(1).

[229] Art. 8(20) of the Comprehensive Economic and Trade Agreement between Canada and the EU (CETA) provides that the disputing parties may at any time agree to mediation.

several recent investment treaties provide for a six-month pre-arbitration period during which the parties "should"[230] or "shall"[231] seek to resolve disputes through consultations. For instance, the Chile–Hong Kong BIT provides that a claimant cannot have recourse to binding arbitration unless it has sought to resolve the dispute with the host State through consultations (that may include "the use of non-binding, third-party procedures, such as good offices, conciliation and mediation") and the dispute has not been resolved after six months.[232] Under the Iran–Slovakia BIT, a claimant "is obliged to submit ... a written request for consultations or negotiations" within three years after the alleged breach, otherwise it will be deemed to have waived its right to arbitration.[233] Some treaties also envisage a more institutionalized ADR process. For example, the Morocco–Nigeria BIT provides that before initiating arbitration, a disputing party must submit the dispute to a "Joint Committee" that will facilitate consultations and negotiations.[234] If the dispute is not resolved within six months, the investor may initiate arbitration.[235]

9.98 The effectiveness of mandatory conciliation provisions in investment agreements is not self-evident. In most treaties, mediation, conciliation, or consultations are an option prior to or instead of arbitration, available only where both parties to the dispute agree. Since mediation and conciliation does not produce a binding award, a final settlement can be reached through such a process only if both sides are willing to participate in good faith. Otherwise, the conciliation process becomes an additional procedural hurdle, adding unnecessary costs and several months of delay. From one point of view, the pre-arbitration conciliation option found in a growing number of BITs and multilateral treaties would appear unnecessary. The parties to an investment dispute are always free to enter mediation at any stage. Even during arbitration, the investor and State can agree to suspend the proceedings to allow a conciliator to work with them toward a settlement. To allow the investor to initiate conciliation proceedings "if both sides agree" gives the investor no additional legal rights. At the same time, the mention of ADR in investment treaties offers affirmation of the efficacy of these tools, and a reminder that less adversarial options are available—particularly before the parties' positions become entrenched in a formal arbitration process.

[230] *See e.g.* Trans-Pacific Partnership Agreement (2016, not yet in force), arts. 9(18) and 9(19)(1).
[231] *See e.g.* Republic of Korea–New Zealand FTA (2015), art. 10(19); Free Trade Agreement between the Eurasian Economic Union and Vietnam (2015), art. 8(38); ASEAN–India Investment Agreement (2014), art. 20(5)–(6).
[232] Chile–Hong Kong BIT, arts. 20 and 21.
[233] Iran–Slovakia BIT (2016), arts. 15–17.
[234] Morocco–Nigeria BIT (2016), arts. 26 and 27.
[235] *Id.*, art. 26(5).

Some references to arbitration, particularly in treaties or investment laws, speak of conciliation and arbitration in the same provision. In *SPP v. Egypt*, arbitral jurisdiction was based on Egypt's Law on Investment, which provided for the settlement of disputes "within the framework of the [Washington] Convention." Since the Washington Convention includes rules on both arbitration and conciliation, Egypt reasoned that it could not be required to arbitrate: it had not agreed to a specific type of dispute resolution. The tribunal held that in the context of the Washington Convention: **9.99**

> Once consent has been given "to the jurisdiction of the Centre", the Convention and its implementing regulations afford the means for making the choice between the two methods of dispute settlement. The Convention leaves that choice to the party instituting the proceedings.[236]

Thus, the reference in a dispute resolution provision to both conciliation and arbitration implies neither that conciliation is a mandatory prerequisite to arbitration,[237] nor that the investor must choose one process to the exclusion of the other.[238] Such interpretations would be contrary to the consensual nature of conciliation, and would unnecessarily limit the parties in their search for an efficient and mutually-acceptable resolution of their dispute. **9.100**

E. Mediation and the Energy Charter Treaty

The Energy Charter Treaty (ECT) encourages amicable settlement of energy disputes. Article 26(1) of the ECT states that investment disputes related to breaches of obligations under Part III of the ECT "shall, if possible, be settled amicably." Article 26(2) provides for a three-month cooling-off period, following which either disputing party may submit the dispute to binding dispute resolution before an arbitral tribunal or the domestic courts of the contracting party involved in the dispute. **9.101**

While there is no *a priori* constraint as to the type of ADR mechanism to be employed, article 26(2) of the ECT makes clear that a party to the dispute needs to **9.102**

[236] *Southern Pacific Properties (Middle East) Ltd. v. Egypt*, ICSID Case No. ARB/84/3, Decision on Jurisdiction and Dissenting Opinion of Apr. 14, 1988, 16 Yb. Comm. Arb. 28 (1991) (excerpts); 3 ICSID Rep. 131 (1995); French translation of English original in 121 J. de Droit Int'l 220 (1994) (excerpts).

[237] A few investment treaties make clear that the investor-claimant retains the right to choose between conciliation and arbitration, where both dispute resolution methods are mentioned. United States–Grenada BIT (1986) art. VI(3)(ii); Israel–Myanmar BIT (2014, not in force), art. 8(2); ASEAN–India Agreement on Investment under the Framework Agreement on Comprehensive Economic Cooperation (2014, not in force), art. 20(7).

[238] UNCTAD Dispute Resolution Course, Module 2.2, available at https://unctad.org/en/Docs/edmmisc232add1_en.pdf.

"request" amicable settlement before proceeding toward international arbitration or the domestic courts. The existence of a prior request for amicable settlement depends on the circumstances of each case and is not as formalistic as the establishment of jurisdiction. In *Petrobart v. Kyrgyz Republic*, for instance, the tribunal found that Petrobart's letters to the Prime Minister constituted requests for amicable settlement for the purposes of article 26(2) of the ECT.[239]

9.103 Previous arbitral tribunals also have stressed the importance of ADR to the ECT system. As explained by the tribunal in *Amto v. Ukraine*, "[t]he request for amicable settlement required by Article 26(2) ensures that a State party is notified of a dispute prior to the initiation of an arbitration and has an opportunity to investigate and take steps to resolve the dispute."[240] To that effect, the tribunal in *Stati Ascom* stayed arbitration proceedings to enable the parties to negotiate towards a settlement.[241] But in *Al-Bahloul*, the tribunal found that the State's unwillingness to settle the dispute made it unnecessary for the claimant to comply with the pre-arbitration requirement of article 26(2) of the ECT.[242]

9.104 The Energy Charter Secretariat plays a key role in the amicable settlement of disputes, by offering good offices to facilitate informal mediation and assistance in pre-trial proceedings through its Conflict Resolution Centre. In 2016, the Energy Charter Conference endorsed a detailed Guide on Investment Mediation as "a helpful, voluntary instrument to facilitate the amicable resolution of investment disputes" under the ECT.[243]

9.105 In parallel, the Energy Charter Conference invited the contracting parties to consider voluntary mediation as one of the options to facilitate the amicable solution of disputes at any stage and to consider using the good offices of the Energy Charter Secretariat. According to the Guide, at least eight ECT cases have been amicably settled, three by way of publicly available awards.[244]

---

[239] *Petrobart Ltd. v. The Kyrgyz Republic*, SCC No. 126/2003, Arbitral Award of Mar. 29, 2005, at para. 73.

[240] *Ltd. Liability Co. Amto v. Ukraine*, SCC Case No. 080/2005, Award of Mar. 26, 2008, at para. 50.

[241] *Anatolie Stati, Gabriel Stati, Ascom Group S.A. and Terra Raf Trans Traiding Ltd. v. Kazakhstan*, SCC Case No. 116/2010, Award of Dec. 19, 2013, at paras. 828–30.

[242] *Mohammad Ammar Al-Bahloul v. Tajikistan*, SCC Case No. 064/2008, Partial Award on Jurisdiction and Liability of Sept. 2, 2009, at paras. 154–56.

[243] *See* Energy Charter Secretariat, Decision of the Energy Charter Conference: Adoption by correspondence of the Guide on Investment Mediation, July 19, 2016, Doc. CCDEC 2016 12 INV, available at https://energycharter.org/fileadmin/DocumentsMedia/CCDECS/2016/CCDEC201612.pdf (accessed Dec. 20, 2017).

[244] *Id.* at 6. These cases are: *ČEZ v. Albania* (2013), *Slovak Gas Holding B.V. et al. v. Slovakia* (2012), *Türkiye Petrolleri Anonim Ortaklığı v. Kazakhstan* (2011), *EVN A.G. v. The Former Yugoslav Republic of Macedonia* (2010), *Vattenfall v. Germany* (2011), *Barmek Holding A.S. v. Azerbaijan* (2006); *Alstom Power Italia S.p.A., Alstom S.p.A. v. Mongolia* (2004), and *AES Summit Generation Ltd. (U.K. subsidiary of U.S.-based AES Corp.) v. Hungary* (2002).

F. The Hybrid Practice of Mediation-Arbitration

Despite the flexibility and reduced expense and time that conciliation entails in comparison with arbitration or litigation, frequently parties invest substantial effort in presenting their positions through conciliation without reaching settlement. In such cases, it may seem natural and efficient, where the parties have agreed to arbitrate should other efforts to resolve the dispute fail, to have the mediator also serve as arbitrator. The mediator would have an advantage over other candidates, alreadying knowing a great deal about the dispute and the interests at stake, and (presumably) enjoying the trust of the parties. In part based upon these considerations, certain legal systems favor the conciliator shifting into the role of arbitrator if negotiations break down.[245] However, the general practice, particularly in international disputes, is to avoid such a "med-arb" procedure. **9.106**

One commentator explains: **9.107**

> The traditional western view is that arbitration and conciliation processes should remain separate, and that the same persons who act as conciliators should not act as arbitrators in the same dispute. It is thought that disclosures of confidential information and offers to compromise made during (and essential to) the conciliation process might affect the ability of the conciliator to act as an arbitrator in the same dispute. Since conciliation is considered to be a completely voluntary process that can be terminated by either party at any time, information acquired by the conciliator during the course of investigation could bias the outcome of an official and binding arbitration. In the western conception of dispute resolution, such information only is discovered through a mutual endeavour to resolve the dispute amicably, and therefore, should be regarded as inadmissible. The United Nations Commission on International Trade Law (UNCITRAL) Rules of Conciliation actually prohibits the combined roles of arbitrator and conciliator.[246]

The ICC Mediation Rules take a similar approach, barring the mediator from later serving as judge or arbitrator in the same dispute, unless the parties otherwise agree in writing.[247] The IBA Mediation Rules also provide that unless the parties agree otherwise, by accepting the designation as mediator, the mediator agrees not to act in any other role, including that of counsel, arbitrator, expert, or witness, in respect of differences or disputes that are the subject of the mediation.[248] **9.108**

A somewhat more controversial issue is whether an *arbitrator* is authorized to act as a conciliator after the start of adversarial proceedings. Here, the problem **9.109**

---

[245] China and Germany appear to be two countries where this practice is prevalent. Trappe, *supra* note 23, at 186.

[246] Neil Sorenson, *Bilateral Investment Treaties and Disputes*, BILATERALS.ORG (2001), available at http://www.bilaterals.org/article.php3?id_article=122. *See also* ALAN REDFERN et al., LAW AND PRACTICE OF INTERNATIONAL COMMERCIAL ARBITRATION 40 (4th ed. 2004).

[247] ICC Mediation Rules, *supra* note 44, art. 10(3).

[248] IBA Rules for Investor–State Mediation, *supra* note 24, art. 7(5).

of disclosed confidential or prejudicial information arises only if the conciliation fails, compelling a return to arbitration before the same arbitrator or tribunal. At the same time, it may be questioned whether settlement proposals outside the framework of the applicable law would be within the arbitrators' authority. Buhring-Ühle explains that on the whole,

> practice seems to vary considerably among countries. Generally, Americans and some Europeans consider it improper for an arbitrator to facilitate a settlement of the dispute. In their view, an arbitrator should do no more than to suggest the possibility of settlement but should not actively engage in mediating efforts. In other cultures, for example China and Germany, arbitrators often take a more active role by proposing at the parties' request possible formula for settlement, by participating in settlement negotiations, and even meeting separately with the parties with their consent. In Asian cultures, which have a particular aversion to confrontation, arbitrators are even more energetic than their European and American counterparts in seeking to facilitate agreement among the disputants rather than merely imposing a decision.[249]

9.110 Buhring-Ühle's observation about arbitrator conduct in Asian countries deserves some elaboration. Many European and North American lawyers engaged in arbitration under Chinese arbitration commission rules such as CIETAC have been surprised to find Chinese arbitrators pressuring the parties to submit to mediation of their dispute by the tribunal.[250] The parties are frequently hesitant to alienate panel members by refusing such a "suggestion," even where they prefer a more structured and law-based solution to their dispute. In such circumstances of compelled mediation, settlement is somewhat unlikely. Since the parties know that the same decision-makers will adjudicate their dispute if mediation fails, they are unlikely to candidly disclose the kind of information that can be central to breaking down entrenched positions through conciliation.[251]

9.111 In any event, parties to an investment dispute should reflect carefully before agreeing that both conciliation and arbitration be conducted by the same person or tribunal. On the one hand, a conciliator's familiarity with the dispute is likely to reduce the costs of arbitration (possibly eliminating the need for initial written submissions), and an arbitrator, having heard the parties' adversarial presentations, may be able to provide creative settlement proposals that would be obscure to the uninitiated. On the other hand, knowing in advance that the same

[249] Buhring-Ühle, *supra* note 7, at 127–217. *See also* Jeswald W. Salacuse, *Mediation In International Business*, in Studies in International Mediation: Essays in Honor of Jeffrey Z. Rubin (Jacob Bercovitch ed. 2003).

[250] Michael Moser, *Dueling with Dragons*, Presentation on Dispute Resolution in China, given in Paris on May 9, 2005.

[251] Nevertheless, arbitrators in East Asia frequently resort to mediation techniques to settle the disputes they are charged to adjudicate. *See e.g.* Kenji Tashiro, *Conciliation or Mediation During the Arbitration Process: A Japanese View*, 12(2) J. Int'l Arb. 119 (1995).

decision-maker will serve as both conciliator and arbitrator can undermine the frankness and flexibility that is the core strength of conciliation.

Moreover, it is by no means self-evident that the qualities that make an individual an ideal arbitrator would also distinguish the exemplary conciliator, and vice versa. Parties tend to select arbitrators based upon their organizational skills, knowledge of applicable law, or precision in legal reasoning. A different set of skills, such as empathy, creativity, and diplomatic communication, may be more important characteristics for successful conciliators. **9.112**

G. Choosing a Mediator/Conciliator or Panel of Conciliators

As with arbitrators, the choice of a mediator or conciliator is one of the most important aspects of the dispute resolution process. But because the tasks of a mediator or conciliator differ starkly from those of an arbitral tribunal, the parties may select a conciliator of a background and personal qualities very different from the ideal candidate to arbitrate the same dispute.[252] **9.113**

1. Number of mediators/conciliators

As is clear from the ADR rules, the most common practice in conciliation today is to engage a single person to lead the parties toward a settlement. The primary reason for this is to improve the economy and speed of the process. It is natural that a sole conciliator will reduce total fees to the parties, one of the more substantial elements of dispute resolution costs—particularly in smaller disputes. Furthermore, a sole conciliator can take decisions and organize the proceedings more quickly than a panel of three, since she need not consult with other panel members, nor coordinate busy schedules for face-to-face meetings. Besides cost concerns, it is also widely believed that a sole mediator or conciliator can foster an atmosphere of informality, which can be essential to creative settlement-building. In particular, a single conciliator may be better able to manage the caucusing process, coaxing the parties to candor and serving as a trustworthy repository for unembellished information about their positions and interests.[253] **9.114**

Furthermore, since conciliation is a consensual process, there is less benefit to be gained from a plurality of decision-makers. A party can simply block the **9.115**

---

[252] It should be noted that ICSID maintains a roster of conciliators specifically designed for use in investor–State disputes. These individuals are appointed to the roster by member States, and many have some former or current connection with the government that appointed them. The roster can be found at https://icsid.worldbank.org/en/Pages/arbitrators/CVSearch.aspx. This roster is updated regularly and new designations to the Panel are published in the ICSID Annual Report.

[253] Hermann, *supra* note 89, at 175.

appointment of a conciliator whom he does not view as sufficiently "neutral," eliminating the need for a "party-appointed" decision-maker who presents the positions of the party who appointed him to the panel chairman. Moreover, the goal of conciliation is not to "get it right" based on the application of rules, but rather to find a solution both sides can accept. The principle that "three heads are better than one" may therefore have less currency in the conciliation context than in arbitration.[254]

9.116 Nevertheless, there are circumstances where a panel of three conciliators may improve the chances of achieving a durable settlement. Where the issues in dispute are highly technical in nature, in particular spanning more than one discipline (*e.g.* geology, taxation, and the environment), more than one individual may be necessary to ensure a full appreciation of the parties' interests, the issues involved, and the architecture of a possible solution. In addition, governments may be better able to accept a mediated settlement and "save face" if the settlement proposal comes from a panel, rather than from a single private person. The presence of at least one government official in the conciliation panel can ease public relations pressure on States, allowing them to avoid the accusation of bowing to purely commercial interests.[255]

2. Nationality

9.117 The citizenship of conciliator candidates is one of the most frequently discussed matters in a conciliation proceeding. It is natural in an international dispute, and particularly in a dispute involving a governmental entity, that the parties will tend to reject any candidates who share the nationality of one of the other parties. From an objective standpoint, this may not be the most effective approach. Conciliation, as a non-binding process, presents fewer concerns of "neutrality" than does arbitration, since the parties are always free to reject recommendations that are unacceptable for any reason, including that they fail to account for the interests of one side. Meanwhile, a conciliator who shares the nationality of one of the parties (and particularly that of the State party), if he is of sufficient stature and independence, may bring important assets to the negotiating table, including cultural and linguistic expertise, deeper understanding of the interests at stake,

---

[254] In international arbitration, three arbitrators are generally preferred over one, because "an arbitral tribunal of three arbitrators is likely to prove more satisfactory to the parties; and the 'quality of justice' is likely to be less subject to the individual pre-dispositions and particular characteristics of a sole arbitrator." This is despite recognition that such a tribunal "is more expensive than an arbitration conducted by a sole arbitrator; and it will usually take longer to obtain an award." Redfern et al., *supra* note 246, at 185.

[255] This may be part of the reason why international treaties providing for State-to-State conciliation tend to stipulate that the process will involve a conciliation commission of three or more members, rather than a sole conciliator. Merrills, *supra* note 13, at 68 ("conciliation . . . carried out by commissions containing several members . . . is the usual arrangement under bilateral or multilateral treaties").

and the possibility of face-saving solutions promoted by the State party as "home grown."[256]

In most circumstances, however, the parties will prefer a conciliator of neutral nationality. In such cases, the parties may wish to select an arbitrator who has significant work experience in the region or country of both sides. **9.118**

3. Lawyer or non-lawyer

Neither the leading ADR rules nor international practice requires that the individual or individuals selected by the parties as mediator be practicing lawyers, or even that they have a legal education. According to one view, a background as a litigator may be more of a liability than an asset in the search for a "win-win" solution. In this assessment, lawyers are "trained to give their clients answers rather than bring them to agreement."[257] At the very least, lawyers have no particular advantage over other professionals in terms of creative problem-solving, diplomatic acumen, or other skills that distinguish a successful mediator.[258] **9.119**

At the same time, the moderation of party positions depends to some degree on the neutral's ability to assess the strengths and weaknesses of each side's legal case in a convincing manner, to demonstrate the real risk of defeat in adversarial proceedings. As a result, the majority of mediators in international disputes, whether purely private or State-related, are probably lawyers.[259] **9.120**

4. Other characteristics

Jean-Pierre Cot, a justice of the International Tribunal on the Law of the Sea and the author of a landmark work on international conciliation, has characterized the choice of conciliator in the international law context as a choice between two archetypes, the "Prince" and the "Wise Man."[260] The Prince impels the parties toward settlement by applying political power and authoritative stature, while the **9.121**

256 On the inter-personal and cultural aspects in the choice of a mediator, *see* Elizabeth Birch, *Practical and Cultural Aspects of International Mediation*, in CONTEMPORARY ISSUES IN INTERNATIONAL ARBITRATION AND MEDIATION: THE FORDHAM PAPERS 2013, 472–79 (2014).

257 *Don't Sue*, THE ECONOMIST, Oct. 26, 2002, at 34. *See also* Hill, *Theoretical Basis, supra* note 2, at 179 (lawyers without mediation experience may be ill-suited to finding "win-win" solutions because they "typically draft arguments based on the absolute frame of reference provided by the law. These arguments attempt to be objective, in the sense that they refer to supposedly provable facts and to supposedly clear interpretations of the law. They typically do not refer to the financial positions of the parties, or the future sales or profits that might disappear or arise depending on the resolution of the dispute").

258 *See* Section G.4, *infra*.

259 Hew Dundas, *Mediation in the Oil and Gas Industry*, 2(3) OIL, GAS & ENERGY LAW INTELLIGENCE 2 (July 2004).

260 JEAN-PIERRE COT, INTERNATIONAL CONCILIATION 1 (1972). *See also* Smith, *supra* note 7, at 238.

Wise Man eschews pressure and influence in favor of equity and the sculpting of creative compromise.

9.122 While this dichotomy may describe well the choice facing governments seeking mediation of their differences with other States, the ideal conciliator for investor–State disputes may be a more complex hybrid of the Prince and the Wise Man. Professor Wälde encapsulates the qualities of the perfect mediator:

> the ideal mediator would be a lawyer (to understand legal argument and litigation implications), a commercial manager (to understand the economics of the issue), an organisation specialist (to understand the inside organisational dynamics of the dispute), a professional negotiator (to know how to bring two sides to a deal), a psychologist (to understand the huge amount of self-love, vanity, competitiveness, love, hatred, jealousy, greed, insecurity that is usually involved in an inter-company dispute), a political scientist (to understand the workings of government bureaucracy and its difficulty in making and maintaining deals with multinational companies), a psychoanalyst (to listen carefully for little noises that indicate suppressed needs and desires), an accountant (to put a value on the various positions being discussed), an engineer (to understand the technical complexity and failure risks in technical project management) and a diplomat (to be able to gently persuade two parties to give up their normal self-righteousness).[261]

9.123 With these considerations in mind, the parties to investor–State disputes may prefer to appoint former government officials, diplomats, or judges from a neutral country. Such individuals, particularly if their career has brought them into contact with commercial issues, may offer the closest approximation of the characteristics needed for the task of mediation/conciliation. Former involvement in government may also give a potential mediator insight into the inner workings of State parties to a dispute, their particular concerns and constraints in reaching a settlement with private foreign investors. At the same time, experienced international lawyers who have represented States may share the same expertise.

H. Why Mediation/Conciliation Is Not More Frequently Used in Investment Disputes

9.124 The discussion in the previous section reveals a paradoxical situation in relation to investment-related conciliation: while less adversarial ADR proceedings can offer distinct advantages over litigated or arbitrated solutions, anecdotal evidence suggests that investors and States rarely engage in conciliation to resolve their disputes.[262] Other sources reveal that very few requests for conciliation have been submitted to ICSID procedures.[263] A review of the most probable sources of this

[261] Wälde, *supra* note 35, at 10.

[262] Mauro Rubino-Sammartano, International Arbitration Law 5 (1990).

[263] *See* August Reinisch & Loretta Malintoppi, *Methods of Dispute Resolution*, in The Oxford Handbook of International Investment Law 702, note 53 (Peter Muchlinski et al. eds.

disuse can serve to alert parties to some of the barriers that may ultimately prevent the initiation of mediation/conciliation proceedings and the amicable settlement of disputes.

Counsel for the investor in the only successful ICSID conciliation to date speculate that "it may be that parties do not resort to conciliation because the ICSID jurisdictional clause in the relevant agreement does not provide for conciliation or because the parties feel that conciliation, since it is not binding, is a waste of time."[264] There is some truth to this assessment, particularly with regard to the importance of parties' perception of the ADR process, but the situation is somewhat more complex. **9.125**

1. Lack of information about mediation/conciliation

It seems clear that there is far less understanding of mediation and conciliation than of more "traditional" forms of dispute resolution, such as litigation and arbitration. This information gap appears to be prevalent not only among government officials, but also among the corporate counsel of major companies engaged in international investment projects, and among litigation practitioners in major law firms.[265] The generalized lack of understanding about ADR techniques is due to a number of factors. **9.126**

First, relatively little has been written about the way mediation works (particularly when compared to the massive scholarly and professional literature treating international arbitration and litigation practice). Much of the literature available is either theoretical or adapted to the domestic contexts in which conciliation is most often used (*e.g.* labor and family disputes).[266] Further, the flexibility of conciliation means that even a close review of prominent rules systems gives users only a very approximate idea of how such systems actually operate. The tight confidentiality of mediation prevents information from reaching the business and government communities about actual instances (both successful and unsuccessful) of such ADR techniques applied in the investment context. **9.127**

Some commentators suggest a more deliberate information-filtering process, by which arbitration and litigation practitioners do not convey the possibilities of **9.128**

2008); *see*, however, Munir Maniruzzaman, *A Rethink of Investor–State Dispute Settlement*, Kluwer Arbitration Blog (May 30, 2013).

264 Nurick & Schnably, *supra* note 43, at 340.

265 *See* Lorraine M. Brennan, *Preparing the Client in an International Mediation: What to Expect from the Process*, in Contemporary Issues in International Arbitration and Mediation: The Fordham Papers 2014 139–51 (Arthur W. Rovine ed. 2015).

266 Susan Franck and Anna Joubin-Bret recognize the gap between theory and practice in investment-related ADR, and offer a role-playing simulation to enable stakeholders to consider how investor–State mediation might function in practice; *see* Susan D. Franck & Anna Joubin-Bret, *Investor–State Mediation: A Simulation*, 29(1) ICSID Rev.—For. Inv. L.J. 90–111 (2014).

conciliation to their clients, favoring more adversarial dispute resolution options. To some degree, such is the natural product of lawyers' "culture," as Professor Wälde explains:

> professional lawyers are in control of disputes, both in government and in the commercial world. They are trained from day one at university to make a "legal" argument about the relative merits of one party over the other one. The legal profession is geared towards litigation. This controls the mindset of most practitioners and academics. Non-litigious ways of settlement tend to downgrade the great value the legal community attaches to the legal argument ...[267]

9.129 Some have also suggested, perhaps too cynically, that outside counsel are less likely to propose or explain ADR options to their corporate and governmental clients because arbitration and litigation promise greater revenues in legal fees.[268]

9.130 Ignorance about the mechanics of conciliation creates striking misperceptions about the variety of roles that a conciliator can play in a dispute. Even the U.S. government appears to have been somewhat misinformed when it declined Switzerland's offer of conciliation in the *Interhandel* case. The United States was apparently operating under the assumption that mediators are restricted to the conduct of an evidentiary inquiry, and demurred because "the facts were clear."[269]

9.131 The previous dearth of information on mediation and conciliation, particularly in the investor–State context, has now been mitigated by increasing attention to ADR in the investor–State context. New ADR rules (such as the IBA Mediation Rules) as well as academic works dedicated to the topic have emerged in recent years, providing investors and governments comprehensive information about the workings of mediation/conciliation and the advantages and disadvantages of such procedures.[270]

---

[267] Wälde, *supra* note 35, at 4.

[268] *Id.* ("There is much less money to be made out of settling a dispute rather than playing it out to the fullest extent ... Payment by time, now the normal way of computing legal fees' income, heavily discourages any action that might cut a legal proceeding short").

[269] *Interhandel (Switzerland v. U.S.A)*, 1959 I.C.J. Rep. 6; Merrills, *supra* note 13, at 85.

[270] *See e.g.* Carrie J. Menkel-Meadow, Dispute Resolution: Beyond the Adversarial Model (1995); Eileen Carroll & Karl Mackie, International Mediation: The Art of Business Diplomacy (2000). Wolf von Kumberg et al., *Enabling Early Settlement in Investor–State Arbitration: The Time to Introduce Mediation Has Come*, 29(1) ICSID Rev.—For. Inv. L.J. 133–41 (2014); Jack Coe, Jr., *Should Mediation of Investment Disputes Be Encouraged, and, If So, by Whom and How?*, in Contemporary Issues in International Arbitration and Mediation: The Fordham Papers 339 (Arthur W. Rovine ed. 2009); Jack Coe, Jr., *Settlement of Investor–State Disputes through Mediation—Preliminary Remarks on Processes, Problems and Prospects*, in Enforcement of Arbitral Awards against Sovereigns 73 (R. Doak Bishop ed. 2009); Jeswald W. Salacuse, *Is there a Better Way? Alternative Methods of Treaty-Based, Investor–State Dispute Resolution*, 31 Fordham Int'l L.J. 138 (2007); Roberto Echandi Priyanka Kher, *Can International Investor–State Disputes Be Prevented? Empirical Evidence from Settlements in ICSID Arbitration*, 29(1) ICSID Rev.—For. Inv. L.J. 41–65 (2014); W. Michael Reisman, *International Investment Arbitration and ADR: Married But Best Living Apart*, 24(1) ICSID Rev.—For. Inv. L.J. 185 (2009).

2. Non-binding nature of mediation/conciliation

As is clear from the foregoing discussion, the unifying feature of all mediation and conciliation techniques is that they are non-binding. Absent particular participation requirements, parties are free to abandon conciliation at any time to opt for more aggressive solutions. Foreign investors who have suffered the manifestations of political risk in the form of expropriation or other interference with property rights are often already seasoned by protracted correspondence, negotiation, and perhaps even administrative battles with the State. They may well feel that the time has come for more forceful steps. Likewise, State parties may be unwilling to participate in a process that will not yield a solution imposed from the outside, for bureaucratic and political reasons. From a certain point of view, after all, conciliation is no more than negotiation in the presence of a neutral third party, which may seem somewhat redundant in light of previous, unsuccessful attempts to negotiate a solution. **9.132**

3. Over-optimism

Studies of psychology and the law reveal that the parties to litigation tend to be overly optimistic concerning their chances of success.[271] Bureaucratic structures (in both private companies and States) evidence a number of structural features that can exaggerate this basic psychological principle. Mid-level bureaucrats and managers often filter information about ongoing disputes before passing it to superiors, offering a partial and overly positive assessment in order to avoid blame for the state of affairs. For disputing States, political pressures can have a similar effect. Both vertical disapproval within the government hierarchy and public opinion can force State entities to overestimate the validity of claims or defenses. Furthermore, individuals within both corporations and States can suffer the side-effects of "corporate" loyalty, which leads them to identify emotionally with their side's positions and to demonize their opponents. All of these forces can result in managers or high-ranking government officials who see no reason to seek an amicable settlement:[272] the more modest results expected from mediation appear outweighed by the more optimistically-viewed results expected from litigation.[273] **9.133**

[271] *See e.g.* Anton van Langelaar, *Establishing Settlement Ranges by using Subject Matter Experts and Probability Analysis*, 71 Arb. 1, 64 (2005); Donald C. Langevoort, *Ego, Human Behavior, and Law*, 81 Va. L. Rev. 853 (1995); Daniel W. Shuman, *The Psychology of Deterrence in Tort Law*, 42 U. Kan. L. Rev. 115, 127–29 (1993) (arguing that deterrence cannot function effectively in torts because of the cognitive biases of potential tortfeasors); Eric Posner, *Probability Errors: Some Positive and Normative Implications for Tort and Contract Law*, U. Chic. L. & Econ., Olin Working Paper No. 161 (2002) (describing how excess optimism might interact with incentives in tort and contract law).

[272] *See Wälde, supra* note 35, at 2 ("The merits of 'our' case increasingly dominate perception; detached critical analysis is absent and discouraged by corporate loyalties ... [and] seen as treason to the evidently morally and legally just cause of each party").

[273] Oddly enough, some observers suggest that the opposite is also true—conciliation is unlikely to be initiated, and less likely to succeed, where one of the parties believes that it will not

4. Governmental constraints

9.134 Government officials, particularly the mid-level bureaucrats who are typically charged with managing disputes with foreign investors, are subject to rather abstract pressures that tend to discourage settlement. Engaging in mediation can be particularly difficult for civil servants. In a litigation proceeding, a result less than a total victory can be blamed on the arbitrator or judge, while the government official himself will have to take responsibility for any concessions included in a settlement agreement. This pressure is increased where public opinion has turned against the foreign investor, and therefore any compromise is viewed as a betrayal of national interests. As a result, despite the advantages of ADR, States—or at least the individuals charged with determining the path of dispute resolution for the State—may prefer litigation or arbitration to engaging in mediation or conciliation with the intent to reach settlement.[274]

prevail in an adversarial dispute resolution forum. As Professor Rubino-Sammartano explains, "the party which knows it is in the wrong generally tries to avoid quick settlement of the dispute. This tendency is unfortunately encouraged by the duration of court and arbitral proceedings and by the financial advantage that the defaulting party can obtain from a delayed payment." Rubino-Sammartano, *supra* note 262, at 5–6.

[274] On the integration of investor–State mediation and dispute-prevention techniques in governmental policies, *see* Silvia Constain, *Mediation in Investor–State Dispute Settlement: Government Policy and the Changing Landscape*, 29(1) ICSID Rev.—For. Inv. L.J. 25–40 (2014).

10

INTERVENTION OF STATES IN INVESTMENT DISPUTES

A. Introduction

Chapters 8 and 9 examined the dispute resolution mechanisms that foreign investors can set in motion at their own initiative, without the assistance of their home State. Direct investor–State mediation and arbitration were covered first because such procedures give investors maximum control over the dispute resolution process—and perhaps the most promising opportunity of a prompt and effective settlement. At the same time, the discussions of international law in the first part of this book underline that States have traditionally played a central role in the defense of their citizens' interests abroad. Indeed, as noted earlier, the investor–State arbitration made available through bilateral investment treaties (BITs) and other international instruments is only a development of the late 1980s, designed by States to mitigate the shortcomings (from both the investor's **10.01** and host State's point of view) of the customary system of State-dominated investment protection.[1]

10.02 In this chapter, we examine the actions that States may take to obtain redress against other States at whose hands their citizens are mistreated. While such remedies have receded somewhat in prominence as a result of the rise of investment treaties at the end of the 1980s, the topic remains an important one.[2] Where no investment treaty binds the home and host States, and where no other instrument (such as a contract or domestic law on investment) offers the jurisdictional foundation for investor–State arbitration, a foreign investor may have no other remedy but to appeal to his government for assistance. The continuing role of State intervention is particularly evident where a host government takes wide-ranging action affecting the property of investors of several nationalities. Consider the position of foreign farmers in Zimbabwe after the land seizures of the early 2000s, as described in this press report:

> About 1,500 commercial farmers who have had their land forcibly and sometimes violently seized by [President] Robert Mugabe's government have taken their case to international arbitration ... The farmers, most of whom are not settlers ... but who acquired their properties after Zimbabwe's independence, are seeking compensation or a return of their expropriated properties. They fall into three different categories: Zimbabwean nationals; foreign nationals whose countries signed bilateral investment treaties ratified by Zimbabwe—such as the Dutch—and foreign nationals whose countries did not have such agreements ... Fifteen Dutch farmers have been notified that their requests for arbitration were registered [at ICSID]. Their assets have been valued at US$15 million. Lawyers acting on behalf of the farmers in the UK ... [stated] that they had plans to persuade other governments that had not signed or ratified bilateral investment treaties with Zimbabwe to espouse claims on behalf of their nationals who have had their property expropriated. "Under international law, harm caused by one state to the nationals of another state is a harm to the state itself," explained a spokesman for the legal firm.[3]

10.03 A State's intervention on its citizens' behalf can take a number of forms, ranging from informal diplomatic discussions to formal adversarial proceedings before ad hoc or standing international tribunals.[4] In the next section we discuss how

---

[1] *See* Chapter 6.

[2] ILC, *Diplomatic Protection: Text of the Draft Articles with Commentaries thereto*, John Dugard, Special Rapporteur 2(2) Yb. ILC 23–55 (2006); *See also* William S. Dodge, *Investor–State Dispute Settlement between Developed Countries: Reflections on the Australia–United States Free Trade Agreement*, 39(1) Vand. J. Transnat'l L. 1–37 (2006); UNCTAD, Dispute Settlement: State-State, UNCTAD Series on issues in international investment agreements, UNCTAD/ITE/IIT/2003/1 (2003), available at https://unctad.org/en/pages/PublicationArchive.aspx?publicationid=323; Georges R. Delaume, *The Finality of Arbitration Involving States: Recent Developments*, 5 Arb. Int'l 21 (1989); Peter Malanczuk, *State-to-State and Investor-to-State Dispute Settlement in the OECD Draft Multilateral Investment Agreement*, in Multilateral Regulation of Investment 137 (E.C. Nieuwenhuys & Marcel M.T.A. Brus eds. 2001).

[3] Wilf Mbanga, *Farmers Are Seeking Compensation*, The Zimbabwean, May 13, 2005.

[4] *See generally* J. Gills Wetter, The International Arbitral Process 27–173 (1962).

individuals can try to set these mechanisms in motion, the possible benefits of State intervention, and the challenges and limits involved.

B. "Espousal" of Claims

Before an investor can rely upon the formal support of its home State, the government must "espouse" his claim, adopting the grievance as its own and raising it to the international plane. Otherwise known as "diplomatic protection," espousal is a completely discretionary right of the State—citizens may request that their claims be espoused, but it is impossible to compel the State to comply.[5] Once a State has espoused a claim, it assumes all related rights and obligations, leaving the investor with little control over the dispute resolution process, and even over the remedy. In the formulation of the Permanent Court of International Justice, by taking up the case of one of its subjects and by resorting to diplomatic action or international judicial proceedings on his behalf, a State is in reality asserting its own right to ensure, in the person of its subjects, respect for the rules of international law.[6] **10.04**

In most countries, diplomatic protection is rather uncommon, in part because an investor must demonstrate to his government that a number of criteria—both formal and informal—have been satisfied. These criteria are discussed below. **10.05**

1. Formal requirements for State espousal

a. Nationality

The most significant formal prerequisite for diplomatic espousal is that the investor to be protected is a "national" of the protecting State. Chapter 7 reviewed some of the complexities of the nationality requirement in the context of investor–State arbitration and the Washington Convention.[7] Within the context of State-to-State investment disputes, the issue of requisite nationality is normally a function of customary international law, according to which a State is only empowered to espouse the claims of its own nationals. There are separate rules in this regard for physical and legal persons. These rules, while still evolving and by no means entirely clear, lay down the first test for investors who seek the protection of their State of origin.[8] **10.06**

i. Physical persons Where the investor is an individual and is recognized as a citizen by only one State, there is nothing to prevent that State from taking up **10.07**

[5] UNCTAD, Dispute Settlement, *supra* note 2, at 52 n.1.
[6] *Mavrommatis Palestine Concessions*, P.C.I.J. Ser. A, No. 2 (1924), at 12.
[7] *See* Chapter 7, Sections B.3.b and D.
[8] For more detail on nationality under customary international law, *see* Chapter 4, section F.

the person's claim as its own.[9] Formalities of nationality, such as passports, voting cards, and the like are less important than the provisions of the host State's law on nationality.

10.08 The more problematic situation under international law is when an individual is considered to be a citizen by more than one State. This is an increasingly common phenomenon in an age of globalization and migration, where prominent businesspeople may hold several passports by virtue of birth, residence, ethnicity, education, marriage, contributions to a country's development, or other reasons.[10] For purposes of customary international law and State espousal, however, it is generally accepted that an individual can have only *one effective nationality*, regardless how many States consider him to be "their own" under local law.

10.09 As is clear from the ICJ's *Nottebohm* decision,[11] the determination of effective nationality involves a case-by-case analysis (in the first instance undertaken by the espousing State internally, and then by a court or tribunal seized of the dispute) of the individual's "genuine link" with the potential claimant State. A number of factors will be weighed in establishing a physical person's effective nationality, with the greatest accumulated connections indicating which citizenship will be dominant.[12] The factual circumstances that are indicative of effective nationality include:

[9] M. SORNARAJAH, THE SETTLEMENT OF FOREIGN INVESTMENT DISPUTES 128, 131 (2000). Stateless persons, even if they reside permanently and exclusively in a particular country, may be barred from seeking espousal from their domicile State. *But see* to the contrary, ILC Draft Articles on Diplomatic Protection, art. 8(1) ("A State may exercise diplomatic protection in respect of a stateless person who, at the date of injury and at the date of the official presentation of the claim, is lawfully and habitually resident in that State").

[10] *See generally* Francisco Orrego Vicuña, *Changing Approaches to the Nationality of Claims in the Context of Diplomatic Protection and International Dispute Settlement*, in LIBER AMICORUM IBRAHIM F.I. SHIHATA: INTERNATIONAL FINANCE AND DEVELOPMENT LAW 503 (S. Schlemmer-Schulte & K.-Y. Tung eds. 2001).

[11] *Nottebohm Case (Liechtenstein v. Guatemala)*, 1953 I.C.J. 111, 20 I.L.R. 567 (1953). *See also* Chapter 4, section F.1.

[12] This approach is reminiscent of the standard analysis that courts apply in many jurisdictions to determine which system of law should apply to a cross-border transaction in the absence of party choice. Restatement (Second) of Conflict of Laws § 188(1) (1971) (U.S. courts generally apply system of law with "most significant relationship" to transaction); JOHN WESTLAKE, A TREATISE ON PRIVATE INTERNATIONAL LAW, WITH PRINCIPAL REFERENCE TO ITS PRACTICE IN ENGLAND 237 (2d ed. 1880) ("proper" law is "the law of the country with which the contract has its most real connection"). The term "proper law" was taken up by John Humphrey Carlile Morris and G.C. Cheshire in *The Proper Law of a Contract in the Conflict of Laws*, 56 LQR 320 (1940) and was later used by John Humphrey Carlile Morris, *Torts in the Conflict of Laws*, 12 MODERN L. REV. 248 (1949) and *The Proper Law of a Tort*, 64 HARV. L. REV. 881 (1951). The "proper law" is arguably the most important concept in contemporary conflict of law theory. *See* WILLIAM TETLEY, INTERNATIONAL CONFLICT OF LAWS 10–11 (1994); *Erie R. R. v. Tompkins*, 304 U.S. 64 (1938); *Amin Rasheed Shipping Corp. v. Kuwait Insurance Co* [1984] A.C. 50; *James Miller & Partners Ltd. v. Whitworth Street Estates (Manchaster) Ltd.* [1970] A.C. 583; *The Assunzione*, [1954] 1 All E.R. 278; *see also* WILLIAM M. RICHMAN & WILLAM L. REYNOLDS, UNDERSTANDING CONFLICT OF LAWS (2002); EUGENE SCOLES et al., CONFLICT OF LAWS (3d ed. 2000); A.V. DICEY & J.H.C. MORRIS, CONFLICT OF LAWS (13th ed. 2000); Dagmar Coester-Waltjen, *German Conflict Rules and the Multinational Enterprise*, 6 GA.

- place of domicile;
- birth;
- family connections;
- economic activity; and
- linguistic or other cultural links.

ii. Corporations In contrast to the rather subjective, multi-factor test applied to physical persons, customary international law defines the nationality of legal entities according to a rather simple and objective rule. Generally speaking, a legal person is considered a "national" of the State under the law of which it was incorporated.[13] Alternatively, a juridical person may be considered a national of the State where it has its effective headquarters (or "siège social").[14] The respect for the corporate form at international law is not normally affected by such factors as the nationality of shareholders, and reflects the reluctance to "pierce the corporate veil" that prevails in many jurisdictions around the world.[15] 10.10

In *Barcelona Traction*,[16] the government of Spain caused the bankruptcy of a Canadian company whose shares were partly owned by Belgian citizens. Belgium espoused the company's claim by virtue of its nationals' equity interest, seeking compensation for the damage caused by the Spanish government in contravention of international law.[17] Spain objected to the jurisdiction of the ICJ, in part on grounds that Belgium had no standing to bring a claim in relation to the dispute. The ICJ accepted the objection and dismissed the case, holding that "the general 10.11

J. Int'l & Comp. L. 197–226 (1976); Volker Triebel, *The Choice of Law in Commercial Relations: A German Perspective*, 37 ICLQ 935–45 (1988).

[13] Christoph Schreuer et al., The ICSID Convention: A Commentary 424 (2d ed. 2009). On corporate nationality under international law, *see generally* Yoram Dinstein, *Diplomatic Protection of Companies under International Law*, in International Law: Theory and Practice 505 (Karel Wellens ed. 1998); Christopher Staker, *Diplomatic Protection of Private Business Companies: Determining Corporate Personality for International Law Purposes*, 61 Brit. Yb. Int'l L. 155 (1991).

[14] *See* Stanimir A. Alexandrov, *The "Baby Boom" of Treaty-Based Arbitrations and the Jurisdiction of ICSID Tribunals: Shareholders as "Investors" and Jurisdiction Ratione Temporis*, 4 L. & Prac. Int'l Courts & Tribunals 19, 34 (2005), available at https://heinonline.org/HOL/Page?collection=journals&handle=hein.journals/lpict4&id=25&men_tab=srchresults; Rudolf Dolzer & Margrete Stevens, Bilateral Investment Treaties 35 (1995); Sornarajah, *supra* note 9, at 136.

[15] *See e.g.* Glenn Morris, *Piercing the Corporate Veil in Louisiana*, 52 La. L. Rev. 271 (1991); *Salomon v Salomon & Co.* (1897) A.C. 22 (H.L.); Carsten Alting, *Piercing the Corporate Veil in American and German Law—Liability of Individuals and Entities: A Comparative View*, Tulsa J. Comp. & Int'l L. 187 (1995); Omar Guerrero et al., *Piercing the Corporate Veil in Mexico*, Comp. L. Yb. Int'l Bus. 375 (Dennis Campbell ed. 2004); *see also* Ignaz Seidl-Hohenveldern, Corporations in and under International Law (1987).

[16] *Case Concerning Barcelona Traction, Light & Power Co. (Belgium v. Spain)*, 1970 I.C.J. 4, 42 (Second Phase), 46 I.L.R. 178. *See also* Chapter 4, section F.2.

[17] For a more detailed description of the case, *see* Rosalyn Higgins, *Aspects of the Case Concerning the Barcelona Traction, Light & Power Company, Limited*, 11 Va. J. Int'l L. 327 (1971); *see also* F.A. Mann, *The Protection of Shareholders' Interests in the Light of the Barcelona Traction Case*, 67 AJIL 259, 272–73 (1973).

rule of international law states that where an unlawful act was committed against a company representing foreign capital, only the national state of the company could sue."[18] At the same time, the Court held that Belgium might have had a sufficient interest in the dispute if the shareholders' rights had been directly infringed, for example their ability to vote or receive dividends.[19]

10.12 Some States have taken the position that diplomatic espousal of the claims of injured shareholders in a foreign corporation is possible, where the company is bankrupt or otherwise unable to procure diplomatic espousal from its home State.[20]

b. Exhaustion of local remedies

10.13 An additional barrier to diplomatic protection is the "local remedies" rule of customary international law.[21] A State is not normally entitled to exercise diplomatic protection in relation to its national's claim if the individual or company has not first attempted to obtain redress through all reasonably available judicial or administrative structures in the host State.[22] The doctrine of exhaustion of local remedies is a concept developed in customary law over several centuries.[23]

10.14 The local remedies rule is based on the premise that "the home government of the complaining citizen must give the offending government an opportunity of doing justice to the injured party in its own regular way, and thus avoid, if possible, all occasion for international discussion."[24] There is some difference of opinion as to whether the aggrieved foreigner must litigate in local courts precisely the claim he seeks to raise through diplomatic espousal, or simply petition for *some* remedy based on the same basic facts. In the *Finnish Ships Arbitration*,[25] the tribunal took

---

[18] Malcolm N. Shaw, International Law 588–95 (7th ed. 2014).

[19] *Barcelona Traction, supra* note 16.

[20] *See e.g.* U.K. Foreign and Commonwealth Office, Rules Regarding International Claims (1985) (espousal of shareholders' claims permissible where company is defunct).

[21] *See* ILC Draft Article on Diplomatic Protection, *supra* note 9, art. 14; C.F. Amerasinghe, Local Remedies in International Law (2004); K. Tamas, *The ELSI Case and the Rule of the Exhaustion of Local Remedies*, in Responsibility of States—Thesaurus Acroasium 341 (1993); *see also* Chapter 4, Section E.

[22] *Interhandel Case (Switzerland v. U.S.A.)*, 1959 I.C.J. Rep. 6, 27 ("the rule that local remedies must be exhausted before international proceedings may be instituted is a well-established rule of customary international law"). The Canadian government openly informs its citizens that it "will not espouse any claim of a Canadian against a foreign State unless the claimant has exhausted all legal remedies provided by the internal law of the country in question (that is all available remedies up to an appeal to the court of last resort in the foreign State) without obtaining redress." Government of Canada, L'Entraide Judiciaire Internationale: Services Juridiques Fournis par le Ministère des Affaires Extérieures Concernant L'Entraide Judiciaire Internationale et Certaines Autres Matières (1987), at 63.

[23] Amerasinghe, *supra* note 21, at 11.

[24] Edwin Borchard, Diplomatic Protection of Citizens Abroad 817 (1915); Amerasinghe, *supra* note 21, at 97; William S. Dodge, *Exhaustion of Remedies and Res Judicata under Chapter Eleven of NAFTA*, 23 Hastings Int'l & Comp. L. Rev. 357, 361–62 (2000).

[25] *Finnish Shipowners Arbitration (Finland v. U.K.)*, Award of May 9, 1934, 3 R.I.A.A. 1479 (1934).

a strict approach, holding that "propositions of law which are brought forward by the claimant government ... must have been investigated and adjudicated upon by the municipal Courts."[26] By contrast, the International Court of Justice has more recently held that an international claim will be admissible as long it is based on the same nexus of facts as a domestic claim pursued to conclusion in the domestic courts.[27]

The basic rule, according to the ICJ, is that the respondent State must first have an opportunity to redress by its own means within the framework of its own domestic legal system the wrong alleged to have been done to the individual.[28] **10.15**

This does not mean, however, that the investor must pursue even those remedies in the local courts that are a mere formality or certain to fail. In the *Finnish Ships* case, for example, the tribunal ruled that the Finnish investor's failure to bring an action in the U.S. Court of Appeal did not prevent espousal of the claim by Finland, because the court would not have had the authority to overturn the offending decision.[29] In the words of the P.C.I.J., "[t]here can be no need to resort to the municipal court if ... the result must be a repetition of a decision already given."[30] **10.16**

2. Informal requirements

Even if an investor satisfies the legal criteria described, there is no guarantee that his claim will be espoused by his home State. Since official representation of private interests entails substantial political costs, many States will refrain from taking up citizens' claims unless the complaining investor and the claim itself present particular importance for the economy of the home country as a whole. To be sure, in some cases interference with the property of a small- or mid-sized company may be symptomatic of a broader pattern of illegal State conduct, which a capital-exporting State may be willing to espouse to prevent harm to other nationals in future, as well as to obtain compensation for investors already harmed. Nevertheless, the investor's economic influence, and even political connections within his home government, may be important factors determining whether his claim will be espoused. **10.17**

Informal elements such as these may be just as prominent in the espousal process for large and politically powerful States as for less influential States. Small States are more dependent on other countries economically and politically, and **10.18**

---

[26] *Finnish Shipowners, supra* note 25, at 1502. *See also Case of Certain Norwegian Loans (France v. Norway)*, 1957 I.C.J. Rep. 9, 41–42 (separate opinion of Lauterpacht, J.); *see also* AMERASINGHE, *supra* note 21, at 176.

[27] *Elettronica Sicula S.p.A. (ELSI) (U.S.A. v. Italy)*, 1989 I.C.J. REP. 1, at paras. 49–50.

[28] *Interhandel, supra* note 22, at 27.

[29] *Finnish Shipowners, supra* note 25.

[30] *Panavesyz-Saldaiskis Railway Case (Estonia v. Lithuania)*, P.C.I.J. Ser. A/B, No. 76 (1939), at 18.

therefore may be reluctant to sacrifice bargaining leverage or risk suffering a deterioration of relations with stronger or wealthier States. But at the same time, larger States tend to have broader political ambitions, covering a wider range of issues and geographical territory. As a result, even an investment dispute involving a far-off host State of relatively little direct importance for the home State's economic or political wellbeing may enter into the home State's long-term strategic policy, and the investor may therefore nevertheless need to demonstrate to his government the importance of his claim from a systemic point of view.

3. How to seek espousal

10.19 A national seeking diplomatic espousal must normally present his case to the Ministry of Foreign Affairs in his State of origin. In the United States, for example, a claim should be presented to the U.S. Department of State, or to the Foreign Claims Settlement Commission, if the investor's claim falls within the scope of the latter body's established claims programs.[31]

10.20 Once an investor has protested expropriation of its property to its government, whether the government then engages in diplomacy for the benefit of the investor is entirely at the home State's discretion.[32] As the court in *Redpath v. Kissinger* held, for example, a U.S. citizen has no legally enforceable right to compel the United States to negotiate on his behalf with a foreign State.[33] As an example of diplomatic protest, the U.S. State Department protested to the Libyan Government following the expropriation of the interests of a company controlled by U.S. investors, the Nelson Bunker Hunt Oil Company, in 1973. The State Department delivered the following message to the Libyan government:

> It is clear from these pronouncements [expropriating the property of the Nelson Bunker Hunt Oil Company] that the reason for the action of the Government of the Libyan Arab Republic against the rights and property of the Nelson Bunker Hunt Oil Company were political reprisal against the United States government and coercion against the economic interests of certain other United States nationals in Libya.

---

[31] The U.S. Foreign Claims Settlement Commission is discussed in Section G.

[32] Brice M. Clagett, *Present State of the International Law of Compensation for Expropriated Property and Repudiated State Contracts*, in PRIVATE INVESTORS ABROAD § 12.05[1][a] (Southwestern Legal Foundation ed. 1989).

[33] *Redpath v. Kissinger*, 415 F. Supp. 566, 569 (W.D. Tex. 1976), *aff'd.* 545 F.2d 167 (5th Cir. 1976). In *Redpath*, the plaintiff sought to compel Executive Branch action to obtain the release of an American citizen from detention in Mexico. The court held that "[t]here is no doubt that a District Court has no authority to grant the requested relief by Writ of Mandamus or otherwise" (415 F. Supp. at 567). This holding was based on the court's view that "commencement of diplomatic negotiations with a foreign power is completely in the discretion of the President . . . The Executive is not subject to judicial control or direction in such matters." *Id.* at 568.

Under established principles of international law, measures taken against the rights and property of foreign nationals which are arbitrary, discriminatory, or based on considerations of political reprisal and economic coercion are invalid and not entitled to recognition by other States.[34] **10.21**

If diplomacy is successful, the home State of the investor may negotiate a settlement with the expropriating State on behalf of the investors. This will typically take the form of a lump sum for the benefit of a class of injured businesses. Under customary international law, a State-to-State settlement of a dispute relating to injury to one State's national by the other State is binding on the individual concerned.[35] This principle was affirmed in a U.S.–Germany Mixed Claim Commission Administrative Decision: **10.22**

> Ordinarily a nation will not espouse a claim on behalf of its national against another nation unless requested so to do by such national. When on such request a claim is espoused, the nation's absolute right to control it is necessarily exclusive. In exercising such control it is governed not only by the interest of the particular claimant but by the larger interests of the whole people of the nation and must exercise an untrammeled discretion in determining when and how the claim will be presented and pressed, or withdrawn or compromised, and the private owner will be bound by the action taken.[36]

It is not surprising that international law should bind individuals to observe settlements negotiated on their behalf by their home States. As noted, a State will normally intervene in investment disputes only upon its national's request. In such cases, the national expects its State to negotiate or assist in achieving settlement. Further, individuals are always, in a sense, "bound" by their State's laws; this is, after all, a necessary outcome of the fact that individuals generally do not have standing under international law to challenge their own State's municipal laws.[37] At the same time, a State's broad-based espousal of a class of claims, such as in the case of a sector-wide nationalization, can foreclose a particular investor's separate settlement on different terms, even if the State espoused claims without the particular investor's participation or request. **10.23**

If a settlement is reached between the expropriating State and the home State of the investor, the manner and amount of distribution of such funds by the home State is a matter of domestic law. In the United States, many of these issues are governed by the Foreign Claims Settlement Act,[38] which is discussed in Section G. **10.24**

---

[34] New York Times, Aug. 8, 1973, at 55, col. 2.

[35] *See infra* note 121 and accompanying text.

[36] *Admin. Dec. V*, Mixed Claims Comm. (U.S.A.–Germany), 7 R.I.A.A. 119, 152 (1924).

[37] *See* Chapter 4, Section F; Chapter 1, Section C.1; Rosalyn Higgins, Problems and Process: International Law and How We Use It, ch. 6 (1994).

[38] Foreign Claims Settlement Act of 1949 (1950), 22 U.S.C. §§ 1621–1645 (1988).

4. Interaction of State espousal with investor–State arbitration

10.25 The procedures of investor–State arbitration described in detail elsewhere in this book are not always compatible with the direct intervention of the State.[39] This is only logical: the right to binding arbitration against States, whether granted through contract, treaty, or domestic investment law, was devised in part to ease the political relations between sovereigns by removing investment disputes from the realm of diplomacy.[40] Depoliticization serves a wide range of interests. Capital importing States can insulate themselves from the political and economic strength of industrialized countries, which could otherwise extract concessions even where investors' complaints lack legal merit. Capital exporting States can extend their influence in the less-developed world and achieve political, security, and overarching economic objectives without the complication of a multitude of domestic investors demanding diplomatic protests or other confrontational actions. Investors also stand to gain: since the lodging of claims (and their satisfaction) no longer depends upon the domestic political influence of the injured foreigner or the power of his home State, disputes are resolved on a more uniform and principled basis. Businesses can therefore better estimate political risk and the probability of redressing its manifestation through dispute resolution mechanisms.

10.26 To further depoliticize investment disputes, the investor–State arbitration system was established in such a way that in many circumstances direct recourse to arbitration will foreclose diplomatic espousal, and vice versa. Most significantly, arbitration under ICSID auspices can *never* be combined with action on the claimant's behalf by his home State. The Washington Convention provides:

> Consent of the parties to arbitration under this Convention shall, unless otherwise stated, be deemed consent to such arbitration to the exclusion of any other remedy …
>
> No Contracting State shall give diplomatic protection, or bring an international claim, in respect of a dispute which one of its nationals and another Contracting State shall have consented to submit or shall have submitted to arbitration under this Convention.[41]

---

[39] *See* Chapter 7.

[40] Horatio A. Grigera Naón, *The Settlement of Investment Disputes between States and Private Parties: An Overview from the Perspective of the ICC*, 1 J. World Inv. 59, 59–60 (2000) ("By advancing the resolution of disputes through the furtherance of principles of justice rather than political accommodation … private international dispute resolution devices provide a better technical and appropriately depoliticized framework for the development of substantive law and principles regarding foreign investment protection likely to enjoy wide international consensus"); Ibrahim Shihata, Towards a Greater Depoliticization of Investment Disputes: The Roles of ICSID and MIGA 1–10 (1992).

[41] Convention on the Settlement of Investment Disputes between States and Nationals of Other States, of Mar. 18, 1965, arts. 26, 27(1), 17 U.S.T. 1270.

While the Convention prohibits home State diplomatic espousal in connection with disputes that have been submitted to adjudication at ICSID, certain specific forms of intervention are allowed. First, an investor's State of origin may engage in informal diplomatic exchanges with the respondent State "for the sole purpose of facilitating a settlement of the dispute."[42] Second, the prohibition on espousal is lifted where arbitration results in an award in the investor's favor, and the respondent State fails to comply with the award.[43] **10.27**

The situation is somewhat less clear with regard to investor–State arbitration conducted outside the ICSID system. Some BITs include a parallel to the provisions of the Washington Convention, which would prevent home States from taking up their citizens' claims in parallel to an ongoing arbitration brought directly by the investor under the UNCITRAL or SCC Rules, for example.[44] Most investment treaties are silent on this point, however, leaving open the possibility of State espousal in parallel to an investor–State claim. Nevertheless, the purpose of investment treaties and the direct right to investor–State dispute resolution that they contain is to insulate investment disputes from the political realm. As a result, many States may be reluctant to espouse the claims of investors who can benefit from such an alternative remedy. Since espousal is purely discretionary, and necessarily entails certain political (and economic) costs for the State, investor–State claims are likely to remain matters between the claimant investor and respondent State, free of direct and formal intervention from the claimant's home government.[45] **10.28**

5. State assistance short of espousal

As explained, not every investor will be able to procure State espousal for his claim. Not only might an investor fail to satisfy the formal requirements of nationality or exhaustion of local remedies, but the business interests at stake or the political balance between his home State and the host State may not favor espousal. Even without such official support, however, investors can benefit in a number of ways from close contacts with diplomatic officials in their home capitals. **10.29**

---

[42] *Id.*, art. 27(2). On less formal diplomatic exchanges, *see* Section B.5, *infra*.

[43] Washington Convention, *supra* note 41, art. 27(1).

[44] Article 8(4) of the 1991 United Kingdom model BIT, for example, prevents signatory States from pursuing "through the diplomatic channel" claims that have already been submitted to investor–State arbitration, unless the tribunal has found that it has no jurisdiction, or the respondent State refuses to comply with a final arbitration award. UNCTAD, Dispute Settlement, *supra* note 2, at 28.

[45] *See* Communication from the European Community and its member States, Doc. WT/WGTI/W/30 (Mar. 27, 1980) ("European BITs and the ECT provide State-to-State dispute settlement. The OECD has a somewhat weaker mechanism to settle disputes at the State-to-State level. In the EC Treaty there is no formal impediment to a foreign country bringing a case before the European Court of Justice, but such cases are unlikely in reality, since the rights granted by the Treaty belong to the investors, and not to their home State").

10.30 It is common practice, for example, for governments to offer "good offices" to their citizens to facilitate the resolution of investment disputes.[46] This entails an informal mediation process where the home State assists the investor in making contact with representatives of the host State (the ambassador or his staff in the home country, for example) and presents a suggestion to meet on the premises of the home State government to discuss possible means of resolving the dispute amicably. While good offices are by definition merely non-binding suggestions to talk, such evidence of the home State's interest in the matter may in itself increase pressure upon the host State to compromise—depending on the relationship between the two countries in question.

10.31 Other types of informal State intervention can also be useful tools to focus the host State's attention on an investment dispute and provoke settlement. These include mention of the dispute during discussions between high-ranking officials of the two States, letters of complaint from the home State's ambassador to the offending State's foreign ministry, and discussion of the dispute by the home State's diplomatic officials during press conferences or in other public fora. Such action need not be taken by diplomatic or executive branch officials to be effective. In 2004, for example, the U.S. House of Representatives held public hearings criticizing Ecuador and Peru for their mistreatment of U.S. investments. Testimony was heard from a number of lawmakers, representatives of the U.S. diplomatic corps, the U.S. Trade Representative's office, and the private sector. In an opening statement, one lawmaker described the difficulties encountered in these countries by specific U.S. companies, and stated that:

> Peru and Ecuador need to know that we are prepared to hold off on further free trade negotiations until they can resolve these investment disputes and ensure that American companies are treated in a fair and equitable manner.[47]

10.32 Often, investors and host States that lack the contacts necessary within the investor's home government to influence that State's intervention in an investment dispute enlist the assistance of political (or "government relations") consultants. These consultants, frequently themselves retired government officials, can help the parties to an investment dispute identify and gain access to the necessary individuals within the home State governmental structure, in order to present the party's view of the dispute and induce the State to intervene accordingly.[48]

---

[46] Raymond R. Probst, *"Good Offices" in International Relations in the Light of Swiss Practice and Experience*, 201 Recueil des Cours 211 (1987).

[47] Opening Statement of Rep. Cass Ballenger, Hearing of the House Subcommittee on the Western Hemisphere, "U.S. Investment Disputes in Peru and Ecuador," Oct. 6, 2004.

[48] *See e.g.* the European Association of Political Consultants (http://www.eapc.eu/), founded in 1996 and including sixty-two members in Austria, Belgium, Canada, Finland, France, Germany, Greece, Italy, Lithuania, Malta, the Netherlands, Russia, Spain, Sweden, Switzerland, Turkey, Ukraine, the United Kingdom, and the United States.

C. Claims before International Tribunals

1. In general

In addition to diplomacy and negotiation, a State may bring a claim against an expropriating State before an international court or tribunal, such as the International Court of Justice or the Permanent Court of Arbitration at the Hague. Such a remedy depends upon satisfying the nationality and exhaustion of remedies requirements at customary international law, and in any event is at the discretion of the claimant State. If the State does advance such a claim, the claim is for the injury to the State itself.[49] **10.33**

Such an action may be based on breach of customary international law on the treatment of aliens (for a denial of justice, expropriation without compensation, or other well-established norms) or for violation of a treaty. In either case, the States involved must either have agreed to submit their disputes generally to international adjudication, be subject to a specific treaty-based submission to arbitration, or enter into a post-dispute *compromis*, consenting to the resolution of their dispute through arbitration. In 1989, for example, the United States filed a claim with the International Court of Justice for violation of a Treaty of Friendship, Commerce, and Navigation (FCN) between the parties based on the requisitioning by Italian authorities of a company controlled by two U.S. companies.[50] The FCN treaty included a clause referring disputes related to performance of obligations under the treaty to the ICJ for adjudication. **10.34**

2. State-to-State dispute resolution under bilateral investment treaties

a. Overview

Chapters 6 and 7 describe in detail the relatively novel phenomenon of BITs and the prominence of their investor–State arbitration provisions in the resolution of investment disputes.[51] Investment-related international treaties pre-date the advent of investor–State arbitration, however. The FCN treaties that formed the structural basis for BITs, for example, relied entirely upon State-to-State mechanisms for the adjudication of disputes related to foreign investment. From 1959 to 1969, BITs were similarly drafted to provide only for arbitration between States.[52] While many of these older treaties have now been superseded by **10.35**

[49] *See Mavrommatis Palestine Concessions, supra* note 6, at 12; *see also* Jacominj J. Van Haersolte-Van Hof & Anne K. Hoffmann, *The Relationship between International Tribunals and Domestic Courts*, in The Oxford Handbook of International Investment Law, ch. 24, 991 (Peter Muchlinski et al. eds. 2008).

[50] *ELSI, supra* note 27.

[51] *See e.g.* Chapter 6, Sections B.1 and C.

[52] The very first BIT that included direct investor–State arbitration was signed in 1969 between Italy and Chad. The dispute resolution clause of that treaty provided that "any dispute related to

modern BITs that include investor–State arbitration provisions, some remain in force today. Just as importantly, nearly all recent BITs establish the possibility of State-to-State arbitration in addition to investor–State arbitration. There therefore remains ample room for direct State involvement in investment disputes today, although in practice such participation is rare.

b. Dispute resolution pursuant to FCN treaties

10.36 While the first FCN treaties, signed during the nineteenth century, dealt primarily with the rights of foreign individuals to due process and physical safety, twentieth-century treaties began to impose substantive obligations upon host States in relation to foreign investment similar to those eventually codified in BITs. These treaties frequently provided that disputes arising out of these obligations would be resolved by State-to-State arbitration or other litigious means, including adjudication before the International Court of Justice.

10.37 A typical State-to-State dispute resolution clause is contained in the 1955 FCN treaty between Iran and the United States:

> Any dispute between the High Contracting Parties as to the interpretation or application of the present Treaty, not satisfactorily adjusted by diplomacy, shall be submitted to the International Court of Justice, unless the High Contracting Parties agree to settlement by some other pacific means.[53]

10.38 In 1992, this clause formed the basis of ICJ jurisdiction in the *Oil Platforms* case, concerning the United States' destruction of certain Iranian offshore oil facilities.[54] The United States filed preliminary objections to the ICJ seeking dismissal of the case on grounds that the Treaty did not apply to issues of the use of force in self-defense. The ICJ rejected this objection in December 1996, finding that the destruction of the Iranian oil platforms was capable of having an adverse effect upon the freedom of commerce guaranteed by article X(1) of the Treaty and that its unlawfulness could be evaluated in relation to that particular paragraph.[55]

10.39 The *ELSI* case was brought before the ICJ by the United States for the alleged breach by Italy of an FCN treaty that prohibited "arbitrary and discriminatory measures" and guaranteed "constant protection and security" to the person and property of qualifying nationals. The case involved the temporary requisitioning of a foreign-owned industrial facility by a local mayor (an action that was later found by Italian courts to be unlawful), who had acted to prevent labor unrest

investments subject to this agreement which may arise between one of the contracting parties (or one of the relevant institutions or organizations of the said party) and a physical or legal person who has the nationality of the other party shall be submitted to the jurisdiction of ICSID."

[53] Iran–United States FCN, art. XXI(2).

[54] *Case Concerning Oil Platforms (Iran v. U.S.A.)*, 1996 I.C.J. 803, Judgment on Merits, Nov. 6, 2003.

[55] Pieter H.F. Biekker, *The Oil Platforms Decision*, 91 AJIL 518 (1997).

when the company announced plans to close the plant. The ICJ held that "protection and security" must conform to the international minimum standard, and that reference to "constant protection and security" cannot be construed as a warranty that property will never in any circumstances be disturbed.[56] Further, the ICJ held that unlawfulness of State action under municipal law did not by itself, and without more, amount to arbitrariness at international law. The ICJ described arbitrariness as "willful disregard of due process of law, an act which shocks, or at least surprises, a sense of judicial propriety."[57]

c. Dispute resolution pursuant to BITs

Many BITs contemplate diplomatic action and, if necessary, State-to-State arbitration by the investor's home State in connection with disputes arising under the treaty. Submission to international adjudication is most commonly to the International Court of Justice or ad hoc.[58] To date there had been very few instances of dispute resolution pursuant to the inter-State arbitration clause in a BIT.[59] As a result, there is some controversy as to the proper scope of such submissions to arbitral jurisdiction. Whether a dispute will be subject to arbitration depends in large part on the wording of the applicable treaty. **10.40**

Most BITs provide for State-to-State arbitration of disputes related to the "interpretation" and "application" of the treaty's provisions. The United Kingdom–Azerbaijan BIT is typical in this regard: **10.41**

> Disputes between the Contracting Parties concerning the interpretation or application of this Agreement should, if possible, be settled through the diplomatic channel ... If a dispute between the Contracting Parties cannot thus be settled, it shall upon the request of either Contracting Party be submitted to an arbitral tribunal.[60]

The dominant interpretation of such a provision is that State-to-State arbitration is available only to determine the proper meaning of treaty terms or the implementation of the treaty, for example if the respondent State fails to pay an investor–State arbitration award. According to this approach, substantive disputes and awards of compensation are left to investor–State arbitration. The official European Commission position, for instance, is that: **10.42**

---

[56] *ELSI, supra* note 27, 1989 I.C.J. Rep. 65, at para. 108.

[57] *Id.* at paras. 124, 129.

[58] For a survey of the various State-to-State arbitration procedures envisaged in BITs, *see* Dolzer & Stevens, *supra* note 14, at 122–29.

[59] One example is the case initiated by Peru against Chile in relation to *Lucchetti S.A. and Lucchetti Peru S.A. v. Peru*, ICSID Case No. ARB/03/4. *See* Jamal Seifi, *Investor–State Arbitration v. State-to-State Arbitration in Bilateral Investment Treaties*, 1(4) Oil, Gas & Energy Law Intelligence (Sept. 2003). For a description of additional cases, *see* Campbell McLachlan et al., International Investment Arbitration: Substantive Principles, paras. 2.33–2.36 (2d ed. 2017); Michele Potestá, *Italy v. Cuba*, 106 AJIL 341 (2012).

[60] U.K.–Azerbaijan BIT, art. 9(1)–(2).

> The main right of the home country in European BITs pertains to the possibility to invoke State-to-State dispute settlement concerning the interpretation or application of the Agreement. This is usually complemented by the home State's right to subrogation, i.e. the right to take over rights and claims of its own investors which it has indemnified (e.g. through an investment insurance payment).[61]

10.43 The narrow interpretation of State-to-State dispute resolution provisions is echoed in the U.S. Model BIT, which specifically relegates disputes over the non-payment of awards to inter-State arbitration, but is silent as to State-to-State jurisdiction over substantive investment disputes.[62]

10.44 An alternative view of BIT State-to-State arbitration provisions is that they cover the full range of substantive rights due to foreign investors under the treaty. According to this approach, the investor–State and State-to-State provisions are alternative means of recourse for the same alleged violations, with the latter establishing mandatory arbitral jurisdiction for investment claims which signatory States have espoused as their own. The broader view is supported by the common inclusion of both "interpretation" and "application" as appropriate subject matter for State-to-State disputes: the "application" of a treaty would appear to include issues related to the host State's compliance with its substantive treaty obligations, in addition to implementation of any investor–State award. Indeed, in BITs concluded before the advent of investor–State arbitration, State-to-State dispute resolution clauses were often identically phrased, and there is little doubt that any disputes arising under those treaties were subject to dispute resolution.[63]

10.45 Regardless of the proper interpretation of State-to-State arbitration clauses in BITs, it is unlikely that they will be invoked frequently in the future. As discussed elsewhere, modern BITs were designed to eliminate the need for State espousal, whether under customary law or specific treaty provisions. Except in cases where the only applicable treaty contains no investor–State provision, the benefit to be gained by the investor through State intervention in an ongoing investment dispute under a BIT is marginal. Further, such intervention is specifically prohibited in the ICSID context. Nevertheless, where specific treaty provisions require definitive interpretation, or where the respondent State refuses to satisfy a BIT arbitration award, the State-to-State provision may serve as a useful supplement to investor–State dispute resolution.

---

[61] Communication from the European Community and its Member States, WT/WGTI/W/30, Mar. 27, 1998 (98-1242), available at https://docs.wto.org/dol2fe/Pages/FE_DownloadDocument.aspx?Symbol=WT/WGTI/W/30&Language=English&CatalogueId=48333&Context=ShowParts.

[62] U.S. Model BIT (2012), arts. 34(8), 37, available at https://ustr.gov/sites/default/files/BIT%20text%20for%20ACIEP%20Meeting.pdf.

[63] *See e.g.* Belgium–Morocco BIT (State-to-State dispute resolution only, with regard to the interpretation or application of the treaty's provisions).

3. Dispute resolution procedures at the International Court of Justice

a. Jurisdiction of the ICJ

The International Court of Justice (ICJ) is the best-known forum for the adjudication of claims between States. The ICJ is an organ of the United Nations, charged by the U.N. Charter with the resolution of legal disputes between States.[64] It is the successor organization to the Permanent Court of International Justice, which was established under the League of Nations framework.[65] The ICJ will exercise jurisdiction over both inter-State "contentious" cases and advisory opinions provided in response to requests from the U.N. General Assembly or the U.N. Security Council.[66] This section concerns only contentious cases between States, the only type potentially related to investment disputes.[67] **10.46**

As is true with all inter-State arbitration, proceedings before the ICJ can only begin with the consent of both States.[68] Such consent can be given after a dispute has arisen, as part of a *compromis*, or before a dispute arises. Pre-dispute submission to ICJ jurisdiction can be general, established when a State registers its consent with the ICJ, or specific, as part of an international treaty. The two types of consent (post- and pre-dispute) give rise to different kinds of jurisdiction, known as "compromissory" and "compulsory."[69] **10.47**

As noted, States submit to ICJ compulsory jurisdiction before disputes arise, either with a blanket submission or with limitations as to the areas of international law, specific treaties, or other circumstances under which disputes will be resolved, at the option of the other State party to the dispute, at the ICJ.[70] Many States limit compulsory jurisdiction on a reciprocity basis, *i.e.* it is effective only for disputes with States that have also consented to ICJ jurisdiction.[71] **10.48**

---

[64] Charter of the United Nations, signed June 26, 1945, amended Dec. 17, 1963, Dec. 20, 1965, and Dec. 20, 1971, ch. XIV, available at https://treaties.un.org/doc/publication/ctc/uncharter.pdf.

[65] James Crawford, Brownlie's Principles of Public International Law 721 (8th ed. 2012).

[66] Statute of the International Court of Justice (1945), arts. 36, 65, available at http://www.icj-cij.org. ICJ decisions rendered in relation to a contentious proceeding have binding effect on the parties to the dispute, whereas advisory opinions have no binding effect. *Id.*, art. 59.

[67] The ICJ is considered as the most prominent option for settling investment disputes between States. *See* August Reinisch & Loretta Malintoppi, *Methods of Dispute Resolution*, in The Oxford Handbook of International Investment Law, ch. 18, 715–17 (Peter Muchlinski et al. eds. 2008). The distinction between contentious and advisory cases has been blurred by the ICJ's advisory opinion *Legal Consequences of the Construction of a Wall in the Occupied Palestinian Territories*, 2004 I.C.J. Rep. 131 (advisory opinion), available at http://www.icj-cij.org. Israel there openly rejected the Court's jurisdiction to hear the case on the basis that the underlying question was contentious, and therefore unfit for an advisory opinion. The Court nevertheless decided to hear the merits of the case.

[68] Crawford, *supra* note 65, at 723.

[69] ICJ Statute, *supra* note 66, art. 36.

[70] *Id.*, art. 36(2).

[71] *Id.*

States can withdraw their submission to compulsory jurisdiction at any time, although such revocation cannot affect cases already pending before the Court.[72]

10.49 Compromissory jurisdiction can be invoked where two States agree to submit an existing dispute to the ICJ on an ad hoc basis, regardless of whether either of them is subject to the compulsory jurisdiction of the Court.[73] The *compromis* between the parties normally sets out the precise legal issues to be submitted to the Court for adjudication, and defines the limits of the ICJ's authority.[74]

10.50 One of the ICJ's more controversial cases serves to underline both the strengths and weakness of compulsory jurisdiction at the Court. The *Military and Paramilitary Activities* case was brought by Nicaragua against the United States based upon the U.S. submission to compulsory jurisdiction.[75] Nicaragua claimed that military assistance rendered by the United States to rebel forces violated principles of customary international law and an FCN treaty between the two countries.[76] The United States objected to the ICJ's jurisdiction, asserting that its submission to the Court did not extend to claims based on violations of the U.N. Charter.[77] The Court nevertheless accepted jurisdiction, reasoning that such claims also sounded in customary international law, which the United States had admitted fell within the scope of compulsory jurisdiction.[78] After the ICJ's decision on jurisdiction, the United States refused to participate in proceedings on the merits, and completely withdrew its declaration of consent to the Court's compulsory jurisdiction for future cases.[79]

b. Procedure before the ICJ

10.51 A State initiates a proceeding at the ICJ by submitting an Application to the Court's Registrar.[80] The Registrar acts as the administering authority throughout ICJ litigation,[81] acknowledging receipt of pleadings, documents, and declarations submitting to jurisdiction.[82] The ICJ rules do not establish any particular timetable for the submission of written pleadings or for oral hearings. The Court has

---

72 *Id.*

73 *Id.*, art. 36(1); ICJ Rules of Court (1973), available at http://www.icj-cij.org, Rule 46(1).

74 ICJ Rules of Court, *supra* note 73, Rule 46(1).

75 *Case Concerning Military and Paramilitary Activities in and against Nicaragua (Nicaragua v. U.S.A.)* (Jurisdiction and Admissibility), 1984 I.C.J. Rep. 392.

76 *Id.* Nicaragua ultimately prevailed on the merits. *Id.* (Merits), 1986 I.C.J. Rep. 14.

77 *Id.* (Jurisdiction and Admissibility), 1984 I.C.J. Rep. 392.

78 *Id. See also* Martin B. Howard, *Military and Paramilitary Activities in and against Nicaragua: The International Court of Justice's Jurisdictional Dilemma*, 7 Loy. LA Int'l & Comp. L.J. 379 (1984).

79 George F. Jones, *Termination of Declarations under the Optional Clause: Military and Paramilitary Activities in and Against Nicaragua*, 20 Tex. Int'l L.J. 557 (1985).

80 ICJ Rules of Court, *supra* note 73, Rule 30.

81 *Id.*, Rule 25.

82 *Id.*

discretion to set any necessary time limits, and tends to honor the parties' requests in this regard.[83]

10.52 The first stage in the ICJ proceedings will be a meeting between the judges of the Court and the parties' agents. This meeting, which takes place in The Hague, is normally scheduled between one and three months after the petitioner's Application is filed, and only rarely more than six months thereafter. At the initial meeting, the Court and the parties' agents discuss a range of procedural matters, and most importantly express their preferences as to the number, sequence, and timing of written pleadings. Absent contrary agreement of the parties, the first exchange of pleadings, called the Memorial (for Petitioner) and Counter-Memorial (for Respondent) is not simultaneous. Rather, the Petitioner is given a certain period after the meeting to prepare the Memorial, after which the Respondent has an equal amount of time to submit its Counter-Memorial. In its initial pleading, the plaintiff State must specify the parties to the case, the subject of the dispute, the legal grounds on which ICJ jurisdiction will be based, as well as its legal claims on the merits and their factual setting.[84] In many cases, the ICJ further orders the parties to submit a second round of briefs, known as the Reply and the Rejoinder, wherein each side responds to the arguments its opponent has presented.[85] All pleadings submitted to the Court must be accompanied by a certified copy of the pleadings, documentary evidence (if appropriate) and translations for the benefit of the opposing party.[86] In most ICJ cases, the timing of the written pleadings is not controversial, and is agreed by the parties. In recent years, the standard amount of time for preparing written submissions appears to be about four months each, but in many cases the time allotted is much longer.

10.53 After written pleadings are completed, the Court will set a date for oral arguments to be held in The Hague.[87] These hearings generally begin three to six months after the end of the written phase, and commonly take between one and four weeks. Once the written part of the pleadings is completed, further documents are only admitted in exceptional circumstances.[88] The oral pleadings consist of two distinct phases: the presentation of evidence and the presentation of arguments.[89] The presentation of evidence is premised on the communication of a comprehensive witness list outlining the points expected to be made by each witness.[90] The Court will decide based on the facts the timeline for the presentation of evidence

[83] In cases begun on the basis of compromissory jurisdiction, the provisions of the compromise will govern the procedural aspects of the proceeding. *Id.*, Rule 46(1).
[84] *Id.*, Rule 38.
[85] *Id.*, Rule 45.
[86] ICJ Rules of Court, *supra* note 73, Rule 52.
[87] *Id.*, Rule 54.
[88] *Id.*, Rule 56(2).
[89] *Id.*, Rule 58.
[90] *Id.*, Rule 57.

and arguments. Parties will always be given a chance to present their views concerning their own and their opponents' evidentiary materials.

10.54 Although the ICJ is a standing body with a permanent roster of judges, the composition of the Court may be temporarily modified in each particular case. The Presidency of the Court must be occupied by a judge who is not a national of either disputing State, and therefore a temporary President may be appointed for any particular case.[91] Furthermore, any State not represented on the Court has the right to appoint one judge ad hoc in proceedings to which it is a party.[92] In order to avail itself of this right, a State must notify the ICJ as soon as possible after proceedings begin.[93] After it provides notification that it intends to name a judge ad hoc, the State has until two months prior to the submission of a Counter-Memorial to provide the name of the individual who will serve in that capacity.[94] The ad hoc judge need not be of the nationality of the State in question.

c. Enforcement

10.55 Judgments of the ICJ are final once rendered, and are not subject to any form of appeal.[95] According to the U.N. Charter, all member States are obligated to observe and implement decisions of the ICJ. Should a State refuse to give effect to an ICJ judgment, the other State party to the dispute may refer the matter to the Security Council for consideration, which may result in a recommendation or even a binding resolution.[96] Absent such a binding resolution, ICJ judgments are not directly enforceable, and as a result there has been mixed experience in the area of compliance.[97] Furthermore, such judgments can only apply to the particular parties to the dispute, and in connection with the specific subject matter that the Court has considered.[98] At the same time, the prestige of the ICJ and its place within the U.N. system can give substantial political force to the Court's decisions, even where formal legal enforcement proves impossible.

D. Economic Sanctions

10.56 Where negotiation toward a settlement or formal dispute resolution are impossible, States sometimes take unilateral, non-military action to influence the

[91] *Id.*, Rule 32.

[92] ICJ Statute, *supra* note 66, art. 31.

[93] ICJ Rules of Court, *supra* note 73, Rule 35.

[94] *Id.*, Rule 35(1).

[95] ICJ Statute, *supra* note 66, art. 60; Shaw, *supra* note 18, at 800.

[96] U.N. Charter, *supra* note 64, art. 94.

[97] *See e.g. Corfu Channel*, Judgment of Dec. 15, 1949, 1949 I.C.J. Rep. 248 (Albania refused to implement judgment); *Fisheries Jurisdiction*, Judgment of July 25, 1974, 1974 I.C.J. Rep. 3 (Iceland refused to implement judgment).

[98] ICJ Statute, *supra* note 66, art. 59.

conduct of other States toward their nationals, or to induce amicable resolution.[99] These options, collectively referred to as economic sanctions, include a variety of measures such as freezing assets, trade embargo, reduction or elimination of financial, military, or humanitarian aid, economic boycott,[100] increased export and import controls, and the severance of diplomatic relations. While some unilateral "self-help" can be problematic from a legal point of view, economic sanctions are not normally considered illegal *per se* under international law. Indeed, States not infrequently apply sanctions for a variety of reasons, including in response to expropriation of their nationals' property.[101]

1. Freezing of assets

One of the more effective forms of economic sanction is the freezing of the expropriating State's assets. By taking such action, the investor's home State can both apply pressure against the offending State in a relatively short period of time, and also create a fund for distribution to injured nationals, should a settlement be reached.[102] In 1979, for example, the United States froze approximately US$12 billion in Iranian government-owned assets located in the United States pursuant to the International Emergency Economic Powers Act.[103] This was one factor that led to the release of the U.S. hostages from Iran and the establishment of the Iran–U.S. Claims Tribunal through the Algiers Accords.[104] **10.57**

2. Vesting

Another remedy used by States following the expropriation of nationals' property is called "vesting." Vesting is the seizure or conversion of assets of the expropriating State that are located in the vesting State, without the consent of the expropriating **10.58**

---

[99] The prohibition against the use of force is discussed in Section F.

[100] For a discussion of the effects of boycott and other economic sanctions imposed on Cuba by the United States following Cuba's confiscation of U.S. nationals' property in the early 1960s, *see* Eric N. Baklanoff, Expropriation of U.S. Investment in Cuba, Mexico, and Chile 117–23 (1975). *See also* Stephen J. Doyle, *International Boycotts*, in The Law of Transnational Business Transactions (Ved P. Nanda ed. 2005).

[101] Ibrahim F.I. Shihata, *Destination Embargo of Arab Oil: Its Legality under International Law*, 68 AJIL 591, 625 (1974). The United States often imposes sanctions to discourage the proliferation of weapons of mass destruction and ballistic missiles, or other reasons related to the promotion of human rights and the support of efforts to combat organized crime and international terrorism; *see* Economic Sanctions and American Diplomacy (Richard N. Haass ed. 1998).

[102] For example, in the mid-1990s the United States agreed to release over US$300 million of Vietnamese assets, frozen after Vietnam seized property belonging to U.S. nationals in 1975. Most of this money was to be used to pay U.S. claimants, pursuant to an agreement reached between the United States and Vietnam; the remainder was to be returned to Vietnam. *Justice Department Announces Progress on Iran and Vietnam Claims*, 6 World Arb. & Mediation Rep. 75 (1995).

[103] Barry E. Carter, *International Economic Sanctions: Improving the Haphazard U.S. Legal Regime*, 75 Cal. L. Rev. 1159, 1173 (1987). *See* 50 U.S.C. §§ 1701 *et seq.* (1982).

[104] For a description of the role of frozen Iranian assets in the establishment of the Iran–U.S. Claims Tribunal, *see Dames & Moore v. Regan*, 453 U.S. 654 (1981).

State. This type of sanction differs markedly from the freezing of assets, since the latter step merely preserves the offending State's property pending the outcome of negotiations or dispute resolution proceedings between the governments involved. Vesting of assets, by contrast, entails the seizure and disposal of assets.

10.59 There is only one instance of the United States vesting the assets of a foreign State in peacetime to pay the claims of its nationals who had suffered expropriation. After the end of World War II, the U.S. government vested steel mill equipment belonging to Czechoslovakia and located in the United States, in order to satisfy the claims of U.S. nationals whose assets Czechoslovakia had expropriated. In that case, the U.S. government decided to vest after ten years of unsuccessful negotiations to obtain compensation for the property in question.[105]

10.60 Vesting is disfavored by most States, and is applied only as a tool of last resort. The redistribution of foreign-owned assets through vesting, even in response to illegal takings by the State owner, may create the impression that the vesting State is not a safe place for foreign governments to maintain or invest capital.[106] Many States are also reluctant to vest assets of another State because it may set a precedent, making other governments more likely to vest their assets in the future.

3. Obligation to impose sanctions

10.61 Economic sanctions can be extremely effective, particularly when applied by a State with significant international influence and substantial trade relations with the offending State. Professor Barry Carter has concluded that "the United States has been successful in as many as eight out of nine uses of sanctions against expropriation," with Cuba the only failure.[107]

10.62 It is important to note that an investor's success in convincing its home State to impose sanctions upon an expropriating State will depend upon the magnitude of the taking, its political ramifications, and the relationship between the investor's home State and the host State, as well as a number of other factors. As in the case of diplomatic espousal, States generally retain complete discretion as to whether or not to impose sanctions against another State following the latter's mistreatment of foreign investors.

10.63 Although international law in no way requires the imposition of sanctions, in a few countries domestic law establishes some requirements in this regard. In

[105] *See* Lori Y. Vassar, *Foreign Assets Control: Proposed Vesting of Viet Nam Assets*, 84 AJIL 539 (1990).

[106] Thomas J. Lang, *Satisfaction of Claims Against Viet Nam for the Expropriation of U.S. Citizens' Property in South Viet Nam in 1975*, 28 Cornell Int'l L.J. 265, 298 (1995).

[107] Carter, *supra* note 103, at 1173 ("The most recent success was against Ethiopia. In December 1985, the United States and Ethiopia signed an agreement providing that Ethiopia pay $7 million to settle claims by U.S. nationals").

the United States, for example, certain statutes mandate that particular actions be taken in response to expropriation deemed illegal under international law.[108] The Hickenlooper Amendment to the Foreign Assistance Act requires, among other things, the cessation of development assistance to States that have illegally expropriated the property of U.S. nationals.[109] This remedy was imposed against Ethiopia following the 1974 nationalization of the property of U.S. nationals.[110] Similarly, the Gonzalez Amendment requires the President to order the Executive Director of the Inter-American Bank (always appointed by the United States) to vote against any loan to a State that has expropriated the property of U.S. nationals in violation of international law, unless arbitration or good faith negotiations are proceeding to resolve the matter.[111] Similar laws are in effect regarding the International Bank for Reconstruction and Development[112] and the Asian Development Bank.[113]

Despite their apparently unequivocal character, these laws and analogues in other countries are applied very rarely. Particularly with the rise of investor–State arbitration, which is viewed as an effective direct remedy for harm to investments abroad, home governments are increasingly reluctant to condition economic and humanitarian assistance and other aspects of diplomatic relations on the treatment of their citizens' business interests. Nevertheless, in at least one instance a U.S. investor was able to overcome this barrier to successfully invoke the Gonzalez Amendment. In *Santa Elena v. Costa Rica*,[114] the government of Costa Rica had, by a 1978 decree, expropriated land for use as part of a national park. The land was owned by CDSE, a development company whose shareholders were mostly American. CDSE had spent about US$395,000 for the property, and had begun development of a luxury resort there. When Costa Rica sought to transform the area into a nature preserve, the government offered CDSE about US$1.9 million as compensation for the property, but CDSE refused, claiming instead that based on its own appraisal, the land was worth US$6.4 million. The parties litigated the issue of compensation before Costa Rican courts for nearly twenty years, without coming to a mutually satisfactory result. At some point in 1994 or 1995, CDSE invoked the Gonzalez Amendment, asking the U.S. government to vote against a pending US$175 million loan from the Inter-American Development Bank. The 10.64

[108] For a discussion of economic sanctions under U.S. law, see generally Carter, *supra* note 103.

[109] 22 U.S.C. §§ 2353, 2370(e) (1983). For a detailed history of the Hickenlooper Amendment through its early versions, *see* Richard B. Lillich, Protection of Foreign Investment 117–46 (1965).

[110] Stefan A. Riesenfeld, *The Ethiopia–United States Compensation Agreement: Dicey Ending to a Spicy Tale*, 5 Int'l Tax & Bus. Law. 239, 240 (1987).

[111] 22 U.S.C. § 283(r).

[112] 22 U.S.C. § 284(j).

[113] 22 U.S.C. § 285(o).

[114] *Compañia del Desarrollo de Santa Elena v. Republic of Costa Rica S.A.* ("*Santa Elena*"), ICSID Case No. ARB/96/1, Award of Feb. 17, 2000.

United States complied, and the loan disbursement was delayed until Costa Rica consented to refer the case to international arbitration.[115] The ICSID tribunal to which the case was presented held that US$4.15 million constituted fair value of the confiscated property, and awarded the claimant an additional US$12 million in interest.[116]

E. Invalidation of Title

1. General rule

10.65 It is often the case that a State will expropriate goods belonging to a foreign business and then sell the goods to a third party. The third party may then export the goods, either to the former owner's home country or to some other destination. In such a scenario, the investor may wish to recover the goods in the courts of the State to which the goods have been transferred.

10.66 The recovery of expropriated property through judicial invalidation of title is based upon the theory that, formally, the goods remain the investor's property if the host State's seizure was illegal. Where the expropriation is illegal under international law (*e.g.* because it was discriminatory or not accompanied by prompt, adequate and effective compensation), the investor may argue that a third party purchaser's title to the expropriated property should be invalidated, because the third party did not receive title from the legitimate owner of the goods.

10.67 This theory enjoys some support under international law.[117] F.A. Mann points out, for example, that "[w]here the foreign state has taken property in circumstances which, for one or the other reason, are contrary to international law, the forum should treat the taking as null and void. In its courts the original owner should continue to enjoy title. The chattel confiscated in a manner considered to be internationally illegal should be treated as having been stolen. The original owner, therefore, has retained his title except where a subsequent purchaser in accordance with the general law of the *lex situs* has acquired it. Where title to stolen property can be acquired at all, the purchaser will usually have to act without actual or constructive notice."[118]

---

[115] *Santa Elena, supra* note 114, at paras. 24–26.

[116] Despite the eminence of the tribunal (Elihu Lauterpacht, Prosper Weil, and Yves Fortier), the basis for the award of interest was unsubstantiated and unexplained.

[117] See Chapter 5, Section B.2.c, for a discussion of the significance of the remedy of invalidation of title to classifying a taking as illegal or legal under international law.

[118] F.A. Mann, *The Consequences of an International Wrong in International and National Law*, 48 Brit. Yb. Int'l L. 1, 47–48, 55 (1977). *See also* Stephen Lee, *Title to Foreign Real Property in Transnational Money Claims*, 32 Colum. J. Transnat'l L. 607 (1995); F.A. Mann, Further Studies in International Law 126 (1990); Marjorie M. Whiteman, Damages in International Law 827 (1937); B.A. Wortley, Expropriation in Public International Law 76 (1959).

How the principle of invalidation of title is applied varies from State to State: **10.68**

> When we come to the effect of the international rule in a municipal system of law, we must look to the latter for the appropriate solution, for international law expects and, indeed requires municipal systems of law to observe and enforce it, but prescribes no method of doing so. International law leaves it to municipal law to decide how obedience is to be achieved.[119]

Thus, although customary international law generally provides that title to goods does not pass to the State as a result of illegal expropriation, only domestic law at the place where the property is located will determine how this rule is applied. Before considering the positions that various national courts have taken, it should be noted that the issue of recognition of title to expropriated goods often involves bringing suit against a foreign State, which may raise important barriers to recovery, such as sovereign immunity. Even if the goods are in the hands of a private third party, the "act of State" doctrine and similar issues may hinder the investor's attempt to obtain judicial relief.[120] Naturally, the investor will be in a stronger position to argue that a national court should assume jurisdiction over such a matter if the original agreement between the investor and the State contained a well-drafted waiver of sovereign immunity clause.[121] **10.69**

The investor should also keep in mind that recovery of property through judicial invalidation of title may be impossible if his home State achieves a settlement with the expropriating State. As F.A. Mann has observed: **10.70**

> The victim's home State, it is true, may at any time dispose of the international claim and thus deprive the victim of any rights in national courts by a waiver of the wrong, by demanding financial compensation and thereby forgoing the nullity or by otherwise disposing of its subject's rights.[122]

Otherwise put, if a private party's claim to compensation or restitution is settled or otherwise disposed of by its home State, the investor may be left with no rights to pursue the claim under international law.[123] **10.71**

Even if the investor does not realistically expect to recover its property, it may use the threat of pursuing the remedy of invalidation of title to force negotiations with the expropriating State.[124] Thus, British Petroleum threatened invalidation of title against Libya following the expropriation of its properties in 1971, insisting **10.72**

---

[119] Mann, *The Consequences of an International Wrong, supra* note 118, at 48 (footnotes omitted).

[120] These issues are discussed in Chapter 4.

[121] *See* Chapter 2, Section E.4.

[122] Mann, *supra* note 118, at 48–49.

[123] *See e.g.* Libby Adler & Peer Zumbansen, *The Forgetfulness of Noblesse: A Critique of the German Foundation Law Compensating Slave and Forced Laborers of the Third Reich*, 39 Harv. J. Leg. 1, 2 (2002); *see also Flatow v. Iran*, 196 F.R.D. 203 (D.D.C. 2000).

[124] *See e.g.* Evrett W. Benton, *The Libyan Expropriation: Further Developments on the Remedy of Invalidation of Title*, 11 Hous. L. Rev. 924, 935–37 (1974), discussing invalidation of title claims brought by the Kennecott Copper Corporation in various jurisdictions.

that it would sue any purchasers of oil from the nationalized concession. British Petroleum actually launched several such suits prior to an arbitration with the Libyan government that settled the dispute.[125]

2. United Kingdom

10.73 If expropriated goods are transferred to the United Kingdom, an investor bringing suit in courts there will face a relatively straightforward analysis. The court will first examine whether the expropriating State has been recognized by the British government. If it has not been recognized, the investor recovers his property, and "[t]he act of the unrecognized foreign sovereign is likened to robbery by bandits."[126] If the expropriating State has been recognized by the British government, the act of taking is held to be valid *prima facie*.

10.74 If the investor is not a national of the expropriating State,[127] the court looks to the customary international law of expropriation. Before there can be a violation of international law for expropriation without compensation, the investor must have exhausted local remedies (or must show that such action would have been futile).[128] The investor must then demonstrate either that it was paid no compensation, that compensation received was insufficient to satisfy the standards of customary international law,[129] or that the expropriating State violated international law in some other fashion (such as by a taking that was discriminatory or not for a public purpose). If the taking of property violated international law, the expropriation "will not be recognized with respect to the property in question and the true owner will be entitled to it."[130]

10.75 The classic invalidation of title case in the United Kingdom is *The Rose Mary*. On May 1, 1951, Iran terminated a concession with the Anglo-Iranian Oil Company (AIOC) and nationalized its interests in Iran, including oil concessions.[131] AIOC subsequently brought suit in various jurisdictions, requesting the remedy of invalidation of title for oil extracted from its former concession territory, which had been sold to third parties. AIOC brought suit in Aden (then a British colony) against the owner of an oil tanker, the *Rose Mary*, to regain possession of crude oil in the tanker.[132] The Supreme Court of

[125] G. Winthrop Haight, *Libyan Nationalization of British Petroleum Company Assets*, 6 Int'l Law. 541 (1972).

[126] George E. Glos, *The Effect of Foreign Decrees of Expropriation in the Courts of the Forum*, 19 S. Tex. L.J. 241 (1978).

[127] International law provides no remedy for expropriation by a State of its own nationals' property. *See* discussion in Chapter 4, Section D.

[128] *See* Chapter 4, Section E.

[129] *Anglo-Iranian Oil Co. Ltd. v. Jaffrate (The Rose Mary)*, [1953] 1 W.L.R. 246, 20 I.L.R. 316, 321–22 (Supreme Court, Aden 1953).

[130] Glos, *supra* note 126, at 242.

[131] *Anglo-Iranian Oil*, *supra* note 129, 20 I.L.R. at 316.

[132] *Id.* at 316, 317.

Aden held that AIOC was the proper owner of the oil, because the government of Iran (and therefore the third-party purchaser) had acquired no title.[133] The court held that the Iranian law expropriating the oil company's property was invalid under international law, because the property had been expropriated without compensation.[134]

3. United States

In the United States, in order to gain jurisdiction over a foreign sovereign, the investor must overcome the act of State doctrine and any sovereign immunity the State concerned may enjoy;[135] otherwise, the courts will not inquire further. But neither the Foreign Sovereign Immunity Act nor the common-law act of State doctrine will protect a sovereign that has, in violation of international law, expropriated property that is located in the United States, or a State that is engaged in commercial activity in the United States related to the expropriated property, even if the property is located outside the United States.[136] **10.76**

Even if the suit is not against a sovereign, but against a third party to whom expropriated goods have been transferred, act of State issues may still be raised. If these barriers are overcome, the U.S. courts will employ an analysis similar to the British approach previously described. In such cases, U.S. courts will generally refuse to recognize the transfer of title to property expropriated from the original owner in contravention of international law.[137] **10.77**

4. Other States

As in the United States and the UK, if suit is to be brought against a sovereign (as opposed to a third party into whose hands expropriated goods have fallen), sovereign immunity may shield the State from court jurisdiction. France and Germany, for example, generally treat an order of expropriation by a sovereign as a public act that is immune from adjudication in their courts.[138] **10.78**

Regarding invalidation of title, many European courts have avoided the issue by finding that the acts in question were not necessarily in violation of international law,[139] and do not violate their own laws to such extent as to require invalidation **10.79**

---

[133] *Id.* at 316.

[134] *Id.* at 323–28. It is unclear how this case would be decided today in light of *Buttres Gas and Oil Co. v. Hammer*, 3 W.L.R. 787 (1978), discussed in Chapter 4, Section G.4.b.

[135] *See* Chapter 4, Section G. *See also* Glos, *supra* note 126, at 243.

[136] U.S.C. § 1605(a)(3) (1988).

[137] *Id.* at 53, 54. Of interest in this regard is the Cuban Liberty and Democratic Solidarity (LIBERTAD) Act of 1996, Pub. L. No. 104-114, 110 Stat. 785 (Mar. 12, 1996). *See* discussion of the LIBERTAD Act in Chapter 4, Section G.2.c.

[138] Joseph W. Dellapenna, *Foreign State Immunity in Europe*, 5 NY INT'L L. REV. 51 (1992).

[139] HIGGINS, *supra* note 37, at 217.

of title. Germany, Japan, and Italy take a similar approach: all regard a taking without the payment of compensation as a violation of international law, yet all reject any corresponding rule of law requiring them to invalidate title to expropriated goods in the hands of the new owner. Each State maintains that title will not be recognized if the expropriation is contrary to its own internal laws or policy. Where the expropriating State has made provision for compensation, even if illusory, these courts have found that the expropriation is not contrary to public policy, and have not invalidated title.[140]

10.80 In a case arising out of the same facts that gave rise to the *The Rose Mary*, AIOC also brought suit in Italy regarding oil that had been shipped from Iran to Venice.[141] The court denied AIOC's request to sequester the oil. The Italian court found that the expropriation was not contrary to Italian public order because there had been an order of compensation, even though no compensation was ever paid.[142]

10.81 French courts tend to show more sympathy to the true owner of property. They do not rely upon international law in deciding invalidation of title issues. Rather, they have held that expropriation without just compensation is contrary to French public policy, and thus title to such property will not be recognized in the hands of the new owner.[143]

5. Conclusions

10.82 Invalidation of title can be a useful threat against an expropriating State, but is sometimes difficult to use in practice due to sovereign immunity and the other legal obstacles previously discussed. Even though courts in some countries, such as the United States, the United Kingdom, and France, have been known to invalidate title as a means of recognizing the property rights of expropriated investors, as a general rule, property rights are sometimes treated with less respect than other rights, such as human rights, under international law or the domestic laws of developed countries. Perhaps one reason for this reluctance is that property rights are not always recognized as being an important "human" or individual right. As Judge Higgins points out:

> It seems that the breaches of international law that most offend national courts—or perhaps are easiest for them to feel confident *do* represent breaches of international

---

[140] In Japan, see *Anglo-Iranian Oil Co. v. Idemitsu Kosan Kabushiki Kaisha*, 20 I.L.R. 305 (District Court and High Court, Tokyo 1953); in Italy, see *Anglo-Iranian Oil Co. v. S.U.P.O.R. Co.*, Civil Court of Venice (Mar. 11, 1953), 22 I.L.R. 23 (1958); in Germany, see *N.V. Verenigde Deli-Maatschappijen v. Deutsch-Indonesische Tabak-Handelsgesellschaft m.b.H.*, District Court of Bremen (Apr. 13, 1959); Court of Appeals of Bremen (Aug. 21, 1959), 28 I.L.R. 16 (1963). *See also* Glos, *supra* note 126, at 252–54; and Mann, *supra* note 118, at 53–54.

[141] *S.U.P.O.R.*, *supra* note 140.

[142] *Id.* at 22–23.

[143] Glos, *supra* note 126, at 254–56.

law—are human rights violations. The familiar hesitation reappears in the face of other aspects of international law.[144]

F. Prohibitions against the Use of Force

1. Overview

Until the early twentieth century, States not infrequently applied military force against other States as a means to resolve investment disputes involving their nationals' property.[145] Under certain circumstances, this sort of "gunboat diplomacy" was considered lawful under customary international law.[146] In his classic treatise *The Law of War and Peace*, the great international law scholar Hugo Grotius opined that the recovery of property was one of three situations justifying the use of force under the law of nations.[147] **10.83**

In 1900, for instance, the U.S. Secretary of State approved the dispatch of a naval vessel to Venezuela to prevent the destruction of property belonging to the New York & Bermudez Company, an American corporation. He instructed the Secretary of the Navy that "the gunboat should also protect all existing rights and maintain the status quo pending an investigation and decision as to an attempt which was alleged then to be in contemplation to deprive the company of its property by executive action."[148] The *Jecker Claim* is another notorious example. There, Mexico obtained a loan from a bank owned by French and Swiss interests. The Mexican government never received more than 5 percent of the face value of the loan,[149] but its subsequent default was one of the primary justifications for France's invasion of Mexico in 1861–62.[150] **10.84**

---

[144] HIGGINS, *supra* note 37, at 218 (emphasis in the original). As the U.S. Supreme Court has recognized: "The right to enjoy property without lawful deprivation ... is in truth a 'personal' right ... In fact, a fundamental interdependence exists between the personal right to liberty and the personal right in property. Neither could have meaning without the other. That rights in property are basic civil rights has long been recognized." *Lynch v. Household Fin. Corp.*, 405 U.S. 538, 552 (1972).

[145] M. SORNARAJAH, THE INTERNATIONAL LAW OF FOREIGN INVESTMENT 19–20 (3d ed. 2010); M. Sornarajah, *Power and Justice in Foreign Investment Arbitration*, 14 J. INT'L ARB. 103 (1997); JAMES CABLE, GUN BOAT DIPLOMACY: POLITICAL APPLICATIONS OF LIMITED FORCE (1981); Matthew B. Cobb, *The Development of Arbitration in Foreign Investment*, MEALEY'S INT'L ARB. REP. (Apr. 2001).

[146] IAN BROWNLIE, INTERNATIONAL LAW AND THE USE OF FORCE BY STATES 289 (1963).

[147] The other two occasions were for defense or punishment. 2 HUGO GROTIUS, DE JURE BELLI AC PACIS, ch. 1, § 2; ch. 2, § 13 (A.C. Campbell trans., 1814), available at http://www.constitution.org/gro/djbp.htm. *See also* HIGGINS, *supra* note 37, at 238.

[148] Letter from Mr. Hay to Sec. of Navy, Dec. 28, 1900, 250 MS. Dom. Let. 8, *reprinted* in 6 MOORE'S INT'L LAW DIGEST 258 (1906).

[149] The loan's face value was 75 million francs, but the Mexicans received only 4 million.

[150] DONALD R. SHEA, THE CALVO CLAUSE: A PROBLEM OF INTER-AMERICAN INTERNATIONAL LAW AND DIPLOMACY 14 (1955); IBRAHIM SHIHATA, TOWARDS A GREATER DEPOLITICIZATION OF INVESTMENT DISPUTES: THE ROLES OF ICSID AND MIGA 1 n.2 (1992).

10.85 Today, some investors hailing from militarily and politically powerful States might favor the threat or use of force to obtain restitution or compensation for expropriated property.[151] Such an option is no longer available, however, due to fundamental changes in international law and politics. In particular, the U.N. Charter has since 1945 prohibited the use of force to resolve disputes, except in the case of self-defense.[152] Today, it is generally accepted that a State may not use force against another State in response to a taking of the property of one of its nationals. This conclusion is reinforced by the modern movement toward "permanent sovereignty over natural resources," which emphasizes the right of a State to control over its own resources and territory.[153] As Professor Brownlie concludes in his important study on the use of force under international law:

> Is nationalization, with or without prompt and adequate compensation, a measure which justifies protection? If so, can a state protect property of nationals threatened not by nationalization but by laws restricting use of currency, discriminating export regulations, or taxation? May the right be exercised in favor of bond-holders? It is submitted that the answer must be negative in these cases since if it were otherwise any state accepting foreign investment or permitting ownership of property by aliens is severely curtailing its sovereignty as a result.[154]

2. The U.N. prohibition against the use of force

10.86 The U.N. Charter prohibits the use of force by any State, except in limited cases for the purpose of self-defense. The general prohibition against the use of force is set forth in Section 2(4) of the Charter. This prohibition is regarded as a principle of customary international law,[155] and is therefore applicable to all nations, not only those that have voluntarily acceded to the Charter by joining the U.N. Article 2(4) of the Charter provides:

> All members shall refrain in their international relations from the threat or use of force against the territorial integrity or political independence of any state, or in any other manner inconsistent with the purposes of the United Nations.[156]

---

[151] *See* Hans-Hermann Hoppe, *Banking, Nation States and International Politics: A Sociological Reconstruction of the Present Economic Order*, 4(1) R. Austrian Econ. 55, 60–61 (1990), available at http://www. mises.org ("The need for a productive economy that a warring state must have also explains why it is that *ceteris paribus* those states which have adjusted their internal redistributive policies so as to decrease the importance of economic regulations relative to that of taxation tend to outstrip their competitors in the arena of international politics. Regulations through which states either compel or prohibit certain exchanges between two or more private persons as well as taxation imply a non-productive and/or non-contractual income expropriation and thus both damage homesteaders, producers or contractors [i.e., those that cause wealth to come into existence]").

[152] U.N. Charter, *supra* note 64, arts. 2(4), 51.

[153] *See* Chapter 5.

[154] Brownlie, *supra* note 146, at 301. *See also* Shaw, *supra* note 18, at 829–31; Higgins, *supra* note 37, at ch. 14. On the doctrine of legislative or parliamentary sovereignty, see Chapter 4, Section B.1.

[155] Shaw, *supra* note 18, at 814–15.

[156] U.N. Charter, *supra* note 64, art. 2(4).

The self-defense exception is set forth in article 51 of the Charter: **10.87**

> Nothing in the present Charter shall impair the inherent right of individual or collective self-defense if an armed attack occurs against a member of the United Nations, until the Security Council has taken measures necessary to maintain international peace and security.[157]

In the present discussion, the relevant question is whether the self-defense exception allows a State to use force against another State in response to interference with or taking of the property rights of its nationals.[158] If property has been illegally taken by a host State, the use of force by a State to recover the property would fall more under the category of "self-help" than self-defense. Self-help has been defined as "the use of force to obtain legal rights improperly denied."[159] Article 51, which allows self-defense, does not permit self-help. In fact, it is nearly universally accepted that it is unlawful for a State to use such self-help to recover property of its nationals.[160] Thus, the self-defense exception to the prohibition on the use of force does not allow the "self-help" necessary to recover property. **10.88**

Although the U.N. Charter prohibits States from using force at their own initiative except in self-defense, the United Nations itself *may* apply force in certain circumstances "for the maintenance or restoring of international peace and security."[161] The use of force by the United Nations, however, authorized under Chapter VII of the U.N. Charter,[162] is unlikely ever to be authorized to recover the property of a private investor.[163] **10.89**

3. The futility of restitution

Because the use of force to recover the property of an investor is both impractical and illegal under international law, it is not surprising that international tribunals rarely award restitution or specific performance. Specific performance is, **10.90**

---

157 *Id.*, art. 51.

158 For a discussion concerning whether an attack against the national of a State constitutes an attack against the State for purposes of art. 51, *see* Higgins, *supra* note 37, at 243–45. *See also* Shaw, *supra* note 18, at 829–30.

159 Higgins, *supra* note 37, at 240. For an analysis of the distinction between self-defense, self-help, and preemptive self-defense, *see* Timothy L. H. McCormack, Self-Defence in International Law 240–83 (1996).

160 Shaw, *supra* note 18, at 829–30.

161 Higgins, *supra* note 37, at 255.

162 U.N. Charter, *supra* note 64, Ch. VII. *See also* Sean D. Murphy, *The Security Council, Legitimacy, and the Concept of Collective Security after the Cold War*, 32 Colum. J. Transnat'l L. 201, 229, 249–51 (1994) (discussing the use of force under international law by individual States and by the United Nations).

163 For further discussions of the collective use of force pursuant to the U.N. Charter, *see* Higgins, *supra* note 37, at 254–66; Julianne Peck, *The U.N. and the Laws of War: How Can the World's Peacekeepers Be Held Accountable?*, 21 Syracuse J. Int'l L. & Com. 283, 291 (1995); Shaw, *supra* note 18, at 814–32, 897 *et seq.*

as a practical matter, unenforceable without the threat of force to back it up, and, as we have seen, such a threatened use of force would be illegal.

10.91 This principle is generally recognized by international arbitrators.[164] Under the "great oil arbitrations,"[165] for example, several important decisions were issued concerning expropriations of foreign investments. None of these tribunals, except the *Texaco Overseas Petroleum Co. and California Asiatic Oil Co. (TOPCO)* panel, awarded relief other than monetary damages as a result of expropriation.[166] The *TOPCO* tribunal did call for "restitution" or specific performance of the contract, but also awarded monetary damages, apparently recognizing that a decision calling for specific performance might be unenforceable as a practical and legal matter.

10.92 The Iran–U.S. Claims Tribunal has reached the same conclusion, declining to award specific performance in response to expropriation. As Charles Brower has explained:

> Theoretically a broad range of remedies is available to claimants whose property interests have been expropriated. These include restitution or specific performance, substitution of the value of the property taken, award of punitive damages, or other measures that may arguable indemnify the claimant for the wrong done, or the property lost … As a practical matter, however, virtually all of the Tribunal's decisions focus solely on the return to the claimant of the value of the property interest lost. Restitution or specific performance has not been discussed or seriously contemplated in any of the Tribunal's awards. The reasons for this are evident: The Tribunal does not have adequate enforcement mechanisms for such restitution, but does have available to it the Security Account established in the Algiers Accord out of which monetary awards can be satisfied.[167]

---

[164] *See generally* Troy Elder, *The Case Against Arbitral Awards of Specific Performance in Transnational Commercial Disputes*, 13 Arb. Int'l 1 (1997).

[165] Higgins, *supra* note 37, at 141 n.29, citing the following cases as the "great oil arbitrations": *Petroleum Development Ltd. v. Sheikh of Abu Dhabi*, 18 I.L.R. 144 (1951); *Saudi Arabia v. Arabian American Oil Co. (ARAMCO)* (1958), 27 I.L.R. 117 (1963); *Sapphire Int'l Petroleum Ltd. v. National Iranian Oil Co.*, 35 I.L.R. 136 (1953); *British Petroleum Exploration Co. (Libya) Ltd. (BP) v. Government of Libya*, 53 I.L.R. 297 (1973); *Texaco Overseas Petroleum Co. and California Asiatic Oil Co. (TOPCO) v. Government of Libya* (1977), 53 I.L.R. 389 (1977), 17 I.L.M. 1 (1978); *Libyan American Oil Co. (LIAMCO) v. Government of Libya* (1977), 62 I.L.R. 141 (1980), 20 I.L.M. 1 (1981); and *Government of Kuwait v. American Independent Oil Co. (AMINOIL)*, 21 I.L.M. 976 (1982).

[166] *TOPCO, supra* note 165, 17 I.L.M. 1 (1978).

[167] Charles N. Brower, *Current Development in the Law of Expropriation and Compensation: A Preliminary Survey of Awards of the Iran–United States Claims Tribunal*, 21 Int'l Law. 639, 658 (1987). *See also* Shaw, *supra* note 18, at 585 ("The problems … of enforcing such restitution awards against a recalcitrant state may be imagined'); A.Z. El Chiati, *Protection of Investment in the Context of Petroleum Agreements*, 4 Recueil des Cours 9, 161 (1987) ("The futility of claiming *a restitutio in integrum* has become so apparent that some litigants do not even bother to claim it"). In the ICSID context, *see Amco Asia Corp. v. Indonesia*, ICSID Case No. ARB/81/1, Award of Nov. 20, 1984, 24 I.L.M. 1022 (1985), at para. 202 ("It is obvious that this Tribunal cannot substitute itself for the Indonesian Government, in order to cancel the revocation and restore the license: such actions are not even claimed, and it is more than doubtful that this kind of *restitutio in integrum* could be ordered against a sovereign state").

Thus, in contrast to provisions of domestic law in many jurisdictions, where specific performance is available to compel the return of property taken by the government in violation of requirements such as non-discrimination and public purpose, failure to comply with these requirements may have little consequence under international law.[168] 10.93

G. The U.S. Foreign Claims Settlement Act

As discussed, when a State successfully negotiates a settlement with another State for interference with the property rights of its nationals, the manner of distribution of the settlement is a matter of the protecting State's domestic law. The Foreign Claims Settlement Act (FCSA) of the United States provides a useful example of how such a procedure might operate. 10.94

1. History and purpose

In the United States, the President has authority to reach binding amicable settlement of claims arising out of expropriation.[169] The controlling statute delegates this power to the U.S. Department of State.[170] The Department of State usually seeks to achieve a lump-sum settlement with the expropriating State, which is then paid on a pro-rata basis to investors whose assets have been interfered with or seized.[171] Settlements concluded by the Department of State are binding on affected U.S. nationals, and constitute their sole remedy.[172] 10.95

While the Department of State negotiates settlements, the U.S. Foreign Claims Settlement Commission (FCSC), an independent quasi-judicial federal agency, is charged with determining the validity and quantum of U.S. nationals' claims for interference with or loss of property rights in foreign countries.[173] The purpose of the FCSC is the 10.96

> adjudication of claims of American citizens, corporations and other legally constituted entities against foreign governments for the nationalization, expropriation or

[168] *See* Chapter 5, Section B.2.c, for a discussion of the significance of the remedy of invalidation of title to classifying a taking as illegal or legal under international law.

[169] *Dames & Moore v. Regan*, 453 U.S. 654, 688 (1981). This authority is limited, however, by the power of the U.S. Congress to enact legislation requiring renegotiation of settlements it considers unsuitable. *Id.* at 687–88.

[170] *Id.* at 680.

[171] Clagett, *supra* note 32, § 12.05[3][a].

[172] *See Dames & Moore*, 453 U.S. at 679–80; *Asociacion de Reclamantes v. Mexico*, 735 F.2d 1517, 1523 (D.C. Cir. 1984); Matias F. Travieso-Diaz, *Some Legal and Practical Issues in the Resolution of the Cuban Nationals' Expropriation Claims against Cuba*, 16 Pa. J. Int'l Bus. L. 217, 225–26 (1995).

[173] 2016 FCSC Ann. Rep. 1.

other uncompensated taking of their property and/or interests, losses or injuries sustained by them.[174]

10.97 The FCSC was created on July 1, 1954 by the President's Reorganization Plan No. 1 of 1954,[175] which abolished its predecessor commissions, the War Claims Commission and the International Claims Commission, and transferred their functions to the FCSC. In 1980, the FCSC was incorporated into the Department of Justice as a separate agency.[176] The Commission comprises a Chair and two Commissioners, who are appointed by the President, and a small staff of legal and administrative personnel.[177]

10.98 The FCSC and its predecessor, the International Claims Commission, had administered forty-seven claims programs by the end of 2016.[178] The FCSC has administered claims arising out of disputes with Yugoslavia, Panama, Bulgaria, Hungary, Romania, Italy, the Soviet Union, Czechoslovakia, Poland, Cuba, the People's Republic of China, the German Democratic Republic, Ethiopia, Iran, Egypt, Albania, and Vietnam.[179]

2. Adjudicatory powers

10.99 The U.S. Congress may establish a claims program either after a lump-sum settlement agreement has been reached with an expropriating State, or in anticipation of such a settlement.[180] In the former case, the State in question pays an agreed-upon lump sum of money in satisfaction of all pending claims presented by U.S. nationals. The FCSC then pays claims from this fund, according to its review of petitions from individual investors. This procedure was put in place to resolve claims arising out of U.S.-owned assets in Egypt, Yugoslavia, and Iran.[181]

10.100 For example, on May 13, 1990, the United States and Iran concluded an agreement for the lump-sum settlement of U.S. nationals' claims valued at under US$250,000 each. These and other complaints had been pending for nearly a decade at the Iran–U.S. Claims Tribunal. This settlement was approved by the Iran–U.S. Claims Tribunal on June 22, 1990, and Iran consummated the agreement

---

[174] Stanley J. Glod, *The Foreign Claims Settlement Commission of the United States: Resolutions of International Claims in the Nineties and Beyond*, 37 Fed. Bar News & J. 140 (1990).

[175] President's Reorganization Plan No. 1 of 1954, 68 Stat. 1279, reprinted in 5 U.S.C. at 1291 (1988).

[176] Mar. 14, 1980, Pub. L. No. 96-209, 94 Stat. 96 (codified as amended at 22 U.S.C. § 1622a (1988)).

[177] FCSC Ann. Rep. 1-3 (2016).

[178] *Id.* at 2 ("The jurisdiction of the Commission and its two predecessor commissions has encompassed the administration of forty-seven claims programs in which more than 740,000 claims were filed and nearly $4 billion in awards were granted").

[179] Glod, *supra* note 174, at 140.

[180] Lang, *supra* note 106, at 285.

[181] James H. Grossman & David M. Frost, *Foreign Claims Settlement Commission of the United States—A Paradigm for International Claims Resolution*, 21 Int'l Bus. Law. 276, 276–77 (1993).

by transferring US$105 million to the United States.[182] Between 1990 and 1995, the FCSC considered over 3,100 individual and corporate claims as part of this program to distribute the Iranian payment to injured U.S. investors.[183] Another FCSC program was initiated in March 1995, after the United States and Albania concluded a lump-sum agreement under which Albania paid US$2 million to dispose of claims raised by U.S. nationals who suffered losses to their property when a Communist regime took power in Albania at the end of World War II.[184]

In other cases, referred to as "pre-adjudication" claims, the FCSC hears and adjudicates the claims of U.S. nationals in anticipation of future settlements between the United States and the expropriating State. This procedure was used in the case of claims against Cuba, East Germany, and Vietnam.[185] For example, in response to the expropriations that followed the Cuban revolution in 1959, the U.S. Congress amended the FSCA in 1964 to establish a Cuban claims program, allowing the FCSC to certify the validity and the quantum of U.S. nationals' claims of compensation for property expropriated in Cuba.[186] Under this claims program, which operated between 1966 and 1972, 8,116 claims were filed with the FCSC (1,146 by corporations and 7,670 by individuals), of which 5,911 were certified (*i.e.* accepted for payment) in an aggregate amount of US$1.8 billion.[187] The FCSC determined that these certified claims should be augmented at a rate of 6 percent simple interest each year.[188] In 2006, the FCSC completed the administration of a second Cuban claims program.[189] U.S. policy continues to link the normalization of bilateral relations with Cuba to payment of U.S. nationals' expropriation claims. **10.101**

Another "pre-adjudication" program concerned Vietnam. Between 1980 and 1986, the FCSC adjudicated 534 claims of U.S. nationals whose property was seized by the Vietnamese authorities in 1975. At the beginning of 1995, the United States and Vietnam concluded a lump-sum settlement, according to which Vietnam would pay a lump sum of US$208.5 million to satisfy these claims.[190] The FCSC adjudicated awards in 192 claims, totaling over US$99 million in **10.102**

---

[182] 1994 FCSC Ann. Rep. 6.

[183] *Justice Department Announces Progress on Iran and Vietnam Claims*, 6 World Arb. & Med. Rep. 75 (1995).

[184] *Foreign Claims Settlement Commission Announces the Commencement of the Albanian Claims Program*, 6 World Arb. & Med. Rep. 171.

[185] Grossman & Frost, *supra* note 181, at 277.

[186] 22 U.S.C. § 1643 (1988) (amended 1994); Travieso-Diaz, *supra* note 172, at 220.

[187] Travieso-Diaz, *supra* note 172, at 220.

[188] *Id.*

[189] 22 U.S.C. § 1623(a)(1)(C) (1988) (amended 1994); in this second program, the Commission evaluated previously unadjudicated claims of U.S. citizens or corporations against the Government of Cuba.

[190] *Justice Department Announces Progress on Iran and Vietnam Claims*, 6 World Arb. & Med. Rep. 75 (1995). *See also* J. Jeffrey Brown, *The Jurisprudence of the Foreign Claims Settlement Commission: Viet Nam Claims*, 27 Va. J. Int'l L. 99, 100 (1986).

principal, with interest to be accrued at 6 percent per year from the date of each award until payment.[191]

3. The claims process

10.103 The FCSC provides claim forms and instructions upon request. The FCSC announces new claims programs through press releases to the news media and notification to relevant organizations and congressional offices. Once a claim is filed, the FCSC may request supplemental information to support the validity or quantification of the claim in question. The claim is then presented to the FCSC for adjudication. At this initial stage, the process is not adversarial, and does not normally involve hearings or other evidence-gathering.

10.104 The FCSC then issues a written "Proposed Decision," which is forwarded to the claimant, who has the right to object within a specific period of time. The claimant may submit additional written information and may request an oral hearing before the Commission. The Commission considers the evidence, reviews the entire record, and issues a "Final Decision." If no objection is received on a claim, the Proposed Decision is automatically entered as the Final Decision.

10.105 Even after the entering of a Final Decision, the FCSC permits claimants to file a petition to reopen a claim for further consideration based on new evidence. Decisions of the FCSC set forth reasons and specific findings of fact and conclusions of law determining each aspect of the claim. The decisions of the FCSC are final on all questions of fact and law, and they are not subject to review by any other official, department, or agency of the United States, nor by any court.[192] However, a claimant who disagrees with the FCSC's decision may request that the FCSC reconsider its initial ruling and obtain an oral hearing, where new evidence and arguments may be entered before a final decision is made.[193]

10.106 Because lump-sum settlements are not usually sufficient to cover the full amount of aggregate claims raised by investors, the FCSC must often fund awards on a *pro rata* basis. In the six cases in which the United States settled with the expropriating State after the FCSC had determined the value of awards to U.S. nationals, claimants received an average of 38.4 percent of the value of their claims.[194] Payment of awards is not made by the FCSC, but by the U.S. Secretary of the Treasury.[195]

191 *Justice Department, supra* note 190, at 76.

192 1994 FCSC Ann. Rep. 2. *See also* Grossman & Frost, *supra* note 181, at 277.

193 Grossman & Frost, *supra* note 181, at 277.

194 Brown, *supra* note 190, at 140–41. The portion of claims satisfied for each program was: Bulgaria—59.3 percent, Romania—28.9 percent, Hungary—26.3 percent, Soviet Union—9.7 percent, Czechoslovakia—73.1 percent, and China—40.0 percent. *Id.*

195 1994 FCSC Ann. Rep. 2–5.

4. Other States' programs

The FCSC process has analogues in a number of capital-exporting countries. In Canada, the claims adjudication process is remarkably similar to that in the United States. **10.107**

When a Canadian citizen submits a prima facie valid claim against a State to the Ministry of Foreign Affairs, and has exhausted all local judicial remedies to no avail, the Ministry can decide to intervene officially ... When a state adopts a policy of general nationalization that effectively attacks the assets of Canadian citizens, it is normal practice to first obtain an agreement of principle with the State concerned to negotiate a general settlement of Canadian claims. This preliminary agreement is then made public and the concerned individuals are invited to fill out claim questionnaires at the Ministry of Foreign Affairs. After a period of assessment and preparation, the claims that are considered valid are brought to the attention of the other State and the negotiations begin in order to achieve a global settlement. If such a settlement is reached, procedures dealing with the distribution of agreed-upon sums are adopted by council resolution, and the claims are then officially transmitted to the Foreign Claims Commission, which prepares a report and recommendations as to the sum to allocate to each claim it has reviewed. Although the question of a particular claimant's inclusion in a settlement of claims between Canada and a foreign State is subordinated to the report and recommendations of the Foreign Claims Commission, approval of the Ministry is required before any compensation can be paid out.[196]

[196] Government of Canada, *supra* note 22, at 66.

APPENDIX I

OPIC Contract of Insurance

Form 234 KGT 12-85 (Revised 12/03) NS

OPIC Contract of Insurance No. ___

OVERSEAS PRIVATE INVESTMENT CORPORATION CONTRACT OF INSURANCE

Against

as defined below,

between the Overseas Private Investment Corporation ("OPIC") and

a corporation organized and existing under the laws of the State of _____

(the "Investor").

TABLE OF CONTENTS

Article I—Subject of Insurance and Exchange of Promises.

1.01 Subject.

1. *Investment.* The Investor promises that the Investor contributed or will contribute $_____ in United States dollars

to

a [type of company] validly organized under the laws of___________________________

(the "foreign enterprise")

for which the Investor has acquired or will acquire

(together, "the investment").

__________ percent of the interests acquired by the Investor is insured under this contract (the "insured investment").

2. *Project.* The investment will be applied to

[project description] in __________ (the "project country")

(the "project").

3. *Foreign Governing Authority.* Foreign governing authority means any of (a) the central government of the project country; (b) the government of any political subdivision of the project country; and (c) any organ, agency, official, employee or other agent or instrumentality of either (a) or (b), acting within the scope of its authority or under color of such authority; and (d) the governmental authorities in de facto control of that portion of the project country in which the project is located.

1.02 Promises.

If acts occur during the term of this contract which satisfy the requirements for coverage in Articles ___, ___, or ___, OPIC shall pay the Investor the amount of compensation provided in Articles ___, ___, or ___, in accordance with the procedures in Article VIII.

The Investor shall comply with each and all of its obligations under this contract, including the provisions of Article I, the procedures in Article VIII, the duties in Article IX[, and the additional provisions in Article X]. If the Investor violates any of those duties, the Investor may lose rights, including the right to compensation.

1.03 Maximum Aggregate Compensation.

OPIC will not pay compensation under this contract in an aggregate amount that exceeds $_____.

1.04 Full Faith and Credit.

The full faith and credit of the United States of America is pledged to secure the full payment by OPIC of its obligations under this contract.

1.05 Term.

This contract shall enter into force on the date it has been signed by both OPIC and the Investor (the "effective date") and shall terminate the day preceding the _____ anniversary of the effective date, unless terminated earlier (§8.07; §9.02).

1.06 Premiums and Active Amount Elections.

This contract shall provide coverage only for those risks set forth on the cover page for which the Investor has made elections of amounts of coverage and paid premiums therefor (§8.06).

The Investor shall elect amounts of coverage (§8.06) and pay premiums on or before each annual anniversary of the effective date of the contract.

The coverages and premiums for the first period shall be as follows:

_____ securities:

	Inconvertibility	Expropriation	Political Violence	
Coverage Ceiling:	$_________	$_________	$_________	
Active Amount:	$_________	$_________	$_________	
Premium Rate is:	x 0.0000%	x 0.0000%	x 0.0000%	
Total Premium is:	$_________	$_________	$_________	$_________

1.07 Underinsurance Premium Surcharge.

If, as of any coverage election date, the Investor has elected, for any coverage, an Active Amount (§8.06) that is less than 50% of the then current book value (§5.01) of the insured investment (§1.01), then the premium rate shall increase for that coverage according to the following Premium Surcharge schedule and the Investor shall pay premiums based on such increased rate:

	Amount of Premium Surcharge		
Active Amount as a % of the current book value of the insured investment	**Inconvertibility**	**Expropriation**	**Political Violence**
35%—49%	10%	10%	10%
15%—34.9%	15%	15%	15%
Less than 15%	25%	25%	25%

The Underinsurance premium increase shall be applied effective as of the coverage election date on which the Active Amount for the coverage(s) is less than 50% of the book value of the insured investment.

Article II—Inconvertibility—Scope of Coverage.

2.01 Inconvertibility of Local Currency.

The lawful currency of the project country that is legal tender for the payment of public and private debt ("local currency") shall be deemed inconvertible and compensation shall be payable, subject to the exclusions (§2.02) and limitation (§3.02), if neither the Investor nor the foreign enterprise is able legally

(a) to convert into United States dollars local currency earnings from or returns of the insured investment through any channel during the days immediately prior to a claim to OPIC, except at an exchange rate that is less favorable than the then-prevailing exchange rate described under §3.01.2, or
(b) to transfer such converted local currency earnings to the United States during such period.

2.02 Exclusions.

No compensation for inconvertibility shall be payable if

(a) *Pre-existing Restrictions.*
  (1) An investor in comparable circumstances would have been unable legally (a) to convert local currency into United States dollars on the date of this contract or (b) to transfer such dollars to the United States on the date of this contract; and
  (2) The Investor knew or should have known about the restriction; or
(b) *Investor Diligence.* The Investor has not made all reasonable efforts to convert the local currency into United States dollars or to transfer such dollars to the United States through all direct and indirect legal mechanisms reasonably available; or
(c) *Reconversions.* The local currency represents funds which were previously converted into another currency; or
(d) *Provocation.* The preponderant cause of the inconvertibility is (i) actions, other than actions taken in the ordinary course of business, attributable to the Investor, the foreign enterprise, or the controlling equity holder of the foreign enterprise, provided such actions are in any way related to the project or (ii) violations of (A) the Foreign Corrupt Practices Act of 1977 (Pub. L. No. 95-213, §§101-104), as amended, or (B) any other applicable law relating to bribery, kickbacks, or similar corrupt business practices (together, "corrupt practices laws") by the Investor, the foreign enterprise, or such controlling equity holder.
(e) *Use Restricted by Expropriation.* The use of such local currency is restricted by an expropriatory action (§4.02).

Article III—Inconvertibility—Amount of Compensation.

3.01 Rate of Compensation for Inconvertibility.

1. *Date.* If the requirements of inconvertibility are satisfied (Article II), subject to the limitation (§3.02), OPIC shall pay compensation
  (a) against prior delivery of the inconvertible local currency, or
  (b) if the Investor is unable legally to deliver the local currency or if OPIC so requests, against prior assignment of the Investor's right to receive the payment that is the subject of the claim.

If the Investor delivers local currency or an assignment of rights denominated in local currency, compensation shall be the United States dollar equivalent of the local currency at the exchange rate in effect ___ days before OPIC receives the completed application for compensation.

If the Investor delivers an assignment of rights denominated in United States dollars, compensation shall be the United States dollar amount of the rights so assigned.

2. *Exchange Rate.*
  (a) The exchange rate shall be the official exchange rate applicable to the type of remittance involved.
  (b) If, however,
    (1) United States dollars were not generally available at the applicable official exchange rate; and
    (2) exchanges of local currency for United States dollars were effected legally and customarily through another channel;

  then the exchange rate shall be the effective rate obtained through that channel.
  (c) In either case, the exchange rate shall be net of all deductions for governmentally imposed charges, such as taxes and commissions.

3.02 Limitation.

Compensation shall not exceed the Active Amount (§8.06) in effect ___ days before OPIC receives the application for compensation.

Article IV—Expropriation—Scope of Coverage.

4.01 Total Expropriation.

Compensation is payable for total expropriation (§5.01), subject to the exclusions (§4.03) and limitations (§5.04), if an act or series of acts of the foreign governing authority satisfies all of the following requirements:

(a) the act(s) (i) constitute an outright taking of the Investor's property or (ii) have the effect of taking the Investor's insured investment in that the acts (A) prevent, unreasonably interfere with, deprive, or unduly delay effective enjoyment of the Investor's fundamental rights in the insured investment (rights are "fundamental" if without them the Investor is substantially deprived of the benefits of the investment) or (B) deny the Investor an adequate, effective forum to review the legality under applicable law of the act(s) that prevents, unreasonably interferes with, deprives, or unduly delays effective enjoyment of the Investor's fundamental rights in the insured investment; and

(b) the taking is not accompanied by prompt, adequate, and effective compensation; and

(c) the act(s) and/or the expropriatory effect thereof continues (§9.01.9) for six consecutive months.

4.02 Expropriation of Funds.

Compensation is payable for an expropriation of local currency or of United States dollars in the project country if

(a) such local currency or United States dollars constitutes a return of or earnings on the insured investment (§5.02); and

(b) an act or series of acts of the foreign governing authority satisfies the requirements of §4.01 and directly results in preventing

  (i) the Investor from converting such local currency into United States dollars or transferring to the United States such converted local currency; and

  (ii) the Investor or the foreign enterprise from effectively controlling such local currency or United States dollars in the project country.

4.03 Exclusions.

No compensation shall be payable if:

(a) *Provocation.* The preponderant cause of the expropriation is (i) actions, other than actions taken in the ordinary course of business, attributable to the Investor, the foreign enterprise, or the controlling equity holder of the foreign enterprise, provided such actions are in any way related to the project, or (ii) violations of (A) the Foreign Corrupt Practices Act of 1977 (Pub. L. No. 95-213, §§101-104), as amended, or (B) any other applicable law relating to bribery, kickbacks, or similar corrupt business practices by the Investor, the foreign enterprise, or such controlling equity holder.

(b) *Government Relationship to the Project.* The act(s) described in §4.01 and §4.02 are those of the foreign governing authority exercising commercial (as distinguished from governmental) functions in relation to the project.

Article V—Expropriation—Amount of Compensation.

5.01 Total Expropriation.

For total expropriation (§4.01), OPIC shall pay compensation in United States dollars in the amount of the book value of the insured investment, subject to adjustments (§5.03) and limitations (§5.04).

Compensation is computed as of the date the expropriatory effect commences (§4.01(c)) and is based on financial statements maintained in accordance with §9.01.6 for the foreign enterprise. However, OPIC may

(1) conform the financial statements to principles of accounting generally accepted in the United States; and
(2) make adjustments (§5.03).

OPIC shall be bound by the Investor's choice among generally accepted accounting principles, if the choice is consistent with the Investor's own accounting, unless such choice results in a substantial overstatement of the fair market value of the insured investment or the foreign enterprise as an independent entity.

5.02 Expropriation of Funds.

For expropriation of funds (§4.02), OPIC shall pay compensation in the amount of the United States dollar equivalent of the expropriated local currency at the exchange rate determined in accordance with §3.01.2, computed as of the date the expropriation begins. For expropriation of United States dollars (§4.02), OPIC shall pay the amount of United States dollars expropriated. (Compensation for expropriation of funds (§4.02) shall be subject to the adjustments and limitations (§5.03 and §5.04).)

5.03 Adjustments.

1. *Investments of Property.* Non-cash items contributed as part of the investment shall be adjusted if necessary to reflect the fair market value of the items furnished at the time of contribution to the project, plus freight, installation and other reasonable direct costs incurred in furnishing the items to the project.
2. *Non-Insured Contribution.* Any direct or indirect contribution (and retained earnings thereon) by the Investor after the insured investment is made shall be deducted from the book value of the foreign enterprise.
3. *Special Accounting Rules.* Dealings among related parties shall be adjusted if necessary to reflect transactions as they would have occurred had they been at arm's length, and forgiveness of obligations shall be disregarded. Each entity shall be accounted for as if it were a separate person for income tax purposes, and the effect of tax shifting arrangements shall be disregarded. Obsolescence or permanent reduction in recoverable values shall be recognized by adjusting the book value of assets to realizable value. OPIC may adjust financial statements to reflect the effect of events that occur before the expropriatory effect commences, such as events of loss which are later confirmed.
4. *Other Compensation and Retained Property.* OPIC may reduce compensation by the amount of
   (a) compensation received from other sources on account of the loss (excluding compensation payable under other insurance policies, except to the extent necessary to prevent the Investor from recovering more than the amount of the loss as recognized under any of the policies under which compensation is due, without regard to policy limits); and
   (b) the book value of commercially viable property which remains subject to the Investor's effective disposition and control after the expropriatory effect commences (unless OPIC requires the Investor to assign the property (§8.02)); and
   (c) any obligation the Investor is relieved of by the expropriation.

The reduction shall be proportionate to the extent that these items are attributable to the insured investment.

5. *Start-up Expenses.* If the book value of the insured investment of a new foreign enterprise in the development stage is less than the insured amount originally contributed, the accumulated loss will be disregarded if
   (a) the foreign enterprise is newly formed for the principal purpose of undertaking the project,
   (b) the foreign enterprise is a going concern as of the date the expropriatory effect commences,
   (c) that date is within three years of the date this contract is issued, and

(d) it is clear that no adjustment to book value is necessary by reason of obsolescence or permanent reduction in recoverable values of productive facilities or assets.

5.04 Limitations.

Compensation shall not exceed any of the following limitations:

(a) *Active Amount.* The Active Amount (§8.06) on the date the expropriatory effect commences;
(b) *Insolvency.* If the liabilities of the foreign enterprise exceed its assets as of the date the expropriatory effect commences, the amount that the Investor would have been entitled to receive in insolvency proceedings with respect to the insured investment if assets had been liquidated at book value on that date;
(c) *Self-Insurance.* The maximum amount which could be received by the Investor from OPIC without breaching §9.01.3.

Article VI—Political Violence—Scope of Coverage.

6.01 Loss Due to Political Violence.

Compensation is payable, subject to the exclusions (§6.02) and limitations (§7.02), if political violence is the direct and immediate cause of the permanent loss (including loss of value by damage or destruction) of tangible property of the foreign enterprise used for the project.

> "Political violence" means a violent act undertaken with the primary intent of achieving a political objective, such as declared or undeclared war, hostile action by national or international armed forces, civil war, revolution, insurrection, civil strife, terrorism or sabotage. However, acts undertaken primarily to achieve labor or student objectives are not covered.

6.02 Exclusions.

No compensation for political violence shall be payable

(a) *Excluded Property.* For loss of precious metals, gems, works of art, money or documents;
(b) *Minimum Loss.* If the amount of compensation payable would be less than $5,000;
(c) *Reasonable Protective Measures.* If the loss results from the failure to take reasonable measures to protect or preserve the property; or
(d) *Provocation.* If the preponderant cause of the political violence is (i) actions, other than actions taken in the ordinary course of business, attributable to the Investor, the foreign enterprise, or the controlling equity holder of the foreign enterprise, provided such actions are in any way related to the project, or (ii) violations of (A) the Foreign Corrupt Practices Act of 1977 (Pub. L. No. 95-213, §§101-104), as amended, or (B) any other applicable law relating to bribery, kickbacks, or similar corrupt business practices by the Investor, the foreign enterprise, or such controlling equity holder.

Article VII—Political Violence—Amount of Compensation.

7.01 Basis of Compensation.

If the requirements of Article VI are satisfied, and subject to the limitations (§7.02), OPIC shall pay compensation for a loss in United States dollars in the amount of

(a) *Adjusted Cost.* Adjusted cost is the Investor's share (§7.03) of the lowest of
    (1) the original cost;
    (2) fair market value; or
    (3) the reasonable cost of repair;

less anything of value received by the Investor on account of the property lost and less the Investor's share of any such receipts by the foreign enterprise; or

(b) *Replacement Cost.* If the Investor so elects, OPIC will pay the reasonable cost to repair any item of lost property or to replace it with equivalent new property, less anything of value received by the Investor or the foreign enterprise on account of the property lost. Such compensation shall not exceed 200% of the original cost of the item. To receive such compensation, the Investor must repair or replace the lost property to the project within three years of the loss.

OPIC shall not reduce the compensation payable under subsections (a) or (b) above by the amount of compensation payable under other insurance policies on account of the property lost, except to the extent necessary to prevent the Investor from recovering more than the amount of the loss as recognized under any of the policies under which compensation is due, without regard to policy limits.

7.02 Limitations.

Compensation shall not exceed any of the following limitations:

(a) *Active Amount.* The Active Amount (§8.06) on the date of the loss.
(b) *Self-insurance.* The maximum amount which could be recovered by the Investor from OPIC without breaching §9.01.3.
(c) *Aggregate Adjusted Cost Compensation.* Aggregate compensation for property compensated at adjusted cost shall not exceed the book value of the insured investment (§7.04) at the time of loss.

7.03 Investor's Share.

"Investor's share" means the ratio that the equity owned by the Investor bears to the total equity of the foreign enterprise.

7.04 Book Value of Insured Investment.

(a) *Book Value.* Book value is based on financial statements maintained by the Investor in accordance with §9.01.6 for the foreign enterprise. However, OPIC may
  (1) conform the financial statements to principles of accounting generally accepted in the United States; and
  (2) make adjustments (§7.04(b)).

OPIC shall be bound by the Investor's choice among generally accepted accounting principles, if the choice is consistent with the Investor's own accounting, unless such choice results in a substantial overstatement of the fair market value of the insured investment or the foreign enterprise as an independent entity.

(b) *Adjustments.*
  (1) *Investments of Property.* Non-cash items contributed to the investment shall be adjusted if necessary to reflect the fair market value of the items furnished at the time of contribution to the project, plus freight, installation and other reasonable direct costs incurred in furnishing the items to the project.
  (2) *Non-Insured Contribution.* Any direct or indirect contribution (and retained earnings thereon) by the Investor after the insured investment is made shall be deducted from book value of the foreign enterprise.
  (3) *Special Accounting Rules.* Dealings among related parties shall be adjusted if necessary to reflect transactions as they would have occurred had they been at arm's length, and forgiveness of obligations shall be disregarded. Each entity shall be accounted for as if it were a separate person for income tax purposes, and the effect of tax shifting arrangements shall be disregarded. Obsolescence or permanent reduction in recoverable values shall be recognized by adjusting the book value of assets to realizable value. OPIC may adjust financial statements to reflect the effect of events that occur before the loss of property, such as events of loss which are later confirmed.
  (4) *Start-up Expenses.* If the book value of the insured investment of a new foreign enterprise in the development stage is less than the insured amount originally contributed, the accumulated loss will be disregarded if
    (a) the foreign enterprise is newly formed for the principal purpose of undertaking the project,
    (b) the foreign enterprise is a going concern as of the date of the loss,
    (c) that date is within three years of the date this contract is issued, and
    (d) it is clear that no adjustment to book value is necessary by reason of obsolescence or permanent reduction in recoverable values of productive facilities or assets.

(e) *Insolvency.* If the liabilities of the enterprise exceed its assets as of the date of the loss, book value of the insured investment shall not exceed the amount that the Investor would have been entitled to receive in insolvency proceedings with respect to the insured investment if assets had been liquidated at book value on the day prior to the loss.

7.05 Appraisal.

If OPIC determines that compensation is payable but OPIC and the Investor are unable to agree on a question of valuation, either may demand the appointment of an impartial appraiser. If the parties are unable to agree on the appraiser, the appointment shall be made by the American Arbitration Association. The appraiser's itemized appraisal shall be binding. Appraisal costs shall be borne equally by OPIC and the Investor.

7.06 Estimated Compensation.

If OPIC determines that compensation is payable but conditions in the project country preclude reasonable efforts by OPIC to determine the precise amount due, OPIC may pay estimated compensation based on the information then available. OPIC may revise its estimate and recover any excess or pay any additional amount due upon receipt of additional information.

Article VIII—Procedures.

8.01 Application for Compensation.

An application for compensation shall demonstrate the Investor's right to compensation in the amount claimed. The Investor shall provide such additional information as OPIC may reasonably require to evaluate the application. The Investor may amend or withdraw an application for compensation at any time, but the right to recover compensation will be lost for any acts covered by a withdrawn application.

(a) There is no time limit on application for inconvertibility compensation (Article III); however, compensation shall not exceed the Active Amount applicable in accordance with §3.02.

(b) An application for expropriation compensation (Article V) must be filed within six months after the Investor has reason to believe that all requirements of Article IV have been satisfied.

(c) A notice demonstrating the Investor's entitlement to political violence compensation for loss of assets (Article VI) must be filed within six months of the loss. The notice together with proof of the amount of compensation due will be considered a completed application, which must be filed within three years of the loss. The Investor may request adjusted cost compensation (§7.01(a)) and later amend the application within three years of the loss to elect replacement cost compensation (§7.01(b)).

(d) OPIC shall have a reasonable time in which to complete processing of any application for compensation.

8.02 Assignment to OPIC.

Within sixty days after OPIC notifies the Investor of the amount of compensation OPIC will pay under expropriation or political violence coverage, and concurrent with payment, the Investor shall transfer to OPIC (a) for expropriation, all interests attributable to the insured investment (§4.01) or funds (§4.02) as of the date the expropriatory effect commences, including claims arising out of the expropriation, or (b) for political violence, claims arising out of the loss due to political violence (§6.01). The Investor shall transfer the interests and claims free and clear of, and shall agree to indemnify OPIC against, claims, defenses, counterclaims, rights of setoff and other encumbrances (except defenses relating to the expropriation).

In connection with an inconvertibility claim, immediately upon receipt of instructions from OPIC together with notification that it intends to pay such claim, the Investor shall deliver the local currency to OPIC by draft subject to collection (or, at OPIC's option, in cash), or, if the Investor is unable legally to deliver the local currency or if OPIC so requests, shall instead deliver an assignment of the Investor's rights with respect to the payment that is the subject of the claim.

OPIC may decline all or any portion of the Investor's interests or claims; if so, the Investor's right to compensation shall be affected only as provided in §5.03.4(b).

8.03 Security.

As a condition for paying compensation (including estimated compensation (§7.06)) prior to a final determination of its liability, OPIC may require the Investor to provide security, satisfactory to OPIC in its reasonable judgment, for repayment pursuant to section 7.06.

8.04 Excess Salvage Value.

With respect to compensated expropriation and political violence claims, OPIC shall pay to the Investor any amounts OPIC realizes in United States dollars from the rights transferred (§8.02) in excess of

(a) the compensation paid by OPIC; plus
(b) reasonable interest; plus
(c) OPIC's out-of-pocket expenses in maintaining and realizing funds from the transferred property.

However, this provision shall not in any way restrict OPIC's discretion to deal with the rights transferred. OPIC shall have no obligation to take action with respect to the rights transferred and shall incur no liability to the Investor for any actions taken or not taken after the transfer.

8.05 Arbitration.

Any controversy or claim arising out of or relating to this contract shall be determined by arbitration in Washington, D.C. according to the then prevailing International Arbitration Rules of the American Arbitration Association. The number of arbitrators shall be three. Unless the Investor initiates arbitration, OPIC's liability shall expire one year after OPIC notifies the Investor of its final determination concerning an application for compensation. A decision by the arbitrators shall be final and binding, and any court having jurisdiction may enter judgment on it.

8.06 Election of Active Amounts and Coverage Ceilings.

By prior notice to OPIC effective as of the next due date for premiums (§1.06), the Investor shall elect an Active Amount for each coverage for the remainder of the election period, subject to the following limitations:

(a) The Active Amount shall not exceed the Coverage Ceiling (§1.06);
(b) (i) The Coverage Ceiling shall be reduced permanently and automatically by compensation paid by OPIC; and (ii) the Active Amount shall be reduced for the remainder of the election period to which the claim for which such compensation is paid relates (§3.02, §5.04(a), or §7.02(a));
(c) The Active Amount shall not be less than the lesser of book value (§5.01) or the Coverage Ceiling;

provided; however, that if the Investor elects an Active Amount that is less than the lesser of the book value (§5.01) and the Coverage Ceiling, then the Coverage Ceiling shall be permanently and automatically reduced to such Active Amount and §1.07 shall apply.

8.07 Termination.

The Investor may terminate this contract by notice to OPIC effective as of any premium due date unless the premium for the contract period commencing on such date has already been paid, in which case the contract shall terminate on the next succeeding premium due date. However, if the Investor elects to terminate this contract within three years from the contract effective date (§1.05), such termination shall not be effective unless and until the Investor pays to OPIC a termination fee in an amount equal to $_____ minus the sum of all premiums paid up to the date of proposed termination. Termination shall not affect any rights or obligations of either party relating to prior periods.

8.08 Governing Law; Integration; Modification.

This contract shall be governed by and construed and enforced in accordance with the law of the State of New York as if all parties were residents of that state. This contract constitutes the entire agreement and understanding between the parties with respect to the subject matter hereof, superseding any prior understandings relating thereto. This contract may be modified or its terms waived only in writing.

8.09 Notices.

Notices must be in writing and shall be effective when received. Notices may be given to the Investor at the address on the title page (unless changed in writing), and to OPIC at

Overseas Private Investment Corporation

Washington, D.C. 20527

Attention: Vice-President, Insurance.

8.10 Refund of Premiums.

Upon timely written request, OPIC will refund premiums *pro rata* if

(a) excess coverage is elected while a valid claim for compensation is pending; or

(b) the Investor becomes ineligible for coverage or ceases to hold all or a portion of the insured investment, in which case any refund shall be calculated from the later of (i) the date the Investor becomes ineligible or ceases to hold the insured investment, or (ii) the date OPIC receives such written request.

Article IX—Investor's Duties.

9.01 Duties.

1. *Representations and Project Execution.* The Investor understands that OPIC has issued this contract based on statutory policy goals (22 U.S.C. §2191) as well as underwriting considerations. All statements made by the Investor to OPIC in connection with this contract are true and complete, and the investment and the project shall be carried out as described.
2. *Ownership and Eligibility.* The Investor shall at all times remain the beneficial owner of the insured investment and shall remain:
   (a) a citizen of the United States; or
   (b) a corporation or other association created under the laws of the United States, its states, territories or the District of Columbia, of which more than 50% of both the total interest and of each class of shares is beneficially owned by citizens of the United States; or
   (c) a corporation created under foreign law in which more than a 95% interest is owned by entities eligible under (a) or (b); or
   (d) an entity created under foreign law which is wholly owned by entities eligible under (a) or (b).
3. *Self-Insurance.* The Investor shall at all times bear the risk of loss of at least 10% of the book value of its interest in the foreign enterprise.
4. *Assignment.* The Investor shall not assign this contract, or any of its rights, without OPIC's written consent, which will not be withheld unreasonably.
5. *Premiums.* In the event the Investor fails to pay when due premiums calculated in accordance with Article I, the Investor shall be in default, but may cure this default by paying the premiums, together with interest as herein provided, within 60 days of the date due. All amounts payable hereunder (§1.06 and §1.07) not paid when due shall bear interest at a rate of 12% per annum.
6. *Accounting Records.*
   (a) The Investor shall maintain in the United States true and complete copies of the records, books of account and current financial statements for the foreign enterprise necessary to compute and substantiate compensation, including
      (1) records documenting the investment;
      (2) annual balance sheets;
      (3) annual statements of income, retained earnings, cash flow and related footnotes.
   (b) ccounting records shall be maintained and financial statements prepared in United States dollars in accordance with principles of accounting generally accepted in the United States (including principles of currency translation), as modified by the special accounting rules (§5.03.3 and §7.04(b)(3)).
   (c) Subject to the obligations of the Investor under Section 9.01.6, the Investor or the foreign enterprise shall retain all accounting records until
      (1) the deadline for filing an application for compensation has expired (§8.01); or

(2) final action has been taken on an application for compensation (including arbitration and judicial appeals).

However, if compensation has been paid, the accounting records shall be retained for three years after the Investor receives the compensation.

7. *Reports and Access to Information.* In order that OPIC may perform its statutory duties, including settling claims and reporting to the Congress (22 U.S.C. §2200a), the Investor shall furnish OPIC with such information as OPIC may reasonably request, including
   (a) making available for interviews any persons subject to the Investor's practical control (including employees of the project and independent accountants);
   (b) making available for inspection and copying all documents and accounting records relating to the project (including workpapers of independent accountants if available);
   (c) permitting OPIC to inspect the project; and
   (d) furnishing available information concerning the effects of the project on the economy of the United States, the environment, and the economic and social development of the country in which the project is located.

The Investor's duties under this paragraph shall continue for the periods specified for retention of accounting records (§9.01.6(c)).

8. *Compulsory Notice.* The Investor shall notify OPIC promptly if it has reason to believe that the Investor or the foreign enterprise will not be able to convert or transfer local currency during the waiting period (Article II). The Investor shall notify OPIC promptly of any acts or threats to act in a manner which may come within the scope of the expropriation or political violence coverage (Articles IV and VI) and shall keep OPIC informed as to all relevant developments.
9. *Preservation, Transfer and Continuing Cooperation.* At OPIC's request, the Investor shall promptly assign rights with respect to the investment, as required by §8.02. Prior to the assignment of rights required by §8.02, the Investor shall, in consultation with OPIC, take all reasonable measures to preserve property, to pursue available administrative and judicial remedies, and to negotiate in good faith with the governing authority of the country in which the project is located and other potential sources of compensation. After a transfer of rights or delivery of local currency, in exchange for reimbursement of reasonable out-of-pocket expenses, the Investor shall take all actions reasonably requested by OPIC to assist OPIC in preserving the property and rights transferred to OPIC and in prosecuting related claims.
10. *Other Agreements.* The Investor shall not enter into any agreement with any foreign governing authority with respect to compensation for any acts within the scope of coverage (Article II, IV or VI) without OPIC's prior written consent.
11. *Other Insurance.* The Investor has notified OPIC of any existing arrangements for other insurance covering the investment against the risks insured hereunder ("Other Insurance") in effect as of the date of this contract. The Investor shall not obtain additional Other Insurance without OPIC's prior written consent, which consent shall not be withheld unreasonably. The withholding of consent by OPIC shall not be deemed unreasonable if, among other things, such other insurer has not entered into arrangements with and satisfactory to OPIC.
12. *Information Disclosure.* The Investor consents to the disclosure by OPIC to the providers of any Other Insurance, and by such providers of Other Insurance to OPIC, of any and all information that the Investor has provided or may provide to any of them in connection with the Investor's application for such Other Insurance, the administration and management thereof, the processing of any claim thereunder, or any salvage efforts in connection therewith.
13. *Worker Rights.* The Investor shall not take actions to prevent employees of the foreign enterprise from lawfully exercising their right of association and their right to organize and bargain collectively. The Investor shall observe applicable laws relating to a minimum age for employment of children, acceptable conditions of work with respect to minimum wages, hours of work, and occupational health and safety and shall not use forced labor. The Investor is not responsible under this paragraph for the actions of a foreign government.

9.02 Default.

Material breach or misrepresentation by the Investor shall constitute default, and OPIC may do any of the following:

(a) refuse to pay compensation,
(b) recover compensation paid which should not have been paid by reason of such default,
(c) terminate the contract effective as of the date of the breach by giving notice to the Investor.

9.03 Non-Waiver.

Neither OPIC's failure to invoke its rights, nor its acceptance of premiums, shall constitute waiver of any of its rights, even though OPIC knows of the Investor's breach.

9.04 Cure.

OPIC may permit the Investor to cure a breach in a manner satisfactory to OPIC, but shall have no obligation to allow breaches to be cured.

9.05 Execution.

This contract may be executed in separate counterparts, each of which shall constitute an original and all of which taken together shall constitute one and the same agreement.

[Article X—Miscellaneous.]

INVESTOR

By:______________________________ Date:____________________________

____

Print Name and Title

OVERSEAS PRIVATE INVESTMENT CORPORATION

By:______________________________ Date:____________________________

____

Print Name and Title

APPENDIX II

Sample Private Contract

Source: The Chubb Group. Private insurance is discussed in Chapter 3, Section D.

General Terms/Conditions Section 1

Limits of Liability

The company shall be liable for no more than the maximum limit of liability stated for each section of this policy and thereunder only for the amount of loss sustained under the authorized coverage. If an aggregate limit of liability is incorporated into this policy, the company shall not be liable for the amount of any loss, however caused, which exceeds the total aggregate limit of liability. Payment of loss will reduce the applicable limit of liability and the aggregate limit of liability accordingly.

Special Terms and Conditions

Except for the General Terms and Conditions of Section 1, the Terms and Conditions of each section of this policy apply only to that section and shall not be construed to apply to any other section of this policy.

Notices

All communications provided for in this policy shall be in writing and mailed to the Insured at its principal address as set forth in the Declarations and to the company at 15 Mountain Vista Road, Warren, New Jersey 07060.

Inspection and Audit

Upon reasonable notice to the Insured, the company shall have the right at all times to inspect and to examine the project insured hereunder and the Insured's books and records, and if practicable, the books and records of any applicable foreign enterprise, as far as they relate to the subject matter of this insurance.

Exchange Rate

Local currency shall be translated by using the average rates for fifteen days prior to the date of expropriation or date of loss as quoted for sale of such currency by the Chase Manhattan Bank N.A. in New York, New York.

Other Insurance

The coverage provided hereunder shall be excess over the applicable limit of, and in no event participate with, any other valid and collectible insurance available to the Insured. Moreover, the company shall only be liable to pay the excess over any applicable Deductible Amount set forth in the Declarations of each section of this policy.

Subrogation

In the event of any claim under this policy, the company shall be subrogated to all rights of recovery which the Insured may have. The Insured shall, within sixty days after receipt of notice from the company of the compensation due hereunder, and prior to the payment thereof, assign and transfer to the company or its designee at the company's sole discretion, including outright ownership of or indirect beneficial interest in: (1) all securities or other title, right, or interest in the project; (2) all assets, currency, or other property received from any party (other than from the company) which are directly or indirectly related to the project; (3) all claims, causes of action, or other rights of the

Insured existing in connection with any of the foregoing; and (4) all bills of sale and other evidence of title to mobile assets. All securities, properties, titles, and/or currencies assigned and transferred to the company shall be validly issued, fully paid and nonassessable, not subject to any defenses, and free and clear of all adverse claims, liens, and encumbrances (excluding those arising solely by reason of loss).

Warranty Agreements

The Insured will indemnify the company for any costs sustained or incurred by the company resulting from (1) any intentional material misrepresentation, breach or inaccuracy of any representation or warranty made by the Insured hereunder or in the application or other written statements made by the Insured with respect to this policy, or in connection with any claim; or (2) any unreasonable failure of the Insured to perform or fulfill any covenant or agreement hereunder.

In addition, the Insured expressly warrants to the company that:

(1) all arrangements, agreements, licenses, permits and understandings applicable to the project have been duly and validly authorized and executed, are and will be available for inspection by the company, and are or will be in full force and effect as quickly as possible;

(2) the Insured has complied and will use its best efforts to continue to comply in all respects with project-related contracts and laws of which the Insured should have reasonably been aware which relate to the project or to the Insured (unless prohibited from such compliance by a law, order, regulation or decree in force in the Insured's country);

(3) the Insured will attempt, as required by law, to extend, renew, or modify licenses and will comply with any non-arbitrary and reasonable licensing requirements relating to the project;

(4) the Insured (A) has no knowledge or information of any matter, fact, or circumstance which may reasonably give rise to a loss, (B) will give written notice to the company within fifteen days after receiving notification or knowledge at its corporate headquarters of any action or event which may give rise to a loss, (C) will diligently monitor and oversee the project, and (D) will not continue to incur expenses or costs associated with operation of the project after knowledge of the circumstances which could result in a loss unless first receiving the prior written consent of the company;

(5) the Insured will not disclose the existence of this policy; and

(6) the Insured, at its own expense, will take all reasonable and ordinary measures to: (a) avoid, prevent or minimize loss; (b) pursue and preserve for the company all administrative or judicial remedies which may be available to contest the loss; (c) cooperate in full with the company in attempting to negotiate a settlement with the government of the project country; (d) will take no action without the prior consent of the company (whether before or after the payment of any claim) which might adversely affect the company's actual or potential subrogation rights; (e) take all action as may reasonably be required (following the payment of any claim) to effect recoveries and assist in preserving and prosecuting any claims transferred to the company including permitting the company, at the company's expense, to bring actions in the name of the Insured; and (f) in all instances, exercise due diligence in meeting all warranties and conditions of this policy.

Recoveries

In the event a loss settlement is negotiated, regardless of any attribution thereof by any other party and for purposes of calculating the loss hereunder, compensation shall be deemed to have been paid and attributable on a proportionate basis between the Insured's uninsured and insured exposures in the project or foreign enterprise.

Amounts recovered for the company's percentage of total recoveries shall be applied: first, to reimburse the company for compensation paid to the Insured; second, to reimburse the company for out-of-pocket expenses incurred in pursuit of recovery; and third, any remaining amounts of recoveries accruing to the company will be given to the Insured.

Appraisal—Waiting Period

Should prevailing conditions in the project country be sufficiently hazardous to preclude an appraisal of physical property damage during the waiting period and for sixty days thereafter, the company will loan to the Insured, interest-free, 75% of the applicable limit of liability, and any adjustments of loss or return payment to the company will be made sixty days after such an appraisal is eventually completed. In the event an appraisal is not possible for a period of one year after the end of the waiting period, the company shall pay the full amount of the loss (up to the limit of liability) and will receive full subrogation rights from the Insured.

The company has the right following the date of loss to waive or reduce the corresponding waiting period.

Loss Reduction—Disputes

The Insured will use its best efforts to reduce the loss. This insurance will pay, subject to the limit of liability, for extraordinary expenses which are necessarily incurred in reducing such loss. In no event shall the aggregate of such expenses exceed the amount by which the loss is reduced.

All disputes which may arise regarding the arbitrariness of action of the government of the project country, shall, if agreed by the Insured and the company, be submitted to the American Arbitration Association. The decision thereby rendered regarding the arbitrariness of action by the government of the project country shall be final and binding.

Claim Procedure—Negotiations

Any claim under this policy must be made in writing to the company no later than six months after the Insured believes a loss has occurred. Such claim shall be in detail satisfactory to the company and shall show the basis for the amount of entitled compensation under all applicable provisions of this policy. Proof of loss at all times rests with the Insured. The Insured shall submit additional information, and use its best efforts to cause others to submit such information, as is required to complete the claim. The company shall have sixty days in which to act upon such claim following completion of the waiting period. The company shall make payment for the loss no later than sixty days thereafter.

In the event a loss is paid, all premium which is payable in installments and/or which has been prepaid shall be fully earned and payable immediately. All company liability arising out of or in connection with any claim for payment hereunder shall cease and expire one year after the company gives notice to the Insured of determination thereof.

If the Insured, within sixty days after a request by the company for additional information, fails to supply or to make reasonable efforts to supply such information, the company may consider the claim as abandoned by the Insured.

The Insured will neither negotiate nor enter into any agreement with the government of the project country nor any other third party concerning compensation for any loss without the prior written consent of the company.

Alteration, Assignment And Waiver

No change in, modification of, or assignment of interest under this policy shall be effective except when made by a written endorsement to this policy which has been signed by an authorized representative of the company.

None of the rights and remedies of the company shall be deemed to have been waived due to any failure of the company to invoke such right or remedy. A waiver in any one instance shall not be deemed to be a waiver in all instances. Any such waiver of rights or remedies must be made in writing by the company to the Insured.

Cancellation

Cancellation of this policy by the company is permitted only for non-payment of premium, and by the Insured only for termination of the project. Such cancellation shall neither discharge nor affect any right or obligation of either party which has accrued prior to the effective date of such cancellation.

If the policy is terminated in its entirety by the Insured, the company shall refund the unearned premium as computed at customary short rates. Under any other circumstances the refund shall be computed pro rata.

Legal Jurisdiction

The construction, validity, and performance of this policy shall be governed by the law of the State of New Jersey, U.S.A.

Project Insurance Section 2

In consideration of payment of the premium, and in reliance upon the statements of the Insured and its representatives and subject to the terms, conditions and exclusions of this policy, the company agrees to indemnify the Insured against loss sustained during the policy period in the manner set forth below.

Expropriatory Action Coverage

The company shall pay the Insured for loss due to expropriatory action, physical property damage incurred during the waiting period, unwanted local currency compensation, and/or third party blockade or quarantine.

Civil War and Insurrection Coverage

The company shall pay the Insured for loss due to physical property damage to insured assets caused solely and directly by civil war and insurrection.

Forced Project Relocation Coverage

The company shall pay the Insured for loss consisting of extraordinary costs incurred solely and directly as a result of and following forced project relocation due to the occurrence of those perils covered.

Valuation

After the designated waiting period has elapsed, subject to the applicable limit of liability, and less (1) proper deduction for the Insured's participation, (2) all amounts recovered, retained, or received by or on behalf of the Insured from any party with respect to the project or to the loss (regardless of attribution therefrom) up to the date of compensation, and (3) all deductions for all applicable policy deductions, the amount which is payable by the company to the Insured shall be established on the following basis.

Claims under expropriatory action shall be valued as follows:

(1) claims for expropriatory action—the insured percentage of the value of the investment as of the date of expropriation;

(2) claims for physical property damage—the insured percentage of the value of the insured assets at their loss value as of the date of expropriation;

(3) claims for local currency compensation—United States' dollars at the exchange rate (as specified in Section 1) existing at the end of the waiting period following an expropriatory action, for any local currency received by the Insured from the government of the project country with respect to such expropriatory action; and

(4) claims for third party blockade or quarantine—for mobile assets involuntarily abandoned in the project country due to military blockade placed on the project country by the armed forces of one or more third-party sovereign nations (including, if applicable, the government of the Insured's country), the loss value of the mobile assets.

Claims under civil war and insurrection coverage shall be valued at the amount of physical property damage suffered, calculated at loss value.

Claims under forced project relocation coverage shall be valued at all extraordinary costs incurred by the Insured in relocating (but not in operating) the project outside the project country with substantially the same physical characteristics as was the case in the project country had no loss occurred; plus, all extraordinary costs actually incurred in meeting binding and non-cancellable third party obligations which pertain to the project and which exist at the date of loss. Costs of rebuilding and/or replacement leasing are hereby included in the loss payment, but such rebuilding or replacement leasing costs will reduce the amount of net loss payments made by the company to the Insured for civil war and insurrection or expropriatory action loss.

Special Exclusions

No action shall be deemed to be an expropriatory action if it occurs or continues in effect during the policy period as a direct or indirect result of:

(1) any law, decree, regulation, or administrative action of the government of the project country which (a) is not by its expressed or implied terms for the purpose of nationalization, confiscation, or expropriation, (b) is not arbitrary, (c) is based upon a reasonable classification of domestic as well as foreign entities to which it applies, and (d) does not violate generally accepted principles of international law;

(2) any action in accordance with any agreement voluntarily made by the Insured or by the foreign enterprise either before or after the date of investment;

(3) any abrogation, impairment, repudiation or breach by the government of the project country (when acting as an equity investor in or lender to the foreign enterprise) of an obligation to the foreign enterprise; or any action which is lawful under the laws of the project country and which is taken by the government of the project country acting in its capacity as shareholder, director, or manager of the foreign enterprise;

(4) a decision by the Insured or the foreign enterprise made prior to expropriatory action to close or suspend (to the level of mere maintenance of the facilities) the operations of the foreign enterprise; or

(5) seizure, impairment, or destruction of the foreign enterprise by revolutionary or insurgent forces or agents unless said seizure or impairment lasts throughout the waiting period.

No loss shall be payable under civil war and insurrection if any such loss is a direct or indirect result of warlike actions within the project country involving organized military forces (other than non-combatant advisors) of a foreign government which exists externally to the territory of the project country.

Notwithstanding anything to the contrary in any documents or agreements relating to the project, guarantees of foreign exchange availability or of the ability to effect foreign exchange convertibility and/or transfer of currency out of the project country shall not be considered fundamental rights of any investment or project in the project country, and by itself any inability to affect foreign exchange and/or transfer shall not be considered an expropriatory action.

Failure of the government of the project country to allow the foreign enterprise or the Insured to obtain production materials or components from locations external to the project country will not, in itself, constitute an expropriatory action unless such refusal, restriction, or limitation is arbitrary, discriminatory, and otherwise constitutes part of an overall pattern of actions that meets all requirements of an expropriatory action.

Accounting Standards

The computation of the investment shall be based upon the audited financial statements of the Insured and the foreign enterprise as prepared in accordance with accounting principles generally accepted in the United States, or adjusted so as to conform to such principles.

Partial Loss

In the event of a partial loss due to forced divestment or seizure of the project, the Insured need only subrogate to the company the pro rata portion of the investment so lost. The amount of loss will be calculated on the percentage of investment so lost and a new limit of liability will be established reflecting the remaining investment.

Debt Securities

In the case of debt securities, the company shall have the right to pay the loss by paying the insured debt securities on the same terms and schedule under which the investment was originally made.

Constructive Total Loss

In the event of ascertained physical property damage to at least 75% of either (1) the total physical assets of the foreign enterprise, or (2) the mobile assets, this policy will indemnify the Insured to the full value of the civil war and insurrection limit of liability hereunder and full subrogation rights (equivalent to the claims payment) will be assigned to the company by the Insured.

Waiting Period Property Damage Provisions

Waiving any additional waiting period requirements, loss payments will be made within sixty days of submission for a valid property damage claim. Property damage loss payment shall be subtracted from the amount of indemnification due the Insured from a valid claim for expropriatory action.

Coverage is granted in consideration of proof by the Insured that a property damage policy is in force and for limits at least equal to coverage hereunder. The Insured shall maintain such policy or policies in force, and such policy terms and conditions for renewal thereof shall not be more restrictive than the expiring policy terms and conditions.

No claims may be made under this coverage until after such claim has been validly denied (due to the invocation of a Government Action Exclusion) by the carrier of the Insured's property insurance. Claim under this present policy will be paid only for perils otherwise covered under the Insured's property policy. Denial of claim by such property insurer shall not be deemed to mean acceptance of liability for such loss by the company.

Forced Project Relocation Requirement

Valid extraordinary costs incurred after the forced project relocation waiting period, as well as unmitigatable third party obligations existing on the date of loss (for which indemnification is due under this coverage), are only covered if and when an expropriatory action is taken against at least 50% of the investment. A valid forced project relocation claim may be filed with the company even if the expropriatory action does not continue for the duration of its waiting period and even if no expropriatory action loss is validly sustained.

Forced project relocation coverage will not apply or respond following physical property damage unless such physical property damage follows an act of civil war and insurrection and entails destruction of or significant damage to at least 50% of either (1) the total physical assets of the foreign enterprise, or (2) the mobile assets.

Compensation in Local Currencies

In the event of any local currency compensation by the government of the project country, right and title to such compensation will be subrogated to the company prior to the payment of any claim.

Limit of Liability, Deductible, and Coinsurance

The company's total limit of liability for any one loss and in the aggregate all losses under Section 2 coverages shall not exceed the amounts set forth in items 2 and 3 of the Declarations page of Section 2.

The company's liability under Section 2 shall apply only to that portion of each loss in excess of the Deductible Amount specified in Item 5 of the Declarations. Section 2, and such Deductible Amount shall be borne by the Insured uninsured and at the Insured's own risk.

With respect to all loss (excess of applicable Deductible Amounts) originating in any one policy year, the Insured shall bear uninsured and at its own risk that percent of all such loss specified as the coinsurance percent in Item 4 of the Declarations, Section 2, and the company's liability hereunder shall apply only to the remaining percent of all such loss.

Key Personnel Insurance

In consideration of payment of the specified premium and in reliance upon the statements of the Insured and its representatives and subject to the terms, conditions, and exclusions of this policy, the company agrees to indemnify the Insured against loss sustained during the policy period in the manner set forth below.

Expatriate Removal Coverage

The company shall pay the Insured, on behalf of designated expatriates, for loss due to politically-motivated endangerment or arbitrary expulsion of such expatriates from the project country, plus any and all extraordinary tax obligations of such expatriates if due to premature expatriate removal caused by war, civil war and insurrection, or expropriatory action.

Transit Insurance Coverage

The company shall pay the Insured, on behalf of designated expatriates, for loss, destruction, or damage to their personal possessions resulting from war, or from civil war and insurrection. The company shall also pay the Insured, on behalf of designated expatriates, for loss due to interruption of their business travel to or from the project country resulting from war or from civil war and insurrection.

Indigenous Key Personnel Expenses Coverage

The company shall pay the Insured, on behalf of designated indigenous employees, for loss expenses incurred as a result of and following forced relocation of designated indigenous employees where such forced relocation is the result of war, civil war and insurrection, or expropriatory action taken against the Insured in the project country.

Valuation

After the designated waiting period has elapsed, subject to the applicable limit of liability, and less (1) proper deduction for the Insured's participation, (2) all amounts recovered, retained, or received by or on behalf of the Insured from any party with respect to the project or to the loss (regardless of attribution therefrom) up to the date of compensation, and (3) all deductions for all applicable policy deductibles; the amount which is payable by the company to the Insured shall be established on the following basis:

(1) claims under Expatriate Removal coverage shall be valued as follows:

- (A) claims for endangerment or expulsion: extraordinary costs (but not payment for the value of abandoned assets) actually incurred in (a) transferring designated expatriates out of the project country, (b) transferring necessary additional personnel into the project country to replace endangered or expelled expatriates, (c) terminating or disassembling and removing the project (but only if expatriate endangerment or expulsion is the sole reason precluding completion of the project), and—if the project is not prematurely terminated—(d) operating the project for the remainder of the policy period or for six months, whichever is shorter, but only those costs and expenses directly resulting from the replacement of designated expatriates who, due to endangerment or expulsion, no longer participate in the project.
- (B) claims for extraordinary tax obligations: that amount of additional taxes on income earned overseas with respect to employment in the project paid by designated expatriates to national or sub-national taxing authorities of the Insured's country, such added tax obligation arising from a premature cancellation or termination of the project in the project country due to war, civil war and insurrection, or an expropriatory action.

(2) claims under Transit Insurance coverage shall be valued as follows:
   (A) claims for loss or destruction of personal possessions: the loss value of personal possessions lost or involuntarily abandoned by designated expatriates following and directly attributable to war or civil war and insurrection in the project country.
   (B) claims due to politically-caused interruption of business travel: extraordinary costs incurred by designated expatriates due to delay or cancellation of business travel to or from the project country, where such delay or cancellation is directly or indirectly caused by war or civil war and insurrection in the project country.

(3) claims under indigenous Employee Relocation coverage shall be valued at the amount of indemnification stated in the Declarations, Section 3 of this policy—which will be payable by the company to the Insured in the event that the Insured can demonstrate to the company that designated indigenous employees must permanently leave the project country due to war, civil war and insurrection, or expropriatory action taken against the Insured with whom the designated indigenous employee is closely identified or associated.

Special Exclusion Section 3

Conditions or the threat of civil war and insurrection, or war, do not alone constitute endangerment of designated expatriates unless (1) the government of the Insured's country formally calls for and also assists in evacuation from the project country or (2) such conditions directly result in the complete and unavoidable cessation of all project activities.

Limit Of Liability, Deductible, And Coinsurance

The company's total limit of liability for any one loss and in the aggregate for all losses under Section 3 coverages shall not exceed the amounts set forth in items 2 and 3 of the Declarations, Section 3.

The company's liability under Section 3 shall apply only to that part of each loss which is excess of the Deductible Amount specified in item 5 of the Declarations, Section 3, and such Deductible Amount shall be borne by the Insured uninsured and at the Insured's own risk.

With respect to all loss (excess of applicable Deductible Amounts) originating in any one policy year, the Insured shall bear uninsured and at its own risk that percent of all such loss specified as the coinsurance percent in item 4 of the Declarations, Section 3. The company's liability shall apply only to the remaining percent of all such loss.

Policy Exclusions Section 4

Coverage under this policy does not apply to any loss directly or indirectly resulting from:

(1) dishonest, provocative, criminal, illegal or malicious acts by the Insured or by the foreign enterprise; or any change, alteration, modification or non-compliance with any significant contracts or agreements relating to the project except when the company has given its prior written consent;

(2) breach or inaccuracy of any representation, warranty, covenant or agreement herein, or in the Application or in other written statements made by the Insured with respect to this policy;

(3) laws, rules, regulations, or administrative actions or policies which exist at the inception of this policy;

(4) currency fluctuations, devaluations, uniform exchange control or taxation restrictions, regulations, or decrees;

(5) physical damage to or destruction of any tangible property (except as specifically insured hereunder) or, for all coverages hereunder, detonation, contamination, or other physical damage or threat thereof, by any nuclear, non-explosive chemical, and/or biological agent, material, weapon or device;

(6) insolvency, bankruptcy, financial default, creditors proceedings, abandonment to the company or otherwise (except for endangerment or expulsion insurance), or loss of market share;

(7) non-procurement of valid and required project permits or licenses which could have been obtained prior to the inception of this policy;

(8) war or military mobilization (whether before of after the outbreak of hostilities) between (a) any of the following Five Powers: China, France, Great Britain, the Union of the Soviet Socialist Republics and the United States of America, or (b) the project country and Insured's country;
(9) any event, act, or occurrence which, but for the existence of this policy, would be or would have been covered by any of the Insured's other insurances;
(10) burglary, theft, unexplained or mysterious disappearance, delay in transit, inherent vice, latent defect, wear and tear, gradual deterioration, termites, insects, vermin, wet or dry rot or contamination; or
(11) loss of future profits or other consequential loss or damage.

Policy Definitions Section 5

When used in this policy:

Act of Sabotage or Terrorism: means politically motivated destruction of or damage to insured assets (1) as a result of state-sponsored and government-directed terrorism, or (2) by an organized political group which advocates the overthrow of the established political authorities in the project country.

Business Travel: means travel undertaken by designated expatriates for the specific purpose of conduction business activities associated with the project or the foreign enterprise.

Civil War and Insurrection: means any mass-based, sustained, non-intermittent and cohesively organized series of actions of insurrection, rebellion, revolution, or civil war which occur within the project country, or acts of sabotage or terrorism (including but not limited to state-sponsored terrorism) which occur directly and explicitly in the project country as part of such insurrection, rebellion, revolution, or civil war. It is agreed that acts of sabotage or terrorism do not in themselves automatically qualify as acts of civil war and insurrection unless such activity occurs within the broader context of mass-based, sustained, non-intermittent, and cohesively organized insurrection, rebellion, revolution or civil war.

Coinsurance Percent: means that percent of the total exposure retained uninsured by the Insured.

Company: means the stock insurance company identified in the declarations, page 1.

Currency Inconvertibility: means the general inability, due to scarcity of hard currency foreign exchange reserves in the project country, to exchange local currency for polity currency and to transfer such policy currency out of the project country.

Date of Compensation: means that date upon which final claims payment is made by the company to the Insured.

Date of Expropriation: means the first day of the occurrence of an action which continues throughout the waiting period and becomes an expropriatory action.

Date of Investment: means each date on which the constituent elements of the investment first come into the control or possession of the foreign enterprise, or in the case of mobile assets, the date such mobile assets are first physically present in the project country.

Date of Loss: means the date during the policy period from which the waiting period begins and on which the occurrence resulting in a loss first happens.

Expropriatory Action: means any action commencing during the policy period of confiscation, expropriation, nationalization, deprivation, or requisition which is taken, authorized, or ratified by the government of the project country, which continues consecutively throughout the waiting period and directly, effectively, arbitrarily and significantly denies or precludes (1) the foreign enterprise from exercising control over the use or disposition of a substantial portion of its property or from conducting any significant economic activities resulting from the investment or (2) denies or precludes the Insured from:

(A) exercising its fundamental rights with respect to the foreign enterprise;
(B) disposing of or, in the case of forced divestiture, retaining the securities of the foreign enterprise;

(C) exercising control over the use of the mobile assets for their intended purpose or removing them from the project country; or

(D) repatriating, and exercising control in the project country over, amounts received with respect to the securities as a return of capital following a voluntary sale of the Insured's interest in the foreign enterprise, which action commences within twelve months immediately succeeding such receipt, unless such return of amounts received is precluded due to currency inconvertibility within the project country.

Extraordinary Costs: means those reasonable, unavoidable, necessary, and extraordinary non-mitigatable costs, penalties, and expenses, net of tax benefit (if any) which are incurred by the Insured as a result of an insured loss hereunder; provided that in no event shall there be included as extraordinary costs any earned or anticipated profits.

Forced Project Relocation: means efforts undertaken by the Insured to re-establish the project or the foreign enterprise in a location other than the project country as a result of a loss amounting to at least fifty percent of the named peril limit of liability.

Foreign Enterprise: means that foreign enterprise identified in Item 1, page 5.

Government of the Project County: means the government effectively controlling that part of the project country where the project is located.

Insured: means, in addition to as specified in the Declarations, any executive officers, director, partner, member, and non-hourly employee of the Insured. If the Insured designated in the Declarations is an individual, the definition of Insured extends to include the spouse, minor age children (as legally defined in the project country), and all employees of such individual when they are acting in an employee capacity.

Insured Assets: means those tangible assets utilized by the Insured in connection with the project, located in the project country, and described in the Application.

Insured Percentage: means the percentage of each and every loss which is Insured under this policy. The remaining amount of the loss is to be borne by the Insured and remain uninsured.

Insured's Country: means the country specified in the Insured's address as set forth in the Declarations, Section 1.

Insured's Participation: means the percentage of the amount of each and every loss which is to be borne by the Insured and remain uninsured.

Investment: means (1) the Insured's book value equity (calculated in accordance with generally accepted accounting principles as practiced in the United States) and/or net debt securities in the foreign enterprise which are owned by the Insured; and/or (2) any mobile assets which are insured hereunder and valued at the appropriate loss value.

Key Person, Key Personnel: means the expatriate(s) and/or indigenous employee(s) designated and identified in the Declarations, Section 3.

Limit of Liability: means the amount stated in the Declarations, after taking into account the Insured's participation, which is the aggregate maximum amount payable under this policy and under specified coverages for any and all claims made under such specific coverages.

Local Currency: means the currency of the project country.

Loss: means those financial liabilities incurred as a result of the occurrence of those perils identified in Item 2, page 5 or Item 2, page 9, and described on pages 6 and 10 of this policy respectively.

Loss Value: means the lesser of replacement or repair cost or actual cash value in the Insured's country on the day immediately prior to the date of loss.

Mobile Assets: means those assets scheduled in the Application which are owned or legally held by the Insured, are not on the books of the foreign enterprise, and are physically present in the project country.

Nuclear: means nuclear reaction, nuclear radiation or radioactive contamination, whether controlled or uncontrolled and whether the loss be direct or indirect, proximate or remote, or if wholly or partly caused by, contributed to, or aggravated by the perils insured against.

Personal Possessions: means those items owned by, or in the personal care of, the Insured while such Insured is either in, or travelling to or from the project country. For the purpose of this policy, the term personal possessions does not include cash, jewelry, or other valuables, contraband, marketable securities, or other financial instruments, but it will include privately-owned and privately-utilized land, buildings, and real estate if they are specifically scheduled for this policy.

Physical Property Damage: means the destruction, loss, impairment, or damage to insured property (excluding cash, jewelry, other valuables, marketable securities, or other financial instruments) of the Insured as a result of the occurrence of covered perils. Under no circumstances is physical personal damage extended to include loss which is the result of the interruption of business or extra expenses incurred due to the occurrence of any peril.

Policy Period: means that period of time identified in Item 6, page 1.

Policy Year: means the twelve month (365 day) period beginning with the Inception Date of the policy, or, if applicable, with any annual anniversary date thereafter.

Project: means that project identified in Item 5, page 1.

Project Country: means any project country identified in Item 4, page 1.

Return of Capital: means (1) the payment of principal or debt securities; (2) dividends or other distributions paid in complete or partial liquidation of equity securities; or (3) proceeds from selling securities.

Securities: means the interest of the Insured in the foreign enterprise acquired as a result of the investment, and all notes, certificates, or other evidence of ownership or financial obligation issued to the Insured by the foreign enterprise.

Third Party Blockade or Quarantine: means the politically motivated use of military force, or the direct threat thereof, by one or more third party sovereign nations, such action preventing the Insured from removing mobile assets from the project country, whether such actions are part of a general blockade or a limited political quarantine.

Waiting Period: means the consecutive period of time, beginning with the date of loss or the date of expropriation, which is required to expire before any action taken or sustained will be deemed to have become a loss.

War: means hostile or warlike action, including action in hindering, combating, or defending against an actual, impending, or expected act by (1) any government or sovereign power or any authority maintaining or using military, naval, or air forces; (2) any military, naval, or air forces; or (3) any agent of any such government, power, authority, or forces.

APPENDIX III

Online Resources

The following is a list of links to various institutions, websites, services, and other resources pertaining to topics discussed throughout the text. They are grouped according to the subject matter of a particular chapter, or under the general section if the link or information is of general applicability or applies to multiple chapters (some links are repeated for convenience). (Note on References: A continually updated list of reference and supplementary materials, as well as errata, external reviews and other resources, is maintained at www.KinsellaLaw.com/iipr. Please feel free to send notes for errata, updates, and other suggestions to the authors at the contact links noted on that page).

General Information

Links, Bibliographies, and General

Electronic Information System for International Law (EISIL): www.eisil.org

Trans-Lex: www.trans-lex.org/

Research Guides on Main Topics of International Law: www.peacepalacelibrary.nl/research-guides/?bibliography=investment

Georgetown Law Library, International Investment Law Research Guide: http://guides.ll.georgetown.edu/InternationalInvestmentLaw

University of Melbourne, International Investment Law Library Guide: http://unimelb.libguides.com/investment_law

European Journal of International Law—Home Page: www.ejil.org/

Legal Research on International Law Issues Using the Internet (Lyonette Louis-Jacques, University of Chicago Law School): www2.lib.uchicago.edu/~llou/forintlaw.html (wide range of selected and annotated international law links)

ASIL Electronic Resource Guide: www.asil.org/resources/electronic-resource-guide-erg (comprehensive international law guide, continuously updated and expanded)

OGEL (Oil-gas-energy law)—the Global Energy Law & Regulation Portal: www.ogel.org/

Eur-Lex: https://eur-lex.europa.eu/homepage.html (access to E.U. law)

International Investment

OECD, Investment Policy: http://www.oecd.org/daf/inv/investment-policy/ (a range of resources and tools for policymakers to enhance the contribution of international investment to growth and sustainable development)

Glossary of Foreign Direct Investment Terms: www.imf.org/external/np/sta/di/glossary.pdf

OECD Working Papers on International Investment:

www.oecd.org/daf/inv/investment-policy/working-papers.htm

Investment Claims: http://oxia.ouplaw.com/ (links to foreign investment law instruments and jurisprudence)

UNCTAD, World Investment Reports: https://unctad.org/en/pages/DIAE/World%20Investment%20Report/WIR-Series.aspx

International Trade

WTO and GATT: www.wto.org

SICE: Foreign Trade Information System: www.sice.oas.org (the "Foreign Trade Information System" [SICE for short from its Spanish acronym—Sistema de Información al Comercio Exterior]—the information technology arm of the Trade Unit of the Organization of American States (OAS). Provides information and documents on trade in the Western Hemisphere).

UNCITRAL (United Nations Commission on International Trade Law): https://uncitral.un.org/

UNCTAD (United Nations Conference on Trade and Development): www.unctad.org

Office of the United States Trade Representative: www.ustr.gov (U.S. trade agreements and other documents)

Cases/Decisions

ICJ cases: https://www.icj-cij.org/en/list-of-all-cases

PCIJ cases: https://www.icj-cij.org/en/pcij

ICSID arbitral decisions: https://icsid.worldbank.org/en/Pages/cases/ConcludedCases.aspx?status=c

European Court of Humans Rights cases: www.worldlii.org/eu/cases/ECHR

Investment Treaty Arbitration: https://www.italaw.com/ (access to all publicly available investment treaty awards; information and resources relating to investment treaties and investment treaty arbitration; and links to further resources)

Investment Claims: http://oxia.ouplaw.com/ (links to foreign investment law instruments and jurisprudence)

U.S. Supreme Court Cases: https://caselaw.findlaw.com/court/us-supreme-court

British and Irish Legal Information Institute (BaILII): www.bailii.org/

Treaties

(See also resources under the Chapters 6 and 7–9 headings, below)

United nations Treaty Collection: https://treaties.un.org/

European Commission, Treaties Office Database: http://ec.europa.eu/world/agreements/default.home.do

ICSID, Database of Bilateral Investment Treaties: https://icsid.worldbank.org/en/Pages/resources/Bilateral-Investment-Treaties-Database.aspx

World LII, International Treaties Collection: http://www.worldlii.org/int/special/treaties/

U.K. Treaties Online: https://treaties.fco.gov.uk/responsive/app/consolidatedSearch/

Bilaterals.org: www.bilaterals.org (information about bilateral trade and investment agreements)

Office of the United States Trade Representative: www.ustr.gov (U.S. trade agreements and other documents)

Eur-Lex: https://eur-lex.europa.eu/homepage.html (access to E.U. law)

U.N. Resolutions and International Organizations

Charter of the United Nations (1945): http://www.un.org/en/charter-united-nations/index.html

ICSID Convention (Washington Convention) (1965): http://icsidfiles.worldbank.org/ICSID/ICSID/StaticFiles/basicdoc/main-eng.htm

U.N. General Assembly Resolutions: http://www.un.org/en/sections/documents/general-assembly-resolutions/index.html

WTO & GATT: www.wto.org

UNCITRAL: https://uncitral.un.org/

North American Free Trade Agreement (NAFTA): www.naftanow.org/; *also* NAFTAClaims.com (AKA NAFTALaw.org): www.naftaclaims.com (information about NAFTA investor–State dispute settlement and copies of recent NAFTA legal documents)

See also USMCA: https://ustr.gov/trade-agreements/free-trade-agreements/united-states-mexico-canada-agreement (provides the text of and statements/fact sheets about the most recent agreement between the United States, Mexico, and Canada in relation to the renegotiation of NAFTA)

Publications/Journals Online

European Society of International Law, International Law Journals: https://esil-sedi.eu/?page_id=54

European Journal of International Law: www.ejil.org

CEPMLP Annual Review (CAR): https://www.dundee.ac.uk/cepmlp/research/cepmlpannualreviewcar/

Harvard International Law Journal, Online Scholarship: www.harvardilj.org/category/content/article-series/

OGEL (Oil-gas-energy law)—the Global Energy Law & Regulation Portal: www.ogel.org/

Oxford university Press, International Law Journals: www.oxfordjournals.org/en/our-journals/law/international.html

Information—by Chapter

Chapter 1: Political Risk

Political Risk and Related Services

The Economist Intelligence Unit, Country Risk Service and Country Reports: www.eiu.com

Marsh, Political Risk Map (2018): www.marsh.com/us/campaigns/political-risk-map-2018.html

The PRS Group: www.prsgroup.com

Control Risks: www.controlrisks.com

Global Risk Management, Inc.: www.grminc.com

Business Environment Risk Intelligence: www.beri.com

Other Information

Export.gov: www.export.gov/Market-Intelligence (U.S. Dept. Commerce and other departments provide information on export promotion programs, regional market information, and international trade agreements)

Chapter 2: Structuring Transactions to Minimize Political Risk

UNIDROIT Principles of International Commercial Contracts 2010: https://www.unidroit.org/english/principles/contracts/principles2010/integralversionprinciples2010-e.pdf

United Nations Convention on Contracts for the International Sale of Goods (1980) (CISG): https://www.uncitral.org/pdf/english/texts/sales/cisg/V1056997-CISG-e-book.pdf

ICSID model clauses: https://icsid.worldbank.org/en/Pages/resources/ICSID-Model-Clauses.aspx

Chapter 3: Investment Insurance

Contact information for various national and other political risk insurers, including OPIC and MIGA, is contained below and available at the Berne Union's list of members at: https://www.berneunion.org/Members. Requests for information concerning private political risk insurance may be made through commercial insurance agents.

Multilateral Investment Guarantee Agency (MIGA): https://www.miga.org/political-risk-insurance (political risk insurance agency). Draft standard terms and conditions for various types of insurance are available at: https://www.miga.org/terms-conditions

MIGA, Annual Reports: https://www.miga.org/annual-reports

Australia: Export Finance and Insurance Corporation (EFIC): www.efic.gov.au/; Germany, AuslandsGeschäftsAbsicherung der Bundesrepublik Deutschland (AGA): www.agaportal.de/en/index.html

Japan, Nippon Export and Investment Insurance (NEXI): www.nexi.go.jp

United Kingdom, Export Credits Guarantee Department (ECGD): www.ecgd.gov.uk

United States, Overseas Private Investment Corporation (OPIC): www.opic.gov

OPIC Annual Reports: www.opic.gov/media-events/annual-reports

OPIC, Political Risk Insurance: https://www.opic.gov/what-we-offer/political-risk-insurance/types-of-coverage

OPIC complements the U.S. Agency for International Development (USAID), which finances projects primarily on a government-to-government basis. See About USAID, USAID History: https://www.usaid.gov/who-we-are/usaid-history

Berne Union: www.berneunion.org/

Chapter 4: State Responsibility and Remedies under Customary International Law

Statute of the International Court of Justice (1945): www.icj-cij.org/en/statute

Vienna Convention on the Law of Treaties (1969): https://treaties.un.org/doc/publication/unts/volume%201155/volume-1155-i-18232-english.pdf

International Law Commission (ILC) Draft Articles on State Responsibility for Internationally Wrongful Acts (2001): http://legal.un.org/ilc/texts/instruments/english/commentaries/9_6_2001.pdf

Chapter 5: History and Development of the Customary International Law of Expropriation and Investment Protection

NAFTA: www.nafta-sec-alena.org; *also* NAFTAClaims.com (AKA NAFTA-Law.org): www.naftaclaims.com

Guidelines on the Treatment of Foreign Direct Investment (Appendix I): www.italaw.com/documents/WorldBank.pdf

Chapter 6: The Substantive Law of Contemporary International Investment Protection

Regional Investment Treaties and General Information

UNCTAD: www.unctad.org

NAFTA: www.naftanow.org/; *also* NAFTAClaims.com: www.naftaclaims.com

See also USMCA: https://ustr.gov/trade-agreements/free-trade-agreements/united-states-mexico-canada-agreement (provides the text of and statements/fact sheets about the most recent agreement between the United States, Mexico, and Canada in relation to the renegotiation of NAFTA)

Energy Charter Treaty (ECT): www.encharter.org

MERCOSUR: Protocol for the Reciprocal Promotion and Protection of MERCOSUR Investments: https://investmentpolicyhub.unctad.org/IIA/treaty/3120

Unofficial English translation done by the University of Oslo available here: www.jus.uio.no/english/services/library/treaties/09/9-02/mercosur_investment.xml

International Law Commission (ILC) Draft Articles on State Responsibility for Internationally Wrongful Acts (2001): http://legal.un.org/ilc/texts/instruments/english/commentaries/9_6_2001.pdf

ILC Draft Rules On Most-Favored-Nation Clauses (1978) with commentaries: http://legal.un.org/ilc/texts/instruments/english/commentaries/1_3_1978.pdf

National Association of Certified Valuators and Analysts International Glossary of Business Valuation Terms: www.nacva.com/content.asp?contentid=166

UNCTAD, Trends in International Investment Agreements: An Overview (1999): www.unctad.org/en/docs/iteiit13_en.pdf

UNCTAD, World Investment Reports: https://unctad.org/en/Pages/DIAE/World%20Investment%20Report/World_Investment_Report.aspx

Bilateral Investment Treaties

UNCTAD, International Investment Agreements Navigator: https://investmentpolicyhub.unctad.org/IIA

European Commission, Treaties Office Database: http://ec.europa.eu/world/agreements/default.home.do

ICSID, Database of Bilateral Investment Treaties: https://icsid.worldbank.org/en/Pages/resources/Bilateral-Investment-Treaties-Database.aspx

List of BITs in force among and between countries in the Free Trade Agreement of the Americas (FTAA): http://www.sice.oas.org/agreements_e.asp

Texts of BITs in force with members of the FTAA: www.sice.oas.org/investment/bitindex_e.asp

Organization of American States, Trade Policy Developments: www.sice.oas.org/tpd_e.asp

Bilaterals.org: www.bilaterals.org (information about bilateral trade and investment agreements) and www.bilaterals.org/rubrique.php3?id_rubrique=29 (other information on BITs and lists of BITs concluded)

Richard Happ's arbitration website: www.happlaw.de/investmentarbitration/index.html (links to various country lists of BITs)

European BITs—links and information: https://www.bilaterals.org/?-europe-bits-&lang=en, including E.U. enlargement: BITs of E.U. accession candidates (April 2004)

Switzerland: www.admin.ch/ch/f/rs/0.97.html#0.975 (links to all BITs entered into by Switzerland (in French))

U.S. BIT program: https://www.state.gov/e/eb/ifd/bit/; U.S. Model BIT (2012): https://www.state.gov/documents/organization/188371.pdf; *see also* https://ustr.gov/trade-agreements/bilateral-investment-treaties

Chapters 7–9: International Arbitration, Mediation, and Conciliation

International Centre for the Settlement of Investment Disputes (ICSID): www.worldbank.org/icsid

ICSID Convention (Washington Convention) (1965): http://icsidfiles.worldbank.org/ICSID/ICSID/StaticFiles/basicdoc/main-eng.htm

ICSID model clauses: https://icsid.worldbank.org/en/Pages/resources/ICSID-Model-Clauses.aspx

Convention on the Recognition and Enforcement of Foreign Arbitral Awards (1958) (New York Convention): www.uncitral.org/uncitral/en/uncitral_texts/arbitration/NYConvention.html

UNCITRAL (United Nations Commission on International Trade Law): www.uncitral.org

UNCITRAL Arbitration Rules: www.uncitral.org/pdf/english/texts/arbitration/arb-rules/arb-rules.pdf

UNCITRAL Conciliation Rules: http://www.uncitral.org/uncitral/en/uncitral_texts/arbitration/1980Conciliation_rules.html

UNCITRAL Model Law on International Commercial Arbitration: http://www.uncitral.org/uncitral/en/uncitral_texts/arbitration/1985Model_arbitration.html

UNCITRAL Notes on Organizing Arbitral Proceedings: http://www.uncitral.org/uncitral/en/uncitral_texts/arbitration/2016Notes_proceedings.html

ICSID Convention, regulations and Rules (present and historical versions): https://icsid.worldbank.org/en/Pages/resources/ICSID-Convention,-Regulations-and-Rules.aspx

ICSID Additional Facility Arbitration Rules: https://icsid.worldbank.org/en/Pages/icsiddocs/ICSID-Arbitration-(Additional-Facility)-Rules.aspx

ICSID Conciliation Rules: https://icsid.worldbank.org/en/Pages/icsiddocs/ICSID-Convention-Conciliation-Rules.aspx

International Chamber of Commerce (ICC): www.iccwbo.org

ICC Dispute Resolution Services: https://iccwbo.org/dispute-resolution-services/

ICC Rules of Arbitration (2017): https://iccwbo.org/dispute-resolution-services/arbitration/rules-of-arbitration/

ICC Mediation Guidance Notes (2013): https://cms.iccwbo.org/content/uploads/sites/3/2014/12/icc-mediation-guidance-notes-english.pdf

ICC Mediation Rules: https://iccwbo.org/dispute-resolution-services/mediation/mediation-rules/

LCIA (London Court of International Arbitration) Arbitration Rules (2014): http://www.lcia.org/dispute_resolution_services/lcia-arbitration-rules-2014.aspx

LCIA Mediation Rules: http://www.lcia.org/Dispute_Resolution_Services/LCIA_Mediation_Rules.aspx#Anchor-Article-33869

Stockholm Chamber of Commerce (SCC) Rules of the SCC Arbitration Institute (2017): https://sccinstitute.com/dispute-resolution/rules/

International Bar Association (IBA) Rules on the Taking of Evidence in International Commercial Arbitration: https://www.ibanet.org/Document/Default.aspx?DocumentUid=68336C49-4106-46BF-A1C6-A8F0880444DC

The IBA Rules for Investor–State Mediation (October 4, 2012): https://icsid.worldbank.org/en/Documents/process/IBA%20Rules%20for%20Investor-State%20Mediation%20(Approved%20by%20IBA%20Council%204%20Oct%202012).pdf

United States Council for International Business (USCIB): www.uscib.org

American Arbitration Association (AAA): www.adr.org

AAA Rules of the International Centre for Dispute Resolution: https://www.adr.org/sites/default/files/ICDR_Rules.pdf

IBA (International Bar Association) Guidelines on Conflicts of Interest in International Arbitration: https://www.ibanet.org/Document/Default.aspx?DocumentUid=e2fe5e72-eb14-4bba-b10d-d33dafee8918

Transnational Dispute Management: www.transnational-dispute-management.com/

International Arbitration Institute: www.iaiparis.com

Singapore International Arbitration Centre—Arbitration Rules (2016): http://www.siac.org.sg/our-rules/rules/siac-rules-2016

World Intellectual Property Organization (WIPO) Arbitration Rules: http://arbiter.wipo.int/arbitration/rules/index.html

WIPO Mediation Rules: http://arbiter.wipo.int/mediation/rules/index.html

United States Uniform Mediation Act (2001): https://www.mediate.com/articles/umafinalstyled.cfm

Hong Kong International Arbitration Centre Mediation Rules: http://www.hkiac.org/mediation/rules/hkiac-mediation-rules

IBA Arbitration Committee, Venezuela Arbitration Guide (2018): https://www.ibanet.org/Document/Default.aspx?DocumentUid=F8363A63-9003-47C2-AB88-D601B4757625

ICSID Members of the Panels of Conciliators and Arbitrators (2018): https://icsid.worldbank.org/en/Documents/icsiddocs/ICSID%2010%20-%20Latest.pdf

Institute for Transnational Arbitration: www.cailaw.org/ita

Chapter 10: Intervention of States in Investment Disputes

Foreign Claims Settlement Commission of the United States: www.usdoj.gov/fcsc

European Association of Political Consultants: www.eapc.eu (consultants used by investors or host States to identify and gain access to the necessary individuals within the home State governmental structure, in order to present the party's view of the dispute and induce the State to intervene [or refrain from intervening] accordingly)

Chapter 11: The Interaction between International Investment Law and Human Rights

European Convention on Human Rights: www.echr.coe.int/Documents/Convention_ENG.pdf

European Court of Human Rights: https://echr.coe.int/Pages/home.aspx?p=home

Charter of Fundamental Rights of the European Union: www.europarl.europa.eu/charter/pdf/text_en.pdf

International Institute for Sustainable Development, International Human Rights in Bilateral Investment Treaties and in Investment Treaty Arbitration: www.iisd.org/library/international-human-rights-bilateral-investment-treaties-and-investment-treaty-arbitration

Trans-Pacific Partnership Treaty: https://ustr.gov/trade-agreements/free-trade-agreements/trans-pacific-partnership/tpp-full-text

The ASEAN Inter-Governmental Commission on Human Rights: http://aichr.org/

INDEX